THE INJURED ATHLETE

Daniel N. Kulund, M.D.

Director of the Sports Orthopaedic Center
Charlottesville, Virginia
Active Staff, Martha Jefferson Hospital
Charlottesville, Virginia
Adjunct Professor of Physical Education
University of Virginia
Charlottesville, Virginia
Fellow of the American Academy of Orthopedic Surgeons
Member of the American Orthopaedic Society for Sports Medicine
Member of the American College of Sports Medicine
Advisory Member, National Athletic Trainers Association
Member, National Strength and Conditioning Association

ILLUSTRATED BY
Ronald J. Ervin, B.F.A., A.M.I.
Charlottesville, Virginia

With 7 Additional Contributors

THE INJURED ATHLETE

SECOND EDITION

J. B. LIPPINCOTT COMPANY
Philadelphia
London · New York · São Paulo
Mexico City · St. Louis · Sydney

Acquisitions Editor: Lisette Bralow
Sponsoring Editor: Sanford J. Robinson
Manuscript Editor: Leslie E. Hoeltzel
Indexer: Ann Cassar
Book Design: Rita Naughton
Cover Design: Anthony Frizano
Design Coordinator: Paul Fry
Production Manager: Kathleen P. Dunn
Production Coordinator: George V. Gordon
Compositor: Ruttle, Shaw & Wetherill, Inc.
Printer/Binder: The Maple-Vail Book Manufacturing Group

Second Edition

1 3 5 6 4 2

Library of Congress Cataloging-in-Publication Data

The Injured Athlete.

  Includes bibliographies and index.
  1. Sports—Accidents and injuries.   2. Sports medicine.   I. Kulund, Daniel N., 1940–
[DNLM: 1. Physical Education and Training—methods.
2. Sports Medicine.   QT 260 I515]
RD97.I55 1988   617′.1027   87–22553
ISBN 0–397–50765–8

The authors and publisher have exerted every effort to ensure that drug selection and dosage set forth in this text are in accord with current recommendations and practice at the time of publication. However, in view of ongoing research, changes in government regulations, and the constant flow of information relating to drug therapy and drug reactions, the reader is urged to check the package insert for each drug for any change in indications and dosage and for added warnings and precautions. This is particularly important when the recommended agent is a new or infrequently employed drug.

Dedicated to my family:
Sandy, Patrick, and David

CONTRIBUTORS

Jana J. Early, P.T.
Director of Sports Physical Therapy
Sports Orthopaedic Center
Charlottesville, Virginia

John N. Gamble, Jr.
Head Strength Coach
University of Virginia
Charlottesville, Virginia

Joe H. Gieck, Ed.D., A.T.C., P.T.
Head Athletic Trainer
Division of Sports Medicine and Athletic Training
Department of Athletics
Associate Professor, Department of Human Services, Curry School of Education
Assistant Professor, Orthopaedics and Rehabilitation
University of Virginia
Charlottesville, Virginia

Frank C. McCue III, M.D.
Alfred R. Shands Professor of Orthopaedic Surgery and Plastic Surgery of the Hand
Director, Division of Sports Medicine and Hand Surgery
Team Physician, Department of Athletics
University of Virginia
Charlottesville, Virginia

Russell R. Pate, Ph.D.
Director, Human Performance Laboratory
Department of Physical Education
Blatt Physical Education Center
College of Health
University of South Carolina
Columbia, South Carolina

Robert J. Rotella, Ph.D.
Associate Professor
Department of Human Services, Curry School of Education
Health and Physical Education
Program Area Director of Sports Psychology Curriculum
University of Virginia
Charlottesville, Virginia

Ethan N. Saliba, M.Ed., A.T.C., P.T.
Assistant Athletic Trainer
Division of Sports Medicine and Athletic Training
Department of Athletics
Instructor, Department of Human Services, Curry School of Education
University of Virginia
Charlottesville, Virginia

PREFACE

Since the publication of the First Edition of *The Injured Athlete*, I have directed The Sports Orthopaedic Center in Charlottesville, Virginia. All of the people I see have athletic or exercise injuries, and my experience with them has influenced the Second Edition of *The Injured Athlete*. As a result, this edition goes far beyond the First Edition as a clinically useful guide for the prevention, diagnosis, and treatment of athletic injuries.

We approach the diagnosis and rehabilitation of injured athletes the "Virginia way." All of the contributors either are or were on the faculty at the University of Virginia, and we all have been influenced by the comprehensive yearly sports medicine meeting held there, *The Art and Science of Sports Medicine*, run by Drs. McCue, Brubaker, and Gieck.

Dr. Joe Gieck, Head Trainer at the University of Virginia and NATA Educator of the Year for 1986, has revised and updated his chapter. In each of the injury chapters, he presents his Rehabilitation Progressions from initial to intermediate to advanced stages.

Ethan Saliba, Assistant Athletic Trainer at the University of Virginia, has written a comprehensive section on the now frequently used electrical modalities.

John Gamble, Head Strength Coach at the University of Virginia, champion power lifter, and the National Strength and Conditioning Association's Strength Coach of the Year for 1985, has written about conditioning programs for the competitive athlete.

Jana Early is the Director of Sports Physical Therapy at the Sports Orthopaedic Center and an advanced back therapist. She describes manual therapy for the injured athlete's spine, including evaluation, rehabilitation progressions, soft tissue mobilization, and intervertebral mobilization techniques.

My mentor in sports medicine, Dr. Frank C. McCue III, is the Team Physician for the University of Virginia. Dr. McCue has added a section on the "sore wrist" to his chapter along with advanced material on carpal instabilities, rehabilitation of the hand, and splinting.

Russell Pate, Director of the Human Performance Laboratory at the University of South Carolina, has added a section on training for distance running to his chapter. He discusses the beginning runner, the fitness runner, the racer, the marathoner, and training for the triathlon.

Dr. Bob Rotella is the Director of Sports Psychology at the University of Virginia and is also well known as the sports psychologist to many professional golfers. He has added to his chapter a section on the psychological attitudes that predispose an athlete to injury and a section on problem patients.

I have revised the preparticipation examination section. Because I see many runners in my practice, I have written about how to examine them and how to evaluate athletic footwear. I also describe how a runner can return "stepwise" to training. In addition, I present detailed descriptions about two special programs for exercising patients: One is Tubics©, an exercise program using a lightweight bicycle inner tube; the other is Poolex©, a pool rehabilitation program for the injured athlete.

In the injury chapters, new information prompted me to rewrite the sections on subacromial impingement, rotator cuff problems and shoulder instabilities, extensor mechanism problems that produce anterior knee pain, arthroscopic surgery for internal derangements of the knee, and anterior cruciate ligament injuries.

A chapter on the leg, ankle, and foot comes last in most books, as it does here, but these problems are seen frequently. In this chapter, I have updated our approach to "shin splints," to "plantar fasciitis," and to matatarsalgia.

Once again, the master of medical illustration, Ron Ervin, has worked his magic. Ron has combined his dynamic illustrations with action photos to depict injury mechanisms, disrupted anatomy, diagnostic methods, and treatments.

Last, but most important, I hope that you learn as much from this book as I have learned from working with the contributors in putting together *The Injured Athlete*.

Daniel N. Kulund, M.D.

PREFACE TO THE FIRST EDITION

In our increasingly athletic society, youths, women, prime-age athletes, older athletes, and handicapped persons are running, swimming, training with weights, and competing in a wide variety of individual, dual, and team sports. Sports medicine, the scientific study and care of people in the context of exercise and sport, has grown with this boom in athletics. Simultaneously, a need has developed for a clinically useful sports medicine book to aid the physician who sees some, many, mostly, or only athletes in his practice, and for other members of the sports medicine team. *The Injured Athlete* has been written to fill this need.

The reader is first shown how to perform a complete preparticipation examination and how to treat the medical problems of athletes. Russell Pate then discusses the principles of training and differences in the training of youths, women, and prime-age and older athletes. Next, Cliff Brubaker describes how to evaluate fitness, and Randy Martin reviews the effects of exercise on the cardiovascular system. After an up-to-date chapter on strength and power training, Professor Töttössy discusses the importance of warming up and provides pictures from which one may design a warm-up program for athletes.

The athletic trainer plays a key role in the rehabilitation of the injured athlete. Joe Gieck describes the trainer's duties, including how to fit protective equipment and the steps in rehabilitating injured athletes. Tom Soos then shows how the trainer uses adhesive tape. There is also a psychological side to athletic injuries, and sports psychologist Bob Rotella details the coping strategies that athletes may use to help in psychological rehabilitation.

The Injured Athlete is foremost a clinically useful guide to the prevention, diagnosis, and treatment of athletic injuries. To this end, Ron Ervin has combined dynamic illustrations and action photographs to depict injury mechanisms, disrupted anatomy, diagnostic methods, and treatment. The injury chapters range from the head to the foot and include a comprehensive chapter on athletic injuries to the elbow, wrist, and hand by Frank McCue and discussions of throwing, running, and cycling. Finally, along with useful tables, the appendices contain the position statements of our American College of Sports Medicine.

Daniel N. Kulund, M.D.

ACKNOWLEDGMENTS

My thanks to Ron Ervin, "the Wizard of Air," for his wonderful illustrations.

Jana Early for her advanced manual therapy and spinal mobilization techniques.

John Gamble for his presentation of the University of Virginia strength programs.

Dr. Joe Gieck for his rehabilitation progressions.

Ethan Saliba, a master of modalities, who detailed the electrical ones.

Professor Miklós Töttössy for sharing his knowledge of athletic conditioning with me.

Eric Fears and Chris Fox, who posed for most of the strength and flexibility pictures.

Jamie Gay, who posed for the rehabilitation pictures.

Dan "Flash" Grogan for taking, developing, and printing the strength and flexibility pictures and most of the rehabilitation pictures, and Buz Goforth for his help.

Chris Dean, Debbie Robinson, Deldora Tuckey, Dr. Steve Early, Lanie Yost, Susan Foreman, Ellen Fox, Merit Brand, Cynthia Lorenzoni, Lou Stephens, Carol Moyers, and Regina Rae, who posed for pictures.

Regina Rae, who typed the manuscript.

Dr. Bob Anderson, Gene Baldwin, Dr. David Brody, Mary Colas, Charlie Feigenoff, Professor Jeff O'Connell, Ed Pierce, Dr. Steve Pohl, Jerry Ratcliffe, and Dr. Austin Sydnor for their help.

My mentors in Sports Orthopaedics: Nicholas Kulund, Dr. A. A. Savastano, and Dr. Frank C. McCue III.

Manuscript Editor Les Hoeltzel.

Sanford Robinson, the "spine of the book" and ever-helpful sponsoring editor for the First Edition and this Second Edition.

CONTENTS

Chapter 1   THE ATHLETE'S PHYSICIAN   1

The Team Physician   2 | Legal Aspects of Sports Medicine   2 |
The Athletic Trainer   4 | Preparticipation Examination   5 |
Emergency Care of Athletic Injuries and Return to the Game   5 |
Explaining Treatment to the Athlete   6 | Releasing Information   6 |
Preseason Examination   6 | Laboratory Tests   29 | Exercise in
Renal Disorders   30 | Paperwork, Permission Slips, and Handouts   30 |
Examining a Runner   30 | How to Return to Running After an In-
jury   34 | Evaluating the Athlete's Footwear   35 | Selecting a
Running Shoe   37 | Other Shoes   39 | Sports Socks   41 |
Shoe Modifications   41 | Caring for Sports Shoes   41 | Learning
About Sports Shoes   41 | Orthotics ("O's")   42 | Balanced Com-
petition (Maturity Matching)   42 | On-the-Field Responsibilities   43 |
Return to Competition   44 | The Young Athlete   44 | The Fe-
male Athlete   46 | The Older Athlete   47

Chapter 2   SPECIAL ATHLETES, MEDICAL PROBLEMS, NUTRITION, AND DRUGS   49

The Handicapped Athlete 49 | The "Special Olympics" 52 |
Ice Skating Therapy 52 | Medical Problems 54 | Sex Before
Sports 60 | The Athlete's Skin 60 | Nutrition 67 | Phar-
macologic Agents 71 | Drug Abuse in Athletics 75

Chapter 3   PRINCIPLES OF TRAINING   81

Russell R. Pate

Physiologic Bases of Exercise 81 | Determinants of Endurance Ex-
ercise Performance 84 | Principles of Training 85 | Stress 87 |
Guidelines for Training the Aerobic System 87 | Specific Training
Techniques 89 | Fitness Programs for Adult Beginners 90 |
Programs for the Elderly 94 | Training the Female Athlete 97 |
Training in Children 101 | Special Problems of Competitive Ath-
letes 108

Chapter 4   STRENGTH AND CONDITIONING FOR THE COMPETITIVE ATHLETE   111

John N. Gamble, Jr.

The Warm-Up 111 | Strength 115 | The Lifting Program 126 |
Free Weights and Machines 127 | Strength-Training Errors 128 |
The Mental Aspect of Weight Training 129 | Conditioning 129 |
Cycle Training (Periodization) 135 | Sport-Specific Strength Train-
ing 137 | Training Injuries 148

Chapter 5   PSYCHOLOGICAL CARE OF THE INJURED ATHLETE   151

Robert J. Rotella

An Athlete's Perception of Injury 151 | Coping with Injury 152 |
Self-Control of Pain 156 | Returning to Competition 159 | The
"Injury-Prone" Athlete 160 | Predisposing Attitudes 161 |
Problem Patients 162

Chapter 6   THE ATHLETIC TRAINER AND REHABILITATION   165

Joe H. Gieck and Ethan N. Saliba

Duties 166 | Playing Field Surfaces 167 | Planning an Athletic
Contest 170 | Athletic Activity in the Heat 171 | Fitting of Pro-
tective Equipment 177 | Taping the Injured Athlete 180 |
Trauma from Acute Injury 183 | Types of Injuries 184 | Treat-
ment of Injury 185 | "ISE" 187 | Electrical Principles 191 |
Electrical Stimulation 196 | Rehabilitation of the Injured Athlete 227 |
Rehabilitation Progressions 234

Chapter 7 MANUAL THERAPY FOR THE ATHLETE'S BACK   241

Jana J. Early

_Evaluation 241 | Treatment of the Acute Injury 242 |
Treatment of the Chronic Back Problem 242 | Soft Tissue Mobiliza-
tions 242 | Intervertebral Joint Mobilization 242 | Home Exer-
cise Program 242 | Evaluation of the Cervical Spine 243 |
Evaluation of the Thoracic Spine 250 | Treatment Modalities for
the Thoracic Spine 251 | Evaluation of the Lumbar Spine 253 |
Sacroiliac Dysfunction 258_

Chapter 8 ATHLETIC INJURIES TO THE HEAD, FACE, AND NECK   267

The Head 267 | The Face 273 | The Neck 287

Chapter 9 THE SHOULDER   301

_Examining the Shoulder 303 | "Backpack Palsy" 304 | Tho-
racic Outlet Problems 305 | The Sternoclavicular Joint 305 |
The Clavicle 306 | Deltoid Strain, Bruised Shoulder, and "Shoul-
der Pointer" 306 | Subacromial Shoulder Pain 307 | "Swim-
mer's Shoulder" 307 | Calcific Tendinitis 309 | Rotator Cuff
Tears 309 | Examining for Subacromial Problems 310 | Treat-
ment of Subacromial Problems 311 | Coracoid Injuries 314 |
Shoulder Separations 323 | Acromioclavicular Arthritis 326 |
Bicipital Tendinitis 327 | Dislocation of the Biceps Tendon 328 |
Rupture of the Long Head of the Biceps Tendon 329 | Partial Avul-
sion of the Glenoid Labrum in Throwing Athletes 330 | Acute Dis-
location of the Shoulder 331 | Recurrent Anterior Dislocations of
the Shoulder 333 | Multidirectional Instability 340 | Inferior
Instability 341 | The Humerus 341 | "Little League Shoul-
der" 341 | Tackler's Exostosis 342 | Tennis Shoulder 343 |
Scapular Pain 346_

Chapter 10 THE ELBOW, WRIST, AND HAND   357

Frank C. McCue III

The Elbow 357 | The Wrist and the Hand 371

Chapter 11 THE TORSO, HIP, AND THIGH   405

_Chest Injuries 405 | Abdominal Injuries in Athletics 409 | Pel-
vic and Hip Injuries 421 | Thigh Injuries 428_

Chapter 12 THE KNEE   435

_Anatomy 435 | Examining an Athlete's Injured Knee 441 |
Running and the Knee 443 | Cutting 444 | Kicking 444 |_

Bicycling 445 | The Knee Extensor Mechanism 446 | Intra-Articular Disorders 466 | Early Postoperative Knee Rehabilitation 481 | Acute Tears of Knee Ligaments 484 | Knee Instabilities 494 | The Dislocated Knee 505

Chapter 13   THE LEG, ANKLE, AND FOOT   513

The Leg 513 | The Ankle 521 | The Feet 536

Appendix 1   SPORTS MEDICINE JOURNALS   565

Appendix 2   SPORTS MEDICINE ORGANIZATIONS   567

Appendix 3   NATIONAL SPORTS ORGANIZATIONS   569

Appendix 4   SPORTS ASSOCIATIONS FOR HANDICAPPED ATHLETES   571

Index   573

THE INJURED ATHLETE

CHAPTER

1

The Athlete's Physician

As athletes of all ages have entered sports in recent years, athletic diversity has become the norm (Table 1-1). Sport beckons young people, prime age athletes, women, older people, the handicapped, and even those who may be suffering from disease. A sports physician will be asked to make evaluations and to treat patients according to the type of athlete, the particular sport, and the athlete's goals; to design fitness programs; and to give advice on cardiovascular fitness, strength training, warming up, and protective gear. The prevention, treatment, and rehabilitation of athletic injuries, including musculoskeletal problems, will be fundamental to one's practice.

The athlete is generally a healthy and well-motivated person. However, an injury that might be insignificant to another patient may be a serious handicap to him, and for this reason the sports physician must appreciate the value the athlete places on sport. For example, an athlete told to stop exercising and to rest will often resist this advice and seek help elsewhere, for "REST" in athletic medicine means to *Resume Exercise below the Soreness Threshold.* Depending on his sport, the athlete may avoid pain-producing activities by decreasing his mileage, by switching to another swim stroke, or by using a temporary orthosis. With an injury to a lower extremity, he may stay fit by exercising in a pool or on a bicycle with his sound leg clipped to a pedal. In general, slings and casts are to be avoided because immobilization reduces proprioception and increases rehabilitation time.

The rehabilitation of an injured athlete is both physical and psychological; unlike a nonathlete, he soon is exposed to the same forces that caused

Table 1-1   THE SPECTRUM OF SPORT AND PHYSICAL RECREATION

Acrobatics	Martial arts
Aerobic dancing	Modern pentathlon
Alpine skiing	Motorcycling
Angling	Mountaineering
Archery	Orienteering
Auto racing	Parachuting
Badminton	Racket sports
Ballooning	Rhythmic gymnastics
Baseball	Road running
Basketball	Rock climbing
Bass fishing (tournament	Roller skating
style)	Rowing
Baton twirling	Rugby league
Billiards and snooker	Rugby union
Bobsledding	Sailing
Bowling	Scuba diving
Boxing	Shooting
Camping	Skateboarding
Canoeing	Skating
Caving	Skiing
Cheerleading	Ski jumping
Cricket	Soccer
Croquet	Softball
Cross-country skiing	Speed skating
Curling	Squash rackets
Cycling	Surfing
Dance—ballet, modern	Swimming
Diving	Synchronized swimming
Equestrian sports	Table tennis
Fencing	Tackle football
Field hockey	Team handball
Figure skating	Tenpin bowling
Fishing	Tobogganing
Flying	Track and field
Gliding	Trampolining
Golf	Triathlon
Gymnastics	Tubics
Handball	Tug-of-war
Hang gliding	Ultimate frisbee
Hiking	Volleyball
Hockey (field, roller, and	Water polo
ice)	Water skiing
Horseshoe pitching	Weight lifting
Hurling	Wind surfing (board sail-
Ice dancing	ing)
Jogging	Wrestling—freestyle,
Judo	Greco–Roman
Kayak	Wrist wrestling
Lacrosse	Yoga
Luge	

his injury. His flexibility and strength, therefore, must be greater when he returns to practice and competition than they were before treatment. His rehabilitation will be aided by his understanding of exercise and by his willingness to work hard. The athlete expects, and should be given, an explanation of his injury and the options for treatment and should be told how he may help his recovery. Psychological rehabilitation is also important, although psychological scars may not be as apparent as physical scars. This effort will be reinforced by systematic desensitization techniques that allow the athlete to relax and to concentrate when he returns to his sport.

THE TEAM PHYSICIAN

The team physician may be a doctor who takes a turn sitting on the bench at Friday-night football games. Occasionally, he may be a parent of one of the players and may attend games and practices, but only as long as his child is on the team. This is not desirable, for the team physician should be under contract to the school. He should be responsible for the athletes' health care and committed to setting up comprehensive programs for preseason evaluation, conditioning, health education, and injury prevention, treatment, and rehabilitation. He is usually a generalist because most problems in sports medicine are common ones, such as upper respiratory infections.[19, 39] The team doctor will, however, need specialist consultants to assist him in treating injuries (Table 1-2).

LEGAL ASPECTS OF SPORTS MEDICINE

Current trends in litigation have made the team physician very vulnerable to legal liability; in fact, awards of up to $2 million have been rendered in sports injury cases. Because the team physician may have to make fast decisions under pressure, he needs to exercise good judgment, to be conscientious, and to follow established guidelines to avoid liability problems.[24, 32, 37, 45]

Table 1-2 THE SPORTS MEDICINE TEAM

The athlete
Athletic trainer
Chiropractor
Coach
Dentist
Equipment manager
Exercise leader
Exercise physiologist
Fitness instructor
Health educator
Kinesiologist
Masseur or masseuse
Nutritionist
Officials
Physical educator
Physician
Podiatrist
Sports physical therapist
Sports psychologist
Strength and conditioning specialist

Negligence

When the physician treats athletes, a doctor–patient relationship is established between him and the members of the team under his care. He must treat the athletes as he would his own private patients. It is immaterial under the law whether diagnoses and treatments are provided for a fee or *gratis*. Moreover the statute of limitations is no safeguard against action by a minor because a suit for negligence can be withheld until the young athlete reaches maturity, at which time he may file suit.

Obviously, sports injuries are common and may be devastating. In one instance, a high school quarterback was tackled on a "quarterback sneak." He lay on the field, and his coach, suspecting a neck injury, checked the young man's grip and found it functioning. The coach then asked eight young men to carry the athlete to the sidelines, which they did without the aid of a stretcher. There the athlete was found to be quadriplegic. Consequently, both the coach and the doctor were found negligent: the coach for failing to wait for the doctor to come onto the field, and the doctor for failing to act promptly after the injury.[45]

The team physician may become involved in legal action through tort liability or direct malpractice suits. Because most courts do not hold coaches and trainees responsible for the diagnosis and treatment of sports injuries, this responsibility must be assumed by a physician. Hence, the team physician will be the major defendant in most cases of litigation. These cases are mostly "tort liability" ones, where liability for personal injury is allegedly a result of the defendant's negligence. Currently, there is a trend to expand the areas in which tort liability is applicable and to increase the size of tort awards. For this reason, the team physician should take every precaution to avoid becoming a defendant in a tort liability case, and he should have liability insurance that covers athletic contests.

The principal charge against which the team physician will have to defend is that of negligence. *Negligence* is defined as failure to act as a prudent physician would under similar circumstances. An example of negligence would be failure to follow standard procedures and established methods for treating an injury. Negligence may consist of inaction as well as action. Actionable negligence comprises four elements, and a cause of action in tort requires proof that all four elements be present: [1] that the defendant had a duty to act to avoid unreasonable risk to others; [2] that the defendant breached said duty with failure to observe that duty; [3] that failure to observe the duty was the proximate cause of the damage; and [4] that actual damage or injury occurred.

A doctor is not an ensurer of the success of all treatments and procedures. He is not held liable for all adverse results. Thus even if an adverse result occurs despite his using a treatment that others might disagree with, if his action conforms to the standards of good medical practice in his community he should not be held liable. However, the standard of care is measured in terms of the doctor's specialty, and the conduct of a physician specializing in sports injuries who treats such an injury could be judged negligent even though the same conduct by a general practitioner might not be.

Legal defenses against the charge of negligence include *assumption of risk* and *contributory negligence*. An athlete, for example, assumes some risk when undertaking to wrestle or to play tackle football, and athletes may act in a negligent manner, thereby contributing to an injury.

To help avoid tort liability, the physician should do the following.

Follow established guidelines.

Have a contract drawn up with the school.

Secure an athletic trainer.

Design and conduct a thorough preparticipation physical examination with attention to disqualifying defects.

Use sound judgment for allowing athletes to return to competition after injury or illness.

Institute proper care early if an injury occurs.

Seek informed consent for treatment.

Be careful about releasing information.

The Contract

When a physician becomes a team doctor, it is often a labor of love. He should, however, insist on an agreement with school officials that spells out his responsibilities. The school must, in turn, vest the physician with the authority to make medical judgments relating to students' participation in school sports. Since the health of the athletes will be the physician's prime concern, his must be the final word on all medical decisions.

Good communication is important, and for this reason the team physician should meet with athletes and their parents before the start of the season. A suit-conscious public may have the notion that protective equipment always prevents injury and may therefore charge negligence if an athlete is injured. This notion can be dispelled at the preseason meeting if the limitations of protective equipment are explained. Athletes and parents should also be told how the doctor, trainer, coaches, and athletes propose to reduce the chance of injury.

At this time the team physician should also meet with the coaches to establish guidelines for injury control and to assist in the development of conditioning programs. Dangerous coaching practices, such as the teaching of head tackling and butt blocking, should be forbidden. Descriptive terms such as "punishment drill," "crucifixion," "suicide," "hamburger," "meatgrinder," and "gauntlet" are best avoided.[4] Athletes must be made aware of the risks of participation, and the mechanics of catastrophic injury should be clearly demonstrated and explained.

THE ATHLETIC TRAINER

The athletic trainer is a key person in the high school athletic program, and if the school does not have a trainer one should be recruited. The trainer's sole concern is safety of the athletes. He carries out injury-control programs and attends practices and games, activities that the team physician often is unable to perform. The trainer fits protective equipment, makes sure it is worn in practices and games, and checks it at least once a week, since the equipment occasionally loosens or parts break. The same good-quality equipment worn in games should be worn in practices. It is also the trainer's duty to be sure that the playing facilities and gymnasium equipment are properly cared for, and he shares with the physician the responsibility to point out dangers in practice areas, on the playing field and in the gymnasium, that may be overlooked by others. The trainer administers first aid with the aim of keeping mi-

Table 1-3   THE SPORTS MEDICINE CURRICULUM

Anatomy	Officiating and rules
Biomechanics	Physiology
Cardiac rehabilitation	Preparticipation examination
Cardiopulmonary resuscitation	nation
Drugs in athletics	Principles of training
Emergency medical care	Protective equipment
Environmental stress	Special problems of
Evaluating fitness	young, female, older,
Exercise physiology	and handicapped athletes
Kinesiology	letes
Injury—prevention, treatment, and rehabilitation	Sports psychology
	Strength training
	Tactics
Medical problems	Transportation of the injured athlete
Nutrition	Warm-up

nor injuries from causing major disability. He should also recognize more serious injuries and take proper first aid steps to avoid compounding such injuries.

The trainer works under, and follows the directives of, the team physician. For this reason, he is almost always regarded as an agent of the team physician; thus negligence on his part is often imputed to the doctor. Good rapport between the physician and the trainer is essential, and guidelines must be clearly established and respected.

PREPARTICIPATION EXAMINATION

The preparticipation examination is an important duty of the team physician, and tort liability may be applied to this procedure. The examination includes a complete history that covers previous illnesses and allergies and that will serve as a base for medical records and may affect later treatment. The examination should be thorough, in accord with guidelines for the examination of athletes, and the findings should be disclosed to the athlete, the athlete's parents, and the athlete's family physician.

Courts have noted that athletes erroneously have been found physically qualified to participate in sports.[21, 25] The physician should avoid guaranteeing or giving assurance that it will be safe for a team member to participate in a sport. Instead he may record, ''I can find no medical reason why the athlete should not participate,'' or, ''The examination failed to disclose anything that would prevent the youngster from participating in athletics.''

If the physician decides that a disqualifying defect, such as one kidney, one eye, or one testicle, warrants that an athlete not participate in a sport, he should not allow anyone to persuade him to change his decision. A defect occasionally may be found in a youngster who has participated in athletics since grade school, and the athlete and his parents may be unable to understand why the defect is now considered disqualifying. Although they may offer to sign a release, the law gives *the parents no authority to release future claims on behalf of the child.* The parents, family doctor, athlete, and school or college should be informed of the findings and the physician's decision. If, contrary to the physician's recommendation, the athlete is allowed to participate in the sport, the physician should repeat his objection to continued participation.

EMERGENCY CARE OF ATHLETIC INJURIES AND RETURN TO THE GAME

The team physician should be available during practice sessions and be present at games, alert for injuries. He should be well versed in the proper care of major injuries, such as those to the head, eyes, neck, and significant musculoskeletal injuries.[12,43] Proper aids, such as backboards and splints, must be available. There should be no hesitation if an athlete needs to be carried from the field on a stretcher. Every athlete should understand that leaving the field on a stretcher is not a sign of weakness.

The team physician often will have to make on-the-spot decisions as to whether an athlete who has been injured during a game should be allowed to continue playing.[18] An overcautious appraisal may mean loss for the team. If, however, the risk of allowing an injured athlete to reenter a game is taken, the injury may worsen and result in permanent harm to the athlete. *''When in doubt, keep the athlete out.''* The team physician must never let anyone pressure him into allowing an athlete who has not fully recovered from an illness or an injury to play. His prime concern must be the health of those under his care. To prevent athletic injuries from going undetected, a firm and inflexible rule should be established that all injuries, no matter how trivial, be reported to the trainer or team physician. An early, accurate diagnosis will ensure prompt treatment and faster recovery.

Transportation for injured athletes, including routes to and from playing and practice fields, should be arranged ahead of need. If an athlete suffers a major injury during a game and must be taken to the hospital, the team physician should accompany him. If the injury is not life-threatening, however, the trainer may accompany the injured athlete; the physician should remain at the field in case a major injury does occur. In most cases, emergency medical technicians will be especially helpful in providing for the care and transportation of injured athletes or ill spectators.

EXPLAINING TREATMENT TO THE ATHLETE

To care properly for an athlete's injuries and to avoid claims of negligence, the nature of the injury and the treatment alternatives must be explained to the athlete and his parents. This information should be sufficient for them to make an intelligent choice as to whether treatment is necessary. The dangers, if any, and the advantages of alternative treatments should be carefully laid out. If drugs are needed, their effects should be described and any alternative measures explained. A new treatment must not be implemented without a full explanation to the athlete and his parents, for a court may regard such treatment as experimentation.

X-rays of the injured area must be taken because their absence may be regarded as negligence. Good medical records are important, and athletes must be followed closely with full control over their treatment. Treatment should not be prematurely ended, but, if an athlete terminates treatment before being medically discharged, he must be persuaded to resume treatment. Failure to follow up an athlete who is under treatment may be construed by the courts as abandonment of treatment. Moreover, athletes should not be allowed to return to competition in any sport after an injury or illness unless recovery is complete. If a case is a difficult one, advice should be sought from a consultant. No firm promise or guarantee of result should be given, nor any assurance that there will be no residual limitations or disabilities.

RELEASING INFORMATION

The doctor–patient relationship is a confidential one, and medical information about the athlete's condition should not be disclosed without his specific written consent. Even with consent, the physician may be subject to liability if his statements turn out to be inaccurate. If an opinion is stated with the knowledge that another will act upon it, the giver of the opinion may be held responsible for damage incurred because of the inaccuracy of his opinion, even though it was rendered in good faith and gratuitously.[42] If consent is given for release of information, any disclosure should be limited to the objective facts of the injury, leaving the team with the burden of determining the current fitness of the athlete.

Obviously, the position of team physician is a demanding one, with liability potential. To render tort liability less likely, the physician must use good judgment, follow established guidelines, and be aware of the latest research and developments in the field of sports medicine. The responsible team physician should also educate athletes and their parents, coaches, and medical personnel about good health practices and the prevention and care of athletic injuries.

PRESEASON EXAMINATION

On first entry into a sports program, each athlete needs a comprehensive history and physical examination.[7, 9, 26, 33] The examination establishes baselines for later comparisons, uncovers deficiencies, and evaluates limitations relative to the given sport. The team physician can locate and quantify inherent or acquired musculoskeletal weaknesses that may predispose the athlete to injury. Also, the injury-prone athlete can be identified, as can those who have histories of concussion or heat stroke, rendering them more susceptible to these conditions.

The examination should be performed before the season starts to allow time to arrange further evaluations and to design and implement exercise programs to remedy deficiencies.[40] When undue risks are anticipated for athletes with potentially disqualifying conditions, the athletes should be counseled and guided into alternative activities. Balanced competition requires that youths be matched according to their levels of maturity.

The preseason examination is a course in health education, especially when youngsters with asthma, diabetes mellitus, or a convulsive disorder are being advised. These children need highly individualized examinations with explanations of how exercise can benefit their asthma or diabetes and how they can help to control the medical condition.

How often should preseason examinations be conducted? As noted above, a comprehensive medical examination should precede the entry of a young athlete, such as a high school freshman, into a sports program. After this examination, problem-oriented medical attention is appropriate, with a check on intervening problems before each new sports season. In this continuing medical care, the emphasis should be on quality, not frequency.

When should the preseason examination be conducted? A good time is 4 to 6 weeks before conditioning programs or preseason practice begins, because early examinations allow time to obtain consultations and accomplish treatment. There are three types of such examinations: the *individual* examination, the *mass* examination, and the *group* examination. A thorough, private individual examination by the athlete's family doctor can provide an excellent assessment of fitness for sport because the doctor knows the youngster's medical history. He may, however, be unfamiliar with the medical aspects of sport, and hence be inclined to be conservative. In other instances, the doctor may pass over health conditions that should limit participation in certain sports. As doctors learn more about sports medicine, better individual preseason examinations will result, reducing the potential for injury as greater understanding of the physical requirements for particular sports events is acquired.

Each year, millions of young athletes undergo hasty and superficial mass examinations by volunteer doctors in noisy, crowded locker rooms. These examinations endanger the athlete, generating a low opinion of doctors and the importance of health care and physical fitness. The place for the examination is usually determined by local conditions, but ideally the examination will be conducted in an appropriate setting by doctors who are trained to administer a thorough examination and who check for those factors that may predispose a young athlete to injury or illness.

Because of the large number of athletes who must be examined and the limited number of physicians qualified to conduct such examina-

tions, a carefully organized group examination with a team approach is recommended. The team should consist of doctors, trainers, nurses, and others who may assist with various routines, such as maintaining discipline and directing traffic. The doctors may include specialists, generalists, residents, and medical students.

The group examination usually is conducted in a large area, such as a physical therapy department.[5] Audiology booths may be used when absolute quiet is needed, as during the heart examination. Boys should wear shorts and girls halter tops or swimsuit tops. An overall health inventory is the first item to be completed. After weights are recorded, the athletes will proceed through a series of stations labeled with large signs. These will include medical, dental, eye and ear, musculoskeletal, orthopedic, and review stations. When the examinations have been completed, the team physician will confer with the school nurse and coaches to review and analyze the findings.

The History for the Preparticipation Examination

Because it will be an important part of the athlete's medical record throughout his career, the history taken at the preparticipation examination must be thorough. A number of typical questions are listed on page 8. Answers should be supplied by the athlete and his parents, and information may also be obtained from the family physician. An instructor will explain the questions, and parents should assist in filling out the form to be certain that all questions are answered properly and no important omissions occur. Any circled answers or "yes" responses should be explained or described. Because there is no standard history form, questions will differ depending on the group examined and the purpose of the examination.

Preseason Examination of the Eyes

Poor vision may account for dropped passes, similar errors, and poor performance, but the athlete may not know that his vision is abnormal. The Titmus machine (Figure 1-1), which may be

(Text continues on p. 10)

PREPARTICIPATION EXAMINATION

Name of Student _____ Grade _____ Age _____

Address _____ Telephone No. _____

Parent's Name and Address: _____

_____

Parent's Phone: Home _____ Work _____
Alternate
Emergency _____
Number

Family Physician _____ Telephone _____

I. Emergency Medical Treatment Form

I, the parent of _____ , give permission for emergency medical treatment of my child for illness or accident if I cannot first be contacted.

Date _____ Parent or Guardian _____

Emergency Phone _____

II. History (To Be Completed by Parent or Family Physician)

1. Has had injuries requiring medical attention	Yes	No
2. Has had illness lasting more than a week	Yes	No
3. Is under a physician's care now	Yes	No
4. Takes medication now	Yes	No
5. Wears glasses/contact lenses	Yes	No
6. Has had surgical operation	Yes	No
7. Has been in hospital (except for tonsillectomy)	Yes	No
8. Do you know any reason why this individual should not participate in all sports?	Yes	No

Please explain any "Yes" answers to the above questions:

_____

_____

_____

_____

9. Has had complete poliomyelitis immunization by oral vaccine (Sabin) or   Yes   No
   inoculations (Salk) Date _____

10. Has had primary series of tetanus toxoid (DPT or DT) and a booster within   Yes   No
    the last year.

Date: _____ Signed: _____

(Parent or Physician)

**III. Emergency Medical
Treatment Form**

I, the parent of _____ , give permission for emergency medical treatment of my child
for illness or accident if I cannot first be contacted.
Date _____ Parent or Guardian_____
                        Emergency Phone_____

IV. Physical Examination (To Be Completed by Physician)
Height: _____   Weight: _____   % Body Fat: _____
Blood Pressure: _____/_____   Pulse:
Eyes R 20/   Lt 20/   ;   Pupils Equal: Yes   No
Ears
Nose
Mouth
Throat
Skin
Lymph Nodes
Heart
Lungs
Abdomen:
    Liver
    Spleen
    Hernia
Genitalia
Neurologic
Musculoskeletal:
    Scoliosis
    Shoulder Strength:
        Abduction R
                      L
        Adduction R
                      L
    Knee Strength on Orthotron at speed 3 or on knee table
        R Quadriceps
            Hamstrings
        L Quadriceps
            Hamstrings
    Back Flexibility
        Distance of knee from chest with
        heel to hip. R
                          L
        Distance opposite knee from exam
        table. R
                    L
    Hamstring Flexibility
        R
        L

(continued)

**III. Emergency Medical
Treatment Form** *(Continued)*

Ankle Flexibility
      Distance of heel from ground R
                                        L

Laboratory Tests:
    Blood test
    Urinalysis

V. I certify that I have on this date examined this student and find him/her physically able to compete in the supervised activities that are not NOT CROSSED OUT BELOW.

Baseball	Field Hockey	Lacrosse	Tennis	Others
Basketball	Football	Soccer	Track	
Cheerleader	Golf	Softball	Volleyball	
Cross-Country	Gymnastics	Swimming	Wrestling	

Date: _____   Signed: _____

found in a Department of Motor Vehicles, should be used for vision tests because youths with poor vision have been known to memorize the Snellen chart to bluff their way through an informal examination

An athlete who has only one useful eye is best excluded from contact sports. Athletes with significant amblyopia should also be barred because trauma to the better eye could be devastating. Athletes with high degrees of myopia may be susceptible to retinal detachment, and this tendency may be brought out by contact sports. Some myopic persons have considerable chorioretinal degeneration, but others with an equivalent my-

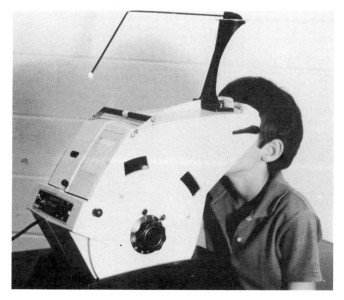

Figure 1-1 The Titmus machine is used for vision testing.

opia have ostensibly normal retinas. Thus, the visually deficient athlete's eyes must be closely examined, and the procedure should include a dilated fundus examination for any spectacle-dependent myopic person. Angioid streaks of retinal degeneration are warnings of an increased danger of detachment, and contact sports are not permitted after repair of retinal detachment.

Preseason Examination of the Teeth

Preventive dentistry includes a mouth mirror examination to reduce the chances that a player will be lost during the season because of a toothache. The preparticipation examination is also a good occasion to check for temporomandibular joint imbalances and to start a mouthguard program.

Preseason Musculoskeletal Examination

The musculoskeletal system examination should draw attention to those areas most prone to injury. Blyth and Mueller found that 46% of all injuries to high school football players were injuries to the lower extremity; 24% to the upper extremity; 13% to the trunk; 13% to the head and neck; and less than 1% internal.[6] More specifically, 19% of the injuries were at the knee; 15% at the ankle; 8% at the shoulder; and 8% involved the hand. Obviously, these areas should be carefully examined because they are high risk for injury. Signs of old injury should not be overlooked because weak links in the limbs may increase the potential for new injury.

Neck

Neck length should be measured with a tape measure from the occiput to the vertebra prominens, which is the spinous process of C-7. The neck circumference is then measured just below the larynx and the neck motion checked. The athlete first must lower his chin to his chest with his mouth closed, because an open mouth will add about 15° to the flexion. If there is a gap of one fingerwidth between the athlete's chin and chest, there will be 10° of restricted motion.

To check neck extension, the athlete should lean his head backwards until his forehead is parallel to the ceiling, a position that yields 35° to 50° of neck extension. For lateral flexion testing, the athlete should bend his head toward his shoulder without shrugging. This measurement depends on the athlete's musculature, which can block the movement, but 40° to 45° of lateral flexion is desirable. For measurement of neck rotation, the athlete should turn his neck as far as he can to each side.

Shoulder

In the preparticipation setting, the shoulder examination is a general one; however, when specific problems such as impingement, rotator cuff tear, or instability are suspected, specific examinations are added, as described in Chapter 9.

Prior subluxation or dislocation may account for apprehension during throwing or a feeling that the arm has suddenly "gone dead." In such cases, x-ray films may show a compression fracture in the humeral head (a Hill–Sach lesion) or calcification at the anteroinferior part of the labrum that may indicate a labral tear (Bankart lesion).

The athlete may say that his shoulder "pops" and "grinds." These sounds may indicate a deranged acromioclavicular joint or a torn rotator cuff. "Pops," "snaps," or "clunks" may signify that a torn glenoid labrum is being caught between the humeral head and the glenoid or that the biceps tendon is subluxing.

The character and location of pain may aid the examiner in arriving at a diagnosis. A deep ache at night may indicate a rotator cuff tear, whereas a stabbing or burning pain is more characteristic of bursitus or tendonitis.

The athlete's normal shoulder should always be examined and compared to the injured one. The examination of an athlete's shoulder may be more difficult than that of a nonathlete's because the athlete's muscles are often hypertrophied. Atrophy, however, will be more evident to the examiner. The examiner checks the shoulder with the athlete standing, supine, and then prone. With the athlete standing, he observes for shoulder drop and muscle atrophy. The right shoulder of a right-handed person is usually lower than his left one. The athlete is then asked to abduct his shoulders while the examiner feels the inferior angle of each scapula. Normally, the scapula will start to move upward and outward significantly at about 90°. In contrast to the normal smooth movement, the athlete will hike a painful, weak, or injured shoulder. The examiner can next get a good idea about the athlete's general shoulder strength and shoulder well-being by having him abduct and adduct his arm against resistance (Figure 1-2 A, B).

The examiner records internal rotation of the shoulder by having the athlete reach behind and touch himself as high on his spine as he can with his thumb. Next, he places his hands on his hips and tightens his shoulder muscles to accentuate the posterior shoulder muscles. Throwing athletes will commonly have a hypertrophied teres minor. The examiner feels for tenderness of these posterior muscles. The athlete then pushes against a wall to see if this produces a prominence or winging of the scapula (Figure 1-3A). Winging indicates a weak serratus anterior muscle, injury to the long thoracic nerve, or both. The acromioclavicular joint is close to the surface and

easily palpated. Pain may be elicited from this joint when the arm is crossed over the chest or horizontally adducted acrosss the body to mimic the follow-through motion of throwing.

With the athlete supine, he abducts his arm to 90° with his elbow bent. The examiner then presses gently at the wrist to rotate both shoulders externally and compares the range of the shoulders. A throwing athlete's shoulder will usually have more external rotation and less internal rotation than a nonthrowing athlete's shoulder. In addition, the shoulders of athletes who do heavy bench presses will often show decreased internal rotation (Figure 1-3B). When the examiner finds these restrictions, he can prescribe corrective exercises. Finally, with the athlete prone and his arm hanging over the side of the table, the examiner holds the scapula fixed and abducts the shoulder to 90°. By externally rotating and internally rotating the shoulder, he may notice contractures of the glenohumeral joint. Further, in this position the shoulder is relaxed and the rotator cuff can be palpated easily.

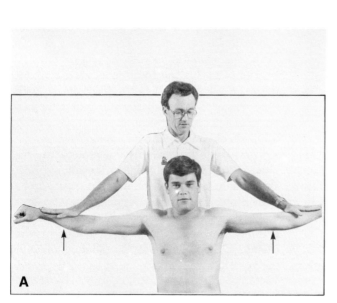
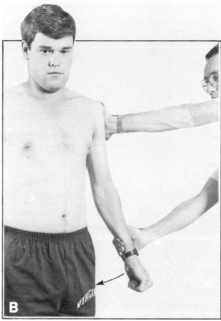

Figure 1-2   To determine general shoulder strength, the examiner resists abduction **(A)** and then resists adduction **(B).**

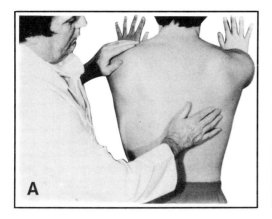
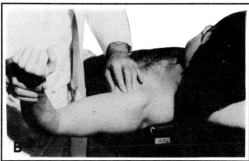

Figure 1-3 The examiner feels for winging of the scapula as the athlete does a wall push-up **(A).** With the athlete supine, he checks for limited external rotation of the shoulder **(B).**

Elbow

The carrying angle of the elbow is usually about 20° of valgus. Some flexion deformity will usually be found in the elbows of pitchers, tennis players, and boxers, and even a Little League baseball pitcher's forearm may lack full supination.

Back

For a back examination, the athlete should bend forward, a position that normally produces a good curve to the spine (Figure 1-4A). If the athlete has tight hamstrings, his lower back will flatten.

The distance between C-7 and S-1 is measured while the athlete is standing straight. The athlete fully flexes forward, and the change in distance between the two points is measured—usually a difference of about 10 cm (4 in). A measurement of less than 10 cm is a sign of decreased flexibility of the lower back, and if the bending measurement remains about the same as the upright one, ankylosing spondylitis should be suspected.

A sit-and-reach test may be used to determine general spinal flexibility. Lordosis (swayback) increases an athlete's susceptibility to lower back strain; when this condition appears, postural exercises are prescribed to help remedy the lordotic posture. The physician checks for leg-length inequality by resting his hands on the athlete's iliac crests and noting whether his hands are at the same level (Figure 1-4B).

Scoliosis

The preparticipation examination is a good occasion to screen for scoliosis or spinal curvature. This condition is seen mostly in 9- to 14-year-old girls, who may even have a substantial curve that their parents may not have noticed. Because secondary curves may balance the head in line with the pelvis, the spine may not, at first glance, appear crooked. The early discovery of scoliosis is essential so that proper bracing and, when necessary, surgery can be done to prevent large curves that may affect cardiopulmonary function and decrease life expectancy.

When checking for scoliosis, ascertain that the shoulders are level before checking elbow height. Waist and flank symmetry are observed, and the subject then bends forward to have the alignment of the spinous processes and the symmetry of the thorax checked. Curves of less than 15° should not limit a youngster's activities. But when a curve exceeds 20°, especially in the lumbar region, contact sports such as football or tumbling may lead to further back trouble. Although scoliosis may produce some disability later in life,

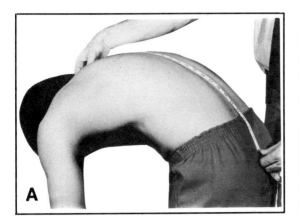 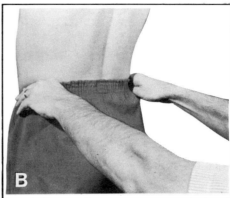

Figure 1-4   The length of the athlete's spine as he stands is compared with that as he bends over **(A)**. A leg-length discrepancy may be found during a check for pelvic tilt **(B)**.

the activity of the young competitor need not be restricted except for contact sports because future problems may bear no relation to earlier sports activities. Youngsters with large curves may wear a scoliosis brace to prevent progression of the curvature. The brace may be removed for bathing and exercise and also for swimming. Full athletics may be permitted with the athlete wearing the brace except for contact sports, in which a brace may be a hazard to opponents. Brace-free athletic participation promotes well-adjusted and physically fit youngsters and need not lead to an increase in the scoliotic curve. The development of better muscle tone through athletics may well hinder curve progression, especially if sport is combined with free gymnastic exercises designed to counteract the curve.

Youngsters with vertebral epiphysitis (Scheuermann's disease) have standing lateral spine films that show vertebral wedging and undulation of their vertebral end-plates. The wedging produces a round back deformity that may be progressive. These youngsters should avoid activities like the butterfly stroke and bench presses, which develop the pectoral muscles and act to increase the humpback. Progression of the deformity is combated by postural and back extensor strengthening exercises and by bracing, when needed.

Hips

Hip flexor strength may be tested with the athlete in a sitting position with arms crossed so that he cannot press down on the examining table. He then lifts his knee against the examiner's resistance while the examiner tries to break the athlete's hip flexion manually. In addition to rating the strength of hip flexion, this test reflects muscular strength around the knee. The examiner then checks for hip adductor tightness (Figure 1-5A) by abducting the athlete's hips without hiking them. When the knee and toes pointing toward the ceiling, each leg should abduct about 45°.

Daily sitting and riding in cars tightens hip flexors, and this can be corrected by stretching. With one knee bent onto the chest, the athlete's other knee is allowed to flex over the table edge. Refusal of the lowered knee to flex to 90°, with some extension of the knee instead, connotes hip flexor tightness. Such tightness resides in the rectus femoris (Figure 1-5B, C), which crosses both the hip and knee joints. Hip flexor tightness may also be tested with the athlete prone. The athlete first maximally flexes his knee, then the examiner passively flexes the knee further to see if the anterior-superior iliac spine on the same side rises. This normally occurs at about 130° of knee flex-

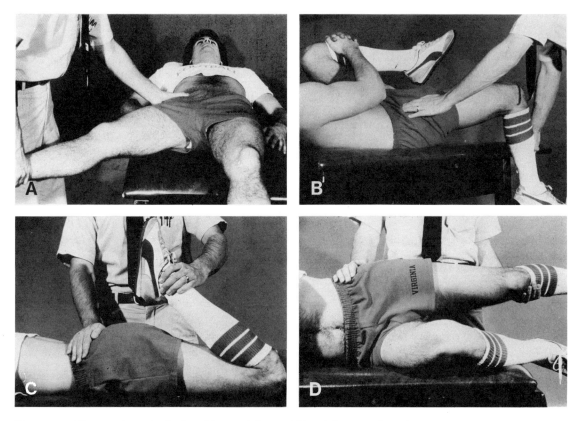

Figure 1-5   The examiner checks for adductor tightness **(A)**, a tight rectus femoris **(B, C)**, and a tight iliotibial band **(D)**.

ion, but if the pelvis rises earlier this indicates that the rectus femoris is tight.

Iliotibial Tract

The iliotibial tract courses from the pelvis to the tibia. In a runner, tightness of this band may lead to lateral hip and knee pain. To test for tightness, the athlete must lie on his side with the tested limb raised (Figure 1-5D). The back is flattened by flexing the lower hip and the tested knee then flexed to 90°, the hip extended, and the knee pressed down toward the table. If the band is not tight, the knee should reach the table without extending. Alternatively, the lower knee may be flexed, with the tested limb allowed to drop. The foot will normally fall below the level of the table if the band is not tight.

Knee

The athlete's hamstrings demand evaluation because tightness or weakness promotes muscle pulls. Tight hamstrings stimulate patella problems, such as tendinitis and chondromalacia, and hinder easy knee extension, causing the knee to follow the path of least resistance into injurious rotary movements.

A neutral pelvis position is needed for hamstring testing, but tight hip flexors will arch the lower back and tilt the pelvis anteriorly. To establish a neutral position, place a pillow under the athlete's thigh to flatten his lower back. The opposite thigh is placed flat on the table to fix the pelvis and to keep it from rotating. The tested hip is flexed to 90°, and the athlete then actively extends the knee (Figure 1-6A), aiming for 180° of knee extension.

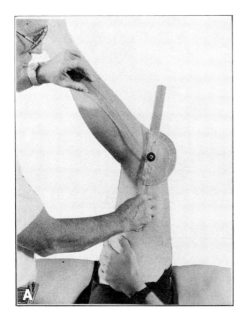
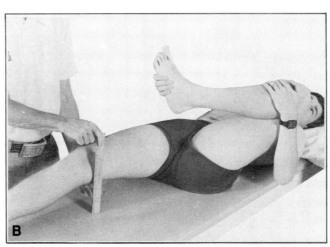

Figure 1-6   The examiner measures hamstring flexibility with a goniometer **(A).** He checks for iliopsoas flexibility by having the athlete pull the opposite knee toward his chest and his heel toward his hip and then measures the distance from the back of the tested knee to the table **(B).**

To test for tightness in an iliopsoas, have the athlete bring his opposite knee to his chest and his heel to his hip. Measure the distance from the knee to the table (Figure 1-6B).

Examine the athlete's ligaments for laxity and check the knee for bowlegs, knock-knees, and recurvatum. Note the patella position and inspect its tracking. Then measure the thigh circumference about 18 cm above the knee joint and also around the kneecap (Figure 1-7A). If there is a difference of more than 2.5 cm (1 in) in the circumference of the thighs, a knee strengthening program is advisable. General knee strength can be estimated by resisting hip flexion (Figure 1-7B). Measure external rotation of the hip as well (Figure 1-8A); if this is limited, the athlete's knee will be more susceptible to injury during cutting maneuvers.

Ankle

A lack of ankle dorsiflexion freedom predisposes the athlete to inversion sprains. Ankle motion should range from 10° to 20° dorsiflexion to about 50° plantar flexion. Dorsiflexion is first tested with the knee flexed to 90° to measure the soleus component of the heel cord. The knee is then fully extended and ankle dorsiflexion retested to measure the gastrocnemius portion. To test ankle dorsiflexion more dynamically, the athlete should crouch and lean forward with his heel on the ground. The angle between the leg and the vertical thus becomes a measure of ankle dorsiflexion (Figure 1-8B).

All athletes, especially those with tight heel cords, should stretch on a stair step or on an incline board and should use a wobble board program to develop and maintain proprioception.

The Feet

The team physician or a team podiatrist can help to prevent foot problems, evaluate footwear, and provide inserts and orthoses. The athlete's feet should be thoroughly evaluated, with checks for imbalances, calluses, corns, warts, blisters, athlete's foot, and ingrowing toenails. A check of

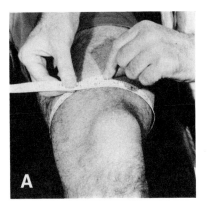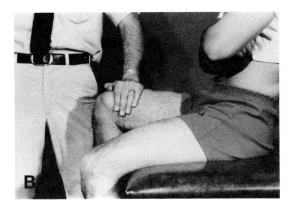

Figure 1-7 The circumference of the athlete's thigh is measured about 18 cm (7 inches) above his knee joint **(A)**. A gross test for knee strength is achieved by having the athlete flex his hip against the examiner's resistance **(B)**.

everyday walking, training, and competition shoes is also recommended.

Loose Joints or Tight Joints

Studies have shown that loose or tight joints in an athlete affect injuries.[30] An increased oc-currence of knee sprains has been found in loose-jointed athletes, whereas more muscle tears have occurred in tight-jointed professional football players.[30] After screening these players, specific exercises have been designed to increase the strength of the loose-jointed players and the flex-ibility of the tight-jointed ones. The flexibility

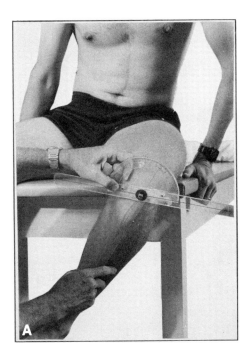

Figure 1-8 With the athlete sitting, the examiner measures external rotation of the hip **(A)**; with the athlete squatting, he measures calf flexibility **(B)**.

screening has served as a means of reducing knee injuries in contact sports and high-velocity athletics. Tests for flexibility include supination of the hand with shoulder rotation, flexion of the spine, assumption of the lotus position, hip rotation, and knee recurvatum.

When systematic flexibility testing was tried with high school players, however, no correlation was found between the frequency of knee and ankle injuries and the looseness of the players' joints. This difference between high school players and professional athletes may be related to developmental phenomena. For example, as the high school athlete matures, his loose joints become tighter, so the loose-jointed sophomore may become a tight-jointed senior.

When joint flexibility was studied in 2817 West Point cadets, no statistical relation was found between joint flexibility and joint injuries sustained in general athletic competition. Also, no relation was found between subjective joint laxity tests and objective biomechanical knee ligament examinations. Because no correlation appears to exist between ligamentous laxity and the type of injury, it may be a disservice to restrict a high school athlete from participating on the basis of ligament laxity testing.

What about psychological factors and injury? Personality factors have been found to correlate well with injury rates and severity,[20] and Cattell's 16-personality factor questionnaire (16-PF) has been useful in assessing this variable. Factor A contrasts reserved, detached, critical, and cool persons to outgoing, warmhearted, easygoing, and participating persons. The former types sustained the most severe injuries. Factor one contrasts dependent, overprotective, sensitive athletes to tough-minded, self-reliant ones. The tender-minded were more likely to be injured. Whether this test has the potential to predict tackle football injuries is not known, but the possibility exists.

Each athlete should possess the essential fit-

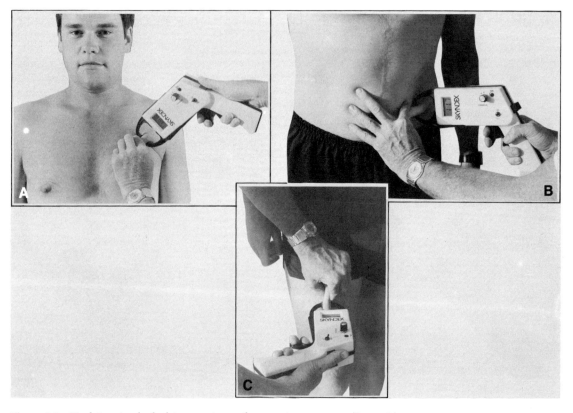

Figure 1-9 To determine body fat percentages, the examiner uses a caliper with a digital readout. Three sites are tested for men and four sites for women.

ness base of strength, flexibility, endurance, and proper warm-up technique because a strong and flexible athlete has the best chance of avoiding injury.

Strength

During the preseason physical examination, in addition to a body fat determination (Figure 1-9A, B, C) the athlete's muscular strength can be measured manually or with weights or machinery. Manual muscle testing requires experience, and gross weaknesses may be noted by comparing sides. A single maximal effort on a particular lift with standard weights or a strain gauge measurement of isometric contractions are the best strength indicators.

The grip dynamometer will provide a rough gauge of overall body strength. In this procedure, the athlete stands with his arm hanging comfortably at his side. After one practice squeeze he is asked to squeeze again and release, and the measurement is recorded.

The Cybex isokinetic machine may be used to measure strength at different speeds and also peak torque, total work, and muscular endurance, but this machine is expensive (Figure 1-10).

Upper abdominal muscular endurance is measured with timed sit-ups, and lower abdominal

endurance with leg raises and abdominal hangs. During a sit-up, the abdominal muscles stabilize the trunk to enable the athlete to sit up. The hip flexors work for the remainder of the sit-up, making it unnecessary for the athlete to do a full sit-up to condition the upper abdominal muscles, since total trunk flexion is achieved by 30°.

Warm-Up

After the preparticipation examination, each athlete should become familiar with simple ways to warm up, to gain and maintain strength, and, for women who are doing aerobic dance, to shape their bodies.

The athlete can best prepare for athletics or exercise by warming up (Figure 1-11A, B, C). He should start by breaking a sweat either by jogging or by pedaling on an exercise bicycle. By raising the body temperature, muscles are heated, tissue fluid becomes less viscous, and nerve conduction velocity speeds up. The athlete is now ready to stretch.

Here are the stretching instructions I give to my patients: Stand straight, feet hip width apart, arms at your sides.

1. *Mandibular motion:* Waggle your jaw to loosen those powerful chomping muscles.

Figure 1-10 The athlete's knee strength may be assessed at both slow and faster speeds on an isokinetic machine.

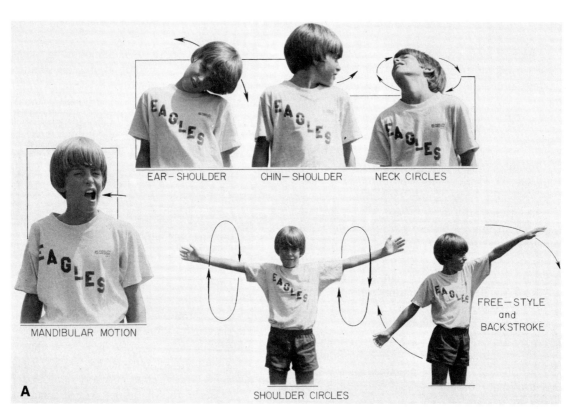

EAR–SHOULDER CHIN–SHOULDER NECK CIRCLES

MANDIBULAR MOTION

FREE–STYLE
and
BACKSTROKE

SHOULDER CIRCLES

A

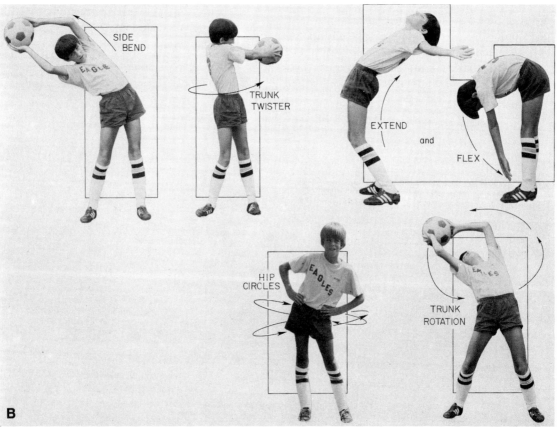

SIDE
BEND

TRUNK
TWISTER

EXTEND

and

FLEX

HIP
CIRCLES

TRUNK
ROTATION

B

Figure 1-11 The athlete begins his warm-up at his head and shoulders. Next, he warms up his torso. Finally, he stretches his lower extremities.

2. *Ear to shoulder:* Try to touch your left ear to your left shoulder without raising your shoulder, then your right ear to your right shoulder.
3. *Chin to shoulder:* Turn your head to the left, touching your chin to your shoulder, then to the right.
4. *Neck circles:* Move your head in a circle to the left, then to the right, looking in the direction your head is going.
5. *Shoulder circles:* Extend your arms straight out to the side at shoulder height with palms up. Rotate your arms in big circles forward and backward.
6. *Freestyle and backstroke:* Swim forward, freestyle. Swim backward, using the back-

stroke. Look back over your shoulder with each stroke.
7. *Side-bend:* With your left arm overhead, stretch and bend to the right. Repeat on the other side with your right arm overhead.
8. *Trunk twister:* Hold your arms out to the side at shoulder height. Swing your arms to the left, then to the right.
9. *Extend and flex:* Hands still overhead, bend backward from the hips, then forward, and then touch the floor.
10. *Hip circles:* With your hands on your hips, make hula-hoop circles with hips clockwise and then counterclockwise.
11. *Trunk Rotation:* Clasp your hands a few inches over your head, look at them, and

swing your upper body around in a big circle from the hips, first to the left, then to the right.

12. *Calf Stretch:* Put your left foot about 18 inches in front of your right, toes forward. Put both hands on the left knee. Lean forward, keeping your right heel glued to the floor, and stretch your right calf for 20 to 30 seconds.

13. *Hip (groin) stretch:* Now extend the left foot out much farther and come up on the toes of your right foot. Lower your body by bending the left knee. *This stretches your groin muscles.* Reverse the feet and do both exercises.

14. *Thigh (quadriceps) stretch:* Put your left hand against a wall or on a chair or fence for support. Reaching down behind you with your right hand, pick up your left foot by the ankle, pull it up behind you, and lean back. Reverse.

15. *Hamstring stretch:* Sit down on the floor or ground. Put the sole of your right foot against your left thigh. Bend your body down over your left knee, reaching for your toes. Reverse.

16. *Adductor (groin) stretch:* Still on the floor, pull your feet up in front of you so that your soles touch. Push your knees out and down with your elbows.

17. *Gluteus and iliotibial band stretch:* Still on the floor, extend your left leg straight out and cross your right leg over it, so that your right foot is on the floor next to your left knee, with your right knee sticking up. Push your right knee back across to the left with the back of your left elbow. Reverse.

Some stretches, however, may be harmful (Figure 1-12). The back arch can hurt the lower back, the "plow" can injure the neck, the standing hamstring stretch can damage

Figure 1-12   Some stretches may cause injury. For example, the back arch can hurt the lower back, the "plow" can hurt the neck, the standing hamstring stretch can hurt the back, and the layback can hurt the knee, as can the "hurdler's stretch."

the back, and the layback and hurdler's stretch can injure the bent knee.

Tubics

The athlete may use a lightweight, bicycle inner tube for various strengthening exercises (Figure 1-13A, B). The simple tube provides resistance that can be varied easily. In each of the exercises, the athlete should keep some tension in the tube throughout the exercise.

Here are the strengthening instructions I give to my patients:

1. *Bench Press:* Stand comfortably, feet placed squarely below the hips, knees bent slightly. Put the tube behind your back, just under your arms. Hold one end of the tube in each hand, and gather it up so that you have a ball of rubber in each hand. Your starting position will be with your hands just in front of your shoulders, thumbs up, elbows out. Now push your hands straight out, to the front, until your elbows are fully extended. Now let the resistance of the tube pull your hands back to the starting position. *This exercise works the pectoral muscles and the triceps.*

2. *Shrugs:* Still standing comfortably, reach down and flip the tube under the instep of both feet. In this exercise you are going to pull up, so remember to have your knees bent slightly. They will act as shock absorbers and take some of the pressure off your spine. With one end of the tube in each hand, gather it up until your hands are at knee level. With elbows straight, raise both shoulders and try to touch your ears with them. Come up smooth and easy, hold for a split second, then let the tube pull your shoulder down. Raise just your shoulders, not your whole body. *This exercises the trapezius muscles.*

3. *Side-bends:* Standing with the tube under your feet, hold each end at the knees. Straighten up and bend first to one side, then the other, pulling against resistance. Do not turn your body, but bend from side to side as though you were moving between two panes of glass. *This exercises the side muscles and helps firm the stomach.*

4. *Stand-ups:* With the tube under your feet, hold the ends below knee level and keep your back straight. Make a deep knee bend and then stand up against the resistance of the tube. If this is too easy, you can get greater resistance by doing a deep knee bend, then grasping the ends of the tube with your hands in front of your shoulder before standing up. *This exercises the quadriceps.*

5. *Hammer curl:* While standing with the tube under your feet, hold each end with your thumbs up so that it runs out the bottomside of your hands. Start with your hands about hip high, and pull up toward your shoulders against the resistance. Remember to keep your elbows against your sides. Bring both hands up at once or alternate. For more resistance, put the tube under one foot, and hold both ends in one hand. To keep your elbow from wobbling, support it with your other hand. *This exercises the biceps and the brachioradialis.*

6. *Overhead press.* While standing with your knees slightly bent, put one end of the tube under your right foot. Hold the other end in your right hand, palm facing toward your face at shoulder level, elbow down against your side. Raise your hand over your head. When you have completed your reps with the right arm, switch the tube to your left foot for left-side reps. *This exercises the deltoid and the triceps.*

7. *Chest pull.* Stand with your legs well apart. Place the tube under the right foot and grasp the end of the tube with your right hand, about knee high. Bend forward from the hips, supporting yourself with your left hand on your bent left knee. Holding the tube in your right hand, bend your right elbow so that it is almost at an angle of 90°. This exercise does not work unless you keep your elbow bent. Starting at a point near your right knee, pull across your chest to your left shoulder, keeping your elbow bent. *This is an exercise that firms and strengthens the pectoral muscles.*

8. *Pull-downs.* Hold one end of the tube above your head a little in front of you with your elbow extended. With your other hand, grasp

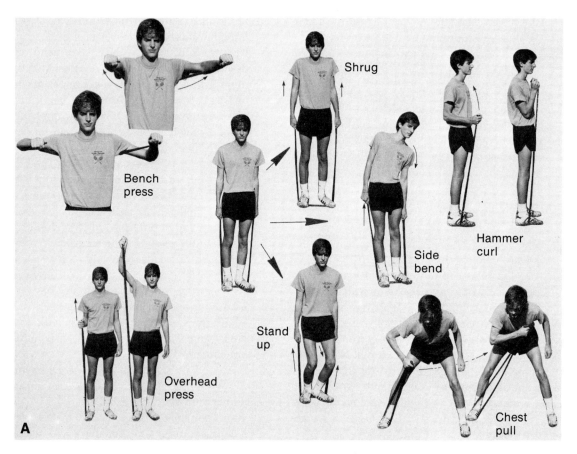

Figure 1-13   For Tubic exercises, the athlete gains strength and power by using a lightweight, inexpensive bicycle inner tube for resistance. He can add exercises by looping the tube around a post or a tree or any other immovable object.

the tube in front of your face. Now, as if you were geting set to shoot an arrow high into the air, pull the tube down toward your waist, keeping your other arm extended above your head. *This exercise works the latissimus muscle.*

9. *Sitting row.* Sit down on the floor. With knees slightly bent, toes up, flip the tube under your feet. Grasp each end of the tube at your knees or wherever is comfortable. Pull your arms back as if you were rowing, bending your elbows. Keep your arms close to your sides, so that your shoulder blades pinch together. *This exercises the rhomboids.*

10. *Sit-ups.* Lie on your back, with knees bent

for comfort. Leave your left foot flat on the floor for support. With the tube under your right foot, move your right foot about 18 inches to the side, toe up. Your right knee is bent, about 6 inches off the floor. Run both ends of the tube around the outside of your right knee and hold both ends with both hands in any grip that is comfortable. Keeping your hips flat on the floor, pull yourself up in line with the tube, twisting your left shoulder toward your right knee. Come up only halfway, *not* to a full sitting position. After doing your repetitions for the right side, repeat with the tube under your left foot, twisting the right shoulder. *This exercise*

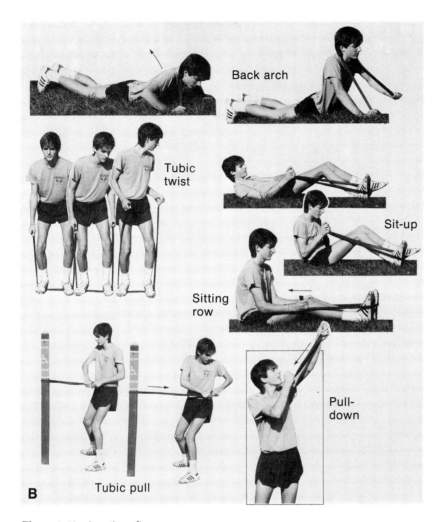

Figure 1-13   (*continued*)

works the rectus abdominus and the oblique abdominal muscles.

11. *Back arch.* Roll over on your stomach and put the tube behind your neck. Put your hands in front of your shoulders, palms down, and hold the tube in each hand. Now, with hips on the floor, raise your head and shoulders and arch your lower back. *This works the paravertebral muscles.*

For strength, do 10 slow reps of each exercise against strong resistance. For power, do 5 rapid reps against strong resistance. For endurance, do 20 or more rapid reps against moderate or light resistance. With all of these goals, the resistance chosen should make the last repetition so difficult that it can barely be accomplished.

Tubic Body Shaping

Bringing out the natural attractiveness of a person's body means more than just losing weight. To become shapely, a woman needs to tone her muscles, too. The best method for losing weight is to combine vigorous exercise with a sensible diet that includes all the necessary foods, vitamins, and minerals to keep her body healthy. She will then lose weight gradually and surely without endangering her health.

Exercise is crucial. It sets her internal thermostat higher. The metabolic rate, the rate at which she burns food, increases; thus she burns more calories even when she is resting. Further, exercise lowers her "set point," which is the weight to which the body naturally returns when no attempt is made to control calories. Vigorous exercise also lessens appetite for several hours after a workout, and thus makes a great substitute for snacking. Finally, exercise is a relaxer, relieving tensions that might otherwise prompt overeating. Despite all of the publicity they receive, fad diets are *not* a good way to lose weight. In fact, these diets may cause a person to look flabbier because she may lose muscle and even gain fat.

Many women are particularly concerned about fat storage in such areas as the buttocks, which droop under the force of gravity; the hips, where fat deposits form "saddle bags"; the abdomen, where many women develop "pot bellies" after childbirth; and the arms, which become loaded down with flabby "bat wings." The only way to eliminate these fatty areas is through general exercise. Spot reduction does not work. The body sheds fat evenly, no matter how much exercise is concentrated on a specific area. Hundreds of repetitions of exercises for the hips, for example, will not make fat disappear from there any faster than a series of fitness exercises designed to work the entire body. In fact, aerobics programs featuring many repetitions in one area can cause bursitis, tendinitis, and strains. A combination approach will, however, produce a more shapely figure.

The seven Tubic exercises listed below should be combined with a sensible diet and vigorous exercise such as aerobic dance, running, bicycling, Poolex, or swimming. The exercises can be done to music as part of the aerobics workout. These Tubics, like all Tubic exercises, are valuable in retarding osteoporosis, the loss of calcium from the bones as a woman ages. The areas most vulnerable to calcium loss are the wrists, spine, and hips. Some of the exercises require a tight grip on the tube, strengthening the wrists. Hip pulses, hip circles, and inner thigh pulls work the hips. Additional Tubic exercises such as shrugs, rowing, and back extensions strengthen the spine.

Here are the instructions I give to my patients:

1. *Elbow straighteners:* Raise your hands and place the tube behind your head. Keep your elbows bent. Straighten your elbows as you move your arms out to the side. *This exercise is excellent for the back of the arms.*
2. *Chest pulls:* This exercise forms shapely breasts by toning the pectoralis major muscle under each breast.
3. *Tubic sit-ups:* These sit-ups flatten the stomach by tightening the oblique muscles that pull the abdomen inward.
4. *Hip circles:* Tie the tube snugly around your thighs just above your knees. Stand with your left side to a ballet bar and hold on to it or support yourself against a wall or the back of a chair. First, raise your right leg to the front in a smooth motion. Do not kick. Then lower your legs. Next, raise it to the side and lower it, then to the back and lower it. Finally, make a big circle with your leg to the front, to the side, to the rear, and down. Turn around and repeat with your left leg. Hip circles work the muscles in front of and at the outside of your hips as well as your buttock muscles.
5. *Hip pulses:* Again tie the tube snugly around your thighs just above your knees, lie on your back, knees up, feet flat on the floor. Keep your shoulders on the floor and raise your buttocks as high as you can. Separate your knees until you have exerted slight tension on the tube. Then separate them a bit more and hold the tension briefly. Ease off slightly, then pulse again. These pulses can also be done standing. With the tube tied around your thighs, face a ballet bar, wall, or chair and support yourself with your hands. Bend your knees until you are in a half-squat. Push your knees out to the sides until there is slight tension on the tube. Now, in a pulsing rhythm, push them out farther. *This works buttocks and outer hip muscles.*
6. *Inner thigh pulls:* Hook the tube around your

right foot. Then lie on your right side, resting on your bent elbow. Put your left foot over your right leg, placing your foot about level with your right knee and on the tube. Now pull the tube up with your right leg, keeping the knee straight. *This works your inner thigh muscles.*

7. *Calf curvers:* Stand up, put the tube under the balls of your feet, and hold the ends at knee level or below. Straighten up and rise up on your toes, as far as you can go. Sink back onto your heels and then rise up again. *This works your calf muscles.*

Preseason Cardiac Examination

A relatively simple cardiovascular screening examination will usually rule out any significant pathologic states.[38, 41] The examiner aims to detect any unusual body build, such as that associated with Marfan's syndrome, or the facial features characteristic of the person with congenital aortic valvular disease. The chest is inspected for abnormal cardiac pulsations or an abnormal chest wall configuration. Substantial moment-to-moment variations in the resting heart rate of the young person are not uncommon.

The sitting blood pressure is a screen for hypertension. Long arms or large biceps, however, may produce abnormal readings if the cuff of the sphygmomanometer is too narrow. The blood pressure bladder should cover at least two thirds of the upper arm and be long enough to circle not less than one half of the circumference of the arm. The total length of the cuff should be long enough to be wrapped around the arm several times.

A child younger than 10 years old should generally not have a blood pressure higher than 130/75 mm Hg.[41] For youths 10 to 15 years of age, the maximum blood pressure should not exceed 140/80 mm Hg. Persons with mild elevation of their blood pressure should be rechecked often to ensure that the elevated blood pressure is not a transient one resulting from anxiety. However, persistent primary hypertension is a sign that further cardiologic evaluation is needed. Youngsters with moderate hypertension must be advised not to engage in primary isometric exercises because these cause marked increases in both systolic and diastolic blood pressures.

Examination for coarctation of the aorta is made by simultaneously palpating the femoral and brachial arteries. A weak or absent lower extremity pulse or a notable delay in the femoral pulse compared to the brachial pulse will alert the physician to this possibility. Also, if the child has high blood pressure in the upper extremities, the femoral pulse and lower extremity blood pressure should be measured to check for possible coarctation of the aorta.

Many youngsters and endurance-trained athletes will normally have a systolic ejection-type murmur. The examiner should listen for the normal first and second heart sounds, ejection and nonejection clicks, and third and fourth heart sounds. If the first heart sound is easily heard and there is no holosystolic murmur, it is unlikely that the youngster has a significant ventricular septal defect. The second heart sound normally splits with inspiration. If both components of this sound are of normal intensity and split normally with inspiration, this will usually rule out a significant abnormality. Aortic insufficiency causes a high-pitched diastolic blowing murmur, whereas a patent ductus arteriosus will produce a continuous heart murmur.

Any situation that increases cardiac output will increase the intensity of heart sounds and murmurs. Thus, harmless small flow murmurs may sound quite prominent in an anxious youngster or in one with an elevated temperature. Also, it is not uncommon for an anxious child to have ectopic atrial beats. There is some ambiguity on the significance of resting premature ventricular contractions (PVCs), and resting PVCs have a variable response to exercise in children and young adults. However, a significant coupling of PVCs, or frequent PVCs, may be associated with a myocarditis. For this reason, any question about the type or significance of premature beats should be referred to a pediatric–cardiologist or cardiologist for evaluation.

The examiner must take care not to create a cardiac neurosis in a youngster. Consultation with a cardiologist familiar with the heart problems of children is suggested by American Academy of Pediatrics experts before excluding any youngster from competition.

Scrotum and Testes

Hydrocele

A hydrocele is an accumulation of straw-colored fluid between the two layers of the tunica vaginalis. A bright light will show through the hydrocele sac, and in larger hydroceles the tunica vaginalis may have to be excised. A hydrocele occurring in a person older than 5 years of age may signal a malignancy.

Varicocele

Scrotal varicoceles contain an abnormally dilated pampiniform plexus of veins. The varicocele is caused by defective valves in the internal spermatic vein and is almost always found on the left side.

The athlete with a varicocele feels dull scrotal pain that disappears when he lies down. Exercise may distend the varicocele to cause pain. When a varicocele is painful, the pain may be relieved by wearing an athletic supporter with the scrotum up front instead of stuck between the legs. If the pain is severe, however, the internal spermatic vein may be ligated near the internal inguinal ring.

The Athlete with One Testis

An athlete is considered to have one testis if the other is maldescended, is atrophied from mumps orchitis, or if there has been torsion of one testis. Some doctors will exclude a youngster with a maldescended testis from contact sports, reasoning that a testis may be easily injured. Contact sports may be allowed after the maldescended testis has been replaced in the scrotum. Other physicians will allow the youngster to enter contact sports on the assumption that injury to a testis is rare if an athletic supporter and protective cup are worn. If an athlete with one testis is allowed to participate, however, the athlete, his parents, and the school authorities should be informed of the risk to the remaining healthy testis.

Cryptorchidism (Maldescended Testes)

The testes normally descend from the gonadal ridge to the inguinal ring, enter the inguinal canal, and, by birth, move into the scrotum. In 3% of all male infants, however, a testis fails to descend. There are three types of maldescended testes: the retractile, the ectopic, and the true undescended. Most are *retractile*, caused by an active cremasteric reflex that draws the testis out of the scrotum during examinations. These testes are histologically normal and usually descend into the scrotum by puberty.

The *ectopic* testis resides outside the normal pathway between the abdominal cavity and the scrotum, near the superficial inguinal ring, pubopenile or perineal. These testes also are histologically normal, requiring surgical placement into the scrotum where they must reside to mature and to produce healthy spermatazoa. Because body temperature is 2° higher than intrascrotal temperature, developing spermatazoa will not mature at body temperature.

The true undescended testis lies outside the scrotum but at some point along the pathway of descent. These testes, unlike other types, are histologically abnormal and have an increased incidence of cancer, regardless of whether they are brought down into the scrotum. Most surgeons prefer to place the undescended testis into the scrotum, where it can be palpated, or to remove it. Surgery should be done before the age of 10 and usually is done in the fifth year, before the child starts school.

Hernia

Hernias should be diagnosed in the preparticipation examination and repaired early to avoid later problems.[18a] If repair is ignored, vigorous athletic activity may force omentum and bowel down into the hernia sac, and both may incarcerate and strangle.

There are several types of hernias, and each type should be searched for. Indirect hernias result from a congenital weakness of the athlete's internal abdominal ring. The neck is narrow, and the bowel may be trapped and can strangle. These hernias should be repaired before allowing competition, especially if the sac comes down into the inguinal canal. Repair is needed even when the sac does not come down to the scrotum. Umbilical and epigastric hernias should also be repaired because omentum may become incarcerated in them. Femoral hernias are relatively more frequent in women than in men and may be responsible for mysterious groin pains. They are difficult to identify but, when found, should be repaired. A graduated exercise program will allow the athlete to return to practice about 5 weeks after hernia repair.

Hemorrhoids

Athletes should be checked for hemorrhoids during the preparticipation physical examination. Hemorrhoidal veins are the only valveless veins below the heart, and, if a contracted sphincter traps some of these veins outside, they may swell and occasionally thrombose. When a thrombosis occurs, the clot must be evacuated and a stool softener prescribed.

Anal fissures and sentinel piles are treated twice a day with a soothing balm and hydrocortisone suppositories. Cold witch hazel packs used externally will help to relieve discomfort.

LABORATORY TESTS

The young athlete's capillary blood hemoglobin must be checked, especially in postpubertal girls and youngsters from low-income families. Athletes who use aspirin occasionally have microscopic blood loss from subacute gastritis that may leave them anemic. Prepubertal youngsters normally have about 11.5 g of hemoglobin/dl of their blood, but a postpubertal boy will have 14 g/dl or more and a postpubertal girl, 12 g or more. If a boy has less than 13 g or a girl less than 12 g, he or she should have a complete blood count.[29]

A dipstick analysis of each athlete's urine is also done at the comprehensive preseason examination.

Proteinuria

Protein in the urine may be related to posture or represent a normal response to exercise.[35] Nonrenal causes of proteinuria include fever, emotional stress, or exposure to excessvie heat or cold.

Postural proteinuria associated with a prolonged exaggerated lordotic posture may be a presenting sign of renal disease. The lordosis may cause renal vasoconstriction and venous congestion leading to renal ischemia, although the condition usually has a good prognosis and most patients do not present with active renal disease. However, renal biopsy will show some changes in about one half of these patients. It is important to follow up on this disorder because treatment may slow the progress of renal disease.

A functional proteinuria normally follows rigorous exercise[8] because blood is shunted to the exercising muscles and renal ischemia results from renal vasoconstriction and venous congestion. The renal blood flow drops together with a smaller drop in glomerular filtration rate and an increased filtration fraction.

During the Commonwealth Games of 1976, proteinuria was often found in athletes after endurance events. Inulin and creatinine clearance of athletes with proteinuria and those without the condition were identical, and hemodynamic changes in renal function were also identical regardless of whether the athletes had proteinuria. The condition was probably a physiologic response of the tubules or glomerulus to the relative drop in blood flow during exercise rather than a pathologic condition. Perhaps the proteinuria reflects a combination of changes in blood flow, pH, and relative hydration states, which in turn effect changes in the basement membrane that allow more protein to pass across the membrane than can be reabsorbed by the tubules.

Urinary Protein

A normal adult passes an upper limit of 150 mg of protein in his urine each day; when reclining, the quantity is much less. Children pass from 35 mg to 70 mg of protein daily. Two thirds of the protein usually is globulin and one third albumin. Heavy outputs of 750 mg or more in 24 hours probably reflect underlying renal disease.

Dipstick Screening

The dipstick is an effective screening test. It contains a pH sensitive dye, tetrabromophenol, that turns from blue to green when albumin in normally acid urine prevents hydrogen ions from acting on the dye. A dipstick "trace" means less than 30 mg/dl of protein. If the urine is strongly alkaline, it may give a false-positive reading. For this reason, when urine is protein positive and alkaline, the result should be checked against a precipitation method such as sulfosalicylic acid. If a dipstick test shows a trace it is usually discounted, but if it is more strongly positive another specimen should be obtained.

What to Do If There Is Protein in the Urine

If an adolescent or a young adult has 1+ to 4+ proteinuria on a routine dipstick analysis, the examiner should determine whether the proteinuria is intermittent or continuous. Serial samples are collected. The athlete voids at bedtime and discards the sample. He then voids on rising and labels his sample #1. His next sample is taken when this daily routine is under way and is labeled #2. The tubes should be left in the refrigerator, not in a freezer, since freezing may confuse the precipitation readings. This schedule is repeated for 2 additional days before the samples are brought to the laboratory.

If there is no protein in the morning sample and later samples are positive, benign orthostatic proteinuria is probable. The urine should be rechecked in about 6 months. The finding of proteinuria in all samples suggests renal disease. Urine sedimentation, blood urea nitrogen concentration, and creatinine clearance should then be ascertained and an intravenous pyelogram performed.

EXERCISE IN RENAL DISORDERS

Renal blood flow decreases by about 50% during exercise and may leave the tubules in a weakened state. Because of this decrease, exercise should be limited for patients with impaired kidney function and those with a history of acute or chronic renal parenchymal disease. A premature return to vigorous exercise after acute nephritis may lead to further kidney damage.

Proteinuria preceded by a severe sore throat leads to a suspicion of postinfectious glomerulonephritis. However, an athlete in training who has a positive throat culture for streptococcus and protein and sediment in his urine may have only a throat infection and a normal renal response to exercise.

PAPERWORK, PERMISSION SLIPS, AND HANDOUTS

By the time of the preparticipation examination, permission slips and information cards must be completed in triplicate, with the original for the school records, a copy for the parents, and another one for the athlete's personal physician. Formal consent must be obtained for the preparticipation physical examination, for emergency care on the field, and to allow treatment of the child at a medical center in the event of injury. Resumes of medical records are kept on 5-inch × 8-inch cards, including listings of previous injuries and treatment, allergies, where to contact parents at work and home, family doctor's phone number, and signed consent for emergency medical care. These cards are carried to all away games.

Each athlete is provided with two instruction sheets: *ICE Treatment for Acute Injury* (Table 1-4) and Home Treatment Program for Chronic Soreness (Table 1-5).

EXAMINING A RUNNER

Sports physicians are often called upon to examine runners. Not all people who run, however, are "runners." A tennis player, in the course of three sets lasting 30 games, may run and walk 7 miles. Soccer players may run and walk about the same distance in a match. Nonetheless, running is the only sport in which you run continuously for periods varying from 20 minutes to more than an hour.

Runners may be categorized as joggers, sports runners, long-distance runners, and marathoners. Joggers run up to 20 miles a week, sports runners 20 to 40 miles, long distance runners 60 to 80 miles, and marathoners 80 to 100 miles or more.

Table 1-4 *ICE* TREATMENT FOR ACUTE INJURY

If you suffer an injury such as a strain, sprain or bruise, use the ICE method as soon as possible. It can prevent or reduce swelling, keep the injury from becoming worse than it already is, and speed up recovery.

ICE stands for *Ice*, *Compression*, and *Elevation*.

1. Make an ice bag by putting ice cubes into a plastic bag.

2. Wet the end of an elastic wrap and wrap the wet part of the wrap around the injured area with gentle firmness.

3. Place the ice bag on the wet wrap over the injured area.

4. Hold the ice bag in place with the remaining dry part of the elastic wrap.

5. Keep the injured limb elevated. For an ankle injury, lie down with your leg propped up on a pillow about 12 inches. For a wrist injury, lie down with your wrist on your chest.

   Apply the ice bag for 20 minutes. Then remove the ice bag and wrap the elastic wrap snugly around the injured area, keeping the limb elevated. Reapply the ice bag for 20 minutes every hour as much as possible during the first 24 to 36 hours after the injury.

Runners are further classifed by age and sex: old, young, or "prime aged," male or female. Each group has special problems. Older runners must compensate for wear and tear on their bodies. Young runners risk injury when they do speed work during growth spurts or if they run more

Table 1-5 HOME TREATMENT PROGRAM FOR CHRONIC SORENESS

1. Every evening treat the injured part with moist heat for 10 minutes. Use either a warm tub, a warm shower, warm and wet towels, or a moist heating pad.

2. Then coat the injured area with a friction fighter such as baby oil, lanolin cream, or Vaseline and massage this area with your fingertips for 7 minutes.

3. Rehabilitative exercises

4. Wash off the friction fighter with rubbing alcohol. If the area is sore, perform ice cube massage.

---

than 70 miles a week. The so-called "prime aged" runner is in the biological prime of life but sometimes trains too hard, too fast, and too often; these errors in judgment lead to injury. Female runners are subject to a characteristic set of injuries for biological and social reasons. Frequently they are new to running, are often "loose jointed," and have a high body-weight-to-bone ratio. They therefore may suffer from strains and sprains, stress fractures, and the consequences of poor running form.

The runner's stride consists of four phases: float, heel strike, pronation, and pushoff. The float phase differentiates running from walking. In walking, one foot is always in contact with the ground; running is a series of leaps. Runners jump from one foot to the other. Each runner has a characteristic manner of landing. Forty percent of runners land on the outside of their heels, whereas another 40% land on the full foot, dropping back onto the inside of their heels. The remaining 20% land on the balls of their feet, their heels never touching the ground. The next stage in the stride is pronation, the process by which the foot absorbs shock by flattening at the subtalar joint below the ankle. The foot unlocks to absorb shock and then locks to become a rigid lever for pushoffs. As the runner's foot pronates, the tibia and knee rotate inward. This winding and unwinding action is rapid, placing extreme torque at the knee. Excessive pronation often produces knee injury. The final stage of the stride is pushoff, which is done through the second toe.

The continuous, fluid motions of the legs produce 47 identifiable stresses with each step. Consequently the cause of a runner's complaint may be distant from the site of the pain.

The evaluation of a running injury consists of such standard procedures as history and physical examination, including x-ray films as needed, a dynamic evaluation of the runner's stride and form, if possible, and an analysis of wear patterns on walking and running shoes. Accordingly, all of our runners are told to come to the examination prepared to run. We also ask them to bring all of the shoes that they wear during the week, including their everyday walking shoes, training shoes (especially old ones), racing flats, and shoes with cleats or other grip aids.

History

The examiner needs to know [1] the length of time the runner has been running, weekly mileage, and the races run in the last 3 months (with dates and mileage); [2] any surgery on the back or legs and any previous injuries; [3] date of onset of the current problem, what happened and what hurts, and what he thinks may be wrong. The runner's own diagnosis may not be correct, but by asking for it you may gain important clues about the injury.

Physical Examination

Begin the physical examination (Figure 1-14) by noting the runner's general alignment. If the right shoulder drops, the runner is probably a "right hander." The right hander's left leg and foot will usually be longer than the right leg and foot, and the right foot will overpronate. The longer leg may suffer lateral problems at the hip and knee, whereas the shorter leg may develop medial knee pain, posteromedial shin splints, and other pronation problems.

Next, check for knocked knees, bowed legs, flat or high arches, bunions, and relative lengths of the toes. In most people, the big toe is the longest. This is called an "Egyptian" foot, because the Egyptians carved their statues this way. In the "Greek" foot, the second toe extends past the first one. This type of foot often overpronates. Corns (calluses over the joints), ingrowing toenails, and "marathon toes" (subungual bleeding) should also be looked for.

The runner is asked to bend over so that the examiner can note how close to the floor he can reach with the knees straight and also check for scoliosis. The experienced examiner can confirm impressions of leg-length difference by feeling the top of the pelvis.

In the second stage of the examination the runner's feet are the focus, with the runner kneeling on the examining table facing away from the examiner. If a knee hurts too much to kneel on, the runner may lie prone on the table. The feet are well relaxed and easiest to examine when the runner is in the kneeling or prone position. First check the Achilles tendon and the area behind the heels and determine the range of motion of the subtalar joint. Then palpate the soles of the feet. Finally, examine the feet for calluses. Pinch calluses on the great toe and alongside the first matatarsal are normal in active people. Calluses under the second metatarsal heads, however, are found in runners with pes planus and overly flexible feet. High-arched runners develop calluses under the first and fifth metatarsal heads. Prominent calluses may act as stones in the shoe and create injury; these are trimmed. Sometimes a callus is invaded by a wart virus, identifiable by little "pepper spots" (capillaries) that are seen when trimming them. In preparation for the dynamic evaluation, mark a straight dark line down the back of the Achilles tendon to the base of the heel.

Ask the runner to lie face up, and check hip rotation. Decreased internal rotation of the hip may be an early sign of osteoarthritis. With the opposite leg bent, the runner's leg is raised to check for hamstring flexibility. The runner should be able to point the leg at the ceiling. Then, with the legs out straight on the table and relaxed, the physician looks for fluid in the knee, checks leg length again, this time by comparing the level of the malleoli, and feels for distal pulses.

In the final stage of the physical examination, the runner sits on the edge of the table with knees dangling off the side so that general stability and kneecap mobility can be noted and troubled areas palpated, such as the iliotibial band and the anteromedial part of the knee. Then palpate the legs over the pes anserinus and the posteromedial part of the leg and anterolaterally for shin splints. Look for ankle swelling and then, with the knee both extended and flexed, check ankle flexibility.

Dynamic Evaluation

A treadmill video evaluation is extremely useful because it enables the examiner to build on the conclusions drawn from the static examination and provides valuable information about the dynamics of the patient's running. It can be performed, however, only if the runner's pain is negligible enough that he is able to run. Running on a treadmill, however, is slightly different from running on an ordinary surface. Most runners are

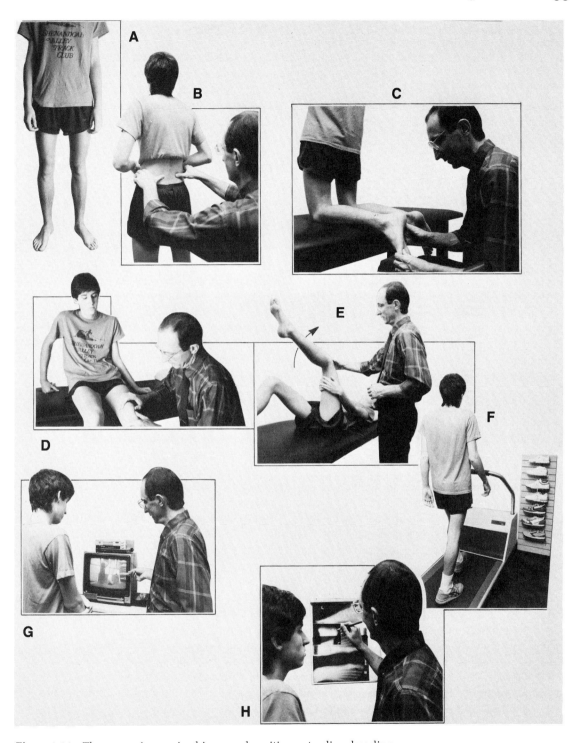

Figure 1-14   The runner is examined in several positions: standing, kneeling, sitting, and lying down. A video is then made of the runner as he runs on a treadmill. He then watches the video in slow motion with stop action and the examiner points out any dynamic problems.

unfamiliar with treadmills and may adopt a cautious gait. They tend to use a shorter stride and run more on the front of their feet than they might normally.

First, ask the runner to walk with running shoes on to get used to the treadmill. To observe running, increase the speed to 5 mph and position the video camera low and behind the runner, focusing on the feet. This gives a "caterpillar's view." Look to see whether the runner overpronates and toes out or lacks pronation and toes in. Note whether the foam midsole of the shoe is collapsing and whether the counter of the shoe deforms as the runner strides. Sometimes the shoes are the cause of the problem. For instance, a runner's stride can be thrown off if the midsole of his shoe collapses during running. A soft orthotic, a heel lift, or a heel wedge may be inserted into the shoes during treadmill running to determine whether they help.

Next, the runner takes the shoes off and walks barefooted. Using the black line as a guide, compare barefooted walking with walking in shoes.

HOW TO RETURN TO RUNNING AFTER AN INJURY

Before an athlete returns to running after an injury, the injured area should not hurt during normal daily activities and should not be tender. Further, he should obtain any needed orthotics or shoe modifications and, if necessary, change shoes.

Swimming is a good way to stay in shape while recovering from an injury. But because swimming is 95% arm work, it is not particularly useful to runners. The runner can try riding a bicycle to maintain endurance, but cycling uphill or against resistance risks overstressing already injured legs. Circuit training with weights may keep the runner fit, but most of these exercises work the arms. The problem with these alternatives is that by the time running can be resumed, the legs are out of shape, and running on poorly conditioned legs invites further injury. Poolex is an answer to this problem.

Poolex

Poolex water exercise is indicated for the athlete suffering from back strain, pelvic stress fracture, hamstring pull, knee sprain, pain behind the kneecap, bad shin splints, plantar fasciitis, stress fracture of the foot, or any other problem that interferes with running. The exercises also allow runners to train when recovering from an operation.

In the pool, resistance is always commensurate with exertion. The harder the runner pushes against the water, the more water resistance is encountered; if the pushing lets up, the water resistance decreases. The water also resists chest expansion, thus building breathing capacity. There are therapeutic benefits as well. While the runner exercises, the pressure of the water acts like a big support stocking. In addition to providing resistance, the constant flow of water provides a massage.

In a whirlpool bath or shallow pool, the runner can rest on his back or hang on to the side and move the legs in a bicycling motion. These exercises are satisfactory, but deep-water running provides a harder and more interesting workout. For deep-water running, the runner dons a water skiing belt, rescue tube, or canoeing vest and "runs" in a diving well or in the deep end of a pool without touching the bottom. The exerciser tries to stay erect while running, bringing one knee toward the chest while thrusting the other leg straight down, and either running in place or moving around. The action is more like bicycling than running. For more intense exercise, the runner may dispense with the flotation device and "run" laps in the deep end of the pool without touching the bottom.

To further increase the intensity of a runner's workout, deep-water Tubic running may be appropriate. The runner buys two used 27-inch × 1¼-inch bicycle inner tubes, cuts out the valves, washes and dries them, joins the two tubes with a square knot, attaches one end of the tubes to a railing or ladder in the diving well, and ties the other end to the ski belt. Thus tethered, the runner can sprint away for the hard part of the workout, letting the tube draw him back as the exercise slacks off. One tube is sufficient, but two tubes give more range.

Poolex offers the runner a variety of training routines. The runner can do endurance work or intervals. Poolex intervals are just like dry-land intervals; the runner alternates all-out runs at top speed for 60 to 70 seconds, with easy runs of 60 to 70 seconds. A standard day consists of ten repeats, but any number of repetitions or any combination of hard and easy work is possible. The purpose is to continue the runner's development and maintain the psychological commitment to training. The deep-water program may be done every day or it can be alternated with an upper-body conditioning program such as Tubics.

The runner should use Poolex with care. Although these exercises only rarely produce soreness, the runner may notice some stiffness in the thighs because the knees are raised so high. If pain is experienced during the pool work, the runner should consult a physician.

Once swelling and soreness in the injured area have abated, the runner may begin shallow-water Poolex. He walks in varying depths of water, starting at armpit depth, where body weight is only about one tenth of normal weight, and advances to chest-deep and then to waist-deep water as the injury clears up.

When the runner can walk on dry land without pain, he may begin a dry land return-to-running program. First, he tries to walk without pain for 30 minutes. If he should have pain after 10 minutes, for example, he should stop and resume walking the next day. Once he achieves 30 minutes of steady walking without pain, he can progress to the walk–jog program supplemented by Poolex.

In the walk–jog program, the runner walks 4 minutes, then jogs 2 minutes. He repeats this five times, for a total of 30 minutes of activity. If this activity does not cause pain and if there is no soreness the next morning, he may proceed to 3 minutes of walking and 3 minutes of jogging, repeating this five times to total 30 minutes. If, after this activity, he has no pain, he may proceed the next day to 2 minutes of walking and 4 minutes of jogging, repeating this five times to total 30 minutes. Now he is up to 20 minutes of jogging.

Once he reaches this level without pain, he may advance to the steady jogging program.

In the steady jogging program, the runner tries to run for 30 minutes without soreness. If soreness does appear, after 15 minutes, for example, he should stop running, take the next day off, and try again the following day. Even if he can run 30 minutes without pain, he should skip a day before running again and do Poolex exercise on the day off. Once he can run 30 minutes without pain he may increase his distance and pace depending on his previous level of training.

EVALUATING THE ATHLETE'S FOOTWEAR

Almost every athlete or exercising person wears shoes, if not during the sport, then at least during the rest of the day. The athlete should bring his shoes to the preparticipation examination in a gym bag or in a box. The shoes should include those that he might wear during an ordinary week: training shoes, competition shoes, everyday walking shoes, casual shoes, and dress shoes. An examination of the shoes may prevent future injury, help in diagnosing a current one, or give clues to abnormalities of gait.

Today's athlete rarely wears "sneakers"; instead, he wears specialty shoes designed for the specific sport. Shoes are made for running, walking, aerobics, tennis, volleyball, basketball, and other sports.

Running Shoes

Every runner wants lightweight shoes that will last forever. Although this goal has not been reached, today's running shoes are superior even to those of a few years ago. Each part of the running shoe has a specific function, and advances in the construction of each part have led to better shoes (Figure 1-15). A runner may be light or heavy, fast or slow, and have narrow or wide, rigid or flexible feet. These differences require that shoes have features best suited for the individual runner.

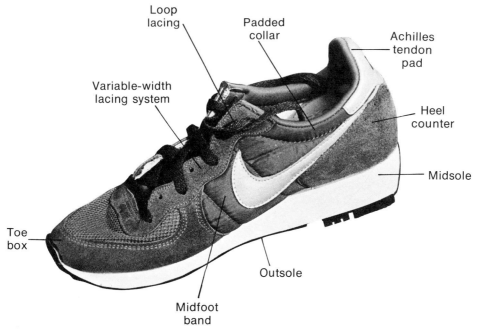

Figure 1-15   Good running shoes help to prevent injuries.

The Shoe Last

A last is the hard plastic or wood over which a shoe is built. It gives a shoe its shape and size. A last may be either straight or curved. A straight last (vector last) shoe controls pronation, providing support medially under the arch like a "Thomas heel." Straight lasted shoes are best for slower runners who land on their heels and for runners who overpronate. Curved lasted shoes are best for runners with supinated or rigid high-arched feet. These shoes are shaped to give support to the outer part of the foot during faster running. They are usually lighter and more flexible than straighter shoes. If a flat-footed person were to wear a curved shoe, his foot might roll in excessively. Normal feet function best in slightly curved or semicurved shoes.

Internal last systems can fine-tune a shoe's flexibility and support. These systems include board lasts, slip lasts, and combination lasts. A lightweight, semirigid, fiberboard insole (boarded last) adds stability. It provides torsion resistance but makes the forefoot stiff, too. To reduce forefoot stiffness, many board-lasted shoes have flex lines across the insole at the ball to encourage motion there. These flexion grooves cross under the metatarsal–phalangeal joints. A slip-lasted shoe is sewn together like a moccasin. It is lightweight and flexible and not as stable as a shoe with a boarded last. A combination last is a hybrid system. Fiberboard extends from the heel to just behind the metatarsal heads. This versatile last provides a stable heel, a stable arch, and a flexible forefoot.

The running shoe should have a soft ankle collar with a well-molded Achilles pad or a notched heel counter to eliminate pressure on the lower Achilles. A thermoplastic heel counter keeps the heel from shifting and prevents shoe breakdown. A firmer plastic or a hard rubber external heel counter extends up onto the counter and sometimes down onto the midsole to reinforce the heel counter. An extended medial counter gives extra stability to runners with flexible feet.

Midsole

The midsole is the resilient material between the upper part of the shoe and the outsole. Training shoes have a full-length midsole that provides shock absorption. Such cushioning is especially important for runners with rigid feet who need a well-cushioned shoe.

Shoe companies are seeking the optimum midsole material to absorb shock and provide stability. These paradoxic roles have prompted the use of multidensity midsoles, composite materials, and multilayered midsole modifications.

Midsole foams are becoming lighter and more durable. The most common foam is ethylene vinyl acetate (EVA). Multidensity midsoles contain materials of different firmnesses in strategic locations. New materials include composite polyethylene-EVA, EVA encapsulated by durable polyurethane, plastic-nylon fibers embedded in polyurethane and surrounded by EVA, and polyurethane encapsulated air or gels.

A multilayered midsole may have a platform-and-pillar design at the heel and channels under the forefoot. A firm sheet of EVA, thicker on the medial side and tapering to the lateral side, adds control and resists pronation. A midsole that bends up around the edges to cup the heel aids stability by offering a better fit and reducing side-to-side motion. Easy extension at the ball of the foot during toe-off is aided by a rippled patch of firmer EVA that extends about ½ inch inward on both sides of the forefoot.

The life span of a midsole, and hence of a shoe, depends on a runner's weight, his running style, and the surface he runs on. The life span is generally from 300 to 500 miles. Therefore, shoes should be replaced about every 400 miles or every 6 months. Air soles, the new composites, and gel soles may last longer.

Outsole

The outsole of a shoe is the part that contacts the ground. It should last long, absorb shock, and afford traction. Carbonized rubber or Vibram outsoles are durable and resist abrasion. The thickest outsoles are not necessarily the best shock absorbers. Shock absorption depends more on the firmness of the rubber used. Expanded (blown) rubber outsoles are less durable but spongier. Firm rubber and blown rubber may be combined to provide the needed wear and shock absorption.

Outsole patterns may be rippled or studded. The ripple or herringbone type has low profile bars that wear longer on hard surfaces such as asphalt or cement. Studs, nubs, or "waffles" give better traction on grass or dirt trails but wear out quickly on harder surfaces.

The outsole of a motion-control shoe may be hollowed out along the center of the rearfoot and midfoot, leaving the edges of the outsole higher than the center. The foot will then fall into place along the midline rather than wander toward the medial edge.

Sock Liners

Sock liners are removable inserts. Some are made of EVA-polyethelene and look like a full-length, soft orthotic. The sock liner absorbs shock and gives extra support and stability. Sock liners can be cut to provide extra space. In addition, shims and lifts may be attached to them. With sock liners removed, the shoes can accommodate orthotics.

SELECTING A RUNNING SHOE

Today's comfortable and lightweight running shoes provide rearfoot stability and impact cushioning, support in midstance, and flexibility in toe-off. Some shoes are made especially to accommodate high or low mileage runners, light or heavy runners, pronators or supinators. They also are designed to prevent injuries. The type of shoe that a runner chooses will depend on the type of foot that he has. To determine his foot type, the runner may wet the bottom of his foot and step onto a flat surface. If the footprint shows the entire foot, it is flat. If about one half of the arch shows, the foot is a normal, neutral one. If only the heel, the ball of the foot, and a thin line on the outside of the foot show, the arch is high.

An overpronater (one whose foot flattens out too much) should select a straight and board-lasted or combination-lasted shoe. The shoe should have a dual-density midsole that is firmer along the medial edge of the shoe and an extended medial counter and external heel counter support. A supinator with high-arched foot should select a curved, slip-lasted shoe with a soft midsole of air or gel that has an external heel counter support.

A woman often has a narrower heel, and wider forefoot than does a man and may have different shoe needs. The midsole of a woman's shoe must be thinner to allow flexibility for her smaller and lighter foot. Lightweight male runners or male runners with small or narrow feet can wear ladies' shoes and big female runners can wear men's shoes. A runner who has wide feet or low arches should select a shoe with a straighter last. The straight last provides more support under the arch. In fact, the runner may have to look twice at the bottom of the shoes to tell the right one from the left.

A runner with sore ankles or sore feet may benefit from a shoe change. If the ankle hurts in front or behind, he should select a shoe with a firmer or higher heel. If the ankle hurts medially or laterally, he should look for a shoe with a firmer counter, an external heel counter support, and a more stable heel. If the pain is in the heel or in the arch, he should purchase shoes that have straight lasts. If the toes hurt or the toenails bruise and blacken, the runner can cut away the end of the sock liner or stretch the toe box with a shoemaker's swan.

In the Running Shoe Shop

Before buying a new pair of shoes, the runner should check for any obvious lapses of workmanship such as loose or uneven stitching or sloppy gluing. He should remove the sock liner to see whether the shoe is board-lasted, combination-lasted, or slip-lasted and then stick his hand deep inside the shoe to feel for rough edges, prominent seams, or loose flaps.

The fit of the shoe is most important. Shoes should be tried on in the afternoon, when the feet are the largest owing to normal swelling, or at the time of day when the runner will ordinarily be wearing the shoes. They should be fit especially to the longer foot. The longer foot is usually the left foot of a right-handed person or the right foot of a left-handed person, probably because these are usually the respective takeoff and balancing legs and hence grow longer and larger. At least ¼

inch of space should be allowed beyond the end of the longest toe. A runner's feet grow both longer and wider during a race or during a long run; thus shoes that are too tight across the forefoot should be avoided.

The runner should try on several pairs of shoes. Once the shoes are laced, he should not be able to slide his feet forward and should not be able to lift his heels out of the shoe. The shoes should feel comfortable right from the start.

If the runner uses orthotics, he should replace the sock liners with them. If the heel counters of his old shoes lean toward the inside, he may need straight-lasted shoes or slightly curved-lasted shoes that provide more support medially. However, even if the runner buys a pair of motion control shoes, he should remember that training on a surface that is too soft may negate the structural benefits of the shoes.

Lacing Tricks

Lacing tricks allow the runner to adjust the width of his shoes, reduce heel slippage, and eliminate pressure points. If the runner uses all of the eyelets, the shoes may be tied too tight and rub on the top of his foot. Shoes with adjustable lacing systems should have shorter laces. If the shoes are too snug, the runner can skip the third and fifth eyelets or skip all of the far eyelets. If the shoes are too loose, he can skip the fourth and sixth eyelets and use the inner eyelets for a snug fit.

Loop lacing can counteract the runner's heel from slipping. The runner crisscrosses the laces until the next-to-last eyelets. The end of each lace is then looped through the next eyelet and the opposite loop used as an eyelet. The laces can then be pulled snugger to provide a more secure fit with less heel slippage.

A runner with high-arched, rigid feet may develop soreness on top of his insteps. The conventional, crisscrossed lacing method only aggravates this condition. The pressure may be relieved by passing the laces under the eyelets rather than across the top of the foot. Some running shoes now even have laces on the side of the shoe rather than on top. Further, cinch-bindings provide a more secure midfoot fit than do laces. Here, a strap extends over the instep and down through a channel in the midsole. The strap supports the midfoot as well as if it were wrapped with tape.

OTHER SHOES

Walking Shoes

An athlete's everyday walking shoes are more likely to cause foot problems than are his high-tech sports shoes. However, high performance walking shoes are now available that have the same technical features, materials, and components as do modern running shoes, including notched heel collars, thermoplastic heel counters, external heel counter stabilizers, dual and triple density midsoles, sock liners, solid rubber heel plugs, padded tongues, and blown rubber outsoles.

The heel of a modern walking shoe is usually a little lower than the heel of a running shoe, and the forefoot is more flexible. Because walking involves less impact than running, the midsole of a walking shoe can be thinner than that of a running shoe. On the other hand, a walking shoe's stiff shank gives better medial and lateral support.

Aerobic Shoes

Aerobic dance combines elements of dance, calesthenics, and stretching into a program performed to music. However, the jogging-in-place and jumping may result in injuries. Instructors suffer more injuries than do their students because they spend more hours doing aerobics.

The most frequent injury in aerobic dance is posteromedial shin splints. Other common injuries are plantar fasciitis, arch strain, and metatarsalgia. Calf strains are also quite common, especially in beginners.

The chances of injury during aerobic dance can be reduced by dancing on a properly cushioned and stable floor, by wearing appropriate footwear, and by following well-designed routines supervised by an attentive instructor. Most of the injuries occur on carpet-covered concrete floors or on linoleum floor. The best surface is a heavily padded concrete floor covered by carpet.

Aerobic dancers can wear court shoes or shoes designed especially for aerobics. Dancing barefoot on a hard floor is not recommended.

An aerobic dance shoe (Figure 1-16) must provide stability. To accomplish this, a shoe may have rubber cantilever outsoles with independently acting, double-tipped lugs to reduce ankle rollover. An exposed molded EVA heel shank will allow the cantilever sole to widen even more on impact for extra shock absorption and stability. A higher-density EVA horseshoe unit at the heel will increase rearfoot stability. An exterior heel counter stabilizer adds support, and stabilizer straps increase midfoot and forefoot support and keep the shoe from stretching out.

A polyurethane forefoot pad will give good cushioning at the ball of the foot. In addition, a polyurethane pad in the rubber sponge sock liner provides extra forefoot cushioning. Forefoot pivotal flex joint bars bend where the foot does, thus reducing fatigue. Board-lasting lends support, and a reinforced toe box gives extra strength. Perforations along the sides of the toe box and along the tongue act as vents for added coolness. The rubber toe bumper should be stitched for durability. A midheight leather padded ankle collar provides ankle support but at the same time allows easy ankle extension and pointing. Supple leather in the upper will make the shoe soft and comfortable yet durable.

Tennis Shoes

Until recently, tennis players have not taken their footwear as seriously as have runners (Figure 1-16). Female players, especially, have often chosen their shoes on the basis of appearance, selecting canvas shoes with soft counters, shallow toe boxes, and no arch support.

A concave, cantilever sole that flares out on impact simultaneously absorbs shock, increases stability, and reduces ankle sprains. Further stability is provided by external heel counters and extended heel counters. For hard-court play, a soft urethane midsole sandwiched in a harder polyurethane outsole gives a mix of cushioning, traction, and durability. The outsole may consist of natural rubber for traction and synthetic rubber for durability. For hard courts, it may have clus-

Running   Aerobic   Aerobic

Tennis   Volleyball   Basketball

Figure 1-16   Today's athlete rarely wears "sneakers"; instead, he has special shoes for each sport, such as running, aerobics, tennis, volleyball, and basketball. Each of these shoes has special features to help the athlete in his sport and to prevent injuries

ters of nubs that look like pencil erasers and for clay courts, a herringbone tread. The rubber bumper should be glued on and stitched. Otherwise, if it were not stitched, it might quickly fall apart. The toe box should be made of reinforced leather. The cushioned sock liner should be elevated at the heel to shift the player's weight to the balls of his feet and to decrease stress on the Achilles tendons.

Volleyball Shoes

Volleyball is a game of starts, stops, jumps, and lateral movement. Consequently, the player's shoes (Figure 1-16) must be lightweight and very durable. Because the game is so hard on shoes, some players wear basketball shoes in practice and lightweight volleyball shoes in games.

The pounding taken by the lower back and knees in volleyball can be lessened by good cushioning. A concave, cantilever sole that flares outward will compress around the outside first and cushion the foot. A player's shoes may also protect against ankle sprains. If the player lands at an angle, the lugs on the cantilever sole keep the foot centered in the shoe and keep the ankle from rolling.

A mesh upper is lightweight yet strong. A

glued and stitched gum-rubber heel wrap enhances rear-foot stability. Stabilizer straps that extend to the eyelets give support and a better fit, and leather reinforcement of the forefoot adds to the durability of the upper and guards against excessive wear from toe drag. The forefoot leather should be backed for further durability.

A gum-rubber outsole provides traction and long wear on indoor courts. The flex joints must bend where the foot bends to allow players to stay on their toes longer with less fatigue. Each shoe should have a sock liner that can be removed while the shoe dries after competition.

Basketball Shoes

Basketball is a game of quick cuts, pivots, and jumps—some of which end in off-center landings. The flared extensions of cantilever outsole stabilizers can keep the ankle from rolling and may prevent a sprain (Figure 1-16).

Dual forefoot straps keep the foot centered during landings and cuts. The straps should extend to the eyelets so that they can be snugged up independently for better forefoot support and to adjust to foot width.

A cantilever sole and tri-layer impact system will absorb shock. The tri-layer consists of a Texon board (for foot stability), a rubber sponge, and a crisscrossed absorption matrix in the rear foot and EVA pad in the forefoot. The shoes should be high topped with flex joints. The joints allow the ball of the foot to bend more easily.

SPORT SOCKS

Shoes and socks form a system to aid athletic performance and protect against injury. Modern sports socks have high-density pads in areas of high stress. They reduce shock, protect against blisters, and reduce compression and pinching of the toes during sudden stops, starts, and lateral movements.

Socks should be checked for holes and for wrinkles before they are put on. Some basketball players wear two pairs of socks to prevent blisters. The inner pair is worn inside-out so that a smooth surface rests against the skin.

SHOE MODIFICATIONS

Running shoes may be modified in the doctor's office. For example, a heel wedge may be added to relieve tension in the Achilles tendon or to equalize leg lengths. If the lift were placed inside the shoe, the athlete's foot might be pushed out or the pad might slip around. To add a heel wedge to the shoe, a cast cutter is first run around the midsole. The rubber wedge is then inserted and glued. To decrease metatarsalgia, a ½-inch rocker can be placed in the midsole under the forefoot.

CARING FOR SPORTS SHOES

Good care of sports shoes is important. They should not be left in a car or in a car trunk on a hot day. The heat will shrink the midsole, and the midsole might then separate from the outsole. If the shoes get wet, they should not be dried in direct sunlight, on a radiator, or with a hair dryer. Instead, the athlete should remove the liner and allow the shoes to dry naturally or in front of a fan. Ideally, two pairs of shoes should be broken in. While one pair is in use, the other pair can be drying or airing out. When not in use, shoes may be left unlaced with absorbent foot powder sprinkled in them. The shoes should not be washed in a machine but may be cleaned with a mild detergent, warm water, and a medium-bristled brush.

Shoes should be used only for the sport for which they were designed. If running shoes were to be worn for a cutting sport, their life and durability would be reduced. Further, the risk of injury would rise. The shoes might roll over sharply because they were made to function straight ahead and not for fast starts, stops, and cutting maneuvers.

LEARNING ABOUT SPORTS SHOES

A comprehensive knowledge of sports shoes may be gained by talking to knowledgeable salespersons in sports shoe stores, by meeting with the regional representatives of sports shoe companies, and by studying the yearly shoe guides and advertisements in sports magazines.

ORTHOTICS ("O'S")

"O's" are devices placed in shoes to correct biomechanical abnormalities, alter biomechanics, or cushion the feet. Some exercising people will bring their orthotics to the examination. Others will need O's.

If a person needs a cushion or a carrier for pads in his sports shoes, I use a Polysorb insert. Pads, such as a Hapad for metatarsalgia, have a sticky side and are glued to the O's. For a heel lift, I place ⅜-inch rubber under the O's. If the athlete wears everyday walking shoes such as loafers that would be too snug for a Polysorb insert, I use a simple Spenco insert as a cushion or as a carrier for pads.

The type of orthotic prescribed depends on the flexibility of the runner's foot. Very flexible feet require more rigid O's. Lifts or wedges are added to these O's medially. Rigid feet require flexible O's that are posted laterally. Interestingly, both the flexible and the rigid foot usually benefit from a heel lift. The flexible foot benefits because the lift reduces pronation, whereas the rigid foot benefits because the lift evens out the rear foot to the forefoot level.

The normal foot should be left alone unless the shoe lacks cushioning, and then a Polysorb cushioning insert may be used.

O's are sometimes improperly used to compensate for anatomic variations in runners who otherwise have no injury problems. In these cases, the runner's body may have already compensated for the abnormal pattern. If the balance of a foot is changed, other X,Y,Z vectors are affected, and the orthotic may cause an injury.[21] For example, borderline knee problems that are not troublesome may become painful because foot compensations are altered by O's.

Lynco inserts are durable and have medial wedges that reduce mild overpronation. However, for the athlete who has a marked biomechanical problem, such as severe overpronation, or for one who has a combined problem, custom-casted cork-latex runner's mold O's with foam covers are best. These are made with deep heel cups for those with a combination of overpronation and heel bruise and with plastazote metatarsal pads for those with overpronation and metatarsalgia.

The slipper casts for custom O's are made with the athlete sitting and putting some weight on his feet. Otherwise, a tight structure such as plantar fascia or flexor hallucis longus might not groove the slipper and the orthotic might rub there, forming a bruise or blister.

The cork-latex O's can also be made with heel lifts, wedges, or extensions and may be reinforced with, for example, nickelplast for heavy heel strikers or padded with plastazote for cushioning. These orthotics are very durable.

The frequently prescribed plastic O's may cost more than $200. Although they may alleviate a runner's current problem such as knee pain, they often provide too much control, which can lead to more serious complications such as an Achilles tendinitis or severe metatarsalgia.

New users of O's are warned that their O's often will not fit into their ordinary walking shoes. I therefore recommend Rocksport and Dressport shoes, which are lightweight and deep. The runner is also given a program for breaking in the O's to avoid pains, bruises, or blisters (Table 1-6).

BALANCED COMPETITION (MATURITY MATCHING)

Although balanced competition reduces injuries, it is difficult to arrange in early adolescence because most school competition is arranged by grade level and most community-sponsored activities are organized by age group. Unfortunately, age is not a completely satisfactory index of the young athlete's physical capability or of his susceptibility to injury.

At age 13, boys may vary physically from 40 kg (90 lb) of baby fat and peach fuzz to 100 kg (220 lb) of muscle and moustache.[17] The early adolescent's strength, stamina, coordination, body composition, and, to some extent, skills are more closely related to sexual maturation than to age. For this reason, maturity matching assumes importance in grades 7 through 12, where youngsters range in age from 12 to 19 years.

Maturity matching of girls is best attained by the menarchal method. Regardless of their chronological age, all girls in the United States are

Table 1-6   ORTHOTICS ("O'S")

Your Runner's Mold Orthotics are made of durable cork-latex covered by leather. The orthotics control excessive foot motion, reduce twisting in your legs and at your knees, and absorb shock.

Break your orthotics in slowly. Otherwise, you may develop foot blisters or soreness anywhere from your feet to your back.

Here is a schedule for breaking in your orthotics:

Day 1—2 hours walking in morning, 2 hours in afternoon

Day 2—same

Day 3—3 hours walking in morning, 3 hours in afternoon

Day 4—same

Day 5—wear your orthotics all day long

Day 6—same

Day 7—add a short training run

Day 8—full use

The transition to wearing orthotics is usually very smooth. However, you may notice a fleeting soreness somewhere. If you have some soreness, drop back to the schedule of the previous day. If the soreness persists, if the orthotics are uncomfortable, or if your problem is not cured, let me know.

Please remember to take any inserts out of shoes in which you intend to wear your orthotics.

---

considered to have a developmental age of 12½ years at the time of their first menstrual period. Thus, a girl who had her first menstrual period 3 years ago is considered to have a developmental age of 12½ years plus 3 years, or 15½ years.

For boys, a series of drawings is used to grade the growth of facial, axillary, and pubic hair on a scale of one to five. The results may be recorded in a master log, and these athletes may then be channeled into competition with others at the same stage of maturity.

Other methods for assessing developmental age are wrist x-rays and grip strength. Wrist x-rays may be compared to skeletal growth x-rays in a radiologic atlas, and grip strength measurement is a fairly reliable index of a person's physical maturity.[13, 40]

Maturity matching should become more popular as more educators and physicians become aware of its benefits in reducing injuries and promoting fair competition.

ON-THE-FIELD RESPONSIBILITIES

The team physician should be readily available before, during, and after games and practices. If he cannot attend, he must delegate authority to another doctor. The team physician should check the training room after each practice and enforce the rule that all injuries be reported. Because athletic injuries demand prompt attention for optimum results, treatment of the injured athlete should not be delayed.

The athlete may return to practice after an injury if he is not favoring the injured part and has met performance criteria. After a knee injury, for example, he must regain full strength and flexibility and run figure-eights, cariocas (cross-over-step-runs) and 40-yard sprints without a limp.

The injured athlete's pain should never be masked by shots, pills, or nerve stimulators to allow him to participate. If a player claims injury and asks to be excused from play, he should not return to the game, no matter what the medical staff and coaching staff think of the injury. It is the team physician's responsibility to analyze the circumstances and suggest preventive programs after every injury.

Contents of The Team Physician's Bag

Stethoscope
Blood pressure cuff
Disposable syringes
Needles
Alcohol swabs
Tourniquet
Intravenous tubing
A large-bore (#15) needle
Two-way radio pager or walkie-talkie
Change for pay phone
Pencils
Notebook or pad of paper
Oral screw
Ophthalmoscope and otoscope

Fluorescein strips
Pen light
Tongue blades
Padded tongue blade
Percussion hammer
Thermometer
Examination gloves
Cotton swabs
Kocher clamps
Tape measure
Aluminum finger splints
Multigadget Swiss army knife
Safety pin
Bandage scissors
Sterile suture set
Sterile gloves
Tincture of benzoin
Band-Aids, butterflies, and Steri-strips
Adhesive tape
Gauze pads, roller bandage, and elastic wraps

Medicines

Ringer's lactate
Dextrose solution
Xylocaine
Epinephrine
Lanoxin
Propranalol
Atropine
Dopamine
Sodium bicarbonate
Lasix
Valium
Dextrose (50% solution)
Decadron
Compazine
Antivert
An antihistamine
Benadryl
Ammonia capsules
Robaxin
Aspirin
Ascription
Acetaminophen
Codeine
Antacid tablets
Maalox
Lomotil
Hydrogen peroxide
Betadine

Neosporin ointment
Xylocaine injectable

On the Doctor's Person

Oral screw
Tongue forceps
Airway
Tongue depressors
Bandage scissors
Penlight
Paper bag (for rebreathing)
Sterile gauze pads
Tape 2.5 to 3.75 cm (1 to 1½ in)
Band-Aids
Multipurpose Swiss Army knife

RETURN TO COMPETITION

It is the team physician's responsibility to decide whether an athlete may return to practice or games after an injury or illness. Overcautious appraisals may mean lost games, but failure to be cautious enough may mean serious harm for the athlete. His injury may worsen with play, converting a minor hurt into a major disability, or the first injury may lead to a second one, as when a dazed athlete is unable to protect himself.

After each injury, a firm diagnosis should be made before the athlete is allowed to return to competition.[16] For example, a single ligament ankle sprain is more informative than a "swollen ankle." Normally, an athlete should not return to the game if he has been knocked out, is dazed, or has inappropriate responses for more than 10 seconds after having been struck on the head. Additional symptoms that bar return to play are numbness, tingling, obvious swelling or bleeding, limited range of motion, or need for assistance to leave the field. Before reentering a game, the athlete must be functioning normally and satisfy performance criteria such as starts, cuts, jumps, and blocks.

THE YOUNG ATHLETE

The growth plates of young athletes, especially at the elbow, hip, and knee, are susceptible to acute injury and overuse, and either type of injury can lead to long-term problems. Further, a youth's ability to develop strength depends on his physical maturity. An immature youth with open epiphyses and a thin, weak neck should therefore refrain from collision sports such as tackle football. A teenager also has less flexibility when going through a growth spurt, and in such periods the youngster should avoid collision sports and speed work but continue to stretch daily. Such immature youths can train on a Hydra-Gym circuit; they may also work on technique for Olympic-style weight lifting with a lightly loaded bar. Power lifting should be disallowed because it emphasizes heavy weights. Other problems for children arise in wrestling, when a grappler tries to make weight, and in gymnastics, where hard training and a low food intake may stunt growth. Each young athlete should wear appropriate top-grade protective gear, such as mouthguards, when practicing or competing in sports.

Based on their own experience and because of budget cuts, many citizens and school boards are questioning the value of physical education in schools, classes that usually include a monotonously repetitive playing of touch football, basketball, and softball. Children often participate wearing their school clothes, do not shower, and return to class sweaty and dirty. Time spent on these traditional team sports should be curtailed and replaced by health education, wherein the youngsters acquire the skills, knowledge, and attitudes for a lifetime of activity (Table 1-7). Physicians may join with health and physical educators in designing and implementing these programs: This marriage was made years ago in Greek mythology when Asclepias, the god of medicine, married Hygeia, the goddess of health.

The fitness concepts of a modern physical education program are best taught through activity, and cognitive material is built into the activity setting. Lecturing is kept to a minimum, and only after a period of vigorous physical activity. The physical educator can systematically incorporate ample cognitive material into the curriculum during just 3 minutes of class. Three minutes twice a week for 40 weeks a year over 10 years adds up to 40 hours of cognitive material.

In addition to the cognitive aspects of the physical education curriculum, some parts may

Table 1-7 COMPONENTS OF A HEALTH-RELATED PHYSICAL EDUCATION PROGRAM

1. Biology of exercise
2. Benefits of regular exercise for men and women
3. How to modify coronary risk factors
4. Principles of endurance training
5. Principles of strength training
6. How to design a personal fitness program
7. Warm-up techniques
8. Nutrition
9. Injury prevention
10. First aid
11. Exposure to a wide variety of recreational and fitness activities that emphasize lifetime body sports, such as cycling, gymnastics, jogging, and swimming
12. Basic movement patterns such as throwing, changing direction (cutting and pivoting) and how to land.

be coordinated with the curricula of other courses. Physical education may also serve as the "lab" for certain topics in biology and health education. Just as in other courses, homework, out-of-class projects, and term papers should be required. Fitness testing can be a cognitive experience if the youth is told why he is being tested, what the results mean, how the results will be used, and how he can improve his performance.

A modern physical education program for young people will produce favorable attitudes toward physical fitness and serve as a base for intramural sports. Quality and quantity are important because a variety of activities will allow each participant to gain from sport at his level. Interscholastic competition allows physically talented athletes to compete against other talented ones, with the better athletes providing examples for others to emulate. Although physicians have given most of their attention to this talented group, intramural athletes need similar supervision because they are generally less proficient, use inferior equipment, and play on poorer fields.

The fitness value of competitive sports is obvious, but there are other lasting benefits. Sports satisfy the young athlete's need for adventure and help him to learn self-discipline and the relation between hard work and success. He also learns how to accept and meet challenges, how to win and lose, and how to work with others toward goals.[9]

THE FEMALE ATHLETE

Because of their social conditioning, most women have been relatively inactive and have shown little interest in athletics. Those who did participate usually did not perform well because they were poorly conditioned and had inexperienced coaches. The larger number of women competing today are stronger, more skillful and agressive, and bringing their physiologic capabilities to a new peak.

Unconditioned women entering athletics have a high injury rate, whereas the injury rate for conditioned female athletes is equal to that of their male counterparts, although the spectrum of injuries differs. The difference in injuries is related to women's anatomic peculiarities and relaxed joints. Shoulder injuries are common because the arms are relatively weak. Lordosis puts more strain on the back, and a wide pelvis requires that the hips move more during walking and running, a movement that puts more strain on the back and promotes pelvic pain and greater trochanteric bursitis.

The female athlete is predisposed to knee problems by knock knees, increased "Q angles" (the angle that the patellar tendon makes with the long axis of the limb), flat kneecaps, and shallow intercondylar grooves. Compared to men, a woman's foot is generally flatter and prone to arch pain. Her metatarsals are smaller, and she suffers stress fractures. A woman also develops bunions more readily and has more frequent pains at the metatarsophalangeal joint of the great toes.

Women normally prefer to wear minimal protective equipment, and the rules are designed to limit contact and injuries. A player in field hockey, for example, may not swat a high ball with her stick, although she may block it. Strict officiating is the key to keeping today's stronger and more aggressive players free of encumbering, unattractive protective gear.

Athletic Infertility

Young women who train strenuously in activities like ballet, modern dancing, running, and gym-nastics often menstruate later than do their less active peers and also have a higher prevalence of menstrual irregularities and secondary amenorrhea. One of five elite female distance runners who train 104 km (65 miles) or more per week will fail to menstruate at all or do so only once or twice a year. These problems may be associated with physical stress or the emotional stress of competition, diversion of blood flow away from the ovaries during exercise, or an altered body core temperature owing to a low percentage of body fat.

A minimum level of about 17% body fat seems to be needed for the onset and maintenance of mensus in the human female, and when body fat is low the reproductive system shuts down, preventing conception. A weight loss of 10% to 15% below normal represents a loss of about one third of body fat and can cause amenorrhea. When weight is regained, the menstrual cycles resume. Many questions, however, remain unanswered: What are the long-term consequences of the athletic amenorrhea? How many female athletes fail to resume menses after hard training? Does the amenorrhea preclude a normal development of the endocrine system or harm the development of the reproductive organs?

Although women show considerable variability in menstrual flow, most need not alter their training, competing, and even swimming during a menstrual period. Although personal records have been set at all phases of the cycle, some women must reduce their activity before and during the menstrual period because they do not feel well.

Pregnancy

Exercise is advisable during pregancy, and a fit woman usually has a better labor. She may, however, be too nauseated to train during the first trimester, and during the third trimester the uterus is large, the fetus bounces, and the breasts swell, making exercise uncomfortable and often causing backache.

As the pregnancy advances, there is a progressive decline in a woman's circulatory reserve owing to peripheral pooling of blood and obstruction of venous return by the large, gravid uterus. If there is already some compromise of the umbilical circulation, moderately severe maternal exercise may harm the fetus by temporarily reducing uterine blood flow and fetal P_{O_2}.

Thus, a pregnant woman should train at a comfortable pace. If she trains too hard, expends too many calories, and fails to gain the recommended 11 kg (25 lb), her baby's nutrition may be compromised. She must therefore be advised to titrate her exercise, cutting back on hard training and avoiding exhaustion and excessive heat.

Although the fetus is well protected by the mother's pelvis and later by a cushion of amniotic fluid, contact sports and downhill skiing are best avoided in the later stages of the pregnancy. Most sports may be resumed about 2 weeks after delivery, and swimming may be resumed at about 3 weeks postpartum when the cervix has closed.

THE OLDER ATHLETE

Older people are now eagerly entering sports, but many of them are unprepared. Even former athletes will find that training techniques have changed. Most injuries in older athletes are due to improper warm-up, training errors, and poor technique.

The older athlete should develop a fitness foundation before competing rather than competing to become fit. Fatigue can result in poor concentration and injury and the older person may also suffer from arthritis and degenerated tendons. He usually has poor flexibility and diminished proprioception. Injuries commonly occur during plyometric activities owing to the switch from an eccentric to a concentric contraction, when stress is the greatest.

The physician often is asked to construct fitness programs for older athletes and to counsel them about competitive sports, such as cycling, tennis, track and field, and swimming. Local coaches and physical educators may instruct the older athlete in warm-up and training techniques and see that they have adequate gymnasium and pool time.

REFERENCES

1. Alyea EP, Parish HH Jr.: Renal response to exercise—renal findings. JAMA 167:807–813, 1958
2. Appenzeller H: Athletics and the Law. Charlottesville, Virginia, The Michie Company, 1975
3. Bailey RR et al: What the urine contains following athletic competition. NZ Med J 83:809–813, 1976
4. Ball RT: Capable coach is best defense against threat of litigation. First Aider, Cramer 48:1, February 1979
5. Blackburn TA (ed): Guidelines for Pre-Season Athletic Participation Evaluation. Ad Hoc Committee on Pre-Season Athletic Participation Evaluation. Alexandria, Virginia, Sports Medicine Section, American Physical Therapy Association, 1979
6. Blyth CS, Mueller FO: When and where players get hurt. Football injury survey: Part I. Phys Sportsmed 2(9):45–52, 1974
7. Clayton ML et al: Football: the pre-season examination. J Sports Med 1:19–24, 1973
8. Collier W: Functional albuminuria in athletes. Br Med J 1:4–6, 1907
9. Craig TT (ed): Comments in Sports Medicine. Chicago, American Medical Association, 1973
10. Fairbanks LL: Return to sports participation. Phys Sportsmed 7(8):71–74, 1979
11. Decof L, Godosky R: Sports Injury Litigation. Litigation and Administrative Practice Series, no. 139, New York, The Practicing Law Institute, 1979
12. Duda v. Baines, 12, New Jersey Superior Court, 326, 79A, 2d 695
13. Fleishman EA: The Structure and Measurement of Physical Fitness. Englewood Cliffs, New Jersey, Prentice-Hall, 1968
14. Flynn TG et al: Injuries to young athletes. Committee on Pediatric Aspects of Physical Fitness, Recreation and Sports. Pediatrics 65:649–650, 1980
15. Gardner KD Jr: "Athletic psuedonephritis"—alteration of urine sediment by athletic competition. JAMA 161:1613–1617, 1956
16. Garrick JG: Sports medicine. Pediatr Clin North Am 74:737–747, 1977
17. Gomlak C: Problems in matching young athletes: Baby fat, peach fuzz, muscle and mustache. Phys Sportsmed 3(5):96–98, 1975
18. Hale v. Davies, 86 Georgia Appellate, 126, 70 S.E. 2d 923
18a. Haycock CE: How I manage hernias in the athlete. Phys Sportsmed 11(8):77–79, 1983
19. Hirsch FJ: The generalist as team physician. Phys Sportsmed 7(8):89–95, 1979
20. Jackson DW et al: Injury prediction in the young athlete: A preliminary report. Am J Sportsmed 6(1):6–14, 1978
21. Kerby v. Elk Grove Union District, 1 California Appellate 2d 246, 36, P. 2d 431
22. Kulund DN, Brubaker CE: Injuries in the Bikecentennial Tour. Phys Sportsmed 6:467–478, 1978
23. Kulund DN et al: The long-term effects of playing tennis. Phys Sportsmed 7(4):87–94, 1979
24. Lowell CH: Legal responsibilities and sports-medicine. Phys Sportsmed 5(7):60–68, 1977
25. Luce v. Board of Education of Johnson City, 2 Ap-

pellate Division 2d 502, 157, New York State 2d 123

26. Marshall JL, Tischler HM: Screening for sports: Guidelines. NY State J Med 78:243–251, 1978

27. Marshall JL et al: Joint looseness: A function of the person and the joint. Med Sci Sports Exerc 12:189–194, 1980

28. Mayne BR: If sports medicine is your bag—equip it well. Phys Sportsmed 3(9):67–69, 1975

29. Nathan DC, Oski FA: Hematology of Infancy and Childhood, p 98. Philadelphia, WB Saunders, 1974

30. Nicholas JA: Injuries to knee ligaments: Relationship to looseness and tightness in football players. JAMA 212:2236–2239, 1970

31. Nicholas JA: A study of thigh muscle weakness in different pathological states of the lower extremity. Am J Sports Med 4:241–248, 1976

32. Obremskey M: Courts set legal guidelines for physical education instructors. First Aider, Cramer 46:4, December 1976

33. Percy EC: The physician and the athlete. Can Med Assoc J 102:137–138, 1970

34. Ryan AJ (moderator): Guidelines to help you in giving on-field care. Phys Sportsmed 3(9):50–63, 1975

35. Ryan AJ (moderator): Proteinuria in the athlete. Phys Sportsmed 6(7):45–61, 1978

36. Ryan AJ (moderator): Qualifying exams: A continuing dilemma. Phys Sportsmed 8(8):10, 1980

37. Savastano AA: The team physician and the law. RI. Med Soc J 51:558–565, 1968

38. Schell NB: Cardiac evaluation of school sports participants. NY State J Med 78:942–943, 1978

39. Shaffer TE: So you've been asked to be the team physician? Phys Sportsmed 4(12):57–63, 1976

40. Shaffer TE: The health examination for participation in sports. Phys Sportsmed 7(10):27–40, 1978

41. Thornton ML et al: Cardiac Evaluation for Participation in Sports. Policy Statement. Evanston, Illinois, American Academy of Pediatrics, 1977

42. Weistart JC, Lowell CH: The Law of Sports. Charlottesville, Virginia, Merrill, 1979

43. Welch v. Dunsmuir. Joint Union High School District, 326, P. 2d 633, California 1958

44. Wilkins E: The uniqueness of the young athlete: Musculoskeletal injuries. Am J Sport Med 8:377–381, 1980

45. Willis GC: The legal responsibilities of the team physician. J Sportsmed 1:28–29, 1972

46. Zaricznyj B et al: Sports-related injuries in school-aged children. Am J Sports Med 8:318–324, 1980

CHAPTER

2

Special Athletes, Medical Problems, Nutrition, and Drugs

THE HANDICAPPED ATHLETE

Handicapped athletes include those who are blind, deaf, or paralyzed; amputees; the mentally retarded; and those with other neuromuscular or skeletal disease. The handicapped person who participates in athletics acquires skills and confidence, drops body weight, subdues depression, increases his mobility and endurance, and rehabilitates atrophied muscles. Handicapped sports are not just rehabilitation but sporting events in their own right. The 1976 Olympiad for the Physically Disabled attracted 1500 athletes from 38 countries.[29] This was the first Olympiad with full competition for blind, paralyzed, and amputee athletes.

When the handicapped athlete competes in his own class, the competition is rewarding for the athlete and exciting for spectators.[13] There is

a tendency, however, for outsiders to compare the performance of the handicapped to that of able-bodied athletes. Even against such standards, the performance of a handicapped athlete may be spectacular.[29] A one-legged high jumper, for example, has hopped up to the bar and cleared 1.85 m (6 ft, 1¾ in), a wheelchair athlete has done a metric mile in 5 hours and 15 seconds, a blind athlete has run 100 m in 11.6 seconds guided by the voice of his coach at the end of the track, and a paraplegic weightlifter has benched pressed 263 kg (585 pounds).

The handicapped person's physician is best suited to channel his patient into sports programs because the physician is best informed about his patient's disabilities.

There is a great need for a national organization to oversee all sport for the disabled and to unify it with able-bodied sport. Pools, gymnasiums, and coaches should be readily accessible to disabled athletes, who are entitled to opportunities for physical education, recreation, and interscholastic and intercollegiate sports comparable to those of able-bodied athletes.

The Blind Athlete

All blind athletes are legally blind, but some are completely blind and others have partial sight. The athlete with partial sight has the advantage of being able to perceive light and dark and appreciate shadows.

Wrestling, track, and swimming have long been the favorite sports of the blind athlete, but other sports for the blind include bowling, skiing, and track-and-field events such as the pentathlon.[46] He may also participate in beep baseball, golf, tandem bicycling, and even archery.

In track, the athlete runs with a sighted companion who holds a short line or the runner listens to his coach calling instructions. Blind bowlers use a portable, 3.6-m (12-ft) long, waist-high guide rail. In downhill skiing, a sighted skier trails closely behind the blind athlete (Figure 2-1). The sighted skier calls signals, touches the blind skier with a ski pole, or uses clap sticks to guide the blind skier audibly. In beep baseball, a regulation softball with a battery in it emits a beep. Although many beep baseball players do not wear protective gear, all players should be encouraged to wear face masks and chest protectors.

The Deaf Athlete

Profound deafness is usually due to sensorineural defects rather than conduction defects. Most often, the athlete's mother had rubella during the first trimester of pregnancy, but sometimes the deafness results from Rh incompatibility of the parents, meningitis, viral infection, or a congenital malformation. If the athlete has cochlear damage but little semicircular canal or vestibular apparatus damage, he probably will escape equilibrium problems.

If his vestibular mechanism is damaged, the deaf athlete must work extra hard to achieve balance and coordination.[51] For example, it will be difficult for the athlete to walk on a balance beam, do rapid spins, or do sharp turns. The deaf athlete may also have major problems with communi-

Figure 2-1 A blind skier **(A)** is guided by instructions from a sighted companion **(B)**.

cation. He must constantly look around to ascertain the position of teammates and has to develop his peripheral vision. Signals, such as dimming the lights in a hockey rink rather than blowing a whistle, are used.

Because deaf athletes appear to be normal, public interest in and support for athletic programs for the deaf are lacking. However, Gallaudet College, a liberal arts college for the deaf in Washington, D.C., sponsors a full athletic program for deaf athletes.

The Paralyzed Athlete

The first international sporting event for paralyzed athletes took place in 1952 at Stoke–Mandeville Hospital in England, the home of The National Spinal Injury Center, directed by Sir Ludwig Guttman. The competition consisted only of archery, but more events and more competitors were added later, and a medical classification system was developed. In 1960, the Wheelchair Olympics moved to the site of the Olympic Games in Rome. In 1964, they were held 1 week after the able-bodied Olympics in Tokyo, and in 1968 the games were held in Israel. In 1972, Heidelberg hosted the games a few weeks before the able-bodied Olympics in Munich. The year 1976 marked the first Olympiad for physically disabled, blind, paralyzed, and amputee athletes held in Toronto 1 week after the Montreal games.[29]

Wheelchair games include track and field, swimming, weight lifting, slalom, archery, pentathlon, and table tennis. There is also competition in fencing, rifle shooting, snooker, precision javelin (throwing a javelin into a large target), darchery (a combination of darts and archery), and basketball. The National Wheelchair Athletic Association is headquartered at the Bulova School of Watchmaking in New York.

Spinal-cord-injured athletes are not the only participants at the wheelchair games; also included are athletes with neurologic or paralyzing disorders, such as polio and meningomyelocele. Some amputees also compete in wheelchairs. Paralyzed persons are introduced to athletics at regional spinal cord injury centers before joining the National Wheelchair Athletic Association or park and recreation department programs.

Doctors and therapists classify paralyzed athletes because proper classification is important to assure fair competition, and the disability of an athlete may improve or worsen with time, requiring reclassification. Quadriplegic athletes are classified according to whether they lack triceps function, have some triceps function, or have some hand function (Table 2-1).[13] The paraplegic's trunk muscles, abdominal muscles, and hip extensors and flexors are also checked, although classification may be difficult when patterns of disability vary so widely. Classification for the National Wheelchair Athletic Association differs from that for the National Wheelchair Basketball Association (Table 2-2). Both equitable team competition and participation in basketball by severely disabled players are encouraged by the rule limiting the number of player points each team may have in a game to 12 (points being equal to the class of each player, that is, class I = 1 point, class II = 2 points, and so forth).[13]

Wheelchair athletes have a low injury rate. At the National Wheelchair Games, the athletes have had very few shoulder problems from propelling the wheelchair (Figure 2-2), but sometimes their skin has broken down in sensitive areas, especially on the hands. Some quadriplegic athletes have suffered heat exhaustion, partly because of their decreased sweating ability.

The Amputee Athlete

Amputee games include track and field, swimming, skiing, slalom, riflery, pentathlon, football-kicking, table tennis, and bowling.

There are 12 categories of amputee athletes, defined by combinations of loss of one or both legs, whether above or below the knee, and by various levels of loss of the upper extremity.[27] Not only do amputee sports benefit the competitors, but also the search for better prostheses for competition may lead to advances in materials and fittings for all amputees.

Although most amputee athletes compete with a prosthesis, some compete without this device, whereas others use a wheelchair. A skier may ski with or without a prosthesis, and some

Table 2-1   CLASSIFICATION FOR NATIONAL WHEELCHAIR ATHLETIC ASSOCIATION COMPETITIONS

Class	Equivalent Spinal Cord Level	Function Present	Function Absent
1A	C-6 or higher	Wrist extensor	No better than fair triceps; nothing distally; no balance or lower extremity function
1B	C-7	Good or normal triceps	No finger flexors of extensors; no balance or lower extremity function
1C	C-8	Finger flexors and extensors	No intrinsics; no balance or lower extremity function
II	T-1→T-5	Normal upper extremity function	No better than poor abdominal muscles; no useful balance or lower extremity function
III	T-6→T-10	Upper abdominal muscles	Some balance but not normal; no lower extremity function
IV	T-11→L-2	Normal abdominal strength	No better than poor quadriceps; nothing distally
V	L-3→S-5	Fair or better quadriceps	Lower extremity weakness "significant and permanent"
VI		Swimming only; ability to push off a wall with lower extremities L-5→S-5)	

skiers "three-track" with outrigger that has a short ski tip and a swivel (Figure 2-3).

THE "SPECIAL OLYMPICS"

The "Special Olympics" are open to all mentally retarded athletes 7 years of age or older,[7] and this group now totals more than 400,000 Special Olympians and 150,000 volunteers. An International Special Olympics is held every 4 years, and each year thousands of local and area meets are conducted. Official sports in the Special Olympics include track and field, swimming and diving, gymnastics, floor hockey, basketball, ice skating, bowling, volleyball, and wheelchair events.

Supervisors at these competitions must be alert for seizures and be sure that the competitors take their preventive medicines. At the 1975 International Games in Michigan, there were 15 recorded grand mal seizures. Also, although some mentally retarded athletes have good control, others may not know when to stop because of a lack of judgment, and therefore need constant supervision in social situations.

ICE SKATING THERAPY

Because balance is lost and regained on a hard and slippery surface, ice skating helps youngsters with physical or mental disabilities to gain confidence and self-control.[1] Their body awareness is enhanced as their anxiety level drops and their muscle tension decreases.

Ice skating therapy benefits children with minimal brain dysfunction because the skating refines precision movement. Obstacle courses may be set up to improve task completion skills for youngsters who have difficulty controlling their behavior and attention. Skating also elevates the kinesthetic awareness of children with learning disabilities and is especially beneficial for youngsters with spastic cerebral palsy and mild to moderate hemiplegia and for the mentally retarded.

Ice skating therapy demands good balance but requires less power and strength than walking.[1] The structural and motor requirements for participation include a stable spine, extensor and abductor stability of the hips and extensor stability of the knee, good quadriceps, and the absence of

Table 2-2 CLASSIFICATION FOR NATIONAL WHEELCHAIR BASKETBALL ASSOCIATION*

Player Points	Class	Equivalent Spinal Cord Level	Function Present	Function Absent
1	I	T-7 or higher		Impaired balance; no lower abdominal muscles or lower extremity function
2	II	T-8→L-2	May have hip flexors graded good, adductors graded fair, and quadriceps graded poor	No useful lower extremity function. (This class includes those with bilateral hip disarticulation but otherwise normal muscles.)
3	III	L-3 or lower	Quadriceps fair or better; all other lower extremity disabilities (including amputation)	

*A team (five players) may not total more than 12 points at any time in a game.

marked knee flexion contractures. Children should have some dorsiflexion and plantar flexion stability of the ankle, which an ankle–foot orthosis could help, and motor power across their ankle joints. Their feet should be relatively plantigrade.

The skate shoes should fit snugly. Off-the-ice walking on perfectly fitted skates is a good exercise before attempting the ice. The skater should use single blades without toe picks. An outrigger skate aid—a figure-skating blade mounted on a Lofstrand-type crutch—can increase his base of support.

The Hein-A-Ken skate aid (Figure 2-4) is based

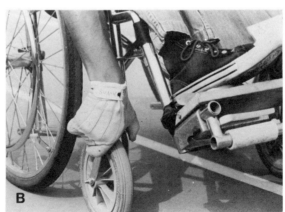

Figure 2-2 A wheelchair athlete **(A),** with just one usable hand, can steer by reaching down to the caster wheel **(B).**

Figure 2-3 An amputee skier can "three-track" with outriggers that have a short ski tip and a swivel.

on the principle of learning to skate with a chair[1] but is more stable than an ordinary chair. It is especially helpful for children who cannot propel themselves with a reciprocal action. The aid allows children to make more effective use of the motor power in the sound leg and to shift their weight away from the affected side in a scooter motion. Eventually they begin stroking and gliding and are gradually weaned from the skate aid.

MEDICAL PROBLEMS

Diabetes Mellitus

Exercise is beneficial for the athlete with diabetes mellitus because it lowers blood glucose levels. Diabetic persons who exercise are usually in better control, and an exercise program often stimulates diabetics to comply with proper manage-

Figure 2-4 The skate aid allows a young skater to develop his skating technique and gain confidence.

ment of the diabetes.[15] Further, the cardiovascular benefits of exercise are especially important to diabetics because they have an increased risk of cardiovascular problems.

Athletes with diabetes are excellent candidates for self-glucose-monitoring. They can use meters or visual strips to check their blood glucose before, during (in the case of prolonged exercise such as marathoning), or after exercise. This will allow them to calculate with some precision the effect of exercise on their blood glucose and adjust their carbohydrate intake appropriately. Self-glucose-monitoring also allows for an accurate discrimination between hypoglycemia and hyperglycemia and lessens the likelihood of inappropriate treatment. Diabetics who have a blood glucose level above 300 mg/dl should not exercise until they have seen a physician and brought it down to 250 mg/dl or less.

Most experienced diabetics do not change their insulin doses with exercise but instead increase their food intake. However, the insulin-dependent diabetic who starts an exercise program should first decrease his insulin by 20% to 40%. Abdominal sites should be used for insulin injection and the diabetic person should avoid injecting into exercised extremities, since increased circulation in the exercised part allows insulin to be absorbed too rapidly. The insulin-dependent diabetic should take glucose supplements every hour during sustained exercise because these athletes are more likely than are other diabetics to become ketoacidotic or hypoglycemic. Insulin is needed to support the life of these athletes, who usually have an onset of the disease at younger than 20 years of age and who do not become very overweight.

A diabetic's precompetition meal should be high in complex carbohydrate and relatively low in fat and protein. The timing of the meal is important: It should be eaten several hours before exercising. If the athlete drinks a strong sugar solution 30 minutes before exercising, his liver will shut off its glucose output. The intestine cannot meet the demands placed on it, and the athlete becomes hypoglycemic after the exercise begins.

Diabetic persons should take responsibility for their own care, bringing food to practices and competitions.[8] The food should be put aside so that others will not snack on it. Doctors, trainers, and coaches should be well informed about diabetes because injuries to diabetics must be treated carefully. Coaches and teammates must be alert for trouble signs and symptoms and be aware of treatment procedures. Trainers must avoid use of excessively hot or cold modalities on the diabetic athlete, and diabetic persons should avoid using counterirritants on their legs. Footwear should be especially checked so that sores may be prevented.

Diabetic coma is caused by too much sugar and acetone in the blood with too little insulin. The athlete may feel sick, have a stomachache, be confused or lethargic, have a fruity breath odor, and have a fast pulse. He should be asked if he has eaten and if he has taken his insulin. Ketoacidosis takes time to develop and this is unlikely to occur during a game.

Insulin shock may be caused by an overdose of insulin, too much exercise, or too little food. The athlete will be fatigued and irritable; he may have slurred speech, a headache, dizziness, hunger, and poor coordination; his hands may tremble; and he will feel faint and may even lose consciousness. In contrast to diabetic coma, there is no fruity breath odor, and the pulse is normal. The athlete should be given sugar in the form of sweet drinks or candy and be allowed to rest so that the sugar can be absorbed.

Addison's Disease

Athletes with well-controlled Addison's disease may participate in all sports. These athletes add extra salt to the evening meal if they have sweated a lot or if they anticipate heavy perspiration. Sometimes extra prednisone is taken before competition.

Hemophilia

Concentrates of Factor VIII are available, as cryoprecipitate or as commercially available products, that will allow hemophiliacs to participate in athletics.[52] However, even though Factor VIII concentrates are effective, hemophiliacs are best advised to participate in noncontact sports and to avoid tackle football because of the danger of intracranial bleeding.

In the past, a cast was applied when a hemophiliac's joint was injured. The limb then quickly atrophied, weakened, and became unstable, further bleeding occurred, and the joint finally collapsed. When a hemophiliac is injured today, he is given an early booster shot of Factor VIII concentrate. There is time for the booster because the athlete's bleeding will be at a normal rate. Factor VIII concentrate averts most serious bleeding and is followed by physical therapy.

Concentrates of Factor VIII may be transported in a small freezer and kept in a refrigerator at camps and gymnasiums. The drug may be infused by a trained layman or by the athlete himself. If the hemophiliac must take other drugs, he should ingest them.

Sickle Cell Trait

Sickle cell disease includes sickle cell anemia (hemoglobin S-S) and the less severe hemoglobin S-C and hemoglobin S-Thal conditions. With two abnormal genes for hemoglobin S, persons with sickle cell anemia will be anemic, with a hemoglobin rarely higher than 7 g. This results in problems before the youth is old enough to consider athletic participation.

The athlete with sickle cell trait inherits one abnormal gene for hemoglobin (S) and one normal gene (A) to form an AS genotype. Ten percent of American blacks have sickle cell trait, which is 50 times more common than sickle cell anemia. The athlete with this disorder is at risk for sickling or sickle cell crisis when at high altitude (greater than 1200 m, or 4000 feet) or under the stress of environmental heat.[56] Decreased oxygen causes red blood cells to deform, elongate, and assume a crescent or sickle shape. These cells then have reduced oxygen-transporting capacity and may lodge in blood vessels and vital organs, such as the spleen, causing pain.

Black athletes and athletes of dark Mediterranean origin may be screened with a simple screening kit test based on turbidity or with a sickle cell preparation test. If the test findings are positive, the athlete should have a hemoglobin electrophoresis done for a definitive diagnosis,

and genetic counseling should be offered. Subjects should be made aware of the early symptoms of sickle crisis, including sudden pain under the lower left ribs, hematuria, weakness, and nausea.

The athlete with sickle cell trait need not be restricted from sports, since he can prevent dehydration by taking fluids before and during practice and contests while avoiding heavy anaerobic work and performing adequate and gradual warm-ups.

Colds

A cold is an infectious disease spread by coughing, sneezing, talking, or contact. The chance of contracting a cold depends on the frequency and degree of exposure to the virus, coupled with the athlete's relative immunity. Colds are not prevented by being in "good shape," and a trained athlete can catch a cold just as easily as a non-athlete.

The chance of a cold spreading through a team can be reduced if athletes avoid community drinking cups, using dispenser squeeze bottles instead. In cold weather, athletes should stay warm and avoid leaving practice sessions with wet hair after showers or saunas. Chills may be prevented by keeping hair shorter during the winter and by using a hair dryer. Wool stocking hats should be worn in cold weather.

Colds cannot be worked off by vigorous exercise. Instead, exercise puts an extra demand on the athlete's body when he needs all his resources to fight the infection. He should rest, eat well, and drink plenty of fluids, keeping away from the team to prevent the cold from spreading. A serious communicable disease may start with symptoms that resemble a simple cold, and pills or capsules will reduce the symptoms of a cold but will not effect a cure.

It is better for an athlete to miss a few practices and return strong than to drag through drills for a week. Athletes with a mild cold may compete but should not do so if fever is present. Poor athletic performance may be due to an illness such as a low-grade tonsillitis. Also, a myocarditis may accompany some viral illnesses, and if the athlete with this disorder trains or competes he may suffer an arrhythmia and die suddenly.

Infectious Mononucleosis

The Epstein–Barr virus causes infectious mononucleosis but only in persons who lack antibodies to this virus. Better sanitation and hygiene have lowered the prevalence of infectious mononucleosis in children, but more mononucleosis is now found in high school and college athletes, whom the virus finally infects at a later age.[48]

The incubation period ranges from 42 to 49 days. Signs and symptoms of the illness include malaise, sore throat, headache, aching, fever (which may be very high), occasionally jaundice, sometimes encephalitis and neuritis, and rarely abdominal pain that mimics acute appendicitis. Early signs include small white spots on the anterior pillars of the tonsils and lymphadenopathy. Toward the 14th day, physical signs are at their zenith. The spleen enlarges and may rupture easily and thus must be examined gently and infrequently.[19, 47]

The blood of an athlete with mononucleosis contains a relative lymphocytosis of at least 50% lymphocytes and a total lymphocytosis. A concurrent acute bacterial infection may abolish the relative lymphocytosis, but the total lymphocyte count will be at least 3500/ml. More than 10% of these lymphocytes are atypical ones. Usually, a positive heterophil test clinches the diagnosis, but the test may not be positive until the third week. Live function test findings are also sometimes abnormal.

The athlete should stay in his room until his temperature falls, whereupon he may return to class. His lymph gland size and breathing should be checked. Although the side-effects of steroids may outweigh their good effects, steroids may be needed if lymph glands block the pharynx. The athlete must be restricted from sports because his spleen may rupture easily owing to lymphocytic infiltration and softness. At the height of the disease, a small increase in intra-abdominal pressure can cause rupture. The spleen must be two or three times larger than normal to be palpated. Its size may be checked with ultrasound or on a plain film of the abdomen, and 3 weeks later the study should be repeated to see whether the size has changed.[11, 55] A radionuclide scan or computed tomography may also be used to determine spleen size.[20, 27, 53]

How long should the athlete be restricted from sports after mononucleosis? Early return is dangerous because a large spleen is more tense than normal and projects below the ribs. It thus loses the natural protection of the ribs, rendering it more susceptible to injury and rupture. For this reason, the athlete may return to sports only when he feels well, laboratory tests findings are normal, and the spleen has returned to a normal size—a recovery that may be delayed for 3 to 6 months.

Infectious Hepatitis

Type A hepatitis virus is transmitted by a fecal–oral route to cause infectious hepatitis.[32] Serum hepatitis, on the other hand, is usually more serious and is transmitted by a type B virus.

The incubation period for infectious hepatitis is 2 to 6 weeks. The *preicteric phase* of fever and gastrointestinal discomforts precedes an *icteric phase* of liver tenderness and jaundice. Bilirubin and liver enzyme levels rise. Jaundice disappears during the *convalescent phase*, and the person becomes immune to subsequent infectious hepatitis but not to serum hepatitis.

In a 1969 college-football-team outbreak, the attack rate of infectious hepatitis was 92%.[12, 40, 60] The team could play only two games the entire season because passive immunization had been administered too late. A football team is a relatively closed population, and if hepatitis occurs all of the other players will need human immune serum globulin injected into each gluteal region to achieve passive immunity to the disease.

Because enzyme changes may be a normal concomitant of vigorous exercise, high creatinine phosphokinase and lactic dehydrogenase levels in a distance runner do not necessarily reflect a pathologic condition but may instead be related to muscle damage from running.

Epilepsy

Epilepsy is not a disease but a symptom. The cause of idiopathic, self-generating seizures and the precise location in the brain where the electrical stimulus begins are unknown.[2]

Genetic factors predispose a person to seizures if he inherits a low seizure threshold. Hypoglycemia, adrenalin release, or cerebral metabolic changes associated with hyperventilation may precipitate seizures. There is no evidence that vigorous physical activity or fatigue after sports precipitates epilepsy.

Head injuries may result in structural alterations in the brain, and stresses to an athlete may trigger seizures from this area. Because seizures arise somewhere in the brain, some doctors consider it unwise for an epileptic person to risk repeated head trauma.[38] Although this seems logical, there is no proof that repetitive physical contact, even to the head as in tackle football, causes more seizures in an epileptic person than usually occur when the same athlete is asleep in bed. In fact, many seizures occur nocturnally as the person sleeps.

Participation In Sports

The supposed adverse effect of head injury on the course of preexisting epilepsy probably has been exaggerated and may not exist.[2] Injury rates for epileptics in full athletic programs are identical to those of nonepileptic persons in full athletic programs—programs that include soccer, tackle football, and boxing.[14] Livingston has studied 20,000 epileptics in his seizure clinic over the past 40 years.[34–36] He allows his patients to participate fully in athletics and has reported no adverse effect from sports activity, including tackle football.

Nonetheless, an individualized approach is still best for determining the suitability of an epileptic for contact sports. No restrictions are recommended for athletes with only nocturnal epilepsy, whereas the frequency of other seizures must first be ascertained. If they are daily or weekly, contact sports should be prohibited. If the seizures are uncontrolled, horseback riding or high altitude climbing should be ruled out even if seizures are infrequent. Partial complex seizures may have bizarre motor or psychic manifestations. If an initial seizure has been clearly associated with head trauma, the physician should be reluctant to allow participation in sports that hold a significant risk of head injury. Also, contact sports should be prohibited when seizures are followed by a prolonged postconvulsive state.

Vigorous physical activity does not alter the metabolism of antiepileptic drugs, which will control about 60% of seizures, although in most instances their site and mode of action has not been ascertained. Epileptic youths should be continued on anticonvulsive drug therapy through adolescence because this is the time when many controlled epileptics have a recurrence of their seizures.

The team physician, trainer, and coach must identify epileptic athletes and be familiar with seizure patterns. When a seizure occurs, the athlete should be kept from hurting himself.

Exercise-Induced Asthma

Exercise-induced asthma is an asthma attack that occurs after exercise. When mild, the athlete may only cough frequently or appear unusually dyspneic, but, when severe, the athlete will wheeze and be very short of breath, with fatigue and anxiety interfering with his athletic activity. Most chronic asthmatics have exercise-induced asthma, as do many people with allergies. The condition also intensifies with seasonal allergies, high pollen counts, smoke and other irritants, fatigue, coldness, emotional upset, stress, and upper respiratory infections. The severely asthmatic person will have a stronger reaction to exercise than will the person with a mild asthmatic condition.

Exercise-induced hyperventilation of the trachea is severer in winter. Normally by the time air reaches the larynx it has been brought to body temperature and is fully humidified. During exercise and dyspnea, however, the lower airway must heat and humidify the air. Mucosal cooling may initiate vagal reflexes that release chemical mediators from mucosal mast cells, with an effect resembling that of an immediate hypersensitivity reaction of the bronchial smooth muscle.

Asthmatic athletes adapt normally to exercise for at least 5 to 10 minutes; as their ventilation rate and tachycardia subside after exercise, they become symptomatic. With longer exertion, symptoms may begin during the exercise period. However, sports help the person with exercise-induced asthma by upgrading his fitness and lowering his heart rate and ventilatory rate.[31] The athlete can then do more without inducing asthma.

Diagnosis

When an athlete wheezes and is very short of breath, his diagnosis presents little problem, but an athlete with mild exercise-induced asthma may have only a hacking cough and mild dyspnea. Pulmonary functions may be diminished by 20% to 30%, yet there may be no frank wheezing. A severe attack, however, may come later. To diagnose exercise-induced asthma, the physician should give the athlete an exercise challenge in the form of the exercise that provoked the attack.

A sound, practical approach to the diagnosis of mild exercise-induced asthma is to assume exercise-induced asthma if an athlete coughs frequently or seems unusually dyspneic. The physician should treat the subject with a bronchodilator and observe him to see if his symptoms resolve. The physician should also bring a stethoscope to practices and listen for wheezes. Special attention must be given to asthmatic athletes who have had a cold because their airway remains irritable and their lung functions are depressed for as long as a week after a cold.

Selection of a Sport

Many asthmatic athletes select sports that emphasize skill and coordination. They tailor their involvement to short activities rather than endurance sports like soccer or time-consuming activities like tennis, which may precipitate exercise-induced asthma.

Endurance sports differ in their tendency to induce asthma, with running and cycling causing asthma twice as often as does swimming. Encouragingly, several world-class swimmers are asthmatic, and asthmatics have won Olympic gold medals. In swimming, regular forced deep breathing promotes maximum emptying of the lungs, and belly-breathing and exhaling against resistance eliminate trapped air; the swimmer also breathes at the water's humid surface.

Coping with the Disorder

Simple breathing methods may prevent asthmatic attacks. The athlete breathes with his diaphragm, forcing expiration against a closed glottis when the first symptoms of asthma appear. During exertion he should breathe through his nose rather than through his mouth to help warm the air. In cold weather, a ski mask may be worn and a lightweight surgical mask added if needed.

"Running through" an attack allows the asthmatic athlete to participate in basketball, hockey, and soccer, as asthmatic attacks are less severe after 12 to 16 minutes of exercise than after 6 to 8 minutes of exercise.[26] The severity of the attack reaches a plateau at about 6 minutes before gradually diminishing. The mechanism for this is poorly understood. In addition, if the athlete resumes exercising in less than 90 minutes, the second exercise bout causes less severe attacks than the first. Thus, by vigorously warming up an hour or so before an event, the asthmatic athlete may compete in a more refractory state.

Drug Treatment

The most effective way to inhibit exercise-induced asthma is by pharmacologic pretreatment.[21] The drug must be taken *before* exercise. The most effective medicines are epinephrine, isoetherine, isoproterenol, metaproterenol, terbutaline, and theophylline. Cromolyn sodium and atropine are effective for some asthmatic persons but not for others. Corticosteroids are not helpful in preventing exercise-induced asthma, nor are antihistamines. Propranolol worsens the condition.

Most drugs are inhaled just before exertion, and the effects may last for hours. Oral drugs are taken 1 to 2 hours before exercise to attain therapeutic levels, and their timing and dosage may be adjusted to produce optimal effects. Inhaled adrenergic drugs are effective in small doses that only occasionally produce paradoxical bronchospasm, tachycardia, and tachyarrhythmia. Oral adrenergic agonists are given in higher doses than when inhaled, but the inotropic and chronotropic effects of these agents increase the risk of tachyarrhythmia during exercise. Among the commonly used drugs, metaproterenol produces fewer cardiac effects, and its duration of action is longer than that of isoproterenol or epinephrine. Athletes in strenuous competitive sport and those with cardiovascular problems should use cromolyn sodium as the drug of first choice. The mechanism of action of cromolyn sodium is unknown, but it is thought to inhibit the release of mediators from mast cells. If the athlete does not respond to cromolyn, an inhaled, selective beta-2-adrenergic agent such as isoethrane may be a second choice. Ephedrine, isoproterenol, and metaproterenol are banned by the Medical Commission of the International Olympic Committee.[41] However, atropine, cromolyn sodium, glucocorticoids, the B_2-agonist terbutaline, and theophylline are acceptable.

Nonprescription medications that contain epinephrine, such as Primatene mist and Bronkaid mist, are usually safe, but these medicines may be abused during strenuous events. Athletes should be cautioned to use good judgment when taking a drug after an attack has started during competition because potentially toxic doses of epinephrine can be inhaled from metered dose inhalers. The combination of lactic acidosis, hypoxia, and increased endogenous catecholamines, plus a burst of adrenergic agonist entering the body by inhalation, may be lethal. The athlete and his parents must be alerted to this combination and the dangers of abusing nonprescription drugs.

SEX BEFORE SPORTS

Some coaches recommend abstinence from sexual intercourse during training or on the night before a contest, believing that it diminishes athletic performance by sapping strength and interfering with the athlete's rest pattern. There is, however, no physiologic evidence that sexual activity saps strength. In fact, a 70-kg athlete expends an average of only 4 to 6 calories per minute during intercourse, an amount roughly equivalent to a brisk walk around a city block. Moreover, sex may be an effective outlet for pre-event jitters and provide the athlete with a good night's sleep.

THE ATHLETE'S SKIN

The athlete's skin may be damaged by heat, cold, viruses, bacteria, fungi, and contact with clothing or other objects. The sun can burn an athlete, and a hot, sweating athlete may develop miliaria or cholinergic urticaria.

Sunburn

Sunburn is generally viewed as a sign of health and vigor, but this condition is actually a dermatitis that damages and ages the athlete's skin. Sunburn is a hazard not only in the summer, but also during sunny, spring skiing if the skier wears only a T-shirt and shorts. There is less atmosphere at pollution-free, high-altitude ski areas to screen out the ultraviolet rays, and the snow also reflects these rays.

Athletes should stay out of the bright sun during the hottest part of the day to prevent sunburn. Gradual adaptation to the sun may be achieved by applying a sunscreen that contains benzoate to partly absorb ultraviolet rays and permit slow tanning. If the athlete is going in and out of water, he should use a sun screen in an alcoholic vehicle that will penetrate the skin and not be washed off by perspiration or swimming. Sun protectors contain para-amino benzoic acid, which blocks most of the ultraviolet light.

If an athlete's skin is burned, a soothing lotion that contains a mild anesthetic should be applied, and soothing tub baths may be taken in boric acid solution. If sunburn worsens after a surface anesthetic has been applied to a sunburn, even though the athlete is avoiding the sun, the surface anesthetic must be discontinued because it may be causing an allergic reaction.

Sunbathing is not recommended, especially on competition days, because prolonged exposure to the warm sun has an enervating effect. Sun screens and sun blockers should be available when athletes travel from one area of the country to another.

Miliaria

Miliaria, or heat rash, may affect well-tanned persons when they sweat. In superficial miliaria, the sweat becomes trapped under layers of the thick stratum corneum to produce a crystalline miliaria. Sterile pustules may form in the deep form of miliaria, miliaria pustulosus. Staphylococcal folliculitis has an identical appearance, but the pustules are, of course, not sterile.

Cholinergic Urticaria

Acetylcholine is important in sweating, and the hot, sweating athlete may develop a cholinergic urticaria. When the skin is stroked, histamine is sometimes released, resulting in dermatographism. These urticarial lesions at the stroked area are sometimes seen in caddies, who rest the golf bag strap over the shoulder.

Cold Urticaria

Cold urticaria may occur when a swimmer jumps into cold water. Histamine is released in reaction to the cold, hives develop, and the histamine may even cause anaphylaxis. History of sudden exposure to cold is important for diagnosis, along with an "ice-cube test" in which an ice cube is placed on the flexor part of the forearm for 2 minutes and the area observed for urticaria for 15 minutes. Affected swimmers may sometimes be desensitized with cold showers, but this treatment must be carefully monitored, with all of the equipment available that may be needed to control a possible anaphylactic reaction.

Equestrian Cold Panniculitis

Young, healthy women who ride horses for at least 2 consecutive hours a day throughout the winter may develop cold panniculitis.[6] They frequently ride in temperatures near or below freezing, and the horses often trot or gallop into heavy winds. As a result, the lateral part of the rider's thighs becomes chilled, and tight-fitting, uninsulated riding pants may slow the blood flow through the skin, further reducing tissue temperature.

Initially, the rider notices several small, erythematous, pruritic papules on the superior-lateral part of one or both thighs. After a week, the lesions progress to indurated, red-to-violaceous tender plaques and nodules. Histologically, there is a panniculitis with very inflamed veins, particularly at the dermal–subcutaneous fat junction.

One who rides in the winter should be advised to ride for shorter periods and to wear looser, insulated, warmer pants.

Frostbite and Frostnip

Frostbite may affect an athlete who is skiing, tobogganing, snowshoeing, ice sailing, ice skating, mountain climbing, or snowmobiling.[23, 24, 62]

"Frostnip" is a mild blanching of the skin that may occur after a downhill ski run. *Frostbite* may be superficial or deep. *Superficial frostbite* involves the skin and the subcutaneous tissue, giving a whiteness or a "waxy" appearance to the skin; blisters may appear after 24 to 36 hours. In *deep frostbite*, the skin, subcutaneous tissue, and deeper tissues, even the bone, are affected, and, as these tissues cool, the blood vessels constrict to conserve body heat. When body tissue temperature drops to 15°C, erythema, burning, and hypoesthesia occur. At 10°C, numbness, redness, and, sometimes, white, patchy areas appear. At −2°C, cellular metabolism stops. Then, as the area begins to thaw, blood vessels dilate, and with this engorgement the capillaries become more permeable. The swelling of the tissues that results may produce gangrene by interfering with the circulation. Moreover, direct cold injury to the cell denatures its proteins and enzymes, and large extracellular ice crystals form, drawing water from the cell.[18]

Peripheral areas such as the earlobes, nose, cheeks, hands, and feet are most frequently frostbitten. Incipient frostbite of the fingers or toes may be recognized by a sudden cessation of cold or discomfort in the injured part, often followed by a pleasant warm feeling. Deep frostbite, however, may occur without this preliminary period of anesthesia.

Wetness, wind, and exercise increase the chance of frostbite. Clothing has an insulating effect, but when the clothing is wet its insulating properties are reduced. The chilling effect increases with wind; thus, the chilling effect of −6°C with a 40-mile-per-hour wind is the same as −40°C with a breeze of 2 miles per hour. This effect is slightly less at high altitude because of reduced air density.[23, 24, 62] If the person exercises too much, he will pant, allowing cold air to enter his lungs and chill his whole body. Similarly, a runner's hands may become frostbitten when he jogs. The reciprocal motion of his hands may produce a 15°F temperature drop. When wind is added, the temperature drops from 20° to 50° lower.

"Instantaneous frostbite" may occur if cold metal is touched with a bare hand, especially if the hand is wet or damp. The skin sticks to the metal and is torn off when the hand is removed. Contact of the skin with gasoline that has been stored outside in the cold may also cause instantaneous frostbite. The freezing point of gasoline lies near −70°F, and its rapid rate of evaporation and extreme chill make it very dangerous.

Frostbite may also result from prolonged direct contact with a synthetic gel pack. If the pack is placed in a freezer and frozen to −15°C, it will remain below freezing for about 15 minutes while retaining its flexibility and conforming to the skin. When used, the pack should be wrapped in a towel and never applied to the skin.

Prevention

Frostnip can be prevented by use of the buddy system with each partner watching the other for telltale signs that cannot be felt. Bathing and shaving the face should be postponed until after the day's outing because these practices remove protective skin oils, and a layer of sun cream should be applied for added protection.

To prevent frostbite, the athlete's body should be warm enough to supply warm blood to his peripheral areas, and perspiring should be avoided. Fishnet underwear will provide a layer of warm air insulation. Light, smooth, clean socks may be worn next to the skin, with one or two heavier socks over these; extra socks and insoles should be carried.

Mittens—not gloves—are best for the cold-weather athlete or mountain climber; if he must use one hand, he should wear a glove on it and a mitten on the other hand. If work must be done bare-handed on metal, he should wear silk or rayon gloves or cover the the metal with adhesive tape. He may intermittently remove his thumb from the mitten-thumb and hold it in a fist in the palm of the mitten to regain warmth for his whole

hand. Extra mittens, removable wool mitten inserts, or glove linings should always be carried.

Treatment

With fast skiing, numb white patches may appear on a skier's face. These areas may be rewarmed with steady pressure from a warm hand but should not be rubbed. Frostnipped fingers may be warmed in an armpit, whereas frostnipped toes or heels may be rewarmed by removing footgear and placing the foot on the abdomen of a friend. Dry socks plus clothing over the foot will restore warmth; when footgear is put on, laces should be loose to assure adequate circulation.

The frostbitten person must remain calm because panic increases perspiration, which evaporates to cause further chilling. The key to the treatment of frostbite is prompt and thorough rewarming. If the area is rubbed with a hand or with snow, the thawing tissue may be irreparably damaged. "Applying ice water or snow to a frostbitten limb makes about as much sense as treating a burned foot by putting it in an oven."[62] Because refreezing of the tissue results in more tissue loss, a frozen part should not be thawed if the thawing may be followed by refreezing. Thus, it is less damaging for a mountaineer to walk to shelter on frozen feet than on feet that have been thawed, and a strong athlete can walk a long way on frozen feet without further injury. A climber should stump down the mountain even if it takes many hours, for if the frozen part is rewarmed on the trail the athlete becomes a litter case who cannot assist in his own rescue, resulting in danger to other climbers.

Frostbitten persons should not be given alcohol because alcohol causes peripheral vasodilation. Although alcohol produces a temporary warm feeling, the blood becomes chilled and body temperature drops further. Marijuana has a similar effect of increasing peripheral blood flow, which then leads to further chilling. The frostbitten climber should also refrain from smoking because smoking causes peripheral vasoconstriction that further decreases blood flow. If the climber must make a long trip on a litter, dry gauze should be placed between his toes but not pulled into his webs. A fluff dressing may then be applied and lightly wrapped with gauze.

Once the base station or hospital has been reached, a warm water bath should be prepared.[23, 24, 62] While the vessel is being filled, the victim's body should be kept as warm as possible with blankets and hot drinks. The water container may be a large bucket or a 19-liter (5-gallon) can that allows room for the frozen part to move without bumping the sides. It should be large enough so that the frozen part itself will not overly cool the liquid, and the affected part should be held in the middle of the fluid, not on the bottom. A duffle bag may be used to support the extremity behind the knee. The water must be kept at a temperature of 40°C to 42°C and monitored with a heavy-duty thermometer. It must not be allowed to rise above 44°C; thus, it should feel warm, but not hot, to a normal hand. The water temperature must never be tested with the frozen part because frozen tissue is insensitive, and even brief exposure to high temperature can cause serious damage. Water hotter than 46°C should never be added to the bath, and hot water must not be added too close to the injured part. No stove should be placed under the warming vessel.

If the container is not large enough to keep the part completely immersed, the part may be wrapped in towels. Water not warmer than 44°C should then be continually poured onto the part. Dry heat is difficult to regulate and will not rewarm evenly, and for this reason the frostbitten extremity must never be exposed to an open fire or an engine's exhaust. However, if dry heat must be used for rewarming, the part may be loosely covered with sterile gauze, placed against another person's abdomen, and covered with warm clothes or blankets. Warming a frostbitten part this way takes three or four times longer than warming with a liquid.

Rewarming in the liquid should be continued until a flush returns to the distal tip of the thawed part—a period of 20 to 30 minutes. There will be little discomfort initially, but pain will increase until it becomes quite intense at the end of the rewarming period. A 25-mg Demerol tablet may be given along with aspirins about 20 minutes before rewarming starts. Heavy doses of pain-killers are to be avoided, especially at high altitudes, where they may cause respiratory depression.

After rapid rewarming, the injured part should be soaked in a whirlpool at 37°C for 20 to 30 minutes twice a day until healing is complete. Hexachlorophine or an iodine prep solution may be added to the bath, and active motion of the part in the bath is allowed. After thawing, the frostbitten area will resemble burned tissue, with blebs and blisters forming. The tissue will be very sensitive to injury and susceptible to infection, and even the slightest abrasion or irritation is dangerous; thus, further cold and weightbearing must be avoided.

The subject should be kept warm at normal body temperature, with frostbitten areas uncovered. If the area must be covered, however, a soft, dry dressing that is changed infrequently is best; wet or greasy dressings should never be applied. Sterile cotton may be placed between the affected fingers or toes. A pillow under the calf will keep the heel off the sheets, but the limb should generally be kept horizontal. A box or a frame placed around the feet will protect against pressure from the sleeping bag or sheets. The frostbitten person should be encouraged to move his other joints to keep them limber.

Gangrene associated with frostbite is often a superficial dry condition that does not require emergency amputation (Figure 2-5). Debridement and amputation are best postponed to allow a natural spontaneous debridement of the dead tis-

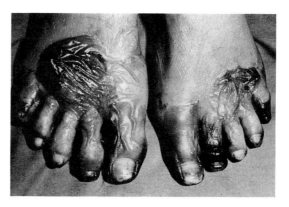

Figure 2-5 Blisters on frostbitten feet should not be debrided.

sue to occur. Patience is needed because recovery takes many months. "The worst *looking* hands and feet, if treated properly and patiently, will shed their shriveled black shells painlessly like a glove, suddenly and unexpectedly revealing healthy, pink skin underneath."[62]

Shoe Boot Pernio (Chilblains)

Children who wear plastic shoe boots in a cold, wet environment may get the linings wet.[16] The waterproof outer covering prevents the evaporation of moisture that has collected. The blood vessels in the child's foot may then go into spasm, reddish-blue patches may appear on his feet, and the dorsum of his toes may turn pink. Twelve to 24 hours after exposure, the foot becomes swollen, itches, and burns, and vesicles may form. To treat this "shoe boot pernio," the foot must be rewarmed, and the subject must avoid further exposure to damp cold.

Skin Infections in Athletics

The skin may be the site of infectious diseases that can be transmitted to other athletes, especially by direct contact. Even minor infections may become major problems, ruining the season for the athlete, his opponents, or his team. The infections may be viral, such as herpes simplex and molluscum contagiosum, bacterial, such as impetigo and acne, or fungal dermatoses, including tinea versicolor, tinea cruris, and candidiasis.

Herpes Simplex

Herpes simplex is a contagious, blistering viral disorder found mostly in athletes engaged in body contact sports, sometimes referred to as "herpes gladiatorum." An infection may spread to an entire team, especially when there is close contact, as in wrestlers (Figure 2-6A). The most frequently affected sites are the right side of the face and the forearm, which are major contact points.

A herpes lesion looks like a fever blister and usually consists of a cluster of vesicles on an erythematous base (Figure 2-6B). The blister breaks to form an itchy, yellowish crust and is infectious during the blistering and ulceration phases, when the athlete may have tender, swollen lymph nodes.

Because some athletes are more susceptible than others to herpes infections, the team physician, the trainer, and the coach must be especially alert for such tendencies. Herpes is also more frequent in athletes who have had previous herpes infections.

Prevention requires athletes in close contact sports to shower before and after practice.[3] Exchanges of towels or clothes between players should be forbidden. All open wounds must be reported, because open skin serves as a portal for infection. Occasionally an athlete may be aware that herpes is beginning 24 hours before he has obvious skin changes. At the first sign of infection, removal from competition is obligatory. Wrestling partners should be advised to check each other for skin lesions to prevent transfer of an infection. Lesions should be caught early, the blisters broken, and a drying agent such as alcohol, silver nitrate, camphor, or alum applied. The area must also be washed frequently with Domeboro solution. The condition is usually self-limiting, lasting about 2 weeks.

A herpes infection can be very dangerous if the athlete has underlying ectopic eczema because the herpes infection may then rapidly disseminate. This is a dermatologic emergency, and antiviral drugs may be needed.

Molluscum Contagiosum

Molluscum contagiosum is a contagious skin infection caused by a wart-like pox virus. It is characterized by umbilicated, pink papules with central gelatinous craters, and the surrounding skin is normally not inflamed (Figure 2-6D). Lesions grow down into the dermis as multiple, closely packed, pear-shaped lobules. Removal may be done by incision of the central punctum, which extrudes the central core of viral bodies. Curettage also destroys these lesions.

Impetigo

Impetigo is a skin infection most often caused by a beta-hemolytic streptococcus, although

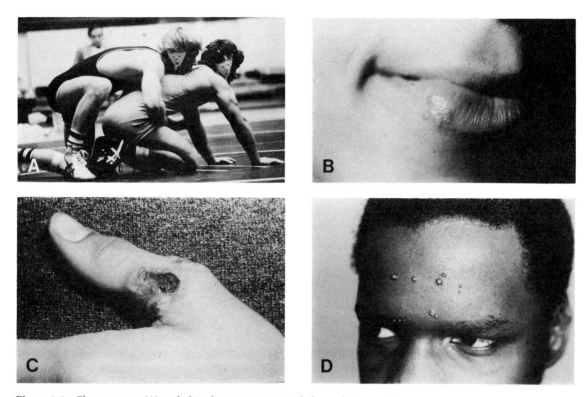

Figure 2-6   Close contact **(A)** and skin damage may spread skin infections. Skin conditions include herpes simplex **(B)**, impetigo **(C)**, and molluscum contagiosum **(D)**.

sometimes the cause may be a staphylococcus. The condition is much more contagious than viral herpes simplex. Groups of blisters are filled with clear fluid and have a similar appearance to the lesions of herpes simplex, but they evolve into sharply demarcated erosions covered with heavy, yellowish, serosanguineous crusts and form pustules (Figure 2-6C).

Athletes must be watched for early lesions, and if they appear the lesions should be cleaned each day with a surgical soap or with Dial soap. The athlete must take a full course of antibiotic therapy because glomerulonephritis will sometimes follow impetigo if it has been undertreated.

Acne

Sporting activity brings physical and emotional stress, increases sebaceous activity in the eccrine sweat glands, exposes the athlete to dirt,

dust, and heat, and causes him to perspire. These conditions combine with the ubiquitous *Staphylococcus albus* and *Corynebacterium acnes* to produce the pustules and small abscesses of acne.

Ambient microparticles, bacteria, and an increased production of sebaceous material block pilosebaceous follicles, setting the stage for inflammation and infection. Chemical changes in the occluded sebaceous material, such as the enzymatic release of irritating free fatty acids, also inflame the walls of the follicles. Surface frictions, as from a shoulder pad strap, may also inflame the skin and lead to an inflammatory papule that ruptures to form a pustule or a small abscess.

"Football acne" affects the skin under a tackle football player's chin strap. Even 10- to 12-year-olds who wear chin straps may suffer mild forms of football acne. The semiocclusive plastic chin strap irritates the player's skin by friction and physical pressure, blocks pores, and rubs in dirt. Patch tests for allergy to the strap in these cases are usually negative.

To treat generalized or localized "football acne," the player must gently wash his face with soap and warm water in the morning, immediately after practice or a game, and at bedtime.[4] A topical cleansing agent or an astringent should be applied; drying lotions or creams may also be used. The pustules should not be squeezed because squeezing only inflames the skin and spreads the infection. If the athlete has acne on his neck, chest, and upper back, he should apply a fungistatic foot powder to absorb the perspiration and skin oils.

If an athlete has had pustules or has a strong tendency to form them, he may be started on tetracycline therapy at the beginning of the season.[5] The bacteriostatic action of low-dose tetracycline hinders the invasion of pathogens. Tetracycline also acts to reduce the hydrolysis of serum triglycerides into free fatty acids.[22]

Fungal Dermatoses

Tinea Versicolor   Tinea versicolor is a yeast infection that usually affects 18- to 20-year-olds. Its lesions may be white on black skin, black on white skin, or pink on skin of any color. Hyphae will be seen on a potassium hydroxide preparation. Selsun shampoo is applied for 10 minutes for ten nights, then once a week to treat this disorder.

Tinea Cruris ("Jock Itch")   Tinea cruris, or "jock itch," is an infectious dermatosis caused by the dermatophyte fungi *Epidermophyton floccosum*, *Tricophyton mentagrophytes*, and *Tricophyton rubrum*. The fungi may be passed from person to person on personal clothing or by direct contact, or it may spread from athlete's foot or fungal involvement of the athlete's nails. Skin lesions on the upper inner thighs are bilaterally symmetrical, with a clearing central area characteristic of "ringworm" and a border sharply demarcated and active. The lesions, however, seldom involve the athlete's genitalia and scrotum. A potassium hy-

droxide wet mount will show true hyphae in tinea cruris, but if the athlete has been treating his infection the scraping may not be a good one. In these circumstances, the treatments are best stopped for a few days before scraping is repeated.

Tinea cruris may be treated with preparations such as tolnaftate (Tinactin), haloprogin (Halotex), miconazole (Mica-Tin), or clotrimazole (Lotrimin). If Tinea unguum is serving as a reservoir for jock itch or athlete's foot, a 6-month or year-long course of systemic griseofulvin therapy may be needed for cure.[10]

Candidiasis   Yeast may be normal flora in the athlete's groin, and they may infect chafed and eroded skin. Candida will turn an athlete's scrotum red. The yeast also produces "satellite lesions" separate from the main lesion. A potassium hydroxide wet mount will show both "pseudohyphae," which are nonseptae, nonbranching, elongated growths, and budding yeast cells. The lesion should be treated with Burrow's solution compresses for 20 minutes three times a day until the acute phase has subsided. Medicines such as nystatin (Mycostatin), amphotericin B (Fungizone), clotrimazole, miconazole, and haloprogin are then used.

Contact Dermatitis

An athlete may come in contact with materials that cause allergic reactions or objects that rub and damage his skin, or he may be allergic to materials that contact his skin, and a dermatitis may ensue. The offending material may be a tape adhesive, a tape adherent such as benzoin, or a counterirritant used in the training room. Also, dyed clothing, or even the rubber in shoes, on balls, and on the handles of exercise equipment, may provoke an allergic response.

When an athlete develops a contact allergy, the examiner must obtain a good history from him concerning contact with substances such as those listed above. The trainer should check the materials used when he is preparing the athlete for his sport. When observing the distribution of the athlete's itchy lesions, the examiner will note whether they occupy a band area where an athletic supporter strap or the stripes on his athletic socks make contact with the subject's skin. Patch testing may be needed to locate the offending material.

The athlete may be allergic to animal dyes or the chromate used in tanning gloves and shoe leather. In such cases, the athlete may have to wear gloves and shoes that have been tanned with vegetable dyes. Because sweat in a hockey glove may also lead to a dermatitis, cotton gloves should be worn under hockey gloves to absorb moisture.

The rubber toebox of tennis shoes or all-purpose gym shoes may cause a contact dermatitis on the toes and dorsum of the foot. The condition is usually bilateral and symmetical, and a potassium hydroxide preparation will be negative. Treatment begins with discarding the offending clothes, gloves, or shoes, and the dermatitis is then treated like poison ivy, with early skin washing, if possible, before the full reaction sets in. A steroid cream is applied after a skin reaction has appeared.

"Strawberries"

"Strawberries," also called floor burns, friction burns, and mat burns, are skin abrasions. The athlete's skin breaks from friction, rubbing off when he slides across a mat, lands on a rocky field, or slides on artificial turf.

An athlete may neglect a strawberry until an infection has set in. For this reason, such abrasions must be reported and promptly and carefully cleaned. While the area is numb, it should be thoroughly scrubbed with a soft-bristled brush that has been dipped in mild soap and water. An antibiotic ointment is then applied and the abrasion is covered with a sterile dressing. The dressing should be changed and the wound checked each day.

Because strawberries are painful if the damaged skin is stretched or stuck, the injured athlete should wear a felt or a foam rubber protective pad over the abrasion. Soccer goalkeepers may wear football pants and hip pads to help prevent this type of injury.

"Saddle Soreness"

A novice cyclist may develop a painful bursitis over his ischial tuberosities, which rest on the bicycle saddle. He may also suffer from irritated, reddened, and itchy skin in his perineum, so-called "pruritis ani." Touring cyclists sometimes have inguinal intertrigo or "cyclist's scrotum." Moreover, friction between a cyclist's skin and his bicycle saddle may produce a panniculitis that could lead to local fat necrosis and boils. Boils may also appear on the backs of athletes doing bench presses. Such boils may be avoided if each lifter wears a shirt or by covering the bench with a towel during weight training.

The novice cyclist's ischial pain usually disappears after about 1 week of riding, and pressure can be reduced if he uses a saddle with softer padding in the ischial area. A cyclist with pruritis ani should be advised to keep the area dry, to use good toilet hygiene, and to apply a hydrocortisone cream or lotion.

Intertrigo is an inflammatory response of the skin to friction and maceration that is associated with a tight athletic supporter or tight cycling shorts. The athlete's skin becomes reddened at friction points, and the diagnosis is based on the exclusion of other groin eruptions. This condition may be prevented by avoiding tight clothes or a tight, rubbing athletic supporter. Talcum powder should be applied to the groin, and the athlete should allow air to reach the area as often as is practical. A 0.5% hydrocortisone cream will alleviate the symptoms, but the cortisone may cause skin atrophy.

The cyclist should smear petroleum jelly or sprinkle baby powder on his skin and wear cycling shorts that contain a built-in chamois to reduce friction between the saddle and his skin.

NUTRITION

Poor knowledge of nutrition may contribute to unbalanced nutrition, with the athlete either underfed or overfed. A swimmer may be trying to keep her weight down, but when she goes to a party with friends, she eats cake and drinks soda pop and later attempts to compensate by omitting more nutritious foods from her diet. Youths who consume soft drinks often cut down on their milk intake. On the other hand, some athletes oversupplement diets with protein powders or tablets, raw blood, vitamins, and minerals. Heavy use of such supplements may lead to kidney trouble, hypervitaminosis, or more severe disorders.

Nutritional counseling for balanced nutrition should begin in grade school. Each young athlete should keep a record of his daily food intake and his activities for a week for review and counseling by a physician or trainer. A team nutritionist is invaluable for dietary counseling, explaining the principles of a balanced diet and discussing dietary misconceptions and the preparation of meals.

The athlete should select food from each of the four basic food groups (Table 2-3).[59] One group consists of fruits and vegetables, such as citrus fruits, carrots, and greens; another includes cereals and grains; a third is the protein group, which includes fish, meat, poultry, and legumes; and the fourth group contains milk and milk products, such as yogurt, cheese, and ice cream. About 50% of the calories the athlete ingests should come from carbohydrates, with less than 10% of these from refined sugar. About 35% should be from fat and 15% from protein, with about half of these from vegetable sources. There is no "best" diet, and variety does not necessarily mean that the diet is balanced. By careful planning to provide all of the essential amino acids, vegetarians can have a very nutritious diet, especially if beans, eggs, nuts, and milk are included to supply high-quality protein.

Athletes usually eat three meals a day, but more frequent, smaller meals eaten when hungry are probably better. The athlete should not skip meals; if he takes snacks, they should consist of fresh fruit—"nature's candy"—vegetables, or a glass of milk.

The caloric needs of an athlete will depend on his body weight and physical activity. For ordinary activity, about 3000 calories per day is needed, containing about 100 g of protein. The hard-training athlete who runs 25 to 35 km (15 to 20 miles) a day, exercises for 3 to 4 hours, or lifts heavy weights may need more than 5000 calories per day. The extra energy needs of these athletes are provided by extra calories and fats, and these and other essential elements should be contained in a balanced diet. Even an outwardly balanced diet may, however, lack sufficient nutritional value. Food processing can destroy much nutritional value: white bread is milled and bleached, and chemicals may be added to foods that come from poor soils. Valuable nutrients may also be lost during canning, freezing, shipping, storage and cooking.

Nutritional supplements have been decried as expensive nutritional nonsense. Although no value is gained by supplementing a nutritionally adequate diet that meets the demands of training, supplements may be needed when an athlete is training hard and his metabolic demands are high. They may also be needed when the athlete is "meeting" weight in wrestling, boxing, or weight lifting. In addition, for various reasons, some athletes cannot eat a balanced diet and may need supplements.

Athletes often select supplements of protein, vitamins, and minerals.[63] Some weight lifters have been known to go into negative nitrogen balance during heavy training. Therefore, the growing athlete or an athlete building muscle may require as much as 2 g of protein per kilogram of body weight each day. Any excess protein intake is excreted as ammonia or converted into fat. Red meats, eggs, and dairy products are high in animal protein but are also high in saturated animal fats. Desiccated liver is a good source of animal protein, and wheat germ supplies plant protein.

Vitamins A, D, E, and K are fat soluble and can be stored in the body, whereas others such as the B-complex vitamins and vitamin C are water soluble and cannot be stored. Vitamin A is found in fish-liver oils, butter, whole milk, cheeses, dark green leafy vegetables, and yellow fruits and vegetables. Cod liver oil is high in vitamin D, as is fortified milk. Vitamin E, or alpha-tocopherol, is an antioxidant found in eggs, nuts, grains, leafy vegetables, and wheat germ oil. Spinach, cabbage, and liver provide vitamin K. The B vitamins are important for carbohydrate and fat metabolism; they are found in protein foods such as liver and whole grains, with wheat germ and brewer's yeast being excellent suppliers of these vitamins. Vitamin C is important in adrenal gland metabo-

Table 2-3 NUTRITION TIPS

Below are the basic food groups. You should eat a *wide variety* of foods from all four groups.

I. Milk and Milk Products	II. Fruit and Vegetables	III. Meats	IV. Cereals
Cheese	Apples	Beef	Breads
Cottage cheese	Bananas	Eggs	Corn
Ice cream	Grapefruit	Fish	Flour
Milk	Oranges	Lamb	Macaroni
Milkshake	Peaches	Liver	Oatmeal
	Pears	Pork	Rice
	Beans	Poultry	Spaghetti
	Cabbage	Veal	Whole grain breakfast cereal
	Carrots		
	Lettuce		
	Potatoes		
	Spinach		
	Tomatoes		

CARBOHYDRATES (CHO)

Starch	*Sugar*
Cake	Candy
Cereals	Fruit
Corn	Honey
Flour	Jam
Noodles	Sugar
Potatoes	Syrup
Rice	

FATS

Animal	*Vegetable*
Butter	Legumes
Eggs	Nuts
Fish	Pastries
Lard	Salad Dressing
Meat	Vegetable Oil

PROTEINS

Animal	*Vegetable*
Eggs	Flour products
Fish	Legumes
Meats	
Milk products	

- Calories should be at least 60% CHO (primarily starch group), only 15% protein
- CHOs are the energy and muscle fuels.
- Performance can be sustained four times longer on a high CHO diet than on a high protein or increased fat diet.
- Protein is for building and repair.
- Vitamin, mineral, and protein supplements have never been shown to improve anyone's performance.
- A normal diet provides all vitamins, minerals, and protein necessary.
- You cannot perform optimally on fewer than three meals daily.
- To add weight, eat light meals six times daily.
- Breakfast provides the fuel for afternoon competition.
- Do not skip a meal, particularly breakfast.
- Do not eat a candy bar; instead, eat fruit.

Pregame Meal

- Eat 3½ to 5 hours before the game.
- The pregame meal should be primarily CHO.

lism, collagen formation, and wound healing and is found especially in citrus fruits. Although the recommended minimal daily requirement for vitamin C is low, some athletes ingest 4 g a day in the belief that it diminishes soreness and speeds healing.

There are some dangers in taking vitamin supplements, as when large doses of the fat-soluble vitamins are stored in the body, leading to hypervitaminosis. Also, large amounts of ascorbic acid may reduce the vitamin C in the athlete's adrenal glands.

When an athlete's vitamin intake is low, his mineral intake also may be low. The important minerals include calcium, phosphorus, magnesium, potassium, sodium, and iron. Iron deficiency is common among young women, especially those menstruating heavily; rapidly growing teenage boys, particularly those in lower income groups; those dieting to lose weight; and vegetarians. The iron-deficient athlete will lose strength and endurance and fatigue easily. A thorough dietary and menstrual history, including whether the athlete is using an intrauterine device that may increase menstrual blood loss, and a history of excess fatigue or lack of endurance may indicate an iron deficiency and the need for an iron supplement.

Intelligent food selection and preparation with an emphasis on fresh food—rather than on canned food that may be deficient—should provide the athlete with a balanced diet for optimum athletic performance. However, hard-training athletes, those meeting weight, those without access to a balanced diet, and those traveling who find it difficult to prepare meals may benefit from properly selected supplements. A blender can be invaluable in preparing nutritious shakes. For example, a combination of milk, eggs, wheat germ, powdered milk, fruit juice, yogurt and fruit (e.g. bananas) can make an excellent, nutritious shake for the athlete.

Carbohydrate Loading

Athletes in endurance events that require more than an hour of strenuous exercise can add glycogen to their muscles by carbohydrate loading. One week before a race, the athlete should train

heavily for more than 2 hours to exhaust his supply of muscle glycogen. Then for 3 days, he should train regularly while on a low-carbohydrate, high-protein, and high-fat diet consisting of meat, bacon, eggs, butter, and vegetable oils. In the final 3 days, he should train lightly while on a high carbohydrate diet of bread, spaghetti, potatoes, sugar, fruit, and fruit juices.

Carbohydrate loading results in extra compensation in the exercised muscles, sometimes almost tripling the muscle's supply of glycogen and enabling the athlete to exercise for a much longer time before muscle exhaustion. The uptake of glycogen, however, is accompanied by an uptake of water, and the muscles may feel heavy and stiff. Some athletes even develop angina, since glycogen and water are added to the heart muscle, causing electrocardiographic abnormalities to appear. If an endurance athlete decides to load with carbohydrates, he should do it only a few times a year for important contests because more frequent carbohydrate loading may disrupt the athlete's metabolic processes.

Dietary Preparation for a Match

Starting a few days before a match, the athlete should be on a balanced diet, stressing carbohydrate intake for glycogen storage. As training is reduced, the muscles recover and store the glycogen. If the athlete eats steaks, bananas, and grapefruits during the week, enough potassium for weekend athletic activity will be stored. When heavy perspiration is anticipated, he may season his food with extra salt, although highly salted foods eaten within a few days of competition may cause fluid retention and sluggishness.

The Precompetition Meal

The precompetition meal should be taken 3 to 4 hours before the match. Moderation is the rule, and the meal should not be too large. Because the athlete is usually tense, less blood will flow to his stomach and small intestine, and there is less motility of the stomach and small intestine. Digestion and gastric emptying are slowed.

The meal should be easy to digest, high in

carbohydrate, but low in refined sugar, protein, and fat. Refined sugar contains only calories and is quickly absorbed to stimulate insulin secretion, which reduces blood sugar. The athlete will be hungry again in a few hours owing to the reactive hypoglycemia. For this reason, refined sugar, although a very quick source of energy, is a poor pregame food. Instead, sugar should be fructose from fruits, which converts to glucose in the liver and is available more slowly.

Before a match, the athlete should avoid food with a high cellulose content, such as lettuce, which can induce defecation. Moreover, spiced foods may irritate the stomach, and high protein foods, such as meat, fish, and eggs, produce fixed acids that use up body water to be excreted. Fatty or fried foods slow stomach emptying. Thus, the athlete should forgo whole milk, which has a high fat content, mayonnaise, and other sandwich spreads high in fat. Coffee, tea, or soft drinks that contain caffeine may increase tension in a nervous athlete. It may, however, be a person's custom to drink a cup of tea, and this psychological need should be respected. The athlete should avoid flatus-producing foods, although gas formation varies among individuals, and athletes have performed well even on pregame diets of sauerkraut.

Some champions ritualistically forgo the pregame meal. The athlete who wins or performs well with a certain pregame routine is not likely to change his habit, but sound nutritional advice may have an important effect over time.

The traditional pregame football steak may impede performance. Fixed acids form and must withdraw water to be excreted, and the fat in the steak slows gastric emptying. A more proper pregame meal consists of clear soup, a lean sandwich, a noncarbonated fruit drink, or cold cereal. Commercially available liquid diets, such as Ensure, SustaCal, and Nutrament make excellent pregame meals, especially on road trips. These liquid meals are high in carbohydrates but contain some fat and enough protein to give a feeling of satiety and relieve hunger. Ordinary liquid breakfasts, however, should not be used as pregame meals because they contain too much protein. The nutritional advantages of liquid meals should be explained to athletes while emphasizing that many successful teams and individuals have benefited from their use.

The athlete should drink about 250 ml of a lightly sweetened fruit juice diluted with an equal volume of water every 15 minutes in hot and humid weather. A small increment in better performance resulting from drinking the diluted fruit juice may mean the difference between winning and losing. A solution containing more than 2.5 g of glucose per 100 ml of water will be delayed in absorption. The hyperosmolar environment in the stomach draws water into the stomach, leaving less water available for sweating, causing the athlete's exercise time to exhaustion to drop. Additives such as sugar pills, honey, or candy draw fluids into the gastrointestinal tract and cause more dehydration.

In prolonged competitions such as tennis matches, track meets, or wrestling tournaments, the athlete should supplement his fluids with sweetened beverages during the contest. These help to maintain hydration, blood sugar, and muscle glycogen. If the competition lasts a few days, the athlete should try to eat regularly scheduled meals, each one similar to a pregame meal. After the game or match, the athlete may be keyed up or depressed and have travel deadlines. Within a few hours, a high-calorie, high-protein, high carbohydrate meal eaten in a relaxed atmosphere—with no caffeine-containing drinks—will help to reduce tension and postgame depression.

PHARMACOLOGIC AGENTS

Pharmacologic agents are sometimes given to athletes to reduce pain and inflammation. Among these are nonsteroidal anti-inflammatory drugs such as aspirin, fenoprofen, ibuprofen, naproxen, indomethacin, sulindac, tolmetin, phenylbutazone local anesthetics, and steroids.[25]

The nonsteroidal anti-inflammatory drugs can be separated into four groups based on their structure: [1] salicylates: [2] proprionic acid derivatives, including ibuprofen, fenoprofen, and naproxen; [3] indole derivatives, including indomethacin, sulindac, and, a close relative, tolmetin; and [4] others such as phenylbutazone. These agents all inhibit prostaglandin synthetase and decrease the local synthesis of prostaglandins, prostacyclins, and thromboxanes.[30] The magnitude of the prostaglandin synthetase inhibition by these drugs correlates with their anti-inflammatory potency. Both aspirin (3 g) and indomethacin (200 mg) have been shown to reduce prostaglandin excretion in humans by more than 75%.[57, 58] The blockage of the formation of these fatty acid derivatives has a widespread effect on the inflammatory sequence. There is less sensitization of pain receptors to chemical and mechanical stimuli, fewer phagocytes are attracted, and less lysozomal contents are released. Chemically induced peripheral pain is also suppressed.

Aspirin and Other Nonsteroidal Anti-Inflammatory Agents

Aspirin is frequently used in sports to treat the pain and inflammation that result from an injury and to forestall the softening of articular cartilage. It is effective against the dull, throbbing pain of inflammation, when prostaglandins sensitize the nerve endings. Aspirin is much less effective, however, against the sharp, stabbing pains from direct stimulation of sensory nerves. To forestall softening of the articular cartilage behind the kneecaps, a runner may take two aspirins about 20 minutes before a run. Aspirin may also be used after a dislocation of the patella to protect against articular cartilage softening, but the aspirin therapy must be started within a few days after the injury, for if the cartilage has already become soft and fibrillated the salicylates will not reverse the condition.

Aspirin therapy is not without dangers. The most common complication is gastrointestinal discomfort, but serious gastric erosions may develop even without symptoms.[33, 50] Although hypersensitivity is uncommon, it may be severe and include vasomotor rhinitis, urticaria, a full-blown acute asthmatic attack, or angioneurotic edema. A combination of dehydration, hyperuricemia, and high-tissue levels of aspirin may produce renal papillary damage. The aspirin may interfere with both the excretion and the reabsorption of uric acid by the renal tubules. For this reason, an older athlete prone to acute gouty attacks should not take aspirin. Further, hemolysis may occur in

black athletes deficient in glucose-6-phosphate dehydrogenase. Acetaminophen may therefore be a better analgesic choice than aspirin for these athletes.

Acetaminophen is effective against chronic low-grade pain but is only weakly anti-inflammatory. Because it makes some athletes relaxed and drowsy, it has a potential for abuse. Although this drug will not irritate the stomach, it may be hepatotoxic if used excessively and and may lead to hepatic failure.[17, 45]

Other nonsteroidal anti-inflammatory drugs besides aspirin include propionic acid derivatives such as fenoprofen (Nalfon), ibuprofen (Motrin), and naproxen (Naprosyn). As a group, they have fewer gastrointestinal side-effects than does aspirin. Indole derivatives include indomethacin (Indocin), sulindac (Clinoril), and tolmetin (Tolectin), a drug related to the indole derivatives. Indomethacin is a potent inhibitor of the formation of prostaglandins, but its gastrointestinal and central nervous system side-effects limit its usefulness against acute inflammation.[42] Sulindac is metabolized to a sulfide that is more active than the parent drug. Naproxen has a longer half-life than does ibuprofen. Piroxican (Feldene) is an oxycayanenoic acid derivitative that has a long half-life. The athlete needs to take only one of these a day.

People have marked differences in response to nonsteroidal anti-inflammatory drugs. If they do not respond to one drug, they may respond very well to one in another class. If a nonsteroidal anti-inflammatory drug does not work, one should not choose another drug in that same class. I prefer starting with aspirin therapy. If it is not effective, I switch to ibuprofen and then to naproxen or piroxicam. Older people have more trouble with salicylates; for them, I usually start with ibuprofen therapy.

The anti-inflammatory activity of these newer drugs is about the same as that of aspirin. In the usual doses, however, they are three to five times more expensive than aspirin. Further, some of their side-effects are quite serious, including asthmatic attacks and aplastic anemia that may occur even with the usual therapeutic doses. It is thus imperative that an athlete given these agents be made aware of possible side-effects and their signs and symptoms.

Phenylbutazone

Phenylbutazone (Butazolidin) is an anti-inflammatory agent that can reduce pain and swelling in equine and human athletes. Oxyphenbutazone (Tandearil), an active metabolite of phenylbutazone, is another often-used anti-inflammatory drug. Phenylbutazone, or "bute," blocks inflammation by inhibiting the synthesis of prostaglandins. The drug is usually given in a dose of 100 mg three or four times a day with meals for a maximum of 7 days.

Given its potency, phenylbutazone is too often casually prescribed. It is, for example, the most commonly prescribed drug in the National Football League.[9] In another instance of its frequent use, phenylbutazone was prescribed for 3300 courses at the United States Naval Academy during a 4-year period for conditions such as painful shoulders, tennis elbow, tenosynovitis at the wrist, inflammation, trochanteric bursitis, jumper's knee, and Achilles tendinitis.

Phenylbutazone can be a very toxic drug with reactions that include aplastic anemia, agranulocytosis, hypersensitivity reactions, and serious skin reactions. It may also limit athletic performance and mask pain, thus leading to further injury. Phenylbutazone has replaced chloramphenicol as the most common cause of drug-related aplastic anemia, in many cases a fatal disease. Although aplastic anemia may follow normal doses, large doses are most often responsible for this toxic effect.[28] Jockeys and exercise boys and girls find that it works so well for horses that they sometimes take it themselves for minor bruises and sprains. In one case, a professional jockey took horse phenylbutazone, ingesting 2 g a day for 3 days. Two weeks later he developed a severe blood dyscrasia. Despite bone marrow transplantation, he died.

Phenylbutazone is also the principal cause of fatal, drug-induced agranulocytosis, a condition in which the leukocyte count drops and the victim notices ulcers in his mouth and pharynx, a sore throat, and, often, a rash. To avoid death in such cases, the patient must have the drug withdrawn immediately and the infection aggressively treated. Thrombocytopenia is another side-effect, characterized by petechiae, ecchymoses, epistaxis, and bleeding from the mucous membranes of the mouth. A hypersensitivity reaction is of most concern with short-term use because it may produce a severe granulocytosis. When an athlete has been sensitized to phenylbutazone, a single subsequent dose may prove fatal. Because allergic reactions cannot be predicted with a routine pretreatment blood test, phenylbutazone should never be prescribed for an athlete who has had any type of previous reaction to the drug. To be safe, a physician should not give the drug to an athlete with a history of an allergy to any drug. Skin reactions to phenylbutazone, such as toxic epidermal necrolysis, may be fatal. An unfortunate athlete may also develop a peptic ulcer, hepatitis, or renal failure. Finally, phenylbutazone should not be given to a pregnant athlete because the drug may be embryotoxic.

In view of these lethal complications, indiscriminate use of this powerful drug in the therapy of trivial, acute, or chronic musculoskeletal disorders can only be condemned. Serious complications aside, athletic performance may suffer while an athlete is using phenylbutazone. The drug blocks enzymes in the Krebs cycle that interfere with the aerobic production of energy. The athlete also retains fluid and gains weight, and his plasma volume expands to produce a dilutional anemia.

Phenylbutazone is especially dangerous for older athletes, particularly older women, who are more susceptible to its toxic effects. Short-term use, for 1 week or less, by young athletes is said not to be particularly hazardous,[9] but the sometimes unpredictable side-effects should eliminate the drug from the physician's repertoire. If used, it should be noted that its toxicity rises if the recommended dosage is exceeded or the duration of its use is prolonged. The athlete should be made aware of the risks and possible complications and their early manifestation. The drug should be stopped immediately if a fever, sore throat, skin rash, pruritis, jaundice, or tarry stools develop.

Local Anesthetics

Local anesthetics, such as short-acting lidocaine (Xylocaine) and long-acting bupivacaine (Marcaine), are sometimes useful in sports medicine. These drugs act as the cell membrane of sensory, motor, and autonomic nerves to block both the generation and the conduction of nerve impulses. Lidocaine produces anesthesia for about an hour, with its duration depending on how long the anesthetic remains in contact with the nerve tissue. If epinephrine is also included in the injection, the duration of anesthesia almost doubles. Bupivacaine anesthesia lasts about 7 hours.

A local anesthetic may be used to block the pain from a rib fracture and may also be injected into an injured area, such as a hip pointer, to relieve acute pain. Infiltration of a trigger point with a local anesthetic can sometimes break a reverberating pain cycle and may serve to distinguish between local and referred pain. A local anesthetic can also lessen the pain of a steroid injection or joint aspiration.

If an anesthetic is injected, the area should first be thoroughly prepared with an iodine solution, not just wiped with an alcohol sponge. On rare occasions, an athlete may be allergic to a local anesthetic. Excessive dosage, even though given locally, may be dangerous, since the drug is eventually absorbed systemically. Numbing injections must be used discriminately, since they mask pain and thus can lead to more serious injury.

Local Steroids

Steroids, like nonsteroidal anti-inflammatory drugs, block the release of arachidonic acid from membrane phospholipids, limiting the formation of inflammatory endoperoxides, prostacyclins, and thromboxanes. Steroids reduce vascular permeability and the number of leukocytes at the inflamed site. They also seem to stabilize the lysosomal membranes of the inflammatory cells. Steroids later inhibit fibroblasts and collagen deposits, reduce capillary proliferation, and thus limit the formation of scar.

Before a steroid is injected, the injection site must be thoroughly cleaned and prepared with an iodine solution. This preparation is particularly important before injecting into periarticular structures because the needle may inadvertently enter the joint and, if the skin is incompletely prepared, bacteria may be transported into the joint.

Injection of a combination of a short-acting and long-acting agent (Celestone, Soluspan) through a fine-guage needle is recommended. This combination contains betamethasone sodium phosphate, a soluble ester that acts promptly, and a betamethasone acetate suspension that is only slightly soluble and affords sustained activity. The injected steroid should bathe the inflamed area, not be injected directly into the tissue. No resistance should be felt as the plunger is depressed. If only a long-acting, repository steroid is injected, it may produce a painful local reaction for the first 24 hours. When this occurs, the athlete should not apply heat because this will increase pain and swelling; instead an ice bag should be used.

Steroid injections must be used with caution because direct injection of a steroid into an inflamed tendon may cause pressure necrosis, inhibit collagen synthesis, and degrade the collagen. The drug may diminish pain to a degree that the athlete exceeds the mechanical tolerance of the tendon, causing a rupture. The athlete who has just had a steroid injection near a weight-bearing tendon, such as the quadriceps, patellar, or Achilles tendon, should be restricted from sports for 2 weeks.

Dimethyl Sulfoxide

Dimethyl sulfoxide (DMSO) is an inexpensive by-product of paper manufacturing and is used as an industrial solvent. Being highly polar, it dissolves many water-soluble and fat-soluble substances. It is also used as a preservative in the freezing and storing of human and animal tissues and cells. Because frozen DMSO does not crystallize, cells and tissues can survive freezing undamaged.

Dimethyl sulfoxide also has the remarkable property of penetrating the keratinized barrier layer of the skin and being absorbed in seconds. Through this action, it may serve as a vehicle for drugs and provide enhanced penetration of local anesthetics and steroids. Dimethyl sulfoxide also has properties of its own to reduce soft tissue swelling and inflammation in acute trauma; DMSO is therefore both a drug-carrier and a drug, although the mechanism for its biologic activity is not fully understood.

Dimethyl sulfoxide is often used by veterinarians to treat inflammatory conditions in horses, such as contusion, sprains, strains, traumatic periostitis ("bucked shin"), "shoe ball," gonitis, blisters, lacerations, hematomas, and fractures and is used postoperatively. The drug is available as a solution and as a gel. Usually, about 100 ml is brushed on the injured area two or three times a day. The most dramatic results are obtained when the drug is applied very soon after trauma. The veterinarian should wear rubber gloves while applying the medicine to prevent the drug from penetrating his skin and producing an unpleasant garlic-like taste in his mouth and an oyster-like breath odor. The horse's skin should be washed, rinsed, and dried before DMSO is applied. If this is not done, the drug will carry in any chemicals that are on the skin. For this same reason, no other topical agents should be applied to the skin until the DMSO has thoroughly dried. A veterinary grade of DMSO is used because industrial DMSO rapidly carries impurities through the skin. The drug is not without irritating effects: It may produce a transient erythema and local skin burning and may also be teratogenic; thus, it is not recommended for horses that are intended for breeding.

Experimentation on the use of DMSO in humans was progressing until the thalidomide catastrophe, whereupon new Food and Drug Administration (FDA) guidelines and policies were instituted. Lens changes appeared in experimental animals that had been treated with DMSO, and, although no eye changes had been reported in humans, the clinical investigation was abruptly discontinued. The drug has been approved by the FDA solely for use in horses as a topical treatment for acute swelling that has resulted from trauma.

The properties of DMSO as a penetrating carrier of other medicines, as a local analgesic, anti-inflammatory agent, and bacteriostatic agent, and as a potentiator of other compounds may someday be helpful to the injured athlete.

Oral Enzymes

Oral proteolytic enzymes are sometimes used in sports medicine to disperse fibrin, hematomas, and inflammatory edema. These enzymes include peptidases, such as chymotrypsin and trypsin, that may be be combined in tablets and taken in a dose of one or two tablets four times a day.

Although the goal of breaking up fibrin deposits that mechanically bar the resolution of edema is desirable, these enzymes seem to work only when given parenterally in large doses to experimental animals *before* the inflammation is produced. Oral enzymes have been found to be ineffective in experimentally produced ringer injuries. As proteins, they probably denatured in the acid environment of the stomach.

Hyaluronidase hydrolyzes hyaluronic acid to decrease the visosity of the cellular-cementing ground substance. One milliliter or 2 ml of hyaluronidase may be injected directly into the injured area, but it may produce a hypersensitivity reaction. If the enzyme is used, the athlete should first be tested for hypersensitivity to it.

These enzymes have little, if any, advantage, and because of the possibility of a hypersensitivity reaction their use is meddlesome and dangerous.

Counterirritants

Moist heat is the warmth producer of choice for athletes. However, counterirritant creams and lotions are sometimes used as components of massage mixtures when the athlete is away from the training room. These rubefacients (L. rubefacere, to make red) irritate the skin and, by an axonal reflex, increase the local circulation to produce warmth and comfort. Counterirritants include methyl salicylate (oil of wintergreen) and camphor, a mild local anesthetic that numbs the skin. They may cause itching and hypersensitivity reactions, and plasma may escape and collect under the epidermis to form blisters.

DRUG ABUSE IN ATHLETICS

Alcohol

Alcohol was formerly used as a general anesthetic until it was found to be too dangerous for that purpose. If alcohol is applied to living cells, the cells' protoplasm becomes dehydrated and precipitates. Ingested alcohol depresses the reticular activating system and the cerebral cortex, represses control mechanisms, and thus frees the brain from inhibition. This depression may cause euphoria and lessen the realization of fatigue, but alcohol does not enhance the mental or physical abilities of an athlete. The drug has been used by marksmen to ease tension and reduce tremor to produce a steady arm, but the eye then loses its alertness for tracking a target.

Although the mechanism for the effect is unknown, moderate alcohol consumption appears to increase high-density lipoprotein levels and may help to protect against coronary artery disease, since myocardial infarction rates are lower in moderate drinkers than in nondrinkers.[64] This does not, however, justify recommending that nondrinkers start drinking moderately.

Caffeine

Coffee, tea, and many soft drinks contain caffeine, a drug related to aminophylline and theophylline. Caffeine may have a direct effect on the brain or act through the reticular activating system to stimulate the cerebral cortex to wakefulness and improve psychomotor performance, unless tremors and agitation supervene. The drug also provokes the vasomotor center in the medulla to induce peripheral vasoconstriction and a rise in blood pressure and may generate an increase in heart rate, extrasystoles, and ventricular arrhythmias.

As an endurance activity progresses, the athlete derives more and more energy from free fatty acids. If a 70-kg athlete ingests 250 mg of caffeine (equivalent to two cups of coffee) 1 hour before competition, he may stimulate the release of free fatty acids. The fatty acids may then spare glycogen, enhance endurance, and reduce the perceived level of exertion.

Most people can tolerate a moderate amount of caffeine; others are more sensitive to the drug, and it may promote cardiac arrhythmias. Caffeine is a powerful diuretic that increases the work of the heart and promotes a loss of fluid that may endanger an endurance athlete. Caffeine can also delay and lighten sleep, promote muscle tenseness, and disturb the athlete's rest periods.

Nicotine

More than one third of the adult population in the United States smokes cigarettes. As the tobacco burns, about 4000 compounds are generated, including carbon monoxide, ammonia, hydrogen cyanide, nicotine and "tar," many carcinogens, and DDT. These noxious ingredients quickly reach the brain, where they stimulate the release of norepinephrine and dopamine from the brain tissue. The heavy smoker pays a high price in toxic effects for this stimulation. The smoke has a ciliotoxic action that paralyzes the cilia in the athlete's respiratory passages, causing normal filtering to fail and the respiratory tract to become susceptible to infection. Maximum ventilatory capacity drops as carbon monoxide enters the blood, resulting in hypoxia, and the products of combustion bind hemoglobin. Along with these immediate effects, the athlete risks deadly long-term hazards from smoking cigarettes, including lung cancer, emphysema, an acceleration of atherosclerosis with coronary artery disease, cerebral vascular disease, and peripheral vascular disease.

Marijuana

Marijuana comes from the hemp plant *Cannabis sativa*. Its psychological effects depend on the compound tetrahydrocannabinol. This drug produces a sedating sense of well-being, with euphoria, relaxation, and sleepiness. The user's balance is disturbed, muscular strength drops, and he becomes less aggressive and loses his motivation to perform.

A few marijuana cigarettes a day may induce subtle personality changes and lower an athlete's interest in achievement and his pursuit of conventional goals, an amotivational state antithetical to athletics. High doses may cause hallucinations, delusions, and panic that resemble a toxic psychosis.

Cocaine

Cocaine, found in the leaves of the coca bush *Erythroxylon coca*, is a local anesthetic that blocks the initiation and conduction of nerve impulses. For recreational use, the drug is inhaled or snorted through the nose to stimulate the user's central nervous system. It potentiates the action of catecholamines in the central nervous system and, like amphetamines, elevates mood, giving an increased sense of energy.

Cocaine seems to stimulate "reward areas" in the brain. Experimental animals will select cocaine over food, lose weight, mutilate themselves, and die. The drug masks fatigue through central stimulation, but the user may become restless and excited. The price paid for the uplifted mood is a depression that follows, and some persons may become paranoid. Higher doses of cocaine produce tremors and even convulsions.

Amphetamines

In the past, some football clubs bought amphetamines in bulk to distribute to their players to allay fatigue, increase alertness, uplift mood, and increase initiative, self-confidence, and ability to concentrate. The athlete may, however, become agitated, overaggressive, hostile, and show confusion and poor judgment—a sorry state for optimal athletic performance. If the dose is high enough, he may even panic and suffer paranoid hallucinations.

The athlete pays for the relief of fatigue and the increased feeling of alertness with subsequent dizziness, mental depression, and fatigue. Further, an overaggressive, hostile athlete with poor judgment may well injure himself or his opponents. These powerful drugs mask or disguise pain and remove the normal psychological and physiologic restraints that prevent overexertion. As a result, the athlete may suffer cardiovascular collapse, arrhythmias, or musculoskeletal damage. Rapid eye movement sleep is reduced, and the athlete's sleep pattern may take a while to return to normal. He soon feels a need for larger and larger doses to produce the euphoric feeling and to blunt pain, and for sedatives to reduce the altered state of alertness.

Anabolic Steroids

Some athletes, especially in strength sports and tackle football, take anabolic steroids to gain a competitive advantage. The athlete may feel at an unfair disadvantage if he is not taking anabolic steroids while other competitors are so doing, and he may then take them for "insurance."[54] These drugs are used almost universally at higher levels of body building and competitive weight lifting. Some athletes have, however, refused to abuse their bodies, becoming champions at the top levels of body building and weight lifting without resorting to drugs.

Do anabolic steroids work? Although many studies on animals and athletes have failed to show strength gains with these drugs, the investigators have used low doses. In reality, weight lifters take high doses of 35 to 100 mg per day, although the optimum dosage range has yet to be established. While on steroids some competitive weight lifters report increases of 9 kg (20 lb) in the maximum weight that they can lift.[61] The anabolic steroids have a euphorogenic effect that aids athletic performance by influencing the athlete's attitude toward training and the quality of his training. By increasing competitiveness and aggression, he can train longer, harder, and more frequently and strenuously with less fatigue. His appetite also increases, and there may be a direct action of the anabolic steroid on the muscle cell that increases the content of skeletal muscle protein by raising the activity of RNA-polymerase in skeletal muscle nuclei.[44] If a particular muscle escapes exercise during training, it will fail to show the improvement displayed by exercised muscles.

On the other hand, these extremely powerful drugs have many severe side-effects. Even though some athletes have been fortunate, taking doses up to 300 mg per day for 2 years without apparent ill effects, jaundice, raised liver enzyme levels, gastrointestinal bleeding, prostatic blockage, sex drive changes, low sperm counts, and fatal primary tumors of the liver are among the dangerous side-effects known to be associated with these drugs. They may stunt the growth of youths by prematurely closing their growth plates. Unfortunately, many female weight lifters and female athletes in strength sports are now taking anabolic steroids. These women may develop permanent vocal cord alterations, hirsutism, and acne while risking the more serious side-effects of reproductive system dysfunction and, in cases of pregnancy, genital malformations in the developing fetus.

Test stations are set up at major competitions to detect whether athletes are using anabolic steroids. However, the drugs pose special problems because they are taken long before competition begins. Since the effect of the steroid is to increase the intensity of training, the athlete has the benefit of a strength gain that lasts through the contest, but the steroid or its metabolites are no longer detectable.

A radioimmunoassay is used to screen for anabolic steroids. If the screening test is positive, gas chromatography and mass spectrometric methods can identify the metabolites of the steroid in the athlete's urine. Some athletes stop taking anabolic steroids about 10 days before a contest and then take instead a natural testosterone to promote high-intensity training and to deceive testers.

Random testing should perhaps be done throughout the year by a detection squad traveling around the world and popping up unexpectedly to check athletes. However, even with such expensive testing as is currently done, an athlete found to be using a drug risks disqualification for only about a year, not a great blow to his career. An alternative approach would be to forgo testing and spend the millions saved on educational programs.

Nonetheless, the drugs are morally and legally unacceptable, conveying an unfair advantage to the taker, who is looking for an "edge." Taking a drug that aids performance is akin to doping an opponent to diminish his performance. Determined effort, dedicated training, good coaching, and proper diet can provide the motivation to increase the athlete's intensity of training, eliminating the need for ergogenic anabolic steroids. The overwhelming majority of great athletic accomplishments reflects this combination, without the use of drugs.

SLEEP

Athletic excellence and strength development rest on systematic training, good nutrition, and proper sleep. An athlete in heavy training needs a lot of sleep, as a lack of rest will show up in poor performance and a great chance of injury. However, he may, for many reasons, be unable to sleep at night. His room may be unfamiliar, he may be suffering from jet lag, or he may be anxious about an upcoming contest.

Drugs are sometimes given to induce sleep. More prescriptions are written in the United States for sedative-hypnotic-antianxiety drugs than for any other class of drugs. These drugs decrease rapid eye movement sleep, disrupt dream time, and may lead to psychological dependence. If they are used the night before and after every contest, the athlete may become addicted to them. Some athletes ride a roller coaster of barbiturates to calm down and amphetamines to train.

The time that passes before the athlete falls asleep—the sleep latency—may seem long but is usually less than 1 hour. This short period of wakefulness is preferable to a dependence on hypnotics. Athletes should be advised that each person's sleep requirements differ, with some not needing the standard 8 hours. Every effort must be made to assist the athlete to meet his sleep requirements. He should avoid food or coffee near bedtime and his bedroom should be cool, with walls painted in subdued colors and the bed furnished with clean sheets and a good mattress and pillow. The worried athlete may use relaxation techniques to calm down, occupying his mind with thoughts of keeping his muscles supple. Breathing rituals and self-hypnosis may also be used.

REFERENCES

1. Adams R et al: Ice skating therapy. Phys Sportsmed 6(3):71–81, 1978
2. Aisenson MR: Accidental injuries in epileptic children. Pediatrics 2:85–88, 1948
3. Anderson S: Four tips that may save your wrestling program. First Aider, Cramer 47:11, November 1977
4. Andrews GC et al: Treatment of acne vulgaris. JAMA 146:1107, 1951
5. Baer RL et al: High dose tetracycline therapy in severe acne. Arch Dermatol 112:479, 1976
6. Beacham BE: Equestrian cold paniculitis in women. Arch Dermatol 116:1025–1027, 1980
7. Bedo AV et al: Special Olympic athletes face special medical needs. Phys Sportsmed 4(9):51–56, 1976

8. Biermann J, Toohey B: The Diabetics Sports and Exercise Book, Philadelphia, JB Lippincott, 1977

9. Black HM et al: Use of phenylbutazone in sports medicine: Understanding the risks. Am J Sport Med 8:270–273, 1980

10. Brodin MB: Jock itch. Phys Sportsmed 8(2):102–108, 1980

11. Brogdon BG, Crow NE: Observations on the "normal" spleen. Radiology 72:412–413, 1959

12. Chang LW, O'Brien TF: Australia antigen serology in the Holy Cross football team hepatitis outbreak. Lancet 2:59–61, 1970

13. Clark MW: Competitive sports for the disabled. Am J Sports Med 8:366–369, 1980

14. Corbitt RW et al: Epilepsy and contact sports. JAMA 229:820–821, 1974

15. Costill DL: Energy metabolism in diabetic distance runners. Phys Sportsmed 8(10):63–71, 1980

16. Coskey RJ, Mehregan AH: Shoe boot pernio. Arch Dermatol 109:56–57, 1974

17. Craig RM: How safe is acetaminophen? JAMA 244:272, 1980

18. D'Ambrosia RD: Cold injuries encountered in a winter resort. Cutis 20:365–368, 1977

19. DeShazo WF III: Case report: Ruptured spleen in a college football player. Phys Sportsmed 7(10):109–111, 1979

20. DeShazo WF III: Returning to athletic activity after infectious mononucleosis. Phys Sportsmed 8(12):71–72, 1980

21. Eggleston PA: Management—not avoidance—for exercise-induced asthma. J Respir Dis 1(1):25–33, 1979

22. Freinkel RK et al: Effect of tetracyline on the composition of sebum in acne vulgaris. N Engl J Med 273:850, 1964

23. Frostbite. Med Lett Drugs Ther 18:25, 3 December 1976

24. Frostbite. Med Lett Drugs Ther 22:26, 26 December 1980

25. Glick JM: Therapeutic agents in musculoskeletal injuries. J Sports Med 3(3):136–138, 1975

26. Godfrey et al: Problems of interpreting exercise-induced asthma. J Allergy Clin Immunol 52:199–209, 1973

27. Heymsfield SB et al: Accurate measurements of liver, kidney, and spleen volume and mass by computerized axial tomography. Ann Intern Med 90:185–187, 1979

28. Inman WHW: Study of fatal bone marrow depression with special reference to phenylbutazone and oxyphenbutazone. Br Med J 1:1500–1505, 1977

29. Jackson RW, Fredrickson A: Sports for the physically disabled. The 1976 Olympiad (Toronto). Am J Sports Med 7:293–296, 1979

30. Katler E, Weissman G: Steroids, aspirin and inflammation. Inflammation 2:295, 1977

31. Katz RM: Asthmatics don't have to sit out sports. A clinical review. Phys Sportsmed 4(4):45–52, 1976

32. Krikler PM, Zilberg B: Activity and hepatitis. Lancet 2:1043–1047, 1966

33. Leonards JR et al: Gastrointestinal blood loss during prolonged aspirin administration. N Engl J Med 289:1020, 1973

34. Livingston S: Should epileptics be athletes? Phys Sportsmed 3(4):67–72, 1975

35. Livingston S, Berman W: Epilepsy and athletics. JAMA 224:236–238, 1973

36. Livingston S, Berman W: Participation of the epileptic child in contact sports. J Sports Med 2:170–174, 1974

37. Marshall E: Drugging of football players curbed by central monitoring play. NFL Claims. Science 203:626–628, 1979

38. McLaurin RL : Epilepsy and contact sports—factors contraindicating participation. JAMA 225:285–287, 1973

39. Meisel A: Pharmacology of anti-inflammatory drugs. Hilton Head Seminar—Resources for Basic Science Educators. Chicago, American Academy of Orthopedic Surgery, 1980

40. Morse LJ et al: The Holy Cross college football team hepatitis outbreak. JAMA 219:706–709, 1972

41. Morton AR et al: Physical activity and the asthmatic. Phys Sportsmed 9(3):51–59, 1981

42. O'Brien WM: Indomethacin: A survey of clinical trials. Clin Pharmacol Ther 9:94, 1968

43. Ramsey R, Golde DW: Aplastic anemia from veterinary phenylbutazone. JAMA 236:1049, 1976

44. Rogozkin V: Metabolic effects of anabolic steroid on skeletal muscle. Med Sci Sports 11:160–163, 1979

45. Rosenberg DM et al: Acetaminophen and hepatic dysfunction in infectious mononucleosis. South Med J 70:660–661, 1977

46. Ross J: Blind break through old barriers to sports. Phys Sportsmed 5(3):98–104, 1977

47. Rutkow IM: Rupture of the spleen in infectious mononucleosis. Arch Surg 113:718–720, 1978

48. Ryan AJ (moderator): Infectious mononucleosis in athletes. Phys Sportsmed 6(2):41–56, 1978

49. Ryan AJ (moderator): Sport and recreation for the handicapped. Phys Sportsmed 6(3):45–67, 1978

50. Samter J, Beers RF: Intolerance to aspirin. Ann Intern Med 68:975, 1968

51. Shapira W: Competing in a silent world of sports. Phys Sportsmed 3(11):99–105, 1975

52. Shapira W: It's a new ball game for hemophiliac youngsters. Phys Sportsmed 3(12):63–64, 1975

53. Sigel RM et al: Evaluation of spleen size during routine liver imaging with 99m Tc and the scintillation camera. J Nucl Med 11:689–692, 1970

54. Stackpole PJ: Effects of anabolic steroids on strength development and performance. Natl Strength Coaches Assoc J 2(2):30–33, 1980

55. Taylor KJ, Milan J: Differential diagnosis of chronic splenomegaly by gray-scale ultrasonography: Clin-

ical observations and digital A-scan analysis. Br J Radiol 49:519–525, 1976

56. The Athlete with Sickle Cell Trait. A Statement of the NCAA Committee on Competitive Safeguards and Medical Aspects of Sports. Athletic Training 10(1):19, 1975

57. Vane JR: Prostaglandins and the aspirin-like drugs. Hosp Pract 7:61, 1972

58. Vane JR: The mode of action of aspirin and similar compounds. J Allergy Clin Immunol 58:691, 1976

59. Van Itallie TB: Nutrition and athletic performance. JAMA 160:1120–1126, 1956

60. Wacker WEC et al: The Holy Cross hepatitis outbreak. Arch Intern Med 130:357–360, 1972

61. Ward P: The effect of an anabolic steroid on strength and lean body mass. Med Sci Sports 5:277–282, 1973

62. Washburn B: Frostbite: What is it—how to prevent it—emergency treatment. N Engl J Med 266:974–989, 1962

63. Werblow JA et al: Nutrition: What's the score? Natl Strength Coaches Assoc J 2(2):20–21, 1980

64. Willet W et al: Alcohol consumption and high-density lipoprotein cholesterol in marathon runners. N Engl J Med 303:1159–1161, 1980

CHAPTER

3

Principles
of Training

Russell R. Pate

Successful participation in athletic activities requires preparation. Such preparation, often called training, might be described as the systematic participation in physical exercise for the purpose of improving performance in an athletic activity. The process of training can be interpreted broadly to include learning of competitive strategies, perfection of motor skills, and establishment of a proper psychologic outlook. I focus here on the physical fitness aspect of athletic performance, provide guidelines for the improvement of basic fitness components in athletes, and give primary emphasis to training for improved endurance performance.

PHYSIOLOGIC BASES OF EXERCISE

Metabolic Systems

Performing an athletic activity depends on the contraction of skeletal muscles, and the energy that fuels these contractions is provided through a complex series of chemical reactions localized in the individual skeletal muscle cells (fibers).[10] The single immediate source of this chemical energy is adenosine triphosphate (ATP). During contraction, ATP, a high-energy phosphate compound, is hydrolyzed to produce adenosine diphosphate (ADP) and phosphoric acid. The

81

breakage of ATP's terminal high-energy phosphate bond releases energy used by the muscle fiber to cause contraction.

Because only a very small concentration of ATP is maintained in the muscle fiber, sustained or repetitive muscle contractions depend on rapid resynthesis of ATP. The energy to support this resynthesis is provided through the biochemical processes of aerobic and anaerobic metabolism. Aerobic metabolism occurs in the presence of oxygen, whereas anaerobic processes function without oxygen.

Anaerobic Metabolism

At the onset of muscular work the available ATP supply is rapidly used. A small amount of ATP may be resynthesized at the expense of another high-energy phosphate source, creatine phosphate (CP), whose role is critical because it provides a reservoir of phosphate bond energy that can be tapped immediately, thereby preventing any lag in the ATP supply. As is the case for ATP, however, only very finite amounts of CP are maintained in the fiber; indeed, at the onset of high-intensity exercise (sprinting) the available supplies of both ATP and CP could, theoretically, be depleted in a few seconds. Clearly the store of energy represented by ATP and CP is too small to support endurance exercise—that is, the *capacity* of the ATP–CP system is low. Its maximum *power* (rate of energy expenditure) is very high, however, and consequently the ATP–CP system is the predominant energy source for high-intensity, short-duration exercise.

Exercise of longer duration but lower intensity is supported, predominantly, by a second anaerobic process, *anaerobic glycolysis*, which involves the breakdown of the carbohydrate glycogen ("muscle starch") through a sequentially arranged series of 11 enzyme-catalyzed chemical reactions. Glycogen is no more than a matrix of individual glucose molecules. In glycolysis the glucose molecules are split from the glycogen matrix and enzymatically altered so as to yield two pyruvic acid molecules. Without oxygen, pyruvic acid is converted to lactic acid. The process of glycolysis releases an amount of energy from the glucose molecule sufficient to resynthesize two

ATP molecules. As compared with the ATP–CP system, anaerobic glycolysis has less power but greater capacity. In anaerobic glycolysis, the rate of energy production is limited by the maximum rate of the individual chemical reactions that constitute the entire system, a rate slower than that of the ATP–CP system. The total amount of energy released, however, is limited only by the amount of glycogen available (usually plentiful) and the person's tolerance for the system's end-product, lactic acid. If lactic acid accumulates in the muscle, tissue acidosis and impaired functioning result, with fatigue being the outcome. Anaerobic glycolysis is a very important supplier of ATP energy during high-intensity work of moderate duration (30 seconds to 2 minutes). In such forms of work the capacity and power of the glycolytic system are well matched to the demands of the activity.

Aerobic Metabolism

The ultimate source of all energy expended by skeletal muscle, aerobic metabolism occurs primarily in the mitochondria and results in the complete oxidation of either carbohydrate or fat while producing two benign end-products, water and carbon dioxide.[7, 13]

As compared with anaerobic processes, the ATP of aerobic metabolism is characterized by a relatively low power but very great capacity. The amount of ATP energy that can be produced through aerobic metabolism is essentially infinite, being limited only by the person's store of food stuffs, such as glycogen and free fatty acids. In contrast, the power of the aerobic system is quite limited because it is restricted by the rate at which oxygen can be delivered to the active tissues by the cardiorespiratory system. The maximal aerobic power is usually expressed in terms of maximum oxygen consumption.

The aerobic metabolic system is used preferentially during low-intensity but sustained exercise. Because the end-products of aerobic metabolism are not fatigue producing and the needed raw materials (*i.e.*, oxygen and glycogen or free fatty acids) are available, for practical purposes, in unlimited quantities, the aerobic process may continue indefinitely.

Relation Between Aerobic and Anaerobic Metabolism

Some athletic activities involve forms of muscular work that derive all the needed ATP energy from a single metabolic process. The long jump in track and field, for example, is an activity that requires a very high rate of energy expenditure for only a few seconds, and consequently the anaerobic processes provide virtually all the required ATP. In contrast, a marathon run involves moderately intense activity sustained for several hours. Many athletic activities, however, require that energy be provided through a combination of the three energy-yielding systems. During the first few seconds of the 400-meter sprint (total duration, 45–60 seconds), for example, most energy comes through the breakdown of available ATP and CP stores. Rapidly, though, anaerobic glycolysis begins to predominate as the provider of ATP energy. Although anaerobic glycolysis continues to function at its maximum rate throughout the run, aerobic metabolism gradually increases to provide, in total, about 25% of the ATP used. Performance in the 400-meter sprint is a function of the maximal power of the three systems in combination and the capacity of the two anaerobic systems. World-class 400-meter sprinters tend to have high anaerobic power, very high anaerobic capacity, and reasonably well-developed maximum aerobic power.

Cardiorespiratory Function

In athletic activities such as distance running and swimming, performance depends on, to a considerable extent, the maximum aerobic power $\dot{V}O_2$max).[2] The higher the $\dot{V}O_2$max, the greater is the rate at which work may be done over extended periods and the longer the work may be done at any submaximal intensity. In activities such as football, aerobic metabolism functions during recovery periods to replenish the stores of ATP and CP and to assist in clearing lactic acid. Thus the development of a high $\dot{V}O_2$ max is probably beneficial in most athletic activities and critical in many.

As mentioned previously, $\dot{V}O_2$ max is limited primarily by the maximum rate at which oxygen can be delivered to the active skeletal muscle tissues. The cardiorespiratory system, which transports oxygen, plays a key role in supporting skeletal muscle metabolism during exercise and comprises four functional components: lungs and respiratory tract, heart, blood vessels, and blood. During exercise the overall system responds in such a way as to increase the rate of oxygen delivery to the active skeletal muscle tissues, where the demand for oxygen increases markedly. Alterations in the functioning of each component contribute to this increased rate of oxygen transport.

Ventilation

As exercise begins, the rate and depth of breathing increase rapidly and substantially. Ventilation, regulated by both neural and humoral factors, increases to a level sufficient to maintain adequate diffusion gradients across the alveolar membrane for both oxygen and carbon dioxide. At very high workloads, arterial blood is maintained at a fully oxygenated level; consequently, for most persons, ventilatory function is not considered to be a factor limiting the $\dot{V}O_2$max.

Cardiac Output

Perhaps the most important determinant of $\dot{V}O_2$max is the maximal cardiac output ($\dot{Q}$max). Cardiac output, the volume of blood pumped by the heart per minute, increases rapidly at the beginning of exercise but takes 2 to 3 minutes to reach a plateau. The level at which $\dot{Q}$ reaches a plateau is highly related to exercise intensity (and $\dot{V}O_2$), and the relation between the two variables is linear up to $\dot{Q}$max. $\dot{Q}$ max is attained at the same exercise intensity as $\dot{V}O_2$max and is equal to the product of maximal heart rate and maximal stroke volume. Heart rate is linearly related to exercise intensity, $\dot{V}O_2$, and $\dot{Q}$; maximal heart rate (HR max) is age related (HR max $\approx 220 -$ age in years) but is not related to fitness level. Stroke volume, the volume of blood pumped with each beat, is a function of heart size, venous filling pressure, and myocardial contractility. Stroke volume increases with exercise but reaches a maximum at workloads requiring about 50% of the $\dot{V}O_2$max. Maximal stroke volume increases with endurance training and results in an increased $\dot{Q}$ max, which in turn is reflected by a greater $\dot{V}O_2$max. Thus adaptations in myocardial function resulting in increased stroke volume represent a critical component of the body's response to endurance exercise training.

Vessels

Vasomotor function supports exercise performance by redistributing the blood flow so as to increase oxygen delivery to the active skeletal muscles. During exercise, dilation of arterioles in skeletal muscle and constriction of arterioles in nonactive tissues (particularly the digestive system) may result in tripling of the blood flow to skeletal muscle. Increased blood flow is also provided to the skin during prolonged exercise, a response that facilitates dissipation of heat to the environment and, in hot, humid conditions, may require a fraction of the cardiac output high enough to decrease significantly the fraction provided to the working muscles. With exercise, the volume of the venous system is reduced through a general vasoconstriction of venules, a response that tends to promote return of blood to the heart.

Arteriovenous Oxygen Difference

As indicated by the Fick equation, VO_2 is equal to the product of cardiac output and arteriovenous oxygen difference (A $-$ VO_2). The oxygen-carrying capacity of the blood is about 20 ml of oxygen per 100 ml of blood; however, under resting conditions only about 25% of this oxygen is removed in the tissues. With exercise, arteriovenous oxygen difference increases as the tissue's demand for oxygen increases. With high-intensity exercise, total body A $-$ VO_2 (left ventricular blood versus right arterial blood) reaches values as high as 75% to 80%. Skeletal muscle tissue A $-$ VO_2 may reach values approaching 100%.

A $-$ VO_2 reflects the ability of the skeletal muscle tissue to use, in aerobic metabolism, the oxygen offered to it by the cardiorespiratory system. Endurance exercise training causes profound adaptations in the skeletal muscle tissue: specifically, increases in mitochondrial density, myo-

globin concentration, and aerobic enzyme activities. These changes are specific to those muscles active during training. Collectively the adaptations contribute to an increased maximal rate of aerobic metabolism in the muscle tissue and an increased whole body $\dot{V}O_2$max.

In summary, the body's physiologic response to acute exercise includes an increased rate of aerobic metabolism in the active skeletal muscles, a metabolic response supported by the cardiorespiratory system, which in turn increases its rate of oxygen delivery to the active muscles. Cardiac, vasomotor, and ventilatory responses contribute to an increased rate of blood flow to the working muscles. The physiologic response to endurance exercise training involves both *central* (i.e., cardiorespiratory) and *peripheral* (i.e., muscle tissue) adaptations: Central adaptation is manifested as an increased maximal cardiac output and thus increased maximal rates of blood flow and oxygen delivery to the working muscles; peripheral adaptation allows an increased rate of oxygen use for the production of ATP energy. The outcome of these adaptations is an increase in the person's tolerance for sustained, whole-body, moderately intense exercise.

DETERMINANTS OF ENDURANCE EXERCISE PERFORMANCE

Maximal Oxygen Consumption

As mentioned previously, VO_2max (ml/kg/min) is a prime determinant of exercise endurance performance. $\dot{V}O_2$max reflects the maximum rate at which ATP energy may be produced aerobically, and thus establishes a maximum rate at which work can be done without tapping anaerobic energy sources. The $\dot{V}O_2$max *per se* is most important as a determinant of performance in activities that require maximal rates of energy expenditure for 4 to 10 minutes. In such activities the athlete is able to work at or near the $\dot{V}O_2$max level throughout the competition, and, although anaerobic sources do contribute to the total energy supply, the aerobic process is predominant, contributing 75% to 90% of the total energy expenditure. Clearly, in activities such as the mile run or the 100-meter swim, $\dot{V}O_2$max should be very highly correlated with performance.

Anaerobic Threshold

In longer duration activities, other variables combine with the $\dot{V}O_2$max to determine the maximum rate at which work can be done. One such variable is the anaerobic threshold. During a graded exercise test, individuals begin to produce and accumulate lactic acid at some characteristic intensity of work. Among different persons, this intensity varies from 50% to 90% of the $\dot{V}O_2$max. Because lactic acid accumulation results in fatigue, exercise cannot be continued for more than a few minutes at workloads requiring oxygen to be consumed at levels above the anaerobic threshold. Thus, the higher the anaerobic threshold, the higher is the $\dot{V}O_2$ and workload that can be sustained for extended periods. Conceivably, then, if two athletes have the same $\dot{V}O_2$max but different anaerobic thresholds, the one with the higher anaerobic threshold will have an advantage in any longer duration activity. The anaerobic threshold tends to increase with endurance training. In the early stages of a training program, the $\dot{V}O_2$max and the anaerobic threshold tend to increase concurrently. Later in a program and in mature athletes who have attained their ultimate $\dot{V}O_2$max, the anaerobic threshold may still be improved through appropriate training procedures.

Efficiency

Another important variable in endurance performance is efficiency. Efficiency, to the engineer, refers to the ratio of work done by a machine to energy used by it. In humans, with activities such as running or swimming, efficiency is often expressed as the rate of oxygen consumption ($\dot{V}O_2$ in ml/kg/min) needed to perform work at a given rate (e.g., running at 9.6 km/h [6 miles/h] or swimming at 6.75 m/min [75 yards/min]). Individual rates of oxygen consumption needed to work at a given pace vary, in part owing to differences in athletes' skill levels. The significance of work efficiency is seen when it is considered in combination with the $\dot{V}O_2$max and the anaerobic threshold. The more efficient athlete needs a

lower $\dot{V}O_2$ at any given work rate, and therefore will work at a lower percentage of the maximal oxygen uptake at any given work rate and experience less fatigue; he also will be able to work at a higher rate before reaching the anaerobic threshold.

Muscle Fiber Types

Physiologic variables such as VO_2max, efficiency, and anaerobic threshold all are subject to improvement through appropriate forms of training; however, each related variable and overall endurance performance are related to inherited, genetic factors. In recent years, studies have shown that a person's distribution of skeletal muscle fiber types is a major determinant of performance potential in certain athletic activities.

Human skeletal muscle fibers may be categorized as either fast twitch (FT) or slow twitch (ST). Fast twitch fibers are particularly well adapted for speed and power activities because they contract rapidly and possess metabolically a high glycolytic capability. In contrast, ST fibers contract more slowly but are quite fatigue resistant because they possess a well-developed aerobic capability. Individuals vary greatly in the relative distribution of FT and ST fibers. Generally persons who inherit a high percentage of ST fibers possess greater potential for development of a high $\dot{V}O_2$max and a high anaerobic threshold, and thus greater potential for performing endurance activities. Those who inherit a high percentage of FT fibers are better adapted to high-power activities. Performance in any athletic activity, however, is multifactorial and is not determined by any single variable. Muscle fiber type is only one variable, and it alone cannot be used to derive an accurate prediction of a person's current ability or ultimate performance potential.

PRINCIPLES OF TRAINING

Typical training programs comprise numerous specific training activities and techniques. Although selecting the proper individual activities is important, combining these activities in a complementary fashion so that the result is an optimal overall training program is crucial. Adherence to the following principles should aid coaches, athletes, trainers, and team physicians in designing proper comprehensive training programs.

Overload

Perhaps the most basic principle of training is overload. Most physiologic systems can adapt to functional demands that exceed those encountered in normal, daily life. Training often systematically exposes selected physiologic systems to intensities of work or function that exceed those to which the system is already adapted. A key, however, is to avoid excessive overload because physiologic systems cannot adapt to stresses too extreme.

Consistency

There is no substitute for consistency in a training program. Successful athletes, almost without exception, adhere to a training regimen with extreme regularity for several years or more. Most physiologic systems require exposure to overloading activities three times a week or more. The required frequency of training, however, depends on the season, the athlete, activity, and the specific component of fitness. Thus a particular athlete might train 12 times a week during certain stages of the year and only three times a week at other stages; he might participate in endurance training six times a week and resistance training (e.g., weight lifting) three times a week.

Specificity

The effects of training are highly specific to the particular physiologic system overloaded, to the particular muscle groups used, and to the particular muscle fibers performing the work. No single training technique can produce any and all desired outcomes; commercial advertising claims to that effect should be rejected.

Because athletic performance usually depends on the development of several physical fitness components, most training programs should include several training techniques and several modifications of each specific technique. The

swimmer's training program, for instance, might comprise a combination of swimming activities using various strokes, intensities, and variations. In addition, the swimmer might participate in stretching exercises for flexibility and resistance exercises for muscular strength and muscular endurance.

Progression

Successful training programs plan for a steady rate of progression over a long period. If an athlete is to improve over several years of participation, his training program must progress so that the appropriate physiologic systems continue to be overloaded. At the same time, however, too rapid an increase of the training stress may lead to exhaustion and impaired performance. The job of the coach or trainer is to structure training programs that continue to challenge the athlete but avoid excessive overload.

Individuality

No two programs are exactly alike physiologically, and thus no two athletes should be expected to respond exactly the same to a particular training regimen. Factors such as age, sex, maturity, current fitness level, years of training, body size, somatotype, and psychological characteristics should be considered by the coach in designing each athlete's training regimen. In large groups in which absolute individualization of training programs may be impractical, the coach should strive for individualization by homogeneously grouping athletes. Successful teams are composed of successful individual athletes, and the optimal training program is that which best fits the needs of each team member.

Periodization

Periodization refers to the tendency for athletic performance to vary cyclically over time. Few athletes can sustain a peak performance level for more than a few weeks, and thus training and competitive schedules should be structured so that peak performances are attained at the desired time. Intense training and competition tends to bring the athlete to his optimal performance level. The key, of course, is to avoid attaining this level too early in the competitive season. Ideally the training program should build to maximum intensity one half to two thirds through the season so that peak performances are achieved during championship competitions at season's end.

Plateauing

In many athletes, performance tends to improve incrementally rather than steadily and smoothly. An athlete may spend weeks, months, or even years on a performance plateau, leading to considerable frustration. If the athlete and trainer are certain that the training program has progressed properly, that illness is not a factor, and that the athlete has not attained his ultimate performance potential, the athlete should persevere and maintain confidence that a substantial improvement could occur at any time.

STRESS

Stress has been defined by Hans Selye, the famous stress researcher, as the body's nonspecific response to external stressors. When the body is exposed to extreme stressors for extended periods, the so-called stress syndrome is elicited, which may lead to a stage of exhaustion typified by fatigue, illness, and injury. Coaches, athletes, trainers, and team physicians must recognize that strenuous training represents a significant stressor which, if combined with other physical or psychological stressors, may lead the athlete into a stage of exhaustion. Such exhaustion, of course, is not consistent with optimal training or performance. Stress-induced exhaustion can be prevented by designing properly individualized training programs, by carefully observing the athlete for signs of fatigue (e.g., upper respiratory illness, blood shot eyes, loss of concentration), and by reducing the training load if the athlete encounters other unavoidable stressors (e.g., examinations, personal conflicts, change of environment). Sensitive coaches and trainers can prevent most stress-related illnesses in their athletes. Programs that subscribe to the "survival of the fittest"

philosophy, however, can expect to lose many athletes to preventable illness and injury.

Competitive Stress

Competition is physiologically and psychologically more stressful than training, and too frequent competitions pose great risk to the athlete. Athletes who compete too frequently are particularly prone to the stress-related difficulties mentioned above. Because sporting activities vary greatly in their physical demands, drawing a generalization on the optimal frequency of competition is not possible. One may conclude, however, that the more strenuous the activity, the less frequently one should engage in competition. Contrasting examples would be golfers who compete 4 days a week over a 30- to 40-week season and marathon runners who compete at the full marathon distance only two or three times a year.

GUIDELINES FOR TRAINING THE AEROBIC SYSTEM

As discussed above, energy used in endurance exercise is provided primarily through aerobic muscle metabolism, which depends on the transport of oxygen by the cardiorespiratory system. Improvements in endurance performance are attained primarily through increases in $\dot{V}O_2$max and anaerobic threshold. These increases are secondary to muscle metabolic and cardiorespiratory functional alternations, which can be generated through proper forms of exercise training. This section summarizes the procedures to be followed in designing training programs for improved performance of aerobic exercise.

Modes of Exercise

Numerous specific forms of exercise may be used to generate improvements in aerobic work capacity. All proper aerobic activities increase the body's rate of aerobic metabolism, increase the heart rate, and allow these increases to be sustained for extended periods. Primary aerobic activities include those that allow metabolic and cardiorespiratory functions to be increased to a particular predetermined level and maintained at that level throughout the activity. Secondary aerobic activities, which include many of the popular recreational games and sports, cause a more intermittent increase in cardiorespiratory functions and are less easily regulated in terms of work intensity.

Primary and Secondary Aerobic Activities

Primary	Secondary
Walking	Tennis
Jogging/running	Handball
Swimming	Racketball
Cycling	Squash
Cross-country skiing	Basketball
Ice skating	Dance

Primary aerobic activities generate a training effect in less time than do secondary activities and are preferred for persons with impaired heart function in whom exercise intensity must be rigorously controlled. Many persons, however, find secondary aerobic activities more enjoyable, and enjoyment, of course, can promote adherence to an exercise regimen. For a given athlete, the ideal aerobic activity is that most similar to the activity for which he is training (principle of specificity) and to which he is most likely to adhere.

Frequency

Improvements in aerobic work capacity may be generated in secondary beginners with as few as two training sessions a week. Sedentary beginners, however, improve at close to the optimal rate with three sessions a week (nonconsecutive days).[1] In some athletes, daily training sessions may be needed to maintain an already high capacity for endurance work. In activities such as distance running and swimming, many athletes train twice a day. The advantages of twice-a-day training sessions have not been clearly documented, but apparently a high frequency of training contributes to a high-exercise caloric expenditure. The continually improving world standards in endurance activities may be partly due to the increasing amount of energy expended in training by today's world class athletes. The optimal training frequency for a given athlete is a function of his current fitness level, the relative importance of aerobic function in the particular activity for which he is training, and individual tolerance for training stress.

Duration

The average person attains an acceptable level of cardiorespiratory fitness by participating in a primary aerobic activity for a duration of 20 to 30 minutes three times a week. Sedentary beginners may need to start with intermittent exercise (e.g., alternate walking and jogging), building gradually to 20 to 30 minutes of continuous activity. Endurance athletes, of course, may need much longer durations of exercise to attain full potential; marathon runners and swimmers, for example, often train for 2 to 3 hours. For most team sports, however, athletes who regularly participate in continuous aerobic activity for one-half hour will develop a cardiorespiratory fitness level consistent with championship caliber performance.

Intensity

Intensity of exercise may be quantified in several ways; perhaps most convenient is heart rate. Because heart rate and rate of aerobic energy expenditure $\dot{V}O_2$) are linearly related and, for each person, maximal heart rate and maximal $\dot{V}O_2$ are attained at the same exercise workload, the percentage of $\dot{V}O_2$max may be accurately estimated from the percentage of maximum heart rate (see Figure 3-1). The threshold for generation of an aerobic training effect is about 60% of the $\dot{V}O_2$max, which corresponds to about 70% of the maximum heart rate.

One technique for estimating the heart rate that corresponds to the training threshold exercise intensity is provided by the following equation:

$$THR = RHR + 0.6 (MHR - RHR),$$

where THR = training heart rate (beats/min), MHR = Maximum heart rate (beats/min), and RHR = resting heart rate (beats/min). Resting heart rate may be determined by counting the radial or carotid pulse while the individual is

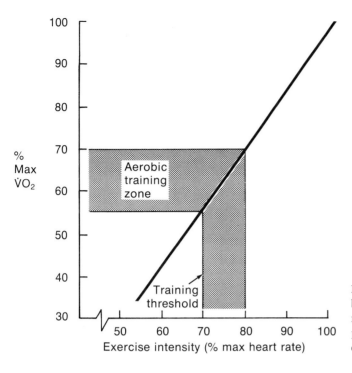

Figure 3-1 Relation between percentage of maximal heart rate and percentage of maximal oxygen content.

resting. Maximum heart rate can be estimated by the following equation:

$$\text{MHR (bpm)} = 220 - \text{age in years}$$

The aforementioned technique provides a lower limit for training intensity. For trained persons, a somewhat higher intensity may be appropriate for sustained, continuous training. Very high-intensity training, at heart rates approaching maximum levels, is appropriate for some endurance athletes and for athletes striving to maximize both aerobic power and anaerobic capacity.

SPECIFIC TRAINING TECHNIQUES

Primary aerobic activities may be used in several specific ways. Of these aerobic activities, running has spawned the greatest range of training techniques, and these methods are discussed below. Many of the techniques described are easily adapted for use by swimmers and cyclists.

Continuous Activity

Perhaps the most commonly used aerobic training technique is continuous activity. With such activ-

ity, the heart rate is increased to a predetermined level and maintained at that level for the duration of the training session. The guidelines presented in the previous section apply most directly to continuous training. The intensity of continuous activity may be varied from one training session to the next. The bulk of the training for endurance activities should consist of continuous activity of moderate intensity (70%–80% maximum heart rate) and relatively long duration, so-called long, slow distance training. The endurance athlete will benefit, however, from occasional bouts of higher intensity continuous training (85% to 90% of maximum heart rate) of moderate duration.

Interval Training

Interval training involves alternating periods of very intense work with periods of active recovery. Interval training is usually done in a controlled environment (e.g., a track) in which the duration of work and recovery periods may be accurately timed. Interval training offers the benefit of allowing the athlete to perform, in total, a considerable volume of very high-intensity exercise in a single training session. An endurance swimmer, for instance, might perform 20 repetitions of a 50-meter sprint with 30 seconds of recovery between each sprint; altogether the swimmer will have covered 1000 meters at very high intensity. All approaches to interval training require that the following variables be designated in advance: duration and intensity of the work interval, duration and intensity of the recovery period, and the number of repetitions. Intensity of exercise may be designated in terms of heart rate. During the work interval, heart rate should increase to 75% or more of the maximum heart rate; during recovery it should fall to about 60% of the maximum heart rate.

Repetition Training

Repetition training differs from interval training only in intensity of exercise during the work and recovery phases. The work phase of repetition training should be almost exhaustive and the recovery phase, almost complete. For instance, in a given repetition training session, an 800-meter runner might perform two 600-meter runs at race-pace with a full recovery intervening between the two.

Fartlek Running

Fartlek running involves a combination of techniques such that continuous, interval, and repetition training are used in a single session. Fartlek is a Swedish term meaning "speed play" and denotes that the various intensities of work are selected by the athlete on an unstructured basis. A typical fartlek running session might involve an hour of continuous running during which the athlete runs, in random order, several fast sprints, interval runs, and repetition runs. Fartlek training may be conducted in an attractive environment (e.g., park or golf course) and thus may be a relatively enjoyable means for the athlete to participate in high-intensity exercise.

Circuit Training, Parcours

Circuit training provides a combination of training techniques and is particularly well adapted for groups. The individual athlete rotates through a series of stations and at each performs a differ-

ent exercise. Circuit routines may include activities to improve muscular strength, muscular endurance, flexibility, and other fitness components. The training session can involve an alternation between continuous aerobic training and a series of strength and flexibility exercises.

A recently popularized modification of the circuit training concept is the parcours. A parcours is, essentially, a graded jogging trail along which exercise stations have been erected. The participant jogs from station to station, performing a different calisthenic exercise at each stop. Often attractive signs and suitable permanent equipment are provided at each exercise station.

In summary, the energy for sustained muscular work is provided through the process of aerobic metabolism. Performance of aerobic exercise depends on the cardiorespiratory system, which provides the active skeletal muscles with needed oxygen. The primary determinant of athletic performance in endurance activities is maximal oxygen uptake; however, efficiency and anaerobic threshold also affect the rate at which work is done for extended periods.

Training programs should be designed in accordance with established principles of training. In training the aerobic system, research indicates that if a primary aerobic activity is used, 20 to 30 minutes of continuous activity three times a week at about 70% of maximum heart rate will result in the desired training effect.

Basic principles of exercise training are similar for everyone. But because each subgroup of the population possesses certain unique characteristics and needs, training programs should be tailored so as to optimize the benefits for the specific participant group. The following sections provide guidelines for the design of exercise training programs for several specific populations, including special training problems encountered by competitive athletes.

FITNESS PROGRAMS FOR ADULT BEGINNERS

Since the early 1970s a rapidly increasing number of adult Americans have begun participating in regular, vigorous exercise. The reasons for this trend are complex, but clearly many adults have begun exercising to control body weight and to reduce the risk of coronary heart disease (CHD). Many Americans now accept regular exercise as an important aspect of a healthy lifestyle. Although a large number of adults begin exercising each year, many no not become habitual exercisers. Many drop out owing to failure to improve fitness; exercise-related injuries; or fatigue and muscle soreness after overtraining. Much of the attrition from personal fitness programs can be ascribed to improper training programs; the information that follows is intended to provide the knowledge needed to prescribe proper exercise programs for adult beginners.

Objectives and Potential Beneifts

Physical fitness is the ability to perform daily tasks with vigor and alertness, without undue fatigue, and with ample energy to enjoy leisure-time pursuits and to meet unforeseen emergencies. This suggests that a person is physically fit if he can readily cope with the physical demands presented by his preferred lifestyle and selected environment. Of course, in our modern technological society, the lifestyle of the typical adult presents few physical challenges. Thus it might seem that the average American would have no need to maintain a high level of physical fitness. Mounting evidence, however, suggests the opposite—that modern man needs, more than ever, to be concerned about his physical activity habits.

Research and clinical evidence strongly suggests that several of the more frequently observed chronic diseases are related to physical inactivity.[6] Sedentary living is itself a risk factor for developing CHD, and some studies have indicated that exercise may ameliorate other CHD risk factors, such as elevated blood lipid concentrations and hypertension. Obesity, a risk factor for CHD, hypertension, and diabetes, is clearly linked to low levels of habitual physical activity and, in most patients, is responsive to exercise therapy. Lower back pain, one of the most frequently reported health problems, is most typically due to inflexibility of the lower back–hamstring region and weakness of the abdominal musculature. An accepted conservative treatment for lower back pain is exercise.

Although regular exercise may aid in the prevention and treatment of certain disease processes, it also contributes profoundly to "positive health," or "wellness." Most sedentary persons who initiate proper exercise programs report "feeling better and more energetic" within a few weeks. Although this effect may be at least partially psychological, a convincing physiologic explanation can be presented. With training, as a person's physical working capacity ($\dot{V}O_2$max) increases, the percentage of his maximum working capacity required by any submaximal level of exertion decreases. Because fatigue is highly related to the percentage of $\dot{V}O_2$max required by physical activities, the fitter person will experience less fatigue in response to standard physical work situations. Greater enjoyment of activities that require strenuous exertion results, as does less fatigue during long duration, low-intensity activity (e.g., occupational endeavors).

The objectives of adult physical fitness programs should focus primarily on the health-related fitness components, including cardiorespiratory fitness, body composition, and neuromuscular function of the lower trunk region.[11, 14] Proper programs can, and should, be structured so as to develop and maintain an acceptable level of fitness in each of the health-related components. Although the designation of any specific fitness level as "acceptable" must be somewhat arbitrary, fitness levels that seem to be consistent with the avoidance of associated health problems and with maintenance of an acceptable physical working capacity may be identified.

Risks and Safety Procedures

For a small percentage of adults, the risks associated with regular exercise outweigh the potential benefits; consequently, those persons must be identified before initiation of a training program. Persons younger than 35 years of age with no history of cardiovascular disease and who show no elevation of CHD risk factors (e.g., smoking, hpertension, serum cholesterol > 250 mg/dl) may safely start exercise programs without medical clearance. Persons older than 35 and sedentary should be advised to consult with a physician before initiating an exercise program. Regardless of age, those with a history of cardiovascular disease or who show significant CHD risk factors should be examined by a physician and, if feasible, complete a graded exercise stress test before beginning exercise. Among properly screened persons, the risks associated with regular exercise are minimal. Serious cardiovascular complications during exercise are exceedingly rare. Indeed, for most of the population, regular exercise is no more dangerous than any other normal activity of daily life. Some physical activities, such as jogging, involve risk of musculosketetal injury. Mostly, these injuries can be prevented through use of proper equipment and training procedures; a small fraction of adults do, however, encounter considerable difficulties with running activities and should be encouraged to try non-weight-bearing activities such as swimming or cycling.

Principles of Adult Fitness Programs

The principles of training outlined previously apply to adult fitness programs. Research has shown that an acceptable level of cardiorespiratory fitness can be developed through participation in a primary aerobic activity three times a week for 20 to 30 minutes a session.[1] Intensity of exercise should be such as to elevate the heart rate to about 70% of maximum. Greater frequencies, durations, and intensities of activities may be safely used by already trained participants; such training will lead to further enhancement of cardiorespiratory fitness.

All the basic tenets of training apply to adult exercisers, but two principles are of particular significance. The principle of *progression* is important for sedentary adults who seek to attain higher levels of fitness. Such persons must be convinced to begin with a very light dose of exercise and then to increase the weekly quantity of exercise very gradually. Many orthopedic injuries experienced by beginning adult exercisers are caused by a training load that increases too rapidly. Also, exercise regimens that begin at too high an intensity contribute to the high rate of recidivism in adult beginners. High-intensity ex-

ercise may contribute to muscle soreness, overuse injuries, and long-term fatigue, all of which lead to lack of adherence to an exercise regimen.

Also of profound importance in adult fitness programs is *individuality*. Training programs for adults must be individualized according to the age, sex, current fitness level, health status, and interests of the participant. The principles of exercise prescribed above contribute to individualization by adjusting the intensity of activity to the current fitness level. Further, exercise programs should be designed so as to optimize the chances of adherence. Personal preference should carry great weight in selecting the mode of activity. The participant's health status may dictate the mode and intensity of exercise: Patients with heart disease should not exercise at intensities so high as to elicit symptoms (e.g., angina pectoris, ischemic electrocardiographic changes), and exercisers with orthopedic limitations may need to use non-weight-bearing or specially modified activities.

Stretching and Strengthening Programs

While focusing on cardiorespiratory fitness, adult fitness programs should include activities that contribute to development and maintenance of adequate muscular strength and flexibility. The primary emphases should be on enhancement of flexibility in the lower back–posterior thigh region and on muscular strength and muscular endurance of the abdominal musculature. In addition, some effort should be dedicated to maintenance of adequate upper body strength.

Generally, the time required to maintain acceptable levels of strength and flexibility is less than that for cardiorespiratory fitness. Usually the use of proper activities three times a week for 10 minutes a session proves adequate. Often calisthenic exercises are used before endurance exercise (e.g., jogging), thereby serving the dual purposes of contributing to warm-up while promoting strength and flexibility.

The preferred technique for improving flexibility is static stretching. First popularized by yoga enthusiasts, static stretching takes advantage of the inverse myostatic reflex that causes relaxation in a stretched muscle. With this technique, the participant stretches a particular muscle group until a moderate degree of tightness is detected (not intense pain). To be effective, the static stretch should be sustained for at least 30 seconds, or longer if tolerable. Static stretching, if used correctly, involves less risk of injury than does the more traditional ballistic stretching (*i.e.,* bouncing) and prevents postexercise muscle soreness.

Muscular strength and muscular endurance are best developed through the use of resistance exercises, which apply significant *overload* to the active muscle group(s). Although free-weights such as barbells or supported weights (*i.e.,* "exercise machines") may be used, calisthenic exercises are usually satisfactory for adult fitness programs. Worthy of particular attention are abdominal strength and endurance exercises because weakness in the abdominal region is associated with lower back pain. Upper body strength may be increased through use of the traditional push-up exercise or modifications thereof.

Weight Control Through Exercise

Regular exercise contributes importantly to the maintenance of an acceptable body weight. *Body composition,* the percentage of total body weight that is fat tissue, is significantly correlated with habitual physical activity levels in all age and sex categories. Moderate obesity can be effectively treated by increasing the daily caloric expenditure through exercise. For most persons, such an approach to weight loss is preferable to dieting because it leads to a loss that is almost entirely fat tissue, whereas dieting alone results in a substantial loss in lean tissue. Moderate exercise combined with mild caloric restriction is most effective because the resultant weight loss is relatively rapid and the regimen involves the adoption of habits that are quite tolerable.

Exercise programs adopted for the purpose of weight loss should adhere to all principles previously discussed. The primary focus, however, should be on expenditure of calories. Thus total amount of work done rather than intensity of activity should be emphasized. In obese adults, intensity of exercise should be reduced so that duration can be increased substantially. For example, an obese person might be instructed to walk for 40 minutes at an intensity that elicits 50% of maximum heart rate. The participants should also attempt to burn additional calories whenever possible—by climbing stairs, mowing a lawn, or walking to work, for instance.

Obesity predisposes the adult exerciser to orthopedic difficulties and may require adoption of non-weight-bearing activities. Because obesity is a risk factor for hypertension, diabetes, and CHD, overweight persons should be carefully screened before initiation of exercise programs.

Sample Programs

In recent years, numerous exercise and weight-control programs have been promoted through the print and broadcast media. Although some of these programs are consistent with the established principles of exercise physiology, many widely advertised programs are not only ineffective but also unsafe. Before adopting or recommending any "prepackaged" exercise routine, one should evaluate a program for its consistency with the principles discussed earlier in this chapter, such as overload, consistency, specificity, and progression. Programs that offer "overnight" results, recommend crash diets, or promise maximum benefits with minimum effort should be viewed skeptically. Other programs are of excellent quality and have benefited many thousands of adult exercisers. Brief descriptions of two recommended programs follow.

Cooper's Aerobic System

In 1968, Dr. Kenneth H. Cooper, then an Air Force cardiologist, published a book entitled *Aerobics,*[3] which is credited by many as being the event that initiated a massive increase in participation in fitness activity by adult Americans. Cooper's "Aerobics System" makes two major contributions: It indicates how much exercise is enough, and it provides an easily understandable method for quantifying an exercise dose. Cooper devised a so-called "aerobic point," which is a unit of energy expenditure derived from the volume of oxygen needed to participate in physical activities. Epidemiologic and experimental studies found that about 30 aerobic points a week are needed to maintain an adequate state of cardio-respiratory fitness. Table 3-1 lists the aerobic point-values of various activities. The activities awarded the most points are those that involve maintenance of high levels of aerobic metabolism.

Another major contribution of the aerobics system has been popularization of the principle of progression. Cooper's training programs begin at a level based on the participant's state of fitness and build gradually, over 10 to 30 weeks, to a maintenance dose of 30 aerobic points a week. The aerobic system also suggests that combinations of activities (e.g., handball and jogging) may be used to achieve fitness, and this approach has proved very popular among adult Americans.

Canadian 5BX Exercise Plan

One of the most popular and enduring of the prepackaged exercise regimens is that developed in the early 1960s by the Canadian Air Force. [12] The 5BX Plan consists of a combination of calisthenics and endurance exercises organized into a long-term progression. Calisthenic activities focus on abdominal, back, and upper arm strength and lower back flexibility. The prescribed endurance activities are walking, running, and running in place. The 5BX Plan has proved successful for many adults because it starts at an acceptably low level, provides a steady yet realistic rate of pro-

gression, focuses on the important health-related fitness components, and is effective in improving these components. The standard 5BX Plan has only one weakness: It calls for only 6 to 8 minutes of endurance exercise and provides no specific guidelines for setting the intensity of this exercise. By applying the guidelines presented earlier in this chapter, however, the 5BX Plan can be modified to meet accepted criteria for cardiorespiratory endurance training. An ideal approach would be to use the 5BX calisthenic routine in combination with the aerobic system for training of the cardiorespiratory system.

PROGRAMS FOR THE ELDERLY

"Aging" is a term often used to describe the biological, psychological, and sociological changes that occur in persons over time. In biology, aging has come to be associated with a gradual decline in the body's functional capacities and a reduction in the system's resistance to stress and disease. Age-related functional changes may, at least in part, be due to genetically coded phenomena, but some biological effects of aging may be due to disease processes as yet unidentified. In addition, much of the age-related decline in physiologic functioning results not from aging *per se* but from the sedentary lifestyle that has come to be associated with advanced age in our society. This section provides insight into the relation between aging and exercise habits as well as information on the design of fitness programs for older persons.

Physiology of Aging

Cross-sectional observations of physiologic variables reveal that many exercise-related functions decline gradually with increasing chronologic age, a decline that begins at about 30 years of age. These changes, however, while consistently observed in American society, may not be "normal." Habitual physical activity often begins a gradual decline in early adulthood, and thus age-related reductions in many physiologic variables may be "abnormal" and reflective of the hypokinesis that is endemic in the older adult population of the United States.

Table 3-1   AEROBIC POINTS

Activity	Points
Walking/Running	
1 mile in 13 min 30 sec	2
1 mile in 10 min 30 sec	3
1 mile in 9 min 00 sec	7
1 mile in 8 min 00 sec	9
Swimming	
100 yards in 2 min 30 sec	1
300 yards in 6 min 00 sec	2.5
600 yards in 12 min 30 sec	7
1000 yards in 20 min 30 sec	9
Handball	
10 min	1.5
20 min	3
30 min	4.5

Cardiovascular Fitness

Aging is associated with marked reductions in cardiovascular functional capacity. Maximum heart rate declines at the rate of about 1 beat a year (maximum heart rate = 220 − age), and although data are scarce, maximum stroke volume and maximum cardiac output also probably decrease substantially. Pathologic conditions such as hypertension, CHD, and peripheral vascular disease are very common in the elderly and may combine with decreased functional capacities to reduce exercise tolerance.

Pulmonary Function

Several pulmonary function variables decline with age. Under resting conditions, vital capacity is reduced, perhaps because of decreased thoracic wall compliance. During exercise, ventilation seems to be increased at standard submaximal work loads but decreased at maximum work levels. Pulmonary diffusing capacity is reduced under both resting and exercise conditions.

Muscle Function

The body's skeletal muscle tissues reflect the aging process through decreases in muscle mass, muscular strength, and muscular endurance. After age 30, although body weight tends to increase, lean body weight decreases by about 3% a decade. This, of course, indicates that percentage of body fat increases with age, as would be expected whenever habitual physical activity decreases without a concomitant decrease in caloric intake. We do not know, at present, how aging affects the enzymatic capabilities of human muscle tissue; however, the well-documented reduction in peak blood lactate after exhaustive exercise suggests that the glycolytic enzymatic pathway may be adversely affected by aging.

Physical Working Capacity

Physical working capacity, as evaluated by maximal oxygen uptake, tends to decline with advancing years. Cross-sectional data indicate that highest mean maximal oxygen uptakes are found in the teenage years (means ≈ 50 ml/kg/min), with values dropping about 50% by the eighth decade of life. As mentioned above, anaerobic capacity, assessed through postexercise peak blood lactate concentration, is markedly reduced in elderly persons. These changes combine to cause a substantial reduction in the capacity for whole body, moderate-to-high-intensity work in older persons.

Training

Training studies conducted by Dr. Herbert deVries of the University of Southern California have shown clearly that elderly exercisers adapt physiologically to physical training in much the same manner as do their younger counterparts.[5] Significant improvement in central and peripheral cardiovascular functions and plumonary functions have been observed. The percentage improvement in $\dot{V}O_2$max generated by aerobic training in older persons ranges from 15% to 20%, about the same as that for younger adults. However, previously sedentary older adults start from a lower baseline, and thus absolute improvement in, and ultimate level for, $\dot{V}O_2$max is reduced.

Available data, although not plentiful, suggest that adults who maintain an active lifestyle through their adult years have much slower rates of decline in exercise-related functional capacities than do sedentary persons. Values of $\dot{V}O_2$max in the range of 40 to 60 ml/kg/min are often observed in habitual joggers older than 50 years of age, values that compare very favorably with mean values for teenagers and young adults. Clearly high levels of physical working capacities can be maintained into later years of life.

Objectives of Exercise Programs

The objectives of exercise programs for the elderly must be established in accordance with the individual participant's age, fitness level, and health status. Each of these factors varies widely within the older population; thus one should never consider the elderly as being one homogeneous group. Although it is always important that adult fitness programs be individualized, individualization with the elderly is critical.

Nonetheless, the general goals of fitness programs for older persons are the same as those for younger adults. The focus should be on health-related fitness components: cardiorespiratory endurance, body composition, flexibility, and muscular strength and endurance. Reduced joint mobility, often secondary to arthritis, is a debilitating malady for many elderly persons, and exercise routines may be devised to aid in retention of adequate levels of static and dynamic flexibility in key joints. Accidents are a major cause of injury and death in the elderly population, and many of these tragedies can be linked to inadequate muscular strength. A strength deficiency impairs the ability to control the body weight (e.g., stair climbing) and to handle external objects (e.g., carrying a bag of groceries). Properly designed and graded resistance exercises can promote maintenance of acceptable levels of muscular strength.

Perhaps the most critical factor in the elderly person's ability to function independently in society is his ability to *move without assistance*.[8] Clearly, older people who maintain good levels of cardiorespiratory fitness and acceptable body composition are more likely to retain the ability to move independently longer than those who become obese or who allow their muscular and cardiorespiratory systems to degenerate. As mentioned previously, the cardiorespiratory system of the older person is trainable, and good levels of aerobic fitness may be attained. Likewise, regular exercise may lead to a loss of fat and maintenance of an acceptable percentalge of body fat.

Risks and Safety Procedures

Advancing age is a highly significant risk factor for CHD and other atherosclerotic diseases. Consequently, older persons must undergo proper medical evaluation, preferably including graded exercise testing, before initiating programs that involve strenuous activity. For those participants who have a history of cardiovascular disease or who manifest signs or symptoms of myocardial ischemia during exercise, intensity of activity should be rigorously controlled and scaled to a level well within personal exercise tolerance. Because many older persons have hypertension, isometric and other heavy resistance exercises should be avoided, since such activities cause elevated blood pressure, which increases the myocardial oxygen demand.

Older persons are more prone to orthopedic difficulties than are younger exercisers. The various overuse syndromes, joint ailments, and musculotendinous injuries may develop rapidly in an elderly person who has been sedentary for several decades. For the most part, however, these problems can be avoided or at least minimized by designing programs that involve a very gradual rate of progression and by selecting modes of activity that avoid stressing tissues particularly vulnerable to injury in specific participants.

Ideally, elderly persons who initiate exercise programs should do so under the supervision of a competent exercise leader trained in emergency procedures such as cardiopulmonary resuscitation, knowledgeable about the characteristics and needs of the elderly, and skillful in designing individualized exercise programs. Preferably, although not always feasible, equipment should be available to allow monitoring of such as the electrocardiograph physiologic variables during training sessions.

Sample Programs

In recent years, exercise programs for the elderly have become commonplace; consequently several standardized programs have been developed and implemented both commercially and through nonprofit agencies.[4] The best of these programs have several characteristics in common.

All activities begin at a low level of intensity and build gradually to suitable maintenance of fitness.

Activities are incorporated that deal with cardiorespiratory fitness, flexibility, and muscular strength, including flexibility, and strength exercises for all major muscle groups and joints (Figure 3-2). The total caloric expenditure involved in each exercise session is high enough to contribute to optimal improvement of the body composition.

Designated activities can easily be scaled to the fitness level and health status of each participant.

Figure 3-2 Senior citizens can exercise on a balance beam.

The program is easily adapted for use in a wide range of physical settings (*e.g.*, home, senior citizen centers, church halls).

The program is organized and presented in a manner that promotes enjoyment and long-term adherence. Often, background music and rhythmic activities are provided.

Brief descriptions of exercise programs designed specifically for older persons follow.

Iowa TOES Program

Developed at the University of Iowa under the direction of Dr. David K. Leslie, the TOES Program comprises a series of calisthenic activities, many of which are performed in the seated position. The exercises are arranged sequentially and are selected so as to enhance flexibility and muscular strength in all body segments.

DeVries Program

Dr. Herbert deVries of the University of Southern California has contributed greatly to our knowledge of exercise programming for older adults.[5] He has devised an exercise regimen that begins with a calisthenic routine such as the 5BX or TOES but that also focuses significantly on cardiorespiratory endurance. Using walking and jogging, the endurance phase of the program builds gradually to an acceptable maintenance level. Each exercise session concludes with a series of static stretching activities.

Gerokinesiatrics

Devised by Lawrence Frankel in Charleston, West Virginia, gerokinesiatrics, a "preventicare" program for senior citizens, comprises aerobic exercises, stretching, and general strengthening.[8] Medicine balls and short broomsticks are used for some exercises, and a subject may do these exercises even while confined to bed or while seated in a chair (Figure 3-3).

TRAINING THE FEMALE ATHLETE

An analysis of existing world record performances in various sporting activities indicates that women have not achieved the same peaks of athletic performance as have men. In track and

Figure 3-3
"Gerokinesiatrics" includes flexibility training with short broomsticks.

field in 1979, for instance, world record performances by women were roughly 10% to 15% lower than those by men (see Table 3-2). At issue, of course, is whether the observed sex differences in athletic performance are due to genetically determined biological factors or to environmental factors such as training and societal attitudes. Available data suggest that some combination of genetic and environmental factors account for these differences. Certainly society has not been totally supportive of the female athlete, and training programs for women have, in many instances, been less vigorous than those for men. In addition, a smaller percentage of women than of men have chosen to participate in athletics, and thus the process of selection has been less demanding among the women. Nonetheless, available physiologic data indicate that certain genetically determined traits do limit exercise performance in women as a group.

Characteristics

As compared with her male counterpart, the female athlete tends to be smaller, lower in metabolic capabilities, and higher in percentage of body fat. The physical performances of highly trained women, however, far exceed those of the average man (see Table 3-3).

The smaller stature of the female athlete has several ramifications. Obviously, performance is adversely affected in those activities in which

Table 3-2 COMPARISON OF WORLD TRACK RECORDS FOR MEN AND WOMEN, 1979

Distance (m)	Men (sec)	Women (sec)	Difference (%)
100	9.95	10.88	9.3
200	19.83	22.06	11.2
400	43.86	48.94	11.6
800	1 min 43.4	1 min 54.9	11.1
1500	3 min 32.2	3 min 56.0	11.2
3000	7 min 32.1	8 min 27.1	12.2
5000	13 min 08.4	15 min 08.8	15.3
10000	27 min 22.5	31 min 45.4	16.0
Marathon	2 h 08 min 34	2 h 32 min 30	19.0

Table 3-3 CARDIORESPIRATORY FITNESS AND BODY COMPOSITION IN FEMALE DISTANCE RUNNERS VERSUS UNTRAINED ADULTS

	Female Distance Runners	Untrained Adult Men	Untrained Adult Women
Maximal oxygen consumption ml/kg/min	60–65	36–40	30–35
Fat, %	10–14	12–16	26–30

height and body mass determine performance. In addition, the smaller body mass of the woman is composed of less lean tissue than that of the man; lower lean body mass dictates lower muscular strength because the strength of a muscle, independent of sex, is highly correlated with its gross size (cross-sectional area). A woman's lower strength-to-body-weight ratio is disadvantageous in activities that involve lifting or rapid propulsion of the body mass. The sex differences in vertical jumping and sprinting ability may be primarily due to this strength and body weight factor.

A high(er) percentage of body fat is a detriment to performance in nearly all athletic activities that involve movement of the body mass. This is particularly evident in endurance activities, such as distance running, because "excess" fat tissue adds to the mass that must be moved but does not contribute to the energy for the performance of work. The suggestion that women may actually be at an advantage in long duration activities since, in such activities, free fatty acids are an important raw material for aerobic metabolism belies an inadequate understanding of exercise biochemistry, overlooking the knowledge that use of free fatty acid is dependent not on the magnitude of the body fat store but rather on the activity of the enzymes of fat metabolism. Thus a woman's higher percentage of body fat tends to affect performance adversely in most athletic activities and accounts for many of the observed differences between men and women in sports.

Women tend to have decrements in cardiovascular function when compared with men of similar competitive standing. Heart size, stroke volume, and maximum cardiac output are smaller in

women than in men even when differences in body size are controlled. In addition, hemoglobin concentration is substantially lower in women than in men, and this represents a limiting factor in a woman's oxygen transport capacity. Indeed, the differences between men and women in endurance performance may largely be accounted for by differences in hemoglobin concentration and body composition. Little is known about the biochemical characteristics of skeletal muscle in female athletes. However, available data suggest that the functional capacities of skeletal muscle are similar in the two sexes as long as muscle mass is not a factor. Muscular strength, expressed per square centimeter of muscle cross-sectional area, is similar in men and women. Maximal oxygen consumption, expressed as milliliters of oxygen consumed per kilogram of lean body weight, is only slightly lower in women than in men, a small difference probably due to cardiovascular, not muscle metabolic, limitations (see Table 3-4). Thus, by inference, skeletal muscle enzyme systems probably are developed about equally in female and male athletes. Likewise, no sex differences are observed in neuromuscular coordination and motor learning ability as long as muscular strength is not a significant factor in the physical skill being performed.

Trainability

At one time women were thought to be less trainable than men, that is, less improvement should be expected in women than in men in response to a training program. Available data now indicate that this premise is false.[15] Training studies have shown that, if exposed to exercise of similar fre-

Table 3-4 MAXIMAL OXYGEN CONSUMPTION*

Age (yr)	Maximal Oxygen Uptake (ml/kg/min)				
	Low	Fair	Average	Good	High
Women					
20–29	<24	24–30	31–37	38–48	49+
30–39	<20	20–27	28–33	34–44	45+
40–49	<17	17–23	24–30	31–41	42+
50–59	<15	15–20	21–27	28–37	38+
60–69	<13	13–17	18–23	24–34	35+
Men					
20–29	<25	25–33	34–42	43–52	53+
30–39	<23	23–30	31–38	39–48	49+
40–49	<20	20–26	27–35	36–44	45+
50–59	<18	18–24	25–33	34–42	43+
60–69	<16	16–22	23–30	31–40	41+

*Standards of the American Heart Association.

quency, intensity, and duration, women exhibit percentages of improvement similar to those observed in men. These observations have been made for strength and cardiorespiratory endurance.

Until recently, heavy resistance training for strength improvement had been rare in female athletes. Misconceptions on trainability and fear of developing masculine characteristics kept many women away from strength training. Fortunately, these reservations are gradually being laid to rest by controlled research studies that have shown women do increase muscular strength through resistance training and do so without developing the heavy musculature of men. Apparently most of a woman's strength gain occurs through neuromuscular adaptations rather than through hypertrophy of skeletal muscle fibers. Lack of hypertrophy in women may be accounted for by lower levels of testosterone, which may be an obligatory intermediate in the anabolic process of hypertrophy.

Cardiorespiratory functions in women seem to be as responsive to aerobic training as do those in men. Although the absolute pretraining and post-training levels of women are lower than those of men, the percentage of improvement tends to be similar. Of course, proper training in women results in attainment of cardiorespiratory capacities that substantially exceed those of sedentary men.

Exercise and Menstruation

The relation between exercise habits and menstruation may be studied from two perspectives: first, if exercise performance is affected in any way by the menstrual cycle. Available data indicate that it is not. Studies in which measures of performance-related physiologic variables have been repeated in the various stages of the menstrual cycle have failed to observe any consistent relationships. This conclusion is based, of course, on group findings. A particular athlete may be affected positively or negatively by the physiologic changes that accompany the stages of a menstrual cycle.

Second, interest has been expressed in the possible effects of training on menstruation. In recent years several published studies have suggested that the incidence of menstrual irregularities, such as amenorrhea and oligomenorrhea, is higher in athletes than in nonathletes. Some investigators have concluded that athletes involved in very heavy training or endurance activities are particularly prone to secondary amenorrhea. At present, the causes of so-called athletic amenorrhea have not been identified. One theory suggests that the reduction in body fat that often accompanies endurance training triggers endocrinologic disturbances that result in absence of menses. Another possibility is that heavy training may be just one of many physical and psychological stressors that can disrupt endocrine functions. Although our current knowledge of athletic amenorrhea is incomplete, amenorrhea appears to be reversible with reduced training.

Exercise and Pregnancy

Beliefs about exercise during pregnancy have changed markedly in recent years among both physicians and the public. At one time, pregnant athletes and fitness exercisers were advised to quit training for the duration of the pregnancy. Current thought, however, is that women should continue to be active during pregnancy unless specific medical complications are apparent. A prudent procedure is to reduce gradually the intensity of exercise as the size of the fetus increases, since the mass of the fetus contributes to the metabolic demands of any weight-bearing activity. Women also should avoid activities that are violent in nature and that may lead to fetal damage.

Maintenance of good fitness during pregnancy probably aids in preparing the prospective mother for the physical demands of delivery. In addition, women should avoid excessive weight gain during pregnancy, and continued activity contributes control of weight.

Pregnancy, of course, need not mean the end of an athlete's competitive career. Although no extensive studies have been done in this area, a considerable volume of anecdotal information indicates that women can obtain the highest performance levels during the early stages of, and after, pregnancy.

Nutritional Considerations

The athlete's diet may affect his exercise performance. In general, the athlete's diet should be well balanced so as to prevent nutrient deficiencies, provide a caloric intake that balances caloric expenditure, and include sufficient amounts of water and electrolytes to offset the loss of these substances through sweating.

Because the caloric intake of the typical athlete is relatively high, nutrient deficiencies are quite rare in athletic populations. One apparent exception to this is iron deficiency, which, several studies have reported, is observed in 10% to 15% of female athletes. *Iron deficiency*, or depletion of the body's iron stores, is best diagnosed by examination of bone marrow samples. Although iron deficiency is observed in about one tenth of female athletes, it is not clear whether this incidence of iron deficiency is higher than in nonathletic groups, as similar rates of iron deficiency have been found in randomly drawn samples of menstruating women. While iron deficiency *per se* involves no known impairment of exercise performance, it may increase the risk of developing iron deficiency anemia, a condition that does reduce endurance performance. Although the incidence of anemia in female athletes is very low, the high incidence of iron deficiency in female athletes has prompted several authors to recommend prophylactic administration of iron supplements. Existing iron supplementation studies, however, have failed to demonstrate that such a practice increases iron storage. Thus, the most prudent course for an athlete may be ingestion of a normal balanced diet that includes adequate sources of dietary iron.

TRAINING IN CHILDREN

Sports programs for children have assumed a high profile in American society since World War II. Organized programs for boys in baseball, football, and basketball have been available for many years. But recently, we have seen large increases in participation in swimming, soccer, gymnastics, and track and field, among others. These expanded opportunities for sports participation are found in both community and school settings. Whereas the typical school system in the 1940s offered interscholastic athletic programs only in a few sports and only for secondary level boys, today many schools offer a wide range of sports activities for both boys and girls beginning at the elementary or middle school level. Clearly, sports programs for children have grown dramatically, and no plateau is yet in sight.

As the number of youthful participants in sports has increased, so has the intensity of their participation. Many of the training and competitive programs to which children are not exposed are far more intense than those designed for mature adults only a few years ago. It is not uncommon, for instance, for a young gymnast to train for 3 hours a day year-round, for a child track star to run 50 to 70 miles a week, or for a youthful football player to undergo a preseason weight-training program. The intensity of athletic training programs and the competitive level in youth sports have risen in parallel, but the side-effects and long-term outcomes of high-intensity training and competition in children may not always be positive. Discussed in this section are goals for youth exercise and sports programs, physiologic trainability of children, proper training techniques for youngsters, and trends in the fields of physical education and physical fitness programming for children.

Purposes of Training Programs

Sports and exercise programs for children come in many different forms. Although the specific purposes of these programs vary according to specific circumstances, certain general goals should provide the philosophical undergirding for all exercise and sports programs for children. These goals should be considered by all persons who serve in leadership roles in youth exercise and sports programs. Such programs should do the following:

· Provide a positive experience in exercise for all children. Exercise and sports activity should be conducted in a supportive, enjoyable environment that engenders positive feelings toward exercise, sports, and physical fitness.
· Provide exposure to sports activities and training procedures. The child's sports experiences should serve to provide him with knowledge of, and basic skill in, a range of sporting activities and exercise training procedures. Acquiring such knowledge and skills is a valuable aspect of acculturation in modern American society.

· Aid in the development of acceptable levels of health-related physical fitness. Youngsters should participate in activities that promote maintenance or development of good cardio-respiratory fitness, body composition, muscular strength, and flexibility.
· Promote acquisition of basic movement skills. Later success and enjoyable participation in sports activities depend on early development of fundamental movement partterns, such as throwing, catching, striking, running, and jumping. Youth exercise and sports programs should attend to these basic skills.
· Expose children to a wide range of lifetime fitness and recreational activities. Studies show that few of the popular competitive sports for youngsters are engaged in by adults. Thus the child's experiences should include exposure to those activities that have potential lifelong usefulness and benefit.
· Provide special remedial fitness and instructional programs for youngsters who manifest fitness or movement deficiencies. Intervention programs in the areas of physical fitness and movement skills are most likely to be successful if they start early in life. Youngsters with low fitness or who fail to develop normal motor functions should be provided with appropriate special corrective programming.
· Promote enhanced athletic performance. Many youth sports programs, although focusing exclusively on this goal, fail to achieve it because of improper teaching techniques. Properly designed training and instructional programs should result in improved performance in children, and such improvements may have important, positive side-effects.

No single exercise or sports program is likely to attain all these objectives. The child's total exercise and sports experience should, however, lead to accomplishment of the stated goals. Thus the youngster's movement experiences at home and in school sports, physical education, and community-based activities, *in toto*, provide a well-rounded and positive lead-up to an adult life characterized by vigor and enjoyable participation in physical activities.

Limits to Performance

A child's body is subject to the same primary laws of physics and chemistry that determine the movement capabilities of an adult. Basically, then, the mechanical and physiologic principles of human movement apply equally across the entire age range. Although the basic principles may be the same, a child's maximal performance capacities differ markedly from those of his older brothers and sisters, and these differences are important in the design of sports and exercise programs for children.

A child becomes an adult through the process of growth and development. Growth, the gradual increase in body size that occurs during the first 15 to 20 years of life, results in marked increases in physical performance abilities. Many anatomic characteristics (e.g., limb lengths, muscle mass, heart volume) can be accurately predicted from height. Likewise, numerous functional variables, such as strength, maximal cardiac output, and $\dot{V}O_2$max (liters/min), are determined largely by gross body size. In many respects, then, the performance capacity of a child is a function of his body size.

In addition, developmental processes independent of variations in body size profoundly affect the functional capacities of a child. For example, increases in certain muscle enzyme activities, hemoglobin concentration, and work efficiency accompany the aging process and serve to expand the physical working capacity at a rate exceeding that predicted from changes in size alone. In addition, muscle strength is known to be lower in younger children even when variations in body size are controlled. Thus a child's states of growth and development are powerful determinants of his physical performance capabilities, and these factors should weigh heavily in the design of exercise programs for children.

Trainability

A fundamental American belief is that hard work pays off. Thus we tend to accept as axiomatic the concept that physical training results in improved performance. For children, however, this may not always be true. As mentioned above, the primary determining factors of a child's functional capacity are his size and developmental state. Although a child's physical activity habits affect his performance capacities, these effects may be manifested only at the extremes of his physical activity range—that is, youngsters who are very sedentary tend to show physical fitness deficiencies, and youngsters who are extremely active manifest higher movement capacities. It is not clear whether moderate doses of exercise generate significant physiologic adaptations in the typical youngster. Some studies of the effects of endurance training in children have reported significant gains in $\dot{V}O_2$max and related variables; these changes, however, have been observed only with very intense and long-term training programs. Other studies have reported that children manifest little or no change in $\dot{V}O_2$max when exposed to training programs that would be expected to yield improved performance in adults. This apparent lack of responsiveness to training may indicate that the habitual physical activity level of the average child is already quite high, since mean $\dot{V}O_2$max values in children approximate 50 ml/kg/min, a value considered quite good in adults.

A well-established principle of exercise physiology is that trainability is a function of initial fitness level. A moderate dose of physical exercise may not provide a significant stimulus to the child's developmental processes, which may already be proceeding at maximal rates.

Responses to other forms of physical training largely have been unexplored in children. Some studies have shown that beneficial body composition changes occur with proper exercise programs. Little is known, however, about the trainability of children in the areas of muscular strength and flexibility.

Training Techniques

Given the dearth of training studies conducted with young subjects, extensive, specific guidelines for training procedures in children cannot be provided. In general, experience indicates that the same basic principles and techniques of training apply to both children and adults. This section emphasizes possible modifications of basic training principles that may be needed when working with youngsters.

Epiphyseal Injuries

The growth plates of the long bones are, of course, active in children. Until the plates ossify, they remain in a cartilaginous state that leaves them vulnerable to traumatic injury and prone to overuse. The vulnerability of the growth plates requires that training programs for children avoid activities that could traumatize these structures. Youngsters should avoid the following forms of physical activity:

· Falling, leaping, or landing in the straight leg position.
· Repeated throwing movements that apply excessive stress to the shoulder and elbow joints (*e.g.*, excessive throwing in baseball or throwing implements whose weight is disproportionate to the youngster's strength).
· Extremely long-duration exercise that involves weight bearing (*e.g.*, marathon running).
· Weight training with very heavy resistances.

Sexual Maturation

Some scientific evidence suggests that heavy training may delay the onset of puberty in girls. Whether this effect, if real, is harmful in the long term is unclear, but coaches, trainers, and physicians should be aware that delayed menarche and late development of secondary sex characteristics may result from heavy training in young girls.

Psychological Burnout

Heavy training and high-pressure competition in youngsters may lead to a loss of interest in sports and exercise. Training programs for children should emphasize enjoyment, wide variation of training techniques, short competitive seasons, moderate numbers of competitions, and frequent breaks from training and competition. For most youths, early specialization in a single sport and year-round training are contraindicated

by the high risks of psychological and perhaps physiologic burnout.

External Rewards

Most children are naturally drawn to sports, games, and exercise; thus, intrinsic motivation is usually more than sufficient to sustain a child's interest in competitive and recreational sports activities. Unfortunately, many current sports programs for children seem to assume the opposite—that numerous and elaborate external rewards (*e.g.*, trophies, uniforms) are needed. Evidence suggests that such external rewards not only are unnecessary but actually have the effect of decreasing the intrinsic motivation that initially existed. The ultimate consequence for many youngsters is failure to participate in exercise when external rewards are missing or removed, as they ultimately will be for most persons. External rewards should be used sparingly, and the highest priority should be placed on rewarding participation rather than competitive success.

Physical Fitness

Nearly everyone agrees that promotion of physical fitness in children is a worthy goal. Few have agreed, however, on how this goal can best be achieved. Indeed, there is considerable disagreement in professional circles about the basic definition of "youth fitness."

Perhaps the most traditional approach to fitness programming for children has been to emphasize *motor fitness*, a broad concept encompassing a wide range of physical fitness components (*i.e.*, movement abilities). Usually included under motor fitness are muscular strength, muscular endurance, cardiorespiratory endurance, speed, flexibility, power, agility, coordination, and balance. The concept of motor fitness is embodied in the American Alliance for Health, Physical Education, Recreation and Dance (AAHPERD) Youth Fitness Test, which, since the 1950s, has been the dominant test of physical fitness in American schools and which is currently the basis for the Presidential Fitness awards offered through the President's Council on Physical Fitness in Sports. The AAHPERD

Youth Fitness Test includes the following test items:

50-yard dash
Agility run
One-minute timed sit-up test
Pull-ups or flexed-arm hang
Standing long jump
600-yard walk/run or optional distance run

An exclusive focus on motor fitness can precipitate certain problems. One problem is that many of the motor fitness components are heavily dependent on genetically determined factors. Thus it seems inappropriate to encourage youngsters to improve in areas in which training has little impact (e.g., speed, anaerobic power). Moreover, motor fitness, although important for the athlete, includes several components that have little import for the typical person. Consequently, emphasizing motor fitness may result in a muddled, inappropriate definition of physical fitness. In response to these perceived problems, the concept of health-related physical fitness came into wide acceptance in the late 1970s (Table 3-5).

Health-related physical fitness is, by definition, narrower than motor fitness and includes only those fitness components significantly related to some aspect of physical health. Typically included in the health fitness category are cardiorespiratory endurance, body composition, strength and endurance of the abdominal musculature, and flexibility of the lower back and hamstring region. Each of these components of

fitness has been found to play a significant role in disease prevention or health promotion.

Health-related physical fitness, long recognized as important for adults, is now receiving great attention with children, a trend manifested by the development and implementation of the AAHPERD Health-Related Physical Fitness Test (see Chap. 4). This new test includes the following items:

Mile or 9-minute distance run
Triceps and subscapular skinfolds
One-minute timed sit-up test
Sit-and-reach test of flexibility

In the future, motor fitness and health-related fitness should receive balanced emphasis in fitness and exercise programs for children. Motor fitness should be presented, evaluated, and interpreted for what it is: a determinant of overall physical ability particularly important in the athletic context. Health-related physical fitness should be presented as an important determinant of physical health, a matter that should concern everyone in our society.

Training for Distance Running

Over the past 15 years distance running has become one of the most popular forms of recreational sport. It has been estimated that about 15% of the American population runs or jogs regularly, and many of these persons participate, at least occasionally, in organized competitions. Rela-

Table 3-5 HEALTH-RELATED PHYSICAL FITNESS COMPONENTS

Fitness Component	Health Factor
Cardiorespiratory endurance	Coronary heart disease risk Physical working capacity
Body composition	Diabetes Hypertension Coronary heart disease
Lower back/hamstring flexibility	Lower back pain
Strength of abdominal muscles	Lower back pain

tively little is known about the risks of participation in competitive running (*i.e.*, injury, illness rates). It does seem clear, however, that appropriate training can optimize the chances for successful, enjoyable participation in distance running competitions and can minimize the attendant risks. In this section, specific training guidelines for various classes of distance runners are provided.

The Beginning Runner

Experience indicates that the transition from a "sedentary" to a "physically active" state involves increased risk for othopedic injury. Because running is a weight-bearing activity that places considerable stress on the tissues of the lower extremity, the beginning runner should be particularly cautious. Some individuals may experience considerable difficulty in starting a running program because of anatomic or biomechanical deficiencies. However, most persons can use running as a primary form of aerobic exercise and can develop a level of fitness that is consistent with enjoyable participation in recreational distance running competitions. The key is *gradual progression*.

The beginning runner should rigorously apply the principles of training described previously in this chapter. It is particularly important that the total weekly dose of running be increased very gradually over the first few months of training. For many persons, 20- to 30-minute walk–jog sessions on alternate days provide an effective initial exposure to regular running. Gradually, the participant should build to 30- to 40-minute sessions of continuous running performed 5 to 6 days per week. During this "start-up period" it is recommended that intensity of exercise be maintained at the low end of the training zone (*i.e.*, 60%–70% of maximal aerobic power).

Proper footgear is critical to successful participation in distance running. Beginning runners should be encouraged to acquire shoes that are designed specifically for running and that are comfortable. Proper running shoes reduce risk of orthopedic injury by absorbing foot-strike forces, limiting pronation and stabilizing the heel.

Beginning runners should participate in competitions sparingly and cautioiusly. As a rule of thumb, a beginner should not enter a competition until he can run the race distance comfortably in training. Initial exposures to racing should be approached noncompetitively with the primary purpose being to finish the race comfortably. The beginner should run the first half of a race at a pace that is slightly slower than the average pace that he projects for the entire race. For example, the runner who projects a comfortable 5-km finish time of 28 minutes should cover the first 2.5 km in about 14 minutes and 30 seconds.

The Fitness Runner

Many regular runners use running primarily as a mode of aerobic activity for the purpose of maintaining adequate cardiorespiratory fitness. Running is a particularly popular fitness activity because it involves minimal skill, is easily accessible, and, for most participants, carries minimal risk.

The regular runner whose primary goal is maintenance of adequate fitness should simply apply the principles presented earlier in this chapter. The health and fitness benefits of aerobic exercise usually accrue to persons who run at least three to four times per week, for about 30 minutes per session at an intensity corresponding to 60% to 75% of maximal heart rate.

Many fitness runners participate occasionally in competitive road races. Such competitions can provide valuable motivation and enjoyable recreation. However, unless approached with caution and restraint, races can carry risks for the fitness runner. The greatest risks are associated with [1] rapid increases in training dose in anticipation of an upcoming race and [2] excessively intense and competitive running in the race itself. These risks can be minimized by ensuring that any changes in training are implemented very gradually and by maintaining a "recreational" attitude toward races. Fitness runners must remember that their training has not been designed to prepare them for the physiologic demands of intense, competitive racing.

The Racer

Competitive road races of distances up to 10 km have become quite popular among runners of all types. Many runners consider performance at the 10-km distance to be a gold standard and, accordingly, train consistently to optimize performance at that distance.

Optimal preparation for racing involves regular participation in several activities that need not be included in the training program of fitness runners. First, the racer should include training sessions that involve running at a pace that is faster than the anticipated race pace. Activities such as interval training, repetition runs, and fartlek running should be done at the rate of once or twice per week. Second, the racer needs "overdistance" runs—steady, moderate-paced runs that cover distances that are 150% to 200% or more of the race distance (e.g., 15–20 km for the 10-km racer).

Also, it is important that the racer organize the various types of training sessions in an optimal pattern. Experience indicates that a so-called easy–hard pattern is successful for many runners. With this approach, very demanding training days (e.g., intervals, overdistance) are alternated with recovery days of no more than easy-paced running. This technique seems to provide the physiologic stimuli needed to induce desirable training adaptations while minimizing the risks of staleness and overtraining.

The Marathoner

For many regular runners, an ultimate goal is successful completion of a marathon race. The marathon, once an obscure sporting event, has become one of the most visible mass participation activities in the United States. Since the standard marathon distance is 26.2 miles (42 km), it is clear that marathon running imposes unique and extraordinary physiologic demands.

Beginning runners should not attempt marathon races. Experience indicates that the vast majority of runners, with proper training, have the potential to complete a marathon run successfully. But proper preparation for a marathon requires at least several months of consistent, appropriate training. It is recommended that a runner not consider participation in a marathon until he is well adapted to participation in shorter races (e.g., 10 km) and has undergone a progressive, marathon-oriented training program.

Marathon training programs should incorporate several key elements. First, the athlete should build gradually to a weekly running mileage of at least 40 to 50 miles. Second, the weekly regimen should include one moderately paced, very long run. The length of this run should be gradually increased over a period of months to distances in excess of 20 miles. Third, the athlete should gain experience in long distance races at distances up to 15 + miles. This is critical to the development of proper pace judgment.

The following tips can aid the well-trained, novice marathon runner in performing well in his initial competition:

1. Wear shoes that are well broken-in.
2. Run the first half of the race at a conservative pace.
3. Drink fluids consistently throughout the race.
4. Eat a palatable, high-carbohydrate diet and perform minimal running for 2 to 3 days before the race.

Training for the Triathlon

In recent years the triathlon has become a very popular endurance athletic event. Triathlons involve sequential bouts of endurance swimming, bicycling, and running. Although these events are conducted over varying combinations of distances, a typical triathlon involves a 1.5-km swim, a 40-km bicycle race, and a 10-km run. The "iron man" triathlon conducted annually in Hawaii covers longer distances (2.4-mile swim, 112-mile bicycle, 26.2-mile run).

The triathlon demands unique physiologic capacities and therefore requires a unique approach to training. All three triathlon activities rely on cardiorespiratory endurance. However, each of the three events imposes physiologic demands that are specific. Swimming is accomplished primarily with arm work, whereas cycling and running are modes of exercise that stress leg work. But even cycling and running differ in the manner in which the leg musculature is used and consequently impose somewhat different physiologic demands.

Optimal triathlon performance requires balance across the three activities. Therefore, successful triathletes dedicate substantial amounts of training time to each of the three subevents. Although training patterns should be individualized in accordance with the athlete's strengths and weaknesses, many triathletes apportion their training time in a ratio approximating 1-hour swimming to 1-hour running to 2-hours cycling. Many triathletes train for two of the subevents each day.

The following weekly schedule is typical of training programs used by many successful triathletes:

Monday:	swimming long intervals (1 h)
	bicycling—steady (½ h)
	running—fartlek (¾ h)
Tuesday:	bicycling—hill repetitions (1½ h)
	running—steady (1 h)
Wednesday:	swimming—intervals (¾ h)
	running—steady (½ h)
Thursday:	bicycling—time trial (1½ h)
Friday:	swimming—long intervals (¾ h)
	running—steady (½ h)
Saturday:	running—road race or intervals (1 h)
Sunday:	swimming—lake swim (½ h)
	bicycling—steady (2 + h)

SPECIAL PROBLEMS OF COMPETITIVE ATHLETES

Sports medicine is rapidly being recognized as a distinct medical specialty. One reason why sports medicine has emerged as a discipline is that athletes often pose medical questions totally unique to the sports environment. This section hopes to address at least a few problems of competitive athletes.

Long-Term Planning of Training Programs

At one time, training for athletic competition was primarily a seasonal activity. Football players, for instance, trained from August to November, basketball players from October to February, and track athletes from March to June. Now, attainment of championship performances requires that athletes, even at the high school level, train year-round. Further, if an athlete is to continue to improve over several years, his training and competitive program must progress in an orderly fashion from one year to the next. These factors suggest that the coach, trainer, and athlete must participate in long-term planning; no longer is it sufficient simply to plan from day to day or game to game.

Long-term planning should involve setting realistic short-, medium-, and long-term goals. Coaches should establish general competitive and training plans for each athlete on at least a yearly and seasonal basis and, in selected situations, for several years in advance. Long-term plans should include goals for training loads, training techniques, physical fitness measures, skill performance, and competitive achievements. Shorter term goals (*i.e.*, seasonal) should be established in each of these areas and should be quite specific. Monthly and weekly plans must be highly specific and individualized.

Staleness

One major reason for developing long-term training plans is to avoid staleness or overtraining. Staleness might be defined as an unexplained dropoff in performance, usually associated with overexposure to highly stressful training and competitive activities. Training plans should incorporate adequate periods of rest and other activities, mainly for psychological reasons but also for physiologic ones. Each athlete possesses a certain tolerance for sustained heavy training and competition. If this tolerance is exceeded, the athlete may lapse into physical exhaustion and psychological depression, circumstances that can be avoided by providing adequate rest periods on a weekly, seasonal, and yearly basis, by designing training programs that involve a variety of activities and environments, and by avoiding an excessive number of competitions.

If an athlete does show signs of staleness (e.g., reduced performance, illness, lack of attention, irritability), the best prescription is either reduced training or total rest. In severe cases of staleness, athletes may need a complete rest and change of environment. Under no circumstances should athletes who are stale increase their training dose. Further competition is not recommended until signs of staleness reverse.

Peaking

A major aim of the competitive athlete is attainment of optimal performances in championship competitions. This so-called "peaking" may be brought about by long-term planning and adherence to the training principle of periodization. Numerous factors combine to bring an athlete to peak performance levels, including training techniques, competitive schedule, psychological outlook, and diet. As the athlete approaches championship competitions, his training should increase in intensity but decrease in total load. Thus, as the swimmer's season progresses, his training might emphasize shorter, faster interval swims rather than total yardage.

Competitions tend to bring an athlete to peak performance; however, too many competitions may cause staleness. The optimal number and rate of competitions are quite specific to the sport and to the individual athlete. The athlete should enter championship competitions with an eager, optimistic outlook and be well rested. Before major competition in endurance activities, 2 to 3 days of significantly reduced training are recommended. During these final days before a championship, the athlete's diet should emphasize carbohydrates so as to fill the body's store of muscle glycogen. Perhaps the most important keys to successful peaking are attempting to peak only once a season and sustaining a peak for no more than a few weeks. Too many coaches and athletes meet with failure in championships because of attempts to peak too often or to sustain a peak too long.

Stitch

"Stitch" refers to pain in the upper abdominal region often reported by endurance athletes, particularly runners and joggers. No definite cause for this problem has been identified, but stiches may be due to muscle spasms in the diaphragm. Often suggested causes are engorgement of blood in the liver and trapped air in the lower sections of the lungs. Beginning exercisers are particularly prone to stitching, and in such persons progressive improvement in overall fitness and in muscular endurance of the abdominal region usually solves the problem. As might be expected, well-trained athletes tend to experience fewer stiches than beginners. Exercising on a full stomach often causes stitching, but this can be prevented by modifying the meal or the training schedule. Stitches often respond to vigorous massage of the affected region and almost always subside with cessation of exercise.

"Second Wind"

Many athletes and fitness exercisers report reduced fatigue and less ventilatory stress after the first few minutes of continuous exercise. This phenomenon, called "second wind," has not been well explained physiologically. Second wind may, in fact, be a warm-up effect resulting from the plateauing of the oxygen consumption rate after about 3 minutes of aerobic activity. At the onset of vigorous exercise, aerobic metabolism is unable to increase rapidly enough to meet the full energy demand. Thus anaerobic metabolism must make up the difference. The lactic acid that is a byproduct of anaerobic glycolosis causes a sensation of fatigue and serves as a stress on ventilation. When aerobic metabolism reaches the requisite level, lactic acid accumulation ceases, thus allowing ventilation to readjust to a less stressful level.

Pacing

In long-duration endurance activities, one of the keys to performance is proper pacing. Research has indicated that even-pacing, perhaps with a "kick" at the end, is most effective and efficient. In moderate-duration activities, even-pacing prevents the premature accumulation of lactic acid which is associated with fatigue. In very long-duration events, even-pacing ensures that muscle glycogen will not be depleted earlier than necessary. Novice competitors often tend to begin races at paces significantly faster than can be sustained for the entire distance, and this always has an adverse effect on performance.

"Hitting the Wall"

"Hitting the wall," a term popularized by marathon runners, refers to the sudden onset of fatigue and depression that may be encountered in later stages of very long-duration exercise. This phenomenon is probably due to depletion of muscle glycogen and blood glucose and thus may be avoided or delayed through proper training, pacing, and nutritional practices. Highly trained athletes seldom report "hitting the wall," suggesting that experience and training adaptations may prevent the problem. Even-pacing, a high-carbohydrate diet for 48 hours before competition, and ingestion of a dilute sugar solution during competition should help the endurance athlete to avoid "the wall."

REFERENCES

1. American College of Sports Medicine position statement on the recommended quantity and quality of exercise for developing and maintaining fitness in healthy adults. Med Sci Sports 10(3):7–10, 1978
2. Astrand PO, Rodahl K: Textbook of Work Physiology, 2nd ed. New York, McGraw–Hill, 1977
3. Cooper KH: Aerobics. New York, Bantam Books, 1968
4. Cundiff DE (ed): Implementation of Aerobic Programs. Washington, DC, AAHPERD Publications, 1979
5. DeVries HA: Physiology of Exercise for Physical Education and Athletics, 3rd ed. Dubuque, Iowa, William C. Brown, 1980
6. Exercise Testing and Training of Apparently Healthy Individuals: A Handbook for Physicians. New York, American Heart Association Committee on Exercise, 1972
7. Fox EL: Sport Physiology. Philadelphia, WB Saunders, 1979
8. Frankel LJ, Richard BB: Be Alive as Long as You Live. New York, Harper-Row, 1980
9. Leslie DK, McLure JW: Exercises for the Elderly. Iowa City, University of Iowa, 1975
10. Margaria R: The sources of muscular energy. Sci Am 226:84–91, 1972
11. Pollock ML et al: Health and Fitness Through Physical Activity. New York, John Wiley & Sons, 1978
12. Royal Canadian Air Force Exercise Plans for Physical Fitness. New York, Simon & Schuster, 1962
13. Sharkey BJ: Physiology of Fitness. Champaign, Illinois, Human Kinetics Publishers, 1979
14. Shephard RJ: The Fit Athlete. New York, Oxford University Press, 1978
15. Wilmore JH: Athletic Training and Physical Fitness. Boston, Allyn and Bacon, 1976

CHAPTER 4

Strength and Conditioning for the Competitive Athlete

John N. Gamble, Jr.

Not so long ago, athletes would prepare for their competitive season a few weeks before the games were to start. Many did not run much, and most did not train with weights. Today's athletes are different. To perform better and to keep up with their competition, they must be bigger, faster, and stronger. To achieve these goals, they follow systematic, year-round strength and conditioning programs that include training in flexibility, conditioning, strength, and power. Further, the competitive athlete must develop or refine skills, be mentally prepared, have sound nutrition, rest well, and avoid staleness or injury.

My job as a strength and conditioning coach is to integrate these activities into a year-round training cycle. By using the principles of periodization, I organize the workouts so that the athlete is in a state of readiness and avoids staleness throughout the year. In this chapter, I discuss

principles of training such as warming up, conditioning, and strength and power and show how they are incorporated into the University of Virginia strength and conditioning program.

THE WARM-UP

The warm-up mentally and physically mobilizes the athlete for practice or competition. The general warm-up consists of jogging and either solo stretching or partner stretches. The sport-specific part of the warm-up includes the movements that the athlete will use in the sport, but not at maximum intensity.

Effects of a Warm-Up

The warm-up, with its psychological, cardiovascular, and muscular effects, has become an accepted way of preparing for athletic activity. Psychologically, it relieves tenseness and tightness and relaxes the athlete so that he is calm and able to concentrate. Physiologically, the warm-up increases circulation and respiration.[6, 15, 18] Oxygen becomes more accessible to the cells because the vascular resistance is lower and hemoglobin gives off oxygen more quickly. Warm-up also reduces the chances of developing myocardial ischemia at the onset of vigorous exercise.

The warm-up literally warms up the muscles, producing faster and more forceful contractions. The metabolic processes involved in contraction and relaxation progress much more quickly. Muscle viscosity drops, making contractions easier and smoother. The heating of the muscles reduces the activity of gamma nerve fibers and lessens the sensitivity of the muscle spindle to stretching, relaxing the muscle.

Muscle soreness can be avoided by a proper warm-up. The warm-up will also promote agility and alertness and decrease movement time. The range of motion of joints increases, and the distance over which force can be applied increases, allowing better technique, new skill acquisition, and a reduction in injuries. In sport, the athlete often has to move from an extreme or unusual position, and it is important that he rehearse these positions during the warm-up.

An athlete should warm-up each day before practice and after breaks in practice, before the start of a game, and before the second half begins. Substitutes should, of course, warm-up before entering a game. The duration of the warmup depends on the sport. The warm-up usually begins 30 to 40 minutes before a contest, and tapers off from 10 to 15 minutes before competition. This allows recovery from any slight and temporary fatigue without the loss of the warm-up effects. An athlete should also try to stretch during the day whenever he finds the opportunity. To be most beneficial, stretching should be done daily.

The Warm-Up Process

The athlete should break a sweat before stretching by jogging to the warm-up area or jogging in place for about 5 minutes or by biking, jumping rope, or doing light calisthenics such as arm rotations.[13]

Then stretching begins, either single or partner stretching.

Solo Stretching

Solo stretching is slow and graceful, since bouncing would set off a stretch reflex and the muscle would then become tighter. The athlete should ease in and out of stretches.[2] An easy, relaxed stretch is held for 15 seconds and should produce a good feeling of mild tension. After 15 seconds, the athlete stretches a little farther for another 15 seconds. Full concentration is needed for these stretches to be effective. He breathes deeply through his nose and concentrates on the muscle that he is stretching; he should not rush or skip steps. When he feels full tension on the muscle, he should exhale.

If a specific area is tight, the athlete should focus on loosening this area. He may have slept in an unusual position. The tight side should always be stretched first. Through stretching, the athlete gets to know his body and its needs. He should stretch within his limits, remembering that stretching is not competitive. All athletes cannot stretch to the same degree: An athlete may even have some tight joints and others that are loose. If the stretching is painful, the athlete is overstretching, and this will produce tightness or an injury.

Partner Stretching (PNF)

At the University of Virginia we prefer a partner stretching program called Proprioceptive Neuromuscular Facilitation (PNF). In sports the athlete often needs to move from an extreme or unusual position. With PNF stretching, we have a method that builds strength as well as flexibility in the extreme leverage positions. Repeated effort and concentration on PNF stretching allow athletes not only to assume the extreme positions at will, but also to exert great force from these positions.

The athlete does partner stretching before and after each workout. He should not compete with his training partner or with teammates. Instead, the competition is with the person he was during the preceding workout. Technique is very important (Figures 4-1, 4-2). An improper stretching position can be painful and may produce an injury. The athlete must concentrate fully for the exercises to be effective, and, if possible, the same partner should be used each time. No "horseplay" is allowed because that is how most injuries arise.

The Four Steps in PNF (Contract–Relax) Stretching Contract–relax stretching is a four-step process:

1. The joint is stretched comfortably just short of pain.

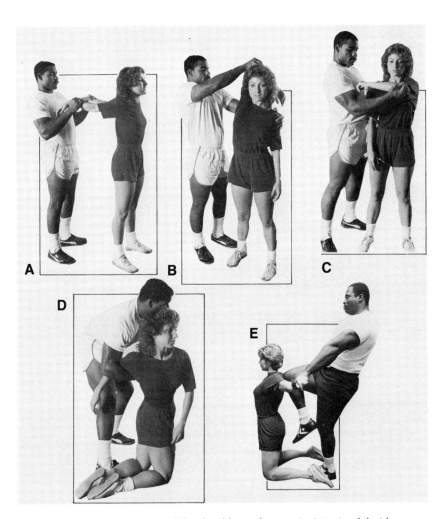

Figure 4-1 Partner stretching of the shoulder and torso. **A.** Anterior deltoid stretch: The athlete's arms should be straight with the palms facing the floor. **B.** Lateral stretch: The athlete starts this stretch with the arm alongside her head. She should not rest her hand on her head and her trunk should not tilt. The partner should concentrate on stretching the latissimus dorsi. **C.** Posterior deltoid stretch: The partner stabilizes the athlete by putting his hand on her shoulder and then pulls her arm toward him. **D.** Trunk twisting stretch: The partner reaches under the athlete's armpit and puts his other hand on her shoulder. The athlete then turns only her trunk, not her shoulders. **E.** Pectoral stretch: During this stretch, the athlete should not sit on her heels but, instead, should keep her body erect, have a slight bend in her elbows, and have her palms facing the floor.

Figure 4-2 Partner stretching of the lower extremity. **A.** Groin stretch: The athlete keeps her knees straight and her toes pointed. **B.** During the contract phase, she squeezes against the partner's ankles. **C.** In the relax phase, the athlete should keep her body erect and not lean back. The athlete stretches both hamstrings first and then stretches each one individually. **D.** Double hamstring stretch: The athlete keeps her hands behind her head and leans forward as far as she can on her own. She should not let her knees bend and should keep her toes up. The partner holds his chest on the middle of her back. He does not press down but just stabilizes her. He places his hands under her legs to give added support. She presses back against his resistance for a 10- to 15-second count and then leans further toward the ground. **E.** Single hamstring stretch: The athlete stretches the right hamstring and then the left hamstring. **F.** Supine single hamstring stretch: The partner places his knee to the inside of the athlete's thigh and his foot to the outside of her leg. This stabilizes the opposite leg, and the athlete can then contract against her partner's shoulder while he holds her knee. **G.** Quadriceps stretch: The partner does not sit heavily on the athlete's buttocks but, instead, applies enough resistance there to keep her hips down.

2. The partner holds the limb in this position while the the athlete applies near maximal isometric force toward the neutral position of the joint, holding for 6 seconds against the partner's resistance.
3. The athlete totally relaxes for 1 or 2 seconds while the partner takes the limb to a new position a few inches farther into the stretched position just short of a painful stretch.
4. The athlete again applies near-maximal isometric force for 6 seconds against the partner's resistance toward the neutral position of the joint.

The athlete performs each stretch three times and eases in and out of the stretches.

Cooling Down

After each practice or competition the athlete should cool down for about 20 minutes to "idling speed." Cooling-down exercises include slow rhythmic activity such as light jogging, walking, partner stretching, or a combination of these. The exercises break down muscle spasm and remove the waste products of exercise. The cool down reduces soreness, and the athlete will feel good when he leaves the field or weight-training room.

STRENGTH

Strength is the ability of an athlete to do work against resistance. It is the force that a muscle group can exert against resistance in a single maximum effort, or the maximum weight that an athlete can lift one time through a full range of motion.

Muscle

An athlete develops strength by working against workloads greater than he normally encounters, responding to the stress of an overload resistance by becoming stronger. Overload is the basis for progressive resistance exercises (PRE) in which the athlete becomes stronger as the resistance against which he works increases. The PRE principle was demonstrated in 6 B.C. by Mylo of Cro-

tona, who is said to have carried a bull calf every day from its birth to its maturity, when he carried it around the stadium at the Olympic games. Progressive resistance exercises are also used to improve muscular endurance, since prolonged repetitions by underloaded muscles have little effect on this factor.[25]

Muscular contractions may be static, concentric, or eccentric. In a static or isometric contraction, the muscle does not shorten. With concentric contraction, the muscle does shorten, as in a biceps curl with a dumbbell. In eccentric contractions, the muscle lengthens while it is contracting, as when lowering a weight during a bench press or while losing at arm wrestling. An eccentric contraction allows the handling of heavier weight.

Muscular strength is a consequence of individual muscle fiber tetanization and the recruitment of a number of muscle fibers that act to lift, maintain, or lower a weight. An athlete may increase his strength by stretching a muscle just before he works with it. Prestretching may be seen in a golfer's backswing, the cocking phase of throwing, and the takeoff in jumping and in a sprint start, where the quadriceps muscle is stretched just before the knee is extended. Such prestretching activates a stretch reflex that summons an added volley of impulses and recruits fibers to supplement the muscular contraction.

Muscles exercised against overload resistance will hypertrophy because of increased cross-sectional diameter of the muscle fibers.[10] Shortening of a muscle is a consequence of interdigitation of actin and myosin protein filaments contained within the membrane of the muscle fiber, the sarcolemma (Figure 4-3). As more myofibrils form per fiber, the total amount of protein increases, especially in the myosin filaments. Some of the gain in the number of fibers may even result from longitudinal fiber splitting. Such splitting may be found in muscles after prolonged weight lifting[9]; the amount of connective tissue and the capillary density in such muscles also increase. Endurance training causes more capillaries to form, improving the blood supply to the active muscles and decreasing the distance over which molecules must diffuse from the blood to the mitochondria.

In addition to the muscular effect of training,

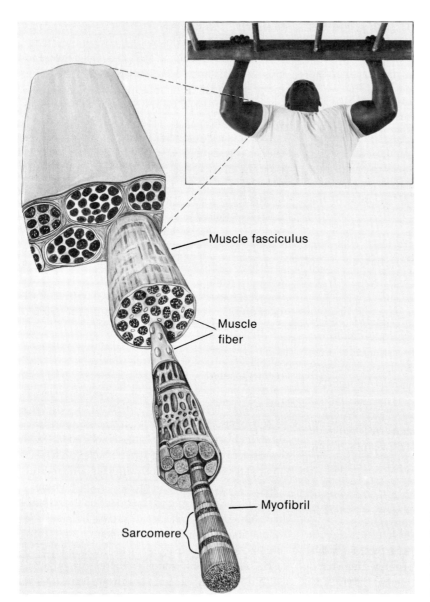

Muscle fasciculus

Muscle fiber

Myofibril

Sarcomere

Figure 4-3 A muscle comprises many bundles of fibers. Each of these fibers, in turn, contains fibrils. The fibrils contain actin and myosin filaments.

there is a neuromuscular effect. Training increases the ease of transmission of nerve impulses across the motor end-plates, which is important because the application of force in athletics demands fine neuromuscular control.

Weight lifters have a higher degree of motor unit synchronization than do nonathletic control subjects.[22, 31] Motor unit synchronization would provide a very rapid rate of maximum tension generation per cross-sectional area per unit of time for a given muscle. To vary the degree of force the athlete applies, he may change the number of motor units that contract together, or he may establish a summation wave by varying the frequency of impulses sent to the muscles. The neuromuscular system probably is inhibited by means of complex nervous system controls, and release of this inhibition may account for extraordinary feats of strength. "Shot and shout" stimuli overcome the inhibition, leading to a stronger contraction.

Strength helps to prevent injury by promoting

increased stability of joints and by enabling the athlete to move faster to avoid injury. The muscle bulk itself protects underlying structures. Strength may be measured with a dynamometer or a cable tensiometer, by the maximal amount of weight an athlete can lift, or on an isometric machine. Developing strength is hard work, but once gained it is relatively easy to retain. If the athlete stops training, he will lose strength at about one third the rate at which it was gained, but as little as one session a week of maximum contractions will prevent such strength loss.

Ligaments and Tendons

Exercise strengthens ligaments and tendons, in addition to muscles. Thus when rats are placed on a systematic running program, the strength of their medial collateral ligament attachments to bone increases. Rabbits trained on a running machine will develop significantly increased strength in their anterior cruciates.

Running on an uneven surface promotes a significantly greater increase in ligament strength than does running on a smooth surface. Thus when an athlete runs on an uneven surface, as in a cross-country race, he enhances his proprioception while increasing his ligament strength to a greater extent than when running on a track.

Exercise also strengthens tendons. When young animals are trained, the cross-sectional area of their Achilles tendon increases; in older animals, however, only the muscle hypertrophies. The tendons become stronger with training, but no quantitative compositional changes occur.

Weight Training for Women

A woman's absolute strength is about two thirds that of a man's, but when strength is related to body weight the difference decreases. In fact, when strength is related to lean body weight, that is, total weight minus fat weight, women are actually slightly stronger than men. A woman's upper body strength is only 30% to 50% that of a man's, but the leg strength differences are minimal. When leg strength is related to body size, a woman's leg strength is nearly the same as a man's. A woman's legs are slightly stronger than a man's when leg strength is related to lean body mass.

Strength differences between men and women probably are related to differences in normal body proportions and the daily activity patterns of men and women. Muscle quality is the same in both men and women in its contractile properties and its ability to exert force. When a woman follows the same strength training program as a man, she can make the same percentage gains in strength that a man can. Weight training will streamline her muscles and improve tone. Low testosterone levels keep her from becoming overmuscled, and subcutaneous tissue conceals muscle definition. Women who do become excessively muscular probably have higher testosterone levels. The female athlete can double her strength over a 10-week period without muscle hypertrophy, a rapid development that is more of a neuromuscular than a purely muscular process.[26, 27] Strength training is a new experience for women, and they start far from their potential level.

Most women are strangers to the weight room, and a strength coach can guide and encourage them. There is nothing feminine about being weak. The lifting frequency, duration of cycle, and intensity of training are the same for women as for men. The only difference is that a woman might increase weight in increments of 2½ pounds rather than by 5 or 10 pounds. A female athlete may have a small decrease in strength on the day before she begins a menstrual period.

Weight Training for Youths

Because many youths are strangers to hard work, they are generally weak, but weight lifting will improve their strength and help prevent injury.

Youngsters should start their general conditioning program with their body weight as resistance. These exercises include leaning, bending, twisting, and hanging from bars, push-ups, dips, and chins. Their weight training should involve a high volume of work with ten repetitions per set using dumbbells, barbells, Tubics, and a wide range of machines. All lifting should be supervised to assure that good technique is being used.

Low-intensity plyometrics can be done throughout childhood. In these exercises, the emphasis is on how to do the exercises properly and on the development of motor skills. The exercises include skipping and jumping and hops off both feet with no added amplitude from boxes or added load from weight vests. Volume should prevail over intensity, and general training should predominate over specific training. These exercises provide variability in training and can make the training fun.

When young men train in Olympic-style weight lifting, they work on speed and technique; such technique can be taught even to 8-year-olds. Some countries hold competitions for youths in which technique is judged. When a youth reaches 12 to 13 years of age and depending on the maturity of his body, weight can be added, but occasionally a young man is only lifting the bar without plates.

Even with good coaching, however, a young lifter may suffer an injury such as a slip of his distal radial epiphysis, dislocate his elbow, or develop spondylolysis. Expert coaching is nonetheless imperative. Youths should avoid power lifting, especially the dead lift, because power lifting emphasizes heavy weights.

Weight Training for Older Athletes

An athlete reaches maximum strength at about 25 years of age. Thereafter, he loses about 1% of strength per year; thus, at age 65, the athlete is about 65% as strong as he was when he was 25 years old. The older athlete's goal should be total conditioning. He should seek to gain and to maintain his strength through lighter loads with dumbbells, barbells, Tubics, or machines. Heavier training loads or bouncing drills may lead to rupture of a tendon, such as the biceps, quadriceps, or patellar tendon.

Training for Strength

The strength program at the University of Virginia is based on three major exercises: the bench press, squat, and power clean. The other exercises are assistive ones, structured to supplement these three.

Bench Press

The bench press strengthens the athlete's pectoral muscles, deltoids, and triceps. To begin a bench press, the athlete lies on the bench with his feet flat on the floor and knees bent to about 90° or less to assure a stable position (Figure 4-4). His head, upper back, and hips should stay in contact with the bench. He should arch his back mildly so that his chest is at the highest possible position and keep his lower back muscles relaxed to prevent a cramp or a strain.

To find the ideal hand position, the athlete places his hands on the bar with elbows bent to 90° and forearms perpendicular to the floor. The bar should rest low in his palms. Athletes with leverage disadvantages, such as basketball players with long arms and narrow shoulders, may start at a 90° elbow angle and then adjust the hand position either out or in to achieve the best position for their anatomy. Most women use less than a 90° elbow angle because of a general lack of shoulder strength.

The Lift   The athlete inhales and takes the bar off the rack. He lowers the bar (eccentric phase) with control to the highest point of his chest. This point is usually at the lower part of the pectoralis major muscle or sternum. He then pauses momentarily but does not relax. Just as the bar touches his chest, he drives it upward (concentric phase) explosively to a lock-out position of full elbow extension at a point in the area of the chin and bridge of the nose. Athletes with longer arms end up at the bridge of the nose while athletes with shorter arms end up at the chin. During this phase, the elbows should be at a 45° angle to the side of the body. Otherwise, if they are too wide or too close, the athlete will have a leverage disadvantage or could possibly sustain an injury.

On each repetition, the athlete exhales just after the "sticking point" where the anterior deltoid and triceps take over from the pectoralis major. If he is lifting high repetitions, he may hold his breath for three repetitions or more before exhaling.

Safety   A spotter monitors the bench press at all times, even while lighter weights are being used.

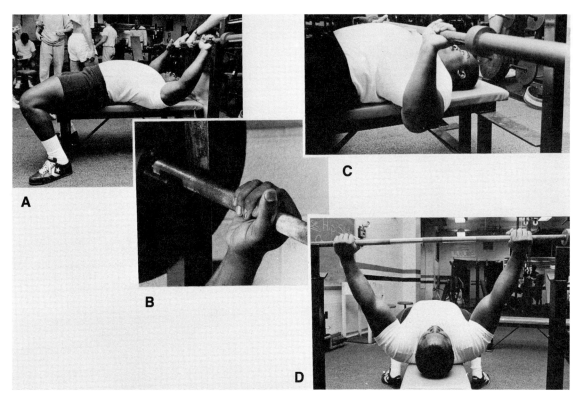

Figure 4-4 **A.** The athlete begins a bench press with his hips and shoulder blades in contact with the bench, his feet flat on the floor with a 90° or less bend in his knees, and a natural back arch. **B.** The bar rests in the base of his palm and he uses a fully wrapped grip instead of a false grip where his thumb would not be around the bar. **C.** He lowers the bar from the rack to the highest point on his chest and **(D)** then presses the bar up to the lockout position, keeping his head down throughout the lift.

The spotter must be ever alert because an injury can happen so quickly. Even an experienced spotter can be too slow to prevent an athlete from being injured.

Variations An athlete sometimes bench presses with his feet up on the bench or on a stool (Figure 4-5). In this position, he can concentrate on strengthening the upper body during the hypertrophy stage of lifting. If the athlete has a lower back injury, this position will reduce stress on the lower back.

Common Bench-Pressing Errors

1. Hand placement too wide or too close.
2. Bouncing the weight off the chest.
3. Kicking feet out during the lift.
4. Raising buttocks off the bench.
5. Improper breathing.
6. Lifting too much weight.
7. If a cambered bar is used improperly, it may cause a pectoralis muscle tear.

The Squat

The squat is the main lift in many weight-training programs. It is basically a deep knee bend performed with a weighted bar resting on the shoulders. The squat primarily develops the quadriceps, hip extensors (gluteus maximus and hamstrings), and trunk extensors. In addition, many other muscle groups are active during the

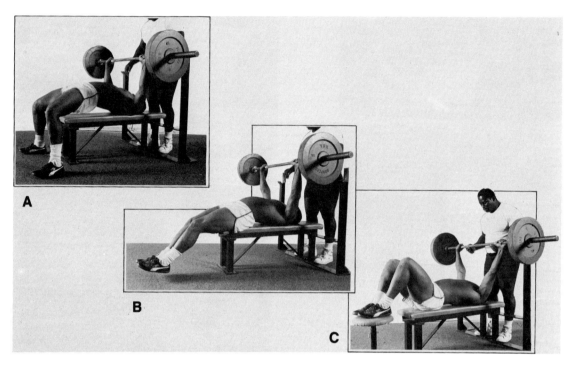

Figure 4-5 Bench press errors. An injury may occur if the athlete arches his back too much **(A)** or keeps his legs off the ground **(B)**, overextending his back. In the hypertrophy stage of cycle training, athletes are concentrating on their upper bodies. They can, therefore, rest their feet on a stool **(C)**, focusing the lift on the upper body.

movement to stabilize the spine, hips, knees, and ankles.

The squat teaches the athlete to consistently bring his hips and legs under his body into a maximum power position. To avoid a lower back strain, the athlete must have full back, hamstring, and calf flexibility, and his back must remain flat throughout the lift. The chance of a lower back strain or abdominal strain can be reduced if a lifting belt is worn. Knee wraps can also be used when heavy weights are lifted. Athletes should wear shoes with wide, solid heels such as basketball, tennis, or weight-lifting shoes. If he squats in running shoes, he may turn his feet over and possibly sprain his ankle. The athlete may also bite down on a mouthpiece during the lift.

The Lift   To start the squat, the lifter positions himself under the bar (Figure 4-6). His feet should be slightly wider than shoulder width apart and his toes turned out about 30° to provide a good base of support. He grasps the bar with a full grip, making sure that he is at the center or midpoint of the bar. The bar should rest on his shoulders no lower than 3 inches below the top of the posterior deltoids. Before beginning the lift, the athlete ascertains that all preparations have been met. He then picks a spot on the wall in front of him above eye level. Focusing his eyes on this spot helps him keep his head up, chest out, and back flat. He is now ready to start.

The athlete inhales and takes the bar off the squat rack. After he is set, the athlete inhales on every repetition just before descending. The descent or eccentric contraction phase is slow. A fast downward movement would produce a bouncing effect and could lead to injury. Throughout the descent, he keeps his knees in line with his ankles. He descends to a position where the top of his thighs are parallel to the floor. He pauses momentarily but does not relax; he then explodes upward. On every repetition,

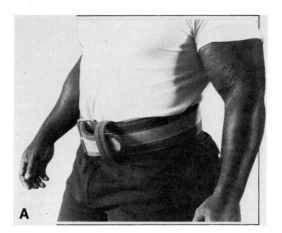

Figure 4-6 The athlete wears a lifter's belt **(A)** to support his lower back and abdomen. The belt should be snug but not too tight. During the squat **(B)**, the athlete keeps his knees in line with his ankles as much as possible. His feet are shoulder width or more apart and his toes turned out slightly. The spotter shadows the athlete **(C)**, underhooking his arms. If the spotter fails to concentrate **(D)**, a missed lift can produce a serious injury. The lifter drops to 90° with his thighs parallel to the floor and his back straight and head up **(E)**. If the athlete is up on his toes with a rounded back **(F)**, his knees will be too far forward and he can develop tendonitis or hurt his back.

he exhales after he has passed the sticking point, which is halfway through the upward phase of the lift.

Common Errors in the Squat

1. Exaggerated forward lean of the trunk
2. Bar too high on neck
3. Feet too far apart or too close together
4. Looking down throughout the lift

The Power Clean

The power clean is a very technical lift that works the athlete's shoulders, arms, forearms, back, hips, thighs, and legs. In fact, all of the muscle groups are involved in the power clean. If only one lift could be chosen for a training program the power clean would be the one. Training for this lift, the athlete begins with a broomstick so that he can concentrate on technique. The lift requires and develops strength, speed, quickness, balance, coordination, timing, and explosive power. It teaches the athlete to consistently bring his hips and legs under his body in a maximum power position.

The power clean comprises five phases:

1. Starting position
2. First pull
3. Transition
4. Second pull
5. Catch

Starting Position   The athlete approaches the bar in a normal stance until the balls of his feet are under it (Figure 4-7). His feet are shoulder-width or slightly less apart and his toes are pointing forward. When he looks down the front of his thighs, he should see the close side of the bar clearly. His weight should be supported by his insteps and heels. He grips the bar with his forearms pronated just outside his legs. He then "sits into the bar" until his thighs are parallel to the floor. His back is flat, head up, and chest out, and his shoulders are directly over the bar. In this position, depending on the anatomic structure of the athlete, his shins may touch the bar slightly or they may be up to 3 inches away.

First Pull   The athlete starts the pull by contracting his quadriceps and gluteal muscles and pushing down on the floor, not by jerking the bar from the floor with his arms (Figure 4-8A). He keeps the bar as close to his body as possible as it travels along the line of his shins to a position just above the knees. His shoulders are over the bar as it passes the knees.

Transition   During the transition phase between the first and second pulls of the power clean, the athlete's balance shifts from near his heels toward his toes. He lifts his shoulders up and back and his body assumes a nearly vertical position. The velocity of the bar decreases slightly during the transition. The lifter is now in a good jumping position.

Second Pull   The second pull is a shrug–pull action. After the transition phase the lifter straightens his back and legs, and his hips and shoulders rise. After he has shrugged his shoulders maximally and straightened his back and legs, he pulls the bar up with his upper back muscles and arms. During the pull, he keeps his elbows flared out and tries to keep the bar as close as possible to his body.

The bar should reach at least the midpoint of his pectoralis major. Because the pull is so explosive, the athlete drives up onto his toes. Olympic-style lifters literally jump during this phase to clean maximum weights in the clean-and-jerk.

The Catch   When the bar has reached the peak of the high pull, the athlete drops his heels quickly to the ground. He bends his knees from 5° to 15° to absorb shock while dropping his elbows under the bar and catching ("racking") it on the front of his shoulders and chest. He should keep his elbows high to prevent the bar from rolling off his shoulders. (Figure 4-8B)

High Pulls

The high pull is a training lift that puts less stress than a power clean on the athlete's lower back and wrists. It is exactly like the power clean except that the weight is not racked on the chest. Beginners perform this lift in the learning (hypertrophy) phase of a training cycle.

Assistive (Supplementary) Exercises

Assistive strengthening exercises supplement the bench press, squat, and power clean. They include upper and lower body exercises:

Upper Body

Front deltoid raises
Flys
Biceps curls
Triceps pushdowns
Cable rows
Chins
Dips

Figure 4-7 The power clean. In the power clean, the athlete grips the bar just outside his knees **(A)** with his feet less than shoulder-width apart or at about shoulder width, if his anatomy dictates. This is not a full grip; instead, the bar hangs in the proximal interphalangeal area. The lifter's back is straight, his head and chest are up, and he looks at a point above his head on the wall. He initiates the lift with his legs **(B).** At the transition phase between the first and second pull **(C),** he is ready to drive his hips into the lift. In the high pull **(D),** the athlete shrugs and pulls with his elbows high and his hands cupped in. To catch the weight, he drops his elbows under and flexes at the knees to absorb the shock **(E).** He then completes the lift **(F).**

Figure 4-8 Power clean errors. The athlete should avoid a rounded back **(A)** at the starting position and should not start with his feet too far from the bar. Further, he should not hyperextend his back **(B)** when catching the weight.

Lower Body

Leg presses
Knee extensions
Knee curls
Calf raises

These exercises can be added to or deleted from the athlete's program depending on individual needs. For example, a basketball player may need cable rows to strengthen weak spinal extensor muscles. In the case of weak hamstrings (less than a 60:40 quadriceps-to-hamstring ratio), knee curls may be added as supplements. Regardless of the phase of the cycle, the athlete does ten repetitions of these exercises. The number of sets may vary but should never exceed four, unless the exercises are being done for rehabilitative purposes.

Midsection Strengthening   After each practice or weight-training session, the athlete does midsection strengthening exercises (Figure 4-9). These exercises begin with low-level bench

---

Figure 4-9 Midsection (abdominal) strengthening. **A.** Ladder crunches (hanging crunch): In this abdominal exercise, the athlete rolls her knees as close as possible to her chest and raises them at least above the horizontal. She works up to two sets of 20 to 30 crunches. The partner should keep his elbows locked. **B.** Straight leg ladder raises: The athlete hangs vertically and, with knees straight, flexes his hips and tries to bring his feet all the way up to his hands. This exercise works the lower abdominal muscles. He starts with two sets of five repetitions and then increases the repetitions as his stomach muscles become stronger. The maximum is from three to five sets of ten repetitions. The athlete can stop the repetitions when he cannot raise his legs past the horizontal. **C.** Bench crunches: Instead of sitting up all the way, the athlete rounds his back during this crunch so that his shoulder blades just leave the floor. With every repetition, however, he should return all the way down to the starting position on the floor. These crunches work the upper abdominal muscles. In a twisting variation, the athlete can also do diagonal bench crunches, bringing his elbow to his opposite knee. **D.** Leg lifts: With his legs straight and his back flat on the floor, the athlete does five sets of as many repetitions as he can, raising his legs for 10 seconds and then lowering them for 10 seconds. If his back arches as he lowers his legs, he should stop at that point and raise his legs again. *(continued)*

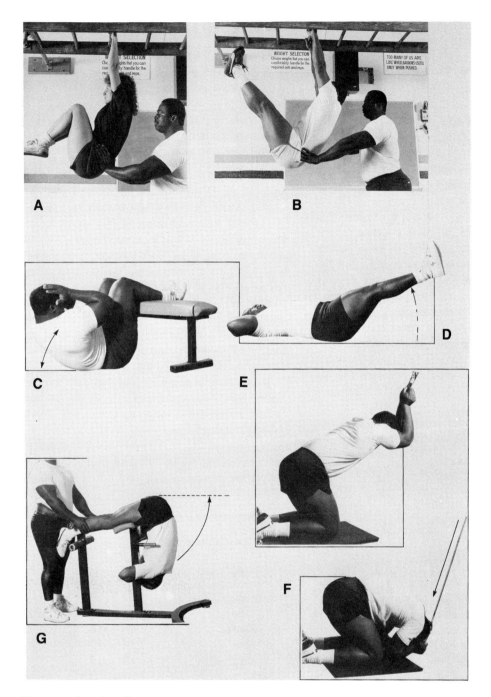

Figure 4-9 *(continued).*
E, F. Cable crunches: Starting with his elbows bent and his hips up, the athlete curls his elbows to his knees, keeping his elbows bent, and then returns to the starting position. Straps hold the athlete's hands together. **G.** Back extensions: Abdominal exercises alone will not strengthen the midsection fully. The athlete should do back extensions, too. He starts from a flexed position and extends his torso until it is parallel to the floor. If he is a very flexible athlete, he can hyperextend slightly. This exercise works the paravertebral muscles, the gluteal muscles, and the hamstrings.

crunches and hanging crunches and progress to the more advanced incline sit-ups and hanging straight leg raises. For the bench crunch, the athlete lies on the floor and places his legs on a bench so that his hips are flexed to 90°. With his hands behind his head, he rolls forward in a crunching action until reaching a 30° angle to the floor. These bench crunches strengthen the upper part of the rectus abdominus.

For hanging crunches, the athlete grabs an overhead bar (ladder, wall bar, or horizontal bar). He raises his knees to his chest and then returns his legs to a hanging position while a partner stabilizes his pelvis. These hanging crunches strengthen the lower part of the rectus abdominus. The athlete does 20 to 30 repetitions of bench crunches and hanging crunches with the number of sets determined by the strength coach. To strengthen the internal and external oblique muscles, the athlete can modify the above exercises by bringing alternate shoulders toward the opposite knee in bench crunches and both knees to alternate shoulders in hanging cruches.

The athlete with a more developed midsection can do incline sit-ups and hanging straight leg raises. For incline sit-ups, the athlete sets a sit-up board at about a 45° angle and lies supine on the board with his hands behind his head. He curls up, touching his elbows to his knees, and then returns to the starting position. He should repeat this exercise for 20 to 30 repetitions with the number of sets determined by the strength coach.

For hanging straight leg raises, the athlete hangs from a bar with his pelvis stabilized and raises both legs as high as possible, trying for a 180° angle. He raises and lowers his legs slowly 10 to 15 times. Incline and hanging leg raises and sit-ups can be modified in the same manner as the hanging crunches and bench crunches to strengthen the internal and external obliques.

THE LIFTING PROGRAM

After warming up, the player begins lifting with the major muscle groups of the chest, legs, or back. He performs the most difficult part of the day's training load first. If he cannot perform all of the required sets and repetitions, he should reduce the poundage to guarantee success.

Selecting Starting Weights and Workout Poundages

To determine what weight to use during the first week of ten repetitions for major exercises, the athlete should pick a realistic goal. Sixty percent of that goal becomes his top set (the heaviest set). The other four sets lead up to it with gradual but consistent poundages. Each week he then adds at least 5 pounds to the top set on the heavy day. For an athlete who has a goal of lifting, say, 400 pounds in the bench press, the top set (heaviest set) in the first week of ten repetitions on the heavy bench pressing day should be 60% of his goal: 400 lb × 60% = 240 lb. He then lifts gradual poundages to lead up to that top set.

In another method for determining starting poundages, the coach picks a fixed weight and has the athlete lift it for three sets of ten repetitions. The athlete then performs a fourth set for maximum repetitions. For each repetition past 10, the coach multiplies by 5 lbs and adds that weight to the fixed weight to give the starting poundage.

Heavy Bench Press Day

SET	WEIGHT REPS
1st	135 × 10
2nd	180 × 10
3rd	205 × 10
4th	220 × 10
5th	240 × 10

Lifting Aids

Lifting aids and proper lifting shoes can add support and increase safety. The aids include wrist wraps, straps, lifting belt, and knee wraps. *Wrist wraps* lock the lifter's wrist while he performs the bench press and power clean. *Straps* help in high pulls, shrugs, and dead lifts. A *lifting belt* supports the lower back and abdomen and keeps the lower back warm. It should fit snugly but not tightly. The belt should be worn for any exercise that is done standing. *Knee wraps* support the lifter's knees. While applying a wrap, the athlete keeps his knee straight and crisscrosses the wrap around the knee. If the wrap were wrapped straight around the knee, it could slip and pinch. If wrapped too tightly, it might inhibit hamstring function and could lead to a hamstring injury. Wraps may be worn for the top sets of squats and for power cleans and high pulls.

Weight lifting shoes have solid heels and are the best shoes for lifting. However, any solid shoe will do, even combat boots. Spongy running shoes are unacceptable.

Spotters

An athlete should come to the weight-training facility with at least one workout partner. The partner serves as a spotter, friend, and motivator. Ideally three athletes train together. When one is performing the exercise, the other two spot for him and load the bar.

During a squat the spotter should stay close behind the lifter like a "shadow" and be constantly alert. If the lifter is going forward, the spotter supports him to keep him from falling forward and injuring his spine and helps him replace the weight on the rack. An unattended lifter could lose a finger by catching it on the rack under a heavily loaded bar. Spotters must work together, especially if they are at opposite ends of the bar. If one spotter were to lift his side of the bar while the other spotter is distracted, the bar would tilt, causing undue stress on the athlete's body.

Because of the heavy poundage, a spotter should be used especially for the following lifts:

Squat
Heavy hip sled
Power clean
High pull

Bench press
Incline bench press
Military press
Seated behind the neck press
Heavy dumbbell fly
Triceps press

At the University of Virginia, we use spotters for *all* lifts for safety and so that our athletes follow good lifting habits.

FREE WEIGHTS AND MACHINES

At the University of Virginia, training with free weights forms the core of our strength program. Free weights include barbells and dumbbells. Machines are used primarily to rehabilitate injuries and to supplement an athlete's workout.

When an athlete trains with free weights, he strengthens not only primary muscles but also synergistic and stabilizer muscles. Because free weights have to be stabilized, stabilizer muscles, ligaments, and tendons are strengthened. Athletic activities may also be simulated against the resistance of free weight and the weights lifted from varying body positions. The strength gained from training with free weights converts well to the playing field. Both arms or both legs can be used or one arm or one leg may be used at a time.

In contrast, the strength-building machines strengthen only the primary muscles. Because the athlete does not have to balance the resistance, he reaps less ligament and tendon strength. Further, the machines are set in a constant movement pattern unrelated to athletics.

The Weight Room

Athletes like to train in a clean, neat environment on well-maintained equipment. The free weight area (Figure 4-10A) is organized as to body parts; the machine area is organized to comprise a circuit (Figure 4-10B). Equipment in the varsity weight room is checked, cleaned, and maintained every day. Checks are made for loose screws, loose chains, and cable wear. The carpet is vac-

Figure 4-10 The weight room: The free weight area **(A)** is organized as to body parts; the machine area **(B)** is organized as a circuit.

uumed three times a week, equipment is painted each year, and coverings are changed every other year or according to wear.

Weight-Training Facility Rules

Strength-training equipment—barbells and dumbbells—can be dangerous. However, an adequate warm-up, proper lifting technique, and good spotting practices will help to prevent injury. In addition, safety is enhanced if lifters adhere to weight-training facility rules.

STRENGTH-TRAINING ERRORS

Common errors in strength training include overtraining, using the wrong sequence of exercises, using the wrong load intensity progression, choosing unrealistic goals, and using improper

Weight-Training Facility Rules

Come in with at least one workout partner.

Do not bring food, drinks, or bags of ice into the weight room.

Chewing gum is absolutely prohibited.

Do not bring in extra clothing, bags, or equipment.

Always wear workout clothes and workout shoes.

Before entering the weight room, be sure that shoes are clean of all mud, grass, and water.

Do not crowd others who are working out.

Replace all dumbbells in rack.

Do not leave plates on any bars or machines.

Be sure that your skin is reasonably dry.

No "horseplay."

technique. When an athlete overtrains, he has probably pushed himself so hard that he peaks prematurely and his body will not allow any more gains. An athlete should follow the prescribed sequence of exercises as closely as possible. If, however, the weight-training facility cannot accommodate a large number of athletes, a lifting station may be occupied, and the athlete then may not be able to follow the best sequence of exercises. Sometimes an athlete will "bounce" up and down his workout sheet, not adhering to the correct order of exercises, and his results will suffer. Further, an athlete may pick unrealistic goals. He may feel peer pressure to lift a certain amount of weight. Failure to accomplish the goal will frustrate him and lead to overtraining and injuries.

One strength-training error, improper technique, stands above the rest. Coaches used to instruct their athletes to "get the weight up the best way you can." With this method of training, it was not long before an athlete would be injured. The athlete should train with good technique so that strength gains will be maximized and translate to his sport.

THE MENTAL ASPECT OF WEIGHT TRAINING

Strength training is hard work. Athletes often look for an edge to aid their performance, but there is no magic or secret to gaining strength and no predetermined optimum combination of sets or repetitions. To maximize strength, the athlete should enjoy lifting. He must concentrate and work intensively for the entire workout and never be interrupted. By achieving daily goals, the athlete will be encouraged to continue his weight training. He should feel that on a particular day, and every day, no opponent could have worked harder to realize his potential.

CONDITIONING

Our conditioning programs at the University of Virginia are designed to build and maintain a cardiovascular base, improve quickness and agility, and develop power (speed-strength). These goals are accomplished through distance running, interval running, form running drills, agility drills, and plyometrics.

Distance Running

The first week of the summer conditioning program for football consists of distance running and form running drills. To avoid shock on the legs, the athlete should run on a grass field. Before running, he should perform a heel cord stretch to prevent tight calf muscles. The distance run is not a race, but the distance should be accomplished in a moderate time. He should run early in the morning before his lifting workout or about 3 hours after and should drink plenty of water. In preparing for a football season, he runs distance 3 days a week on nonlifting days until the last 4 weeks of the precompetition phase, at which time the Monday run is discontinued. After each running workout, the players run up and down the stadium steps for 10 minutes: full speed up and slow speed down.

Interval Running

Interval running means that bouts of hard running are separated by rest periods or lighter exercise. Athletes training in hot and humid climates may have to take a little more rest between intervals. Interval running should be done in the early evening. The distance the athletes run will vary from 5 yards to 660 yards. During rest intervals between sprints he should not sit down and should try mentally to bring his pulse rate under control, rather than letting his mind wander.

Form Running Drills

Because speed is an essential part of most athletic contests, the athlete should develop it maximally. Not everyone is blessed with blazing speed, but, through concentrated work on form and technique, all athletes can improve their running speed.

Two main factors dictate how fast an athlete can run: stride rate and stride length. Great sprinters have a stride rate of 4½ to 5 strides per second and a stride length of 7½ to 8 feet regardless of their height. The stride rate depends on muscle contraction. The speed of contraction can be increased by improving the strength of the muscle. The stride length can be improved by increasing muscular elasticity and range of motion in the joints (PNF stretching) and by doing form and technique drills. Optimum speed requires proper running technique, and the running should be done as efficiently as possible. We use the following form running drills at the University of Virginia.

The Stance The football stance is different from a sprinting start in that the athlete's weight is more evenly distributed rather than forward over his shoulders. His head is up, his buttocks are down, and his back is flat (Figure 4-11). His feet should never be more than shoulder-width apart, and one foot should be slightly behind the other. The hand on the same side of the foot that is farther back should be on the ground; that is, if the right foot is farther back than the left one, then the right hand should be placed on the ground.

1. *High knee lifts and run*—In this drill, the ath-

Figure 4-11   The athlete assumes a stance with his buttocks low. His feet should not be too far apart. If the back foot is too far behind, motion is wasted behind the athlete and he slows down. If the athlete is right-handed, the first step is off his left leg. He stays low during the first two steps and then comes up gradually. Some athletes keep their hands closer to the body to give more power.

lete lifts his knees to waist level and maintains proper head and body alignment. The arms should swing forward and back, and the fists should travel from the hips to shoulder height. The athlete concentrates on proper running form and arm swing. He performs this exercise over a distance of 25 yards at half speed, rests, and repeats the drill.

2. *Rapid-fire knee lifts*—The athlete runs in place for about 10 seconds and then runs forward. The object is to go about 10 yards and get in as many steps as possible. Rapid high knee movement and arm speed are emphasized in this drill. After the first 10 yards, the athlete finishes in a jog. This exercise should be performed twice.

3. *Footfire*—The footfire drill increases stride rate and quickness. The athlete moves his feet as quickly as possible, raising them only an inch or two off the ground with each step. His weight is on the balls of his feet and his toes are pointed straight ahead. He thinks only of

picking up his feet. He avoids lifting his feet too high, shuffling his feet, angling his toes out, tensing his face and hands, and using arm action. This exercise should be performed twice at a distance of 5 yards each, then he strides for 25 yards.

4. *Ankle flips*—Ankle flips develop power in the calf muscles. *Using only ankle action*, the athlete alternately explodes from foot to foot as high as possible (usually only about 6 inches off the ground). He keeps his knees and hips rigid, landing high on the toes and settling down to the heel. Arms are kept relaxed at the sides. The athlete should avoid achieving too much distance on each explosion, flexing knees and hips, swinging feet out to the side, and using his arms. This exercise should be performed twice at a distance of 30 yards each.

5. *Heel-ups*—Heel-ups develop hamstring strength and active flexibility in the quadriceps. The athlete alternately swings the heel of each foot up to his buttocks. This is a quick, smooth swinging motion produced largely at the knee joint. He should avoid moving forward too fast and using his arms and should not lift his knees by flexing his hips. This exercise should be performed twice at a distance of 30 yards each. The athlete should finish with a jog.

6. *Stride-outs*—Stride-outs improve the athlete's stride length and flexibility. For 30 yards, he tries to improve the distance of the previous stride at three-quarters speed while maintaining a consistent arm swing. This exercise should be performed twice at a distance of 30 yards each.

In training for football, form running drills are performed on Mondays and Thursdays. They last 20 to 30 minutes the first week and are reduced to 5 to 10 minutes when plyometric training starts.

Agility Drills

Agility drills help the athlete develop balance, coordination, and mobility and keep him from becoming "stale" while performing the same routine. Before beginning the drills, the athlete warms up, stretches, and then jumps rope. Agility drills are always done *before* running so that the athlete is fresh. The drills involve the skill movements needed to play the sport. Jumping drills alternate with sliding and balance drills. At the University of Virginia we select from the following nine drills for football:

1. *Jumping rope*—After warming up and stretching, the athlete jumps rope for 10 minutes using various speeds and footwork.

2. *Harness drill*—The athlete runs with good form in a harness against the resistance provided by a partner (Figure 4-12).

3. *In-and-out bag drills*—The athlete runs forward between bags, and then alternates this with backward and sideways run-throughs. The athlete performs five sets lasting 30 seconds each, with a 30-second rest between runs.

4. *Nebraska agility drill*—This cone drill combines forward running, turning, bending, and backward running. At the end of the winter football workouts, we time the athletes for quickness.

5. *Bag or box hops*—In this drill, the athlete jumps over bags or boxes. He performs five sets lasting 30 seconds each, with a 30-second rest between sets.

6. *Combination drill*—The combination drill includes a variety of challenges: crawling, one-legged hops, bear crawl, cross-over run (carioca), backward run, and two-legged hops around a 10-yard square.

7. *Dot drill*—The athlete jumps back-and-forth or side-to-side quickly. He performs five sets lasting 30 seconds each, with a 30-second rest between sets.

8. *Cone drill*—The athlete "slides" laterally around cones. This drill is performed around a 7-yard square. He performs five sets lasting 30 seconds each, with a 30-second rest between sets.

9. *Rope drill*—The athlete runs over a series of strung ropes, lifting his knees high.

For football training in the winter, the athlete

Figure 4-12 Harness drill: The athlete runs with good form—head and chest up, arms pumping, knees driving, and body leaning slightly forward. The partner varies the resistance on the reins. This exercise is done at the beginning of conditioning workouts for four sets of 20 yards each.

performs all of these drills. In the summer, he does at least four of the drills each session. Before the precompetition period is over, he should try to do all of the drills at least twice. All of the agility drills are timed. For best results, the athlete should concentrate totally on the exercise.

Power (Speed-Strength) and Plyometrics

Power is the linking of sheer strength with speed of movement to produce an explosive-reactive type of movement. It is the ability of a muscle to reach a maximum level of strength quickly. An athlete develops power by training with high-intensity bouncing drills (plyometrics). These exercises train the neuromuscular system to react

quickly and forcefully during stretch-shortening actions.

Plyometrics depend on the stretch reflex to produce an explosive reaction. The stretch reflex responds to stretching of a muscle. When a muscle is stretched rapidly, the stretch reflex causes the muscle to contract. How fast the muscle switches from an eccentric (lengthening) contracting to a concentric (shortening) contraction will determine the athlete's speed-strength or power. The force of a concentric contraction of a muscle can be enhanced if it is immediately preceded by a rapid eccentric contraction of the same muscle. During the eccentric contraction, elastic energy is stored in the contractile elements of the muscle. This stored energy is released as mechanical work during the concentric contraction.

The aim of plyometric exercises is to train the athlete's nervous system to react with maximum speed to the lengthening of muscle and to develop the muscle's ability to shorten rapidly with maximal force. In sports, there is seldom enough time to develop maximum strength or maximum speed. It takes 0.5 to 0.7 seconds to develop maximum strength. However, there are few explosive movements in athletics that take this long. For example, ground contact time in sprinting takes only 0.1 to 0.15 seconds. Therefore, a tremendous amount of force must be developed in an extremely short time.

By mastering plyometrics the athlete will become a better athlete. Any sport skill that requires power or the application of maximum force in the shortest time will benefit from this training. Further, the athlete's running form and running speed will improve. These drills also raise skill levels by enhancing both motor coordination and hand–eye coordination.

Plyometric Training

To train for power, the coach should select a progressive series of plyometric exercises for his athletes that will mimic movements in the particular sport. The exercises must be done properly to ensure maximum gains and to lower the chance of injury. Because plyometrics require flexibility and agility, the athlete should prepare for them adequately with a light jog, PNF stretching, form-running drills, and a few low-intensity jump-throughs.

Plyometrics complement the weight-training program for the development of explosive power. The exercises range from the simple to the complex and can be designed for the beginner to the elite athlete. Certain exercises are specifically for the hips and legs, the trunk (midsection and chest), and the shoulders and arms.

An athlete can generally begin a basic plyometric program during his sophomore year of high school provided that he has had at least 1 year of supervised weight training. A basic rule-of-thumb strength base for plyometrics would be the ability to perform a one repetition maximum (1RM) in the squat of 1½ times his body weight. Beginners should start with low-intensity, simple plyometrics such as basic rope jumping, jumps from the ground, and double-leg bounds and hops. As power increases and technique improves, more advanced drills may be added, such as one-legged drills and depth jumps. Power gains will result as the exercises increase in intensity and difficulty and the progressive overloads force the athlete's muscles to work harder.

Because the exercises are demanding, the athlete must be fresh for each set. He should rest for 1 or 2 minutes between sets. The rest periods should be active ones with light stretching, shaking, and loosening of the muscles. The athlete should not rush into another set unless he is physically and psychologically ready. If he becomes tired, the risk of injury is high and the training effect will be minimal.

Explosive-reactive power is the athlete's goal. He can achieve this goal only by treating each exercise as an all-out, maximal effort. Each effort requires the utmost concentration and physical effort. The exercises are done quickly, never slowly and lazily. Beginners often spend too much time absorbing the impact of landing. To correct this fault, they should think of the ground as a "hot stove" and spring off it quickly.

Safety Tips

During plyometrics the athlete should wear supportive shoes. The landing surface can be a smooth, resilient grassy field that is free of ruts or holes, or it can be a wrestling mat. Hopping, jumping, and bounding on hard or slippery surfaces such as concrete or gymnasium floors will cause injuries. On the other hand, if the landing surface is too soft it will absorb the impact too much, and the elastic recoil and training effect will be reduced.

The following plyometric exercises for the hips and legs are some of the ones that we use at the University of Virginia.

Jumps

1. *Double-leg-tuck jumps*—From a standing position, the athlete springs from the ground, flexing his hips in the air until his thighs are parallel to the ground (Figure 4-13). He then grasps his knees briefly with both hands, ex-

Figure 4-13 Double-leg tuck jump: With his hands up and touching at shoulder level, the athlete jumps ten times, bringing his knees up to his hands, and lands with a slight bend in his knees.

tends his legs to the ground, and repeats the exercise. He should perform two sets of ten jumps with a 1-minute rest between sets.

2. *Standing triple jump ("hop, step, and jump")*—The athlete jumps forward off both legs and lands on one foot (the hop). He then lets his momentum carry him forward to land on his opposite foot (the step) and concludes by jumping from that foot to a two-footed landing (the jump). He should perform five full triple jumps with a 1-minute rest between each jump.

3. *Standing long jump*—The athlete begins these jumps from a starting line with his feet shoulder-width apart. He leaps forward as far as he can using his arms to assist in this movement. He should perform five full jumps, rest 2 minutes, and repeat.

Hops

1. *Double-leg-speed hops*—The athlete stands erect and hops forward on both legs, concentrating on height rather than distance. He should perform two sets of ten consecutive hops, with a 1-minute rest between sets.

2. *Single-leg-speed hops*—Starting with a two-legged pushoff, the athlete lands on a single foot and takes off from that foot. He should perform two sets of ten consecutive hops (each leg), concentrating on height rather than distance, with a 1-minute rest between sets.

3. *Bag, box, cone, hurdle, tire, or cinder block jumps*—With feet together, the athlete clears the first cone and then goes forward over the next ones. He should perform two sets over at least six cones, with a 2-minute rest between sets.

4. *Bag, box, cone, hurdle, tire, or cinder block hops*—The athlete stands beside a cone with his feet together. He then hops over and back repeatedly. He should perform two sets for 30 seconds each, with a 2-minute rest between sets.

Bounds

Bounds are exaggerations of the normal running stride that lead to faster running and higher jumping by improving stride length (Figure 4-14). Each drill should be followed by a 1-minute rest between sets.

1. *Single-leg bounds*—With a running start, the athlete bounds on a single leg for 25 yards. He shortens the radius of movement of his leg by tucking his heel against his buttocks and moves his thigh forward rapidly, extending his knee and reaching for a landing on the same

Figure 4-14 Power skipping (bounding): The athlete keeps the body erect and skips, driving the knees up as high as possible with power and good arm action, for two sets of 20 yards.

leg. He should perform two sets at a distance of 25 yards each.

2. *Alternate-leg bounds*—The athlete uses the same "reaching and pulling" technique as in the single-leg bound, but the landings are on alternate feet. He should perform two sets at a distance of 25 yards each.

3. *Combination bounds*—The athlete does combinations of single-leg bounds or combines alternate and single-leg bounds rhythmically, for example, L-L-R, R-R-L, or LL-RR-LL patterns. He should perform two sets at a distance of 25 yards each.

Depth Jumps

The athlete begins depth jumps from 12-inch high boxes and works up to 16-, 20-, 24-, 26-, and 30-inch boxes. During the foundation phase, he does depth jumps from boxes up to 24 inches high. In the preparation phase, he does depth jumps twice a week, working up to the highest possible box. He should perform three sets of ten repetitions.

For forward depth jumps, the athlete drops off a low box onto a mat or grass and leaps up onto a higher box. He can hold his arms still by placing his hands on his hips. Otherwise the arm movement will transfer momentum from his legs to his torso. The athlete should not allow his legs to "give" before rebounding. Instead the rebound or "explosive reflex" should be immediate from knees that are flexed. He should not do depth jumping if his knees are sore.

Upper Body Plyometrics

The athlete can gain upper body power by doing plyometric exercises. These exercises are simply an extension of lower body plyometrics. They are especially important for baseball and basketball players, field-event participants in the shot, discus, javelin, and pole vault, football linemen, gymnasts, and wrestlers.

Upper body plyometrics can duplicate any sport movement with an intensity that is equal to or greater than that which occurs in the sport. The plyometric principle is applied when the ath-

lete catches a heavy object and then immediately pushes it away or throws it. The catching and throwing motions are performed at high levels of concentration and intensity.

The baseball player can practice his swing with a heavier-than-normal bat. He starts the bat back quickly and then reverses the direction suddenly to swing it forward. A gymnast can do drop push-ups, rebounding off the ground onto low boxes. This exercise builds the power needed to push off during vaulting or to work on the pommel horse or to do free exercise. The athlete can also catch and throw medicine balls, weighing from 3 to 15 pounds or more, against a wall or catch and throw them with a partner. He can do this while standing, kneeling, sitting, or lying down.

The athlete can also catch and throw a weight, such as a heavy punching bag or an automobile tire. that is suspended by a rope from the ceiling. The athlete swings the weight away from him. As it swings back, he catches it at shoulder height, allowing it to stretch his throwing arm, shoulder, and torso muscles. He then quickly follows the catch with a throwing motion and projects the object in the opposite direction. The intensity of the workout can be increased by increasing the weight, by increasing the distance thrown, or by increasing the length of the rope.

CYCLE TRAINING (PERIODIZATION)

My job as a strength and conditioning coach is to develop programs for our athletes that will enable them to be in an optimum state of readiness for the competitive season. To do this, I use a system of long-range planning called periodization or cycle training that was developed in the 1950s by sports scientists in the Soviet Union. The program sets specific objectives or short-range goals during a yearly training program. By following this program, an athlete can be at physical and mental peaks when necessary. It should be noted, however, that an athlete can peak only twice a year. If the frequency, duration, and intensity of training are too great, the athlete will overtrain, peak prematurely, and suffer from fatigue. His nervous system then shuts down, strength gains stop, performance suffers, and the athlete may even become ill or injured.

Signs of overtraining include the following:

1. Excessive soreness
2. Decreased body weight
3. Decreased tolerance to illness
4. Increased injury rate
5. Increased resting and working heart rates
6. Lift plateaus
7. Decreased quality of sports performance

To allow peaking and to avoid overtraining, we build sharp breaks in the types of exercises, sets, and repetitions into the training program at regular intervals. These sharp breaks or changes in volume and intensity stimulate or "shock" the athlete's nervous system, causing positive adaptations in his body. Variation is the key. The program uses a wide variety of equipment—free weights and machines—and exercises with multiple sets at varying speeds.

I divide each year into training blocks or phases: foundation phase, preparation phase, precompetition phase, in-season maintenance phase, and active rest phase. The athlete starts with general exercises at low intensity and progresses to higher and higher intensities, with a 2-minute rest between each.

Because I am responsible for designing strength and conditioning programs for 600 athletes in 23 varsity sports, a computer is a great help (Figure 4-15). The computer saves time and shows goals and projections. If the immediate projections seem low, the goals can be changed easily and a new projection entered promptly.

Training Phases

Foundation Phase

During the foundation phase, the athlete establishes a fitness base. He builds a foundation of strength and conditioning so that he can reach performance peaks when necessary. In addition, injuries are rehabilitated, weaknesses strengthened, and imbalances diagnosed and rectified. The exercises are of low intensity with a high volume of work and high repetitions with gradually increasing poundage (see Displayed Extract below). The athlete starts at about 60% of his maximum repetition goal and tries to increase his major exercises by 5% each week. He establishes a conditioning base by distance running. This phase lasts 4 weeks in football.

Figure 4-15 Strength coach and athlete use a computer to check the athlete's workouts. The coach can thus make changes quickly for the many athletes for whom he is responsible.

Example of a 10-Week Cycle for the Bench Press, Hip Sled, or Squat, Power Clean, or High Pulls and Dead Lift

2 weeks of 10 repetitions
2 weeks of 8 repetitions
3 weeks of 5 repetitions
3 weeks of 3 repetitions

Preparation Phase

During this phase, the athlete builds basic strength through muscle hypertrophy. He increases intensity to medium level with a medium volume of work with midrange repetitions. The fitness base is built up further to ready him for the higher intensity work and power specialization of the later stages. All sets for major exercises during this phase are performed for five repetitions with increases of 5% per week. The athlete also starts interval sprints and agilities, and hopping and bounding exercises are worked in gradually. This phase lasts for 3 weeks in football.

Precompetition Phase

In this phase, the athlete is brought to a peak in strength, power, and conditioning. All activities become sport-specific, and he works at a very high intensity. Assistive exercises are reduced, poundage is increased, and repetitions are reduced to three. At the end of this period, all athletes are tested for maximum lifts. The athlete now performs maximum speed and agility drills, and these drills are timed. This phase lasts for 3 weeks in football.

In-Season Maintenance Phase

The last phase is the in-season maintenance phase. All activities are now specific to the speed of movement of the particular sport. The volume of training is reduced to what is necessary to maintain what was built during the first three phases. The number of repetitions will vary according to the needs of the athletes in their respective sports.

Active Rest Phase

The in-season maintenance phase is followed by 2 weeks of "active rest." During this phase, the athlete engages in activities other than his sport. For example, a football player might play basketball or volleyball or swim. This rest is important for long-term progress.

SPORT-SPECIFIC STRENGTH TRAINING

Each sport has specific strength needs, and a coach must be able to design programs that meet these needs. The following sections introduce some of the training programs for various sports.

Baseball

Baseball players used to concentrate only on the skills and techniques of the game itself. But baseball requires the ability to sprint, change direction quickly, and move laterally along with the unique activities of swinging a bat and throwing the baseball. Strength training improves these abilities and enhances the unique skills.

In batting, the athlete drives forward with his legs, rotates his pelvis, and transfers momentum through the midsection to his shoulders. His wrists then swing into ulnar deviation. Tubic pulls simulate the baseball swing. Other exercises include arm crosses with pulleys and dumbbell flys. Forearm and wrist strengthening exercises include pronation and supination, wrist curls, and reverse curls. Batters will usually use heavier weights for upper body work than will pitchers.

A pitcher lifts his forward leg with his hip flexors and abdominal muscles. He then strides forward to shift his weight, and his pelvic girdle rotates with a further weight shift into a lunging position. His shoulder then rotates, and he follows through with internal rotation of the shoulder and flexion of the wrist.

CYCLE TRAINING YEARLY OVERVIEW CHART FOR FOOTBALL

Cycle Phase	Strength Training	Conditioning	Goal
FOUNDATION (hypertrophy) 4 weeks * †	General work—very little actual event participation High volume work High repetition lifting (10 reps) Longer duration and frequency of training sessions Four times a week	General work High volume work Distance running	Fitness base
PREPARATION 3 weeks football * †	Specific work on all factors affecting football performance Moderate event participation Medium volume Higher-intensity midrange repetitions in lifting (5 reps) Moderate duration and frequency	Specific work Medium volume Higher intensity 12-minute run Agilities—220s begin	Basic strength
PRECOMPETITION 3 weeks football A transformation phase †	Very specific work on factors affecting football performance High-volume event participation Low-volume work Assistive exercises reduced Very high intensity Low repetitions but heavy weights ending in maximum workout (3 reps)	Very specific work Low volume work Very high intensity Agilities, sprints High event participation All-out effort	Strength-power
IN-SEASON MAINTENANCE	Very sport-specific work Low volume Lower intensity 70% to 80% of maximum load (10 reps)	On-field conditioning by coaches Maintain fitness level achieved in former three phases	Win football games

*Build-up phase.
†Off-season preparatory phases.

At the end of the season the athlete rests and does no weight training at all. When he begins the new cycle, he is tested and evaluated comprehensively. New daily goals are set. He starts the new cycle at a higher point than his beginning efforts of the last cycle.

Exercises for pitchers work the hips, legs and midsection, shoulder, forearm, wrist, and hand. During barbell or dumbbell lunges, his forward leg bends to a 90° angle while his back knee almost touches the floor. He strengthens his midsection with supine twists or "Russian twists." He strengthens his shoulders with pull-downs, pull-overs, and bent-over rows. The deltoid has three important parts: anterior, middle, and posterior. Each part must be strengthened. He strengthens the anterior part by doing front raises with his elbow bent and thumb up, the middle part by doing lateral raises with his palm down, and the posterior part by bent-over raises with his thumb down. A strong posterior part of the deltoid is particularly important for a pitcher because this part of the muscle is often underdeveloped and overbalanced.

Basketball

Basketball is a game in which the athlete needs power to jump for rebounds, to take jump shots, and to block shots and strength to block out and hold position under the backboard. The strength program should take into account the number of games to be played and the need for recovery.

Jumping employs the same plyometric moves used by Olympic-style weight lifters in high pulls and power cleans. Because these lifters develop great vertical jumping ability, basketball players profit from adopting some of the lifters' training techniques, including the high pull, power cleans, and squats. Players are taught to skillfully perform the rotary hip jerk. Starting with the bar in the catch position, he dips about 15 cm (6 in), and, as his legs push off, the weight goes up.[20, 21] Other lifts include latissimus pulls for rebounding, bent-over rowing for grabbing the ball off the floor, and triceps extensions and wrist curls for increasing the shooting range.

The basketball player needs strong wrists and hands for shooting, dribbling, passing, and rebounding. This strength is gained by rope climbing, fingertip push-ups, and catching and passing a medicine ball. With a medicine ball, an eccentric contraction occurs during the catch and becomes a concentric one during the pass. Trunk curls and back hyperextensions with weights are very important because they tie the upper and lower body together.

To improve agility, the athlete may perform bench jumps, jumping back and forth sideways over a narrow 45-cm (18 in)-high bench for 30 seconds, do forward and backward runs, cuts, and shuffle drills, and jump rope.

Field Events

The shotput, discus, hammer, and javelin events require great body control because the athlete must throw with his whole body. To develop a strength base for power, he should start his training by concentrating on the three core lifts—the bench press, squat, and power clean. The shot putter strengthens his trunk rotators and abdominal muscles by means of twisting sit-ups and twists with a loaded bar. Rotational training is important for the throwing sports and for the rotational and lateral movements needed in most other sports. Explosive one-arm jerk presses help the athlete develop power, and incline presses serve his needs better than standard bench presses. Fingertip push-ups strengthen his hands.

A strong midsection is especially important for the discus thrower, and for this reason trunk exercises make up nearly half of his strength workout. Trunk curls and back hyperextensions "tie" his upper and lower body together, and twists help to develop his midsection. To perform twists, the athlete lies supine with his upper body and midsection extending over the edge of a high platform while a partner holds his legs down. The athlete holds a weight plate to simulate a discus and twists, reaching his throwing arm down toward the floor, then twists up again, doing maximinal repetitions in good form. He may also do twists while holding a plate with both hands. Side cleans are like power cleans, but the athlete stands sideways to the barbell and twists while lifting it.

The discus thrower also does dumbbell flys and pulley work. During flys, he keeps his elbow almost straight and his palm down. When he simulates the throw against pulley resistance, his hip must always lead. To develop lower extremity power, he does double-leg bounds over hurdles, one-legged bounds, and box jumps.[19]

Lunges are especially good for shot putters. Hammer throwers use pulleys, and javelin throwers do pull-overs on a cam machine and Tubics. The field-event athlete also benefits from trampoline work that teaches him how to handle his body in space. "Gaming," or free play in basketball, soccer, or racquetball, gives practice with starts, stops, jumps, and lateral movements.

Football

Football requires short and explosive bursts of energy for running, blocking, and tackling. My job is to coordinate a proper training cycle with the goal of improving each player's explosive power. The exercises develop flexibility, endurance, speed, agility, strength, and power. The athlete should build up safely to high-intensity, explosive bursts.

Football players lift four times per week because strength is a primary factor in their sport. Hip and leg power is emphasized in football, but upper body strength is important too, especially for players such as offensive linemen who are allowed to use their hands for blocking. Football players also follow a strict neck-strengthening program (Figure 4-16). Athletes in most other sports, such as basketball, swimming, or wrestling, lift three times per week during preseason. For these athletes, the major emphasis is on the sport itself, and the weight training is used as a supplement.

The preseason training last 10 weeks and usually ends the week before the athletes return for summer camp. The athlete's strength and power are then tested in the bench press, hip sled, power clean, vertical jump, and standing long jump (Figure 4-17). Winter max-outs are more extensive.

After testing, we refrain from lifting again until after two-a-day practices to avoid muscle fatigue. After two-a-days have ended, the players begin in-season maintenance by lifting four times per week, just as in the preseason—the only difference being that during preseason they lift for 1 hour and 15 minutes compared to only 15 minutes during the season. The in-season weight training maintains the strength level that was built during the preseason.

Once the football season has ended there is a period of 3 to 4 weeks of "active rest." During this low-intensity stage, the athlete maintains some level of conditioning by performing anything but a sport-specific event while preparing for examinations.

During the winter training program, the athlete increases his overall skill level and performance. His weaknesses are overcome and his strength is maintained. He also works on gaining maximum speed and strength. In addition to the strength work, he does sprints, distance running, and agility drills, which maximize explosive power, agility, and quickness.

Gymnastics

A gymnast may use free weights to develop strength, but his coach may also weave strengthening exercises into his practice sessions. This approach develops coordination and agility along with strength.

MONDAY	TUESDAY	WEDNESDAY	THURSDAY	FRIDAY	SATURDAY
Distance running	Chest	Distance running	Legs	Chest	Distance running
Legs	Shoulders	Plyometrics	Back	Shoulders	Plyometrics
Back	Arms	Skill work	Arms	Arms	
Skill work	Interval running			Interval running	

MONTH	PRACTICE	STRENGTH	CONDITIONING
January	Active rest Winter workouts Jan 18—March 26	Active rest 2 weeks foundation	Active rest Form running
February		2 weeks preparation 2 weeks precompetition	Agilities Plyometrics Timed distance runs
March	 Spring break	Testing Spring break	 Spring break
April	Spring football March 21—April 19	In-season maintenance (sport-specific training)	On-field conditioning with coaches
May	April 20—June 6 Exams and active rest		
June	Summer training June 9—August 9	Foundation—4 weeks Preparation—3 weeks	Form running and distance running Interval sprints and agilities
July		Precompetition—3 weeks testing	Plyometrics
August	Summer camp (2 a day) August 10—August 29	No lifting	On-field conditioning with coaches
September	In season August 30—November 28	In-season maintenance (sport-specific training)	On-field conditioning with coaches
October			
November			
December	Exams, break and active rest		

The gymnast first establishes a standard routine. Then, to tax him, the coach may increase the number of skills in his routine, increase the number of times the routine is executed, decrease the rest interval time, or speed up the routine. If the coach detects a specific weakness, that area in the routine may be isolated for strength work. For example, if a gymnast lacks the strength to press into a handstand on the parallel bars, he may increase his strength by an assisted swing or by handstand push-ups. Plyometic drills prepare the gymnast for tumbling runs.

Soccer

Soccer demands endurance, agility, and lower extremity power. Because soccer is such an aerobic sport, heavy leg training is not advised and brute strength is not necessary. The soccer strength-training program emphasizes exercises such as

Football Winter Max-outs

Name _____
Height: _____
Weight: _____
Body fat%: _____

Flexibility:
    Lower back: _____
    Hamstrings: _____
    Hips: _____
    Ankles: _____

Speed, agility, and power:
    300-yard shuttle run: _____
    40-yard dash: _____
    20-yard dash: _____
    Agility run: _____
    Vertical jump: _____
    Standing long jump: _____

Strength and power:
    Bench press: _____
    Bench press (max. reps.): _____
    Hip sled: _____
    Power clean: _____
    Dips: _____
    Chin-ups: _____

push-ups, dips, and chin-ups that are performed with the player's body as resistance. Soccer players train for strength only 2 days a week, as compared to 4 days a week for football players. Plyometrics are emphasized to develop power and agility. In these drills, the player uses total body movements that are specific to soccer movements.

Swimming

A swimmer pulls himself through the water, doing 90% of the work with his arms. He may use aids such as hand paddles, tubes, and floats to improve his upper body strength (Figure 4-18). Hand paddles add more resistance to the pull, and a tube and float restrict the swimmer's leg motion, requiring that his arms take up the slack.

Latissimus pull-downs and a back program are important for swimmers. Some swimmers enjoy the Nautilus pull-over machine that features a prestretch, although a swimmer may sublux his shoulders on this machine. A swimmer may also train on an isokinetic swim bench to develop powerful starts and push-offs, duplicating strokes in a horizontal position. Strong swimmers, however, usually overpower these machines and need too many repetitions for a good workout.

Circuit training is used by swimmers and wrestlers during the season and by other athletes in off-season conditioning programs to develop

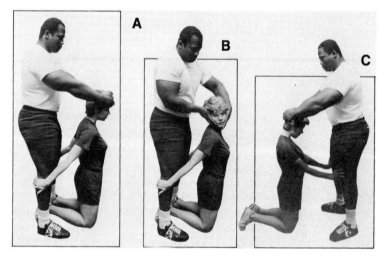

Figure 4-16 Neck strengthening through a complete range of motion: The athlete stabilizes herself by holding the coach's legs. She then brings her neck through a full range of motion against moderate resistance: first in flexion **(A)**, then in rotation **(B)**, and finally in extension **(C)**. There is no time limit for this exercise. Unlike the other partner exercises, this one is performed after the workout rather than before.

Figure 4-17 Vertical jump: The athlete's vertical jump is tested during summer testing and at winter max-outs. With his feet flat on the floor, and together, he first determines his reach **(A).** He keeps his hand flat with fingers together and reaches as high as he can on the vanes of the Ver-tec machine. He then assumes a quarter-squat, power takeoff position **(B).** He jumps up, fully extending to touch the highest possible vane **(C).** If he tries too hard, however, he will bend his arm and lose jumping height.

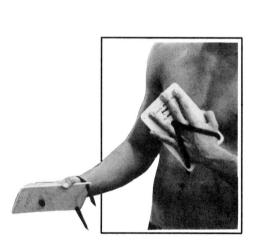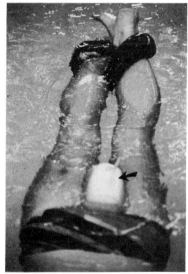

Figure 4-18 A swimmer can use hand paddles, a tube, and a float (*arrow*) to tax his arms.

muscular strength, power, and muscular and cardiovascular endurance. A circuit may consist of six to ten exercise stations set up so that the same group of muscles is not exercised at two consecutive stations; thus one muscle group will be recovering while another muscle group is being exercised. An athlete should do as many repetitions as possible with good form at 50% of one-repetition maximum in 30 seconds. He then should rest for 15 seconds to recover partially before advancing to the next station. With ten stations, the total time needed to perform three full sets will be just over 20 minutes. At the University of Virginia, our swimmer's circuit consists mainly of free weights and tapers as the swimming meets approach.

A swimmer can also have an intensive workout by swimming against Tubic resistance with lightweight bicycle inner tubes tied around him and around the starting platform. Special tanks have been developed to allow a swimmer to swim against a current, much as a salmon swims upstream. Lower extremity plyometric drills improve a swimmer's starts and turns.

Volleyball

The volleyball player needs lower body power for jumping and upper body strength for blocking and spiking. Exercises also protect the shoulders, back, knees, and ankles from breakdown injuries. The exercises are performed in a circuit and include rotary hip jerks and Tubic jumps. In Tubic jumps, the athlete jumps against Tubic resistance to simulate blocking moves. The player does the jumping drills twice a week during the off-season (first two phases only) for 12 to 15 minutes each session. The jumps are discontinued at the end of the off-season preparation part of the cycle.

Weight Lifting

How do weight lifting and weight training differ? Weight lifting is a competitive sport, whereas weight training is part of the preparation for sports. The yearly workload of weight lifters has increased sharply, with some men lifting 2000 to 2500 tons per year. For a lifter to train at this level, his coach must adjust the training program

and make changes at optimal times to produce the best results. Sound recovery methods for repair and recuperation, such as good food, adequate rest, and skilled massage, are equally important.

The lifter trains year-round, and his training cycle is divided into three periods: preparatory, competitive, and transitional. At the start of the preparatory period, he works on general conditioning to develop his strength, speed, endurance, agility, flexibility, and motor skills. He thus creates and improves the foundation on which to develop competitive form. His volume and intensity are gradually increased, with volume emphasized more. Later during this preparatory period, the lifter works proportionally more on competitive lifts and hones his technical skills in simulated practice competitions. Microcycles of heavier and lighter work, the "lead-up phase," bring the lifter to competition in optimal form.

During the competitive period, the lifter's objective is to achieve his best performance. He polishes his technique and mobilizes his physical and mental powers maximally. A postcompetitive microcycle follows immediately after competition for up to a week. During this time, he can rest and correct technical errors.

Weight lifting includes Olympic-style weight lifting, power lifting, and body building. The Olympic-style lifts are the snatch and clean-and-jerk (Figure 4-19). Power lifters perform the bench press, dead lift, and squat. Body builders "pump iron" to define and to proportion their muscles in preparation for posing.

Olympic-Style Weight Lifting

In the snatch, the athlete lifts the barbell, with his arms locked, from a position in front of his legs to above his head in a single, uninterrupted motion. He must then hold the barbell overhead for 2 seconds to receive the referee's signal.

The clean-and-jerk consists of two distinct moves, one to the chest and the second over the head. The pull from the floor places the barbell at the lifter's shoulders (the clean), and from this point he must lift it to an overhead, locked-arms position (the jerk).

Injuries to Olympic-style weight lifters may

Figure 4-19 Olympic lifting includes the snatch and the clean-and-jerk. The snatch **(A)** is an especially quick lift, whereas the clean-and-jerk **(B, C)** is slower but more weight is lifted.

include fractures, dislocated elbows, forearm tendon strains and forearm fractures, slipped distal radial epiphyses in young lifters, blisters, spondylolysis and spondylolisthesis, quadriceps or patella tendon ruptures, and knee problems, such as chondromalacia and meniscal tears.

As a heavy barbell is pressed overhead, the lifter's serratus anterior contracts to protract his scapula and hold it against the chest wall. The upper slip of the serratus anterior jerks on the first rib, and the rib cracks in its weak part at the subclavian groove. During the snatch, the weight lifter may dislocate his elbow, since the elbow is hyperextended when he holds a heavy weight. If his elbow strikes his thigh, his forearm tendons may be strained, or both bones of his forearm may break. A youth with poor lifting technique may slip his distal radial epiphysis as he catches the weight during the clean. Weight lifters often compete with painful blisters caused by calluses being ripped by the knurling on the bar. These may be prevented by good hand care and the use of hand wraps while training.[16]

Hyperextension of the weight lifter's spine may lead to spondylolysis and spondylolisthesis. The main offender, the Olympic press, is no longer included in weight-lifting competitions. Olympic-style weight lifters may also suffer quadriceps and patellar tendon ruptures. In one case of rupture, the force on the lifter's patella tendon was calculated to be more than 17 times his body weight with his knee flexed to 90°.[29] If a lifter has soreness in a major weight-bearing muscle group or tendon, he should refrain from training and from competing until the soreness has been alleviated through hot and cold applications and stretching in order to avoid a major rupture. Weight lifters develop knee problems from ballistic movements, such as squat snatches and the split in the clean-and-jerk. Barbell plates are 45 cm (18 in) in diameter; thus the bar is about 22.5 cm (9 in) above the platform. If a lifter slips under the bar, his raised knee may be caught and injured. Although Olympic lifters handle heavy loads, their injury rate is low because they train hard to develop technique, and their flexibility is exceptionally high.

Improper technique and inflexibility account for most of the injuries in Olympic-style weight lifting. A lifter needs full shoulder flexibility to "rotate out," that is, rotate his shoulders behind his back if the weight gets behind him. He may practice shoulder "dislocates" with a broomstick, starting with his hands out comfortably on the stick and moving them in a bit each week until the snatch grip is comfortable.

Weight lifting should be done only on a lifting platform. The area on and around the platform should be cleaned to give the lifter a clear area in which to bail out from an unsuccessful lift. In gymnasiums that lack a platform, mats are sometimes placed under the weights, but these may encourage a conscientious young lifter to fight the weight in an attempt to place it down properly, and he may injure himself.

A lifter is well advised not to perform maximum squats without a safety rack or spotters because he may fall forward and be badly injured. He should also wear weight-lifter's shoes with good midfoot support and a heel that aids his balance.

Power Lifting

Power lifters compete in three lifts: the bench press, the dead lift, and the squat. In the dead lift, the lifter stands up while holding the weight, using a combination overhand and underhand grip to keep the bar from rotating. A super heavyweight can deadlift more than 405 kg (900 lb). In the bench press, the lifter lowers the bar to his chest and waits for the referee's signal before pressing it up. Although super heavyweight power lifters can bench press more than 225 kg (500 lb), their pectoralis major sometimes tears. If the tear is in the muscle mass, it is not repaired; if the tendon of the pectoralis major rips, however, it should be repaired. In squats, the loaded bar is on the lifter's shoulders, and he must bend his knees to more than 90°, then stand up. Power lifters take a deep breath and execute before breathing again. The power lifter is handling very heavy weights; thus technique must be mastered to limit injuries.

Body Building

Body builders lift weights to develop all of their muscle groups in proper proportion and symmetry.[23] They assess their development with mirrors, like sculptors observing the progress of their work.

A body builder enters a contest shaved, oiled, and "pumped," and his definition, proportion, symmetry, and posing determine his score. He must be flexible because he needs a good range of motion for posing. These athletes are strong, but the strongest body builder is not necessarily the most successful. They sustain few musculoskeletal injuries in competition but do strain muscles when training, and their cardiovascular endurance is similar to that of healthy sedentary subjects. If a body builder stops training, his muscles will shrink about 50%, but if he maintains only a light training schedule, good musculature will remain.

Many body builders take anabolic steroids despite the dangers of liver cancer and shrunken testes. Some athletes, however, reach the highest levels of body building without using these drugs. Female body builders tone up and develop bulk that is dependent on their testosterone level, and those who take anabolic steroids risk damage to complex hormonal mechanisms.

Weight-Lifter's Blackout

A weight lifter may become dizzy and confused and suddenly fall to the floor while lifting a heavy barbell. This occurs most commonly after a hard stand-up while cleaning a weight in the clean-and-jerk. Such blackouts are caused by a combination of events that lead to a fall in cerebral blood flow, including hyperventilation, squatting, and lifting the weight and holding it while breathing again.[5]

Many competitors overbreathe just before lifting in the belief that this will help to produce a maximum effort. Such hyperventilation, however, reduces a lifter's cerebral blood flow by dilating muscle vessels while constricting cerebral vessels. If the lifter remains in a squatting position for a long time while preparing for the stand-up that must follow, he may suffer peripheral vasodilation and may become dizzy as both his peripheral resistance and the venous return to his heart drop.

Esophageal pressure ballons record that the lifter's thoracic pressure rises greatly (in the range of 60 mm Hg) when weight is lifted. Without this climb in intratruncal pressure and added pneumatic support, the forces on the lifter's spine would exceed his capacity to resist them. Raised intrathoracic pressure is initially transmitted to central vessels and to the arterial pulse. The high pressure, however, also obstructs venous return so that the cardiac volume, stroke volume, and pulse pressure soon begin to fall. If the lift takes a long time to perform, even more time is available for reflex vasodilatation in response to the initial rise in arterial pressure. Cineradiography shows that the heart size becomes greatly reduced during the lifting phase, and the pulsations of the heart, pulmonary artery, and aorta are barely visible.

At the end of the clean, the lifter holds the weight and catches his breath in preparation for the jerk, causing the intrathoracic pressure to drop acutely. The arterial blood pressure falls steeply to as little as 50 mm Hg. Simultaneously, the great veins and splanchnic vessels expand, and the filling of these expanded vessels causes a lag in blood reaching the left ventricle. Three or four electrocardiographic complexes go by unaccompanied by an arterial pressure wave, suggesting the absence of ventricular ejection. Cineradiography shows that the pulmonary artery pulsates almost immediately but aortic pulsation is delayed. The lifter's heart has "pumped dry," and he faints from cerebral ischemia.

Spirits of ammonia will usually be helpful in reviving an unconscious lifter. Inhalation of the irritating vapor reflexly stimulates his medullary centers by way of the trigeminal, and perhaps the olfactory, nerves.[30] Resistance blood vessels in his limbs constrict, his systemic blood pressure rises, and his capacitance vessels reflexly constrict, all serving to raise his cardiac filling pressure and to revive him.

A lifter is less likely to "black out" if he avoids hyperventilation. Squatting should be as brief as possible, with the weight quickly raised and normal breathing resumed. When a lifter feels that he is losing the weight, he can back out from under it by pushing the bar. Experienced lifters know when a lift is lost, whereas a novice may fight the weight and be injured. A competitive lifter must occasionally fight lifts that are not in perfect balance, but he is aware when he is going to lose the lift.

Wrestling

Wrestling is explosive work in all directions against resistance. A wrestler pushes, pulls, lifts, and uses leg action; thus the muscles involved in these movements are worked during a weight program.[3, 4, 7, 8, 14, 24] Strength training for wrestling should be explosive and of high intensity. In the off-season the wrestler works for strength and power, and in the preseason and in-season he works with more repetitions for muscular stamina. Strength, however, is often lost over a wrestling season because workouts are continuous for 5 ro 6 days a week and the wrestler is trying to control his weight. The strength decline is tempered by two-man resistive drills, chinning, rope climbing, and specific wrestling exercises, such as body lifts. Because strength can be increased only by overload, a wrestler must work with weights at least two times a week during the season to maintain his strength. Pulling movements are emphasized with dumbbells, pulleys, and Tubics serving as resistance. Hands can be strengthened by climbing a rope, doing fingertip push-ups, and by throwing and catching a medicine ball.

The wrestler should establish an aerobic base with distance runs before the season; during the season, he may sprint, run stairs, and run short hills. Circuit weight training also helps to provide needed endurance. "Burnouts," or high-intensity weight-training workouts until exhaustion, are excellent but may be too grueling for most wrestlers. Burnouts bring out a wrestler's competitive instincts much as a match does and may give him a psychological edge, especially in the final period of a match. They should not, however, be done more than once every few weeks.

A wrestler can perform some of the moves normally used in a match by practicing against Tubic resistance. A Greco–Roman wrestler can practice his throws on a dummy usually 25% lighter than his weight class. With this preparation, the wrestler enters the match fully warmed up and ready to use all his moves right from the start, thus lowering his chance of injury.

TRAINING INJURIES

Muscle Soreness

Acute muscle soreness starts during or immediately after exercise and may persist for a few hours. Stress-induced ischemia impairs the muscle's ability to quickly remove metabolic waste products, such as lactic acid and potassium, and these accumulate to cause pain. When the athlete stops exercising, blood flow increases, and his pain soon disappears.

Delayed soreness appears from 8 to 48 hours after exercise[12] and may result from tears of tissue, tissue irritation, local muscle spasm, or eccentric work. Violent exercise may tear muscular or tendinous tissue. High hydroxyproline levels are found when there is delayed soreness; thus connective tissue irritation may be a factor. During less vigorous exercise, local muscle spasm will produce ischemia, releasing pain substances that stimulate pain endings and provoke further local muscle spasm. Finally, heavy eccentric work may generate a diffuse, delayed soreness.

A full warm-up will help the athlete prevent soreness. He should follow the training principle of *progression*, with gradual increases in his workload and its duration. Athletes are also advised to warm down to dissipate waste. Ice can be applied to exercised areas to lessen muscle spasm, followed by massage to rid the area of wastes and a pneumatic, intermittent pressure device to press out edema.

The athlete with muscular soreness should stretch statically to the point of pain onset and hold the stretch there. If the soreness is severe, he may be given cryotherapy with ice massage or ice packs. When ice is applied, he will first feel coldness and then aching. The area soon becomes numb, and he may then begin stretching, performing 1-minute stretches in sets of three, separated by 5 minutes of ice massage.

Muscle Cramps

Muscle cramps may be due to electrolyte depletion or to fatigue where partial relaxation causes spasm. When an athlete changes from everyday walking shoes with heels to sports shoes with no heels, running on soft ground may cause increased tension in his calf muscles, generating fatigue and cramps. Athletes salt their food or eat potato chips during two-a-day workout periods to replace the salt that they have lost through sweating and to prevent muscle cramps. Moreover, they should follow a good stretching program and avoid fashionable high-heeled footwear to help keep cramps to a minimum.

When a cramp occurs, the athlete should lie down while the examiner grasps the affected muscle and squeezes it firmly from the sides. When the spasm stops, the muscle should be stretched through its normal range of motion and massaged to help restore circulation. An athlete may stop his own cramps by squeezing the muscle firmly or, in the case of calf cramps, by grabbing his toes and pulling them toward him, then releasing and repeating this procedure. An unusual but often effective method for relieving a cramp is to pinch the athlete's upper lip.[1]

Returning to Weight Training After an Injury or After Surgery

An injured athlete can return to the weight room after he has reached a predetermined level of rehabilitation in the sports medicine department. However, an athlete who returns to major lifts too soon after an injury risks further injury. My responsibility, therefore, is to individualize his program, making sure that he resumes his training gradually, and to encourage patience and determination. By following a systematic exercise program, we can determine his readiness for return to full training.

Grade II Acromioclavicular Sprain

A typical case might involve an athlete with an acromioclavicular sprain who wishes to return to bench presses. He begins resistance exercises with shoulder flexion, extension, and abduction while holding a 1-pound weight. When he can perform 20 repetitions of these exercises painlessly with a 10-pound dumbbell, he can return to the bench. He then selects a weight he can bench press for ten repetitions without pain.

From this point, he increases gradually to his previous level.

<u>Arthroscopic Selective Meniscectomy</u>

Another example is the athlete who has had an arthroscopic selective meniscectomy. When this athlete is permitted to return to the weight room, he usually can do knee extensions with about 45 pounds. He continues the knee extensions for the first week with small increases in weight and then progresses to the leg press machine with light weights for about a week in addition to continuing the knee extensions and

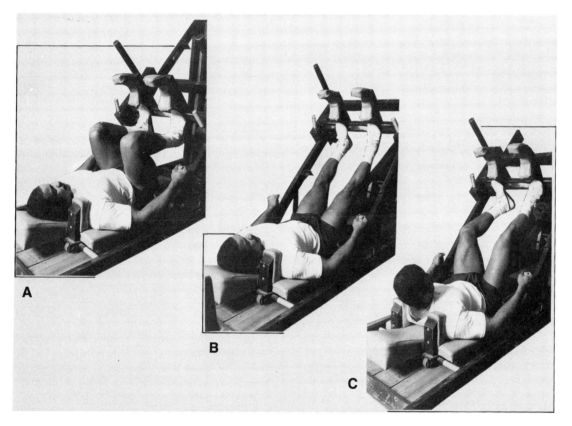

Figure 4-20 The hip sled. The athlete uses the hip sled during in-season strength training and when recovering from an injury. The hip sled puts less stress on the back than do squats. On the sled, the athlete keeps his head on the pad and his back down. He starts the lift with his hips at a 45° angle from his chest **(A).** The balls of his feet are on the foot plates and he extends his hips and knees **(B).** Common errors on the hip sled include raising the head **(C)** and having the feet either turned out too much or turned in.

some hamstring curls. By the third week, he may be ready for the hip sled, which is used in place of squats. The hip sled involves little technique compared to the squat and is safer for an injured athlete (Figure 4-20). The carriage alone on the hip sled weighs 150 pounds, which compares to a squat of about 60 pounds. If the athlete were doing squats, the knee problem might cause him to change his lifting technique and he could injure the knee. By week four, he may be ready to do a full leg workload. When he has worked up to 60% of his best effort on the hip sled in addition to still doing the knee extensions and hamstring curls, he has recovered enough to return to full training on the playing field.

REFERENCES

1. Allen MF: Acupinch. First Aider, Cramer 50(4):11, 1980
2. Anderson B: Stretching. Bolinas, California, Shelter Publications Random House, 1980
3. Bolkavadze TA: Strength preparation of the wrestler. NSCA J 8(6):71–73, 1986
4. Christensen C: Relative strength in males and females. Athletic Training 10(4):189–192, 1975
5. Compton D et al: Weight-lifter's blackout. Lancet 2:1234–1237, 1973
6. De Bruyn–Provost P: The effects of various warming up intensities and durations upon some physiological variables. Eur J Appl Phys 43:93–100, 1980
7. Dziedzic S, Farrell W: USA National Weight Training and Conditioning Program for Wrestlers: Part II. Natl Strength Conditioning Assoc J 1(5):14–17, 1979
8. Dziedzic S, Farrell W: USA National Weight Training and Conditioning for Wrestling: Part III. Natl Strength Conditioning Assoc J 1(6):16–19, 1979
9. Gonyea WJ et al: Skeletal muscle fiber splitting induced by weight-lifting exercise in cats. Acta Physiol Scand 99:105–109, 1977
10. Gonyea WJ: The role of exercise in inducing increases in skeletal muscle fiber number. J Appl Physiol 48:421–426, 1980
11. Hoolahan P: Strength and conditioning for basketball. Natl Strength Conditioning Assoc J 2(5):32–34, 1980
12. Hough T: Ergographic studies in muscular soreness. Am J Physiol 7:76–92, 1902
13. Jensen C: Pertinent facts about warm-up. Athletic J 56(2):72–75, 1975
14. Johnson M, Yesalis C: Strength training and conditioning for wrestling: The Iowa approach. NSCA (4): 56–59, 1986
15. Karpovich PV, Hale C: Effect of warming-up upon physical performance. JAMA 162:1117–1119, 1956
16. Kulund DN et al: Olympic weight-lifting injuries. Phys Sportsmed 6:11, November 1978
17. Lorette LH: Strength training modalities: The medicine ball. NSCA 7(2):18–19, 1985
18. Martin BJ: Effect of warm-up on metabolic responses to strenuous exercise. Med Sci Sports 7:146–149, 1975
19. McDermott A: Plyometric training for the throwing events. NSCA J 8(4):52–55, 1986
20. Miller C: Rotary action of leg and hips common to many sports. Natl Strength Conditioning Assoc J 1(6):20–22, 1979
21. Miller C: Sequence exercise to learn the rotary action of the legs and hips common to many sports. Natl Strength Conditioning Assoc J 2(3):38–39, 1980
22. Milner-Brown HS et al: Synchronization of human motor units: Possible roles of exercise and supraspinal reflexes. Electroencephalogr Clin Neurophysiol 38:245–254, 1975
23. Pipes TV: Physiologic characteristics of elite body builders. Phys Sportsmed 7(3):116–121, 1979
24. Stucky J, Palmieri GA: Strength and conditioning for wrestling. NSCA J 7(5):40–42, 1985
25. Stull GA, Clarke DH: High-resistance, low-repetition training as a determiner of strength and fatigability. Res Q 41:189–193, 1970
26. Wilmore JH: Alterations in strength, body composition and anthropometric measurements consequent to a ten-week weight training program. Med Sci Sports 6:133–138, 1974
27. Wilmore JH: Exploding the myth of female inferiority. Phys Sportsmed 2:54–58, 1974
28. Yessis M: The key to strength development: Variety. Natl Strength Conditioning Assoc J 3(3):32–34, 1981
29. Zernike RF et al: Human patellar tendon rupture. A kinetic analysis. J Bone Joint Surg [Am] 59:179–183, 1977
30. Zitnik RS et al: Hemodynamic effects of inhalation of ammonia in man. Am J Cardiol 24:187–190, 1969
31. Zorbas W, Karpovich P: The effect of weightlifting upon the speed of muscular contractions. Res Q 22:145–148, 1951

CHAPTER

5

Psychological Care of the Injured Athlete

Robert J. Rotella

After an injury, an athlete typically undergoes a sequence of predictable psychological reactions similar to those of a person facing death.[16]

1. Disbelief, denial, and isolation
2. Anger
3. Bargaining
4. Depression
5. Acceptance and resignation while continuing to remain hopeful

An athlete initially responds to an injury by saying that there is no damage, that the injury is less severe than originally thought, or that it will probably be better tomorrow. When tomorrow comes and the injury remains, the athlete feels isolated and lonely. Once the athlete begins attending to the injury, he commonly becomes irritated with himself and others. Anger is followed by a true sense of loss. With his arm in a sling or

his leg in a cast, he lacks his ordinary comfort and freedom. He is well aware that the injured limb makes the difference between actually competing and merely watching from the sidelines. Ideally, this depression stage should be followed by that of acceptance and hope, but various factors may intervene to delay or prevent this from happening.

AN ATHLETE'S PERCEPTION OF INJURY

Athletes perceive injuries in different ways. One may perceive the injury as a disaster, another may see it as an opportunity to show courage, and yet another may find it a welcome relief from the embarrassment of poor performance, lack of playing time, or a losing season. The injured athlete may wonder whether he will completely recover.

151

He must be prepared for the end of participation and yet remain positive and enthusiastic about the prospect of total recovery. Because of his injury, his self-image is attacked, and he loses the opportunity to display prowess. If the injury should end his athletic career, he may suffer an "identity crisis."

Emotional and irrational thinking may take over. The injured athlete may become lost in "the work of worry," excuse his own mistakes and responsibilities, and be overwhelmed by anxiety. These self-defeating thought patterns may interfere in his recovery.

When an athlete is thinking irrationally, he may exaggerate the meaning of an event, disregard important aspects of a situation, oversimplify events as good or bad, right or wrong, overgeneralize from a single event, or draw unwarranted conclusions, even though evidence is lacking or contradictory.[3] He may, for example, decide that the trainer is giving preferential treatment to "major-sport" athletes over "minor-sport" ones. He may exaggerate the meaning of an event, thinking his athletic career has been ended by the injury. He may disregard important aspects of a situation and become terribly discouraged after, for example, 10 days of therapy, even though he was told it would take at least 2 or 3 weeks to complete. The injured athlete may oversimplify events or overgeneralize from a single event. He may, for instance, know of another athlete who had a similar injury and, despite intensive rehabilitation, failed to recover. Because of this, he may believe that nothing can help him to recover. Moreover, an athlete who is injured once may decide that he is "injury prone." This thought may cause him to be more anxious, and as a result he may well become more frequently injured.

COPING WITH INJURY

When injury occurs, the athlete should be encouraged to view it in a rational, self-enhancing way rather than from a self-defeating perspective. He should understand that when an injury blocks the attainment of important goals, it is reasonable and appropriate to think that the injury is unfortunate, untimely, and inconvenient and to feel irritated, frustrated, and sad. It is unreasonable, however, for an athlete to convince himself that the situation is hopeless, that the injury should be hidden from his coach or trainer, that the season or his career has ended, and that he will never again be able to perform effectively.

An athlete with emotional self-control will be able to cope with his injury by responding rationally to it, and not being overwhelmed by it. He can best exert self-control if he has knowledge of his injury and the rehabilitation process. He cannot be positive and relaxed if he is unknowledgeable, anxious, and wondering. Much of an injured athlete's anxiety results from uncertainty, misconceptions, or inaccurate information. If uncertainty persists, he may have trouble getting through the denial and isolation states. Honest and accurate information, padded with hope, helps him move into the acceptance stage.[15] Further, the athlete who understands what he is doing in rehabilitation, and why, is more likely to work hard and be able to provide useful information to the trainer about his progress.

What an athlete says to himself and imagines after an injury has occurred helps to determine his behavior. Fortunately, he can learn coping skills to control his thoughts and what he says to himself. When he notices faulty or self-defeating internal dialogues, he can use his coping strategies to change his thinking.[3,20–23] He may use an intervention strategy such as "thought stoppage."

When his faulty thinking is recognized, the athlete says "STOP" and then repeats self-enhancing thoughts. A sports psychologist can help him recognize faulty thought patterns and anticipate destructive thoughts and can "inoculate" the athlete with coping strategies. Team physicians and trainers can also learn to teach these strategies that may shorten the time the injured athlete needs to progress from disbelief to acceptance, to productive rehabilitation, and to a safe, successful return to competition.

In addition to coping with faulty thinking, the injured athlete will have to cope with the conditions of the hospital and training room and the stress of special treatment procedures. He is encouraged to express his feelings, to establish rapport with hospital and training room staffs, and to balance accepting help from others with re-

Controlling Inner Dialogue
with Thought Stoppage

Injury-related situation (potential source of stress): The extent of the injury is explained to the athlete and a rehabilitation program outlined.

Self-defeating inner dialogue: The athlete worries about the injury and feels sorry for himself. "I'll never play again this year, if ever." "There's no sense listening to this; it will heal itself eventually anyway. I know others who went to therapy, and it didn't help them." The athlete is so preoccupied with self-defeating thoughts that he does not even hear the rationale for rehabilitation or the program outlined. He gives himself excuses for missing treatments.

Self-enhancing inner dialogue: The athlete recognizes that worrying and feeling sorry for himself have no value. He stops thinking negatively and redirects his thoughts to listening closely to the rehabilitation program outlined. He asks questions about the exercises he is unsure of. He directs his thoughts to preparation for tomorrow's first treatment session. He plans his schedule for tomorrow and looks forward to rehabilitation in a positive manner.

7:30 A.M.

Injury-related situation: The athlete gets up and limps to the training room for rehabilitation exercises, but the training room is locked with no trainer in sight.

Self-defeating inner dialogue: The athlete gets mad at the trainer for not showing up for the therapy session. "This is typical. He never shows up. He gives me a big talk on the importance of rehabilitation and then he doesn't show up. To hell with him! I won't show up anymore either until he comes and apologizes to me." The athlete, seeing only the negative side, accepts no responsibility for himself. He fails to realize that he will be the one who will suffer by not getting therapy.

Self-enhancing inner dialogue: The athlete gets mad but then recognizes that this is self-defeating. He relaxes, takes a deep breath, and thinks: "I wonder what happened. He never misses a treatment. Something important must have happened. I know he wants me to get better, and if I'm going to get better, I will need my treatments. If I don't get them, I will be the loser. I'll wait or stop by later to get another meeting time for my treatment." The athlete attempts to understand why the trainer did not show up. He recognizes the importance of taking responsibility for therapy and makes sure that he gets it, so that he can return to action sooner.

10:30 A.M.

Injury-related situation: In class, the athlete is getting constant attention from his classmates about his injury.

Self-defeating inner dialogue: The athlete enjoys the attention. "This is nice. I enjoy the attention. I feel special. Gosh, many people who never recognized me before now know who I am." The athlete begins to enjoy the attention of others that comes from being injured. Consciously or unconsciously, he may begin to like being injured and to question the value of a speedy rehabilitation.

Self-enhancing inner dialogue: The athlete enjoys the attention but recognizes that this may work to his disadvantage by decreasing his motivation to get better. The athlete thinks, "It's nice to know that others care, but I don't want their sympathy; I want their respect as an athlete. The best way to get it is to rehabilitate myself and get back into competition." The athlete feels good that others care about him and uses these thoughts to motivate himself to return quickly to competition.

2:30 P.M.

Injury-related situation: The athlete is in the training room receiving treatment and going through rehabilitation exercises while experiencing a great amount of pain and little apparent improvement in the injured part.

(continued)

Controlling Dialogue with Thought Stoppage (*Continued*)

Self-defeating inner dialogue: The athlete worries and questions the benefit of treatment and exercise. "This is awful. This hurts too much to be beneficial. These exercises will probably cause me more harm. Besides, I've been doing this for 3 days now, and I can't see any progress. It would be a lot easier to just let it heal on its own. I don't think I'll go in tomorrow. If it's really important, the trainer will call me. If he doesn't, it will mean I was right. It really doesn't matter if I get treatment." The athlete does not get as much out of today's treatment and begins to develop excuses for not continuing therapy.

Self-enhancing inner dialogue: The athlete worries and questions the benefits of treatment and exercise. He thinks, "STOP. These exercises hurt, but it's OK—they'll pay off. I'm lucky to have knowledgeable people helping me. I'll be competing soon, because I'm doing these exercises. I must not let the pain bother me. If the pain gets too severe, I'll speak up and tell the trainer. He'll want to know. Otherwise, I'll live with it and think about how happy I'll be to be competing again." The athlete has a good treatment session and prepares himself to continue for as long as necessary. He develops rapport with the trainer, who feels good about the athlete.

4:00 P.M.

Injury-related situation: The athlete watches the practice session.

Self-defeating inner dialogue: The athlete sees other athletes practicing and feels sorry for himself. "Why me? Why am I the one who has to be injured? I was in better shape than anyone. I'll probably lose my position on the team by the time I'm healthy again. I hope the team doesn't play too well without me. I hope I'm missed." The athlete gets more discouraged with himself. He is seen by his teammates negatively. He is obviously more concerned with himself than with the team.

Self-enhancing inner dialogue: The athlete observes others practicing. He starts to feel sorry for himself but recognizes these inappropriate thoughts and stops and redirects them. "I wish I hadn't been injured. The fact that I'm in really good shape will help me get back on the field a lot faster. I hope everyone plays well without me so we can still go to the tournament. I'm going to do everything I can to help. I'll go to practice and help out and cheer for my teammates. I'll make sure I know what's going on, so that when I'm healthy again I'll be ready to return." The athlete feels good as a result of enthusiasm during practice. Teammates are happy to see him and encourage him to stick with his treatments and to get back soon because the team needs him.

taining independence. With safety considered, the athlete will gain confidence by mastering skills such as ice massage, ultrasound, and crutch-walking.

Visual Imagery as a Coping Skill

The athlete's imagination can greatly influence his response to an injury. Often he imagines the worst thing that could happen. Athletes can be taught to control their visual images and to direct them productively to reduce anxiety and to aid in rehabilitation. Visual imagery strategies include emotive imagery, body rehearsal, mastery rehearsal, and coping rehearsal.

Emotive Imagery

In *emotive imagery*, a technique that helps the athlete to feel secure and confident that his rehabilitation will be successful, scenes are imagined that produce positive, self-enhancing feelings, such as enthusiasm, self-pride, and confidence. Some athletes, for example, can recall success in recovering from an earlier injury and returning to competition. Others may think of the admiration that coaches, teammates, and friends will have for them when they have overcome the injury. The athlete is instructed to think of other athletes who have overcome the same injury and to generate other scenes that produce positive feelings.

Body Rehearsal

In *body rehearsal*, a mental rehearsal technique now being investigated, the athlete is given a detailed explanation of his injury. Whenever possible, colored pictures are used to help him develop a mental picture of the injury. The healing process and the purpose of the rehabilitation techniques are then explained to him so that he can envision what is happening internally to the injured part during the rehabilitation process. After the athlete has clearly visualized the healing process, he is asked to imagine it occurring in color during his treatments and at intervals throughout the day. Body rehearsal may become a way of influencing healing.

Mastery Rehearsal and Coping Rehearsal

Mastery rehearsal and coping rehearsal are used to prepare the athlete for difficult situations and to achieve important goals. *Mastery rehearsal*

Mastery Rehearsal for Knee Surgery

"I'm looking forward to surgery and feel great about the upcoming operation and rehabilitation. I'm glad I'll no longer be bothered by my knee. I have a well-qualified surgeon who'll perform the operation successfully. I'll begin rehabilitation shortly afterward with a caring and talented athletic trainer. Rehabilitation will be short and successful. Each day, I'll make progress. In a few weeks, I'll be training again. I'll feel good and be excited. I know I'll be successful."

Coping Rehearsal for Knee Surgery

"I'm looking forward to surgery, but I'm anxious. I'm likely to become even more anxious as the day of surgery approaches. Whenever I realize that my mind is running wild with anxiety, I'll 'STOP' and replace these thoughts with helpful thoughts and 'let go' and relax.

"Rehabilitation will be long and demanding, challenging my self-discipline and willpower. But if I want to reach the goals I've outlined for myself, I can't let the injury stand in my way. I must have confidence in my ability to overcome this challenge.

"What must I do? I'll work out a plan that will prepare me for successful rehabilitation. I must keep cool and not respond emotionally. If I find myself responding emotionally, I'll relax and become more aware of my self-statements. If I'm thinking self-defeating thoughts, I'll 'STOP' them and repeat helpful thoughts to myself. If I become discouraged, I'll think of athletes who have overcome far worse injuries than mine. An injury such as mine has ruined some athletes' careers, but successful athletes realize that successful management of injuries and rehabilitation is part of becoming a successful athlete.

"There will be many excuses for not going to therapy: 'I can't find time,' 'I'm too busy,' 'I have a test tomorrow,' 'the training room hours are ridiculous.' I will make sure that I'm ready for these excuses and realize that they will only work against me. I will always find a way to get my treatments.

"There will be days when I'll see little or no progress in therapy. I will also probably experience pain that is likely to make me tense, irritable, and frustrated. When this occurs, I must remember to stay calm and positive and to keep my sense of humor. Then the trainer will enjoy helping me more, and I'll feel better about myself. Think how good I'll feel when my rehabilitation is successful."

is a positive imagery technique that builds confidence and provides a motivational framework for the athlete's rehabilitation. In mastery rehearsal, the athlete only imagines the successful completion of tasks, whereas in *coping rehearsal* he actively anticipates potential problems. By using his imagination to anticipate problems and appropriate responses to these problems, he can plan effective measures to cope with the difficulties. Coping rehearsal is the more realistic of the two rehearsal methods and prepares the athlete for difficulties that might realistically occur. Coping rehearsal does include some anxiety itself, however, and in some cases may overwhelm an injured athlete.

SELF-CONTROL OF PAIN

Pain is influenced by motivational and cognitive factors. The athlete can be taught nonimagery and imagery strategies to control or to eliminate pain.[22, 23] He must be careful, of course, not to completely block out pain signals that could otherwise warn him of danger.

Pain has three dimensions: the sensory–discriminative, motivational–affective, and cognitive–evaluative. Different coping skills are needed for each of these dimensions. For the sensory–discriminative dimension, relaxation techniques can control the sensory input of pain and reduce the tension that otherwise magnifies the intensity of the pain. Other strategies include attention diversion, somatization, imaginative inattention, and transformation of context.

The athlete can exclude the sensation of pain by diverting his attention to other stimuli in the external environment. He can, for example, do mental arithmetic, count ceiling tiles, or plan his daily schedule. Another nonimagery strategy is somatization. Here the athlete focuses directly on the pain at the injured area and ignores other sensations. When, for example, his foot is placed into ice water, he focuses on a feeling of pleasant dampness and numbness.[6] Imaginative inattention requires the athlete to imagine "goal-directed fantasies" that are usually pleasant and allow him to ignore the pain. The athlete becomes totally absorbed in the guided fantasy, such as a perfect performance in an upcoming contest.[5] He may also imagine the injured or painful part to be numb or minimize the pain as being insignificant or unreal.[4, 8]

The athlete may also imaginatively transform the context in which he is feeling the pain. He acknowledges the pain and includes it in a fantasy, transferring the context or the setting in which the pain occurs. He may, for instance, imagine himself to be a spy who has been shot and is now in a car that is being chased down a winding mountain road by enemy agents. The car chase should require more attention than the pain. Relaxation can also reduce the sensation of pain. The athlete imagines that it is a summer day and he is relaxing in a rowboat on a calm pond, or that the injured part is warm and heavy.[6, 14]

A second dimension of pain is the motivational–affective. Negative feelings of anxiety and helplessness may increase the perception of pain, whereas positive feelings of confidence and control decrease it. Thought stoppage techniques and positive self-statements may help.

The third dimension is the cognitive–evaluative. How intense the athlete expects the pain to be will usually influence how much pain he will report. Thought stoppage and self-instruction statements are valuable.

Biofeedback is another way to gain control over pain.[27] The athlete's awareness is raised and his self-control improved by listening to recordings of psychophysiologic processes. Biofeedback may also be used to show the athlete the effectiveness of his self-control strategies.

Relaxation Training

The injured athlete may use relaxation training to help manage stress and anxiety and to control pain. The relaxation techniques allow him to develop more vivid and productive visual images. The athlete learns how to relax deeply by systematically tensing and releasing muscle groups and by learning to differentiate between the tense and relaxed feelings.[11, 12] Progressive relaxation techniques may not, however, be equally effective for all athletes. Those who tend to be anxious about an injury or who have insomnia, tension headaches, or general tightness benefit most. Many other athletes have learned on their own how to cope with stress and have been coping well for years. They should not be forced to spend extra time on relaxation training.

Introducing the Athlete to Relaxation Training

At the beginning of the relaxation training session, the sports psychologist explains the reasons for, and the benefits of, relaxation training and conveys his enthusiasm for the technique. Then he answers any questions that the athlete may have. Relaxation training takes place in a quiet, calm, comfortably warm, and dimly lit area. The sports psychologist will need some light to ascertain that the athlete is following directions correctly and relaxing his body properly. The athlete should wear loose, comfortable clothing, should unbutton his collar, and loosen his belt. Female athletes should wear a shirt or blouse and slacks. Contact lenses, eyeglasses, and watches should be removed.

The athlete's body should be completely supported in a recliner chair that has well-padded head, arm, and leg rests. Pillows are placed under the athlete's head and behind his knees to further relax these areas. Some athletes prefer to recline on a wide couch or on a carpeted floor; others lie in a position that appears to be quite uncomfortable but may be the athlete's most comfortable position.

As the athlete reclines in the chair, the therapist stands nearby and gives directions. For the first few exercises, the therapist speaks in a conversational tone. As relaxation progresses, his voice becomes softer, and he speaks more slowly. When the athlete is instructed to tense his muscles, the therapist speaks louder and faster. He might say the following to the athlete.

"Focus your attention on the way your body feels. If your mind wanders onto other things, calmly tell yourself 'STOP,' push those thoughts away, and concentrate on your body's feelings. These exercises will teach you to recognize muscle tension and muscle relaxation so that you will become more aware of them. You will then be able to eliminate muscle tension once you recognize it, and so be able to relax.

"Close your eyes but do not force them shut. Hold them comfortably closed. With your heels about 6 inches apart, point your toes away from your body and tighten the muscles in your calves, thighs, and buttocks. Feel the tension as you hold it. Remember this feeling. 1 . . . , 2 . . . , 3 . . . , 4 . . . . Repeat the words 'let go' to yourself, and slowly let the tension flow out of your body. Again concentrate on your calves, thighs, and buttocks. Let your toes point upward and flop to the outside. Feel the relaxation. Remember how good it feels. Feel the heaviness and the warmth flowing through your lower body. Let it feel good. If you have any tension anywhere in your lower body, 'let go.'

"Now, concentrate on your stomach. Tighten your stomach muscles as much as you can. Feel the tension as you hold the tightened position. Remember the feeling. 1 . . . , 2 . . . , 3 . . . , 4 . . . . Repeat the words 'let go' to yourself, and slowly let the tension flow out of your body. Again concentrate on your stomach muscles. Feel the relaxation and remember how good it feels. Let it feel good for a moment. If there is any tension anywhere in your body, let it go.

"Now concentrate on your chest muscles. Tighten them as much as you can. Take a deep breath through your mouth, and then hold it. As you hold it, you may feel tension spots in your chest. Remember where they are—they may surface when you are stressed. Now, slowly 'let go'—very slowly. Breathe normally and comfortably as if you were sleeping or resting. Make sure you have eliminated the tension spots. Completely relax your entire body.

"Tighten all of the muscles from the tips of your fingers to your shoulders in both arms as much as you can. Raise your arms about one foot off the floor. Clench your fists. Feel the tension in your fingers, hands, arms, and shoulders. Hold it. 1 . . . , 2 . . . , 3 . . . , 4 . . . , and feel the tension. Slowly 'let go.' Let your arms drop and your fingers spread, and completely relax. Concentrate on how your hands and arms feel. If there is any remaining tension, remember where it is. You are likely to have tension there when you are in a stressful situation. Now, 'let go,' and completely relax. Once again, concentrate on just your fingers. Relax them completely. Feel how warm and heavy they are. Relax your upper arms completely. Eliminate any excess tension.

"Now concentrate on the muscles of your upper back—the muscles between the shoulder blades and

the neck. These muscles are very sensitive to tension. You may have often experienced soreness here. Tighten these muscles as much as possible. Feel the tension and hold it. 1 . . . , 2 . . . , 3 . . . , 4 . . . . Slowly 'let go.' Dwell on the feelings of relaxation as you do so. Concentrate on these relaxed feelings, and remember them.

"Now, tighten your entire body as much as you can from the tips of your fingers to the top of your toes. Hold it. 1 . . . , 2 . . . , 3 . . . , 4 . . . . Slowly 'let go,' and completely relax your entire body. If you have any tension remaining anywhere in your body, let it go.

"Imagine a pleasant scene, such as walking on a beach or lying in a rowboat on a calm pond—any place that you feel completely relaxed. Let your whole body feel calm and relaxed. Enjoy the feeling. Take a couple of very deep, slow breaths. Inhale deeply into your stomach: 1 . . . , 2 . . . , 3 . . . , 4 . . . ; then exhale slowly: 1 . . . , 2 . . . , 3 . . . , 4 . . . . Feel your body become more and more relaxed. Breathe normally, smoothly, and calmly. Continue to feel your body, and let go of any remaining tension."[11]

After the first relaxation session, athletes have generally related positive experiences. Some problems, however, have arisen during relaxation training.

Anticipating and Solving Problems

Some problems that may arise while relaxation skills are being taught are laughter, falling asleep, muscle cramps, and mental distractions.

Laughter   Younger athletes may think that relaxation training is humorous and begin laughing. The laughter may be due to something that the therapist said or did, a distracting thought that crossed the athlete's mind, or to self-consciousness. If the athlete is self-conscious, let him know that he is doing the exercises right. Encouraging statements give him comfort and confidence.

Falling Asleep   An athlete sometimes falls asleep during relaxation training. Unfortunately, he cannot practice the skills while asleep. There may be some difficulty in determining whether an athlete is practicing relaxation techniques or

is sleeping. The therapist must watch closely to see if his directions are being followed. An athlete who tends to fall asleep may be asked to give a signal to indicate whether a particular muscle group is relaxed or not. If there is no signal, the athlete may be asleep.

Failure to Relax Certain Muscle Groups   An athlete may have difficulty in completely relaxing an area, such as his shoulders, hamstrings, or jaw muscles. Clearly, extreme tension in any of these areas will affect performance adversely. He should spend extra time learning to relax these muscles.

Muscle Cramps   Relaxation training is sometimes interrupted by muscle cramps, particularly in the calves and feet. These cramps can usually be eliminated if the athlete tenses less during the tensing phase of each exercise. If this strategy does not prevent cramping, the athlete may massage the cramped muscle. While he massages, he should keep his eyes closed and remain as relaxed as possible. The interruption is followed by a review of the last few exercises and extra work on relaxation. With practice, the athlete will learn to tense just below the level that causes cramps. Occasionally, however, the athlete will have to skip the tensing phase for a particularly troublesome muscle group.

Mental Distractions   An athlete may have trouble paying attention to the skills being presented to him. Perhaps he is distracted by a fear of forgetting, anxious thoughts, overanalysis, or sexual arousal. The athlete may be worried that he will not remember the exercises when he is home alone. To relieve this fear of forgetting, the relaxation training session may be taped for the athlete to take home.

Some athletes are distracted by anxious thoughts related to the injury or to some aspect of their athletic performance. Athletes should be reminded before and after each relaxation session that the relaxation exercises they are learning will facilitate a successful rehabilitation and return to sports participation. Other athletes overanalyze or worry about whether they are doing the exercises correctly. The therapist must be certain that he is giving clear and consistent directions. The athlete should be reminded to focus on the body parts being tensed or relaxed. Encouraging and supportive feedback is helpful.

An athlete may question the value of relaxation training before giving it a chance. As a result, his mind may wander to other activities that he finds more enjoyable. Sometimes an athlete becomes sexually aroused during a relaxation training session. Certain aspects of the environment may have to be changed. The athlete can be shown thought stoppage techniques to redirect thoughts in a more appropriate direction. If the problem persists, the only solution is to find another therapist.

Home Practice

The athlete should leave the relaxation training session with a well-thought-out plan, enthusiastic about practicing and using the relaxation skills. Athletes usually learn the skills quite easily, as sport has given them good control of their bodies and minds. Whenever possible, the athlete should take a tape recording or a written copy of the exercises home. His room should be free of distractions from other people or sounds. This may take some planning: The telephone may have to be taken off the hook, a "quiet please" sign put on the door, or relaxing music played to help block out noise.

Relaxation skills are practiced twice a day for about 20 minutes each time. Usually, one session is in the middle of the day and the other late at night. The night session may help the athlete get to sleep, especially when pain is associated with the injury. (Later, relaxation skills may be used to enable the athlete to fall asleep before an important contest.) If, however, the athlete has homework due or a test to take the next morning and he does not wish to fall asleep, an alarm clock should be set for ½ hour.

RETURNING TO COMPETITION

Despite the great advances in physically preparing an athlete for a return to sport after an injury or surgery, little use has been made of systematic psychological rehabilitation. As a result, psychological scars may be overlooked. These "scars" may be rational or irrational anxieties that cause him to lose his ability to concentrate and may lead to reinjury or to an injury of another area. It also may take a long time for the athlete to regain his confidence for peak performance.

Systematic Desensitization

Systematic desensitization may be used psychologically to rehabilitate the injured athlete. Desensitization helps the athlete handle anxiety[28] by combining relaxation training and visual

---

Football Running Back's Fear Hierarchy for a Shoulder Injury*

1. You are told by the trainer that you are ready to return to practice.
2. In the huddle for the first time after return to practice and you must block.
3. In the huddle for the first time after return to practice and you must carry the ball on a sweep play.
4. In the huddle for the first time after return to practice and you must carry the ball on a dive play.
5. You must jump high in the air to catch a pass with a defender about to tackle you on the side of the injured shoulder.
6. Your must jump high in the air to to catch a pass with a defender about to tackle you on the side opposite the injured shoulder and you are about to land on the injured shoulder on a turf field.
7. Imagine successfully running the ball on various plays and avoiding or breaking tackles. (This was the state of the athlete's mental process before his injury.)

*The athlete imagines doing each step successfully over and over while maintaining a relaxed state before moving to the next step.

**Basketball Player's Fear
Hierachy for an Ankle Sprain***

1. You are going on the basketball court to practice.
2. You begin practice by running windsprints.
3. You are now in a "wave" drill and you practice your defensive step slide.
4. You are going to practice shooting with no defense.
5. You are running layups in practice.
6. You are in a scrimmage and you shoot over a defensive player.
7. You shoot over a defensive player and you are fouled.
8. You are in practice and will rebound a ball to start a fastbreak, and there is no defense.
9. You rebound a ball during a scrimmage and turn to give an outlet pass.
10. In a scrimmage, you jump high to rebound a basketball; when you come down you land on another player's foot, but you still turn and throw an outlet pass.

*The athlete imagines doing each step successfully over and over while maintaining a relaxed state before moving to the next step.

imagery. It should be, when possible, supplemented by biofeedback training.

At the onset of rehabilitation, the sports psychologist should encourage the athlete to talk about anxieties over the injury and his return to competition. The athlete should then be introduced to relaxation training techniques and practice them by using a tape recording each day at home or in a private room next to the training room. When the athlete becomes skilled at relaxing on cue, he should then start desensitization procedures.

Systematic desensitization lasts for 20 to 30 minutes a day. It is timed so that psychological rehabilitation is completed when the athlete is physically ready to return to playing sports. A fear hierarchy should be established that applies specifically to the athlete's fears or to his anticipated fears. This hierarchy is a list of five to ten situations that elicit a progressive increase in his anxiety.

Desensitization starts with step one on the fear hierarchy. As the athlete imagines the first step, he tries to remain as relaxed as possible. Electromyography or thermal biofeedback may be used to measure muscle tension and relaxation. If this equipment is not available, the athlete should indicate his degree of relaxation on a scale of 1 through 10 (1 = very tense; 10 = very relaxed). The therapist calls off the numbers 1 through 10, and the athlete raises his index finger at the appropriate number. He may proceed to the next step after indicating deep relaxation and confidence while imagining the previous step on the fear hierarchy. The process is repeated until the athlete can relax on cue and stay relaxed while imagining each step on the fear hierarchy. After successfully completing the fear hierarchy, he should be ready mentally to return to athletics. In addition to mental desensitization, he should physically go through each step of the fear hierarchy before returning to competition.

THE "INJURY-PRONE" ATHLETE

Some athletes seem to be more prone to injury than are others, perhaps for physical reasons, such as limb malalignment, joints too loose or too tight, poor strength, or strength imbalance. Perhaps the athlete is not fully fit; his poor endurance leads to fatigue, a slower reaction time, and reduced coordination. In addition, he may not be warming up correctly.

Mentally, the athlete may be tense, depressed, or preoccupied with problems in school, social problems, or problems at home. The mental changes may be subtle, but the team physician, trainer, or sports psychologist can often tell that something is wrong. The athlete may uncharacteristically jump the gun, start fights, miss foul shots, or otherwise not be concentrating on his task. He may have trouble sleeping, show a changed behavior pattern, and have mood changes. Talking with the athlete will sometimes uncover the source of the problem, and the difficulty can then be resolved.

PREDISPOSING ATTITUDES

In addition to the predisposing personality factors presented, there are also potentially predisposing attitudes that have been fostered by many coaches. These attitudes usually "sound good," and athletes who accept them typically "look tough" and appear to have "great attitudes." Unfortunately, when taken too far, as is often the case for many highly motivated and coachable athletes, these well-learned attitudes become counterproductive and predispose athletes to injury.

The False Image of Invulnerability

Athletes have been systematically taught that mental toughness and giving 100% effort all of the time are necessary for success in sport. Athletes must be taught that "trying your hardest" is not the same as "doing your best" and that giving 100% all of the time will simply guarantee mental weakness rather than mental toughness. The reality is that it is impossible to give 100% all of the time. A full acceptance of the false attitudes or an extreme reaction to these attitudes may increase the likelihood of injury and failure.

Many highly motivated athletes can learn to "play through" almost any kind of pain. Developing such an ability may make for an often injured athlete who seldom, if ever, performs in a fully healthy state. Such athletes will commonly have short-lived athletic careers and lives filled with pain and suffering from masked injuries that they were tough enough to "play through."

Unfortunately, in sports and especially in contact sports, an abundance of rewards is provided to athletes who accept these attitudes. Such rewards often lead to an extreme psychological reaction by athletes wishing to win the admiration and respect of coaches, trainers, teammates, and fans. As the rewards for displaying these attitudes are enjoyed, athletes become increasingly willing to do whatever is necessary to earn them.

Gradually, the well-intentioned appearance of mental toughness and dedication evolve into the projection of a false image of invulnerability. As athletes strive to live up to this impossible image, problems begin to appear. Gradually it is accepted as fact that "tough" athletes never need a rest, never miss a play, never go to the training room, and never let a "minor" injury keep them from playing. Failure to live up to this image of invulnerability would be judged a sign of weakness. Unfortunately, for athletes with this belief system their self-pride is attached to never missing a practice or game. Their bodies are therefore left extremely vulnerable to injury. Their minds are left unprepared for the incapacitating injury or life-long pain that may follow.

A major change in attitude is required to ensure a healthy adaptation to injury and life. Without such change athletes who hold such views will not accept the reality that they are vulnerable, that they are human and can get hurt physically and scared psychologically. This change of attitude is crucial if athletes are to accept injuries as a natural occurrence in sport and be capable of responding positively to them. Such acceptance will enable athletes to come closer to developing to their fullest ability and allow coaches, trainers, and physicians to effectively fulfill their respective roles. The hazards of these past mistaken attitudes must be realized before the specific psychological strategies presented can be most fully utilized.

Some leaders of sport have been led to believe that the best way to foster a rapid recovery from injury is to make injured athletes feel unimportant as long as they are injured. This is, to say the least, a counterproductive approach. Leaders who hold this view clearly communicate to their athletes that they care only for them as performers. Some leaders communicate this message by isolating injured athletes from healthy team members. Some refuse any form of verbal communication while using body language to suggest that injured athletes should feel guilty for being injured and not helping the team win. Others suggest that these athletes are malingerers, lack mental toughness and desire, or are not fully committed to the success of the team.

Leaders in sport must realize that the time during which athletes are recovering from injury is crucial for either developing or destroying *trust*. It is during this time that leaders have a chance to demonstrate *care* and *concern* and show that they are as committed to their athletes as they ask their athletes to be to them.

Successful leaders of present-day athletes must help them realize that attitudes such as desire, pride, and commitment are beneficial at the right time and place but that these attitudes may also be hazardous to present and future health if taken to the extreme. The key is for leaders to do what is in the *best interest* of injured athletes. When this approach is followed, athletes, coaches, trainers, and teams alike will have the best possible chance of attaining their fullest potential. When this approach is not followed, there is still a chance that the athletes themselves will put sport in proper perspective. They will do so, however, out of *distrust* rather than trust, often leading them to decide that sport is unimportant and a place for personal abuse rather than positive growth and fulfillment.

PROBLEM PATIENTS

All sports medicine specialists must recognize that there are certain athletes who are particularly difficult. A brief description of five of the most typical problem types is presented below. Some practical ideas of communicating with these patients are suggested. Understanding and empathy are crucial.

A central feature of successful rehabilitation requires a positive relationship between the parties involved in that their roles are interrelated. Staff members must at all times remain professional, helpful, and friendly while not allowing such closeness to interfere with effective feedback and treatment. When the relationship becomes too close, objectivity in assessment and treatment is lost.

Experiencing an array of human emotions does not make a relationship ineffective. Such shared emotions are normal and often allow for the empathy necessary for the ideal relationship.

Dependent Attention-Loving Patients

Athletes with needs for attention who enjoy being dependent upon others frequently make constant and extreme demands on the training room staff.

Their behavior breeds dependency. These athletes seem to have mastered the ability to make others feel responsible for them and their health. The normal services provided to other athletes on a day-to-day basis are never good enough: These athletes always want more attention, time, and help.

In general, athletes of this type have refused to accept the responsibility of taking care of themselves. They want to be taken care of by others and, often as a result of their athletic abilities, have always been able to find others quite willing to do so. These athletes have developed innocent and devious behaviors for attaching themselves to giving people in the helping professions.

The training room staff members with the greatest need to help others will usually allow themselves to be taken advantage of by such athletes. It is important for the trainers to set limits for athletes and for themselves or such athletes will constantly overwork them. When such limits are set the unhappy athlete will look for another staff member to take over. This must not be allowed to happen.

For these athletes their problem must be recognized. Reasonable time limits must be set when working with dependent attention-loving patients. A firm stand must be taken or the patient will try to receive the time, energy, and attention desired and the helping professional will give until worn out and unable to help others. Some athletes will respond with frustration, hostility, and hurt feelings. In the past these responses have commonly helped them get the attention they desire. In some cases athletes with such needs will not be content to live within the stated boundaries. Sports medicine specialists must be willing to let the athletes go, which will usually cause the athlete to accept the limits.

Resistant Athletes

Athletes who resist treatment make the training room staff's job most difficult. Whereas it is common for the dependent type to make the staff feel needed and respected, the resistant athlete is perceived as showing no respect or appreciation for their rehabilitation skills. Although there are various reasons for the resistant behaviors of such athletes, it is usually best to avoid psychological interpretations unless guided by a trained psychologist.

For most athletes of this type, the staff must not take personal offense at the athletes' attitudes. Many athletes will change their attitudes and behaviors when the staff's responses are combined with humor. After trying these strategies without satisfactory results, the staff should employ a more straightforward approach. It is best simply to tell these athletes that it is their decision, they can live with their injuries, suffer through an extremely slow recovery, or follow the recommended rehabilitation regimen. Make it clear that the training room staff can live with the injury and the lack of treatment if the athlete is able to do so. Letting the athlete decide often leads him to make a commitment to rehabilitation. Too often training room staff members are hesitant to leave such decisions in the hands of athletes who might choose to continue to refuse treatment. This response will not encourage the development of the necessary self-responsibility.

Staff members who become impatient with resistant athletes may show signs of fatigue, overwork, or burnout. Some resistant athletes need to be referred to a different staff member who might communicate more effectively with this type of problem patient.

Childlike Patients

It is not uncommon for even the toughest and most mature athletes to regress to a more childlike state when they are injured. This reality makes sense, particularly for athletes with disabling injuries that require a prolonged rehabilitation period, when it is understood that, as with young children, many everyday activities require help from another adult.

Depending on the athlete's personality, a variety of behavior patterns will occur. Some athletes will like being waited on, some will withdraw and become quiet and shy, some will lose their tempers, and others will whine and get lost in self-pity.

When such behaviors occur, training room staff members should recognize and accept them while helping athletes to anticipate what is coming. It is then appropriate to give the athletes

control and self-responsibility over their rehabilitation to foster more adult-like behavior.

Angry Patients

Obviously no training room staff member enjoys being verbally attacked or ridiculed by athletes receiving treatment. Athough an athlete's normal response to injury makes it easy to understand, occasional displays of prolonged anger or persistent displays of anger, particularly when directed at the training room staff members, should not be tolerated.

Anger is best responded to immediately and directly. Rather than attempting to explain the anger, it is best for training room staff members to show empathy and firmness while asking questions of the athlete intended to facilitate an understanding of the response in question.

The major goal in working with an angry athlete is to establish a workable relationship between the parties involved. To do so the staff member involved must stay calm while establishing the necessary boundaries.

Staff members who respond to such athletes by attacking back and acting irrationally will only ensure that there will be no resolution. Likewise, allowing oneself to display bitterness toward the angry athlete will further hinder the desired relationship. In any case the sooner a calm and objective relationship is established, the better it will be to achieve rehabilitation goals.

Unmotivated Athletes

Athletes display a lack of motivation for many reasons. Some athletes arrive in the training room for treatment with an extremely negative attitude, which hinders progress. Other are injured for the first time and know of friends who, despite efforts to rehabilitate themselves, did not make a healthy return to competition. As a result these athletes assume that there is no reason to be motivated. Still others are despondent about their injury and have developed a counterproductive habit of complaining and questioning everything they are asked to do.

In all cases the underlying problem must be addressed. Athletes cannot be forced to have a great attitude; they can, however, be helped to develop a positive outlook toward their treatment. Athletes can be given numerous examples of other athletes with similar injuries who, as a result of a positively motivated attitude, successfully recovered. A variety of strategies are useful, including motivational tapes, stories, or videos that help inspire athletes to think about how good they will feel upon their return to competition.

Training room staff members must accept the fact that while they may be able to *inspire* athletes for a short time they cannot make athletes *want* something that they do not want. But unmotivated athletes can be taught *how* motivated athletes think when they are going through rehabilitation. Once such thinking patterns are understood, athletes will be able to motivate themselves. When all other attempts fail, it is crucial for the training room staff to remember the importance of always maintaining an enthusiastically optimistic attitude so as to serve as effective role models.

REFERENCES

1. Averill J: Personal control over aversive stimuli and its relationship to stress. Psychol Bull 80:286–303, 1973
2. Bean KL: Desensitization, behavioral rehearsal, the reality: A preliminary report on a new procedure. Behav Ther 1:525–545, 1970
3. Beck A: Cognitive therapy: Nature and relation to behavior therapy. Behav Ther 2:194–200, 1970
4. Blitz B, Dinnerstein A: The role of attentional focus in pain perception: Manipulation of response to noxious stimulation by instructions. J Abnorm Psychol 77:42–45, 1971
5. Chavers J, Barber T: Cognitive strategies, experimental modeling and expectation in the attention of pain. J Abnorm Psychol 83:356–363, 1974
6. Evans M, Paul G: Effects of hypnotically suggested analgesia on physiological and subjective responses to cold stress. J Consult Clin Psychol 35:362–371, 1970
7. Foreyt JP, Rathjen DP (eds): Cognitive Behavior Therapy. Research and Application. New York, Plenum Press, 1978
8. Greene R, Reyher J: Pain tolerance in hypnotic analgesia and imagination states. J Abnorm Psychol 77:42–45, 1977
9. Hamburg D, Adams JE: A perspective on coping behavior. Arch Gen Psychiatry 17:277–284, 1967
10. Jacobson E: You Must Relax. New York, McGraw–Hill, 1934
11. Jacobson E: Progressive Relaxation. Chicago, University of Chicago Press, 1938
12. Jacobson E: Anxiety and Tension Control. Philadelphia, JB Lippincott, 1964
13. Janis IL: Psychological Stress: Psychoanalytic and Behavioral Studies of Surgical Patients. New York, John Wiley & Sons, 1958
14. Johnson R: Suggestions for pain reduction and response to cold-induced pain. Psychol Rep 18:79–85, 1966
15. Kavanaugh RE: Facing Death. Los Angeles, Nash Publishing, 1972
16. Kübler–Ross E: On Death and Dying. New York, Macmillan, 1969
17. Lazarus RS: Psychological stress and coping in adaptation and illness. Int J Psychiatry Med 5:321–333, 1974
18. Lindmann B: Symptomatology and management of acute grief. Am J Psychiatry 101:1–11, September 1944
19. Lipowski ZJ: Physical illness, the individual and the coping processes. Psychiatry Med 1:91–102, 1970
20. Mahoney M: Cognitive and Behavior Modification. Cambridge, Massachusetts, Ballinger, 1974
21. Mahoney MJ, Thoreson CE: Self-Control: Power to the Person. Monterey, California, Brooks/Cole, 1974
22. Meichenbaum D: Cognitive Behavior Modification: An Integrative Approach. New York, Plenum Press, 1977
23. Meichenbaum D: Cognitive Behavior Modification. Morristown, New Jersey, General Learning Press, 1978
24. Melzack R, Casey K: Sensory motivational and central control determinants of pain. A new conceptual model. In Kenshalo D (ed): The Skin Senses. Springfield, Illinois, Charles C Thomas, 1968
25. Melzack R, Wall P: Pain mechanisms: A new theory. Science 150:197, 1965
26. Moss RH: The Crises of Physical Illness: An Overview in Coping with Physical Illness. New York, Plenum Medical Book Company, 1979
27. Reeves J: EMG-biofeedback reduction of tension headache: A cognitive skills training approach. Biofeedback Self Regul 1:217–225, 1976
28. Rotella RJ: Systematic desensitization. Psychological rehabilitation of injured athletes. In Bunker L, Rotella R (eds): Sport Psychology: From Theory to Practice. Charlottesville, Virginia, Department of Health and Physical Education, University of Virginia, 1979
29. Selye H: The Stress of Life. New York, McGraw–Hill, 1956
30. Sternback R: Pain: Psychophysiological Analysis. New York, Academic Press, 1968
31. Vanderpool JP: Stressful patient relationships and the difficult patient. In Krueger D, Collins L (eds): Rehabilitation Psychology: A Comprehensive Textbook. Rockville, Maryland, Aspen Publications, 1984

CHAPTER 6

The Athletic Trainer and Rehabilitation

Joe H. Gieck and Ethan N. Saliba

Sports, by their very nature, invite injury. Each year, millions of injuries occur to more than 4 million boys and almost 1½ million girls who participate in interscholastic and intercollegiate athletics. More than 1 million boys at 14,000 high schools participate in football alone. Yearly, these players sustain more than 110,000 major injuries that result in 3 weeks or more of inactivity. Most of these injured athletes never see a physician.

Some high schools have a physician in attendance at games, but more than 65% of athletic injuries occur in practice. Who will aid these athletes? Good medical care is especially important in high schools because these youths are often uncoordinated and are only beginning to mature physically and mentally. Moreover, only 5% of high school health care personnel are certified athletic trainers. About 75% of health care is given by coaches, and more than 80% of these coaches do not meet any standards for health care personnel.

The overworked coach assigned the duties of an athletic trainer may lack knowledge of emergency first aid, cardiopulmonary resuscitation (CPR), and transportation procedures. The coach is also placed in a conflict-of-interest situation when he must decide whether a young athlete may return to competition. Some high schools have student trainers, but these students lack supervision and often overstep their abilities. The student trainer may lack sports medicine knowledge and jeopardize the athlete by not referring him to a doctor. Because optimal health care is not provided by coaches or rendered by student trainers who lack first aid skills, negligence is likely to occur. Although the blame lies with the school system, the coach often ends up in court. Athletes should not participate in interscholastic or intercollegiate sports without optimum health care. Without a certified athletic trainer, optimum health care is impossible.

To assure basic competency and the finest health care for athletes, some states now require that athletic trainers be licensed. Certification is another answer. One possible route to certification is through a National Athletic Trainers Association (NATA)-approved undergraduate or graduate program. Another route is through an apprenticeship.

All applicants for certification must have at least a bachelor's degree, have a current CPR and first aid card, be a NATA member, be recommended by a certified athletic trainer (ATC), and pass the written and oral tests developed and administered by an independent board of the NATA.

Curricula approved by the NATA provide 1 to 4 years of experience with a certified athletic trainer. The candidate must have a minimum of 800 hours of practical experience with a certified trainer. Required courses are anatomy, physiology, physiology of exercise, kinesiology, psychology, first aid and safety, nutrition, remedial or adapted exercise, personal, community, and school health, and techniques of athletic training.

Serving an apprenticeship requires 2 to 4 years of work under a certified athletic trainer and the amassing of more than 1800 hours of clinical work.

DUTIES

The athletic trainer is responsible for athletes in his trust receiving excellent health care. The trainer not only works with members of athletic teams, but also may provide medical emergency care in physical education and school situations. A student who falls down a flight of stairs, for example, or is otherwise injured benefits from the emergency medical skills of the athletic trainer. The trainer administers first aid ranging from the treatment of simple abrasions to splinting, CPR, and other life-saving techniques.

The athletic trainer is charged with the prevention, treatment, and rehabilitation of athletes

in his athletic setting. Preventive measures are taught for avoiding injury. If injury has occurred, however, proper care reduces recovery time, and the athlete may enjoy a quicker return to competition. The athlete is rehabilitated for a return to competition, not just back to the activities of daily life; this requires greater levels of strength, flexibility, power, endurance, speed, and skill. The trainer uses heat and cold but employs exercise as the major modality. Under the care of an athletic trainer, an athlete is less likely to return to action before being ready, thereby reducing the chance for reinjury.

The trainer is a link between the team physician and coach, the athlete and coach, and others. He is responsible administratively to the athletic director for policies and budget items and medically to the team physician. The team physician cannot be at all practices and games; thus the athletic trainer refers the athletes to the doctor as necessary. The trainer is also responsible for carrying out the team physician's instructions.

The athletic trainer sets up and directs conditioning programs for flexibility, strength, and endurance that will help prevent injury. He also may advise coaches as to the safety of their practice procedures, inspect playing facilities for safety, and fit and check protective equipment. He serves too as a health counselor to athletes, especially those who lack family health care. Personal counseling is also an important role.

In addition to health care duties, the trainer is the administrator of the health care facilities and personnel and is involved in purchasing. Some trainers are faculty members who work mornings in the school's student-health physical-therapy department or teach courses.

When school administrators are asked why their high school does not employ a certified athletic trainer, the reply is often, "We cannot afford one," or, "We haven't had one before, so why do we need one now?" Granted, many schools cannot afford a full-time athletic trainer, but the trainer can be a full-time faculty member with training in the principles of athletic training, CPR, first aid, and transportation of the injured. Such a faculty member could receive supplemental pay, like a coach's supplemental pay, for athletic training. The prevention of even one serious injury because of the presence of a trainer would justify allocation of the necessary funds. Courts are expecting optimum athletic health care: Schools without certified athletic trainers are not meeting this need adequately and thus leaving themselves open to liability.

The trainer is also involved in purchasing equipment for the training room, trainer's kit, and travel trunk and in making sure that the equipment stays in good condition (Table 6-1).

PLAYING FIELD SURFACES

Artificial Turf

Artificial turf initially was designed for indoor use. It provides a uniform playing surface for athletic contests under many playing conditions and allows intensive and varied use of the stadium.[40] Artificial turf has its critics, however; one has said that "the only good thing about artificial turf is that it keeps uniforms clean."[7]

Not all artificial turfs are the same; they have different types of pile fibers, backing fibers, and pads.[37] Astroturf, for example, has 1.3-cm (0.5-in) nylon pile on a polyester nylon mat bonded to a 1.6-cm (0.63-in) closed-cell nitrile rubber and polyvinyl chloride pad. The pad rests on an asphalt base. Just as brands differ, old artificial turf differs from new artificial turf.[5] As the pad wears out, the aging turf has a diminished impact-absorbing capacity and different traction qualities.

Are these surfaces as safe as, or safer than, natural grass? The Stanford Research Institute (SRI) study compared injuries on artificial surfaces and natural grass in the National Football League.[12] More major ligamentous injuries occurred on artificial surfaces than on natural grass. The investigators concluded that, generally, natural grass is safer and recommended a return to natural grass in all undomed stadiums. However, a study by the National Athletic Injury/Illness Reporting System (NAIRS), a computerized data-gathering system located at Pennsylvania State University, concluded that no surface is an inherent hazard to the athlete and that "artificial turf did not constitute an imminent hazard to the college tackle football and soccer football teams using it in 1975."[40] Further, in a study at the University of Wisconsin that compared Tartan-Turf to natural grass, more serious sprains occurred on the natural surface, and investigators concluded that this specific brand of turf may be a good surface.[15]

There are many disadvantages to the use of artificial turf. Purists, for example, are often unhappy about the changes that occur in their sport because of the artificial surfaces. In baseball, the ball travels dangerously fast and bounces high on artificial turf, sometimes making a mockery of a great game. Soccer football on artificial turf differs markedly from the same game on natural grass; on artificial surfaces, the athletes refuse to risk the "turf burns" from sliding tackles. With the exception of the goalkeeper, referees will not allow the players to wear 'long johns" on this surface. Moreover, the touch line is often dangerously close to the asphalt.

An artificial surface allows increased running speed. Perhaps the "uniformity of these synthetic surfaces accounts in part for the increase in speeds, since no adjustment is needed to compensate for perturbations on the playing surfaces."[37] This increased speed results in increased collison forces, which cause more serious injuries. The SRI study showed 33% more concussions on synthetic turf than on natural grass, and these concussions may be fatal.

"Turf burns" are the common abrasions from artificial turf; "green dust" is ground into the wounds and may become secondarily infected. Turf burns are often over joints, where bending causes the wound to stay open. A physician cannot aspirate or operate on the joint through or near the damaged skin. Thus a turf burn may ruin the chance for early repair of a torn ligament. Many turf burns can be prevented with extra pads, and some athletes smear petrolatum on their legs so that they can, for example, tackle in soccer.

Leg fatigue and shin splints are common problems on artificial surfaces. Traction is greater, and, if the player's feet slide in his shoes, blisters will form. Many players wear shoes that are too light and too flexible, and they may sprain the metatarsal–phalangeal joint of the great toe when it is hyperextended or hyperflexed. This debilitating sprain can be avoided by wearing a protec-

(*Text continues on p. 170*)

Table 6-1   EQUIPMENT FOR TRAINERS

Basic Training Room Equipment

Examination tables
Refrigerator
Sink
Therapeutic modalities
Scales
Weight charts
Stethoscope and blood pressure cuff
Locked cabinet for medications
Bulletin board (for emergency telephone numbers)

Trainer's Side Table (out of the way)

Gauze pads (4 in × 4 in and 2 in × 2 in)
Band-Aids
Tongue depressors
Cotton buds (Q-tips)
Buffered salt tablets
$AlCl_2$ solution (30%) (aluminum chloride)
Petrolatum
Analgesic cream (gold)
(Heavy) skin lubricant (green)
Foam pads for tapings
Tape remover
Bandage scissors
Callus file
Electric hair clipper

Trainer's Kit

Oral screw
Tongue forceps
Airways
Tongue depressors
Paper bag (hyperventilation)
Contact lens case, contact lens solution, contact lens
    extractor
Eye cup and eye wash
Eye drops
Toothache kit
Oral thermometer
Flashlight
Scalpel
Bandage scissors
Surgical scissors
Hemostat
Forceps
Hand mirror
Safety pins
Razor with blades
Nail clippers
Callus file
Sling
Finger splints

Trainer's Kit (*continued*)

Transcutaneous electrical nerve stimulator (TENS)
    unit and cream
Plastic ice bags
1-oz cups
Tape measure
Marking pen, paper, pencils
Shoe horn
Coins for pay phone
Nonadhering sterile pads
Gelfoam
Band-Aids
Butterfly closures and Steri-Strips
Roll of cotton and cotton balls
3 in × 3 in sterile gauze
2 in × 2 in nonsterile gauze
3-in roller gauze
Felt horseshoe
Tape adherent
Skin lubricant
Foam heel and lace pads
Underwrap
½-in adhesive tape
1-in adhesive tape
1½-in adhesive tape
3-inch elastic tape
Elastic tape
Conform tape
Waterproof tape
Tape cutter
Tape remover
2-in elastic wrap
3-in elastic wrap
4-in elastic wrap
Ankle wrap
Ear drops
Nose drops
Throat lozenges
Cough syrup
Cold tablets
Aspirin
Motion sickness tablets
Antacid tablets
Salt tablets
Sun lotion
Envelopes for pills
First aid spray
Ointment for minor skin irritations
Zinc oxide ointment
Betadine
Liquid soap

Table 6-1 EQUIPMENT FOR TRAINERS (*continued*)

Trainer's Kit (*continued*)

Tinactin
Ethyl chloride
Ammonia capsules
Nasal tampons
Pocket knife
Can opener
Blue light (ophthalmic)
Fluorescein strips
Eye patches
Flexible collodian
Petrolatum
Saline in plastic squeeze bottle
Alcohol
Alcohol prep sponges
Cotton buds
First aid manual

Travel Trunk

Dental kit
Tongue depressors
Mouthpieces
Cotton buds
Examination gloves
Towels
Plastic ice bags
Drinking cups
Calamine lotion
Talcum powder
Analgesic balm
Telfa pads
Nonsterile gauze pads: 2 × 2, 4 × 4
Roller gauze
Sterile gauze roll
Assorted pieces of foam rubber
Orthopedic felt
Felt horseshoes
Tape adherent
Skin lubricant
Adhesive tape (1 in and 1½ in)
Elastic tape (3 in), Lite Flex (2 in)
Elastic wraps (2 in, 3 in, 4 in, and 6 in)
Tape remover
Moleskin
Stockinette (3 in and 6 in)
Rolls of plaster (3 in, 4 in, and 6 in)
Neck collars
Thomas collars
Assorted protective pads
Acromioclavicular pads

Travel Trunk (*continued*)

Sternum pad
Thigh caps
Heel cups
Ensolite (¼ in, ⅜ in, ½ in)
Orthoplast
Slings
Hexcelite
Thermafoam
Band-Aids
Rib belts
Knee immobilizer
Air splints
High-intensity lamp
Equipment hardware
Spare parts
   Chinstraps
    Shoulder pad straps
   Clips
    Screws
Pliers
Screwdrivers
Collapsible cane
Shoe horn
Knee braces
Metal innersoles
Shoulder straps
Tape cutters
Heel pads
Heel/lace pads
Groin wraps
Tape underwrap

Sidelines

Two spine boards, with neck traction unit or four 5-lb
   sandbags
Bolt cutter (taped to spine board)
Stretcher
Crutches
Blankets
Ice chest
Ice
"Magic sponge"
Ice water bucket for cold towels
Plastic bags for ice
Water containers
Water squeeze bottles
Cups and racks
Fans (2), 4 in

tive stainless steel or orthoplast splint inserted between the midsole and the insole of the shoe. Many players prefer a soccer-style shoe with molded cleats when they play on artificial turf, but a basketball-type shoe with a ribbed, elasto-meric sole has as much traction as does the cleated shoe.

Heat builds up tremendously on artificial turf, especially near the surface, and in the summer months heat exhaustion is a constant danger. The players become fatigued more easily, reducing their coordination and increasing the chance of injury. The heat that builds up on a synthetic field is related to a lack of moisture. Natural grass absorbs moisture from its roots and evaporates it into the air, cooling down the field. If artificial turf is wetted down, the surface will cool, and the coefficient of friction decreases. If the wetting is not uniform, however, the resultant wet and dry areas may increase the chance of injury. More-over, tackle football fields are built over a crown, and it takes longer for the edges to dry out than the center. In areas of the country with high humidity, wetting the field may increae the incidence of heat illness.

Natural Grass

Just as the brands of artificial turfs differ, the quality of grass field varies. A natural grass field is only as good as its groundskeeper, and even parts of the same field may vary. Some "grass" fields are in fact grass, others are grass and dirt, some are dirt or clay, and some are rocky. Many fields are poorly maintained. When the top layer of dirt becomes maximally compacted, water cannot go through this layer.

Durable, fast-draining natural grass surfaces are now available. They have the safety advantages and aesthetic qualities of grass and a cumulative cost less than that of the artificial surfaces. A good strain of natural grass is used with a 2.5-cm (1-in) layer of topsoil. Underlying this soil is a deep, sandy, porous base for deep root development. Pumps work through perforated pipes to irrigate or, by suction, to dry the field through the roots. Subterranean heating cables may be used in colder climates to prevent the field from freezing.

The well-being of the athlete should come first, and an excellent natural surface is the best surface to spare them injuries. An artificial surface has a place indoors, where grass will not grow, and outdoors when extremely heavy use under poor weather conditions would quickly ruin a natural field.

PLANNING AN ATHLETIC CONTEST

Track Meet

Advanced planning is the key to a safe athletic contest for athletes and spectators. Planning for a track meet, for example, includes space allotments, scheduling, and safety instructions. The field-event danger zones must be roped off and must not overlap when one station is in use. Field-event warm-ups are especially dangerous because the athletes may not be fully ready or concentrating. Concurrent activities, moreover, may cause crowding.

At all-comers meets, athletes of different skill levels compete. Each athlete, however, should have a skill level that enables him to keep the discus or javelin, for example, within the competitive corridors. In a poorly run track meet, a javelin may land on the timer's table or on the pole vault cushion. If an athlete lacks skill in the discus, he should practice by throwing a rubber discus into a net or canvas.

Dangers in the vaulting area are reduced by good spotting and proper care of the landing cushion and poles. Spotters should be alert to break the fall of a vaulter if he misses the landing area and keep the crossbar from landing on the athlete. Another spotter catches the vaulting pole so that it is not scratched or otherwise damaged. If the air cushion has separate side cushions, the athlete may catch his leg or arm in one of the gaps. On hot days, the cushion may actually burn the athlete; thus water should sometimes be splashed on it.

The overloading of a fiberglass vaulting pole may cause it to break and to impale the vaulter. Safe force limits for the vaulting pole are determined by the weight of an athlete, the speed of his run, and his hand-hold position. Each pole has a definite weight limit usually specified for the vaulter's weight. The faster athlete has a greater plant force, and the pole should be correctly placed in the emplacing box. Proper hand position is crucial to achieve a maximum safe bend of the pole. An unsafe position of the hands may cause an awkward vault and a loss of control.

There should be at least one trained person whose only duty at the meet is safety. All athletes must completely understand and respect the safety regulations. If an accident does occur, a causal analysis should be done.

Rebound Tumbling

Rebound tumbling is the most likely sports activity to produce a spinal cord injury. Most injuries occur on the trampoline bed, even when spotters are in proper position and alert.

A trampoline should never be used in a routine physical education class; there are many less dangerous things for youngsters to learn. With proper coaching and spotting, however, the trampoline may be used as an integral part of the training and conditioning of some athletes. Divers, for example, may practice flips and twists on it. Safety belts may be used for difficult or new stunts. The tumbling belt has rings, and the twisting safety belt has slots for twisting.

To increase safety in rebound tumbling, the trampoline must have safety side pads or frame pads and safety spotting decks on the ends. The rebound tumbler should master the basic landing positions and progress systematically. If the trampoline is used in a physical education class, no somersaults or tricks with inversion of the head should be allowed, and only basic skills and twisting routines should be done. Somersaulting is only for the advanced athlete who uses overhead spotting devices, except in elite performances.

Exercise programs should be brief because fatigue increases injury potential. Two-and-three-quarter forward and two-and-three-quarter backward somersaults should be banned, except in elite performances. In these somersaults, a gymnast may not see his position until it is too late to correct a wrong landing. Rebound tumbling should be judged as an art form.

Rebound tumbling requires great concentration; therefore, no children should be allowed near the apparatus to distract the gymnast, and there should never be more than one person on the trampoline. "Minitramps" should not be used for complicated tricks. The trampoline must always be folded and locked when not in use.

If an athlete's neck is injured and he is lying on the trampoline, the elastic trampoline bed may cause movement of his head and neck if standard methods of removal are used. To prevent excessive movement, a plank and plywood rescue method should be used.[2] This framing technique uses four wooden planks and a sheet of plywood. The wood should be stored near the trampoline along with a scoop stretcher.

To facilitate a rescue, the boards should be placed on the bed, extending a foot beyond each side of the trampoline. These boards form a frame around the athlete, and the rescuers support the injured athlete on the trampoline by holding the plywood under him with their upper backs or legs. While the athlete's head is being held steady, the trainer directs four assistants to place the athlete on the scoop stretcher. Head straps are then applied, the athlete's wrists are secured, and he is transferred from the trampoline without commotion.

ATHLETIC ACTIVITY IN THE HEAT

As early fall and late spring football practice necessitate participating in weather of high heat stress, and with artificial turfs compounding the problem, it is wise for all personnel to review the literature pertaining to the problems associated with heat. It is important to remember that *humidity must be considered* in heat stress, since cases of fatal heat stroke have been recorded in an environnment of 64°F with a humidity reading of 100%.

Physiologic Response to Heat

The nervous control and coordination of thermoregulation is located in the hypothalamus. Heat conservation and heat dissipation are subcenters in the hypothalamus that regulate the body's reaction to cold and heat, heat dissipation being regulated by cutaneous vasodilation and sweating. Increased blood temperature from the periphery causes the hypothalamus to respond to the environmental temperature. Sensitive hypothalamic receptors and indirect afferent impulses of the thermoreceptors are responsible for this response. Other centers for homeostasis located in the hypothalamus are water balance, vasomotor activities, and humoral activities. *Temperature of up to 110°F in heat stroke* can often damage the hypothalamus. The athlete with a defective hypothalamus becomes more susceptible to heat disorders.

The results of heat disorders are most pronounced on the cardiovascular system. The heart must pump a greater supply of blood in order to cool the body. For each degree of rectal temperature increase, there is a 7% additional demand for oxygen to maintain body processes. The heart must also increase its blood supply to the lungs. As is sometimes the result, particularly in the unacclimated person, *heat stroke results as the cardiovascular system is overloaded.* Circulatory failure is attributable to the exhaustion and cessation of the myocardium. Pulse rate is said to be an indicator of cardiovascular response, with a resting rate of 110/minute associated with tolerable body temperature.

Body fluid lost through perspiration and not replaced is derived mainly from interstitial fluid osmotically drawn by the plasma to keep plasma water content normal. During heat stress, secretion from the pituitary gland of an antidiuretic hormone conserves fluid by the reabsorption of water in the renal tubules, thus diminishing urine flow. One-hundred fifty liters of fluid or more may pass through the kidneys with only 1.5 liters excreted and not reabsorbed back into the body. Salt in the perspiration is conserved, after a period of acclimation, by adrenocortical activity, which provides for its reabsorption in the kidneys. Na^+ and Cl^- are the ions primarily responsible for maintaining the water content of the extracellular compartment. A potassium deficit may arise as this sodium-conserving process increases the loss of potassium from the body. Large quantities of water are lost in heavy daily activities, and up to 20 g of salt may accompany this fluid loss (1 g being 15 grains). During these activities, athletes regain their fluid balance only by rehydrating after the activity. *Fluid is lost more rapidly than it can be taken in during exercise.* Thirst accounts for only 50% of body needs.

Heat is gained or lost through *conduction, radiation, convection, and evaporation.* Conduction may cause a rise in body heat of a football player through his contact with hot pads and helmets. The drinking of cool water causes the body to lose heat by conduction because this water must be warmed to body temperature. Cold water empties more rapidly from the stomach as the cooler temperature increases the smooth muscle activity. Sweat loss is often more than a quart/hour, where maximum replacement is less than a quart/hour.

Surrounding temperatures may cause a rise in body heat from radiation. Athletes can gain as much as 250 cal/h in the sun (radiation), *but the wearing of white clothing reduces this gain by one-half.* Hot air flow increases body temperature through convection means.

When the environmental temperature is below 87°F (skin temperature), 70% of body heat is lost through radiation, conduction, and convection and 30% by evaporation. *Once the temperature rises above 87°F, heat is added to the body temperature as heat is supplied more rapidly to the body than can be eliminated by evaporation (perspiration).* In areas of high heat stress, sweating provides the primary protective mechanism of the body against overheating. As the humidity rises, the amount of body heat lost by evaporation decreases to almost zero at 100% humidity. With an exchange of cool air by ventilation, the heat elimination of convection and evaporation is greatly increased. Hot air exchange may often offset the benefits of evaporative cooling.

Heat Disorders

The classification of heat disorders is *circulatory instability, water and electrolyte balance disorders, and heatstroke or heat hyperpyrexia.* Of these, one group may predispose to another. Circulatory instability is often characterized by heat syncope of fainting and has been more commonly observed in women. Other symptoms are lightheadedness, dizziness associated with postural change, long standing, or exercise, nausea, and weakness. Because football linemen are constantly changing postural movements, they are particularly susceptible to heat syncope, a form of exercise-induced heat exhaustion. In circulatory instability, peripheral vasodilation occurs with a tendency toward venous pooling and hypertension. The pulse blood pressure immediately drops with a rise in pulse rate. Recovery is rapid if the athlete spends a few minutes in a reclining position.

In disorders of water and electrolytes that lead to heat edema, water depletion heat exhaustion, salt depletion heat exhaustion, and heat cramps, *unlimited access to the ingestion of water is the major preventative* of heat illness. Frequent copious urine flow is a sign of adequate hydration. Heat edema results in swelling of the feet and ankles during early exposure to heat, probably because of the pooling of blood in the area.

Water depletion heat exhaustion often occurs early and is caused by a loss of body fluid from diarrhea as well as sweat loss. Rectal temperature increases, as do pulse rate and respiration, leading to hyperventilation. The skin becomes hot and inelastic, cheeks hollow, eyes sunken, and the victim exhibits symptoms of tingling, paresthesia, restlessness, hysteria, giddiness, and uncoordination. Water depletion heat exhaustion

sometimes leads to cyanosis, hypertension, circulatory and urinary failure, heat stroke, coma, and death. An early weight loss of 2% may be followed by a severe 7% weight loss. For this reason weight charts are useful to prevent this heat disorder. Rehydration in a cool area is necessary. Salted drinks are of no use in this instance.

Cutaneous blood flow decreases drastically as exhaustion appears during exercise in heat, thus jeopardizing the ability of the body to dissipate heat from the skin. As a result the athlete may become hypothermic and begin shivering. Slow runners in cool weather may also become hypothermic with a resultant excess heat loss.

Although water depletion heat exhaustion and salt depletion heat exhaustion may coexist (Table 6-2), the chemical picture of the latter is somewhat different. A large intake of unsalted fluid predisposes to salt depletion heat exhaustion. Less water is reabsorbed from the renal tubules, and water depletion is secondary.

Salt depletion heat exhaustion generally progresses over 3 to 5 days with a normal or slightly elevated temperature. Symptoms are cool clammy skin, weariness, headache, nausea, vomiting, diarrhea or constipation, and muscular cramps. Cramps from heat stress are caused by water intoxication into the intracellular fluid, resulting in dilution of the sodium chloride content. Despite statements that extra salt in the diet is unneces-

Table 6-2 DIFFERENCE IN WATER DEPLETION VERSUS SALT DEPLETION HEAT EXHAUSTION

Water	**Salt**
Urgency of thirst	Slight or no thirst
Predisposes to heat stroke	Does not predispose to heat stroke
High intake of salt without water danger	High intake of water without salt danger
May occur immediately	Generally progresses over 3 to 5 days
Fatigue less prominent	Fatigue prominent
Muscle cramps absent	Muscle cramps present
Vomiting usually absent	Vomiting present
Skin inelastic, usually dry	Skin clammy, moist
Temperature high	Temperature near normal
Death occurs generally as a result of heatstroke	Death rare
Treat by cooling and rehydration	Treatment by cooling and saline drinks

sary, some individuals need enteric salt with meals or extra salting of food to prevent cramps. Saline is also necessary for treatment. Beef tea, consomme, and tomato juice are fluids that can mask the salty taste (1 tsp/pint) needed to treat or prevent.

Heat stroke and heat hyperpyrexia are the result of thermoregulatory failure that too often results in death. Physical exercise is the most common cause of this type of reaction to heat stress. There is a primary failure to produce sweat by water depletion, the fatigue of the sweating apparatus being unknown. It is postulated that circulatory collapse from high output leads to cardiac failure, and cessation of sweating from increased venous pressure. Heat stroke often progresses from water depletion heat exhaustion.

The individual may have sudden coma onset, delirium, central nervous system disturbance, convulsions, disorientation, incontinence, involuntary limb movements, plus the usual milder symptoms of heat stress. The skin, usually hot and dry, may be pale and cool. Temperature will be high. Cyanosis and lack of pupil coordination and reaction to light may be noted. The pulse rate is often 130/minute with a rapid, labored, gasping respiration of 35/minute. Renal failure and shock may develop.

Effective cooling is the treatment for heat stroke and heat hyperpyrexia. The patient with heat stroke is unconscious, irrational, and has a temperature of at least 105°F, whereas the individual with heat hyperpyrexia is conscious, rational, and has a temperature below 105°F. If the temperature is reduced within an hour to 102°F, the cooling is usually effective. If cooling is not effective, heat stroke is fatal in 20% to 75% of the cases, depending on complications. Heat hyperpyrexia fatality rate is about 5%. *Untreated cases of both are fatal.*

Various modalities for cooling may be used. A special slatted table designed to spray cool water (44°F) on all sides of the patient is effective. So also is the use of wet sheets, submersion in cold water, and the "cold blanket" used in heat surgery. Probably the most practical of all is the use of a fan blowing across the athlete who is lying on a slotted deck lounger while at the same time his extremities are being vigorously massaged

with cool wet towels. Care should be taken not to over chill because shock or shivering (vasoconstriction), or both, may occur. The extremities should be massaged to promote circulation. Chlorpromatine is often administered by medical personnel to depress the hypothalamic center for heat to promote vasodilation and to prevent shivering.

Heat affects performance, and there is a direct correlation between heat and minor injuries, illnesses, and irritability. Studies have shown a 15% decrease in weight lifting ability when the temperature was elevated from 68° to 75°F. Manual dexterity also deteriorates. Heat, however, seems to decrease a person's willingness to work rather than his capacity to work.

Prevention

Individuals susceptible to heat disorders include the aged, obese, unacclimated, the dehydrated whether from vomiting, diarrhea, or alcohol, and those with cardiovascular disorders. The physically unfit, those just recovering from a febrile illness, and those with a history of heat illness are also prone to heat illness. The implications for athletes is clear: *Exercise is a must for full development of physical adaptation to heat.* Acclimation to heat allows an individual to work effectively in heat of 80°F +, whereas the physically unfit cannot perform in environments in which the temperature is much above 65° to 75°F. For full benefits of acclimation, two sessions of 2 hours daily are best employed. One session should be during the heat of the day. Longer sessions only put excessive strain on the athlete. Most acclimation occurs in 4 to 7 days and is usually complete by 12 to 14 days. Deaths usually occur in the first 3 to 5 days among the dehydrated who may lose 20 or more pounds during a practice. Heat illness may be accumulative, so be aware of those who show increasing effects of the heat.

The individual who is highly competitive and overenthusiastic should be watched carefully during periods of heat stress because he is often the one doing more than the rest of the team. Consequently, he is overtaxing his system in the heat and is usually the player with the dry uniform at the end of practice because he has exhausted his perspiration. As the individual matures, he learns to pace himself and thus does not suffer the effects of heat as does the inexperienced athlete.

When the athlete becomes acclimated, his rectal temperature and pulse rate recede to near normal from an initial increase during heat stress. Cardiac output, blood volume, and venous tone are increased. Less blood is needed by skeletal muscle; therefore, the skin can get more blood to the surface for body cooling. The basal metabolic rate is reduced. The initial sweat rate may increase up to several liters per hour for improved cooling capacity. The acclimated individual will tolerate dehydration better than the unacclimated. After about 2 weeks the sweat rate then returns to near normal. With this massive dehydration, cool water and salt tablets or a saline solution (1–2 tsp salt/gal) should be available every 30 to 90 minutes of exercise. It is recommended, however, that the athlete have access to unlimited water at all times. The athlete should drink several glasses of fluid just before competition. Increased cold fluid in the gut causes more rapid absorption.

Five to 15 g of salt/day may be needed at the start of the acclimation process. Vitamin C, potassium, and calcium are also useful to the diet at this time. It has been suggested that potassium deficiency leads to depressed muscular activity. Tablets are available that contain salt, potassium dextrose, ascorbic acid, and calcium* to prevent an excess loss of any of the above.

As indicated by Mayer and Costil, there is no benefit in using electrolyte solutions for the individual who has a normal diet and participates in sports, except for perhaps the marathon runner. Some commercial electrolyte solutions have such a high concentration of sugar that they actually interfere with the emptying of the gastrointestinal tract. A 10% glucose concentration decreases gastric emptying by one half. The primary aim of any replacement fluid is to maintain blood volume, and water does this best. No more than 2.5 mg/dl

of sugar is indicated. Soft drinks need 3:1 dilution with water, and Gatorade, 2:1.

Players should weigh out and in for each practice, and these charts should be examined for athletes losing 2 to 5 lb/24 h. *These are the candidates for heat illness* and ideally should be excluded from practice for 24 hours. A 4% to 5% body weight loss results in a 20% to 30% decline in hard muscular work. Also, exclude those with minor heat problems for 24 hours. Vomiting and diarrhea further dehydrate the body and should be contraindications for heavy workouts in the heat. Clothing should be light, loose, and white whenever possible. Mesh or net jerseys further help in body cooling. A cold shower taken before competition will also increase the body's resistance to heat.

The use of the wet bulb globe thermometer or sling psychrometer is a useful index as to the number of salt and fluid breaks and the length of practice times (Table 6-3). In many instances the physically fit acclimated athlete has participated above these standards without any seemingly ill-effects.

Physical fitness tests that measure endurance (e.g., 3–300 yard sprints, 1–1½ minute rest between; accumulative times depend on 40 yard times) at the beginning of hot weather training will indicate to the trainer who is in poor physical condition and thus is a candidate for heat illness. It is unfortunate that these individuals are not motivated enough to report in good condition. Athletes in this condition should probably be worked by themselves or in selective drills until they are ready to participate. Rubber sweat suits must not be used for obvious reasons.

A common error in conditioning in early practice is to overwork the athlete. The poorer the physical condition of the athlete, the less work he can tolerate. Here is another instance in which the cardiovascular physical fitness test plays an important part in determining the amount of physical conditioning needed. Conditioning beyond the point of fatigue only results in an overall decline in fitness as food stores are depleted. Once liver and muscle glycogen stores are exhausted, usually about the third or fourth day of two-a-days, work capacity rapidly diminishes. Thus by the first game the question often is not

---

*Thermotabs.

Table 6-3A   PRACTICE IN THE HEAT

Attire	Length of Exercise (min)	WBGT	Length of Water Break (min)
Full pads	45	84 or below	5
Full pads	45	84–85	10
Full pads or	30	85–88	10
Helmet, shoulder pads, shorts, shoes	30	85–88	5

The above is for a 2-hour practice session once daily. No more than one 2-hour practice session a day should be undertaken in the heat.

The use of managers to give each group continuous and unlimited cold fluids is to be considered the ideal.

Table 6-3B   UNIVERSAL WBGT INDEX

WBGT Index for Outdoor Activities
(Wet Bulb Global Temperature)

Range	Signal Flag	Activity	Wet Bulb Temperature Guide	
82–84.9	Green	Alert for possible increase in index	Under 60°F	No precaution necessary
			61–65°F	Alert all participants, especially heavy weight losers
85–87.9	Yellow	Active practice curtailed (unacclimated men)	66–70°F	Insist that appropriate fluids be given in the field
88–89.9	Red	Active practice curtailed (all men — except most acclimated)	71–75°F	Alter practice schedules to provide rest periods every 30 min, plus above precautions
90 +		All training stopped, skull session — demonstrations	76°F and up	Practice postponed or conducted in shorts

Whenever relative humidity is 97% or higher, great precaution should be taken.

who is in the best shape, but who is the least tired and worn out.

The ideal diets for work in the heat are ones high in carbohydrates, because carbohydrates are high in water content. Proteins require a great amount of water for digestion, thus adding to fluid imbalance. It is important for the athlete to maintain his normal calorie intake. The intake of large amounts of fluids leads to loss of appetite, and thus to diarrhea and vomiting. The athlete should drink just enough fluid to satiate his thirst before eating. After he has eaten a good meal, he may then take extra fluids.

Alcohol is to be avoided during periods of

heat stress because it causes dehydration and increases the metabolic load. All medications should be evaluated for possible deleterious effects. Medications that reduce sweating are phenothiazines, which include the major tranquilizers; antihistamines; diuretics such as chlorothiazide; and anticholinergics such as atropine and belladonna, usually taken for the treatment of gastrointestinal disorders. Athletes taking diuretics for control of high blood pressure should be closely observed. Heavy meals before exercise are contraindicated so that maximum circulation may be used for cooling.

Air conditioning with dehumidifiers for off-practice hours benefits acclimation because the body processes do not have to constantly be active in order to cool the body. Sweating is reduced, and dehydration is therefore not as much of a problem. Skin disorders from chronic wetness are also avoided, and the athletes are better able to rest in a cool environment, thus diminishing fatigue and additional cardiovascular strain.

All team physicians, trainers, and coaches should be familiar with the prevention and treatment of heat disorders. A yearly review of existing literature is to be encouraged. With the use of sound practices, athletes will be able to compete safely in times of heat stress.

FITTING OF PROTECTIVE EQUIPMENT

Helmets and shoulder pads are the primary pieces of protective equipment in tackle football and are worn by more than 1 million high school players. Today's football equipment can provide adequate protection for these players. With all of the contact in high school and college football, professional ranks, and assorted leagues, it is amazing that there are not more serious injuries. The equipment so fully protects the wearer, however, that he plays with much more abandon. Thus extra torque and velocity increase the likelihood of certain types of injury.

Even with excellent protective equipment, a proper fit is important. Improperly fit equipment may cause injury or increase the severity of an injury. To assure that the equipment will provide the optimum protection for which it was designed, all personnel who fit protective equipment must be extremely knowledgeable about fitting. Improper fitting is especially a problem at the high school level, where coaches, managers, and student trainers often lack proper knowledge of fitting. Sometimes, first-string players are given the best equipment, although it is not necessarily properly fitted, and the rest of the squad takes what is left. Not only do all of these athletes need the best equipment, but also these players must be fitted individually for each piece of equipment.

Football Helmet

The football helmet distributes and attenuates shocks and recovers rapidly. Shock reduction is optimal only when the helmet is properly fitted.[10] All football helmets bearing the National Operating Committee on Standards for Athletic Equipment (NOCSAE) seal provide adequate protection if they are properly fitted. When a school purchases a particular brand of helmet, the sales representative should demonstrate proper fitting technique to those persons charged with fitting the helmets.

Basic Guidelines

Short hair allows a better fit of the football helmet.[18] If an athlete has long hair, he should wet his hair before trying on the helmet. The fit will then be a proper one for sweaty competition. The helmet should fit snugly on the athlete's head and not slide excessively from side to side, forward, or backward. To check for excess motion, the fitter should grasp the face mask, with the chin strap fastened, and apply pressure while the player holds his neck stiff (Figure 6-1). If the helmet slides excessively, it is improperly fitted, regardless of whether the size corresponds to the player's head size. A special fitting will usually be needed to ensure a proper fit in an athlete with a long, oval head. Jaw pads should be of the proper size—for example, thick pads for a thin-faced player.

The frontal crown of the helmet should be one or two fingerbreadths above the eyebrows. This position should remain the same when the player overlaps his fingers on top of the helmet and presses down (Figure 6-2).

The padding on the front lip of the helmet reduces lacerations and abrasions of the nose. If, however, the posterior tails of the chin straps are loose, the helmet may still slide forward over the player's nose. Proper tension on the anterior straps keeps the helmet from sliding backward during contact (Figure 6-3). The back edge of the helmet should not impinge on the player's neck when he extends it.

Players should be advised that a properly fitted helmet may feel slightly tight for the first few days of practice, especially if the helmet is new. If a player feels that the fit of his helmet is unsatisfactory, he should report back promptly to the person in charge of fitting. All players should be shown how to put on a helmet correctly. First,

Figure 6-1   To check for excess motion of the helmet, grasp the face mask with the chin strap fastened and apply pressure while the player holds his neck stiff.

the player puts his thumbs in the earholes, with the helmet tilted back. He then rolls the helmet forward onto his head. He removes it in the reverse order. The helmet must not be jammed onto the head or jerked off because this causes discomfort and external ear damage. Each player's number should be marked inside his helmet, and players should never swap helmets.

A player should never wear a cracked helmet. Cracks may appear in the helmet at areas of stress

Figure 6-2   The helmet should not slip down when the player overlaps his fingers on top of the helmet and presses down.

where facemask hardware has been attached. The helmets should be checked for soundness during and after the season and after reconditioning. The examiner looks for cracks in the shell, rusted or loose rivets, and loose or bent facemasks. During the season, padded suspensions tend to bottom out, and air pads and fluid pads may leak.

Shoulder Pads

The two basic types of shoulder pads are flat pads and cantilever pads.[10] Flat pads are worn by players in limited contact positions who need more glenohumeral motion—for example, quarterbacks and receivers. Cantilever pads are named for the bridge that extends over the shoulder and are worn by players who are in constant contact. Most flat pads are less protective than cantilever pads but, when properly constructed, can afford excellent protection for linemen and linebackers. Of the cantilever pads, the inside cantilever is the more common. The outside cantilever affords somewhat more protection with a larger blocking surface and is the most popular for offensive linemen. The pads for linebackers and for players receiving blows in a standing position are larger anteriorly and slanted forward.

The neck opening of shoulder pads should

Figure 6-3 Anterior and posterior chin straps (a four-way chin strap) keep the helmet from shifting forward or backward.

have enough room for the player to extend his arm overhead without the pad's impinging on his neck. However, the neck opening should not be so large as to allow excessive sliding around on the shoulders, as in the case of oversized pads. A pad too large will slide to one side and invite neck injury, and an improperly fitted shoulder pad may allow injury to the player's acromioclavicular joint.

The tip of the shoulder pad should reach just to the lateral edge of the shoulder, and the flaps, or epaulets, should cover the deltoid area (Figure 6-4). A pair of calipers may be used to speed proper fitting (Figure 6-5). The fitter should measure from the edge of one shoulder across to the other shoulder.

The elastic axilla straps that hold the pads to the chest and to the back must be tight but comfortable. These straps allow the impact of a blow to be distributed onto the chest and back. If the straps are loose, the pad may flatten out and press over the acromioclavicular joint.

Shoulder pads should be inspected constantly for cracks, frayed straps and strings, loose rivets, and other failures. At the end of the season, all equipment must be inspected. Defective equipment should be discarded, but if the equipment is salvageable it may be sent to a reputable athletic equipment reconditioner. When the equipment has been returned from the reconditioner, it must again be inspected carefully.

Special Pads

Often pads need to be made for areas for which commercial pads are unavailable. A soft silicone cast may be made from GE-RTV-11 and will allow the necessary protection while at the same time allowing a greater degree of comfort and functional participation. Since a hard cast is illegal in secondary school competition, this material allows the athlete with carpal and metacarpal injuries to continue playing.

Other products often used for a hard protective outer shell are Lightcast, Hexcilite, and Orthoplast. Ensolite and Therm-O-Foam are used for inner padding.

Figure 6-4 The shoulder pad should extend to the tip of the shoulder.

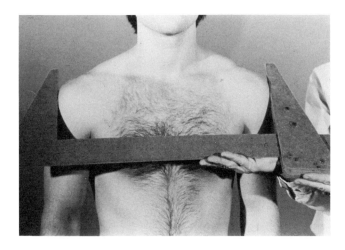

Figure 6-5   Calipers help in the proper fitting of shoulder pads.

TAPING THE INJURED ATHLETE

Adhesive Tape

Adhesive tape may be used to prevent excessive motion in injured and normal joints. The tape relieves pain by splinting injured soft tissue and aids healing by approximating torn tissue. In some fractures, taping is preferable to a cast because the tape may be removed to allow applications of cold or heat and exercise of the limb. Tape may also be used to cover blisters and secure player protective equipment.

Adhesive tape varies in color, width, strength, and the nature of the backing to the adhesive material. The tape must be strong enough to withstand the rigors of athletics. Its strength is determined by the thread count (the number of threads per inch). Cotton- or cloth-backed, rubber-based white adhesive tape is the most commonly used tape in athletics and is available in speed packs or tubes. A speed pack is wound more loosely, and the roll is bigger than a tube; it bruises easily, however, and may dent while traveling. Generally, 3.8-cm (1.5-in)-wide white cloth-backed adhesive tape, although inelastic, meets most needs at a school with a limited budget. If more funds are available, elastic tapes may be considered.

Elastic tape stretches and may be used when gentle compression, which reduces muscle spasm and the sensation of instability, is required. The elastic tape may also be used to support damaged tissue, such as strained muscles. More rugged elastic tapes are needed for shoulder and hip injuries. Elastic tape is also used to secure protective pads, especially in areas such as the shoulder, upper humerus, forearm, hand, thigh, and shin. A gymnast may use elastic tape for hand taping: His fingers are passed through holes cut in the tape, and the tape is then pulled down and secured at the wrist with white adhesive tape. The weaker elastic tapes are preferred when tissue must be protected, but free movement is needed. A waterproof, hypoallergenic, plastic-backed tape may be used to secure bandages and dressings and to approximate wound edges, but this tape is not as durable as cloth tape. Moleskin tape is designed with a soft, thick-napped cotton cloth for cushioning.

Taping Technique

Taping is an art, and the trainer must be proficient at preparing and protecting the athlete's skin, applying the tape properly, and removing the tape with care (Table 6-4). The taping job must be effective and comfortable and should conform with consistent pressure. For taping to be effective, the trainer must know which motions should be limited to reduce the stress on the injured body part. The function of taping should be explained to the athlete, along with how it should feel.

The athlete is positioned for taping with the injured part at a comfortable working level. For a

Table 6-4   TAPING RULES

1. Prepare skin—wash, shave, apply tincture of benzoin

2. Position properly

3. Use proper-sized tape

4. Anchor and work toward heart

5. Angle the tape to fit the contour of the body

6. Apply snug, but not constrictive, even tension

7. Apply tape neatly, thoroughly, cleanly, simply

knee taping, for example, the athlete stands up on the trainer's table with his heel raised and his knee slightly flexed. A band of hair should be shaved at either end of the area to be taped to serve as an anchoring base. The anchor area should be wide so that the anchoring point may be moved each day. Otherwise, if the same anchoring point were used for consecutive tapings, the skin might become irritated, eroded, and infected. An electric clipper is preferable to a razor for shaving because the razor may cause cuts. If a razor must be used, the shaving should be done the night before.

The skin in the taped area should be carefully cared for, since the athlete may have to be taped two or three times a day. Sweaty and dirty feet should be cleaned and dried before being taped. The skin should not be prepped with irritating organic solvents that remove all of its natural oils, but it must be free of oily contamination before taping because the tape will not adhere well to skin to which ointments have been applied. If the skin is sweaty or if an athlete must be taped in the midst of competition, a tape adherent may be needed to prevent slippage and to help prevent mechanical erosion. Tincture of benzoin, or Friar's balsam, will improve adhesiveness; however, it is not generally necessary to use it with the more adhesive modern tapes, and the benzoin itself may cause irritation. If a skin preparation is needed, a fast-drying, less irritating, non-benzoin-containing material may be used.

Adhesive tape should be applied only to skin that is at room temperature. If placed on skin that is too hot or too cold after a treatment, the skin

may be damaged as the tape is removed. To protect the skin, the tape may be placed over an underwrap or prewrap, which is a thin, porous, polyurethane foam wrap. The prewrap may, however, limit the supportiveness of the tape, and, in some cases in which more support is needed, it may be necessary to shave the entire area and apply the tape directly to the skin.

The first straps of a taping are applied parallel (or vertical) to the injured muscle, tendons, or ligaments, and no more than a few inches of the tape are pulled from the roll at a time while the tape is being applied. The continuous wrapping of a part is not the most effective way to support the underlying tissue, and the tape may cause constriction. If the part must be encircled, the tape is applied in single strips, with each strip circling the injured part just once. This method produces uniform pressure and avoids constriction.

Adhesive tape is torn by rapidly twisting the tape as it is held tightly between the thumb and index finger. The right and left hands twist quickly in opposite directions. Another useful tearing method is to lay the thumb of one hand firmly across the tape as it lies in position on the body part being taped. The roll of tape is then rapidly rotated with the other hand. Beginners learn how to tear tape by tearing it into very small pieces.

Gaps and Wrinkles

The trainer must avoid gaps between strips of tape or wrinkles in the tape, especially the vertical strips, that may cause blisters and new areas of discomfort. Gaps are avoided if each strip overlaps the preceding strip by about one half (Figure 6-6). Gaps are most common in the Achilles tendon region and anterior tibialis; thus these areas should always be inspected before the athlete leaves the taping table. Wrinkles generally result from carelessness. All layers of tape, especially the innermost, should be neat and free of wrinkles by applying it with smooth, even tension. The site of application may itself, of course, favor wrinkles because most body parts are not cylindrical but conical.

To avoid wrinkles when tape is being applied

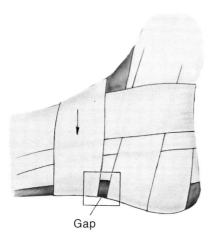 

Gap

Figure 6-6 Gaps may occur, especially in the Achilles tendon area, causing blisters and new areas of discomfort. Gaps may be avoided if each strip overlaps the preceding strip by about one third the width of the tape. The tape job should be checked for gaps and wrinkles before the athlete leaves the taping table.

to these curved surfaces, the trainer may use several narrow strips instead of one wide strip. Sometimes a wide strip may be torn at either end to make several narrow tabs, which unite at the middle of the strip. Wrinkles normally occur in places such as in front of the ankle or behind the heel where the skin itself must wrinkle to allow movement. These areas may be protected with a cushioning pad of gauze, cotton, felt, or foam that has been covered with a skin lubricant. To prevent tape from splitting at bending areas, such as near the kneecap, the edges of the tape may be rolled or doubled over.

A taping should be comfortable. If it aggravates pain, it has been improperly applied or not indicated. If the strapping itself produces undue tension and pain, numbness, or pinching, then the tape must be reapplied.

Removal of Tape

Just as there is a proper way to apply tape, there is a proper way to remove it. "If you don't want it to hurt, rip it off" is bad advice. As much care should be taken in removing tape as in applying. Tape is best removed by gently pulling along the long axis of the strapping, not across it. It is usually easier to push the skin away from the tape than to rip or pull the tape away from the skin. A solvent may make removal easier. If tape has been applied to an area where there is still some hair, the tape should be removed in the direction of the hair growth, it should not be jerked or

yanked because this increases the amount of hair removed and mechanically irritates the skin.

Most tapings will develop a natural crease while being worn. These creases are convenient places to cut through for removal of the tape. A sharp-tipped implement should never be used to remove tape. Instead, the trainer should use bandage scissors or a special commercial tape cutter. He may dip the scissors into skin lubricant, which will allow them to slide. The tape is then cut away from the injury site. In removing an ankle strapping, vertical and horizontal cuts may be made with the bandage scissors. Once the tape has been cut, it is gently removed from the skin, and after the athlete has showered he should rub massage lotion into his skin to restore its moisture.

Tape Rash

Tape rash occurs most commonly right after summer, when the player's skin is not ready for two-a-day tapings. Most reactions to tape come from mechanical irritation and, to a lesser degree, from chemical irritation. Daily tapings especially cause moisture to build up under these occlusive tapings, which softens the stratum corneum and reduced cohesion between cells. When the tape is removed, the soft stratum corneum is stripped away with the adhesive tape mass. This separation does not occur at the skin-adhesive interface but deeper, to cause irregular delamination of the stratum corneum.[2] The more adhesive the tape, the more cells are removed. After the tape has been removed, the adhesive surface of the tape may be covered with a film of desquamated epidermis. In this case, the skin should be cleansed with a neutral soap and thoroughly dried before the tape is reapplied. If hair follicles and the skin that surrounds them have been irritated from the tape being pulled away from the skin, the irritated area is treated like an abrasion, and the part is not taped for a few days. The tape also blocks sweat pores, and, within 3 days, explosive bacterial growth will occur under occlusive tape and an infection may start. Fortunately, tape is usually worn only for a short time in athletic activities.

Acrylate tapes allow for long-term adhesion. Their molecular structure permits water vapor to pass through so that the statum corneum is not overhydrated from perspiration.[1] With these tapes, only a small amount of statum corneum is lost during tape removal. The plane of separation develops near the surface of the stratum corneum in the region of the naturally desquamating cells. Thus, these tapes may be used repeatedly with only minimal skin damage. Itching may be from mechanical or chemical factors, or both. There seems to be little correlation between the presence of visible skin lesions and itching. The athlete may have bad lesions without itching or may itch without a single visible lesion.

Only infrequently are athletes truly allergic to adhesive tape. An allergic reaction includes erythema, edema, papules, vesicles, and, in severe cases, desquamation. The response becomes more severe the longer the tape is left on and usually intensifies for some time even after the tape has been removed, requiring days to subside completely.

The allergic athlete may react to an individual ingredient of the tape or to the component mass. If an athlete is allergic, he should be patch-tested with different brands of tape. Conventional rubber-based adhesives have many ingredients, including elastomers, plasticizers, tackifiers, pigments, and stabilizers.[2] There may be source variation and the potential for introducing irritants and sensitizing agents. Acrylate adhesives do not have as many components, and thus are hypoallergenic.

TRAUMA FROM ACUTE INJURY

The inflammatory consequences of acute injury are pain, erythema and warmth, loss of function, and hematoma. This outcome encourages the formation of fibrous tissue in the area. Cellular debris and red blood corpuscles hemorrhage into the interstitial spaces to organize and form the hematoma and possible myositis ossificans.

Fibrin in the blood becomes fibrous tissue as early as the fourth day. Hemarthrosis destroys articular cartilage, and resultant edema stretches capsular and ligamentous tissue. Edema and fibrous tissue are the greatest enemy of healing as joint and muscular motion are impaired, followed by atrophy.

With acute injury there are cellular changes. Cell death occurs, and with the cell degeneration histimine is released, which induces vascular changes. There is an increase in capillary permeability as a result, with a reversal of osmotic reaction within the body. Plasma proteins, colloids, and water flow into interstitial spaces from normal vessels, leading to edema in the area.

Soon thereafter, white blood cells migrate to the traumatized area. Neutrophils arrive first and die. They also release active proteolytic enzymes into the inflammatory process. The enzymes attach joint tissues, with resultant degenerative change from prolonged inflammation. The neutrophils are then phagocytized by the macrophages, along with cellular debris, fibrin, and red blood cells. The amount of exudates in the area is directly related to healing time. With pain, joint edema, and inflammation, muscle tone is inhibited and atrophy results.

A sequence of events begins in 1 to 3 days. Capillary buds begin to appear, as does collagen. Granulation tissue then fills the collagen matrix, the main supporting protein of body tissue. Fibroblasts, the connective tissue cells, proliferate, laying down collagen matrix. Reepithelialization begins, and by the fifth day a loose mesh of fibrous connective tissue, vascular with abundant collagen fibers, is laid down.

During the second week, fibroblasts proliferate further with collagen being oriented along normal stress lines if proper therapeutic exercise has begun. Otherwise an excess is produced with structures becoming stuck together. This excess bramble-bush effect is produced with inactivity. Edema vascularity decreases, and tensile increase of scar tissue allows removal of sutures in areas of stress. There is also an increase of fibrous connective tissue devascularization with increased healing by scarring.

Fibroblast proliferation slows by the end of the first month. There is then a maturing of fibrous tissue until the end of the second year with devascularization of scar tissue. This explains why it is often necessary to wait 1 or 2 years until full result is seen after injury.

TYPES OF INJURIES

Contusions

A blow to an athlete's body may damage tissue and cause swelling, bleeding, and pain. These bruises are especially painful at the shoulder and iliac crest where large muscles arise. Blows to the front of the arm or front of the thigh may result in myositis ossificans traumatica. Initial treatment is ice, compression, and elevation. If the injured area is very fluctuant, the team physician may decide to aspirate it. Once the reaction has died down, cryotherapy is used, and, when the danger of further hemorrhage is over, the region may be massaged. The area is taped to reduce abnormal motion and a protective pad applied.

Open Wounds

If an abrasion is considered trivial, it is sometimes treated inadequately. Wounds should be treated promptly, and if suturing is needed it should be done before swelling occurs. After an athlete sustains an open wound (Figure 6-7) such as a slide burn, he should scour all dirt from the wound with soap and water during his shower and then scrub the wound with sterile gauze pads. A surgical antiseptic such as Betadine O is then used. The wound should be covered with a protective Telfa dressing. Zinc oxide, a drying agent, may be applied beneath the Telfa. An infection may set in if the wound is inadequately cleaned. There is no such thing as a "mild" infection. Signs of infection may include soreness and redness around the wound, red streaks, and swollen lymph nodes.

Figure 6-7   A goalkeeper's abrasion should be treated promptly.

Sprains and Strains

A sprain refers to a damaged ligament and a strain to a damaged muscle or tendon. Sprains and strains are graded as either first, second, or third degree or mild, moderate, or severe. A mild sprain or strain is damage to the tissue but no loss of continuity of the fibers. The area will be tender and may be swollen. These mild and moderate sprains are treated by cryotherapy, and the athlete may experience an early return to athletics.

A moderate injury, a partial tear that allows increased laxity with some "give" on testing, is treated with ice, rest, and crutches to prevent extension to a complete tear. A severe sprain or strain is a complete tear, producing instability and often necessitating surgical repair.

Diagnosis of a sprain is made with pain/instability of a ligamentous area with stress. A strain is indicated when the athlete has pain with muscle/tendon stretching or resistance.

Fractures

Fractures are immobilized to prevent further damage and compounding of the injury. The joints above and below the fracture are splinted. Early treatment of a fracture also includes ice, compression, and elevation. The ice is left on until after x-ray films have been taken. An open fracture should be covered with a sterile dressing.

TREATMENT OF INJURY

Ice

Ice, by delaying or minimizing swelling, decreases pain and muscle spasm and limits the magnitude of an injury. The lower tissue temperature induces local vasoconstriction, which lessens capillary permeability, making the blood more viscous. Less blood flows into the injured area, and the hematoma is smaller.

The ice dulls peripheral pain by interfering locally with nerve impulses and decreasing nerve conduction velocity. It relieves spasm by decreasing muscle activity, muscle spindle firing, and acetylcholine levels so that ischemia is prevented. Ice limits the magnitude of an injury by lowering metabolism in peripheral, uninjured cells. By decreasing the cellular demand for oxygen, cells are put in partial hibernation, and thus extension of the injury is avoided. Otherwise cells that have survived the initial trauma may not be able to withstand the lack of oxygen imposed by the disruption of local circulation.

Initial treatment of an injury follows the acronym *ICE*, meaning *I*ce, *C*ompression, and *E*levation (Figure 6-8). The injured part should also be protected from painful stimuli. Ice may be applied initially for 30 minutes. The athlete may then shower before receiving another 30-minute

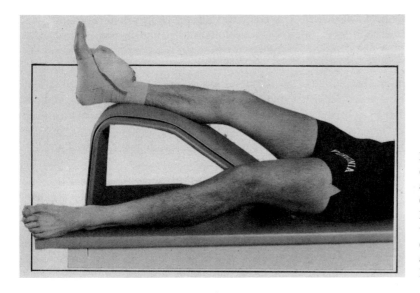

Figure 6-8 Initial treatment of a new injury follows the acronym ICE: *I*ce, *C*ompression, and *E*levation. In this case, the ankle is wrapped with a cold, wet elastic wrap, an ice bag is applied to the ankle, and the leg is elevated.

icing. If a fracture is suspected, ice is left in place until x-ray films are taken. Ice keeps the swelling down so that a better-fitting cast may be applied. Ice may then be used for 20 minutes each hour as necessary.

There are many ways to apply ice, including ice wraps, icepacks, ice slush, or a cold whirlpool. Elastic wraps are kept in a water bucket, and the bucket is placed in an ice chest. After injury, a cold, wet ice wrap should be applied initially. (If the wrap were dry, it would act as an insulator.) When ice is not available immediately, use cold water.

An icepack should be placed over the cold wrap. Chipped or crushed ice conforms better than cubes. The ice may be put in a plastic bag to prevent dripping or be placed in a towel that is moistened only on the skin side. The dry side acts as an insulator over the ice. Chemical icepacks are expensive and can be used only once; ethyl chloride and other cold sprays are expensive, too, and may cause skin reactions, but all are useful until something better is available. The spray may temporarily relieve the pain from a hard blow by superficially cooling the skin. It does little, however, to control internal bleeding. Synthetic gel packs stay below freezing for about 15 minutes but remain flexible and conform to the injured area. These reusable frozen gels are dangerous because they may cause frostbite. If one is used, it should be wrapped in a towel and not applied directly to the skin.

Ice slush is made by mixing chips or flakes of ice in water to produce a temperature of 13°C to 18°C (55°F–65°F). Because the limb hangs down into the slush, it should be wrapped with a wet elastic wrap to provide some comfort. The athlete may wear a neoprene cap over his toes.

Care should be used in applying ice because it is not without its deleterious effects. Documented cases of neuropraxia and axotomesis have occurred, especially when applied in the ulnar groove and fibular head.

Cold

Physiologic Effects

Vasoconstriction
Decreased local temperature to a depth of up to
   10 cm

Less blood flow to the area and less edema
Less venous and lymphatic drainage
Slowing of nerve conduction and muscle depolarization
Less muscular excitability and spasm
Breaking of pain cycle by analgesia
Reduced cellular metabolism
Increased muscle viscosity

Methods of Application

Ice bags
Ice slush in a bucket
Cold sprays
Ice massage
Contrast treatments (iced whirlpool)

Indications in Athletes

Prevention of swelling after acute injury
Reduction of muscle spasm and pain
Reduction of inflammation
Treatment of heat illness, minor burns, and blisters
Preexercise to allow exercise and increased range of motion (cryotherapy)

Contraindications

Circulatory insufficiency
Hypersensitivity to cold
Hyposensitivity to cold

Compression

A cold, wet elastic wrap provides comfort and stops swelling and hemorrhaging mechanically. Elastic wraps work best on cylinders, and, because the wrap will not compress in hollows, a felt horseshoe or foam rubber pad should be placed in these areas. For an ankle sprain, an open basket-weave taping is applied to prevent limping.

Some areas, such as where the trunk muscles insert into the iliac crest, are harder to compress than others. For a thigh bruise, an elastic thigh sleeve provides even compression. For a knee injury, the limb may be wrapped with an elastic wrap from the toes to the upper thigh.

Intermittent compression serves as a valuable adjunct to cold in reducing edema (Figure 6-9). Some of these units even combine a refrigerant fluid with the compression. The extremity is en-

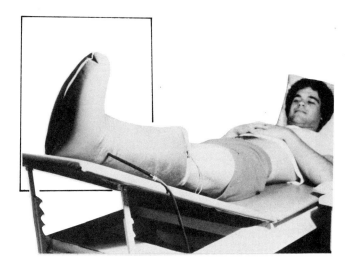

Figure 6-9 An intermittent compression device is combined with elevation to treat an ankle sprain.

cased in an air-filled glove. Pressure is then alternately applied and released to force edema from the limb. Whenever a snug wrap has been applied or when an intermittent compression device is being used, the limb should be elevated, which decreases blood flow to the limb, limits venous pooling, and encourages and assists venous return to the heart. An elevation block should support the entire limb. The commonly used smaller blocks or pillows placed under the distal part of a limb are uncomfortable and place a strain on the knee.

"ISE"

For grades 1 and 2 mild or moderate injuries, next day treatment of ISE (Ice, Stretching (range of motion), Exercise) is begun. The ice allows the athlete to exercise pain free because muscles relax and the ice blocks painful nerve impulses. With less pain and muscle spasm, the athlete exercises better, which in turn retards the adverse effects of immobilization.

Resistance exercise, even if isometrical, begins the next day after the injury and is the most important modality. Pain-free exercise increases range of motion and prevents disuse atrophy.

The athlete begins ISE with the application of ice for 20 minutes. He first feels coldness, then burning, aching, tingling, and finally numbness. The numbness stage is usually reached in 7 to 10 minutes. As the athlete is icing for 20 minutes,

he is moving the part through a pain-free range of motion (Figure 6-10). As the part becomes numb, range of motion increases.

At the end of the 20-minute session the athlete begins a resistance exercise for three sets of ten repetitions. Ideally the resistance exercises should be the maximum he can do comfortably. If resistance exercises are uncomfortable, isometrics may be substituted provided that they are pain free. The athlete should be advised that he may feel some slight discomfort as the blood flows back rapidly into the injured area when he returns the lower extremity to a dependent position. If the lower extremity is involved, walking may begin if it is pain free and not of a limping nature.

After the ISE treatment has been terminated, a compression wrap is reapplied if swelling is present. If the individual is limping with a lower extremity injury, he should use a crutch or crutches even though the limp may be slight.

ISE should be repeated three to four times daily and may be adapted to a home program. The athlete may fill a paper cup with water and place it in the freezer, or a salt/water or alcohol/water solution in a plastic bag may be used. The last two solutions keep the water in a slush consistency to conform better to an irregular body part.

Using the ice cup, strip back the cup to expose the ice (Figure 6-11). Massage the injured area until it feels numb and the skin has turned bright

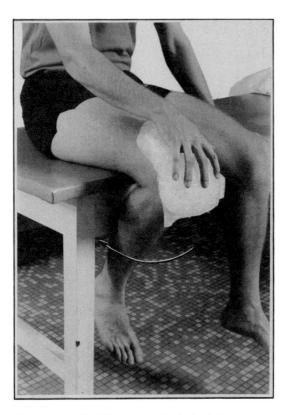

Figure 6-10   The ISE program includes Icing, Stretching, and Exercise.

red, usually 20 minutes. The injured part is again brought through a normal range of motion and pain-free resistance exercise program (cryokinetics). This ISE regimen may be used throughout the entire treatment program. In any case, ice should be used until the criteria to begin heat are reached. Whenever in doubt as to whether to use cold or heat, use cold because there is less chance of a problem developing.

Ice will not numb an area, in grades 1 and 2 injuries, to allow further injuries to occur if pain-free exercise is used. Soreness after the ISE session or on arising the next morning should indicate that the initial session may have been too vigorous and should be modified accordingly. Exercise is the ultimate modality. Ice, heat, electrotherapy, and massage allow the athlete to exercise within a pain-free range to retard atrophy and the effects of immobilization.

Contrast

Contrast treatments of hot and cold may begin when the athlete's progress with ice has plateaued, edema has stabilized, and there is no hyperemia in the injured area. Contrast treatments provide an alternating vasodilation–vasoconstriction effect that mobilizes edema.

Treatment begins when the ankle, for instance, is placed in a warm tub or whirlpool of 39°C (102°F), followed by a session in cold water of 13° to 18°C (55°–65°F). Temperatures colder than 55° are not beneficial physiologically and only cause patient discomfort. Times of treatment begin with 2 minutes in warm water and 2 minutes in cold water and may progress to 4 minutes warm and 1 minute cold. The athlete begins with the warm and ends in the cold water for a total of four repetitions. The last treatment with cold prevents edematous effects from heat and allows more pain-free exercise, the ultimate modality.

Figure 6-11   For ice massage, a paper cup is filled with water and then frozen. When the ice has formed, the cup is partly peeled back and the injured area gently massaged.

Contrast treatments may be repeated three or four times daily.

In the treatment area, each electrical outlet should have a ground fault breaker that automatically shuts off current within 1/40th of a second if there is an interruption of current within the circuit. Wall circuit breakers are not adequate.

There should also be full visibility of the treatment area and adequate ventilation, especially in the hydrotherapy area. Whirlpool turbines should be bolted to their shafts. Support bars and fish-eye mirrors also add elements of safety to treatment areas.

Heat

Heat is used only in rehabilitation, whereas ice may be used to treat acute injuries and in rehabilitation (Table 6-5). Some athletes are averse and sensitive to cold. The choice of heat for rehabilitation, then, may be based on the athlete's comfort; the athlete's cooperation may be difficult to obtain if comfort is not considered. Both ice and heat are analgesic and reduce muscle spasm, but in most cases heat produces more comfort as a result of its sedating properties. Heat induces vasodilation and increases blood flow, resulting in an influx of oxygen and nutrients to the injured area and waste products being carried away. Cellular metabolism increases, leading to rapid repair and healing. Regardless of whether heat or cold is used, however, it still takes time for an injury to heal.

After acute symptoms have subsided, the recovery rate with heat or cold is about the same. The modality of prime importance is exercise. Cold or heat allows exercise to be more pain free.

The many methods of applying heat include whirlpools, hot packs, heating pads, and analge-sic balms. The injured part may be placed in a warm, soothing whirlpool for 20 minutes. The water temperature may range from 37°C (98°F) for subacute injuries to 41°C (106°F) for chronic injuries. Heat packs are segmented canvas bags filled with a heat-absorbing silicone gel. These packs are stored in a water-filled stainless steel container and wrapped in towels for use. Water-proof heating pads are also useful. A moist towel is placed underneath the pad against the skin to provide heat. Analgesic packs that contain an analgesic balm are also used. The analgesic balm may be an external analgesic, such as methylsalicylate. The analgesic is usually applied to the skin and covered with an insulating cover, such as an old towel. Only mild surface analgesics should be used, since the stronger ones may be dangerously irritative.

Heat

Physiologic Effects

Vasodilation and increased blood flow
Increased local temperature
Increased swelling
Rise in influx of oxygen and nutrients; also in venous and lymphatic drainage
Increased local metabolism
More permeable capillaries to leukocytes
Sedative effect
Less pain and muscle spasm
Increased elasticity of muscles, tendons, and ligaments, capsule

Methods of Application

Heating pad
Moist hot packs
Whirlpool
Ultrasound
Infrared lamp
Counterirritants

Indications in Athletes

Reduction of muscle spasm and pain after acute phase of injury
Preexercise, allowance of increased range of motion
Increased local blood flow
Facilitation of wound healing

Table 6-5 CRITERIA TO BEGIN HEAT

1. Edema stabilized
2. No hyperemia at injury site
3. Almost full range of motion
4. Pain-free range of motion
5. Progress with ice has plateaued

Contraindications

Acute injury
Diminished sensation
Circulatory problems
Hypersensitivity to heat
Hyposensitivity to heat
Febrile conditions
No diathermy if athlete has metal implant

Massage

Massage, a manipulation of soft tissue that can benefit an athlete mechanically, physiologically, and psychologically, may be used before competition as part of the warm-up, during breaks, during time-outs, or at halftime, after a workout, for rehabilitation from an injury, and after a cast has been removed.

Before competition, a pitcher's arm or a runner's or cyclist's legs are massaged to produce the peripheral vasodilatation that warms up these parts. During breaks in competition, such as between periods in a Greco–Roman wrestling match, a wrestler's arms are massaged and shaken to break muscle spasm and remove waste products.[16] After a race, a runner's or cyclist's legs are massaged to break spasm, remove wastes, and reduce swelling. As a substitute for massage, inflatable boots can be used for the athlete's legs. The intermittent pneumatic compression unit will reduce swelling and the fatigued feeling in the athlete's legs and feet. After a day of activity, all athletes benefit from automassage of their feet. The long arches of the feet should be massaged at bedtime, too. Circular motions up and down the long arch will relax the feet. A massage after exercise is restorative in that it promotes relaxation,[13] reduces muscle tension, relieves swelling, and helps prevent soreness. Massage is especially useful in rehabilitation after sprains, strains, or fractures, stimulating both the arterial and venous circulation, accelerating the flow of lymph, reducing edema, breaking up undesirable fibrosis, relaxing muscle spasm, and relieving discomfort by increasing the pain threshold.[35]

Muscles thrive on all forms of massage: friction, stroking, kneading, percussion, and shaking (Figure 6-12). A friction massage is done with circular motions of the fingers or thumb and is especially useful over joints, where there is not much soft tissue. The circular motions loosen scars and adhesions and can break muscle spasm. A stroking masage has a sedative effect, relieves pain and swelling, and diminishes muscular tension. Both friction and stroking massages are useful after a cast has been removed. This combination breaks adhesions and reduces swelling. Kneading massage relieves cramps and keeps tissues supple. Skin and muscles are lifted, rolled, squeezed, and twisted. Percussion is a technique of hacking, cupping, or slapping that is invigorating and stimulating before a competition.

Massage is an art that demands a confident approach. The athlete should take a shower beforehand or otherwise clean the area to be massaged. He should rest in a comfortable position, with the area accessible and relaxed. The trainer stands with his knees bent, back straight, and legs turned out to allow him to swing up and down the length of the training table by shifting his weight from one foot to the other.

The trainer applies a generous amount of lubricant to his hands and to the athlete's skin; otherwise, the skin will become irritated. The lubricant may be a liniment, any petroleum-based material, a vegetable oil, or a powder. A favorite massage mixture is a combination of olive oil and methyl salicylate (oil of wintergreen). The ratio of these two ingredients depends on the purpose of the massage and the size of the area to be massaged. The ratio is generally one to one. For a pitcher's warm-up massage, however, it is three parts methyl salicylate to one part olive oil. For massage of very large areas, the ratio is three parts olive oil to one part methyl salicylate.

The trainer directs all his attention to the massage. Talking, which detracts from the athlete's relaxation, is kept to a minimum. Flowing music may assist the rhythm of the strokes and add to the relaxation. All movements are centripetal, following the course of the lymphatics to the heart. The trainer notes any knots, nodules, or tender areas and focuses attention on those areas.

Massage is contraindicated directly over a new injury because it may create additional hemorrhage. The area around an injury, however, can be stroked to eliminate some of the swelling. The

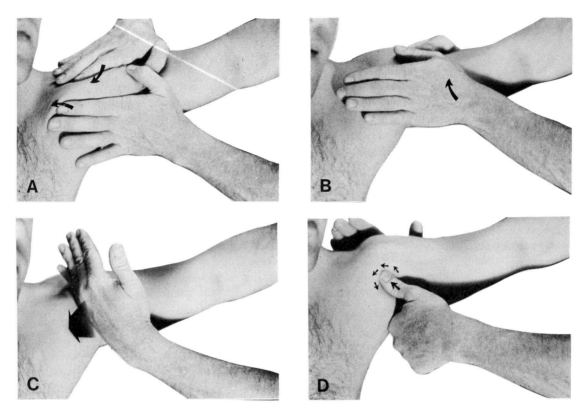

Figure 6-12   Massage techniques include stroking **(A)**, kneading **(B)**, percussion **(C)**, and friction **(D)**.

trainer should record the presence of any skin lesions, moles, or lumps. Massage is not done in the presence of skin rashes, eczema, herpes, or other skin infections.

Cross-friction massage is a valuable adjunct in inflammatory conditions. The operator uses his thumb or fingers to rub across soft tissue fibers. The duration of treatment is usually 3 to 20 minutes every other day. Cross-friction massage may be slightly uncomfortable during treatment and often the next day. Some conditions that respond well to this method of massage are lateral humeral epicondylitis, rotator cuff inflammation, and postsurgical adhesions.

Massage is a very effective modality, but its use has generally been supplanted by machinery, such as ultrasound, electrical stimulation and whirlpools, mainly because of time constraints on athletic trainers. However, once an athlete experiences an effective massage, he will always want one. To satisfy this demand, athletes can be taught automassage and partner-massage. In addition, a professionally trained massage specialist can be an invaluable member of the sports medicine team.

ELECTRICAL PRINCIPLES

Often a clinician can recognize the capability of an electrical modality by the manufacturer's name or by what the sales representative states that the unit is capable of doing. The better the clinician can understand and recognize the effects of current parameters on biological tissues, the more appropriately the equipment can be used, and with greater versatility. It is difficult to address all the concepts and terms relevant to the area of electrotherapy, but the following may clarify some of the confusion.

Neurophysiology

A thorough understanding of muscle physiology and neurophysiology is helpful when addressing the effect electrical stimulation has on a biological system. Whenever the nervous system is intact and an electrical current is applied, the muscular response is through the nerve. The basic unit of the peripheral nervous system is the neuron, with its dendrites and axons (Figure 6-13). Neurons make up an extensive network of relay systems that conduct both sensory information (afferent fibers) from the periphery to the spinal cord and motor stimulation (efferent fibers) from the spinal cord to the muscles. The dendrites take in information from other neurons and receptors, and the axons direct the stimulation to other neurons, muscles, or the spinal cord, depending on their type. Nerve fibers are classified as either myelinated or nonmyelinated, depending on the presence of a phospholipid-insulating membrane, the myelin sheath. Myelinated fibers carry their impulses faster, since the impulse jumps from node to node (interruptions in the membrane). Larger diameter fibers tend to have more myelination, and therefore transmit an impulse faster than smaller, less myelinated fibers.

Nerve fibers are also classified by their function: pain, sensory, or motor. The largest nerve fibers are the "A"-fibers, and they are the fastest conducting motor and sensory nerve fibers. This group is subdivided into A-alpha, A-beta, A-gamma, and A-delta, depending on their size. These larger fibers have a lower capacitance and are the most quickly stimulated. The functions of the A-fibers are summarized in Table 6-6.

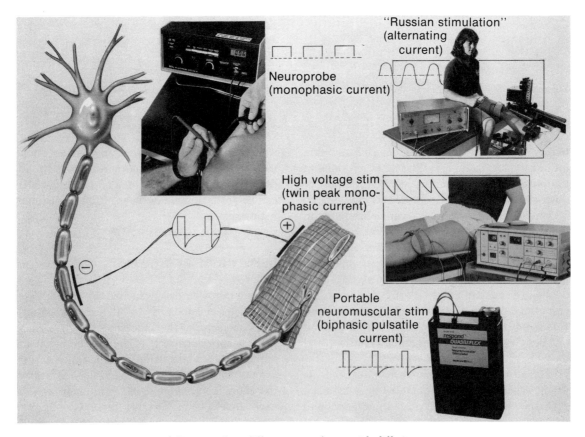

Figure 6-13   The electrical modalities produce different wave forms with differing physiologic effects. The electricity can depolarize a nerve to produce a muscular contraction.

Table 6-6 CLASSIFICATION AND FUNCTION OF NERVE FIBERS

"A" Fibers A-alpha:	Largest motor nerves. Their function is to innervate skeletal muscle fibers.
A-beta:	Large sensory fibers, dealing largely with fast touch and proprioception, e.g., joint position, and movement sense. These fibers transmit sensory information very quickly and are associated with the gate theory of pain modulation.
A-gamma:	Fibers that innervate the muscle spindle and Golgi tendon and function primarily for proprioception.
A-delta:	Transmit quick pain, temperature, and light-touch sensation.
"B"-Fibers Preganglionic autonomic fibers.	
"C"-Fibers Transmit slow pain, temperature, and are mechanoreceptors. These fibers also transmit postganglionic autonomic impulses.	

The "B"-fibers are the smaller myelinated fibers and are generally the efferent fibers of the autonomic nervous system. These fibers are not usually associated with direct responses of electrical stimulation but may act indirectly as an important link between some of the physiologic effects of electrical stimulation. The "C"-fibers are unmyelinated and include the efferent postganglionic fibers of the sympathetic nervous system and the smallest afferent peripheral nerves usually associated with pain. The C-fibers are the slowest in conduction and take more stimulation to elicit a response. Because the A- and C-fibers have sensory components, they play the largest role in both pain and pain control. Many of the pain control theories and electrical stimulation protocols utilize the properties of these nerve fibers to produce their results.

An excitable membrane has an active transport system of sodium and potassium, as well as an electrical gradient of other ions to create a membrane resting potential or voltage in nerve and muscle tissue. A large-enough stimulation, either hormonal, thermal, chemical, mechanical, or electrical, causes a change in the membrane's permeability, resulting in the depolarization of the tissue. When a threshold level is surpassed by this stimulation, an action potential results (see Figure 6-15), which can lead to a sensory or motor response, depending on the fiber stimulated. This response can occur naturally or can be induced through some exogenous application of a stimulation, such as electricity. The current applied to biological tissues causes an ion migration, which induces a current to be generated inside the body. Depolarization is most prominent where the current leaves the nerve membrane.

The biological effects of electrical stimulation are physiologic, thermal, and physiochemical and are influenced by type of electrical current used and its parameters. The physiologic effects refer to the changes on membrane potentials and the subsequent action potentials. The thermal response occurs as electrical energy is converted to heat. However, the average current of most electrical stimulators used in physical therapy is too low to cause a substantial temperature change. Diathermies, which use high-frequency radio waves, create their thermal effects in this manner. The physiochemical response is usually associated with galvanic or D.C. currents and also is a result of the average current. The chemical response that occurs depends on the polarity of the electrode, since it is the result of an ion flux or electrophoretic effect.

Electrophysiology

Several factors affect the flow of current through the body, including tissue impedance, electrode size and placement, and the current stimulation parameters. The current parameters include waveform, amplitude (intensity), pulse duration (pulse width), pulse rise time, frequency, and duty cycles.

Impedance includes resistance to the flow of current and follows Ohm's Law:

Voltage = Current × Resistance ($V = IR$).

For a given voltage, the more resistance that is met, the less current is delivered to the tissues.

The body does not have uniform conductivity because of varying amounts of tissue resistance. This resistance is strongly affected by the tissue's water content. Tissues with high water content, such as blood or muscle, have less resistance than does fat or bone, therefore conduct the current much more easily.

Another factor that affects tissue impedance is the capacitance of the tissues. Capacitance is the ability to store and separate charge. The greater the capacitance of a tissue, the longer the current must flow in one direction (either positive or negative) before the fibers discharge. The larger the nerve fiber, for example, the motor nerve or proprioceptive fiber, the smaller is its capacitance. This means that large fibers are more responsive to a stimulus than are the smaller nerve fibers, for example, "C"-pain-fibers. The tissue with the largest capacitance of all excitable tissue is the muscle membrane. It requires a very long pulse duration (several milliseconds) to exceed the capability of the membrane to store that charge and elicit a response. Therefore, owing to capacitance, a motor response is elicited through the intact nerve, which would have discharged much sooner than the duration necessary for the muscle membrane to respond. Because different-sized nerve fibers, each with their own functions, have different capacitances, modulating the electrical currents can alter which fibers are recruited. The practitioner can therefore target specific tissues to elicit the desired effects.

The electrode size and orientation also affect the flow of current through the body. The electrodes and their placement ultimately affect the current density and therefore the degree of response that occurs. Current density is the amount of current delivered per unit of surface area. Unequal-sized electrodes result in a greater current density under the smaller electrode. The smaller electrode is classically called the "active" electrode for that reason. The electrode termed the "dispersive" is appropriately named, since this electrode spreads the same amount of current as its smaller counterpart over a larger area, resulting in a less stimulating effect.

The distance between electrodes influences which tissues are affected and the depth of stimulation. When the electrodes are placed closely together, the current flows more superficially. As the electrodes are spread apart, the current can spread and reach the deeper fibers, although the current density is still greater in the more superficial tissues immediately under the electrodes.

Within the stimulus parameters, the waveform describes the configuration of the pulses of the electrical current. Waveforms are considered to be of two major classifications: monophasic or biphasic. Classic waveforms are the direct and alternating currents, which have very specific definitions and are categorized as monophasic and biphasic, respectively. With the progression of current modulation, the pulsatile currents have evolved. Pulsatile currents have various shapes, pulse durations (usually short), and interpulse spacings. The pulsatile currents have created a confusion in the classic terminology. Within the biphasic and monophasic categories, alternating and direct currents are appropriate terms. However, their names are often inappropriately used to designate pulsatile current types.

An alternating current is one in which the polarity continuously shifts from positive to negative, or *vice versa*. The classic alternating current is the sinusoidal wave, which has symmetrical shapes in its biphasic pattern. Another A.C. current, which is less frequently used in modalities today, is the faradic wave. A faradic wave is an alternating current but is asymmetrical with regard to its phase configuration. A current induces a flow of ions in a membrane, and, because an A.C. current periodically shifts the direction of this flow, all polar effects to the tissues are eliminated. Use of A.C. current also causes both leads of the circuit to have identical effects. The chief distinction between alternating currents and other biphasic pulsatile currents is that the inverse relation between frequency and wavelength is maintained with the A.C. As the frequency of the A.C. increases, the pulse widths must decrease within a specific time segment. Pulsatile currents generally have very short pulse widths and have an interpulse interval that disrupts this normal frequency/wavelength relationship. The frequency of the pulses can change without affecting the pulse widths because the length of interpulse interspace can be changed.

A D.C. is monophasic and utilizes a unidirectional flow of current for an unlimited time duration. An example is the classic galvanic current. In physical therapy and sports medicine modalities, an interrupted D.C. is used, but to be classified as D.C. the current must flow in one direction for a minimum of 300 msec (msec = 1/1000 sec). Physiochemical reactions can take place with this type of current because the polarity of the electrodes stays constant and the average current delivered is higher. Different chemical effects occur at opposite poles. (These will be elaborated on in the electrical stimulation section.) Monophasic pulsatile currents, with their very short pulse durations, do not fit into the classic D.C. category and have a significantly less physiochemical effect. This short pulse width, along with the interpulse intervals frequently associated with pulsatile currents, further diminishes the chemical influences.

Pulsatile currents include both monophasic and biphasic currents and can be of any pulse duration or frequency. The waveforms are usually rectangular and can be modulated to have various duty cycles (on–off times). An example of a pulsatile waveform is the twin peak monophasic current, used with high-voltage units and others with portable transcutaneous electrical nerve stimulators.

Other parameters that need to be considered are the pulse duration, intensity, and pulse frequency. The duration, as discussed previously, affects the type of fiber recruited and is the length of one pulse. The intensity refers to the amplitude or magnitude of the current. The peak current is the maximum amplitude of the current at any point during the pulse without regard to its duration. A high peak current allows more fibers to be recruited owing to a potentially greater depth of penetration. Average current refers to the amount of current supplied over a period of time. Depending on the waveform, it is possible to have a high peak but low average current, which is usually associated with high-voltage stimulators. The average current ultimately determines the physiochemical response of a tissue and, if too high, can damage tissue. Often, the average current is lowered to safer levels by modifying the waveform or parameters, namely, pulse widths and interpulse intervals.

The frequency of the stimulation is the number of pulses generated per second (pps or Hertz). The frequency affects the number of action potentials elicited during the stimulation. Although the same number of fibers is recruited, a higher frequency causes them to fire at a more rapid pace, which ultimately increases the tension generated. Nerve membranes must repolarize, however, after discharging. There is an absolute refractory period in which the resting membrane potential is reinstated, and another action potential cannot be elicited during this time. The absolute refractory period is ultimately the rate-limiting factor of the impulses that can be generated by a nerve.

Rise time is also a parameter incorporated into the current waveform. The rise time references the duration it takes to get from zero to maximal intensity within each pulse. Short rise times are necessary, especially with low capacitance tissues, namely, large motor nerves. The low capacitance membrane cannot store charge and quickly accommodates to a stimulus. These nerves can dissipate the charge from a pulse with a slow rise time, and the ion flux needed to alter the voltage to exceed threshold is never reached. Generally, tissues with low capacitance have higher accommodating abilities, whereas high-capacitance tissues, because they store the charge, do not accommodate or dissipate the charge readily.

Pulses are also incorporated into duty cycles which create envelopes or packages of pulses. Duty cycles have an on–off time and are measured as the percentage of time the current is allowed to flow. Any waveform can have its pulses modulated into a duty cycle. The Russian stimulator uses this principle to create an interrupted sine wave. Pure sinusoidal waveforms, which have relatively high average currents, can be modulated into safer modalities in this manner. The off time lowers the net average current that is delivered.

In summary, there are three important considerations when determining the efficacy of an electrically induced response: First, within each individual pulse of an electrical current, the stimulus must be of adequate intensity to reach the threshold level of excitatory tissues. Second, the rate of voltage change must occur rapidly enough so that tissue accommodation cannot take place. If the potential difference (voltage) is of gradual onset, then the tissues have time to redistribute the induced ion migration. Therefore, the tendency for the electrical charge to reach threshold is decreased because the nerves accommodate to the stimulus. Third, the length of the stimulus or the pulse duration must be considered. Each pulse must be of adequate duration so that an action potential may take place. Different-sized nerve fibers have different capacities to store charge before an action potential results. If the pulse duration is not long enough, the charge build-up never exceeds this capacitance. The law of DuBois Reymond addresses these three factors and refers to each pulse in the electrical waveform. The current must meet specific criteria to elicit a physiologic response within the tissue. The waveform of the individual pulses can have an effect on the amount of average current that is delivered. One waveform is not necessarily more advantageous than another. (The different shapes will be elaborated on later under each modality.) The individual pulses are packaged and modulated to modify the effect of each of the individual pulses. The modulation is controlled by the frequency and by incorporating duty cycles (on–off times).

ELECTRICAL STIMULATION

The interest in and use of electrical stimulation have been reborn in the United States over the past few years. There has been an expansion not only in the number of units and parameter controls, but also in the awareness of the many inconsistencies in understanding stimulators. Much of this confusion is due to terminology and to the expansion of parameter controls allowed to the practitioner.

The units can be categorized into different groups according to their specific applications or unique features. One category includes transcutaneous nerve stimulators such as conventional TENS, high voltage, interferential, Electro-Acuscope, and point stimulator. Another category includes neuromuscular stimulators such as

"Russian Stimulation," portable stimulators, and low-voltage units.

Transcutaneous Electrical Nerve Stimulation

Historically, electrical stimulation has been used by applying electrical eels to injured parts for the management of painful conditions. Electrical stimulation has been used under much more refined conditions during the past few years. It is no longer a question of whether transcutaneous electrical nerve stimulation (TENS) works, but how the response can be optimized under the stimulation parameters and application techniques offered. TENS is much more than the small portable unit that attaches to the patient's belt; by definition TENS is any stimulation in which the current is applied across the skin to stimulate nerves. TENS is most commonly classified by the unit's function to provide pain relief. Various manufacturers have modified the current and the packaging of the current parameters to create a multitude of units, each purporting to elicit unique results attained only by their unit. The categories of stimulators that can be included under this heading are high-voltage stimulators, interferential units, Acuscopes, and some low-voltage A.C. stimulators.

The following section addresses the variations of TENS that can be achieved by adjusting the current parameters. Levels of pain modulation appropriate for each type of electrical stimulation are also discussed. Finally, the different units, the manner in which they are categorized, and their rationale are addressed.

Because therapy with electrical stimulation treats the symptoms of an ailment and not the cause, proper evaluation of the etiology and rectification of the cause is important. Modalities are often considered to mask symptoms, so management of the condition with any modality while the patient maintains an active lifestyle often brings about ethical scrutiny. It is often difficult to convince an injured athlete to accept the ideal healing conditions needed to eliminate the problem, which often includes rest. The modalities discussed in this chapter provide a noninvasive method of pain relief, but it is our belief that they will not enable the athlete to tolerate activity beyond a significant stress level. The modality is not worn during competition, and the athlete must be in a competitive state before activity is allowed.

Classic TENS was initially devised as a screening device to assess individual responses to implanted electrodes along the spine in patients with chronic pain. Proper electrode placement was ascertained using the cutaneous leads. It was discovered that the cutaneously applied electrodes provided pain relief as well, and there was no threat of surgical complications using this noninvasive technique. The recent developments of pain theories and methods of pain modulation have also vastly expanded the acceptance and use of TENS.

Because many TENS applications are with portable units and the athlete may be operating the unit independently, electrode placement and preparation are important. As with all electrical stimulation, the skin should be clean and inspected for any abrasions to ensure good conduction. If carbon rubber electrodes are being used, sufficient gel should be applied to cover the entire surface of the electrode. Disposable electrodes with preapplied gel and adhesive are expensive but convenient and effective. Excessive gel increases the size of the conductive surface and therefore should not extend beyond the size of the electrodes.

Electrode placement is generally applied over the pain site but can also include dermatomes, myotomes, trigger-acupuncture points, peripheral nerve trunks, or spinal nerve root levels (Figure 6-14). Paresthesia should be perceived in the painful region. Two or four electrodes can be used, and their placement is readjusted if a poor response occurs. At a minimum, the electrodes and skin should be inspected daily.

The athlete is instructed in the operation of the unit because adjustments in parameters, namely, amplitude, will be necessary over time. Parameters such as frequency and pulse width would have been preset before the unit was turned on. The athlete is to note how long it takes for pain relief to occur. A response to the conventional mode of stimulation should be noticed within the first 10 to 15 minutes of the treatment.

If no reduction in the symptoms is noted, either parameter or electrode adjustments should be made. Once relief occurs, the athlete is to keep the unit on for 1 hour. After 1 hour, the unit is then turned off and the duration of relief monitored. This process is continued as frequently as necessary to maintain as pain free a state as possible.

Physiology

There are three theories of pain control, each of which can be recruited by selecting the proper stimulation parameters with TENS. In the first level of pain control, pain is modified by the gate theory and the production of neurohumoral substances (enkephalins). In this theory, TENS operates by stimulating afferent sensory nerves ("A" beta) which, through a mechanism in the spinal cord, inhibit pain from A-delta or C-fibers. As discussed previously, the afferent sensory nerves are larger and have a lower capacitance; they therefore can be stimulated more easily. When the larger A-beta fibers are selectively stimulated, this causes the stimulation of the substantia gelatinosa, a structure in laminae II and III in the spinal cord. The substantia gelatinosa in turn inhibits the transmission of pain to the brain so that the pain is not perceived to be as great. Neurohumoral substances such as enkephalin are released at interneurons of the spinal cord and sensory nerves. Enkephalin has a very short half-life (45 seconds–2 minutes); pain relief therefore does not last long when the stimulation ceases.

The second level of pain is thought to include more of the midbrain and the descending spinal tracts. Inhibition of pain transmission occurs primarily through excitation of the raphe nucleus and periaqueductal gray matter (PAG). This causes a release of neurotransmitters such as serotonin, norepinephrine, and enkephalins that inhibit transmission of impulses in the dorsal horn similarly to the previously mentioned gate closing. To elicit this response, the C-fibers should be stimulated.

The third level of pain control is through higher levels in the brain and has an influence on the pituitary gland. Endorphins, which are naturally produced opiates, are released by stimula-

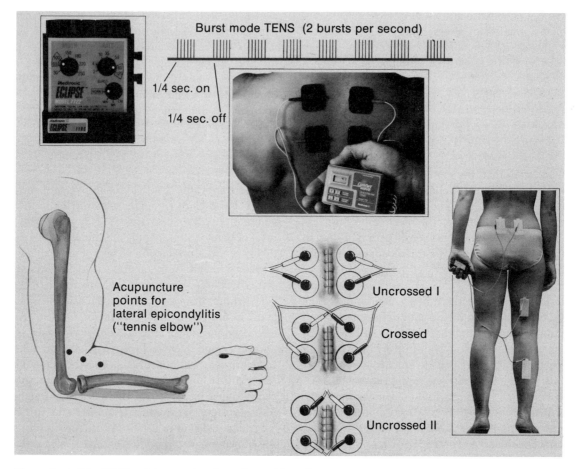

Figure 6-14   The TENS unit has settings for pulse width, pulse rate, and mode. Electrode placement can be crossed or uncrossed across a painful area, a wound, or an incision. For sciatica, the electrodes may be placed on the back and along the sciatic nerve. Acupuncture points, in this case for a tennis elbow, are usually close to the painful area, but some may even be distant from the painful area.

tion at this level. Cortisol may also be released, causing an anti-inflammatory effect at the tissues. Prostaglandin synthesis is also inhibited through this system.

Four modes of TENS application have different stimulation parameter settings that attempt to initiate the different pain modulation processes. The current parameters that are varied are the amplitude, frequency, and pulse durations. These techniques include the following:

Conventional or high-frequency TENS
Acupuncture-like or low-frequency TENS
Brief-intense TENS
Burst mode

Conventional High-Frequency TENS (High TENS)

The high TENS mode is perceived as a comfortable "pins and needles" sensation that does not elicit any motor response. There should be a strong but comfortable stimulation. High TENS incorporates the first level of pain control, which provides the fastest relief of all the techniques of TENS application. However, because of the short half-life of enkephalin, the pain relief does not last for a long time. High-frequency TENS can be applied from 30 minutes up to 24 hours if advocated by the practitioner. The prolonged benefit is attained by disrupting the pain-spasm cycle, which then allows the the body to contend with the condition more readily.

Application

Application

The parameters can be preset on the unit and the intensity adjusted. The pulse rate should be high, between 60 and 150 and most commonly around 60 to 80 pulses per second. The pulse width should be narrow, less than 200 μsec—usually about 60 μsec. If no pulse width control is available, preset the rate and adjust only the amplitude. The intensity should be increased so that the stimulation is strong but comfortable and so that no muscle contraction is elicited.

Modifications in the parameters can be made to increase the effectiveness of high TENS. For example, the pulse width can be increased gradually and the athlete is asked if the perception of the stimulation is getting wider or deeper. This could provide a broader area of stimulation, but if it is only perceived as getting stronger, then the shorter pulse width is used. Another modification in the stimulation is the frequency. If little or no reduction in pain is experienced, the pulse rate can be increased gradually to see whether the sensation has changed other than just being stronger. A submotor response should be maintained.

Acupuncture-Like Low-Frequency TENS

The pain modulation that occurs with this type of stimulation is attributed to the endogenous opiate beta-endorphin. This technique requires the elicitation of motor responses so that larger nerve fibers are stimulated. The duration of the stimulation is less than that for conventional TENS, lasting only 30 to 60 minutes. The onset of pain relief is latent, usually occurring 20 to 30 minutes after the onset of stimulation. The pain relief attained from low-frequency TENS is much longer, since the half-life of beta-endorphins is about 4 hours.

Application

The stimulation parameters are the opposite of high TENS—low frequency, long pulse width. The pulse rate should be from 1 to 5 pulses per second, and must be below 10 pps. To elicit a muscular contraction more easily, a longer pulse width of 200 to 300 μsec is used. The intensity should be adjusted to elicit strong, rhythmic contractions within tolerable limits.

Especially with acute injuries, it is sometimes recommended to begin the treatment using the high-frequency TENS technique to obtain the rapid onset of pain relief. After 10 to 20 minutes of this mode, low-frequency TENS is administered because it has more prolonged, although latent, pain relief. There is less nerve accommodation with this transition protocol. It is generally not advised to apply low-frequency TENS in the region of acute trauma. The contractions may be painful, and there is the threat of causing further irritation owing to the muscle activity.

Electrode placement and skin preparation are done in the usual manner. Placement is either over dermatomes, myotomes, paraspinal regions, or peripheral nerve trunks, but most commonly over motor, trigger, or acupuncture points.

Brief-Intense or Hyperstimulation Analgesia

There is some discrepancy in the literature as to the exact settings of the unit when attempting to elicit this mode of TENS. The confusion occurs predominantly when referring to the pulse rate. This mode of TENS is called hyperstimulation analgesia because a noxious stimulus is applied for a short duration to elicit the second level of pain relief. This stimulation is often applied through point stimulators, which also contain Ohm meters to allow the clinician to locate more accurately the treatment points. Points of low resistance that correlate highly with motor or acupuncture points are the optimal treatment sites. The pain relief attained is through descending tract inhibition, which is mediated by the neurohormones mentioned above, that is, serotonin and enkephalin.

The pulse rate for brief-intense TENS depends on the type of stimulator being used. Some units supply a galvanic current; the pulse rate is therefore set at 1 to 5 pps, which results in pulse widths of significant duration to stimulate small pain fibers. Typical TENS units have a pulse rate of 150 pps, which allows a larger average current to be delivered to provide a stronger stimulation.

The intensity should be adjusted to allow muscle fasciculation or a tetanic contraction if the typical TENS unit is being used. Duration of application can last up to 15 minutes and can be repeated after a 2- to 3-minute rest period. If the point stimulators are being used, trigger points are stimulated for 30 seconds per point at maximum tolerance. Treatment can follow meridians for acupuncture points, or selected trigger points appropriate for regional pain areas can be stimulated.

Burst Mode

The fourth method of TENS incorporates two of the previously discussed techniques. The parameters are modulated using a carrier frequency of 50 to 100 Hz packaged into bursts of current using a duty cycle. This modulation ultimately allows a burst frequency of 2 to 4 bursts per second. The individual pulses are imperceptible, and thus a single pulse is felt by the athlete. This, therefore, utilizes a carrier frequency like the conventional TENS (high-frequency), which is modulated to provide a low TENS effect. The intention of this technique is to allow a strong muscle contraction at a low intensity of current, resulting in a more comfortable sensation (Figure 6-14).

Application

Stimulation parameters of the burst mode may vary with different manufacturers. The pulse rate generally is from 50 to 100 pps with a pulse width of 75 to 100 μsec. The intensity is then adjusted so that a strong but comfortable stimulation is perceived, with muscle contractions occurring.

The duration of this treatment lasts anywhere from 20 to 60 minutes. Results are achieved through the same mechanisms as the low-frequency TENS.

In general, the classic TENS units have evolved into a diversity of modifications by the various companies. Some of these modifications have been very beneficial, whereas others merely create confusion. Numerous waveforms are present, none of which has proved to be more effective than another. The essential consideration of the waveform is that there is no net ion flux, which can cause skin irritation and other chemical effects. A biphasic current prevents ion migration.

The contraindications of TENS rarely involve the athlete but include the following:

Patients with demand pacemakers
Over the carotid sinus
During pregnancy
Over the chest if there are cardiac problems
Any kind of cerebral vascular disorders
Over eyes or mucosal membranes

Overall, TENS is an invaluable modality in the treatment of athletes with acute or chronic pain. It enables them to continue care at home and throughout the day to help expedite the resolution of their symptoms and their subsequent return to activity.

High-Voltage Pulsed Galvanic Stimulators

High-voltage pulsed galvanic stimulators (HVPGS) are classified by having two distinct specifications: They must be able to transmit a voltage in excess of 100 V (some references state

Table 6-7   PARAMETERS FOR TENS APPLICATION

	Frequency (pps)	Pulse Width (μsec)	Intensity
High TENS	75–150 (pps)	60	Submotor
Low TENS	2–4	200–300	Contraction
Brief-Intense TENS	1–5 (point stim)	150 or galvanic	As strong as
	125–150 (TENS unit)		tolerable
Burst Mode	50–100 modulated	75–100	Muscle contraction
	1–5 pps		

150 V) and must use a twin-peaked monophasic current (see Figure 6-13). The 100 V delineation is an arbitrarily set value that demarcates high and low voltage units. Most electrical stimulators have the capability to exceed 100 V; therefore, the chief distinction of the HVPGS is the twin peak monophasic waveform. The major claims of these units are that the high peak current associated with the high voltage allows deeper penetration of the energy and that the short pulse widths do not allow the capacitance of smaller sensory fibers (C-fibers) to be exceeded, resulting in less cutaneous sensory stimulation and therefore more comfort. High-voltage units are used clinically for pain, edema reduction, tissue healing, circulation improvement, increases in joint mobility, muscle spasm reduction, and muscle reeducation.

Pulse Parameters

The key parameters associated with this type of stimulator include high voltage, short duration, monophasic, twin-peaked waveform, and low average but high-peaked current.

High-voltage stimulators are constant voltage units, meaning the amount of stimulation reaching the tissues varies according to the current's conductive conditions present during a treatment. If, once the intensity is set, the conduction is altered during the treatment, the voltage intensity does not adjust itself to maintain the preset level of stimulation. For example, if the electrode-surface impedance increases during the treatment, there is a reduction in current flow, and therefore a different clinical response. The constant voltage unit is contrasted to the constant current unit in which the preset intensity is maintained throughout the treatment. If the resistance increases the voltage also increases, so that the original level of stimulation is maintained despite the increase in current delivered. The relationship between current and voltage is further described by addressing Ohm's Law (current equals voltage divided by resistance, $I = V/R$). Constant current units usually require a voltage limit to prevent injury.

The voltage intensity available with HVPGS ranges from 0 to 500 V. The intensity, as with most of the electrical stimulators, is determined by patient comfort but is also adjusted to meet the desired objective of the treatment, that is, sensory or motor response. One of the purported features with this unit is that although the voltage is high, the average current generated is minimal. It is thus a very safe modality. This unit is able to have high voltage and a low average current because of the waveform used. The current generated by the high-voltage unit can reach up to 2.0 amps, but the interpulse interval and the very short pulse width allow an average current flow of up to only 1 to 2 milliamps (mAmps = 1/1000 ampere). This ensures the safety of the patient and minimizes any ion flux, which is also dependent on average current.

The short pulse duration accounts for much of the confusion with this modality. The confusion extends even to the name of the unit, which implies that a galvanic current is being used. The unit was likely to have been given the name galvanic because a monophasic current is used. Galvanism is an uninterrupted unidirectional current that flows for an indefinite duration. A galvanic current can be modulated so that it is interrupted at specific time intervals, but the current maintains its unidirectional flow. If interrupted, its pulse duration is generally longer than the 300 msec required to be classified as direct or galvanic current. The stimulators that use this type of current are those that elicit the physiochemical responses in biological tissues. The short pulse durations used with the HVPGS range from 20 to 200 μsec (microsecond = 10^{-6} sec.) and thus do not qualify as galvanic current. This discrepancy in the terminology of the HVPGS has been addressed by interjecting the word "pulsed" into the unit's name. Preferably, the word "galvanic" is excluded entirely when referencing this type of stimulator, more correctly calling them high-voltage stimulators. The short pulse duration makes any physiochemical response negligible, unlike the low-voltage galvanic stimulators, for reasons previously stated.

Many claims were made initially as to the relevance of the polarity control of the HVPGS but have since been deemphasized. During tissue healing, the wound emits a charge potential, depending on the stage of healing. This potential is believed to be reinforced by applying the polarity of a like charge, either positive or negative, from a stimulator. This process promotes a stronger physiological response, which enhances healing. However, the electrophoretic response with this type of unit is negligible, especially with short treatment durations. The net ion flux across the cell membrane is minimal and is self-limiting. The short pulse widths cause only a minor shift in the ion migration, and with the interpulse interval the membrane can neutralize any change in the normal ion status. Iontophoresis cannot be performed with this unit because no net ion flux occurs. The polarity is therefore not a concern with the HVPGS as it is with the low-voltage direct current stimulators. The short pulse widths

of high-voltage units do not allow current flow in one direction long enough to exceed the capacitance of muscle membranes, which is why denervated muscles cannot be stimulated with this type of unit.

The need for a twin-peak waveform is explained by the strength–duration principles of stimulation (Figure 6-15). The classic strength-duration curve shows the relationship of the strength of a stimulus to the duration that the stimulus must be applied to obtain a specific response, that is, motor or sensory stimulation. If the intensity of a stimulus is decreased, the initial level of response can be resumed if the duration of the stimulus is extended, and *vice versa.* Therefore, with the shorter pulse widths charac-

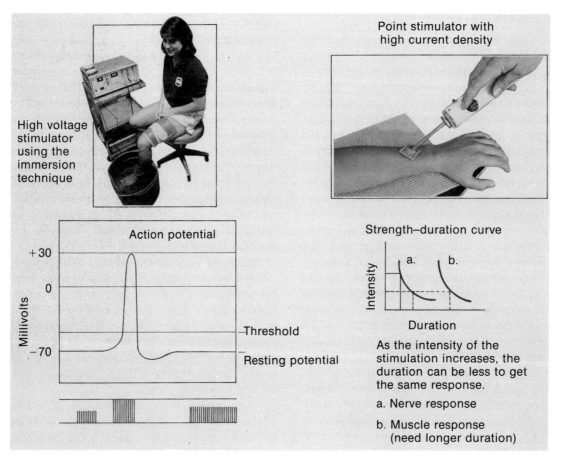

Figure 6-15 High voltage stimulation may be used with the ankle immersed in water. The point stimulator provides a high current density.

teristic of high-voltage units, a higher intensity would be needed to reach the threshold of excitatory tissues. The high voltage is compensated for by using two peaks that allow temporal summation, which is an additive effect of a repeated stimulation. Therefore, the intensity does not have to be as high to elicit a response. Overall, the pulse duration is still so small that neither nonmyelinated nerve fibers (C-fibers) nor direct muscle fibers with their higher capacitance can be stimulated. The need for the second peak in the waveform has been questioned, since the same response can be elicited with a single peak by itself.

Intrapulse spacing is a feature provided by some of the units that allows the clinician to spread the space between the two peaks of a pulse. This parameter purportedly allows the adjustment of the stimulus to ensure greater comfort to the patient. When the intrapulse spacing is increased, the intensity is perceived to have decreased, and therefore becomes more comfortable. By spreading the twin peaks farther apart, less of the temporal summating effect occurs. This feature is easily countered by again increasing the intensity to its initially perceived level of stimulation.

Some units that are constant voltage stimulators, such as the Soken, are very similar to the high-voltage units but have single pulsed monophasic currents. The pulse durations of the Soken are longer and have a greater potential for a net ion flux; therefore, precautions that consider polar responses should be exercised if prolonged treatment durations are intended. The voltage capacity is not as high with the Soken as with typical high-voltage units.

The frequency range offered by most HVPGS is from 2 to 100 cycles per second (Hz). The frequency adjustments allow the incorporation of either low or high TENS principles when pain modulation is intended. Higher frequencies are used initially in the acute phases when the primary intention is to elicit submuscular threshold to attain pain relief. If autonomic nerve responses are elicited directly or indirectly to aid in edema reduction, it is considered an added benefit. In the subacute phases of injury, lower frequencies with muscular contractions are used to aid in vascular flow or for trigger point stimulation.

Electrode placement when using high-voltage units usually employs the monopolar technique (Figure 6-15). This procedure uses one or more active electrodes and a larger dispersive electrode. The active electrodes are smaller in size and concentrate the current, and therefore the level of stimulation. As its name implies, the dispersive electrode spreads the same amount of current over a larger surface area. This should result in a minimum, if any, sensory perception. The active electrodes are placed over the treatment site, and the dispersive electrode is placed on a site distant to the treatment area. The bipolar technique, which uses equal-sized electrodes over the same treatment area, can also be used. This is not as frequently used with the high-voltage unit and would most likely be used while incorporating a muscle exercise program.

A key feature of the HVPGS is its ability to be used with appendage submersion treatments (Figure 6-15). Submersion is our preferred method of treatment because of its circumferential and irregular surface coverage. This method also allows the athlete to perform active motion during treatment. The active electrodes are placed in the cold water bath (55°–65° F), and a 20-to 30-minute treatment is applied. The treatment is followed by other modalities and exercise, as indicated for the specific condition. The treatment can be repeated several times throughout the day.

HVPGS are very versatile in their applications. We primarily use them for pain and edema reduction. The claims for polarity control are not a concern, for reasons mentioned previously. The negative polarity is generally used because it has a greater excitatory capability, and therefore a lower intensity of current can generate the same response.

The modality can be used as long as discomfort is present throughout the duration of the acute injury.

Interferential

Interferential stimulation is another form of transcutaneous electrical nerve stimulation used for pain relief, increased circulation, and for muscle stimulation (Figure 6-16). This unit simultaneously applies two medium-frequency currents to allow a deeper penetration of the stimulation.

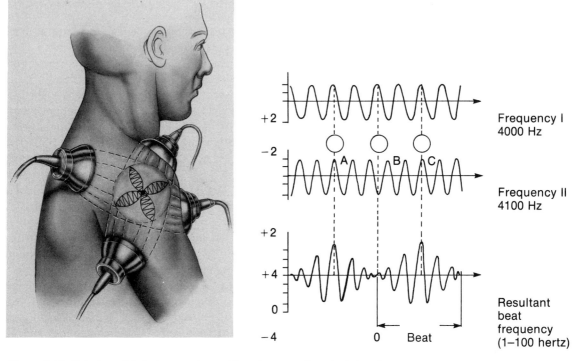

Figure 6-16   Interferential devices produce a "beat frequency" at the injured area.

Higher-frequency currents overcome some of the skin impedance encountered by low-frequency currents but cause minimal or no response in the tissues. Low-frequency currents within the range of 1 to 100 Hz, have a biological effect on the tissues but create more surface resistance. In theory, to overcome some of the resistance yet still provide a stimulation that benefits the body, two different medium-frequency (within the range of 1,000–10,000 Hz) sinusoidal wave currents are applied. Their waveforms become superimposed on each other, which causes an interference. Interference creates points of augmentation and attenuation of the phases where peaks and valleys are added together. The interference results in the modulation of a "beat" mode with a frequency that ranges from 1 to 100 beats per second, which is well within the conventional low-frequency range (Figure 6-16). Therefore, with the higher-frequency carrier currents, the stimulation now has the capability of reaching deeper tissues and is as biologically active as other low-frequency currents.

The carrier frequencies of an interferential unit generally range from 4000 to 5000 Hz, which allows a stronger perception at a lower intensity and deeper stimulation. The medium-frequency carrier currents reduce skin impedance but also shorten the pulse widths because they are sinusoidal waves, allowing more comfort. A more comfortable stimulation allows more current to be tolerated—so much that there is a threat of delivering too high an average current.

The frequency of the beats can vary by changing one of the two carrier frequencies. The beat frequency, not the carrier frequencies, affects the tissues, and changes in this parameter alter the stimulation responses. The number of muscle twitches is greater as the beat frequency increases, until a tetanic contraction is attained. Some units have a feature that constantly changes the frequency of one of the carrier currents while the other remains constant. This mode is a "sweep frequency" that causes a rhythmic change throughout a range of frequencies. The purpose of the rhythmic mode is to reduce accommodation: Because the stimulation continuously changes, the body cannot adapt to it. The sweep frequency provides a more effective stimulation in this manner.

Some models include a rotating vector system that rotates the electrical field 45° and then back to further reduce nerve accommodation. The efficacy of this modification has not been substantiated.

The beat frequency is selected according to the condition being treated. A frequency of 100 beats per second (bps) is used for pain management (high TENS effect), 50 to 60 bps for tetanic muscular contractions, and 1 to 50 bps for muscular activity that enhances venous return and minimizes circulatory congestion. This unit is not an effective neuromuscular stimulator because there is no control of on–off time. To allow for prolonged passive exercise, interruptions in stimulation are needed or else fatigue results. The unit can, however, be used to induce fatigue in a spasmodic muscle group. Denervated muscle cannot be treated with interferential stimulation because the unit uses sinusoidal currents with very short pulse durations. Therefore, no physiochemical effects take place.

Four electrodes can be used for an interferential treatment, two for each carrier current. The electrodes of each current are placed diagonally facing each other on opposite sides of a body part (Figure 6-16). The part to be treated should be surrounded by the electrodes if it is an extremity or joint, or the electrodes should be placed all on one surface, such as the back, if the treatment area is large.

The interferential units also offer suction electrodes in which a mild vacuum is created under the electrode to allow it to stick to the body part. The electrodes provide a convenient method of application because they do not have to be tied down, and they stay in place throughout the treatment.

The passage of current through the tissues does not occur linearly between electrodes but creates an electrical field. This field is purported to be shaped in a "cloverleaf" pattern situated three dimensionally between the electrodes (Figure 6-16). If the conductivity of the tissues were uniform, this perfectly formed electrical field

would occur with the maximal current concentration in the central region between the electrodes. However, differences in tissue impedance affect the location of the electrical field and the degree of superposition of currents. Therefore, the concentration of current is not always centralized. To maximize the probability of properly placed electrodes and subsequent electrical fields, adjust the electrodes so that the maximal intensity is perceived in the painful region.

Interferential stimulation can be used with other modalities. Although sometimes difficult because of the suction electrodes, ice or heat can be used in conjunction with the stimulation. Treatment durations last from 20 to 30 minutes, and intensities can be submotor or cause muscular contractions, depending on the desired effects. The intensity should always be comfortable throughout the range of beat frequencies when using the sweep mode.

Contraindications to using this unit are the same for other forms of TENS, which include pregnancy, cardiac pacemakers, thrombophlebitic conditions, and acute infections.

Point Stimulators

A proposed mechanism for pain reduction called hyperstimulation analgesia uses point stimulators or locus stimulators. This is considered to be a form of electroacutherapy. These units are used similarly to acupuncture except that the points are stimulated with an electrical current instead of needles. Point stimulators used in this manner can potentially help any painful condition. Point stimulators can indirectly encourage the resolution of these conditions by interrupting the pain—spasm—pain cycle.

Monophasic or biphasic current of significant duration is used to stimulate the small C-afferent-nerve fibers. A small tip electrode that stimulates a well-defined focal region delivers the current. The stimulation of localized points is often analogized to a "bee sting" sensation and is considered uncomfortable but should not be unbearable. This noxious stimulation elicits a pain fiber excitation that prompts a level of pain modulation associated with descending tract inhibition. This is believed to occur in the midbrain and uses various neurohormones such an enkephalin, sertonin, and norepinephrine, which decrease pain impulses in the dorsal horn of the spinal cord.

Technique

Ancient acupuncture points, trigger points, or motor points, which correlate highly with one another, are found on the body as points of low skin resistance. Charts are available to indicate these treatment points and their relevant landmarks. An ohmmeter measures skin resistance and makes the location of these points easier and more accurate. The ohmmeter is incorporated in the electrode tips of some units. A second dispersive electrode must be held by the athlete to complete the electrical circuit for both the resistance detection and stimulation to occur. The unit responds by signifying with an audible beep or on a meter when the probe is over these points of low resistance. The practitioner should look for a sudden increase in the meter reading beyond the patient's baseline skin resistance to determine the location of the appropriate point. The detection sensitivity can be adjusted to accommodate variations in each athlete's skin resistance to make detection of the appropriate points more accurate.

The stimulation is applied for 30 seconds at the patient's tolerance once the point is located. The patient's first perception of any sensation should be acknowledged. Frequently, the current flow is enhanced when the initial skin resistance breaks down; therefore, what was first perceived to be a tolerable intensity quickly becomes too noxious. The initial intensity may have to be reduced shortly after stimulation begins, and the patient should be warned that this may occur. Again, the treatment is often perceived to be uncomfortable but should not become unbearable.

Acupuncture master and associated points recommended for the involved region are treated, as are points on the meridians that travel through the painful area. It is recommended that the practitioner work from the distal to proximal points and that he treat an average of eight points per session. Auricular points (points in the ear) can also be stimulated, although the efficacy of this is controversial. Treatments can be given as often

as once a day, causing almost instantaneous pain relief for some athletes. A three-treatment trial is recommended before an inadequate response is determined when a patient does not feel he is benefiting from this treatment. Treatments can last up to 2 weeks, although athletes during their season often exceed this duration because of the need of continued activity. Our experience has found that athletes with overuse injuries, especially swimmers and throwers, find an extreme attraction to this unit because of success in managing the dull, aching pain. This unit is helpful in reducing pain so that rehabilitative exercises can be performed to strengthen the overstressed body part.

Other modalities may be used in conjunction with the point stimulator but, because of the difficulty in delineating the treatment points afterwards, it is recommended that the point stimulator be used first. The efficacy of this treatment is significantly reduced if pain medications, especially those containing opiate derivatives, are being taken. Demand pacemakers and pregnancy are the only contraindications when using this unit.

Electro-Acuscope/Myopulse

A relatively new electrical stimulator was made available in 1978: the Electro-Acuscope and its companion, the Myopulse unit. These units are referred to by the manufacturer as "intelligent TENS" modalities. They function by monitoring the level of electrical stimulation that the injured tissue requires and by reinstating the tissue to a normal, homeostatic state. These units have received much publicity recently after world-class and professional athletes responded to this treatment when more conventional modalities were deemed ineffective.

The information available on the intrinsics and mechanics of these units is vague. The manufacturer is especially evasive when attempting to contrast the Acuscope and the Myopulse. The Acuscope is called an electrical neural stimulator that works on all body systems. It is recommended for arthritic and orthopedic discomfort. Its benefits include increasing range of motion, muscle reeducation, and stress reduction. The

Acuscope can also be used for various musculoskeletal disorders such as bursitis, tendinitis, muscle strains, and sympathetic reflex dystrophy. The microchips are programmed to monitor neural tissue activity. In contrast, the Myopulse is purported to be an electrical muscle stimulator whose microchips are "tuned" to treat muscle and connective tissue only. Information on the research gathered to program the microchips is vague, especially when questioning the values used for normal tissue electrical activity.

Physiology

The units enhance pain relief and healing through a biofeedback mechanism. Conventional TENS sends an electrical signal that disrupts pain impulse propagation. The Acuscope measures the amount of electrical activity present in an area, compares it to a preprogrammed reference level, and adjusts the waveform so that a specific amount of current or electromagnetic energy is delivered.

The theory is consistent with the "tissue resonance–oscillation theory," which implies that tissue functioning in a normal metabolic state generates and maintains an electrical equilibrium. When injury occurs, the electrical activity is disrupted and tissue resistance increases in the injured region. This diminished activity alters the resonant frequency and slows the regenerative capabilities. This also allows metabolite congestion to occur within the cells. Although not stated in the manufacturer's literature, the Arndt Schultz principle seems to be applied with this modality. One of its features is that the unit delivers microamperes (10^{-6}) to reinstate the normal level of electrical activity into the affected area. By applying similar levels of energy and frequency, it enhances ATP production and reduces the increased resistance that resulted from the injury. The increased ATP allows the active transport of wastes away from and nutrients to the cell, thereby allowing a homeostatic condition to resume. The normal electrical activity that was circumvented from the area owing to the increased resistance is then returned. This increased natural electrical activity then allows the healing processes to occur.

Equipment

It is reported that four components work together with this modality: a monitoring and reading device, computer microprocessor, electrical generator, and information-gathering device. The monitoring device picks up the tissue's activity and delivers it to the microprocessor, which recognizes abnormal activity. The abnormal activity is processed, and the microprocessor directs the electrical generator to deliver the optimal waveform, frequency, and intensity that duplicates a homeostatic condition. This process is continuous and cycles periodically depending on the parameters selected.

The current specifications of these units are vague. The stimulation parameters actually used for treatment are difficult to ascertain, since oscilloscope readings have been inconclusive.

The Acuscope incorporates two modalities primarily so that the modality would be approved by the FDA. Mode I is the "sophisticated TENS" component that identifies the activity present and provides the corrective treatment. Mode II is a regular TENS unit. Mode I uses a carrier current that monitors the tissue. It is an alternating current with a frequency range of 0.5 to 320 Hz—the higher frequencies monitoring the more superficial tissues. The carrier current has an intensity capacity of 25 to 600 microamps and controls the strength of the carrier current, not the stimulation. These parameters deal only with monitoring the biological system, not with the treatment. The parameters of the carrier current can be adjusted so that the most information can be read from the body with the greatest sensitivity. The waveform of the second current delivered is modulated according to what the unit perceives as necessary to return the system to normal.

The control knobs on the unit do not affect the treatment delivered but affect the monitoring process, or the carrier current of the unit. The controls affect the gain setting and adjust the scanning frequency, monitoring duration, and intensity of the carrier current. The timer affects the monitoring duration in which the sampling of the tissues and subsequent treatment take place cyclically. This current deals with monitoring and not treatment intensity. The most commonly used settings are timing duration of 12 seconds, at a frequency of 0.5 Hz, and an intensity of 500 microamps. These parameters optimize the feedback that the unit can obtain from the body.

Mode II is more of a standard TENS unit, using a monophasic current with a frequency range of 1 to 20 Hz. The monophasic current has a pulse range from 50 to 200 μsec. Mode I is more frequently advocated by the manufacturer because it provides a treatment unique to the Acuscope unit.

Various treatment probes are used in the treatment applications. These have different sizes and shapes and are composed of unique alloys that enhance the efficacy of the specific treatment situation.

Several companies and researchers have attempted to analyze this unit and have not been able to substantiate or duplicate fully the claims purported by the manufacturer. The parameters used in the treatment current are virtually unobtainable. The above information is the recommended technique and rationale used by the manufacturer's specifications. We have not been able to formulate personal impressions with regard to efficacy and rationale.

Low-Voltage Stimulators

The treatment of painful conditions, stimulating innervated and denervated muscles, iontophoresis, and electrodiagnosis have been the classic applications of low-voltage stimulators in the physical therapy environments. The waveforms associated with low-voltage stimulators are faradic, sinusoidal, and galvanic (direct) currents. Faradic, an asymmetrical biphasic waveform, is rarely used today.

Chemical, thermal, and physiologic events may occur when an electrical current is applied to the body. The result ultimately depends on the average current and pulse charge that is delivered. Electrical stimulators that deliver more than 100 to 150 V are classified as high-voltage stimulators. These high-voltage units are associated with having high peak but low average currents. In contrast, low-voltage stimulators deliver only up to 100 or 150 V. Low-voltage units utilize waveforms that maintain low peak currents but have the capability to deliver high average cur-

rents. The potential for chemical and thermal responses with the low-voltage stimulators is much greater. Although these responses are desired in several therapeutic situations, if not controlled they can have adverse effects on biological tissues.

Alternating currents or modified biphasic currents are used primarily to stimulate innervated muscles. Classically and almost exclusively present for many years was the low-voltage A.C. muscle stimulation termed *electrical muscle stimulation* (EMS). EMS is used to treat pain, myofascial dysfunction, and muscle spasms and to enhance venous return. It is sometimes combined with ultrasound to provide a massaging effect while attaining the vascular responses with thermal responses. The muscle stimulation can be obtained in a tetanic, surged, or pulsed mode. Contemporary electrical stimulators, namely, the interferential and "Russian" stimulators, use the true A.C. or sinusoidal waveform. The interferential unit is a TENS unit and the latter, a neuromuscular stimulator. Both of these units are scrutinized for having the potential to deliver too much average current because of the higher frequencies that they use.

Galvanic or direct current is the other waveform that the low-voltage category incorporates. Galvanic current allows the stimulation of denervated muscles and the application of iontophoresis, a technique that uses a current to drive ions through the skin directly to the problem area. The term *galvanic* is appropriately used with this type of stimulator, as contrasted to the units labeled high-voltage galvanic stimulators. A galvanic current is unidirectional and flows for an indefinite duration, usually in excess of 300 msec. The galvanic current makes it possible to stimulate denervated muscles, since the muscle membrane must be stimulated directly when the motor nerve is not intact. The much longer pulse width available with this type of current is necessary to overcome the high capacitance of the muscle membrane, allowing its depolarization.

Polarity affects the chemical responses from low-voltage D.C. stimulators. If enough average current is supplied, a significant electrophoretic response can occur. Under the positive electrode, an acidic reaction occurs, along with a tissue-hardening effect and diminished nerve tissue irritability. At the negative electrode is an alkaline reaction in addition to a tissue-softening effect and an increase in nerve tissue irritability.

There are few applications for low-voltage direct current in the treatment of athletic injuries. Occasionally peripheral nerve damage results, and the atrophic responses of the muscles can be reduced with direct muscle stimulation. Iontophoresis is a noninvasive procedure in which a medication can be administered into a local region using an electrical current. The electrophoretic principle that "like charges repel and unlike charges attract" is used with iontophoresis. The electrolytes of similar charge are repelled away from medium source by applying an electrical current of a specific polarity. In this manner, the ions of the medication are driven into the body. Although iontophoresis has been used for many years, problems such as poor electrodes, determining drug dosage, unsafe electrical instrumentation, and inconvenience have made its reliability and safety questionable.

A transistorized galvanic generator called the Phoresor (Figure 6-17) has recently been developed to alleviate some of the problems originally encountered with iontophoresis. The generator produces up to 5 mAmp of current with a built-in shut-off device if the skin resistance is too great or too low. An injectable cell with a sterile porous membrane is the active electrode and allows the diffusion of ions into the body part. The unit is designed primarily to deliver a combination of anesthetic agents: xylocaine or lidocaine, and a corticosteroid, that is, dexamethasone sodium phosphate. The mixture is 1 ml of corticosteroid and 2 ml of anesthetic and is injected into the electrode cell. The medication is delivered by means of the positive electrode for 20 minutes and is usually applied every other day.

Animal studies have found that iontophoresis is an effective means of delivering the chemicals even into deeper tissues. The purported advantages of using iontophoresis follow:

It is noninvasive means of administering medication, so there is less chance of infection.

The application of the medication is localized.

No carrier fluid is needed with the medication and there is less tissue tension and pain from the volume expansion.

Caution is advised, however, when using the modality over abraded skin, anesthetic areas, and recent scars, near metal implants, on patients with demand pacemakers, when there is sensitivity to the medication, or with electrically sensitive patients.

Other medications can be used for different conditions, and these can be administered using conventional low-voltage D.C. stimulators or by using an adapter with the Phoresor that alters its polarity. Medications can be driven into the body

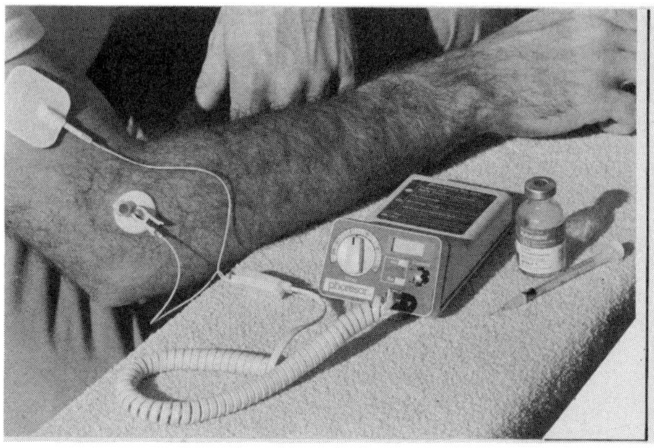

Iontophoresis Medications

Condition	Medication	Polarity
Fungal infection	Copper sulfate	Copper (+)
Keloids	Potassium iodide	Iodide (−)
Recent scars	Sodium chloride	Chloride (−)
Calcium deposit	Acetic acid	Acetate (−)
Strain-sprain	Hydro-cortisone	Hydro-cortisone (+)
Pain	Salicylate	Salicylate (−)

Figure 6-17   The "Phoressor" provides for the percutaneous transport of medicines.

with the D.C. stimulator by applying the medication to the appropriate electrode in a gel or solution or by using a solution bath. Conditions that include epicondylitis, tendinitis, bursitis, fascitis, arthritis, and myofascial trigger points can be treated with this modality. Each condition has its recommended medication (and polarity) and dosage guidelines for both concentration of medication and electrical stimulation.

The application guidelines for both the Phoresor and conventional D.C. stimulators are given below:

1. The procedure is explained to the athlete.
2. Treatment surface is cleaned.
3. The anesthetic and corticosteroid are injected into the active electrode and placed over the treatment site.
4. The dispersive pad is applied, usually proximally.
5. The unit is turned on and is set for 20 minutes.
6. Always using patient comfort as a guideline, the current is increased 1 mAmp per minute up to 4 to 5 mAmp.
7. The skin is inspected and the electrodes disposed of after the treatment.

When using the conventional D.C. low-voltage stimulator for iontophoresis, the following protocol should be considered:

1. Ensure that the skin integrity is good and the skin is clean.
2. Explain the treatment to the athlete.
3. Prepare the electrodes or treatment baths. The dispersive electrode should be twice the size of the active. The electrode pads should be clean, since any ions present on their surface will inadvertently be driven into the body. The pads should be well moistened (saturated, but not dripping) in tap water or saturated with the solution. The ointment, if used, is applied underneath the electrode.
4. Check the drug polarity and use the electrode of like charge as the active electrode.
5. Use a solution strength of 1% or less, since higher concentrations have been found to be less efficacious.
6. Make the athlete comfortable and tell him that he may experience a sensation of pins and needles that evolves into a warmth. No discomfort or burning sensation should occur.
7. Determine the dosage by the current intensity and duration. Once the paresthesia is perceived, the intensity is increased 1 mAmp per minute. Generally the current should be at least 0.5 to 1 mAmp per square centimeter of electrode surface area to allow adequate penetration. Skin resistance may decrease after several minutes of treatment, and the intensity may have to be decreased.
8. When terminating the treatment, slowly reduce the intensity. Rinse off the remaining solution and inspect the skin. An erythmatic patch may be present under the electrode, but this is normal and should resolve.

As an example of a treatment involving calcific deposits, a negative polarity may be applied using a 2% aqueous solution of acetic acid. The intensity is set to tolerance and is maintained for up to 20 to 30 minutes. The treatment can be administered three times a week.

Neuromuscular Stimulators

Neuromuscular stimulators in sports medicine are primarily used to maintain strength and flexibility or to reduce atrophy in an injured area while healing is taking place. These units are directed toward stimulating muscles with an intact nervous system and act to reeducate the muscle after trauma. If peripheral nerve damage has occurred, the muscle membrane has to be stimulated directly to achieve a contraction; therefore, most neuromuscular stimulators cannot be used for this purpose. Electrical stimulation employed with muscle contractions was used almost exclusively to prevent muscle atrophy. Recent claims about the use of electrical stimulation for muscle strengthening have brought about an expansion in the interest and types of units available. Because many of the current parameters for muscle stimulation are similar to those used for pain management, the units can often be used interchangeably. Constant stimulation of the TENS units, however, causes muscular fatigue. To prevent fatigue and maximize strengthening, an interruption (on–off) mode in current delivery should be made available. There is much controversy in the literature as to the types of training programs and current parameters needed to optimize the results of a neuromuscular stimulator.

Application

Many types of units currently available claim similar results. Portable units enable the patient to continue treatment independently throughout the day, although the stronger clinical models are usually more effective. The portable units are also invaluable, for example, while the athlete is immobilized. The cast can be windowed over motor points and electrical stimulation applied to unused muscles to reduce atrophy and to provide a trophic action on articular cartilage.

Neuromuscular stimulators can be used to isolate specific muscles that cannot be isolated and strengthened volitionally. For instance, with patellofemoral problems, the vastus medialis muscle is emphasized during quadriceps stimulation to aid in patella tracking changes. Rehabilitation problems such as inhibition can also be overcome in this manner. When the patient can volitionally exercise the muscle, these units can be used to increase the effectiveness of the contraction by superimposing the electrical contraction.

Several factors make the electrically induced contraction different from the volitional contraction:

1. When the muscle is stimulated electrically, all motor units fire in synchrony.
2. There is no inhibitory reaction with the electrically induced contraction. Normally, the Golgi tendon organs at the musculotendinous insertion react to a potentially threatening contraction by reflexively relaxing the muscle; this is not present with the stimulation. This potentially creates a stronger contraction but removes a normal protective reflex.
3. Larger nerve fibers are recruited first with electrical stimulation, which is the opposite of what the body would preferentially do.
4. The frequency of the nerve fiber firing is also affected by electrical stimulation. Muscle tetany normally occurs when a nerve fires at a frequency between 25 and 50 pulses per second. Electrical stimulators often operate at higher frequencies than those needed to achieve tetany; they will thus cause fatigue to occur much more rapidly.

These factors provide the benefits found with the neuromuscular units but should always be a consideration, especially with the more powerful machines. It has been claimed that a stronger contraction occurs with stimulation than one volitionally maintained, causing greater strengthening. However, because of the uninhibited contraction, joint jamming may occur. This problem arises when the knee, for example, attempts to prevent hyperextension because of the strong contraction when the quadriceps are stimulated. Joint jamming can be prevented by blocking terminal extension mechanically so that the pressure is removed from the joint.

Instrumentation

The "Russian" stimulator is one of the more popular classifications of neuromuscular stimulators currently available. Many models provide similar parameters, including Electrostim 180, Omnistim, and Multiflex. Their parameters include a medium-frequency sinusoidal wave carrier current (2500–4000 Hz) modulated into bursts of 10 msec on and 10 msec off. This modulation results in 50 bursts per second, which allows a tetanic muscle contraction (see Figure 6-13). These units are modeled from the Russian design that was purported to result in significant strength gains in world-class athletes. Studies performed in the United States using this type of unit have found strength gains in a normal population, but its efficacy is no greater than that of volitional exercise. Treatment of atrophied muscles has resulted in 10% to 20% gains in strength, but these figures are consistent with the results of other electrical stimulators that cause vigorous contractions.

Physiology

The relatively high average currents provided by the neuromuscular stimulators mentioned have the ability to stimulate large muscle groups such as the quadriceps. The high average current can become uncomfortable and potentially dangerous when treating certain areas, especially over the thorax. The portable units have the same milliampere output (100 mAmp), but because of their much lower frequencies, the average current is less. Strength gains or atrophy reduction can occur with these portable units, although longer treatment times are required. All treatments should be within the athlete's tolerance and a shut-off switch within the athlete's reach if the stimulation becomes uncomfortable.

Various protocols purport to be the most effective in strengthening isolated muscles. The parameter considerations, as with most TENS units, include amplitude, pulse duration, pulse frequency, and duty cycle (on–off time). With the duty cycle, an important factor in neuromuscular stimulation is the rest phase. These units create a tetanic contraction which is often combined with a volitional contraction. If the cycle does not allow an adequate rest phase, the muscle becomes fatigued too quickly for strengthening to occur. On–off ratios should allow a rest phase of three to five times the "on time" to prevent fatigue, especially as the training program begins. As the stimulation program progresses, the duty cycle can change from a 1:3 to a 1:1 on–off cycle.

Current Parameters

The parameter settings recommended for effective neuromuscular stimulation of large muscles follow.

Frequency

Frequency depends on the goal of the stimulation. To increase range of motion or if a sustained stimulation session is desired, the frequency should be adjusted just above that necessary to create a tetanic contraction. This frequency is generally around 20 to 35 Hz, which allows a tetanic contraction while minimizing the onset of fatigue. If the goal is to get a few repetitions of strong maximal contractions, as recommended by some training programs using the larger stimulators, then higher frequencies (50 Hz) can be used.

Pulse Duration

Many neuromuscular stimulators have fixed pulse widths in the range of 50 to 500 msec, and thus pulse duration is not a consideration. If variations of this parameter are available, it is generally recommended to have shorter pulse durations. This allows excitation of large motor nerves without depolarizing many of the smaller sensory nerves. The stimulation therefore will be more comfortable.

Amplitude

Amplitude is interrelated with the pulse width control as indicated by the strength–duration curve. Amplitude affects the peak intensity and therefore the depth of penetration of the current. Greater penetration of the current allows recruitment of additional nerve fibers, resulting in an increase in the strength of the contraction.

The waveform of the current must be considered primarily for electrode placement. If the unit is a monophasic current or an asymmetrical biphasic current, then it will have a positive and negative electrode. Polarity is often designated by red and black leads, which are the positive and negative electrodes, respectively. This color scheme should be confirmed for each unit. The negative electrode is placed over the nerve trunk and the positive electrode over the motor point of the target muscle. The symmetrical biphasic currents do not have a specific polarity; thus either electrode can be used on the above sites.

Technique

The following is an example of a stimulation protocol for the quadriceps muscles:

1. The treatment protocol is explained to the athlete, who is encouraged to increase the current intensity according to his tolerance. It is desired to produce a contraction as strong as possible that remains comfortable. The athlete is also encouraged to superimpose a volitional contraction in conjunction with the stimulation.
2. One electrode (negative) is placed over the femoral nerve in the femoral triangle and the

other (positive) over the distal quadriceps proximal to the patella. Ideally the athlete has isometric resistance to the contraction which limits the complete excursion of the limb. Terminal extension should be avoided to prevent joint "jamming" and damage to soft tissue.

3. Treatment parameters are adjusted and may vary according to the type of unit used:

> Amplitude—adjusted and increased to tolerance
>
> Frequency—often preset, otherwise 30 to 50 Hz
>
> Pulse duration—often preset, otherwise 200 to 300 μsec
>
> Duty cycle—15 seconds on/50 seconds off (preset on some units; otherwise on a 1:3 on–off ratio)
>
> Rise time—3 to 5 seconds

4. The treatment durations vary according to the type of neuromuscular stimulator being used. The larger clinical models may require only 10 to 15 contractions. The home portable units should be worn up to three times a day for up to 1 hour.

Electrical Safety

The safety of the patient when using electrical current is always a concern to the practitioner, a concern frequently reinforced by an apprehensive patient who is about to have his foot submerged into a bucket of water that has electrical wires from a modality draped into it. Certain factors must be considered when trying to determine whether the patient is in a threatening situation. Many of the specific principles will be discussed in the electrical stimulation sections of this chapter, but the general factors will be addressed now.

In the United States, commercially delivered electrical current operates at a constant frequency of 60 cycles per second (Hz). The voltage is dropped to ranges of 110 to 240 from initially high voltages of over 200,000 volts (Ritter, p 302). This is accomplished by using transformers. Individual electrical modalities must also increase or decrease the voltage within the unit, depending on the power required for its operation.

The power supplied to a unit travels through the electrical plug's "hot" and "neutral" prongs. The same amount of power that enters the unit through the hot line should exit the unit through the neutral line. A certain amount of current will leak out of the circuit to conductive material in the vicinity. This current will travel through any grounded conductive object. The term *ground* usually references the earth and has a zero-voltage potential that can safely accommodate this voltage conduction. The path that current leakage travels will be that of least resistance. The third prong on the electrical plug, the ground, is the usual source of accommodating the current leakage. The ground is usually an access for the current leakage because of the minimal resistance it offers when compared to biological tissues. This is true unless there is a defect in the receptacle's grounding, if the individual is in a wet environment, or if there is an insulation breakdown in the equipment. An excessive amount of current could be leaked, and, if a grounded individual comes into contact with this current leakage, a shock could result.

The purpose of circuit breakers is to monitor the amount of current that passes through a circuit and the amount of current that returns. If there is any significant reduction in the amount of current returning to the breaker, the circuit will switch off. In conventional breakers, as much as a 15-amp loss is required to switch it off. Even if a modality has an internal fuse that also serves as a safety feature, a significant amount of current can be leaked before the circuit is shut off, potentially causing harm to the patient. This is especially true in wet environments, since water is an excellent conductor of electricity. In a whirlpool, the patient in the water becomes part of the circuit; thus in the process of having the conventional circuit breaker respond, a lethal current can flow before the current is shut off. Health care facilities are now required to add "ground fault circuit breakers" into the receptacles of hydrotherapy equipment. These are more delicate in the perception to current loss, switching off with the loss of 4 to 6 mAmp of current, because this is believed to be the maximal transthoracic current that is safe. Monthly checks of the working status of the ground fault circuit breakers should be performed.

The amount of leakage allowable is 100 µAmp (micro = 1/1,000,000) for the chassis leakage and 50 µAmp leakage from an electrode. The allowable currents are those delivered through intact skin. If there is the possibility of bypassing the skin, as when a patient is on a cardiac monitor or using needle electrodes, the natural resistance of the skin is gone, and minute amounts of current can be lethal. The following list shows the physiologic responses that can occur if current is passed through the chest:

1 to 15 mAmp	tingling, muscular contractions
15 to 50 mAmp	labored breathing, pain, exhaustion
50 to 100 mAmp	tetanic contractions, ventricular fibrillation, burns
100 to 200 mAmp	unconsciousness, cardiac or respiratory arrest
Above 200 mAmp	death

The degree of the shock that occurs depends largely on the current allowed to flow through the body. Currents as small as 20 mAmp have resulted in fatalities. Although the voltage delivered could be high, the amount of tissue resistance present may significantly reduce the current generated. Skin resistance varies according to the degree of oil and moisture present but can range from 1,000 to 500,000 ohms. This relationship of voltage, resistance, and resulting current is described in Ohm's Law:

$$\text{Current} = \frac{\text{Volts}}{\text{Resistance}}$$

The resulting current, therefore, is the critical factor to consider.

Various sources of current may result in an electrical shock to the patient. Very commonly the defect is in the power cord of the modality. Also if moisture gets into the unit, the insulation is damaged through rough handling, or, if the three-prong plug is diverted through an adapter, the grounding becomes ineffective and a shock may result. Several suggestions may help to reduce the chance of an electrical shock or injury:

1. Make sure the ground on three-prong outlets is connected and that the electrical system has been evaluated so that it can accommodate the various modalities.
2. Extension cords or multiple adapters can increase current leakage and should not be used.
3. Avoid placing electrical equipment near radiators or pipes because it may serve as a grounding source if the patient were to come into contact with it.
4. If a circuit breaker is tripped more than once, it should be checked by an electrician before being used again.
5. Ground fault breaker circuits should be checked monthly and calibration checked annually.
6. Modalities should be checked annually for the amount of leakage that occurs from the chassis so that it does not exceed the allowable 100 mAmp. This is required by several health-care-certifying agencies.
7. Ultrasound units should be calibrated for timers and power output annually. Federal performance standards do exist for ultrasound.
8. Do not wind cables or leads tightly because this can damage their insulation.
9. Thermometers should be checked for accuracy.
10. Units that have thermostats such as paraffin or moist hot pack units should be calibrated periodically.

Ultrasound

Ultrasound is the application of high-frequency sound waves beyond human audible perception. Although ultrasound is used diagnostically for various medical purposes, it has become an important therapeutic modality in both physical therapy and sports medicine. The high-frequency sound waves emitted from early underwater communication networks were found to have an effect on the biological tissues of fish and other marine life. Further development of ultrasound began near the end of World War I, primarily with the advent of sonar radars that were used to detect enemy submarines. The uses of ultrasound then began to be researched extensively in Europe. Therapeutic application of ultrasound on soft tissues began in the United States in the 1950s and is now purportedly the most effective deep heat modality in the physical therapy realm.

Ultrasound is very effective in providing heat to soft tissues because it operates with a minimal increase in superficial temperature. Ultrasound can be used to treat chronic tendinitis, muscle spasms, strains, and sprains, among other conditions. Ultrasound provides both thermal and nonthermal effects that can relieve pain and promote tissue healing. These effects can also help increase range of motion and tissue extensibility, reduce inflammation, and break up scar tissue and muscle spasms.

Frequency

Unlike most other modalities that operate in the electromagnetic spectrum, ultrasound uses mechanical energy that is part of the acoustical spectrum. The frequency of ultrasound is above the audible ranges for humans, which is normally 15 Hz through 20,000 Hz. Therapeutic ultrasound operates at the frequencies of 0.8 to 1.1 MHz (mega = million) and is most commonly used at 1 MHz. Recently, an ultrasound unit that provides up to 3.3 MHz frequency has been produced commercially. The higher frequency of this unit allows treatment of more superficial areas.

There is an inverse relationship between the frequency of the sound and the energy's depth of penetration into the soft tissues. For example, 1 MHz frequency, which is generally used in physical therapy, has been found to have 50% of the energy penetrating a depth of 5 cm into the soft tissues. A frequency of 4 MHz, however, has 50% of the energy penetrating a depth of only 1 cm. Therefore, higher frequencies have less ability to penetrate to deep tissues. This inverse relation is caused by an increase in molecular resistance as the frequency increases. Application of ultrasound causes the molecules of tissues to vibrate at a rate proportional to the frequency of the sound. At high frequencies, more energy is required to maintain the more rapid molecular oscillations. The increased resistance causes an attenuation of energy with the high frequencies,

therefore less energy for deeper penetration. The 3.3 MHz unit enables a more superficial application of ultrasound so that there is a lessened chance of periosteal irritation. Application with a frequency this high is useful in conditions involving areas of relatively thin soft tissue coverage, such as superficial bones and joints.

Equipment

The components of an ultrasound unit consist of the following: an electrical generator, an oscillating circuit, a pulse/continuous mode selector, a coaxial cable, and sound head or transducer (Figure 6-18). The unit contains a timer that regulates the duration that energy is supplied to the transducer. A power meter is also present to provide information about the total watts (power) and watts per square centimeter (intensity) that the unit is generating.

Ultrasound is produced by the machine through the conversion of electrical energy to sound energy. The generator supplies the electricity for the system, and the amount of voltage it provides depends on the type of crystal that the system utilizes. In the original ultrasound units, natural crystals were used to create the sonar reverberation but required up to 4000 V because of their high impedance. Synthetic ceramic crystals are now being used that may require as little as 30 V to operate but commonly use about 300 to 400 V.

The electrical energy is transmitted to the transducer or sound head by means of a coaxial cable. The cable's primary functions are to minimize the loss of energy and to minimize any variations in the frequency of the current as it travels to the sound head. Electricity is converted to mechanical energy in the sound head by a reverse piezoelectric effect. A piezoelectric effect, as observed by the Curies in the late 1800s, is the production of an electrical current by rapid vibrations of a crystal. A reverse piezoelectric effect is the opposite—the production of mechanical deformations of a crystal by the introduction of an electrical current. The compression and the expansion of the crystal result in a vibrational activity that ultimately creates the therapeutic effect of ultrasound. Each crystal has an inherent

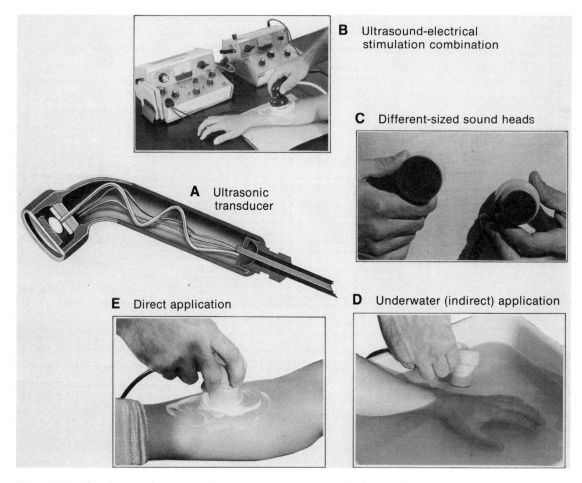

Figure 6-18   The ultrasound transducer **(A)** contains a quartz crystal. Ultrasound may be accompanied by electrical stimulation **(B)**. The sound heads may be of various sizes **(C)**. The ultrasound may be applied underwater **(D)** or it may be applied directly with cream serving as an interface **(E)**.

resonating frequency depending on its composition, diameter, and width. This resonating frequency occurs when the crystal's deformation and subsequent vibration is at a maximum for a given amount and rate of energy applied.

Two other factors that must be considered when referencing the sound head are the effective radiating area (ERA) and the beam nonuniformity ratio (BNR). These address the output characteristics of the ultrasound transducers.

The ERA is always smaller than the actual size of the transducer. Assessing the output intensities of the radiating surfaces discloses that many irregularities are present in the region 10 to 30 cm (near-field) from the transducer. The output may

range from no intensity to extremely high intensities. The ERA is calculated by scanning the sound head 5 mm from the radiating surface and measuring the areas that emit higher than 5% of the maximal power output anywhere over the surface of the transducer. The area that delivers this amount of intensity is considered the ERA of the crystal. The clinician should be aware of the ERA when determining the dosage of the ultrasound treatment. Intensity is determined by taking the total watts delivered divided by the ERA and is measured in watts per square centimeters.

$$\text{Intensity} = \frac{\text{Total power (watts)}}{\text{ERA (cm}^2)} = \text{watts/cm}^2$$

Beam nonuniformity ratio (BNR) is another measure of the consistency of the crystal in the sound head. Ultrasound energy is not consistent as it is being delivered away from the sound head. The meter displays the average intensity being delivered (watts/cm²) but may have regions that are delivering much higher intensities in the beam. The BNR is the ratio of the highest intensity found in the ultrasound beam compared to the average intensity indicated on the power meter. A BNR of 6:1 indicates that intensities of 6.0 W/cm² can be found in the near-field region when the intensity is set on 1.0 W/cm². The lower the BNR the better, although a BNR of 6:1 is generally considered to be acceptable. The higher the BNR, the greater the chance for "hot spots" to be encountered so that the movement of the sound head becomes more important.

The oscillating circuit tunes the frequency of the electrical current to the natural resonating frequency of the crystal being used. The amount of voltage applied to the crystal ultimately determines the intensity of the ultrasound. The oscillator also has another circuit added that creates a duty cycle by interrupting the power at specific intervals and durations, allowing for the pulsed mode of ultrasound.

Modes of Transmission

Ultrasound can be delivered in a continuous or a pulsed mode. Continuous ultrasound has an uninterrupted tranmission of sound vibrations. It is primarily associated with the thermal responses generated from ultrasound, although nonthermal responses may occur as well. With pulsed ultrasound, however, the sound intensity is interrupted at specific intervals. The interruptions in the sound that create the pulsed mode of ultrasound are specified by a designated duty cycle. The duty cycle is the ratio of the amount of time the pulses are on over a designated period of time (Table 6-8).

The typical duty cycles are 20% and 50%. Because the energy is delivered only a portion of the time, pulsed ultrasound provides a lower average intensity over a specified time, causing negligible thermal responses. For example, a 50% duty cycle with an intensity of 1.5 W/cm² would

Table 6-8   DUTY CYCLE OF PULSED ULTRASOUND

$$\text{Duty cycle} = \frac{\text{On time}}{\substack{\text{Total pulse time} \\ \text{(on + off time)}}} = \frac{2 \text{ msec}}{10 \text{ msec}} = 20\% \text{ duty cycle}$$

A 20% duty cycle with a pulse duration, which is the combined "on" and "off" times, of 10 msec (msec = 1/1000 sec). Energy is delivered for 2 msec of the cycle, which is on the "on" time, and there is a duration of 8 msec when no energy is transmitted through the sound head.

---

deliver only 0.75 W/cm² (1.5 × 50%) or half of the temporal average current that continuous ultrasound at the same intensity would provide. The thermal responses are also dissipated by the "off time" of the pulsed mode.

Application

The patient receiving ultrasound treatment should be positioned for comfort with the target area exposed. The duration of treatment runs from 3 to 10 minutes depending on the surface area to be covered. A recommended guideline to treatment time is 5 minutes for a 5-square-inch area or for an area two to three times the size of the sound head. Covering too much surface area at one time or moving the sound head too fast minimizes the amount of energy exposed per unit area, causing decreased effects. Speed of the sound head is recommended to be 1 to 4 cm/sec. Ultrasound can be applied using either linear or circular motions of the sound head, with each stroke overlapping the previous one.

A conducting medium is required to allow adequate transmission to the sound waves to the treatment area. Acoustical energy travels poorly through gases, and the therapeutic value of the energy would otherwise be lost to the environment during the application of ultrasound. Even with direct contact to the skin's surface, air present in the pores of the skin results in poor transmission and less absorption in the soft tissues. Therefore a liberal amount of a conducting agent should be applied to the treatment area. In addition, this inability of sound waves to be transmitted through air makes it essential that contact be maintained throughout the treatment so that the sound head does not become damaged. The sound waves can be reflected back onto the crystal, and, because there is no mechanism to dissipate the energy, the crystal may be damaged.

Commercial gels, lotions, mineral oil, or water can be used as the conducting medium with equally beneficial results, unless a combination of ultrasound and electrical stimulation is given. In this case, mineral oil is not as effective because it is not a good conductor of electrical current. When treating irregular surfaces such as the hands or feet, a submersion technique or "indirect ultrasound" can be used to maintain contact throughout the treatment. Ideally, degased water is used for this technique, since ultrasound travels poorly through gases. Water can be degased by allowing tap water to sit for several hours before use. The clinician should wipe away bubbles that appear on the sound head or on the patient. Using ultrasound in a whirlpool just after agitation is not advised because of the aeration that has occurred.

During the application of indirect ultrasound, the sound head and treatment area are submerged. The administration of ultrasound is the same except that the sound head should be kept 1 to 2 cm away from the surface to be treated. The intensity usually must be increased by 0.5 W/cm^2 to compensate for the absorption of ultrasound by the water and for the increased distance from the sound head. When using this technique, electrical safety should be considered, making sure all cables to the machine are sealed.

During the treatment of ultrasound, the patient should not experience discomfort or excessive warming of the area. If an increase in surface temperature is sensed or if the conducting medium is becoming heated, one should question the effectiveness of the sound penetration. This situation may indicate that the energy is being absorbed at the surface of the skin, leaving less energy to be delivered to the deeper tissues. It has been found that the use of water as the conducting medium has minimized this concern. The sound head should be inspected for damage or the submersion technique should be considered if increased surface temperatures continue.

Treatment Parameters

As the instrumentation, regulation, and materials of ultrasound become more refined, treatments are becoming more specific. The classic factors to consider when determining the treatment parameters include duration, intensity, and mode of transmission—pulsed or continuous. One must also consider the type of injury, the stage of healing, the part being treated, and the amount of surface area to be treated.

Intensity or strength of the ultrasound energy is referenced as watts per square centimeter (W/cm^2). This is the total power emitted over the crystal's radiating surface. The average output of an ultrasound treatment ranges from 0.5 to 3.0 W/cm^2. Newer units may have lower peak intensity outputs owing to the refinement of the synthetic crystal's composition and the equipment regulations that enhanced the efficiency and accuracy of the units.

The intensity of an ultrasound treatment depends on the desired results, the stage of the injury, and the amount of soft tissue covering on the target area. When treating chronic conditions, it is generally desired to create a vigorous heating in the tissues with deep penetration. To achieve these results, higher intensities of ultrasound ranging from 1.5 to 2.0 W/cm^2 should be used. In more acute conditions, lower intensities are recommended (0.5–1.0 W/cm^2). When treating areas with a minimal soft tissue coverage of bony parts, lower intensities should be used to reduce the possibility of periosteal irritation. As discussed previously, the depth of penetration of energy depends on the frequency of the sound, which is a preset variable of the ultrasound unit. Lower intensities are required to treat superficial areas because the depth of penetration is a function of the frequency and cannot be altered.

Suggestions for selecting treatment intensities range from eliciting periosteal irritation and then decreasing the intensity 10%, to having the patient perceive only mild warmth, to having no sensory perception at all. There should be no discomfort to the patient during the application of ultrasound. The treatment intensity should be decreased or the speed of the sound head movement increased, or both if the patient perceives any discomfort or notable warmth. Pain during the application of ultrasound may indicate periosteal irritation, in which case treatment parameters should be adjusted or the use of ultrasound discontinued.

There is some concern expressed for using ultrasound after a cryotherapy technique. It is believed that the anesthetic effect that results from ice application will not allow the patient to detect excessive energy levels. Ultrasound has been reported to have a more effective deep heating by maintaining cooler surface temperatures. The cooler surface temperatures allow greater heat loss at the skin and higher peak temperatures in the deeper tissues. The concern for the hypesthetic state after cryotherapy can be decreased by routinely decreasing the intensity of ultrasound initially. The technique of using ice followed by ultrasound has been found empirically to be effective. Ultrasound may be used when thermal agents are indicated for an injury, but a cutaneous sensitivity is elicited when a more superficial application of heating occurs. The potential for rebound hyperirritability after use of superficial heat is avoided. The hypesthetic benefit of cryotherapy along with getting therapeutic heat in the deeper target tissues can be attained.

Thermal Responses

The thermal responses that occur with ultrasound include increased collagen fiber extensibility, changes in nerve conduction, increased pain thresholds, increased enzymatic activity, and changes in contractile tissue. Tissue temperature ranges from 40° to 45° C after an ultrasound treatment with a depth of penetration of more than 5 cm. The degree that the tissues are heated depends on several factors, including the absorptive capacity of the tissues to ultrasound, the dosage (intensity and duration) of ultrasound delivered to a given surface area, and the mode of transmission.

The ultrasound energy can be either absorbed or scattered by the tissues being treated. The better the absorptive capacity of the tissue, the more ultrasound energy can be delivered to the tissues. If scattered, the energy is lost to the surrounding areas and is of minimal benefit. Absorption of

ultrasound energy is greatest in tissues with a high collagen content. These tissues, namely, muscle, nerve, capsule, and bone, are therefore selectively heated. The selective heating of these tissues occurs with a minimum of superficial tissue heating, which is one of the chief advantages ultrasound has over the shortwave and microwave diathermies. The latter modalities often heat superficial tissues to a dangerous level before significant penetration occurs.

Ultrasound has excellent penetration through homogeneous tissues such as adipose, causing minimal absorption and subsequent heating in these superficial regions. However, at tissue interfaces, standing or shear waves develop, creating a concentration of energy that generates heat. The standing waves are found to be most significant at the bone–muscle interfaces. This concentrated heating is thought to be the cause of the periosteal pain or burning that can occur with ultrasound treatments.

Selective heating has been shown to increase collagen extensibility. The most effective method to achieve an increase in extensibility of the tissues is to combine ultrasound with stretching. The heating of the tissues increases the molecular bonding activity, therefore allowing plastic deformation to occur when that body part is placed under a stretch. This method can be used to help increase range of motion and flexibility.

Studies of the effects of ultrasound on blood flow have produced varied results, largely due to the variations of treatment parameters used by the researchers. Some authors have concluded that high intensities of 2.0 W/cm² or greater and of longer durations (10 minutes or more) are needed to attain an increase in blood flow to the treatment area. The increase in blood flow supports the moving technique of application (linear or circular) versus the stationary technique. Stasis of blood flow, blood cell aggregation, and endothelial damage of blood vessels were found to occur at therapeutic dosages with the stationary technique.

The mechanism by which ultrasound decreases pain is uncertain. Ultrasound has been found to increase the pain threshold of peripheral nerve fibers. This effect was attributed to the generation of heat that transpires and to a nonthermal mechanism. The nonthermal effect is hypothesized to result by mechanically stimulating the superficial sensory fibers that would decrease the nerve transmission along the course of the nerve fiber. Results of the effects of ultrasound on nerve conduction velocities are inconclusive. Some authors have reported that the dosage of the ultrasound treatment ultimately affects nerve conduction. Dosages of 1 to 2 W/cm^2 caused a decrease in nerve conduction, whereas dosages below 0.5 and above 3.0 W/cm^2 caused an increase in nerve conduction. As the nerve conduction decreases, the patient's perception of pain diminishes.

A similar explanation is given for the effect of ultrasound on muscle spasms. Ultrasound decreases the conduction of secondary afferent and gamma nerve fibers as a result of the thermal response. Heating decreases the sensitivity of the muscle to stretch, causing a reduction in muscle tone.

Nonthermal Effects

The nonthermal effects of ultrasound may be presented in conjunction with the thermal responses or may be present alone, as with the pulsed mode of ultrasound transmission. These nonthermal responses are cavitation and acoustical streaming. As sound is transmitted through the tissues, it causes regions of molecular compression and expansion (condensation and rarefaction). The molecular oscillations affect small gas bubbles present in the blood or tissues. This vibrational effect on gas bubbles is cavitation. Cavitation may be stable, creating positive effects by increasing cellular activity, or can be harmful (transient) if the gas bubbles become too large and collapse suddenly. The transient form of cavitation can be minimized by the atmospheric pressure and by maintaining contact on the treatment surface with the sound head.

Acoustical streaming is a microstreaming event that produces velocity gradients and subsequent fluid movement along cell membranes. This movement results from mechanical vibrations caused by the sound waves or from the stable cavitation's vibrating bubbles. Changes in chemical gradients result in ion migration through cell membranes and vessel walls. This stimulates protein synthesis, which is responsible for tissue regeneration. This effect, caused by an increase in fibroblast activity, was found with low-intensity ultrasound (0.1 W/cm^2) and is attributed to acoustical streaming. Tissue healing was not found at higher intensities and could not be attributed to thermal factors.

Therapeutic Effects and Uses of Ultrasound

Ultrasound may be indicated for numerous problems encountered in a sports medicine environment. The therapeutic uses of ultrasound include pain relief, decreasing muscle spasms, promoting tissue healing, increasing range of motion, reducing inflammatory conditions, and phonophoresis. Therefore ultrasound can potentially benefit a multitude of entities.

Methods of pain relief and the reduction of muscle spasms have been addressed previously. The treatment of inflamed soft tissues with ultrasound has not been studied extensively, but empirical findings substantiate its use with this type of problem. We believe that caution should be used when employing continuous ultrasound over an area of inflammation. On several occasions a latent exacerbation in pain was experienced by athletes, even with moderate dosages (1.0 W/cm^2 for 5 minutes) of continuous ultrasound. Using a pulsed mode of ultrasound, with its less thermal effect, was initially found to be more advantageous, even though more superficial heat was tolerated by the patient.

When treating scar tissue, dosages that elicit a thermal response are most effective in increasing range of motion. As discussed previously, flexibility exercises should be used to optimize the effects of ultrasound on connective tissue extensibility and range of motion.

Plantar warts are frequently encountered in athletes. Ultrasound has been used to provide relief of pain and to help resolve this condition, with questionable results. Numerous techniques and treatment parameters have been attempted to optimize the effects of ultrasound on this entity. The intensity of 0.1 W/cm^2 is most frequently used but may progress to 1.5 W/cm^2 as the treatment sessions continue. Ultrasound is applied for 15 minutes once a week for up to 15 sessions.

Young lesions and those with no prior intervention of acid, cauterization, or surgery respond most favorably to treatment. Although placebo treatments result in similar benefits, ultrasound is generally believed to be a benign attempt to resolve the condition. This treatment can be given without any adverse side-effects and without interrupting the athlete's participation.

The effect of ultrasound on mineral deposition in soft tissues is inconclusive at present. Although significant pain reduction occurred with conditions suspicious of having calcific deposits present (calcific tendinitis, bursitis, or heel exostoses), no radiologic confirmation has shown a reduction in calcium deposits.

A condition very controversial with regard to ultrasound is application to a large hematoma. A complication that can result from this type of injury, especially to the quadriceps or anterior arm, is myositis ossificans. Theoretically, ultrasound would be very effective in helping to resolve a large organized clot because of its penetrative ability. Clinicians have reported significant progress in range of motion when ultrasound was used in the treatment of a resolving severe contusion. It is proposed that ultrasound may cause deionization of calcium ions such that fewer calcium ions are deposited in the forming fibrin matrix needed for clotting. However, if the injury caused periosteal disruption and osteoblast proliferation within the hematoma, ultrasound may only exacerbate the condition from the mechanical agitation. Further stimulation of osteoblasts is why ultrasound is contraindicated in a condition when myositis ossificans is suspected until the condition is radiologically diagnosed as mature.

The time after injury is an important factor to consider when using ultrasound to promote tissue healing. Tendon repair in animals was inhibited when ultrasound was administered immediately after surgery. It is recommended to wait 2 weeks after an acute injury before ultrasound is used when attempting to promote tissue healing. Low-intensity ultrasound in the pulsed mode of transmission is found to be most effective for this type of result. The healing is attributed to a nonthermal response because the optimal intensities used are very low (0.25 W/cm^2–1.0 W/cm^2 at a 20% duty cycle and 0.1 W/cm^2 continuous at 3.5 Hz). Higher intensities may result in tissue edema. Therefore, delayed application of ultrasound at low intensities has been found to be most effective in promoting tissue healing.

Phonophoresis

Phonophoresis is a technique in which chemicals, usually anti-inflammatory or analgesic medications, are driven into tissues by means of ultrasound. The thermal response and acoustical streaming are thought to be the reasons the ions are driven through cell and organelle membranes. Repeated studies revealed that therapeutic responses with phonophoresis, especially pain relief and improved range of motion, were superior to those with placebo treatments or ultrasound alone. Treatments using 10% hydrocortisone ointments were found to be more effective than 1% oinments. Phonophoresis has been found to be more efficient than the iontophoretic (electrical driven) means of chemical transmission. To minimize the possibility of trapped air bubbles that impede transmission, the ointment is massaged onto the treatment surface. Conventional treatment parameters are used with phonophoresis.

Electrical Stimulation and Ultrasound

Ultrasound is often combined with some form of electrical stimulation. The sound head becomes the active electrode while administering ultrasound. This technique provides a mechanical massage in conjunction with the thermal response of ultrasound. The combination of modalities is believed to enhance circulation, help relieve muscle spasms, and loosen fibrotic tissues, although these results have not been found in controlled studies. In our clinic, electrical stimulation has been a valuable adjunct, especially in treating the sore arm of a baseball pitcher.

Contraindications

Contraindications to ultrasound include the following:

Ischemic areas.

Areas of decreased sensation—ultrasound must be administered within pain-free limits to avoid burning of tissues or irritating the periosteum. In anesthetized regions, the patient cannot perceive these potential side-effects.

Over the eyes—the danger to eyes includes retinal damage and lens opacities as a result of the selective heating of these tissues.

During pregnancy—temperature elevation in fetuses has caused numerous adverse effects that range from central nervous system to orthopedic abnormalities. It is not advised to treat females in the low back or abdominal regions if there is any chance of pregnancy.

Cancer—because of the threat of metastases if neoplasms are present, ultrasound is contraindicated in these situations. This similar concern is present with infections because ultrasound may cause them to spread.

Active infections

Over fracture sites—application of continuous ultrasound over healing fractures is not advised because a demineralization process can occur, affecting the callous formation. Also a disrupted periosteum can easily be agitated with ultrasound, causing pain. Ultrasound can therefore be an effective tool when attempting to diagnose stress fractures.

Caution over spinal cord—transient cavitation, which may damage cells, is especially a concern with the central nervous system tissues because of the inability to regenerate. Caution should be exercised when sonating over the spinal cord, especially after laminectomies. It is generally believed, however, that with the bony protection the spinal cord is afforded, minimal sound reaches the neural tissue.

Over open epiphyses—caution should be exercised when sonating in regions of open epiphyses. Selective heating of the cells at the bone interface can cause abnormal growth patterns. Although therapeutic dosages are believed to be safe, adverse effects can occur.

Over cervical and stellate ganglia

Around pacemakers—sonating directly over or around a pacemaker is contraindicated because of the chance of electrical interference. With a pacemaker, ultrasound to other parts of the body is not a problem as it would be with the diathermies. Ultrasound directly over the heart has found EKG changes in canine studies and should also be avoided.

Metallic implants and polyethelene and methyl methacrylate associated with joint prostheses have not produced adverse reactions to ultrasound treatments and are not contraindicated.

Lasers

Lasers (light amplification by stimulated emissions of radiation) are light amplifiers that emit energy in the visible and infrared region of the electromagnetic spectrum. There are high- and low-power lasers that are classified by their intensity and wavelength. High-power lasers whose intensities can be as high as 100 million W have numerous applications in industry, military, engineering, and medicine. Some of the medical specialties that utilize high-power lasers include dermatology, surgery, ear–nose–throat, rheumatology, and immunology. The emphasis of this section, however, deals with low-power lasers that are also known as cold or soft lasers. The maximal output of cold lasers is less than 1 mW (1 mW = 1/1000 W). As the name implies, the low intensity results in a prethermal effect in which no tissue warming occurs. Cold lasers are used for relief of acute and chronic pain and for soft tissue healing in rehabilitative environments.

Cold lasers have been used in the United States for the last 7 to 8 years. They have been researched extensively and incorporated clinically in Europe for many years before this date. The use of light as a healing aid has a long history, dating back to 1500 B.C. when its therapeutic effects were attributed to a sun god, Sanitir. The application of light was included in treatments of mental illness, smallpox, rickets, and other ailments. Light therapy has become more sophisticated and includes the use of ultraviolet light and lasers, which have various uses in rehabilitation. The first successful operational laser was a ruby laser, invented in 1960. The applications of lasers in physical therapy and sports medicine continue to be explored.

Therapeutic Uses

Cold lasers can benefit many entities in the sports medicine environment, ranging from the treatment of carpal tunnel syndromes and tendinitis to joint sprains. Potentially, any condition that involves pain, inflammation, and damaged tissues can be aided by this modality. Although a laser can promote the healing of injured tissues and reduce pain, it will not correct anatomic or mechanical dysfunctions. In these conditions, one must eliminate the cause while attending to the effect of the injury.

The results we have seen in our clinic have been exciting, especially in reducing edema and ecchymosis in acute injuries. The classic method of acute injury management (Rest, Ice, Compression, Elevation—RICE) can thus be expanded to include laser, enhancing a quicker return of the athlete. Acute injuries are lasered as soon as possible with an emphasis on a gridding technique unless the region of involvement is large or the injury diffuse. In diffuse conditions such as a strain, the trigger/acupuncture points are treated. Often a point stimulator such as the neuroprobe is combined with the laser when treating distal trigger points. The impressions of both the practitioner and the athlete have been positive with regard to ultimate effectiveness.

Production of Laser Light

Laser light is produced by a sequence of reactions that cause the "stimulated emission" of photons which are light energy. An electrical discharge or light flash ionizes a gas, raising its electrons to a higher valence level, thus creating an excited state of the atoms. As the ionization process continues, most atoms reach an excited state by absorbing a specific level of energy. The energy, in the form of photons, is naturally released from the excited atom in its attempt to reach a more stable configuration. As the photons are released, the electrons return to their ground state, a process call spontaneous emission. This emitted energy stimulates adjacent atoms, causing them to release photons (stimulated emissions). The photons continue to be released, each stimulating subsequent atoms of a gas (Figure 6-19).

Types of Lasers

The amplification process occurs as a result of the type of laser used. Two types of cold lasers are used in the United States: the helium neon (HeNe) and the gallium arsenide (GaAs). Each is given its name by the type of atoms used to elicit the stimulated emission. Amplification in the HeNe laser occurs as the photons reflect between two resonating mirrors. This laser uses a glass chamber that contains the gas and reflecting mirrors. One of the mirrors is a semipermeable silver resonating mirror that allows photons of a very specific wavelength to escape when the energy attains a certain level. The photons emitted from the HeNe laser travel through a fiberoptic tube that directs them to the applicator.

The GaAs laser is a semiconductor laser and uses a diode in the tip of the applicator. A diode allows current to flow in only one direction. The diode comprises two semiconducting materials with different electron densities entwined. Electrical energy is applied to the system, and, as enough energy is generated between the semiconducting materials, a unidirectional flow of light energy with a specific wavelength is emitted.

The two types of lasers use different atoms that result in different wavelengths of light to be emitted. Specific wavelengths of laser light affect the tissues differently, causing variations in tissue responses. As will be discussed later in this section, wavelengths affect tissue penetration and the effectiveness of the laser in pain reduction and tissue healing.

Characteristics of Laser Light

The three major characteristics of laser light are monochromaticity, coherence, and divergence. Monochromaticity implies that the light is a single well-defined wavelength. Visible light covers a spectrum of wavelengths ranging from 400 to 770 nm (nm = 10^{-9} meters). The infrared (GaAs) laser has a specific wavelength of 904 nm. Because its wavelength is beyond the visible range, it is therefore imperceptible. The HeNe's wavelength is 632.8 nm, which is in the visible region. This type of device gives off a characteristic red beam often associated with lasers.

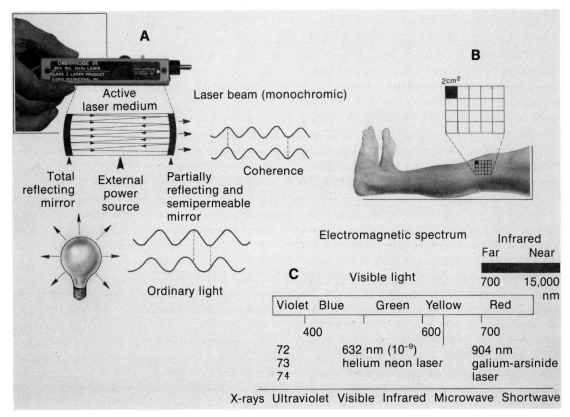

Figure 6-19   A laser beam consists of parallel waves **(A)**. The laser applications may be given in a "grid" pattern **(B)**. Note the point at which laser light fits into the electromagnetic spectrum **(C)**.

A second characteristic of lasers is the light waves' coherence or phase relationship. Normal light has numerous wavelengths that superimpose their phases on one another. Lasers, in contrast, have a specific wavelength and travel with their phases in synchrony. The light waves from a single laser source progress unidirectionally and symmetrically (Figure 6-19).

The third major characteristic of lasers is the minimal divergence of emitted light. The photons travel together in a parallel fashion, thereby concentrating the beam of light.

Frequency

The light that is emitted from the laser devices is delivered in pulses. The frequency output of

the laser refers to this pulsed mode and affects the average power of the laser. The energy of both the GaAs and HeNe lasers is delivered in pulsed frequencies of 73,142 and 292 Hz that correspond to natural resonating frequencies of the tissues. Injured or diseased tissue oscillates at a different frequency than healthy tissue, and the laser units allow variations in frequencies so that the frequency closest to that of the tissue may be selected. Therefore, the recommended frequencies for treatment may vary according to the stage of injury. With more acute pain, lower frequencies are recommended. As the stage of the injury progresses, higher frequencies should be used. Changing the frequency allows the laser to be more effective throughout the rehabilitative process.

Physiologic Effects of Lasers

The proposed physiologic mechanisms of how lasers work are the bioluminescence and cellular oscillation theories. A Russian researcher has documented that ultraviolet light is emitted with mitotic and meiotic cell divisions. This energy emission promotes the division of adjacent cells in the tissue, producing a state of natural metabolic activity. In a homeostatic state, the biological system assumes a natural frequency of activity. In a disease state, however, this frequency is disturbed. It has been purported that by applying energy with a similar intensity such as the laser, the homeostatic state of the tissue will be resumed. This theory can also be applied to neuronal activity. A German researcher theorized from results of animal studies that nerve conduction and transmission are propagated by means of photon emission and not strictly from a histochemical response. The purported benefit of the laser's effect on neural tissue is that it would help normalize the membrane potential in the axons. Bringing the membrane potential to normal helps relieve muscle spasms, reduce arteriole spasms, which therefore enhances microcirculation, and influences active transport and the metabolic processes of the mitochondria.

Various researchers using cold lasers of varying intensities have found the following:

Increased mitochondrial activity with elevated ATP production.

Higher levels of RNA in the endoplasmic reticulum of animals with a subsequent increase in DNA replication. There were no genetic or histochemical changes in the DNA.

Elevated blood cortisol levels that enhance the anti-inflammatory effect.

Prostaglandin production was lowered, resulting in less pain from tissue irritation.

Edema reduction occurred that was attributed to the laser's effect on membrane potentials, active transport, and microvascular dilation. This response was most evident in acute phases of injury.

Increased collagen formation and increased vascularization in the lasered wounds. The fibroblasts proliferated for the first 10 to 12 treatments, then progress plateaued and began to decline. Initially laser enhanced collagen generation, and then a degradation began. However, the tensile strength of the collagen was increased after the laser treatments.

Several other studies have been performed that used low-powered lasers but were beyond the range of class I and II lasers. The results of these studies are interesting in the areas of bone healing, bacteriocidal effects, and microvascular proliferation.

Application of Laser

Several factors influence the effectiveness of laser therapy, including tissue composition; laser wavelength (using either the HeNe or GaAs laser); time of application; and intensity.

Tissue composition affects the amount of light absorbed during a treatment. Generally, the higher the water content of a given body part, the greater is the absorption. For example, tissues such as mucus membranes and epithelium absorb light much better than does eschar or heavy scar tissue. Laser is also thought to be absorbed better through more darkly pigmented skin, although research findings are inconclusive at present.

Lasers with longer wavelengths have a greater depth of penetration. The HeNe laser, with a wavelength of 632.8 nm, has a direct penetration of 0.8 mm and an indirect penetration of 10 to 15 mm. Direct penetration refers to the level of the tissue that an unaltered form of laser energy reaches. An indirect effect occurs when the tissues respond to the absorbed energy of the light. The GaAs laser, whose wavelength is longer, has a direct penetration of 15 mm and an indirect penetration of up to 5 cm. The greater penetration makes the application of the GaAs laser more efficacious in treating musculoskeletal problems.

The intensity of the cold lasers is preset by the manufacturer according to the Food and Drug Administration's (FDA) classification of the laser. In rehabilitative applications, the laser is delivered in a pulsed mode. As the frequency of the output decreases so will the average power or intensity. Therefore a unit with a peak intensity of 1 mW at a high frequency may have an average power of less than 0.5 mW when the frequency is reduced.

Tissue Healing

The duration of treatment times depend on the type of laser being used and whether the laser's desired effect is to provide pain relief or to promote tissue healing. When applying laser for tissue healing, the wound can be treated either directly over the lesion or around its perimeter. Lasering directly over a wound, contusion, or injured body part is termed *gridding*. The technique is analogous to placing a piece of graph paper over the site with a 1-cm scale (Figure 6-19). The wound receives the laser treatment for 10 to 15 seconds per each square centimeter using the GaAs laser or 20 to 30 seconds per square centimeter using the HeNe device. A multiple head laser that emits a laser over a broader area has been developed to reduce treatment time. The gridding technique does not require the laser tip to touch the wound, making the treatment of infected areas safer. Because lasers have minimal divergence, the applicator can be held to 1-2 cm away from the skin during treatment with beneficial results but should be held as close as possible. If the wound contains eschar or scar tissue, it is advisable to laser around the wound instead of directly over it. The energy is not absorbed well in these conditions, and thus lasering directly over a scar is less effective.

Pain Management

For pain management, the painful site itself, the nerve root levels, or trigger and acupuncture points can be lasered (see Figure 6-14). Each point is lasered for 15 to 20 seconds with the GaAs or 30 seconds with the HeNe laser. It is advisable to treat the area as close to the injury as possible and to limit exposure to only a few areas. The same gridding technique can be used for localized pain areas, or specific acupuncture points can be lasered to treat the desired body part. Ideally the treatment is limited to 25 points, but the surface area should be covered. The Arndt–Schultz Principle is very applicable with the laser and implies that more is not necessarily better. The principle states that "weak stimuli excite physiologic activity, moderately strong ones favor it, strong ones retard it and very strong ones arrest it." Therefore too much energy results in a diminished response. In determining the number of laser treatments, this principle should be implemented. The frequency of treatments should not exceed one per day, and it is sometimes recommended to use laser every other day. In Europe, laser treatments can be as infrequent as once or twice a week, although they use stronger lasers. If the rate of tissue healing begins to diminish, a reduction in the frequency of treatments is advised.

It may take two to three treatments before a response to laser treatments is noted. It is purported that the GaAs laser is more effective in treating acute and deep pain and provides more immediate relief, whereas the HeNe device has a better effect on chronic pain but may have latent results. Occasionally a rebound phenomenon can occur in which the pain is perceived to be of greater magnitude after laser treatment. Although the active pain decreases with treatment, the patient does not experience relief because of the existence of a pain memory. When the acute pain relief subsides, its resumption is noted as an increase in pain because of the additive effect with the pain memory. It is generally believed that 8 to 12 treatments are sufficient to produce the desired results. If the condition persists, it is recommended to interrupt the treatments for 1 week. Another suggestion is to decrease the output frequency of the laser. The reduced frequency results in a lower average power output, which further implements the Arndt–Schultz Principle.

Safety

Safety considerations concerning the use of therapeutic lasers are few. The FDA still has the cold lasers classified as an investigational device. The FDA categorizes lasers according to their maximal output, which is less than 1 mW in both the GaAs and HeNe lasers. Cold lasers are considered to have low risks and are categorized as class I and II laser devices and class III medical devices. These lasers are used in various settings under an investigational device exemption (IDE).

A proposed investigation must be approved through an investigational review board of the manufacturer, a university, or a hospital. An IDE requires the patient to be informed about what the laser is, its potential side-effects, and available alternatives for treatment. The practitioner must also keep records that include the results of the treatment and any side-effects experienced by the patient. Side-effects are to be reported promptly (within 10 days), and treatment results are to be reported monthly to the review board. The IDE is to allow clinical collection of data to aid the FDA in determining the efficacy of lasers as well as their potential harm.

Contraindications

The contraindications and precautions of therapeutic use of lasers are also few. They should not be used in the following situations or conditions:

During pregnancy
While taking photosensitive medications
Over the unclosed fontanelles of infants
If prolonged nausea or dizziness (exceeding 5 minutes) occurs during or immediately after the treatment. This condition occurs in only a very small proportion of the population.
In patients with cancer
After prolonged exposure to the eyes

REHABILITATION OF THE INJURED ATHLETE

The team physician can do only so much; the remainder, in the form of rehabilitation, must be done by the athlete. The athlete must not just be given a list of exercises and sent away: The best effects are achieved when the trainer shows concern and gives individual attention to the athlete from the time of injury to his return to practice and competition.

Each injury to an athlete has both physical and emotional effects, and emotional conflicts may undercut rehabilitation (see Chap. 5). Thus the athlete must be both physiologically and psychologically rehabilitated. At first, the athlete

may not accept the diagnosis. "It can't happen to me." He then becomes angry: "Why did this happen to me?" This anger may be vented on the athletic trainer. The trainer should listen and avoid being offended, because anger cannot be matched with anger. If the trainer were to react defensively, the trainer–athlete relationship would be strained, making successful rehabilitation a trying experience. Later the athlete may feel that "I'll never be able to play again." However, in the final and desirable phase, the athlete decides that "I accept what I've been dealt, but I shall overcome the effects."

Initially, the athlete may not listen to or believe what the trainer says. Repetition, patience, and reinforcement are important. The athletic trainer seeks to guide the athlete into the final acceptance phase as rapidly as possible, and his interest helps to heal the athlete's shattered sense of worth. The trainer should be nonjudgmental, show empathy, concern, and understanding, and give encouragement. Lack of interest and beratement result in mutual frustration and paranoia for the athlete. If the trainer fails to be positive, the athlete may never emerge from one of the first three phases and may never reach full potential.

The athletic trainer should not make too many promises. He should not, for example, give a specific time for healing. His goal is to return the athlete to the same activity level as before the injury in the shortest possible time.

Goal Setting

After injury, the athlete is apprehensive and anxious about his return. The athlete must be an active participant in goal setting because it increases his involvement in the rehabilitative process. The athlete then assumes responsibility for his progress, shifting it from the physician and athletic trainer. The medical staff thus assumes the supervisory role within the rehabilitative process.

The subjective, objective, and functional criteria previously mentioned are all long-term goals. The immediate goal is pain-free exercise within the limits of functional activity—it may be simply to complete a straight leg-raise exercise. Short-term goals must be constantly reinforced to the athlete to maintain his motivation and give him the emotional rewards of attaining success in each phase of his relationship.

Effects of Exercise After Injury

After injury adhesions form in and around muscles, tendons, and ligaments, binding these soft tissue structures to bony structures and obliterating otherwise the normal smooth gliding surfaces of joints. Active exercise increases blood flow to injured areas and mechanically stretches and softens fibrous scar tissue, resulting in regained range of motion, strength, and endurance.

Functional inactivity from immobility causes joint stiffness. Lymphatic and venous stasis lead to articular surface breakdown as the joint is without synovial lubrication. The resultant edema from sluggish circulation allows adhesions to form from the serofibranous fluid leading to decreased tendon, muscle, and ligamentous strength as well as possible osteoporosis. Ligamentous strength may decrease 40% as a result of an 8-week immobilization.

Functional activity improves blood flow, relieving stasis and resultant edema. The more prolonged and strenuous the exercise within pain-free limits, the greater are the aftereffects of exercise. The cast/brace concept is an especially valuable concept because exercise is permitted within the physiologic range of motion. As strength and range of motion are regained concurrently, the capacity for strong functional activity within the new range is simultaneously restored. Joint motion regained passively cannot be used with sufficient strength in a newly gained range. Because early active exercise is not always possible because of injury, early passive motion is preferable to inactivity, since studies have indicated strength increases in ligaments and tendons with early passive exercise.

Resistance exercise as tolerated further reduces adhesions. Fibroblasts become oriented along lines of stress with collagen laid down along these lines instead of a disorganized alignment as seen in fibrous scar. Thus Wolf's Law of tissue reacting to the stress placed upon it is implemented.

The body's response to overexercising results in inflammation. The histamine response to such abuse reverses the osmotic process with a result as shown in Table 6-9.

Acutely the skin is warm and moist as contrasted to dry, smooth, shiny skin in chronic inflammation. With inflammation, rest is required to allow recovery from abuse.

Muscular strength is important in preventing degenerative change of loose joints by preventing excess motion. However, early excessive weight-bearing exercises lead to early degenerative changes. Early exercise must be within the pain-free range.

Objectives

The objectives of rehabilitation are to regain range of motion, strength, flexibility, muscular endurance, power, cardiovascular endurance, speed, balance, agility, and skills. The rehabilitation process comprises many steps, and each one must be successfully completed, pain free, before the athlete returns to competition. Criteria for return are established for each injury in terms of skills and abilities that the athlete will need to regain before returning to his sport. He may return only when near-normal strength, flexibility, speed, power, endurance, and agility have been regained. The athlete must be told what these criteria are so that he can strive for concrete goals (Table 6-10).

Return to competition will demand agreement from team physician, athletic trainer, coach, and athlete. The athlete must be involved in this decision so that maximum performance can be achieved; otherwise, he may lack confidence and aggressiveness, which will result in subpar performances and possible reinjury.

Healing and rehabilitation take time. When mild or moderate injuries are properly treated,

Table 6-9   INFLAMMATORY RESPONSE

Heat	Loss of motion
Redness	Swelling
Pain	Malfunction
Crepitation	Atrophy

Table 6-10 CRITERIA FOR RETURN TO COMPETITION: SUBJECTIVE–OBJECTIVE–FUNCTIONAL

An athlete who returns to competition before being ready may be more easily reinjured and consequently hurt all season. Fulfillment of the following objectives before his return will reduce the chance of reinjury.

- Reabsorption of acute swelling
- Full pain-free range of motion of the injured part
- Normal strength and power as compared to the opposite side (80% + may be used in season)
- Normal size of muscular mass as compared to the other side
- Normal endurance of the injured part
- Normal cardiovascular endurance
- Regaining of previous speed and agility for lower extremity injuries:
  - Running full speed straight ahead without a limp
  - 90° cuts left and right from full speed without a limp
  - Full speed cross-over carioca without a limp
- All exercise is pain free (exercise with pain increases recovery time)
- Dynamic control of any instability
- Cerebromuscular rehabilitation complete
- Athlete can perform tests appropriate to physical demands of the sport
- Strong positive desire of the athlete to return
- Physician, trainer, and athlete agree on return to activity

the athlete may lose up to 3 weeks from competition. Reinjury and possible early joint deterioration may result if the athlete returns to competition too soon. Further, if rehabilitative procedures are inadequate, reinjury is more likely to occur.

Strength

Isometrics are the exercise of choice early in rehabilitation, when movement may be undesirable. A single isometric will aid in strength development within a 20° range of motion. Therefore several isometrics within the normal range of motion are necessary.

Initially, the athlete needs to hold only a 40% to 50% contraction for a few seconds to gain strength. As his strength increases, however, he needs more forceful contractions to further his strength development. He should hold these maximal contractions for 6 seconds.

Isotonic exercise with free weights is started as soon as possible to strengthen gaps left by isometric exercise. In regular strength training, repetitions are usually done with maximum weight. In rehabilitation, however, the athlete should go through a range of motion with submaximal weight to prevent the edema and soreness that would develop with three sets of maximum lifts. The part to be exercised should be isolated to prevent accessory motion from other muscles. Momentum and inertia are minimized by doing the exercises slowly during the early phases.

Early in rehabilitation, strength is gained from daily work efforts. As strength gains peak, weight training should be done every other day. Three sets of repetitions are needed for good strength and bulk gains. The repetitions are done slowly with a two or three count through a range of pain-free motion and a two or three count while returning the weight to the starting position.

Exercise

Exercise is the ultimate modality. Cold, heat, and electrical modalities aid in enabling exercise to become pain free and accomplish their physiologic objectives but do nothing to aid in regaining strength or endurance. Injuries require a certain time in which to heal. When that time has been reached, the athlete should be ready to return to competition. If, however, he has not been exercising or the exercises are painful, he will require extra time to return (Figure 6-20 A).

Exercise is begun the day after injury even if only isometrically. In this manner strength loss is retarded. Exercise progresses pain free to recovery (Figure 6-20 B). The athlete often overdoes his rehabilitation program, which results in a peak-and-valley sequence as he exceeds pain-free lim-

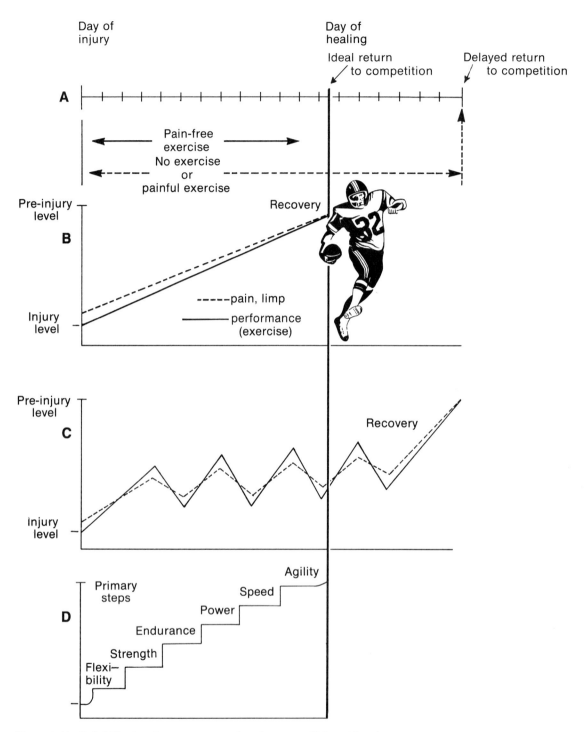

Figure 6-20 Rehabilitation time sequence and performance. If the athlete has pain during flexibility work, vary the degrees of motion. If there is pain with strength and power work, vary the repetitions and weight. If there is pain with endurance or speed work, vary the distance or time. If there is pain with agility drills, vary the quickness and time. The athlete must rehabilitate to his pre-injury level or higher or to the same level as his healthy side.

its (Figure 6-20 C). The athlete should experience no undue pain or swelling after each exercise session or upon arising the next morning. Ice is often used after exercise to prevent pain or edema from excessive exercise.

In all exercises the athlete works just below the point of pain and without limping in the case of lower extremity injury. The philosophy of no pain, no gain is extremely inappropriate in acute rehabilitation. Even a minor limp retards time of return. A cane or crutches should be used until gait is normal. The athlete should bear weight as much as possible within pain and physiologic limits. A cane or single crutch is used on the side opposite the injury to simulate normal gait mechanics.

The first two goals in rehabilitation are the regaining of flexibility and strength (Figure 6-20 D). Strength and flexibility gains must progress together. Strength programs must not wait until flexibility returns. Strength can actually help improve flexibility.

A certain amount of neural learning takes place in early phases of rehabilitation. The athlete who can lift 50 pounds with his quadriceps and the next day after a mild medial-collateral sprain can lift only 5 pounds has not lost this strength. Pain from soft tissue injury causes a reflex inhibition of strength to prevent further injury by limiting functional activity of the athlete. The return of strength must thus be relearned. This is accomplished by using a maximal pain-free weight done in multiple sets of usually ten repetitions per set. Four to eight sets are commonly used. As the athlete begins to plateau using multiple sets, a program modified from the original DeLorme system may be established.

The athlete's ten-repetition maximum (10-RM) is determined by the maximal amount that he can lift through a complete range of motion ten times. The athlete first performs ten repetitions at one half of the 10-RM, then does ten repetitions at three quarters of 10-RM, and ends with repetitions at the 10-RM. A fourth set comprises ten repetitions at the 10-RM plus 2.5 to 5 pounds. When this new weight is achieved, it becomes the 10-RM.

Repetitions and sets are changed as the athlete peaks with a certain routine. He may begin with eight sets of ten repetitions, progress to four sets of ten, peak out, switch back to eight sets of ten, and so forth. Endurance exercises may be added to his routine to aid in his progress.

Initially a slow pain-free pattern should be used to develop a good base for neural learning to take place. Later isokinetic exercise may be added as tolerated pain free. However, excessive torque may cause joint effusion, especially in the case of joint instability; thus care should be used in beginning this form of exercise. Isokinetics are especially valuable in the later phases of rehabilitation because they more closely resemble speeds used in competition. Because isokinetics may not load the muscle eccentrically, isotonic exercise is continued for successful rehabilitation. This is especially true in overuse syndromes often caused by lack of eccentric muscle strength. Isokinetics as well as isotonics that utilize machines unfortunately train only one motion. For this reason free weights that simulate actions necessary in competition are necessary in final phases of rehabilitation.

Isokinetics

Isokinetic means constant speed. Isokinetic training provides an accommodating resistance that allows the athlete to maximally load his dynamically contracting muscles at each point of a joint's range of motion, thus enabling him to do more work than is possible with either constant or variable resistance. Skilled trainers have used the isokinetic concept for years, applying manual resistance. Today, isokinetic machines may be used to condition, rehabilitate, screen, and test athletes.

When an athlete trains on an isokinetic machine, the machine automatically adjusts to, and matches, the force that he applies,[43–45] causing his muscular contractions to remain constant. The harder he pushes, the harder it gets; it should therefore be possible to do voluntary maximal contractions on each repetition, with resulting maximal strength gains. To achieve this accommodation, some machines use hydraulics (Orthotron, Hydra-Gym), and others have a motor, gear box, and clutches (Cybex-II). There is no "sticking point" with isokinetics because the tension developed by the muscle as it shortens is maximum at all joint angles. More motor units are thus activated to provide a maximum contraction for each repetition.

Strength gained at slow speeds does not carry over to fast speed. Strength gained at high speeds, however, converts to fast movement on the playing field and carries over to a strength gain at slower speeds. A variable adjustment allows the speed of the machine to be preset at slow, intermediate, or fast, and the velocity of movement may be varied from 0°/sec (isometrics) to 300°/sec.

Isokinetic machines allow the athlete to work on quickness and power, and he may be less likely to be injured on them because inertia is eliminated. Further, he will not meet more resistance than he can handle. As he tires, he applies less force, and the machine matches this reduced force with less resistance. His angular velocity, however, remains constant, and his joint range of motion stays the same. This contrasts with isotonic work, where inertia is brought in and the resistance is fixed, with the last repetition being as heavy as the first. In isotonics, the speed is variable and unknown, and as the athlete tires he slows down and his range of motion lessens. Another advantage of isokinetic machines is that the athlete uses his limbs independently against their own maximum resistance, with less soreness resulting because only concentric contractions are used. A disadvantage of the machines is that the athlete might not be sufficently motivated because he cannot perceive movement of a weight.

The Orthotron device is a hydraulic machine with a variable speed adjustment (Figure 6-21). It has two gauges: one to record flexion torque, and the other to record extension torque. The machine is most useful in the rehabilitation of the knee, ankle, and shoulder and, like other isokinetic devices, accommodates for pain and fatigue. If isokinetics are begun too early in knee rehabilitation, however, soreness may be produced as the athlete kicks out. Isotonic work thus remains the best way to gain important terminal extension of the knee.

The Cybex-II isokinetic machine may be used for the screening, rehabilitation, and testing of athletes and will isolate and test joints and muscle groups at many speeds.

Line other isokinetic devices, it accommo-

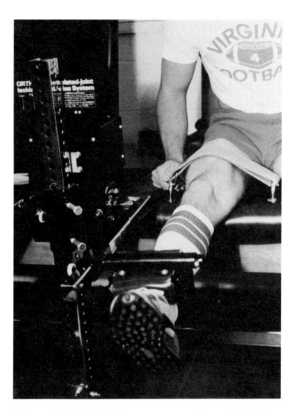

Figure 6-21   The Orthotron system allows isokinetic rehabilitation and training at many speeds.

dates for pain and fatigue. The Cybex-II contains a motor, gear box, and two clutches (one for each direction). The athlete moves a lever to engage the clutches, and, as he tries to increase speed, resistance increases. The trainer can speed up the motor to allow the clutch to go faster.

The Cybex-II provides a digital and graphic read-out of key measurements, including peak torque that the athlete can generate at speeds ranging from 60°/ sec to 300°/sec, peak torque at various joint angles, the speed at which the athlete can develop peak torque, and his endurance, total work, and joint range of motion (Figure 6-22). The examiner may also locate and analyze variations in torque at specific points in the range of motion caused by pain, weakness, or instability. The balance between muscle groups and both sides of the body can also be tested at various speeds.

Some isokinetic devices are especially useful for conditioning an athlete. The isokinetic swim

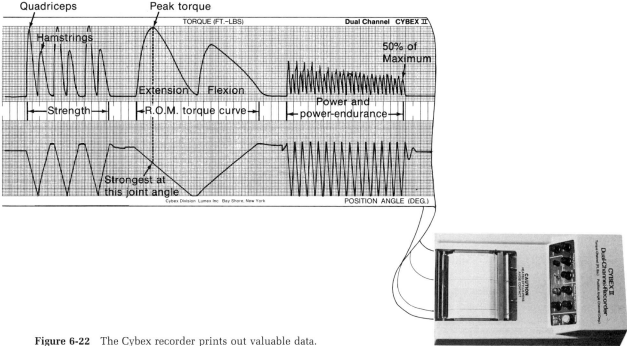

Figure 6-22 The Cybex recorder prints out valuable data.

bench allows a swimmer to lie prone and duplicate his swim strokes. A strong swimmer, however, may overpower the machine and must do hundreds of repetitions for a good workout.

Flexibility

Joint degeneration can be retarded if the athlete regains strength and flexibility early. Slow, static stretching, proprioceptive neuromuscular facilitation, and joint mobilization techniques are methods that may be used to help gain flexibility. The goal is a normal joint, not a hypermobile one. A corresponding gain in strength provides joint stability so that a normal range of motion may be achieved without producing abnormal motion. Strength and flexibility parallel one another. An increase in strength will facilitate range of motion; by the same token, an increase in motion needs an accompanying increase in strength within the newly gained range.

Capsules and ligaments have proprioceptive properties that are interrupted with injury. This may explain why some clinical degrees of instability become disabilities as more proprioceptive training is begun early in rehabilitation and em-

phasized heavily in the later stages in agility, speed, coordination, and skill exercises. These activities should be sport specific and graduated as the athlete enters his final phase of rehabilitation.

Power

An athlete must regain power before returning to competition. If he trains only with slow repetitions, he will gain strength but will not be ready for the rapid speeds of competition. The athlete should start high-speed power training as soon as his strength is adequately developed. For power training, a weekly one-repetition maximum (1-RM) should be determined first. Then, the athlete should train three times a week with three sets of 30-second repetitions with one half of this 1-RM, and rest for 20 seconds between sets. These sets are done explosively with proper technique.

Isokinetic machinery is used in power training. With isokinetics, the speed of muscle contraction remains constant as the load changes throughout to adapt to different strength levels at each point in the range of motion. Isokinetics may also be used for "cross-training," wherein exercise of the sound limb helps to maintain strength in the injured limb. Isokinetics, however, need isotonic supplementation, especially in knee rehabilitation. In an isokinetic quadriceps exercise as the knee reaches terminal extension, the stimulus is least where it is needed most. Strength gain is therefore lacking in terminal motion because resistance is not provided once the joint is "locked out."

Endurance

Muscular

Rehabilitation for muscular endurance should not be neglected, although it takes time and can be monotonous. Endurance training may be done during the intermediate phases of rehabilitation in the intervals between strength exercises. Underwater exercises in a pool are one way to regain both strength and endurance early. The athlete can usually begin these exercises as soon as his cast is removed. The buoyancy of the water allows him to perform exercises that would otherwise be painful. These exercises are especially beneficial in the rehabilitation of injuries to weight-bearing joints (Table 6-11).

Cardiovascular

An injured athlete should strive to have better cardiovascular endurance upon return to competition than he had at the time of injury. If the athlete were just to rest or if he performed specific exercises without regard to cardiovascular endurance, he would be more likely to be reinjured as a result of fatigue. The injured athlete is considered successfully rehabilitated only after he has competed at least one season in his sport.

Exercise Progressions for Lower Extremity Injury (EPLEI)

The endurance exercise goals are short-term goals. In this way the athlete does not overdo the exercise and get injured. This is an easily reachable goal. Instead of the first goal being, for example, to return to the basketball court, the first goal is to do low step-ups. (Table 6-12). By reach-

Table 6-11   POOL REHABILITATION FOR KNEES

Exercise	Water Depth
Walk	Waist to neck
10 laps, down and back	
Front–back kick	Waist
30, rest, 30	
Flutter kick	On Back
2 min, rest, 2 min	
Scissors	On back
35, rest, 35	
High step	Armpit
8 laps	
Walk–run	Waist to neck
10 laps	
Tucks	6 ft
10, rest, 20	
Sitting kick	N/A
1 min, rest, 1 min	
Body lifts	8–10 ft
15	
Squats	Waist
15, rest, 15	

ing it, the athlete sees improvement and develops confidence in his ability to recover from the injury. The athlete should first warm up and stretch and then do the endurance exercises. After exercising, he should again stretch and, if he is having some pain or swelling, apply ice for 30 minutes. As the goal levels increase, the exercises become more demanding. By the time the athlete reaches goal 8, he may return to his sport.

REHABILITATION PROGRESSIONS

In upcoming chapters, you will find rehabilitation progressions for specific body areas and for specific injuries. For example, the shoulder chapter contains a general rehabilitation program and a listing of the parts of the general program that are of particular importance in the rehabilitation of a rhomboid strain, anterior dislocation of the shoulder, acromioclavicular sprain, subacromial impingement syndrome, "tennis shoulder," and rotator cuff problems. There are also rehabilitation progressions for the neck; elbow, forearm,

Table 6-12 EXERCISE PROGRAM FOR LOWER EXTREMITY INJURY (EPLEI)*

Phase I	Step-ups (4″ step)	60 × daily
	Walk	30 minutes—M,W,F
	Swim	30 minutes—T,Th,Sat
Phase II	Step-ups (8″ step)	60 × daily
	Walk rapidly	30 minutes—M,Th
	Bike (when 90° + ROM attained at knee)	30 minutes—T,F
	Swim	30 minutes—W,Sat
Phase III	Step-ups (12″ steps)	60 × daily
	Walk/jog (stairs)	30 minutes—M,Th
	Bike	30 minutes—T,F
	Swim	30 minutes—W,Sat
Phase IV	Step-ups (18″ steps)	60 × daily
	Jog (PRE quad strength 20% body wt)	30 minutes—M,W,F
	Bike	30 minutes—T,Th,Sat
	Swim (optional)	
	Quadriceps PRE (30 lb)	10 repetitions
Phase V	Full speed sprints	30 minutes—M,W,F
	Swim (optional)	
	Bike	30 minutes—T,Th,Sat
	Quadriceps PRE (25% body wt)	10 repetitions
Phase VI	Full speed sprints/ cutting	30 minutes—M,W,F
	Bike	30 minutes—T,Th,Sat
Phase VII	Return to sport	

*In progression of activity, all exercise should be pain free, without a limp. In patellofemoral problems, eliminate step-ups over 8 inches. Stretch again after exercising. Apply ice for 30 minutes for pain or swelling.

and wrist; fingers; the lower back; the hip; the knee, including a progression that would follow an extra-articular knee reconstruction for an anterior-cruciate-deficient knee; and ankle and arch.

Stages of Rehabilitation

All rehabilitation progressions have the same format. They start with a listing of the objectives for flexibility, strength, and endurance. Rehabilitation progresses through three stages: initial, intermediate, and advanced. Each stage contains specific exercises for flexibility, strength, and endurance. Along with pictures of each exercise, the number of sets and repetitions is given.

The initial stage includes the acute phase and usually encompasses the time when ice is used. The athlete can usually leave the initial stage and enter the intermediate stage when the five criteria for using heat have been reached: Edema has stabilized, there is almost a full range of motion, the range of motion is pain free, there is no hyperemia at the injury site, and progress with ice has plateaued. The intermediate stage might also be called the preparticipation stage. The advanced stage is a participation level stage during which the athlete can return to practice.

When to Move to the Next Stage

In each stage, the exercises increase in intensity as if there were an initial, intermediate, and ad-

(Text continues on p. 238)

REHABILITATION PROGRESSION FOR GRADE I OR II STRAIN OF THE LOWER EXTREMITY

OBJECTIVES

To strengthen: hip flexors, adductors, quadriceps, hamstrings, gastrocnemius
Flexibility: same
Endurance: same

STAGES

Initial
Cryokinetics—ISE (ice, stretching, exercise)
Flexibility (Figure 6-23)—hip flexors (Figure 6-23 A), adductors (Figure 6-23 B), quadriceps (Figure 6-23 C), hamstrings (Figure 6-23 D), gastrocnemius (Figure 6-23 E)
Strength (Figure 6-24)—Hip flexors (Figure 6-24 A), adductors (Figure 6-24 B), quadriceps (Figure 6-24 C), hamstrings (Figure 6-24 D), gastrocnemius (Figure 6-24 E)

Intermediate
Flexibility—continue the above with increased resistance
Strength—increase resistance
Endurance — EPLEI goals 1,2

Advanced
Flexibility—apply heat and continue the stretching
Strength—increase resistance, leading to normal levels
Endurance—EPLEI goals 3–8

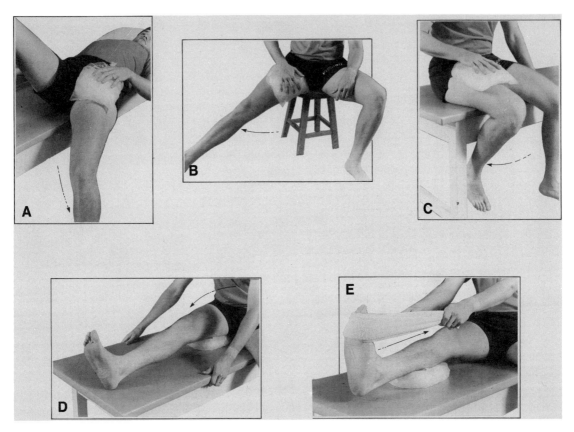

Figure 6-23   Ice and stretching for a lower extremity injury.

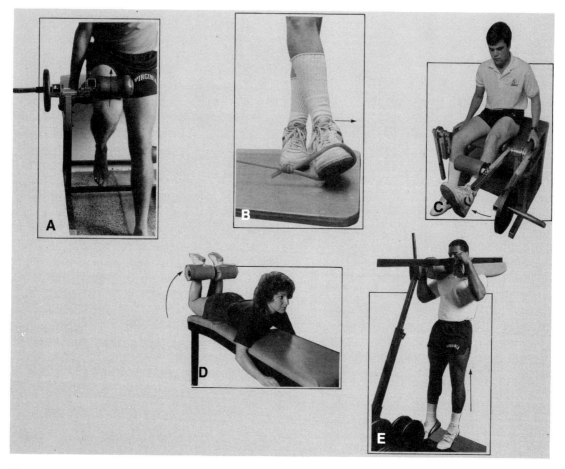

Figure 6-24   Strengthening techniques for a lower extremity injury.

vanced level within each stage. When the athlete reaches the advanced level within a stage, he is ready to move to the initial level of the next stage. But how do we know when the athlete is ready to move to the next stage? Pain is the best guideline.

If the athlete has pain while doing the exercises and awakens with soreness the next morning, he should drop back to easier exercises. If there is no undue pain or swelling and he feels about the same the next day, he should stay at that same level of exercise. If he has no pain during or after exercise or upon waking the next morning and he is comfortable and the injured area feels better in daily activities the next day, then he can increase the intensity of the exercises or move to the next stage.

REFERENCES

1. Anderson DG et al: Analgesic effects of acupuncture on the pain of ice-water: A double-blind study. Can J Psychiatry 28:239–244, 1974
2. Baggett R et al: Successful trampoline extrication. Athletic Training 14(2):74–76, Summer 1979
3. Balagura S, Ralph T: The analgesic effect of electrical stimulation of the diencephalon and mesencephalon. Brain Res 60:369–379, 1973
4. Boname JR, Wilhite WC: The acute treatment of heat stroke. South Med J 60:885–887, 1967
5. Bowers KD, Martin RB: Aging astroturf: A threat to safety and performance. Phys Sportsmed 3(10):65–67, 1975
6. Consolazio CF et al: Environmental temperature and energy expenditures. J Appl Physiol 18:65, 1963
6a. Emerick CE: Ankle taping: Prevention of injury or waste of time? Athletic Training 14:186–188, 1979

7. Epstein RK: The case against artificial turf. Trial 13(1):42–45, January 1977
8. Fox RJ, Melzack R: Transcutaneous electrical stimulation and acupuncture: Comparison of treatment for low-back pain. Pain 2:357–373, 1976
9. Gieck JH: Influence of environmental factors: Temperature. In Encyclopedia of Sports Medicine, pp 1120–1123. New York, Macmillan, 1971
10. Gieck JH, McCue FC III: Fitting of protective football equipment. Am J Sports Med 8(3):192–196, 1980
11. Gold J: Development of heat pyrexia. JAMA 173:1175–1182, 1980
12. Grippo A: NFL Injury Study 1969–1972. Final Project Report (SRI-MSD 1961). Menlo Park, California, Stanford Research Institute, 1973
13. Hall D: A practical guide to the art of massage: Anyone can administer a good massage that will give relief to a tired body. Runner's World 14(10):85–89, 1979
14. Hardy JD: Physiology of temperature regulation. Physiol Rev 41:521–606, 1961
15. Keene JS et al: Tartan Turf® on trial. Am J Sports Med 8(1):43–47, 1980
16. Kopysov VS: Use of vibrational massage in regulating the pre-competition condition of weightlifters. Sov Sports Rev 14(2):82–84, 1979
17. Knochel JP et al: The renal, cardiovascular, hematologic and serum electrolyte abnormalities of heat stroke. Am J Med 30:299–309, 1961
18. Malacrea R: Protective Equipment Fit. Proceedings of the NATA Professional Preparation Conference. Nashville, NATA Professional Education Committee, 1978
19. Mayer DJ, Liebeskind JC: Pain reduction by focal electrical stimulation of the brain: An anatomical and behavioral analysis. Brain Res 68:73–93, 1974
20. Melzack R, Wall PD: Pain mechanisms: A new theory. Science 150:971–979, 1965
21. Melzack R: Phantom limb pain: Implications for treatment of pathologic pain. Anesthesiology 35:409–419, 1971
22. Melzack R: The Puzzle of Pain. New York, Basic Books, 1973
23. Melzack R, Melindoff DF: Analgesia produced by brain stimulation: Evidence of a prolonged onset period. Exp Neurol 43:369–374, 1974
24. Melzack R: Prolonged relief of pain by brief, intense transcutaneous somatic stimulation. Pain 1:357–373, 1975
25. Melzack R et al: Trigger points and acupuncture points for pain: Correlations and implications. Pain 3:3–23, 1977
26. Monkerud D: Put your health in your hands. Runner's World 11(12):32–37, 1976
27. Monkerud D: Putting your finger on the source of pain: The solution to many of the pains running cause may already be at your fingertips. Runner's World 14(8):59–61, 1979
28. Oliveras JL: Behavioral and electrophysiological evidence of pain inhibition from midbrain stimulation. Exp Brain Res 20:32–44, 1974
29. Parsons CM, Goetzl FR: Effect of induced pain on pain threshhold. Proc Soc Esp Biol (NY) 60:327–329, 1945
30. Prentice BE: Acupressure massage to relieve menstrual cramps. Trainer's corner. Phys Sportsmed 9(3):171, 1981
30a. Professional Uses of Adhesive Tapes, 3rd ed. New Brunswick, New Jersey, Johnson & Johnson, 1975
31. Rossi GF, Zanchetti A: The brainstem reticular formation. Arch Ital Biol XCV (Fasc 3–4):199–435, 1957
32. Rutherford GW Jr: Injuries Associated with Public Playground Equipment. HIA Hazard Analysis Report. Washington, DC, U.S. Consumer Product Safety Commission, 1979
33. Ryan R (moderator): Artificial turf: Pros and cons.. Phys Sportsmed 3(2):41–50, 1975
34. Ryan R (moderator): Artificial vs. natural turf. Phys Sportsmed 7(5):41–53, 1979
35. Ryan J: The neglected art of massage. Phys Sportsmed 8(12):25, 1980
36. Sola AE, Williams RL: Myofascial pain syndromes. Neurology 6:91–95, 1956
37. Stanitski CL et al: Synthetic turf and grass: A comparative study. J Sports Med 2(1):22–26, 1974
38. Tovell J: Ice immersion toe cap. Athletic Training 15(1):33, Spring 1980
39. Travell J, Rinzler SH: The myofascial genesis of pain. Postgrad Med 11:425–434, 1952
40. Troy FE: In defense of synthetic turf. Trial 13(1):46–47, 1977
41. Veghte JH, Webb P: Body cooling and response to heat. J Appl Physiol 16:235–238, 1962
42. Wand–Tetley JI: Historical methods of counter-irritation. Ann Phys Med 3:98, 1956

Suggested Readings: Electrical Modalities

Alon G: High Voltage Stimulation. Chattanooga, Chattanooga Corporation, 1984

Assimacopoulos D: Low intensity negative electric current in the treatment of ulcers of the leg due to chronic venous insufficiency. Am J Surg 15:683, 1968

Baker LL, Binder SA: Applications of low- and high-voltage electrotherapeutic currents. In Wolf SL (ed): Electrotherapy. New York, Churchill Livingstone, 1981

Baker L: Lecture notes from symposium on Functional Electrical Stimulation. Des Moines, Iowa, 1981

Benton LA, Baker LL, Bowman BR et al: Functional Electrical Stimulation. Downy, California, Rancho Los Amigos Rehabilitation Engineering Center, 1980

Bertolucci LE: Introduction of antiinflammatory drugs by iontophoresis: Double blind study. J Orthop Sports Phys Ther 4(2):103–108, 1982

Burdick Syllabus: A Compendium on Electromedical Therapy. Milton, Wisconsin, Burdick Corporation, 1969

Castel JC: Pain Management with Acupunture and Transcutaneous Electrical Nerve Stimulation Techniques. Lake Bluff, Illinois, Pain Control Services, 1979

Dunn F, Frizzell LA: Bioeffects of ultrasound. In Lehmann JA(ed): Therapeutic Heat & Cold, 3rd ed. Baltimore, Williams & Wilkins, 1982

Fact Sheet: Laser biostimulation. Clin Management 5(2), 1983

Gamaleya NF: Laser biomedical research in Tae-USSR. In Wolbarsht ML(ed): Laser Applications in Medicine and Biology. New York, Plenum, 1977

Gersten JW: Effect of ultrasound on tendon extensibility. Am J Phys Med 34:662, 1955

Gieck J, Bamford M, Stewart H, Ferguson B: Therapeutic Ultrasound: Technology, Performance Standards, Biological Effect, and Clinical Application. Washington, DC, HHS Publ FOA 84-XXXX, August 1984

Greathouse DG, Currier DP, Gilmore RL: Effects of clinical infrared laser on superficial radial nerve conduction. Phys Ther 65:1184, 1985

Griffin JE: Physiological effects of ultrasound as it is used clinically. J Am Phys Ther Assoc 46:18, 1966

Harris PR: Iontophoresis: Clinical research in musculoskeletal inflammatory conditions. J Orthoped Sport Phys Ther 4(2):109–112, 1962

Hayes KW: Manual For Physical Agents. Evanston, Illinois, Northwestern University, 1984

Killian C, Malone T, Carroll W: High Frequency and High Voltage Protocols. Minneapolis, Medtronic, 1984

Kleinkort JA, Wood F: Phonophoresis with one percent versus ten percent hydrocortisone. Phys Ther 55(12):1320–1324, 1975

Kleinkort JA, Foley RA: Laser: A preliminary report on its use in physical therapy. Clin Management 2(4), 1983

Kots YM: Notes from DeKot's (USSR) lectures and laboratory periods. Canadian–Soviet Exchange Symposium on Electrostimulation of Skeletal Muscles, 1977

Kovacs IB, Mester E, Gorog P: Laser-induced stimulation of the vascularization of the healing wound: An ear chamber experiment. Experienta 4:341, 1974

Kramer JF: Ultrasound: Evaluaton of its mechanical and thermal effects. Arch Phys Med Rehabil 65:223, 1984

Lampe GN: TENS Technology and Physiology. Codman & Shurtleff, 1984

Lappin PW: Ocular damage thresholds for the helium-neon laser. Arch Environ Health 20:2, 1970

Laser Fundamentals and Experiments. Washington, DC, U.S. DHEW Publ 70-1, 1971

Lehmann JA, De Lateur Bj, Silverman DR: Selective heating effects of ultrasound in human beings. Arch Phys Med Rehab, 47, 1966

Lehmann JF, De Lateur BJ: Diathermy and superficial heat and cold therapy. In Kottke, Stillwell, Lehmann: Krusen's Handbook of Physical Medicine and Rehabilitation, 3rd ed, pp 275–350. Philadelphia, WB Saunders, 1982

Lehmann JF, De Lateur BJ, Stonebridge JB, Warren CG: Therapeutic temperature distribution produced by ultrasound as modified by dosage and volume of tissue exposed. Arch Phys Med Rehabil 48:662–667, 1967

Lehmann JF, Guy AW: Ultrasound therapy. In Ried J, Sikov MR (eds): Interaction of Ultrasound and Biological Tissues. Washington, DC, DHEW Publ (FDA) 73-8008, Session 3:8, 141–152, 1971

Mannheimer JS: Electrode placement for transcutaneous electrical nerve stimulation. Am J Phys Ther 58:1455, 1978

Mannheimer JS, Lampe GN: Transcutaneous Electrical Nerve Stimulation. Philadelphia, FA Davis, 1984

Matteson JH, Eberhardt T: Pain management and the new generation of "intelligent" TENS devices. Am J Acupuncture 13:149, 1985

Meyer FP, Nebrenski A: Electro-Acuscope and placebo effect. Calif Health Rev 2(1), 1983

Mortimer AJ, Roy OJ, Taichman GC, Keon WJ, Trollope BJ: The effects of ultrasound on the mechanical properties of rat cardiac muscle. Ultrasonics 16:170–182, 1978

Newton R: Electrotherapy Update Lecture Notes. Clifton, New Jersey, Preston Corp, 1983

Newton RA: Electrotherapeutic Treatment: Selecting Appropriate Waveform Characteristics. Clifton, New Jersey, Preston Corp, 1981

Nippel FJ: Interferential Current Therapy: An Advanced Method in the Management of Pain. Nemectron Medical, 1979

Protocol: Stimulation for Patients with Knee Disorders. Minneapolis, Medtronic, Neuro Division, 1982

Ritter HTM III: Instrumentation consideration: Operating principles, purchase, safety, and management. In Michlovitz (ed): Thermal Agents in Rehabilitation. Philadelphia, FA Davis, 1986

Seitz LM, Kleinkort JA: Low power laser: Its application in physical therapy. In Michlovitz (ed): Thermal Agents in Rehabilitation. Philadelphia, FA Davis, 1986

Sokoliu A: Destructive effect of ultrasound on ocular tissues. In Reid JM, Sikow MR (ed): Interaction of Ultrasound and Biological Tissues. DHEW Publ (FDA) 73-8008, 1972

Stratton SA: Role of endorphins in pain modulation. J Orthop Sports Phys Ther 3:200, 1982

Warren CG, Koblanski JN, Sigelmann RA: Ultrasound coupling media: Their relative transmissivity. Arch Phys Med Rehabil 57, May 1965

Wolf SL, Gersh MR, Kutner M: Relationship of selected responsiveness to transcutaneous electrical nerve stimulation. Phys Ther 58:1478, 1978

Wolf SL: Electrotherapy: Clinics in Physical Therapy, vol 2. New York, Churchill Livingstone, 1981

Wolf SL: Perspectives on central nervous system responsiveness to transcutaneous electrical nerve stimulation. Phys Ther 58:1443, 1978

Ziskin MC, Michlovitz SL: Therapeutic ultrasound. In Michlovitz (ed): Thermal Agents in Rehabilitation. Philadelphia, FA Davis, 1986

CHAPTER

7

Manual Therapy for the Athlete's Back

Jana J. Early

An athlete may seriously injure his back in sports. The pain may be short-lived or may become chronic. Other chronic back problems result from poor body mechanics, poor posture, and a sedentary life-style. The poor mechanics produce imbalances in spinal flexibility and strength.

The athlete with a back problem often "bounces" from one health care professional to another. The treatments are all too often nonspecific: shots, modalities, and a handout sheet of standard exercises. In some of these cases, a cure can be effected with manual therapy to restore proper mechanics.

EVALUATION

To begin a back evaluation, the examiner takes a thorough history. The athlete fills out a back form that asks questions such as, What hurts? How did it start? What can you not do that you would like to do? Any old back trouble? Where does the pain go? Does sneezing make it worse? Any numbness? Any weakness? Are your bowels and bladder working OK? Then the examiner can ask specific questions about the history.

Next, the examiner performs a comprehensive examination of the athlete. He observes, checks active motion and bony landmarks, performs passive motion tests to check for tightness of soft tissue and tightness of intervertebral joint ligaments, and performs a sensory evaluation and manual muscle testing. When the examiner knows which structures are painful, which soft tissues are tight, and which spinal segments have increased or decreased movement, the dysfunction will be clear and the treatment will then be obvious. Therefore, as a result of the systematic evaluation, the treatment can be individualized and be more effective.

TREATMENT OF
THE ACUTE INJURY

In an injury such as an acute back strain, treatment involves ice and electrical stimulation and sometimes point stimulation. The athlete also applies ice to his back for 20 minutes every 2 hours and wears a TENS unit. Active range-of-motion exercises in the pain-free range prevent the athlete's ligaments and muscles from becoming tight. The athlete avoids passive stretching during the first 10 to 12 days after a neck injury. His activities must stay within a pain-free range.

TREATMENT OF THE CHRONIC
BACK PROBLEM

With a chronic back problem, treatment starts with the application of moist heat. The moist heat can take the form of hydrocollator packs over electrical stimulation or a warm whirlpool. The examiner explains the treatment goals to the athlete and answers any questions the athlete may have. When the back is warmed up, the athlete is ready for soft tissue mobilization.

SOFT TISSUE MOBILIZATIONS

Soft tissue mobilizations are steady, forceful stretching movements of musculofascial tissue through restricted areas. They begin with the most superficial layers and progress to deeper layers. The techniques correct musculoskeletal asymmetries, normalize tissue quality, and increase range of motion. The therapist mobilizes the skin to assure good movement between superficial and deeper layers. Deep strokes will free fascial adhesions from the periosteum or from bony prominences. Inhibitive techniques relax muscles, and cross-friction massage frees the muscles. The soft tissues are treated before intervertebral joint mobilizations. Otherwise tight soft tissue would resist the joint mobilization.

INTERVERTEBRAL JOINT
MOBILIZATION

When the examiner notes decreased passive intervertebral movement, he proceeds to stretch the tight ligaments. To do this, he needs a thorough schooling in spinal anatomy and advanced manual therapy skills. These techniques are harder to learn than soft tissue stretches because they are more specific and involve deeper structures. Sometimes practitioners of manual therapy use nonspecific thrusting, high velocity manipulations that produce "pops" and relaxation of the spine. These techniques should, however, be used judiciously and only for specific areas of tightness or for acute facet blocks.

Contraindications to intervertebral joint mobilization are infrequent in athletes. The contraindications include hypermobile joints, fractures, severe osteoporosis, inflammatory stages of arthritis, bleeding disorders, any progressive neurological deficit, Paget's disease, spinal cord tumors, and multiple myeloma.

HOME EXERCISE PROGRAM

A customized home exercise program allows the athlete to take an active part in his rehabilitation program. The exercises include techniques to correct any abnormalities found in the evaluation. The therapist can show the athlete how to perform a Home Mobilization Program. This program includes solo soft tissue and spinal ligament stretches, proprioceptive neuromuscular facilitation (PNF) stretches, and strengthening exercises. However, this program is not as specific as the soft tissue and intervertebral joint mobilizations that are performed by the therapist. The exercises are not presented as a standard sheet of exercises but instead are individualized. Each exercise is pictured on a sticky label, and only those that apply to the athlete in question are stuck on his exercise sheet. If the athlete is not getting ongoing therapy, he should be checked every few weeks to make sure that he is complying with the program, to note his progress, and to make any needed alterations in his exercise program.

EVALUATION OF THE CERVICAL SPINE

To evaluate an athlete with cervical pain, the examiner should take a thorough history, observe the athlete's movements, and perform a hands-on evaluation. Special attention is directed to medical history, the mode of onset, and any radicular component of the pain. Have the patient describe the location and nature of his pain. Do any positions relieve the pain or increase it? Note particular times of day when the pain is better or worse. If the problem is a chronic one, past treatments should be discussed, including heat or cold, medications, and evaluations by physicians, chiropractors, therapists, or trainers.

When introducing himself and while taking the history, the examiner observes the athlete's general movements and mobility and any signs of tension, nervousness, or pain. All of our male patients wear shorts, and our female patients wear shorts and a halter top. If a patient forgets to bring shorts, we have clean ones available.

The examiner evaluates the athlete's posture, including the entire body from in front, from behind, and from the side. The side view is most important as the examiner checks for a forward head and rounded shoulders. Note the head position, shoulder position, spinal curves, scoliosis, muscle symmetry, body somatotype, weight, and soft tissue bulk. Check the level of posterior landmarks, including scapular spines, axillary folds, and inferior scapular angles, and anterior landmarks, including shoulder height and upper trapezius height.

The examiner palpates all surrounding musculature and structures, including borders of the clavicle, interscalene triangle, upper trapezius, rhomboids, levator scapulae, suboccipital muscles, temporalis, and masseter. For example, a tight lower one third of the scalene muscle can press on the dorsal scapular nerve, sending pain down the scapula. Note any tender points, spasm, fibrous nodules, and tenderness along facet joint lines and interspinous ligaments.

Active Range of Motion

To assess active range of motion, have the patient perform forward-bending, side-bending, rotation, subcranial nodding, and subcranial side-bending. For every degree of rotation in the cervical spine, there must be an equal and opposite rotation at the atlantoaxial joint. If nodding is limited but rotation is normal, the problem is at the occipital-atlas joint.

Passive Motion Tests

The examiner should evaluate passive intervertebral motion at each level of the cervical spine. The examination starts with the athlete supine. The therapist supports the head in a neutral position.

1. *Subcranial Side-Bend*—This test is important after a neck injury for determining the integrity of the alar ligament. The examiner palpates anterior to the mastoid process and feels the atlas move to the concavity as it disappears on the convexity. The atlas should move in the same direction as the head, and the spinous process of the axis should roll in the opposite direction.

2. *Side-Bend with Rotation*—To evaluate tightness at the atlantoaxial joint, the examiner bends the athlete's head to one side and then rotates it in the opposite direction from this side-bent position.

3. *Unilateral Passive Nod*—To determine which side is tight, the examiner grasps one side of the athlete's occiput and rhythmically nods the head. He assesses the ease of movement and any differences in the two sides.

4. *Side-Glide*—To assess the midcervical spine, the examiner performs a side-glide at each facet joint. To do this, he places the palmar side of the metacarpophalangeal (MP) joint of his index finger on the facet at the level to be tested and pushes it medially at a 45° angle toward the opposite hip. He notes the excursion, any tenderness, and the end feel.

5. *Head Roll*—To assess the ability of the facets to move up, the examiner rolls the athlete's head to one side while palpating the facet joint line on the other side, noting any asymmetry or restrictions.

REHABILITATION PROGRESSION FOR A NECK STRAIN

OBJECTIVES

Strengthen: cervical flexors, extensors, rotators
Flexibility: cervical extensors, rotators
Endurance: cervical flexors, extensors, rotators

STAGES

Initial

Pain control using cryokinetics and modalities, including TENS
Flexibility: Frequent cervical range of motion within pain-free limits every 20 or 30 minutes (Figure 7-1).
Gentle supine stretch with head resting on a book (Figure 7-2). Start with 5 minutes and work up to 20 minutes.
Posture: Sitting (Figure 7-3)—head back, ears over shoulders, shoulders back, arms supported, and supported lumbar lordosis *(arrow)*. In an automobile, the athlete should use a lumbar support and keep the headrest up and his head back against the headrest.
Standing—head back, eyes forward, shoulders back, and normal lumbar lordosis.
Lying—supine with a small cervical pillow under the neck for comfort; avoid the prone position.

Intermediate

Flexibility (Figure 7-4):
Supine neck press (Figure 7-4A)—tuck the chin and press the neck to the table. Do three sets for 10 seconds each.
Rotation to the left and to the right (Figure 7-4B)—rotate the head to the left and then to the right. Do three sets for 10 seconds each.
Sitting chin tuck (Figure 7-4C). Hold for 6 seconds three times.
Shoulder rolls—tuck the chin and roll the shoulders down and in, holding this position for 10 seconds. Then contract the shoulders and bring the head and neck up and back (chin tucked), holding this for 10 seconds. Repeat this sequence twice.
Supine chin tuck (Figure 7-4D)—pinch the shoulder blades together, tuck the chin, and roll the chin to the chest. Hold this position for 6 seconds three times.
Sitting diagonal stretches (Figure 7-4E)—hold onto the side of a chair or table to enhance this stretch.
Corner stretch (Figure 7-4F)—lean into a corner. Hold this position for 15 seconds three times.
Strength:
Apply manual resistance to the head in the ten positions (see Figure 7-1). Hold each contraction for 10 seconds twice. If any of these positions hurts, for example, extension, then avoid the painful position until the soreness subsides.
Arm circles (Figure 7-5A)—rotate the arms clockwise and then counterclockwise for 15 seconds each way three times.
Bring the elbows up and then back (Figure 7-5B). Hold for 5 seconds ten times.

REHABILITATION PROGRESSION FOR A NECK STRAIN (*continued*)

STAGES

Intermediate (*continued*)

Bring the elbows up, move to the hands-up position, and bring the elbows back (Figure 7-5C). Hold for 5 seconds ten times.

Avoid abdominal work during this stage. Tightening the abdominal muscles with sit-ups can strain the neck.

Advanced

Flexibility: The neck is moved through a full range of motion.

Side-bending and rotation stretches with overpressure.

Strength (Figure 7-6):

Shoulder shrugs with weights in hands (Figure 7-6A). Shrug to the ears, then lower the weights and rotate the head to the right and then to the left. Do three sets of ten each.

Wrestler's bridge (Figure 7-6B)—After the athlete balances himself, the partner provides resistance at the hips.

Commercial neck strengthening machines (Figure 7-6C).

Strength of the upper extremities and neck musculature should be thoroughly evaluated. Any weakness should be correlated with neurologic levels for diagnostic purposes.

Vertebral Artery Test

With the patient supine, the examiner rotates the head and neck to end-range and then side-bends it in the same direction. He holds this position

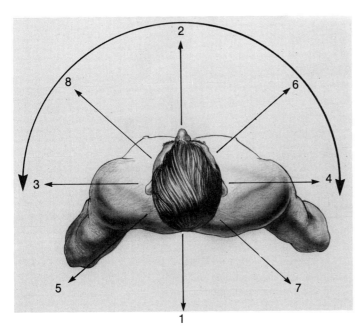

Figure 7-1   Major neck motions.

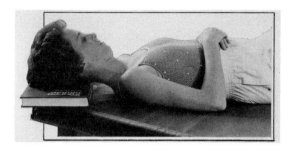

Figure 7-2   The athlete rests her head on a book to self-stretch the suboccipital region. While in this position, she concentrates on relaxing.

for 12 seconds and watches for any of the following symptoms: nystagmus, dilated pupil, slurred speech, slowness of response, ringing in the ears, dizziness, nausea, or any other unpleasant sensation. If the vertebral artery test is positive, the athlete should not be treated with cervical spinal mobilization; otherwise, the artery might become occluded.

TREATMENT OF THE CERVICAL SPINE

Acute Phase

Acute injuries of the cervical spine are usually treated early with modalities to decrease pain and promote healing. Cervical traction or manual distraction is not performed immediately after a whiplash injury because of the risk of overstretching an injured ligament. This principle becomes more obvious when thinking of a knee sprain in which traction on that ligament would clearly damage the already stretched ligament.

On the second day after an acute injury, the athlete may begin gentle active range of motion

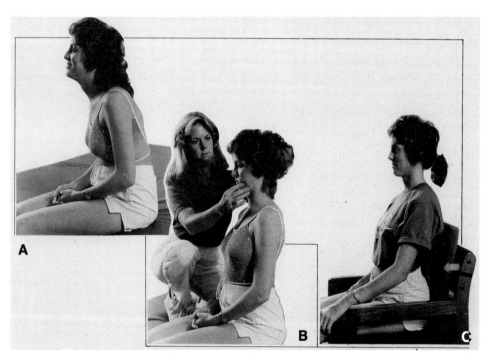

Figure 7-3   Posture reeducation: **A.** The athlete has a forward head posture. Her cervical spine is forward, her occiput is hyperextended, and her shoulders are rounded. **B.** The therapist assists posture correction. Now the cervical spine is straight with easy-over shoulders, occiput is in neutral position, and shoulders are square. **C.** A lumbar support helps improve cervical posture by supporting the normal spinal curve.

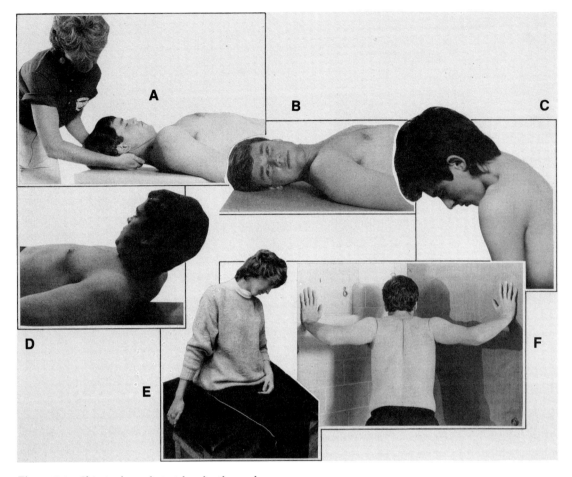

Figure 7-4   Chin tucks and stretches for the neck.

within the pain-free range. By moving within the pain-free range, he can avoid the soft tissue tightness that would result from immobilization. Treatment becomes the same as that for a chronic cervical problem usually about the 12th day after the injury.

Subacute and Chronic Phases

In chronic neck pain, moist heat, point stimulation, and ultrasound relieve pain, relax muscle spasm, and make ligamentous tissue more supple. When moist heat is applied before a mobilization treatment, the athlete will relax more and the treatment will be more effective.

Electrical stimulation can effectively decrease cervical muscle spasm. However, electrode placement may be difficult because of the contour of the neck and because the location of motor points in the upper trapezius produces muscle contraction too easily. Point stimulation is very effective for acute and chronic cervical pain. The following points are most helpful for relieving localized cervical pain: Gb20, B10, Gb21, Li10, Gv14; for radicular pain, Gb20, B10, Gb21, Li4, Li10, Li5, Li11, Li15.

Transcutaneous electrical nerve stimulation (TENS) can control both acute and chronic pain. The electrodes are placed at the four most sensitive points, as found with electroacupuncture or point stimulation.

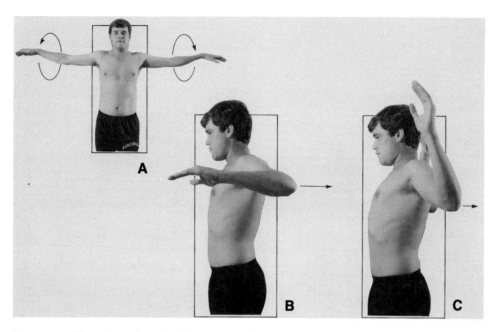

Figure 7-5   The athlete does shoulder circles and stretches his arms back.

Soft Tissue Mobilization and Stretching

1. *General Distraction* (Figure 7-7 A)—With the athlete supine, the examiner places one hand on the occiput and the other hand on the forehead and applies gentle, longitudinal traction. He avoids pulling on the chin because such pulling disturbs the temporomandibular joint. The examiner can make longitudinal distraction more specific by blocking a spinous process (e.g., holding the spinous process of C-6 with a finger) and applying traction to stretch above that level.

2. *Side-bending Diagonal Stretches* (Figure 7-7 B) —With the athlete supine, the examiner places one hand on the occiput and the other hand on the shoulder for counterpressure. Diagonal patterns irritate the facets less than do pure side-bends because of the plane of the joints.
   a. The examiner stretches the athlete's neck in a lower diagonal of side-bending and extension while turning the face toward the stabilized shoulder.
   b. The examiner stretches the neck in the upper diagonal of side-bending and flexion while turning the face away from the stabilized shoulder.

3. *Inhibitive Distraction* With the athlete supine, the examiner places his fingertips under the occiput at a 90° angle. He then applies gentle traction while the athlete relaxes.

4. *Muscle Energy Techniques*—As the athlete begins to improve, the examiner can use hold–relax techniques to relieve soft tissue tightness, having him contract isometrically into a restriction and also away from a restriction.

5. *Resisted Backward Nod*—With the athlete supine, he presses his head isometrically back into the examiner's hand. The direction of resistance from the examiner's hand can guide the athlete and fine-tune muscle firing.

Intervertebral Joint Mobilization

With these techniques, the examiner can stretch tight spinal ligaments specifically.

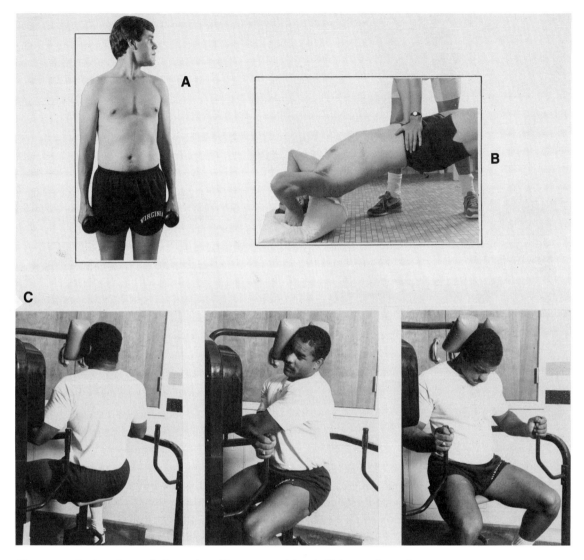

Figure 7-6   In the advanced phase, the athlete uses weights, bridging, and a neck strengthening machine.

Atlanto-Occipital

1. *Unilateral suboccipital stretch*—With the athlete supine, the examiner places his middle finger over the arch of the atlas just off the midline. With the other hand, he depresses the athlete's forehead diagonally downward toward the opposite hip.

2. *Lateral atlas press*—With the athlete supine, the examiner holds the athlete's head in a neutral position. He first bends the head to the left and then uses the MP joint of his right hand just anterior to the mastoid process to press the atlas laterally to the left.

Atlantoaxial Area

1. *Axis block*—The axis block helps to restore motion in all directions. With the athlete sitting, the examiner grasps the axis by blocking

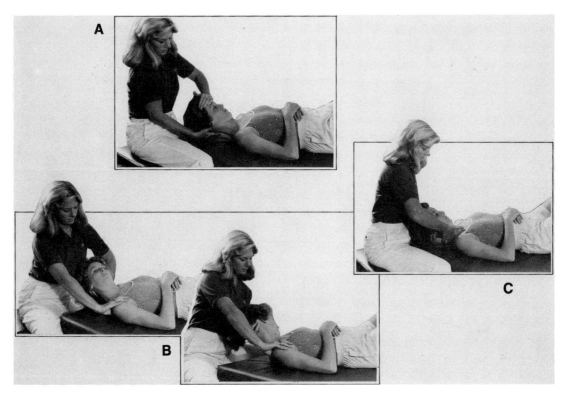

Figure 7-7 **A.** General distraction. **B.** Lower diagonal and upper diagonal stretches. **C.** Side gliding.

the lamina beside the spinous process and then rotates the head in the same direction.

Midcervical Area

1. *Side-gliding*—Side-gliding improves downward glide of the facet on the treated side. With the athlete supine, the examiner places one hand under the occiput to hold the head in a slightly forward bent position (Fig. 7-7 C). With the MP joint of his index finger on the facet joint, the examiner pushes it medially at a 45° angle toward the opposite hip in the same manner as when evaluating passive mobility. He exerts three short-amplitude thrusts, each going farther into the range, without letting up totally between thrusts.

2. *Massage hook technique*—With the athlete supine, the examiner holds the athlete's head in a neutral position with one hand under the occiput. Using the index finger of the other hand, he reaches under the neck and hooks around the spinous process of one vertebra. To promote upward glide of the facet, he then pulls this vertebra into side-bending and rotation. To make this technique more specific, the examiner positions the head in a neutral position with a pillow. This position frees the examiner's other hand to apply pressure on the anterior neck. The anterior hand placement should be lateral to the trachea on the same side as the direction to which he will be pulling. With the palmar aspect of the MP joint of the index finger of his hand, he blocks the level above the one that he is stretching.

EVALUATION OF THE THORACIC SPINE

When evaluating the thoracic spine, the examiner looks for the normal kyphosis and for scoliosis and rib humps and also observes the cervical and lumbar spine. He checks for body type, soft tissue bulk, and bony landmarks and also looks for paraspinal muscle asymmetry. Next, he assesses the pain pattern, strength, sensation, and range of motion. The active trunk range of motion includes forward-bending, side-bending, and rotation. He then palpates for muscle spasm and ligamentous tenderness.

Passive Intervertebral Motion Test

With the athlete prone, the examiner assesses intervertebral motion.

1. *Spinous process spring*—To assess the ability of the vertebrae to glide anteriorly, the examiner applies pressure with the palmar aspect of his pisiform posteriorly to anteriorly (PA) directly over the spinous process of each vertebra. This test must be done carefully because the long spinous processes create a long level arm and excessive pressure could produce a fracture.

2. *Transverse process spring*—To assess rotation, the examiner springs in a PA direction on the transverse processes of adjacent levels. He places his index finger on one transverse process and his middle finger on the adjacent one on the opposite side. With his other hand on top of these fingers, he applies steady downward pressure.

3. *Posterior–anterior glide*—Using the same hand position as for transverse process springs, the examiner springs on the bilateral transverse processes.

TREATMENT MODALITIES FOR THE THORACIC SPINE

Moist heat and high-voltage electrical stimulation will relax spasm of the thoracic muscles. Ligamentous stiffness responds well to ultrasound. Point stimulation (electroacupuncture) is extremely beneficial in acute conditions in which there is a high level of pain. Important points include GV13, GV14, B11, B12, B13, B14, B15, B17, B18, B19, B20, and B21. TENS electrodes

are applied for home carry-over with settings adjusted to the conventional high-rate mode. However, the modalities alone can rarely accomplish what manual therapy can.

Soft Tissue Mobilization

Soft tissue mobilization techniques precede joint mobilization. These soft tissue techniques include laminar release, J-stroking, cross-friction massage, and scapular framing.

1. *Laminar release*—The examiner uses his proximal interphalangeal (PIP) joint area to stroke firmly along the groove beside the athlete's spinous processes and directly over the lamina to elongate the tissue.

2. *J-stroking*—With the tips of the middle and ring fingers, he strokes across tight tissue in a "J" while stabilizing the tissue at the top of the "J" with his other hand.

3. *Cross-friction massage*—This massage method consists of deep, short amplitude strokes perpendicular to the muscle fibers.

4. *Scapular framing* (Figure 7-8 A)—The examiner uses cross-friction massage and J-stroking to frame the borders of the scapula and massage strokes to protract the scapula from the chest wall.

Intervertebral Mobilization

Intervertebral mobilization techniques are similar to those used for evaluating passive intervertebral motion.

1. *Posterior–anterior spring on spinous processes.*
2. *Posterior–anterior spring on bilateral transverse processes.*
3. *Rotation spring on adjacent transverse processes on opposite sides. Rotation occurs to the side of the lowest finger (Figure 7-8 B).*
4. *Rotation sitting*—While the athlete sits with his arms folded across his chest, the examiner guides him into rotation.
5. *Side-bending sitting*—While the athlete sits with his arms folded across his chest, the examiner side-bends him.

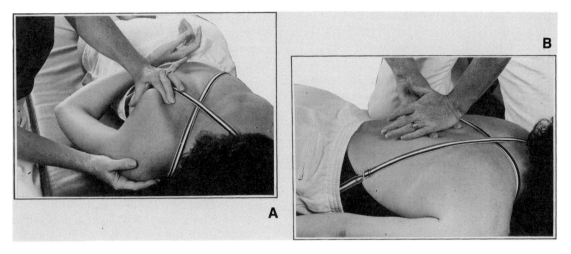

Figure 7-8   In the thoracic spine, the therapist mobilizes the soft tissue around the scapula **(A)**. This technique is called "scapular framing." To mobilize the thoracic spine and correct rotational faults, the therapist performs posterior–anterior (P–A) springs on the transverse processes of adjacent levels **(B)**.

6. *Rotation thrust*—With the athlete in the long-sitting position, the examiner places the flexed PIP joint of his middle finger and the base of his first metacarpal on the transverse processes of adjacent levels. He then lowers the athlete to a supine position and presses downward on his chest.

Home Exercises

1. *Thoracic range of motion*—The athlete begins this exercise sitting comfortably with his feet resting flat on the floor. He then slumps gently forward and then sits erect with squared shoulders.
   a) Sitting erect and facing forward, the athlete reaches his right hand down toward the floor, sits up again, and then repeats the process with his left hand.
   b) Sitting with his buttocks squared in a chair and his arms crossed on his chest, he gently rotates his upper body to look over his right shoulder.
2. *Upper back stretch*—Sitting with his buttocks squared in a chair, he slowly rotates around to the right until he can grasp the back of the chair. He holds this position for 10 seconds and then repeats the stretch to the other side.

3. *Shoulder pinches*—The athlete pinches his shoulder blades together.
4. *Thoracic isometrics*—Lying supine with arms at sides, the athlete presses his shoulders and elbows into the surface of the mat, holds for 6 seconds, and relaxes.
5. *Upper back extensions*—Lying prone with arms at sides, he slowly lifts his head, shoulders, chest, and arms.
6. *Scapular strengtheners* of increasing difficulty.
   a) Lying prone with arms at sides, lift about 10 inches.
   b) With arms straight out from shoulders, lift about 10 inches. Light weights will strengthen the rhomboids (Figure 7-9 A).
   c) With arms stretched overhead, lift about 4 inches.
7. *"Paint the wall"*—Sitting with arms at sides, the athlete pretends he has a paint can near his left foot and a wall to his right. He reaches his right hand down and across to the paint can and then reaches up and over to the right as if painting the upper part of the wall. Or the athlete can "paint the wall" from a three-point starting position (Figure 7-9B).

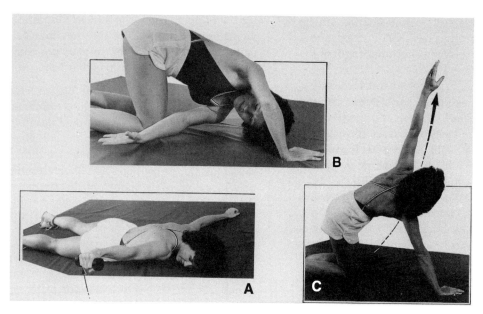

Figure 7-9   The athlete strengthens her posterior scapular muscles with a dumbbell **(A)**. She "paints the wall" by reaching down and under and then reaching up and out **(B)**.

EVALUATION OF THE LUMBAR SPINE

To evaluate an athlete's lumbar spine, the examiner first assesses posture, observing the athlete from the front, back, and side. He notes the stance, somatotype, weight, muscle balance, symmetry, and abdominal tone. Further, he observes the cervical lordosis, thoracic kyphosis, and lumbar lordosis and looks for scoliosis. He checks the following landmarks: shoulders, scapulae, axillary skin folds, iliac crests, posterior superior iliac spines, anterior superior iliac spines, sacral sulci, ischial tuberosities, greater trochanters, popliteal creases, and gluteal folds and notes the biomechanics of the lower extremity chain.

The examiner next performs a manual test of the trunk muscles and all muscle groups of the lower extremities. A finding of muscle weakness in the distribution of a specific nerve root will aid in diagnosis. Further, weakness around a joint may connote a muscle imbalance that can cause a strain or an abnormal gait.

The examiner measures the range of motion of the trunk and joints of the lower extremities. Hip motion measurements are very important because a hip contracture in any direction can in-fluence the position of the plevis. The straight leg raise test can reveal sciatic nerve irritation and show the flexibility of the hamstring muscles.

Straight Leg Raising Test

If the sciatic nerve is irritated, straight leg raising will produce severe pain in the sciatic distribution of the affected leg. For testing straight leg raising, the examiner raises the athlete's leg with the knee straight and the ankle relaxed. If there is no irritation, the athlete will feel only hamstring tightness at 90°. Pain produced in the sciatic distribution can be confirmed by lowering the leg about 2 inches to a point at which the pain stops, then dorsiflexing the ankle. This move stretches the posterior tibial branch of the nerve and renews the sciatic pain. After reaching the limit of the straight leg raise, flexion of the athlete's neck will increase the pain in the sciatic distribution as the dura stretches.

The straight leg raising test may also be performed with the athlete seated with his legs dangling over the edge of a table. The test is positive if pain is produced in the sciatic nerve distribution when the examiner straightens the athlete's knee. In doing this test, be sure that the athlete does not rock his pelvis back into a sacral sitting position because this may affect the length of the nerve.

In the Lasègue test, another test for sciatica, the examiner flexes the athlete's hip to 90° and then extends his knee. The test is positive if this knee extension produces pain in the sciatic nerve distribution. The straight leg raise test is probably more accurate than this test, however, because it involves movement of only one joint.

The active motion assessment includes forward-bending, backward-bending, side-bending, and rotation. The examiner checks the quality of movement and looks for appropriate curve reversal, deviations, and fulcrums.

Forward-bending is observed from behind. During forward-bending, the lumbar lordosis normally reverses to a mild kyphosis. Muscle and ligamentous tightness in the lumbar area, however, can prevent this reversal, causing the lordosis to remain when the athlete bends forward. These athletes typically can touch their palms to the floor because they have worked hard to stretch their hamstrings, but they have only minimal flexibility in the lumbar area.

The examiner should also note the direction of any arc of movement away for the midline. A deviation occurs toward a tight or restricted side. Fulcrums may be observed in side-bending and result from more motion occurring at hypermobile segments and little or no motion occurring at hypermobile segments. In such cases, the lumbar spine side-bends in an ''L''-shape rather than in a smooth curve.

Limitations of side-bending in one direction and rotation in the opposite direction may indicate a facet restriction in the lumbar spine. In such cases, passive intervertebral motion (PIVM) must be assessed in forward-bending, side-bending, and rotation to localize the level that is involved.

Passive Intervertebral Motion

1. *Forward bending*—The athlete lies on his side close to the edge of the treatment table facing the examiner. The examiner holds the foot of the top leg and places the knee of that leg on

his own upper thigh. The athlete's top hip is then flexed further while the examiner palpates the movement of the spinous processes in the lumbar spine with his other hand.

2. *Side-bending*—The athlete lies on his side near the edge of the table facing the examiner. Both of his hips and knees are then flexed to 90°. The knees rest on the examiner's thigh as the feet are lowered toward the floor and then raised toward the ceiling. Throughout this maneuver, the athlete's thighs remain parallel to the floor. The examiner palpates along the side of the spinous processes for movement into side-bending.

3. *Rotation*—With the athlete prone and his knees flexed to 90°, the examiner rocks the feet to one side and then the other while palpating the spine.

Acute Lower Back Pain

The athlete with acute lower back pain often may have spent an extended time in a forward flexed position, such as on a long drive, or may have reached suddenly for something and then could not straighten up. In such cases, a facet joint may have been sprained and the capsule pinched. He often presents with a forward flexed posture, some scoliosis from spasm, and tender lumbar spine muscles but usually does not show radicular symptoms. Motions that slide the facets downwards will hurt.

In acute injuries, a complete evaluation may have to be delayed because of the pain. The examiner should apply modalities for symptomatic relief as soon as possible after the injury.

Ice reduces pain and spasm and allows active range of motion and isometrics. Electrical stimulation of the paravertebral muscles will also reduce muscle spasm and pain. The examiner also gives point stimulation, or electroacupuncture, to reduce pain. Acupuncture points in the lumbar area include B23, B25, B27, and GV4; local trigger points may also be used. The acupuncture points to diminish the radicular components of back pain include B61, B60, Sp6, B57, B54, B51, and B50 for posterior leg pain and B60, Gb38, Gb34, St36, Gb31, and Gb30 for lateral leg pain. TENS should be used on the most sensitive points found when treating with point stimulation.

The lower back can be passively stretched to relieve a restriction of lateral flexibility or a scoliosis. Warm whirlpool and modalities will relax the soft tissue. The examiner follows these modalities with mobilization, usually the lumbar roll as described below. The athlete can also be instructed in soft tissue stretching. He leans sideways against a wall with his feet far enough from the wall to allow the pelvis to drop toward it. This movement will stretch the paraspinal muscles on the side toward the wall.

Acute lower back pain may also result from a bulging lumbar disk. In this case, the exercises should feature lumbar extension and avoid lumbar flexion. Extension of the lumbar spine "milks" the disk anteriorly while closing the posterior area where the bulging has occurred. Extension exercises should not, however, be performed if they increase radicular pain but should be used in situations in which they cause the pain to become more centralized.

Intermediate Stage

When the acute pain has subsided somewhat, the athlete can tolerate a more thorough evaluation and more active treatment. In this stage, heat will relax the soft tissues. Hot packs and whirlpools relax the superficial layers and ultrasound reaches the deeper ligamentous structures to increase their extensibility.

Soft Tissue Mobilization

Stretching of superficial and deep layers of muscles and fascia around the spine and hips increases flexibility and precedes joint mobilization.

Deep Stroking Massage. To increase sidebending of the trunk, the examiner does soft tissue work along the superior aspect of the iliac crest and at the lower border of the 12th rib. With the athlete lying on his side, the examiner uses his thumb to apply deep stroking massage to the quadratus lumborum, the iliolumbar ligament and over the transverse processes.

Laminar Release. To increase forward-bending, the examiner may have to free adhesions that lie along the laminae. Such adhesions form frequently after injury or as a result of chronic abnormal postural conditions. For laminar release, the athlete lies on his side with his hips and knees flexed to place some stretch on the paraspinal muscles. The examiner then strokes firmly downward along the groove between the spinous process and the paravertebral muscle mass. The laminar release can also be performed with the athlete kneeling or with him sitting and leaning forward.

Lumbar Intervertebral Mobilization

1. *Lumbar roll* (Figure 7-17)—The lumbar roll is a complex maneuver that can stretch the facet joints at L-2–3, L-3–4, or L-4–5. The athlete lies on his side near the edge of the table facing the examiner. The examiner localizes the level to be treated by palpating the spinous process (Figure 7-17A). He then holds the athlete's top leg at the ankle and, while keeping the leg low near the table, flexes the hip and knee. The examiner increases the flexion until he feels motion at the proper interspinous space. He then lowers the leg to rest at exactly that position. Next, the examiner grasps the athlete's lower arm and pulls that shoulder and the trunk into rotation toward a supine position (Figure 7-17B). During this rotation movement, the examiner continues to palpate the interspinous space. The end-point is when the rotation reaches the lumbar level that he is palpating.

For the lumbar roll part of the maneuver, the examiner drapes the athlete's upper arm over his with the examiner's forearm and elbow resting in the anterior part of the athlete's axilla (Figure 7-17C). The examiner places his other forearm on the posterior aspect of the iliac wing. With his cephalic middle finger on the top side of the spinous process above the interspace and his caudal middle finger on the bottom side of the spinous process below the interspace, he palpates the segment that is to be stretched.

The athlete is told to take a deep breath. As

REHABILITATION PROGRESSION FOR LOWER BACK STRAIN

OBJECTIVES

Strengthen: Abdominal muscles, lumbar extensors
Flexibility: Lumbar extensors, psoas, hamstrings, gastrocnemius, adductors
Endurance: Lumbar extensors, abdominals

STAGES

Initial
Pain control using modalities, TENS, and cryokinetics.
Flexibility (Figure 7-10):
    Pelvic tilt (Figure 7-10A)—The athlete rolls his hips back and presses his back
        into the table for 10 seconds, four times every hour.
    Knee drops (Figure 9-10B)—Lying supine with his knees flexed, he gently rolls
        his knees side-to-side.
    Knee to chest and ankle to hip, left and right, holding for 4 seconds six times.
    Both knees to chest (Figure 7-10C), holding for 4 seconds six times.
    Prone lying—The athlete may need a pillow under his abdomen for comfort. He
        rests this way for 1 to 5 minutes.
    Supine hamstring stretch (Figure 7-10D)—The athlete grabs behind his thigh
        with the hip flexed to 90° and gently straightens his knee, holding this stretch
        for 10 seconds three times.
    Lean left and then right (Figure 7-10E) for 30 seconds each way twice.
Strength (Figure 7-11):
    One-half sit-ups (Figure 7-11A): three sets.
    Forearm bridging (Figure 7-11B) for 15 seconds twice.
    Hip raise (Figure 7-11C) for 15 seconds twice.
    Heel press (Figure 7-11D): 6 seconds four times for each leg.
    Multifidus exercises—The athlete lies prone and lifts his opposite arm and leg
        five times to a point at which there is some muscle recruitment.
Endurance
    Swimming
Posture
    Supported lumbar lordosis
    Correct head position with the shoulders up. Incorrect position is with the
        shoulders dropped forward.

Intermediate
Flexibility (Figure 7-12):
    Prayer stretch (Figure 7-12A) for 30 seconds.
    Prayer stretch to diagonals (Figure 7-12B) for 30 seconds each way.
    Prone prop with straight arms (Figure 7-12C) for 5 minutes. The athlete can
        prone prop on straight arms or on his elbows (Figure 7-12D). If he cannot keep
        his pelvis down on the mat, he can stabilize his pelvis with a belt (Figure 7-
        12E).
    Long sitting rotation (Figure 7-13A) for 15 seconds, twice to each side.

REHABILITATION PROGRESSION FOR LOWER BACK STRAIN (*continued*)

STAGES

Intermediate (*continued*)

Cross-stretch (Figure 7-13B) for 15 seconds, twice to each side.

Groin stretch (Figure 7-13C) for 15 seconds, twice on each side.

Thigh stretch (Figure 7-13D) for 15 seconds, twice.

Calf stretch (Figure 7-13E) for 30 seconds.

Cat and camel (Figure 7-14A) five times.

Standing lumbar extension (Figure 7-14B) ten times.

Bar hang (Figure 7-14C), inversions (Figure 7-14D), or chair hang (Figure 7-14E) for 30 seconds.

Strength (Figure 7-15)

One-half sit-ups to diagonals (Figure 7-15A).

Upper back raise (Figure 7-15B): hold for 10 seconds, twice.

Prone single leg lifts (Figure 7-15C) for 10 seconds, twice.

Endurance

EPLEI goals 1,2

Advanced

Strength (Figure 7-16):

Lower/upper back raises.

Tubic back extensions (see Tubics).

Side-lifter (Figure 7-16A).

Arm and leg lifts with weights while in the all-four's position

Commercial back machine

Commercial leg press machine (Figure 7-16B)

Endurance

Mountain climber (Figure 7-16C)

EPLEI goals 3–8

Nordic track

---

the athlete exhales, the examiner takes up the slack by pressing back on the athlete's chest and pulling his ilium forward. The examiner maintains firm pressure at all times with his fingers. In addition, the examiner can perform a thrust with his forearm and fingers at the end-range in the direction of rotation.

2. *Lumbar side-bending* (Figure 7-18)—The athlete lies on his side near the edge of the table with hips and knees flexed to 90° facing the examiner. The examiner palpates with one hand along the upper side of the spinous processes. He grasps the athlete's feet with his other hand while supporting the athlete's thighs on his thigh. Then he creates a fulcrum on the upper side of the spinous process above the space to be stretched by first lowering the feet to the floor and then raising them to the ceiling. The side-bending may also be performed with the athlete prone. The examiner again creates a fulcrum at a spinous process and abducts the leg.

3. *Lumbar rotation*—With the athlete prone, the examiner grasps the anterior–superior iliac spine and raises the pelvis while palpating beside the spinous process with his other hand. He blocks the spinous process above the level to be stretched as he creates lumbar ro-

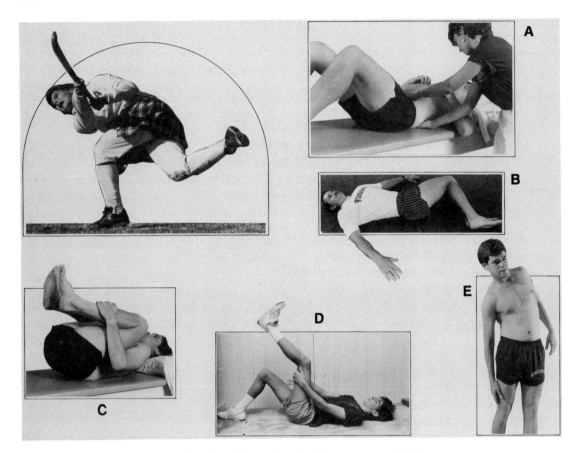

Figure 7-10   In the initial stage, the athlete does pelvic tilts, knee drops, and back rolls.

tation. In an alternative method the athlete is prone, and the examiner flexes the knees to 90° and rolls the legs to one side while palpating the spinous process as before.

4. *Transverse process springs*—The examiner can use this springing technique at L-2, L-3, and L-4 to produce motion and check for a healthy rebound. He applies pressure with the pisiform area of his palm directly over the transverse process in a PA direction to take up soft tissue slack. Then he applies four short thrusts or springs to produce a rotary motion. Springing of a transverse process on the left gaps the facet joint on the right. To gap the facet at L-5, the examiner springs on the iliac crest on the same side.

5. *Positional distraction*—To open intervertebral foramina, the examiner can place a bolster un-

der the athlete while the athlete is lying on his side. He localizes the level using the lumbar roll technique. He rotates the upper body down to the level desired and flexes the hips and knees up in forward-bending to the level below. The upper side is the side that gaps. The examiner can apply traction by pulling on the iliac crest using his finger as a fulcrum. At home, the athlete can assume the same position over the bolster while resting. He starts with 5 minutes and works up to 30 minutes.

SACROILIAC DYSFUNCTION

Anatomy

The sacroiliac joints join the first three sacral vertebrae and the ilium on each side. They contain

Figure 7-11   Strengthening includes "crunch" sit-ups and heel presses.

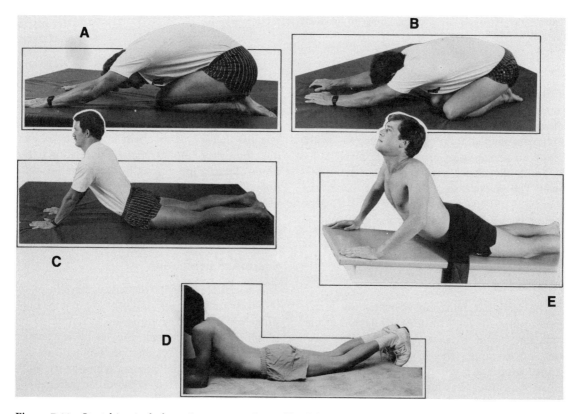

Figure 7-12   Stretching includes a "prayer stretch" and back hyperextensions.

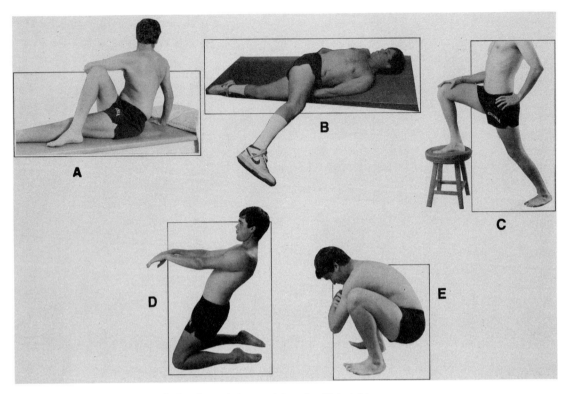

Figure 7-13   Stretches also include a long-sitting stretch and calf stretching.

cartilage, a synovial lining, a joint capsule, and ligaments. The wedge-shaped sacrum fits tightly between the ilia. From a lateral view each joint is crescent-shaped, forming an inverted ''L'' with a superior and inferior projection. Viewed from the front, the upper aspect is wider than the lower. The sacral surface of the joint is convex, whereas the ilial surface is concave. This configuration confers some stability, and the joint is reinforced by many strong ligaments.

Biomechanics

The sacroiliac joint moves when the lower spine or hips move. With forward flexion of the trunk the sacrum extends especially. This happens, for example, when a person goes from a sitting to standing position. With trunk extension, the sacrum flexes. Raising a leg up or flexing a hip way up with the opposite leg extended stresses the sacroiliac joint.

During walking and running, the ilium rotates posteriorly at heel strike on the weight-bearing side. During midstance it rotates anteriorly and remains that way until the next heel strike. Further, the sacrum moves caudally in relation to the ilium. Translation normally accompanies rotation. Therefore, whenever the ilium rotates posteriorly, it also glides posteriorly. When it rotates anteriorly, it also glides anteriorly.

Sacroiliac Evaluation

The sacroiliac area is frequently the site of referred pain from the lumbar spine and hips. Therefore, before beginning the examination for sacroiliac malalignment, the examiner should rule out facet joint dysfunction, lumbar disk protrusion, or hip malalignment. The history helps to differentiate the causes. Sacroiliac pain usually is increased while walking, especially during the stance phase and while walking down stairs or

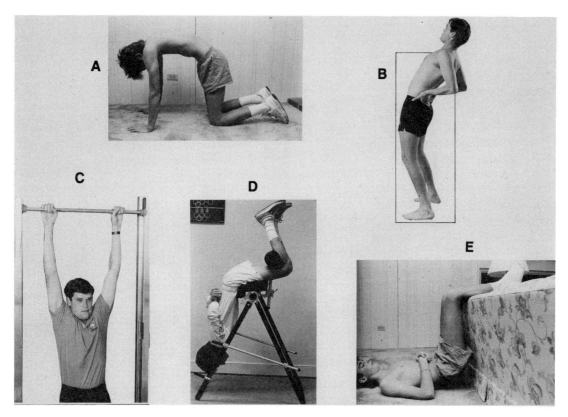

Figure 7-14   The athlete does the "cat and camel" exercise by first letting his back sink like a camel's and then raising it like a cat's **(A)**. Traction methods include a bar hang **(C)**, an inversion machine **(D)**, and a chair hang **(E)**.

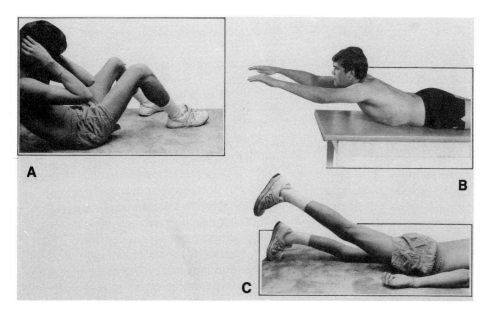

Figure 7-15   For abdominal strengthening, the athlete can do sit-ups to diagonals **(A)**. For back strengthening, he can do upper back extensions **(B)** and prone leg raises **(C)**.

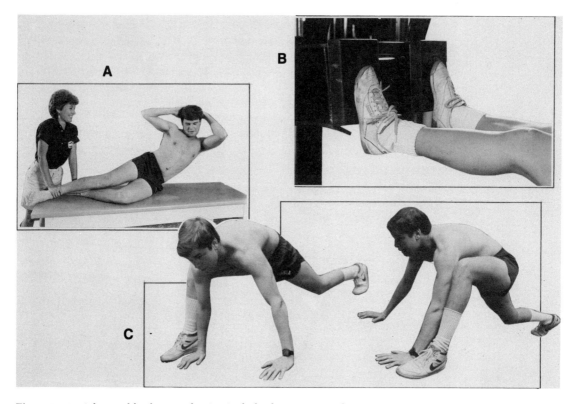

Figure 7-16 Advanced back strengthening includes leg presses and a "mountain climber" exercise.

stepping up on the affected leg. It may also hurt when bending toward the painful side but even when rolling over in bed or lying on the affected side. On the other hand, pain from lumbar disk protrusion increases if the athlete sits for a long time or takes a long drive because trunk flexion raises intradiskal pressure.

Postural Screening

Before beginning the sacroiliac examination, the examiner checks for lumbar problems and other lower extremity abnormalities. For the spine, he inspects all curves, noting any deviation from the normal lordosis and kyphosis and any scoliosis. He checks active motion of the spine, straight leg raising, and deep tendon reflexes, sensation, and muscle strength. Next he looks for lower extremity postural abnormalities such as genu varum, genu valgum, genu recurvatum, and excessive subtalar joint pronation or supination.

The examiner then proceeds to evaluate landmarks, including the shoulders, inferior scapular angles, iliac crests, anterior–superior iliac spine, posterior–superior iliac spines, greater trochanters, and popliteal creases. Leg lengths are measured standing and supine. The examiner palpates the sacral sulci, noting their depth and distance from the midline. He also notes the position of each anterior–superior iliac spine on that side and its distance from the midline.

The assessment of pelvic landmarks in both height and distance from the midline helps the examiner diagnose anterior or posterior rotation as well as inflares or outflares of the ilium. An outflare will also be obvious if there is more external rotation of the lower extremity in the relaxed supine position. More obscure sacroiliac problems may occur with sacral side-bending, more obscure rotation, and torsion.

Before performing the sacroiliac joint tests, the examiner must check active and passive motion

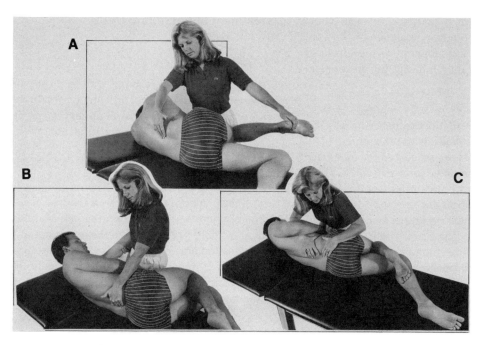

Figure 7-17   Lumbar roll: **A.** The examiner maneuvers the athlete's upper leg to localize the appropriate spinal level. **B.** She rotates the athlete's upper body down to the level to be stretched. **C.** The athlete exhales as the examiner stretches the lumbar segment into rotation.

of the hips and hip strength and perform the Scour test to rule out an intra-articular hip problem.

The examiner checks external and internal rotation of the hips with the athlete supine. Tight muscles can affect the sacroiliac area. For exam-

Figure 7-18   The therapist moves both of the athlete's legs to assess side-bending motion and to mobilize the lumbar spine.

ple, a tight quadratus lumborum causes the ilium to ride up; adductor muscle tightness pulls the ilium downward. Tight hamstrings rotate the ilium posteriorly; a tight iliopsoas rotates the ilium anteriorly on that side. A tight or spastic pyriformis can pull the sacrum down and into rotation on the opposite side.

Testing Sacroiliac Joint Motion

1. *The march test*—In addition to posture evaluation and palpating of landmarks, the examiner will have to evaluate sacroiliac joint motion. He performs the march test with the athlete standing. The examiner palpates just below the posterior iliac crest. While the athlete flexes one leg to about 90°, the examiner notes the degree of downward excursion as the ilium on that side rotates posteriorly. A hypermobile sacroiliac joint will move quicker and farther than normal, whereas a hypomobile joint will move slower because it has to pull the sacrum along with it. The examiner

should also watch for poor balance, which may indicate abductor weakness of the other hip, and note any vibration as the hip is extended, which may indicate hip flexor tightness.

2. *Bending*—The examiner palpates the posterior iliac crests bilaterally while the athlete bends forward, and checks the feel as the movement is started. A restricted joint will move first as the ilium is carried with the sacrum. The examiner also checks for deviation toward the restricted side. On backward bending, the examiner palpates the sacral sulci. The sacrum should flex as the spine extends, causing the sacral sulci to deepen. A sulcus that does not deepen may indicate a hypomobile area.

3. *Provocation tests*—The examiner uses provocative tests to isolate sacroiliac joint problems. With the athlete supine, the examiner pushes the iliac crests laterally near the anterior–superior iliac spines bilaterally in an attempt to gap the sacroiliac joint anteriorly. Pain indicates a problem in the anterior ligaments. To stretch the posterior ligaments, the examiner applies a medially directed compressive force near the anterior–superior iliac spines bilaterally. In big athletes, this compressive maneuver is easier to do with the athlete lying on his side and the examiner pressing down on the ilium.

4. *Long-sitting test*—Although the long-sitting test for determining iliac rotational faults is commonly performed, it is not always accurate. The athlete lies supine, and the examiner pulls on the legs, positions them, and notes the relative levels of the medial malleoli. The athlete then sits up with his legs still extended, and the examiner again observes the malleoli to see whether they have changed position with respect to each other. An anteriorly rotated ilium causes an apparent lengthening while supine, and shortening while long-sitting. A posteriorly rotated ilium causes an apparent shortening while supine and lengthening while long-sitting.

Treatment of Sacroiliac Dysfunction

Modalities

Sacroiliac sprains respond well to pulsed ultrasound with 10% hydrocortisone cream. In addition, point stimulation at acupuncture points B60, Sp6, St36, B25, B27, and local points will reduce pain.

Muscle Energy Techniques The examiner can use muscle energy techniques so that the lower extremity muscles will pull on the pelvis to correct positional faults. While the examiner immobilizes the area of insertion of muscle to prevent joint movement, the athlete contracts the muscle maximally, which results in a reverse pull of the muscle at its origin.

1. *"Upslip" of the ilium*—"Upslip" means that the pelvis is elevated on one side. To correct this, the athlete is asked to lie on the unaffected side. The examiner then grasps the iliac crest and the ischial tuberosity and glides the crest and tuberosity inferiorly. During this maneuver, the examiner notes the end feel as well as the recoil.

2. *"Downslip" of the ilium*—"Downslip" means that the pelvis is depressed on one side. To correct this, the athlete is asked to lie on his unaffected side. The examiner then contacts the iliac crest and the ischial tuberosity and glides the crest and tuberosity superiorly. During this maneuver, the examiner notes the end feel as well as the recoil

3. *Anterior rotation of the ilium*—The examiner can use mobilization techniques and muscle energy techniques to treat rotational faults of the ilium.
a) With the athlete lying on his unaffected side, the examiner flexes the hip and knee of the involved side as far as possible. He then places one of his hands on the ischial tuberosity and the other hand on the anterior iliac crest and applies pressure to rotate the ilium posteriorly.
b) With the athlete prone, he hangs the involved leg over the edge of the treatment table

and "walks" that leg as far as possible up toward his head (Figure 7-19A). While the athlete is in this position, the examiner can apply pressure to rotate the ilium posteriorly as above. The athlete can also use the walking part of this technique as a self-mobilization.

c) If the athlete maximally contracts his gluteus maximus while the examiner immobilizes its insertion, the ilium will rotate. This muscle energy technique is performed in a side-lying or a supine position with the hip and knee flexed as far as possible. The contraction is held for 6 seconds, and the examiner can apply pressure between contractions to rotate the ilium posteriorly.

4. *Posterior rotation of the ilium*—The mobilization and muscle energy techniques used to correct a posteriorly rotated ilium are the opposite of those used for an anteriorly rotated one.

   a) With the athlete lying sideways on the non-affected side, the examiner grasps the ischial tuberosity with one hand and the anterior crest with the other hand. He then applies pressure to rock the ilium anteriorly.

   b) With the athlete supine, the athlete hangs his affected leg gently over the edge of the table while the examiner presses the ilium anteriorly. In such cases, an assistant may be needed to stabilize the unaffected side.

   c) A maximal contraction of the origin of the hip flexors in the supine position will rotate the ilium anteriorly. The athlete drops his affected leg off the edge of the table with his hip hyperextended and his knee passively flexed. The examiner then stabilizes the unaffected side while resisting maximal isometric hip flexion on the affected side. The isometric contraction lasts for 6 seconds, and the examiner can apply pressure between contractions to rotate the ilium anteriorly.

5. *Outflare faults of the ilium*—To treat an outflare, the examiner applies a medially directed compressive force near the anterior iliac crests of the pelvis bilaterally. This creates a bilateral inflare by stretching the posterior sacroiliac

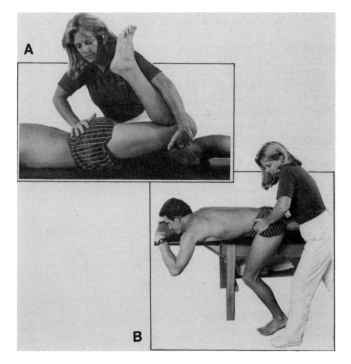

Figure 7-19 Sacroiliac joint mobilization: **A.** To treat a posterior rotational fault of the ilium, the therapist applies overpressure into the direction of anterior rotation. **B.** To treat an anterior rotational fault of the ilium, the therapist presses on the ilium to rotate it posteriorly.

ligaments. The muscle energy technique requires that the athlete contract maximally into internal rotation while the examiner resists. An athlete who has pain caused by an outflare fault can relax the posterior ligaments by lying with his legs externally rotated. Outflare faults can also be corrected by adducting and internally rotating the hip passively.

6. *Inflare faults of the ilium*—In an athlete who has an inflare fault, the examiner pushes the iliac crests laterally near the anterior iliac crest bilaterally to stretch the anterior sacroiliac ligament and gap the sacroiliac joint anteriorly, creating an outflare. If this outflaring causes pain in the person with an inflare fault, he should be encouraged to lie with his hips externally rotated to relax the anterior sacroiliac ligament. The muscle energy technique requires that the athlete contract maximally into external rotation while the examiner resists.

Treatment of Sacral Problems

Pyriformis Tightness

To stretch his tight pyriformis, the athlete flexes, adducts, and internally rotates his hip while lying on his back. Contraction of the pyriformis causes extension, abduction, and external rotation of the hip and flexes the sacrum on that side. The muscle energy technique requires that the athlete lie on his unaffected side and contract maximally in these combined directions while the examiner resists.

Excessive Sacral Extension

To create more sacral flexion, the examiner presses on the base of the sacrum with the heel of his hand. He applies pressure to take up slack and then springs. While doing this, he notes any stiffness and the ease of movement. The athlete can increase sacral flexion by doing prone press-ups on his elbows or with outstretched arms. This technique is contraindicated, however, in a person who has a spondylolisthesis.

Excessive Sacral Flexion

To create sacral extension, the examiner springs on the apex of the sacrum to pull the base into extension. While doing this, he notes any stiffness and the ease of movement. The muscle energy technique to create sacral extension requires that the athlete contract the paraspinal muscles and multifidi on the same side and then pushes back with a maximal contraction against the resistance of the examiner's hand toward the side of the excessive sacral flexion.

RECOMMENDED READING

Cailliet R: Low Back Pain Syndrome. Philadelphia, FA Davis, 1983

Cyriax J, Coldham M: Textbook of Orthopaedic Medicine, vol 2: Treatment by Manipulation, Massage, and Injection. London, Bailliere–Tindall, 1984

Finneson B: Low Back Pain. Philadelphia, JB Lippincott, 1980

Macnab I: Backache. Baltimore, Williams & Wilkins, 1977

McKenzie R: Treat Your Own Back. Auckland, New Zealand, Spinal Publications, 1985

Paris SV: Course Notes—The Spine: Etiology and Treatment of Dysfunction, Including Joint Manipulation, 1979

Yessis M: Absolutely ripped. Sports Fitness 2:7, 14–20, July 1986

Yessis M: Back in shape. Sports Fitness 2:642–647, June 1986

CHAPTER

8

Athletic Injuries to the Head, Face, and Neck

THE HEAD

In some sports, the athlete must use his head as a prime impact area—for example, when heading a ball in soccer or landing on the forehead while carrying an opponent in Greco–Roman wrestling. In tackle football, the helmet and facemask system is now so effective that some players illegally use the head as a battering ram and an offensive weapon. The risk of neck injury thus rises, especially if the player's neck is weak.

Although the number of fatal head injuries in tackle football has dropped over the past two decades, the number of paralyzing neck injuries has risen.[76] Moreover, although there are now fewer head injuries, such injuries are devastating. The doctor, trainer, coach, and athlete must try to prevent these injuries, recognize the danger signs of head injury, and be able to care for the head-injured athlete. Every effort must be made to protect the athlete's brain because brain injury may lead to epilepsy, dementia, or death.

Concussions

A *concussion*, derived from the Latin *concussus*, meaning "to shake violently," is a temporary disturbance of brain function that occurs without a structural change in the brain. About 50,000 concussions occur each year in tackle football as a result of blows to the head, and about one of eight collegiate football players sustains a concussion during his career. Although a concussion does not produce gross changes in the brain, it may produce neuronal, chemical, or neuroelectrical changes. This "scrambling of connections" takes time to reorganize.

Concussions may be graded as mild, moderate, or severe. The severity of a concussion seems to correlate best with the duration of unconsciousness.[66] A mild concussion produces a stunned, dazed athlete. The athlete is "out on his feet" but promptly regains awareness of his surroundings; no confusion, headache, dizziness, nausea, or visual disturbance results. The athlete feels well in 1 or 2 minutes and exhibits no unsteadiness or lack of coordination. It is easy for the athlete to hop on one foot and tightrope-walk a straight line. Neurologic examination findings are normal.

The football player with a mild concussion should be kept out of action for a series of downs, a cautious approach that benefits both the athlete and the team. A dazed athlete is extremely vulnerable to further injury because his coordination is abnormal. Moreover, if the player returns to the game dazed, he may drop passes, miss handoffs and assignments, and fumble. The examiner should observe, examine, and question the athlete but should not return him to the lineup immediately. The player must be able to demonstrate that he can fully perform the techniques he must use in the game; when he does resume play, he should continue to be observed from the sideline.

A moderate concussion results in loss of consciousness, some mental confusion, and retrograde amnesia. Injured athletes sometimes have ringing in their ears, dizziness, and unsteadiness. Recovery may be fast, and after a few minutes the athlete may demonstrate good skill performance. But because he was knocked out and has amnesia for the plays and other events accompanying his injury, he should remain out of the game. He may return to the next practice if he is mentally clear, free of headache, and not confused, dizzy, or nauseated.

The severely concussed athlete will remain unconscious longer than the moderately concussed one. When he awakens, he will have a headache, dizziness, ringing in his ears, and be confused and unsteady. Memory is lost for the events associated with the injury, and he may have other recent memory loss. Of course, he must not return to play. If the athlete remains groggy or if his condition worsens, he should be hospitalized for observation. If he suffers a con-

cussion and the examiner believes that he should be awakened at night for a check, the player had best be observed at the hospital.

Other players sometimes notify the trainer or physician that a teammate is acting strange in the huddle. The athlete may be able to walk normally but still have a concussion. If concussion is suspected, the player should be examined. He will usually be able to do simple mathematics and reverse spelling and follow commands. The questions put to him, however, should involve recent memory. "What play was run when you were injured?" "Were you blocking or tackling?" "What happened at impact?" "What is the score?" The memory loss associated with concussion contrasts with the memory of the limb-injured athlete, who retains a lucid, explicit memory of the play and impact, as if the activity had occurred in slow motion.

The fixation of memories is an ongoing process that is damaged by the effects of a concussion. As information on the injury begins to be stored, the concussion disrupts the storage process. A player will recall the play signal or concussive impact when asked about it seconds after injury but lose this information permanently within minutes. It is thus important to sit the player out for a few minutes and to ask him again questions connected with recent memory.

In addition, the athlete should be asked if he has a headache, nausea, ringing in his ears, or dizziness. Inequality of the pupils should be checked for, keeping in mind that some athletes have anisocoria (unequal pupils) normally. A baseline blood pressure and pulse rate should be recorded and the player then asked to close his eyes and hold his arms out to his side with palms up. Downward drift of an arm is a sign of hemiparesis. More subtly, a forearm may pronate—the "pronator drift." The finger-to-nose test should be done, and, as another test of control, the athlete should be asked to reach out his foot to touch the examiner's hand.

If the athlete can easily hop on one foot, there probably is no corticospinal or corticocerebellar damage. He should be asked to tightrope-walk along a line and then stand with his eyes closed. If he wobbles, he should not be allowed to reenter the game. Of course, waxing and waning of consciousness and continued grogginess are signs necessitating immediate hospitalization.

After a concussion, the athlete may be allowed to return to practice when he has no headache, has no trouble remembering, and is not irritable or tired.

Return to Contact Sports

The athlete must be thoroughly evaluated by a physician before being allowed to return to contact sports after a concussion. The dictum "three concussions and you're out" is too simple. One severe concussion may be sufficient for the team physician to recommend that the athlete avoid contact sports. Some doctors will not allow the athlete to play contact sports after he has had four moderate or two severe concussions. There is no simple rule, however, that applies to all athletes. Consciousness should be graded and a decision made based on severity of the concussions, their aftermath, and the risk to the athlete of serious, permanent brain damage.

"Knockout"

The most common knockout blow is to the chin or "button." This twists and distorts the brain stem and overwhelms the reticular-activating mechanism (sleep–wake center), sending a sudden bombardment of impulses to the brain and rendering the boxer, for instance, unconscious. When a boxer is knocked down, striking the ring floor may cause more serious damage than the blow from his opponent. Ring floors are more safely constructed today than before, being made of canvas stretched over shock-absorbing Ensolite. The boxer may also be knocked out as his head strikes the cable ropes or ring posts or from a succession of hard blows. A blow to the eye or neck may produce severe pain, causing loss of consciousness, and a blow to the carotid sinus, heart, or solar plexus may block blood flow and cause the boxer to lose consciousness. Punches to the thin-walled temporal area may lead to loss of balance and dizziness.

Unfortunately, former fighters or steeple chase jockeys who have suffered many blows to the head may develop brain-stem hemorrhages that result in diffuse neuronal destruction and the clinical appearance of dementia pugilistica ("punch drunk").[51] Such persons become irritable and depressed, with slurred and monotonous speech. They move slowly with an unsteady gait, have tremors, and must endure dull headaches and seizures.

Stroke

In young athletes with little or no atherosclerosis, brain-stem stroke may result from vertebral artery trauma after neck rotation and extension. In this condition, the rotation or extension of the spine compromises vertebral artery blood flow.

The vertebral arteries ascend in transverse foramina up to the level of the axis. They then abandon their vertical course and are susceptible as they pass upward and outward to reach the transverse foramina of the atlas, from which point they enter the skull to form the basilar artery.

Most of the movement during neck extension and rotation occurs at the atlantoaxial and atlanto-occipital joints, where the vertebral arteries lie unprotected. Excessive rotation may sublux the atlantoaxial joint, and the contralateral vertebral artery may be especially vulnerable to stretching and compression within the transverse foramen of the atlas, reducing blood flow to the brain.[35] Two thirds of all persons have significant discrepancies in the size of their vertebral arteries, with the left usually being larger than the right. Ischemia is more likely when the smaller vessel is compressed than when the dominant artery is compressed. Hyperextension causes the atlas to slide forward and stretch and compress the vertebral arteries within the transverse foramen of the atlas.

In one case, a wrestler who hyperextended and rotated his neck while bridging had several half-Nelsons applied to him shortly thereafter.[63] He then developed vertigo, ataxia, numbness of the left side of his face, and tingling in his body. Transient singultus prevented him from swallowing when he tried to drink water. Similar neck manipulations in yoga may also cause a stroke involving the brain stem.

Other Severe Injuries

One blow to the head, or the cumulative effect of many blows, may tear veins that pass from the brain to the dura, producing a subdural hematoma. Veins are usually torn on the side opposite the blow, a "contrecoup" injury. Veins may also be ripped when the brain strikes the sharp sphenoidal ridge, the bony prominence of the anterior fossa, or the free edge of the tentorium. The blood collects slowly over hours or weeks. The injured person has a headache, intermittent drowsiness, lack of concentration, mild confusion, and slow deterioration of consciousness, and death may ensue. These persons should be examined serially, and the blood may require evacuation. A chronic subdural hematoma may be subtle, causing headache, nausea, blurred vision, irritability, and personality changes.

A skull fracture that extends across the groove of the middle meningeal artery may sever the artery, causing a rapid epidural accumulation of blood. Initially, in the so-called "lucid period," the athlete may seem well. Ten to 20 minutes later, however, danger signs of decreased consciousness and motor problems appear. X-ray films may show a fracture line that is usually more lucent than vascular markings because it extends through the entire thickness of the skull. The line also is usually sharply angled or straight, unlike the gentle arcs and branchings of vascular markings. Immediate surgery is imperative because an epidural hematoma is life-threatening.

A basilar skull fracture may cause periorbital ecchymosis, or "raccoon eyes." Other signs of this fracture are subcutaneous ecchymosis in the mastoid area, or "Battle's sign," and blood that lies behind the tympanic membranes to produce a blue and bulging eardrum. The basilar fracture may be seen on a Towne's x-ray view that shows the vault of the skull without overlap from the facial bones. A petrous bone fracture may cause bleeding from the ear if the tympanic membrane has been ruptured. In these cases, a speculum should not be inserted into the ear canal because it may cause contamination. Serious brain injury

with herniation of the uncus produces a palsy of the third cranial nerve and anisocoria. Vertical nystagmus also connotes injury to the brain.

On-the-Field Evaluation of Head Injuries

If an athlete is lying on the field unconscious, a head and neck injury should be assumed until proven otherwise. The rescuer should grasp the athlete's jaw and pull it forward to protect him from swallowing his tongue. This should be done gently because there may be a major neck injury. Ammonia ampules should not be placed under the athlete's nose because they may cause him to jerk his head away and damage his spinal cord.

The athlete is placed on a backboard with his head immobilized between sandbags or held fixed with a four-way strap. The facemask should be removed; the helmet usually is not removed because improper removal may cause undue neck motion. Some masks are hinged, or the rubber facemask mounting loops may be cut to allow the mask to swing away. If the facemask must be cut, heavy-duty bolt cutters will do the job efficiently. Bolt cutters should always be at hand, taped to the headboard. If the player's helmet must be removed, two persons must do the job[43]: One applies longitudinal traction while the second places his one hand behind the player's neck and grasps the player's jaw with his other hand. He maintains traction while the first rescuer spreads the helmet and removes it from the injured player's head.

Athletes who wear contact lenses should be identified so that the lenses may be removed if the athlete is knocked unconscious.

Footballer's Migraine

Blows to a player's head from a soccer ball, especially unexpected and accidental blows, may initiate migraine headaches by distorting the player's intracerebral vessels.[50] At the beginning of a match, the soccer ball will weigh 400 g, but old leather balls become much heavier on a wet pitch. The balls may travel at 50 km/h (30 miles/ h); thus they have a heavy impact. Migraine headaches have also been reported after blows to the side of the head in wrestling, a condition attributed to trauma-induced cerebral vasospasm. Tunnel vision, tingling in the hands, general headache, and vomiting may accompany a migraine headache. These cases demand a careful neurologic examination.

Helmets

Tackle Football

Tackle football helmets have changed dramatically since the 1890s, when the first unpadded leather headgear was worn. In the late 1930s internal suspension systems were added, and in 1950 rigid outer shells with pneumatic and hydraulic inner suspension systems became available. The air-padded helmets are preferred by professional tackle football players today (Figure 8-1).

Better energy-absorbing systems are being placed into helmets to protect against brain injury, and helmets have become so sophisticated and protective of the head that they now endanger the wearer's neck and his opponent's body.[59,75] One study showed that helmets were responsible for 12% of the total injuries in high school football.[7] Similarly, almost 10% of professional tackle football injuries are produced by a blow from an opponent's helmet.

Minimum protective standards are now compiled by the National Operating Committee on Standards for Athletic Equipment (NOCSAE). Helmets are tested by dropping them from heights of 3, 4, and 5 feet to land on an Ensolite-covered steel block. The helmet is positioned to land on its top, front, rear, right and left front, and right and left rear sections under varied environmental conditions.[61] Football helmets must have rebound capabilities, unlike those used in motor sports racing that are designed to absorb a high impact only once. All National Collegiate Athletic Association institutions now require that helmets meet NOCSAE standards, and high schools must also meet these minimum standards.

A poorly fitted helmet is a dangerous piece of equipment, but when properly fitted it affords the athlete a remarkable degree of protection. Faulty technique and improper fit are the real villains in

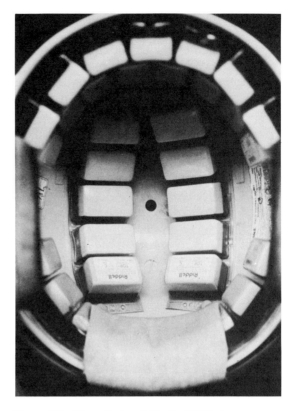

Figure 8-1 The interior of this football helmet contains individual vinyl foam air cushions that conform to the shape of the player's head and absorb shock. Other helmets have inflatable air cells, liquid cells, and suspension systems.

the risk of neck injuries. Most legal claims have been associated with such injuries, even though the helmet was not shown conclusively to be at fault. As a result of legal judgments against helmet manufacturers, about one half of the cost of a helmet is absorbed by liability premiums.[59]

Motorcycle

Although motorcross competitors are required to wear crash helmets, motorcyclists are not required to wear a helmet on the highways in most states. Motorcycle crash helmets are designed to absorb a high impact only once, and they have poor rebound capability. The helmet also serves as a place to attach the facemask that prevents stones and bugs from striking the driver's eyes.

The best protection against facial injury is a full-face helmet.

Laws requiring the use of crash helmets by motorcyclists have been repealed in many states, and deaths have doubled where such laws have been repealed.[37] Those who argue for repeal claim that a helmet decreases the driver's ability to hear, lowers his peripheral vision, and increases neck injuries and that the requirement is a violation of a person's rights.

These arguments are countered by studies showing that hearing is not reduced because there is no change in the signal-to-noise ratio.[37] Even wrap-around, full-face helmets allow 109° of peripheral vision on each side of the nose, an amount that satisfies Department of Transportation safety standards. There is no evidence of increased neck injuries. With respect to the rights issue, taxpayers must often underwrite lifelong medical bills and maintenance costs for head-injured cyclists, who frequently do not have insurance.

Bicycle

Many bicyclists forgo helmets, even though they achieve high speeds on hard roads with potholes and traffic dangers. Among head protectors, the "leather hairnet" can prevent scrapes but provides only minimal shock absorption. Vegetable bowl-shaped styrofoam helmets are better and can protect the cyclist's head in a fall from saddle height. They do not, however, cover the vital temporal region that can strike curbs. In addition to protecting the head, a white or fluorescent helmet helps to identify a cyclist.

Equestrian

Almost all serious head injuries in our equestrian study occurred to helmetless riders.[34] Fewer than 20% of all horseback riders wear a helmet, and even if they do the helmet usually flies off when the rider falls because most riders fail to attach the chin strap. Most helmets are little more than decorative shells anyway and afford little protection if they do stay on the rider's head.

Steeplechase jockeys who suffer many falls may, like boxers, become "punch drunk" with traumatic encephalopathy and epilepsy.[46] The Jockeys Association in Great Britain and the British Standards Association have cooperated in the design of helmets for jockeys and for exercise boys and girls. These rigid shells contain energy-absorbing liners and floating cushions with temple protection and a secure cap retainer. Wearing this headgear has resulted in dramatically reduced numbers of severe, and sometimes fatal, head injuries.[34]

Baseball and Cricket

Little League baseball rules require protective helmets for batters, catchers, baserunners, first and third base coaches, and on-deck hitters. These helmets have saved many lives, as a pitched ball may travel 112 km/h (70 miles/h) and a batted ball more than 160 km/h (100 miles/h). For further protection, the on-deck circle should be in a safe location and all dugouts fenced in. Major leaguers usually wear a modified batting helmet while at bat, but the helmet only protects one side of the head, and if the batter ducks the wrong way he can be struck in the bare temple.

A cricket cap may soften a blow from the 154-g (5.5 oz) leather cricket ball. The bowler stands only 6.6 m (22 ft) from the batter, and the ball may bounce unpredictably at the batter from the turf or may glance off his bat. Peaked caps, such as baseball and kayak caps, block the sun's rays from striking the athlete's forehead and help to prevent headaches. The kayak cap may also be dunked in water and put on as a refreshing headpiece.

Hockey, Lacrosse, and Jai Alai

A hockey helmet should have a shock-resistant lining and padding in the temporal regions. The helmet not only protects a player's head but also serves as an anchor for the facemask. A hockey helmet with a suspension system but without padding leaves the player's head susceptible to a depressed skull fracture from the hard puck. Lacrosse helmets, although only thin shells with a small visor, serve to anchor the facemask. Jai alai players also wear hard, plastic caps that are unfit to protect their heads from balls almost the size of baseballs and harder than golf balls that travel faster than 160 km/h (100 miles/h).

THE FACE

Facemasks have helped significantly to reduce the number of facial injuries in tackle football, hockey, lacrosse, and motorcross. In the 1950s most tackle football injuries were to the face, such as bloody noses, cut lips, and dental injuries. In 1955, facemasks and mouthguards were recommended for high school football; by 1960 a facemask was required, and in 1962 the mouthguard was made mandatory. Players at first wore a single bar facemask, then a double bar. A vertical bar was added later, and more recently the birdcage facemask has become popular.

Quarterbacks, wide receivers, and running backs will often sacrifice protection for an unobstructed view. Faceguards do restrict the visual field slightly at knee level and below, making it harder to see a low opponent.[67] Special facemasks help to reduce injury; if a player must wear eyeglasses, for example, a specially designed facemask may be used. Mounting loops on a helmet allow the facemask to absorb blows.

The facemask must fit properly. If the bar style is fitted too low, it provides little protection for the facial area. If fitted too high, the bars obstruct vision and the mandible is exposed. By placing the facemask closer to the face, leverage is reduced if the facemask is grabbed by an opposing player. When a cage mask is fitted too close to the face, however, the angle of the mandible may be lacerated during violent contact as the cage is driven back and bent. Facemasks should be checked each week for loosened screws and bolts. If no facemasks were worn, the large number of severe neck injuries probably would be reduced, because a player wearing only a helmet and mouthguard would be less likely to head-tackle, butt-block, or spear.[66] Lost teeth or facial scarring would be a reasonable tradeoff for serious head and neck injuries. Without a facemask, however, the player might tend to close his eyes and drop his head, and even more injuries could result.

Before introduction of the facemask, eye injuries were common in ice hockey.[58] Two thirds of those injuries were caused by the stick and the rest by the puck, but blindness resulted equally from both objects. Full-face wire mesh and polycarbonate hockey masks reduce facial injuries by preventing the stick or puck from penetrating. Although goaltenders often wear an expensive, molded fiberglass mask, the puck can still get through to cause a hyphema or worse injury. Plastic shield face protectors are satisfactory if kept in good condition but may fog up and scratch.

When lacrosse facemasks had only horizontal bars, the number of facial injuries was large because the stick and balls could squeeze through (Figure 8-2). The addition of a mandatory vertical bar has helped to reduce the number of facial injuries (Figure 8-2).

Serious motocross competitors wear a face-

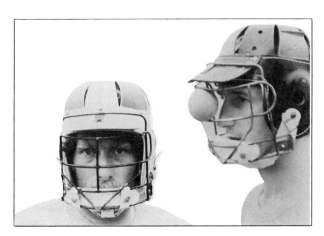

Figure 8-2 A lacrosse ball could enter the old-style lacrosse mask to damage a player's eye *(right)*. The recently mandated vertical bar should reduce the number of facial injuries *(left)*.

mask, and such masks and helmets should be worn by all motorcyclists. The motorcyclist's mask keeps flying objects, stones, and bugs from injuring his eyes and helps a driver avoid losing control of his vehicle. A full face helmet will give even better protection against severe facial injuries from motorcycle crashes.

Eye Injuries in Athletes

Because the opening to the eyeball is small, large objects, such as soccer balls and basketballs, may be deflected before their kinetic energy reaches the eye.[14] Almost any kind of ball, however, may become deformed and seriously contuse the globe, despite protection provided by the skull's bony rims. Moreover, although the eyeball is surrounded by bony rims and is elastic and embedded in a resilient fat pad, minor trauma may cause eventual blindness, as when glaucoma develops after an injury.

Facial Cuts

The boxer's face may be cut by friction from laces rubbed over it, by pinching of the skin between the boxing glove and the orbital bone, and by head-butting. The cuts usually occur in the supraorbital region but may occur infraorbitally and in the lid. A supraorbital cut may trickle blood into the eye, interfering with the boxer's vision.

Cuts cannot be treated between rounds in the Olympic games, but a cut can be fixed in other amateur and professional bouts. The periorbital cut should be wiped clean and pushed shut and pressure applied: the cut should then be coated with an astringent. Pressure should not be used, however, if there is a chance that the globe has ruptured. A layer of flexible collodian is next applied and Vaseline smeared around the cut so that further blows will slide off. After the fight, the cut should be minimally debrided and closed in layers to keep it from scarring down to bone. If not thus treated, the cut will open easily. Stitches should be placed about 2 mm apart, tied loosely, and a pressure dressing applied. To minimize scarring, the stiches may be left in only 3

to 5 days, and the athlete should not box for 4 weeks.

The eyelid consists of two halves: The anterior half contains skin and orbicularis muscle; the posterior half contains the tarsus and conjunctiva. Vertical lid lacerations, and lacerations that include the canthal tendons and lacrimal drainage system, should be treated by a practitioner with experience in oculoplastic surgery. A thorough eye examination, including dilated fundus examination, should be done to exclude damage to the eyeball.

Boxers should wear headgear while sparring and during collegiate and service team bouts. The soft leather boxing headgear is padded with latex foam rubber or animal hair to protect the boxer's eyes, temples, and base of the skull; some models even protect the jaw.

Conjunctival Irritation

Dust and dirt from playing surfaces irritate an athlete's eyes, while sweat may be rubbed into his eyes by dirty fingers. If the conjunctiva becomes irritated, foreign bodies or corneal abrasions might be suspected. Antibiotic drops should be administered only by an ophthalmologist after a slit-lamp examination; they should never be given at the time of an initial corneal abrasion.

After a few hours in bright and reflected sun, a skier or yachtsman's cornea may suffer sunburn in which the eyes become irritated and the athlete is then unable to tolerate bright light. Dark glasses or goggles will prevent this type of sunburn.

Finger in the Eye

In basketball, fingers are sometimes poked in the eye while players scramble for the ball, and a fingernail may scrape the eyeball. During cross-country skiing, a skier's cornea may be abraded by a tree limb. Such minor accidents may result in serious injury to the eye, including hyphema (blood in the anterior chamber), dislocation of the lens, and a retinal detachment. These conditions should never be overlooked on examination. All fingernails should be inspected and trimmed before games and practices and players required to remove rings and other jewelry that may endanger opponents or their teammates. Cross-country skiers are advised to wear eyeglasses or goggles while skiing in the woods.

To assess eye problems and to protect an injured eye, the physician should carry a local anesthetic, fluorescein strips, a concentrated light source, a small, near-vision card, eye patches, hard protective shields, and tape.

Fluorescein drops demonstrate superficial eye scrapes as bright green marks where the epithelium is absent. The marks are especially easy to see when a cobalt blue light is used for the examination. Scratched eyes should be patched. In this procedure, a pad is folded into the hollow of the orbit and then topped with a second pad. The athlete should be instructed to keep both eyes shut while wearing a patch, because blinking only futher irritates the eye. Corneal injuries should be checked by an ophthalmologist because the abrasion may be a laceration. The eye patch should be worn for 24 hours, then the eye rechecked and patched for another 24 hours, which is usually sufficient time for healing to take place.

Foreign Body in the Eye

If a foreign body enters the athlete's eye, it may lodge in the upper or lower fornix or on the conjunctival or corneal surfaces, producing the sensation of being under the upper lid. Oblique illumination from a concentrated light source may be needed to determine its precise location. A foreign body at the lower lid is easily removed by pulling the lower lid down and gently wiping it away with a cotton bud.

When a foreign body is under the upper lid, an attempt should be made to move it to the lower lid. The athlete should first be asked to look down, and the upper lid should then be gently pulled over the lower lid to produce tears that may flush the object to the lower part of the eye. If the foreign body remains under the upper lid, the lid should be pulled out before folding it upwards over a cotton bud to expose the tarsal conjunctival surface. Another cotton bud may be used to wipe away the object.

Tennis Eye

Eye injuries may occur unexpectedly if an athlete is off guard, as in tennis when a player's eye is struck during a warm-up when more than one ball is in play (Figure 8-3). When volleying, players' eyes are vulnerable to hard-hit balls and to balls that skip off the net. Balls hit in anger or frustration after a player loses a point may strike an opponent who is not alert. Players with poor vision may have difficulty following the flight of the ball and be injured.

Squash balls and racketballs are especially dangerous because they are small enough to fit into the orbit of the eye. The wild swings of inexperienced players send balls flying off at dangerous angles and velocities. In badminton, the 1.9-cm (0.75-in) diameter striking end of the shuttlecock similarly endangers the eyes.

In the excitement of a racket game, the player may underestimate the severity of a blow to his eye. The blow may cause temporary blurring with rapid recovery, but weeks or even years later the player may have serious vision loss from a detached retina that progressed from an asymptomatic peripheral break. For this reason, when a player's eye is struck by any small ball, an ophthalmologic checkup is desirable to rule out intraocular damage. An early fundoscopic examination, with the pupil fully dilated, may reveal hemorrhage and edema in the peripheral retina, indicating a small tear. Proper observation and treatment will prevent extension of the tear. Any player with subjective disturbance of vision, altered visual acuity, loss of visual field or diplopia, excessive edema, and chemosis or hemorrhage into the anterior chamber should consult with an ophthalmologist.

A player looking around at a partner who is serving should have his racket up as a guard. Ordinary eyeglasses will not protect the eyes in tennis, since the lens may be pushed against the eye. To prevent this, tennis players should wear either an eyeguard or a sports frame with popout lenses and rotating earpieces (Figure 8-3). Closed eyeguards should be mandatory for squash and racketball players, and novice badminton players are especially well advised to wear safety glasses

Figure 8-3   The tennis player should not look around while his partner is serving. Closed frames will keep out a racketball or squash ball, and skiing goggles protect against the sun's glare and tree branches.

because inexperienced players frequently suffer eye injuries.

"Black Eye"

Blows to a boxer's eye may rupture small blood vessels in the subcutaneous tissue of the eyelid. This skin is the thinnest in the body, and the subcutaneous supporting structures are equally tenuous. Hemorrhage here causes rapid and extensive swelling, shutting the lid. The eyeball shold be checked for blood before it swells shut and the orbital bones palpated. A swollen eye should not be dismissed as a minor contusion because a blow may dislocate the lens or produce a hyphema, retinal edema, retinal hemorrhage, vitreous hemorrhage, retinal tear, or retinal detachment. The globe may have ruptured, causing intraocular hemorrhage and loss of vision. If the lids are swollen shut or if the eye is difficult to examine, it should not be forced open, and an ophthalmologist should be promptly consulted.

Swelling is usually self-limiting, and ice bags may be applied during the first 24 hours. Instant cold packs should not be placed over the eyes because they occasionally leak small amounts of chemicals through tiny holes. Some boxing handlers will cut a boxer's eyelid with a razor blade to evacuate blood, an unacceptable practice with little practical value, as the blood has spread diffusely through the tissues and is not located. The blood supply to the lids will help resorb such interstitial blood within a few weeks.

Hyphema

A blow to the eye may damage small vessels of the ciliary body, which hemorrhage into the anterior chamber between the cornea and the iris. The athlete reports blurred vision, photophobia, and aching eye pain. The eye reddens and blood appears, producing a fluid level in the anterior chamber. Eyes with this condition should be shielded immediately and the athlete placed under the care of an ophthalmologist. Bed rest is obligatory, since further hemorrhage occurs in the first few days and the second hemorrhage may be worse than the first. The hyphema may prevent a clear view of the retina for several days, but most hyphemas are absorbed within a week. After absorption takes place, the ophthalmologist can dilate the pupil to check for retinal damage, and the patient should be followed for life to avert the development of secondary glaucoma.

Retinal Detachment

A blow to the eye may be followed by detachment of the retina, especially in athletes with a predisposing familial history. Detachment is most likely to occur in persons with retinal degenerative lesions, such as myopia. Constant agitation of the vitreous body may be accompanied by retinal traction sufficient to cause breaks in a retina that is thin or diseased. For this reason, some ophthalmologists caution myopic people, especially those who have had previous retinal detachment, against jogging. A retinal detachment may occur weeks or months after an injury. Retinal breaks, with or without detachment, require the expertise of an ophthalmologist for full assessment and appropriate treatment.

Blow-Out Fracture of the Orbit

If a fist, elbow, or ball strikes the orbit, blunt trauma may increase intraorbital hydrostatic pressure and break the inferomedial margin of the orbit. Because this weak bone may fracture even without an associated orbital rim fracture, the athlete should be sent to an ophthalmologist with the eye shielded after any blunt trauma.

An athlete with a blow-out fracture of the orbit will develop periorbital edema and hemorrhage; when this subsides, he may have double vision. The infraorbital rim may feel abnormal, and the inferior rectus muscle may become tethered to the fracture, interfering with ocular movements.

Water's x-ray view, Caldwell view, and a coned-down view of the orbital floor will reveal bone fragments that have been driven into the maxillary antrum from the orbital floor. Tomography is the best means to evaluate the extent of the damage, and surgery is usually performed in 7 to 14 days.

Contact Lenses

Many athletes wear contact lenses to avoid the disadvantages of spectacles, which may have heavy frames, fog up, and require cages, masks, and elastic straps.[28] Spectacles can also be knocked off or a spectacle lens pushed into the orbit. Although hard contact lenses are particularly beneficial to athletes who have astigmatism, such lenses may slide off center, pop out, and be lost. Moreover, wind and dust particles may slide under them to cause serious eye abrasions. These sudden and often painful distractions may be dangerous in some sports, negating the advantages of such lenses. For the athlete who wears contact lenses, a cage or mask is still advisable because a broken contact lens may be more dangerous than a shatterproof spectacle lens.

Soft contact lenses are generally more comfortable than hard contact lenses.[70] Vision is often not as crisp, however, and astigmatism not as well corrected with soft lenses. Swimmers usually can wear the soft lenses if goggles are used. These lenses require considerably more care than hard lenses and are more expensive. Proper care of soft lenses requires distilled water, saline solution, special lens cases, and a heating unit. The team physician and trainer should know which athletes are wearing contact lenses, and if a wearer is knocked unconscious the lenses should be removed immediately.

Eyeguards

Because a badminton bird, squash ball, or racketball may cause eye injuries, some clubs require players to wear eye protectors. Such protection is important not only for myopic and novice players but also for skilled players. The skilled player is less likely to give up control of center court, thus increasing the risk of eye injury from the racket or ball.

A myopic athlete's eyeglass lenses are concave, with the center section of the lens thinner than the outer edge, subjecting it to easy breakage. To give optimum protection, the lens center should be at least a 3-mm thick CR39 plastic or polycarbonate plastic.[17] Plastic lenses have a higher resistance to breakage than do glass lenses and are lighter, give less surface reflection, and are less likely to fog.

Although plastic lenses do not easily break, they can be broken and may pop through an ordinary frame. Such lenses should be mounted in a sports frame made of nylon with a steep posterior lip. When a lens in a sports frame is struck, it projects forward instead of being driven toward the eye. The athlete should wear a nylon frame with temples that rotate about 180°. Currently popular metal frames should be avoided because they can cut the face or damage the eye easily.

All open eyeguards do not provide equal protection, and direct shots from a racketball or squash ball can strike and damage the eye through the space between the upper and lower rims of some guards. Closed eyeguards with either plain or prescription lenses will prevent such injuries. An open eyeguard is, however, better than none because it will prevent slashes from rackets and damage from off-center hits.[17] Sturdy goggles are recommended for skiers because cheap plastic goggles can shatter into tiny pieces.*

Facial Bone Fracture

A blow to the angle of the jaw, the point of the chin, or the side of the chin may break an athlete's jaw and fracture the thin facial bones (Figure 8-4).[24] Although the mandible is stronger than the maxilla, it is weak at the canine teeth, the third molars, and the condylar necks, the places where most mandibular fractures occur.

To diagnose a facial bone fracture, the physician should palpate the bone edges for a step-off or crepitus. He should then place traction on the chin to elicit condylar neck pain. To detect a midthird facial bone fracture, the examiner should press down on the vertex of the athlete's head while pressing upward in the vault of his palate with the index finger. These maneuvers will produce pain and bony movement at the fracture. The upper incisors may be grasped with one hand and the nose with the other; the incisors

are then wiggled. Facial bone fracture must be diagnosed early, as the excellent blood supply of the facial bones will otherwise allow them to heal rapidly in a poor position, resulting in an unacceptable malocclusion of the teeth.

Facial bone fractures may be wired and healing achieved in about 6 weeks. Most athletes may resume sports after 8 weeks, but a boxer must wait 3 months before returning to the ring. A special facemask will afford protection to an athlete after a facial bone fracture. In football, for example, an extra face bar may be added to the helmet to protect the player's injured jaw (Figure 8-5).

Ear Injuries in Athletics

"Scrum Ear" and "Wrestler's Ear"

When an athlete's ear is repetitively rubbed or when it absorbs many blows or a single blow, blood may leak between the skin and the perichondrium. The ear then becomes throbbingly painful, tender, and swollen. After a few hours, a well-defined, smooth, rounded mass forms within the helix fossa. Blood and serum collect on both sides of the ear cartilage, isolating the cartilage from the soft tissue upon which its nutrition and vitality depend. The cartilage may then die and collapse. If the ear is not properly treated, the hematoma will organize and scar down within a few weeks, pulling the ear into a contorted, cauliflower-like configuration—the gnarled ear of a boxer, the scrum ear of a rugby player, or wrestler's ear.

Hot spots from friction during wrestling practice may be prevented by smearing Vaseline on the ears. The lubricant is, however, prohibited during matches. Wrestlers should wear earguards, especially during wrestling practice, where the wrestler spends 95% of his time (Figure 8-6). The headgear must be well fitted because poor-fitting or loose headgear may rub and cause wrestler's ear.

If an ear has been rubbed and becomes hot, an ice pack should be applied promptly. Any hematoma should be aspirated sterilely because infection in this region may lead to chondritis, a

---

* For a copy of eye protection recommendations or other information on eye safety in sports, contact the National Society to Prevent Blindness, 79 Madison Avenue, New York, NY 10016.

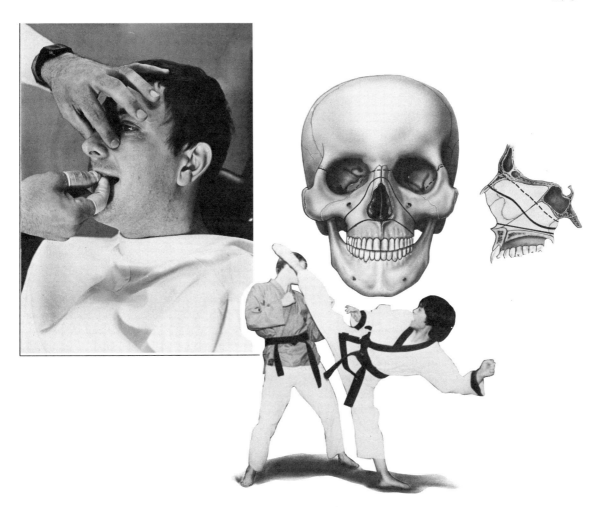

Figure 8-4   A blow to the face *(lower right)* may produce a facial bone fracture (lines on the skeleton). One diagnostic maneuver to diagnose a facial bone fracture is for the examiner to grasp the upper incisors with one hand and the nose with the other, and then wiggle the incisors to elicit motion and pain at the fracture *(left)*.

long-lasting problem. After the hematoma has been aspirated, the region may be compressed with a collodion pack, plaster of Paris cast, mineral-oil-soaked cotton balls, or silicone mold. The collodion pack is a cast of cotton or strips of gauze soaked in flexible collodion.[12] The collodion applicator should be kept well saturated to place collodion on the ear before the layers of gauze are started. After 24 to 48 hours, the pack may be removed and the ear checked for any reaccumulation before being repacked. The new pack should be left in place as long as possible, and

repeated if needed. Plaster of Paris may also serve as a packing, but a Q-tip should be placed in the ear canal while the plaster sets. Another technique uses a cotton "stent" moistened with mineral oil and placed into all of the convolutions of the auricular folds and also postauricularly. A mastoid dressing holds the stent in position for 10 days. As an alternative to aspirating the hematoma, it may be evacuated by making multiple incisions through the skin and perichondrium.[19] Dental rolls are then sutured in place and a mastoid dressing applied.

Figure 8-5   An extension on the face mask protects the player's injured mandible.

These techniques are not without problems, as the collodion pack may easily dislodge and the collodion pack and plaster of Paris cast usually lack a vent. The problems may be avoided by fashioning a silicone mold pressure dressing around the end of an applicator stick, providing a tunnel through the mold that equalizes pressure between the external auditory canal and the outside atmosphere.[33]

"Swimmer's Ear"

Swimmer's ear is an acute, diffuse external auditory canal infection usually caused by the bacterium *Pseudomonas aeruginosa* or, sometimes, by *Proteus, Escherichia coli,* or fungi.[18,64] Humans lack the adaptations diving mammals have to prevent external ear problems. Porpoises, for example, have no external auditory canal opening, and a seal's ears are covered during dives by external skin flaps.

Swimmer's ear may develop even if pool water is sparkling clean,[73] because water washes away the ear's natural cerumen and the skin in the canal becomes irritated and itches. If the athlete then scratches in his ear, he may disrupt the continuity of the lining cells of the ear canal. These cells produce a protective acid mantle that retards bacterial growth, and individual variations in the mantle may explain why some athletes are more prone to develop swimmer's ear. An excessively curved, narrowed, or partly obstructed ear canal may trap water. Trapping also occurs when cysts, bone growths, ear wax, ear plugs, allergies, or dermatitis blocks the canal. In some cases, the infection moves inward to cause a middle ear infection or to interfere with balance and hearing, or the infection may even advance to infect the brain.

Because the latency period for swimmer's ear is about 3 days, the association between swimming and swimmer's ear is sometimes overlooked. When the ear hurts and itches, the swimmer pulls the earlobe and rocks his jaw from side to side. On examination, the external ear canal is swollen and tender. Less often the infection is caused by a fungus; *Candida* produces yellow or white dots, and *Aspergillus nigra* forms a grayish-black membrane that coats the canal.

An infected ear canal should be reacidified with a solution of acetic or boric acid in alcohol.[18] Antibiotic and cortisone drop combinations may also be used, and alcohol and glycol drops will decrease the moisture. A cotton wick that has been soaked in Burrow's solution (alumninum acetate) should be inserted to limit further swelling. The ear debris is then carefully removed, and acid–alcohol drops are instilled. The wick should be kept moist with drops of Burrow's solution applied to it every 2 hours to bring the solution to the full length of the ear canal and keep the canal open.

The swimmer can remove trapped water and prevent swimmer's ear by vigorously shaking his head and jumping with his head tilted to one side. The ears should then be fanned or blown dry with a hair dryer. Three drops of 3% boric acid in alcohol may be put into the ear canals before and after each swim to dry the canals. For good aural hygiene, three drops of glycerin may be placed in each ear canal after a shower and the canal covered with a cotton pledget that is removed after 1 hour.

Vinegar dropped into an ear may macerate the ear canal. If cotton buds are stuck into the canal or if the concha or tragal areas are vigorously rubbed with a hand or a towel, the delicate skin

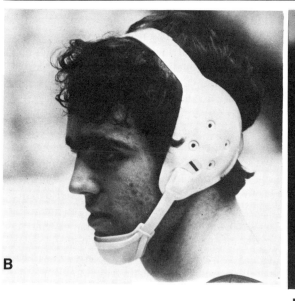

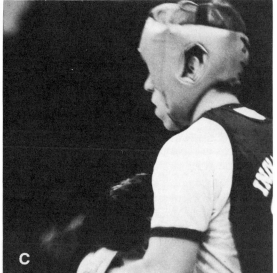

Figure 8-6 Wrestlers **(A, B)** and boxers **(C)** wear ear protectors to protect against an auricular hematoma and a deformed ear **(D)**.

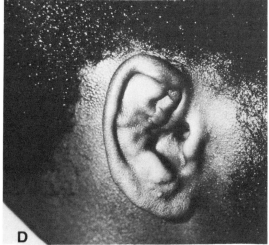

surface may break. Cotton buds may also push wax against the tympanic membrane or remove too much of the protective wax. Ear plugs should not be used because they are not water tight and may trap water and cause pressure necrosis.

Osteomas and Exostoses

Some swimmers and surfers develop small, bony masses in front of the tympanic membrane.[15, 18, 23] Such growths are endemic in swimmers in cold California water but are not usually found in the ears of swimmers who swim in heated pools. Swimmers in cool ocean water should wear headgear to protect their ear canals.

A growth may be an attempt to protect against the cold water that bathes the tympanic membrane and may be an osteoma or an exostosis. An *osteoma* is a solitary unilateral bone growth attached to the tympanic squamous suture superficial or lateral to the canal isthmus. Exostoses are broad-based elevations of the bony canal that are usually multiple and bilaterally symmetrical. They lie deep or medial to the canal isthmus at the upper edge of the tympanic bone. These multilobed tumors of the external ear canal, unlike swimmer's ear, are painless but progressive. First, the inner bony part of the canal thickens with cobblestone-like swellings, and after further exposure to cold water the swellings become knuckle-like. Eventually, they completely block the ear canal to produce a conductive hearing loss.

Osteomas and exostoses may be excised. If a defect remains that rings more than one third of the circumference of the ear canal, it may be closed with a skin graft.[15].

Barotrauma

Divers may experience serious problems such as cerebral arterial air embolism, joint pains (the "bends"), or venous gas pulmonary embolism (the "chokes").[78] Divers who have chronic obstructive pulmonary disease, bronchial asthma, or lung blebs sometimes trap air when they ascend from deep water, causing a pneumothorax.

More common problems affect the air-filled cavities of the sinuses and the middle ear spaces of divers.[73] These very susceptible air-filled structures have rigid walls and small openings, and the air within them must be equilibrated, continuously, with the external air pressure. Proper equilibration demands that Eustachian tube and sinus ostia be patent.

The barometric pressure outside and inside the body at sea level is 14.7 lb/in², and for every 33 feet of descent in sea water the pressure increases by this amount. Barotrauma may occur even in relatively shallow dives because the greatest volume changes within tissue cavities per foot of descent occur near the surface.

"Ear squeeze" may develop during the descent phase of diving as pressure differentials cause vascular tissues to dilate and the epithelium of the sinuses and middle ear to swell. This swelling is an autoregulatory mechanism that functions to lower the pressure differential. The engagement of the tissues decreases air volume in the cavity but may further occlude the ostia and prevent equalization of pressures. The pressure differential may then increase to produce transudation and, finally, blood vessel rupture, which reduces the pressure differential by adding blood to the cavity. With ear squeeze, the diver notices ear pain, decreased hearing, ringing in his ears, inability to clear his ears, and, sometimes, blood-tinged sputum.

When the external canal is blocked by cerumen, an osteoma, the diving hood, or an earplug, an artificial air-filled cavity external to the tympanic membrane is created. The middle ear becomes overpressurized in relation to the closed cavity between the plug and tympanic membrane, and the tympanic membrane distends outward to produce a "reverse ear squeeze."

Inexperienced divers may not be able to equalize pressure.[78] Infection, allergies, or vasomotor rhinitis may also swell the mucus membranes. Large adenoids, scarring from adenoidectomy, or congenital obstruction of the openings prevents pressure equalization.

The diver should keep the openings to his middle ear and sinuses clear by removing impacted cerumen. The ears should be checked for osteomas or exostoses, and pharangeal masses that block air passages should be removed. Divers are advised to practice equalizing pressure and are cautioned not to dive when suffering from sinusitis or during a seasonal flare-up of allergic rhinitis. Persons with disorders that might interfere with consciousness, such as seizure disorders or potential insulin reactions, should not dive.

A diver who takes a decongestant or antihistamine before diving should be aware that a "rebound" phenomenon may occur that produces swelling of the mucus membranes and barotrauma.

Tympanic Membrane Rupture

A blow to the ear in water polo, surfing, or water skiing may rupture the athlete's tympanic membrane. This injury used to be common in water polo, but players now wear caps with ear protectors, and thus the disorder is seen less often.

In competitive water skiing, the maximum boat speed is 58 km/h (36 miles/h), although the skier may go faster than the boat and a fall may rupture his tympanic membrane. The rupture occurs with a pop, and the athlete notices a decreased ability to hear. A ruptured membrane may admit cold water to produce a dangerous cold water caloric effect on the labyrinth, causing dizziness and nausea, which may panic the diver, water skier, or swimmer.

A ruptured tympanic membrane should be observed each day for signs of infection. If infection is present, antibiotic therapy should be administered; alternatively, antibiotic drops or systemic antibiotics may be given from the start to prevent infection. Steroid drops should be avoided because they retard healing. The membrane usually closes spontaneously within a week, although some otolaryngologists recommend early surgical closure of the rupture.[57]

Caloric Labyrinthitis

Stimulation of the labyrinth of the ear by cold water produces caloric labyrinthitis with vertigo, loss of balance, and nausea.

Pipkin reported on caloric labyrinthitis in an otolargyngologist who dove from a dock into a lake.[60] As cold water suddenly filled his external

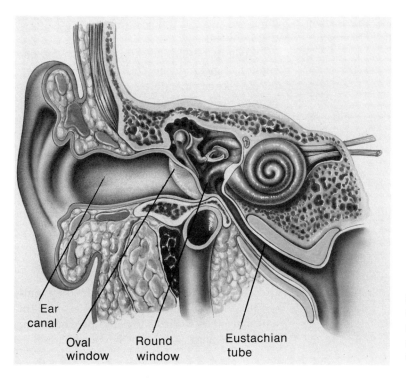

Ear
canal

Oval
window

Round
window

Eustachian
tube

Swimming and diving can damage the athlete's ear canal, the oval window, the round window, and the sinuses.

auditory canal, the doctor developed vertigo and lost his sense of balance. He understood, however, what was happening and, using his sense of touch, he crawled on the lake bottom to safety.

Ninety percent of all drowning victims drown within 9 m (10 yd) of shore; why so many strong swimmers drown is uncertain. Because caloric labyrinthitis may cause some of these drownings, no one should swim alone or in unfamiliar water and all boaters should wear life preservers.

Round Window Rupture

The round window membrane may rupture in skin divers, free underwater divers, snorkelers, scuba divers, and weight lifters.[18] The athlete's ear pops and a leakage of perilymph causes sudden deafness. This type of rupture demands prompt closure of the fistula, which may save some hearing. Unfortunately, the sudden hearing loss is often irreversible, making prevention essential.

Divers should be advised to avoid wearing earplugs and to forgo diving if they have an upper respiratory infection or allergic flare-up. Also, divers and weight lifters with already damaged ears should be advised that they risk more serious damage when they perform a Valsalva maneuver, which is increased pressure by forcible exhalation against a closed glottis.

Hearing Loss from Firearms

Repetitive impulse noise from the sudden explosive force of gunfire may produce hearing loss in marksmen and officials who must fire a starting gun at track meets. The "near ear" is subject to the greater acoustical trauma because it is closer and at a more direct angle to receive the assault.[56] The left ear is the near ear of a right-handed rifleman, whereas the right ear is the near ear of a right-handed pistol shooter.

The noise from most guns is loud enough to cause hearing loss.[55] The peak sound pressure level (PSPL) for the maximum endurable threshold of repeated impulses for ears of normal sensitivity is 150 dB. All shotguns and center-firing and rim-firing weapons have been found to ex-

ceed the damage risk level of 150 dB, except for the smaller 0.22 cartridges.

Less noise would preserve hearing and would allow marksmen to be more relaxed and to shoot more accurately.[74] The amount of powder in the cartridge and its characteristics could be reduced to decrease the PSPL, but this would alter ballistic findings.[55] Therefore, the most practical solution would be a modification of the gun barrel. In the absence of such a change, marksmen can help to reduce their hearing loss by firing on flat, open terrain and by wearing earmuffs that reduce noise by 20 to 45 dB.[56]

Nose Injuries in Athletics

Nose Bleed

The athlete with nose bleed should sit or kneel in front of the physician and bend his head slightly forward. This position keeps him from swallowing blood, which may produce nausea and vomiting, and also lessens bleeding, since the head is above the heart. The physician places his thumb along the outside of the bleeding nostril and his index finger on the opposite side of the athlete's nose and applies steady pressure for several minutes.

When persistent bleeding occurs, the nose should be packed, but cotton ball packings are unsafe because the athlete may inhale a piece of cotton. A regular-sized tampon will serve as packing and may be referred to as a "nose plug."[4] The tampon must be cut to fit inside the nose. Once in the nose, the material expands and conforms to the nostril. The athlete may return to the game, since the tampon is too large to be inhaled, and the nose plug can be removed later. Several tampons, with strings removed, may be carried in the trainer's kit.

Broken Nose

A nasal fracture may be determined by gently wiggling the athlete's nose at the cartilage line and above it on the bone to detect pain or grating. If displacement is noted, the nose should be splinted, and the fracture will need to be reduced. When swelling prevents a proper evaluation of external nasal deformity, ice should be applied and the nose reevaluated in 3 days. If the diagnosis of a nasal fracture is delayed for 2 weeks, the fracture may no longer be reducible by closed means. Even though the nose contains very little bone, nasal defects may affect the Eustachian tube, making clearing of the ears by inflating the middle ear difficult or impossible.

A hematoma in the nasal septum is an emergency and must be incised or aspirated and the nose packed to prevent cartilage destruction, necrosis, and development of a saddle nose deformity. A bulge may also cause nasal obstruction.

Mouth Injuries in Athletics

Mouthguards

Before facemasks were added to football helmets, 50% of football injuries were in or around the mouth; after the addition of facemasks, mouth injuries fell to 25% of the total. The facemask, however, offers little protection against blows under the chin from forearm blocking, from knees, or from kicks and does not block blows to the top of the head that snap the jaws shut.

Mouthguards were recommended for high school tackle football players in 1955 and made mandatory in 1962 but were not required to collegiate tackle football players until 1973.[40, 42] Today's combination of facemask and mouthguard has made mouth injuries very rare. Mouthguards not only have reduced injuries to the mouth, such as split lips and broken teeth, but also have helped decrease concussions by absorbing the energy from blows, thus damping the transmission of forces to the brain. [45, 71, 72]

Whether playing in recreational or competitive sport, every athlete should wear a mouthguard as a routine safety item,[41] whether in practices or in an actual game.

The major types of mouthguards include custom-made, mouth-formed, and stock. Custom-made mouthguards are heavy-duty ones, made of dental vinyl or plastic pulled by vacuum over a plaster mold of the athlete's teeth. A mouth-formed, thermal-set, boiled, pliable, plastic mouthguard (Figure 8-7A) is satisfactory, but the stock rubber mouthguard is unacceptable because it may be a very poor fit. A well fitted mouthguard is comfortable and offers very little interference with the athlete's speech and breathing. The volume of air intake in an athlete pushed to exhaustion decreases only by about 5% with a custom-made mouthguard (Figure 8-7B).[36]

In tackle football, the mouthguard is often attached to the player's facemask or chin piece to keep him from misplacing it. A safety strap feature allows the strap to be pulled free of the mouthguard under unusual pressure to avoid stress injury to the player's teeth. Mouthguards must be checked for wear; many injuries occur when the guard has worn down.

Temporomandibular Joint

In addition to absorbing shocks, a mouthguard may also help to preserve an athlete's energy and to increase his strength by balancing the temporomandibular joints. When this joint is imbalanced, the nervous system picks up the fact of the malalignment when the athlete swallows and his teeth touch. As reflexes are activated, energy-sapping compensations for the malalignment occur in the athlete's back and limbs.

Some athletes have large mandibles with equally large mandibular condyles. If a large condyle is cradled in the base of an average-sized skull, there is less tolerance in the joint and a greater susceptibility to concussion. Athletes with deep overbite occlusion problems usually have small condyles and average-sized heads. These persons lack anterior muscle supports for thier heads and necks, resulting in an overuse of the posterior cervical muscles and more strained necks and pinched nerves.[71, 72]

An orthodontist can place a resilient bite plate between the occlusal surfaces of the upper and lower teeth to suspend the condyle away from the fossa, providing the temperomandibular joint with more tolerance. The plate also gives posterior occlusal support needed to balance the head.

Richard Kaufman, a sports orthodontist, fit the

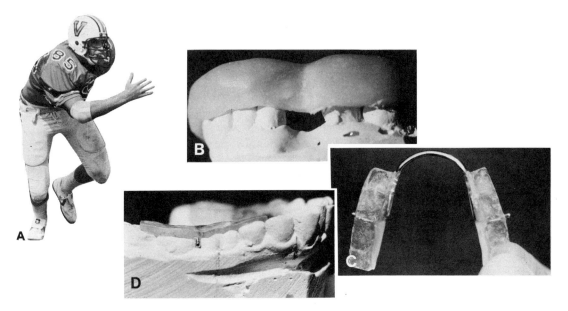

Figure 8-7   A mouth-formed mouthguard attaches to the face mask **(A)**. A latex mouthguard is custom-made and even fills in gaps **(B)**. The MORA **(C)** is an acrylic device that corrects temporomandibular joint dysfunction; it rests on the lower teeth **(D)** to produce proper occlusion.

American luge team with mandibular orthopedic repositioning appliance (MORA) mouthpieces to relax their tense head and neck muscles and reduce headaches and back pain.[80] The MORA mouthpiece (Figure 8-7C) comprises two strips of acrylic that fit precisely over the lower molars and bicuspids (Figure 8-7D). The mouthpiece is held painlessly in place by two small stainless steel clasps that latch between the first and second bicuspids. The orthodontist adjusts the appliances, repositioning the condyles and balancing them from left to right as needed. With the MORA mouthpiece in place, the athlete can speak and breathe normally. The temporomandibular joint is thus balanced, reflex activity at the joint is reduced, and the athlete has added strength and endurance.[80]

Tooth Problems

Tooth problems may be prevented by preseason checkups and early dental care. Equipment for dental emergencies should include a kit containing forceps, sterile cotton, sterile saline, oil of clove (Eugenol), calcium hydroxide (Dycal), and temporary filling material (Cavit).

If an athlete loses a filling, forceps and sterile cotton may be used to clean the area and oil of clove and calcium hydroxide placed in the hole before a temporary filling is added. When a toothache accompanies the lost filling, the area should be cleaned with sterile cotton and a small ball of oil-of-clove-wetted cotton placed into the cavity. The cotton is then covered with temporary filling material. The subject then bites down to compress the temporary filling. When a tooth is chipped and the nerve exposed, calcium hydroxide may be applied to the uncovered nerve area.

When knocked out, a tooth should be promptly washed with sterile saline but not rubbed. An ice pack may be applied to the face, with the athlete holding the tooth in its bed with his fingers or by keeping his mouth closed. He should then see a dentist, who may be able to align the tooth and keep it in place with arch bars or dental bands. If the periodontal membrane heals, the tooth will be reattached solidly.

A Panorex x-ray film should be taken to rule

out alveolar or mandibular fracture after all moderate or severe injuries to the mouth.

Swallowed Bubble Gum or Chewing Tobacco

If an athlete chews gum or tobacco, his temperomandibular joint becomes overworked, and the chewing induces fatigue by sapping strength and endurance. The chewing athlete also risks aspirating the gum or tobacco and strangling.

The Heimlich or abdominal-thrust maneuver may save a choking athlete.[38, 39] Using this technique, the rescuer wraps both of his arms around the victim, and the victim's head and torso are allowed to slump forward. The rescuer then clasps the back of his wrist with his other hand so that the fist is pressed against the victim's diaphragm just below the ribs with a quick, hard squeeze. The squeeze is repeated as needed until the foreign body pops out like a cork. The victim should *not* be slapped on the back to dislodge the foreign body because such a slap may cause further inhaling of the foreign body.

If an athlete is knocked out and has gum or tobacco lodged in his throat, an oral screw may be used to force the mouth open to remove the foreign body. For an athlete who has an uncorrectable upper airway obstruction to breathing, a cricothyreotomy may be lifesaving.

Laryngeal Injury

A laryngeal injury may threaten the athlete's life; for this reason, a boxer keeps his chin tucked in. Blows may otherwise cause swelling and spasm of the larynx, and the thyroid cartilage (Adam's apple) may be contused or fractured. Trail bike riders risk laryngeal injuries when they ride on trails where wires, ropes, or chains may be strung. The threat of such injury requires baseball catchers and hockey goaltenders to wear throat flaps to block the ball or puck (Figure 8-8). An inexpensive flap can be made by attaching the spine pad from a football girdle to the catcher's mask by leather lacing.[52] The pad will also serve as a target for the pitcher. Full-contact karate participants shun neck protection, risking fractures of the larynx from kicks or punches.

Laryngeal injury produces voice changes. Crepitus is felt and landmarks are lost. Stridor may be delayed, and a laryngeal hematoma may expand to obstruct the airway completely.

THE NECK

The neck is subject to some of the most devastating injuries in athletics, and sports rank second only to automobile accidents as a leading cause

Figure 8-8 The goaltender's protective gear includes a throat flap that attaches to his face mask and protects his larynx.

of injury to this area. Three of four fatalities in organized tackle football are associated with head and neck injury, and one half of wrestling deaths follow a broken neck.

The National Athletic Trainer's Association (NATA) and the University of Pennsylvania Sports Medicine Center have established a National Head and Neck Injury Registry* that solicits information on head and neck injuries in sports.[76] Injuries qualifying for the Registry include head and neck fractures or dislocations, injuries that require hospitalization for more than 72 hours or that require surgery, and those that produce permanent paralysis or death. The Registry provides information forms to record the diagnosis, treatment, disability, and current status of the athlete. The Registry also requests a record of the place of injury, the position the athlete played, and how the injury occurred—whether in a game, practice, or scrimmage, the mechanism of injury, and how it was verified. Other information requested includes the height, weight, and age of the player, whether he had a previous injury, the helmet manufacturer (if applicable), the type of field, and weather conditions at the time of injury.

Deadly head injuries in tackle football have declined over the past two decades, but neck injuries have risen during the same period.[7, 76] The helmet-facemask system effectively protects the player's head, but by so doing it allows the head to be used as a battering ram in tackling and blocking. Luckily, the helmet's slick outer plastic shell sometimes enables the head to glance off an opponent. At first, the proposal to place a soft outer lining on the football helmet may seem sound, but such a lining would produce increased friction, and the tackler's head would stick to his opponent and absorb more force.

Football helmets are not designed to protect a player's neck; thus most fatal or paralyzing injuries occur when the player's neck is hyperflexed as he spears, head tackles, or butt-blocks. In head tackling and butt-blocking, the top of one's head is used as the contact point, hitting the opponent "in the numbers." Knee blows to the head or grabbing of the facemask tilts the facemask violently and hyperextends the neck. Tacklers sustain more than 70% of all neck injuries; specifically, defensive backs, who must tackle bigger running backs and ends, suffer the largest number of head and neck injuries.

Philo and Stine assert that the grave risk of quadriplegia in tackle football has been concealed from players and parents.[59] Feldick and Albright further state that "unless changes in technique are taught and rules are enforced, continued neck injuries and catastrophic paralysis will put football in severe jeopardy.[21] If the number of neck injuries does not decrease appreciably, litigation against equipment manufacturers could conceivably remove helmets from the market, and football could end by default."[21, 79] Such criticism has resulted in a change in the definition of spearing, tightening of the rules, and a reappraisal of blocking and tackling techniques. Spearing, for example, formerly referred to the impaling of a player who is out of the action or the use of one's helmet after a blown whistle. It is now redefined as intentional use of the helmet to punish an opponent, and no player may now deliberately butt, ram, or stike an opponent with the top of his helmet. In "head tackling," the tackler drives in with his face to his opponent's numbers, propelling his helmet upward to the opponent's chin. Officials are now empowered to penalize players who use the head as a primary contact point. Instead of a 15-yard penalty for use of the head, the player should be banished from the game. Officials who neglect to call penalties for spearing and butting should be replaced, and coaches who teach spearing should be fired.

Running backs should run with their heads up, avoiding the dangerous, flexed position.[47] If the head nods slightly forward, the neck becomes a vulnerable straight column. In the correct "bulled" position, the player holds his head back some 10° and tucks his chin so that shocks are absorbed by the neck muscles and upper back muscles. Proper tackling is done head to side, with the tackler's head up, his eyes open, and initial contact made with the hands. The head slides up along the opponent's side, and chest-

---

*National Athletic Head and Neck Injury Registry, University of Pennsylvania Sports Medicine Center, 235 South 33rd Street, Philadelphia, Pennsylvania 19104.

to-chest contact is made. Strong leg drive is needed. Players should work on their tackling form in preseason practice. Shoulder blocking and tackling with the neck extended and tucked in a "bulled" position must be taught, and players must be trained to fall forward and backward, rolling on their shoulders and quickly getting up.

Types of Injuries

Diving

Immature, reckless young men with impaired judgment who lack training are the ones most likely to suffer a neck injury while diving, often ignoring warnings of shallow water. The water slows a diver's speed of fall, but only when a depth of 1.5 m (5 ft) has been reached. The force of the water spreads the unskilled diver's arms apart, and his head may strike the bottom.[1] Many drownings may be due to tetraplegia, when the diver strikes his head on the bottom, resulting in wedge or burst fractures of C-2.[8]

Recreational divers rarely even lock their thumbs, but this precaution is insufficient to prevent their hands from pulling apart on entry. A stronger grasp may be achieved by holding the thumb with the opposite fist or by using the competitive diver's interlocking technique (Figure 8-9).

Safety efforts are best directed toward the prevention of diving accidents, with widely publicized warnings about the hazards of diving into shallow water, including the fact that underwater rocks may not be clearly seen with changing light conditions later in the day.[1]

Equestrian

A fall from a horse may result in a cervical spine fracture and tetraplegia. Such injuries are a significant problem for steeplechase riders, who often tumble from their mounts.[46]

Equestrian athletes should practice dressage to bring the horse's hindquarters underneath the body and to achieve balance. As the horse's gymnastic skill increases, the horse should move more easily. Riders should stay on familiar terrain and check tack routinely. Learning how to fall and roll to protect the neck is advisable. A few steeplechase jockeys wear spinal protectors to prevent neck injury.

Young Tackle Football Players

Death rates do not accurately reflect the incidence of neck injuries in high school tackle football,[2] and juniors and seniors have especially high rates of injury. Many injuries in this age group go unrecognized; thus when the symptoms of neck injury, such as radiation of pain into an arm or numbness and tingling in a limb, are explained to high school players, they frequently reveal a history of such injury.

Of 108 college freshmen tackle football recruits in one study, 35 showed x-ray evidence of previous injury, such as old compression fractures, posterior element fractures, disk narrowing, and ligamentous instability.[21] Only about half of these athletes had been seen by a doctor and x-ray films had been taken only in 13 cases.

Youths who complain of neck pain should be examined. The examiner sometimes may find congenital instability in an immature neck. Lack of an odontoid, for example, puts the player at great risk for serious injury. Players should be informed about the symptoms of neck injury, and any player who misses a practice or game because of neck pain should have an x-ray taken. The player must have full, pain-free range of motion in his neck before returning to practice.

Fractures

The head weighs about 4.5 kg (10 lb) and is supported by the smallest, most delicate part of the spine. The first cervical vertebra, the atlas, comprises a ring with lateral masses and no central body. Its articulations are curved to provide flexion and extension between the overlying occiput and itself. The second cervical vertebra, the axis, has curved articulations that allow rotation between the atlas and the axis. Most of the rotation in the cervical spine occurs in this area.

The odontoid is the superior projection of the body of the axis. The transverse ligament holds the anterior tubercle of the atlas adjacent to the odontoid. Stability of the atlas and axis depends

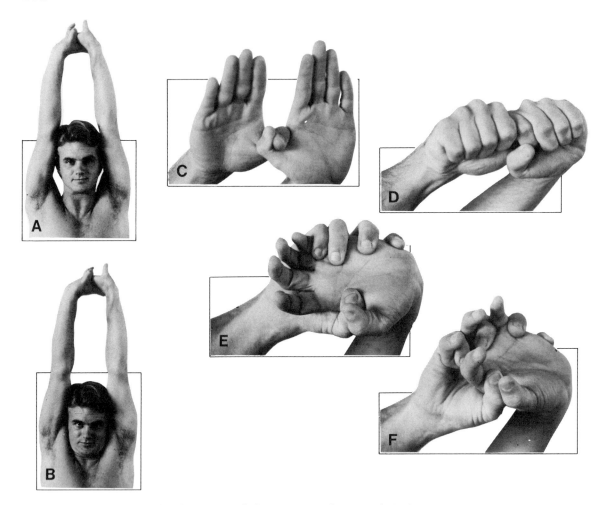

Figure 8-9   Proper arm and hand positioning help to protect a diver's neck. In **A,** the shoulders do not cushion the neck as they do in **B,** the correct position. Locked thumbs **(C)** can be easily pulled apart, exposing the diver's head. A better grip is to grab a thumb **(D).** The best grips are with overlapping hands **(E)** or intertwining fingers **(F).**

on the transverse ligament of the atlas and the odontoid process of the axis. The third through seventh vertebrae are similar to each other, providing some flexion, extension, tilt, and rotation. the vertebral arteries ascend in the vertebral foramen of each lateral mass from C-6 through C-1.

X-ray films of the cervical spines should include anteroposterior, lateral, and oblique views and an open-mouth view to show the odontoid and the lateral masses of the atlas. Sometimes the lower cervical spine is especially difficult to vi-

sualize after an injury because muscle spasms cause the shoulder shadow to obscure the region. In these instances, the athlete's head is stabilized, and his arms are gently pulled down to allow this area to be seen. If this technique is unsuccessful, a "swimmer's view" is obtained in which one arm is abducted 180° and the other arm is pulled down along the athlete's side (Figure 8-10). To obtain a clear view of the lower cervical spine, the beam is then directed at a 60° angle to the neck.

Prevertebral soft tissue swelling of 5 mm or

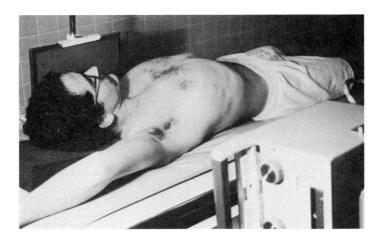

Figure 8-10 Sometimes, lower cervical vertebrae are not seen on a standard lateral x-ray film. The swimmer's view, with one arm raised, equalizes soft tissue densities and allows a clear view of these vertebrae.

more at the anterior–inferior border of C-3 provides indirect evidence of a cervical spine injury. Although an x-ray film may show normal alignment, momentary subluxation may have occurred at the time of injury, causing severe damage to the spinal cord. The mechanisms of cervical spine injury include neck compression, pure flexion, flexion and compression, flexion and rotation, hyperextension, and lateral flexion.

Compression Injuries

Compression injuries to the cervical spine occur in diving accidents and from head-on tackles.[5, 26] An axial load on the head causes the occiput to drive the atlas down onto the axis, producing a burst fracture of the ring of the atlas (Jefferson's fracture). The ring usually fractures posteriorly in two places weakened by grooves of the vertebral arteries. The atlas is a fragile ring, but fortunately its opening for the spinal cord is wide. This fracture is diagnosed on an open-mouth view by noting that the articular facets have slid laterally on the axis.

Vertical compression may also produce a comminuted, explosion fracture of a vertebral body and a posterior subluxation of the body. Even though the fracture itself is stable, serious neurologic damage may result. With the aid of tomograms or a computed tomography scan, fragments may be found in the spinal canal. Such fragments may be pressing on the anterior spinal artery, producing cord ischemia. This ischemia

leads to an anterior cervical cord syndrome consisting of complete motor paralysis and sensory anesthesia with dorsal column sparing so that proprioception and deep pressure sensation from the trunk and lower extremities are retained.

Flexion Injuries

In a pure flexion injury, the athlete's chin sometimes strikes his sternum before his neck breaks. A facemask such as the birdcage facemask used in tackle football blocks further flexion (Figure 8-11). Flexion of the neck may produce a stable wedge fracture of a vertebral body. A pure flexion injury, as from a fall on the back of the head, may also rupture the transverse ligament. The odontoid then is no longer restrained, and an atlantoaxial dislocation results. After such an injury, as the athlete leans his head forward, the atlas slides forward, and he becomes dizzy, developing a headache from pressure on the greater occipital nerve and a tingling in his feet. As he leans backward, the dislocation reduces.

If the distance between the odontoid and the anterior arch of the atlas on a lateral x-ray film exceeds 5 mm, the supporting structures probably have failed. A distance of more than 10 mm implies the loss of all ligamentous stability. A lateral x-ray film with the neck flexed is most important, since overlooking this instability could result in an athlete's death. If he survives this dislocation, his neck is firmly immobilized, and an early oc-

Figure 8-11   Head tackling *(left)* can seriously damage the tackler's neck and even paralyze him. The "bird-cage" mask *(right)* can help to block full flexion.

cipitoaxial fusion or an atlantoaxial fusion with wire and an iliac bone graft is performed.

When an athlete falls on the back of his head, he may fracture his odontoid. Such fractures usually occur at the weakest part of the dens, its base. A slight tilt of the odontoid on the open-mouth view will serve as a clue to a fracture and is an indication for tomograms and flexion and extension films. When a fracture is suspected but no fracture line is seen, the lateral film should be checked for prevertebral soft tissue swelling as a clue to the presence of a fracture.

Flexion/Compression fractures

A player's neck may buckle during head tackling (see Figure 8-11). This happens most commonly in high school defensive backs who wear single- or double-bar facemasks, the kinds least likely to block flexion. Major stress occurs at the C-5–C-6 level, where the mobile part of the cervical spine joins the less mobile part. Flexion and compression forces produce a wedge-shaped or a teardrop fracture, which is a chip broken off the anterior lip of C-5. The injured athlete's neck will be unstable if his posterior soft tissue elements are completely torn, but otherwise the compression fracture may be stable. The entire vertebral body may crumble, with the posterior part split

off and displaced posterolaterally and the posteroinferior margin fracture pushed into the spinal canal. The disk between C-5 and C-6 may also be expelled back into the spinal canal. These fractures frequently produce a transverse lesion of the cord and tetraplegia.

Flexion and Rotation Injuries of the Cervical Spine

A combination of neck flexion and rotation may dislocate or fracture one or both facet joints. If a player is lying on the field with his head locked in one position, no attempt should be made to straighten it, since his facet joints may be locked. If the rotational component of the injury force is great, the pedicles may be fractured. With complete unilateral facet dislocation, x-ray films show the vertebral body to be subluxed about 25% anteriorly. When both facets are locked, the body is displaced anteriorly about 50%. Traction may unlock the facet joints, but sometimes operative unlocking is needed.

Hyperextension Injuries

When a player's facemask is grabbed and levered backward or an athlete's face is struck by a knee, his occiput may actually contact his thoracic spine, causing neck injury (Figure 8-12). The force needed to hyperextend the neck is not too great, since the anterior muscles of the neck are far weaker than the posterior muscles. Such injuries may produce vertebral artery ischemia or thrombosis, with a momentary feeling of paralysis or tingling in the limbs. Compression and spasm of spinal arteries produce acute paralysis, numbness, and tingling in the lower limbs, then in the upper limbs, but the athlete may recover even before he is transported from the field.

Hyperextension is the most common mechanism of nerve root injury. Injury to the C-5 root affects the shoulder and deltoid muscle; the C-6 root controls the biceps and conveys sensation from the radial aspect of the arm and thumb; C-7 conducts sensation from the index and middle fingers; and C-8 controls the intrinsic muscles of the athlete's hand and innervates his ring and little fingers and his inner arm.

Hyperextension of an athlete's neck may fracture the laminas or pedicles of the axis, or a lamina may fracture along with an avulsion of an anterior–superior chip of a vertebral body. Tomograms and oblique x-ray films may be needed to diagnose such a fracture. The athlete may have a complete cord injury, but an x-ray film may show only a widened interspace anteriorly. Hyperextension may also produce an odontoid fracture; the only external sign of the injury may be a bruise on the athlete's forehead or face.

Hyperextension may produce a central cord syndrome, the most common incomplete cord syndrome. This occurs mostly in middle-aged persons who have osteoarthritic spines. The spinal canal is narrow, and the cord is crushed between anterior osteophytes and an infolded ligamentum flavum posteriorly. Central spinal cord vessels are injured, venous circulation is impaired, and there is progressive hemorrhage and thrombosis of vessels, with edema ensuing. Damage to the anterior horn cells in the central gray matter of the cord will produce a severe, flaccid, lower motor neuron paralysis of the upper extremities, whereas damage to the central part of the corticospinal and spinothalamic long tracts in the white matter produces upper motor neuron spastic paralysis of the trunk and lower extremities. The medial parts of the lateral pyramidal tracts are affected, but there is sacral sparing. Motor and sensory function often return to the athlete's lower exremities and trunk, but recovery of hand function is poor.

Cervical collars will limit extension of the neck, but defensive backs and wide receivers object to collars, arguing that a collar restricts their movements.

Lateral Flexion Injuries

Lateral flexion of an athlete's neck may cause a fracture through the lateral mass of a pedicle, a vertebral foramen, or a facet joint. Such an injury may produce a Brown–Sequard syndrome in which damage is limited to the lateral half of the athlete's spinal cord, producing an ipsilateral corticospinal muscle palsy and contralateral hypesthesia to pain and temperature. Lateral flexion may also produce a nerve pinch.[10]

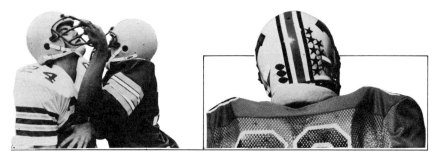

Figure 8-12 A player's neck may be hyperextended by leverage on his face mask *(left)*. A neck roll *(right)* can help to block hyperextension.

"Burners" and Nerve Pinch

An athlete may stretch his cervical plexus or his brachial plexus, damage a nerve root, or rupture a cervical disk that will press on a nerve root. These upper extremity nerve injuries are especially common in wrestling, hockey, and tackle football, as when a linebacker's neck is bent to the side when he tackles. Nerve injuries in motocross are quite severe and may include nerve root avulsions. Other athletes who may injure their upper extremity nerves are skiers whose poles catch on trees, diving soccer goalies, and mountaineers and hikers who carry heavy backpacks.

A "burner," also called a "stinger" or a "hotshot," is a stretching of the cervical plexus, the supraclavicular nerves, or the brachial plexus that occurs when the athlete's head is bent away from the side of his arm pain.[11] Supraclavicular nerves convey sensation from the top and front of the athlete's shoulder, and injury to them produces a sensory loss but no motor loss. An athlete's brachial plexus may be contused (neurotmesis) beneath his clavicle on the surface of the first rib. If a nerve root is avulsed (axonotmesis), the axon degenerates distally. A nerve root may be pinched when an athlete's head is abruptly flexed laterally, and pain then radiates down the arm on the side to which his head was bent.

Knowledge of neuroanatomy is essential when examining the athlete's arm for nerve damage. The first and second cervical nerve roots contribute to the spinal accessory nerve. This is the motor nerve to the trapezius, but it lacks a sensory part. The contour of the trapezius should be examined and compared to its counterpart. Trapezius strength may be tested by having the athlete shrug his shoulders against manual resistance. The rhomboid muscles are innervated by the nerve to the rhomboids from the C-5 nerve root; the examiner should observe for wasting of this muscle. The serratus anterior receives its nerve supply by way of the long thoracic nerve; the athlete should perform a wall push-up as a check of his serratus anterior's ability to protract the scapula. The suprascapular nerve supplies motor impulses to the supraspinatus and infraspinatus muscles; atrophy of these muscles should be

looked for. For evaluation of the muscles supplied by the brachial plexus, the examiner should ask the athlete to abduct his shoulder, flex and extend his elbow, and pronate and supinate his forearm against resistance. The examiner should note any numbness or tingling in the arm and do a pinprick sensory examination.

If the athlete's neck is extended and tilted toward the involved side during an examination after a nerve pinch or cervical disk rupture, his symptoms are aggravated. After a brachial plexus injury, pain will increase when his neck is tilted away from the symptomatic side. An electromyogram may help in differentiating between a cervical disk protrusion and an injury to the brachial plexus. With cervical disk protrusion, the electromyogram will show fibrillation in the athlete's paraspinal muscles. When the injury is to the brachial plexus, the paraspinal muscles are normal.

If an athlete suffers a burner or a nerve pinch, his protective gear should be checked. His shoulder pads should be in good condition, fit correctly, be worn separately, and protect him from lateral flexion beyond safe limits. When he shows signs of clinical recovery, his neck, shoulders, and upper back should be restrengthened. He must recover full sensation and strength before being allowed to return to practice, and he may need protective straps or a neck roll. His blocking and tackling technique should also be reevaluated.

If an athlete feels well after a burner and the clinical examination findings are normal, he may return to the game. He should, however, be checked after the game, the next day, and several days later because there may be ischemia and delayed nerve damage. After neuropraxia, with damage only to the myelin sheath, the player may return to practice in 2 days to 2 weeks.

After the first injury, an athlete is more easily reinjured, possibly because of less space in the foramen owing to swelling and fibrosis. The nerve root remains trapped and vulnerable to movement that may stretch or compress it. An athlete may also have less range of lateral flexion toward the injured side and impaired facet joint function. Long after nerve pinches and burners, he may have neurologic changes and limited neck flexibility and note persistent weakness in his extensor–supinator or flexor–pronator groups of muscles, along with patches of radial or ulnar nerve numbness.

An athlete who suffers recurrent burners in a high-velocity collision sport may have an underlying cervical sagittal stenosis.[32] The stenosis is usually asymptomatic until spondylolysis develops or a hyperextension injury or vertebral subluxation occurs, whereupon the subject may become transiently or permanently quadriplegic. If sagittal stenosis is suspected, a lateral cervical spine film should be taken. The examiner measures the cervical canal width from the middle of the posterior surface of the vertebral body to the nearest point on the ventral surface of the spinous process. From C-3 through C-6, a sagittal diameter ranging from 14.5 mm to 20 mm is within normal limits.

On-the-Field Care of Neck Injuries

The team physician must be constantly alert for the mechanism of injuries. If a player is knocked out, it should be assumed that he has a neck injury.[47] Ammonia capsules should not be used because the injured player may jerk his head away and injure his spinal cord. If he is conscious, a rapid sensory and motor examination should be done to rule out spinal cord injury.

If an athlete has neck pain or a tender neck, he is assumed to have a fracture or a fracture-dislocation. His neck should be supported manually in a neutral position with his head and neck aligned with his spine. Forceful traction is unnecessary, and a pillow should *not* be placed under his head. If he holds his neck in a fixed position, he may have locked facets; no attempt should be made to straighten the neck out, maintaining it instead in the position in which he is holding it.

The player's helmet should remain on, with his facemask swung away or the bars cut with a high-quality, heavy-duty bolt cutter. If the helmet must be removed, two persons should do the job.[43] One rescuer applies inline traction by placing his hands on each side of the helmet with his fingers on the player's mandible, a position that prevents slippage if the chin strap is loose. The chin strap is unsnapped, and a second rescuer places one of his hands at the angle of the player's mandible, the thumb on one side, the long and index fingers on the other. With his other hand, he applies pressure from the occipital region. This maneuver transfers the inline traction responsibility to the second rescuer. The rescuer at the top then removes the helmet, which must be expanded laterally to clear the ears. Throughout the procedure, inline traction is maintained from below to prevent head tilt. After the helmet has been removed, the rescuer at the top replaces his hands on either side of the injured player's head with his palms over the player's ears. This traction is maintained from above until a backboard is in place.

A backboard, rather than a stretcher, should be used for transporting the neck-injured athlete, because it can be placed under him with minimal movement, is rigid, and has an outrigger and buckles that form a four-tailed chin strap. Five men carry the board while a leader at the head gives commands.

Neck Straps and Neck Rolls

To prevent excessive neck motion, a 3.8-cm (1.5-in)-wide semielastic strap may be snapped to the shoulder pad from the rear of the football helmet.[3] Potential liability exists, however, when a helmet is altered in this manner.

Neck collars are the most common shoulder-pad accessories and include standard types, inflatable types, and custom-made models that consist of a rolled towel in stockinette with a string through it. Some players wear an inexpensive collar made of pipe insulation with a shoestring running through it. Stockinette is placed around the pipe insulation and taped.

A cervical collar should encircle the entire neck rather leaving a "V" in the front. Interior linemen, linebackers, and especially those athletes who have had a neck injury should wear collars. A loose-fitting collar has little value, but a properly applied collar will prevent excessive neck motion.

The edges of poorly fitted shoulder pads may drive into the base of the wearer's neck in a pileup. If the pads are too low, they will allow excessive neck motion. On the other hand, a high cantilever pad may be struck by a player's neck and cause injury if he has increased his neck size through strengthening exercises. For this reason, the cantilever pads should be lowered when the player's neck size increases.

Many nerve pinches are associated with wearing professional-type shoulder pads.[10] These pads protect the shoulders adequately, but players of average build and flexibility are especially prone to lateral neck sprain while wearing them. The neck motion of bull-necked players is limited when they wear either high or low shoulder pads, whereas one half of those with average neck length get no protection for lateral flexion from professional shoulder pads. Long-necked, limber athletes receive more protection to lateral flexion than do athletes with average-size necks, since long-necked athletes have greater ranges of motion.

Neck Strengthening

All tackle football players must have strong and flexible necks. Thus, before the season begins, long-necked athletes should add at least 2.5 cm (1 in) of circumference to their necks. Weak-necked athletes should not play football. A strong neck will not prevent a neck fracture from occurring if great force is applied to the bone, but it will aid the athlete in keeping his head in a stable position.[47] This position prepares his neck musculature for contact: He holds his head in about 10° of extension with the occipital line about 10° above the horizontal and his shoulders elevated—

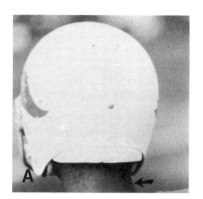
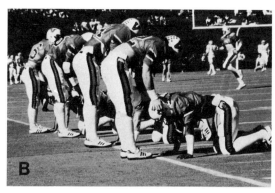

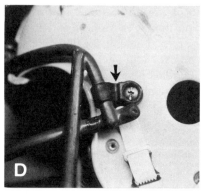

Figure 8-13   Young football players often lack good neck development **(A).** Neck exercises **(B)** play an important part in an athlete's preparation for tackle football. Bridging prepares and protects the athlete's neck but should not be done with a helmet on **(C).** Some face masks can swing away when rubber mounting loops (*arrow*) are cut **(D).**

Bridging

Figure 8-14 "Bridging" is taught stepwise by a skilled instructor.

the "bulled position." Players who tend to duck their heads need special coaching to lessen their chances of injury. Strong neck muscles also prevent fatigue that results from wearing a heavy helmet.

The athlete may strengthen his neck by isometric, isotonic, Tubic, or functional bridging methods. Isometrics may be performed either against the athlete's own hand resistance, the resistance of a hand-held towel, or the hands of a partner during buddy exercises. The contraction is held for 6 seconds and released; three sets of six repetitions should be done.

Isotonic strengthening is achieved with weights attached to the athlete's head by a halter and strung over a wall pulley. The athlete flexes, extends, and obliquely and laterally flexes his neck. A 6-week isotonic wall pulley program can add 3 cm (1.25 in) of circumference to the neck,

compared to a gain of only 1 cm (0.4 in) after an isometric program.[49] Because the shoulder is the base of support for the neck, the athlete should also do shoulder shrugs and high pulls with barbells.

A broad bicycle innertube may be used to resist neck motion. The athlete assumes the positions that may be encountered in his sport and strengthens his neck in these positions. Wrestlers may also perform neck strengthening against the resistance of a knowledgeable partner, with the athlete stopping his neck motion for a brief isometric contraction, then resuming the motion against his partner's manual resistance. This technique simulates the common stops and starts at the different positions encountered in athletics.

Bridging is an athlete's best all-round neck strengthening and flexibility exercise because it tunes his neck to absorb shocks and develops proprioception. Bridging has been criticized unjustly as emphasizing excursion of the neck, causing ligamentous loosening, and "grinding up the neck." Equipment managers oppose bridging in tackle football because it damages helmet suspensions. Bridging on the top of the head in a football helmet produces shearing stress and damages the helmet and the player's neck (Figure 8-13). A correct program will allow the athlete to bridge on his forehead and develop a strong, supple neck (Figure 8-14).

REFERENCES

1. Albrand OW, Corkill G: Broken necks from diving accidents: A summer epidemic in young men. Am J Sports Med 4:107–110, 1976

2. Albright JP et al: Nonfatal cervical spine injuries in interscholastic football. JAMA 236:1243–1245, 1976

3. Andrish JT et al: A method for the management of cervical injuries in football. A preliminary report. Am J Sports Med 8:89–92, 1977

4. Baker TE: A quick and easy method for controlling nosebleeds. First Aider, Cramer 48(5):14, January 1979

5. Bailey RW: Fractures and dislocations of the C-spine. In Adams JP (ed): Current Practice in Orthopedic Surgery. St Louis, CV Mosby, 1969

6. Bennett DR et al: Migraine precipitated by head trauma in athletes. Am J Sports Med 8:202–205, 1980

7. Blyth C, Mueller F: An Epidemiological Study of High School Football Injuries in North Carolina. Final Report of PHS Grant No. FDA00032-02, 1 Washington DC, U.S. Public Health Service

8. Burke DC: Spinal cord injuries from water sports. Med J Aust 2:1190–1194, 1972

9. Carter DR, Frankel VH: Biomechanics of hyperextension injuries to the cervical spine in football. Am J Sports Med 8:302–309, 1980

10. Chrisman OD, Snook G: Lateral flexion neck injuries in athletics. JAMA 192:613–615, 1965

11. Clancy WG et al: Upper trunk brachial plexus injuries in contact sport. Am J Sports Med 5:209–216, 1977

12. Cooper DL, Fair J: Treating "cauliflower ear." Phys Sportsmed 4(7):103, 1976

13. Danielson LG, Westlin NE: Riding accidents. Acta Orthop Scand 44:597–603, 1973

14. DeVoe AG: Injuries to the eye. Am J Surg 98:384–389, 1959

15. DiBartolomeo JR: Exostotic ear tumors—sea water sport peril. Phys Sportsmed 4(7):60–63, 1976

16. Dove A: Case report: Rotary subluxation of the first cervical vertebra. Phys Sportsmed 7(9):115–119, 1979

17. Easterbrook M: Eye protection for squash and racquetball players. Phys Sportsmed 9(2):79–82, 1981

18. Eichel BS: Otologic hazards in water sports. Phys Sportsmed 2(7):43–45, 1974

19. Eichel BS, Bray DA: Management of hematoma of the wrestler's ear. Phys Sportsmed 6(11):87–90, 1978

20. Farber GA: Football acne—an acneiform eruption. Cutis 20:356–360, 1977

21. Feldick HG, Albright JP: Football survey reveals "missed" neck injuries. Phys Sportsmed 4(10):77–81, 1976

22. Fowler BJ: Ocular injuries sustained playing squash, Am J Sports Med 8:126–128, 1980

23. Fowler EP Jr, Osmum PM: New bone growth due to cold water in the ears. Arch Otolaryngol 36:455, 1942

24. Frackel WH: Facial injuries in sports. Am J Surg 98:390–393, 1959

25. Funk FJ, Wells RE: Injuries of the cervical spine in football. Clin Orthop 109:50–58, 1975

26. Garber JN: Fracture and fracture-dislocation of the cervical spine. In Hoyt WA Jr (ed): Symposium on the Spine. St Louis, CV Mosby, 1969

27. Garner AI: Correct eye disorders to improve performance. First Aider, Cramer 46(8):2–3, 1977

28. Garner AI: Athletes are endangered by unsafe eyewear. First Aider, Cramer 47(3):3, 1977

29. Garner AI: Can your athletes really see? Athletic Training, 14:156–157, 1979

30. Gierup JM et al: Incidence and nature of horse-riding injuries. Acta Chir Scand 142:57–61, 1976

31. Good RP, Nickel VL: Cervical spine injuries resulting from water sports. Spine 5:502–506, 1980

32. Grant TT, Puffer J: Cervical stenosis: a development anomaly with quadriparesis during football. Am J Sports Med 4:219–221, 1976

33. Gross CG: Treating "cauliflower ear" with silicone mold. Am J Sports Med 6:4, 1978

34. Grossman JAI et al: Equestrian injuries: Results of a prospective study. JAMA 240:1881–1882, 1978

35. Hardesty WH et al: Study on vertebral artery blood flow in man. Surg Gynecol Obstet 116:662–664, 1963

36. Hayes D et al: Effects of intraoral mouth guards in ventilation. Phys Sportsmed 5(1):61–66, 1977

37. Head Protection for the Cyclist: A Medical Inquiry. American Medical Association Meeting. Washington, DC, 14 April 1977

38. Heimlich HJ: The Heimlich Maneuver: Where it stands today. Emergency Med 10:89, 1978

39. Heimlich HJ, Uhley MJ: The Heimlich maneuver. Clin Symp 31(3):3–32, 1979

40. Heintz WD: Mouth protectors: A progress report. J. Am Dent Assoc 77:632–636, 1968

41. Heintz WD: The case for mandatory mouth protectors. Sports Med 3:61–63, 1975

42. Heintz WD: Mouth protection in sports. Phys Sportsmed 7(2):45–46, 1979

43. Helmet Removal from Injured Patients: American College of Surgeons Committee on Trauma. QJ Am Assoc Automotive Med 2(4):2, 1980

44. Herrick RT: Clay-shoveler's fracture in powerlifting: A case report. Am J Sports Med 9:29–30, 1981

45. Hickey JC et al: The relation of mouth protectors to cranial pressure and deformation. J Am Dent Assoc 74:735–740, 1967

46. Landro L: Riding injuries stir British medical concern. Phys Sportsmed 4(10):125–129, 1976

47. Leidholt JB: Spinal injuries in athletes: Be prepared. Orthop Clin North Am 4:691–707, 1973

48. MacFie DD: ENT problems of diving. Med Serv J Can 20:845, 1964

49. Maroon JC et al: A system for preventing athletic neck injuries. Phys Sportsmed 5(10):77–79, 1977

50. Matthews WB: Footballer's migraine. Br Med J 2:326–327, 1972

51. Mawdsley C, Ferguson FR: Neurological disease in boxers. Lancet 2:799–801, 1963

52. Middleton J: Football spine pad protection for baseball catchers: Athletic Training 15:82, 1980

53. Nelson WE et al: Syncope, bradychardia and hypotension after a lacrosse shot to the neck: Management and prevention. Phys Sportsmed 9(8):94–97, 1981

54. Odess JS: The hearing hazard of firearms. Phys Sportsmed 2(10):65–68, 1974

55. Odess JS: Acoustic trauma of sportsman hunter due to gun firing. Laryngoscope 82:1971–1989, 1972

56. Ogden FW: Effect of gunfire upon auditory acuity for pure tones and the efficacy of ear plugs as protectors. Laryngoscope 60:993–1012, 1950

57. Oppenheimer P et al: Repair of traumatic-myringoruptue. Arch Otolaryngol 73:328–333, 1961

58. Pashby TJ: Eye injuries in Canadian amateur hockey. Am J Sports Med 7:254–257, 1979

59. Philo H, Stine G: The liability path to safer helmets. Trial Magazine 13:38–40, 1977

60. Pipkin G: Caloric labyrinthitis: A cause of drowning. Case report of a swimmer who survived through self-rescue. Am J Sports Med 7:260–261, 1979

61. Reid SE et al: Head protection in football. Phys Sportsmed 2(2):86–92, 1974

62. Richards RN: Rescuing the spine-injured diver. Phys Sportsmed 1(9):63–65, 1973

63. Rogers L, Sweeney PJ: Stroke: A neurological complication of wrestling. A case of brainstem stroke in a 17-year-old athlete. Am J Sports Med 7:352–354, 1979

64. Roydhouse N: Earaches and adolescent swimmers. In: Swimming Medicine IV. International Series on Sport Science. vol 6, pp 79–85 (Eriksson B, Durberg B, eds). Baltimore, University Park Press, 1977

65. Ryan AJ (moderator): Round table discussion: Eye protection for athletes. Phys Sportsmed 6(9):43–67, 1978

66. Schneider RC: Head and Neck Injuries in Football. Baltimore, Williams & Williams, 1973

67. Schneider RC, Antine BE: Visual fields impairment related to football headgear and face-guards. JAMA 192:616–618, 1965

68. Schwartz R, Novich MM: The athlete's mouthpiece. Am J Sports Med 8:357–359, 1980

69. Seelenfreund MH, Freilich DB: Rushing the net and retinal detachment. JAMA 235:2723–2736, 1976

70. Smith M: Contact lenses and athletes. Trainer's corner. Phys Sportsmed 6(4):124, 1978

71. Stenger JM et al: Mouthguards. J Am Dent Assoc 19:263, 1964

72. Stenger JM et al: Mouthguards. J Am Dent Assoc 69:273–281, 1964

73. Strauss MB et al: Swimmer's ear. Phys Sportsmed 7(6):101–105, 1979

74. Taylor GD, Williams E: Acoustic trauma in the sports hunter. Laryngoscope 76:863–879, 1966

75. Torg JS: Unusual fractures caused by football helmet impact. Phys Sportsmed 4(11):73–75, 1976

76. Torg J et al: The National Football Head and Neck Injury Registry: Report and Conclusions 1978. JAMA 241:1477–1479, 1979

77. Torg JS et al: Collision with spring-loaded football tackling and blocking dummies. Report of near fatal and fatal injuries. JAMA 236:1270–1271, 1976

78. Turcotte H: Scuba divers answer the challenge of the sea. Phys Sportsmed 5(8):67–68, 1977

79. Underwood J: The Death of an American Game: The Crisis in Football. Boston, Little, Brown, 1979

80. Verschoth A: Weak? Sink your teeth into this. Sports Illustrated 54:36–42, 1980

81. Vinger PF: Sports-related eye injury. A preventable problem. Surv Opthalmol 25:47–51, 1980

82. Virgin HH: Cineradiographic study of football helmets and the cervical spine. Am J Sports Med 8:310–317, 1980

CHAPTER

9

The Shoulder

The shoulder comprises four joints: sterno-clavicular, acromioclavicular, glenohumeral, and scapulothoracic (Figure 9-1). Although it serves as a base for the upper extremity, the shoulder is the most mobile of joints, with relatively little bony stability except that lent by the capsular and musculotendinous structures. Many shoulder injuries in athletics occur to these soft structures.

The sternoclavicular joint is stabilized by ligaments and often contains a fibrocartilaginous meniscus. The acromioclavicular joint may also contain an intra-articular disk that degenerates with age. The joint capsule is weak but is strengthened by fibers of the deltoid and trapezius muscles. The coracoid process of the scapula is closely related to the acromioclavicular joint and extends forward like a crow's beak—hence the term "coracoid" from the Greek "korax," "the crow." Arising from the coracoid are the pector-

alis minor, the conjoined tendon of the coraco-brachialis and short head of the biceps, the coracohumeral ligament, the coracoacromial ligament, and the coracoclavicular ligaments. The coracoclavicular ligament comprises conoid and trapezoid portions that strengthen the nearby acromioclavicular joint and lend vertical stability to the clavicle. The coracoid and its attached muscles and ligaments stabilize the scapula while muscles flex the arm and forearm.

The glenohumeral joint is the major shoulder joint. The humeral head is three times larger than the glenoid socket, and the arcs of the joint surfaces differ. The socket is shallow but is deepened by the glenoid labrum, the fibrocarti-laginous origin of the joint capsule. The tendon of the long head of the biceps starts at the supro-glenoid rim of the scapula and extends extrasy-novially, but intracapsularly, through the shoul-

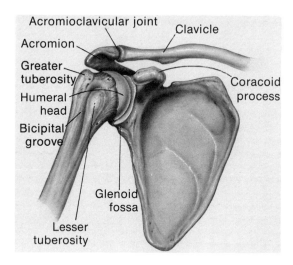

Figure 9-1   The humerus and scapula join at the glenohumeral joint to form the true shoulder joint. The acromioclavicular joint is a satellite joint of the shoulder.

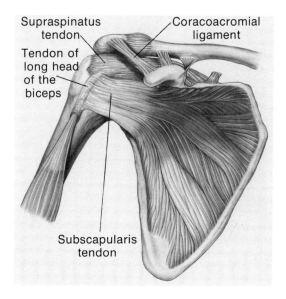

Figure 9-2   The rotator cuff "captures" the humeral head and can rotate it. The supraspinatus part of the cuff passes under the acromion and the strong, flat coracoacromial ligament.

der joint. It then passes into the bicipital groove under the transverse humeral ligament. The bicipital groove angles medially about 30° from the course of the biceps tendon in the arm, and its medial wall may vary from steep to shallow. A supratubercular prominence on the humerus will sometimes irritate the biceps tendon above the point where the tendon passes into the groove.

The short rotators of the shoulder comprise the rotator cuff (Figure 9-2). They retain the humeral head in the glenoid and maintain the instant center of rotation in a fixed position while the deltoid abducts the shoulder. The supraspinatus does not initiate abduction of the shoulder but instead has a quantitative action throughout abduction and forward flexion. This may be proved by paralyzing the supraspinatus muscle with local anesthesia around the supraspinous nerve.[58] The completeness of the paralysis is checked by electromyography. Even though the supraspinatus is paralyzed, the subject will be able to move his shoulder against gravity through a full range of motion. His abduction power and endurance, however, will decrease with his arm held in 90° of abduction and with weights in his hand. Because the same results hold for forward lifting, the supraspinatus has only a quantitative

role in shoulder abduction and flexion. It functions to retract the joint capsule and to hold the head in the glenoid while the deltoid abducts the arm.

The bony acromion and the coracoacromial ligament compose the coracoacromial arch (Figure 9-3). The ligament forms a soft roof for the rotator cuff, intra-articular portion of the biceps tendon, and humeral head. It may also be a stabilizer that counteracts the pull of the conjoined tendon during the skeletal development of the coracoid process. The underlying subacromial bursa and supraspinatus tendon may, however, impinge on this ligament and become irritated.

As the athlete abducts his shoulder, the humerus is depressed by the rotators so that the tuberosities may pass under the coracoacromial arch. If the arm is kept in internal rotation during abduction, the greater tuberosity impinges on the arch, and the arm can only abduct to about 60°. When the athlete externally rotates his arm, however, the greater tuberosity may pass under the arch.

Scapulohumeral motion should be smooth and coordinated. During the first 30° to 60° of

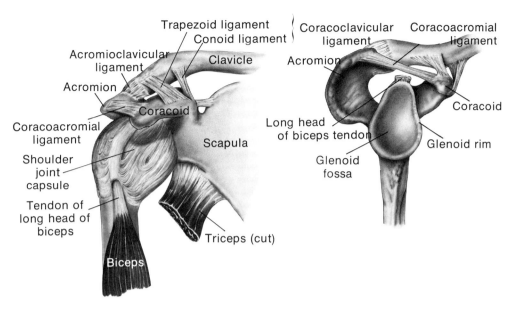

Figure 9-3   A shoulder seen from the anterior aspect *(left)*, and then looking into the glenoid *(right)*.

abduction or forward flexion—the "setting phase"—the scapula seeks a stable position. The scapula then moves laterally with the humerus in a ratio of 1° of scapular movement for every 2° of humeral movement. Thus for every 30° that the arm is elevated, the humerus moves 20° and the scapula 10°. This scapular movement preserves the resting length of the deltoid.

EXAMINING THE SHOULDER

The athlete's shoulder should be examined systematically, with the examiner first observing for undue prominences, as from an acromioclavicular separation and for muscular hypertrophy or atrophy. Some athletes have normally hypertrophied muscles, as in the case of the latissimus dorsi of a baseball pitcher or of a veteran tennis player. Scapulohumeral rhythm is next assessed as the athlete abducts his shoulder to determine whether there are any hitches, hiking, or substitutions in this motion.

The athlete's neck should always be examined during a shoulder evaluation, since a neck disorder may be causing the shoulder pain. As the athlete rotates his neck, and with his neck turned

to one side, the examiner presses on the vertex of the athlete's skull to see if he reports any discomfort or arm pain that may indicate a disk problem. Adson's maneuver is done by having the athlete turn his head away from the arm to be tested; the examiner then raises the arm to see if the radial pulse disappears, an indication of a possible thoracic outlet problem.

A systematic shoulder examination should start in front and work around the shoulder to the back. The sternoclavicular joint is first palpated. If the athlete has landed on his hand, forces may have been transmitted up to this joint; blows from the lateral side of the shoulder may also disrupt it. The examiner next walks his fingers along the entire clavicle, checking the area of insertion of the trapezius into the clavicle and the medialmost origin of the deltoid from the clavicle. The coracoclavicular ligament area and the acromioclavicular joint are palpated, and the clavicle is pressed at the acromioclavicular joint to see whether it moves. The coracoid process is next felt; even a normal coracoid, however, may be tender to deep pressure.

The anterior capsule of the shoulder lies about one fingerbreadth lateral to the coracoid. While this area is being palpated, the athlete's arm should be rotated internally and then externally. If the tender spot does not move, the anterior capsule may be implicated.

The stability of the athlete's glenohumeral joint may be tested with the subject supine by pulling and pushing the humerus forward and back, trying to produce subluxation. In a more dynamic test for shoulder stability, the athlete externally rotates his arm and then presses forward against the examiner's manual resistance while the examiner pushes the humeral head forward. The examiner next feels over the bicipital groove for the long head of the biceps tendon, first with the shoulder rotated internally and then with it rotated externally. If the tender area moves with shoulder rotation, the biceps tendon is the probable structure involved. A test for a dislocating biceps tendon may also be made with the arm abducted to 90° and the examiner rotating it from internal to external rotation. If a slip is felt or a pop heard, the tendon of the long head of his biceps may be dislocating. The examiner next abducts the athlete's arm to 70° and palpates under the acromion for a tender supraspinatus tendon or subacromial bursa. At this level of abduction, the greater tuberosity is just passing under the coracoacromial arch where impingement may occur.

The rotator cuff may be tender, and sometimes the shoulder will pop when the arm is rotated. A roughened or torn anterior part of the cuff may be detected by rotating the arm and feeling under the deltoid. The arm is extended to palpate the anterior part of the cuff, and when the athlete grasps his opposite shoulder with his hand or lies prone with his arm hanging over the examining table, the posterior part of the cuff is uncovered and may be palpated. The examiner should ask the athlete to simulate the shoulder motion that hurts, and by offering resistance to this movement the examiner may be able to locate the trouble spot.

Throwers may develop latissimus dorsi tightness, and athletes who do heavy bench presses in the off-season may have pectoralis major tightness, resulting in an internal rotation contracture. This may be checked with the athlete supine: His chest is held down on the examining table and the shoulder rotated externally.

The scapula is examined with the subject prone and his arm hanging over the examining table. The short rotators and the large muscles that anchor the scapula to the thorax may then be palpated from behind. The shoulder is moved to uncover the region under the scapula, and the chest wall may be palpated.

"BACKPACK PALSY"

Campers, hikers, and mountain climbers often wear heavy backpacks, and the infantry type—lightweight aluminum frame with heavy web shoulder straps (Figure 9-4)—may damage the upper trunk of the backpacker's brachial plexus, producing a severe and prolonged disability. There is a striking predilection for damage to the nondominant side, perhaps because it is relatively weak. Such damage is similar to Erb's pa-

Figure 9-4   A heavy backpack may cause "backpack palsy."

ralysis from breech deliveries or from lateral flexion injuries of the neck. An affected backpacker may have significant radial and musculocutaneous nerve dysfunction but usually only minimal median nerve deficit. The ulnar nerve is spared.

Early diagnosis allows a good recovery. The suprascapular and axillary nerves are checked by ascertaining the strength of the supraspinatus and deltoid muscles. Sensory changes are checked over the lateral upper arm in the sensory region of the C-5 and C-6 nerve roots.

A backpacker with a nerve injury should refrain from wearing the backpack and should strengthen his shoulder muscles, especially on the nondominant side. When the hiker resumes wearing the pack, he should limit the weight he carries.

THORACIC OUTLET PROBLEMS

Many anatomic abnormalities and some injuries may narrow the space through which an athlete's arteries, veins, and nerves enter his arm. These may include cervical ribs, a prominent transverse process of C-7, anomalies of the first rib, excessive callus around a clavicle fracture, or a malunited clavicular fracture intruding on this space. A shoulder drooped from heavy use may also narrow this space. Moreover, during the abduction, extension, and extreme external humeral rotation phase of throwing, the pectoralis minor stretches, transiently occluding the second portion of the axillary artery.

The symptoms of thoracic outlet compromise may be neurologic, venous, arterial, or a combination of these.[54] Venous compromise produces edema, limb stiffness, venous engorgement of the arm, and sometimes thrombophlebitis.[59] Arterial involvement may produce a cool, pale limb with claudication.[57] The sympathetic nerves may also be irritated, causing a Raynaud's phenomenon, with worsening after prolonged activity. Irritation of the brachial plexus produces numbness and tingling, and the arm feels weak and heavy and tires easily. The pain is usually around the elbow but may also be in the chest, neck, shoulder, forearm, or hand.

Arterial occlusion may occur in baseball pitchers,[57] resulting in a painful, weak, and tired pitching arm. Arteriograms will show the occlusion, and thrombectomy and bypass vein graft, followed by rehabilitation, may enable the player to return to high-level pitching. In one case, a shortstop developed acute swelling and numbness in his throwing arm. Cinevenogram revealed acute occlusion of the subclavian vein from compression by his first rib. The compression was relieved by resection of the first rib.

Tennis players with a heavy, drooped, and internally rotated racket arm shoulder may develop neck and arm pain owing to nerve compression.[47] This "tennis shoulder" may be helped by shrugging exercises that strengthen the shoulder elevators, elevating the shoulder to relieve the compression.

When examining athletes for thoracic outlet compromise, the examiner should ask them to mimic the activity that produces the discomfort. Local problems must first be ruled out before checking for referred causes. A cervical disk or compression in the quadrilateral space, for example, may be causing the shoulder or elbow pain. Tests such as a cervical myelogram, a Doppler examination of arterial and venous blood flow, cinevenography, arteriography, electromyography, or nerve conduction studies may be needed to ascertain the diagnosis.

Most compression problems may be initially managed nonoperatively with a sling, anti-inflammatory medicine, and exercises. The athlete's upper, middle, and lower trapezius muscle fibers are strengthened, along with the serratus anterior and erector spinae, to elevate the drooped shoulder.[7] Thrombectomy, bypass graft, or first rib resection may be needed.

THE STERNOCLAVICULAR JOINT

The sternoclavicular joint is located at the base of the shoulder strut. Forces from landing on the hand may be transmitted to this area, and blows to the side of the shoulder may even dislocate this joint. In an anterior dislocation, the joint capsule is torn and may interpose to block reduction. This dislocation may be seen when a tangential view of the sternoclavicular joint is taken with the beam angled along the opposite clavicle. The dislocation may result in grating, clicking, and popping when the athlete moves his arm overhead or rotates his shoulder.

An anterior dislocation may be reduced by abducting the athlete's arm and pulling the shoulder girdle backward with arm traction and then manipulating the clavicle. These reductions are often hard to hold with the usual figure-eight bandage; some surgeons, therefore, use a fascial sling between the clavicle and the first rib or perform a subclavius muscle tenodesis to hold the clavicle in place.

Upon returning to athletic activity after anterior dislocation of the sternoclavicular joint, the athlete may note aching and swelling, grating, clicking or popping, and fatigue in that area. When these signs appear, a short portion of the inner end of the clavicle may be resected.

Retrosternal dislocation of the clavicle at the sternoclavicular joint may exert pressure on the trachea and great vessels, threatening the athlete's life.[1, 25] It may produce dysphagia, a snorting type of breathing, and even neurovascular trouble in the upper extremity. The dislocation should be reduced immediately. For this procedure, the athlete lies supine with a sandbag between his shoulders or with his shoulder extended over the table edge. Traction is then applied to his arm with his shoulder abducted and extended. His clavicle may have to be grasped through the skin with a towel clip and then maneuvered up and forward so that it snaps into place. After reduction, the athlete must wear a Velpeau bandage for 3 to 4 weeks and then begin motion exercises. Because of the contour of the joint and the ripped ligaments, these reductions are often unstable. Even so, pins should not be used to hold the reduction because they may migrate.

THE CLAVICLE

When an athlete falls, he may extend his arms to absorb the shock. The clavicle may snap, however, especially in jockeys, equestrians, or motocross racers who fall from a height or are thrown into the air. Rodeo cowboys who ride broncos and bulls, rope calves, and wrestle steers commonly fracture their clavicles. These men, however, usually know from experience how to fall, and they try not to land with their arms outstretched.

In youth ice hockey, broken clavicles are common, not so much from direct contact but from indirect transmitted force, when the skater falls on the ice or crashes into the boards.[40] Shoulder pads with a polyethylene cap protect the players from direct trauma but are not effective against forces transmitted up the arm.

An angled clavicle x-ray film, with the athlete bowed backward, will reveal any displacement. Clavicle fractures are usually treated with a figure-eight bandage and a sling with an icebag wrapped over the fracture. While wearing the figure-eight, the athlete must work to maintain the strength and endurance of his other limbs to avoid falling behind during the treatment phase.

DELTOID STRAIN, BRUISED SHOULDER, AND "SHOULDER POINTER"

Arm tackling may cause an anterior deltoid strain; these strained shoulders should be iced and taped before the athlete goes home and iced as needed later. Heat should *not* be applied. Shoulder bruises may follow firearm recoil in marksmen, but most marksmen wear a shoulder pad to prevent such bruising.

Shoulder injuries account for one third of all injuries in rugby union, and many of these impairments are bruises.[35] A "shoulder pointer" is a contusion to the trapezius or to the deltoid muscle around the shoulder. Trapezius fibers may be avulsed where the muscle inserts into the posterior edge of the clavicle close to, but not at, the point of the acromioclavicular joint. Cryotherapy is effective for shoulder pointers, and a local anesthetic and steroid may be injected, as in a hip pointer.

Modifications of rugby have led to tackle football. In rugby union, however, blocking is not permitted, and the object is to go after the ball rather than the runner. Some rugby players wear soft foam shoulder pads, and rugby forwards may have light felt pads sewn into the jerseys over the point of the shoulder. Rigid protective equipment probably would be counterproductive, because players would then increase their impact speed.

SUBACROMIAL SHOULDER PAIN

Repetitive overhead movements can lead to sub-acromial shoulder pain. (Figure 9-5). Swimmers develop tendinitis, older athletes develop calcific tendinitis and bursitis, and throwing athletes may erode and tear a rotator cuff. The acromion and coracoacromial ligament overlie the humeral head with the subacromial bursa and supraspinatous tendon in-between. The bursa is a large and redundant one. The supraspinatus tendon is the superior part of the rotator cuff. The suba-

cromial area can become crowded if bone spurs form (Figure 9-6), soft tissue structures swell, or a tear occurs.

"SWIMMER'S SHOULDER"

A swimmer who trains by swimming up to 18,000 meters a day may develop shoulder pain, since 80% of the power in swimming comes from arm action. If we assume 15 strokes for each 22.5 meters and if the swimmer trains at 9000 meters a

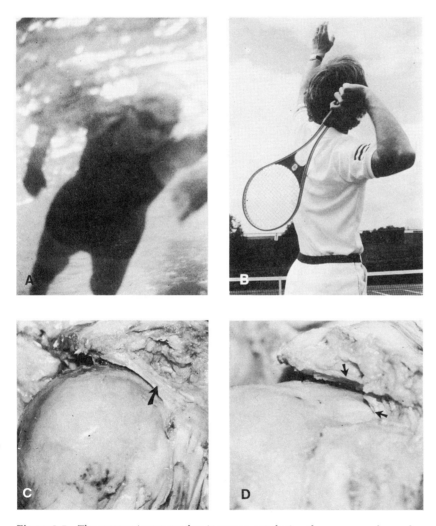

Figure 9-5   The supraspinatus tendon is wrung out during the recovery phase of the freestyle stroke **(A).** Subacromial impingement may occur during overhead activities in tennis **(B).** The coracoacromial ligament **(C)** is responsible for many impingement problems. After the ligament has been resected **(D),** the supraspinatus moves much more freely.

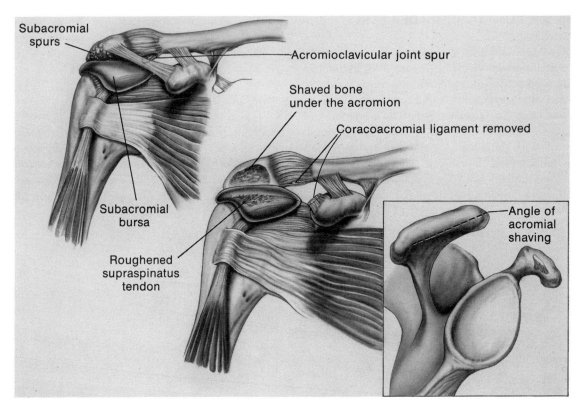

Figure 9-6 A spurred acromion or spurred acromioclavicular joint can produce subacromial bursitis or roughen the supraspinatus tendon to produce a tendinitis. In pitchers, the spurs may be removed and the acromion beveled. In swimmers, the coracoacromial ligament is removed.

day, with 60% freestyle, butterfly, or backstroke, each arm goes through about 10,800 repetitive motions a week. The butterfly stroke is similar to the freestyle stroke except for the body roll, and the backstroke is remarkably similar to the freestyle stroke. As the arm is near the swimmer's side or as the forward-flexed shoulder is rotated internally, the humeral head abuts against the acromion and the coracoacromial ligament. This impingement may irritate subjacent structures. The microvascular pattern of the rotator cuff has been studied with micropaque injections. The supraspinatus tendon is wrung out, especially when the swimmer adducts and then internally rotates his arm. During internal rotation and forward flexion, the greater tuberosity abuts against the acromion. The supraspinatus tendon also has an avascular zone when the arm is abducted. This

has been found to be true even in cadavers of persons younger than 20 years of age. The avascular zone is about 1 cm proximal to the point of insertion of the supraspinatus. The intracapsular part of the biceps becomes stretched over the humeral head and also has an avascular zone. These are vulnerable vascular patterns, in which chronic irritation leads to a death of cells and inflammation, subacromial bursitis, calcific tendinitis, and rotator cuff tears.

The incidence of painful shoulders in swimmers ranges from 40% to 60%. It is slightly more common on the breathing side and most likely to occur in sprinters and middle-distance swimmers because of the "explosiveness" of each stroke. Women suffer from painful shoulders more often than do men, perhaps because of their higher stroke turnover rate. The condition is rare in swimmers younger than 10 years of age, probably because of shorter workouts. More than 50% of 13- to 18-year-old swimmers, however, complain of shoulder pain, mostly those not doing weight training or flexibility work.

The classification system that defines the severity of swimmer's shoulder is similar to that used to classify jumper's knee. In phase I, the swimmer has pain only after activity; in phase II, he has pain both during and after activity but still can compete normally and his condition is not disabling; in phase III, the swimmer cannot compete at his normal level; and, in phase IV, he has pain even with everyday living.

CALCIFIC TENDINITIS

As the athlete abducts his arm, especially with the palm down, the greater tuberosity moves under the arch and the bursa, the biceps tendon, and the critical zone of the supraspinatus tendon can be impinged upon. Impingement occurs against the anterior edge of the acromion and the coracoacromial ligament and not, as was earlier thought, against the lateral edge of the acromion. This friction leads to inflammation and edema, which in turn leads to more friction in a cycle of discomfort and attrition of the midportion of the tendon and deposition of calcium in the degenerated tissue (Figure 9-7). The calcium deposit enlarges and may become the size of an acorn. When the athlete abducts his shoulder the deposit will crunch, catch, and hurt. Inflammation in the bursa around the calcium deposit may make the shoulder so sore that it cannot be abducted. A frozen shoulder may result.

ROTATOR CUFF TEARS

When a baseball pitcher's hypertrophied rotator cuff passes through the confined subacromial place, it can become inflamed. A pitcher's cuff will be physiologically older than the pitcher's chronological age.

There are four stages to rotator cuff problems leading to cuff tears. In stage I, the cuff is inflamed and swollen, and the supraspinatus becomes con-

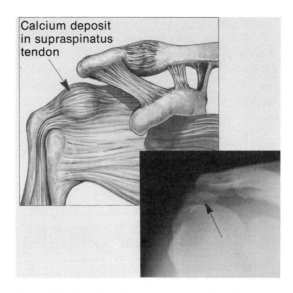

Calcium deposit in supraspinatus tendon

Figure 9-7   Calcium *(arrow)* may deposit in the relatively avascular "critical area" of the supraspinatus tendon. A true anteroposterior x-ray film taken with the arm externally rotated and the x-ray tube angled down 20° shows the deposit best.

tracted and atrophies. Later, collagen fibers are damaged but not yet torn and the bursa becomes thickened. In stage II, collagen fibers break down within the substance of the tendon. This intratendinous horizontal cleavage tear can cause pain, swelling of the cuff, and subacromial impingement. They are the most common tears and are forerunners of the undersurface tears and complete tears.

Pain is the predominant symptom of the rotator cuff tear. It begins as a deep ache in the shoulder, especially at night. Because of pain, the athlete may have to stop throwing, but this layoff may lead to weakness of his rotator cuff. When he returns to throwing his cuff fatigues, and the athlete may drop his elbow and substitute other shoulder muscles. This can lead to further impingement as the shoulder is pushed up and jammed against the acromion.

In stage III, the deep part of the tendon may break and form a flap. The bursa will be thickened. Because of the flap the athlete may now report catching in addition to the pain. In stage IV, the tear extends through the substance of the tendon completely and the bursa is thickened. A cuff will only rarely tear acutely. If this happens, it is usually in an older athlete (over age 40). It may occur during a fall in skiing or when an equestrian's arm is jerked by a horse while the reins are wrapped around her hand.

EXAMINING FOR SUBACROMIAL PROBLEMS

To examine the subacromial region of the shoulder, the examiner tests for impingement and a "painful arc" and assesses the rotator cuff.

Impingement

Subacromial impingement may be reproduced by either raising and rotating the shoulder or by raising the shoulder and jamming it. In the first case, the athlete abducts or flexes his arm to 90°. With the arm so elevated, he adducts it across his chest and rotates it inward. This movement may be painful as the subacromial structures are pressed against the coracoacromial ligament.

Alternatively, the athlete raises his arm with his palm down while it is positioned 30° in front of the plane of his body. The examiner depresses the scapula manually by holding the top of the shoulder and at the same time raises the arm. These maneuvers jam the subacromial structures against the coracoacromial ligament and the anterior acromion, and the resulting pain may make the athlete grimace.

"Painful Arc"

Calcific tendinitis may produce a "painful arc." To test the smoothness of abduction, the examiner can place a finger at the inferior angle of each scapula. During normal abduction, the scapula does not shift much during early abduction and then moves suddenly and significantly upward and laterally at about 90°. In the case of a painful arc, the athlete will hike the shoulder rather than abduct it smoothly. Once the inflamed part of the tendon has passed proximal to the coracoacromial arch, abduction will again become smooth.

The Rotator Cuff

When the rotator cuff tears, the supraspinatus muscle atrophies in the suprascapular fossa. The examiner may elicit grinding, crepitus, or clicking by placing his palm over the painful shoulder and then should compare this shoulder to the normal one. Most of the shoulder weakness comes from deltoid atrophy from reduced use of the arm owing to pain.

Specific weakness of the supraspinatus muscle would indicate a tear in the supraspinatus tendon. To test the supraspinatus the examiner stands behind the athlete with one hand on his elbow and the other on his opposite hip. The athlete then raises his arm with his thumb down 30° in front of the plane of his body. In this position the supraspinatus is straight and isolated on top of the humeral head. The examiner should advise the athlete that he will not be too strong in this position and should, therefore, not start the movement too vigorously.

For the examiner to palpate the rotator cuff, the overlying deltoid must be relaxed. If the athlete lies on his side and supports his head with the affected arm, the deltoid will relax and the front and top of the cuff can be easily palpated. This is the head rest or "TV watching" position. To palpate the back of the cuff, the examiner asks the athlete to lie prone with his arm hanging over the edge of the examining table. In this position, the posterior deltoid moves forward to allow easy palpation of the posterior part of the cuff. The posterior joint capsule may also be felt just above the teres minor. In this prone position, the examiner can fix the scapula and measure internal and external rotation of the shoulder.

X-ray Films, Arthrograms, and Magnetic Resonance Imaging (MRI)

A plain x-ray film may show spurs under the acromion, sclerosis or cysts at the area of insertion of the supraspinatus into the greater tuberosity of the humerus, or a calcium deposit in the supraspinatus tendon. The film should be taken with the tube angled slightly downward to show the acromion best and with the arm externally rotated to expose a calcium deposit.

A shoulder arthrogram can reveal whether an athlete's rotator cuff is torn. However, the arthrogram will be negative in stage I. In stage II, the test will also be negative because the dye cannot leak through the tendon into the intratendinous tear. In a stage III tear, the dye will indent the tendon and the tear will also be visible at arthoscopy. In a stage IV tear, the dye will leak through the torn tendon into the subacromial bursa (Figure 9-8). Sometimes, however, a thin layer of tissue covers the tear and the dye cannot leak through. This is why it is important to exercise the shoulder after the dye has been instilled so that the dye can work its way through the tear.

Magnetic resonance imaging (MRI) can also reveal whether an athlete's rotator cuff is torn. Further, an MRI may reveal stage II intratendinous tears.

TREATMENT OF SUBACROMIAL PROBLEMS

The treatment of subacromial problems ranges from rest and exercise to injections, relatively minor operations, and even to major operations.

"Swimmer's Shoulder"

Treatment of a swimmer's shoulder pain should begin at phase I or II rather than at an advanced phase. During the early phases, a swimmer may be switched to sprints to decrease his training distance. In addition, a change to another stroke allows cardiovascular conditioning and avoids the aggravating movement. For example, the butterfly stroke may be free of pain even though the freestyle stroke hurts. The swimmer should be on a full range-of-motion program during his training and should ice his shoulder immediately after a workout. There is a great reduction in swimmers' shoulder problems when swimmers stretch thoroughly before entering the water. The stretching increases the blood flow, lubricates, and gently stretches the rotator cuff. A short course of phenylbutazone is sometimes used in diminishing doses to reduce the inflammation.

If the swimmer needs rest in phase III, he is put on dry-land exercises and a kickboard program. A steroid injection is sometimes given if a vital meet is upcoming. The swimmer may work on a high arm recovery technique because this technique seems to produce fewer shoulder problems. Bilateral breathing also helps; otherwise one arm always catches deeper than the other.

Surgery is recommended in phase IV.[45] The swimmer's coracoacromial ligament should be resected, for if merely transected it will grow back. Older swimmers may need some bony decompression, achieved by shaving the undersurface of the acromion without disrupting the deltoid.

The coracoacromial ligament may be resected before chronic changes occur. X-ray films usually

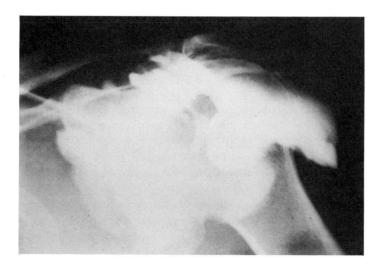

Figure 9-8 In this arthrogram, a full-thickness rotator cuff tear allows injected dye to escape from the shoulder joint.

show normal findings, there is good shoulder strength and motion, and the cine studies and clinical examinations do not show instability. Arthrograms do not reveal any communication with the subacromial space, and subacromial bursagrams show the bursa to be normal or small. If these subjects do not significantly improve after a rest, including a minimum of 6 weeks free from the aggravating activity, they should undergo an operation.

In this procedure, a strap incision is made under local anesthesia, extending from the acromioclavicular joint to the coracoid process. The deltoid is split and then detached for about 2 cm along the acromion. The athlete is asked to reproduce the pop, and the ligament is then cut and partly excised. He is then asked to reproduce the motion again and should volunteer that the impingement is no longer present. Postoperatively, he gradually regains motion, followed by strengthening. Although the shoulder pain and popping are relieved after resection of the coracoacromial ligament, some athletes will feel a lack of constraint of the humeral head, as when spiking a volleyball.

Calcific Tendinitis

A calcium deposit in the supraspinatus tendon may inflame the surrounding tissue, click, crunch, pop, and impinge and reduce shoulder motion to produce a "frozen shoulder." Rest, antiinflammatory medicine, and pulsed ultrasound may reduce the inflammation. Hydrocortisone or acetic acid iontophoresis may reduce the size of the calcium deposit, and the deposit may even disappear. If the calcium is in a less chalky form it may sometimes be aspirated and the subacromial space decompressed by a double-needle technique.

A large, painful, and impinging calcium deposit may have to be removed surgically. Through a short, deltoid-splitting approach, the surgeon exposes the deposit, which is usually the size of a marble. The deposit is excised elliptically, and the more normal edges of the tendon are sutured longitudinally. The surgeon then checks for impingement. If the repaired area still impinges under the acromion, the anterior undersurface of the acromion is shaved.

Postoperatively, the athlete's shoulder is moved passively after a few days, and by the seventh day he is usually doing Poolex.

Rotator Cuff Tears

Stage I rotator cuff tears (Figure 9-9) with swelling and fibrous disruption are treated by rest, antiinflammatory medicine, pulsed ultrasound, and rehabilitation of the shoulder. The supraspinatus pulls the humerus down into the glenoid and maintains the correct center of rotation of the humeral head. While pitching, the rotator cuff and even its individual components become independently fatigued, atrophied, or injured. If the rotation is not maintained correctly, humeral motion becomes abnormal, and the "critical zone" of the rotator cuff may rub against the acromion and coracoacromial ligament. The tendon will then swell and wear out in the relatively avascular substance of the supraspinatus. The rotator cuff can be rehabilitated independent of the deltoid. Strengthening exercises in the "empty the can" position are performed against Tubic resistance or with dumbbells.

In stage II, where there is degeneration within the tendon, the arthrogram will be negative and arthroscopy will not show a tear. These cases should be rehabilitated as above, but, if symptoms persist, decompression by partial acromionectomy and removal of the coracoacromial ligament is indicated. The surgery starts with a short anterior saber cut that can be extended more posteriorly if an osteotomy is needed[15a, 54a]. The thickened subacromial bursa is removed to allow an examination of the rotator cuff. If a defect is felt in the cuff, the area is incised longitudinally in line with the supraspinatus fibers to identify the incomplete horizontal cleavage tear and then removed elliptically, and the edges of healthier tendon are sewn together.

In stage III, where the unhealthy tissue has been broken through and formed a flap at the deep surface, arthroscopic trimming may be curative. At arthroscopy, the rotator cuff flap is removed. Not only does this remove the catching fragment,

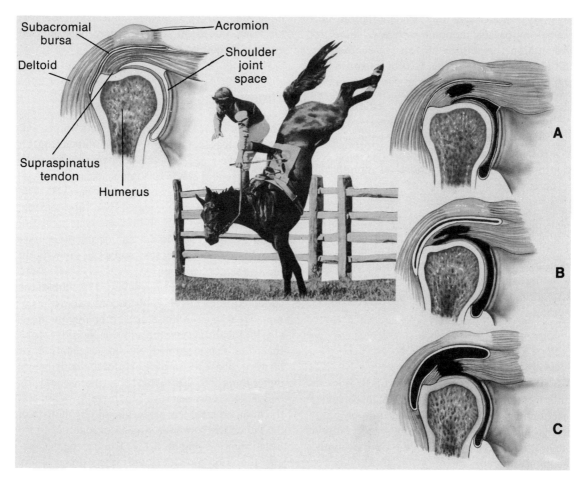

Figure 9-9   A rotator cuff tear may result from chronic overuse, as in baseball pitching, or from an acute injury, such as while riding horseback, skiing, or body surfing. The cuff tear may begin as intrasubstance degeneration **(A).** It then breaks through into the joint, producing a flap **(B)** that can catch and produce pain. If the tear is complete **(C),** it will often allow dye that is injected into the joint to escape into the subacromial bursa.

but also the tendon is rendered less bulky. The swelling above it is reduced, with consequent reduction of impingement symptoms. If symptoms should persist or recur, an open operation as used for a stage II tear is performed.

If a stage IV full-thickness tear is diagnosed, the unhealthy tissue is debrided from around the edges of the tear and the torn part approximated with nonabsorbable sutures with the knots buried. In addition to the repair, a partial acromionectomy and removal of the coracoacromial ligament will eliminate impingement from these overlying structures.

Rehabilitation After Rotator Cuff Repair

After a rotator cuff has been repaired, rehabilitation proceeds slowly and systematically, especially if the surgeon had to detach the deltoid and then reattach it to the acromion. Passive range of motion may begin as early as the fourth postoperative day, and Poolex may begin on the seventh postoperative day. Rehabilitation proceeds from passive motion to active-assistive, active motion, light throwing, and strengthening. Not until after more than a year of rehabilitation is the pitcher ready to return to competition.

Month 1—Passive abduction and external rotation and Poolex

Month 2—Dry-land active-assistive exercises and Poolex.

Month 3—Gain full active range of motion and do stretching

Month 4—May toss baseball 30 feet and increase the distance

Month 5—Pitch 60 feet slowly

Month 6—Increase to three-quarter speed

Months 7–12—Endurance exercises and strengthening with light weights

After 12 months—Return to competition

CORACOID INJURIES

A marksman's coracoid may be bruised from recoils in target or game shooting. A more severe reaction may occur during the acceleration phase of the tennis serve or when a young athlete pitches. Excessive traction on the tip may avulse the coracoid.

Because even a normal coracoid tip is usually tender to deep palpation, the one opposite the injury should be palpated for comparison. An axillary view will help to locate the avulsed fragment, but the examiner should be aware of secondary ossification centers to avoid misinterpreting the x-ray films.

A fresh avulsion of the coracoid need not be fixed internally. If it later becomes symptomatic, however, the distal fragment may be exercised and the conjoined tendon reattached.[3]

Throwing

Throwing is an integral part of many sports, but different techniques are needed, depending on whether the object propelled is heavy or light and on the size and shape of the object.[18]

The baseball pitcher flings the baseball. The phases of pitching are stance, windup, cocking, acceleration, and follow-through (Figure 9-10). During stance, the pitcher stands on the rubber and obtains signs from his catcher. In the windup phase, the pitcher steps back with his rear leg and extends his arms. During cocking, the shoulder is abducted in extension and marked external rotation. This prestretching phase prepares the muscles for the throw, and the anterior shoulder structures are also stretched. In the acceleration, or forward, phase, the arm is behind the body before being flung forward toward the catcher, and the ball is released at ear level. In the follow-through, the humeral head leaves the glenoid by more than 2.5 cm as the shoulder goes from external to internal rotation (Figure 9-11). The triceps decelerates the arm, and the thumb turns down as the forearm pronates. A unique aspect of baseball is the pitcher's need to master several pitches and different types of arm motions. The stress on the pitcher's shoulder is increased by having to throw from a pitcher's mound.

The football pass is a pushing motion in which the cocking phase and follow-through are shorter than in a flinging motion. While the bi-

Stance   Wind-up   Cocking   Acceleration   Follow-through

Figure 9-10 Phases of throwing.

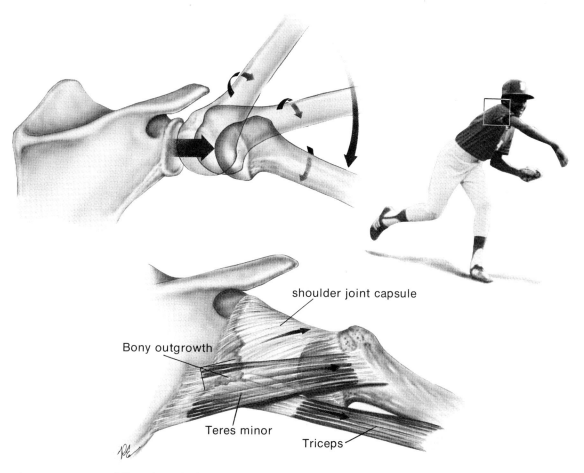

Figure 9-11   During follow-through of a throw, the humeral head leaves the glenoid. The humerus pulls on the capsule, triceps, and teres minor, causing a bony outgrowth.

ceps tendon is tight, the quarterback is especially vulnerable to opponents' attacks on his throwing arm. Unlike a baseball pitcher, the football quarterback uses the same type of motion for each pass, with little variation.

Field event throws include the javelin, shotput, discus, and hammer. Javelin throwers with good technique throw over the shoulder with elbow extension. "Round arm" throws are incorrect, and these throwers tend to develop shoulder and elbow problems similar to those of baseball pitchers. A shotputter's fingers support the heavy shot, and the large, scapular-anchoring muscles must slow the arm down after the shot has been released. Discus and hammer throws are centri-fugal motions that do not produce as many shoulder problems as do overhead events.

Softball pitchers, hurlers, and ten-pin and duck-pin bowlers stress, and sometimes rupture, their biceps tendons during their underhand, flexion activities.

The Tennis Serve

The tennis player differs from the baseball pitcher in serves per match versus pitches per game, pace versus speed, recovery time, amount of external rotation of the shoulder, and rotator cuff problems (Table 9-1).

Table 9-1 Comparing the Tennis Player and Baseball Pitcher		
	Tennis	**Baseball**
Serves per match versus pitches per game	135	120
Pace versus speed	>120 mph	<95 mph
Recovery time	Same day	3–4 days
External rotation	Slight	Marked
Rotator cuff problems	Older players	Younger players

A hard-fought three-set singles tennis match with scores of 6-4, 4-6, 6-4 requires that each player serve 15 games. Taking nine serves per game as an average, each player would hit 135 serves. In contrast, a major league baseball pitcher averages about 120 pitches in a game Further, the serves of many leading tennis players are timed consistently at more than 120 miles an hour, whereas the fastest pitchers throw around 95 miles an hour but most do not reach 90 miles an hour.

The tennis player after serving 135 serves in a match may the same day play the next round of the tournament and serve the same number of serves or may play doubles and come right back the next day without shoulder trouble. On the other hand, the baseball pitcher's arm may be so sore the next day that he can hardly raise it and then the following day may be able to throw easily.

The tennis player allows the racket to drop down behind his neck in the "back scratch position." There may be slight external rotation but much less than the amount of external rotation that the baseball pitcher has in his cocking phase.

Young tennis players often have good coaching in the service motion from a certified tennis professional. The player learns to hit up and out and extend the elbow (Figure 9-12). In contrast, coaching of young baseball players is generally by unskilled volunteers. Baseball pitching appears to be a more forceful motion in which the arm is brought forcibly into internal rotation and adduction in the acceleration phase as the ball is released. The pitcher attempts almost literally to throw the arm away from the body toward the catcher's mitt. The marked internal rotation in adduction forces the anterior part of the rotator cuff against the coracoacromial arch.

Few young tennis players have major shoulder problems. Most rotator cuff problems occur in tennis players who are 40 or 50 years of age who have played for a long time. Players with shoulder problems are often those who learned the game late. They tend to use a baseball throwing, "waiter's position" motion for the service, a habit retained from their baseball throwing days. In baseball each year a number of pitchers in high school, college, and the professional ranks have rotator cuff problems that end their baseball pitching careers.

Diagnosis and Treatment of Throwing Injuries

When diagnosing a throwing injury, the examiner should obtain a detailed history to determine which phase of the throwing motion is involved. During windup, the head of the humerus wears and roughens from leverage on the posterior glenoid, and the tendon of the long head of the biceps stretches. In the cocking phase, the shoulder moves from internal to external rotation. Pitchers have increased external rotation of the shoulder and decreased internal rotation, but their total range of motion is usually normal. The cocking phase produces anterior shoulder pain sometimes associated with anterior cuff irritation, anterior "cuffitis," or subluxation of the long head of the biceps. Because both biceps and triceps are contracted, bicipital tendinitis and tricipital tendinitis may occur.

When his arm is abducted and rotated externally, the athlete who has had injury to the glenohumeral joint may have laxity of the anterior complex of the shoulder, consisting of the capsule and the subscapularis. A pitcher will note an unstable feeling as his humeral head begins to slip forward out of the socket and then pops back again. As the examiner pushes the humeral head forward, the athlete may wince in apprehension of the feeling of instability. This is the "apprehension shoulder" of anterior subluxation. Some

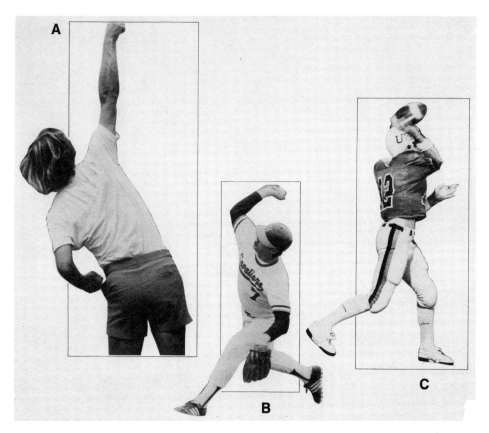

Figure 9-12 The tennis serve is an upward and outward motion. Compare this to the forward flinging motion of the baseball pitch or the forward pushing motion of the football pass.

pitchers normally sublux their shoulders and develop posterior shoulder pain first as their muscles go into spasm to prevent the humeral head from sliding forward. They later develop anterior shoulder pain.

At the start of acceleration, the pitcher's body is "opened up" and his arm is left behind. Strong internal rotation of the shoulder then begins, a movement so forceful that a young pitcher may even avulse the coracoid tip. Apprehension shoulder may occur at the beginning of the acceleration phase, and anterior capsular pain may be reproduced when the examiner manually resists the acceleration motion.

Repetitive throwing too hard and too often may produce subacromial pain with subdeltoid and subacromial bursal adhesions. Frequently pitchers with these adhesions exhibit poor form, opening up too soon; that is, the pitcher leaves his arm behind his body after bringing his trunk around. As his arm drags behind, he tries to rush it forward to catch up by dropping his elbow, "short-arming" the ball.[41]

Subacromial symptoms subside with rest, but once mature adhesions form the pain returns whenever throwing is resumed. At surgery, the subdeltoid and subacromial bursa are often obscured by a thick adhesion that involves the whole bursal complex. The bursae are thick and show myxoid degeneratoin. Unfortunately, all modes of treatment for fully developed subdeltoid bursitis seem to fail.[41] For this reason, a pitcher should not be asked to pitch through a painful shoulder and to risk irreparable damage from formation of dense adhesions. The pitcher's motion should be analyzed by a pitching coach to identify and correct flaws in the delivery.

The force of strong internal rotation in the acceleration phase may rupture the pectoralis major or latissimus dorsi or fracture the pitcher's humerus. A pectoralis major rupture leaves a gap in the axillary fold.[60] Tears of this tendon should be repaired, but tears within the muscle will heal themselves.

A pitcher releases the baseball at ear level, and his arm then follows through toward the plate. The arm continues to rotate internally, soon catching up with the body. Now the arm must be decelerated by the long head of the triceps, which acts as a rein, putting traction on the area of origin of the triceps at the inferior lip of the glenoid. This traction may produce triceps origin microtrauma and the formation of new bone at this site. A traction spur may later break off, move, and cause pain. To demonstrate this bone formation on x-ray film, the pitcher lies supine and externally rotates and abducts his shoulder 90° (Figure 9-13) as the x-ray beam is angled from his axilla to an x-ray plate placed above his shoulder.

Ossification at the posteroinferior part of the glenoid—"Bennett's lesion"—is often associated with tears of the glenoid labrum and posterior capsule. The ossification is, in part, an inflammatory response to microtrauma and is also caused by posterior subluxation of the humeral head and posterior cuffitis in the region of the teres minor.

If a pitcher develops posterior shoulder pain and x-ray films show bone at the posteroinferior glenoid, his arm should be rested, and oral anti-inflammatory therapy or a steroid injection may be given. A pitching coach should later evaluate his follow-through mechanics. Sometimes, the pitcher stays closed too long, not opening up to face the target, and his arm gets ahead of him. In addition, he should stop throwing sidearm. If the pain persists, the bony overgrowth may have to be excised. In this procedure, the surgeon makes an incision over the scapula spine with the pitcher prone. The deltoid is reflected from the spine, and the posterior capsule and glenoid are then reached through the interval between the infraspinatis and teres minor. The capsule is

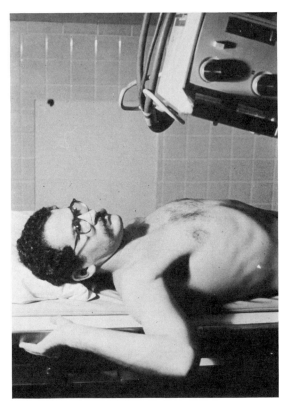

Figure 9-13 Subglenoid bone growths are best seen on x-ray films taken with the pitcher's shoulder externally rotated and the tube angled upward.

opened longitudinally and the lesion noted and removed. After operation, the athlete must wear a sling for 1 week before beginning a strength and flexibility program. Light throwing resumes about 8 weeks after the procedure.

If a pitcher is not fit, fatigue will decrease his coordination and change his pitching motion. If he is overweight, the excess fat serves as a brake on his contracting muscles. "A pitcher's legs go fits": If his legs are not strong for pushoff and balance, his pitching power will drop. This disrupts his delivery, and the change in his throwing motion may lead to injury.

Warming-Up

A complete warm-up before pitching helps to prevent injury to a pitcher's throwing arm.[2,6] The trainer first applies moist heat to the pitcher's arm for about 20 minutes, followed by an ice rub or a cold, wet towel rub. The pitching shoulder may also be massaged with an analgesic rub. The trainer then stretches the pitcher's arm (Figure 9-14).

After the massage and stretches, the pitcher suspends his full body weight from a bar by one arm and revolves slowly for 30 seconds. He may also hang from the roof of the dugout later to achieve the same stretching effect. Hanging

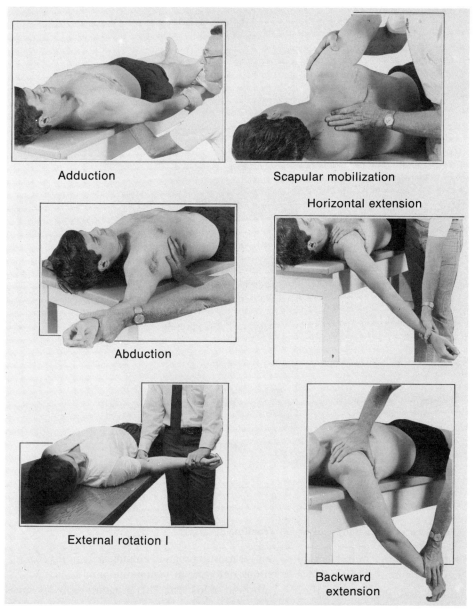

Adduction

Scapular mobilization

Horizontal extension

Abduction

External rotation I

Backward extension

A

Figure 9-14   A. The trainer begins pitcher stretches at the shoulder. These stretches were designed by Don Fauls, ATC, Head Athletic Trainer (retired), Florida State University. **(continued)**

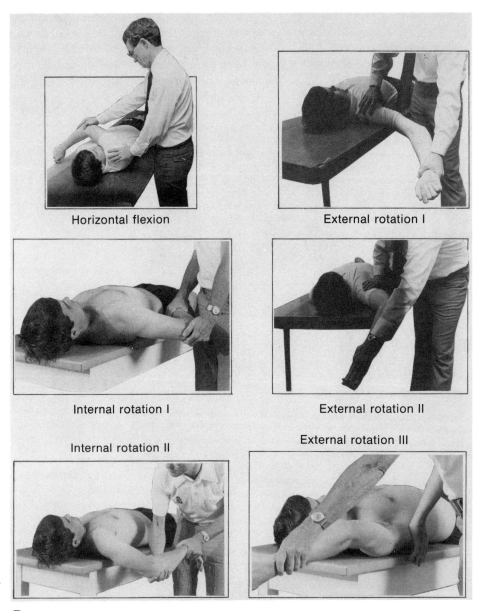

Horizontal flexion

External rotation I

Internal rotation I

External rotation II

Internal rotation II

External rotation III

B

Figure 9-14   B. The trainer works on motion in all planes. **(continued)**

stretches his shoulder and arm muscles and opens the joint to loosen the joint structures. He shold not do chin-ups or pull-ups because they cause tightness. Once the shoulder is stretched and before the pitcher begins his warm-up throws, he performs a general warm-up, working up a sweat before stepping on the rubber.

The moist heat, massage, stretching, and gen- eral warm-up program enhances flexibility for op- timal delivery, allowing the pitcher to get the most out of his arm. This program probably saves as many as 20 pitches from pregame warm-up throws, giving the pitcher an extra boost late in the game.

When warming up, the pitcher should remove his jacket and throw in the direction he will be

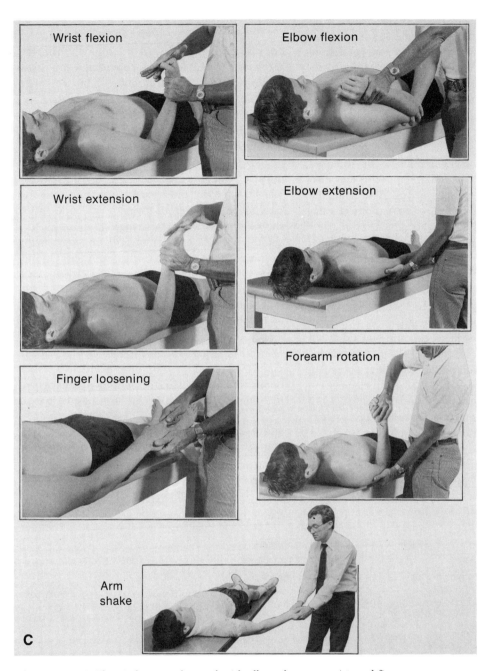

Figure 9-14 C. The pitcher stretches end with elbow, forearm, wrist, and finger mobilizations and, finally, a shaking of the arm while the shoulder is being abducted.

facing in the game.[6] He should begin at a distance shorter than the rubber to home plate, gradually moving to the full distance. The first pitches should be straight slow balls, with no curves thrown until the arm is fully warmed up. The pitcher should not throw hard until the umpire is on the scene.

A pitcher's normal 15 to 20 minute warm-up may start with 30 straight balls at medium velocity, then adding 10 curves, 10 sliders, and 10 fast balls of increasing speed. He finishes with sets of 5 pitches of various types, to total 80 pitches. The pitcher then rests for 5 minutes before game time but keeps his warm-up jacket on until he is ready to pitch, regardless of climatic conditions.

Arm Care After Pitching

After repetitive hard throwing in a game, edema and a fibrin exudate accumulate in the shoulder tissues. Some bleeding into the muscles may also occur that could result in scarring. After firing the last pitch, or after throwing a football or a javelin, the athlete can lessen this accumulation and assist in waste product removal by warming down, stretching the shoulder, and moving it through its range of motion. Pitchers who do not complete a game and relief pitchers who pitch only to a few batters need the same postgame arm care as pitchers who pitch complete games.

After the game, the arm should be iced down with a large ice pack held over the player's shoulder by an elastic wrap and the elbow soaked in cold water (Figure 9-15). The ice is analgesic, decreases swelling, and is antispasmodic. Cold reduces the metabolism of the tissues and lessens cellular damage and the inflammatory response. The ice should not, however, be left on for more than 15 to 20 minutes, or a strong reflex vasodilitation may occur.

Sore Arm

Because throwing too hard or too soon during the early season may lead to a sore arm, a good way to start the season is to throw without wearing a glove. If a sore arm occurs, the cause of the soreness should be diagnosed carefully. Pitchers must not be allowed to pitch through sore arms because this may worsen any condition.

The pitcher with a sore arm will experience a drop in strength with each day of rest. For this reason, a pitcher must exercise outside the soreness range to maintain strength and to keep his shoulder loose with a full range of motion. A sore shoulder exercise program will include sawing exercises, cross-overs, shrugs, and circumductions. The circumductions are first done in a clockwise and then in a counterclockwise direction, making the largest possible circles. Each exercise should be repeated 50 times three times a day.

Anti-inflammatory medicines such as aspirin may be given 20 to 30 minutes before exercising. Some physicians give a decreasing dosage schedule of butazolidine, 200 mg four times daily for 2 days, then 200 mg three times daily for 2 days, and finally 100 mg three times daily for 3 days. Others use indomethacin (Indocin), ibuprofen (Motrin), tolmetin sodium (Tolectin), or naproxen (Naprosyn) for an anti-inflammatory effect.

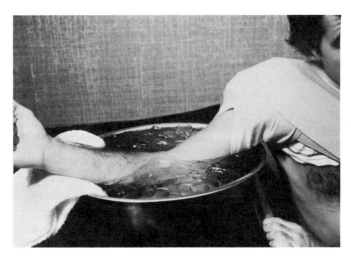

Figure 9-15   After a game, the pitcher has an ice bag placed on his externally rotated shoulder and rests his elbow in ice water.

The Fungo Routine

If a thrower is sidelined for a lengthy period and begins his return to throwing with short throws, neither a full range of motion nor a natural throwing motion will be achieved. A "fungo routine" of long easy throws is a better beginning. In this program, the fungo hitter bats balls to the player, who throws them back from the outfield in an easy manner, bringing his arm through a full range of motion. The arm is thus stretched and strengthened without placing too much stress on the shoulder. The throws must be pain free with normal form, and if the player substitutes movements or deviates from normal form the workout should be halted.

The program starts with long easy throws from the deep outfield, and the ball should be allowed to roll into the plate, just reaching the fungo hitter. The sessions last 30 minutes for 2 days, then the player's arm is rested for 1 day. The player next moves to the middle of the outfield, making stronger throws into the fungo hitter on about five bounces. These sessions last for 30 minutes over 2 more days, followed by another day of rest. Next come stronger, crisp throws from the short outfield, with a straight trajectory, on one bounce to the fungo hitter. These sessions also last 30 minutes for 2 days, followed by 1 more day of rest. The pitcher should now be ready to return to the mound with a full windup, throwing at about half speed before increasing to three-quarter and then to full speed. The full program takes 3 to 4 weeks until the pitcher returns to the pitching rotation.

SHOULDER SEPARATIONS

The acromioclavicular joint is a satellite joint of the shoulder that moves throughout shoulder abduction, especially during the early and late stages of this motion. As it shifts and rotates, much of its stability is afforded by the deltoid and trapezius origins that surround it. With damage to the supporting ligaments of the acromioclavicular joint, the muscles may pull the distal clavicle into a dislocated position. If an athlete falls on the point of his shoulder or lands on the ground with an opponent on top, as in rugby, wrestling, or tackle football, the clavicle hits the first rib and is driven upward, and the acromioclavicular ligaments or the acromioclavicular and coracoclavicular ligaments may be disrupted, springing the joint.[35, 46]

Acromioclavicular separations are graded I, II, and III (Figure 9-16).[4] A grade I separation connotes damage to the acromioclavicular ligament fibers but no laxity. If an athlete comes to the sideline with shoulder pain, the examiner should feel under his shoulder pads for tenderness over the acromioclavicular joint. Before he is sent back into the game, his shoulder should be completely examined with the shoulder pads off. Otherwise, if the acromioclavicular joint has been damaged and the player is returned to the game, a second hit may transform a grade I separation into a grade II or grade III sprain. Ice and a sling are used in the initial symptomatic care of a grade I sprain, followed by cryotherapy and isodynamics or weight lifting out of the soreness range. The player may return to competition when soreness diminishes and he has gained full strength and flexibility. For added protection he may wear a foam donut pad or a plastic cup under his shoulder pads (Figure 9-17).

A tear of the athlete's acromioclavicular ligament, combined with a grade I sprain of the coracoclavicular ligament, ranks as a grade II shoulder separation. An x-ray film may show the distal clavicle to be elevated by about one half the width of the joint, and there is a slight increase in coracoclavicular distance. The resulting prominence at the acromioclavicular joint is sometimes obscured by swelling, but the distal clavicle is movable.

The risen clavicle may be best seen on x-ray film when the tube is tilted up 15° and the exposure is decreased. Sometimes the athlete is asked to hold weights in his hands, or the weights may be strapped to his wrists to bring out the subluxation. These weights may, however, cause him to shrug his shoulder and reduce the subluxation. If weights are needed to demonstrate the separation, the treatment is usually no different from that for a grade I separation.

A grade III, or major shoulder, separation con-

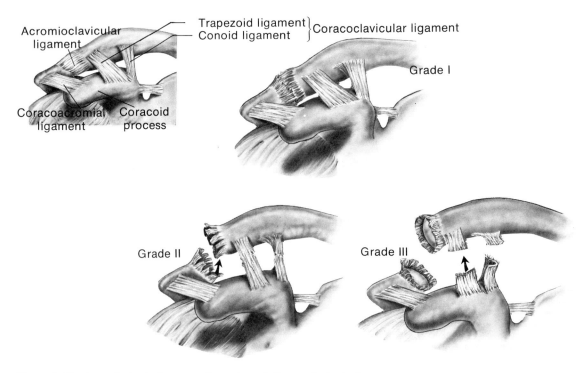

Figure 9-16   Acromioclavicular separations. A grade I acromioclavicular separation implies damage to the acromioclavicular ligament without displacement of the clavicle. A grade II separation means subluxation of the acromioclavicular joint and an increase in the coracoclavicular distance, owing to disruption of the acromioclavicular ligament and damage to the coracoclavicular ligaments. Both the acromioclavicular and the coracoclavicular ligaments are ruptured in a grade III separtion, allowing the clavicle to ride high.

notes rupture of the athlete's acromioclavicular ligament and the conoid and trapezoid portions of the coracoclavicular ligament. The distal clavicle is movable, and, because of swelling or spasm of the surrounding muscles, this type of separation may appear clinically to be a mildly elevated grade II separation. With the athlete in a supine position, the prominence may not be very apparent, but when he sits up the clavicle may be strikingly elevated. Some surgeons inject the injured area with lidocaine to see whether the athlete can abduct the shoulder completely or if there is abutment. If shoulder motion is blocked, the surgeon may decide to operate.

The treatments for grade II and grade III shoulder separations are subjects of controversy, varying from symptomatic programs and early motion

and strength work, to special slings or tape jobs and operations to hold the clavicle down.

The nonoperative program emphasizes exercises. During the early sore period, while the athlete is lying down, he uses active-assistive overhead motion. About 5 days after injury, he may begin a trapezius and deltoid strengthening cryotherapy program that includes abduction against resistance and shoulder shrugs. Early strengthening of these muscles produces a strong shoulder, and there is usually not much functional difference between this early activity, a nonoperative program, and operative treatment. Allowing the distal clavicle to remain in a dislocated position may cause the athlete no trouble. Later, if the distal clavicle abuts in overhead activities, such as pitching a baseball, throwing a

Figure 9-17   Shoulder pads or a plastic and felt pad can protect an injured acromioclavicular joint.

football, or grabbing rebounds in basketball, the distal clavicle may be resected.

The examiner may decide to inject a local anesthetic into the painful area, relocate the clavicle with the patient supine, and hold the reduction with an acromioclavicular sling until the ligaments have healed. In practice, however, this technique is painful, prolonged, and only occasionally successful. Even if reduction is achieved and the coracoclavicular ligaments heal, the damaged acromioclavicular joint may become painfully arthritic.

The clavicle functions mainly as an attachment for the deltoid, trapezius, and sternocleidomastoid muscles. To maintain the effective length of these muscles, some surgeons pull the clavicle down and reconstruct the coracoclavicular ligaments. Occasionally, an athlete will not want a bump, preferring instead to trade the bump for a scar. There are many ways to stabilize the acromioclavicular joint (Figure 9-18). Wires may be passed through the acromion into the clavicle, but they must be bent so that they will not migrate. Some surgeons place a lag screw through the clavicle into the coracoid, but the

screw must be removed in 6 to 8 weeks or it may break owing to rotary motion between the coracoid and clavicle. To eliminate the need for removal of the fixation device, the clavicle may be lashed down to the coracoid with a 5-mm polyethylene fiber tape. Range-of-motion exercises and rehabilitation may start a few days after the operation. The tape does not stretch and need not be removed, and the athlete may return to sports as soon as the wound has healed. Before all operations that use the coracoid as a stabilizing post, the surgeon should take an x-ray film along the spine of the scapula to show the entire coracoid. If the coracoid has a fracture through its base, it could dislodge after the operation. Another operative approach entails attaching the short head of the biceps or the coracoid process itself as a "dynamic transfer" to the undersurface of the clavicle.

An important consideration in these operations is the disposition of the acromioclavicular joint when the clavicle has been reduced. The damaged acromioclavicular joint may become a trouble spot; thus an arthroplasty may be done in which 1 cm of the distal clavicle is resected (see

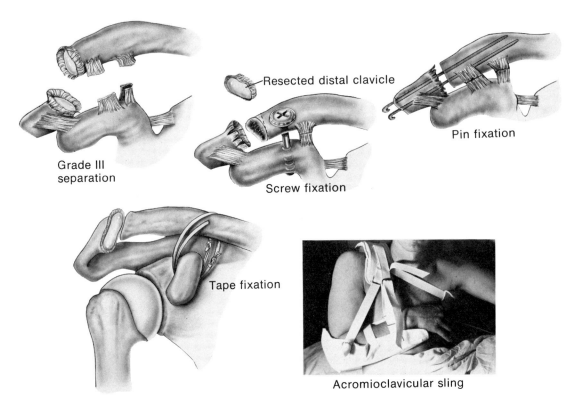

Figure 9-18 Acromioclavicular repairs. A grade III acromioclavicular separation
may be treated with a special sling or operatively with a screw, pins, or tape. In
each operation, a short piece of the distal clavicle is also resected.

section on Acromioclavicular Arthritis below).
Some surgeons sever the acromial attachment of
the coracoacromial ligament and use it to reinforce the shredded coracoclavicular ligament.
However, unless the athlete is a swimmer, a
throwing athlete, or a volleyball player who has
been having subacromial trouble, the coracoacromial ligament is usually left in place to act as
a soft cushion, preventing upward placement of
the humeral head.

ACROMIOCLAVICULAR ARTHRITIS

Heavy use of the shoulder may cause the acromioclavicular joint to break down with arthritis,
especially in athletes who use across-the-body
motions, such as golfers, baseball players, and ice

and field hockey players.[12] Osteoarthritic changes
of narrowing and osteophyte formation are apparent on x-ray film. The x-ray tube should be
tilted up at an angle of about 15° and the exposure
decreased to show the acromioclavicular joint,
since the joint may be washed out in an ordinary
shoulder x-ray.

With proper operative technique, a resection
of the distal clavicle solves the problem of acromioclavicular joint arthritis. If too much of the
distal clavicle and the posterior capsular ligament
is removed, however, the distal clavicle will become hypermobile. No more than 1 cm of bone
need be resected, and the resection should be
angled wider posteriorly, with the posterior capsular ligament retained. The shoulder is then
brought through a full range of motion to ensure
that there will be no impingement during overhead activities. It is mobilized a few days after

operation, and the athlete may return to contact sports in about 6 weeks.

BICIPITAL TENDINITIS

The tendon of the long head of the biceps arises at the supraglenoid tubercle and passes at an angle of 30° into the bicipital groove, where it lies deep to the transverse humeral ligament. During shoulder motion, the tendon does not glide but remains fixed as the humerus slides along the tendon. During the follow-through in throwing, the humerus actually leaves the socket by as much as 2.5 cm to 3.75 cm (1 in–1.5 in). Rubbing

of the tendon by the groove and ligament is worsened by a tight groove, especially if the channel has a steep medial wall (Fig. 9-19). In addition, many shoulders have a rough supratubercular area that irritates the tendon.[24]

The athlete with bicipital tendinitis usually reports a prodrome of shoulder pain. There is tenderness over the bicipital groove, and this area moves when the shoulder is shifted from internal to external rotation.[15] The examiner can press over the bicipital groove to locate the tender spot. The athlete's elbow is then flexed, with his arm at his side, and the shoulder is rotated. In bicipital tendinitis, the tenderness follows the movement of the bicipital groove. With the shoulder rotated

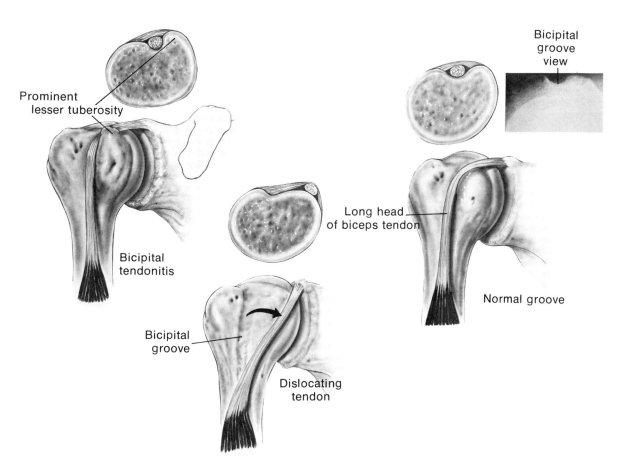

Prominent lesser tuberosity

Bicipital tendonitis

Bicipital groove

Dislocating tendon

Long head of biceps tendon

Bicipital groove view

Normal groove

Figure 9-19   The tendon of the long head of the biceps may be irritated in a bicipital groove that has a prominent lesser tuberosity. If the groove is too shallow, the tendon may dislocate.

internally, the tenderness is medial; at neutral position it remains medial. When the shoulder is externally rotated, however, the groove lies in front or even lateral to the midline, and this becomes the tender area.

In examining for bicipital tendinitis, the athlete should be supine so that he is relaxed and his shoulder can be maneuvered easily. The examiner abducts the shoulder to 90° and holds it in neutral rotation. He supports the elbow and then rotates the shoulder internally about 15° so that the bicipital groove points toward the ceiling. He can now palpate the bicipital groove and the anterior deltoid easily. Further, by lowering the arm off the table, the biceps tendon bowstrings somewhat, becoming even more prominent. Next, the examiner rotates the humerus from external rotation to internal rotation and then back with the elbow flexed. If the tendon is subluxing, a snap or a pop may be heard or felt. If the athlete puts his hand on his head and then contracts his biceps, he may produce bicipital groove pain.

In supination test for bicipital tendinitis, the athlete supinates his forearm against resistance. The examiner stands to the side and just behind the athlete. The athlete has his arm at his side and then flexes the elbow to 90° with his thumb up. The examiner's hand is placed on the back of the athlete's hand and shadows his forearm; he asks the athlete to supinate against the resistance. In bicipital tendinitis, this movement will cause pain at the bicipital groove. To balance the athlete for this exercise, the examiner places his free hand on the athlete's opposite hip.

The straight arm flexion test or "bowling" test is performed with the athlete standing and his arm at his side. The examiner stands on the affected side, putting one hand on the front of the athlete's forearm and the other hand on the back of the athlete's hip for balance. The athlete is then asked to flex his arm, with his elbow straight, to perhaps produce pain at the bicipital groove.

Ice may be used in the early treatment of bicipital tendinitis and the athlete given a nonsteroidal, anti-inflammatory medicine. Painful maneuvers should be avoided, and if the pain persists the arm should be rested. A local steroid deposit around the tendon often relieves the pain,

but if it is injected into the tendinous substance it may provoke rupture. The surgical procedure for recurring bicipital tendinitis is identical to that for ruptures of the tendon of the long head of the biceps.[11]

DISLOCATION OF THE BICEPS TENDON

A checked swing in baseball, with a sudden forceful jerking back of the bat, or an attack on a quarterback's externally rotated passing arm, with the biceps tensed, may tear the transverse humeral ligament from its insertion on the lesser tuberosity. Where the transverse humeral ligament peels off, the long head of the biceps tendon can slide up and over the tuberosity, especially when the medial wall of the bicipital groove is shallow, with an inclination of 30° or less (Figure 9-19).[42]

The athlete with a dislocating biceps tendon has anterior shoulder pain with popping, cracking, and occasionally a locking sensation. The tendon slips and rolls over during throws, sometimes snapping back during internal rotation.

Shoulder pain may occur when the shoulder is abducted to 90° and then rotated externally and internally. The tendon dislocation can sometimes be brought out by manually resisting the throwing motion. Tenderness follows the movement of the bicipital groove. When the arm is internally rotated the tenderness is medial, and in neutral position the tenderness remains medial. When the arm is externally rotated, however, the groove lies in front of, or even lateral to the midline, and the tenderness shifts to this position.

A tunnel x-ray view may be taken to evaluate the bicipital groove. The x-ray plate is placed at the top of the athlete's shoulder and the beam directed along the line of the groove. The picture provides information on the configuration of the groove and may reveal osteophytes at the edges of the groove.

For acute biceps tendon dislocation, the shoulder is iced and the arm rested in internal rotation. When dislocations recur, the repairs are the same as those for biceps tendon rupture.

RUPTURE OF THE LONG HEAD OF THE BICEPS TENDON

The biceps tendon becomes worn by persistent rubbing in a tight, steep-walled groove that has supratubercular rough spots. Further degeneration of the tendon occurs in swimmers as an avascular zone of the intracapsular part of the tendon is stretched over the humeral head. Rupture of the biceps tendon is not uncommon in the degenerated tendons of older athletes: It may follow an underhand delivery in fast-pitch softball or a snappy, underhand basketball pass (Figure 9-20). Even young athletes, especially gymnasts and weight lifters, may rupture the tendon of the long head of their biceps. This type of rupture produces a bulging biceps in the arm.

The biceps spans two joints, and repairs usually restore only the part near the elbow. If the tendon is left unrepaired, the athlete will lose about 20% of his elbow flexion power. Repair is usually not recommended for nonathletes, but repair may restore needed elbow flexion and supination to competitive athletes.[14]

In repairing this condition, the surgeon enters the shoulder joint through a small split in the rotator cuff. The intra-articular part of the tendon is then removed from the glenoid to prevent a buckling tendon remnant from interfering with shoulder action. Some surgeons roughen the floor of the bicipital groove and suture the tendon into the groove with mattress stitches.[24] Others use a staple, but the staple may loosen.[15] Still others choose a "trap door" technique in which the

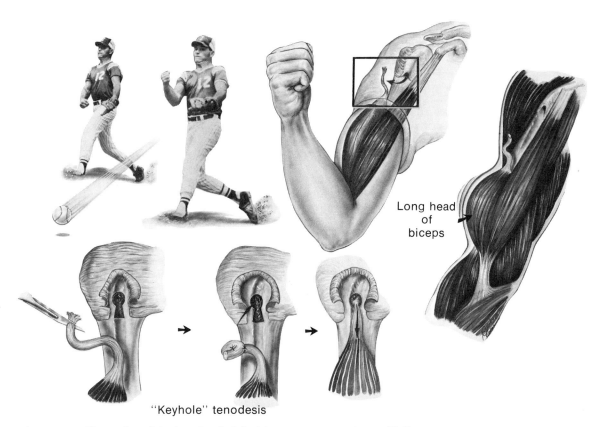

"Keyhole" tenodesis

Long head of biceps

Figure 9-20 The tendon of the long head of the biceps may rupture in a softball pitcher, leaving him with a weakened arm. Some elbow power may be regained by reattaching the tendon in the bicipital groove.

tendon is placed under an osteoperiosteal flap near the bicipital groove. After most of these operations, the shoulder must be rested. Because such long restriction of motion may freeze the shoulder, a keyhole technique that allows postoperative shoulder and elbow motion and rapid resumption of activities may be preferred (Figure 9-19).[17]

PARTIAL AVULSION OF THE GLENOID LABRUM IN THROWING ATHLETES

As a pitcher releases the ball, his biceps contracts strongly.[1] This contraction may avulse the *upper* portion of his glenoid labrum from the glenoid rim[2a] (Figure 9-21). In contrast, when a football player dislocates his shoulder while arm-tackling, the *lower* portion of his glenoid labrum is avulsed.

The pitcher's tear may extend to become a long, bowstring tear. It can catch in the shoulder joint just like a bowstring tear of a knee meniscus. When a pitcher who has an avulsed labrum throws, his shoulder will catch and pop and feel unstable.

Clunk Test

To determine whether a glenoid labrum tear is impinging in the shoulder, the examiner performs the ''clunk test,'' a test similar to the click test in the knee. In both tests, the examiner tries to catch a torn piece of fibrocartilage between two bones.

With the athlete supine and relaxed, the examiner supports the elbow with one hand and places his other hand behind the humeral head. He then raises the athlete's arm fully overhead and pushes the shoulder anteriorly while rotating the humerus. The test is positive if it produces a clunk or grinding, which may be associated with apprehension and pain as the humeral head strikes or snaps over the labral tear.

The surgeon may debride a bowstring or flap tear of the labrum arthroscopically. Although the operation does not stabilize the shoulder, it removes the offending labral tear. Postoperatively, the athlete may begin passive range of motion the

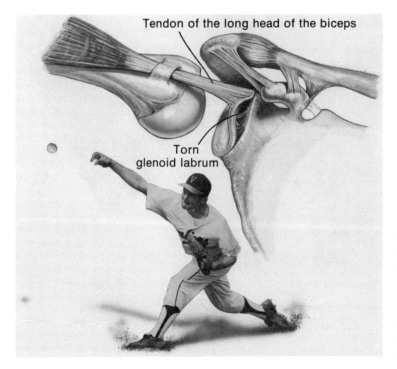

Tendon of the long head of the biceps

Torn glenoid labrum

Figure 9-21 After a baseball pitcher releases the ball, his biceps muscle contracts strongly. This contraction may result in the long head of the biceps pulling the upper part of the glenoid barium from the glenoid.

day after surgery and then strengthen his arm. By 3 weeks, he should be throwing easily and by week 7 he should be ready to return to competition.

ACUTE DISLOCATION OF THE SHOULDER

In an anterior dislocation of the shoulder, the shoulder abducts and rotates externally, and the acromion acts as a fulcrum on the humeral head, which breaks through the weak anterior capsule.

The labrum rips from the glenoid, and the subscapularis and supraspinatis stretch. The humeral head then slides below the coracoid and sometimes pops back into place but more frequently stays dislocated (Figure 9-22).

A player typically comes off the field supporting his arm and usually has a hollowed-out area at the shoulder. In a muscular athlete, this sign may be less apparent when the two shoulders are compared. However, an athlete with an anterior dislocation will usually not be able to touch his other shoulder.

Although the shoulder will sometimes pop

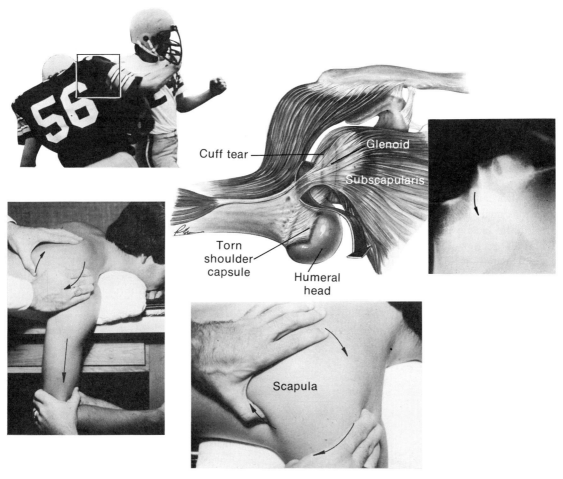

Figure 9-22 Forces applied to the externally rotated and abducted arm during arm tackling may wrench the humeral head from the glenoid, ripping the capsule. A rotator cuff tear sometimes accompanies the dislocation. The dislocation, usually an anterior, subcoracoid one, is best reduced by traction and scapular rotation.

back after gentle traction on the field or sidelines, in most cases the athlete must be taken from the playing field for reduction of the dislocation.

Early on, there is not much spasm. An ice bag on the shoulder will provide analgesia and muscle relaxation. The athlete is then helped to a prone position on the training table or on a car fender, with his arm hanging over the side. The physician gently pulls downward, with the athlete's elbow flexed to 90° and his forearm supinated to relax the biceps (Figure 9-22). An assistant then rotates the inferior angle of the scapula toward the spine so that the glenoid faces the humerus. The combination of traction and scapular rotation allows the humeral head to slide easily back into the socket. A dislocation will sometimes even reduce spontaneously when the athlete lies prone on the examining table with a pillow under his chest and his arm hanging over the edge of the table.

The "Hippocratic" is an alternative method of reduction. While an assistant applies countertraction around the chest, the athlete's arm is pulled at about 30° of abduction in line with the trunk (Figure 9-23). If the examiner's foot is placed against the athlete's chest for countertraction, it may slip into the axilla to damage the brachial plexus. In a muscular athlete, a wrist-lock technique may be used with the athlete's elbow flexed to relax the biceps tendon and forestall fatigue during the traction phase. The dislocated shoulder will usually reduce, but, in some muscular persons seen late and who have strong muscle spasm, a narcotic medicine and an intravenous relaxant, or even general anesthesia, may be needed to facilitate reduction.

Once the dislocation is reduced, a true anteroposterior x-ray film of the shoulder should be taken. An axillary lateral or a transthoracic lateral view is also needed to be certain that the dislocation has been reduced. An ice bag is placed on the shoulder over a towel, held with a figure-eight elastic wrap.

An athlete's first anterior dislocation should be immobilized for 3 to 4 weeks. Special immobilizatoin devices or advanced exercise programs appear to have no effect on the recurrence rate.[50, 51] The arm is usually placed in a sling, with abduction and forward flexion resistive exercises starting as soon as the early pain subsides. Otherwise, the anterior deltoid will atrophy rapidly. The athlete should also perform shrugs but should avoid external rotation early in retraining.

A fracture of the humerus or of the scapula sometimes accompanies a shoulder dislocation, and nerve damage may account for slow progress in regaining strength. In this situation, an arthrogram may be needed because a rotator cuff tear may also be present, causing shoulder pain and a poor return of strength.

A blow to the front of the shoulder may drive the humeral head out of the socket posteriorly, or, when a lineman comes up with shoulders abducted 90° and flexed forward, his humeral head may slip out posteriorly. This type of dislocation also occurs after falls on ski slopes. The athlete

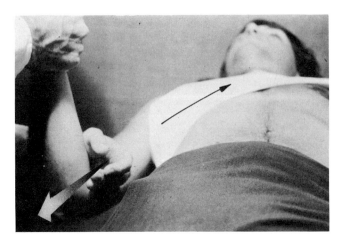

Figure 9-23 An anteriorly dislocated shoulder may be reduced with sustained straight traction *(arrow)* against the countortraction of a sheet around the chest *(smaller arrow).*

who has sustained a posterior dislocation will have his arm internally rotated and adducted at his side. The coracoid is prominent and the anterior part of the shoulder flat. He will have limited ability to abduct and to rotate his shoulder externally, and the humeral head may often be felt posteriorly, below the acromion.

An anteroposterior x-ray film may look almost normal (Figure 9-24A), but close inspection will show the medial margin of the humeral head to be overlapping the glenoid abnormally. Posterior dislocation should be suspected if there is a fracture of the lesser tuberosity. A lateral x-ray view along the spine of the scapula will reveal the humeral head to be dislocated posterior to the Y axis of the scapula (Figure 9-24B).

Gentle traction is applied in line with the internally rotated, adducted humerus to reduce a posterior dislocation. Sometimes the internal rotation may have to be increased to disengage the head. Pressure is then applied to the humeral head from behind to push it forward. After the dislocation has been reduced, the humerus is most stable at midrotation and slight extension. If the arm is placed in a sling and rotated

internally across the chest, the chance of redislocation increases to about 30%. Thus, a splint that will hold the shoulder in the internally rotated and slightly extended position for 3 weeks should be applied.[9] If an athlete should suffer recurrent posterior dislocations or subluxations, a posterior osteotomy and bone graft will change the angle of the glenoid, checking posterior dislocation.

RECURRENT ANTERIOR DISLOCATIONS OF THE SHOULDER

The "essential lesion" and the humeral head wedge defect both promote recurrent dislocation of the shoulder. The "essential lesion" is a tear of the fibrocartilaginous glenoid labrum that occurs during the initial dislocation and does not heal back to the glenoid. As a result, the anteroinferior part of the shoulder joint capsule is not able to block redislocation of the shoulder and the humeral head may slide out through the gap. The torn labrum is not visible on a plain x-ray film, but an arthrogram of the shoulder will show

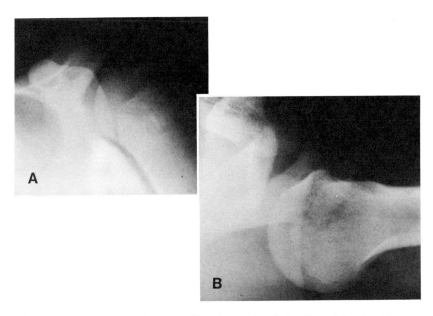

Figure 9-24 Anteroposterior x-ray film of posterior dislocation of the shoulder looks convincingly normal **(A).** The axillary view, however, shows the humeral head to be dislocated posteriorly **(B).**

dye leaking from the shoulder joint through the defect into a bursa. The lesion may also be inspected athroscopically.[37, 55]

The wedge defect of the humeral head is visible on plain x-ray films taken with the shoulder rotated internally.[13] As the humeral head dislocates from the glenoid, it jams against the anterior glenoid rim. The firm cortical rim crushes the soft cancellous bone in the posterolateral part of the humeral head, producing a defect that appears on plain x-ray film as a posterolateral wedge of compressed bone.

Anterior dislocation of shoulder recurs frequently in contact sports that require abduction and external rotation of the arm. In ordinary activities, persons younger than 45 years of age have an 80% recurrence rate.[50, 51] The lower rate in older persons may be due to fibrosis at the glenoid rim and to less activity. These statistics, however, may not apply to older athletes.

Some football players who have had an anterior dislocatoin of the shoulder may compete while wearing a shoulder strap that prevents redislocation (Figure 9-25). Gieck uses a 1.5-inch wide elastic belt,[19] riveting the buckle to the shoulder pad on the side opposite the dislocation.

The remaining part of the belt is then looped around the affected arm while the arm is held adducted and flexed slightly forward. The belt has several notches to allow the athlete to adjust the tension. Because it tends to stretch, the belt must be adjusted every week or two.

The belt system is good for receivers, running backs, and defensive backs by allowing forward flexion of the shoulder for pass receiving and defending while limiting external rotation from a horizontal, extended, and abducted position. If the belt cannot be worn and dislocations recur, one of many surgical options may be recommended,[32] including capsulorrhaphies with sutures or a staple, transfer of the subscapularis, and transfer of the coracoid process.

A capsulorrhaphy is a replacement of the torn shoulder capsule to the glenoid rim from whence it came. Techniques for this procedure include the Bankhart, DuToit, and Putti-Platt operations.[43] In the Bankhart operation, the surgeon drills holes through the glenoid rim and reattaches the torn labrum to the rim by means of sutures. After the operation, the athlete wears a sling for 3 days before advancing to full range-of-motion exercises. Recurrences of dislocations are

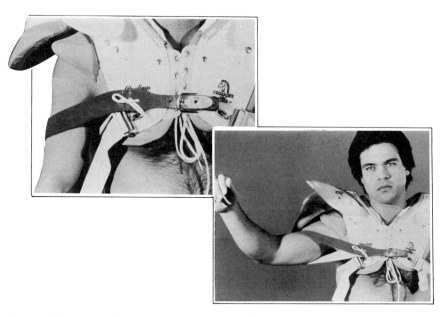

Figure 9-25 An elastic strap attached to the shoulder pad *(left)* prevents full abduction and external rotation *(right).*

infrequent unless the athlete has a large defect in the humeral head (a Hill–Sachs lesion). The staple capsulorrhaphy (DuToit operation) requires a longitudinal incision through the subscapularis tendon (Figure 9-26). The surgeon then peels the capsule off the subscapularis and staples the torn capsule to the glenoid. This corrects the essential lesion, but the staple may loosen. In the Putti-Platt operation, the capsule and distal part of the subscapularis tendon are attached to the soft tissue around the glenoid rim. This operation limits external rotation of the shoulder.

The surgeon may elect to perform a subscapularis transfer (Magnuson and Stack operation), which entails transferring the subscapularis tendon from its insertion into the lesser tuberosity of the humerus, laterally across the bicipital groove to the greater tuberosity, about 1.5 cm distal to the original level of insertion (Figure 9-27). The tendon may be placed into a trap door of bone, or the surgeon may use a serrated staple to secure the tendon. This operation also restricts external rotation, and the staple may loosen.

The Bristow operation is a coracoid transfer that protects against dislocation while allowing good external rotation (Figure 9-28). In this procedure, the surgeon removes the tip of the coracoid process with the coracobrachialis and short head of the biceps still attached to it. He then roughens the bone at the junction of the middle third and lower third of the anterior glenoid rim and places the coracoid there. As the athlete abducts and rotates his shoulder externally after healing, the coracoid tip serves as a bone block, and the conjoined tendon of the coracobrachialis and short head of the biceps work as a dynamic sling that prevents the humeral head from dislocating.

Some surgeons modify the coracoid transfer operation by using a screw to attach the coracoid tip to the glenoid, but the screw may loosen and even damage a blood vessel to produce an aneu-

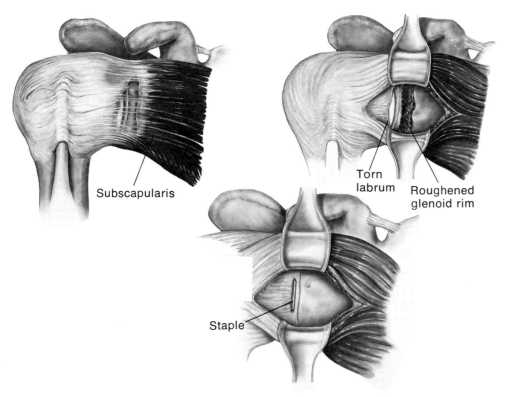

Figure 9-26 The shoulder capsule may be repaired by reattaching it to the roughened glenoid rim with a staple.

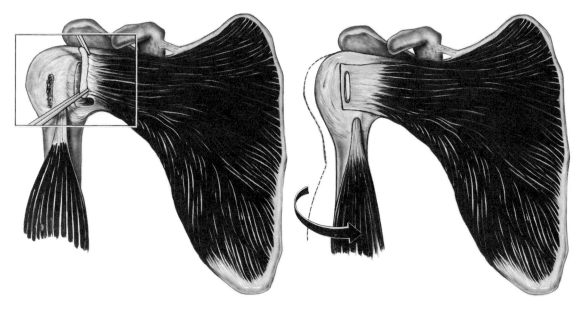

Figure 9-27   The subscapularis tendon may be transferred from the lesser to the greater tuberosity, thereby limiting external rotation of the shoulder.

rysm. Although a coracoid transfer will sharply reduce dislocation, it limits external rotation to some extent. Because a throwing athlete needs the fullest external rotation of his throwing arm shoulder, only rarely can he return to the highest levels of performance and competition after repair of a recurrently dislocating shoulder.

Anterior Subluxation

A young athlete's shoulder may sublux anteriorly, the shoulder slipping somewhat out of the socket and then popping back in.[5] An athlete with this problem may recall having wrenched his shoulder, for example, when sliding headfirst into a base or diving back to a base. Others report having had a direct blow to the shoulder or a history of heavy throwing or hard serving.

Subluxation may produce a "dead arm" syndrome. In the cocked position of throwing, the arm goes dead with a sharp paralyzing pain. The arm "goes out" or feels numb after a throw, and the thrower cannot come forward vigorously with the ball. In short, he cannot use the arm forcefully in abduction and external rotation. In fact, the athlete may even drop the object he is throwing or holding. The quarterback will be unable to throw the "long bomb" and the volleyball player will be unable to spike. In a swimmer, the humeral head may slide partly out of the glenoid during a turn in the backstroke (Figure 9-29A).

Some athletes are clearly aware that the shoulder is slipping out of the socket or catching on the edge and popping back in. Others experience only the sharp, paralyzing pain and are unaware that the shoulder is subluxing. A correct diagnosis is difficult to arrive at in a patient like this who is unaware that the shoulder is subluxing. Another group of people with shoulder subluxation are those who have had a previous shoulder operation. For example, a partial acromionectomy for relief of impingement or a transplant of the long head of the biceps tendon may have been performed. The diagnosis in these cases may have, in fact, been a subluxing shoulder, and the operation was of no help.

In a subluxing shoulder the inferior glenohumeral ligament is usually incompetent. This thickened area of the capsule is the prime anterior stabilizer of the shoulder. It is the strongest of the

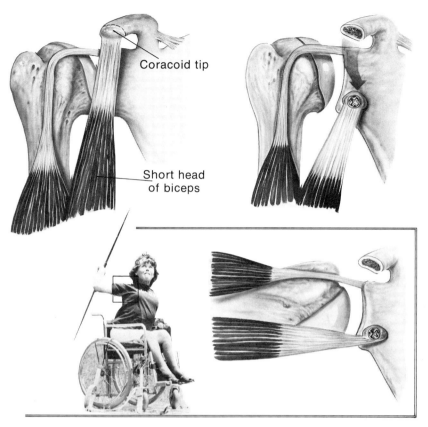

Figure 9-28   The coracoid tip and its conjoined tendon may be transferred to the glenoid rim. When the arm is abducted, the tendon blocks dislocation of the humeral head.

Examination

In patients with glenohumeral subluxation, the anterior glenoid rim may be tender. However, the tenderness and pain are often posterior. For the shoulder to slide anteriorly, the tissues on the opposite end of the joint may be stressed, producing a posterior capsulitis or tendinitis. This explains the frequent posterior shoulder pain and tenderness in patients with anterior subluxation.

three anterior ligaments and bends with the glenoid labrum anteriorly. The discomfort in shoulder subluxation occurs as the humeral head hangs on the glenoid rim and then slides back. Such trouble can be tolerated better in the athlete's nondominant extremity.

Further, some posterior laxity may be found in patients with anterior subluxation because the posterior capsule has been stretched.

The examination begins with the athlete sitting. Anterior instability is reproduced best when the shoulder is stressed in an anteroinferior direction. Have the athlete elevate his arm above 90° in line with the scapula (Figure 9-29C). Hold the arm with one hand at the elbow and press the humeral head forward, displacing it anteroinferiorly. At this time, the athlete may grimace and tighten his shoulder muscles because he feels pain or is apprehensive that the shoulder is about to dislocate. Next, with the athlete supine on the examining table, externally rotate his shoulder. Excessive external rotation is common in anterior subluxation and in multidirectional shoulder in-

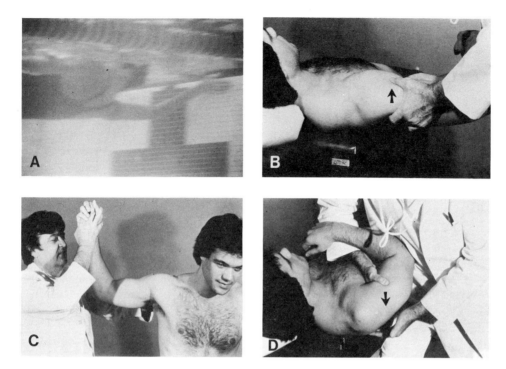

Figure 9-29   The humeral head may slide partly out of the glenoid during a turn in the backstroke **(A)**. The examiner tries to duplicate this subluxation by pulling the humeral head forward **(B)**. In throwing athletes, the feeling of instability recurs when the athlete "throws" against resistance **(C)**. The examiner may also test for posterior subluxation by pressing the humeral head posteriorly **(D)**.

stability. Sometimes, however, because the athlete is apprehensive, the affected shoulder may show decreased external rotation compared to the normal side or compared to an earlier baseline examination. As the shoulder is externally rotated, the pectoralis major may fasciculate. This sign is almost pathognomonic for anterior subluxation.

Next, abduct the shoulder to 90° with the elbow bent at a right angle. Place your hand posteriorly at the glenohumeral joint with your fingers on the humeral head and your thumb anteriorly with your other hand supporting the arm at the elbow and try to lever the humeral head anteriorly (Figure 9-29B). Repeat this maneuver at varying degrees of abduction up to full overhead position. Stressing the shoulder at varying degrees of abduction is important because the shoulder may slip forward only at the same angle of abduction that the arm was in at the time of

the initial injury. A labral tear is probable if these tests or internal rotation of the shoulder produces a clicking sensation.

Diagnostic Tests

An x-ray film may show a mild Hill–Sachs lesion. This may be seen in an internal rotation view but even better with an x-ray film taken with the athlete supine, arm flexed 100°, and elbow flexed. The x-ray film is taken from above and will show a divot or notch in the humeral head clearly.

An x-ray film may also show changes along the anteroinferior glenoid rim where periosteum may have been stripped from the anterior scapular neck, there may be avulsed bone chips, or there may be calcification. They are best seen on a "West Point view" taken with the athlete prone and his arm abducted to 90° and elbow flexed off the edge of the table. The x-ray plate is placed above the shoulder and the x-ray beam shoots into the axilla. This x-ray may also be taken with the athlete supine.

Arthrography may show dye extravasating into a large subscapular pouch that has resulted from avulsion of the glenohumeral ligaments from the glenoid. During this test, the athlete should abduct and rotate his shoulder inward. The subscapularis is tense in external rotation, and the underlying pouch might not be seen. Arthrotomograms may also be helpful in delineating labral tears.

If apprehension is the only positive instability finding when the arm is abducted and externally rotated, impingement must be excluded as the cause. Impingement and instability overlap in this position. They may be differentiated, however, by injecting 10 ml of lidocaine (Xylocaine) subacromially. An acromioclavicular joint sprain may confuse the diagnosis, too. In such cases the joint will be tender, and injection of 1 ml of lidocaine into the acromioclavicular joint should render it pain free. In some cases, all tests may be negative but suspicious. An examination under interscalene block anesthesia may then be indicated. If the shoulder is unstable during the examination under anesthesia, an arthroscopic assessment is indicated. However, many shoulders have a normal laxity that may be misinterpreted as abnormal.

Most people with anterior subluxation have been found to have a lesion. This is an avulsion of the labrum and capsule from the anterior glenoid rim. However, some have only laxity of the capsule and others have only a large opening between the tendons of the supraspinatus and subscapularis.

Treatment of Anterior Subluxation

After the first subluxation, the shoulder should be immobilized with a sling and swath for 2 weeks to decrease the possibility of a recurrence. Along with this rest, nonsteroidal anti-inflammatory drugs lessen the inflammation. The athlete may then restrengthen the shoulder, balance the muscles, and work to regain flexibility. Many will respond to a 2-month long exercise program with no further trouble. The athlete is allowed to abduct up to 50° against Tubic resistance. To do this, he places his forearms palms down into a looped tube and abducts both arms against Tubic resistance. With his elbow at his side he externally rotates against the tube, which is held in the other hand. He internally rotates against a tube that passes around his back or is attached in a door. Special problems demand special solutions; if a backstroke swimmer, for example, has anterior capsular derangement, he may have to change his turning technique to a front flip turn wherein he reaches across but remains on his back at the touch to avoid disqualification.

If subluxations persist and interfere with athletic performance, an operation may be needed.[51a] A Bankart lesion requires a Bankart repair. Here, the conjoined tendon of the biceps is released to be attached later. After a Bankart procedure, the athlete wears a sling for a few days. On the third or fourth postoperative day, he begins pendulum exercises. By the third month he may swim or row, and by the sixth month he may return to contact sports and throwing.

When there is no Bankart lesion but only a lax capsule, a modified capsulorrhaphy may be used to reef the capsule. In case of a large opening between the supraspinatus and the subscapularis tendons, the gap may be partly closed with interrupted sutures, care being taken not to limit the division of the two tendons around the coracoid. The Bristow procedure (coracoid transfer to the anteroinferior glenoid rim) had gained favor in throwing athletes with anterior derangement. However, it may limit rotation because the graft traps the subscapularis. Hence, the Bristow is now used only in persons with deficient glenoids.

Arthroscopic surgical procedures are gaining popularity for treating anterior subluxations and someday may replace the Bankart procedure. Under arthroscopic control, a staple or a screw is inserted to reattach the labrum and reef the anterior capsule and has the virtue of not being a major open operation. Along with the capsular repair, arthroscopy allows a surgeon to treat bicipital lesions, remove loose bodies, trim areas of chondromalacia, and repair labral damage or rotator cuff tears.

Posterior Subluxation

Sometimes an athlete will feel shoulder pain during deceleration in the follow-through phase of throwing and pain when the shoulder is flexed, adducted, and internally rotated. The tenderness may be posterior or anterior. A history of a fall on the flexed arm or of a blow to the shoulder, driving the shoulder posteriorly, is common. Athletes who perform heavy bench presses may also develop posterior subluxation. Some athletes are more uncomfortable when the humeral head leaves the glenoid, whereas others have discomfort when the head relocates. Pain results from the humeral head pressing against the posterior capsule and the cuff tendons of the infraspinatus and teres minor.

The examination for posterior subluxation begins with the athlete supine. This position calms the patient, relaxes the shoulder muscles, and eliminates the effects of gravity. The examiner first palpates the scapular neck and humeral head and controls the arm by supporting it at the elbow. The arm is flexed to 90° and then horizontally abducted about 20° (Figure 9-29). A posterior force applied to the arm may then sublux the shoulder. Often there will be a posterior bulge below the acromion. As the shoulder is horizontally abducted about 20° more, the humeral head will reduce suddenly and the humeral head prominence will disappear. Remember that a shoulder may normally show considerable posterior laxity in fact, one can normally get up to 50% posterior movement of the humeral head on the glenoid. Posterior subluxation may also be tested for by abducting the shoulder to 90°, externally rotating it, and then horizontally adducting it. In posterior subluxation, the examiner will then feel the humeral head posteriorly. The athlete will usually say that this is the type of discomfort he feels in his sport. As the arm is returned to neutral position at 90° of abduction, the humeral head will reduce.

The shoulder will sublux at a level of abduction that depends on the position of the arm at initial injury. Therefore, the probability of detecting a subluxation problem will increase if the amount of humeral rotation and the amount of abduction are changed and the examination repeated.

An axillary lateral x-ray film may show evidence of damage at the glenoid, such as a posterior capsular spur, bone chip, or calcification from throwing, or it may show a wearing away or erosion of the posterior glenoid with insufficiency of the posterior glenoid owing to repetitive heavy bench presses.

Treatment of Posterior Subluxation

The athlete should avoid bench presses and heavy pushing and pulling while the shoulder is symptomatic. Shoulder flexion should be avoided, too, so that the humeral head will stay in the center of the glenoid away from the posterior aspect of the glenoid labrum and cuff. To strengthen the shoulder, the athlete does Tubic external rotations, starting the exercises at 45° of external rotation with his arms at his side. If he were to perform the exercises with less external rotation, the humeral head would shift posteriorly. The athlete should also strengthen his supraspinatus (with empty-the-can Tubics) and trapezius (with shrugs).

In adolescents, strengthening will reduce the laxity as the posterior shoulder tightens and the shoulder matures. The older athlete with subluxation, however, is less likely to recover fully.

MULTIDIRECTIONAL INSTABILITY

Multidirectional instability is a combination of anterior and posterior instability. In addition, significant inferior instability is the hallmark of generalized shoulder laxity with multidirectional instability. In fact, the inferior laxity may be such that even the unsupported arm with no additional weight may slip down.

On examination, athletes with multidirectional instability will commonly have excessive external rotation at 90° of abduction. Further, a "sulcus sign" may be elicited in multidirectional instability and inferior instability. When the examiner pulls straight down on the arm while feeling in the axilla, a sulcus appears between the humeral head and the acromion.

At surgery on a patient with multidirectional instability who has inferior instability, the surgeon must carefully evaluate all components of the instability. An inferior capsular shift procedure can snug up these shoulders.[36a] In this operation, the capsule is pulled upwards and reefed as one component of the repair.

INFERIOR INSTABILITY

Inferior instability is noted in multidirectional instability. It is not a common isolated finding but often presents as a residual instability after surgical repairs. Therefore it is important to elicit this finding before repairing a shoulder so that an inferior capsular shift can be done to snug it up. Otherwise the patient may have pain even when doing something as easy as lifting light objects, since his humeral head catches on the glenoid rim.

As another method for determining inferior instability, the patient's elbow rests on the examiner's forearm and the examiner applies downward force on his proximal humerus. Inferior capsular laxity may also be elicited by placing the patient's arm directly over his head and directing a longitudinal force inferiorly.

Voluntary instability of the shoulder may be found in people with very lax shoulders. The treatment includes exercises to snug up the shoulder muscles and reassurance of the patient that this laxity will not ruin his shoulder. Before deciding on a surgical approach for voluntary dislocations, the motivational status of the individual must be assessed.

THE HUMERUS

Hypertrophy of the humerus is a normal response to prolonged heavy arm exercise,[22] and the cor-

tical thickness of the humerus on the playing side of top-level male tennis players is thus 35% greater than on their nonplaying side. Top-level female players have a cortical thickness 28% greater on their playing side than on their control side.[47]

One half of a large group of college gymnasts showed an asymptomatic cortical irregularity of the proximal humerus that simulates the cortical desmoid often found at the distal medial femoral condyle. This benign reactive process is located at the insertion of the broad, strong pectoralis major on the anteromedial cortical border of the humerus. Most athletes with this irregularity are all-around gymnasts who regularly perform strength moves, especially on the rings—hence the term "ringman's shoulder."

The proximal humeral epiphysis of a young thrower may become disrupted, or a cyst in the proximal humerus may weaken the bone, making it more vulnerable to fracture. The normal humerus of a child may also fracture if it is subjected to excessive torque, and exostoses may develop from direct trauma to the arm.

"LITTLE LEAGUE SHOULDER"

Injury to the proximal humeral growth plate in a young pitcher is called "Little League shoulder." This injury also occurs in catchers who throw as often as pitchers but use less windup. Rotary torques are applied to the humerus during the acceleration phase, and decelerating distraction forces are applied during the follow through.[8]

If the proximal humeral growth plate is injured, the youngster's shoulder may swell and hurt. The examiner may reach into the player's axilla and feel for tenderness of the bone,[56] and an x-ray film may show "preslip" changes. These changes include a wide epiphyseal line, with demineralization and rarefaction on the metaphyseal side of the growth plate. A young pitcher's proximal humeral epiphysis may also slip off his humeral shaft. The x-ray film will sometimes show a triangular chipped-off piece of metaphyseal bone that indicates a grade II epiphyseal fracture. New bone appears about 10 days after these fractures, which quickly heal with rest.

A fracture may also occur in youths through a thin-walled unicameral bone cyst just distal to the proximal humeral growth plate. This fracture produces a painful, swollen shoulder, and an x-ray film will show the cyst. The natural course of a cyst is to disappear in the diaphyseal region as the epiphysis grows away from it. The cyst may spontaneously fill in after a fracture as the callus forms. If fractures recur through a cyst, the surgeon may elect to curette out the cyst wall and insert a bone graft. The growth plate must first, however, be allowed to move away from the cyst before surgery is done.

Fractures of the humeral shaft have been reported in throwing athletes and wrist wrestlers.[20] During the acceleration phase of throwing, the latissimus dorsi and the pectoralis major strongly rotate the athlete's shoulder internally, leaving his elbow behind. This torque may produce a spiral fracture of the humerus, especially in weak-armed but hard-throwing teenage pitchers with unrefined deliveries. When an outfielder throws from next to a fence or wall, he cannot use his body but must throw with his arm only. The torque may be so great as to fracture his humerus. Similarly, an arm wrestler may fracture his humerus during the losing phase of a contest. In the losing position, his elbow extends progressively, and there are changes in the direction of applied force during this eccentric muscle contraction. The humerus fractures spirally in its middle third and lower third with or without a butterfly fragment. These fractures are treated with a hanging arm cast.

TACKLER'S EXOSTOSIS

In tackle football, a linebacker's internally rotated and abducted arms receive direct blows from the helmets of players he is tackling. The linebacker also sustains blows as he holds his arms internally rotated to ward off blockers, and the arms are bruised from direct blows or blows that slide off his shoulder pads.

The player may develop a painful bony prominence at the subcutaneous part of the anterolateral humerus, just distal to the edge of the shoulder pad (Figure 9-30). This "tackler's exostosis" results from damage at the insertion of the deltoid or at the brachialis origin with tearing of the periosteum. Bone forms in continuity with the cortex and grows by accretion. The athlete's upper arm swells acutely, and within 4 weeks a hard mass can be felt. The elbow range of motion usually is full. Early x-ray films show swelling, and at 2 or 3 weeks the accretion of bone is confirmed as a "dotted veil" that later evolves into a mature exostosis. Because the exostosis may be disabling, early recognition and treatment are important.

When a blow to the arm brings tenderness and swelling, the area is iced and the arm rested. If a large hematoma develops, it is aspirated and a compression wrap applied for 10 days. The contusion should not be massaged soon after injury because this may cause further bleeding and irritation. If the arm is seen for the first time at 2 weeks after injury and bone is noted, the arm should be rested in a plaster splint. Sometimes, the bone will then spontaneously resorb. If mature bone forms, the area will be sore, despite extra padding. If the region continues to be painful, the mass may be removed surgically.

At surgery, a tackler's exostosis may be differentiated from myositis ossificans. A tackler's exostosis has no cleavage plane between it and the cortex of the humerus, and the anterior mass of the brachialis is not involved. The exostosis usually occurs in older players, whereas myositis ossificans occurs more frequently in high school players. The connective tissue associated with the bruised brachialis muscle becomes ossified in myositis ossificans.[23] A mature myositis ossificans lesion may be resected if it is large and painful, predisposes to further injury, has a pointed end that is easily reinjured, or restricts elbow motion to the point of being a functional handicap.

Tackler's exostosis can be prevented by requiring offensive linemen and linebackers to wear fiber doughnut pads attached to their epaulets or separate from the shoulder pads to cover the lateral humerus.

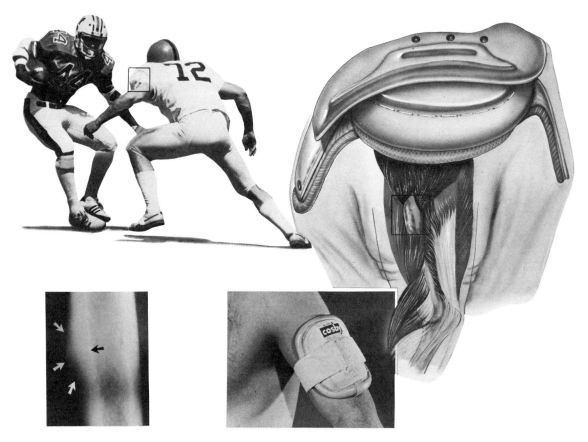

Figure 9-30   Tackler's exostosis (see text for description). Blows that slide off a shoulder pad may damage the humerus. An extra arm pad can protect the area from these blows.

TENNIS SHOULDER

In the tennis serve, the racket is thrown up at the ball and decelerated over a very short distance from a speed of about 480 km/h (300 miles/h).[38] The forces generated in this movement stretch the scapular-anchoring muscles, and the shoulder then droops, rotating forward from the pull of gravity on the increased mass of the arm (Figure 9-31).

The player with a drooped shoulder may develop anterior rotator cuff symptoms. A relative abduction of the shoulder is produced as the scapula tilts downward. There is less room for the rotator cuff, and it may be impacted, especially during serves and overhead returns. The player may also have pain on the backhand side when the arm ends high, especially with backhand volleys.

Signs and symptoms of compression at the thoracic outlet are thought by some to be associated with the drooped "tennis shoulder," causing neck and arm pain.[47] However, we have studied over a period of 5 years the players who compete in the United States Tennis Association National Clay Court Championships.[28] These players have an average of 50 years of playing experience. All have drooped racket arm shoulders, but none have had symptoms of an outlet syndrome. We therefore conclude that the "tennis shoulder" of a veteran player is a normal response to exercise and generally will not produce outlet difficulties.

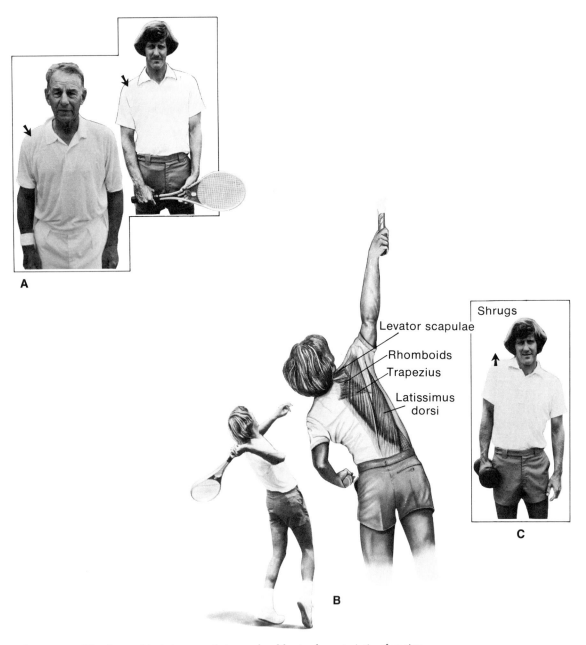

Figure 9-31   The drooped but strong racket-arm shoulder is characteristic of senior tennis players and young professionals **(A)**. It follows a stretching-out of the scapular-anchoring muscles from repeated serves **(B)**. These muscles may be strengthened with shrugging exercises **(C)**.

REHABILITATION PROGRESSION FOR THE SHOULDER

OBJECTIVES

Strengthen: shoulder girdle in ten motions (Figure 9-32)
Flexibility: shoulder girdle in ten motions
Endurance: shoulder girdle in ten motions

STAGES

Initial
Cryokinetics with range of motion within the pain-free limits
Active/resisted (isometric) exercises in the affected motion

Intermediate
Flexibility (Figure 9-33)
"Pendulums":

Forward and back (Figure 9-33A)
Side-to-side
Clockwise circles (Figure 9-33B)
Counterclockwise circles (Figure 9-33B)
The athlete holds a small weight while doing exercises 25 times in each direction.

Lean on hands. Shift to the right and then to the left 25 times (Figure 9-33C)
Stick swing (Figure 9-33D) 25 times.
Corner stretch and pulley stretch (Figure 9-34A) for external rotation, 25 times each.
Towel stretch (Figure 9-34B) for internal rotation. Stretch and hold for 15 seconds three times.
Table stretch (Figure 9-34C) for internal rotation—bend knees for 15 seconds three times to slowly stretch the shoulder.
Pitcher stretch (Figures 9-34D–G)—The athlete reaches across his chest and then back for 15 seconds three times; he then stretches forward and back for 15 seconds three times.
Strength:

Isometrics in the ten motions, holding for 6 seconds three times.
"T" exercises (Figure 9-35)—These exercises are done in a pattern with forward flexion (Figure 9-35A), backward extension (Figure 9-35B), and then abduction to the horizontal and swing up (Figures 9-35C–E). The abduction to horizontal exercise is a most important part of the exercise because it reestablishes a useful pattern of movement. The athlete externally rotates his arm while coming forward and up, as if he is tracing a reverse "C" on a wall at his side. All "T" exercises start with three sets of ten repetitions and no weight or a light dumbbell and increase to five sets of ten. When the athlete reaches five sets of ten, he may substitute surgical tubing for the weight or increase the weight and cut back to three sets of ten. He again progresses with a goal of five sets of ten with a 10-lb weight.
The athlete uses hand weights or surgical tubing as resistance for adduction (Figure 9-36A), abduction (Figure 9-36B), internal rotation (Figure 9-36C),

(continued)

REHABILITATION PROGRESSION FOR THE SHOULDER (*continued*)

STAGES

Intermediate (*continued*)

external rotation (Figure 9-36D), horizontal extension (Figure 9-36E), horizontal flexion (Figure 9-36F), and to strengthen the supraspinatus. In the supraspinatus exercise (Figure 9-36G), he raises the dumbbell from his pants crease to the horizontal with his thumb down or may do horizontal extension with the thumbs up.

Shoulder shrugs: The athlete shrugs his shoulders to his ears, then lowers his shoulders and rotates his head and neck to the left and then to the right for three sets of ten repetitions.

Advanced

Flexibility: "Devastator" T-bar exercise (Figure 9-37)—these external rotation stretches at the side (Figure 9-37A) and above the head (Figure 9-37B) are held for 15 seconds three times. A pitcher should strive to rotate his throwing arm so that his forearm is perpendicular to the floor because he will need this external rotation when pitching.

Strength (Figure 9-38)

Barbell weights

Dips (Figure 9-38A) ranging form one quarter to full

Chins (Figure 9-38B) ranging from one quarter to full

Push-ups (Figure 9-38C)

Run with weight cuff on wrists (Figure 9-38D)

The younger and harder-hitting tennis professional may, however, develop outlet problems. If such a play is symptomatic, shrug exercises will help to elevate his shoulder, and if the symptoms persist a thorough workup should be conducted.

SCAPULAR PAIN

The athlete's scapula is surrounded by muscles to stabilize his upper extremity. Several bursae between the scapula and the chest wall may become irritated.[52]

Periscapular pain is frequent in shotputters, tennis players, and weight lifters. In putting the shot, the scapula muscles anchor the arm and must restrain the scapula during the follow-through. Pain in the rhomboids and scapulocostal bursitis are treated with massage, ultrasound, and, occasionally, steroid injections. During the backscratch position of the tennis serve, the inferior angle of the scapula may jam against the ribs to produce a bursitis, and the rhomboids may also be strained during the follow through. Treatment is similar to that given for the shotputter's shoulder.

A weight lifter must strongly protract his shoulders. During this activity, the serratus anterior holds the scapula firmly to the lifter's chest wall. The muscle arises from his first eight ribs and inserts into the medial border of the scapula. A strong contraction of this muscle may fracture the first rib through the weak subclavian groove.

In weight training, standing pull-overs may place traction on the long thoracic nerve, paralyzing the serratus anterior. This injury may be diagnosed by having the athlete do a wall push-

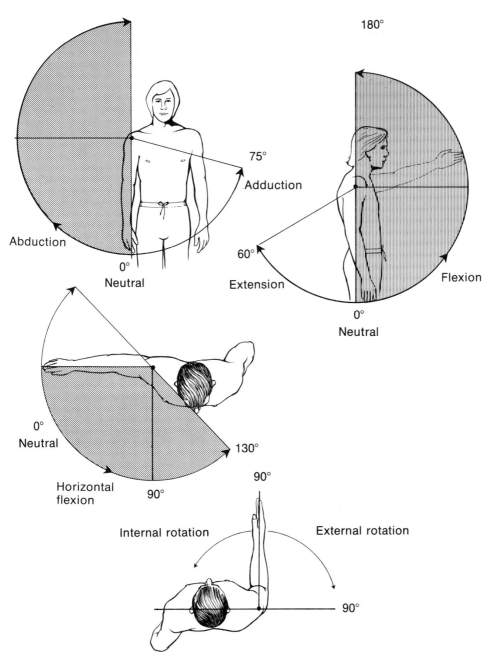

Figure 9-32 Planes of shoulder motion.

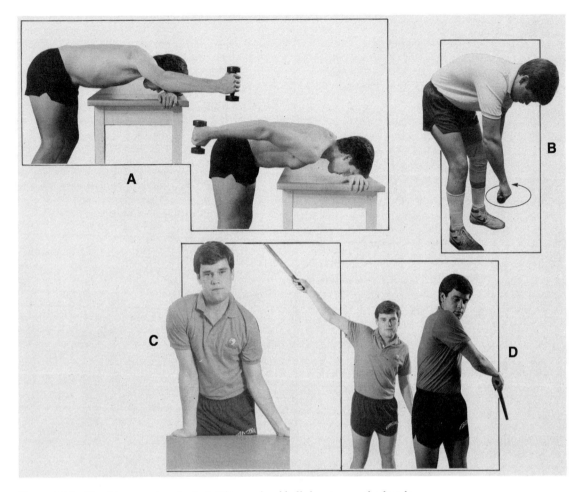

Figure 9-33   Shoulder exercises include lifting a dumbbell, leaning on the hands and shifting from side to side, and moving a stick in a pattern.

up to elicit scapular winging. An electromyogram will show serratus anterior denervation. This injury may be prevented if pull-overs are done while the athlete is supine.[53]

A snapping scapula may be due to a prominent superomedial border of the scapula that passes over the underlying muscles and ribs. The examiner may move the scapula around and feel under it while the athlete lies prone with his arm hanging over the side of the examining table. If the snapping is painful and persists after a rest period, the superomedial angle may have to be resected.

When an athlete has intractible periscapular pain, the examiner should look to the neck for diagnosis because the pain around the scapula may have a radicular origin in the neck.[10] The athlete may report recurrent stiff necks but usually without neurologic or electromyographic changes. Pain in his trapezius or other shoulder muscles or at the occipital–cervical junction may be due to nervous tension or afternoon fatigue or may follow prolonged flexion and extension of the neck. In these cases, the athlete should strengthen his neck muscles and try neck traction for relief of the shoulder pain.

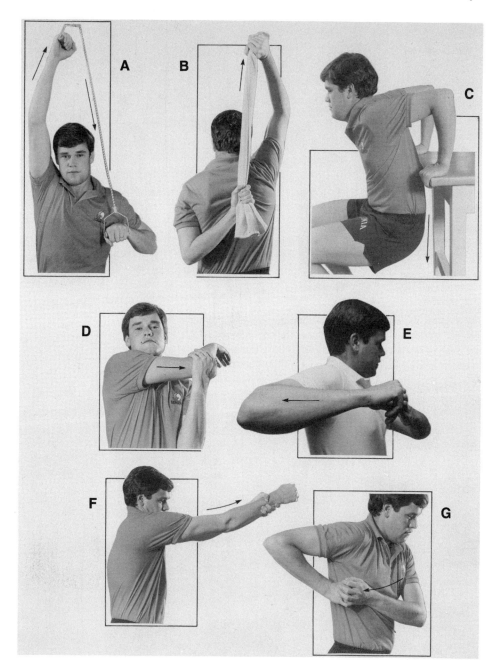

Figure 9-34   Shoulder flexibility may be gained by using pulleys or a towel. A baseball pitcher stretches his shoulder across his body and back and then forward and back.

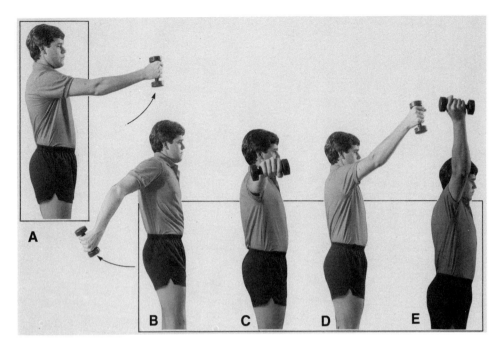

Figure 9-35 In "T" exercises, the athlete moves his shoulder forward and back and then abducts it to 90°. From this position, he rotates the shoulder externally while bringing it into forward flexion directly overhead. During this movement, he should imagine that he is tracing a backwards "C" on a wall at his side.

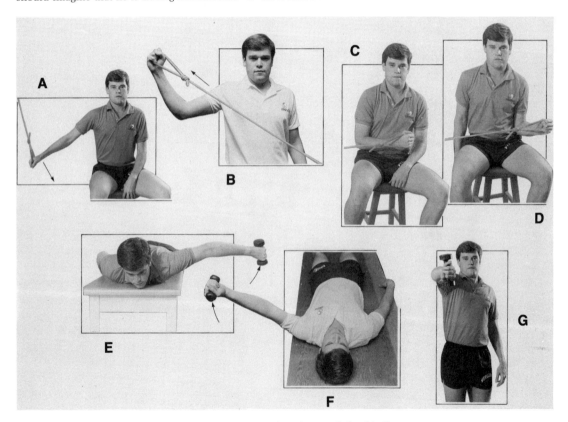

Figure 9-36 The athlete strengthens his shoulder with Tubics and dumbbell exercises.

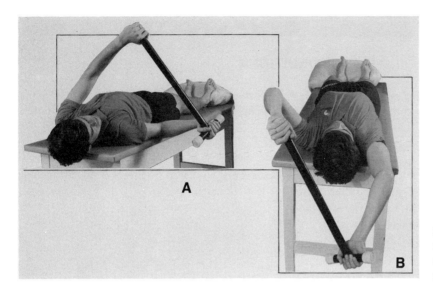

Figure 9-37 A T-bar helps the pitcher stretch his shoulder into external rotation.

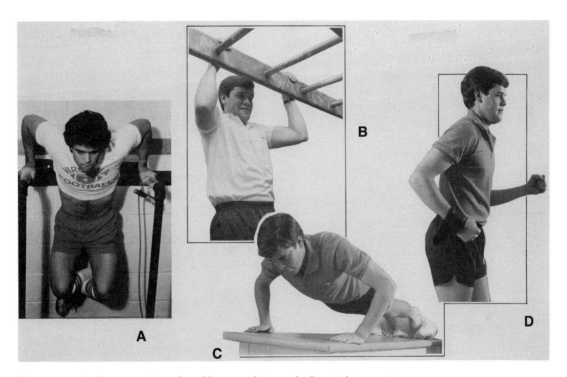

Figure 9-38 In these exercises, the athlete uses his own body weight as resistance.

SHOULDER EXERCISES FOR SPECIFIC CONDITIONS

The following are common shoulder injuries along with the exercises that are of prime importance in their rehabilitation. A description of each exercise can be found in the general shoulder rehabilitation progression.

Rhomboid strain (Figure 9-39):
    Forward flexion (Figure 9-39A), backward extension (Figure 9-39B), horizontal
        extension (Figure 9-39C), and elbow lift (Figure 9-39D)
Anterior dislocation of the shoulder
    "T" exercise
    Horizontal flexion
    Adduction
    Internal rotation
Acromioclavicular sprain
    "T" exercise
    Adduction
    Shoulder shrugs with weight in hand
Impingement syndrome
    Neck posture routine (see neck section)
    Flexibility:
        Corner stretch
        Pulley stretch
        Towel stretch
        Table stretch
    Strength:
        "T" exercise
        External rotation
        Rhomboid exercise
Tennis shoulder (slouch)
    Flexibility:
        Corner stretch
    Strength:
        "T" exercise
        Adduction
        Shoulder shrug
        Horizontal extension
Rotator cuff problems
    Flexibility:
        Corner stretch
        External rotation with a "devastator" T-bar and with pulleys
        Internal rotation with towel stretch and table stretch

SHOULDER EXERCISES FOR SPECIFIC CONDITIONS (*continued*)

Strength:
    "T" exercise
    Adduction
    Supraspinatus
    External rotation
    Horizontal extension with the thumb up (strengthens supraspinatus as well)

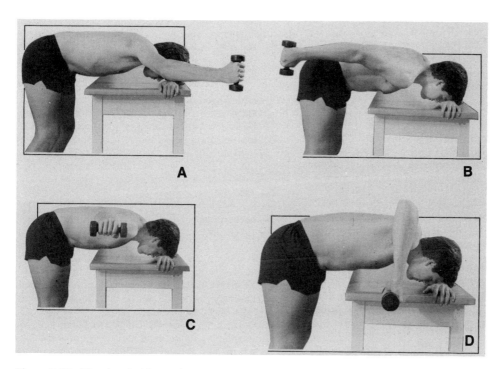

Figure 9-39   The rhomboid muscles are strengthened with dumbbells.

REFERENCES

1. Allman F: Symposium on sports injuries to the shoulder. Contemp Surg 4:70–109, 1975
2. Andrews JR et al: Musculotendinous injuries of the shoulder and elbow in athletics. Athletic Training 11(2):68–70, 1976
2a. Andrews JR et al: Glenoid labrum tears related to the long head of the biceps. Am J Sports Med 13(5):337–341, 1985
3. Benton J, Nelson C: Avulsion of the coracoid process in an athlete: Report of a case. J Bone Joint Surg [Am] 53:356–358, 1971
4. Bergfeld JA et al: Evaluation of the acromioclavicular joint following first and second degree sprains. Am J Sports Med 6:153–159, 1978
5. Berson BC: Surgical repair of pectoralis major rupture in an athlete—case report of an unusual injury in a wrestler. Am J Sports Med 7:348–351, 1979
6. Boyd R: Gradual warmup routine helps pitchers avoid arm injuries. First Aider, Cramer 47:6, February 1978
7. Britt LP: Non-operative treatment of the thoracic outlet syndrome symptoms. Clin Orthop 51:45–48, 1967
8. Cahill BR et al: Little League shoulder. Am J Sports Med 2:150–154, 1974
9. Cautilli RA et al: Posterior dislocations of the shoulder: A method of post-reduction management. Am J Sports Med 6:397–399, 1978
10. Coventry M: Recurring scapular pain. JAMA 241:942, 1979
11. Crenshaw AH: Surgical treatment of bicipital tenosynovitis. J Bone Joint Surg [Am] 48:1498, 1966
12. Cox JS: The fate of the acromioclavicular joint in athletic injuries. Am J Sports Med 9:50–53, 1981
13. Danzig LA et al: The Hill-Sachs lesion—an experimental study. Am J Sports Med 8:328–332, 1980
14. Del Pizzo W et al: Rupture of the biceps tendon in gymnastics: A case report. Am J Sports Med 6:283–286, 1978
15. Depalma AF, Callery GE: Bicipital tenosynovitis. Clin Orthop 3:69, 1954
15a. Ellman H et al: Repair of the rotator cuff. J Bone Joint Surg 68A(8):1136–1144, 1986
16. Fowler P: Swimmer problems. Am J Sports Med 7:141–142, 1979
17. Froimson AI, Oh I: Keyhole tenodesis of biceps origin at the shoulder. Clin Orthop 112:245–249, 1975
18. Gainor BJ: The throw: Biomechanics and acute injury. Am J Sports Med 8:114–118, 1980
19. Gieck JH: Shoulder strap to prevent anterior glenohumeral dislocations. Athletic Training 11(1):18, 1976
20. Gregerson HN: Fracture of the humerus from muscular violence. Acta Orthop Scand 42:506–512, 1971

21. Hawkins RJ, Kennedy JC: Impingement syndrome in athletes. Am J Sports Med 8:151–158, 1980
22. Huddleston AL et al: Bone mass in lifetime tennis athletes. JAMA 244:1107–1109, 1980
23. Huss CD, Puhl JJ: Myositis ossificans of the upper arm. Am J Sports Med 8:419–424, 1980
24. Hitchcock HH, Bechtol CO: Painful shoulder. J Bone Joint Surg [Am] 30:263–267, 1948
25. Kennedy JC: Retrosternal dislocation of the clavicle. J Bone Joint Surg [Br] 31:74, 1949
26. Kennedy JC, Hawkins RJ: Swimmer's shoulder. Phys Sportsmed 2(4):35–38, 1974
27. Kennedy JC: Orthopedic manifestations of swimming. Am J Sports Med 6:309–322, 1978
28. Kulund DN et al: The long–term effects of playing tennis. Phys Sportsmed 7(4):87–94, 1979
29. Kulund DN et al: Tennis injuries: Prevention and treatment. Am J Sports Med 7:249–253, 1979
30. Kummel BM: Arthrography in anterior capsular derangements of the shoulder. Clin Orthop 83:170–176, 1972
31. Kummel BM: When shoulder complaints limit athletic performance. Phys Sportsmed 2(8):46–51, 1974
32. Lipscomb AB: Treatment of recurrent anterior dislocation and subluxation of the glenohumeral joint in athletics. Clin Orthop 109:122–125, 1975
33. Mariani PP: Isolated fracture of the coracoid process in an athlete. Am J Sports Med 8:129–130, 1980
34. Macnab I, Rathbun JB: The microvascular pattern of the rotator cuff. J Bone Joint Surg [Br] 52:524, 1970
35. Micheli LJ, Riseborough EM: The incidence of injuries in rugby football. Am J Sports Med 2:93–98, 1974
36. Neer CS: Anterior acromioplasty for the chronic impingement syndrome in the shoulder. J Bone Joint Surg [Am] 54:41–50, 1972
36a. Neer CS II, Foster CR: Inferior capsular shift for involuntary inferior and multidirectional instability of the shoulder. J Bone Joint Surg [Am] 62(6):897–907, 1980
37. Nelson CL: The use of arthrography in athletic injuries of the shoulder. Orthop Clin North Am 4:775–785, 1973
38. Nirschl RP: Throwing or swinging the shoulder pays. Phys Sportsmed 2(12):20–27, 1974
39. Nixon JE, Disterano V: Rupture of the rotator cuff. Orthop Clin North Am 6:423–447, 1975
40. Norfray JF et al: The clavicle in hockey. Am J Sports Med 5:275–280, 1977
41. Norwood LA et al: Anterior shoulder pain in baseball pitchers. Am J Sports Med 6:103–106, 1978
42. O'Donoghue DH: Subluxing biceps tendon in the athlete. Am J Sports Med 1:20–29, 1973
43. Osmond-Clarke H: Habitual dislocations of the

shoulder. The Putti-Platt operation. J Bone Joint Surg [Br] 30:19, 1948

44. Park JP et al: Treatment of acromioclavicular separations. Am J Sports Med 8:251–256, 1980

45. Penny JN, Welsh RP: Shoulder impingement syndromes in athletes and their surgical management. Am J Sports Med 9:11–15, 1981

46. Pettrone FA, Nirschl RP: Acromioclavicular dislocation. Am J Sports Med 6:160–164, 1978

47. Priest JD, Nagel DA: Tennis shoulder. Am J Sports Med 4:28–42, 1976

47a. Protzman RR: Anterior instability of the shoulder. J Bone Joint Surg 909–918, 1980

48. Richardson AB: The shoulder in swimming. Swimming World 29:33–34, 1979

49. Richardson AB: The shoulder in competitive swimming. Am J Sports Med 8:159–163, 1980

50. Rowe CR: Prognosis in dislocations of the shoulder. J Bone Joint Surg [Am] 38:957–977, 1956

51. Rowe CR, Sakellarides HT: Factors related to recurrence of dislocations of the shoulder. Clin Orthop 20:40–48, 1961

51a. Rowe CR, Zarins B: Recurrent transient subluxation of the shoulder. J Bone Joint Surg [Am] 63:863, 1981

52. Russek AS: Scapulo-costal syndrome. JAMA 150:25–27, 1952

53. Stanish WD, Lamb J: Isolated paralysis of the serratus anterior muscle: A weight training injury. Case report. Am J Sports Med 6:385–386, 1978

54. Strukel RJ, Garrick JG: Thoracic outlet compression in athletes: A report of four cases. Am J Sports Med 6:35–39, 1978

54a. Tibone JE et al: Surgical treatment of tears of the rotator cuff in athletes. J Bone Joint Surg [Am] 68:887–891, 1986

55. Tirman RM: Shoulder arthography. Contemp Orthop 1(2):26–32, 1979

56. Torg JS et al: The effect of competitive pitching on the shoulders and elbows of pre-adolescent baseball players. Pediatrics 49:267–272, 1972

57. Tullos HS et al: Unusual lesions of the pitching arm. Clin Orthop 88:169–182, 1972

58. Van Linge B, Mulder JD: Function of the supraspinatus muscle and its relations to the supraspinatus syndrome: An experimental study in man. J Bone Joint Surg [Br] 45:750–754, 1963

59. Wright RS, Lipscomb AB: Acute occlusion of the subclavian vein in an athlete: Diagnosis, etiology and surgical management. Am J Sports Med 2:343–348, 1974

60. Zeman SC et al: Tears of the pectoralis major muscle. Am J Sports Med 7:343–347, 1979

CHAPTER

10

The Elbow, Wrist, and Hand

Frank C. McCue III

THE ELBOW

Anatomy

The elbow joint consists of three articulations: the humeral-ulnar, the capitellar-radial, and the radial-ulnar. The humeral-ulnar articulation determines the carrying angle of the elbow. When the elbow is flexed, the forearm is in line with the arm; as it extends, the trochlear course allows the forearm to move into valgus, producing the "carrying angle." Fractures at the elbow may alter this carrying angle. Pronation and supination take place around the capitellar-radial articulation, an area jammed during throwing. The radial-ulnar articulation is a small one that moves during pronation and supination.

The medial collateral ligament of the elbow is deep to the flexor mass. It has two parts: an an-

terior band and a posterior band. The thick anterior band is a major static stabilizer of the elbow, arising from the medial epicondyle to insert on the medial side of the coronoid process of the ulna. Some of its fibers are taut in all degrees of flexion and extension. The thinner and weaker posterior band functions only when the elbow is flexed to more than 90°. The medial collateral ligament is stretched in baseball pitchers and round-arm-style javelin throwers, all of whom put extreme valgus stress on their elbows. Medial collateral ligament laxity may result from poorly reduced medial epicondyle fractures.

The flexor carpi radialis, palmaris longus, and parts of the flexor carpi ulnaris and flexor digitorum sublimis originate from the medial epicondyle. One head of the pronator teres arises from the metaphyseal flare just proximal to the epicondyle. The flexor muscle mass exerts a strong pull

357

on the epicondyle and may be partly avulsed in the young thrower. Because it is not yet fused to bone, the epicondyle sometimes is jerked from its bed and pulled into the elbow joint. Older tennis players, especially professionals who use spin serves, develop a large medial epicondyle as a response to heavy use.

The extensor muscles of the wrist and fingers arise from the lateral condyle of the humerus. The origin of the extensor carpi radialis brevis is often the site of damage in tennis elbow. It inserts at the base of the third metacarpal, the center of the hand. A fracture through the lateral condyle into the elbow joint sometimes heals slowly because the fracture site is bathed in synovial fluid containing fibrinolysin that prevents organization of the fracture hematoma.

The bony structures of the elbow joint are the capitellum, trochlea, and radial head. The capitellum lines up with the radial head on a lateral x-ray view of the elbow. If the radial head repeatedly jams against the capitellum, as in baseball pitching, capitellar avascular necrosis and osteochondritis dissecans may ensue. The trochlear sweep controls the carrying angle, and pieces from the medial edge of the trochlea may be chipped off during throwing.

Incongruity of the radial head after a fracture may result in osteoarthritis of the elbow with pain during pronation and supination. The orbicular or annular ligament arises from the humerus to surround the radial head. Adhesions between this ligament and the capsule of the elbow joint are responsible for some cases of tennis elbow.

When the elbow is fully extended, the olecranon fossa accepts the olecranon tip. The common supracondylar fracture in children extends through the very thin bone of this fossa and may lead to a bony build-up within the fossa that blocks full extension. Such a bony block affects throwing and also hinders a good follow-through in basketball shooting.

A posterior fat pad resides in the olecranon fossa just external to the elbow joint.[67] Intra-articular injury pushes this fat pad up so that it may be seen on a lateral x-ray film as evidence of intra-articular swelling. During throwing, the fat pad is normally pulled up by a slip of triceps, such as the articularis genu muscle of the knee, to prevent trapping and painful pinching of the fat pad between bone surfaces during rapid extension.

The biceps muscle is the main supinator of the forearm. Strong flexion of the elbow against resistance may avulse the biceps brachi from the bicipital tubercle of the radius. The brachialis muscle inserts into the coronoid process of the ulna. This muscle pulls chips from the coronoid in boxers, pitchers, and wrist wrestlers.

The major nerves near the elbow are the radial, median, and ulnar nerves. The deep and recurrent branches of the radial nerve may be trapped as they pass between the two parts of the supinator muscle. The median nerve may be impinged upon proximally in a tunnel under the ligament of Struthers, which sometimes runs from a supracondylar process of the humerus down to the medial condyle. Distally, the nerve may be trapped between the humeral and ulnar heads of the pronator teres as it seeks to lie on the substance of the flexor digitorum superficialis. The ulnar nerve courses behind the intermuscular septum and enters the forearm between the humeral and ulnar heads of the flexor carpi ulnaris. It may be trapped and irritated by fascial thickenings in the ulna groove behind the medial epicondyle; in such a case, the ulnar nerve may be decompressed or transplanted to the anterior compartment above the level of the medial epicondyle.

Fibers of the interosseous membrane descend medially from the radius to the ulna. If the athlete falls on his hand, the compression forces can be transmitted through this membrane from the strong lower radius to the strong upper ulna and humeral-ulnar joint. The triceps insertion fans out over the olecranon, and chips may be pulled off the olecranon tip in over-the-shoulder javelin throws or during missed jabs in boxing. The olecranon bursa lies at the elbow tip. It may become inflamed from repeated landings on the point of the elbow or after forceful elbow extensions. Sometimes loose bodies form within this bursa.

Fractures

Supracondylar

A fall from playground apparatus may fracture the thin bone in the supracondylar region of a child's humerus (Figure 10-1). The fracture ends may then damage the intima of the brachial artery. Although the intima is torn, it may take days for it to block the circulation completely. If the brachial artery is blocked, Volkmann's ischemic contractures of the forearm may occur, wherein the muscles die and the nerves fibrose, producing a useless limb. The vascular status and the nerve function of the limb should be evaluated both before and after reduction of the supracondylar fracture. The fracture is carefully reduced under axillary block or general anesthesia by applying traction and then flexing the elbow. The elbow should not be flexed initially without first applying traction, or else the brachial artery may be pinched.

A splint may be applied with the elbow in a flexed position for undisplaced or minimally displaced supracondylar fractures. If the elbow is flexed too much, however, the radial pulse may disappear. If this happens, it should be extended somewhat until the pulse returns. To treat a fully displaced fracture, a pin may be placed through the olecranon for overhead traction, and 10 days later a cast may be applied.

If there is no radial pulse and the youth has pain, pallor, paresthesia, and pain on passive extension of the fingers, overhead traction should be instituted. If pulse and feeling fail to return, then the brachial artery should be explored. Resection of a segment of the artery that contains the torn and folded intima may be needed to

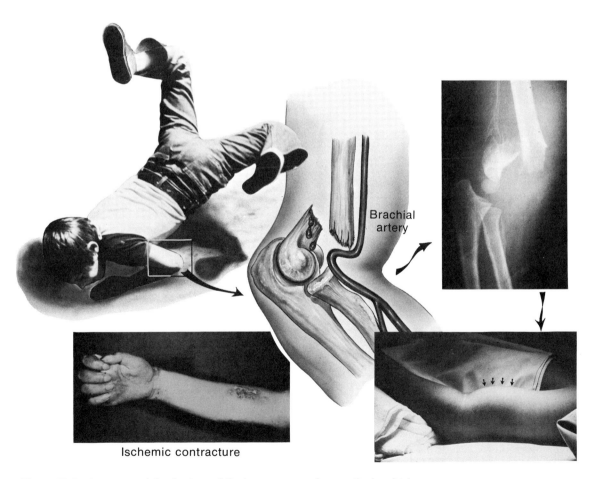

Ischemic contracture

Brachial artery

Figure 10-1 A supracondylar fracture of the humerus may damage the brachial artery and lead to a severe ischemic contracture of the forearm and hand.

reduce the circulatory spasm. Prompt treatment of an elbow with danger signs may avoid the terrible complication of Volkmann's contracture.

Medial Epicondyle

The medial ligament of the elbow and flexor origin may be disrupted in a young thrower, gymnast, or wrestler who fractures the medial epicondyle (Figure 10-2). Medial elbow stability depends on an intact medial collateral ligament and forearm flexors. Fibrous union of a displaced medial epicondyle fracture may cause chronic medial instability of the elbow and end a throwing career.

A routine elbow x-ray may not show much displacement of the medial epicondyle, compared to that which occurred at the time of injury. On x-ray film, the epicondyle may appear to be reduced, but in fact it may be rotated 90°. This change in position of the medial epicondyle alters medial collateral ligament function and lessens the stability of the medial side of the elbow.

There are three types of medial epicondylar fractures.[91] Type I occurs in youths who have open epiphyses. Here, the entire apophysis is avulsed, along with the forearm flexors and the medial collateral ligament. In type II fractures, the young athlete's epiphyses have closed. If the fragment is large enough to include the proximal attachment of the anterior band, the medial collateral ligament will be intact. Marked displacement, however, may tear the ligament. Type III fracture occurs in older children and adults. Here, a small chip is avulsed from the posterior aspect of the medial epicondyle with part of the musculature, and the midportion of the medial collateral ligament tears.

A gentle test, the gravity stress test, is available for diagnosing acute medial instability of the elbow. With the athlete supine, the shoulder is rotated externally. Then his elbow is flexed 20° to bring the olecranon clear of its fossa. The weight of the forearm and hand will usually exert enough valgus force to open the medial side. In larger, more muscular persons, a 0.45 kg or 0.9 kg (1 lb or 2 lb) weight may be strapped around the wrist. If the elbow is unstable, gravity stress test x-rays will show that the joint has opened and

the medial epicondylar apophysis has become displaced distally.

Exploration of the medial side of the elbow is indicated if the medial epicondyle is displaced more than 1 cm or if it lies in the elbow joint. Moreover, a throwing athlete's elbow is usually explored if it is unstable on the gravity stress test. Exploration is also indicated with a posterior or posterolateral dislocation, since the epicondyle was probably very displaced and is now rotated.

Lateral Condyle

Fractures of the lateral condyle of the elbow are intra-articular ones that heal slowly and may become displaced (see Figure 10-2). Synovial fluid seeps from the joint into the fracture site and contains fibrinolysin, which disrupts the fracture hematoma and may lead to a delayed union or to a nonunion.

A displaced fracture of the lateral condyle demands pin or screw fixation. Even if a lateral condylar fracture is undisplaced, however, the elbow should be x-rayed intermittently until it has healed, because an initially undisplaced fracture of the lateral condyle may become displaced. A malunited fracture alters the carrying angle of an athlete's elbow, and his range of elbow motion may also suffer.

Dislocation

Most elbow dislocations are posterior or posterolateral ones. Both of these types may have associated fractures of the medial epicondyle. Fortunately, even if the elbow is unstable medially, the forearm flexors are usually functionally intact and give satisfactory dynamic support for most elbow activities. In a thrower, however, a ligamentous repair is more likely to restore optimum function. Operative exploration is indicated in throwing athletes if the medial epicondyle has been fractured, since the epicondyle was probably very displaced and is now rotated.

The dislocation may be reduced on the field or in the locker room before muscle spasm sets in. It is best performed, however, with the athlete lying prone on an examining table with his elbow hanging off the side. First the lateral displacement is reduced and then straight traction applied. The elbow should not be directly flexed before reduc-

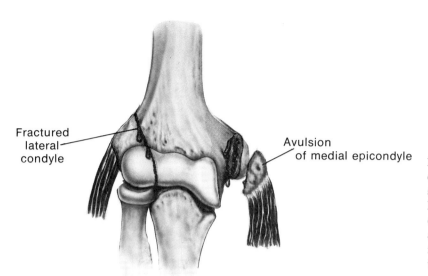

Fractured lateral condyle

Avulsion of medial epicondyle

Figure 10-2 A lateral condyle fracture allows synovial fluid to flow in and hinder healing. The medial epicondyle may be avulsed and even rotate from its normal position, obstructing the joint.

tion because this flexion maneuver could damage the brachial artery.

The athlete's elbow is rehabilitated with active range-of-motion exercises. Passive stretch should be avoided because it may cause elbow stiffness or myositis ossificans. When the athlete it ready to return to practice, the elbow should be taped in slight flexion, or a custom-made padded elbow strap may be wrapped around the arm and forearm and connected to allow full flexion but prevent hyperextension (Figure 10-3).[36]

The Elbow in Throwing

During the acceleration phase of throwing, the thrower's arm is pulled forward dramatically. The forearm lags behind, and thus a valgus stress is placed on the elbow (Figure 10-4). The forearm flexors then flex the wrist and fingers to propel the baseball, which is released in a flinging motion at about ear level. During follow-through, the forearm pronates and the olecranon jams into the olecranon fossa.[2]

Types of Elbow Injuries

"Little League Elbow"

Young baseball players may develop elbow problems from a heavy pitching schedule.[55] The Little Leaguer is allowed to pitch as many as six innings per week and averages 18 pitches per inning. A professional pitcher throws about 120 pitches in a nine-inning game, averaging 11 to 15 pitches per inning. Although a Little Leaguer throws fewer pitches than does a professional pitcher in a week of competition, he may throw hard on days between games. He may be a catcher for his team as well, and thus throw even more.

Adams studied the x-ray films of both elbows of 162 boys, aged 9 to 14 years, and compared pitchers to nonpitchers and to youngsters who were not playing organized baseball.[1] He found that changes at the medial epicondyle, the radius, and the capitellum were in direct proportion to the amount of throwing and whether the youngster threw curve balls. All of the 80 pitchers that he checked had some degree of bony hypertrophy and separation and fragmentation of the medial epicondyle apophysis. Only a small number of the x-ray films of nonpitchers and control subjects showed these changes.

In the "Houston study," 595 Little League pitchers were examined.[34] Seventeen percent had elbow symptoms, and 12% had a limitation of elbow extension. Many radiologic "anatomical variants" were noted at the elbow. The medial epicondylar lesions were thought to be stress fractures, and if the youngster rested his arm these lesions were said to result in no functional deficits. The bony hypertrophy and enlarged medial epicondyles were considered to be normal anatomic variants.

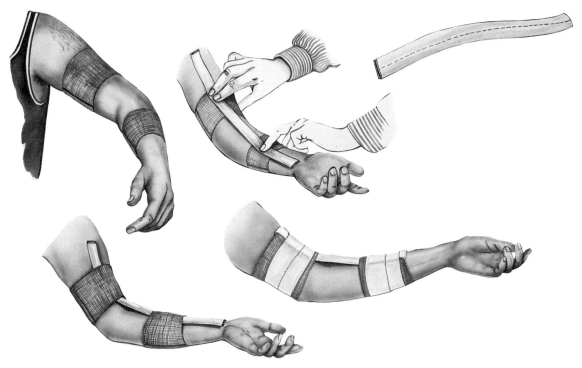

Figure 10-3 Taping may prevent hyperextension of the elbow. Elastic tape serves as an anchor. Four strips of 3.8-cm (1.5-in) white tape are then stacked and folded longitudinally to form a strong band, which is held in place with more elastic tape. The ends of the band are folded over and secured with white tape.

In the "Eugene study," 120 pitchers, aged 11 and 12 years, were examined.[51] Twenty percent had elbow symptoms, and 23% had x-ray changes related to traction on the medial epicondyle. Ten percent of these pitchers had limitation of elbow extension. Five percent of these youths had more serious lateral compartment x-ray changes, but none of them had symptoms related to that area. The investigators concluded that the elbow symptoms of Little League pitchers did not correlate with the x-ray findings.

Studies that show negligible epiphyseal involvement in Little League baseball players may be misleading, since the youths present to physicians with symptoms when they are 13 or 14 years old and have already graduated from Little League baseball.[11] The elbow trouble has an insidious onset, symptoms being early but subtle.[5] These young athletes may fail to report elbow pain to the coach, and even if they do the coach may not have the soreness thoroughly investigated.

Most problems are at the medial side of the elbow, and Little League elbow has been defined as an avulsion of the ossification center of the medial epicondyle.[9, 25, 84] The valgus stress of throwing may cause fragmentation, irregularity, mild separation, enlargement, or breaking of the medial epicondyle. The worst, chronic problems, however, are found on the lateral side of the elbow where repeated jamming of the radial head against the capitellum may cause osteochondritis of the capitellum, avascular necrosis of the radial head, osteochondritic loose bodies, and osteoarthritis.[86] Eight percent of young pitchers have lateral changes, and it is not uncommon to see loose bodies in the olecranon fossa of teenagers who began pitching at a young age.

The most serious of the elbow findings in young pitchers is osteochondritis dissecans of the

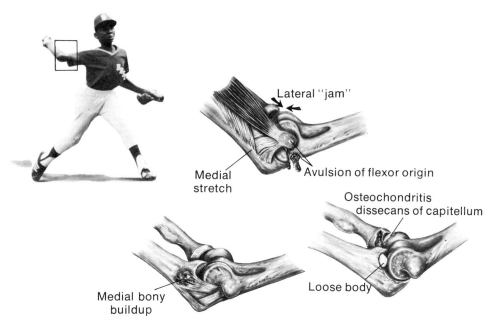

Figure 10-4 Thrower's elbow. Valgus stress to the elbow stretches the medial side and jams the lateral side, producing avulsions, bony build-ups, osteochondritis, and loose bodies.

capitellum. Valgus elbow stress during the acceleration phase stretches the medial collateral ligament of the elbow, and ultimately the radial head impinges against the capitellum. Osteochondritis dissecans occurs mostly in pitchers but does occur in some catchers. The average age of onset is 12.5 years, with the youths having played organized baseball for an average of 3.5 years.[11]

X-ray films show ill-defined, patchy decalcification or cystic areas on the capitellum, radial head irregularity and hypertrophy, and early partial closure of the proximal radius growth plate. In contrast to normal closure, however, the fusion of the radial head growth plate begins on the lateral aspect and proceeds medially. These conditions are not benign but mark the end of hard, painless throwing for the teenage athlete. The prognosis is poor despite treatment, and these lateral side problems may reduce the athlete's ability to participate in throwing or racket sports later in life.

When elbow symptoms are marked and rest measures fail, the most consistent results follow curettage of the fragmented capitulum down to bleeding bone and removal of all fragments that are either loose or attached to bone. In a study of young throwers with osteochondritis of the capitellum, 13 of 15 operated on had loose bodies.[31] Surgery will not produce a normal elbow, but the pain does lessen and the youngster usually regains more elbow extension.

To prevent elbow problems in young pitchers, good throwing mechanics must be taught, and youngsters should especially avoid just "throwing with the arm." Proper pregame warm-up is important, and the pitcher should ice his shoulder and elbow after the game. Young pitchers should be encouraged to report elbow soreness. In youth baseball, sore arms are often treated like the sore arms of professional players with ice, reducing the pitching, or missing a rotation. Soreness in youngsters, however, is more likely to be due to epiphysitis, and thus x-ray films are needed. If x-ray findings are abnormal, the youngster should refrain from pitching during that season.

Little League pitchers are at a disadvantage

compared to their Big League counterparts. Foremost, the Little Leaguer's elbow is always immature. Professional pitchers have skilled pitching coaches who emphasize good body mechanics, using the large muscle groups, body turn, and proper push-off and follow-through. The professional pitcher has conditioning programs for muscle strength, endurance and flexibility, postgame icing, and expert medical care. The Little Leaguer usually lacks these advantages. Coaching is not expected to improve because there is no requirement that these well-meaning coaches be trained and certified to instruct their young players.

"Baseball Elbow"

When pitchers throw hard for years, their elbow joints wear out. Veteran pitchers develop an elbow flexion contracture, medial collateral ligament traction spurs or medial collateral ligament rupture, tardy ulnar nerve palsy, articular cartilage degeneration, posterior compartment lesions, and loose bodies.

The flexion contracture results from traction on the anterior capsule, biceps, and brachialis, microtears of the wrist and finger flexors, and pronator tears with resulting fibrosis.[5, 37, 42] Bone may build up on the coronoid process and chip off to cause acute elbow pain.[19]

Reactive bone spurs form in the distal part of the medial collateral ligament owing to valgus overload. Sometimes a spur breaks off to entrap and irritate the ulnar nerve. Spurs can be removed before they break off.

Medial Collateral Ligament Tears

A throwing athlete may rupture the medial collateral ligament of his elbow.[90] He may report that he has had soreness medially for years. Suddenly, however, he feels a snap in the elbow; it gives way and he is unable to throw. Then when he makes a fist, he has pain in the flexor muscle mass or over the anterior oblique ligament. The examiner may find valgus instability, and x-ray films may show calcification or ossification medially. To check for stability, the examiner first flexes the elbow to about 50° and then applies a

valgus stress. Tears of the medial collateral range from complete ruptures, some of which are repairable and some of which are not, to chronic problems that result in attenuated ligaments.

If the ligament has been chronically stretched, the humeral portion may be moved up and forward on the humerus and fixed with a screw and washer. In tears that are unrepairable and in the case of ligaments that are stretched and markedly attenuated, the palmaris longus tendon may be transferred to the elbow and tied as a figure-of-eight.

In this tendon transfer operation, the surgeon incises the flexor muscle mass longitudinally to expose the ligament and its pathology.[37] He frees the ulnar nerve and holds it aside with care to preserve muscular branches of the nerve. He then harvests the palmaris longus tendon from the same side, drills holes in the humerus and ulna through which he passes the tendon, and then ties it. He then transfers the ulnar nerve anteriorly; otherwise the nerve may become encased in scar tissue.

After palmaris longus substitution for the medial collateral ligament, the athlete is not permitted to throw for about 5 months. He then throws for 15 minutes a day for about 2 months and then increases to three-quarter speed; by 12 months he may be back pitching. During rehabilitation, the tendon assumes ligamentous properties and becomes stronger.

Ulnar Nerve Entrapment

The throwing athlete with ulnar nerve entrapment may give a history of having fallen on his elbow or may report a twang at the elbow during pitching. He will have soreness near the ulnar groove (Figure 10-5), and numbness of the little finger and the lateral side of his ring finger and may have some weakness of grip. An EMG test may be positive and x-ray films may show spurs.

If the ulnar nerve subluxes during pitching, it may produce a traumatic twang with tingling pain in the ring and little fingers with each pitch. If chronic neuritis develops, the nerve may be transferred anteriorly. With the nerve in this new anterior position, the pitcher can usually continue at a high level of throwing.

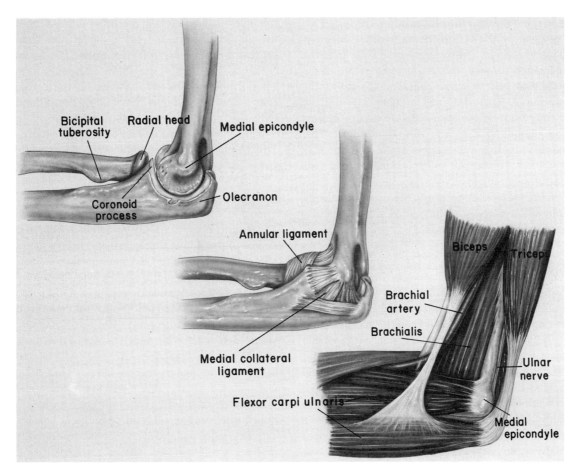

Figure 10-5   At the medial side of the elbow, the ulnar nerve passes in a groove behind the medial epicondyle.

In transferring the ulnar nerve anteriorly, the surgeon should free the nerve all the way up to the arcade of Struthers and remove the intermuscular septum. He should also free the nerve all the way down through the fascial covering in zone III.

In a baseball pitcher, the transplanted ulnar nerve should be positioned under the muscle. If it is placed just on top of the muscle, it will probably twang when he throws. A little carpet of muscle should be left along the course of the nerve to prevent scar tissue from forming. When the nerve is transferred, the surgeon should also look for reactive bone spurs and posterior loose bodies.

Articular Cartilage Degeneration

Articular cartilage degeneration at the radiohumeral joint may disable a player. Moreover, in the acceleration phase, as valgus stress is applied to the elbow and it rapidly extends, an osteocartilaginous piece may be chipped from the trochlea, and the athlete will feel an acute, severe pain.

"Olecranon Fossitis" and Posteromedial Olecranon Bone Spurs

Posterior compartment lesions may be equally disabling. The olecranon process jams into the fossa, especially in pitchers with a poor follow-through who snap the elbow into extension. This jamming produces "olecranon fossitis" and new bone formation. The overgrowth of bone from the olecranon tip may fracture, causing severe elbow pain and leaving loose bodies at the tip of the olecranon. There is a toggle effect at the elbow during throwing as the olecranon bumps against the medial side of the olecranon fossa. This bumping may produce spurs at the olecranon tip and medial olecranon spurs. Further, the cartilage of the olecranon fossa may become soft. The spurs can be removed by resecting the tip of the olecranon and a portion of the medial side of the olecranon with an osteotome.

Surgery for Loose Bodies

Surgery on a pitcher's elbow usually comprises a combination of medial soft tissue surgery with removal of spurs and posterior intraarticular surgery. A posterolateral incision is generally chosen so that after the olecranon is observed and the loose bodies removed, the radial head and capitellar articular surfaces can be evaluated. The operation may well be effective if only one loose body is found and removed. The prognosis for a pitcher, however, is generally not good when many loose bodies are found because of coexisting traumatic arthritis. The surgeon's observations of the radiohumeral joint allow a prognosis as to when the pitcher may return to competition and a realistic appraisal of his future in baseball.[37]

"Javelin Thrower's Elbow"

A javelin thrower may develop elbow trouble with either the correct arm action or an incorrect, round-arm method.[65] The types of injuries suffered with each of these throwing styles, are, however, different.

The correct arm action for throwing a javelin is an over-the-shoulder throw with a bent-arm carry. The elbow is flexed and held well above and in front of the shoulder and close to the head. The elbow is then brought forward early and forcibly extended to launch the javelin. This violent extension may fracture the olecranon tip.[88]

When the javelin is thrown with an incorrect round-arm method, the elbow comes around at the level of the shoulder, and internal rotation of the shoulder transmits force to the javelin. These throwers, like baseball pitchers, sprain the medial collateral ligament of the elbow and spurs form. The athlete may be able to develop the correct arm action by changing to a middle-finger hold, with the index finger extended under the javelin and the middle finger placed behind the binding. This change twists the hand inward to reduce the stress on the medial collateral ligament.

"Tennis Elbow"

"Tennis elbow" most often refers to pain at or near a player's lateral epicondyle[76] and is generally caused by faulty backhand stroke mechanics.[35, 74] The player with a faulty backhand often uses an Eastern forehand grip or a fistlike grip with the thumb extended behind the handle for more power (Figure 10-6). His stroke usually starts high with a hurried backswing. His body weight is on the back leg, and power is generated at the wrist and elbow. As the elbow extends, the wrist strongly hooks into ulnar deviation, which is a strong, commonly used motion for opening doors, chopping wood, and swinging a baseball bat. The beginner, however, may incorporate this motion, which comes so easily, into his stroke as a bad habit. His follow-through usually will be short and low and end with a jerk.

Combined elbow extension and ulnar hooking of the wrist cause the extensor mass, especially the deeply located extensor carpi radialis brevis, to rub and to roll over the lateral epicondyle and the radial head. Along with this irritation from rubbing over bony prominences are tugs on the extensor origin resulting in microtears. Rubbing, rolling, and microtears result in a painful elbow.

In an attempt to heal the damage, nerve-laden granulation tissue forms. This tissue is ill-suited to withstand constant use because it swells, stretches, and becomes painful. Adhesions also form between the annular ligament and the joint capsule. The pain worsens from the constant strain of the faulty backhand and the transmission of vibrations to the elbow from a too tightly strung racket with too small a handle or from heavy, wet balls and off-center hits.

Players with tennis elbow have pain in the

Figure 10-6 A good backhand will have a relaxed backswing, low starting position, weight transfer, "L position" of the wrist at contact, and a full follow-through **(A, B)**. The novice who has poor technique starts high with a leading elbow and a hammer grip and hooks his wrist **(C)**. A two-handed backhand may improve the mechanics of the stroke **(D)**.

region of the common extensor origin, especially when they try to extend their middle finger against resistance with the elbow extended. The extensor carpi radialis brevis inserts into the base of the third metacarpal, and extension of the middle finger tightens the fascial origin of the muscle. The lateral epicondyle is tender, and the player notes pain when he grips the racket and extends his wrist.

For a quality backhand, either an Eastern backhand or a Continental grip is used. The arm and racket form an "L."[81] The racket is unhur-

riedly taken back low, and the stroke starts low. The player's other hand can help support the racket during the backswing. He then shifts his body weight and swings from the shoulder to achieve pace. At impact, his weight has been transferred to his front foot. His wrist is firm and locked in a cocked position, a position that corrects the hooked wrist, which in turn cures the leading elbow. The ball is met in front, and the follow-through is long and high.

The player with a faulty backhand should be taught proper form and master the wristcocked

"L" position (see Figure 10-6). If this cannot be learned, then he should work on a two-handed backhand, since tennis elbow only rarely affects players who use a two-handed backhand. A right-handed player hits a two-handed backhand like a one-handed left-handed forehand, with the right elbow slightly bent at contact. The player's left hand prevents the right wrist from hooking and also absorbs most of the impact and vibration. The player follows through by driving with the left arm.

A proper grip size prevents torque. A player determines his grip size by measuring from the proximal palmar crease to the tip of the ring finger, along the radial side of the ring finger (Figure 10-7). More simply, he can grip his racket and then place the free index finger between the ring finger and the base of the thumb. If the index finger just fits, then the grip size is usually correct.

A player with "tennis elbow" should avoid a rigid racket.[33] A racket with a large sweet spot or a fiberglass or graphite racket helps to reduce

vibration. Some metal rackets vibrate like a tuning fork. A racket should not be strung too tightly; usually between 50 and 55 pounds of tension is best.

Stretching and strengthening the wrist extensors are effective and major parts of the treatment for tennis elbow.[6, 47] Soreness is a guide for all stretching, isometric, and weight work. If the elbow becomes sore, the player has done too much exercise. The player's elbow is first immersed in a 40°C (104°F) whirlpool before he begins his exercises. He then performs isometric radial deviation-extension wrist cocking, holding each contraction for 6 seconds. When he can do these at full force without pain, he advances to cocking a tennis racket. Next, a 0.67 kg (1.5 lb) weight is added to the neck of the racket. More weight is added slowly until the player is lifting 2.25 kg (5 lb). He may have been lifting 6.75 to 9 kg (15–20 lb) before this episode of tennis elbow; thus it must be explained to him that he should start off with lighter weights.

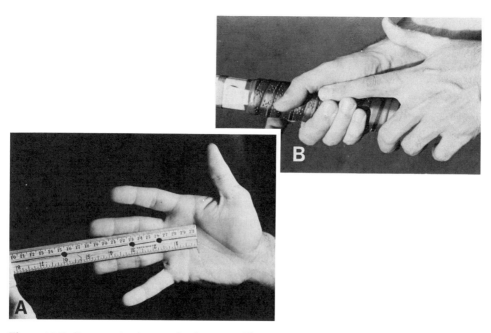

Figure 10-7   Proper grip size may be determined by measuring along the radial side of the ring finger, from the proximal palmar crease to the fingertip **(A).** Another way to determine grip size is to hold the racket and see whether a finger fits in the gap between the thumb and fingers **(B).**

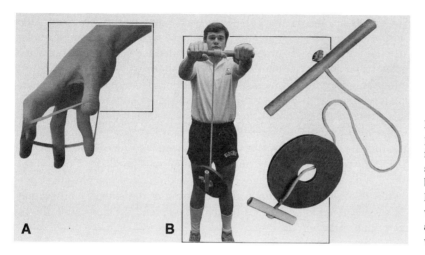

Figure 10-8 The tennis player can strengthen his forearm muscles by stretching a large rubber band called "Tubics Jr" **(A)**. For more strength, he can wind up a weight that is attached to a broomstick with a rope **(B)**.

The tennis player may also wind up a weight attached to a broomstick by a rope (Figure 10-8). He starts with 20 repetitions of 0.56 kg (1.25 lb) and then gradually increases to 2.25 kg (5 lb), or he can twist a towel. After the acute period, deep friction massage is an excellent way to break up adhesions at the elbow, to increase circulation, and to eliminate wastes.

After doing well in flexibility, isometrics, and weight programs, the player may hit against a wall for 5 minutes and then build up to 7.5 minutes, 10 minutes, and 15 minutes a day. It is important that he use an Eastern backhand or Continental grip, hold his wrist cocked, and that his arm and racket form an "L". Theoretically, however, hitting against a wall invokes a longer grip time than hitting with a partner, and therefore places a prolonged stress on the extensor origin. The grip pressure of better players is of short duration and peaks just before ball impact and then immediately relaxes. In average players the grip lasts longer. If there is no soreness after hitting against a wall for 15 minutes a day, the player may begin rallying. His elbow should be iced for 15 minutes after the stroke work.

Tennis players should keep their elbows warm, especially on cool or windy days. Some tennis players cut the toe section out of a wool sock, place the sock around their elbows, and secure it with a light strip of adhesive tape to prevent it from sliding down. Neoprene elbow sleeves perform the same function. While the player sleeps, he should wear a splint that cocks his wrist up, as he may otherwise be flexing his wrist at night and stressing his extensors.

The symptoms of tennis elbow may resolve with rest, but they are sure to recur unless the player starts a strengthening and flexibility program and hits with a cocked wrist. If his arm were put in a cast, his muscles would atrophy, his proprioception would decrease, and recovery would take longer.

The "counterforce brace," a nonelastic, curved strap that the player fastens around his upper forearm,[26] is supposed to remove stress from the extensor origin. When his extensor muscles contract during the stroke, the brace serves essentially as a new origin for the muscles. It may reduce the sliding of the extensors over the lateral condyle. The brace also acts as a flag, reminding the player to concentrate on his backhand stroke mechanics.

A short, tapering course of phenylbutazone will usually alleviate the symptoms of acute tennis elbow. The chance that the drug may cause aplastic anemia or other serious problems is, however, too great for routine use. A white, chalky residue may accrue if a long-acting steroid is injected, and steroid injections may cause some of the tissue necrosis seen at operation for tennis elbow.

If tennis elbow does not resolve after the above

changes have been made and the player has followed a complete flexibility and strengthening program and improved the mechanics of his stroke, an exploration of his lateral epicondyle region and an extensor slide operation may be proposed.[47, 77] The extensor origin is explored and the extensor carpi radialis brevis exposed. This muscle lies under the extensor carpi radialis longus. Damaged tissue is removed from its undersurface. The elbow joint is then entered and checked for adhesions and synovial pannus. Any adhesions that bind the capsule to the orbicular ligament are lysed, and a partial synovectomy is performed. The extensor origin is then allowed to slide distally and left in this position. After operation, the player resumes the same exercise program recommended for the treatment of acute tennis elbow. Less successful operations include removal of the "radiohumeral meniscus"—a pannus of synovium growing between the radial head and the capitulum—which may be pinched, excision of the orbicular ligament to relieve tension in the elbow joint, and a procedure to elongate the extensor carpi radialis brevis. However, if the soreness is only at the lateral epicondyle, a percutaneous sectioning of the extensor origin may relieve the pain completely (Figure 10-9, dotted line).

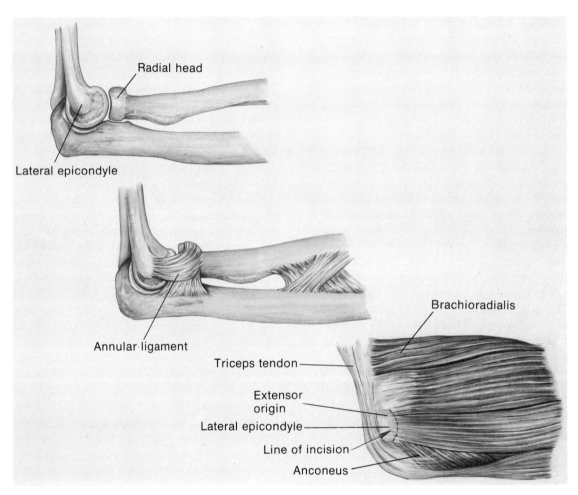

Figure 10-9   Intractable pain at the lateral epicondyle may be relieved by percutaneous sectioning (*dotted line*) of the extensor origin.

A medial tennis elbow most commonly affects veteran tennis players and professionals who hit hard with good stroke mechanics.[70] Their strong wrist flexion in the tennis service and forehand ground strokes leads to medial epicondylar hypertrophy, avulsion of chips of bone from the medial epicondyle, and tears at the flexor origin. In the acute phase, rest and anti-inflammatory drug therapy may be beneficial. A player's warm-up procedures should be checked, especially his shoulder warm-up. The elbow must be iced after practice and after matches. Massage to the sore area rids it of waste products and breaks up scar tissue.

"Boxer's Elbow"

When a boxer misses a jab, pieces of bone may chip from the tip of his olecranon process as it jams into his olecranon fossa.[32] These chips may then become loose bodies in his elbow joint. Direct impacts of the olecranon against the trochlea may shear off pieces of the trochlea, and traction on the coronoid process may avulse bone. Elbow pain is usually not related to one specific blow and is most painful when a jab is missed.

These elbows are operated on arthroscopically if the loose bodies cause locking or catching. The joint is irrigated, loose bodies are removed, and any pieces of articular cartilage that are partly attached but appear ready to break free are removed.

Olecranon Bursitis

Direct blows to the point of an athlete's elbow, or repetitive rubbing there, may irritate the olecranon bursa to produce synovial fluid that swells the bursa.[24] Olecranon bursitis is common in football receivers who land on hard artificial turf and also has been noted in recreational dart throwers trying to throw the darts *through* the board.[52] If the bursa is often irritated, the bursal wall will thicken. Fibrinous or cartilaginous loose bodies may form within the bursa and feel like bone chips.

An acutely swollen olecranon bursa should have an ice pack. The bursa is then sterilely aspirated of fluid and an elastic wrap snugly applied over a cotton roll for 24 to 48 hours. If the wall of the bursa has been thickened from recurrent bursitis or if it contains cartilage chips, the bursa may have to be removed. The incision should not be placed over the point of the elbow because such placement may produce an adherent, painful, and easily bumped scar. Olecranon bursitis may be prevented by wearing well-fitting elbow pads.[73]

THE WRIST AND THE HAND

Injuries of the hand are common in athletics, probably because the hand is characteristically in front of the athlete in most sports and frequently absorbs the initial contact.[64] Further, the hand is used in almost every sport in one way or another. There is a tendency to minimize the severity and importance of these injuries because the hand does not bear weight and injuries to the hand usually do not totally disable the athlete. This is particularly true of young, poorly supervised athletes who may return to vigorous activity and unprotected use of the extremity long before adequate healing.

The key to proper care of hand injuries is early, accurate diagnosis and precise and proper treatment, which must be followed by an appropriate rehabilitation program.[13] Conservative treatment measures are preferable for most injuries of the hand, and most athletes can be rapidly returned to their normal activities.[23] Primary surgical repair is indicated, however, in a small number of cases, and secondary reconstructive surgery may be needed in injuries that have been neglected or improperly treated.

The wrist is probably the most complex joint in the human body because of its multiple joints and their varied anatomic configurations. Reaching an accurate diagnosis necessary for proper treatment can be difficult in many cases. In many of the more significant problems, however, a specific treatment of choice has not yet been perfected; despite the growing realization about the functional importance of the wrist, there has been a dearth of optimal results of treatment of many of its disabilities. There is still need for further research and study in this area. As in all examinations, a careful history is important and should include the location, duration, and intensity of pain, whether repetitive activity or a single traumatic event has occurred, the mechanism of injury, the previous treatment program, what activity aggravates the problem, a medical history (including previous diseases, past surgeries and injuries) and what specific activities are limited and to what degree.

A complete physical examination of the upper extremity should include examination of the appearance of the extremity, localization of the tenderness, measurement of strength of grip and pinch, and examination of all involved structures. The presence of instability and any "click," particularly if it is reproducible, is extremely helpful and important, particularly in light of recent awareness of the various instabilities that can occur in this intercalated joint. A knowledge of the kinematics and biomechanics of this complicated joint is also extremely important, and our knowledge of these components has significantly increased over the past several years.

A basic radiographic profile will include many views, depending on the individual problem. It is more efficient to have a basic series of wrist views supplemented by clinical findings. A basic profile may include a neutral PA view, and AP or PA views in radial and ulnar deviation. A true lateral view in the neutral position is particularly important in potential instabilities involving the lunate. Occasionally, laterals in palmar flexion and dorsiflexion are also indicated. A carpal tunnel view is particularly important to visualize the tunnel itself and the hook of the hamate for possible fracture. A closed-fist view with the forearm in supination allows axial compression and also increases the instability at the scapholunate joint in rotatory instability of the scaphoid. Obtaining a carpal tunnel view after an acute injury may be difficult because of the pain, and an oblique view with the forearm in midsupination or in pronation with approximately 20° of elevation from the flat surface and the wrist in some dorsiflexion may be helpful in visualizing the hook of the hamate. Other oblique and rotational views, as indicated by the specific problem, are often valuable.

Also often necessary are secondary diagnostic studies, including wrist arthrography which, under fluoroscopic control, often shows perforations in the various ligamentous structures. However, some communications are a normal variant, some are found in increasing numbers with age, and there is difficulty in correlating the findings as a potential source of the patient's disability. The perforations at the radiocarpal joint and the radioulnar joint increase with age, whereas those at the scapholunate and the triquetral-lunate joint almost always denote pathology. Because of the high percentage of false-positives, the information must be carefully correlated with other findings of the examination in order to be helpful.

Bone scan may be helpful, but the generalized findings are not specific, with two abnormal patterns commonly seen: the diffuse pattern of increased uptake with generalized metabolic diseases, osteoporosis, rheumatoid and synovitis-type involvement; and a localized pattern seen in specific degenerative arthritic changes, fractures, tumors, and other vascular problems of the bone, such as Kienbock's and Preiser's diseases.

The CT scan has been particularly helpful in evaluating distal radioulnar stability and is the single most accurate study to determine incongruities at this joint. The plane lateral radiographs are accurate only in the perfectly neutral position, but the CT scan demonstrates dislocation or incongruity in all degrees of pronation and supination and also gives an accurate picture with a plaster cast on the extremity.

Cineradiography is very useful in localizing wrist instability, especially when the patient has a "snapping" wrist and the normal synchronous motion is broken by the instability. This study is particularly enhanced by combination with arthrography.

Tomograms, particularly trispiral tomograms, have been helpful in visualizing irregularities, such as seen in Kienbock's disease, fractures, displacements, angulation, cysts, and other similar problems.

Arthroscopy has been of limited value, but, as experience, technique, and equipment improve, this study may increase its diagnostic benefits.

Some areas of confusion show up on radiography, such as accessory ossification centers, congenital absences and traumatic fusions, variation in size and shape of the bones, periarticular calcific deposits, cystic deformities, and tumors.

Injuries to the Wrist

Most wrist problems in athletics are produced by acute falls on the outstretched hand or result from repetitive stress with the wrist in extension.[54] These injuries are frequent in weight lifters during the catch in the clean-and-jerk, gymnasts during floor exercise, and wrestlers and push-up enthusiasts. When the wrist is extended to extremes, the dorsal articular surfaces impinge and are compressed. If the wrist is forced beyond this point, the compressed contact areas are sheared. This force may pinch the synovium or produce osteocartilaginous damage. These extension forces may produce scaphoid impaction, triquetral-hamate impaction, or synovial cysts. More serious injuries include fractures and instabilities.

Radial-Scaphoid Impaction

With extension and radial deviation, the dorsal rim of the radius and the dorsal scaphoid rim collide (Figure 10-10), resulting in pain, weakness, and tenderness at the dorsoradial aspect of the wrist aggravated by wrist extension.

The examiner tells the athlete to point to the site of discomfort with one finger and should then ascertain the point of maximum tenderness carefully. The wrist may be tender over the dorsal scaphoid rim with the wrist in moderate flexion and ulnar deviation. A radiographic film, taken with a "skin-pin" (a small piece of paper clip) over the tender point, may show a bone spur or a little, loose piece of bone over the dorsal aspect of the scaphoid. In this case, the athlete should rest the wrist. When he returns to practice and competition, he may have to change his wrist position for the exercise and have his wrist taped. If the disability is protracted, a surgical explora-

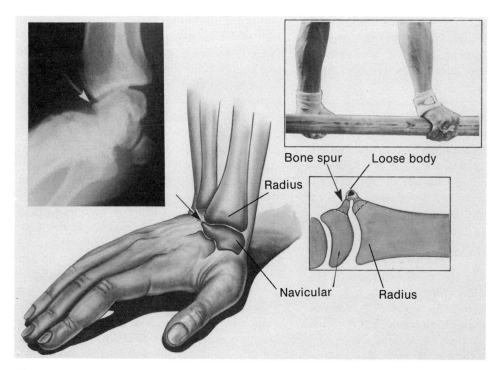

Bone spur   Loose body
Radius
Navicular   Radius

Figure 10-10 Acute or repeated hyperextension of the wrist may produce dorsal wrist pain. As a result, a spur may form on the navicular and on the distal radius, producing a synovial cyst between them. These spurs can be resected *(dotted lines)* and the cyst removed.

tion may be needed. The surgeon may find synovitis dorsally and an area of chondromalacia and early osteophyte formation on the dorsal rim of the scaphoid. The rim may be hypertrophied, and the contiguous area of the dorsal radial rim may show chondromalacia. Sometimes, impaction of the scaphoid against the radius may avulse the osteocartilaginous fragment.

If a hypertrophic ridge on the scaphoid blocks extension, a cheilectomy (spur removal) of the dorsal rim of the scaphoid, synovial debridement, and perhaps removal of the dorsal radial lip are indicated (Figure 10-10). This operation is similar to the cheilectomies performed for impingement at the anterior aspect of an ankle or at the big toe metatarsal–phalangeal joint. Postoperatively the athlete wears a splint for 2 weeks and then begins gradual range-of-motion and strengthening exercises.

Triquetral-Lunate Impaction

Forceful extension with ulnar deviation may occur in pile-ups in contact sports, during landings in floor exercise, with moves on the side-horse, or swings in racket sports. Impingement occurs between the dorsal aspects of the triquetrum and the hamate.

Treatment includes rest and pulsed ultrasound, anti-inflammatory medicine, a change of wrist position, and taping of the wrist. Exploration is indicated if the symptoms are unremitting. The surgeon may find inflamed synovium and chondromalacia at the hamate or triquetral rim and may need to remove the synovial infoldings and perform a synovectomy.

Occult or Overt Synovial Cysts

After damage to the wrist joint capsule, synovium may herniate to form a synovial cyst, expecially in young female gymnasts. Wrist soreness is usually maximum in extension, but occasionally there is discomfort in flexion. The wrist is usually tender over the scapholunate interval, and sometimes the examiner can feel a mass there. Radiographic films are generally negative, and an arthrogram is usually not helpful.

Treatment includes rest in a splint, anti-in-

flammatory medicine, a change of hand grip position, and taping. Aspiration rarely results in release of a jelly-like material and decompression of the cyst.

In recalcitrant cases, percutaneous needling may decompress the cyst and scar may form to prevent a recurrence. The cystic area is numbed and then stuck about 20 times with an 18-gauge needle. The athlete wears a splint for a few days and then resumes activities. If the needling does not work, an exploration may be necessary. The surgeon excises the cyst as it protrudes from the scapholunate ligament and sutures the ligament. The athlete should be informed that the cyst will sometimes, nonetheless, recur.

Radioulnar Joint

The distal radioulnar joint (DRUJ) allows forearm rotation of about 150° in pronation and supination, with the radius and hand rotating around the ulna, with some associated glide of the ulnar head in the radial sigmoid notch. The radius carries approximately 80% of the axial load of the forearm and the ulna, with the associated connections with the triangular fibrocartilage complex carrying 20%.

Understanding and knowledge of the ulnar aspect of the wrist have increased greatly in recent years, allowing greater awareness of proper diagnosis and thus more effective methods of treatment. A problem occurs in differentiating ulnar wrist pain from that arising from the radioulnar joint, and that from the ulnocarpal complex. Painful pronation–supination of the forearm designates radoulnar involvement and, when painless, implies pain of ulnocarpal origin. Point tenderness, pain, subluxation with crepitus, and clicking, with or without stress, along with general hand and wrist examination, are important to localize the lesion.

Plain films, especially a direct lateral with the forearm in neutral position, are important, as are specific views to rule out other causes of pain. The CT scan is the most accurate method to evaluate the distal radioulnar joint, since it is easier to interpret and can be done with the cast in place. Arthrography may be helpful here as well.

Treatment of acute displacement of the distal

ulna, where accurate reduction can be obtained, consists of closed manipulation and reduction, held with a long arm cast for 4 to 6 weeks. The forearm should be positioned in full supination for dorsal displacement and in full pronation for volar displacement.

In chronic cases, many alternative methods of treatment are available, including ligamentous reconstructions, fusion of the DRUJ, proximal resection arthroplasty, ulnar shortening, and direct ulnar excision.

Triangular Fibrocartilage Complex (TFCC)

The mechanism is usually an ulnar blow to the hand, forcing the wrist into dorsiflexion and pronation. Local tenderness at the DRUJ, painful click or catch, or both, and occasionally radioulnar instability are diagnostic aids. Other causes of local pathology must be excluded, including subluxation of the extensor carpi ulnaris, lunatotriquetral instability, piso-triquetral degeneration, and general ligamentous laxity.

Partial ligamentous injuries may occur, and these should respond to protective casting until healing has occurred. If there has been a complete tear, however, repair with or without augmentation should be carried out in order to preserve the function of the TFCC in wrist stability, load resorption, axial compression, and motion of the wrist. Locking or intermittent catching may occur. Owing to injury and to the confined space, excision of the injured tissue may be indicated but should be carried out with caution and appreciation of its functional importance.

Carpal Instabilities

Stability of the wrist as an intercalated segment depends on the configuration of the joint surfaces in their articulation, plus the multiple ligaments connecting the bones. There are three longitudinal bony columns: thumb; radial force-bearing; and ulnar control. The force-bearing column, which transmits the force generated by the hand to the forearm, consists of the distal radial articulation, the lunate, the proximal two thirds of the scaphoid, the capitate, the trapezoid, and the bases of the second and third metacarpals. The control column on the ulnar side of the wrist consists of the distal ulna with its styloid and attached triangular fibrocartilage continuous to the distal radius, plus the triquetrum, the hamate, the capitate, and the bases of the fourth and fifth metacarpals. The thumb column comprises the distal third of the scaphoid, the trapezoid joint, and the base of the first metacarpal. Less force will be transmitted to the carpus with greater mobility at the carpometacarpal joint of the thumb.

The major ligaments of the wrist are intracapsular. They consist of the interosseous ligaments contained within the carpal row and the ligaments that cross the carpal row to guide the excursion of the proximal row upon the distal row. The volar ligaments are more substantial than the dorsal ligaments, with the prime stabilizer of the proximal pole of the scaphoid being the volar radioscaphoid ligament. Rotary subluxation of the scaphoid cannot occur unless this ligament is torn. The deep radiocarpal ligament is actually three ligaments: the radiocapitate, the radiolunate, and the radioscaphoid ligaments. The scapholunate interosseous ligament is a short, stout ligament standing dorsal to the palmar. These ligaments are difficult to repair individually, and repairs are carried out as complexes. The degree and the type of injury are determined by the position of the hand at the time of impact, the severity and velocity of the force involved, the type of loading of the joint surfaces, and the natural anatomic and biomechanical laxity of the individual involved. Most commonly, a fall occurs with the wrist in extension and pronation, with the impact on the thenar side. The force carries the wrist into hyperextension, ulnar deviation, and intercarpal supination. The radiocapitate ligament is tightest in extension and ulnar deviation, whereas the radioscaphoid ligament is maximally taut in extension, with the proximal row stabilized to the forearm by five ligaments and the distal row by only the radiocapitate ligament. It has been shown that partial ligament failure can occur without complete disruption, and grossly intact ligaments can be associated with various carpal instability patterns. Also, in loose-jointed individuals, certain instability patterns can be seen, and it is often necessary to obtain stress views of the normal extremity as well.

Carpal Instability Patterns   The most frequent pattern is the dorsal intercalated segment instability (DISI) pattern in which the lunate is displaced volarward and flexed dorsally. In the volar intercalated segment instability (VISI) pattern, the lunate is displaced dorsally and flexed volarward. The DISI pattern can occur when the normal volar tilt of the distal articular surface of the radius is reversed, in addition to the ligamentous injuries. It is helpful to remember that, when a fracture of the radial styloid is present, the associated carpal instability pattern may be present as well. To determine these instabilities, a true lateral view of the wrist in neutral position is imperative.

The normal scapholunate angle averages 47° (30°–60°), with greater than 70° suggesting carpal instability and greater than 80°, diagnostic. The capitolunate angle greater than 20° is strongly suggestive of carpal instability. A scapholunate space of 1 to 2 mm is normal and greater than 3 mm abnormal, although occasionally this may be present bilaterally.

Diagnostically, the DISI shows a scapholunate angle of greater than 70° to 80°, a capitolunate angle of greater than 15° to 20°, the lunate is dorsiflexed, and there is increased overlap of the lunate and capitate on the AP view. The VISI shows findings of a palmarflexed lunate, a capitolunate angle of greater than 30°, dorsal subluxation of the lunate on the radius, overlap of the lunate and capitate on the AP view, and a scapholunate angle of less than 40°.

The rotary subluxation pattern (supinated fist view, Figure 10-11A) shows a scapholunate joint space of greater than 2 mm (Figure 10-11B), a shortening of the scaphoid due to vertical position with increased volar tilt, and a cortical ring sign, which is due to axial projection of the abnormally oriented scaphoid.

In the midcarpal instability pattern, the wrist assumes a VISI configuration until the final degrees of ulnar deviation, when the proximal row abruptly reaches dorsiflexion rather than making a smooth transition.

Carpal Instability Treatment   Subluxation, in some cases, may be reduced and held in radial deviation and dorsiflexion, closing the scapholunate gap and restoring the alignment of the lunate and capitate. Usually, however, some type of fixation, open or closed, is necessary, since reduction may be difficult not only to obtain but especially to maintain in a satisfactory position. If the injury is fresh and normal alignment is obtained, it is generally better to use percuta-

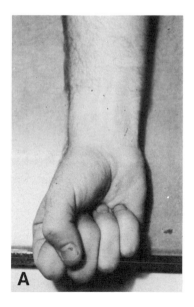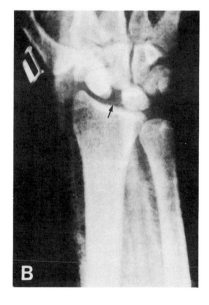

Figure 10-11   A supinated x-ray view with the athlete's fist clenched may show the gap between the scaphoid and lunate *(arrow)*.

neous K-wire fixation under the image intensifier, after which a short arm cast is worn full-time for 6 to 8 weeks and then a removable splint for an additional 4 weeks. In the complete scapholunate instability, I approach the injury through both dorsal and volar incisions with repair of the anterior ligamentous complex and decompression of the median nerve and repair of the remnants of the dorsal interosseous ligaments, either directly or by roughening a bone and attaching through drill holes with a reefing of the dorsal capsule, using a flap of the dorsal carpal ligament routed beneath the extensor tendons. K-wire fixation is then carried out between the lunate and radius, between the scaphoid and radius, and between the scaphoid and capitate. The postoperative immobilization is essentially the same as for the closed reduction, with or without pinning. In deformity in which the normal volar tilt of the distal radial articular surface has been reversed, corrective osteotomy may be indicated.

In injuries seen after 2 months, before the appearance of degenerative changes, there are three main types of reconstruction. The first is repair of the ligament with grafting between the navicular and lunate, using a portion of a wrist extensor or flexor as a transfer. Most of these ligamentous structures do stretch out in time, but in most of our cases there was clinical improvement, especially in pain relief, and most of the individuals believe that they benefited functionally from the surgical procedure. Second, the tri-scaphe fusion between the distal scaphoid and trapezoid and trapezium, as described by Watson, did correct the increased gap on the neutral radiograph, but there tended to be a recurrence of the gap on ulnar deviation, as the lunate fails to rotate on the fixed navicular. Also, a more rapid radioscaphoid arthrosis is seen in some cases. Third, a scapholunate fusion may be performed. This is logical but may be difficult to achieve; it certainly causes more stress on the adjoining articulations. Fourth, complete intercarpal fusion and, fifth, Silastic implant of the scapholunate may be used.

If degenerative changes are present, arthrodesis, proximal row carpectomy, or Silastic prosthesis may be the treatment of lunate triquetrum instability (VISI). In acute injuries, early treatment with casting for 6 to 8 weeks plus protective splinting until 3 months postinjury may be satisfactory. In chronic cases with dorsal subluxation and volar angulation of the lunate with compensatory dorsiflexion of the capitate, fusion of the triquetro-lunate joint is necessary. In most cases, ligamentous reconstruction eventually attenuates, although, again, symptomatic improvement may occur after these operations. When there is marked dorsal subluxation, soft tissue reinforcement is warranted postfusion.

Midcarpal Instability Treatment All patients are started on a trial of conservative management, including immobilization, subjective symptomatic treatment, and anti-inflammatory agents. In patients in whom these measures have failed, arthrodesis of the triquetro-hamate joint should be performed. Ligamentous structures have been used, but secondary attenuation tends to occur here as well.

Scaphoid Fracture with DISI

Most of these are fractures of the scaphoid waist, with the force causing dorsiflexion with collapse of the volar cortex. In acute cases, open reduction and internal fixation with a graft are carried out if volar collapse is present. In cases of scaphoid nonunion, treatment with electrical stimulation or bone graft can be carried out. It is important to correct this scaphoid angle with volar grafting if there is more than 30° of angulation. The correction of this angulation will aid in the reduction of the lunate to a neutral position.

Lunate Dislocations

A lunate dislocation is seen more commonly than the perilunate dislocation; however, we believe that the lunate dislocation is secondary to a perilunate dislocation, which reduces spontaneously. With the reduction, the lunate is rotated and pushed volarly, where it may give symptoms of median nerve compression. The palmar radial lunate ligament remains intact, preserving the blood supply to the lunate. Diagnosis is easily made with lateral roentgenograms of the wrist..

The lunate is reduced with longitudinal traction, extension of the wrist, and pressure on the lunate from the palmar surface toward the dorsum. It is not unusual to have to recreate a perilunate dislocation to reduce the lunate, and then reduce the perilunate dislocation itself.

We protect wrist dislocations by holding them for 4 weeks in a cast with the wrist in slight flexion. At that time, we allow asymptomatic athletes to resume competition if they are protected for 4 more weeks in a silicone cast.

If an acute lunate dislocation is not diagnosed, open reduction is usually necessary. Median nerve palsies and flexor tendon constrictions are complications often seen and must be dealt with accordingly. The most common complication of this injury is late rotatory instability of the scaphoid.

Avascular Necrosis of the Lunate

Avascular necrosis of the lunate is also known as Kienbock's disease. The decreased blood supply to the lunate may be due to [1] primary circulatory problems; [2] traumatic interference with circulation; [3] ligament injury with subsequent degeneration and collapse; or, more often, [4] single or multiple fractures with vascular impairment. This has not been found to be a common complication of lunate dislocation because blood supply is usually preserved. Repeated compression sprains or occasional single compressive episodes may be a cause.

The initial complaint is a weak wrist, with stiffness and pain with motion and on use, with the discomfort in the area of the lunate dorsally. There is weakness of grip, and early radiographs may be negative, except for an ulnar minus variant. It has been shown that, among randomly x-rayed wrists, about 51% have normal variance and 23% an ulnar minus variance. A relatively high percentage of individuals with Kienbock's disease show the ulnar minus variant of 2 mm or more. Over time, the typical x-ray findings of sclerosis, loss of lunate height, fragmentation, and proximal migration of the capitate may be seen, along with local and regional degenerative joint changes. The trispiral tomogram may be of diagnostic value to determine the degree of involvement and degenerative changes.

Treatment   The intra-articular effusion and reaction with unavoidable continuous stress on the "carpal keystone" interfere with attempts at healing. It has been postulated that, once the process of lunate collapse has begun, there is a progressive sequence of destruction in the face of anything other than operative treatment. However, I have seen a number of cases that have responded to splinting and conservative treatment over time without significant collapse or roughening of the articular surface. These, however, may be compression-type fractures, and thus conservative treatment is successful.

The search for an acceptable treatment plan continues, and many operative procedures have been described. One, a Silastic lunate implant, has been successful in our hands. The new Silastic is more resistant to wear. It is important to close the anterior structures, along with reinforcing the dorsal structures, to maintain the position, since the most common complication is subluxation of the implant. Even a subluxed implant, if not severely displaced, can be successful.

Intercarpal fusion is another treatment option. In cases in which there is less than 2 mm of collapse, there is fusion of the capitohamate joint only, and there is a collapse greater than 2 mm, a capitohamate fusion with a Silastic lunate implant has been advocated. Also, fusion of the triquetrum and hamate has been described.

Ulnar lengthening and radial shortening to alleviate the stress of the ulnar minus variant allow revascularization of the bone. Various methods of wrist fusion and proximal row carpectomy are indicated as salvage procedures in cases in which there is degenerative arthritis of the wrist. Total wrist arthroplasty has also been used in cases of this type. The multitude of operative procedures reveals that an ideal method of treatment has not yet been found, but recent advances have shown a significant improvement in the knowledge and treatment of Kienbock's disease.

Tendinitis near the Wrist

Overuse of the wrist and hand in athletics may result in tendinitis near the wrist. The athlete will complain of an aching pain and the involved tendon will be tender. The pain is accentuated by passive stretching of the affected tendon or by contraction of the associated muscle against resistance. X-ray films will usually have normal findings but may show a calcium deposit within the tendon sheath.

"Oarsman's Wrist"

Rowers, canoeists, and weight lifters who do curls may develop a traumatic tenosynovitis of the radial extensors of the wrist. This chronic and disabling overuse condition results in localized pain, tenderness and a squeaky crepitus and swelling over the radial dorsal aspect of the forearm about 7 cm proximal to Lister's tubercle. The tenosynovitis results from hypertrophy of the abductor pollici longus and the extensor pollicis brevis muscles that overlie the radial extensor tendons in the distal forearm and cross these underlying radial wrist extensor tendons obliquely.[89] The extensor tendons and their enveloping paratenons are compressed against the deeper structures.

Treatment includes splinting, nonsteroidal anti-inflammatory medicines, and, sometimes, a steroid shot. If pain persists, surgical decompression of the sheath of these muscles will relieve the pressure on the underlying paratenons of the radial wrist extensors. The release incision is made parallel to the muscle bellies of the abductor pollicis longus and extensor pollicis brevis obliquely over the dorsum of the distal forearm. This incision is dorsal and proximal to the site for decompression of these tendons for deQuervain's tenosynovitis. The APL and EPB are found to be hypertrophied where they cross the radial extensor tendons. The paratenons of the underlying extensor tendons are inflamed and adherent. The surgeon divides the sheath longitudinally from the musculotendinous junction to where the muscles disappear deep into the forearm. After a few days, the splint is removed and the athlete can exercise back to normal.

DeQuervain's
Stenosing Tenosynovitis

Ulnar deviation of the wrist angles the tendons of the abductor pollici longus and the ex-

tensor pollicis brevis under the retinaculum covering the first dorsal compartment of the wrist at the level of the radial styloid. Repetitive angulation produces tenosynovitis in this fibro-osseous tunnel. The area will be tender and Finkelstein's test positive. In this test, the wrist is ulnar deviated passively while the thumb is held adducted in the palm. This movement produces pain at the radial styloid. Treatment includes resting the wrist, putting the thumb in a splint and prescribing a nonsteroidal, anti-inflammatory medicine. In chronic cases, however, the roof is thick and pain persists. In such cases, decompression is indicated. While releasing the roof, the surgeon takes care to avoid the sensory branch of the radial nerve. He searches for a separate canal for the extensor pollicis brevis. Sometimes a synovial cyst is found in the compartment. The tendon may exhibit a fusiform enlargement just distal to the site of compression. After tendons are released, the wrist is splinted for a few days, then early motion begins.

Flexor Carpi Ulnaris Tendinitis

The flexor carpi ulnaris dominates wrist activity, and tendinitis of it is not uncommon after repetitive activity. The tendon of the flexor carpi ulnaris will be tender at the wrist, and wrist flexion or ulnar deviation against resistance will hurt. X-ray films usually have normal findings but may show a calcium deposit in the paratenon or tendon itself. Splinting, pulsed ultrasound, and nonsteroidal anti-inflammatory medicines are usually effective.

The flexor carpi ulnaris inserts into the hook of the hamate and the bases of the fourth and fifth metacarpals. The pisiform bone is a sesamoid bone in the tendon. A synovitis may develop around the pisiform, or the pisiform-triquetral articulation may become arthritic.[69] In such cases, the pisiform will be tender. With the wrist held flexed, pain is produced when the examiner pushes the pisiform laterally on its articulation with the triquetrum. A lateral x-ray film of the wrist may show a narrow joint space. In cases of arthritis of the pisiform, the surgeon may have to excise calcium deposits, lyse peritendinous adhesions, and excise the pisiform bone subperiosteally, leaving the insertion of the flexor carpi ulnaris intact. Postoperatively the wrist is splinted for a week, and then the athlete begins range-of-motion exercises and soon returns to his sport.

Flexor Carpi Radialis Tendinitis

Tendinitis is less common at the radial side of the wrist joint than at the ulnar side because motion is less frequent there. Wrist flexion against resistance will hurt, as will passive extension of the wrist. Resistant cases of stenosing tenosynovitis at the fibro-osseous tunnel of the flexor carpi radialis may be relieved by releasing the tunnel.

Scaphoid Fractures

The scaphoid spans the proximal and distal carpal rows. The proximal part of this bone is intracapsular, and the distal portion has many soft-tissue attachments. The vulnerable waist of the scaphoid is adjacent to the styloid tip of the radius, and most of the scaphoid fractures occur here. A fall on the outstretched hand or direct impact on the hand may fracture the scaphoid by forcing it against this styloid process. The athlete notes pain on power grip and is tender over the "anatomic snuffbox."

Scaphoid fractures often are diagnosed inaccurately as sprains, and inadequate treatment may result in nonunion. If an athlete has the above symptoms but x-ray findings are negative, a cast is applied, which incorporates the proximal phalanx of the thumb. Then, in about 2 weeks, the wrist is reexamined and another x-ray film taken. If a fracture is noted, another cast is applied that extends from three fourths up the forearm down to the interphalangeal joint of the thumb and is carefully molded about the base of the thumb.

Most scaphoid fractures are through the waist, some are through the proximal pole, and the least frequent are of the distal pole. Fractures of the distal pole heal fast because of good blood supply. Fractures at the waist or proximal pole may require prolonged immobilization, and nonunion, avascular necrosis, and collapse may occur.

Those scaphoid fractures that are unstable and displaced need primary open reduction and fixation and sometimes primary grafting. Delayed unions require prolonged casting; a decision should then be made as to whether the fracture should be grafted. If the decision is made to treat the fracture with a bone graft, I favor a volar approach and use the volar aspect of the distal radius as a donor site. Postoperatively, patients with these fractures are treated with the standard scaphoid cast, and postoperative healing still takes about 3 to 4 months. While the fracture is healing, the athlete may sometimes play his sport wearing a silicone rubber splint.

Protective Splint of Silicone Rubber   Under the rules of collegiate tackle football, sole leather or other hard or unyielding substances are prohibited on the hand, wrist or forearm no matter how well they are covered or padded. Mindful of this rule, a protective silicone rubber splint has been developed.[4] The splint allows the safe return to competition of athletes who have had wrist sprains or fractures, such as a healing scaphoid fracture.

The silicone rubber protective splint (Figure 10-12) is constructed with gauze impregnated with silicone rubber-RTV 11. The splint is easy to apply, conforms to the injured part, and is durable. First, a thin coat of lubricant cream is applied to the skin, and the gauze is wrapped smoothly on the body part. A catalyst is mixed with the silicone and a generous first coat of silicone applied. Usually three or four thicknesses of gauze are used, and the silicone is worked into each layer of the gauze with a spatula. The silicone takes about 3 hours to cure at room temperature. For removal, the splint is cut along the ulnar side. It can be secured again with adhesive tape. Because the silicone splint does not breathe, it is not used as a permanent cast but may be worn during practice and competition. A bivalved hard cast is worn at other times.[4]

Hamate Hook Fractures

The hook of the hamate projects toward the palmar surface of the hand as a long, thin process of bone. The transverse carpal ligament and the pisohamate ligament both attach to the hook, and

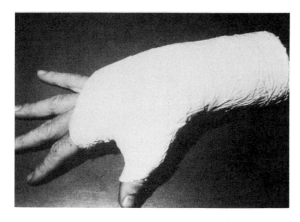

Figure 10-12 A silicone cast may allow an earlier return to practice and competition.

the flexor digiti minimi brevis and opponens digiti both arise from it. The tendon of the flexor digitorum profundus to the little finger lies on its radial side, and the motor branch of the medial nerve on its ulnar side.

The hook of the hamate may be fractured in a fall, but it breaks more commonly during a tennis, baseball, or golf swing (Figure 10-13).[85] The butt of the handle may strike the hook and fracture it, or a violent contraction of the flexor carpi ulnaris can pull through the pisohamate ligament and jerk the hook.

An athlete with a hook of the hamate fracture will have wrist pain, a poor power grip, and a

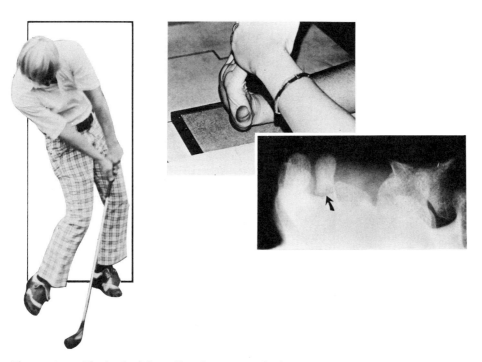

Figure 10-13 The hook of the golfer's hamate may be fractured during a swing. The fracture line may be seen on a carpal tunnel view. The fracture sometimes fails to unite and irritates the nearby motor branch of the ulnar nerve; it may also cause a rupture of the flexor profundus to the little finger.

tender hook of the hamate. Routine x-ray films often do not show the fracture; thus a carpal tunnel view should be included with the wrist in maximum dorsiflexion. If the wrist is too painful for this view to be obtained, a maximum radial deviation view, with the wrist partly supinated, may show the fracture.

A short gauntlet cast, with an extension to the little finger, is applied for acute undisplaced fractures of the hook of the hamate. The nonunion rate for this fracture is high, owing to the intermittent pull of the muscular attachments. For a badly displaced fracture or a symptomatic nonunion, the displaced hook is removed.

The ulnar nerve or the flexor digitorum profundus to the little finger may become irritated at the fracture site and give symptoms of ulnar nerve neuritis or flexor tendinitis. To prevent a later tendon rupture, some surgeons remove the hook of the hamate even in painless nonunions. So that the ulnar nerve is not damaged during this procedure, it is exposed in the canal of Guyon and carefully followed.

Nerve Compression

An athlete's median nerve may be compressed in a tight carpal tunnel, or the ulnar nerve may be compressed in the canal of Guyon. In the young, healthy athlete, rest and an anti-inflammatory medication will usually relieve median nerve compression, but sometimes surgical decompression is needed.

Touring cyclists, especially on bumpy gravel roads, often develop numbness of the little finger and the ulnar half of the ring finger, with associated ulnar intrinsic muscle weakness.[20, 45] The numbness and weakness are caused by pressure from the handlebars on the ulnar nerve (Figure 10-14) and may be relieved by wearing cycling gloves and thickly padding the handlebars. The ulnar nerve may also be compressed after a fracture of the pisiform or the hamate bone, and blunt trauma to the heel of the palm may also result in scarring within the canal of Guyon. This acute trauma may even produce a false aneurysm of the ulnar artery that may compress the ulnar nerve. Treatment consists of release of the ligament

Figure 10-14   A cyclist's ulnar nerve may be compressed at the wrist from pressure on the handlebars.

overlying the canal of Guyon and appropriate measures for the underlying lesion.

"Bowler's Thumb"

The hard edge of the thumbhole in a bowling ball may press against the base of a bowler's thumb during delivery and cause perineural fibrosis of the relatively subcutaneous ulnar digital nerve of the thumb.[20, 21, 44, 56, 57, 78] If fibrosis develops, the bowler will note pain, paresthesia when pressure is applied to this region, numbness of the ulnar-volar aspect of the thumb, and a fusiform mass.

If "bowler's thumb" is detected early, the bowler should modify his grip and use a larger, padded thumbhole. If the condition is noted later, after a mass has formed, the thumb is operated on. The thick, perineural sheath is incised and meticulously dissected free from the nerve fascicles. After neurolysis, the nerve may be transposed to a more dorsal-ulnar aspect of the thumb. Awareness of the entity of bowler's thumb neuroma prevents unnecessary removal of the digital nerve. The symptoms may be relieved without excising the neuroma, and the critical sensation is maintained along the medial border of the thumb.

REHABILITATION PROGRESSION FOR THE ELBOW, FOREARM, AND WRIST

OBJECTIVES

Strengthen: Elbow flexors, extensors, pronators and supinators; wrist flexors and extensors; radial and ulnar deviators

Flexibility: Elbow flexors and extensors
Wrist flexors and extensors

Endurance: Elbow flexors and extensors
Wrist flexors and extensors

STAGES

Initial

Cryokinetics (ice, pain-free active range of motion and resistive exercise—ISE.)

Intermediate

Flexibility: Stretch the wrist into flexion for 15 seconds three times (Figure 10-15A). Stretch the wrist into extension for 15 seconds three times (Figure 10-15B).

Strength: All of the following strength exercises begin with three sets of ten repetitions and progress to five sets of ten repetitions. When the athlete can handle five sets of ten, he then adds weight and begins again at three sets of ten repetitions.

Holding a dumbbell, flex the elbow from the extended position (Figure 10-16A). Then extend the elbow while forward flexing the shoulder (Figure 10-16B) and repeat.

Use the T-bar to supinate (Figure 10-16C) and pronate (Figure 10-16D). Choke up on the bar to flex the wrist (Figure 10-16E) and extend the wrist (Figure 10-16F) holding a dumbbell. Radially deviate (Figure 10-16G) and ulnar deviate (Figure 10-16H) with the T-bar.

Advanced

Progress to weight machines and other upper extremity exercises with barbells.

Thumb Metacarpal Fractures

Axial compression may injure a hockey player's thumb metacarpal when he takes off his gloves to throw a punch. The thumb may be driven down to shear off the base of the thumb metacarpal. A small medial fragment remains hooked to the strong volar ligament as the abductor pollicis longus pulls the main portion of the metacarpal proximally. This Bennett's fracture–dislocation may be treated by closed reduction and percutaneous pin fixation. In some cases, however, open reduction is needed to approximate the articular surfaces accurately. A Rolando's fracture is a proximal, intra-articular, T-shaped fracture of the first metacarpal. Here the flexor and extensor muscles pull the fracture fragments apart over the trapezium.

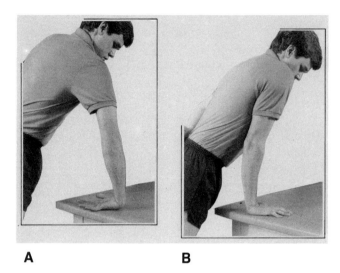

A   **B**

Figure 10-15 The player stretches his elbow extensors **(A)** and flexors **(B)** by leaning on a table.

Although fractures of the metacarpal shaft are often angulated by muscle pull, a well-molded gauntlet cast can usually hold the reduction. Fractures of the proximal phalanx of the thumb may follow a twisting injury, such as when an equestrian's thumb becomes caught in a halter as the horse rears. These fractures are usually treated by a closed reduction and a gauntlet cast. Internal fixation may be required if the fracture slips.

Thumb Metacarpophalangeal Joint Dislocation

When the metacarpophalangeal joint of the thumb is forcefully hyperextended and dislocates, the membranous part of the volar plate may tear (Figure 10-17). In a simple dislocation, the proximal phalanx lies dorsal to the metacarpal head and is standing straight up. Longitudinal traction should be avoided because the volar plate may slip between the metacarpal and the proximal phalanx, converting the simple dislocation into a complex one. Instead, the physician should push against the dorsal surface of the proximal phalanx and push the metacarpal dorsally.

When the volar plate is caught between the metacarpal and the proximal phalanx, the dislocation may be irreducible. X-ray films show a sesamoid bone within the widened joint space, and there is a dimple in the palmar skin. To reduce such a dislocation, the thumb metacarpal

is first adducted and the thumb flexed to relax the intrinsics. Then the proximal phalanx is hyperextended, and the physician pushes against the dorsal surface of the proximal phalanx and pushes the metacarpal up. If closed reduction fails, open reduction may be performed through a volar or dorsal approach.

After reduction, the thumb is immobilized in a plaster splint for about 2 weeks. The athlete often is allowed to resume competition while wearing a silicone splint. When the joint is completely stable and has a full range of motion, the immobilization may be discontinued.

Ulnar Collateral Ligament Injury of the Thumb

Ulnar collateral ligament injuries of the thumb are often overlooked in young, poorly supervised athletes.[62, 63] There is a tendency to minimize the injury, but it may lead to a weakness of pinch and instability when the thumb is stressed in abduction. The injury occurs mostly in tackle football, from forced abduction of the thumb, but also in hockey players, who take off their gloves to fight, and in soccer goalkeepers, skiers, wrestlers and baseball players.[10, 15, 16, 27, 28, 75] The skier's pole strap allows him to plant the pole harder by pulling down on the strap, and thus the pole need not be gripped as tightly. When the strap is wrapped around the wrist, discarding the pole is

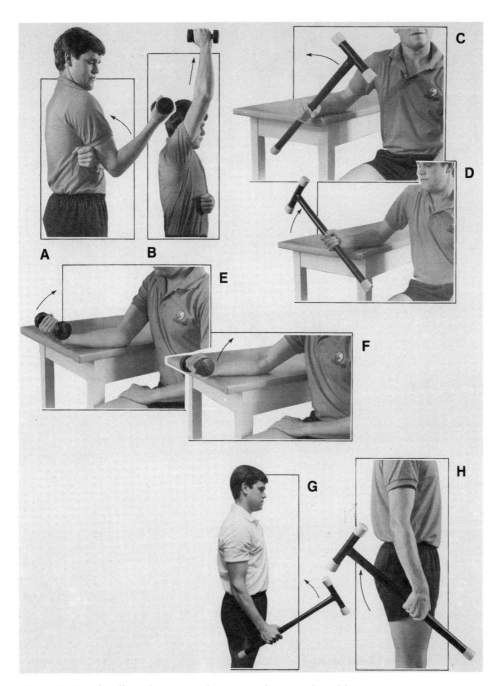

Figure 10-16   The elbow, forearm, and wrist may be strengthened by using dumbbells and a T-bar. The T-bar, or "Devastator," is an easy-to-hold, 5-pound bar that fits into the palm of the hand. It has lines on it that denote resistance from 1 to 5 pounds. The baseball pitcher needs especially to regain external shoulder rotation; thus he should seek to stretch to the point at which his forearm is perpendicular to the floor. (Devastator information is available from Tab Blackburn at Rehabilitation Services of Columbus, Columbus, Georgia.)

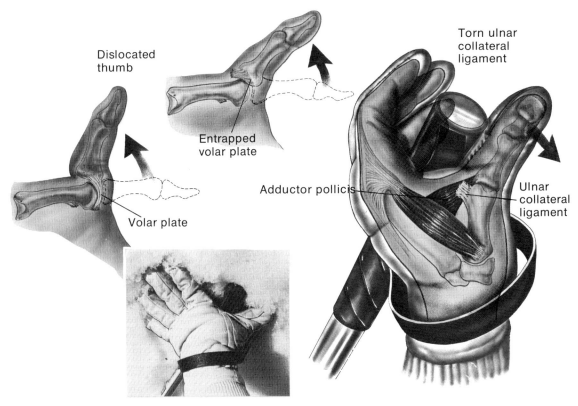

Figure 10-17   Landing on a ski pole may dislocate the metacarpophalangeal joint of the thumb, and the volar plate may become trapped in the joint. In other instances, the ulnar collateral ligament of the thumb may tear from its insertion into the proximal phalanx, and the tendon of the adductor pollicis may interpose to prevent healing.

difficult, and the skier may land on it in trying to break the fall (Figure 10-18). A better method of holding the pole is with only the hand put through the loop.

The ulnar collateral ligament is usually torn from its attachment to the proximal phalanx. Sometimes a displaced rotated chip from the proximal phalanx may be seen on x-ray films. Most of the tears are partial and can be treated by closed means, but acute, complete tears are treated with open repair and reconstruction. In more than half of these complete tears, the intrinsic aponeurosis is found to be lying between the ends of the ulnar collateral ligament and would block healing.[62] The avulsed ulnar collateral ligament is reattached by a pull-out wire technique.

If the ligament has been torn in its midportion, sutures are placed in it with the metacarpophalangeal joint flexed to 15° to 20°, and the athlete must wear a splint or a thumb spica for 5 weeks.

Taping of the thumb allows an athlete to continue playing without jeopardizing a mild or moderate sprain and to play after surgery (Figure 10-19). First the metacarpophalangeal joint is stabilized with the tape, and then the athlete's index finger is taped to his thumb, holding the thumb adducted and preventing abduction at the metacarpophalangeal joint. Alternatively, elastic tape may be used to hold the thumb adducted (Figure 10-20).

An athlete with an old ulnar collateral ligament injury may have a long history of pinch

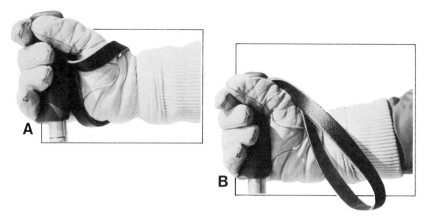

Figure 10-18   If a skier wraps the pole strap around his wrist **(A)**, he may injure his thumb in a fall. If he does not use the pole strap **(B)**, however, another skier may be injured by the lost pole.

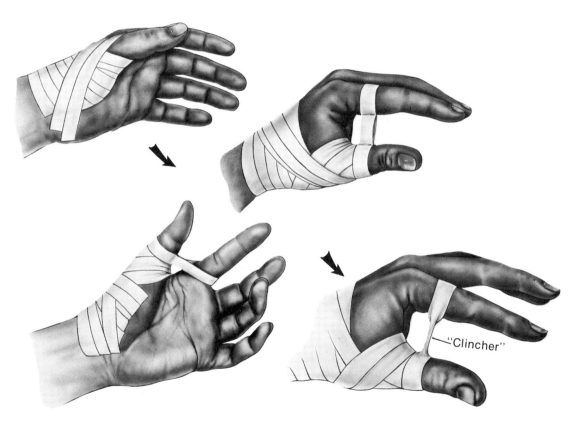

"Clincher"

Figure 10-19   A thumb taping with a "clincher" strap restricts thumb movement.

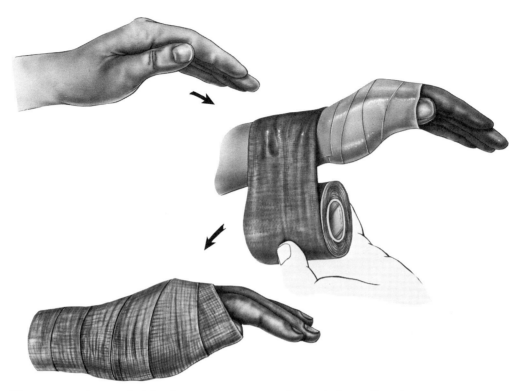

Figure 10-20   A "pancake" thumb taping may protect a damaged ulnar collateral ligament of the thumb.

weakness, pain, and instability at the metacarpophalangeal joint of the thumb. When the ulnar collateral ligament is thin or missing, it can be replaced by a slip of the abductor pollicis longus, or a slip of the adductor pollicis may be advanced to the proximal phalanx as a dynamic repair.

Soft Tissue Injuries at the Metacarpophalangeal Joint of the Fingers

What may at first appear to be a dorsal dislocation of the proximal phalanx of a metacarpophalangeal joint is actually a volar dislocation of the metacarpal head. The head breaks through a buttonhole rent in the volar plate and is caught in this rent and between the lumbrical tendon and long flexors. This dislocation is usually referred to as an "irreducible dislocation" because closed reduction often fails. Although the index finger is most often affected, the little finger metacarpal or other metacarpals may also be dislocated. The affected finger is generally angled toward the ulnar, overlapping the adjacent finger, and a dimple appears in the skin at the midpalmar crease. Longitudinal traction actually prevents reduction, as the surrounding structures form a nooselike constriction around the metacarpal neck. An acute dislocation may sometimes be reduced by increasing the deformity and attempting to return the proximal phalanx through the tear in the volar plate. Once swelling has occurred, however, an open reduction is usually needed.

The dislocation may be reduced surgically through a volar approach (Figure 10-21). Great care must be taken to avoid damaging the very prominent palmar structures, especially the digital nerve and artery. Once reduced, the joint is surprisingly stable. The metacarpophalangeal joint is kept flexed about 30° for 7 to 10 days, and then active flexion is begun from this position.

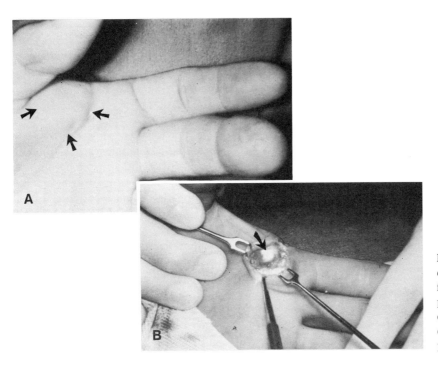

Figure 10-21 A volar dislocation of the index finger metacarpal head presents as a bulge and a dimple in the palm **(A)**. At operation **(B)**, the metacarpal head *(arrow)* is reduced.

An extension-block splint is worn, and extension and hyperextension are not permitted until 5 weeks after surgery. Nearly full flexion has usually been accomplished by the time the splint is removed.

A collateral ligament injury of a metacarpophalangeal joint is not nearly as common or as disabling as one involving a proximal interphalangeal joint. However, a piece of the proximal phalanx may be avulsed by the collateral ligament into the joint. Swelling, thickening, and the possible inclusion of the collateral ligament in the joint are the most disabling findings. Lateral instability is usually not a functional problem, since radial or ulnar control is maintained by the intrinsics.

Another soft tissue injury at the metacarpophalangeal joint is rupture of the extensor hood of the extensor digitorum communis. The extensor tendon can then slip into the valley between the metacarpal heads and produce a disabling snapping. A large mass of granulation tissue may form from hypertrophic synovium in the tear, preventing an athlete from gripping. The mass should be removed and the extensor hood repaired.

Hand Injuries in Karate

Karate means "empty hand" in Japanese. The fighting technique began in India more than 1500 years ago for self-defense against bandits, was later taught to Chinese monks, and developed further in Okinawa. In 1920, the martial art was exported to Japan and, after World War II, to the United States.[17, 29]

Karate enthusiasts scar their limbs, converting them into weapons to strike the sensitive areas of their opponents. This toughening may be achieved by striking a straw-covered, pliable post over a number of years, or the hands and feet may be driven into sacks of sand, gravel, grain, or leather scraps.[49] Scar tissue slowly increases, but, if rigid adherence to this program is replaced by a desire for quick results, the hands may be damaged.[82]

Hypertrophic infiltrative tenosynovitis may develop around an extensor tendon that is greatly enlarged proximal to where it is trapped by a mass of scar tissue at the metacarpophalangeal joint.[29] The scar tissue may be removed, but the incision should be placed so that it does not interfere with striking.[29]

A correctly executed thrust and hand strike uses the index and middle finger metacarpal heads. Axial compression forces are transmitted from these metacarpals to the distal carpal row, which is dynamically splinted by the taut wrist extensors and flexors. These forces may produce intra-articular fractures.[46] In contrast to correct technique, inaccurate thrusts, roundhouse blows, and the blocking of kicks will transmit angular torsional forces to produce oblique diaphyseal fractures of the metacarpals.[41]

To lessen the chance of hand injury, a fist must be made properly (Figure 10-22). A loose fist leaves the second and third metacarpals unsupported, and only their thick cortex and shaft may save them from breaking. To make a proper fist for karate, the interphalangeal joints are first maximally flexed. Then the metacarpophalangeal joints are flexed so that the thenar eminence gives support. The thumb is tucked out of the way.

Striking is done only with the index and middle finger knuckles and with a maximally tightened fist. At impact the wrist is pronated, reminding the striker to maximally tighten the fist and also tearing an attacker's skin.

Metacarpal Fractures

Fractures of the finger metacarpals include proximal fracture–dislocations at the base of the fifth metacarpal that may be similar to a fracture–dislocation of the first metacarpal; metacarpal shaft fractures; fractures through a metacarpal neck, the "fighter's fracture"; and intra-articular fractures at the metacarpophalangeal joint.

A proximal fracture–dislocation of the fifth metacarpal may behave like an unstable Bennett's fracture–dislocation of the first metacarpal. Such a fracture is reduced and fixed with pins. Fracture–dislocations of the second, third, or fourth

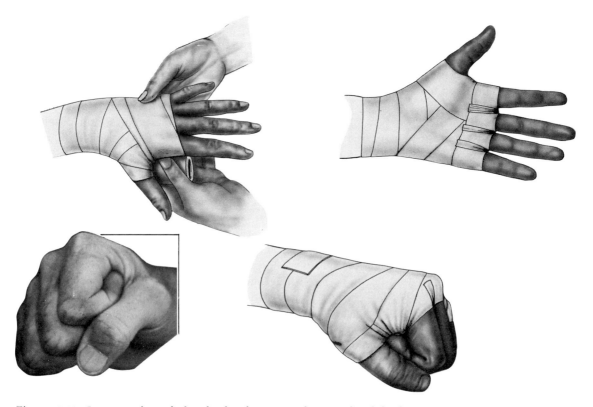

Figure 10-22 In a properly made fist, the thumb supports the second and third metacarpals, but the lateral two metacarpals remain unsupported, allowing a fracture to occur. The taping supports the boxer's metacarpals.

metacarpal are extremely rare, and the treatment must be individualized. Fractures of the proximal shaft of the metacarpals are controlled by metacarpal ligaments and are generally stable. They are protected in a short arm cast.

A fracture of a metacarpal shaft is usually only minimally displaced and may be controlled in a well-molded short-arm cast that is worn for 4 to 6 weeks. Occasionally percutaneous pins or an open reduction is necessary. Long, spiral fractures are more likely to require internal fixation to avoid compounding, rotatory deformity, and shortening of the metacarpal. When these fractures are treated closed, care must be taken to control the rotation of the digit, and it is often taped to an adjacent finger. Open reduction of a metacarpal shaft fracture may produce complications such as compromise of the bone's blood supply, fibrosis of the interosseous muscles, adherence of the extensor tendons, and local infection.

A "fighter's fracture," or "punch fracture," through the neck of the fifth metacarpal may follow a roundhouse punch. A boxer, with proper punching technique and taped hands, will more often fracture his second or third metacarpal than his fifth metacarpal. The boxer has the advantage of good technique, bandaged hands, and boxing gloves. His hands are bandaged with his fingers spread. When he flexes his fingers, the metacarpals are held strongly together. A boxing "glove" is really a mitten, with a firm leather band in the palm of the glove that supports all four finger metacarpals.

The fourth and fifth metacarpals are structurally weak, the fourth being the most slender, while the fifth is shorter and has a paper-thin cortex. The thenar eminence supports only the second and third metacarpals, leaving the lateral two metacarpals without support in a bareknuckled fist. The volar articular ridge of the metacarpal heads acts as a reinforcement and explains the obliquity of the fracture lines.

A fighter's fracture is common and often overtreated. Any rotation can usually be corrected by closed reduction with the metacarpophalangeal joint flexed so that the fragment is controlled by a tightening of the collateral ligament. Volar and dorsal felt pads are placed after the reduction.

Then a molded plaster cast is applied, with an outrigger or with the little finger buddy-taped to the ring finger. Up to 40° of angulation is acceptable in the more mobile fourth and fifth metacarpals. Holding the metacarpophalangeal and proximal interphalangeal joints in flexion with pressure over the dorsum of the proximal phalanx is unnecessary. Serious secondary stiffness and skin problems frequently follow such treatment. A fracture that is very unstable may require percutaneous pinning and, occasionally, open reduction with internal fixation.

If an appreciable part of the articular surface is involved in a fracture, the fracture must be anatomically reduced, usually by open reduction. An arthroplasty with a Silastic prosthesis may be needed in a joint that has been left grossly deformed by an old injury.

The complications of metacarpal fractures include rotatory deformity, localized Volkmann's ischemic contracture, limitation of flexion and extension at the metacarpophalangeal, proximal interphalangeal, or distal interphalangeal joints, and nonunion of the bone. In these cases reconstructive procedures may be needed to improve function.

Fractures of the Proximal Phalanx

The periosteum of the proximal phalanx is in contact with the extrinsic extensor and flexor tendons and the lateral bands. Because of this close association, these tendons readily adhere to fractures of the proximal phalanx, especially if they have been imperfectly reduced. Tethering of the tendons limits active and passive motion at the proximal interphalangeal and distal interphalangeal joints. Moreover, a fracture of the proximal phalanx may affect the metacarpophalangeal or the proximal interphalangeal joint. Restricted motion in either of these joints is disabling, but restriction of motion in both joints is disastrous.

The intrinsic and extrinsic muscles exert deforming forces on the fracture fragments. The proximal fragment is flexed by the intrinsics, and the distal fragment is controlled by the extrinsic flexors and extensors that span it. The collateral ligaments of the metacarpophalangeal joints aid closed reduction, controlling the metacarpophalangeal joint when it is flexed and maintaining control of the proximal fragment. A flexed position also lessens the deforming force of the intrinsic muscles, and flexion of the proximal interphalangeal joint relaxes the extrinsic flexors, reducing their deforming force.

An epiphyseal fracture of a young athlete's proximal phalanx may be angulated. Closed reduction is usually successful. The tough periosteum is often intact and aids in obtaining and maintaining the reduction. After reduction the finger is splinted, and when the reaction has died down the injured finger is taped to an adjacent finger.

Inherently stable fractures of the shaft of the proximal phalanx and those that are stable after reduction may be controlled by splinting. After a thin felt pad is placed between the fingers, the injured finger is taped to an adjacent finger. For less stable fractures, a forearm splint is applied with an outrigger that holds the finger in the position of greatest stability. Remember that all the fingers should point toward the proximal tubercle of the scaphoid. Malrotation will occur if this relationship is not maintained. Early motion is particularly important after a fracture of the proximal phalanx to regain optimal finger motion.

Some proximal phalanx fractures present special problems. The spike of an oblique fracture may encroach upon the proximal interphalangeal joint just proximal to the articular surface and severely disrupt joint function. A spiral fracture can easily rotate and shorten to produce a deformity if it is not held well reduced. These are usually fixed percutaneously with pins, but when a closed reduction is not possible open reduction and pin fixation are done. A fracture involving the articular surface must be reduced anatomically and held with pins. When a proximal phalanx fracture is treated by open reduction and internal fixation, incisions must be placed properly and the tissue handled gently; otherwise, functional loss may be even greater than that after closed treatment. Prompt, appropriate treatment for proximal phalanx fractures is imperative. Secondary reconstructions for nonunions or for other bony or soft tissue abnormalities may not produce a fully functional finger.

Injuries to the Proximal Interphalangeal Joint

The anatomy of the proximal interphalangeal joint is complex for such a small articulation and must be understood for correct diagnosis and effective treatment of injuries to this joint. A hinged joint, it has a range of motion of from 0° to 120° in the plane perpendicular to the palm. The lateral ligaments and volar plate are thick and strong. They are supplemented dorsally by the central slip of the extensor tendon and by the flexor tendons, less closely on the volar surface. The lateral bands and their extensions, the oblique and transverse retinacular ligaments, and Cleland's ligament radiating dorsal to the neurovascular bundle add some stability and must move and glide freely to allow proper motion. The volar cul-de-sac must be free of scar to allow full flexion of the finger, during which the base of the middle phalanx glides into the sac.

The proximal interphalangeal joint has limited lateral mobility and is particularly vulnerable because of its relatively long proximal and distal lever arms that transmit lateral stress and torque.[60] Any fixed deformity of the proximal interphalangeal joint, either in flexion or extension, is extremely disabling. Because it is a small, non-weight-bearing joint, there is a tendency to minimize the severity of injuries to it. Poorly supervised athletes often return to unprotected use of the digit long before adequate healing has taken place.

Injuries to the proximal interphalangeal joint include articular fractures, fracture-dislocations, dislocations, collateral ligament injuries, buttonhole deformities, and volar plate injuries such as hyperextension and pseudobuttonhole deformities.

Articular Fractures at the Proximal Interphalangeal Joint

Commonly seen articular fractures at the proximal interphalangeal joint include those that pass through one condyle of the head of the proximal phalanx, long and short oblique fractures, T fractures that split the condyles, fractures of the base of the middle phalanx, avulsion fractures of the articular surface, and comminuted fractures.

Stable fractures with little or no ligamentous instability, such as small chip fractures and avulsion fractures, should be splinted for 3 weeks with the proximal interphalangeal joint flexed to about 30°. In most cases, the athlete may return to competition, wearing the splint for protection. Early protected flexion begins as soon as the acute reaction abates. Either a dorsal or volar splint should be worn during sports and other strenuous activities for an additional 4 to 6 weeks or until a full range of motion has been regained.

The indications for open reduction and internal fixation include displaced articular fractures that constitute more than one fourth of the articular surface, displaced volar lip fractures that invite subsequent dorsal subluxation, comminuted or displaced fractures, and dorsal avulsion fractures that include the insertion of the central slip of the extensor tendon into the base of the middle phalanx. Accurate restoration of the articular surface in this little, tight-fitting joint is important for a maximum return of function. Secondary reconstructive procedures, including Silastic implant arthroplasty, give less predictable results. Arthrodesis is a treatment of last resort and is rarely indicated.

Fracture–Dislocations of the Proximal Interphalangeal Joint

The most common fracture–dislocation of the proximal interphalangeal joint is one through the volar lip of the proximal phalanx (Figure 10-23A). Here the buttressing effect of the volar lip is lost, and, if untreated, the finger becomes stiff and painful and its function greatly impaired. The volar fragment may vary in size and comminution. If the joint is stable, the digit may be splinted in flexion with a splint that blocks extension; if unstable, operative reduction and pinning are needed (Figure 10-23B). Early flexion exercises should begin in 3 weeks, and the finger should be protected during sports activity for an additional 4 to 6 weeks.

An avulsion of the central slip of the extensor mechanism, with or without a bony fragment, and volar subluxation of the middle phalanx are rare injuries. They often demand an open reduction because the head of the proximal phalanx may be entrapped by the lateral bands to block a closed reduction.

Dislocations of the Proximal Interphalangeal Joint

If the proximal interphalangeal joint is hyperextended, the volar plate may rupture at its distal attachment, with or without an avulsion fracture from the base of the middle phalanx, and the middle phalanx will dislocate dorsal to the proximal phalanx (Figure 10-23C). Reduction is usually easy and the joint generally stable because the collateral ligament system has usually remained intact. Once reduced, the joint is immobilized in 20° to 30° of flexion for 3 weeks, whereupon the splint is removed and the athlete begins an active exercise program. The finger should be taped to an adjacent normal digit during sports activity for at least 2 more weeks until it is asymptomatic. With proper care and protection, full recovery should be expected, with an asymptomatic finger and a full range of motion.

For a lateral dislocation of the proximal interphalangeal joint to occur, a collateral ligament and the volar plate must tear. The method of treatment for these dislocations depends on what instabilities exist after reduction. Some dislocations have a rotatory component, and the head of the proximal phalanx may become buttonholed between the central slip and the lateral band. These dislocations usually require open reduction. Open dislocations are meticulously cleaned, and then the torn tissues may be repaired. The athlete may begin active protected motion as soon as his skin heals.

"Buttonhole Deformity"

A disruption of the central slip of the extensor digitorum communis tendon over the proximal interphalangeal joint produces a classic buttonhole (boutonnière) deformity (Figure 10-23D) that consists of hyperextension at the distal interphalangeal joint.[59] A central slip rupture is diffi-

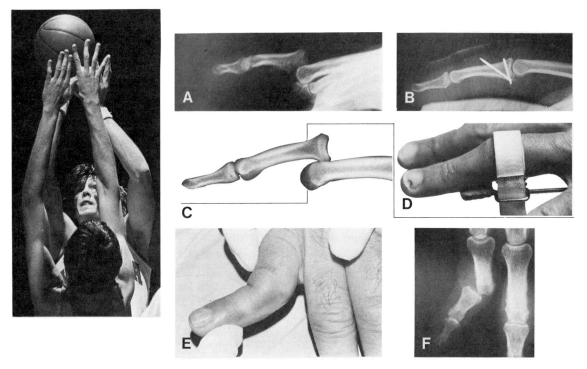

Figure 10-23   A fracture of the volar lip of the middle phalanx may allow dislocation **(A)**. Pins are used to fix this fracture **(B)**. A dislocated proximal interphalangeal joint **(C)** may yield a buttonhole deformity that can sometimes be corrected with a safety-pin splint **(D)**. In a collateral ligament tear **(E, F)**, the proximal end of the ligament catches within the joint and may need to be removed operatively.

cult to diagnose accurately. Unopposed pull of the flexor digitorum sublimis and pain and swelling at the proximal interphalangeal joint keep the joint flexed. The athlete's inability to extend his proximal interphalangeal joint is often attributed to the pain and swelling from the injury. The finger is splinted in the usual semiflexed position. When the extensor tendon is disrupted, however, this position favors a continued separation of the central slip and prevents healing. Later, as the athlete attempts to extend the finger, the tension on the lateral bands increases, causing them to drop volarly. These bands then become flexors, aggravate the deformity, and produce hyperextension at the distal interphalangeal joint.

To avoid developing a buttonhole deformity, a person with any injury associated with a lag of more than 30° in proximal interphalangeal exten-

sion and tenderness dorsally directly over the base of the middle phalanx should be treated for an acute extensor rupture. The digit should be splinted with the proximal interphalangeal joint in full extension, and this splint should be worn for 6 to 8 weeks. Protective splinting should be continued during competition for another 6 to 8 weeks or until full flexion and maximum extension of the finger have returned. The metacarpophalangeal and distal interphalangeal joints may be left free to move. If there is residual restricted passive extension at the proximal interphalangeal joint, correction with a safety-pin splint is needed. In many of these cases, however, surgical reconstruction will be required. Many surgical procedures have been designed to correct chronic deformities, but owing to a variety of findings the results of these procedures are not predictable.

Volar Plate Injuries

The volar plate of the proximal interphalangeal joint has a proximal membranous portion attached to the proximal phalanx and a thick, cartilaginous distal portion attached strongly to the base of the middle phalanx. An acute volar plate injury requires splinting for at least 5 weeks. The athlete may begin early protected motion at 3 weeks, wearing an extension-block splint to prevent extension of the digit.

An injury to the volar plate may result in either a hyperextension deformity or a flexion deformity at the proximal interphalangeal joint. Distal disruption of the plate may produce a "swan-neck" deformity. Surgical reconstruction is indicated only if the proximal interphalangeal joint locks in extension and interferes with normal function of the hand.

Damage to the proximal, membranous part of the plate may produce a "pseudoboutonnière deformity." This resembles the classic boutonnière deformity, but the central extensor slip is intact. With a pseudoboutonnière deformity, there is usually a history of a hyperextension or a twisting injury to the proximal interphalangeal joint. The signs of a pseudoboutonnière deformity include a flexion contracture of the proximal interphalangeal joint, which is more resistant to correction by passive extension than is the typical boutonnière, slight hyperextension of the distal interphalangeal joint, and radiologic evidence of calcification under the distal end of the proximal phalanx.

Static safety-pin splinting is used in subacute, less-fixed pseudoboutonnière deformities. After correction, these fingers must still be followed closely because the deformity may recur. Chronic pseudoboutonnière deformities are much more resistant to extension with a safety-pin splint. If the deformity is disabling—usually past 40° of flexion—or if it progresses or is a problem to the athlete, surgery is indicated.

Collateral Ligament Injuries

Collateral ligament injuries to the proximal interphalangeal joint are most common on the radial side of the digit (Figure 10-23E,F). The proximal attachment of the collateral ligament is avulsed, and the volar plate may be partly or completely ruptured, depending on the magnitude of the injury force. If part of the collateral ligament is intact, as evidenced by some stability, the joint may be splinted in 30° of flexion. The finger is splinted protectively for at least 3 weeks, but active motion exercises may begin at 10 to 14 days after injury. The splint is worn for another 4 to 6 weeks during athletic activity or until the joint becomes asymptomatic.

The treatment of choice for complete collateral ligament tears at the proximal interphalangeal joint is controversial. Some surgeons maintain that nonoperative treatment is satisfactory; however, the proximal end of the ligament frequently folds into the joint at the time of injury and remains stuck there. Thus, closed treatment often leaves the athlete with a swollen, tender, and unstable joint susceptible to further injury and prone to develop degenerative changes. Surgery allows inspection of the joint and repair of the torn ligament. The surgeon must, of course, be well versed in surgery of the hand, or further damage may result from the operation. Reconstructive surgery may be needed in chronic cases, but the results are less satisfactory and less predictable than after a primary repair.

Fractures of the Middle Phalanx

Fractures of the middle phalanx are usually slow healing, oblique, or transverse through the hard cortical bone in the narrow waist of the shaft. The central slip of the extensor tendon inserts dorsally into the base of the middle phalanx, whereas the two slips of the flexor digitorum sublimis insert further distally into the volar surface of the shaft. This anatomy accounts for the characteristic deformities seen in the fractures.

The most common fracture site is distal to both insertions. In these, the stronger flexor sublimis tendon flexes the proximal fragment. Longitudinal traction and flexion of the distal fragment align the fracture, especially if there is an intact periosteal bridge. When a fracture occurs more proximally in the shaft, between the central slip of the extensor tendon and the insertion of the flexor digitorum sublimis, the proximal fragment will be extended and the distal fragment flexed. These fractures are reduced with longitudinal traction without flexion.

Fractures of the middle phalanx are held in a splint for about 3 weeks, whereupon exercises are begun. When the athlete is engaged in athletic competition, however, the splint must be worn for 6 to 8 more weeks or until the fracture is healed completely. Unstable fractures are fixed with percutaneous K wires and protected similarly. Occasionally, when satisfactory alignment cannot be obtained by closed means, open reduction and internal fixation are needed.

Avulsion of the Flexor Digitorum Profundus

Avulsion of the flexor digitorum profundus, "football finger," is more common than was earlier thought. [8, 14, 53, 72] The injury was misdiagnosed after or missed entirely, but increased suspicion and thorough examinations have led to an appreciation of its true incidence. The injury may occur in any digit but is most common in the ring finger. When a football player grabs an opponent's jersey, his little finger may slip, leaving only his ring finger holding on, the finger least able to be extended independently. The pull of the jersey forcibly extends the distal phalanx while the finger is being flexed actively. As a result, the flexor digitorum profundus is pulled from its insertion on the distal phalanx.

Even though the flexor digitorum is avulsed, it does not produce a diagnostic deformity. The examiner may decide wrongly that the athlete's inability to flex the tip of his finger is due to the marked soft tissue swelling and pain. The athlete's grip is weak and his proximal interphalangeal joint motion limited. The examiner should feel for a tender mass where the avulsed tendon has reacted into the proximal part of the finger or into the palm. X-ray films may show a small, avulsed fragment of bone.

The three common levels of retraction of the profundus tendon depend on the force of the avulsion. The least retraction occurs with an avulsion fracture of the volar lip of the distal phalanx as the volar plate remains attached to the fracture fragment. The plate tethers the flexor tendon near the distal interphalangeal joint to prevent further retraction. Greater force produces an avulsion of the tendon itself, which retracts to the level of the hiatus of the flexor digitorum sublimis and is held there by the vinculum longum. Intense force will completely avulse the tendon, and it will retract up into the palm.

The surgeon who treats these injuries must be familiar with the principles of hand surgery and well versed in the techniques of flexor tendon repair. Treatment must be individualized and adapted to each situation. In injuries that cause a large fracture through the volar lip of the distal phalanx with the volar plate attached, the fracture fragment is replaced. This reestablishes the continuity of the flexor digitorum profundus tendon. Postoperatively the finger is splinted in flexion for 3 weeks. The athlete then begins protected range-of-motion exercises, and the finger is splinted for another 2 weeks.

If the tendon has retracted to the hiatus, it still may be reattached for up to 3 weeks after the initial injury, and in some cases up to 6 weeks. If the injury is missed or neglected for a longer time, however, contractures will necessitate a secondary reconstructive procedure. When the tendon has retracted all the way into the palm, it may be reattached if the athlete is seen within 7 to 10 days after injury. However, the complete retraction of a sublimis tendon may disrupt its blood through the vinculum longum, and the tendon may die. By 10 days after these injuries, contractures develop, and a secondary repair is then indicated. The surgeon uses a free tendon graft because a primary repair at this time would result in a permanent flexion contracture of the digit. In reconstructing the tendon, any method that entails acute flexion of the finger must be avoided because this would produce a flexion contracture. For some surgeons, a fusion of the distal joint may be the treatment of choice. A solidly fused, pain-free distal interphalangeal joint at the end of a proximal interphalangeal joint that has a normal range of motion is far better than a stiff finger.

Distal Interphalangeal Joint Dislocation

In the usual dislocation of the distal interphalangeal joint, the phalanx dislocates dorsally. The injured athlete himself or a teammate usually reduces the dislocation by traction and manipulation before the trainer or doctor sees it. After the reduction, the distal interphalangeal joint is generally stable; however, collateral ligament damage or interposition of the volar plate must be checked for carefully. After the dislocation has been reduced, a splint is worn during athletic activity for at least 3 more weeks or until tenderness is gone and a good range of motion regained.

Volar dislocations of the distal phalanx are much less common than dorsal ones. They are associated with damage to the extensor tendon mechanism or fracture of the dorsal lip of the distal phalanx. Open wounds are not uncommon with distal interphalangeal joint dislocations; they are cleaned and closed whenever possible and treated appropriately to prevent infection.

Injuries to the Extensor Mechanism of the Distal Interphalangeal Joint

Extensor mechanism injuries at the distal interphalangeal joint are common in athletics, expecially in football receivers, baseball catchers or fielders, and basketball players (Figure 10-24). Compared to flexor tendon injuries, however, these extensor mechanism injuries are often in-

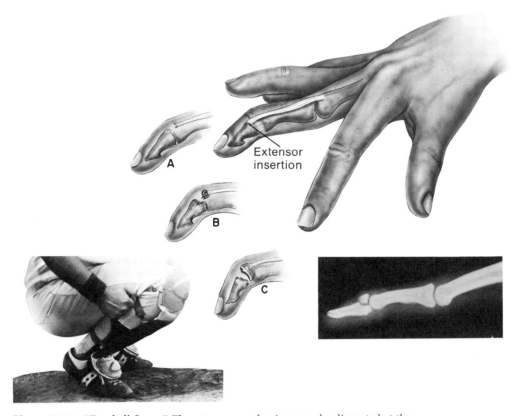

Extensor insertion

Figure 10-24 "Baseball finger." The extensor mechanism may be disrupted at the distal phalanx by being stretched or torn **(A)**. A bony fragment may be avulsed **(B)**, or, in a youngster, a fracture may occur at the growth plate **(C)**. Flexible catchers' mitts reduce the incidence of baseball finger by allowing the catcher to keep his throwing hand protected.

appropriately minimized. Two types of forces may cause extensor mechanism injuries: An extrinsic force can flex the distal interphalangeal joint against the active contraction of the extensor mechanism and rupture the extensor mechanism; and an extrinsic hyperextension can compress the athlete's distal phalanx against his middle phalanx. The middle phalanx then acts like an anvil to break off a large fragment of the articular surface, disrupting the extensor mechanism. In any type of drop finger deformity, the proximal interphalangeal joint must be examined clinically and roentgenographically. An injury to this joint frequently accompanies a drop finger injury and may result in serious residual disability if unrecognized and untreated.

The extensor tendon most commonly ruptures at the insertion of its conjoint tendon into the base of the distal phalanx to produce a "mallet" or drop finger deformity. The flexion deformity of the distal interphalangeal joint is, in many cases, associated with a hyperextension deformity of the proximal interphalangel joint.[1] The proximal interphangeal joint deformity develops after the central slip of the extensor mechanism has been disrupted distally. As the athlete repeatedly attempts to extend his distal interphalangeal joint, he has increased extension at the middle joint, with resultant dorsal subluxation of the lateral bands and a stretching of the volar plate. The intrinsic muscles thus gain a mechanical advantage, and the deformity increases. The flexor digitorum profundus, now lacking an antagonist at the distal joint, is placed under increased tension owing to the hyperextension of the middle joint. This gain in the mechanical advantage of the profundus produces an even greater flexion force across the distal joint.

There are several distinct anatomic types of distal interphalangeal joint extensor mechanism injuries, and the treatment needed depends on the type of injury. In some instances, the fibers of the extensor mechanism have been stretched and attenuated without being divided completely. In other cases, the tendon itself may rupture or may be avulsed from the base of the distal phalanx without any bony involvement (Figure 10-24A). The tendon may also be avulsed with a small fragment of bone attached to it. This bony frag-

ment appears on the x-ray film and may be used to localize the distal end of the retracted tendon.

A fracture may involve the articular surface of the distal phalanx (Figure 10-24B). The fragment is usually large enough to affect the collateral ligaments of the distal interphalangeal joint and allow volar subluxation of the distal fragment in addition to the dropped finger deformity. Children may sustain a fracture–dislocation through the growth plate, which often involves the nail bed (Figure 10-24C). The nail bed must be replaced to prevent later deformity and to facilitate healing.

A mallet finger, particularly in a young athlete, is usually treated by splinting alone if a large fragment of bone has not been avulsed. Stretching injuries often correct with time, but reinjury with complete rupture is a danger; thus they are treated like true ruptures. The distal joint is splinted in full extension or very slight hyperextension. If the distal joint were placed in extreme hyperextension, the blood supply to the skin might be impaired, resulting in a skin slough over the distal joint. Immobilization of the distal joint alone is satisfactory, allowing increased use of the hand and preventing proximal interphalangeal joint stiffness that follows use of a longer splint (Figure 10-25A). I have used this method successfully to treat mallet fingers that were first seen up to 12 weeks after the injury had taken place.

An athlete may continue to participate in sports with the finger splinted. I use either a custom-molded aluminum splint covered with moleskin or a thermoplastic orthoplast splint. The splint is worn continuously for 6 to 8 weeks and then for an additional 6 to 8 weeks only during athletics. The splint may be placed either volarly or dorsally. A dorsal splint allows more fingertip sensitivity, which is particularly important for football receivers and basketball players (Figure 10-25B). The splint must be kept dry to prevent skin maceration and should be checked at regular intervals. When the splint is changed, however, the finger must not be allowed to drop down into any flexion.

When the articular surface of the distal joint is involved significantly, an open anatomic reduction with internal fixation is needed to correct the deformity, forestall volar subluxation, and

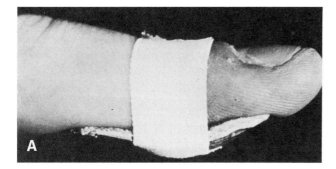

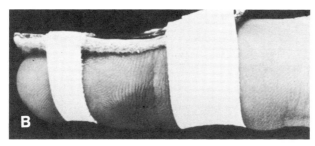

Figure 10-25 A short splint **(A)** is used for "baseball fingers." The splint is worn dorsally **(B)** by ball handlers.

prevent later traumatic arthritis. If there is any question about being able to maintain the splint properly, a thin wire is passed across the distal joint as an adjunct to the splint. The pin is removed after 4 weeks, but the finger must be splinted for an additional 3 to 4 weeks during athletic activity.

If an untreated drop finger is disabling to the athlete, a secondary surgical reconstruction may be indicated. Although these procedures are not technically difficult, the results are not entirely predictable. A good alternative for the symptomatic athlete is a fusion of his distal interphalangeal joint.

Fractures of the Distal Phalanx

Fractures of the distal phalanx mostly are direct crush injuries and usually are not displaced. If the fragments are displaced, the displacement is due to the initial traumatic force, since no deforming tendons span the fracture site. The distal phalanx is covered dorsally by the nail bed, which rests directly on the periosteum, and volarly by the fingertip pulp.

Undisplaced fractures of the distal phalanx are treated with a compressive dressing and splint. A painful subungual hematoma can be drained aseptically by piercing the nail with a heated paper clip. If the fracture of the distal phalanx is a displaced one, the nail and matrix may be disrupted. The matrix may lodge between the fracture fragments, block healing, and even cause a nonunion. A disrupted nail matrix must be replaced and repaired anatomically to allow proper healing and to prevent a nail deformity. The edges of the nail bed are approximated and repaired with fine absorbable sutures.

A nondisplaced nail may be used as a splint but should be removed unhesitatingly if the nail bed needs to be repaired. In addition, a nail may act as a foreign body or as a sequestrum. Although a nonunion is unusual in this area, it may occur, and reconstruction may be needed.

Hand Blisters and Calluses

Friction of the palm may cause blisters, which are collections of fluid between separated layers of epidermis, or produce calluses, which are protective build-ups of epidermis at friction areas.

During the season, calluses build up on a gymnast's hands.[7] They should be kept trimmed or else will catch on the equipment and rip. They may be shaved down with a safety razor or reduced with sandpaper or a callus file. Ideally,

REHABILITATION PROGRESSION FOR THE FINGERS

OBJECTIVES

To strengthen flexors and extensors to normal. Tone is more important than strength.
Flexibility: Flexibility is more important than strength. The MP, PIP, and DIP joints should be worked individually.
Endurance: Athletes should seek more synchronous motion.

STAGES

Initial

Ice and active range of motion in an ice cup (Figure 10-26A).
Splinting as necessary (Table 10-1).

Intermediate

Isolated active and passive joint motion with the uninvolved joints stabilized (Figure 10-26B).

Advanced

Grip-strengthening exercises such as gathering and squeezing a bicycle inner tube, winding a wrist roller, or climbing a rope.

---

calluses should be trimmed to the level of the surrounding skin. If they are completely removed, the underlying skin will be left tender and may tear.

Gymnasts follow a daily routine of cleansing and moisturizing their hands and controlling calluses. To keep rips to a minimum, a gymnast changes apparatus if his hands begin to feel hot from friction. If his hands begin to feel hot while he is working on parallel bars, for example, he may switch to floor exercises to rest his hands. After a workout, he washes his hands to remove the gym chalk, which would otherwise dry his skin and increase its susceptibility to blisters and rips. He also applies a hand cream or a glycerin-based massage lotion a few times daily.

A gymnast's hands need protection, but to perform well he must have a feel between his hands and the bar. A leather hand protector may be worn, or one may be fashioned out of tape. Holes are cut through the elastic tape for the index and middle fingers, and the tape is placed over his benzoin-coated palm. The elastic tape is anchored at the wrist with adhesive tape and can be chalked with magnesium carbonate.

If the skin rips, it should be cleaned and an antiseptic applied. The skin should then be kept clean and should be moistened with massage lotion to decrease the chance of the underlying skin's cracking.

Weight lifters suffer blisters, especially when they use a bar that has deep knurling. Blisters may also trouble baseball pitchers.[87] A curve ball may cause a blister to form on a pitcher's thumb, and a fast ball may cause blistering on his fingertips. Although blisters on his fingertips indicate that the pitcher is releasing the ball correctly, they can certainly interfere with his throwing.

To prevent finger blisters, ballplayers can apply benzoin to their fingers, especially during layoffs from pitching. All players are advised to report blisters early because an ice cube applied to a hot spot or to a blister may reduce the formation of fluid. A blister may also be aspirated sterilely.

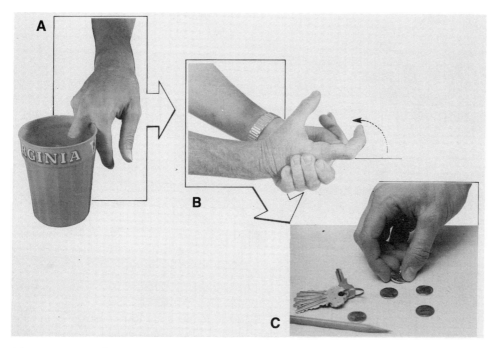

Figure 10-26 To decrease finger pain and swelling, the athlete can place his finger in cold water **(A)**. To regain joint motion, he should "block" the more proximal joint **(B)**. For dexterity, he picks up objects such as coins and keys **(C)**.

Table 10-1   SPLINTING OF FINGER INJURIES

Injury	Constant Splinting (wk)	When to Begin Motion (wk)	Splinting During Competition (wk)	Joint Position
MP fractures	3	3	+4–6	30° flexion
Phalangeal fractures	4–6	4–6	+3	N/A
DIP, PIP fractures	9–11	3	+3	30° flexion
DIP and PIP dislocations	3	3	+3	30° flexion
Boutonnière deformity	6–8	6–8	+6–8	PIP in extension; DIP, MP not included
Volar plate injuries	5	3	+3	30° flexion
Collateral ligament	3	2	+4–6	30° flexion
FDP repair	3	3	+3	
Mallet finger	9	9	+3	Slight DIP hyperextension

(Gieck JH, McCue FC III: Splinting of finger injuries. Athletic Training 17:215, Fall 1982)

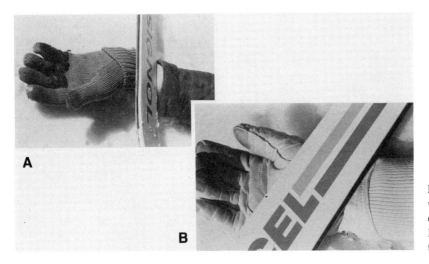

Figure 10-27 If a skier wears short gloves, a ski edge can cut the wrist. Longer gloves will prevent this injury.

If a blister tears, it is cleaned, and the shreds are removed. The main covering is then replaced and attached with benzoin adherent.[71]

Gloves for Athletes

Gloves protect an athlete's hands. Lacrosse gloves have a flexible thumb and extra padding over the scaphoid. The palm is open so that the lacrosse player has a feel for his stick. To gain an even better feel for the stick, some players cut out the fingers of their gloves up to their fingertips, but a finger may then slip out and be injured.

The baseball catcher's mitt is now flexible so that the catcher may catch one-handed, thus protecting his ungloved hand from damage. The catcher may wear a pad inside his mitt to absorb shocks and to help prevent thromboses or aneurysms of the radial and ulnar arteries. An aneurysm occurs most commonly at the hook of the hamate where the vessels are least protected.

The boxer's glove is actually a mitten, since the thumb is separated from the other fingers. An extra pad guards the thumb, and a firm leather pad in the palm of the glove supports all four finger metacarpals. Football linemen wear boxing gloves and linebackers wear gloves that leave their fingers free so they can intercept passes. Skiers should *not* wear short gloves. A young skier's gloves should be checked to be sure that he has not outgrown them, leaving his wrists susceptible to a sharp ski edge. (Figure 10-27A). Long ski gloves protect a skier's wrists from cuts from a ski edge (Figure 10-27B).

Platform tennis enthusiasts, who play in cold weather, may wear a mitten or a wool sock that has a hole cut in it to receive the handle of the paddle. While wearing this ingenious glove, the player's hand stays warm, yet he retains a feel for the paddle.

Still other athletes use golves. Cyclists may use cycling gloves or, alternatively, pad their handlebars to avoid pressure on the ulnar nerve as it passes through the canal of Guyon. Fencers use a gauntlet to protect their wrists from blows. Wheelchair racers wear gloves to prevent possible damage to hands that have impaired sensations. Tennis or racketball players may wear light, cotton gloves inside outer gloves to prevent skin irritation when the player sweats. They should carry a number of these as replacements when one pair becomes wet.

REFERENCES

1. Adams JE: Injury to the throwing arm: A study of traumatic changes in the elbow joints of boy baseball players. Calif Med 102:127–132, 1965
2. Albright JA: Clinical study of baseball pitchers: Correlation of injury to the throwing arm with method of delivery. Am J Sports Med 6:15–21, 1978
3. Barnes D, Tullos H: An analysis of 100 symptomatic baseball players. Am J Sports Med 6:62–67, 1978
4. Bassett FH et al: A protective splint of silicone rubber. Am J Sports Med 7:358–360, 1979
5. Bennett GE: Shoulder and elbow lesions of the pro-

fessional baseball pitcher, JAMA 117:510–514, 1941

6. Berg K: Prevention of tennis elbow through conditioning. Phys Sportsmed 5(2):110, 1977

7. Black SA: Blistered and torn hands disrupt gymnast's training. First Aider, Cramer 48(6):10–11, 1979

8. Blazina ME, Lane C: Rupture of the insertion of the flexor digitorum profundus tendon in student athletes. J Am Coll Health Assoc 14:248–249, 1966

9. Brogdon BG, Crow NE: Little Leaguer's elbow. Am J Roentgenol 83:671–675, 1960

10. Browne EZ Jr et al: Ski pole thumb injury. Plast Reconst Surg 58:17–23, 1976

11. Brown R et al: Osteochondritis of the capitellum. Am J Sports Med 2:27–46, 1974

12. Buckhout BC, Warner MA: Digital perfusion of handball players: Effects of repeated ball impact on structures of the hand. Am J Sports Med 8:206–207, 1980

13. Burton RI, Eaton RG: Common hand injuries in the athlete. Orthop Clin North Am 4:809–838, 1973

14. Carroll RE, Match RM: Avulsion of the flexor profundus tendon insertion. J Trauma 10:1109–1118, 1970

15. Commandre F, Viani JL: The football keeper's thumb. J Sport Med Phys Fitness 16:121–122, 1976

16. Curtin J, Kay NR: Hand injuries due to soccer. Hand 8:93–95, 1976

17. Danek E: Martial arts: The sound of one hand chopping. Phys Sportsmed 7(3):140–141, 1979

18. Dangles CJ, Bilos ZJ: Ulnar nerve neuritis in a world champion weightlifter. A case report. Am J Sports Med 8:443–445, 1980

19. DeHaven KE, Evarts CM: Throwing injuries of the elbow in athletes. Orthop Clin North Am 4:801–808, 1973

20. Dobyns JH et al: Bowler's thumb: Diagnosis and treatment: A review of seventeen cases. J Bone Joint Surg [Am] 54:751–755, 1972

21. Dunham W et al: Bowler's thumb. Clin Orthop 83:99–101, 1972

22. Eckman PB et al: Ulnar neuropathy in bicycle riders. Arch Neurol 32:130–132, 1975

23. Ellsasser JC, Stein AH: Management of hand injuries in a professional football team. Am J Sports Med 7:178–182, 1979

24. Farnum S: Traumatic bursitis. Phys Sportsmed 6(5):147, 1978

25. Francis R et al: Little League elbow: A decade later. Phys Sportsmed 6(4):88–94, 1978

26. Froimson AI: Treatment of tennis elbow with forearm support band. J Bone Joint Surg [Am] 53:183–184, 1971

27. Gamekeeper's thumb on the ski slopes (editorial). Br Med 1:213–214, 1974

28. Ganel A et al: Gamekeeper's thumb: Injuries of the ulnar collateral ligament of the metacarpophalangeal joint. Br J Sports Med 14(2–3):92–96, 1980

29. Gardner RC: Hypertrophic infiltrative tendinitis (HIT syndrome) of the long extensor. The abused karate hand. JAMA 211:1009–1010, 1970

30. Gieck JH, McCue EC III: Splinting of finger injuries. Athletic Training 17:215, Fall 1982

31. Grana WA, Rashkin A: Pitcher's elbow in adolescents. Am J Sports Med 8:333–336, 1980

32. Grenier R, Rouleau C: Boxer's elbow: An extension and hyperextension injury. Am J Sports Med 3:282–287, 1976

33. Gruchow HW, Pelletier D: An epidemiologic study of tennis elbow: Incidence, recurrence and effectiveness of prevention strategies. Am J Sports Med 7:234–238, 1979

34. Gugenheim JJ et al: Little League survey: The Houston study. Am J Sports Med 4:189–200, 1976

35. Gunn CC, Milbrandt WE: Tennis elbow and the cervical spine. Can Med Assoc J 114:803–809, 1976

36. Harris G: Elbow flexion strap for dislocated elbows. Athletic Training, 13(1):12, 1978

37. Indelicato PA et al: Correctable elbow lesions in professional baseball players: A review of 25 cases. Am J Sports Med 7:72–75, 1979

38. Jobe FW et al: Reconstruction of the medial collateral ligament in athletes. J Bone Joint Surg [Am] 68:1158–1163, 1986

39. Kalenak A et al: Athletic injuries of the hand. Am Fam Physician 14:136–142, 1976

40. Kaplan EB, Zeide MS: Aneurysm of the ulnar artery: A case report. Bull Hosp Joint Dis 33:197–199, 1972

41. Kelly DW et al: Index metacarpal fractures in karate. Phys Sportmed 8(3):103–106, 1980

42. King JW et al: Analysis of the pitching arm of the professional baseball pitcher. Clin Orthop 67:116–123, 1969

43. Kirk AA: Dunk lacerations—unusual injuries to the hands of basketball players (letter). JAMA 242:415, 1979

44. Kisner WH: Thumb neuroma: A hazard of ten pin bowling. Br J Plast Surg 29:225–226, 1976

45. Kulund DN, Brubaker CE: Injuries in the Bikecentennial Tour. Phys Sportsmed 6(6):74–78, 1978

46. Kulund DN et al: The long term effects of playing tennis. Phys Sportsmed 7(4):87–94, 1979

47. Kulund DN et al: Tennis injuries: Prevention and treatment. Am J Sports Med 7:749–753, 1979

48. Larose JH, Sik KD: Knuckle fracture: A mechanism of injury. JAMA 296:893–894, 1968

49. Larose JH, Sik KD: Karate hand-conditioning. Med Sci Sports 1(2):95–98, 1969

50. Larson RL, McMahan RO: The epiphyses and the childhood athlete. JAMA 196:607–612, 1966

51. Larson RL et al: Little League survey: The Eugene study. Am J Sports Med 4:201–209, 1976

52. Leach RE, Wasilewski S: Olecranon bursitis (dart thrower's elbow): A case report illustrating overuse/abuse in the sport of darts. Am J Sports Med 7:299, 1979

53. Leddy JP, Packer JW: Avulsion of the profundus tendon insertion in athletes. J Hand Surg 2:66–69, 1977

54. Linscheid RL, Dobyns JH: Athletic injuries of the wrist. Clin Ortho 198:141, December 1985

55. Lipscomb AB: Baseball pitching injuries in growing athletes. Am J Sports Med 3:25–34, 1975

56. Marmor L: Bowler's thumb. J Trauma 6:282–284, 1966

57. Marmor LL: Bowler's thumb. J Bone Joint Surg [Am] 52:379–381, 1970

58. Match RM: Laceration of the median nerve from skiing. Am J Sports Med 6:22–25, 1978

59. McCue FC III, Abbott JL: The treatment of mallet finger and boutonniere deformities. Va Med Monthly 94:623, 1967

60. McCue FC III et al: Athletic injuries of the promixal interphalangeal joint requiring surgical treatment. J Bone Joint Surg [Am] 52:937–956, 1970

61. McCue FC III et al: The coach's finger. Am J Sports Med 2:270–275, 1974

62. McCue FC III et al: Ulnar collateral ligament of the thumb in athletes. Am J Sportsmed 2:270, 1974

63. McCue FC III et al: Ulnar collateral ligament of the thumb in athletics. Am J Sports Med 2:70–80, 1975

64. McCue FC III et al: Hand injuries in athletics. Am J Sports Med 7:275–286, 1979

65. Miller JE: Javelin thrower's elbow. J Bone Joint Surg [Br] 42:788–792, 1960

66. Minkow FV, Bassett FH III: Bowler's thumb. Clin Orthop 83:115–117, 1972

67. Norell HG: Roentgenologic visualization of the extracapsular fat: Its importance in the diagnosis of traumatic injuries to the elbow. Acta Radiol 42:205–210, 1954

68. Norwood LA et al: Acute medial elbow ruptures. Am J Sports Med 9:16–19, 1981

69. Palmieri TJ: Pisiform area pain treated by pisiform excision. J Hand Surg 7:477–480, 1982

70. Priest JD et al: Elbow injuries in highly skilled tennis players. Am J Sports Med 2:137–149, 1974

71. Raymond P: Care of the hands. Oarsman 9(2):40–41, 1977

72. Reef TC: Avulsion of the flexor digitorum profundus: An athletic injury. Am J Sports Med 5:281–285, 1977

73. Reichelderfer TE et al: Skateboard policy statement. Pediatrics 63:924–925, 1979

74. Roles NC, Maridsley RH: Radial tunnel syndrome: Resistant tennis elbow as a nerve entrapment. J Bone Joint Surg [Br] 54:499–508, 1972

75. Rovere GD et al: Treatment of "gamekeeper's thumb" in hockey players. Am J Sports Med 3:147–151, 1975

76. Ryan AJ (moderator): Round table: Prevention and treatment of tennis elbow. Phys Sportsmed 5(2):33–54, 1977

77. Savastano AA et al: Treatment of resistant tennis elbow by a combined surgical procedure. Int Surg 57:470–474, 1972

78. Siegel IM: Bowling thumb neuroma. JAMA 192:163, 1965

79. Slager RF: From Little League to big league, the weak spot is the arm. Am J Sports Med 5:37–48, 1977

80. Spinner M: The arcade of Froshe and its relationship to posterior interosseous nerve paralysis. J Bone Joint Surg [Br] 50:809, 1968

81. Stolle F: How to put topspin on your backhand. World Tennis 27:85–88, 1980

82. Steetong JA: Traumatic hemoglobinurina caused by karate exercises. Lancet 2:191, 1967

83. Tivnon MC et al: Surgical management of osteochodritis dissecans of the capitellum. Am J Sports Med 4:121–128, 1976

84. Torg JS et al: The effect of competitive pitching on the shoulders and elbows of preadolescent baseball players. Pediatrics 49:267–272, 1972

85. Torisu T: Fracture of the hook of the hamate by a golfswing. Clin Orthop 83:91–94, 1972

86. Tullos HS: Unusual lesions of the pitching arm. Clin Orthop 88:169–182, 1972

87. Vere–Hodge N: Injuries in cricket. In Armstrong JR, Tuckers WE (eds): Injury in Sport, pp 168–171. Springfield, Illinois, Charles C Thomas, 1964

88. Waris W: Elbow injuries of javelin throwers. Acta Chir Scand 93:563–575, 1946

89. Williams JGP: Surgical management of traumatic common noninfective tenosynovitis of the wrist extensors. J Bone Joint Surg [Br] 59:408–412, 1977

90. Wilson FD et al: Valgus extension overload in the pitching elbow. Am J Sports Med 2(2):83–88, 1983

91. Woods W, Tullos HS: Elbow instability and medial epicondyle fractures. Am J Sports Med 5:23–30, 1977

CHAPTER

11

The Torso, Hip, and Thigh

CHEST INJURIES

Runner's Nipple

Friction from a runner's shirt may cause nipple irritation, pain, and bleeding in both women and men.[47, 48] For protection, a Band-Aid or a piece of tape may be placed over the nipples. Alternatively, the nipples may be coated with petrolatum or talcum powder and a silk shirt or a shirt made of synthetic material worn in place of a T-shirt.

Breast Pain from Jogging

A woman's breasts bounce when she runs, contusing the breast tissue and causing soreness. When a brassiere is not worn, the breasts may slap against the chest wall with as much as 70 foot-pounds of force. Bouncing and bruising are

problems especially for large-breasted women, just before menstrual periods, during pregnancy, in women with fibrocystic breasts, and for those who run braless or who wear a nonsupportive brassiere.

A sports brassiere may help to prevent premature ptosis of the breasts by reducing the stress on Cooper's ligaments, which hold the breasts to the chest wall (Figure 11-1).[30, 31] The supportive brassiere should prevent motion of the breast relative to the body and should contain at least 55% cotton for absorbency. The brassiere's elasticity should be minimal, although some elastic is needed to allow easy breathing. Wide, nonelastic straps will stay on the shoulders but should not be the entire support the brassiere, as the brassiere should be designed to provide some lift from below. All hooks should be well covered to prevent scratches; if the cups have seams, the seams

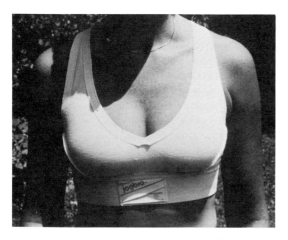

Figure 11-1   A sports bra should have wide straps and no seams against the skin. In addition, an elastic wrap may help to hold the breasts against the chest wall.

should not pass over the nipples or should be reversed to avoid nipple irritation. The female athlete should wear a sports brassiere and wrap a 10-cm (4-in) elastic wrap binding over the brassiere for the best control of breast motion. The binding will provide additional support for the breasts, reducing motion by almost 50%.[30]

Rupture of the Pectoralis Major

The powerful pectoralis major muscle arises from the medial part of the clavicle, the sternum, the first six ribs, and the aponeurosis of the external oblique. The strong tendon of this muscle has a twisting insertion into the humerus, and the clavicular and upper sternal part attach distally on the humerus while the lower sternal and abdominal portion cross over the upper part to insert higher up on the humerus. The pectoralis major adducts, flexes, and rotates the shoulder internally.

Rupture of the pectoralis major results from excess tension on the muscle. It may occur in a power lifter, wrestler, or athlete doing bench presses with a heavy barbell, and it is not unusual for a champion power lifter to have had many of these muscle tears. The tear may be within the muscle itself, at the musculotendinous junction, or an avulsion of the tendon from bone. The symptoms of a tendinous injury are a "snap" or a "pop," sudden sharp pain in the upper arm or chest, ecchymosis, and swelling. Adduction, flexion, and internal rotation of the arm are weakened, and the pectoralis muscle belly bulges on the chest with resisted adduction. With tendon avulsion, a defect can usually be felt in the anterior axillary fold. With a tear at the musculotendinous junction, however, continuity may seem intact when the fascial covering remains intact. A chest film will usually show an absent pectoralis major shadow.

An injured person can do normal activities after a pectoralis major tendon rupture but has much less strength for strenuous activities. Surgery is advised for professional athletes or young athletes in strenuous sports to restore full strength and function.[73] In this procedure, a deltopectoral incision is made, the large hematoma evacuated, and the tendon reattached with sutures through bone. The athlete then wears a shoulder harness for 3 weeks, gradually increases his range of motion, and does progressive resistance exercises. A power lifter must be restricted from heavy training for 3 to 6 months after surgery.

Rib Fractures

Because the athlete's first ribs are protected by the muscles and bones of the shoulder girdle, direct trauma usually will not produce a fracture. Nonetheless, first rib fractures do occur, generally from indirect forces. The scalene muscles and the upper slip of the serratus anterior muscle insert on the first rib, exerting opposing traction forces at the subclavian sulcus. When the athlete throws a ball or serves in tennis, a sudden strong scalenus anterior muscle contraction, combined with traction on the arm, may crack the first rib. As a weight lifter presses the barbell overhead, strong protraction of the scapulae fixes them against the thorax to form a solid base for the arms. The first rib may snap from overpull of the serratus anterior during this maneuver (Figure 11-2).

As the rib fractures, the athlete usually feels an acute, knife-like pain, although some rib fractures are stress fractures, which produce relatively little pain. An x-ray film will show a crack through the weak subclavian groove. A fracture

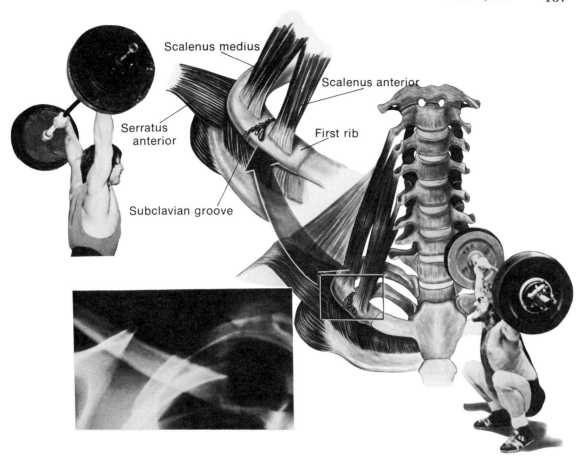

Figure 11-2 A weight lifter may sustain a fracture through the weak subclavian groove of his first rib as he protracts his scapula.

through the groove is rarely a surgical emergency unless the subclavian artery is torn. More commonly, first rib fractures are treated with a sling followed by a graduated exercise program.

In contrast to first rib fractures, fractures of other ribs usually result from direct blows to the chest by balls or implements. The fastpitched, 154-g (5.5 oz) cricket ball may fracture a wicket keeper's ribs, and jabs from the upper end of a hockey stick or blows from the head of a lacrosse stick may cause a similar fracture. Indirect forces may also cause rib fractures, as when a novice golfer fractures the posterior part of an upper rib during his golf swing, and a fracture may even occur in a pitcher while throwing.[32]

Diagnosis of a rib fracture is most often clin-ical with tenderness or crepitus over the involved rib. Such fractures are mostly of the crack type and may not be seen on initial films. Focal, spot films may be needed, and a chest x-ray film should also be taken to check for underlying lung damage or a pneumothorax.

Protective equipment such as the rubber chest protector of the lacrosse goalie (Figure 11-3) or the tackle football blocking vest serves to cushion blows to the chest. When a rib is fractured, the area is usually taped to reduce motion and to support the segment. The older athlete with ob-structive lung disease should not be taped, how-ever, because taping restricts tidal air and en-courages the retention of secretions. Intercostal nerve blocks will help to control pain. Protective

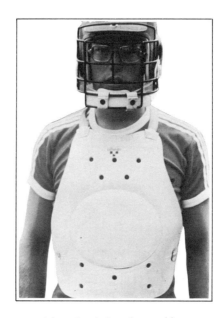

Figure 11-3   A lacrosse goalie's chest is protected from hard shots by a rubber chest protector.

padding or a ''flak vest''—a rubber air bladder covered with a plastic shield—may be worn to block blows to the injured chest (Figure 11-4).

If an athlete's sternum is fractured, the heart may also be contused, the aorta may tear at the left subclavian, or a hemopericardium may follow. A baseline electrocardiogram should be obtained for comparison with changes that may later occur. Aortography is needed if the athlete is in shock or if a chest film shows mediastinal widening.

Costochondral Separation

A deforming force to the chest may cause a rip to separate from the costocartilage that attaches it to the sternum. A blow to the anterolateral part of the chest and a twisting injury in wrestling or in a rugby scrum all may lead to this type of separation.

With separation, the costochondral region is very tender, and trunk motion causes sharp pain. The athlete may feel a ''slipping-out'' and snapping sensation or a popping with crepitation.

The acute injury may be so painful that a local anesthetic must be used to dull the pain. An elastic rib belt is applied to support the chest, and the player is kept out of contact activities until he is almost totally asymptomatic—a period of 3 to 4 weeks for wrestlers, although the pain sometimes lasts more than 6 weeks.

Rib separation may also occur at a transverse process. The paravertebral area will be locally tender. Rarely, if the pain persists, the junctional area is restricted.

Pneumothorax

A pneumothorax may occur during strenuous activity or even at rest without a direct blow to the chest.[57] If a lung bleb breaks, air is released into the pleural cavity.

The onset of symptoms may be insidious, with shortness of breath and vague chest discomfort, or the subject may have acute and dramatic shortness of breath. Diagnosis is made by percussing the chest and listening to the breath sounds. In a small pneumothorax, the chest film has an arc of

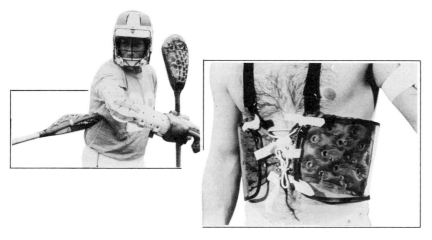

Figure 11-4 A rib may be fractured by a blow from an implement. The sore area may be protected by a "flak vest," an inflatable bladder with a plastic shield.

lucency peripheral to the lung margin, while the lung may be partially collapsed in a larger one, and there may be a mediastinal shift.

The athlete with a small pneumothorax should avoid unnecessary physical activity and should be followed with serial chest films. The lung reexpands as free air is absorbed. If the lung has collapsed more than 30%, the athlete should be admitted for the placement of an intercostal catheter, which allows reexpansion, and the leak usually seals spontaneously after 24 hours. After discharge from the hospital, the athlete should be restricted from sports for 2 or 3 weeks to allow healing, and he should be warned that recurrence on the same or opposite side is quite possible. A third episode usually calls for operative intervention, at which time the nest of blebs in the apex is selectively resected and the parietal pleura abraded to promote adherence.

Hyperventilation

The injured and upset athlete may breathe too fast and hyperventilate. Carbon dioxide is lost and the blood becomes more acidic. Dizziness develops, and the athlete's fingers, toes, and lips tingle. These symptoms lead to greater apprehension, faster breathing, and panic. The athlete should be reassured that there is no cause for alarm and advised to breathe slowly and to hold his breath intermittently. He should then breathe in and out of a paper bag placed over his mouth and nose to effect rebreathing of exhaled carbon dioxide. The bag may be removed when the athlete is calm and breathing properly.

ABDOMINAL INJURIES IN ATHLETICS

The athlete's abdomen is usually not covered by protective gear and therefore is susceptible to injury in most sports. Fortunately, the lower ribs and strong abdominal and back muscles help to protect abdominal organs from blows. Although an alert athlete will tense the abdominal muscles to guard the underlying viscera, internal damage may occur as a player reaches over his head for a pass or is otherwise not on guard for a blow.[69]

In the case of a blow to an athlete's abdomen, the physician should suspect an injury to the spleen, liver, or small bowel. Apparent rapid recovery in a healthy young athlete after an abdominal blow does not exclude internal injuries. Even a small laceration within the abdominal cavity may lead to considerable intraperitoneal bleeding because resistance to blood flow in the abdominal cavity is very low. Solid organs and hollow viscera may both be injured, but the former are more often injured than the latter.

A high index of suspicion, coupled with careful repeated examinations, will assure early diagnosis and avoid the overlooking of serious injury. At examination, the athlete should lie on his back and bend his knees to relax the abdominal muscles. The abdomen may then be checked for tenderness, guarding, absent bowel sounds, rigidity, and rectal bleeding.

Peritoneal lavage may help in the diagnosis of intra-abdominal injury when the athlete has associated injuries that preclude serial physical examinations or when the neurologic status of the injured athlete makes abdominal findings difficult to evaluate. In this procedure, a liter of fluid is instilled into the abdomen, and the fluid that is siphoned back is placed in a glass test tube. When the examiner is unable to read newsprint through the fluid-filled tube, a positive tap is indicated. This degree of haziness of the fluid is considered significant, indicating that there are at least 20,000 to 30,000 cells/ml of fluid. Isotope scans and computer tomography (CT) scans have also been used as aids in the diagnosis of internal injuries but have limited value in acute cases. Repeated physical examinations are the best means of diagnosing intra-abdominal injury.

Abdominal Wall Contusion and Muscle Tears

An abrupt twist, as in fast bowling at cricket, may rupture the rectus abdominus muscle. A hematoma then forms, and the pain that accompanies any motion restricts all activities.

For early treatment, ice should be applied, along with a compressing elastic wrap. The region is taped to appose the torn muscle ends. Infrequently, the athlete's inferior epigastric artery may also tear, and the hematoma will rapidly expand. In this case, the artery should be ligated. Isometrics will help to restrengthen the athlete's abdominal muscles, and with soreness as a guide the athlete may progress to sit-ups, abdominal hangs, and leatherball raisers.

Blows to the Solar Plexus

When an athlete is not on guard, a blow to his upper abdomen by an opponent or from an implement or ball may "knock his wind out." He may be unable to catch his breath and feel as if he is in danger of death. In such cases, the phy-

sician or trainer should hurry to make certain that the athlete's airway is not being blocked by his mouthpiece, his tongue, or some turf. His belt should be loosened and his knees bent. A cold towel or "magic sponge" should be applied to his forehead, and he must be quietly reassured that he will recover in a short time.

Even when recovery from a solar plexus blow is rapid, a high index of suspicion should be maintained, along with repeated examinations for intra-abdominal injuries, such as a hematoma of the mesentery, pancreatic damage, or an injury to a solid or hollow organ.[69] A laparotomy is probably indicated if recovery is slow and the athlete has persistent local pain, tenderness, or shock.

Ruptured Spleen

The spleen is usually protected by the left lower ribs. It may, however, be injured as a player extends his arms overhead to receive a pass, when the muscles are relaxed and not guarding the abdomen, or when the spleen is enlarged from mononucleosis and extends beyond the protective ribs.[24, 59]

In mononucleosis, the spleen is made large and weak from white pulp hyperplasia and extensive lymphocytic infiltration into the trabeculi and into the cores of the red pulp. The capsular and trabecular changes take 14 to 28 days to advance; thus the soft spleen probably will not rupture during the first 2 weeks of the disease. After 2 weeks, however, it may rupture from even the slightest blow or from a Valsalva maneuver that suddenly compresses it by diaphragmatic and abdominal wall contraction. Thus, when mononucleosis is diagnosed, the athlete should be restricted from contact activities to protect the spleen from injury.

Infectious mononucleosis mostly affects athletes of high school and college age. The cardinal signs are lymphadenopathy, sore throat, fever, and fatigue. A positive mono spot test clinches the diagnosis. The examiner should gently palpate for an enlarged spleen. Care must be taken because repeated examinations, especially forceful ones, may rupture a large, soft spleen.

Mononucleosis should not be overtreated. The subject should rest while he has a fever, but when the fever abates he should resume ordinary activities. Before he returns to sport, however, he should feel well, have normal strength, normal spleen and liver size, a normal serum glutamic-oxaloacetic transaminase, serum glutamic-pyruvic transaminase, bilirubin, complete blood count, erythrocyte sedimentation rate, and urinalysis.[66] Return to noncontact sports is usually possible in 3 to 4 months, but the athlete may have to be barred from contact sports for about 6 months, since delayed rupture of the spleen is a persisting danger. A ruptured spleen is, in fact, the most frequent cause of death in abdominal injuries. In one study, 17 of 22 splenic ruptures occurred football, and, in 8 of these cases, mononucleosis had been diagnosed *before* the rupture occurred.[25] The physician therefore must be alert to *delayed rupture* of a weak, large spleen of an athlete with mononucleosis. Such a rupture may occur even after all clinical, hematologic, and serologic criteria appear to be normal. Obviously, the athlete with mononucleosis should be instructed to seek immediate medical consultation if he develops any abdominal pain.

When an athlete receives a blow to the left upper quadrant of the abdomen, the spleen may rupture without a rib being fractured.[33] Initially, the left side will have a dull pain, but sometimes the symptoms quickly disappear and the player can return to the game. Thirty minutes later he may develop left shoulder pain, called "Kehr's sign," as free intraperitoneal blood irritates the diaphragm and excites the phrenic nerve reflexly. Less often, the blood will irritate the athlete's right diaphragm and pain will be referred to the right shoulder, or the spleen may be injured in the absence of any shoulder pain.

A delayed rupture of the spleen may follow an injury that produces a subcapsular hematoma. Such a spleen is highly susceptible to blows or strains, and the athlete may suddenly bleed to death days or weeks after the injury. The diagnosis of a subcapsular hematoma depends on a high index of suspicion and repeated abdominal examinations.[24] Radionuclide scans and CT scans help in the diagnosis by showing a definite separation of the capsule from the spleen.[13, 63] If the spleen is removed, the abdominal muscles require about 3 months to heal. Reconditioning is achieved by a graduated program, from isometrics to weighted abdominal hangs. The athlete should refrain from contact sports for about 6 months after splenectomy.

Ruptured Hollow Viscus

Rupture of a hollow abdominal organ, although uncommon in sports, is so dangerous that the medical team should have a high index of suspicion for such damage after a blow to the abdomen. A blow to a soccer player's unguarded abdomen may rupture a segment of bowel fixed across the spine. The abdomen is also a target in karate, where kicks may rupture a viscus. During hip circles on the uneven parallel bars, a gymnast's iliac bones normally bear the brunt of the force (Figure 11-5), but intra-abdominal injury may occur if the bar strikes the abdomen above the iliac crests.[23] Visceral injuries also occur in equestrian accidents; thus a rider should be carefully checked for internal injuries after a fall from a horse.

A ruptured viscus usually produces pain, guarding, tenderness, loss of bowel sounds, abdominal rigidity, clammy, sweaty skin, and shock.[7] In addition, blood may irritate the diaphragm and cause shoulder pain from reflex stimulation of the phrenic nerve. A symptom-free interval after the injury may occur, however, as in the case of retroperitoneal injury, for which it may

Figure 11-5 A gymnast may injure her abdomen on the uneven bars.

take hours, or even days, for pain, guarding, and shock to develop.

If a ruptured viscus is suspected, an upright or right-side-up decubitus abdominal x-ray film should be taken and examined for free air under the diaphragm.[70] For the x-ray film to have maximum value, the athlete should remain in the upright or decubitus position for at least 3 minutes before the film is shot. The athlete's stool should also be checked for blood, since a submucosal bowel hemorrhage may leak into the stool.[23]

Solid abdominal organs, especially the soft and vulnerable spleen in mononucleosis, are more frequently injured than hollow organs.[59] Hemorrhage from a solid organ is more life-threatening than peritoneal contamination or bleeding from an injury to a hollow viscus. The liver may be torn or "fractured," especially when enlarged by hepatitis. Most liver lacerations will respond to simple tamponage, but, if the liver is severely damaged, part of it may have to be resected. Also, an athlete's pancreas may rupture if it is stretched over the spine. This type of injury will reveal all the usual signs of intra-abdominal injury, but these signs sometimes appear late. Serial determinations of serum amylase may be helpful in diagnosing pancreatic injury.

The duodenum is vulnerable where it crosses the spine. If an athlete sustains severe, blunt trauma to the abdomen, the examiner should suspect a retroperitoneal rupture of the duodenum. The signs of intra-abdominal disorder or shock may take days to appear, and a late diagnosis may have a fatal outcome. Even during an abdominal exploration, there may be no intraperitoneal signs of duodenal damage; for this reason the surgeon should take care to examine the retroperitoneal portion of the duodenum. Suspicion of intra-abdominal injury is the key to its diagnosis, and methodical reexamination is the best way to uncover these serious injuries.

"Stitch in the Side"

A "stitch in the side" refers to sharp pains in an untrained runner's right side, behind his lower ribs. Possible causes of a stitch include gas in the large bowel, local anoxia of the diaphragm, dia-

phragmatic spasm, and liver congestion with stretching of the liver capsule. A runner may be able to "run through" the pain by breathing out forcefully through pursed lips or by breathing deeply and regularly. If the pain persists, the runner should lie on his back with his arms raised above his head, or a stitch can sometimes be relieved by the opposite movement of flexing the chest toward the thighs. When the pain leaves, the runner is usually able to resume his workout without a reccurrence during the training session, and, as fitness improves, stitches become less common.

Genitourinary Injuries

The athlete's kidneys, bladder, and genitals are relatively well protected from injury. The upper third of the right kidney and the upper half of the left kidney lie above the 12th rib, and there are three layers of abdominal muscle anterior to the kidneys. When these muscles are tensed, they help to protect the kidneys. Splenic and hepatic flexures of the colon lying between the kidneys and the abdominal wall also cushion the kidneys. The kidneys rest closer to the posterior abdominal wall than to the anterior wall, and the psoas muscles cushion them from the vertebrae. These organs are covered posterolaterally by the lower ribs and the paravertebral and flank muscles and rest in shock-absorbing pericapsular fat. They are fixed only by their vascular attachments to the aorta and vena cava, affording an ability to move that reduces the impact of external blows.

An athlete's bladder is rarely injured in its protected location. When there is an urge to urinate, the bladder still lies below the pubis, protected by the pubic bones. Urinating before going out to the field empties the bladder, leaving the thickness of the bladder wall in its maximum and most protective state. The penis and testes are protected from injury by the athletic supporter, which holds them close to the body.

Renal Injury

A blow to the flank may damage a kidney, but abdominal blows, as when a player is tackled as he reaches up to catch a pass, are more often responsible for such injuries.[61] Injury to a kidney produces pain and tenderness, sometimes ecchymosis, and often hematuria, but the examiner may be fooled unless he is aware that normal urinalysis findings do not rule out renal injury, since the damage may not have interfered with the collecting system. Although kidney injury will usually produce hematuria, correlation between the degree of hematuria and the degree of kidney injury is weak. An indication of bleeding is loss of the kidney outline and obliteration of the margin of the psoas muscle on a plain x-ray film of the abdomen. If an athlete's urinalysis findings are normal and kidney injury is doubtful, however, there is no need for special studies.[71]

If an athlete has flank pain but the urine is normal, successive urine studies should be done to ensure that the urine remains clear. If kidney injury is strongly suspected, however, an intravenous urogram should be performed. Such a study certainly is needed if an athlete complains of flank pain and develops hematuria after a blow to the flank or abdomen.

Most kidney injuries are intracapsular and usually heal without complications or sequelae, but an athlete should be placed at complete bed rest until the urine is clear. Half of the athletes with extracapsular injuries respond well to bed rest and close follow-up. The other half may continue to bleed or leak urine. If the intravenous urogram shows a nonfunctioning kidney or a major injury with extracapsular extravasation, a renal angiogram should be done. The angiogram can pinpoint and elucidate the lesion, resulting in more surgical repairs of kidney lacerations and fewer losses to nephrectomy.

The athlete's lumbar and flank muscles guard the kidneys, and protection is gained by strengthening these muscles.[52] Hip pads do not extend high enough to protect the kidneys, but the kidneys may be protected by kidney pads hung by straps from the shoulders. The flak vest is an excellent kidney protector.

Hematuria

Hematuria commonly accompanies or follows vigorous athletic activity. During intensive exercise, blood is shunted to active muscles, and renal blood flow decreases by about 50%, leading to relative renal ischemia and hematuria.[4] Other possible causes of exercise hematuria include direct kidney damage, renal vein kinking, damage to the kidney tubules, and bladder contusion.[3, 10, 44]

Erythrocytes, albumin, and erythrocyte casts have been found in the urine specimens of 80% of lacrosse players, swimmers, and runners and in 55% of tackle football players and oarsmen.[6] Distance swimmers and long distance runners show greater abnormality than do other athletes, but the urine usually clears within 48 hours.[27, 62] After a heavy football scrimmage or game, the player's urine sediment resembles that of a person with acute glomerulonephritis, containing erythrocyte casts, epithelial casts, and leukocyte casts.[12] Such findings have been termed "athletic pseudonephritis."[29] The frequency of abnormal urines parallels the severity of exertion, and the abnormalities disappear with reduction of the athlete's daily exercise load.

Although a boxer's urinalysis must be normal before he is permitted to enter the ring, after a fight most boxers have hematuria and albuminuria and their urine sediment may contain granular or hyalin casts.[4] These findings are related to exertion, the boxer's crouched position, his "grunt reflex," and direct damage from body blows. The more rounds boxed, the more chance that the boxer will have blood in his urine. The boxer assumes a crouched position for better balance, but his position increases intra-abdominal pressure and compresses his renal vessels. Boxers emit a loud grunt during attacks—the grunt reflex—that is timed with the delivery of a punch, causing the diaphragm and abdominal muscles to contract. The diaphram may partially displace the kidneys and perhaps cause ptosis.

Effective body blows are infrequent in boxing. About 85% of all blows are directed to the head and face, and many body punches are blocked or slipped. Loin blows usually land near the left kidney, but they are indirect, and their force is thus attenuated. Blows to the right upper quadrant of the abdomen, however, are transmitted to the right kidney, making renal damage to this area more common.

Punches to the kidneys may produce recurring

capillary damage that leads to scarred distortions. The term "athlete's kidney" refers to an impaired contour of the upper calyx, mostly of the right kidney, resulting from such scarring.[44] Many boxers with hematuria also have congenital anomalies, particularly hydronephrosis. Incompressibility of contained urine makes the hydronephrotic kidney more susceptible to injury than a normal kidney. A study of retired boxers might elucidate whether residual renal changes follow a boxing career.

Bladder trauma is another cause of hematuria in athletes, especially distance runners. The long distance runner with hematuria—"10,000 meters hematuria"—may pass small clots and have dull suprapubic discomfort and mild dysuria. What causes this bladder trauma in a runner? The pelvic floor muscles contract and intra-abdominal pressure simultaneously increases with exertion, forcing the flaccid, mobile posterior wall of the bladder against the bladder base. The base is a thicker, more rigid structure than the bladder wall and is relatively fixed by the ureters of lateral ligaments and continuous with the prostate. In an empty or near-empty bladder, the bladder surfaces are in contact, and minor impacts can summate to produce contusions, loss of the urothelium, and formation of a fibrinous exudate.

Blacklock performed cystoscopy on distance runners within the first few days after the onset of hematuria.[10] The bladder sites affected included the posterior rim of the internal meatus, the interureteric bar, and the area overlying the intramural ureter on each side. A mirror image of these lesions was found on the lower half of the posterior wall of the bladder. These findings suggest that there was contact of the posterior wall with the prominences of the interureteric bar and intramural ureter on each side and with the raised rim of the internal meatus. The rim of the internal meatus is rigid, prominent, and fixed because of the immediately underlying prostate. In some cases, the midline lesion on the posterior bladder wall featured a ring of contusion with a central area of normal urethelium. This pattern suggested contact of the posterior wall with the firm rim of the internal meatus, the island of normal urethelium being accommodated in the central depression of the meatus. Cystoscopy 1 week later showed only mild hyperemia at the affected sites.

Even when bladder knocking is presumed to be the reason for an athlete's hematuria, other potentially progressive abnormalities must be searched for, such as tumor, polycystic kidney, or renal cyst.

Investigating Hematuria

A fresh urinary sediment should be checked for erythrocytes, since hematuria may be the first sign of serious urinary tract disease. A count greater than one to two erythrocytes per high-power field is considered microscopic hematuria. The supernatant should also be checked with a dipstick for hemoglobin and for proteinuria. The sediment is then examined for bacteria, since infection may cause hematuria, erythrocyte casts, and leukocyte casts. Black athletes with hematuria should have a sickle cell preparation because hematuria may accompany each variety of sickle cell disease.

A complete history affords clues to the source of the hematuria. The athlete may have injured his flank or pelvis or may have engaged in heavy exercise. Does the hematuria appear at the beginning of urination? If so, "initial hematuria" indicates a urethral source. If the blood is noted chiefly at the end of urination, "terminal hematuria" connotes a source near the bladder neck or in the posterior urethra. Uniformly bloody urine, "total hematuria," indicates a source in the bladder, ureters, or kidneys.

An examination of the urine with the naked eye may produce a clue to the source of the bleeding. The longer the blood has been in contact with urine, the more it changes from bright red to a rusty or smoky brown, owing to the formation of acid hematin.[71] Upper tract bleeding produces dark brown urine and, sometimes, wormlike clots molded by the ureter. Lower urinary tract bleeding produces a pink-red or salmon-pink urine and irregularly shaped clots.

If a person has asymptomatic gross hematuria, the probability of a tumor is about 20%, whereas with microscopic hematuria the possibility is less than 2%. An exercise history, however, lowers the probability for tumor because hematuria is so common in athletes. A person's exercise program may have to be revised or even stopped briefly to eliminate the possibility of exercise-induced hematuria.

The athlete with hematuria should also be checked for high blood pressure, and the flank and pelvis should be examined for a mass or tenderness. In addition, skin abnormalities should be noted, including signs of injury and evidence of renal disease, such as purpura, edema, hemangiomas, or telangiectasia. The athlete with hematuria may need an intravenous urogram to determine the cause of the disorder.

Exercise After Kidney Transplantation and for Persons with End-Stage Renal Disease

A person with a new kidney should refrain from engaging in contact sports because the transplanted kidney is much more vulnerable to damage in its new pelvic location than is a kidney in the normal retroperitoneal position. Transplant recipients should, however, be encouraged to pursue endurance activities. Maximal comfortable exercise is appropriate to improve the appetite and retard muscle wasting in subjects on dialysis and in those with end-stage renal disease.

Hemoglobinuria

Runners sometimes pass a dark red urine that contains hemoglobin pigment. The source of this hemoglobin pigment has been elucidated by placing narrow, soft, compressible polyvinyl chloride tubes in the insoles of three runners.[62] Each runner had a tube of his own blood placed under one foot and a tube filled with another runner's blood placed under his other foot. As a control, another sample of his own blood was attached to one of his legs. Hemoglobinemia constantly appeared in the tubes underfoot if these runners ran on hard surfaces. When they switched to soft grass surfaces, the hemoglobinemia ceased. The test indicated that hemoglobinuria is probably due to mechanical damage to the erythrocytes in the soles of the runner's feet. The condition can be eliminated by running on softer surfaces and using a light foot fall with a sliding style and cushioning shoes.

Traumatic hemoglobinuria may also follow ill-designed karate exercises, in which the enthu-

siast pounds his hand for a long time against a firm object. When a foam cushion is interposed, the hemoglobinuria ceases.

Myoglobinuria ("Squat-Jump Syndrome")

Myoglobin may appear in the urine of an athlete who performs squat jumps. In this exercise, the athlete starts from a squatting position and jumps into the air. Myoglobin, hemoglobin, albumin, erythrocytes, and erythrocyte casts are found in the urines of military recruits who perform squat jumps. The hemoglobinuria may come from hemolysis of extravasated erythrocytes in the swollen muscles. The squat-jump syndrome is distinguished from acute glomerulonephritis in that the dark urine follows excessive exertion, the muscles are sore and swollen, and there is myoglobinuria and a normal anti-streptolysin O titer.

Acute tubular necrosis may follow rhabdomyolysis, the breakdown of muscle. Acute tubular necrosis has been noted in a young wrestler, with elevated serum glutamic-oxaloacetic transaminase, creatinine phosphokinase, lactic dehydrogenase, and aldolase enzymes after vigorous exertion. He had severe myalgia, muscle tenderness, dark brown urine, and clear blood plasma. The diagnosis of myoglobinuria may be missed, however, if the examiner always expects to see gross pigmenturia.

Torsion of the Spermatic Cord

The scrotal ligament normally prevents mobility of the testis by attaching the lower end of the spermatic cord and epididymis to the scrotum. If the tunica vaginalis is loosely attached to the scrotal lining, however, *extravaginal torsion* may occur as the spermatic cord rotates above the testis. With *intravaginal torsion*, the tunica vaginalis attaches unusually high on the spermatic cord, allowing freer motion of the testis below—the "bell clapper" deformity. Forceful contraction of the athlete's cremasteric muscle may draw his testis up over the pubis and twist the cord. Torsion is unlikely, however, if the athlete wears an athletic supporter.

Wyker and Gillenwater cite the primary physician's failure to suspect torsion of the spermatic cord as the most frequent cause of delayed treatment of testicular torsion.[66] This diagnosis must be kept in mind whenever an athlete has scrotal pain or swelling. Testicular torsion usually occurs in a young athlete who develops slowly increasing abdominal or groin pain. The athlete will sometimes, however, suffer abrupt, excruciating testicular pain, vomiting, and collapse. He also may convey a history of a mobile testis. The examiner should check for local tenderness, edema, and hyperemia of the scrotal skin with the scrotal contents adherent to the skin. Also, the vas deferens will be inseparable from the swollen, twisted cord. In epididymitis, elevation of the scrotum usually relieves the pain. In contrast, when a twisted testis is manually elevated, the pain increases.

If testicular torsion can be reduced by external manipulation, an orchipexy should be performed later. If the torsion is irreducible, early operative exploration is necessary to save the testis, since infarction of the testis can occur within hours of the onset of torsion. At surgery, the testis is fixed to the scrotum with sutures. Because the anatomic defect is most often bilateral, an orchipexy should be done on both sides.

Hematocele

A kick in the groin or a straddle injury on a motorcycle, or on a bike with a long, thin saddle, may trap a testis against the thigh or bony pubis. Blood can collect in the tunica vaginalis, and a testis may be ruptured. Hematoceles do not transilluminate. A tense hematocele is treated at bed rest with scrotal elevation and an ice pack. If a hematoma is rapidly developing, a bleeding vessel may have to be ligated.

Gynecologic Injuries in Water Skiers

Although the female athlete's sex organs are well protected behind the pubis, the vagina, uterus, and fallopian tubes may be injured in water skiing. Inexperienced water skiers have difficulty standing up, and, as the skier squats, water may damage the vulva and enter the vagina or the rectum. Such injuries may also cause incomplete abortions and salpingitis. Salpingitis, with right upper quadrant and iliac fossa pain, may begin about 3 days after a forced vaginal douche from

squatting in the water, and the skier may be unaware of the association between water skiing and the disorder.

To avoid injection injuries to the vagina or rectum, water skiers should wear rubber pants while skiing. In the case of vulvar hematoma, ice packs should be applied.

Penile and Urethral Injuries

The athlete's penis is only rarely injured because his athletic supporter holds it firmly against his body. Traumatic irritation of the pudendal nerve in bicycle racers or touring cyclists may, however, cause priapism or ischemic neuropathy of the penis. Priapism and the numbness from ischemic neuropathy resolve when the race or tour is over. Cyclists should be advised to use a furrowed saddle (Figure 11-6) and not to squeeze the saddle on uphills, which can cause irritation from the saddle and numbness.

A fall astride a fixed object may rupture an athlete's urethra partially or completely, result in immediate pain, swelling, and perineal ecchymosis. Straddle injuries on motorcycles may produce a pelvic diastasis, rupture of the driver's bulbous urethra, and extravasation of the urine into the scrotum, perineum, and lower abdominal wall.

The early passage of a catheter into the bladder may obscure a complete rupture of the urethra after a urethral injury and may convert a partial urethral rupture into a complete one. A diagnostic retrograde urethrogram should therefore be done

Figure 11-6   A padded bicycle seat with a longitudinal furrow *(arrow)*.

before a urethral catheter is passed. A catheter may be inserted if a minor injury is diagnosed. The completely ruptured urethra should be operatively repaired and a suprapubic cystotomy added for urinary diversion.

Lower Back Injuries

Lower Back Pain

An athlete's lower back pain usually results from a strain or sprain with muscle spasm. If the pain persists, however, the examiner must look for a more serious condition.[65]

Runners may develop lower back pain. On downhill runs, the lumbar spine is hyperextended and the pelvis tipped posteriorly, occasionally generating pain, especially in the runner with lordosis. There is excessive forward flexion of the lumbar spine during uphill runs, as the runner "leans into the hill." The pelvis tips anteriorly, limiting forward hip flexion and putting greater stress on the lower back muscles. In the midstance phase of running, the unsupported side of the pelvis tilts downward, bringing a shearing force to the sacroiliac joint.

The runner with one leg shorter than the other may develop lower back pain with shearing at the sacroiliac joint. One leg may be functionally shorter than the other because one foot pronates excessively. The feet should be put into a neutral, balanced position. If one leg is still shorter after balancing with an orthosis, a heel lift should be prescribed. Limb shortness of one-quarter inch may not be a problem while walking but should be treated with a lift in a runner.

Adolescents may have a functional hyperlordosis while standing that may cause lower back pain.[54] The combination of a tight lumbodorsal fascia and tight hamstrings posteriorly with weak abdominal muscles anteriorly may be corrected by proper stretching of the lower back and the hamstrings, strengthening the abdominals, and attention to proper posture. Moreover, an athlete's iliopsoas muscles may be tight if he has been doing sit-ups with his legs straight, and these muscles should be stretched.

Almost half of all young athletes with lumbar pain for more than 3 months are found to have spondylolysis.[38, 40, 41] A few have spondylolisthesis with segmental instability, and some have a symptomatic disk rupture. End-plate fractures, growth plate injuries, altered disk spaces at many levels, and even neoplasms are also found. In some cases, however, a specific diagnosis is never confirmed.

The differential diagnosis of back pain in an adolescent athlete may include spondylolysis, spondylolisthesis, Scheuermann's epiphysitis, a mild vertebral body fracture, ruptured disk, disk space infection, ankylosing spondylitis, gynecologic problems, and aneurysmal bone cysts or tumors, such as osteoid osteoma or chondroblastoma. In older athletes, rectal tumors and myeloma sometimes occur.

Epiphysitis of vertebral end-plates in the thoracic region is known as Scheuermann's disease and mostly affects young males from 10 to 25 years of age. X-ray films show irregularities in the superoanterior part of the epiphyses that result in vertebral wedging. Subjects with this disorder report back pain during sitting and lying and after sports, but the pain often decreases during sports activities. With kyphosis, long-term back pain develops, along with increasing thoracic spine deformity. Subjects' activity should be limited, especially avoiding the butterfly stroke during swimming and activities such as bench presses and dumbbell flies that strengthen the pectoral muscles but accentuate the kyphosis. Sometimes these youngsters require a kyphosis brace to halt progression of the deformity.[55]

Mild vertebral body fractures may go unrecognized because x-ray films of the back are not often taken; these fractures may cause lower back pain later in life. Preflexion of the spine on a toboggan (Figure 11-7) reduces the force needed to produce a fracture at the vulnerable T-12 and L-1 level. If the toboggan hits a bump or a rough area, the rider may be thrown into the air and strike down with compressive loading on his preflexed spine. This force bursts the vertebra, driving bone and disk material into the spinal canal, perhaps paralyzing the athlete or leaving him with long-term back pain.

A ruptured disk usually occurs in an athlete who has had repeatedly injured disk and disk degeneration, but a disk rupture may hamper a young athlete for whom spontaneous recovery

Figure 11-7   In sledding or tobogganing, the preflexed spine is susceptible to compression fractures.

has been the rule. The ruptured disk is usually first diagnosed as a back sprain or strain; however, intermittent lower back pain and stiffness develop, usually without sciatica, although true sciatica may develop years later. Pain extending to the knee but not beyond is usually due to hamstring spasm. The straight-leg-raising test that produces pain only to the knee indicates hamstring tightness. The pain of true sciatica goes all the way to the foot. Water-soluble agents are now used for diagnostic myelograms, and epidural cortisone may hasten recovery in young athletes with chronic radicular symptoms.

The examiner should look for ankylosing spondylitis in older adolescents and young adults who have lower back pain as well as dorsal spine and sacroiliac area pain, with or without sciatica. Both hips are forcibly abducted to stress the sacoiliac joints for sacroiliitis. Oblique x-ray films of the sacroiliac joints are then taken and a sedimentation rate and histocompatibility antigen (HLA) typing obtained.

Because a gynecologic problem may also present as lower back pain, the female athlete should be examined for an ovarian cyst or gynecologic tumor.

An older athlete's back pain may be caused by facet overload with disk degeneration or may result from myeloma.[65] A rectal examination to check for a rectal tumor or a tumor of the prostate is also appropriate for older athletes with lower back pain.

Distant problems may be responsible for lower back pain.[36] The latissimus dorsi muscle, for example, which arises from the pelvis and spine and extends to the arm, may become strained because of poor use of the throwing arm. In such cases, good coaching in throwing technique helps to reduce back trouble. When an athlete sits on the bench, his hip flexors, hamstrings, and calf muscles are shortened, causing him to become more susceptible to a muscle pull or back strain if he enters the game without proper warm-up. Coaches can help to prevent injuries by advising athletes well in advance that they may be entering the game to allow time for adequate warm-up.

Lower Back Strain and Treatment

For a discussion of lower back strain and its treatment, see Chapter 7: Manual Therapy for the Athlete's Back.

Spondylolysis

Spondylolysis is a break in the narrow bony neck (the pars interarticularis) between the articular process of the vertebrae. It commonly occurs in the lower lumbar region where high shearing forces tend to generate stress fractures resulting from repeated hyperextension of the athlete's lumbar spine. Hyperflexion may also cause stress fractures by placing great leverage on the neural arches, with the vertebral bodies serving as fulcra. A dysplasia in the cartilage model of the arch probably combines with these overbendings to render the pars susceptible to the physical forces.

Spondylolysis had been thought to result from

a congenital defect in the pars, a dual ossification zone. Now that we know that there is only one ossification center, a congenital cause seems less likely, but there does appear to be a hereditary predisposition to this defect. Persons with a family history of spondylolysis need only the trauma of normal living to produce a defect. A defect is sometimes noted on x-ray films, although no pain is reported by the subject. Stressful athletic competition may, however, produce pain in such cases.

Spondylolysis most often affects athletes who must hyperextend their spines (Figure 11-8). Young female gymnasts performing front and back walkovers, vaults, flips, and dismounts have a high incidence of the condition. Defects in the pars interarticularis occur in 2.3% of the general white female population, but 11 of 100 young female gymnasts were found to have these defects.[38, 40, 41] Football linemen, butterfly-stroke swimmers, and weight lifters hyperextend their spines.[26] Hyperextension also accompanies the hiking in sailing, the tennis serve, the volleyball spike, hurdling, pole vaulting, and high jumping. Even divers who hyperextended on entry into the water, or jerkily distort their lumbar spines on entering the water after an imperfectly executed dive, show spondylolysis.

The athlete with spondylolysis has aching lower back pain that is usually unilateral or has started on one side. The pain is worsened by twisting and hyperextension, and there may be hamstring spasm and limited extension of the spine. Oblique x-ray films may show a lucent line in the pars interarticularis, but a cephalad-angled oblique view or a tomogram may be needed to

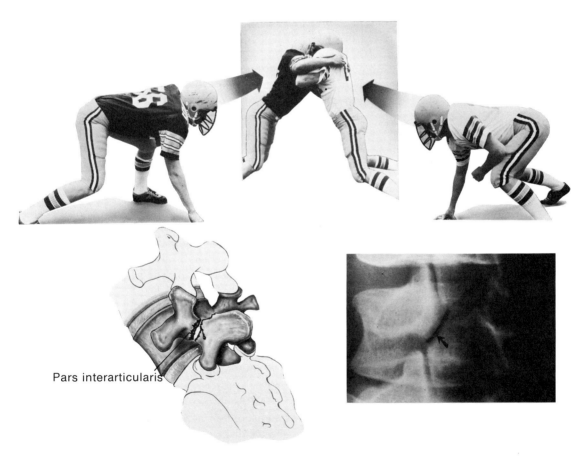

Pars interarticularis

Figure 11-8 Spondylolysis, a break in the continuity of the pars interarticularis, follows repeated hyperextension of the spine, as in football linemen.

demonstrate the defect. The first films may be normal. If pain persists after a rest period, the films should be repeated 6 weeks later. These serial films may show a developing defect. In contrast to these subtle defects, a defect may sometimes be so prominent as to be easily visible on a lateral film of the lower lumbar spine. Some athletes have a unilateral pars fracture with hypertrophy of the opposite pars.

If successive oblique x-ray films do not show a defect but lower back pain persists, an oblique technetium bone scan may be done that will show the developing defect as a "hot spot." A positive scan is usually associated with the athlete's being disabled for 3 months or more.[40] Resolution of the pain closely corresponds with resolution of the bone scan activity, although the athlete usually returns to competition before the bone scan activity returns to normal.

Lower back pain and muscle spasm in young athletes should always be heeded. Restricting vigorous activity may allow a stress facture or fatigue fracture to heal, thus preventing a subroentgenographic reaction from becoming an x-ray detectable defect. Some defects heal without restriction of activities, whereas others require bed rest. If restriction or bed rest is required, the athlete should perform hamstring stretching and antilordotic abdominal strengthening exercises. A polypropylene antilordotic brace may allow a hyperlordotic youth to participate in sports.[50]

Spondylolisthesis

Spondylolisthesis (Figure 11-9) is a slippage of one vertebra on another, and the disorder may occur in senior athletes with facet joint degeneration. It is more often seen, however, in youngsters between the ages of 9 and 14 years, and it is usually L-5 that slips forward on S-1. High-grade slips are more common in females, although pars defects are more likely in young male athletes.[40]

When the lumbosacral joints are loaded, a bilateral spondylolisthesis may convert to a spondylolysis. X-ray films should be taken while the athlete is weight bearing.[6] A first-degree slip means that a vertebra has slipped 25% over the body of the vertebra underlying it. A second-degree slip denotes that the vertebra has slipped 25% to 50%. About 5% of the general population have some degree of spondylolisthesis, but few have significant disability at a young age. If a slip reaches 50%, the athlete's sacrum becomes vertical. His flexibility lessens and his hamstrings become tight, making him incapable of high-level gymnastic performance. Pars defects in older athletes have rounded edges. Flexion and extension views should be taken or cineradiography used to see if motion is occurring at the defect.

With "spondylolisthesis crisis," an acute slippage of one vertebra over another, there is pain, tight hamstrings, and a peculiar gait, since the hips do not fully extend owing to the vertical sacrum. Nerve root tension may produce a sciatic scoliosis.

A high-grade slip produces a typical spondylolisthesis build with a short torso and heart-shaped buttocks.[40] The rib cage looks low, the iliac crests are high, and, because of the vertical sacrum, the buttocks are flat. If a preadolescent or adolescent athlete has slippage and lower back pain, he is restricted from vigorous activity until pain and muscle spasm abate. He may then resume all sports, but if the pain and spasm recur he must stop activity. X-ray films are repeated at 4- to 6-month intervals to rule out any further slip. A spine fusion may be needed when there is a spondylolisthetic crisis or nerve root irritation, a significant slip, or progression of the slip. The surgeon uses a paraspinal approach rather than a midline approach, so that the athlete may be up immediately after the operation. Heavy contact sports, skiing, or gymnastics are not allowed after the fusion.

The college athlete with spondylolisthetic lower back pain may engage in contact sports provided that he has no nerve root irritation. Younger athletes with grade II or greater slips are, however, usually barred from skiing or contact sports.[54]

Although pars defects alone do not seem to predispose an athlete to later significant degenerative disk disease, those who have defects with slipping have more chronic pain and future disability.

Figure 11-9 Repeated hyperextension of the spine may produce a defect in the pars interarticularis. Further damage may cause spondylolisthesis, a sliding forward of one vertebra on the subjacent one.

PELVIC AND HIP INJURIES

The powerful hip and buttock muscles are the body's "seat of power." From here power radiates outward like a pebble dropped in a pond, with muscle groups generally growing weaker with greater distance from the center of the body.

The pelvic muscles are links to the limbs. The latissimus dorsi, for example, arises on the iliac crest and spine, inserting into the humerus to rotate the arm internally. The hip abductors arise on the ilium and insert on the greater trochanter of the femur. The hip adductors arise on the pubis and insert on the femur. The gluteus maximus, a strong hip extensor, arises on the ilium to insert on the femur and is also extended to the tibia by way of the iliotibial band. The iliopsoas arises from the lumbar spine and ilium and inserts at the lesser trochanter to flex the hip.

The strong rectus femoris part of the quadriceps arises from the anterior–superior and the anterior–inferior iliac spines to insert on the tibia, flexing the athlete's hip and extending his knee. The hamstrings arise from the ischium to insert on the tibia and fibula to extend the hip and flex the knee. Thus muscles arising from the pelvis have distant action, and damage to these powerful muscles greatly limits athletic activity.

"Hip Pointer"

A direct blow to the iliac crest, as when a football helmet mashes muscle against bone, may painfully contuse the rim of the iliac crest. Such "hip pointers" may also result from a separation of muscle fibers pulled from the crest.

When an athlete is warmed up and involved in a match, a bruised iliac crest may not cause him immediate concern. Without first aid, however, slow internal bleeding overnight will result in swelling and pain the next morning. For this reason these injuries should be noted and treated early. An x-ray film is taken to rule out an iliac crest fracture, especially in high school athletes who may avulse the iliac crest apophysis.[15] A fluctuant hematoma should be aspirated, an ice pack applied, and the area compressed with an elastic wrap over a felt pad.

As soreness, swelling, and ecchymosis subside, contrast treatments are begun with ice massage for 10 minutes, moist heat for 10 minutes, ultrasound for 10 minutes, and ice massage once more. The area is then covered with a wide elastic wrap; the player should also change from girdle pads to old style hip pads.

Hip pads are now mandatory in college tackle football and are usually constructed of hard polyethylene sandwiched between layers of Ensolite. The pads protect a player's iliac crests, greater trochanters, and coccyx. Three types of hip pads include snap-in, girdle, and wrap-around pads. Snap-in pads fit on the belt in the player's pant and are most effective if the pants are pulled up to keep the pads in place. The girdle pad is the most diffcult to keep in place, and players should be advised to keep these pads from sliding over their iliac crests or they will lose protection. A popular trend today is to imitate professional players by removing the coccyx pad and using only a light foam padding over the iliac crest. This, however, means a loss of needed protection.

Iliac Apophysitis

The ossification center of the iliac crest first appears anterolaterally, and as the athlete matures it advances posteriorly until it reaches the posterior iliac crest. The average age of closure of this ossification center is 16 years for boys but may range up to 20 years. The age of closure for girls is 14 years but may range to 18 years.

High school runners now train harder than ever. Whereas they formerly ran 3 miles a day, they now run 6 to 8 miles, and some youths are running more than 80 miles a week. Repetitive contractions by the oblique abdominal muscles, gluteus medius, and tensor fascia lata on the iliac apophysis as the pelvis swings and tips may cause an inflammatory response, an iliac apophysitis, or a subclinical stress fracture at the iliac apophysis.[18] This occurs especially in runners with cross-over arm swings, and the athlete usually cannot relate the onset of pain to a specific injury.

Iliac apophysitis presents as local pain over the anterior iliac crest while the athlete runs. To diagnose the condition, the examiner checks for tenderness at the origin of the tensor fascia lata, the gluteus medius, and the abdominal obliques. When the athlete abducts his hips against the examiner's resistance, the pain worsens. X-ray films may, however, show normal findings.

A young runner may also develop a posterior iliac crest apophysitis. He will have pain when he tries to abduct his hip against manual resistance as he lies on his sound side with his affected upper hip flexed. A fracture should always be suspected and an x-ray film taken to rule it out.[15, 18] Both types of iliac apophysitis, anterior and posterior, resolve with 4 to 6 weeks of rest. Running resumes with less mileage, fewer hills, and care to avoid arm swings across the body.

"Pyriformis Syndrome"

Buttock pain may be caused by a "tight pyriformis" muscle. The pyriformis (L. *pyrum* = pear) usually crosses the sciatic nerve, but there are many variations of its relationship to the nerve. Whether or not there is such an entity as "pyriformis syndrome," tight external rotator muscles should be stretched (Figure 11-10).

Avulsion Fractures of the Pelvis

The sartorius muscle originates from the anterior–superior iliac spine, the rectus femoris from the

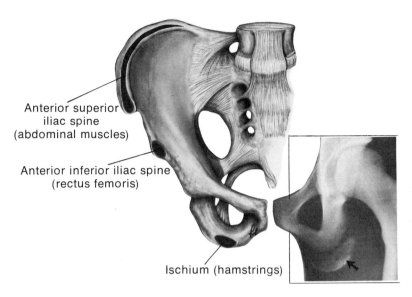

Anterior superior
iliac spine
(abdominal muscles)

Anterior inferior iliac spine
(rectus femoris)

Ischium (hamstrings)

Figure 11-10 Strong muscles may avulse bony fragments from the sites of their origin or insertion on the pelvis. In this case, the ischial apophysis has been avulsed *(arrow)*.

anterior-inferior iliac spine, and the hamstrings from the ischial tuberosity. If a place kicker's cleats catch in the turf, his rectus femoris may be pulled from his pelvis to produce a defect in his upper thigh. A strong hamstring muscle contraction may similarly avulse a large bony fragment from the ischium (Figure 11-11). If the fragment is separated far from its source, operative replacement may be needed.

Osteitis Pubis

Although muscle attachments cover the pubic symphysis externally, a large area on its internal aspect is covered only by periosteum and parietal fascia. The pubic symphysis has a poor blood supply, and this region is not well equipped to withstand irritation or infection.[1]

While an athlete runs, jumps, and kicks, the symphysis moves up and down, forward and backward, and rotates. Shear forces are transmitted to the symphysis, especially in soccer players and race walkers.[37] In the midstance of running, the unsupported side of the pelvis tilts downward, producing a shearing force at the pubic symphysis. Tension from the rectus abdominus or adductors or direct trauma may produce periosteal or subperiosteal damage to this weak bone, causing a subacute periostitis.[19, 34] Thromboembolic occlusion of the end vessels may allow a

subsequent transient bacteremia to cause an infection there and accelerate bone absorption.

Osteitis pubis is common in soccer players and race walkers[46] and is also seen in runners who abruptly increase their mileage or add interval training with speed work. The onset is usually gradual, with local pain and tenderness at the symphysis. Sudden tension may, however, produce intense pain at the symphysis and groin pain. The athlete may think that he has strained a muscle and do stretching exercises that only aggravate the problem.

The pain of osteitis pubis may also be confused with an inguinal hernia, prostatitis, orchitis, urolithiasis, or a groin pull. Although a digital examination of the prostate may be painful, the pain may be due to pressure on the athlete's underlying pubic symphysis. Ankylosing spondylitis may also produce a periostitis of the pubic symphysis; thus an HLA-B27 antigen study should be done before affixing a trauma diagnosis to the osteitis.[34] A pulled groin muscle will be tender.

Changes seen on x-ray film at the symphysis sometimes lag about a month behind the onset of pain. The lower half to lower two thirds of the symphysis should be checked for widening, loss of definition of the bones with demineralization, sclerosis, and periosteal reaction. The examiner should keep in mind, however, that marked os-

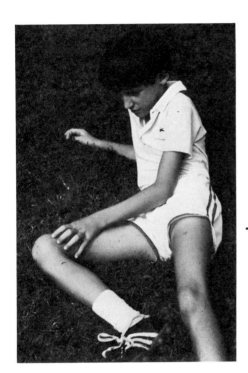

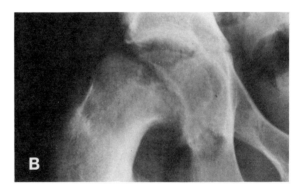

Figure 11-11   A youth who complains of knee pain should have his hip examined. The hip should flex normally. External rotation of the thigh during hip flexion **(A)** may connote a major slip of the capital femoral epiphysis **(B).**

teoporosis with rarefaction is a normal x-ray picture in a 20-year-old whose pubis is ordinarily weak at this time.[67] A technetium pyrophosphate bone scan may allow early detection of inflammation around the symphysis.

After infection is ruled out, the athlete rests and uses an anti-inflammatory agent, such as aspirin or phenylbutazone (Butazolidin), then begins an adductor stretching program and returns, in a graded fashion, to running.

A soccer player may develop an unstable symphysis pubis in which the symphysis becomes tender, and he may also have lower abdominal pain. "Flamingo views" may show a shift of his symphysis. X-ray views should include an anteroposterior taken with the subject standing on one leg and another anteroposterior view taken with the subject standing on his other leg.

Groin Strain

An athlete may strain his groin if the thigh is violently rotated externally while his leg is widely abducted. This injury is commonly seen during early workouts in tackle football when players are raising their legs and in slips on muddy fields. Groin strains are common in ice hockey players who forcefully adduct the thigh in the pushoff and rapidly shift their weight to the opposite leg to initiate the glide stroke.[53] Middle-aged bowlers may also strain their adductor muscles if they slip or stop suddenly. Bowlers at cricket suffer groin strains, especially at the beginning of the season when the ground is quite firm.[68]

An adductor strain is especially painful when the athlete adducts his thigh against the examiner's manual resistance. A psoas muscle strain produces deep groin tenderness and pain that radiates to the lower abdomen, and external rotation of the hip in extension worsens the pain. A very severe psoas strain may avulse the lesser trochanter.

All athletes should stretch their adductors diligently to prevent groin strain. This is best done with a partner stretching program. A gymnasium floor should be swept with a damp towel before each practice and game to clear it of dust that may cause players to slip.

If an athlete strains his groin, any fluctuant hematoma is aspirated and ice applied. Four days later, the strained region should be treated with heat and low-intensity ultrasound. The groin may be stretched with ice on it. For practices and games, a felt pad should be placed over the region and snugly wrapped with a spica wrap. An extra long elastic wrap is best. The athlete's adductors, iliopsoas, and rectus femoris may be strengthened by squeezing and lifting a medicine ball with his legs. Hip flexion may be strengthened by lifting weights with the hip muscles on a knee table.

Stress Fractures of the Hip and Femur

Stress fractures of the femur are most common in the femoral neck and in the upper, medial part of the femoral shaft.[11, 51]

Subcapital Fractures

A subcapital stress fracture can be a compression type or tension type. In younger patients, the compression type occurs in the inferior cortex of the femoral neck. The earliest x-ray evidence is a "haze" of internal callus in this area. Eventually, a small fracture line shows. A tension fracture of the femoral neck is more dangerous. It occurs in older patients usually and is on the tension side of the femoral neck (laterally), showing as a small crack in the superior cortex.

An athlete with a subcapital stress fracture may have achy hip pain, groin or thigh pain, or even knee pain that many times is noticeable on awakening in the morning but improves somewhat with activity. However, continued activity usually results in worsening of the discomfort and the athlete may limp. Because the complaints are often vague and findings few, the examiner must have a high index of suspicion for these fractures if there is to be an early diagnosis.[50] A diagnosis is important, however, because a tension fracture may become displaced. Once displaced, the fracture may be difficult to fix because of the high density of the bone in these athletic people. Treatment of an undisplaced femoral neck tension stress fracture is by non-weight-bearing and not even swimming or biking to start.

Subtrochanteric Fractures

A subtrochanteric fracture may be produced when the runner changes running surfaces or increases the intensity of workouts or does bounding exercises, which are repetitive jumps with or without weights.[50] When a runner has vague pain around the knee or in a glove-type distribution, the examiner should suspect a fracture. Palpation or precussion over the bone may cause pain.

An x-ray film may show normal findings. However, when pain persists, despite a normal x-ray, a bone scan is indicated.[16] In a highly competitive, intercollegiate runner, there is pressure for an early diagnosis. In such a case, a bone scan is done after at least 2 weeks of conservative treatment have failed to improve the condition.

The athlete who has a subtrochanteric stress fracture should use crutches until there is no pain. He should not even swim or cycle.[51] The pain should go away in 2 or 3 weeks; by that time, an x-ray film may show some callus. When the athlete can walk without pain and has full range of motion, he may begin a walk–jog program (see Chap. 1) and then increase his running. During rehabilitation he should be alert for groin

REHABILITATION PROGRESSION FOR HIP STRAIN

OBJECTIVES

Strengthen: Hip flexors, hip extensors, hip abductors, hip adductors, hip external rotators, and hip internal rotators
Flexibility: Same motions as strength
Endurance: Same motions as strength

STAGES

Initial

Cryokinetics: Ice is combined with active range of motion toward the motion of discomfort and with resisted exercise.

Intermediate

Flexibility
Hip flexion, hip extension, hip adduction, hip abduction, hip external rotation, and hip internal rotation.
Strength
Hip flexion, hip extension, hip adduction, hip abduction, hip external rotation, and hip internal rotation
Endurance
EPLEI Goals 1, 2

Advanced

Flexibility: Continued efforts from the intermediate phase
Strength: Continued efforts from the intermediate phase
EPLEI Goals 3–8.

pain or decreased hip range of motion, which would indicate a need to cut back on the running program.

Dislocated Hip

Major trauma or a high-velocity collision in a sport such as tackle football will dislocate an adult athlete's hip, but a youth's hip may dislocate with much less force. Because the hip usually dislocates posteriorly, the subject lies with his hip in a flexed and adducted position. Oblique x-ray films are taken to see whether any fragments of bone have been knocked from the posterior lip of the acetabulum. The dislocation may sometimes be immediately reduced by holding the athlete's pelvis down, flexing his hip to 90°, and then pulling up. However, because of the strong muscles in spasm around his hip, anesthesia is often needed. When the hip has been relocated, it may be tested for stability by trying to press it back out of the socket, and, if stability has been restored, skin traction is applied to the leg to decrease muscle spasm around the hip.

The main danger of dislocation is the possibility of damage to the blood supply to the femoral head, which may cause part or all of the head to die. Long-term crutch walking is therefore prescribed, with only a gradual return to athletic activity.

Avascular Necrosis of the Femoral Head

Hip pain in a young athlete between 5 and 12 years of age may be due to synovitis, an irritation of the hip joint with inflammation. As the hip joint fills with reactive synovial fluid, pressure from the fluid may occlude the blood supply to the femoral head, and part or all of the femoral head may die.[42]

The youngster with a complaint of pain in the hip must be evaluated fully. X-ray films should be taken and examined for rarefaction of the head characteristic of Legg–Calvé-Perthes avascular necrosis. Avascular changes usually involve the superior and anterolateral weight-bearing part of the head, and in later stages this area becomes irregular, collapsed, and sclerotic.

Because synovitis of the hip may be a cause of avascular necrosis, subjects should be put at bed rest. Skin traction will relax muscle spasm around the hip. These problems should be dealt with early to prevent the development of an incongruent hip, which leads to later osteoarthritis. Depending on the age of the subject, the stage of the process, and its severity, a special brace may have to be worn or an operation may be needed to realign the joint.

If a youth develops severe hip pain with a marked limitation of hip motion, he may have a pyarthrosis. Hip aspiraton will prove the diagnosis.

Slipped Capital Femoral Epiphysis

A young athlete's capital femoral epiphysis may slip even after a minor injury. The disorder occurs mostly in lanky or heavy youngsters between the ages of 9 and 15 years of age who are entering a growth spurt or who have an endocrine imbalance. There is often a prodrome or "preslip" phase, with vague aching around the hip or knee for weeks and a limp. X-ray films at this stage show widening of the growth plate and rarefaction at the metaphysis just below the physis.

The youngster with hip or knee pain should be checked to rule out a preslip phase or slippage of the femoral head. Although he reports knee pain, examination of the knee may be normal, with pain originating in the hip and referred to the knee by way of the obturator nerve. Youngsters with hip pain and x-ray evidence of preslip should be put at bed rest to prevent a slip. In some cases, prophylactic pinning may be needed.

Minor slips of the capital femoral epiphysis in childhood have been found to cause idiopathic osteoarthritis of the hip in adulthood.[56] Adults who were quite active in sports as children often show evidence of old slips, whereas such slips are infrequent in less active, age-matched control subjects. Many former athletes have old slipped capital femoral epiphyses that reduce joint congruence and presage osteoarthritis. A measurement technique and index to check for early slips will show the femoral head to be in a slightly drooped position. Care should be taken to catch these slips in the preslip phase by attending to hip or knee pain in youngsters, with the aim of preventing slippage and later arthritis.

A major slip of the capital femoral epiphysis may occur on the playing field, followed by hip or knee pain. When the hip is flexed, it swings into external rotation instead of flexing (Figure 11-12). The player should be transported carefully from the field to have a hip x-ray, as he may have a major slip that movement could convert into a disastrous full slip.

The slipped capital femoral epiphysis may be seen best on a frog-leg lateral view. The slipped femoral head is tilted or in a drooped position, the "tilt deformity," and is eccentrically placed on the femoral neck (Figure 11-12B). The head slips posteromedially on the neck, or, as some describe it, the neck slips anterolaterally from the head.

Major slips deserve a short course of traction that may gently reduce the slip, and the head may then be stabilized with pins. If traction is unsuccessful, the head should be pinned *in situ* to prevent further slippage. A later osteotomy will restore good hip mechanics. Attempts to manipulate the head back onto the femoral neck may, however, cause the head to die.

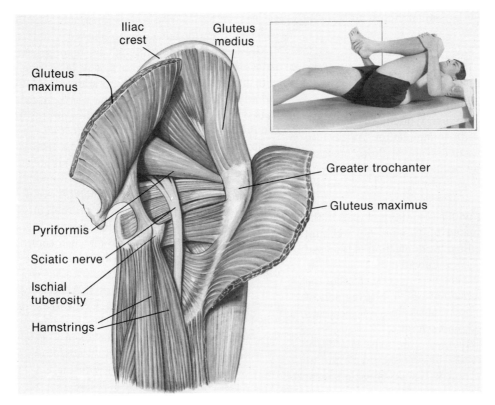

Figure 11-12   To stretch the external rotator muscles of his left hip, including the pyriformis, the athlete brings his left knee to his chest and his heel to his opposite hip and pulls into internal rotation with his left hand.

Hip Cysts

Unicameral bone cysts are sometimes noted in the femoral neck of youngsters and in older athletes. A fracture through this weakened area may jeopardize the femoral head. Steroid injections have been recommended as a means of obliterating the cysts, but the cysts often remain after such injections. Filling the cyst with a bone graft is the surest way to reduce the risk of a fracture.

Greater Trochanteric Bursitis

Inflammation of the bursa overlying the greater trochanter commonly occurs in female runners who have a broad pelvis and increased Q angle. The condition also occurs in runners who have a leg length discrepancy, which causes the pelvis to tilt abnormally. It is not uncommon in novice

runners whose feet cross over in the midline, thus increasing the adduction angle. More experienced runners my develop a greater trochanteric bursitis when they train or compete on banked surfaces. Treatment includes rest, ice, and sometimes a steroid injection to reduce the inflammation. Leg length discrepancy and faulty running technique should also be corrected.

THIGH INJURIES

Quadriceps Contusion ("Charley Horse")

A blow to the front of an athlete's thigh may produce a contusion with bleeding into the quadriceps.[60] The more relaxed the quadriceps at the moment of contact, the severer is the injury. Such blows are most often anterior or anterolateral, since the medial part of the thigh usually is protected by the athlete's other leg. If the thigh is struck dead-center on a thigh pad, it is safe, but if the periphery of the pad is struck the pad edge is driven against the thigh.

The severity of a quadriceps contusion is nearly always underestimated. There may be little pain or discomfort while the athlete is warm and competing, but stiffness and pain develop within hours of the injury.

If a player receives a sharp blow to his thigh in football, treatment should be started at half time. If he is limping, immediate attention is needed to prevent worsening. The player should not try to run out the quadriceps contusion. These injuries deserve respect because they may be followed by myositis ossificans, a bony growth within the muscle.

Initial hemorrhage and muscle spasm may be reduced by stretching the quadriceps. The athlete's knee should be flexed and held in flexion with an elastic wrap until the next day and an ice bag placed over the wrap.[22] Early heat, massage, and whirlpool treatments should not be used because these will bring in more blood and produce further swelling. The athlete may, however, take a shower as long as he keeps ice bags in place over the area.[43]

A mild quadriceps contusion produces little pain and swelling and some tightness but leaves a normal range of knee motion.[22] The athlete is able to flex the knee to 90° or more. For treatment, ice is applied for 10 minutes, followed by a transcutaneous electrical nerve stimulator for 20 minutes, and the quadriceps is stretched by slow, full knee flexion until the tightness is gone. A foam pad is then secured over the area with an elastic wrap.

A moderate quadriceps contusion produces more severe pain and swelling and limits the range of knee motion. The muscles are in spasm, and the athlete will not be able to flex his knee to 90°. Treatment comprises cold towels applied for 72 hours with the leg up and resting, and the athlete then uses crutches.[43] The athlete may return to practice when his thigh is pain-free and he has normal range of knee motion and normal

muscle power and can fully perform functional exercises such as jumps and cuts.

A hematoma and muscle herniation exist in severe quadriceps contusions. If swelling has occurred very rapidly or is extreme, a bleeding diathesis or a significant vascular injury must be suspected. Clotting studies should be performed when there is a markedly swollen thigh. Minor clotting deficiencies are probably more common than is realized, and partial deficiencies of varying degrees may be noted in all types of hemophilias. If there is fluctuance, some physicians try to aspirate or remove the hematoma surgically, since the removal of a large blood clot may minimize subsequent fibrosis. Even when the thigh is quite swollen, blood often resists aspiration because it is contained in the muscle, much as if it were in a sponge. Local anesthetics, enzymes, and steroids are sometimes administered to aid in the absorption of the hematoma, but these injections always pose danger of infection.

The athlete with a severe quadriceps contusion should remain at bed rest with his thigh wrapped and iced. The circumference of the thigh should be checked serially. The athlete may do quadriceps sets for 5 minutes each hour but should avoid flexing the knee until the soreness diminishes. A plaster splint will keep the knee from bending while the athlete is up; otherwise, traction on the quadriceps will increase the inflammation. A pair of cutout sweatpants will allow the plaster slab to fit comfortably.

An elastic thigh support will provide constant circumferential pressure and support during recovery. A foam rubber pad or an air pad covered with a football thigh pad will give added protection, and the player's pants should be tight enough to keep this pad from slipping.

Myositis Ossificans Traumatica

A blow from a helmet to another player's thigh or a knee to the thigh, or even a quadriceps muscle strain, may cause bleeding into the quadriceps. Heterotopic bone may later form adjacent or attached to the femur[39] (Figure 11-13). Although the swelling usually stabilizes in about 24 hours, the hemorrhage may be followed closely

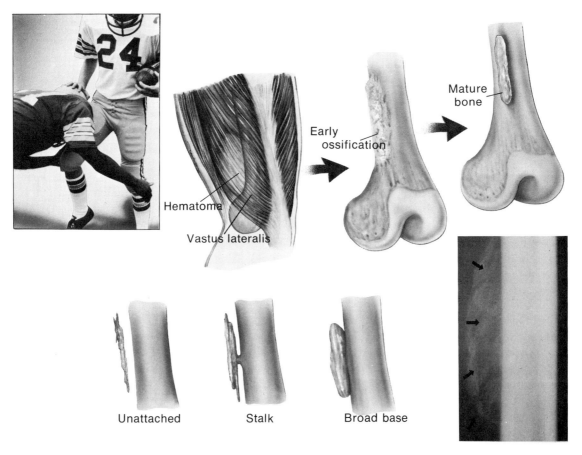

Figure 11-13   A blow to the thigh may produce a hematoma that ossifies. It may take many forms as it matures and may need to be excised (see text for description).

by acute inflammation. The thigh will be tender, firm, and hot the next day, and the athlete's body temperature may even be elevated. Fibroblasts from the endomysium or primitive mesenchyme from the injured fascia and connective tissue may then form osteoid and chondroid tissue. The reaction is similar to callus formation, and experiments show that the periosteum plays a role. Trauma to rabbit periosteum produces periosteal bone proliferation, but myositis ossificans does not occur without injury to the periosteum[72].

In developing myositis ossificans, initial x-ray films will show a soft tissue mass. After 2 to 4 weeks, flocculations will be noted, and these evolve into of three types of bone formation[39]:

The stalk type is connected to the adjacent bone; the broad-based, periosteal type is more broadly connected, and the third type has no direct connection to the bone.

Bony myositis ossificans masses have been mistaken for a malignant bone tumor, the juxtacortical osteogenic sarcoma. The tumor differs in many ways, however, from myositis ossificans. Fifty percent of the sarcomas occur in people older than 30 years of age, and there is often pain with activity and at night. The tumor usually is located in the distal and posterior one third of the femur, the alkaline phosphatase level in the blood is raised, and the tumor expands in size. Histologically, the juxtacortical osteogenic sarcoma has wild bone at its periphery, in contrast to the mature peripheral bone of myositis ossificans.

Myositis ossificans usually follows significant trauma by 2 to 4 weeks, often occurring in a young athlete who has active bone turnover. After the acute phase, the mass is usually painless and is typically anterior to the midshaft of the femur. The alkaline phosphatase level is usually normal, and the mass decreases in size, becoming more compact and rounding off at the edges. Histologically, the ominous fields at the interior proceed to a more innocent osseous tissue at the periphery in a centrifugal pattern of maturation.

After 3 to 6 months, the myositic bone mass usually stabilizes, remaining unchanged, or it may shrink. If the mass is in a muscle belly, it sometimes is almost fully resorbed. When it is near a muscle origin or insertion, it is less likely to be resorbed and more likely to cause functional impairment. If the mass is tender or inhibits motion after 1 year, it may be removed.[39, 49] Earlier removal may provoke unwanted bone to recur in even greater amounts. Clotting studies should be performed if an athlete has recurring myositis ossificans because the athlete may have a clotting deficiency.

Hamstring Strain

The hamstring muscles decelerate hip flexion, extend the thigh, and flex the leg when the foot is not weight bearing. The hamstrings antagonize the quadriceps during most of leg extension in running and assume an extensor action with footstrike. The sudden change from a stabilizing flexor to an active extensor may cause a hamstring strain.

Quick starts with sudden, violent hamstring contraction or stretching may tear an athlete's hamstring. A strain may occur as a sprinter leaves the starting blocks, in the lead leg of a hurdler, or in a jumper's takeoff leg. It may also occur when a football lineman charges, especially late in a game if the player has failed to warm up properly before the beginning of the second half.

The short-head of the biceps femoris is of little help in the running pattern and is the most fre-

quently strained hamstring.[14] It arises from the linea aspera, the upper part of the supracondylar line, and the lateral intermuscular septum and has two motor points, one innervated by the tibial part of the sciatic nerve, the other by the peroneal division of this nerve. This dual innervation of the biceps femoris causes problems because the short head of the biceps may contract at the same time as the quadriceps, resulting in a hamstring pull.

Hamstring strains are associated with poor flexibility, inadequate warm-up, fatigue, deficiency in the reciprocal actions of opposing muscle groups, and imbalance between quadriceps and hamstring strength. With conventional isotonic testing, an athlete's hamstrings should have 60% to 70% of the strength of his quadriceps. Cyclists are an exception because their hamstring strength is roughly equal to their quadriceps strength. Strength ratios change with isokinetic testing at higher speeds, when the quadriceps and hamstrings of most athletes balance out.

In a mild hamstring strain, there is no tear, only spasm of the hamstrings. The thigh usually does not hurt until the athlete cools down. In moderate pulls the athlete feels a "pop" or a snap, and there is immediate pain and loss of function. The examiner should palpate the hamstrings to see if there is a gap resulting from torn fibers. There may also be a lump or a hematoma. Severe pulls generally occur at the origin or at the insertion of the hamstring into bone.

Athletes should not try to "run out" a hamstring strain.[21] Instead, an elastic wrap and an ice bag should be applied. Crushed ice will conform to the shape of the thigh. A felt or foam rubber pad may be cut out and wrapped over the injured area with an elastic wrap to provide compression overnight. With varying effects, some physicians have the athlete ingest trypsin–chymotrypsin enzyme tablets or inject enzymes locally to help decrease the hematoma. Once further swelling has been controlled, cryotherapy and contrast treatments of ice massage and ultrasound may begin. The athlete may work through an active range of motion in chest-deep water. When the soreness is gone, he may begin knee curls, knee extensions, and high-speed cycling. Later, light massage will break up intramuscular adhesions that exercise and heat cannot handle.

Mild pulls heal in a few days to a week, and moderate pulls heal in 1 to 3 weeks. Avulsion fractures at the ischial tuberosity or at the head of the fibula, however, take a month or more to heal.

On returning to practice, the athlete should wear an elastic support around his thigh. The support has a seamless circular knit and a rubber-elastic construction, is sized to fit tapered circumferences, and will help to keep the area warm and lessen swelling. Adhesive tape is too restricting, and elastic wraps may work loose.

REFERENCES

1. Adams RJ, Chandler FA: Osteitis pubis of traumatic etiology. J Bone Joint Surg [Am] 35:685–696, 1953
2. Allman FL: Problems in treatment of athletic injuries. J Med Assoc Ga 53:381–383, 1964
3. Alyea EP, Parish HH Jr: Renal responses to exercise—urinary findings. JAMA 167:807–813, 1958
4. Amelar RD, Soloman C: Acute renal trauma in boxers. J Urol 72:145–148, 1954
5. Bailey RR et al: What the urine contains following athletic competition. NZ Med J 83:809–813, 1976
6. Bailey W: Observations on the etiology and frequency of spondylolisthesis and its precursors. Radiology 48:107–112, 1947
7. Baker B: Jejunal perforation occurring in contact sports. Am J Sports Med 6:403–404, 1978
8. Benson DR et al: Can the Milwaukee brace patient participate in competitive athletics? Am J Sports Med 5:7–12, 1977
9. Berson B: Surgical repair of pectoralis major rupture in an athlete. Am J Sports Med 7:348–351, 1979
10. Blacklock NJ: Bladder trauma in the long-distance runner. Am J Sports Med 7:239–241, 1979
11. Blatz DJ: Bilateral femoral and tibial shaft stress fractures in a runner. Am J Sports Med 9:322–326, 1981
12. Boone AW et al: Football hematuria. JAMA 158:516–517, 1955
13. Brogdon BG, Crow NE: Observations on the "normal" spleen. Radiology 72:412–413, 1959
14. Burkett LN: Investigation into hamstring strains: The case of the hybrid muscle. Am J Sports Med 3:5, 1975
15. Butler JE, Eggert AW: Fracture of the iliac crest apophysis: An unusual hip pointer. Am J Sports Med 3:192–193, 1975
16. Butler JE et al: Subtrochanteric stress fractures in runners. Am J Sports Med 10:228–232, 1982

17. Castenjors J: Renal clearance and urinary sodium and potassium excretion during supine exercise in normal subjects. Acta Physiol Scand 70:204–214, 1967
18. Clancy WG, Foltz AS: Iliac apophysitis and stress fractures in adolescent runners. Am J Sports Med 4:214–218, 1976
19. Cochrane GM: Osteitis pubis in athletes. Br J Sports Med 5:233–235, 1971
20. Collier W: Functional albuminuria in athletes. Br Med J 1:4–6, 1907
21. Cooper DL, Fair J: Trainer's corner. Hamstring strains. Phys Sportsmed 6(8):104, 1978
22. Cooper DL, Fair J: Trainer's corner. Treating the charleyhorse. Phys Sprotsmed 7(6): 157, 1979
23. Dauneker DT et al: Case report: Intra-abdominal injury in a gymnast. Phys Sportsmed 7(6):119–120, 1979
24. DeShazo WF II: Case report: Ruptured spleen in a college football player. Phys Sportsmed 7(10):109–111, 1979
25. DeShazo WF III: Returning to athletic activity after infectious mononucleosis. Phys Sportsmed 8(12):71–72, 1980
26. Ferguson RJ et al: low back pain in college football linemen. Am J Sports Med 2:63–80, 1974
27. Fred HL, Natelson EA: Grossly bloody urine of runners. South Med J 70:1394–1396, 1977
28. Funk FJ Jr: Injuries to the extensor mechanism of the knee. Athletic Training 10:141–145, 1975
29. Gardner KD Jr: "Athletic pseudonephritis"—alteration of urine sediment by athletic competition. JAMA 161:1613–1617, 1956
30. Gehlsen G, Albohm M: Evaluation of sports bras. Phys Sportsmed 8(10):89–98, 1980
31. Gehlsen G, Albohm M: Evaluating sports bras. First Aider, Cramer 50(4):4–5, 1980
32. Gurtler R et al: Stress fractures of the ipsilateral first rib in a pitcher. Am J Sports Med 14:277–279, 1985
33. Hahn DB: The ruptured spleen: Implications for the athletic trainer. Athletic Training 13(4):190–191, Winter 1978
34. Hanson PG et al: Osteitis pubis in sports activities. Phys Sportsmed 7(10):111–114, 1978
35. Heymsfield SB et al: Accurate measurements of liver, kidney and spleen volume and mass by computerized axial tomography. Ann Intern Med 90:185–187, 1979
36. Horner DB: Lumbar back pain arising from stress fractures of the lower ribs—report of four cases. J Bone Joint Surg [Am] 46:1553–1556, 1964
37. Howse JJG: Osteitis pubis in an Olympic road walker. Proc R Soc Med 57:88–90, 1964
38. Jackson DW, Wiltse LL: Low back pain in young athletes. Phys Sportsmed 2(11):53–60, 1974
39. Jackson DW: Managing myositis ossificans in the young athlete. Phys Sportsmed 3(10):56–61, 1975

40. Jackson DW et al: Spondylolysis in the female gymnast. Clin Orthop 117:68–73, 1976

41. Jackson DW: Low back pain in young athletes: Evaluation of stress reaction and discogenic problems. Am J Sports Med 7:361–369, 1979

42. Jacobs B: Legg-Calvé-Perthes disease, the "obscure affection." Contemp Surg 10:62, 67, 1977

43. Kalenak A et al: Treating thigh contusions with ice. Phys Sportsmed 3(3):65–67, 1975

44. Kleiman AH: Athlete's kidney. J Urol 83:321–329, 1960

45. Knochel JP et al: The renal, cardiovascular hematological and serum electrolyte abnormalities of heat stroke. Am J Med 30:299–309, 1961

46. Koch RA, Jackson DW: Pubic symphysitis in runners—report of two cases. Am J Sports Med 9:62–63, 1981

47. Levit F: Nipple sensitivity. Med Aspects Hum Sex 12:135, 1973

48. Levit F: Jogger's nipples. JAMA 297:1127, 1977

49. Lipscomb AB et al: Treatment of myositis ossificans traumatica in athletes. Am J Sports Med 4:111–120, 1976

50. Lombardo SJ, Benson DW: Stress fractures of the femur in runners. Am J Sports Med 10(4):219–227, 1982

51. McBryde Jr AM: Stress fractures in runners. Clin Sports Med 4:737–752, 1985

52. Melvin M: Trainer's corner. Protecting the kidney. Phys Sportsmed 7(3):161, 1979

53. Merrifield HH, Cowan RF: Ice hockey groin pulls. Am J Sports Med 1:41–42, 1973

54. Micheli LJ: Low back pain in the adolescent: Differential diagnosis in low back pain in athletes. Am J Sports Med 7:361–369, 1979

55. Micheli LJ et al: Use of modified Boston brace for back injuries in athletes. Am J Sports Med 8:351–356, 1980

56. Murray RO, Duncan C: Athletic activity in adolescence as an etiologic factor in degenerative disk disease. J Bone Joint Surg [Br] 53:406–419, 1971

57. Pfeiffer RP, Young TR: Case report. Spontaneous pneumothorax in a jogger. Phys Sportsmed 8(12):65–67, 1980

58. Priest JD, Nagel DA: Tennis shoulder. Am J Sports Med 4:28–42, 1976

59. Rutkow IM: Rupture of the spleen in infectious mononucleosis. Arch Surg 113:718–720, 1978

60. Ryan AJ: Quadriceps strain, rupture and charley-horse. Med Sci Sports 1:106–111, 1969

61. Ryan AJ (moderator) Round table: Diagnosing kidney injuries in athletes. Phys Sportsmed 3(1):48–49, 1975

62. Siegel AJ et al: Exercise-related hematuria. Findings in a group of marathon runners. JAMA 241:391–392, 1979

63. Sigel RM et al: Evaluation of spleen size during routine liver imaging with 99m Tc and the scintillation camera. J Nucl Med 11:689–692, 1970

64. Smodlaka VN: Groin pain in soccer players. Phys Sportsmed 8(8):57–61, 1980

65. Stanish W: Low back pain in middle-aged athletes. Am J Sports Med 7:361–369, 1979

66. Taylor KJ, Milan J: Differential diagnosis of chronic splenomegaly by gray-scale ultrasonography: Clinical observations and digital A-scan analysis. Br J Radiol 49:519–525, 1976

67. Todd RW: Age changes in the pubic symphysis. Roentgenographic differentiation. Am J Anthropol 14:255–271, 1933

68. Vere–Hodge N: Injuries in cricket. In Armstrong JR, Tucker WE (eds): Injuries in Sport, pp 168–171. Springfield, Illinois, Charles C Thomas, 1964

69. Williams RD, Sargent FT: The mechanism of intestinal injury in trauma. J Trauma 31:288–294, 1968

70. Wyman AC: Traumatic rupture of the spleen. Am J Roentgenol 72:51–63, 1954

71. Wyker AW Jr, Gillenwater JY: Method of Urology. Baltimore, Williams & Wilkins, 1975

72. Zaccalini PS, Urist MR: Traumatic periosteal proliferations in rabbits. J Trauma 4:344–357, 1964

73. Zeman SC et al: Tears of the pectoralis major muscle. Am J Sports Med 7:343–347, 1979

CHAPTER

12

The Knee

ANATOMY

The knee joint is a large, complex one in which the medial femoral condyle extends more distally than the lateral femoral condyle and prominence of the lateral femoral condyle serves to block the patella from sliding laterally out of the femoral groove. The lateral plateau of the tibia is convex, and the medial plateau is concave.

The quadriceps muscle group comprises the rectus femoris, vastus lateralis, vastus intermedius, and the vastus medialis and serves to extend the knee. These muscles join to form the quadriceps tendon, which is central to a fascia-like retinaculum that is lateral and medial to the patella (Figure 12-1). The articularis genu is a small part of the quadriceps that extricates the suprapatella pouch to prevent its being pinched during knee motion. The oblique part of the vastus medialis usually inserts about half-way down the medial side of the patella. Because this part rapidly atrophies after a knee operation or immobilization, and terminal extension of the knee weakens, it had been thought that this part of the quadriceps was solely responsible for the last 15° of knee extension. It has since been shown that such limited extension is related to total quadriceps strength and is not an indication of selective weakness of the vastus medialis obliquus.[83]

Thus, the vastus medialis obliquus serves a patella-centering function.[82] In amputated limbs, a solitary vastus medialis obliquus will not extend the knee, whereas all of the long components of the quadriceps—the vastus lateralis, vastus intermedius, vastus medialis longus, and rectus femoris—effect full extension. Normally the last 15° of knee extension require 60% more force than is needed for extension up to the 15° position. When a weight is attached to the vastus medialis obliquus to keep the patella centered in the femoral

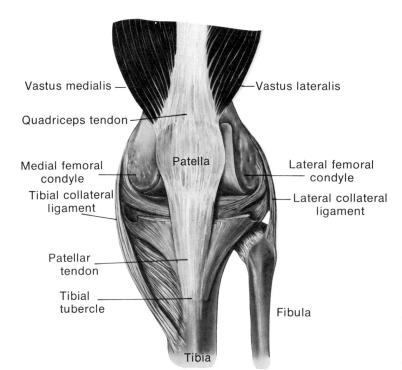

Vastus medialis —

—Vastus lateralis

Quadriceps tendon —

Patella

Medial femoral
condyle

Lateral femoral
condyle

Tibial collateral
ligament

Lateral collateral
ligament

Patellar
tendon

Tibial
tubercle

Fibula

Tibia

Figure 12-1   Anterior aspect
of the knee showing the
extensor mechanism (see
text for description).

groove, however, the force needed for the vastus lateralis to extend the knee decreases by 13%.

The patella usually has two major facets: a large lateral facet and a smaller medial one. The smallest facet is a medialmost "odd facet" of the patella, where osteoarthritis begins. The articular cartilage at the apex of the patella, the junction between the medial and lateral facets, is the thickest patellar cartilage. The earliest softening and chondromalacia appear here because it is so thick that diffusion of nutrients to its depths is difficult. Patellar-femoral, patellar-meniscal, and patellar-tibial ligaments arise from the patella. These ligaments sometimes hold the patella laterally and may be sectioned to relieve patella subluxation and to allow it to glide better in the femoral groove.

The patellar tendon passes from the distal pole of the patella to the tibial tubercle, where it has a sinuous insertion. The usually prominent tibial tubercle is the tongue portion of the tibial epiphysis, which eventually fuses to the rest of the tibia. There are two bursae in this region, one lying between the patella tendon and the tibia just before the tendon inserts into the tibial tu-

bercle, and a second resting subcutaneously just anterior to the patella tendon.

Ligaments

The knee is encased in a fibrous capsular sleeve, weak in its anterior half and strong in its posterior part. Ligaments, menisci, and bone of the knee joint are responsible for the static stability of the knee, whereas muscles and tendons provide dynamic stability. The ligaments work as an integrated network of bundles and fans with complex functions. In full knee extension, the cruciates and collateral ligaments are taut and the knee cannot rotate, but when the knee is flexed the tibia may rotate as the lateral ligaments relax. Although the ligaments work as a unit, they may be divided into a medial complex, a lateral quadruple complex, and the cruciates.

The Medial Side of the Knee

The medial capsular ligament comprises three parts: an anterior capsule, the medial capsular ligament, and the posterior oblique ligament. It

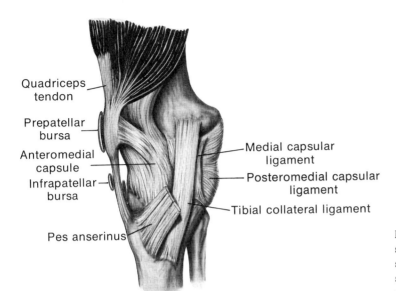

Quadriceps tendon

Prepatellar bursa

Anteromedial capsule

Infrapatellar bursa

Pes anserinus

Medial capsular ligament

Posteromedial capsular ligament

Tibial collateral ligament

Figure 12-2   The medial side of the knee contains static and dynamic structures (see text for description).

joins with the medial meniscus by way of the coronary ligament and has a strong meniscal-femoral and a weaker meniscal-tibial part (Figure 12-2).

The tibial collateral ligament is phylogenetically a remnant of the adductor magnus tendon, arising high on the medial femoral condyle, separated from the medial capsular ligament over the joint line. It inserts into the medial face of the tibia beneath the pes anserinus and is the strongest medial structure and the primary stabilizer of the medial side of the knee. Its tension is maintained during the entire range of knee motion by a reciprocal tightening and loosening of its fibers (Figure 12-3). This ligament stabilizes the knee against excessive external rotation and against

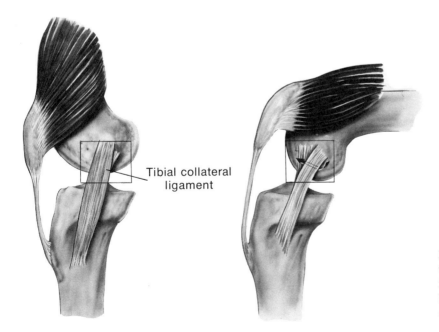

Tibial collateral ligament

Figure 12-3   Some part of the tibial collateral ligament is always taut as its fiber bundles shift with flexion and extension.

valgus forces and resists rotational forces better than the more centrally located cruciates. If the deep ligament and posterior capsule are resected to the midline of the popliteal space but the long tibial collateral ligament is left intact, the knee is still stable to valgus and rotatory stress.[90]

The posterior oblique ligament is strong, forming a sling around the medial femoral condyle.[53] It might better be termed the posteromedial capsular ligament to avoid confusion with the oblique popliteal ligament, a part of the insertion of the semimembranosus into the posterior capsule. The semimembranosus, through its capsular arm, tightens the posteromedial capsular ligament and retracts the posterior horn of the medial meniscus during knee flexion. The semimembranosus also has a direct head that inserts into the tibia and one to the oblique popliteal ligament that tenses the posterior capsule.

The Lateral Retinaculum

The iliotibial band or fascia lata attaches to the lateral intermuscular septum and inserts into Gerdy's tibial tubercle. By being fixed both proximally and distally to the knee joint, it lends both static and dynamic support to the lateral side of the knee.

The superficial oblique retinaculum extends from the iliotibial band to the lateral side of the patella and to the lateral side of the patellar tendon. The transverse retinaculum lies deep to the superficial retinaculum, extending from the deep aspects of the fascia lata to attach to the lateral side of the patella. The synovium of the knee joint adheres to the thin capsular layer that is under the transverse retinaculum.

The epicondylopatellar band extends from the lateral intermuscular spectum and lateral epicondyle to the superolateral pole of the patella near the insertion of the vastus lateralis. A patellotibial and meniscopatellar band extends from Gerdy's tibial tubercle and the lateral meniscus to the inferolateral part of the patella.

The Lateral Quadruple Complex

The lateral quadruple complex consists of the iliotibial band, lateral collateral ligament, popliteus tendon, and the biceps femoris.

The iliotibial band has a dynamic proximal origin as the fascial extension of the tensor fascia lata and the gluteus maximus. It attaches to the intermuscular septum at the level of the lateral femoral condyle and proceeds to insert into the lateral epicondyle of the femur and the lateral

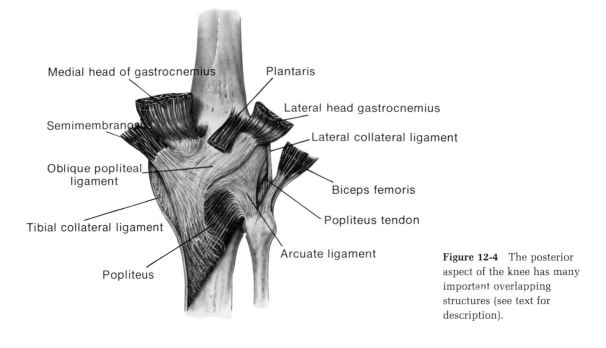

Figure 12-4 The posterior aspect of the knee has many important overlapping structures (see text for description).

tibial tubercle of Gerdy. The iliotibial band is a static lateral stabilizer of the knee but, owing to its tensor fascia lata origin, has some dynamic function as well. It is tense as it moves forward in extension and back in flexion.

The lateral collateral ligament, shaped like a pencil, arises at the lateral femoral epicondyle and inserts on the fibular head. It is tight in extension but relaxes as the knee flexes. The popliteus muscle is peculiar, arising from the lateral femoral condyle as a tendon that passes deep to the lateral collateral ligament, and also from the posterior horn of the lateral meniscus and the posterior aspect of the fibula and inserting on the tibia (Figure 12-4). This muscle stabilizes the knee in flexion and helps govern movement of the lateral meniscus. A popliteus bursa lies between the popliteus tendon and the lateral collateral ligament.

The biceps femoris, an important lateral stabilizer, inserts at the fibular head, the posterolateral tibia, the joint capsule, and the iliotibial tract. The lateral capsule, with its strong mid-third capsular ligament, completes the lateral structures. In flexion, the iliotibial band, poplit-eus tendon, and lateral collateral ligament cross each other to enhance lateral stability.

The Anterior Cruciate Ligament

The anterior cruciate ligament is intracapsular but extrasynovial. It has a crescentic origin from the lateral femoral condyle behind the intercondylar shelf, extending forward and medially into the medial plateau of the tibia in front of the intercondylar eminence (Figure 12-5). The blood vessels course up into the ligament from the infrapatellar fat pad and the synovium, and the nerves in the ligament probably relay position sense.

The anterior cruciate contains three coiled bundles: anteromedial, intermediate, and posterolateral. In extension, the anterior bundle is tight against the intercondylar shelf of the femur; in flexion, the anterior bundle relaxes while the posterolateral becomes tight.[113] Most of the anterior cruciate fibers are longitudinally oriented, but they also spiral from one insertion to the other; for this reason, the geometry of the ligament

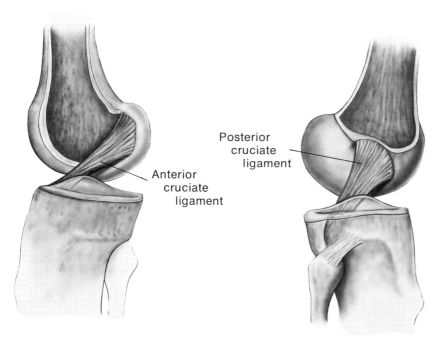

Figure 12-5 The anterior and posterior cruciate ligaments form axes for knee rotation (see text for description).

would be difficult to duplicate with an artificial ligament.

The anterior cruciate is tightest at the extremes of motion, full extension, and full flexion. In midflexion, it is tight when the tibia is internally rotated, but it is otherwise lax. Tightness in various parts of the anterior cruciate at all degrees of flexion acts reciprocally with the posterior cruciate, so that some cruciate fibers are tight at all times.

The anterior cruciate ligament prevents the athlete's femur from sliding backward during weight bearing while also preventing abnormal internal rotation of the tibia by tightening up and twisting on the posterior cruciate. In addition, this ligament exerts control over abnormal external rotation of the tibia. During external rotation of the tibia on the femur, as in a side-step cut, the cruciates unwind. With continued external rotation, the anterior cruciate wraps around the medial side of the lateral femoral condyle to limit further external rotation.

The Posterior Cruciate Ligament

Like the anterior cruciate, the posterior cruciate ligament is intra-articular but extrasynovial, with a crescentic insertion into the medial femoral condyle and a complex architecture (Figure 12-5). Its thin posterior part fans out on the femur. It is twice as strong as the anterior cruciate working reciprocally with the anterior cruciate.[46]

The posterior cruciate ligament is a basic knee stabilizer that is tightest in the midranges of motion. Because of its fan-shaped insertion, some part of it is tight during each degree of knee motion, and it becomes tighter with internal rotation of the tibia, resisting anterior slide of the femur when the athlete is bearing weight. The posterior cruciate also resists hyperextension and contributes to medial stability of the knee.

Posterior Capsule

The posterior capsule helps to stabilize the knee in extension. It is reinforced by the oblique popliteal ligament, an expansion from the semimembranosus tendon. The capsule is governed by a complex system of dynamic motors that include the popliteus, biceps, gastrocnemius, and medial hamstring muscles.

Menisci

The menisci of the knee arise from wedge-shaped condensations of mesenchyme between the developing femur and tibia,[93] whereas the remaining mesenchyme forms the cruciate ligaments. The menisci are mobile buffers with a circumferential arrangement of collagen fibers that suits them to their weight-bearing, shock-absorbing function. They also help to guide and to synchronize knee motion and are important for knee stability. The outer third of each meniscus has a blood supply that accounts for the healing of some peripheral tears and the regeneration of a tough, fibrous meniscus after some meniscectomies. The nonvascularized part of the meniscus receives its nutrition through the diffusion of synovial fluid.

The medial meniscus is C shaped, covering 30% of the surface of the medial tibial plateau (Figure 12-6). It is firmly attached anteriorly and posteriorly to the tibia and securely attached peripherally to the joint capsule by the coronary ligament.

The three types of medial menisci[19] include type I menisci with anterior and posterior horns of equal size; type II with large posterior horns; and type III with a very large posterior horn. The posterior horn is thick, making diffusion of nutrients into the depths of this horn difficult; hence degeneration is likely to occur here.

The blind side of the medial meniscus is an area that is not easy to see from an anterior operative approach to the knee joint.[44] It includes the posterior horn and its capsular and synovial attachments and the meniscal attachment to bone. The meniscus dives into a deep, wide hole behind the intercondylar eminence to attach posteriorly. This strong attachment is best seen through an arthroscope. When the meniscus is completely freed from the joint capsule, it pops straight up, owing to its vertical deep hole attachment.

The lateral meniscus is O shaped, covering 50% of the lateral tibial plateau. Its anterior and posterior horns attach to the tibia, whereas the meniscus is only loosely attached to the capsule.[78] The popliteus tendon arises partly from

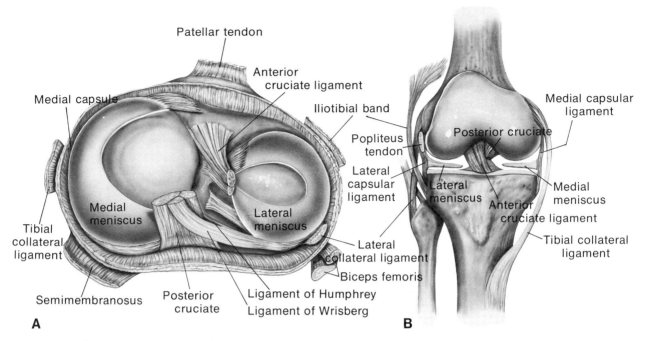

Figure 12-6 The many structures in and around the knee joint are each important in athletic injuries. (**A**) Coronal view of the tibial plateaus. (**B**) Frontal view of the knee joint.

the posterior part of the lateral meniscus and is probably important in coordinating meniscal motion with knee joint motion.[49]

Pes Anserinus

From above downward, the pes anserinus is the combined insertion of the sartorius, gracilis, and semitendinosus on the anteromedial face of the tibia. Although the tendons insert individually, they are connected by an aponeurosis, the combined structure resembling a pes anserinus, or "goose's foot." The pes works mainly as a flexor of the knee but also rotates the leg internally. The pes anserinus bursa sits between the pes, near its insertion, and the overlying tibial collateral ligament.

EXAMINING AN ATHLETE'S INJURED KNEE

When examining an athlete's knee, the physician should first ask whether the athlete has had pre-vious injury to the knee and what sort of treatment he has received. Then, how was the knee hurt this time, and what was the mechanism of injury? What did the injury feel like? Did the knee pop or give way? Was the athlete able to stand up immediately after the injury? Did the knee swell, and, if so, when did it swell—immediately or overnight? Swelling is estimated by a comparison to the sound knee. Is the athlete bowlegged or knock-kneed, or does he have recurvatum or external tibial torsion? The quadriceps must be checked for wasting and the thigh circumferences measured.

The sound knee should be examined first to establish baselines for strength and stability and to observe whether the athlete is tight jointed or loose jointed. This procedure tends to increase the athlete's confidence in the examiner. The dynamic Q angle—the angle that the patella tendon makes with the long axis of the thigh with the knee flexed 30° and the tibia rotated externally—is also measured.

The examiner should feel along the distal femoral growth plate of the young athlete, searching for a fracture. He should also palpate the adductor tubercle for an osteochondroma or bone spikes and bursae. With the athlete sitting, hip flexion strength should be manually tested, furnishing a good guide as to whether the athlete has been favoring the knee. The tone of the quadriceps is felt, the quadriceps is palpated, and the knee is extended against the examiner's manual resistance. The examiner next feels around and under the patella and over the femoral condyles for defects or tender areas.

The athlete is then asked to flex and extend his knee. While the knee is being flexed and extended, the examiner may cover the patella with his palm and feel for crepitus. At less than 30° of flexion, the patella is mobile and all of its facets may be felt, including the most medial portion, or odd facet, where osteoarthritis commonly begins. Next, with the knee extended and the examiner's thumbs placed laterally, the patella should be pressed medially at the same time as the fingers press it into the groove. This maneuver may bring out the pain of chondromalacia. The examiner then palpates the athlete's patella tendon from its patellar origin to its insertion at the tibial tubercle. With the knee flexed to 45°, the examiner should try to sublux the patella by pressing it laterally. An athlete whose patella has previously been dislocated may reach down in fear that his patella is sliding out laterally, a positive apprehension sign. The lateral capsule is considered tight if the examiner is unable to push the patella more than 1 cm medially with the knee flexed to 30°.

With the athlete's knee flexed over the table, the examiner next feels along the medial and lateral joint lines for tender areas or bulges that may mean meniscal cysts. Such cysts usually are posteromedial or posterolateral, bulging through a weak area in the capsule. The examiner then feels the pes insertion on the medial face of the tibia for a swollen and tender pes anserinus bursa. The athlete is asked to assume a figure-four position with his knee bent to 90° and his ankle placed on his other knee. In this position, the examiner may feel the prominent lateral collateral ligament and the popliteus tendon that passes deep to it. The iliotibial band, which may be snapping over the lateral femoral epicondyle, is examined at this juncture. The athlete then lies prone with his feet hanging over the examining table as he is checked for a popliteal cyst, and his hamstrings are palpated as they course toward their insertions.

The athlete should be asked to do a deep squat, and, if there is pain as he goes down or comes up, patellar femoral problems are indicated. Pain at the deepest part of the squat, usually posteromedial, is characteristic of a posterior horn tear of the medial meniscus. To bring out the symptoms, the athlete may be asked to duck-walk and do squat jumps. The click test is next performed. The athlete's hip is first flexed and then his knee fully flexed. The examiner rotates the leg with one hand, and with the other feels over the joint line for any clicks or pops. Any knee can be made to click, but a painful click is evidence for a meniscal tear. A similar analysis, the compression grind test (Apley), may be made with the athlete prone, with the examiner holding the athlete's thigh in place with one hand while his other hand flexes the knee and rotates the leg. If the grinding phase hurts, the leg is pulled up and the same maneuver performed. The grinding may disappear when the leg is lifted, signaling that the pain and the crunching on the grind test were probably due to a meniscal tear. The athlete may also sit in a yoga position with soles together while the examiner presses his knee downward, a maneuver that sometimes causes the meniscus to be caught, eliciting pain.

With the athlete supine and relaxed, his injured leg is gently lowered over the side of the examining table to relax his muscles for valgus and varus stress tests. With the knee fully extended, the leg should have good stability unless there is major ligamentous damage. The knee is then flexed to 30°, and the same valgus and varus stress tests are performed to measure any damage to the medial and lateral sides.

Testing for anterior cruciate integrity was formerly done by flexing the knee to 90°, sitting on the foot, and checking that the hamstrings were relaxed before pulling the leg forward. Now, a more accurate way to test for anterior subluxation of the tibial plateau is the pull test (an anterior drawer with the knee flexed 15°. The examiner holds the thigh steady with one hand while pulling the tibia forward with the other. This test is more accurate than the drawer test because it is not hindered by hamstring contraction and the concavity of the posterior horns of the menisci that lend stability and act as secondary restraints to the drawer. To test for posterior cruciate integrity, the examiner flexes the knee to 90° and firmly pushes the tibia backward. At this time he should also observe whether the tibia sags backward compared to the sound side.

Because some muscles cross both the hip and the knee and the knee and the ankle, it is important during a knee examination to examine the hip flexors, extensors, abductors, and adductors and to perform a thorough examination of the foot and a check of heel-cord flexibility.

To study the knee with plain x-ray films, anteroposterior, lateral, tunnel, sunrise, oblique, and "skin pin" views may be taken. The anteroposterior and lateral views are taken with the athlete bearing weight. The tunnel view is taken with the knee flexed 45° to show the intercondylar notch, which may house the lesion of osteochondritis dissecans, most often noted on the lateral side of the medial femoral condyle. "Sunrise" views, taken with the knee flexed to 30°, 60°, and 90°, reveal the position of the patella in the femoral groove, the slope of the femoral groove, the form of the lateral condylar buttress, the patellar shape, and whether the patella is tilted. Oblique views may be needed to show avulsion fractures. If a tender spot is noted, a pin is taped to the skin at the site and a "skin pin" x-ray film taken.

RUNNING AND THE KNEE

A runner's knee problem may be caused by an abnormality of the leg or foot, such as a tight heel cord, a pronated foot, or a cavus, high-arched foot. Shocks are normally absorbed at the knee by knee flexion, at the ankle by dorsiflexion, and in the foot by pronation. A tight heel cord puts a burden on the knee to flex further to absorb shock. As a result, even when the runner is on a flat surface the knees are flexed, putting extra strain on the quadriceps, which presses the patella painfully against the articular surface of the femur. A pronated foot leads to valgus forces at the knee, putting stress on the medial knee capsule. In this condition, the foot stays on the ground longer,

and the patella may thus translate, or slide side-to-side, to produce shearing stress. Lateral capsular knee sprains are caused by jamming of the inflexible cavus foot. Tight hamstrings may also produce knee problems because the quadriceps must work harder against these tight hamstrings, and the kneecap is thus further compressed against the femur. To prevent or to treat these problems, the athlete should stretch his heel cords, use orthotic devices for pronated feet, wear padding for cavus feet, and stretch his hamstrings.

The surface on which the athlete runs may affect his knees. Subchondral bone trabeculae absorb shock at the knee, amounting to a force of about three times that of body weight during running. These trabeculae may fracture and cause knee pain, although the fractures are too fine to be seen on x-ray films. Healed microfractures cause increased density in the subchondral region and decrease its shock-absorbing capacity. The articular cartridge must then absorb the shocks, a job for which it was not designed and which causes the cartilage to break down, resulting in incongruities and arthritis.

A 59-kg (130-lb) person puts about 390 pounds of force on his tibial plateaus with each walking step. If an average day of walking consists of about 8000 steps, the knees must accept more than 3 million pounds of force a day.[104] If the person weighs 200 pounds, almost 5 million pounds of force reach the plateaus of the knees each day. These forces are much greater in running than in walking because, while walking, one supportive foot is always on the ground, whereas running is a series of jumps. These figures underline the value of weight loss in the heavy person to avoid arthritis of the knee.[79]

The terrain on which the athlete runs may affect his knees. On crowned roads or banked tracks, the uphill leg pronates to cause medial knee pain, and the downhill leg jams to produce lateral knee pain (Figure 12-7). During downhill runs, quadriceps contractions decelerate the runner's femur, pressing the kneecap against the articular cartilage of the femur and possibly causing retropatellar pain. The popliteus also aids in holding the femur back during downhill runs, and popliteus tenosynovitis may arise. A temporary change to flat terrain will often correct some

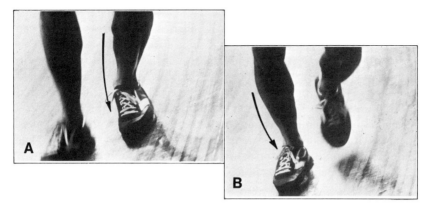

Figure 12-7   The uphill leg on a banked track **(A)** pronates *(arrow)* and places stress on the medial side of the knee. The downhill foot **(B)** jams and supinates *(arrow)*, stressing the lateral side of the knee.

of these problems, and stretching, orthoses, or shoe changes may effect a cure.

Unusual running styles sometimes promote knee problems. Some inexperienced runners run with their knees turned in, externally rotating their legs to clear the ground. This style may result from femoral anteversion and tibial torsion, but it can be improved by lifting the knees to clear the ground. Strange running styles may be quite effective, however, for some athletes.

CUTTING

Cutting is the term used to describe an athlete altering his running gait and changing direction by a few degrees or as much as 90° or more.

Cuts involve three phases.[3] The first is preliminary deceleration. There is no foot descent phase. Instead, the heel jams into the ground, and the foot flattens. The quadriceps and hamstrings provide the power for deceleration, which is achieved by knee flexion instead of the normal dorsiflexion of the foot. After deceleration, the plant and cut involves a twist toward the new direction. In the final phase, takeoff, the athlete pushes off and moves in the direction of the cut.

There are two major cuts: the sidestep and the crossover (Figure 12-8). In the sidestep cut, the foot opposite the direction of the cut is planted, and the other foot then takes the first step in the new direction. In the crossover cut, the athlete plants the foot that is on the same side as the new

direction. The opposite leg then crosses in front of the planted one to move in this new direction.

Because there are such strong forces on the knee, many athletic injuries occur during cutting. The sidestep cut stresses the medial knee ligaments of the planted leg. Also, the twisting motion of the planted leg in this cut and quadriceps contraction at pushoff may snap the patella laterally into a dislocated position. In a crossover cut, the lateral knee ligaments of the planted leg are stressed.

During cuts, the athlete's knee is placed in a vulnerable, partly flexed position in which its inherent stability drops and a blow from an opponent may damage the knee. The ligaments are further loaded if shoe cleats catch in the turf. Cutting drills come last in knee rehabilitation programs because they are the most stressful moves. Thus, one of the prime determinants as to when the athlete may return to practice or games is how well he performs cuts.

KICKING

The energy contained in an athlete's leg just before a kick is equivalent to the energy of a fall of almost 1 m by a 90-kg person.[36] During a kick, 15% of the leg's kinetic energy is transferred to the ball to accelerate it. Most of the remaining 800 pounds of force is dissipated by knee flexion and a pulling back of the leg by the hamstrings.

Figure 12-8   A cross-over cut **(A)** and side-step cut **(B)** affect the pivoting knee differently.

Hamstring strains are common in kicking, as the forces on these structures are very strong and there is not much time in follow-through to dissipate the energy.

Flexibility and good technique are important in preventing injuries in kicking sports. In the martial arts, many American enthusiasts suffer knee injuries, whereas these are only minor problems in Asiatic competitors.[70] Some have attributed this injury distribution to racial differences in knee anatomy,[70] but the variations more likely are related to the athlete's technique and flexibility, since white European competitors also have a low knee injury rate.

The athlete may injure an opponent or himself while kicking and may develop quadriceps tendinitis or pes-anserinus bursitis. If a placekicker's foot catches in the turf or strikes an opponent, he may strain a muscle or avulse a piece of bone. For this reason, soccer cleats are stubby at the toe to avoid catching. Medial hamstring strain is commonly seen in older persons new to soccer football, resulting from attempts to kick with the medial side of the foot.

BICYCLING

Bicycling is safe and beneficial for the knees. It develops the thigh muscles, improves muscular endurance and flexibility, enhances the nutrition of knee cartilage, and possibly postpones arthritis. The hamstrings of a cyclist often are equal in strength to his quadriceps because toe clips allow him to pull, and, when the crank is just 15° past the horizontal, the vastus muscle group is turned off but the hamstrings continue to act. Cycling also enhances muscular endurance by stimulating mitochondrial enzyme systems.[29] In addition, the cyclist nourishes the knee by gently pumping in nutrients, rather than jamming the knee, as in running.

Knee safety in cycling depends on proper saddle height, avoidance of pushing too hard in high gears, proper cleat placement, and keeping the knees warm. In a study of persons of all ages who participated in the Bikecentennial 80-day tour from Reedsport, Oregon, to Yorktown, Virginia,[73] it was found that each cyclist used about 2 million pedal strokes to pedal the 7200 km (4500 miles) over varying terrain. Knee pain was rare, however, and was easily relieved by altering the saddle height. Older cyclists with osteoarthritis reported that their knees vastly improved during the tour.

Proper saddle height is determined by placing the heels on the pedals and pedaling backward while the bicycle is supported. The cyclist's knee should be slightly bent when the pedal is at its lowest point. If the pelvis rocks, the seat is too high, causing the rider to reach for the pedals. To be sure that the saddle is not too low, it should be run up until the pelvis starts to rock and then should be slightly lowered.[151]

Another method often used to measure saddle height is the crotch-to-heel measurement.[36] One-hundred-nine percent of the cyclist's inside leg measurement is transposed along the tube from the pedal surface to the top of the saddle. The 109% value serves as a starting point. The saddle is then lowered a bit, and the cyclist keeps it at this height for about 150 km (100 miles). A mark is placed on the post, and the saddle height is changed again. Eventually, the most comfortable position will be found, and the saddle height is set at this point. This method may, however, result in the saddle's being placed too high.

Knee pain frequently occurs from pushing too hard in high gears. Many cyclists have their saddles too high and cannot pedal fast enough because they cannot reach the pedals. Instead of spinning, they end up pushing gears that are too high. Ideally, cyclists maintain the same revolutions per minute in different gears. Bicycle tour riders may strive to maintain an 80-per-minute cadence.

A cyclist's knee pain may often be relieved by a slight change in the saddle height, thus altering the contact points on the patella. Even a 2.5-cm (1-in) change of saddle height, up or down, alters the action of almost every muscle in the lower extremities involved in pedaling. For this reason, the saddle must be adjusted carefully to avoid knee soreness.

Proper adjustment of the saddle on a stationary exercise bicycle is as important as it is on a touring bicycle. This is evident during bicycle ergometer graded exercise testing of noncycling subjects, when quadriceps muscle soreness sometimes prematurely ends the test. A proper saddle height adjustment before the test begins will avoid the problem

Faulty placement of the feet on the pedals or incorrect cleat placement may stress the knee. The cyclist's toes should point slightly medially. Medial knee pain may result when the foot is turned out, and lateral pain occurs if the foot is pointed in too far.[39]

Proper cleat placement may be determined by having the cyclist ride a good distance in his new shoes so that an impression of the pedal forms on the bottom of the shoe. The cleat is then aligned to this impression to orient the shoe properly. Although the cyclist's tibia rotates in when the knee is flexed and rotates out when the knee extends, the cleats do not hinder this movement, since flexibility at the ankle and foot adapts to these movements.

Cyclists tend to think like runners. Just as runners often wear shorts at air temperature of 10°C (50°F), so do some cyclists, overlooking the wind-chill factor. Shorts should not be worn until the temperature reaches about 18°C to 21°C (65°F–70°F). When the temperature drops to −7°C to −1°C (20°F–30°F), the wind-chill factor on a bicycle is −18° to −12°C (0°–10°F), making long underwear obligatory. When a cyclist pedals home on cool evenings, he should wear a cut-off wool sock around each knee to keep them warm. Cyclists should stretch before cycling, just as runners stretch before running.

Knock-knees, bowlegs, and foot pronation cause knee stress in cyclists, and these problems must be balanced with shims or orthotic devices in the shoes or with shims affixed to the pedals. A bowlegged cyclist's lateral knee pains may be eliminated by building up the lateral side of the pedals, and medial ligament pains may be relieved by building up the medial side of the pedals or by adding arch supports to the shoes.

THE KNEE EXTENSOR MECHANISM

Quadriceps Tendon Rupture

Quadriceps tendon rupture is most likely to occur in an older athlete with a degenerated tendon.[35] Soreness often precedes the quadriceps tendon rupture, and in this phase the athlete's activity level should be reduced and a gentle quadriceps cryotherapy stretching program begun. If the athlete is taking anti-inflammatory drugs, he must not be allowed to use the affected part in training or competition during the course of treatment because the drugs mask pain. Steroids should not be injected into or around this major weight-bearing tendon[64] because they will mask pain and may cause collagen necrosis, which can weaken the tendon.

The quadriceps tendon usually ruptures when the knee is flexed to about 90° and is subjected to abnormal stress, as when an older athlete slips on sand or leaves on an unswept tennis court or the Olympic-style weight lifter does a split in the clean-and-jerk.

Although it is a major injury, quadriceps tendon rupture is sometimes overlooked. Initial x-ray films may fail to show a fracture; an athlete's knee may then be wrapped, only to give out a day later. Careful examination will prevent such delays in diagnosis. The examiner should feel for a gap above the patella and test for knee extension. X-ray films may show a low patella, and occasionally a fragment of bone is seen to have avulsed from the superior pole of the patella.

If a quadriceps tendon rupture occurs, the tendon is reattached to the patella through drill holes, or the avulsed fragment of bone is replaced on the patella and the rest of the tendon attached through drill holes. In recurrent or old quadriceps tendon ruptures, some of the proximal tendon is reflected distally and incorporated into the repair.

Postoperatively, a major goal is to restore the fullest flexion to the knees without damaging the repair. Full flexion is especially important to collegiate and freestyle wrestlers, rodeo cowboys, and hockey defensemen, who must drop their knees into acute flexion. A bicycle is used in rehabilitation, and the contract–relax stretching method usually obtains further flexion. In this technique, the athlete first contracts his quadriceps isometrically against resistance, then relaxes as the trainer passively flexes the knee.

Prepatellar Bursitis

Inflammation and swelling of the prepatellar bursa may follow a single blow to the kneecap from a lacrosse stick or when the athlete lands on

synthetic grass that rests on asphalt (Figure 12-9). Repetitive rubbing of the knee in collegiate or freestyle wrestling sometimes inflames the bursa. The prepatellar region becomes puffy, and flexion of the knee decreases as the skin becomes tense over the tender, swollen bursa.

The prepatellar bursa may also become infected from a "turf burn," as "green dust" is ground into the abrasion.[76] An acutely or chronically inflamed prepatellar bursa may occasionally be contaminated from an overlying infected artificial turf burn. In such cases, the red, inflamed, and contaminated bursa may be hard to differentiate from an abrasion with cellulitis.

An inflamed prepatellar bursa usually is aspirated and an elastic wrap applied. If the needle is placed into the bursa through cellulitis, however, the bursa may become infected. Thus, if cellulitis is suspected, warm, moist packs should be placed around the knee, the knee immobilized, and antibiotics started. The knee must then be systematically reappraised to arrive at a precise diagnosis.

To prevent prepatellar problems, an athlete may smear petroleum jelly on his legs to ease a slide on artificial turf. Knee pads should be worn when repetitive knee contact is anticipated on hard surfaces or in tackle football, where forces on the prepatellar area are increased by the weight of other players piling on.

The most widely used knee pad is flat and fits in the front knee pocket of the pants. Basketball players use an elastic sleeve with a flat insert. The pads should be large enough to cover the knee region, and athletes should not be allowed to cut them down for any reason.

The athlete's pants must be long and tight enough to prevent the knee pads from sliding. Newer stretch materials allow players to select pants as tight as may be comfortable, but sometimes pants are too short and the patellar area is exposed as the knee pads ride up. This causes the pants to become too tight in the popliteal region, and when the player cuts the back of the pants the knee pads flop around.

Subluxation of the Patella

During the pushoff phase of a sidestep cut, extension and valgus forces act on the knee of the

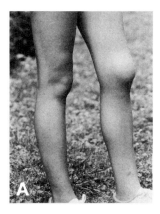
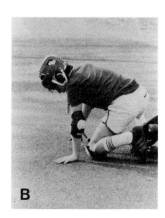

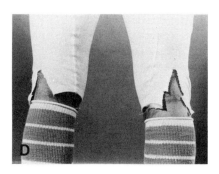

Figure 12-9   Prepatellar swelling may be quite marked **(A)**. Knee pads **(B, C)** may prevent such damage. If, however, a player's football pants are too tight and he cuts them **(D),** the knee pads will slide up and lose their protective value.

planted leg. The kneecap may then slide out laterally, especially in a female athlete who has a weak vastus medialis obliquus or a high insertion of this muscle. Many female athletes have a wide pelvis and anteverted hips, a shallow femoral groove and a flat lateral femoral condyle, a high-riding and flat patella, and ligamentous laxity with recurvatum and externally rotated tibias, all favoring subluxation. However, the male athlete may also sublux his patella with hard cuts. In the past, this condition was often overlooked in male athletes, resulting in unnecessary meniscectomies.[52] In younger athletes, the sliding often disappears as the sulcus deepens and the shape of the patella changes as the bones mature.

The athlete with subluxation of the kneecap reports "catching," "giving way," and medial knee pain, a symptom complex that resembles that of a medial meniscus tear. The laterally sliding patella causes pain by tugging on and tearing the medial capsular structures. On examination

of the seated athlete, the kneecaps sometimes point laterally like "grasshopper eyes," often with more mobility than is normal and occasionally more proximally than normal. To ascertain whether the kneecap is abnormally high (patella alta), the athlete should sit with his knee flexed to 90° over the edge of the table. If his kneecap faces upward, it is high; if it faces straight ahead, it is at a normal level. On a lateral x-ray view, the patella and the patellar tendon should be about the same length. The Q angle, the angle that the patellar tendon makes in reference to the long axis of the thigh, is usually more than 15°, however, a large Q angle is not diagnostic of subluxation, since even Q angles of more than 20° may not be associated with subluxation. The dynamic Q angle is found by flexing the knee to 30° and rotating the tibia externally. It is more significant than the static Q angle because it shows what happens when the athlete cuts.

The sunrise x-ray view of the knee is very

helpful because it yields a tangential view of the flexed knee that shows the intercondylar sulcus, the shape of the lateral condyle, how the patella sits in the sulcus, and whether it is in a tipped position. The view may be taken with the athlete sitting and his knees flexed to 30° (Figure 12-10). The cassette is placed proximal to the knees and the x-ray tube positioned between the ankles, or the film may be put in a cassette holder distal to the knees and the x-ray tube positioned proximally. If the knee is flexed more than 50° to 60°, the patella shifts away from the femur. The intercondylar sulcus may also be viewed with the athlete prone and the cassette placed under the knee with the tube positioned near the toes.[47] Although this technique is commonly used, it necessitates placing the cassette at a distorting angle, and the patella is artificially pressed into the sulcus. Instead of a set angle for the x-ray, several angles of flexion are better, including the angle of flexion where the athlete has pain.

The treatment of patellar subluxation ranges from exercises, orthotics, and braces to operative ligament releases and reconstruction of the knee. Since a youngster may outgrow the problem, the quadriceps should be strengthened and balanced with the hamstrings, and the quadriceps, hamstrings, and gastrocnemius should be stretched for flexibility. The feet of an athlete whose patella is subluxing should be checked. Excessive pronation prolongs the stance phase to allow translation of the patella. A lightweight orthosis or shoe wedge will serve to limit pronation and reduce sliding of the patella.

Recurvatum of the knee reduces the buttressing action of the lateral femoral condyle; a felt pad may be used as an external buttress. A neoprene knee sleeve that contains a buttress pad is more effective than wrapping the felt pad with an elastic wrap, since a wrapped-on pad often slips. A dynamic patellar stabilizing brace is preferable to these padding methods.

Palumbo Dynamic Patellar Stabilizing Brace

The effectiveness of the padding methods used to prevent lateral sliding of the patella is inconsistent because the pads are hard to maintain in a functional position during activity, are bulky and uncomfortable, and sometimes cause skin problems. A dynamic patellar stabilizing brace has been developed to overcome these deficiencies.[123] The brace is consistently effective throughout the full range of knee motion, is comfortable, simple to use, available in various sizes, and inexpensive. It applies an active, medially displacing force to the lateral border of the patella and improves patellofemoral seating while maintaining constant pressure during flexion, extension, and rotation.

The brace consists of an elastic sleeve with a patellar cutout and two circumferentially wrapped "live" rubber arms that apply dynamic tension to a crescent-shaped lateral patellar pad (Figure 12-11). The arms are contoured and directed so as to avoid patellar tilting and irritation of the popliteal area. An elastic circumferential counterarm maintains the pad in proper position, preventing the brace from rotating. Each of the arms is attached by a Velcro fastener. The dynamic brace is measured by taking the circumference of the athlete's knee at the kneecap, 7.5-cm (3-in) above it, and 7.5-cm (3-in) below.

The dynamic brace may be used for the diagnosis, treatment, and rehabilitation of the athlete who has a subluxating patella. Its effectiveness is

Figure 12-10 The sunrise view is taken with the athlete sitting with her knees bent to about 30°. If the x-ray were taken with the athlete prone, the kneecaps would be jammed into the femoral sulcus artificially, distorting their position.

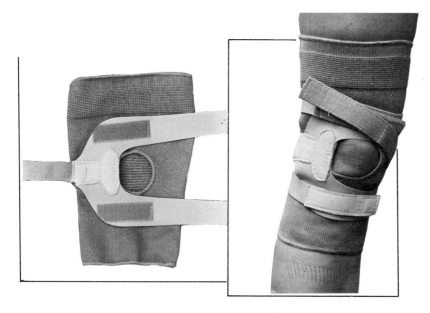

Figure 12-11   The Palumbo dynamic patellar brace is a diagnostic and therapeutic aid.

tested by asking the wearer to perform the activities, such as sidestep cuts, that would ordinarily cause knee pain or instability. If the brace relieves the pain or improves stability, patellofemoral dysfunction is suspected. Early use of this brace during patellofemoral development may improve patellar posture and prevent irreversible soft tissue and skeletal changes. By the time the skeletal structures mature, the subluxation may have ceased. The brace also allows skeletally immature youths who will need surgery to participate in athletics until they reach maturity and until a distal realignment is possible.

The brace can be used therapeutically to prevent contracture of the lateral retinaculum and deters stretching of the medial retinaculum, thus simulating the effect of a lateral release. It may even afford permanent relief and obviate the need for surgery. Such surgery is reserved for athletes who do not respond to a trial of dynamic patellar bracing and vastus medialis rehabilitation. After a realignment operation, use of the brace may reduce the stresses on the realigned structures. The brace can also be used to alleviate patellar tendinitis, tibial epiphysitis, and localized chondromalacia patella. In these conditions, it acts to diminish stress on the patellar tendon and on the tendon's insertion. The brace also seems to alter the pathologic contact points of the patella, thus

decreasing symptoms from localized chondromalacia patella.

Operations for Patellar Subluxation

An athlete with a recurrent painful patellar subluxation may need an operation if the quadriceps cannot overcome the lateral capsular ligaments, especially the patellofemoral ligament that tethers the patella laterally. The lateral tilt test may be used to check for tight lateral structures. In this test, the knee is first flexed to 45° over the examiner's knee; the examiner then uses both thumbs to push the patella medially in an attempt to set it in its groove. If this cannot be accomplished, the lateral side is considered to be tight, and a lateral retinacular release is indicated.

When planning a lateral release, the surgeon should first assess the articular surface of the patella and analyze patellar tracking arthroscopically. If the medial facet of the patella shifts too far laterally and is soft, the surgeon makes a short skin incision lateral to the patella, dissects below the subcutaneous tissue with scissors, makes a nick in the capsule into which he inserts a straight meniscotome, and passes the meniscotome distally, lateral to the patellar tendon, to release the tight lateral ligaments. He then dissects superiorly with scissors, severs the vastus lateralis tendon insertion into the patella, and continues the incision in the quadriceps 5-cm (2-in) proximal to the patella. A hemarthrosis may complicate this procedure owing to bleeding from a severed superior genicular artery. To reduce the incidence of this complication, the surgeon may place a foam pad over the line of incision and insert a drain through a superomedial portal, removing it on the second postoperative day.

A more extensive reconstruction may occasionally be needed to correct lateral patellar subluxation, especially in athletes with ligamentous laxity or when a lateral release has proved ineffective. Reconstruction includes a lateral release, examination of the joint interior, advancement of the vastus medialis obliquus, reefing of the anteromedial capsule, and transfer of the pes anserinus into the medial side of the patellar tendon (Figure 12-12). This operation must be a meticulous one on the dynamic knee mechanism, for if the vastus medialis obliquus is advanced too distally the patella will rotate. After reconstruction, the athlete's pes is trained by conscious use during cuts to reduce the Q angle and prevent lateral patellar slide.

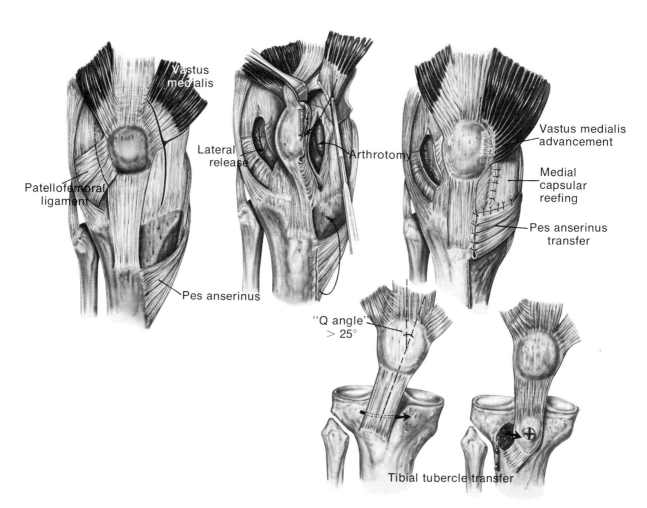

Figure 12-12 The extensor realignment comprises a lateral release, arthrotomy, vastus medialis advancement, medial capsular reefing, and pes anserinus transfer. If the Q angle is greater than 25°, the tibial tubercle is transferred medially.

Dislocated Patella

During a sidestep cut or while swinging a baseball bat, an athlete may suppose that someone has struck his knee or that it has been hit by the ball. What has happened is that as the quadriceps has contracted with the knee in valgus, the kneecap has completely pulled out of its sulcus, causing it to lodge laterally to the lateral femoral condyle, locking the knee in flexion (Figure 12-13).

To reduce this dislocation, the hip is first flexed to relax the quadriceps and the knee then gently extended to effect reduction. To enhance the ease of reduction, a local anesthetic may be injected around the kneecap and into the joint. Gentle reduction is important to allow the kneecap to relocate without chipping off bone or damaging articular cartilage. As the kneecap snaps back into the intercondylar sulcus, the lateral femoral condyle occasionally fractures, or a medial patellar facet may be chipped off. For this reason, the knee should be x-rayed after reduction and checked for chips. Chips should be replaced if they come from the buttressing area of the lateral femoral condyle or from the medial facet of the patella.

The knee can be aspirated if it is moderately swollen after reduction of the dislocated kneecap; this prevents further ligamentous laxity and allows the athlete to initiate an effective quadriceps strengthening program. He then wears a cast for 5 weeks while starting an intensive rehabilitation program. Some surgeons recommend acute reapproximation of the torn capsular structures to avoid future laxity.

An athlete who has suffered recurrent dislocations of the patella may show apprehension as the examiner presses the patella laterally to sim-

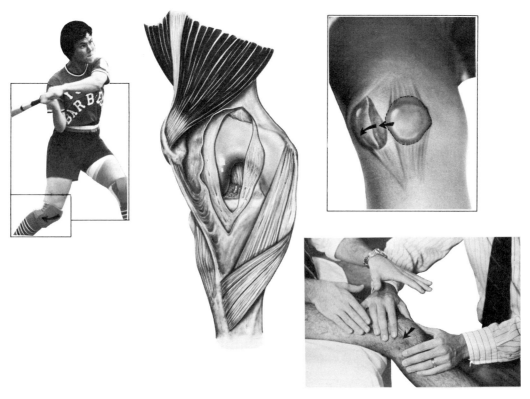

Figure 12-13 A batter's patella may dislocate laterally during a swing, ripping the medial capsule. To test for an unstable patella, the examiner presses it laterally. The athlete reaches down apprehensively, feeling as if his patella is once again dislocating.

ulate an impending dislocation. The athlete with recurrent dislocations of the patella usually benefits from an extensor mechanism reconstruction.

"Runner's Knee"

"Runner's knee" refers to pain in the front of a runner's knee. It may be anteromedial, anterolateral, or retropatellar (behind the kneecap). Anteromedial pain may be caused by the stretching or catching of a fold of synovium called a plica (Latin, fold). Anterolateral pain may be caused by nerve degeneration in the lateral retinaculum or by excessive pressure of the lateral facet of the patella against the lateral femoral condyle. Retropatellar pain is most often caused by a softening of the articular cartilage behind the kneecap.

Traumatic synovitis is an especially common cause of knee pain in young people. The injured synovium is leaky; thus, the knee may swell and be painful for months. Arthroscopy is sometimes needed to rule out an internal derangement. If the problem proves to be only a synovitis, the arthroscopic irrigation may cause it to resolve.

Excessive Lateral Facet Pressure

Eccentric impingement of the patella against the lateral femoral condyle during knee flexion and extension produces both compression and shearing.[30] In such cases, the laterally directed forces and medial stabilizers have lost their equilibrium. This is not a subluxation. A *subluxation* means a tendency to luxate or dislocate. In the case of lateral patellar pressure, the patella is not unstable but, instead, is tethered laterally and excessively stable (Figure 12-14). This excessive loading of the articular cartilage or excessive tension in the lateral joint capsule leads to lateral facette pain. Nerve damage has been found in the lateral retinacula of knees exhibiting the excessive lateral pressure syndrome.[33] The damage includes demyelination and perineural fibrosis similar to the changes observed in cases of Morton's interdigital neuroma.

The diagnosis of excessive lateral pressure is a clinical one. Sometimes, but not always, there is a history of a direct injury to the kneecap. The athlete will report aching at the lateral side of the patella. The pain is aggravated by bent-knee activities. The lower extremity, and particularly the extensor mechanism, will be malaligned. Flexion and extension of the knee may produce crepitation. The parapatellar region may be tender (a sign of synovitis), and medial excursion of the patella with the knee relaxed in extension will be decreased. The examiner may find lateral retinacular tightness when he tries to tilt the lateral edge of the patella up.

Sunrise-view x-ray films may show patellar subluxation laterally or lateral tilting of the patella. The films may also show signs of excessive pressure on the lateral facet. Specifically, the subchondral bone of the lateral facette may be sclerotic and the medial facette more radiolucent than normal. Further, stress lines in the lateral facet may be vertical rather than perpendicular to the patellar articular surface.

Most young patients respond to a conservative treatment program to relieve excessive lateral pressure. This program includes rest, anti-inflammatory medicine, isometric quadriceps contractions, and limitation of bent knee activities. If the patient does not respond to conservative treatment, an arthroscopic assessment may be needed along with a lateral release.

The Lateral Release

The percutaneous procedure[50] is performed under an epidural anesthesia or a light general anesthesia of Brevital Sodium and nitrous oxide. Through a lateral suprapatellar approach, the surgeon assesses the articular surface of the patella, its line of tracking across the femoral condyle, and any lateral patellar displacement. In cases of excessive pressure, the space between the lateral facet and the patella will be tight, but chondromalacia will not necessarily be present.

Before doing the release, the surgeon may infiltrate the expected line of lateral release with 20 ml of 0.5% bupivocaine containing epinephrine. This step promotes hemostasis and relieves postoperative pain. He then nicks the retinaculum and introduces heavy scissors. He begins the release at the level of the tibial turbercle just lateral to the patellar tendon and extends the release along the lateral border of the patella, sectioning

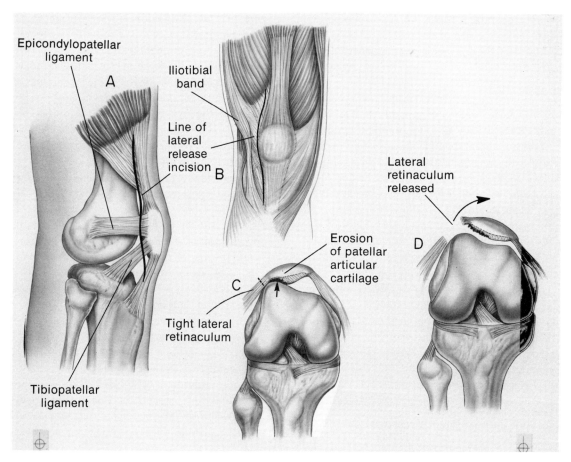

Figure 12-14   Anterolateral knee pain may be produced when the epicondylopatellar ligament **(A)** is stretched. As the iliotibial band **(B)** sweeps to-and-fro over the lateral epicondyle, it too may produce pain. A tight lateral retinaculum holds the patella over the lateral condyle and produces erosion of the articular cartilage that covers the lateral facet **(C).** After release of the lateral retinaculum, the patella fits better in the femoral sulcus **(D).**

the meniscopatellar and epicondylopatellar ligaments. The incision then curves slightly medially at the superolateral corner of the patella to release the insertional fibers of the vastus lateralis. Before the lateral release can be considered complete, the incision must be carried proximally along the lateral side of the tendon of the rectus femoris. The incision ends about 5 cm above the patella, and the surgeon must then ascertain by feel that no fibers of the vastus lateralis remain inserted into the patella.[99] This superior part of the procedure can be monitored through a small incision at the superolateral part of the patella.

Because the deep fibers of the retinaculum are immediately adjacent to the thin capsulosynovial layer, the joint is frequently entered during a lateral release. Some surgeons purposely divide the synovium, believing that it will otherwise tether the patella. I try not to divide it because entering the joint may lead to a synovial fistula. Further, bleeding from the vascular synovium may produce a hemarthrosis.

After completing the release, the surgeon flexes the knee fully to ascertain that there is no further lateral tightness. The lateral side of the patella should now be easily movable to the center of the femoral sulcus. He places a drain along the line of the incision in the capsule. After skin closure, he wraps a foam rubber compression pad snugly over the line of incision with an elastic wrap.

The percutaneous lateral release is favored by some surgeons over an open method because it is simple, the area of skin laterally will be supple, there is little soreness, and only the little arthroscopy nick scars. After an open release, a skin scar occupies the area that had been contracted and tethered. Complications of the percutaneous method include hematoma, hemarthrosis, and synovial fistula. To help prevent bleeding, the athlete should not use aspirin for 3 weeks before to 3 weeks after the operation.

Postoperative Care

Postoperatively, the athlete wears a knee immobilizer and may bear weight immediately. After 24 hours, the surgeon removes the drain and the athlete begins active range-of-motion exercises. Early motion prevents adhesions and regrowth of tissue across the gap produced by the released incision. The athlete also begins isometric quadriceps and hamstring exercises and uses a neuromuscular electrical simulator (NEMS) for 20 minutes every 2 hours. He rewraps the compression pad snugly each day for 7 days. At 1 week postoperatively, most patients can flex the knee to 90° and they may begin bicycling.

The success of the dynamic realignment depends on the athlete's willingness and ability to build up his weak medial thigh muscles in a progressive resistance program. He is also taught how to mobilize his patella. With his knee extended, he pushes it medially and also tilts up the lateral side.

Open Lateral Release

Some surgeons favor an "open" lateral release because some lateral support can be retained. The open method also has the advantages of allowing direct vision, easy checking for bleeding points, and less chance of the formation of a synovial fistula. Disadvantages include the possibility of infection, lateral tethering of the patella by scar tissue, and cosmetic considerations.[77]

The surgeon makes a 6-cm incision just lateral to the patella. He then incises the superficial oblique retinaculum longitudinally, retracts the retinaculum, and incises the deep transverse retinaculum anteriorly. Next, he sews the anterior edge of the deep transverse retinaculum to the posterior edge of the superficial layer, which results in a lengthening of the retinaculum yet maintains its continuity.

Retropatellar Arthralgia

Pain behind an athlete's kneecap usually comes from chondromalacia patella, a softening of the articular cartilage. The cartilage may have been damaged by a fall on the knee or by the repetitive stress of patellar malalignment.

Articular cartilage receives its nutrition by a diffusion of nutrients, which is enhanced by a compressive, milking action. Pressure stops absorption of nutrients into its deeper layers. As the pressure releases, nutrients flow in. The cartilage functions well in compression, but translation causes shearing, as in the side-to-side use of a pencil eraser. Whether caused by foot pronation, congenital malalignment, or muscle weakness, translation of the patella produces a pathologic state of articular cartilage softening or chondromalacia of the patella.[55] Stress-loading also produces microfractures of the subchondral bone and subchondral sclerosis. The less resilient bone places a greater shock-absorbing burden on the articular cartilage. The increased density of the subchondral bone also alters its vascular pattern, further decreasing articular cartilage nutrition.

In grade I chondromalacia, the ground substance of the articular cartilage swells and soft blisters form, but the articular surface is intact (Figure 12-15). In grade II, the surface breaks down with fissuring and fragmentation. In grade III, the cartilage has been eroded and the subchondral bone is exposed.

Chondromalacia of the patella may precede osteoarthritic change. However, the anatomic location of the two conditions differs. Chondromalacia is most often found near the median ridge, where the patella cartilage is thickest, and on the

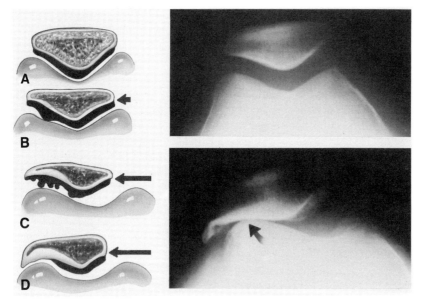

Figure 12-15
Chondromalacia is progressive. The coronal sections of the patella show the articular cartilage in black **(A)**. A "blister," or soft area, forms initially **(B)**. If the blister breaks, chunks erupt to produce an ulcer **(C)**. As the kneecap slides laterally, the chunks are eroded to expose bone **(D)**.

medial and lateral facets. In contrast, osteoarthritis first appears on the least frequently loaded area of the patella, the "odd facet" at the most medial side of the patella. The odd facet contacts the femur only during a full squat.

The athlete with chondromalacia patella may complain of a dull and disagreeable aching pain behind the kneecap, worsened by bent knee activities. The knee is commonly sore while he sits watching a movie or while on an airplane. Since articular cartilage is devoid of pain nerve endings, how is the pain in chondromalacia of the patella generated? Perhaps the loading and the shearing action affect nerves in the subchondral region, or perhaps cartilage waste products, lysosomes, and proteoglycans irritate the synovium.

The examiner can reproduce the dull and disagreeable aching pain by pressing the patella into the femoral sulcus. During flexion and extension, the examiner can sense a coarseness behind the patella and hear a grating or crunching. The examiner assesses the quality of the crepitation. A brush-like feel suggests fibrillation. A crackling and popping sound is more likely due to fissuring, chondral fractures, and greater articular cartilage damage.

X-ray films may show bony changes. A U-shaped indentation and sclerosis of the posterior surface of the patella on the lateral film denotes excessive pressure and healed microfractures. As in the lateral pressure syndrome, the sunrise view may show sclerosis of the lateral facet and median eminence and rarefaction or lucency of the medial facet. Further, the trabeculae in the lateral facet may be oriented vertical to the patellar articular surface rather than perpendicular. The sclerosis and altered traveculae also denote excessive pressure.

Treatment of Retropatellar Arthralgia

Runner's knee is sometimes cured by correcting abnormalities of the foot, changing training techniques, or stretching out tight structures. Flexible orthoses or wedges built into the training shoes and into everyday shoes will limit abnormal pronation, and foam rubber inserts absorb shock and alleviate the lateral knee pain from cavus feet. The runner should avoid crowned roads and indoor banked tracks and omit downhill runs until his hamstrings and heel cords are loose.

It is very important to advise runners to stretch out their hamstrings to reduce the load on the quadriceps and the resulting patellar pressure. Heel cord flexibility will also lessen the need for shock-absorbing knee flexion and pronation of the feet.

An infrapatellar knee brace or strap, snugged over the patellar tendon, will occasionally relieve the pain behind the runner's kneecap.[81] The brace displaces the patella upward and tilts it slightly anterior, altering patellofemoral relationships without impeding patellar mobility.

The rehabilitation program for an athlete with chondromalacia of the patella comprises four phases.[24] In phase I, symptomatic control is gained by activity modification and taking an anti-inflammatory medicine regularly. The athlete takes two aspirin four times a day or ibuprofen to arrest cartilage degradation by inhibiting proteoglycan synthesis and cathepsin.[132] He may need to walk with crutches until the knee pain abates.

In phase II, strengthening exercises begin, starting with isometrics for the quadriceps and isotonic exercises for the hamstrings. When he begins short arcs on a knee table, they are in the ranges that do not produce knee pain. The first 30° are usually pain free because the patella does not seat itself in the femoral groove until this angle has been reached. If the athlete has pain throughout the range of motion, he does the resistive exercises only with his knee in full extension. Phase III begins when symptoms are under control and the athlete is lifting a predetermined weight calculated from his sound side strength. In this activity phase, he begins a graduated straight-ahead running program. Cuts, hard stops and starts, jumps and figure-eight runs are added when he has reached the weight goals. In phase IV, the athlete follows a maintenance program of resistance exercises two or three times a week.

Case Report

A female runner has developed retropatellar right knee pain after increasing her mileage. She is right-handed with right shoulder droop. She has bowed legs, pes planus, and "Greek" toes (the second toe is longer than the great toe), conditions that indicate a hypermobile foot. Her left leg is from ¼ to ½ inch longer than her right one. A ¼ inch difference is perfectly normal, but even this mild difference can contribute to running injuries. The callus under her right second metatarsal head is more prominent than the one on her left foot. Her knee is tender when the kneecap is pressed into the sulcus and crunches during flexion and extension against resistance.

During treadmill testing, her right foot turns out and overpronates. The outsole of the heels of her running shoes has worn down on the lateral sides nearly to the midsole, and the shoe counters have collapsed medially. She wears very flexible walking shoes and sneakers. X-ray films show a normal AP and sunrise view, but the lateral view shows sclerosis in the middle of the kneecap just beneath the articular surface.

She has typical signs and symptoms caused by excessive pronation. As her foot collapses, her knee flexes and turns in. When her foot straightens, her knee then extends and turns out. All of this activity within a fraction of a second overloads her knees. Repeated a thousand times a mile, this stress may produce pain by shearing the articular cartilage and stressing its junction with the subchondral bone.

To help this runner understand her problem, I show her the treadmill video, pointing out the overpronation on the right. I describe how overpronation produces a sideward slide of the patella. To reduce the pronation, I advise her to purchase a new pair of running shoes. The shoes should have straight lasts, extended medial counters, and dual density midsoles. If she had already had a good pair of shoes, I would have provided her with a pair of Lynco orthotics with medial heel wedges. I also stress the importance of wearing firmer street shoes with good counters.

The therapist instructs her in how to do a progressive resistance knee-strengthening program and outlines a return-to-running program. She learns how to strengthen her arch and how to do a home treatment program, including moist heat, massage, and icing. Before long walks, she will take two buffered aspirin or ibuprofen.

Surgery for Chondromalacia Patella

If symptoms persist despite the rehabilitation program, arthroscopic surgery may be indicated.[122] Softened blisters of articular cartilage may be punctured at surgery and the area shaved. Fibrillations and chunks and the softened cartilage at the edge of the lesions may be removed with a side-biting basket forceps, a pituitary rongeur, or power-shaving equipment. This procedure makes the knee less noisy and usually gives temporary improvement.

Although long-term improvement is less likely, the removal of catching chunks may lessen the pain and stop the knee from catching. Further, the debridement should allow more aggressive rehabilitation, a stronger knee, and perhaps long-term relief of symptoms.

An arthroscopic lateral release is indicated in chondromalacia if there is excessive lateral tightness. However, the finding of a subluxed patella during arthroscopic surgery, for a torn meniscus, for example, does not mandate a lateral release. Some patellar subluxation is asymptomatic, and a preventive lateral release is not justified in asymptomatic cases.

Bipartite Patella and Patellar Fracture

Occasionally an extra ossification center of the patella may be seen in its supralateral segment on an anteroposterior x-ray film of the knee (Figure 12-16). This segment is separated from the rest of the patella by a lucent line of fibrocartilage, producing a "bipartite patella," and the extra ossification center may sometimes be lateral or distal. Three percent of the population have separate patellar ossification centers, and 30% of this proportion have bilateral, bipartite patellae.

A bipartite patella may be painful,[150] with pain sometimes arising from direct injury to the knee, or the onset may be gradual. The quadriceps tendon usually attaches to these segments, and mobility in the synchondrosis produces pain. The segment may abut against the lateral femoral condyle or ride over it to contribute to abnormal motion of the kneecap in the intercondylar sulcus, producing chondromalacia. Kneeling hurts, and the athlete's kneecap may catch. The area of the separate ossification center is tender, and a cylinder cast may be applied; however, if pain recurs and the area remains tender, the segment may have to be resected. A fracture line may pass through the synchondrosis of a bipartite patella, and healing with callus may occur.

The patella protects the femoral condyles. If it is struck by a baseball, for example, a stellate fracture may result. However, because cancellous bone heals quickly, early motion is allowed. Transverse fractures of the patella are not common in athletes, since they usually affect porotic bone. The tendinous extensor mechanism of the athlete will usually rupture before a transverse fracture can occur, and, if there is separation or a step-off of the articular surface of a patella fracture, it should be fixed with an encircled wire or pins.

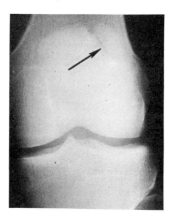 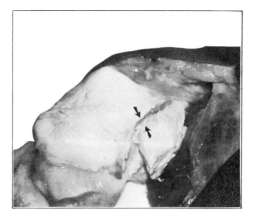

Figure 12-16   A bipartite patella may be painful at the fibrous union and may lead to chondromalacia because of abnormal tracking of the patella. At operation, the fibrous union may be separated (*arrows*). Note chondromalacia of the patella at the left of the arrows.

"Jumper's Knee"

"Jumper's knee" is a patellar or quadriceps tendinitis that results from traction stress[10] when overload produces focal degeneration of the tendon and a tearing of its fibers. There may also be some local circulatory impairment, as in the supraspinatus tendon or biceps tendon ischemia of swimmers. Some athletes also may have an aberrant immunologic response to injury that worsens the condition.

The symptoms of jumper's knee may appear after jumping or kicking, climbing or running, and although the pain may start after only one jump it more often follows repetitive activities. The aching and tenderness reside just above the patella or inferior to the patella along the patellar tendon.

In the initial phase of jumper's knee, pain appears only after athletics, with no functional impairment.[10] In phase II, the pain occurs during the activity and persists after it, but the athlete still can perform satisfactorily. Phase III is characterized by pain that occurs during activity and is prolonged afterward, making it difficult for the athlete to perform at his accustomed level.

To diagnose jumper's knee, the examiner feels for point tenderness near the patella and notes pain when the athlete extends his knee against manual resistance. On x-ray film, a search is made for a lucency in the inferior pole of the patella, a prolonged patellar pole, a fracture or irregularity in the inferior pole, some calcium within the tendon, or an avulsion of bone from the patella. Jumper's knee must not be seen as a benign, limited condition, for it results in some loss of continuity of fibers, and then mucoid degeneration, fibrinoid necrosis, and scarred nodules may develop.[133] Soreness sometimes presages rupture of the extensor mechanism if heavy plyometric stress is applied during this period.

To treat jumper's knee in phases I and II, have the athlete warm up his knee before exercise in a warm whirlpool or with warm packs. After exercise, he should use ice massage, an ice towel, or an ice whirlpool. If he is given phenylbutazone, he should not be allowed to exercise against resistance, and he must stop plyometric exercises and running. Local steroids are effective in reducing inflammation and pain but are dangerous because they act to degrade the collagen in the tendon. Steroids may also mask symptoms so completely that the athlete may overuse the limb, rupturing a major tendon.

A phase III jumper's knee should be rested. If pain persists while walking, curative surgery may be recommended. Granulation tissue and mucoid degeneration occasionally occupy a hole in the distal pole of the patella, a deposit similar to that residing under and in the extensor carpal radialis brevis of a tennis elbow. The material may be scraped out through a longitudinal slit in the patella tendon without otherwise disrupting the tendon. The precise area of tenderness may be located under local anesthesia, but the procedure is ordinarily done under general anesthesia.[133] Percutaneous "needling" of the area of soreness sometimes is curative (Figure 12-17). The tendon is stuck 20 times but is never injected with cortisone. Five weeks after needling, the athlete may be symptom free.

Patellar Tendon Rupture

Patellar tendon soreness sometimes precedes a catastrophic major tendon rupture, since the tendon may be pulled from its origin at the inferior pole of the patella (Figure 12-18). Only rarely will it rupture through its midportion.

In one instance while cinematographic data were being accumulated for a biomechanical analysis of Olympic-style weight lifting, the patellar tendon rupture of an American light-heavyweight national champion was photographed.[157] The rupture occurred as he attempted to clean a weight more than twice as heavy as his body. Kinetic analysis of the lift established that when the tendon failed, patellar tendon tension was about 18 times the lifter's body weight and the angle of his knee joint was about $90°$.

The best approach to major tendon rupture is a preventive one, since major tears can retire an athlete. Complete warm-up and the purest technique are encouraged, and an athlete with major tendon soreness or who is being treated with an anti-inflammatory medicine should avoid heavy training.

Major tendon tears are operated on early to

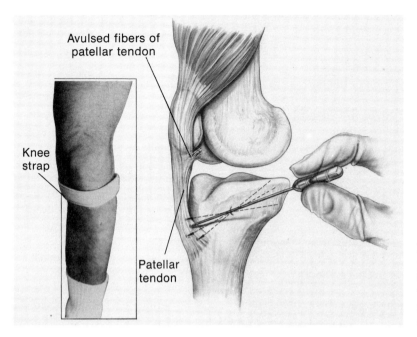

Avulsed fibers of
patellar tendon

Knee
strap

Patellar
tendon

Figure 12-17   Intractable
patellar tendinitis may
respond to "needling." The
tendon is stuck 20 times but
is never injected with
cortisone.

allow anatomic repair before the tissue swells and weakens. The distal pole of the patella is freshened and the tendon reattached through drill holes. A pin is then placed through the tibia and a wire looped around the patella and attached to the pin to prevent any separation from occurring at the anastomosis (Figure 12-18).

Rehabilitation after a repair of the patellar tendon, as in that after repair of a quadriceps tendon, demands a fine tuning of the flexion program. For athletes such as collegiate and freestyle wrestlers, rodeo cowboys, hockey defensemen, and Olympic-style weight lifters, restoration of deep knee flexion is extremely important. Bicycle riding and contract–relax techniques are effective aids in restoring flexion.

Traumatic Tibial Epiphysitis (Osgood–Schlatter's Condition)

The powerful quadriceps complex inserts into a small area of the tibial tubercle. Sudden contraction of this complex, as in plyometric exercises, may avulse some formative tissue, and the epiphysis may separate, resulting in knee pain at the tibial tubercle and development of the "knee knob" seen in many athletically active youths.

There are four stages of change in the proximal tibial epiphysis during adolescent growth,[102] beginning with the cartilage stage followed by the apophyseal stage. In the apophyseal stage, ossification centers form within a cartilage plate that projects down like a tongue in front of the tibia. The third phase is the epiphyseal, in which the ossification centers fuse to the rest of the epiphysis. Stage four is closure of the growth plate.

Disruptions at the plate usually occur when girls are between the ages of 8 and 13 years and boys, between 10 and 15 years. At one time boys with tibial tubercle epiphysitis outnumbered girls with this condition, but the ratio is changing as more females participate in athletics.

To diagnose tibial epiphysitis, the examiner observes for tenderness and swelling at the tibial tubercle and for pain when the young athlete extends the knee against his manual resistance. The x-ray picture will depend on the stage of development of the epiphysis. A true lateral view of the tibial tubercle with the knee turned slightly inward should be taken.

In the early stages of tibial epiphysitis, there may be no apparent change except for swelling visible on x-ray film. Avulsed fragments of various sizes can be observed during the apophyseal or epiphyseal stages (Figure 12-19). These findings are not the main criteria for a diagnosis or

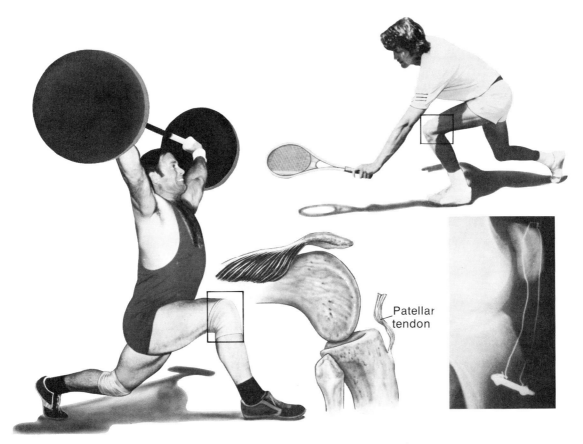

Patellar
tendon

Figure 12-18   The patellar tendon may rupture during a plyometric activity with the knee bent to about 90°. It usually rips from the patella, producing a patella alta. Wire and bolt are used to reduce tension from the repair.

for the selection of treatment for tibial epiphysitis. X-ray films of the two knees should be compared. Although the symptomatic epiphysis looks disrupted, the opposite epiphysis will sometimes look the same. Occasionally, the worst looking x-ray changes will be on the asymptomatic side. X-ray films are still important, however, in evaluating traumatic tibial epiphysitis, since more serious conditions may cause pain, tenderness, and swelling in this region.[22] Osteomyelitis and arteriovenous malformations, for example, although uncommon may be found here, and the dreaded osteosarcoma remains a remote possibility.[22]

Ice and compression are used during the acute phase of tibial tubercle epiphysitis, and a reduction of athletic activity will usually allow healing. When the soreness leaves, quadriceps stretching is begun, and a free knee strap can then be worn over the painful region as a counterforce brace

(Figure 12-19). If the young athlete will not slow down, a lightweight cylinder cast may be applied. Local steroids should not be used because these will degrade the tendon. Any avulsed piece of bone seen on x-ray film, or a palpated loose piece, should be removed (Figure 12-20). Most youngsters will have tight quadriceps from sitting all day in school. To prevent tibial tubercle epiphysitis, they should stretch their quadriceps during the warm-up before practices and games, just as they must stretch heel cords to avoid runner's bumps.

Tibial Tubercle Fractures

When a kick is interrupted by striking an opponent or by catching one's cleats in the turf, the patellar tendon may overpull and fracture the tibial tubercle. There are three types (Figure 12-21)

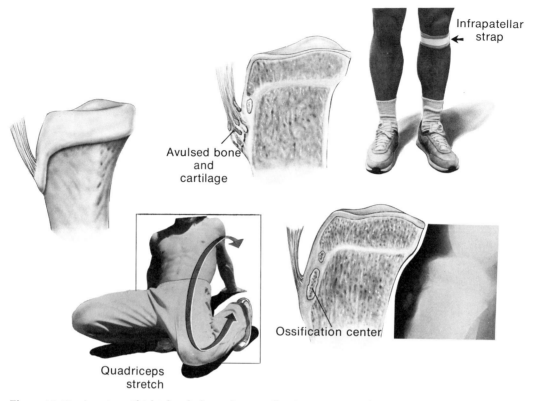

Infrapatellar
strap

Avulsed bone
and
cartilage

Quadriceps
stretch

Ossification center

Figure 12-19   A mature tibial tubercle forms from ossification centers in the epiphysis. Tugs by the patellar tendon may avulse cartilage and bone from the developing tibial tubercle. This irritation may be prevented by quadriceps stretching. An infrapatellar strap may take some strain off the tubercle.

of tibial tubercle fractures.[149] Type I is an avulsion of the tubercle, and the avulsed piece may be pulled up to the level of the knee joint. A type II fracture is a type III epiphyseal fracture that does not enter the knee joint but allows the tubercle to hinge upward. A type III tubercle fracture is a progression of a type II fracture into the knee joint. Again, the fragment may be displaced proximal to the tibia.

If a tibial fracture occurs during the cartilage stage, there may be no x-ray sign of the condition other than patella alta.[80] The radiolucent cartilage may have been pulled up to the level of the joint, and the young athlete will be unable to extend his knee. Distantly displaced avulsion fractures and displaced type III fractures require reattachment of the piece to its original site.

Lateral Side Problems

The Iliotibial Band Friction Syndrome

The iliotibial band, a thick extension of the fascia lata, is attached to the lateral intermuscular septum and the quadriceps muscle fascia, inserting at the tibial tubercle of Gerdy. With the knee extended, the iliotibial band lies anterior to the axis of knee flexion, and when the knee is flexed the band passes posterior to this axis (Figure 12-22).

During downhill running, the iliotibial band overrides and rubs on the prominent lateral epicondyle to produce a bursitis, a condition that mostly affects distance runners and some cyclists and skiers. The runner often has bowlegs or has

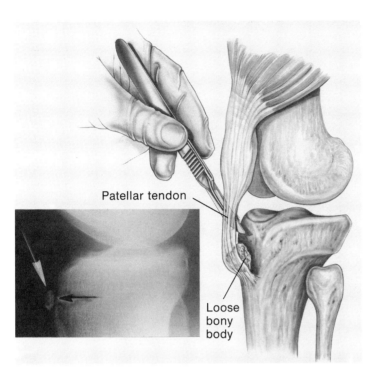

Patellar tendon

Loose
bony
body

Figure 12-20 A loose bony body behind the patellar tendon near its insertion into the tibial tubercle can best be seen *(arrow)* on a lateral x-ray film with the leg rotated inward about 10°. The bony piece is removed by sharp dissection.

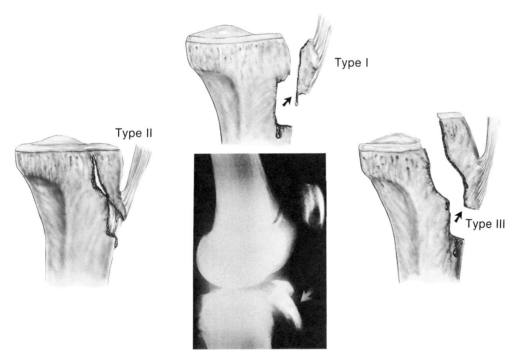

Type I

Type II

Type III

Figure 12-21 The tibial tubercle may be partly or completely avulsed. If fully avulsed, it should be replaced and fixed with a screw.

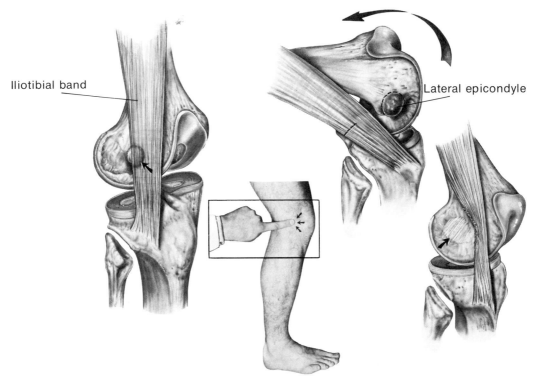

Figure 12-22   With flexion and extension of the knee, the iliotibial band moves back and forth over the lateral epicondyle. There is tenderness over the epicondyle when the knee is flexed to 30°; the condition may be relieved by sectioning the posterior third of the band and resecting the bony prominence.

allowed the outer side of his shoes to wear down. The pain starts or is worsened by running on banked surfaces, where overpronation produces obligatory internal tibial rotation. The friction syndrome is less frequent in racket sports, in which running is not continuous.

Flexed-knee activities hurt, and the lateral femoral condyle is tender. The knee creaks, resembling the sound of a finger rubbing over a wet balloon.[131] For diagnosis, the knee is flexed to 90°, and the examiner presses on the lateral epicondyle or 1 cm to 2 cm proximal to it (Figure 12-22). As the knee is gradually extended, the epicondylar area will become painful at 30°. The pain may also be produced by having the athlete support all his body weight with his knee flexed to 30°.

The athlete with iliotibial band friction should reduce his training mileage and avoid downhill runs, and the pain can be relieved by walking with the knee straight. An oral antiinflammatory drug or a local steroid may be given. If the condition fails to respond to these measures, the posterior 2 cm of the band may have to be sectioned across the line of its fibers, leaving a gap over the epicondylar prominence at 30° of flexion.[107]

Popliteus Tenosynovitis

The popliteus muscle arises from the lateral femoral condyle as a pencil-sized, synovium-ensheathed tendon. It passes deep to the fibular collateral ligament in a recess that separates the lateral meniscus from the ligament (Figure 12-23). The tendon also attaches to the lateral meniscus and the fibula to form a conjoined tendon whose muscle belly inserts on the tibia.[78] This muscle assists the posterior cruciate in retarding forward

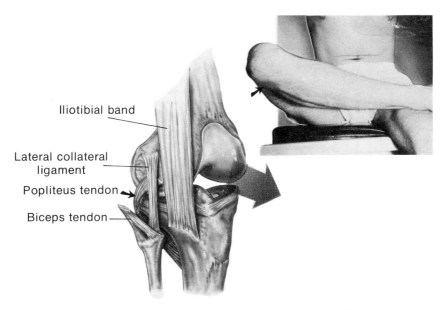

Iliotibial band

Lateral collateral
ligament

Popliteus tendon

Biceps tendon

Figure 12-23 The popliteus helps to restrict forward motion of the femur. The tendon is subjected to increased stress and becomes irritated during downhill runs. The figure-of-four position makes the lateral collateral ligament prominent. The tender popliteus tendon lies just anterior to this ligament.

displacement of the femur on the relatively fixed tibia during the stance phase, especially during downhill running.[5] It helps to bring about and maintain internal rotation of the tibia on the femur shortly before heel strike and continuing through three fourths of the stance phase.[89] This action prevents the lateral femoral condyle from rotating off the lateral tibial plateau. The popliteus also retracts the posterior arch of the lateral meniscus.

Tenosynovitis of the popliteus tendon may produce pain at the lateral side of a runner's knee.[91] The subject will often relate a recent history of downhill work. Overpronation on banked surfaces produces obligatory internal tibial rotation that places more traction on the popliteus, causing backpackers, for example, to report lateral knee pain and a peculiar crunching sound while descending from mountains. Cutting athletes have pain and sometimes describe the same crunching sound during sidestep cuts, when the femur is rotated internally on the tibia.

To diagnose popliteus tenosynovitis, the examiner should have the athlete sit in the figure-four position with the lateral side of the ankle of his affected leg resting on his opposite knee (Figure 12-23). This position makes the lateral collateral ligament prominent, and the popliteus may be palpated just anterior to the ligament and above the joint line. The symptoms of this disorder must be differentiated from those of a lateral meniscus tear. The athlete with popliteus tenosynovitis will not report the acute injury, the giving-way, or the locking that is characteristic of a worn lateral meniscus.

Oral nonsteroidal anti-inflammatory medicine may be given to an athlete with popliteus tenosynovitis, or a steroid may be instilled into the bursa about the tendon. If the athlete must run hills, he should run up the hills and ride down; changing the side of the road on which he runs may also help.

The Proximal Tibiofibular Joint

A violent twist, as in water skiing, may disrupt an athlete's proximal tibiofibular joint. The fibula may also be dislocated posteriorly when a rider's knee is caught between a gate or tree and the horse. If there is pain at the proximal fibula, it may also mean a fracture or dislocation of the upper fibula.[121]

The examiner must be especially alert for these injuries, comparing symmetrical x-ray views of both knees. If an athlete develops chronic subluxation or chronic postinjury arthritis of the proximal tibiofibular joint, the fibular head may have to be resected. Care to protect the peroneal nerves must be taken during this procedure.

INTRA-ARTICULAR DISORDERS

The Swollen Knee

Immediate Swelling

If an athlete's knee swells with blood immediately after an injury, he probably has ruptured his anterior cruciate ligament. Other causes of acute hemarthrosis include peripheral meniscus tears, a dislocated patella with rupture of the medial retinaculum, osteochondral fractures, and grade II or grade III collateral ligament sprains. If the injury is a seemingly mild one, a bleeding diathesis must be suspected. Arthroscopic evaluation of the acutely swollen knee allows the surgeon to remove the blood, define the abnormality, perform any needed repairs, and provide a prognosis for the athlete. Combinations of injuries are sometimes found, such as when a meniscus tear is associated with an anterior cruciate rupture.

Delayed Swelling

An athlete's knee may be injured and swell slowly to melon size overnight. This delayed swelling may be due to diffuse irritation of the synovium, pinching or bruising of the villi, a meniscal tear, a chondral fracture, or a grade I capsular sprain, causing the synovium to react and produce synovial fluid.

The synovium is a loose arrangement of cells: Some are synthesizing protein and glycosamino-

glycans, whereas others are phagocytes.[136] It is highly vascular with many nerve endings, although most nerve endings at the knee are in the capsule. A knee normally contains only about 1 ml of synovial fluid. This fluid sweeps over 28 cm^2 (43 sq in) of synovial surface to lubricate the joint and also provides nutrition for the articular cartilage and the fibrocartilaginous menisci. Because synovial fluid does not contain fibrinogen, it normally cannot clot.

Diffuse irritation of the synovium and pinching or bruising of the villi cause the synovium to react and produce synovial fluid. Early in a traumatic effusion, the transudation of fluid into the joint is so pronounced that it outruns the hyaluronate-synthesizing capacity of the lining cells; thus the viscosity of this fluid is low.

A large knee effusion inhibits quadriceps contraction and makes exercise difficult, resulting in a rapid decrease of quadriceps strength. The moderately to severely swollen knee should be sterilely aspirated to reduce capsular tension and relieve pain. This procedure also helps to establish a diagnosis and allows early effective quadriceps exercise.

The examiner first prepares the swollen knee with iodine. After injecting a local anesthetic by means of a 25-gauge needle into the skin and subjacent tissues near the superolateral pole of the patella, he aspirates the knee with an 18-gauge needle (Figure 12-24). After aspirating, he wraps the knee in a cotton roll and holds the roll in place with an elastic wrap. The athlete then uses crutches and starts setting his quadriceps to pump out the remaining fluid, to prevent muscle atrophy, and to give a head start to rehabilitation. On the day after the aspiration, the compressive cotton roll should be removed and cryotherapy begun.

In a traumatic synovitis, the aspirated fluid is initially clear and straw-colored, but during the aspiration it turns pink as blood from the needle puncture is added. If the fluid is drawn up in a plastic syringe, the walls of the syringe will give it a cloudy appearance. The fluid should be transferred to a clear test tube to allow the examiner to determine whether it is cloudy by attempting to read print through it. Because episodes of gout, pseudogout, or rheumatoid arthritis are some-

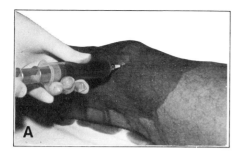

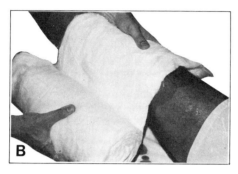

Figure 12-24 A swollen knee joint may be aspirated with little pain through a superolateral puncture **(A)**. The knee is then wrapped with a snug, but comfortable, cotton roll **(B)**. Extensions from the catcher's shin guards are now available to protect the suprapatellar area of the knee **(C)**.

times associated with a joint injury, a wet smear should be done when fluid appears abnormal and the sample sent to the laboratory for synovianalysis. A bloody effusion indicates a damaged joint lining and possible torn ligaments. If a fracture enters the joint, fat droplets will be found in the bloody fluid.

The Knee Plica

In the embryo, a septum normally separates the suprapatellar pouch from the major part of the knee joint. This usually disappears, but in one of five knees it will persist into adult life as a fibrous band, beginning at the undersurface of the quadriceps tendon just above the patella and extending transversely in this region to insert on the medial wall of the knee joint[29] (Figure 12-25). The inner edge of the band may be round, smooth, sharp, or transparent. Loose bodies may hide behind it, but it rarely causes snapping or pain.

A medial plica is found in 50% of knees and is clinically more significant. This synovial fold begins on the medial wall of the knee joint, proceeding obliquely downward to insert into the synovium covering the infrapatellar fat pad. Most plicas, however, are soft and pliable synovial folds that are asymptomatic. A large, thick medial patella plica is like a fibrotic shelf and may produce chondromalacia of the medial femoral condyle and of the medial facet of the patella.

The athlete with a symptomatic medial plica will often give a history of having fallen onto the knee. The anteromedial pain increases with activity. The plica also provokes pain when the athlete sits for a long time with this knee flexed, stretching the plica across the medial femoral condyle. This stretching may occur while sitting in a movie theater, or on an airplane flight, or during yoga exercises. A fenestrated plica may snap or produce pseudolocking, a catching sensation that mimics the symptoms of a torn meniscus.

When the athlete is asked to point to the site

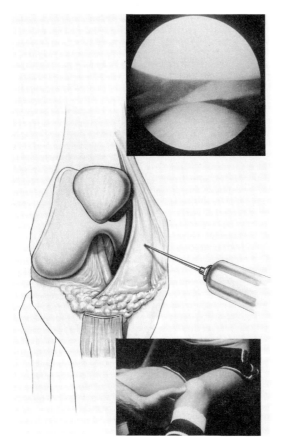

Figure 12-25   A medial plica may be injected with cortisone.

creased stretch on the plica. The athlete should also use the Home Treatment Program (see Chap. 1). A local steroid shot into the plica at varying angles may relieve symptoms (Figure 12-25). However, if faulty mechanics are the cause of the problem, the pain will recur. If corrective exercises and a local steroid injection prove ineffective, an arthroscopic assessment may be indicated.[135]

The surgeon should remove a 1-cm segment of plica down to, but not through, the synovial wall. If the surgeon merely divides a plica, it may rejoin and symptoms will recur. If the fold is incised down into the subcutaneous fat or if the plica is completely excised into the subcutaneous fat, a tight, fibrous scar may form, causing more symptoms than did the plica.

Just because a plica is seen at arthroscopy does not mean that it is the cause of symptoms or will cause symptoms. If there are no anteromedial symptoms, the plica need not be removed. If the plica is a fenestrated one, however, it should be removed because it may otherwise produce catching. Inflamed plicas are often broad and fibrotic. The severity of symptoms, however, is not always proportional to the thickness or width of the fold. In fact, removal of a very thin plica in a distance runner with anteromedial pain may relieve the symptoms.

of the discomfort with one finger, he will point to the plica area. The examiner can sometimes feel the plica, and it may be tender as he rolls it under his thumb. To roll the plica, the examiner flexes the athlete's knee to about 40° and rolls his thumb over the medial femoral condyle adjacent to the medial side of the patella, just above the joint line.

A notch in the medial femoral condyle on a sunrise x-ray film may indirectly indicate the presence of a plica. Further, a lateral x-ray film taken during an arthrogram may show dye outlining the plica.

An athlete with bowed legs or flexible flat feet and anteromedial knee pain may be cured with a pair of orthotics. Balancing the foot in neutral position results in less knee rotation and de-

Chondral Fracture and Osteochondral Fracture of the Patella or of the Femoral Condyle

A fall on the knee or a dislocation of the patella or a twisting injury to the athlete's knee can produce a chondral or an osteochondral fracture of the patella or of a femoral condyle. In a skeletally mature person, a chondral fracture is more commonly seen than an osteochondral one.[51] The cartilage breaks across calcified cartilage at the "tidemark" or transition zone. In an adolescent, the same injury force is more likely to produce an osteochondral fracture as the force extends vertically into the subchondral bone.

The symptoms produced by either type of fracture may mimic a meniscal tear, plica, a retropatellar disorder, or knee joint instability. These symptoms may include catching, giving way, and

joint line tenderness. If the examiner is not suspicious of a fracture, treatment is likely to be delayed and the athlete may suffer chronic disability.

A chondral fracture may produce an effusion but usually not a hemarthrosis. An x-ray film will not show the fracture, but an arthrogram may show a slight irregularity of the articular surface. If the examiner suspects a chondral fracture, the best diagnostic tool is arthroscopy. In contrast to a chondral fracture, an osteochondral fracture usually produces a hemarthrosis that contains fat droplets. The fracture can be seen on x-ray films as a sliver of bone. A small chondral fracture will heal only incompletely, if at all, and a larger one will not heal. At arthroscopy, the loose fragment may be removed with a basket forceps or with a rongeur. If the cartilage separates deeper, cortical bone may be exposed. In such a case, the surgeon can assist healing by drilling or excising the bony base, in effect converting the lesion to an osteochondral fracture with a floor of cancellous bone. Fibrocartilage may then grow into the defect, filling it somewhat and rounding it off.[88]

To treat an osteochondral fracture, the surgeon assesses the crater and determines whether to replace the fragment. An osteochondral fracture can heal, especially if it is reduced and fixed; however, if the fragment is not at a weight-bearing area or is otherwise unsuitable for replacement, it is removed.

Osteochondritis Dissecans

Osteochondritis dissecans is a separation of an osteocartilaginous piece of joint surface from subjacent bone. Teenagers and adults with this condition often relate a history of knee injury,[139] such as compression fracture, when the tibial spine jams against the lateral side of the medial femoral condyle. Osteochondritic lesions are most often on the medial femoral condyle near the insertion of the posterior cruciate ligament.[120] The posterior cruciate ligament is a possible culprit, pulling up an osteochondral flap. The defect often extends to the weight-bearing surface, as if the cartilage were on a hinge. In younger children, the defects may be associated with a growth variance

resulting from an obstruction to blood flow in the region.

Athletes with osteochondritis dissecans report knee pain, catching, recurrent swelling, and occasionally a mobile loose body in the knee. The defect may often be felt and rocked on the femoral condyle with the knee acutely flexed. To aid in the diagnosis of this condition, the knee should be flexed to 90° and the tibia rotated internally as the examiner slowly extends the knee.[152] At 30° short of full extension, a pain may occur that is quickly relieved by externally rotating the tibia at the same angle of flexion. The pain presumably arises from a lesion of the medial femoral condyle that presses on the tibial spine.

On a tunnel view (notch view) of the knee, the lesion appears as a semilunar lucent line or as patchy bone (Figure 12-26). Although most of these lesions reside on the lateral side of the medial femoral condyle, others occupy the weight-

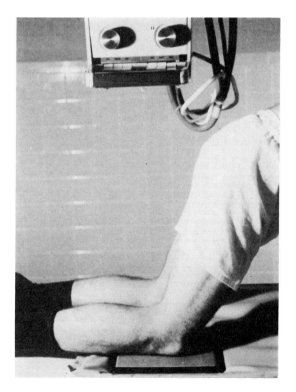

Figure 12-26   A "tunnel view" of the knee may reveal an osteochondritis dissecans at the lateral side of the medial femoral condyle.

bearing area of the medial femoral condyle, the lateral femoral condyle, or the patella.

If osteochondritis is diagnosed in a youth's knee, his activity should be limited. A lightweight cylinder cast or a splint may be needed that can be removed for active range-of-motion exercises. The lesion may take as long as a year to heal. In teenagers and adults, the surgeon should examine osteochondritic lesions through an arthroscope to determine the condition of the articular cartilage. If the fragment is stable, he may drill holes through it into the underlying bone under arthroscopic control to stimulate healing.[47] If the fragment is movable in its bed, it should be drilled and pinned. Long pins may be passed through the fragment and into the femoral condyle under arthroscopic control until they are felt beneath the skin. The pins should then be pulled further until they disappear just beneath the surface of the cartilage. These pins are removed readily through a nick in the skin after 8 weeks.[84]

A loose fragment that protrudes above the surrounding weight-bearing surface requires open surgery. The surgeon prepares a bed for the fragment by removing fibrous tissue and "freshening" the defect in the femoral condyle with many drill holes. If the fragment does not fit into the prepared defect, however, the bed should be packed with cancellous bone to make the fragment level with the surrounding joint surface, and the fragment should be secured with pins.

Loose Bodies

When a soft piece of articular cartilage frays off, or when a knee joint injury chips off a piece of cartilage or a chunk of cartilage and bone, the fragment may assume a life of its own, absorbing nutrients from the synovial fluid and growing in size. A loose body may also arise from an osteochondritis dissecans as a freed osteochondral disk. Such a loose body may move around in the joint, becoming a "joint mouse." Pieces of cartilage attached to the synovium receive nutrition through the synovium and sometimes have a bony center. An unattached, freely moving type of loose body, however, acquires a calcified center as it enlarges and its central part degenerates. Loose bodies may also include structures that can

catch in the joint, such as synovial chondromatosis, cartilage flaps, and the ends of a torn cruciate ligament.

A loose fragment may cause the knee to catch, click, pop, lock, and give way, and its elusive symptoms may lead to a misdiagnosis of a meniscal tear. Occasionally the athlete can grasp the loose body and show it to the doctor. For diagnosis, x-ray films that include oblique views are taken to track down any loose bodies with bony or calcified centers. The suprapatellar pouch region must be included in these x-rays films because a loose body sometimes finds its way into the pouch and then slips back into the knee.

A loose body may be located by arthroscopy or on an arthrogram. A positive-contrast arthrogram or an air arthrogram is preferable to a double-contrast arthrogram because bubbles may form during a double-contrast arthrogram and be mistaken for the loose body. The object may then be removed by arthroscopic surgery.

An elusive loose body may lodge in a recess, such as the lateral recess, or may hide under a meniscus or glide into the posteromedial part of the knee joint. The fluoroscope can be useful in locating a radiopaque loose body.

Arthroscopic surgery obviates the need for an arthrotomy to remove a loose body. In this procedure, the skilled arthroscopist examines the knee systematically, and if he finds a single loose body he continues his search because there may be more. The loose bodies are seized with a backbiting "jaws" forceps to prevent them from squirting away. Small loose bodies are usually removed first because larger ones can be relocated to a convenient place, such as the lateral gutter, or stabbed with an 18-gauge needle and retrieved last. The larger loose body is tucked away in this manner because its early removal may generate a "fountain" of saline through the exit wound for the entire procedure.

Intercondylar Eminence Fractures of the Tibia

When a child falls from a bicycle, the anterior cruciate ligament may yank up a piece of intercondylar eminence, causing the knee to hurt, swell, and assume a more comfortable flexed position with the hamstrings in spasm. There are three types of intercondylar eminence fractures[101] (Figure 12-27). Type I is minimally hinged; type II has a significantly hinged beak of intercondylar eminence; and type III presents a completely displaced, rotated, free-floating anterior cruciate insertion. If a displaced avulsion fracture is overlooked on x-ray films, a serious disability may result, with instability of the knee and a mobile intercondylar piece of bone.

For nondisplaced type I fractures, the hemarthrosis is aspirated so that the knee may be extended. The aspirated blood will contain fat globules, and this type of fracture will heal in an extension cast. When the x-ray film shows a type II fracture, the knee is aspirated and immobilized in extension. These knees must be handled carefully because disruption of the cartilage hinge may convert a type II to the dangerous type III. If there is doubt as to whether the fracture should be graded as type II or type III, arthroscopy of an arthrotomy should be done and the piece replaced in its bed. In type III fractures, the fragment is accurately replaced into its bed and sewn in place through drill holes in the tibia.[38]

Meniscal Tears

Meniscal tears include bowstring tears, flaps, degenerative tears, and radial and oblique tears (Figure 12-28). Tears may be solitary or there may be double or triple bowstrings or more than one type of tear in either meniscus or both menisci. The

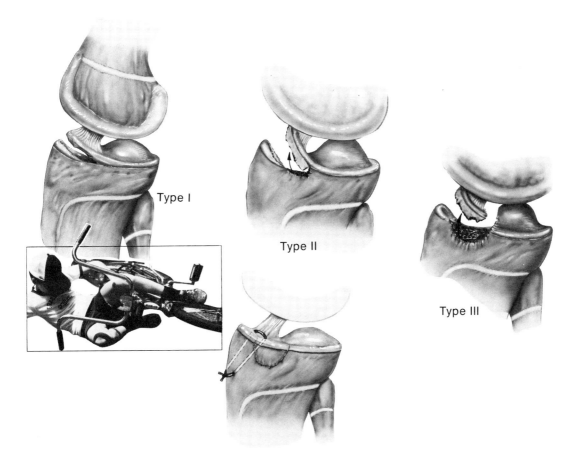

Figure 12-27 An avulsion of the intercondylar eminence, depending on the type, may need operative replacement.

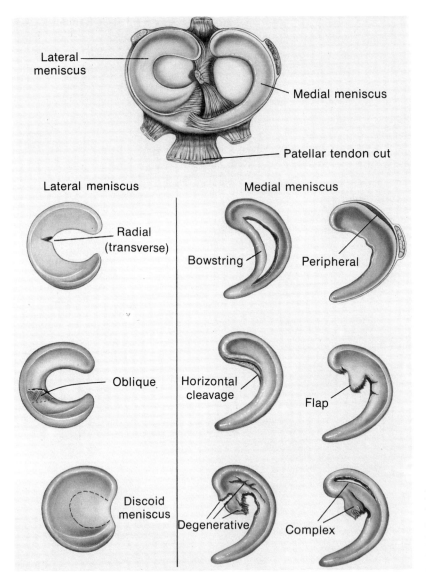

Figure 12-28 *Meniscal tears may be of many different types. Some patterns, however, are most common in either the lateral or medial meniscus.*

bowstring tear and flap tear are the major tears of the medial meniscus. Oblique tears and radial tears are more common in the lateral meniscus.

Bowstring Tears

A young athlete may suffer a bowstring tear when a blow from another player buckles his knee or when his foot catches in the turf as he cuts (Figure 12-29). During such cutting, the meniscus twists and distorts, the anterior and pos-terior horns move with the tibia, but the body of the meniscus moves with the femur. The thick femoral articular cartilage drives into the menis-cus, shearing it vertically between circumferen-tial fibers.

The tear may be one of three types, classified according to the length of the tear. Type I is a short tear, concealed under the medial femoral condyle. This tear may cause the knee to lock during a full squat and emit a thud as the knee is straightened. On the other hand, such a tear may

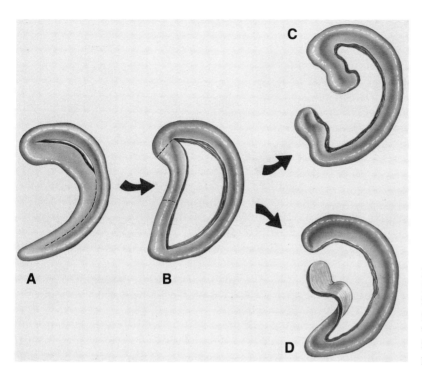

Figure 12-29 A short bowstring tear **(A)** may tear further **(B).** If the bowstring part breaks in the middle, it will produce two flaps **(C).** If it breaks at an end, it will produce one long flap **(D).**

be asymptomatic until a later injury extends it (Figure 12-29A).

A type II tear is most common. The anterior extent of the tear falls short of the anterior meniscal insertion. The bowstring piece (also called a "bucket handle") of the meniscus blocks full extension of the knee by catching between the femoral condyle and tibial plateau.

In type III tears, the split extends to the anterior tibial insertion of the meniscus. Because the bowstring lies in the intercondylar notch, it may not cause locking.

In type IV tears, the bowstring detaches at one end or breaks in the middle. The ends become round and smooth, like a bell clapper, and can catch in the knee.

Flap Tear

In older athletes, posterior horn flap tears are common. Years of friction from the femur and tibia stress the meniscus. Athletes who must move around in a crouched position, such as baseball catchers or collegiate and freestyle wres-tlers, grind the thick posterior horn of the meniscus. The horn has trouble securing nutrients, and mucoid degeneration occurs in its depths.[139] The degenerated meniscus may then split and the upper or lower piece tear loose to form a flap.

Flap tears are like loose bodies tethered at the joint line. They cause predominantly mechanical problems. When this flap catches in the joint, it produces clicking, popping, giving way, slipping, and sliding. The athlete may feel as if he is walking on uneven ground or in a plowed field. The knee may catch or give out after a minor twist. In contrast, in order for a ligamentous injury to produce these symptoms, the knee must be twisted sharply.

Not every torn meniscus produces pain and swelling because the meniscus itself does not contain pain fibers. If the meniscus catches in the joint, however, it tugs on the sensitive synovium and capsule to produce pain and swelling. Sometimes the torn part of the meniscus will remain in its normal position, with no pull on the synovium and capsule. In such cases, pain and swelling may be absent, even though the athlete has a large tear of his meniscus.

Discoid Meniscus

A discoid meniscus is one that lacks the normal concavity, instead covering most of the tibial plateau. This disorder is found in children but also may occur in older athletes.[9] A lateral discoid meniscus is the most common type, although a torn discoid medial meniscus may be found in some athletes. The disorder may produce a loud "clunking" at the lateral side of an adolescent female athlete's knee joint. It is more likely than is a normal meniscus to develop intrameniscal degenerative changes, tears, and cysts because it is pushed, pulled, and crimped between the tibia and femur. A meniscal cyst may be felt at the joint line as it becomes prominent with knee extension and recedes with knee flexion.[72]

Diagnosis

To diagnose a torn meniscus, as for any knee injury, the examiner should ask the athlete, "How, what, when, where?" Did the knee twist or give way while cutting? Was there a sharp pain or tearing sensation? Perhaps the athlete noted a momentary locking with a quick recovery of full extension as a bowstring snapped back into place.

The athlete is asked whether his knee clicks, pops, or slips. Does he feel as if he is walking on uneven ground? Such symptoms indicate catching of a meniscal flap between the femur and tibia, particularly if the athlete squats or changes direction. Giving way may also be caused by weak quadriceps, a loose body, or the proprioceptive deficiency that follows immobilization of a knee. The knee should be x-rayed to ensure that there are no loose bodies or fracture.

The examination begins with the athlete sitting with his knee extended. If there is a rubbery block to the last 15° of extension, a freed bowstring may be interposed. The blocking, however, may also be due to hamstring strain or spasm, a loose body, or, in youths, a distal femoral growth plate fracture. The examiner then checks for tenderness over the joint line. On flexion and extension of the knee, the tender spot will move as the meniscus moves. Any tenderness will usually be posteromedial, the site of most flap tears.

The three main tests for a flap tear are the squat test, the click test, and the grind test. In each of these, the examiner tries to catch the torn meniscus between the femoral condyle and tibial plateau and elicit a click, pop, and pain.

The athlete does a *deep squat*. With a meniscal tear, pain occurs at the lowest part of the squat as the posterior horn is ground between the femur and tibia. Pain that occurs while going down into the squat or coming up from it suggests a patellofemoral problem.

The *click test*, or McMurray test, is performed with the athlete on his back and begins with the knee fully flexed. The examiner's fingers feel over the joint line while the foot is held by the other hand (Figure 12-30). The leg is then rotated in an attempt to catch the flap. As the knee is extended, a click may be felt, which at times may be audible. However, any knee may be made to click or pop. A positive click test should bring pain along with the click.

The *grind test* is done with the athlete prone. The knee is flexed and traction applied to the leg, which is then rotated. This maneuver is usually painless. Then, with the knee flexed, the leg is pressed down to compress the knee joint and rotated in an attempt to catch the torn meniscus between the tibia and femur.

Arthrography

The clinical examination may complemented with an arthrogram to give the examiner more information about the integrity of the menisci. When dye is injected into the knee joint, it may leak into a meniscal tear to provide an x-ray diagnosis.[61] Single- and double-contrast arthrography with fluoroscopic and spot film techniques by experienced arthrographers have been up to 95% accurate in diagnosing meniscal tears and slightly higher for the medial meniscus.[32, 36] False-positive arthrograms are rare, but a few false-negatives do occur if a tear cannot be opened to run the dye through it.

To inject dye, the examiner should make a lateral needle puncture and aspirate the knee joint to produce a clear study. Three milliliters of a contrast medium and 30 ml of room air are then injected. If the athlete is allergic to contrast medium, an air arthrogram may be done.[32]

After injection of the dye, an elastic wrap is wound over the suprapatellar pouch to prevent

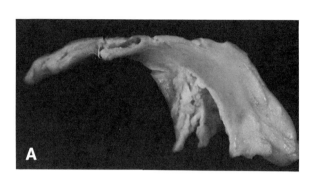

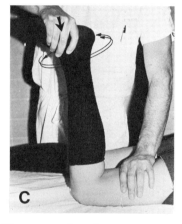
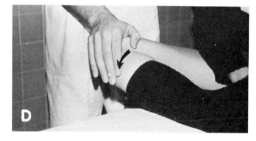

Figure 12-30 When testing for a flap tear **(A)**, the examiner tries to catch the flap between the femur and the tibia. In the click test **(B)**, the examiner first rotates the leg and then extends it. For the grind test **(C)**, he uses rotation and compression. Sometimes, the pain from a torn medial meniscus is reproduced when the knee is pressed into varus **(D)**.

the pouch from filling with contrast material. The subject then walks with the wrap on to disseminate the dye throughout the joint before multiple views of the knee, stressed and unstressed, are taken under fluoroscopic control.

If the meniscus is intact, no air or contrast material will be seen within the meniscal substance or at its periphery (Figure 12-31). Any dye that enters the meniscal wedge indicates a tear regardless of whether it is a large amount of dye or merely a veiled streak of contrast.

The frequently torn posterior horn of the medial meniscus is easily studied by arthrography. Although arthrography shows whether a tear exists, it is less helpful in depicting the configura-

tion or extent of the tear. The examiner can be misled by recesses in the anterior horn of the lateral meniscus or in the posterior horn of the medial meniscus and dye collections at the popliteal sheath. The recesses are rounded, whereas tears are sharper. Collections of dye around the sheath of the popliteus tendon make posterior longitudinal tears and the common transverse tears of the middle third of the lateral meniscus more difficult to detect.[112]

The medial meniscus is usually wedge shaped, and a tear is indicated if it appears rounded. It is also wider from front to back in most persons. If its width remains the same on each film, a meniscal tear is probable. In some

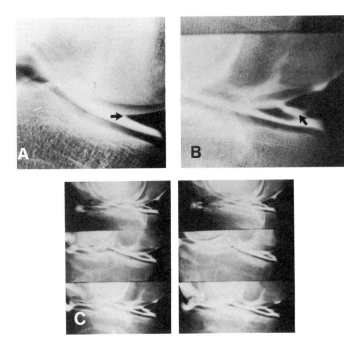

Figure 12-31 A normal meniscus appears as an uninterrupted dark wedge *(arrow)* on an arthrogram **(A)**. An arthrogram of a torn meniscus **(B)**, however, shows streaks of dye *(arrow)* within the wedge. An extensive tear is revealed by streaks of dye that invade the meniscus on many views **(C)**.

cases, however, menisci are not wider posteriorly, and the arthrographer can be fooled when this condition appears.

Arthroscopic Selective Meniscectomy

The symptoms of a meniscus tear are mostly caused by the interference of a meniscal fragment with knee mechanics. The surgeon generally removes only the offending bowstring part or the flap of the meniscus, leaving the healthy part of the meniscus behind. Compared to an open operation, operative trauma is reduced, postoperative bleeding is rare, convalescence is rapid, and the remaining part of the meniscus serves a useful function[88]—transmitting about one third of the load of a normal meniscus across the joint.

Medial Bowstring Tears

The arthroscopic surgeon may use a two portal avulsion method to remove a bowstring tear (Figure 12-32). First, he probes the meniscus to be sure that all of the necessary work areas can be reached. The meniscus tear can usually be reduced with a probe or with a #18 spinal needle. If the athlete has been walking, there may be

synovitis. If the anterior horn cannot be seen well, the synovium in that area may be trimmed with a shaver. The surgeon then uses a straight basket punch as scissors to cut partially across the posterior attachment of the bowstring. He leaves a small bridge of meniscal tissue. Next, he cuts the anterior attachment with the basket punch or scissors. The surgeon then grasps the anterior cut end with a "jaws" forcep and avulses and removes the piece. He inspects and trims the remaining rim with a power cutter to achieve a balanced and stable rim. He need remove only the fibrillations that could catch and offend the joint.

Some surgeons prefer to cut the anterior attachment first, and move the bowstring into the notch, and then cut the posterior horn, or they may free the anterior horn and use a power meniscal cutter to take out the fragment.

Horizontal Cleavage Tear

To eliminate the shearing in a horizontal cleavage tear, the surgeon may resect just the smaller leaf or the more unstable leaf. If the tear extends to the rim of the meniscus, some surgeons remove only the bottom leaf; however, the thin

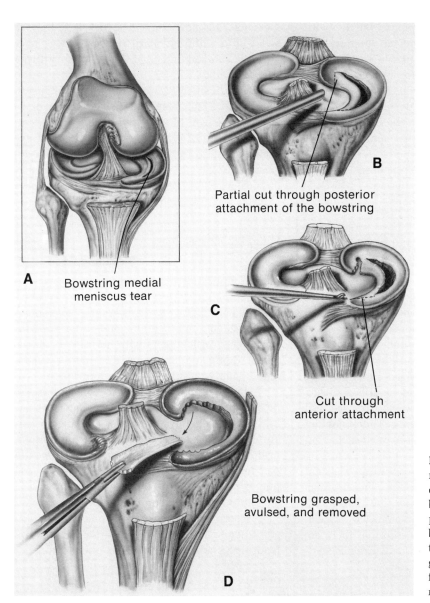

A Bowstring medial meniscus tear

B Partial cut through posterior attachment of the bowstring

C Cut through anterior attachment

D Bowstring grasped, avulsed, and removed

Figure 12-32 The surgeon may remove a bowstring tear of the medial meniscus **(A)** by partially cutting the posterior attachment of the bowstring **(B)**. He then frees the anterior attachment **(C)**, grasps the bowstring with forceps, avulses it, and removes it **(D)**.

remaining leaf may become trapped and then catch and tear. To prevent this further tearing, the upper and lower cleavage components should be resected back to normal tissue. In contrast to the above larger tears, small cleavage tears in the peripheral rim of bowstring tears are usually stable.

Medial Flap Tears

A flap tear is flat, broad, and loose at one end. Either the upper or lower leaf of a horizontal cleavage tear may become a flap. Other flaps begin as bowstring tears that, with use of the knee, split to produce one large flap or two smaller flaps (Figs. 12-29 C, D).

Flaps cause pain by catching in the joint and pulling on the sensitive capsule. A flap that flips under the meniscus will cause intermittent symptoms. Removing a flap stops the pain and catching and slows degenerative joint changes.

A flap may be partially sectioned at its base with a basket forceps or scalpel and avulsed (Figure 12-33). There is no need to hold the flap with a grasper because the meniscus has inherent tension. Further, if a clamp is placed in the joint, there is not much room left for cutting. The surgeon may also use a power meniscal cutter to remove some flaps easily. After avulsion of the flap, he must inspect and trim the rim and assess the integrity of the rest of the meniscus. What looks like a flap tear may actually be a complex degenerative tear of the posterior horn. The flap is just the "tip of the iceberg."

Degenerative Tear

If the surgeon sees that the femoral articular cartilage is worn out, he must be alert to a possible underlying degenerative meniscal tear. When badly damaged articular cartilage obscures a tear, the articular cartilage should be shaved so that the meniscus can be better seen.

The surgeon uses a basket forceps to cut nonpliable, degenerative meniscal tissue crisply. Then he employs a mechanized instrument to debride freed-up fragments of mobile meniscal tissue. Most small pieces of freed cartilage will exit through the vacuum tubing. The synovium probably can handle any small pieces that remain.

Toward the end of the procedure, an assistant can press from the outside of the knee to push the posterior rim forward a few millimeters so that the trimming can be completed. The surgeon then probes the rim to make sure that there are no nicks in the meniscus that may serve as start-ing points for new tears. If a nick is found, he bevels it to round off sharp angles.

If the surgeon finds that the articular cartilage has been eroded down to bone, he abrades the bone with a small curet or burr. This "abrasion arthroplasty" can result in the formation of fibrous tissue over the exposed bone.

Care should be taken particularly when applying stress to the knee of a person with a degenerative tear. Otherwise, in an effort to see better posteriorly by stressing an older knee, the surgeon may tear the medial collateral ligament.

Lateral Meniscus Tears

Tears in the lateral meniscus are generally more complicated than medial meniscus tears because of the mobility of the lateral meniscus and the influence of the popliteus hiatus.[78] Even bowstring tears are more complicated, often containing several vertical tears with horizontal components. Compared to the medial meniscus, the lateral meniscus suffers more anterior tears.

A radial tear of the lateral meniscus is the most common type and results from meniscal mobility. The surgeon uses basket punches to balance these tears, going from the more rigid, healthy part of the meniscus to the more mobile part near the tear (Figure 12-34). He uses a side punch to scallop the anterior postion and a straight punch to scallop the posterior part.

A lateral meniscus tears often near the popliteus tendon. Oblique tears, in particular, may extend to this area. The meniscus bridges over the

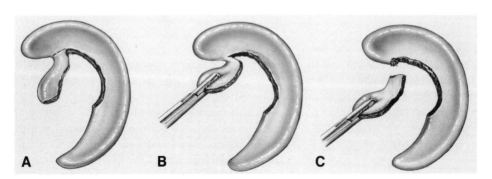

Figure 12-33   To remove a flap, the surgeon cuts its base partially (**A**—*dotted line*) with a punch. He then grasps the flap **(B),** avulses it **(C),** and trims the base.

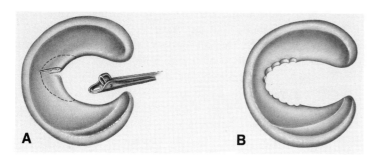

Figure 12-34   To eliminate a radial tear, the surgeon "balances" it (**A**—*dotted line*) with basket punches to produce a scalloped edge (**B**).

popliteus hiatus where the popliteus tendon lies. This bridge should be left intact. Even if a few millimeters of bridge are left, it will thicken later. If this bridge is broken, however, two large, mobile meniscal fragments are produced, destroying the peripheral hoop and allowing the meniscus to spread out. The hoop or rim of the meniscus has a containing effect on the knee joint. In cases where the popliteus bridge is lost, an almost total lateral meniscectomy is needed to remove the remaining pieces from the joint.

For lateral meniscus work, the knee is usually kept near full extension with the tibia internally rotated. The "figure-of-four" position allows an easy examination of the lateral compartment, but this position is not as good for meniscal work because fluid flow is poor and instrument breakage is possible. A posterolateral puncture is needed only rarely on the lateral side because the surgeon can see so well from the front.

Discoid Lateral Meniscus

An asymptomatic discoid meniscus should be left alone. If it is catching or producing pain, however, it may be sculpted with a basket punch to produce a C-shape. Although a thick edge is left, this edge triangulates later to become a thin, leading edge.

Meniscal Cyst

An asymptomatic meniscal cyst may be left alone or may be debrided with a mechanical cutter. In the case of a solitary cyst and meniscal tear, the tear should be resected and the cyst aspirated and trimmed.

Arthroscopic Meniscal Repair

The outer third of each meniscus has a blood supply (the red area), and tears in this area can heal. The inner two thirds (white area) are avascular and have less healing potential. Surgeons repair tears in the red area and in the red–white area. Some even repair the meniscus in the white area. Just because a meniscus repair can be done, however, does not mean that it should be done. By reattaching tears in the white area, we subject the patient to the technical problems of the repair, to immobilization, and to the possibility of future tearing through scar tissue. Further, the athlete is denied a rapid return to activity.

If the surgeon decides to repair a meniscus, he freshens the torn edges with a curet or power trimmer to stimulate healing. Suturing may be performed either "outside-in" or "inside-out." To perform an outside-in repair, the surgeon passes a spinal needle from the outside of the knee at the joint line through the tear. He threads a strand of nonabsorbable suture material through the needle, grasps it, pulls it out, and ties a knot in it. He then pulls the thread back into the joint to appose the edges of the tear. This suture is tied to an adjacent suture just outside the capsule. Nonabsorbable suture is needed because the meniscus takes about 6 weeks to heal.

To perform an inside-out repair, the surgeon places a double-barreled needle carrier into the joint and passes needles through the tear. He then ties a knot just outside the capsule. Although inside-out techniques require special equipment, they have the advantage of not leaving a small knot in the joint. After a meniscus has been repaired, the knee is immobilized in 30° to 40° of flexion for 6 weeks.

Meniscus mending demands great care because the sutures may endanger the saphenous nerve on the medial side or, when suturing in the posterior portion of the lateral meniscus, the peroneal nerve.

Open Total Meniscectomy

With the advent of arthroscopic surgery, open total meniscectomy is being used far less commonly. It is, however, sometimes necessary if a meniscus is totally torn or contains cysts that leave no healthy meniscal tissue.

A total meniscectomy removes an important shock absorber, increasing the compressive forces on the articular cartilage. The medial meniscus normally carries 60% of the load on the medial side of the knee, and the lateral meniscus carries 75% of the lateral load.[137] If the medial meniscus is removed, the force on the condyle increases threefold. It is normally 15 kg/cm^2 during walking, but after a total meniscectomy the contact area must absorb 60 kg/cm.[2,104] Further, after total meniscectomy, the semimembranous insertion into the posteromedial capsular ligament and into the posterior arch of the medial meniscus may be disrupted, rendering the corner lax and promoting giving way and a feeling of instability. The integrated motion of the knee is affected, leading to later degeneration.

The most common incisions used in this procedure are short anteromedial or short transverse incisions. The anteromedial incision may easily be extended if necessary, but a short transverse incision leaves less scar while affording excellent exposure. Some surgeons use an anteromedial skin incision with one vertical capsular incision anterior to the tibial collateral ligament and another behind the ligament.[11] Others prefer a horizontal skin incision and two capsular ones.[18]

After entering the knee joint, the surgeon searches for a fibrotic medial shelf, examines the articular cartilage of the patella and the femoral condyles, and analyzes the integrity of the anterior cruciate ligament. Both menisci are then examined, since the signs and symptoms of a medial meniscus tear may override those of a lateral meniscus tear. The ligamentum mucosum is pulled out of the way to enable the surgeon to look across the joint to the lateral compartment. This step demands skill and patience; sometimes, a transverse or longitudinal tear of the lateral meniscus is then inspected with a probe.

A posteromedial incision will allow an analysis of the posterior horn, where 75% of medial meniscus tears occur. This incision starts at the adductor tubercle region and extends along the back side of the tibial collateral ligament down to the tibia. The joint is entered through a weak spot, or "back door," between the tibial collateral ligament and the posterior oblique ligament. The meniscus is then carefully separated from the deep capsular ligament, leaving a small rim or coronary ligament to help prevent anteromedial instability. Next, the meniscus is pushed through the back door and the meniscectomy completed under direct vision. Free fragments that might have been left behind if an anterior approach only had been used are sometimes found.

After the meniscus has been removed, the knee is tested to see whether the tear has masked any instability; if so, the surgeon must deal with the instability through an extended incision. In this procedure, before the wound is closed, the posteromedial capsular ligament is pulled forward and snugged up to provide a stable knee.[54] This step is very important to the athlete, who depends on a stable knee for cuts, jumps, and stops.

Some surgeons may use an anteromedial incision for medial meniscectomy routinely. The knee is flexed and stressed to allow more of the meniscus to be seen. After the meniscotome has been passed around the periphery of the meniscus, the meniscus is pulled into the intercondylar notch (Figure 12-35). If it still lies horizontal when pulled into the notch, part of the posterior capsule is still attached. To facilitate removal of the meniscus, the vertical attachment is cut at the deep hole and the meniscus pulled forward on stretched synovium. It may now be removed easily under direct vision.

If the meniscus pops up into a vertical position when transferred to the notch—the "flip sign"—the surgeon knows that synovial attachments already have been severed fully. Only the strong vertical meniscal fibers now hold the meniscus and account for the vertical position. The flipped meniscus may be removed simply by placing the meniscotome horizontal to cut the vertical attachment.

In the knees of some older athletes, an exostosis extends posteriorly from the intercondylar eminence. This restrains the meniscus and keeps it from flipping, and the surgeon may think that the posterior capsular attachment remains. If he presses the meniscus posteriorly, however, it will pop free over the exostosis and may then be removed easily by severing its vertical attachment.

Open Lateral Meniscectomy

A lateral meniscectomy is facilitated by acutely flexing the athlete's knee, placing his foot lateral to his opposite knee, and firmly pusing the foot toward his opposite hip, a maneuver that opens the lateral joint space.[12, 13] The meniscus is removed through an incision just anterior to the iliotibial band. Another incision may be made parallel to the popliteus tendon between the iliotibial band and the fibular collateral ligament to view the entire meniscus. Meniscal cysts and tears in the posterolateral corner may also be analyzed through this incision.

Complications of Open Total Meniscectomy

The complications of open total meniscectomy may limit the future function of an athlete's knee, with complications such as instability, retained posterior horn fragments, hemarthrosis, infrapatellar numbness, and postoperative arthritis. The knee is checked for instability under anesthesia before surgery begins. After the torn meniscus has been removed, knee stability is rechecked because the meniscus may have been masking an instability.[54] To aid in preventing laxity after a total medial meniscectomy, the posteromedial corner should be advanced.

A retained posterior horn of the medial meniscus may be stable, with no attendant problems, or it may catch and tug the capsule to cause pain. The posteromedial corner should be examined through a posteromedial approach to remove these potentially catching posterior fragments.

Because hemarthrosis is common after an open meniscectomy, all bleeders should be stopped at operation and the postoperatively swollen knee aspirated early to allow effective quadriceps setting. If a painful hemarthrosis follows an open lateral meniscectomy, the surgeon should suspect that the lateral geniculate artery has been cut. This requires an operation to ligate the vessel.

The infrapatellar branch of the saphenous nerve is sometimes sectioned during an open medial meniscectomy, resulting in numbness distal to the kneecap or a painful neuroma. Athletes should be advised that such numbness may occur. Deep friction massage of the scar may prevent neuroma formation and a painful scar. If a neuroma does appear, however, it may be resected.

Half of the subjects will have normal knees after a total meniscectomy, and half will develop varying degrees of osteoarthritis[143] (Figure 12-36). After meniscectomy at a young age, those who had undergone another arthrotomy were found to have developed cartilage damage within 2 years of the first operation.[31] This arthritic aftermath attests to both instability and increased forces on the bone and cartilage.

The athlete who develops osteoarthritis of the knee after a meniscectomy may have pain and swelling. His knee will feel insecure and moments of instability will be painful, followed by additional aching. The narrow joint space implies a certain measure of instability, but dramatic improvement results if the athlete wears a helical glide brace.

Postmeniscectomy weight-bearing x-ray films often show compartmental narrowing, subchondral flattening of the distal end of the femur, and peripheral tibial spurring.[28] Valgus deformity often develops after a total meniscectomy in persons older than 40 years of age.[59] These persons should be followed up with weight-bearing x-ray films for early degenerative signs, since valgus proximal tibial osteotomy may add athletic life to the knee.

EARLY POSTOPERATIVE KNEE REHABILITATION

The Early Postoperative Knee Exercise Program

To achieve the goals of restoring muscular strength, power and endurance, flexibility, agility, and cardiovascular fitness after a knee operation,

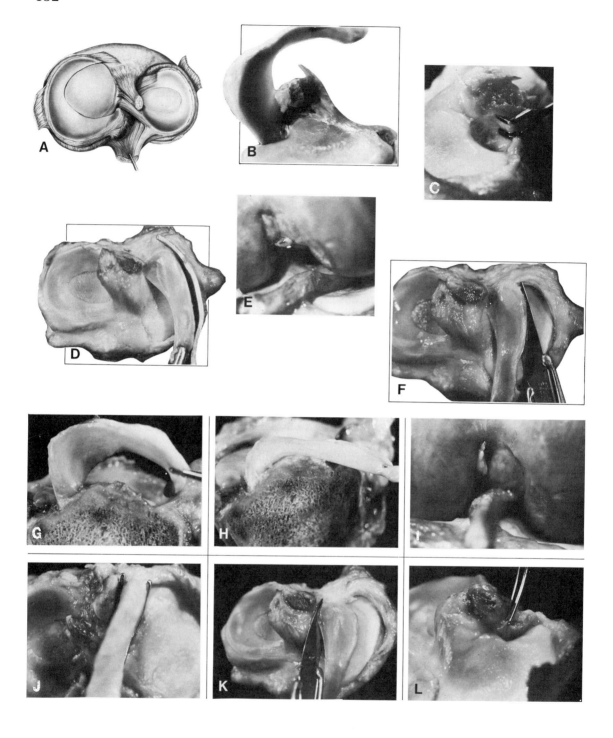

Figure 12-35 Open total meniscectomy. The medial meniscus inserts posteriorly into a deep hole behind the intercondylar eminence **(A–C).** During an open meniscectomy, the meniscotome may not cut all of the peripheral attachments of the meniscus **(D),** and the meniscus will appear to be horizontal **(E)** when it is pulled into the notch. The surgeon sometimes can sever these remaining peripheral attachments by stressing the knee into valgus and inserting the meniscotome at a different angle **(F).** Once these attachments are severed, the meniscus, owing to its remaining vertical attachment, pops up **(G).** This new vertical position is called the "flip sign." The meniscus is then pulled forward **(H),** and the surgeon knows that only the vertical attachment remains because the meniscus has "flipped" **(I).** The meniscotome now fits easily around the meniscus **(J)** over its insertion into the deep hole, and the meniscectomy may then be completed. Sometimes the surgeon may complete a medial meniscectomy wherein some peripheral attachments remain intact by first cutting the vertical attachment **(K).** The meniscus may then be easily pulled forward on its peripheral attachments, whereupon these are severed. All that is left after a "total meniscectomy" is a thin rim of meniscus and a nubbin of meniscus in the deep hole **(L).**

therapeutic exercise is the most important modality. The athlete should begin isometric exercises before the operation and reinstitute them in the recovery room to prevent a dissociation of quadriceps function and to ensure muscular stability of the joint.[155] Initially 50% contractions are performed for a few seconds before advancing to more forceful contractions, which are held for 6 seconds, 20 times a hour. Pillows are not permitted under the knee, which should be placed out straight while the subject reclines. Next comes active hip extension, with the sound foot on the floor while the upper body rests, chest down, on the training table as the hip of the operated side is extended. Hip adductors may be strengthened while sitting by squeezing a basketball between the thighs, and hip adductors may be exercised by abducting the hip while lying on the unoperated side. Ankle flexion and extension and ankle circles will also provide a beneficial calf-pumping action.

Straight Leg Raise

To assist himself in straight leg raising, the athlete places his sound leg under the ankle of his operated extremity. This technique will often permit an independent straight leg raise on the same day as the operation. A sling is also provided, or the leg may be held up so that the subject can lower the leg eccentrically with his hip flexors. The lowering technique is usually easier than raising the leg, since more eccentric than concentric work can be performed.

Walking

When the athlete can do a single leg lift, he is allowed to walk with two crutches, advancing to a single crutch on the sound side for 2 or 3 days after a week has passed. This aid should be used until he can walk unassisted without limping.

The athlete should never be allowed to limp

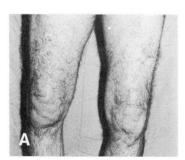
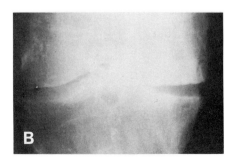

Figure 12-36 Knee arthritis may follow meniscectomy. In this case, varus deformities **(A)** have followed medial meniscectomies. An x-ray **(B)** shows that the bone is squared-off and sclerotic and the joint space is narrowed.

because even a slight limp will result in a longer period of rehabilitation. While using a cane or a single crutch, he should be instructed to bear as much weight as possible and to put pressure on the hand grips to prevent a limp. The knee is kept straight and locked when walking, and the athlete should concentrate on heel strike rather than walking flat-footed with his knee bent. He may usually begin jogging when he can lift 20% of his body weight and may run when he can lift 30% of his weight. If he does limp when running, his activities should be reduced.

Crutches

Proper crutch fitting and crutch-walking instruction and gait instruction when the athlete is ready to put the crutches aside are important.

Crutch Fitting

The athlete can be fit with crutches without having to stand on an injured leg. To obtain the length of the crutch, ask him to reach both arms straight out to the side and then to bend one of his elbows. Measure the distance from the fingertips of his extended arm to the tip of his bent elbow (Figure 12-37A). To obtain the hand grip height, have the athlete reach one arm out again and bend his elbow to 90° with his thumb up. Measure from the tip of his elbow to the tip of his thumb (Figure 12-37B).

Crutch Walking

When the athlete walks with crutches, he should advance both crutches with the injured leg (Figure 12-38A). If he is using just a single crutch, he should use it on the side opposite the injured leg (Figure 12-38B). When the athlete ascends stairs, he should lead with his uninjured leg followed by the crutches and his injured leg (Figure 12-38C). When he descends stairs, he should lead with his crutches and his injured leg (Figure 12-38D).

When the athlete is ready to walk without crutches, he should walk with his shoulders level. To check this, he can watch his shoulders as he walks toward a mirror (Figure 12-39A). When he strikes his heel, he should keep his knee straight. If he strikes his heel, keeps his knee straight, and then toes off, his shoulders will stay level (Figure 12-39B). If, however, he walks with a flat-footed gait, even though it may be faster, his shoulder will drop (Figure 12-39C). Limping is not allowed because it can aggravate the injury and set up a bad gait pattern. If the athlete limps, he should return to using a crutch or crutches.

ACUTE TEARS OF KNEE LIGAMENTS

All of the knee ligaments are involved in knee stability, and if a ligament is completely torn other supporting structures are usually damaged

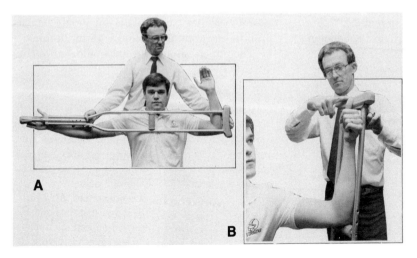

Figure 12-37 The athlete can be fit for crutches without having him stand on his injured leg. Using this technique, the length of the crutches **(A)** and the hand grip setting **(B)** are determined from upper extremity length.

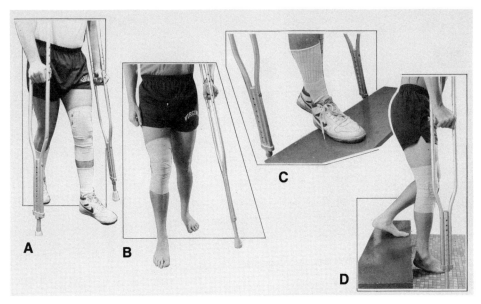

Figure 12-38   The trainer teaches the athlete how to walk with two crutches **(A)** or with one crutch **(B)** and how to walk up **(C)** and down **(D)** stairs.

too. The examiner should try to gauge the extent of the damage, since early knee ligament repair is superior to later reconstruction. Occasionally, the severest knee ligament injury does not cause much swelling, as when a tear through the capsular ligament decompresses the knee. If the knee is tense and painful, the capsule probably is intact, and, if the knee swells acutely with a hemarthrosis, the athlete probably has torn his anterior cruciate ligament.

An injured knee should be examined before it swells and muscle spasm sets in. If the knee is already swollen and the muscles are in spasm, the knee can be aspirated and some local anesthetic instilled to allow a complete examination. If there is any question about the adequacy of the examination, it should be done under general anesthesia.

Diagnostic aids such as arthroscopy and arthrography are useful in many acute knee ligament injuries.[25, 118, 146] With major ligament damage, however, the instillation of an irrigant fluid into the knee joint must be done carefully because it may lead to further swelling and produce nerve and vascular damage that endangers the limb. An arthrogram is useful for collateral ligament tears during the first 48 to 72 hours, but after this time the joint seals and dye cannot extravasate beyond the ligament. Arthrograms are not very helpful in cruciate ligament tears because the cruciates are covered by synovium, and a cruciate tear with intact synovium produces a false-negative arthrogram.

Acute Medial Ligament Tear

An acute medial knee ligament tear may be produced by forced abduction of the flexed knee with external rotation of the tibia—the "clipping" injury (Figure 12-40). As the knee is twisted, its capsular sleeve shortens to increase the pressure between the tibia and femur and to stop the external rotation. If external rotation stretches beyond this point, however, the medial capsular ligament tears and the tibial collateral ligament will also tear, especially if valgus stress is added. After the medial structures have torn, external rotation may continue along with anterior subluxation of the tibia. The anterior cruciate ligament then angles over the lateral femoral condyle and may tear, resulting in a triple lesion, including tears of the deep capsular ligament, tibial collateral ligament, and anterior cruciate ligament.

The site of a medial rupture will be tender

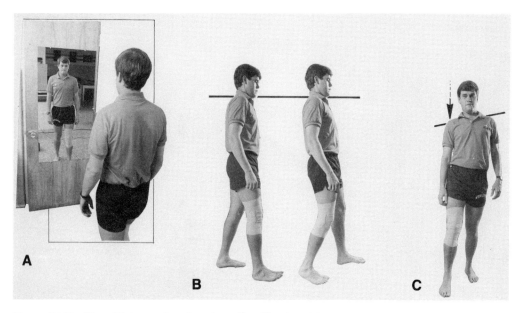

Figure 12-39   The athlete practices how to walk without crutches.

and swollen locally. The examiner tests for the integrity of the medial ligamentous structures with the athlete supine on the examining table, first examining the sound knee for baseline laxity. The knee is flexed to about 30° and valgus force applied to check the medial side (Figure 12-41).

A slight opening of the medial side to valgus stress means a medial ligament rupture; a gross test indicates a medial ligament and either an anterior cruciate or posterior cruciate rupture. If the knee opens to abduction stress in extension, the medial ligaments and both cruciates are ruptured. The knee should be examined under anesthesia if the degree of sprain is hard to determine. A young athlete's swollen and deformed knee may be caused by a fracture of the distal femoral epiphysis; thus an x-ray film should be taken before stress tests are performed (Figure 12-42).

Mild Medial Collateral Ligament Sprain

A mild (grade I) medial collateral ligament sprain indicates microscopic tearing of the ligament fibers without gross laxity. This is the most common knee injury in downhill skiing.[90] The inside edge of a ski catches, leaving the trailing limb with the leg rotated externally and the knee in

valgus. As the skier's body continues forward, the medial side of his knee is stressed.

"Breaststroker's knee" is a grade I medial collateral ligament sprain that results from the "whip kick."[65] As the swimmer's knee moves from flexion to extension during the "whip kick," his tibial collateral ligament tension increases markedly. Valgus knee stress and external rotation of the tibia accentuate the tenson. The femoral origin of his tibial collateral ligament will be tender, but the knee is stable. Ice and compression are used, and ultrasound will remove accumulated waste products. The athlete may then resume his flexibility and weight-lifting program while being advised to change his kick to a flutter kick for a time. The swimmer's breaststroke kick should be assessed, making sure that he is not abducting his hips during the recovery phase and then rapidly extending his knees with his legs apart during the thrust phase of the kick. Instead, his heels should be together during recovery and his knees apart only slightly during the thrust.

Moderate Medial Collateral Ligament Sprain

A moderate (grade II) medial collateral ligament sprain denotes a gross disruption of fibers and

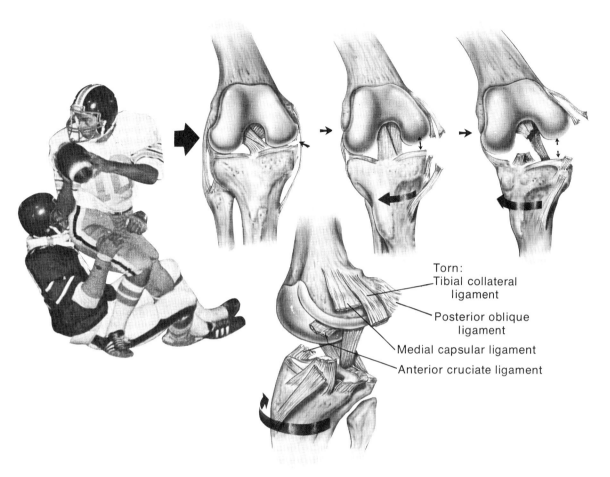

Torn:
Tibial collateral ligament
Posterior oblique ligament
Medial capsular ligament
Anterior cruciate ligament

Figure 12-40   Medial ligament tears. A "clipping"-type injury applies a valgus force to the knee. First, the medial capsular ligament tears, then the tibial collateral, and, with further force, the anterior cruciate. The medial meniscus and the posteromedial capsular ligament also usually tear during this serious injury.

loss in integrity of the substance of the ligament. The injured ligament lengthens just enough to allow moderate instability with 5° to 15° more laxity than on the sound side; however, a definite resistance end-point is felt to valgus stress. Arthroscopy will reveal whether there are any associated injuries, such as meniscal tears.

If a knee with a grade II medial collateral ligament sprain is put in a cast, muscle function deteriorates and the athlete suffers a major setback. Experimentally, the strength of intact or repaired dog medial collateral ligaments is influenced by exercise,[145] and immobilization means lack of strength. When the knees are exercised, the medial collateral ligaments show larger-diameter collagen fiber bundles and significantly higher collagen content. Moreover, immobilization leads to significant weakening of monkey ligaments, and ligament strength will not return to normal even after 20 weeks of resumed activity.[116, 117] For these reasons, many grade II medial collateral ligament sprains are treated with a brace and graded exercise rather than immobilization of the knee in a cast. A functional program will give the athlete a head start toward a return to action, since the ligament is strengthened during the recovery period.

Moderate sprains fall into two groups, de-

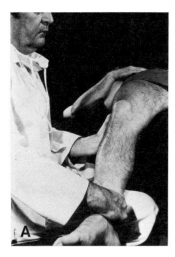
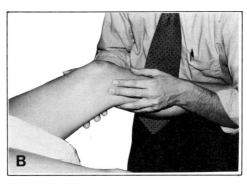

Figure 12-41   Valgus stress is applied to the knee **(A)** as the athlete allows his leg to hang comfortably over the table. This test may also be done while one hand feels for an opening of the joint **(B).**

pending on their severity,[8] and both types are initially placed in soft casts. Within a day, the last severe sprains are put in a knee immobilizer and the severer ones in a lightweight cast with a hinge. Athletes use two crutches and begin isometrics, while a maintenance strength program is begun on the sound side, along with hip flexion, extension, and abduction on the injured side. The knee immobilizer is removed three or four times a day to begin gentle knee range of motion.[26] The athlete whose knee is in a hinge cast also works on active range of motion in his cast, advancing from isometrics to isometrics against resistance around the fourth day. He then uses one crutch on the side opposite the injury. Around the sixth day, he will no longer need the crutch, and he should then concentrate on walking without a

limp while landing heel first. After 1 week, if an athlete with either of these injuries is pain free, he may begin isotonic work. When the athlete begins isotonic work, he may also start a bicycle program. This is prescribed because immobilization significantly depletes type I endurance muscle fibers of oxidative enzymes,[21] which drop even in well-controlled, progressive resistance exercise programs. Bicycle riding, or a high-speed isokinetic program, helps to maintain the enzyme levels. When the athlete can perform well on his isometric and isotonic programs, he may begin isokinetic speed work, and when the latter program is underway he may advance to graduated functional activities.

For protection against further valgus stress, a hinged, single-side knee brace has been devel-

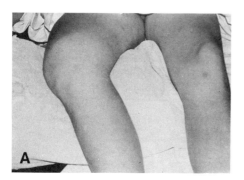
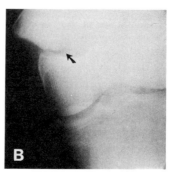

Figure 12-42   A young athlete's swollen and deformed knee **(A)** may be caused by a fracture of the distal femoral epiphysis **(B).**

oped that allows full flexion and extension of the knee while preventing stress.[125] This brace is designed to avoid the restrictions of mobility, speed, and performance commonly associated with cumbersome braces. It is useful when the athlete reenters collision sports during the period of more than 1 year when the ligament remains weaker than normal.[117] If the knee is taped, the patella must be allowed to move freely, and the popliteal region is left open. Elastic tape without underwrap is usually the most secure taping method around the knee.

Unwanted Bone in the Medial Collateral Ligament (Pellegrini–Steida's Disease)

After a partial avulsion of the medial collateral ligament from its femoral origin, heterotopic ossification may appear in the upper fibers of the medial collateral ligament.[147] Such ossification is known as Pellegrini–Steida's disease. The new bone may appear as a hard, tender swelling at the femoral origin of the medial collateral ligament, and there is pain when the knee joint is sprung with valgus stress. A local steroid injection may relieve the symptoms, but if it fails to do so the heterotopic bone may have to be resected.

Major Medial Collateral Ligament Sprain

A major (grade III) medial collateral ligament sprain may occur from being "clipped" in tackle football (see Figure 12-40).[127] The severe sprain produces an alarming instability with a mushy end-point, and the rupture will require surgical repair. The medial meniscus is first checked, and if it is torn peripherally it can be sutured to the capsule. All torn ligaments are replaced or reapproximated, and if the posteromedial capsular ligament is torn it is reinforced with the semimembranous or the medial head of the gastrocnemius.[53] A pes anserinus transfer is added to increase dynamic internal rotatory stability.

Pes Anserinus

The pes anserinus is the combined insertion of the sartorius, gracilis, and semitendinosus tendons that insert in a row down the proximal anteromedial face of the tibia. The tendons may be transferred to help control some rotatory instabilities of the knee and as an adjunct to extensor mechanism reconstruction (Figure 12-43A).[138] To transfer the pes, its insertion is dissected free, and the inferior portion is shifted superiorly. It is sutured to the patella tendon and under the metaphyseal flare. Such a transfer significantly increases its internal rotatory effectiveness.[115] Before transfer, the sartorius and gracilis, acting through greater moment arms over the wider proximal metaphysis than the short moment arm of the semitendinosus, provide three fourths of the rotatory force. The semitendinosus is normally the most efficient flexor of the three. After transfer, the semitendinosus becomes a better internal rotator, and the combined muscle moment arms are lengthened, almost doubling rotation forces at 30° and 60° of knee flexion.

After a pes transfer, the pes is strengthened isometrically, isotonically with a weight on a rope, and against the spring resistance of a pes plate (Figure 12-43B). Thereafter, when the ath-

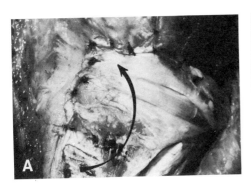
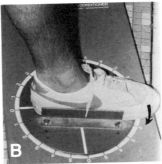

Figure 12-43 A pes anserinus transfer includes a semitendinosus transfer to just below the metaphyseal flare of the tibia **(A)**. The muscles may be restrengthened against spring resistance **(B)**.

lete cuts, he consciously "thinks internal rotation" to contract his pes.

The Acutely Torn Anterior Cruciate Ligament

The anterior cruciate ligament may tear when an athlete decelerates and changes direction (Figure 12-44). He may hear or feel a "pop" and report that his knee "slipped out." The hallmark of an acute anterior cruciate tear is, however, a rapidly developing, tense hemarthrosis.

The type of treatment decided upon for an acute tear depends on the results of the clinical examination, determination of the knee "at risk," a stability examination under anesthesia, and an arthroscopic assessment.

Clinical Examination

The injured athlete will usually have his knee flexed to about 20°. The knee holds the most fluid at this angle; this position is, therefore, most comfortable. To decompress the knee joint and ascertain the nature of the fluid contents, the examiner numbs the skin superolateral to the kneecap, aspirates the fluid cleanly through a #18 needle, and injects a local anesthetic into the joint. He checks the aspirated bloody fluid for fat droplets that would indicate a fracture.

To test for anterior cruciate ligament integrity, the examiner first performs the pull test, which is an anterior drawer test at 25° of knee flexion (Figure 12-44). This test is almost always positive in acute anterior cruciate tears. Rarely, however, it can be negative if intact menisci and intact

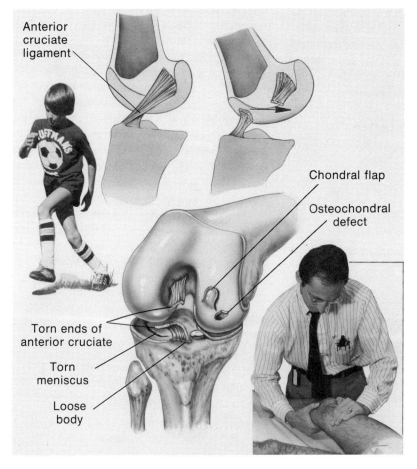

Figure 12-44 An acutely torn anterior cruciate ligament will usually produce a hemarthrosis and a positive pull test. Associated internal derangements are common such as a meniscus tear, articular cartilage fracture, osteochondral fracture, loose body, or a combination of these.

secondary restraints prohibit the tibia from coming forward.

For stability testing, the athlete should be lying on a *sturdy* examining table, or on the floor, with his back resting against the wall. His patellar tendon and hamstrings should be relaxed. If he tightens his patellar tendon, his tibia will already be subluxed forward and no excursion will occur. If the hamstrings are tight, they will prevent the tibia from moving forward. After checking for tendon tightness, the examiner pulls the tibia forward with one hand while holding the femur still with the other. If the anterior cruciate has been torn, the tibia moves forward much more than on the uninjured side.

The Knee "at Risk"

An athlete who suffers an acutely torn anterior cruciate ligament may have a knee that is "at risk." Whether a knee is at risk depends on the functional demands of the athlete, the construction of his particular knee, and the amount of additional injury that the knee sustained when the anterior cruciate was torn. A knee at risk requires a stabilization procedure to reproduce the function of the lost anterior cruciate and prevent instability, recurrent effusions, meniscal and articular damage, and arthritis.

A knee is at risk if the athlete competes in a high-performance sport. High functional demands necessitate a stabilization procedure to ensure a stable knee. The athlete should be asked about his goals. Athletes with lower functional demands may do well with exercise and bracing.

Some people have "anterior cruciate dependent" knees. This type of knee has thin capsular ligaments that serve only as weak secondary restraints, allowing the knee to go easily into recurvatum. Such a knee depends on the anterior cruciate ligament for stability. Therefore, a stabilization procedure is indicated when this kind of knee suffers an anterior cruciate ligament tear.

A stabilization procedure is also indicated if the examination under anesthesia reveals a positive pivot shift test or if the arthroscopic assessment shows meniscal or articular cartilage damage.

Arthroscopic Assessment

At arthroscopy, the injured knee is first examined under anesthesia. The examiner tests stability by stressing the knee into valgus and varus and performing a push test (posterior drawer). He then focuses on the anterior cruciate by performing a pull test and a pivot shift test. A positive pivot shift indicates severer damage to secondary restraints, raises the likelihood that there has been intra-articular damage, and warrants a stabilization procedure.

An arthroscopic assessment allows the surgeon to ascertain the amount of intra-articular damage, permits him to perform debridement or repair, and provides information for the surgeon to give a prognosis to the athlete. The surgeon may find meniscal tears or articular cartilage divots or flaps indicating that the injury was a severe one. Tears in the body of the lateral meniscus and peripheral tears of the medial meniscus are especially common.

Conservative Treatment of the Acute Anterior Cruciate Tear

If the pivot shift is negative and only minimal damage is found at arthroscopy in an otherwise normal knee with low functional demands, the treatment may be conservative. The athlete works to regain motion and performs progressive resistance exercises to strengthen his quadriceps and especially his hamstrings. He then returns to athletics wearing a protective brace (Figure 12-45).

Extra-Articular Reconstruction in the Acutely Torn Anterior Cruciate

An extra-articular lateral stabilization procedure is indicated to prevent further knee damage in the athlete with an acutely ruptured anterior cruciate ligament and a knee at risk. These include high-performance athletes with a positive pivot shift and damaged menisci or articular cartilage and those people with hypermobile knees with positive shifts and cartilage damage. The stabilization procedure is performed immediately after the intra-articular lesions have been dealt with arthroscopically.

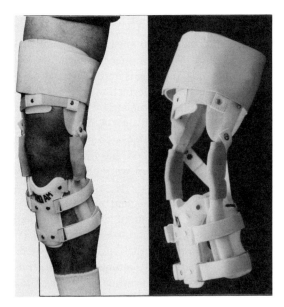

Figure 12-45 A hinged brace with hyperextension straps can prevent abnormal mobility of a knee that lacks an effective anterior cruciate ligament or may be used to reduce abnormal stresses after reconstructive surgery.

An extra-articular reconstruction creates a "lateral cruciate" external to the knee joint but parallel to the intra-articular route of the anterior cruciate ligament. The extra-articular reconstruction has a mechanical advantage over an intra-articular one by being further from the center of rotation. This gives the replacement an increased rotational moment arm and creates a "lateral dominant knee." The extra-articular replacement avoids the hostile intra-articular environment of synovial fluid and collagenases and does not produce a hemarthrosis.

The extra-articular reconstruction can be made stronger than an intra-articular one so that there will be less stretching out. Tensile strength is related to cross-sectional area. Cross-sectional area, and hence tensile strength, may be increased by braiding the extra-articular cruciate substitute.

To optimize biomechanics and graft strength, the surgeon may perform an extra-articular reconstruction using a braided portion of iliotibial tract (Figure 12-46). He divides the iliotibial tract longitudinally along its fibers for 10 cm, about 3 cm

anterior to its posterior margin. He then separates the strip into three tails and may suture a Mersiline tape to the origin of the tract and incorporate it to make four tails. The tails are then braided.

Next, the surgeon creates an osteoperiosteal tunnel in the lateral femoral condyle. He passes the graft through the tunnel and weaves it through the tendon of the lateral head of the gastrocnemius. This weaving reefs the posterolateral capsule. He then pulls the graft anteriorly and staples it to Gerdy's tubercle. He closes the defect in the fascia lata in all but the distal 6 cm.

Postoperative Care

After a stabilization operation, the athlete wears a cushioned brace. Motion is allowed into flexion, but the brace is locked so that he cannot extend the last 30°. Once out of the soft brace, he follows a graduated, supervised knee rehabilitation program. Progressive resistance quadriceps and hamstring exercises are allowed in the 30° to 90° range, and he gains extension slowly. Athletic drills are usually started about 5 months after the operation, and the athlete wears a protective brace.

Acute Posterior Cruciate Ligament Tear

An athlete's posterior cruciate ligament may tear when his knee is hyperextended severely (Figure 12-47). The anterior cruciate ligament tears first, followed by a tear in the posterior cruciate. A blow to the front of a flexed knee, a fall on the flexed knee with the ankle in plantar flexion, or a hook slide in baseball may also rupture the posterior cruciate. The ligament is usually torn from the tibia, and a bone chip visible on x-ray film may be avulsed.

The knee joint usually will not swell after a rupture of the posterior cruciate because the capsule is often damaged, allowing blood and synovial fluid to escape. The popliteal fossa will be tender and the posterior drawer test positive if both the posterior cruciate and the posterior capsule are torn. Posterior motion of the tibia on the

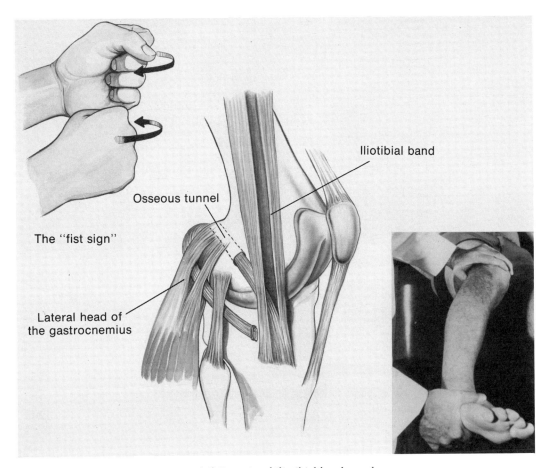

Figure 12-46 To eliminate a "pivot shift," a strip of iliotibial band may be woven through the tendon of the lateral head of the gastrocnemius and stapled into the tibia.

femur is prevented mainly by the posterior cruciate, with little help from the posterior capsule. If the capsule is intact, however, there may be no posterior drawer sign.

Recurvatum of the knee is evidence of a posterior cruciate rupture, and a posterior sag with the knee flexed also indicates posterior cruciate insufficiency. The examiner should be aware that a posterior sag may masquerade as a positive anterior drawer because the tibia is being drawn forward from an already posteriorly subluxed position.

If the posterior drawer test is only up to 5 mm, an operation is not needed because a reconstruction cannot improve on this amount of drawer.

Surgery is indicated when the posterior drawer is 5 mm to 15 mm. In this procedure, the cruciate ligament is approached through a posteromedial incision and the bone fragment secured with a screw or the ligament repaired with sutures passed through drill holes in the tibia (Figure 12-47). The repair may be augmented with the tendinous medial head of the gastrocnemius. Postoperatively, the athlete wears a knee brace with an extension stop and promptly works his quadriceps. He should refrain from early hamstring work because the hamstrings pull the tibia backward, antagonizing the effect of the posterior cruciate that holds the tibia forward. If both anterior cruciate and posterior cruciate ligaments have

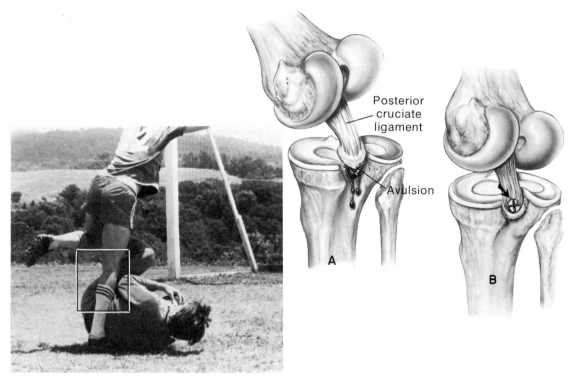

Figure 12-47 If the tibial attachment of the posterior cruciate ligament is avulsed **(A)**, it may be reattached with a screw **(B)**.

been torn, a medial incision will allow repair of both structures.

KNEE INSTABILITIES

Late Instabilities and Knee Reconstruction

An athlete's knee may become unstable months or years after a knee ligament injury, give way, and start hurting. Such instabilities are defined during an examination by the direction of the tibial displacement—the opposite of what happens in athletics, during which the femur is usually moving on the fixed tibia of the planted leg. The instabilities are classified as either straight, rotatory, or combined.

If the athlete's muscles are strong enough to provide dynamic stability, an unstable knee may not bother him. Surgery is reserved for functional instability, and before it is suggested the athlete should undergo a 3-month rehabilitation program of his entire lower limb while wearing a helical glide brace. This type of brace allows proper muscle action, whereas hinge braces and derotation braces decrease the athlete's mobility and do not help to guide the knee helically. Knee taping provides support but must be applied skillfully; when elastic tape must be applied frequently, it becomes very expensive. Reconstruction of the knee is indicated only if the exercise and bracing programs are unsuccessful, with the knee still painful and giving way.

If an operation is decided on, the deficient ligament may be substituted for directly, or reinforcement may be established at a distance from the deficient ligament. In either case, adjunctive active tendon transfers are used to "back up" the repair.

Straight Instabilities

Straight instability means an instability in one plane and consists of six different kinds (see list).

REHABILITATION PROGRESSION FOLLOWING EXTRA-ARTICULAR RECONSTRUCTION FOR A TORN ANTERIOR CRUCIATE LIGAMENT

WEEKS 2–3

Electrical muscle stimulation
Hip flexion exercise
Toe-touch weight bearing (10% body weight) with crutches
PRE opposite leg
Bike opposite leg
Isometrics (see Rehabilitation Progression for the knee)
Double-leg knee bends from 30° to 60° (three sets of ten repetitions, four times a day) in the brace, which is set to move only between 30° and 60°

WEEKS 3–4

Add active motion in the brace as tolerated but only to − 30° of extension

WEEKS 5–6

Whirlpool with active range of motion to − 30° of extension
Limited PRE. Exercise from 90° to 30°; eight sets of ten repetitions

WEEK 7

Flat footed, full-weight bearing with crutches
High knee steps in the pool; the athlete takes the brace off and works in the pool for 30 minutes

WEEK 8

The brace is off, and, if he is not limping, he no longer uses crutches
Propriception exercises working on standing balance
Stationary bicycle when the athlete can achieve 90° to 95° of knee flexion
Tubic single-leg knee bend program. These exercises produce a co-contraction of the quadriceps and hamstrings
Tubic, surgical tubing, or "Fit Kit" half circles. The athlete side steps in a semicircle. These exercises produce co-contractions of the quadriceps and hamstrings. If the right knee is the one that has been operated on, when the athlete moves to the right that knee will be especially stressed and strengthened

WEEKS 9–12

Work toward full extension. If the knee is stable (a solid repair with negative anterior drawer), then the athlete may begin to work toward full extension in the ninth week. If the knee is a little loose and there is a positive anterior drawer, he must wait until the 12th week before starting to work toward full extension
Begin EPLEI Goal 1

WEEKS 10–12

The athlete may start jogging if he can lift 20% of his body weight
Work the quadriceps and hamstrings with PRE and isokinetics

Straight anterior instability results from a tearing of the medial collateral ligament and the anterior cruciate. Straight medial instability in flexion is produced by a torn medial capsular ligament combined with a torn anterior cruciate or posterior cruciate. Straight medial instability in extension is produced by a torn medial collateral ligament and both cruciates. Straight lateral instability in flexion results from a lateral ligament tear along with an anterior cruciate or posterior cruciate rupture. Straight lateral instability in full extension means a lateral ligament tear and tears of both cruciates. This type of instability is a special hindrance to full athletic participation because the athlete must adduct his limb while running, and the lateral instability causes his supporting leg to give out.

Posterior cruciate insufficiency produces a straight posterior instability. The knee may be generally stable at examination but eventually breaks down with osteoarthritis. Even if the athlete has a posterior drawer sign, an operation is not indicated unless he has functional instability and the drawer is more than 5 mm, since repair will not yield a result better than this.

At operation, the medial meniscus may be substituted for the posterior cruciate (Figure 12-48). Alternatively, the semitendinosus tendon may be rerouted as a cruciate substitute. Also, the medial third of the patellar tendon may serve as a replacement because it approaches the strength of the posterior cruciate. Any one of these transfers may die, and for this reason the best replacement for the posterior cruciate probably is the tendinous part of the medial head of the gastrocnemius, extended by an artificial leader through a hole in the femur.[153]

Because a plaster of Paris cast alone will not prevent postoperative posterior sag, a Steinman pin should be placed up the center of the knee joint. In postoperative rehabilitation, the quadriceps is a dynamic stabilizer that aids the posterior cruciate in preventing the tibia from dropping backward. Thus, after replacement, the athlete should work his quadriceps but refrain from strengthening his hamstrings because they pull the tibia backward, antagonizing the posterior cruciate replacement.

Rotatory Instability

The rotatory instabilities of the knee include anteromedial rotatory instability, anterolateral rotatory instability, and posterolateral rotatory instability (see list). Whether there is such an entity as posteromedial rotatory instability is debatable.

Anteromedial Rotatory Instability

When a knee with anteromedial rotatory instability is tested, the medial tibial plateau moves anteriorly and laterally with respect to the femur. The anterior drawer test and valgus stress test in flexion are positive. Medial capsular ligament damage permits this instability, and since the anterior cruciate supports the capsular structure the instability worsens when the anterior cruciate is ruptured. The athlete usually walks well but cannot sprint or cut, and in time his medial meniscus will tear. The posterior horn of the medial meniscus may block the instability, and if a total medial meniscectomy is performed the removal of this block will unveil a full-blown anteromedial rotatory instability. The examiner must be alert for this condition because its presence makes reconstruction mandatory. The examiner should also check for an accompanying anterolateral rotatory instability in knees that show anteromedial rotatory instability.[114] To counter the instability, the posteromedial capsular ligament should be tightened and a "dynamic sling" established by a pes anserinus transfer or an advancement of the semimembranosus.[53]

Anterolateral Rotatory Instability

Anterolateral rotatory instability refers to anterior and medial displacement of the lateral tibial plateau on the femur during testing of the knee. With an incompetent anterior cruciate ligament, the lateral femoral condyle glides posteriorly on the lateral tibial plateau. This displacement is reduced by a tightening of the iliotibial band when the knee is flexed. The athlete may report that his knee "comes apart." The midlateral capsule eventually stretches out, and the athlete's lateral meniscus may tear.

Causes of Straight Knee Instabilities

INSTABILITY	TORN OR INCOMPETENT
Anterior instability	Medial ligament and anterior cruciate
Posterior instability	Posterior cruciate
Medial instability	
Opening with valgus stress in slight flexion	Medial ligament
Opening with valgus stress in more flexion	Medial ligament and either the anterior or posterior cruciate
Opening with valgus stress in extension	Medial ligament and both cruciates
Lateral instability	
Opening with varus stress in slight flexion	Lateral ligament
Opening with varus stress in more flexion	Lateral ligament and either the anterior or posterior cruciate
Opening with varus stress in extension	Lateral ligament and both cruciates

Testing for this type of instability will depend on the posterior subluxation of the lateral femoral condyle in extension and reduction of the subluxation with flexion of the knee. These tests include the pivot-shift and the jerk test, the cross-over test, a side-lying test, and the flexion–rotation drawer test. All of these tests should be tried to determine which ones work best for the examiner.

To elicit a *pivot-shift*, the examiner cradles the athlete's heel with one hand and rotates the tibia internally. He also applies a valgus force to the extended knee with his other hand before passively flexing the knee while applying an axial load. At 0° to 5° of flexion, the lateral aspect of the tibia will be subluxed anteriorly and the iliotibial band shifted forward. As the knee is flexed to 30° or 40°, the subluxation suddenly reduces with a thud or a clunk as the iliotibial band pops back into position, a movement that reproduces what the athlete feels during competition when his knee buckles.

The *jerk test* is a variant of the pivot-shift. "Jerk" is an engineering term for a sudden rate of change of acceleration. The examiner begins the test with the athlete's knee flexed and presses forward under the fibular head (Figure 12-49). A jerk will be felt at about 30° of knee flexion as the lateral tibial plateau subluxes anteriorly, jumping out of place when the iliotibial band shifts forward.

The *cross-over test* may be used in athletes to duplicate statically a cross-over cut and bring out anterolateral rotatory instability.[4] For this test, the examiner stands on the foot of the involved limb and has the subject cross over with his other leg, turning his torso as far as possible while contracting the quadriceps of the fixed limb. This test may reproduce the athlete's feeling of instability on the playing field when his quadriceps contracts, his iliotibial band slides forward, and his lateral tibial plateau subluxates.

In the *side-lying test*, the athlete first lies on his unaffected side, then rolls back about 30° and

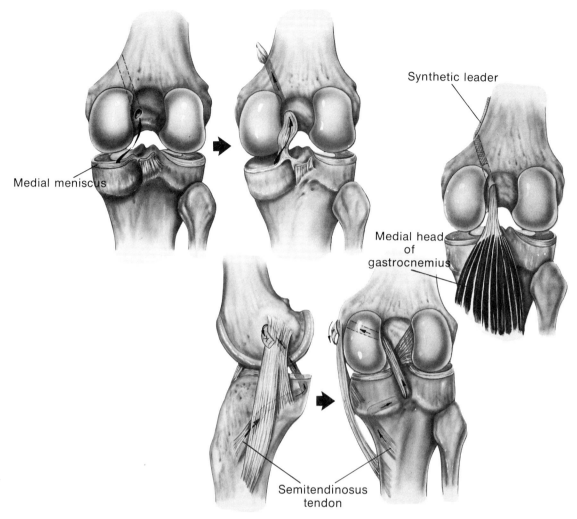

Figure 12-48   The posterior cruciate ligament may be replaced by the medial meniscus, the tendon of the medial head of the gastrocnemius, or the semitendinosus tendon.

flexes the hip and knee of his uninjured leg. His weight now rests on the medial border of his heel. The examiner places one thumb behind the fibular head and the other behind the athlete's lateral femoral condyle, with his fingers over the anterior aspect. The knee is then pushed from full extension into flexion and some valgus force applied. As the knee is flexed, the tibia jumps back onto a reduced position, and as the knee is extended the tibia subluxes.

To perform the *flexion–rotation drawer test*, the examiner holds the athlete's leg in a neutral position behind the calf, cradles the ankle, and lets the hip fall into external rotation. He then pulls the leg forward slightly and flexes and extends the knee with axial loading and valgus stress, movements that will accentuate the instability.

Treatment of Chronic Anterolateral Rotatory Instability

Anterior cruciate reconstruction is indicated in chronic cases only if the instability is func-

Causes of Rotatory Knee Instabilities

INSTABILITY	TORN OR INCOMPETENT
Anteromedial rotatory instability	Medial ligament or medial ligament and anterior cruciate
Anterolateral rotatory instability	Anterior cruciate (the instability is increased by posterolateral capsular incompetence)
Posteromedial rotatory instability	Posterior cruciate and medial ligament
Posterolateral rotatory instability	Posterior cruciate and lateral ligament

tionally disabling. In such cases, the athlete may say that his knee gives out when he cuts or when he lands from jumps. He may have effusions and hemarthroses, and x-ray films may show progres-

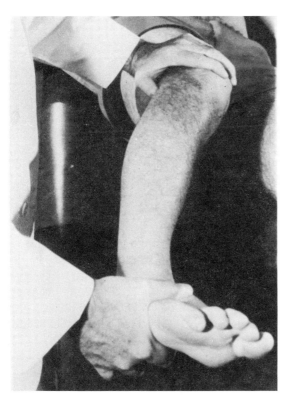

Figure 12-49   The jerk test may be used to diagnose anterolateral rotatory instability. With this instability, the lateral tibial plateau will sublux as the examiner extends the athlete's knee.

sive arthrosis. A stabilization is especially indicated in the anterior-cruciate-dependent knee with weak secondary restraints and recurvatum.

Before a stabilization procedure is performed, an arthroscopic assessment is essential to determine the integrity of the menisci and the state of the articular cartilage. In some patients, symptoms are primarily due to an internal derangement such as a meniscal tear or chondral fracture. Such a person may benefit substantially from arthroscopic removal of the damaged parts of the menisci, extraction of a loose body, or trimming of long or swollen ligament stubs. These lesions should be treated before embarking on a ligament reconstruction.

To restrain anterior subluxation of the tibia, the surgeon may perform an intra-articular replacement or perform an extra-articular reconstruction. The extra-articular procedure has been described previously in the section on the acutely torn anterior cruciate.

Arthroscopic Anterior Cruciate Replacement

To perform an anterior cruciate replacement under arthroscopic control (Figure 12-50), the surgeon first makes a 1-cm incision medial to the tibial tubercle. He passes a drill bit through the tibia to enter the knee at the anterior edge of the anterior cruciate ligament. Under arthroscopic control, he bevels the edges of the femoral notch and widens the notch. Otherwise, if a graft im-

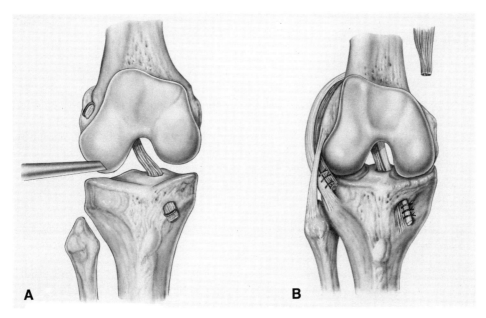

Figure 12-50   An anterior cruciate ligament substitute may also be inserted under arthroscopic control, and stapled at both ends **(A)**. In a "combined" reconstruction, the iliotibial band and the tendon of the semitendinosus are substituted for the cruciate ligament **(B)**.

pinges in the notch, it will fail and block knee extension.

Under continued arthroscopic control, the surgeon passes the graft material through the drill hole in the tibia and "over the top" of the lateral femoral condyle. This technique obviates the need for a femoral drill hole. The graft is tightened so that it is "isometric" and attached with a staple.

Arthroscopic replacement of the anterior cruciate lowers the chance of hemarthrosis or infection compared to an open procedure. Postoperatively, the knee need not be immobilized. Psychologically, the patient benefits because he may go home the same day, the scars are small, and he can move the knee right away. However, the ideal graft material has not yet been found.

Cruciate Ligament Replacement Materials

The fibers in a normal anterior cruciate ligament have a fan and spiral arrangement. Each fiber has a unique origin and insertion, and the fibers are not the same length and not under the same tension. Each fiber can elongate to allow an even distribution of loads through the ligament, which is isometric throughout the entire range of motion.

In searching for a reliable technique to replace the anterior cruciate ligament, almost every expendable structure around the knee has been used (Figure 12-51). Some of these structures are quite strong. A 1.5-cm wide strip of patellar tendon is almost twice as strong as the anterior cruciate, and a 4.5-cm wide strip of the iliotibial band is about equal in strength to the anterior cruciate.[119] However, these structures are subject to enzymatic degradation in the hostile environment of the knee joint and they stretch out. Surgeons are looking for a suitable synthetic material as a substitute.

Synthetic materials under clinical investigation include braided carbon fiber coated with polylactic acid or medical-grade gelatin, woven high-strength Dacron (polyglycolic acid), Dacron-dexon composite, braided polypropylene, expanded polytetrafluorethylene (Teflon), and bovine xenograft consisting of animal-tendon collagen

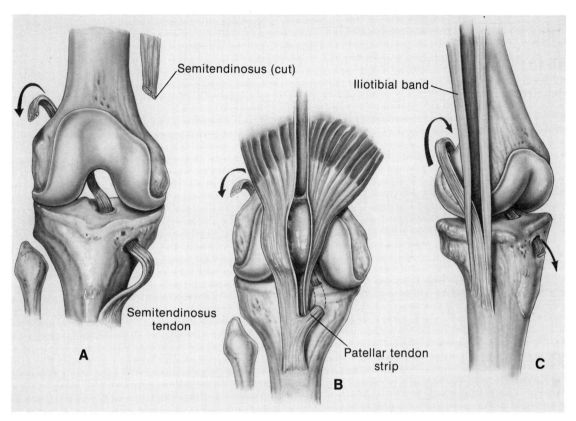

Figure 12-51 The tendon of the semitendinosus **(A)**, the medial part of the patellar tendon **(B)**, or a portion of the iliotibial band **(C)** may be used as an intra-articular substitute for the anterior cruciate ligament. In such cases, the transferred piece is passed through a drill hole into the tibia and "over-the-top" of the lateral femoral condyle.

fixed in glutaraldehyde. However, these materials share some of the same disadvantages as autogenous tissues used in the intra-articular environment. Further, these materials possess undesirable characteristics unique to themselves.[34] Their stiffness prevents them from elongating and returning to resting length without permanent deformation. Stress can concentrate at a single point and the device may fail. Sharp edges or ridges of bone make abrasion likely, which can weaken the material and spread particles of the material throughout the joint to produce synovitis.

With the above deficiencies in mind, intra-articular replacement of a torn cruciate with either an allograft or synthetic material is far from ideal. As tissue-typing techniques develop, perhaps human cadaver cruciates with bone at both ends for strong fixation will become the preferred replacement.

Complications of Intra-articular Anterior Cruciate Surgery

Probably as many disabled knees result from intra-articular anterior cruciate ligament repairs, augmentation, and reconstruction as result from the absence of an anterior cruciate ligament.[34] Ankylosis is the major complication of anterior cruciate ligament reconstruction. Excellent surgical technique is most important in preventing this complication. The surgeon should learn the details of reconstructive procedures firsthand

REHABILITATION PROGRESSION FOR THE KNEE

OBJECTIVES

Strengthen: Knee extension, knee flexion, hip abduction, hip adduction

Flexibility: Knee extension, knee flexion, hip extension, hip external rotation, and patellar motion.

Endurance: Lower extremity

STAGES

Initial

Cryokinetics with active knee extension and flexion range of motion followed by resisted extension and flexion

Flexibility: Quadriceps, hamstrings, gastrocnemius. Patellar mobilization, if patellar motion is compromised. The patella is moved proximally and distally (Figure 12-52A) and also medially and laterally (Figure 12-52B).

Strength

Quadriceps setting (Figure 12-52C).

Isometrics (Figure 12-53)—hold each contraction for 6 seconds, ten times an hour. These exercises may be done while seated—the right leg over the left one in three positions, and the left leg over the right one in three positions (Figures 12-53A,B,C)

Hip abduction (Figure 12-53D)

Hip adduction (Figure 12-53E)

While standing, the athlete can work on isometric hip flexion, hip extension, hip abduction, and hip adduction (Figure 12-54C,D,F).

Straight leg raise (Figure 12-54A)—the athlete locks his injured knee, dorsiflexes his foot, and then raises the leg to a level parallel to his opposite thigh (which is kept flexed 45° to flatten his back). He then returns the leg to the mat, relaxes, and repeats the exercise for eight sets of ten repetitions. His goal is to do this with a resistance of 5% of his body weight.

Electrical muscle stimulation (see modality section)

Opposite leg progressive resistance exercises (PRE) to gain a "cross-over effect" (Figure 12-54A).

Endurance

Bike with the opposite leg. In addition to building cardiovascular and muscular endurance, there is a cross-over effect to the injured leg.

Intermediate

Flexibility

Continue the above with increased effort.

Strength

PRE knee extensions: eight sets of ten repetitions to a goal of doing this with a resistance of 5% of body weight.

Quadriceps extensions to lock out. Terminal extension is the most important aspect of these exercises. A pad under the thigh will help the athlete achieve this. He can start the exercise with his foot resting on a stool (Figure 12-

55A). The Knee Table has markings that indicate the degree of extension (Figure 12-55B). On each repetition, he should reach the fully extended (180°) mark. If the athlete has had an anterior cruciate injury, the pad is placed at the proximal tibia to reduce forward movement of the tibia (Figure 12-55C).

Hamstrings—for a medial hamstring injury, the foot is turned out; for a lateral injury, the foot is turned in (Figure 12-55D.)

Tubic squats using a bicycle innertube, surgical tubing, or the Pro "Fit Kit." The athlete does these exercises within the pain-free range of motion and goes no further than a half squat (Figure 12-55E).

Endurance
   Begin EPLEI Goals 1, 2

Advanced
Flexibility

   Continuation of above.

   Hip external rotation—if an athlete has limited external rotation of his hip, his knee will give way when he plants his foot. Good flexibility in external rotation of the hip will relieve valgus and external rotation stress at the knee (Figure 12-56A).

   Transverse friction massage over the painful area with passive mobilization. The trainer puts one finger over the other so that he can exert uniform pressure (Figure 12-56B).

   Leg press (Figure 12-56C)

Progressive resistance knee extensions—On Mondays, Wednesdays, and Fridays, the athlete does four sets of ten repetitions using the table shown on page 504 to determine the resistance load and progression. On Tuesdays and Thursdays, he does one set of 200 repetitions with the maximum weight that he can handle for that many repetitions. He may begin isokinetic exercises when he has reached a resistance of 20% of his body weight in the quadriceps progressive resistance exercises.

   Endurance goals—EPLEI Goals 3–8

from surgeons skilled in them. He should then perform the procedures on anatomic specimens to develop finesse before applying them to an injured athlete's knee.

Posterolateral Rotatory Instability

A tear of the arcuate complex, consisting of the arcuate and lateral collateral ligaments and the popliteus tendon, allows the athlete's lateral femoral condyle to slide backward on his convex lateral tibial plateau. The external rotation recurvatum test is used to diagnose this instability. The athlete lies relaxed on his back, and the examiner then raises the athlete's leg by his big toe. If there is posterolateral rotatory instability, the tibia will rotate externally and drop back. The knee assumes a position of recurvatum, varus, and excessive external tibial rotation, findings opposite to those in anterolateral rotatory instability.

To stabilize these knees, the surgeon advances the popliteus tendon insertion on the lateral femoral condyle to a more proximal and anterior position. The lateral tendon of origin of the gastroc-

PROGRESSIVE RESISTANCE KNEE EXTENSION

	1st Set 10 Reps@	*2nd Set* 10 Reps@	*3rd Set* 10 Reps@ MAX	*4th Set* 10 Reps@ OVER MAX
1.	5 lb.	7½ lb.	10 lb.	15 lb.
2.	7½	12½	15	20
3.	10	15	20	25
4.	12½	18¾	25	30
5.	15	22½	30	35
6.	17½	26¼	35	40
7.	20	30	40	45
8.	22½	33¾	45	50
9.	25	37½	50	55
10.	27½	41¼	55	60
11.	30	45	60	65
12.	32½	48¾	65	70
13.	35	52½	70	75
14.	37½	56¼	75	80
15.	40	60	80	85
16.	42½	63¾	85	90
17.	45	67½	90	95

nemius is also transferred anteriorly, and because this tendon blends with the posterior capsule its advancement tightens the posterior capsule. Finally, the lateral collateral ligament and the biceps tendon are advanced. Postoperatively, the quadriceps is strengthened to hold the tibia forward. Hamstring strengthening is pursued late in rehabilitation because early training of the hamstrings will pull the tibia backward and work against the transfer.

Combined Instabilities

The most common combined rotatory instability of the knee is anteromedial–anterolateral instability. To stabilize these knees, the surgeon must prevent the tibia from sliding both ways. A pes anserinus transfer may be performed medially. Laterally, an iliotibial band rerouting under the lateral collateral ligament acts as a check rein, preventing forward subluxation of the tibia when full extension is approached. A dynamic biceps advancement also is added on this lateral side. For combined anterolateral–posterolateral instability, a dynamic biceps femoris tendon transfer

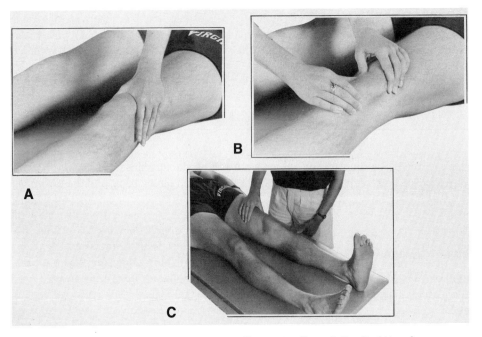

Figure 12-52   The trainer can mobilize the patella proximally and distally **(A)** and laterally **(B)** and supervise quadriceps setting.

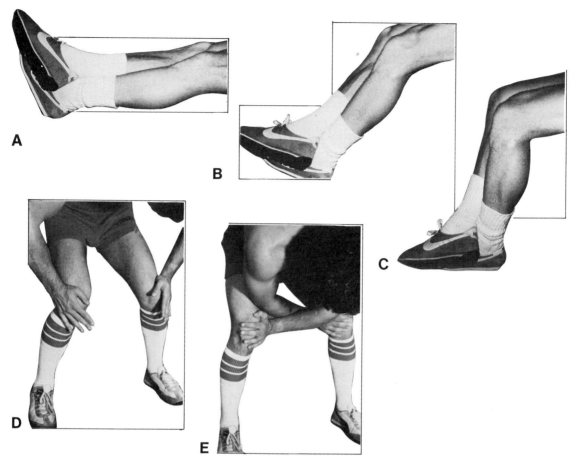

Figure 12-53   Postoperative knee exercises. The legs are squeezed against one
another at varying angles to strengthen isometrically the quadriceps and hamstrings
(A–C). The hip abductors and adductors can also be strengthened isometrically by
working against hand pressure on the outside and the inside of the legs,
respectively **(D, E).**

is performed, along with an advancement of the
lateral collateral ligament, the popliteus tendon,
and the lateral head of the gastrocnemius to
tighten up the posterolateral capsule.

THE DISLOCATED KNEE

A dislocated knee is classified according to the
position of the tibia in relation to the femur. Thus
an anterior dislocation of the knee means that the
tibia is dislocated anterior to the femur. A dislocation may be anterior, posterior, lateral, medial,

or rotatory. Anterior dislocations resulting from
hyperextension of the knee are the most common
type.

Many dislocated knees probably reduce spontaneously at the time of the injury, and if the knee
has not already relocated it should be reduced
immediately. To reduce an anterior dislocation,
the examiner should apply longitudinal traction
and add the appropriate push or pull. If the ligaments have been torn from the bone, there is a
better chance for a stable result. Eventual stability
is less likely, however, if the ligaments have ruptured in their midsubstance. Sideways disloca-

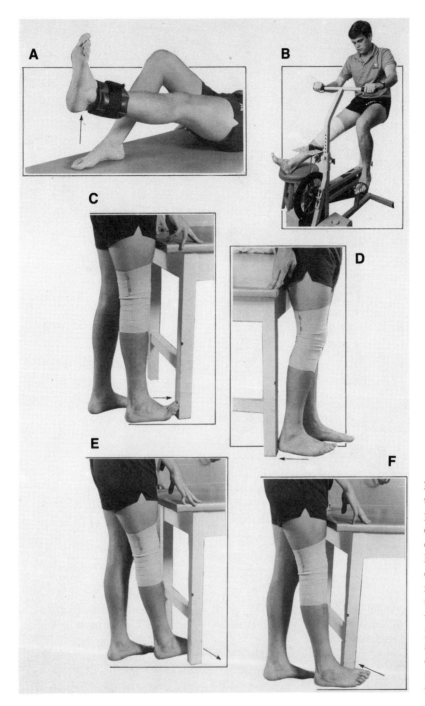

Figure 12-54 Strengthening the uninjured knee with progressive resistance exercises provides a "cross-over effect" for the injured knee. To maintain endurance, the athlete can ride an exercise bicycle using the uninjured leg, which is clipped onto the pedal. He maintains hip strength with isometric contractions against an immovable object such as a table leg.

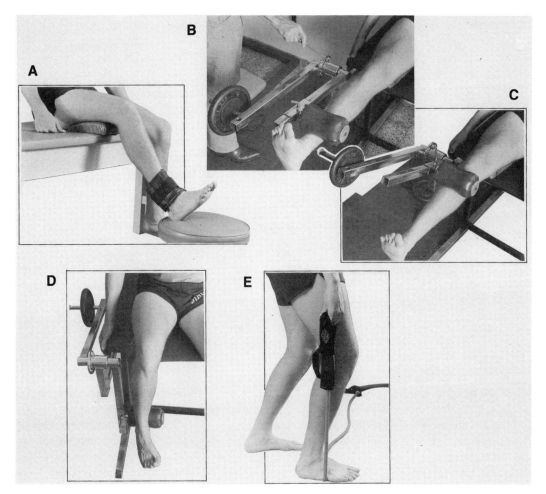

Figure 12-55   During short arcs, the athlete can set a stool under his heel to prevent excessive knee flexion **(A)**. A gauge on the knee table indicates the degrees of knee extension. The athlete should aim for full extension **(B)**. In the anterior cruciate deficient knee, shear can be prevented by placing the knee pad high on the tibia **(C)**. In addition to strengthening his quadriceps, the athlete should strengthen his hamstrings **(D)**. Co-contractions during a Tubic squat **(E)** strengthen both his quadriceps and hamstrings.

tions will need ligament repairs, but anterior or posterior dislocations may eventually become quite stable without surgery, since the collateral ligaments remain intact and the posterior cruciate heals back to bone. In some dislocations, reduction is maintained by flexing the knee and placing a heavy pin down through the distal femur into the tibia.

A knee dislocation may result in damage to the popliteal artery, which is tethered between the adductor canal and the tendinous arch of the soleus. Although nerves may also be injured, the tibial and common peroneal nerves are more mobile than the popliteal artery and can stretch. Arterial trouble appears in about one third of knee dislocations, and about the same proportion of subjects develop nerve trouble, usually of the traction type.

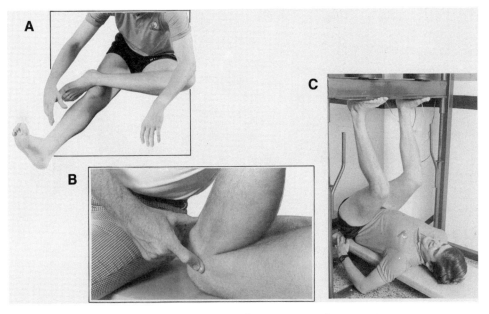

Figure 12-56   An external rotation stretch of the hip can prevent knee injuries during cutting **(A)**. The trainer massages with one finger behind the other for support **(B)**. Leg presses **(C)** strengthen the lower extremities.

After the dislocation has been reduced, the examiner should check for fullness in the popliteal area. If there is any question as to the patency of the popliteal artery, an arteriogram should be performed and, if damage is noted, the vessel explored. An anterior dislocation of the knee is the condition most often associated with vascular problems. Even though there may be no detectable arterial damage on early examination and the foot is warm and looks well, the intima of the vessel may be damaged. Within days an intimal flap may block the flow of blood. If an arterial procedure is needed, it is best performed under spinal anesthesia because this provides good relaxation and the accompanying lumbar sympathetic block increases circulation to the leg.

Major ligament damage is best repaired at the time of injury. If there is vascular damage that requires attention, the experienced surgeon can take care of that simultaneously.

Figure 12-57   "Tubic arcs" help the injured athlete to recover strength and balance.

REFERENCES

1. Anderson G et al: The Anderson knee stabilizer. Phys Sportsmed 7(6):125–127, 1979
2. Andrews JR et al: The double bucket handle tear of the medial meniscus. Am J Sports Med 3:232–237, 1975
3. Andrews JR et al: The cutting mechanism. Am J Sports Med 5:111–121, 1977

4. Arnold JA et al: Natural history of anterior cruciate tears. Am J Sports Med 7:305–313, 1979

5. Basmajian JV, Lovejoy JF Jr: Functions of the popliteus muscle in man. J Bone Joint Surg [Am] 53:557–562, 1971

6. Behrens F et al: Intra-articular gluco-corticoids and cartilage damage. J Rheumatol [Suppl] 1:109, 1974

7. Bentley G, Goodfellow JW: Disorganization of the knees following intra-articular hydrocortisone injections. J Bone Joint Surg [Br] 51:498–502, 1969

8. Bergfeld J: First, second and third-degree sprains. Am J Sports Med 7:207–209, 1979

9. Berson BL, Hermann G: Torn discoid menisci of the knee in adults. Four case reports. J Bone Joint Surg [Am] 61:303–304, 1979

10. Blazina ME et al: Jumper's knee. Orthop Clin North Am 4:665–678, 1973

11. Bosworth DM: An operation for meniscectomy of the knee. J Bone Joint Surg [Am] 19:1113–1116, 1937

12. Brown CW et al: Simplified operative approach for the lateral meniscus. Am J Sports Med 3:265–270, 1975

13. Bruser DM: A direct lateral approach to the lateral compartment of the knee joint. J Bone Joint Surg [Br] 42:348, 1960

14. Cahill BR: Stress fracture of the proximal tibial epiphysis: A case report. Am J Sports Med 5:186–187, 1977

15. Cabaud JE, Slocum DB: The diagnosis of chronic anterolateral rotary instability of the knee. Am J Sports Med 5:99–105, 1977

16. Cabaud HE et al: Exercise effects on the strength of the rat anterior cruciate ligament. Am J Sports Med 8:79–86, 1980

17. Cargill AO, Jackson JP: Bucket-handle tear of the medial meniscus: A case for conservative surgery. J Bone Joint Surg [Am] 58:248–251, 1976

18. Cave EF: Combined anterior-posterior approach to the knee joint. J Bone Joint Surg 17:427–430, 1935

19. Charles CM: On the menisci of the knee joint in American whites and Negroes. Anat Rec 63:355–364, 1935

20. Cooper DL, Fair J: Trainer's corner: Stationary cycling for post-op fitness. Phys Sportsmed 4(6):129, 1976

21. Costill DL et al: Muscle rehabilitation after knee surgery. Phys Sportsmed 5(9):71–74, 1977

22. D'Ambrosia RD, MacDonald GL: Pitfalls in the diagnosis of Osgood-Schlatters disease. Clin Orthop 110:206–209, 1975

23. DeHaven DE, Collins HR: Diagnosis of internal derangements of the knee. The role of arthroscopy. J Bone Joint Surg [Am] 57:802–810, 1975

24. DeHaven DE et al: Chondromalacia patella in athletes. Clinical presentation and conservative management. Am J Sports Med 7:5–11, 1979

25. DeHaven KE: Diagnosis of acute knee injuries with hemarthrosis. Am J Sports Med 8:9–14, 1980

26. Ellsasser JC et al: The non-operative treatment of collateral ligament injuries in the knee in professional football players. J Bone Joint Surg [Am] 56:1185–1190, 1974

27. Euckerman J, Stull AG: Effects of exercise on knee ligament separation force in rats. J Appl Physiol 26:716–719, 1969

28. Fairbank TJ: Knee joint changes after meniscectomy. J Bone Joint Surg [Br] 30:664–670, 1948

29. Faria IE, Cavanagh PR: The Physiology and Biomechanics of Cycling, American College of Sports Medicine Series. New York, John Wiley & Sons, 1978

30. Ficat RP, Hungerford DS: Disorders of the patello-femoral joint. Baltimore, Williams & Wilkins, 1977

31. Fox JM et al: Multiphasic view of medial meniscectomy. Am J Sports Med 7:161–164, 1979

32. Freiberger RH et al: Arthrography of the knee by double contrast method. Am J Roentgenol 97:736–747, 1966

33. Fulkerson JP et al: Histological evidence of retinacular nerve injury associated with patello-femoral malalignment. Clin Orthop Rel Res 197:196–205, July–August 1985

34. Fullerton LR Jr, Andrews JR: Mechanical block to extension following augmentation of the anterior cruciate ligament—a case report. Am J Sports Med 12:166–168, 1984

35. Funk FJ Jr: Injuries of the extensor mechanism of the knee. Athletic Training 10:141–145, 1975

36. Gainor BJ et al: The kick: Biomechanics and collision injury. Am J Sports Med 6:185–193, 1978

37. Galway RD et al: Pivot shift: A clinical sign of symptomatic anterior cruciate insufficiency. J Bone Joint Surg [Br] 54:763, 1972

38. Garcia A, Neer C II: Isolated fractures of the intercondylar eminence of the tibia. Displaced fractures reduced by extending the knee. Am J Surg 95:593, 1958

39. Gaston EA: Preventing bikers' knees. Bicycling 20(7):50–53, 1979

40. Gieck J et al: Treatment of pain in athletes by the use of transcutaneous nerve stimulation. Athletic Training 14(2):97–101, 1979

41. Ginsburg JH et al: Nutrient pathways in transferred patellar tendon used for anterior cruciate ligament reconstruction. Am J Sports Med 8:15–18, 1980

42. Glein GW et al: Isokinetic evaluation following leg injuries. Phys Sportsmed 6(8):75–82, 1978

43. Godshall RW: The predictability of athletic injuries: An 8-year study. Am J Sports Med 3:50–54, 1975

44. Goldner RD et al: The "blind side" of the medial meniscus. Am J Sports Med 8:337–341, 1980

45. Grana WA, Moretz JA: Ligamentous laxity in secondary school athletes. JAMA 240:1975, 1976

46. Grood ES, Noyes FR: Cruciate ligament prosthesis: Strength, creep and fatigue properties. J Bone Joint Surg [Am] 58:1083–1088, 1976

47. Guhl JF: Operative arthroscopy. Am J Sports Med 7:328–335, 1979

48. Hardaker WT Jr et al: Diagnosis and treatment of the plica syndrome of the knee. J Bone Joint Surg [Am] 62:221–225, 1980

49. Heller L, Langman J: The menisco-femoral ligaments in adults less than fifty-five years old. J Bone Joint Surg [Am] 59:480–482, 1977

50. Henry JH et al: Lateral retinacular release in patellofemoral subluxation—indications, results and comparisons to open patellofemoral reconstruction. Am J Sports Med 14:121–129, 1986

51. Hopkinson WJ et al: Chondral fractures of the knee: Causes for confusion. Am J Sports Med 13:309–312, 1985

52. Hughston JC: Subluxation of the patella. J Bone Joint Surg [Am] 50:1003–1026, 1968

53. Hughston JC, Eilers AF: The role of the posterior oblique ligament in repairs of acute medial collateral ligament injuries of the knee. J Bone Joint Surg [Am] 55:923–940, 1973

54. Hughston JC: A simple meniscectomy. Am J Sports Med 3:179–187, 1975

55. Insall J: "Chondromalacia patellae": Patellar malalignment syndrome. Orthop Clin North Am 10:117–127, 1979

56. Ireland J et al: Arthroscopy and arthrography of the knee: A critical review. J Bone Joint Surg [Br] 62:3–6, 1980

57. Ismail AM et al: Rupture of patellar ligament after steroid infiltration: Report of a case. J Bone Joint Surg [Br] 51:503–505, 1969

58. Jackson DW: Video arthroscopy: A permanent medical record. Am J Sports Med 6:213–216, 1978

59. Jones RE et al: Effects of medial meniscectomy in patients older than forty years. J Bone Joint Surg [Am] 60:783–786, 1978

60. Kalenak A, Morehouse CA: Knee stability and knee ligament injuries. JAMA 234:1143–1145, 1975

61. Kaye JJ, Himmelfarb E: Knee arthroscopy in symposium on disorders of the knee joint. Orthop Clin North Am 10:51–59, 1979

62. Keene JS: Surgical injury to the lateral aspect of the knee—a comparison of transverse and vertical knee incisions. Am J Sports Med 8:93–97, 1980

63. Kennedy JC: Complete dislocation of the knee joint. J Bone Joint Surg [Am] 45:889–904, 1963

64. Kennedy JC, Willis RB: The effects of local steroid injections on tendons: A biomechanical and microscopic correlative study. Am J Sports Med 4:11–21, 1976

65. Kennedy JC et al: Orthopaedic manifestations of swimming. Am J Sports Med 6:309–322, 1978

66. Kennedy JC et al: Anterolateral rotatory instability of the knee joint. J Bone Joint Surg [Am] 60:1031–1039, 1978

67. Kennedy JC et al: Posterior cruciate ligament injuries. Orthop Digest 7(8/9):19–31, 1979

68. Kennedy JC et al: Presidential address: Intra-articular replacement in the anterior cruciate ligament-deficient knee. Am J Sports Med 8:1–8, 1980

69. Klein KK: Full squats loosen the knee joint. Preventive conditioning and reduction of knee injury. Athletic J 40:7–28, 1960

70. Klein KK: The martial arts and the caucasian knee: "A tiger by the tail." Am J Sports Med 3:440–447, 1975

71. Knight KL: Testing anterior cruciate ligaments. Phys Sportsmed 8(5):135–138, 1980

72. Kulowski J, Rickett HW: The relation of discoid meniscus to cyst formation and joint mechanics. J Bone Joint Surg 29:990–992, 1947

73. Kulund DN, Brubaker CE: Injuries in the bikecentennial tour. Phys Sportsmed 6(6):74–78, 1978

74. Kulund DN et al: Olympic weightlifting injuries. Phys Sportsmed 6(11):111–119, 1978

75. Kulund DN: The foot in athletics. In Helfet AJ (ed): Disorders of the Foot. Philadelphia, JB Lippincott, 1980

76. Larson RL, Osternog LR: Traumatic bursitis and artificial turf. Am J Sports Med 2:183–188, 1974

77. Larson RL et al: The patellar compression syndrome: Surgical treatment by lateral retinacular release. Clin Orthop 134:158–167, 1978

78. Last RJ: The popliteus muscle and the lateral meniscus. J Bone Joint Surg [Br] 32:93–99, 1950

79. Leach R et al: Obesity: Its relationship to osteoarthritis of the knee. Clin Orthop 93:271–273, 1973

80. Levi JH, Coleman CR: Fracture of the tibial tubercle. Am J Sports Med 4:254–263, 1976

81. Levine J: A new brace for chondromalacia patella and kindred conditions. Am J Sports Med 6:137–140, 1978

82. Lieb FJ, Perry J: Quadriceps function: Anatomical and mechanical study using amputated limbs. J Bone Joint Surg [Am] 50:1535–1548, 1968

83. Lieb FJ, Perry J: Quadriceps function: An EMGic study under isometric conditions. J Bone Joint Surg [Am] 53:749–758, 1971

84. Lipscomb PR Jr et al: Osteochondritis dissecans of the knee with loose fragments: Treatment by replacement and fixation with readily removable pins. J Bone Joint Surg [Am] 60:235–240, 1978

85. Losee RE et al: Anterior subluxation of the lateral tibial plateau: A diagnostic test and operative repair. J Bone Joint Surg [Am] 60:1015–1030, 1978

86. Lutter LD: Foot-related knee problems in the long-distance runner. Foot Ankle 1:112–116, 1980

87. Lyons R: Bicycle ergometer for injured athletes. Trainer's corner. Phys Sportsmed 2(8):218, 1974

88. Mankin HJ: The reaction of articular cartilage to

injury and osteoarthritis. N Eng J Med 291:1285–1292, 1974

89. Mann RA, Hagy JL: The popliteus muscle. J Bone Joint Surg [Am] 59:924–927, 1977

90. Marshall JL, Johnson RJ: Mechanisms of the most common ski injuries. Phys Sportsmed 5(12):49–54, 1977

91. Mayfield GW: Popliteus tendon tenosynovitis. Am J Sports Med 5:31–35, 1977

92. McDaniel WJ, Dameron TB Jr: Untreated ruptures of the anterior cruciate ligament. J Bone Joint Surg [Am] 62:696–705, 1980

93. McDermott LJ: Development of the human knee joint. Arch Surg 46:705–719, 1943

94. McGinty JB et al: Partial or total meniscectomy. A comparative analysis. J Bone Joint Surg [Am] 59:763–766, 1977

95. McLeod WD, Blackburn TA: Biomechanics of knee rehabilitation with cycling. Am J Sports Med 8:175–180, 1980

96. Medlar RC et al: Meniscectomies in children. Am J Sports Med 8:87–92, 1980

97. Merchant AC et al: Roentgenographic analysis of congruence. J Bone Joint Surg [Am] 56:1931, 1974

98. Merchant AC, Mercer RL: Lateral release of the patella. Clin Orthop 103:40–45, 1974

99. Metcalf RW: An arthroscopic method for lateral release of the subluxing or dislocating patella. Clin Orthop Rel Res 167:11–18, 1982

100. Meyers E: Effect of selected exercise variables on ligament stability and flexibility of the knee. Res Q 42:4, 1971

101. Meyers MH, McKeever FM: Fractures of the intercondylar eminence of the tibia. J Bone Joint Surg [Am] 41:209, 1959

102. Mital M: Osgood-Schlatters disease: The painful puzzler. Phys Sportsmed 5(6):60–73, 1977

103. Moore HA, Larson RL: Posterior cruciate ligament injuries. Results of early surgical repair. Am J Sports Med 8:68–78, 1980

104. Morrison JB: Bioengineering analysis of force rations transmitted by the knee joint. BioMed Eng 3:164, 1968

105. Nicholas JA, Minkoff J: Iliotibial band transfer through the intercondylar notch for combined anterior instability. Am J Sports Med 6:341–353, 1978

106. Nitter L: Arthrosis in the knee after meniscectomy. Acta Chir Scand 93:483–494, 1946

107. Noble CA: Iliotibial band friction syndrome in runners. Am J Sports Med 8:232–234, 1980

108. Noble J: Clinical features of the degenerate meniscus with the results of meniscectomy. Br J Surg 62:977–981, 1975

109. Noble J, Hamblen DL: The pathology of the degenerative meniscus lesion. J Bone Joint Surg [Br] 57:180–186, 1975

110. Noble J: Lesions of the menisci: Autopsy incidents in adults less than fifty-five years old. J Bone Joint Surg [Am] 59:480–482, 1977

111. Noble J, Erat K: In defense of the meniscus. A prospective study of 200 meniscectomy patients. J Bone Joint Surg [Br] 62:7–11, 1980

112. Norwood LA Jr et al: Arthroscopy of the lateral meniscus in knees with normal arthrograms. Am J Sports Med 5:271–274, 1977

113. Norwood LA Jr, Cross MJ: Anterior cruciate ligament: Functional anatomy of its bundles in rotary instabilities. Am J Sports Med 7:23–26, 1979

114. Norwood LA Jr, Hughston JC: Combined antero-lateral-anteromedial rotatory instability of the knee. Clin Orthop 147:62–67, 1980

115. Noyes FR, Sonstegard DG: Biomechanical function of the pes anserinus at the knee and the effect of its transplantation. J Bone Joint Surg [Am] 55:1225–1241, 1973

116. Noyes FR, Grood ES: The strength of the anterior cruciate ligament in humans and rhesus monkeys. J Bone Joint Surg [Am] 58:1074–1082, 1976

117. Noyes FR: Functional properties of knee ligaments and alterations induced by immobilization: A correlative biomechanical and histological study in primates. Clin Orthop 123:210–239, 1977

118. Noyes FR et al: Arthroscopy in acute traumatic hemarthrosis of the knee—incidence of anterior cruciate tears and other injuries. J Bone Joint Surg [Am] 62:687–695, 1980

119. Noyes FR et al: Biomechanical analysis of human ligament grafts used in knee ligament repairs and reconstructions. J Bone Joint Surg [Am] 66:344–352, 1984

120. O'Donoghue DH: Treatment of chondral damage to the patella. Am J Sports Med 9:1–10, 1981

121. Ogden JA: Subluxation and dislocation of the proximal tibiofibular joint. J Bone Joint Surg [Am] 56:145–154, 1974

122. Ogilvie–Harris DJ, Jackson RW: The arthroscopic treatment of chondromalacia patella. J Bone Joint Surg [Br] 66:660–665, 1984

123. Palumbo PM Jr: Dynamic patellar brace: A new orthosis in the management of patellofemoral disorders—a preliminary report. Am J Sports Med 9:45–49, 1981

124. Patel D: Arthroscopy of the plicae: Synovial folds and their significance. Am J Sports Med 6:217–225, 1978

125. Paulos LE: Lateral knee braces in football: Do they prevent injury? Phys Sportsmed 14(6):119–124, June 1985

126. Pease RL, Flentje W: Rehabilitation through underwater exercise. Trainer's corner. Phys Sportsmed 4(10):143, 1976

127. Peterson TR: Knee injuries due to blocking: A continuing problem. Phys Sportsmed 3(1):440–447, 1975

128. Pevey JK: Out-patient arthroscopy of the knee un-

der local anesthesia. Am J Sports Med 6:122–127, 1978

129. Pipkin G: Knee injuries: The role of the suprapatellar plica and suprapatellar bursa in simulating internal derangements. Clin Orthop 74:161–176, 1971

130. Puddu G: Method for reconstruction of the anterior cruciate ligament using the semitendinosus tendon. Am J Sports Med 8:402–404, 1980

131. Renne JW: The iliotibial band friction syndrome. J Bone Joint Surg [Am] 57:1110–1111, 1975

132. Roach JE et al: Comparison of the effects of steroid aspirin and sodium salicylate on articular cartilage. Clin Orthop 106:350–356, 1975

133. Roels J et al: Patellar tendinitis (jumper's knee). Am J Sports Med 6:362–368, 1978

134. Roeser WM et al: The use of transcutaneous nerve stimulation for pain control in athletic medicine. A preliminary report. Am J Sports Med 4:210–213, 1976

135. Rovere GD, Adair D: Medial synovial shelf plica syndrome: Treatment by intraplical steroid injection. Am J Sports Med 13:383–386, 1985

136. Schumacher HR: Traumatic joint effusion and the synovium. Am J Sports Med 3:108–114, 1975

137. Seedhom BB: Loadbearing function of the menisci. Rotterdam, International Congress on the Knee Joint, September 1973

138. Slocum DB, Larson RL: Pes anserinus transplantation: A surgical procedure for control of rotatory instability of the knee. J Bone Joint Surg [Am] 50:226–242, 1968

139. Smillie IS: Injuries of the Knee Joint, 4th ed. New York, Churchill Livingstone, 1975

140. Starr W: The Strongest Shall Survive: Strength Training for Football. Annapolis, Fitness Products, 1976

141. Steadman JR: Rehabilitation after knee ligament surgery. Am J Sports Med 8:294–296, 1980

142. Stulberg S: Breaststroker's knee: Pathology, etiology and treatment. Am J Sports Med 8:164–171, 1980

143. Tapper EM, Hoover NW: Late results after meniscectomy: 10–30 year follow-up after uncompli-

cated meniscectomy. J Bone Joint Surg [Am] 51:517–526, 1969

144. Tegtmeyer CJ et al: Arthrography of the knee: A comparative study of the accuracy of single and double contrast techniques. Radiology 132:37–41, 1979

145. Tipton CM et al: Influence of exercise on strength of medial collateral knee ligaments of dogs. Am J Physiol 218:894–902, 1970

146. Tongue JR, Larson RL: Limited arthrography in acute knee injuries. Am J Sports Med 8:19–30, 1980

147. Tucker WE: Post-traumatic para-articular ossification of medial collateral ligament of the knee. Br J Sports Med 4:212, 1969

148. Wang JB et al: A mechanism of isolated anterior cruciate ligament rupture. J Bone Joint Surg [Am] 57:411–413, 1975

149. Watson–Jones R: Fractures and Other Bone and Joint Injuries, 2nd ed. Baltimore, Williams & Wilkins, 1941

150. Weaver JK: Bipartite patellae as a cause of disability in the athlete. Am J Sports Med 5:137–143, 1977

151. Weaver S: Don't wait until your knees hurt—check positioning now. Bicycling. 20(7):52–53, 1979

152. Wilson JN: Wilson's sign. A diagnostic sign in osteochondritis dissecans of the knee. J Bone Joint Surg [Am] 49:477, 1967

153. Woods GW: Proplast leader for use in cruciate ligament reconstruction. Am J Sports Med 7:314–320, 1979

154. Woods GW: Synthetics in anterior cruciate ligament reconstruction: A review. Orthop Clin North Am 16:227–235, 1985

155. Yocum LA et al: The deranged knee: Restoration of function. A protocol for rehabilitation of the injured knee. Am J Sports Med 6:51–53, 1978

156. Youmans WT: The so-called "isolated" anterior cruciate ligament tear or anterior ligament syndrome. Am J Sports Med 6:26–30, 1978

157. Zernicke RF et al: Human patellar-tendon rupture: A kinetic analysis. J Bone Joint Surg [Am] 59:179–183, 1977

CHAPTER

13

The Leg, Ankle, and Foot

THE LEG

Skiing Fractures of the Tibia

When a skier falls or has a collision on the slopes, the usual mechanism of leg injury is external rotation.[130, 131] The ski becomes fixed, and the skier falls to the side and forward. Such falls often resulted in ankle fractures when skiers wore low boots, but, with today's higher, rigid, molded boots, fractures occur mostly at the junction of the middle third and lower third of the tibia—the "boot top" fracture.[41, 42, 62, 64] The "skier's fracture" is a comminuted, spiral fracture of the tibia usually accompanied by a fracture of the fibula.[133] Whereas female skiers suffer knee ligament injuries more often than do male skiers, especially grade II sprains of the medial collateral ligament, the rates of tibia and fibula fractures are about the same for men and women. The spiral fracture occurs more often in a young skier who moves slowly, with shorter skis and lower, softer boots. Although the skier's tibial fracture is usually considered to be a spiral one, oblique and double-oblique types with a butterfly are also common. Fortunately, such injuries are relatively low-energy fractures and rarely open, and internal fixation is usually not needed.

Most tibial fractures result from binding failures. This problem is aggravated when the common toe and heel release systems are poorly adjusted. When properly set, bindings can reduce ski injuries, but most skiers tend to set their bindings too tight. Since the two-mode release bindings are insensitive to several loading configurations, multimode release bindings that allow release by roll, shear, and twist methods at the heel, as well as conventional release modes (twist at the toe and forward lean at the heel), are needed. These would help protect both the knee and the leg.[63] As a practical test of bindings, the skier should be able to twist out of the bindings painlessly.

If a skier injures his leg, his boot should not be removed on the slope. Ice should be applied to the region and the leg placed into a splint. The fracture may then be reduced at the orthopedic area and a long-leg cast applied that can usually be changed to a short-leg cast relatively soon. The short cast has lateral extensions around the knee, allowing the skier to walk and permitting knee flexion and extension while keeping the knee from rotating.

The question as to when the skier may resume skiing after a fracture of the tibia and fibula must take into account that the stresses of skiing make refracture a problem. Tomography may reveal gaps or defects in the cortex, and, if such gaps or defects are found, skiing may have to be proscribed for an additional 6 to 12 months.[16]

Skiers can prepare for the ski season by doing plyometric jumps in all directions over boxes, "Tubic skiing" against the resistance of a light-weight bicycle inner tube or surgical tubing, or hiking over rough terrain. The skills of water skiing and surfing also transfer to skiing. Each of these activities demands muscular endurance, requiring the athlete to react to momentary losses of balance and shifts of his center of gravity.

Stress Fractures of the Leg

As a runner trains, osteoclasts and osteoblasts remodel his weight-bearing bones to accommodate stress. The osteoclastic action may be so rapid that a defect forms in the bone, producing a loss of continuity or a "fracture before a fracture."[43] Muscle spasm then splints the painful area. Stress fractures occur not only in beginning runners, but also in champions often after an abrupt increase in training mileage, a change in running surfaces, an injury such as an ankle sprain or a blister that changes the running gait, or a recent layoff.

During the pushoff phase of running the leg rotates externally, and the foot supinates to become a rigid lever. The plantar flexors of the toes and the great toe flexor arise from the fibula, drawing it toward the tibia.[30, 31, 39] The fibula also moves rhythmically to and fro, especially when the runner runs on the balls of his feet on a hard surface. The point of greatest stress is near the inferior tibiofibular joint, where the cortex may break about 6 cm above the tip of the malleolus. A runner may also suffer a stress fracture through the posteromedial cortex of his upper or lower tibia.[30, 31, 40] Stress fractures are often found in the upper third of the tibia in military recruits. These appear as a dense condensation of bone just below the medial tibial plateau. Ballet dancers usually develop stress fractures in the middle third of the tibia.[14, 39, 41, 42] These appear as a lucency extending about 20% through the cortex. Tibial stress fractures are most common in athletes with cavus feet. Fibular stress fractures are more common in athletes with pronated feet.

To diagnose a stress fracture of the tibia or fibula, the examiner may strike the runner's heel sharply. If there is a stress fracture, this maneuver will elicit pain at the fracture site. The bone may be tender to direct pressure as well. To check further for a fracture, the examiner may use his own knee as a fulcrum to spring the tibia. In any instance of leg pain, a stress fracture should be suspected and an x-ray film obtained. A magnifying glass may be needed to see the stress fracture. The fracture may not be visible immediately but may appear about 2 weeks later under bright light as a local surface haze or even a line of condensation in the bone. If the fracture callus does not appear on the film, it may be seen on a film taken at a different angle. Soft tissue x-ray films or xeroradiographs are sometimes taken to reveal the fracture.

A technetium diphosphonate bone scan may also be done 1 to 3 hours after radionuclide injection to diagnose a stress fracture. The isotope uptake is more than 300% greater at a stress fracture site than on the sound side.[125]

If a stress fracture is suspected, the athlete should be treated as if one has been confirmed, and strapping, brace, or light cast applied. Running must not be allowed until x-ray films show healing and the bone is no longer tender. A fibular stress fracture usually takes 6 weeks and a tibial one, 8 to 10 weeks to heal. While the fracture is healing, the athlete may stay in condition by cycling and doing circuit training; he may also wear a flotation device and run in the swimming pool.

Shin Splints

Shin splints refer to a periostitis, myositis, or tendinitis, or a combination of these in an athlete's leg. Some shin splints are anterior and some posteromedial.

Anterior Shin Splints

The anterior tibial muscle raises the foot during each step and keeps the foot from slapping down after heel strike. This muscle action is stressful, especially in the untrained runner, whose anterior tibials are much weaker than his calf muscles. Even trained runners, however, may develop anterior shin splints if they overexert. Shin splints are common during sprinting, running uphill, and on hard surfaces and in those runners who wear stiff training shoes. In sprinting, the runner must lift the foot after a strong pushoff, and when slowing down he begins to heel run. Because this forceful heel placement leads to strain of the anterior tibial muscle, many runners have the most pain when sprinting or while slowing down after a sprint. Also, uphill cross-country running creates a tight gastrocnemius, and the forward body lean for balance increases the stress on the leg. Moreover, shin splints are likely if a runner overstrides (e.g., on downhills) or runs on hard surfaces such as asphalt. Anterior shin splints are common when the athlete changes to a hard playing surface or goes from natural grass to synthetic turf, especially if his shoes are rigid and the heel firm and not rounded. In addition, street shoes with high heels will tighten the athlete's heel cord and further stress the anterior tibial muscle.

With anterior shin splints, the runner notes pain, tenderness, and tightness along the lateral border of the tibia and at the distal third of the tibia along the medial crest. The pain increases with active dorsiflexion and passive plantar flexion of the ankle.

Anterior shin splints are treated with ice to reduce swelling, and an elastic wrap is used for compression. The runner rests while strengthening his anterior muscles and stretching his heel cords. He may dorsiflex the ankle against a weight sleeve placed over his foot, beginning with three sets of ten repetitions of 2.5 lb and working up to three sets with 10 lb. In addition, a lightweight bicycle inner tube or surgical tubing may be used to provide resistance and develop anterior tibial and peroneal strength. A plywood box measuring 12 inches by 12 inches by 6 inches may be used for heel cord stretches for periods of 5 minutes, three times a day. Ideally, all athletes should stretch their heel cords before practice and should perform a soleus crouch to stretch the soleus component of the heel cord.

As soreness is relieved, the athlete may resume training by walking 2 miles. He then moves to a walk-and-jog, progressing to a 7.5- to 8-minute-mile pace. A flat running surface, such as grass or wood chips, is preferable, and hills should be avoided until the soreness has gone. During these initial walks and runs, the leg is taped with elastic tape and the mileage increased by 5 miles per week for the next 6 weeks, up to 40 miles a week. Athletes should wear shoes with a normal height rather than high heels. If a runner's training program must be changed, the change should be gradual. He should also take time to adjust to new surfaces.

Posteromedial Shin Splints

Posteromedial shin splints most often affect athletes who have pronated feet and those who run on crowned roads or on an indoor track with banked turns. On turns, the inside hip is adducted and the foot must pronate more. In addition, these athletes often have a significantly higher adduction angle of the inside leg. The uneven terrain of a cross-country course and beaches also increases such pronation.

The pain of medial shin splints is located in the posteromedial compartment, 10 cm to 15 cm proximal to the tip of the medial malleolus. This is where the thickened band at the lower edge of the soleus fascia inserts into the posteromedial angle of the tibia.[98a] Tugs from this band from overpronation probably produce a periostitis.

Treatment is with pulsed ultrasound and the

home treatment program. Reduction of the pronation may be achieved by strengthening the arch and taping the arch or by using a pair of Lyncos with medial wedges or a pair of runners molds. In recalcitrant cases, the soleus band may be released through a short incision (Figure 13-1).

Compartment Syndromes

Anterior compartment syndrome is a dangerous complication of leg injury. It usually follows a blow or repeated blows to the shin but also may follow a heavy early training schedule. As swelling increases within the tight fascial covering that invests the muscles in the anterior compartment, the web space between the great and second toes becomes numb and the extensor hallucis longus weakens. The condition does not improve with

rest and ice application. Serial wick catheter determinations of compartmental pressure will help the physician to determine whether the condition is progressing or resolving and aid him in deciding whether a fasciotomy is needed.

A more common compartment problem in runners is chronic compartment ischemia in which the strong fascia that invests the leg muscles is unyielding. It does not accommodate to the 20% increase in muscle mass that typically occurs with heavy exercise. As the muscle volume increases, pressure in the leg compartments rises, collapsing the veins and increasing capillary resistance. Edema is produced, adding to compartmental pressure to produce an aching, ischemic pain.

Chronic compartmental ischemia may affect any of the compartments, and the onset of pain

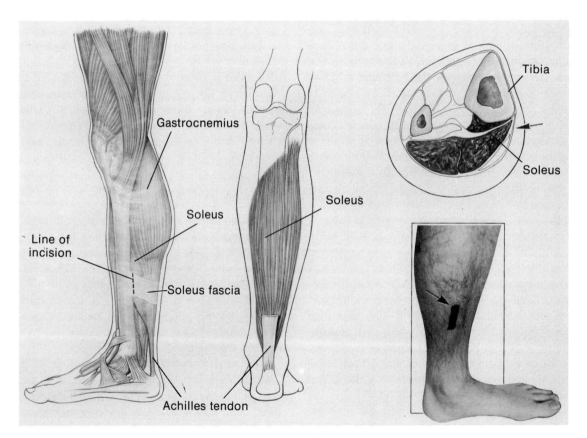

Figure 13-1   The most common shin splints hurt posteromedially *(arrow)*. To cure this condition, the surgeon may have to release the soleus fascia *(dotted line and arrow)*.

is usually gradual over 1 year or more.[68a] The runner usually must cover a certain distance to bring on the pain, which may persist into the night. The condition is usually bilateral but worse on one side than on the other. On examination, the involved muscle mass may be tender, although the runner may be asymptomatic if he has not exercised before the examination. Chronic compartmental ischemia and a stress fracture may give the same symptoms in the same area in the same type of patient. Although the bone scan in compartmental ischemia generally shows some increased uptake of isotope compared to the healthy side, it is much less than the 300% increase seen in a stress fracture. A saline technique may be used to measure superficial compartment pressure for a baseline, and the runner then runs on a treadmill until he becomes symptomatic or tires out. The pressure is then remeasured with 30 mm Hg to 40 mm Hg, indicating a compartment syndrome.

A chronic superficial compartment syndrome in a runner is treated with a subcutaneous fasciotomy performed under local anesthesia. Three small incisions are made, and the fascia is stripped longitudinally and divided transversely at the level of the three incisions to leave a wide-open compartment. Running may be resumed in 1 week. Fasciotomy of the deep posterior compartment produces more soreness after the operation, but the runner is usually running again in 6 weeks.

"Tennis Leg"

When a middle-aged tennis player develops soreness in his calf, he may have "tennis leg,"[49, 88, 126] a strain of the medial head of the gastrocnemius near its musculotendinous junction. The gastrocnemius works across two joints, which confuses the muscle and predisposes it to tearing. A tear may occur as the player with low-heeled tennis shoes approaches the net, dorsiflexes his ankles, and suddenly extends his knees. The pain may be sharp and acute, and the player may think that a ball from an adjacent court has struck his calf. The area becomes swollen and ecchymotic, signs that years ago would have been attributed to a plantaris rupture. However, the plantaris tendon usually stays intact even if the heel cord has completely ruptured.[1, 127] The athlete with mild strain notes a generalized aching in his calf and more calf pain when he dorsiflexes his ankle. The medial belly of his gastrocnemius is tender. The soreness should be a warning that continued vigorous activity may produce complete tearing.

For mild strains, the calf is iced for 20 minutes and a strap looped around the foot for passive stretching.[89] The player stretches, for 10 seconds, to discomfort but short of pain, then relaxes for 10 seconds. This activity is continued for 10 minutes. After 5 minutes of ultrasound, the player does isometric and intermedialis exercises in a program that is repeated three times a day. An equinous taping is applied to the calf (Figure 13-2), and the player wears a shoe with a low heel that provides comfortable calf shortening and promotes a more correct walking style than if he were to wear a higher heel. As swelling and soreness lessen, the player advances to standing calf stretches, returning to competition in about 1 week.

After a moderate strain of the medial head of the gastrocnemius, the muscle partly retracts, leaving a small gap. Soft tissue x-ray film or xerograms will show the gap and the soft tissue swelling. If the player can raise himself on the toes of his injured leg, he should wear a long-leg cast for 4 weeks with his knee flexed to 60° and his ankle in gravity plantar flexion, and then wear a short-leg cast in neutral position for 3 more weeks. If the medial head of the gastrocnemius has completely ruptured at the musculotendinous junction, the athlete will not be able to stand on his toes on the involved leg. In addition, the gap will not fully close with knee flexion and ankle plantar flexion. These tears are repaired, and the limb is then immobilized as if for a moderate strain.

Achilles Tendon Rupture

The Achilles tendon is the conjoined tendon of the gastrocnemius and soleus muscles, the latter being the major contributor to plantar flexion strength. Much of the blood supply for the Achilles tendon reaches it through its anterior mesentery, and blood supply is poorest in the region 2 cm to 6 cm above the os calcis.[72, 127]

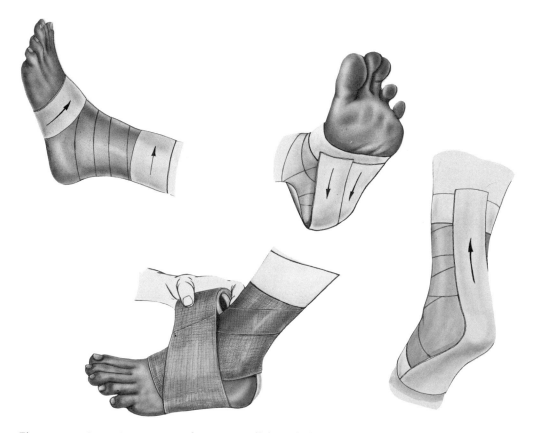

Figure 13-2   An equinous taping takes tension off the Achilles tendon.

The normal Achilles tendon is very strong, withstanding forces up to 2000 lb during fast running.[33] The usual tearing mechanism is a stress applied to the already contracted musculotendinous unit, usually the pushoff foot, most often the left foot (Figure 13-3). The biarticular nature of the tendon makes allowance for the athlete to push off at the ankle while extending the knee joint with the Achilles tendon unit. Rupture may occur during sudden dorsiflexion of the ankle or a moment of motor uncoordination. A football player may be pushing against the blocking sled as another athlete falls on his calf, further dorsiflexing his ankle.

Ski boot pressure may cause ischemia of the Achilles tendon, and when a tendon strain is added the tendon may rupture. A heel cord may also rupture after local injection of symptom-relieving cortisone when an athlete increases his activity as a result of feeling much better. The tendon tears in the critical zone of poor circulation 2 cm to 6 cm above the os calcis (Figure 13-3).

Athletes with Achilles tendon rupture are usually older than 30 years of age, with regressive changes in the tendon from lessened blood flow. Typically, they feel a snap during pushoff, have pain, and then limp. Examination will reveal swelling, a gap, and increased passive dorsiflexion, but in about one fourth of all ruptures the diagnosis is overlooked[56] because there may have been only mild trauma and pain and the athlete may be able to stand on his toes. He can weakly plantar-flex his foot with the long toe flexors, tibialis posterior, and peroneals. The Achilles tendon appears to function normally, even if only one fourth of its fibers remain in continuity. The outline of the tendon is also lost in diffuse swelling, and the gap may fill with a hematoma and be obscured. Thus a swollen lower leg should always be tested for an Achilles tendon rupture.

The "squeeze test" is the definitive test for

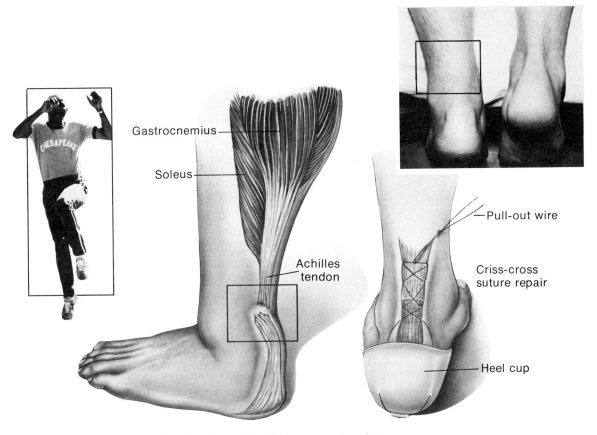

Figure 13-3   The degenerated tendon of an older athlete may rupture during a plyometric activity such as long jumping. It usually tears 5 cm to 10 cm (2 in–4 in) above its insertion into the calcaneus, and the entire region swells, obscuring the normal tendon outline. Repair is done with a criss-cross stitch, and the plantaris tendon is usually woven into the repair.

complete rupture of the Achilles tendon[127] (Figure 13-4). The injured athlete lies prone or kneels on a chair. The examiner squeezes the athlete's calf in the middle third, just below the place of the widest girth. The examiner's hand must be distal to the apex of the curve of the soleus because even a normal ankle will not plantar-flex if squeezed proximal to the apex of the soleus curve. If the ankle fails to plantar-flex when the calf is squeezed, the rupture is complete.

Lateral x-ray films of the heel area normally show a triangular, low-density region occupied by fat. The triangle is bounded anteriorly by the flexor tendons, posteriorly by the Achilles tendon, and inferiorly by the os calcis. After a complete rupture of the Achilles tendon, the triangular area becomes more dense, as it does in Achilles tendinitis and partial ruptures of the heel cord. After a complete rupture, however, the triangle is also distorted.[1]

Treatment of an Achilles tendon rupture is determined on an individual basis, ranging from nonoperative treatment to surgery.[59] The Achilles tendon has a considerable ability to heal itself, and if the ends are opposed it will heal, avoiding the problems of skin slough, tendon slough, or infection in this ideal culture medium of edema, hematoma, and poor blood supply.[118] If, however, the ends are not opposed, the athlete loses strength and pushoff power and risks rerupture.

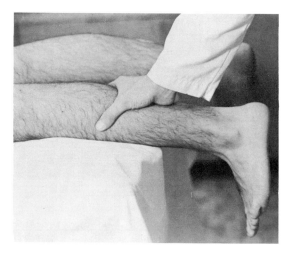

Figure 13-4 To test for a ruptured heel cord, the examiner squeezes the athlete's calf and pushes toward the knee.

It is therefore important to separate cases that will benefit from closed treatment from those needing operation.[80]

After Achilles tendon rupture, the proximal fragment retracts, and reduction of the tendon requires moving *both* ends. Five milliliters of contrast medium is injected into the gap under fluoroscopic control, and the ankle is then exercised. The athlete rests his foot on a chair with his ankle at 90°, a position that straightens the sheath and minimizes its tendency to collapse. The calf is next wrapped with an elastic wrap from the knee crease downward to force the retracted upper tendon down for better contact. The athlete then lies on his side while the heel cord is fluoroscoped. If the tendon is opposed, the wrap should be removed and a long-leg gravity equinous cast applied and left on for 6 weeks, then changed to a short-leg equinous plaster for 2 weeks, followed by a short-leg walking plaster for 2 additional weeks.[74] Once out of plaster, the athlete wears a 2-cm heel lift for 3 months. Failures and poor results from closed treatment occur if the tendon ends have not been opposed and, when opposed, if immobilization has been for too short a time.[59] If the tendon ends remain separated after the elastic wrap maneuver, the tendon should be remanipulated or the ends opposed operatively.

At operation, surgeons choose from medial, lateral, S-shaped, or zig-zag incisions.[100] The skin and subcutaneous tissue are preserved as one layer, and the laterally situated sural nerve is avoided. Vigorous retraction is also avoided, and the sheath is opened away from the line of the skin cut. On opening the sheath, the surgeon will find the tendon ends shredded into mop-like frazzles. The surgeon may use a pull-out wire technique and end-to-end anastomosis along with an interwoven, distally based plantaris tendon graft to reconstruct the tendon.[32, 33, 35] Lack of tension on the muscle may cause marked calf atrophy; thus extreme plantar flexion should be avoided. The ankle is immobilized in as much dorsiflexion as the tendon suture can bear. At 3 weeks, the cast is changed and the foot dorsiflexed within the athlete's pain and motion range. This usually will place the foot at 90° to the leg, and this new cast should be worn for 4 more weeks. The pull-out wire is removed at 7 weeks and a high heel worn for 2 months.

Partial Achilles Tendon Rupture

Partial rupture of the Achilles tendon may occur in young, fully grown athletes who are at their highest levels of performance.[29] It occurs especially with increased training loads, presenting immediately or gradually as sharp, stabbing pain in the lower calf. The athlete limps, and the area is tender locally.

Electrophysiologic studies may be used to diagnose partial ruptures. Potentials are reduced in the muscle of the torn tendon, and the large potentials that usually appear with moderate and strong contractions are absent. Magnetic resonance imaging may also reveal a partial tear.

The athlete with a partial Achilles tendon rupture is first treated with cryotherapy, strapping, and a heel lift. Steroid shots are not given because they mask symptoms and may cause a complete rupture. If the rupture is not cured by a conservative program, an operation is done to close the defect. The surgeon splits the tendon to inspect its central parts and excises pathologic granulation tissue and devitalized tissue. Multiple longitudinal incisions are also made in the tendon to encourage revascularization. Postoperatively, the athlete may exercise his ankle immediately.

Achilles Tendinitis

A runner's Achilles tendon may become inflamed if he wears high-heeled dress shoes and then trains in low-heeled shoes, or when he changes from training shoes to competition shoes without heels. It may also happen when a runner switches from cross-country running to a track with more elastic recoil. In each instance, an increased pull on the Achilles tendon occurs. Moreover, if a runner has a sore arch, his tendon may become strained as he dorsiflexes his ankle to avoid pronating his foot.

The runner with a rigid, cavus foot is predisposed to Achilles tendinitis. Uphill runs in stiff shoes will also produce the condition. On the other hand, overpronation in a shoe with a soft heel counter will twist the tendon and produce a tendinitis. The condition may also occur in cyclists who "ankle" too much, although the pain and swelling usually abate when they reduce their ankle motion while pedaling.

Repeated strains produce degeneration of the tendon and granulation tissue forms, usually about 3.75 cm (1.5 inches) above the tendon's insertion into the os calcis. The degeneration may be focal or diffuse. In addition, adhesions may develop between the paratenon and the tendon, becoming constricting bands. If a steroid is injected within the paratenon, collagen synthesis is suppressed, further weakening the tendon. Moreover, pressure within the paratenon from the injected material may embarrass the tendon's blood supply and lead to ischemic necrosis. It must be kept in mind that the tendon's blood supply reaches it from its sheath and is tenuous.

A heel pad will lessen the stretching of the Achilles tendon, and a wider, or flared, cushioned heel will limit side-to-side shifting and irritation of the tendon. Arch soreness must be treated early to prevent Achilles tendon problems. If an athlete has chronic tendon pain, the surgeon may have to strip his paratenon if it is obviously diseased. Although the surface of the tendon may look perfectly normal, it should be opened longitudinally

and inspected for focal degeneration and areas of degenerated granulation tissue removed.

THE ANKLE

The ankle works as a hinge with dorsiflexion and plantar flexion. Because the talus is wider anteriorly than posteriorly, there is some play in other planes during plantar flexion. Inversion and eversion occur at the subtalar joint.

The ligaments of the ankle include the distal tibiofibular ligaments, the deltoid ligament on the medial side, and the anterior talofibular, calcaneal-fibular, and posterior talofibular on the lateral side (Figure 13-5). The distal tibiofibular ligaments strongly bind the tibia and fibula together anteriorly and posteriorly just above the joint line. On the medial side, the deltoid ligament arises from the medial malleolus and fans out to attach on the talus and calcaneus.

The fibula provides muscular attachments and also has a weight-bearing and dynamic, stabilizing function, bearing one sixth of the weight supported by the leg. It changes position, moving to and fro and bowing to stabilize the ankle mortise in response to weight bearing, ankle motion, and the muscular tractions of plantar flexion. The fibula is pulled distally and medially during contraction of the foot and toe flexors, a shift that deepens the ankle mortise and stabilizes the talus in stance and pushoff.

The lateral ankle ligaments arise on the fibula, and the anterior talofibular ligament runs medially, reinforcing part of the weak anterior capsule. It becomes vertical during plantar flexion to serve as a collateral ligament. The distinct, cord-like calcaneal-fibular ligament lies under the sheath of the peroneal tendons. In neutral position, it is vertical and serves as a collateral ligament, but in plantar flexion it is more horizontal. This ligament stabilizes both the ankle and subtalar joints. The posterior talofibular ligament stabilizes against posterior displacement of the talus but is rarely torn unless the ankle is completely dislocated. A lateral talocalcaneal ligament lies between the anterior talofibular and the calcaneal-fibular ligament, and its fibers blend with both of these ligaments and the joint capsule.

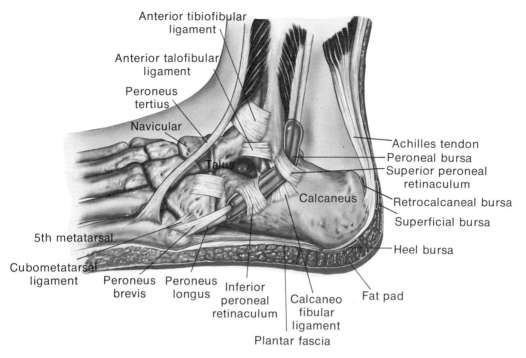

Figure 13-5   The lateral side of the ankle and foot contains many structures that may be injured during sports.

Sprains

Anterior Capsular Sprain

During a hook slide in baseball or when a player's plantar-flexed ankle suffers impact in football, the anterior capsule may tear. This injury produces pain on resisted dorsiflexion and passive plantar flexion, and a long course of rehabilitation is needed to restore full function. To prevent this type of sprain in baseball, a lower, breakaway base with a Velcro strap may be substituted for the standard, high, stationary base.

Medial Eversion Sprain

External rotation and abduction at the ankle may produce a medial eversion sprain. These sprains are less common than lateral sprains, occuring in soccer if the player kicks an opponent and in wrestling when pushing off the medial side of the foot. If the force is continued, the distal tibiofibular ligament may tear, and the interosseous ligament may be damaged. X-ray films should be repeated 24 to 48 hours after this injury to be certain that there is no diastasis of the tibia and fibula. In young athletes, the deltoid ligament may snap off the medial malleolus like a rubber band and stick in the joint to produce a widened mortise. This ligament must then be extracted from the joint and replaced on the medial malleolus. For ankle support and to keep the ankles from turning out, wrestlers must wear high-top shoes.

Lateral Ankle Sprains

A lateral ankle sprain is by far the most common sprain, easily accounting for the most time lost from injury in athletics. As a result of the normal adduction in running and the weaker lateral ligaments, an athlete is more likely to turn his foot in than out. These sprains occur commonly on an irregular surface, such as a rutty football field or when landing on another player's foot in basketball. A tight heel cord predisposes to lateral sprains by forcing the foot into inversion and turning the lateral side of the foot under. Most lateral sprains are isolated anterior talofibular injuries.

The mild, moderate, and severe grading system for sprains is hard to apply to lateral ankle sprains because two ligaments are involved. The terms "single ligament tear" and "double ligament tear" are preferable. Lateral ankle ligaments usually tear in a predictable sequence (Figure 13-6). With plantar flexion and inversion, the anterior talofibular ligament is vertical and tight and tears. This is a single ligament tear. With further inversion, the athlete's full body weight falls on the more dorsiflexed ankle. The calcaneal-fibular ligament is now vertical to the ground, tight, and it also tears, the combination becoming a "double ligament tear."

Signs, Symptoms, and Diagnosis   In most sprains, the ankle plantar flexes and inverts. Severe sprains may be accompanied by an audible pop or tearing sensation, pain, and inability to bear weight. The skin around the lateral ligaments is loose and swells easily, and the most swollen ankle may be the least severely injured. Blood may appear around the heel or even around the toes from leaking, damaged vessels.

Sprained ankles should be examined before swelling and muscle spasm set in to mask the signs, and the ankle should also be viewed from behind. A hemarthrosis will fill in the cavities at either side of the tendo Achilles, whereas an extra-articular hematoma will leave the tendo Achilles defined. The examiner presses on the tibia and fibula to check for fractures and also checks for tenderness at the base of the fifth metatarsal. He then palpates over the ligaments. A palpable sulcus appearing when the ankle is inverted is more conclusive evidence of a complete ligament tear than x-ray studies will provide. Gross instability indicates a tear of both ligaments, but the subject should always be asked whether the instability results from an old injury.

To help in giving a prognosis, the athlete should be asked to stand on his toes. If he is able to stand with ease, the prognosis is good, but if he has difficulty standing the prognosis is less promising. Proprioceptive defects are next sought

with a modified Romberg test. The athlete stands on his sound foot with his eyes open and then closed, then repeats this test on the injured side. Impaired stability that is obvious to the examiner is objective evidence of a proprioceptive defect. If the athlete notes impaired stability that the examiner cannot confirm, the evidence is considered to be subjective.

X-ray films may show a flake of bone that has been avulsed from the fibula.[4] In children, a distal fibula epiphyseal fracture should be checked for, and the examiner should also look for osteochondral fractures in the talar dome. These are best seen on an internal rotation view of the ankle, mostly at the lateral side of the dome of the talus. If an athlete is not improving as well as expected after an ankle sprain, a talar dome osteochondral fracture should be suspected.

Stress tests include the anterior drawer test and the talar tilt test. But because swelling and spasm may mask results from these tests, a peroneal nerve block or hematoma block may be needed.[9] The ankle anterior drawer test is similar to the anterior drawer test of the knee. The athlete sits with his knee flexed to relax his calf, and the examiner gently pulls his heel forward. In functionally normal ankles, the anterior drawer does not exceed 3 mm, and the right and left ankles are roughly equal. When the foot moves forward with crepitation at the ankle, the anterior talofibular ligament is torn, and if the test is grossly positive the calcaneal-fibular ligament is also torn.

To check for talar tilt, the examiner should let the foot fall into normal plantar flexion. The examiner then places one hand medially over the tibia while pressing the other lateral to the heel. The degree of talar tilt produced is influenced by the ankle position at the time of stress. Testing at neutral position analyzes the calcaneal-fibular ligament, whereas a plantar-flexed talar tilt test assesses the anterior talofibular ligament. There is no clear-cut amount of tilt that distinguishes between single and double ligament tears, with most results in the 10° to 20° gray zone. There is a wide normal range, with some subjects showing more than 20°. A positive test is considered to be 10° more talar tilt than is found in the normal joint,[120] although there are right and left differ-

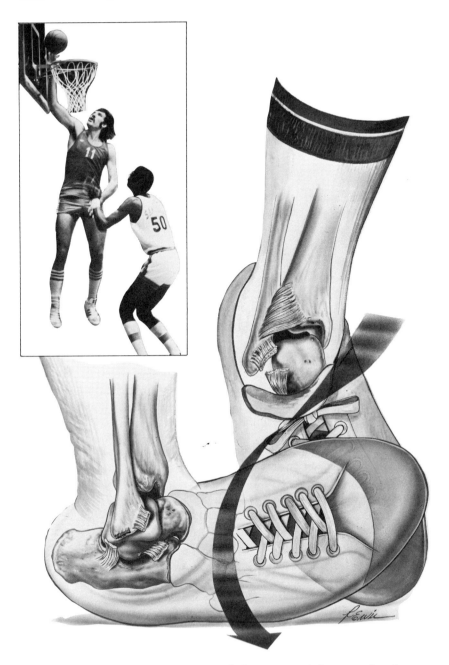

Figure 13-6   Lateral ankle sprains. A "single-ligament sprain" occurs when the player's plantar-flexed ankle is inverted, tearing the anterior talofibular ligament. If the inversion continues when the whole foot has reached the ground, the calcaneal–fibular ligament rips, producing a "double-ligament sprain."

ences with talar tilt and the sound side may open more than the injured side.[110]

An ankle arthrogram may help in the diagnosis of double-ligament tears. The calcaneal-fibular ligament lies deep in the peroneal tendons and is closely associated with the peroneal tendon sheath. An arthrogram may show dye leaking from the joint into the peroneal sheath, indicating a calcaneal-fibular ligament tear. If the dye leaks through a large anterior talofibular tear, however, it may not pass through an associated smaller calcaneal-fibular ligament tear. To avoid this deficiency, dye may be injected directly into the peroneal sheath, along the anterior border of the peroneus brevis tendon, just behind the fibula about 4 cm proximal to the lateral malleolus.[6, 11] If the calcaneal-fibular ligament is torn, dye will pass into the ankle joint. If the arthrogram is done more than a week after the injury, however, it will be invalid because the tear will have sealed. Arthrograms are useful diagnostic adjuncts but are not as reliable as the palpation of a sulcus with the ankle inverted.

Prevention Many ankle sprains can be prevented with heel-cord stretching, proprioceptive training, and proper footwear. Sitting causes the heel cords to tighten and resist ankle dorsiflexion, whereupon the foot inverts. For this reason, all athletes should stretch their heel cords on a step or an ankle board before and after practice.

If an athlete walks and runs only on flat surfaces, a proprioceptive deficiency will develop. Proprioceptive ability can be gained by running on uneven surfaces or on a trampoline or by using a foot seesaw or wobble board each day. Although some athletes train with ankle weights, these may throw off their coordination and produce more sprains due to fatigue.

Proper footwear can also reduce the incidence of ankle sprains. Thus training shoes should not be worn for cutting sports, since they are made for straight-ahead movement. Hightop shoes are best but are not considered stylish today. Wrestlers wear them because they stay on the feet and resist abrasions to the ankle. If the athlete wears a low-cut shoe, tape may be applied firmly around it. X-ray films show that such taping lessens slipping and sliding between the foot and the shoe,

making the foot and shoe a single functional unit and simulating the stability of high-top shoes. The position of cleats on the soles also may influence ankle sprains. Cleats located a distance from the edge of the shoe offer a narrow base of support. For broader support, cleats should extend to the lateral margin of the shoe.

"Preventive" Ankle Taping

Adhesive tape is the biggest item in the training room, and miles of tape are used each year.[40] A hundred million dollars is spent on tape each year for high school tackle football, and its cost is soaring. Elastic tape costs even more than cloth-backed tape.

Even though taping dominates much of the trainer's time, the athlete loses support from the

---

ANKLE TAPING TIPS

1. Table height is important—36″ desirable.
2. Anterior tibial tendon should stand out with dorsiflexion.
3. Tape different-shaped ankles.
4. Identify common areas of tightness and lacerations:
   a. Anterior tibial tendon
   b. Achilles tendon
   c. Base of fifth metatarsal
5. Secret to taping is practice and correct angles:
   a. Angles of heel lock
   b. Horizontal strip angles change with each strip.
6. Pull tightly on vertical strips.
7. Lay on horizontal strips.
8. Pull tightly for heel lock.
9. Overlap strips one-half.
10. Place an X across anterior tibial.
11. Practice heel locks with ankle wraps.
12. Hold skin as tape is removed.

---

tape almost as soon as he walks out of the training room, and after the practice or contest the tape is discarded. Unfortunately, athletes often become psychologically dependent on taped ankles. A poor taping job can restrict the athlete's running speed and vertical jump height and may even cause injury by restricting a normal range of motion. If normal subtalar motion is blocked, its safety-valve action is compromised, and ankle sprains increase. Skillful strapping, however, may reduce such sprains.

During running, the foot comes down inverted, and the peroneus brevis contracts just before heel strike to evert the foot and to place it into a more stable position. A simple lateral loop, or a heel lock over the sock, may prevent some ankle sprains by its action on the peroneus brevis. The loop of tape may excite the peroneus brevis to contract earlier and stabilize the ankle in swing. A more complete taping job is not needed to serve this function. Routine festooning of sound, healthy ankles with adhesive tape often is unnecessary. The motto "never sprained, never taped" makes good sense.

Playing fields should be maintained and policed so that they have no rocks, divots, or potholes. In one instance, a coach improved the condition of his field by banning local rodeos and livestock shows that had been held on the football field for decades.[134] Good maintenance of the playing field will do more to prevent ankle sprains than will taping jobs and shoe changes. With respect to indoor courts, more sprains occur on artificial floors than on wood courts, and for this reason players should wear worn gym shoes to decrease friction.

Acute Treatment of Ankle Sprains

Swelling of an ankle sprain is controlled with "ICE"—*Ice, Compression,* and *Elevation*—and must not be accepted as a part of the injury. Wet elastic wraps kept in a bucket of ice water in an ice chest should be wrapped from the toes up over the sprain. An ice bag is then applied and kept in place with another elastic wrap over it and the leg elevated. Alternately, the ankle may be placed in a bucket of ice slush and a neoprene toecap worn to warm the toes, since the slush is shockingly cold. The ice is left on for 30 minutes, taken off for an hour, and then reapplied. A transcutaneous electrical nerve stimulator can be activated for 30 minutes during the off hour. If the ankle is very painful, a local anesthetic and Wydase may be injected.[9]

A note should be sent home with the athlete describing the injury and its treatment, and the athlete and his parents should be cautioned against using a home remedy, such as hot Epsom salts, which will cause the ankle to blow up. An open, basket-weave taping job is applied for support and an elastic wrap applied for compression.[79] Because the elastic wrap works best on cylinders and will not compress in the hollow around the malleolus, this area should be filled with felt, or a foam horseshoe pad, to establish even compression. The elastic wrap should be removed at night because the wrap could change position and act as a tourniquet if the foot slips off the pillow. A suitcase placed under the foot of the mattress offers better elevation.

The athlete may be permitted to bear weight a bit within his pain tolerance to retain his proprioceptive sense. Also, early cryotherapy range-of-motion exercises and isometrics prevent atrophy. Contrast baths may usually begin 48 hours after the injury; they alternately dilate and constrict the vessels, producing a pumping action[22] that drains edema, lymph, and residue and relieves pain and stiffness. Moreover, blood flow is increased for 45 minutes after a treatment, helping to repair damaged tissue. Contrast treatments are given three times a day in a whirlpool or in a galvanized tub. The cold phase is in a slush made with water and ice cubes with a temperature of about 16°C (60°F). The warm phase is in water with a temperature that ranges from about 38°C to 41°C (100°–105°F). The athlete may follow a 10-minute program, starting with 1 minute in cold water and 3 minutes in warm water. He then does 1 minute in the cold and 2 in the warm, followed by 1 in the cold and 1 in the warm, finishing with a final minute in the cold. Cryotherapy with ice massage or in a 60° whirlpool will also promote recovery, and exercise may be permitted after the skin turns pink and becomes numb.

Foot and ankle exercises include foot circles

and writing the alphabet with the big toe while the ankle extends over the edge of the table. For foot exercise, the athlete picks up tape rolls and other objects and pulls in a towel with his foot. As he improves, a weight may be added to the towel for resistance. Resistance exercises are begun when he has pain-free ankle motion, starting with isometrics (Figure 13-7). He may perform these alone, and his parents or friends may also be taught to help. A lightweight bicycle inner tube may be used for isodynamic resistance. Cryotherapy permits toe raisers on a 2-inch × 4-inch board or on a step performed with the toes turned out. As swelling and soreness disappear, power work may begin on the Orthotron isokinetic unit. Isokinetic training is important because fast contractions are needed to resist inversion.

When ankle ligaments are torn, proprioceptive nerve endings are also torn. These nerves normally provide feedback that signals the need for appropriate muscle action. Once torn, these nerves do not heal. The athlete may, however, restore his sense of balance and coordination by a mechanism similar to that involved in learning to ride a bicycle or to walk on a tightrope. The reeducation process may be performed on a seesaw block or on a tilt board curved in one plane. The board imposes passive displacements on the athlete's foot similar to uneven ground as the athlete stands at varying angles to its axis of movement. While maintaining his balance on one leg, he tries to prevent either end of the block from touching the floor. He advances next to a wobble board (Figure 13-8), a plywood disk

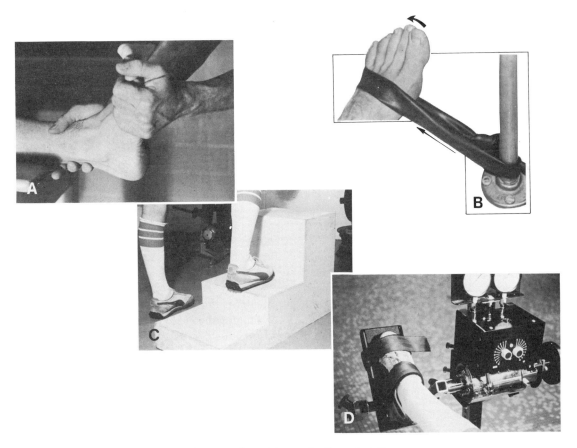

Figure 13-7 A sprained ankle may be strengthened isometrically against the trainer's manual resistance **(A)**, with Tubics **(B)**, by side step-ups **(C)**, and isokinetically **(D)**.

Figure 13-8 A "wobble board" allows the athlete to regain proprioception. Weights may be added **(A)** to strengthen the ankle. The board wobbles on a doorknob or on half a croquet ball **(B)**.

placed on half a croquet ball or a doorknob, leaving the board free to tip in all planes. The athlete balances on the board untaped, since the board will hit the ground before the ankle inverts too much.

The next step in rehabilitating the ankle is special training on walking style. With restricted ankle motion, the athlete will tend to abduct and rotate his leg externally with his knee extended, using his heel as a pivot point. This naturally protective gait minimizes ankle motion and allows long strides with the sound limb. To walk fast, he carries his injured limb through in abduction. The injured athlete should be taught to walk with a short step, with his feet about 10 cm (4 in) apart and his toes pointing forward. True ankle motion is used with the heel striking first. The quadriceps and gluteus maximus waste, however, if an athlete uses this short step walk; for this reason, isometric and resistive hip and knee extension should be added to the exercise program.

Stress can be taken off the lateral ligaments with a heel wedge. A 1.25-cm (0.5-inch) lateral wedge made of felt may be placed inside the athlete's toe, or a 0.63-cm (0.25-inch) neoprene lateral heel wedge may be glued in. The athlete should not wear cleats in the early rehabilitative phase, and the ankle should be taped for exercise. The athlete may begin to jog straight ahead with his ankle taped when he can walk with a normal pushoff and without a limp, taking care to walk the turns. Then, if he has no limp, he may jog the turns. When turns can be jogged without a limp, he may increase to one-half-speed runs and then full speed. When he is able to run turns without a limp, he may start running circles of progres-

sively smaller diameters clockwise and counterclockwise. He then runs a zigzag course and progressively tighter figure-eights. Isodynamic running is superior to running in place or jumping rope because the tubing allows body lean. Because jumping rope demands great proprioception, it is not included in the early rehabilitation of an athlete with an ankle sprain.

The advanced program includes side step-ups, progressing from 5-minute endurance bouts on a 4-inch block to the 8-inch block, the 12-inch step, and finally the 18-inch bench. Next come runs up the stadium steps sideways, half-speed cuts, and finally right-angled cuts, stops, starts, and jumps. Tackle football players also use a cross-over step run.

Running on the fairway of a golf course or on a cross-country course will strengthen the athlete's ankle ligaments and enhance proprioception. He should also be encouraged to ride a bicycle, and his ankle range of motion can be increased by adjusting the saddle. More plantar flexion occurs as the saddle is raised.

Protective Taping A complete rehabilitation program is the key to restoring full ankle function. Festooning the ankle with tape is not a substitute for functional strength; it gives only a false sense of security. Damaged ankles should be protectively taped for contact or heavy activity for the rest of the season, however, because the collagen in the ligaments takes about 7 months to mature. The ankle need not be taped routinely the following year, since the rehabilitation program should return it to normal. A skillful and correctly applied taping will limit abnormal extremes of motion but should not influence the normal range of motion. If normal subtalar motion is limited by taping, the ankle may be sprained again.

When a damaged ankle requires daily taping, the athlete should shave the area the night before so that the skin will not be too sensitive. If taping is needed two or three times a day, a polyurethane foam underwrap material should be applied first (Figure 13-9). Tape should be applied only to skin that is at room temperature. Taping done just after cold or heat treatment may damage the skin when the tape is removed. After the tape is removed, a skin lubricant should be used to restore moisture to the dry skin.

A protective taping for an ankle may include two stirrups and two heel locks (one in each direction) and a figure-eight (Figure 13-10). The components of an ankle taping vary from school to school and from trainer to trainer. The order of application of the specific features is not important as long as the taping limits only inversion

and not plantar flexion, dorsiflexion, or eversion.[1] To help achieve this goal, the tape is applied with the ankle at maximum dorsiflexion and slightly everted.

Standard ankle wraps do not enhance ankle stability. If they are used, benzoin should first be applied to the skin. A sock is then pulled on and sprayed with benzoin, and the ankle wrap is applied over the sock. I prefer to use a brace that contains a lateral plastic strut.

Surgery for an Acute Lateral Ankle Sprain
When an athlete sustains a serious double-ligament ankle sprain, he may note a tearing sensation and will have difficulty if asked to stand on his toes. The examiner can feel a gap laterally when the ankle is stressed, and the tear produces gross instability.[25, 117]

If the torn ends are not grossly separated, the sprain will heal well without operation. The lig-

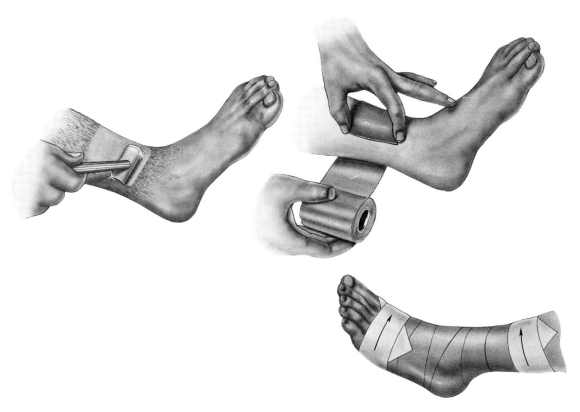

Figure 13-9 The athlete's ankle is shaved at the anchoring area *(left)*, a foam prewrap applied *(right, top)*, followed by anchor strips *(bottom)*.

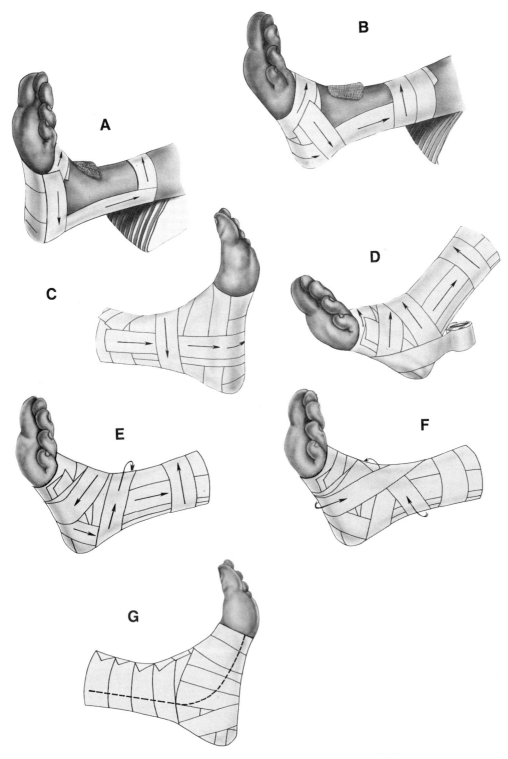

Figure 13-10   Ankle taping starts with "stirrups" and "horseshoes" **(A, B)**. The trainer then applies a figure-of-eight, two heel locks, another figure-of-eight **(C–F)**, and closes the tape job with separate strips **(G)**.

ament will fail to heal, however, if the ends are grossly separated, even if the leg is encased in plaster. Operation guarantees approximation, even when the ligament is originally grossly separated.[120]

The operation is performed through a short oblique incision and the skin gently retracted. In about one half of these cases, the surgeon will find that the torn calcaneal-fibular ligament is sufficiently approximated to have allowed healing with closed treatment. Only by exploring the region, however, can the surgeon determine whether the ligament edges are adequately opposed. Sometimes, the calcaneal-fibular ligament will be found to have pulled from its fibular attachment under the peroneal sheath to lie on top of the sheath. In such cases, closed treatment will not effect reattachment. Instead, reattachment is accomplished by means of holes drilled through the fibula. After operation, the leg is kept in a cast for 6 weeks, and the athlete then follows a rehabilitation program similar to that for the treatment of single ligament sprains.

Chronic Ankle Instability

Chronic instability in a golfer after an ankle sprain may result in his left ankle giving out or in repeated sprains in running and jumping athletes. Foot and ankle inversion before heel strike is accentuated, and the chronically unstable ankle suffers unbalanced loading. The medial aspect of the talus also develops arthritic wear.[52]

Before the surgeon decides to operate on a chronically unstable ankle, the athlete should complete a 3-month rehabilitation program while wearing proper shoes. Some athletes will have "stable instability" in which the ankle gives way during activity, although it is stable when examined. In place of surgery, neuromuscular reeducation on a wobble board is needed. Surgery is also deferred if the ankle causes no functional problems but is unstable only when it is stressed. Operative repair of the ankle is indicated if it remains sore and continues to give way despite full rehabilitation.

Late direct repair, tenodesis, and reconstruction are among the procedures designed to stabilize these ankles. In late repairs, the ligaments are reefed and tightened.[5] For a tenodesis (the Evans procedure), the surgeon sections the tendon of the peroneus brevis and reroutes the distal portion of the tendon through a hole in the fibula, reattaching it to its proximal part.[43, 44] The rerouted tendon then provides a vector between the two stretched-out ligaments but does not restore the function of either directly. In most cases, the tendon will scar down as a tenodesis, but sometimes it may continue to move.

Among the reconstructive procedures performed for chronic ankle instability are the Watson–Jones operation, the modified Watson–Jones, and the Chrisman–Snook procedure (Figure 13-11). In the Watson–Jones, the surgeon transfers the tendon of the peroneus brevis.[48, 136] He passes the tendon through a hole drilled in the fibula. The tendon is then continued through a drill hole in the talus and passed back to the fibula. In a modified Watson–Jones, instead of directing the tendon through the talar tunnel from above to below, it is brought from below to above to better resemble an anterior talofibular ligament.[52, 120, 141] If the tendon of the peroneus brevis is too small, the peroneus longus is used.

The Chrisman–Snook reconstructive procedure is a modification of the Elmslie procedure[17, 38] in which the tendon of the peroneus brevis is used rather than the fascia lata strips used in the Elmslie. The surgeon first sections the tendon of the peroneus brevis proximally and frees it to the base of the fifth metatarsal. It is next passed under the talocalcaneal ligament and sutured to remnants of the anterior talofibular ligament or passed through a slit in the anterior talofibular ligament. After feeding the tendon through a hole in the distal fibula, the surgeon brings it downward to replace the calcaneal-fibular ligament and sets it into a tunnel in the calcaneus. This reconstruction thus replaces both the anterior talofibular and the calcaneal-fibular ligaments.

After an ankle reconstruction, the athlete's leg is placed in a walking cast for 7 weeks. The rehabilitation program should be the same as that for an athlete with a single ligament sprain.

Peroneal Tendon Dislocation

The tendons of the peroneus longus and brevis run in a groove behind the lateral malleolus. If an athlete's ankle is dorsiflexed forcefully and his

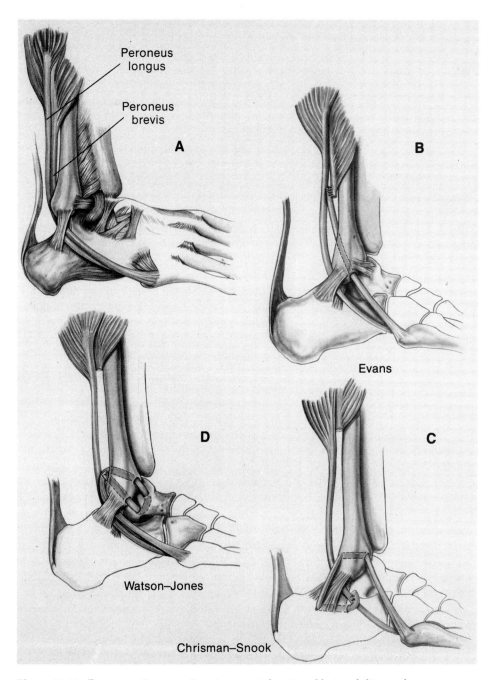

Figure 13-11   Reconstructive operations to correct chronic ankle instability, such as the Evans **(B)**, the Chrisman–Snook **(C)**, and the Watson–Jones **(D)**, generally include a weaving of the tendon of the peroneus brevis through bone. In each of these operations, the tendon of the peroneus brevis is passed through the fibula.

peroneal tendons contract, the peroneal retinaculum may rupture about 2 mm from its insertion into the fibula, freeing the tendons. This occurs when a skier falls forward, loading the inner edge of the lower ski. This type of dislocation was more frequent when low ski boots were worn, but it still occurs when higher boots are buckled improperly.

Early diagnosis of peroneal tendon dislocation is important so that the retinaculum can be repaired.[121] It may mimic an ankle sprain, but, with the tendon dislocation, tenderness is felt behind the lateral malleolus rather than over the lateral ligaments. The examiner may even be able to reproduce the dislocation of the tendons by dorsiflexing the athlete's ankle.

An athlete with recurrent peroneal tendon dislocation reports ankle pain, snapping, and instability. In late cases, the retinaculum may be so atrophied as to be irreparable.[9] Several operations have been designed to solve this problem. A periosteal flap may be swung back over the tendons to hold them in place, or the tendons may be rerouted deep to the strong calcaneofibular ligament.[107] In the Ellis–Jones procedure, a tendon strap is constructed to hold the peroneal tendons medially.[65, 68] A strip of the Achilles tendon 5 mm wide is freed proximally and left attached to the os calcis. It is then passed over the peroneal tendons and through a hole drilled deep in the peroneal groove. The tendon strap is next sutured back on itself and pulled snug with the ankle in dorsiflexion. Sometimes the surgeon selects the plantaris tendon as the tendon strap. If he finds that the groove for the peroneal tendons is very shallow, he may elect to deepen it.

Osteochondral Fracture of the Talus

A cross-country runner may step in a hole, twist his ankle, hear a pop, and develop ankle pain. The injury is usually treated as an ankle sprain, but later the athlete may develop a "weak ankle" with deep ankle pain, recurrent swelling, and a grating sensation. Such slow improvement or worsening after an ankle sprain may be due to an osteochondral fracture of the talus.

An osteochondral fracture in the dome of the talus may follow a compression injury to the sub-chondral bone.[82, 95, 140] A fragment may partly detach (stage III) and later become completely detached (stage IV). Even though it becomes completely detached, however, it may remain in place, never moving from its normal position.

Lateral lesions, produced by shearing forces, are shallow and are more likely than medial lesions to displace and to cause symptoms. They are also "wafer" shaped, located in the midportion of the talus (Figure 13-12), and are best seen on an anteroposterior x-ray view with the ankle in neutral position and rotated internally about 10°. Some medial lesions probably have a traumatic origin, but others may have been present since childhood. Their depth is often greater than their width, and they are less likely to displace and less symptomatic than lateral lesions.[3, 15] Medial lesions are cup shaped, located on the posterior surface of the talar dome, and best seen on an anteroposterior plantar-flexed view. Tomograms are sometimes needed to discern lateral and medial osteochondral lesions.

The athlete with a stage I or stage II lateral or medial lesion should wear a cast for 12 to 18 weeks, until healing is noted between the fragment and the underlying bone. A stage III medial lesion is treated initially with a cast, but if symptoms persist the fragment is excised and the crater curetted. Early operation is indicated for stage III lateral lesions and all stage IV lateral and medial

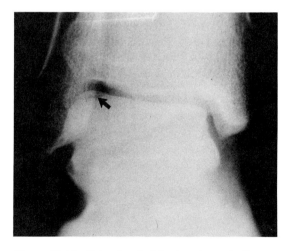

Figure 13-12 Osteochondral fracture is most often seen as a "wafer" on the lateral dome of the talus.

REHABILITATION PROGRESSION FOR THE ANKLE

OBJECTIVES

To strengthen the dorsiflexors, plantar flexors, invertors, and evertors of the ankle

Flexibility: Dorsiflexion and plantiflexion

Endurance: Dorsiflexors, plantiflexors, invertors, and evertors

STAGES

Initial

Cryokinetics in cold water (55°–65°F) wearing a neoprene toe cap to make the cold more tolerable. The athlete does active dorsiflexion, plantar flexion, inversion, and eversion in the water and resisted exercises in these four main directions

Intermediate

Flexibility (Figure 13-13)

Manual passive plantar flexion (Figure 13-13A) for 30 seconds, three times

Towel stretch (Figure 13-13B) straight and with the foot inverted and then everted

Lean forward (Figure 13-13C) with the knee locked (and later with the knee bent), then lean back (Figure 13-13D) with the knee locked for 30 seconds, three times. These exercises stretch the gastrocnemius (knee locked) and soleus (knee bent).

Toe walk (Figure 13-13E) and heel walk (Figure 13-13F)

Strength

Isometrics held for 6 seconds each time. Dorsiflexion, plantar flexion, inversion, and eversion (Figure 13-14A–D)

Cross-legged isometrics to strengthen both dorsiflexion and eversion (Figure 13-14E). The athlete presses the outer border of the affected foot against his other foot

Tubics (Figure 13-15A–D) using the same four motions for three sets of ten repetitions

Heel raises (Figure 13-15E) and heel walks

Endurance: Begin EPLEI Goals 1, 2

Balance: The athlete balances all of his weight on the affected ankle (Figure 13-15F) for 30 seconds, three times each hour, holding onto a bar or table for support, if necessary

Advanced

Flexibility

Stretching off a step with the knee locked (Figure 13-16A) and then with the knee bent (Figure 13-16B) for 30 seconds, three times

Stretching against a wall with the knee locked and feet turned in and then with the knee bent and feet turned in (Figure 13-16C)

Walking down stairs keeping the heel of the injured leg on the upper step until the other foot hits the lower step (Figure 13-16D)

REHABILITATION PROGRESSION FOR THE ANKLE (*continued*)

> Strength
>> Orthotron (Figure 13-16E) or Cybex
>> Multiaxial (Figure 13-16F)
>> Exercise disk (Figure 13-16G)
>> Heel raises with weights
>> Leg press
> EPLEI Goals 3–8
> Balance: Standing only on the injured leg, with eyes closed, the athlete bends down and reaches out to pick up objects
>> Exercise disk

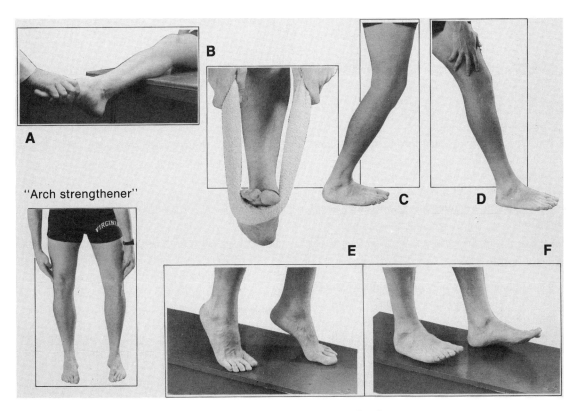

Figure 13-13 The athlete can stretch his ankle manually with a towel or by using his own body weight.

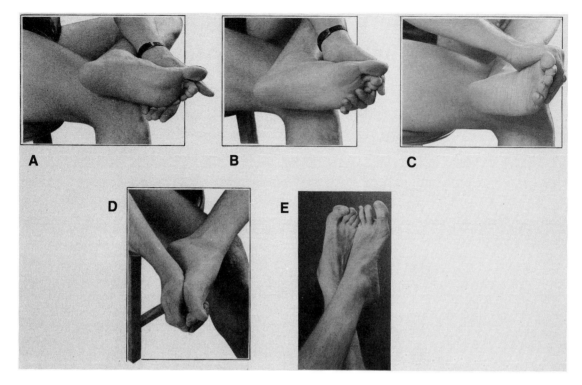

Figure 13-14　The athlete does isometric ankle exercises in all directions.

lesions. The lateral lesions are best approached through an anterolateral incision because the fibula is posterior and the lesion is in the middle third. An osteotomy of the medial malleolus may be needed to provide adequate exposure of a medial lesion.

"Soccer Ankle"

A soccer player's ankle may be extremely plantar-flexed when kicking a heavy ball on a wet pitch. He may note that his ankle becomes painful with kicking and with sudden stops and starts, and he may have swelling and tenderness at the anterior aspect of his ankle joint. An x-ray film may show that new bone has formed on the upper surface of the neck of the talus as a result of traction at the insertion of the capsule.[87, 94] Painful capsular bone spurs may be removed because pain will be persistent and the spurs may even chip off into the joint.

To help prevent capsular sprains and the development of soccer ankle, young players should use a number-3 ball, advance to number-4, and,

finally, when their feet are large and strong, use a full-sized soccer ball.

THE FEET

The foot comprises 26 bones (Figure 13-17) and acts, at times, as a supple shock absorber and, at other times, as a rigid lever.

Problems Around the Heel

Problems affecting the athlete's heel include Achilles tendinitis, subcutaneous bursitis, "runner's bump," retrocalcaneal bursitis and bony prominence, stress fracture of the calcaneum, pinch of the os trigonum, "black dot heel," heel bruises, plantar fasciitis, and pronation neuritis.[109]

Subcutaneous Bursitis

An unpadded, thin shoe counter, such as may be found in some cycling and running shoes, will

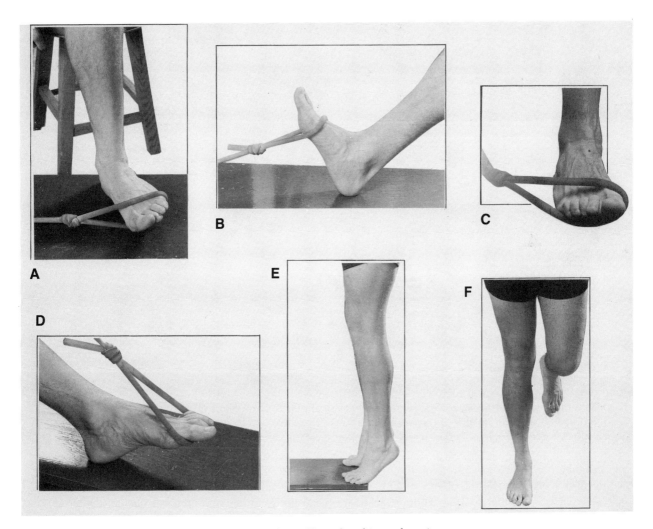

Figure 13-15   The athlete can also strengthen his ankle with Tubics and regains balance by standing on one leg with his eyes closed.

irritate the subcutaneous bursa behind the lower part of the Achilles tendon, causing redness, swelling, and pain. To avoid this problem, or at the first sign of irritation in this region, the athlete should apply a Band-Aid, tape, or "second skin" and change to a shoe with a soft counter.

"Runner's Bump"

A prominence at the back of an athlete's heel may be a "runner's bump." This bump is a bone spur produced by tugging of the heel cord on the os calcis. A lateral x-ray film will show a stalagmite of bone extending from about 1.5 cm below the posterior–superior tip of the os calcis upward into the Achilles tendon. To prevent these spurs from occurring or enlarging, the athlete can work on heel cord stretching, use a heel lift, and wear shoes with a wider heel that will limit rocking. If the spur remains painful, it may be excised. The surgeon exposes it by splitting the Achilles tendon longitudinally.

Retrocalcaneal Bony Prominence

The heel cord begins its insertion to the os calcis about 1.5 cm distal to the uppermost posterior part of the bone. The bony area above the insertion is smooth and occupied by a retrocalcaneal bursa. This area is sometimes prominent

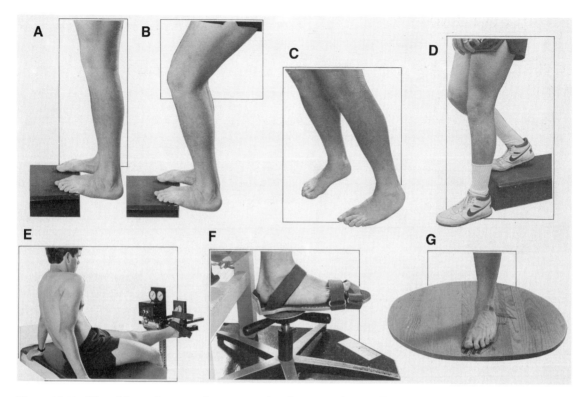

Figure 13-16   The athlete gains strength, power, and endurance isokinetically on the Orthotron and with weights. He regains balance on the ankle disk and by standing on the injured leg and then reaching for objects on the floor.

and may rub against the bursa and the heel cord to cause pain and swelling (Figure 13-18).

To lessen this irritation, the runner can wear training shoes with a flared heel to reduce rocking at heel strike. If symptoms persist, an oblique osteotomy of the prominent bone may be performed. At operation, the surgeon retracts the heel cord and removes the bump obliquely down to the level of the heel cord insertion. Early postoperative motion is allowed, and the athlete can usually expect a good result.

Os Calcis Stress Fracture

A ballet dancer, especially one who has a long, thin os calcis, may note a gradual onset of pain and swelling at the back of her heel.[55, 135, 138] This may be caused by a stress fracture of the os calcis that can be mistaken for Achilles tendinitis. With a stress fracture, however, the bone will be tender.

X-ray films of the bone may not show a fracture line initially, but one may appear later at the upper posterior margin of the os calcis, just anterior to the apophyseal plate at a right angle to the trabeculi. These fractures are immobilized in a walking plaster cast for 5 weeks.

Os Trigonum Pinch

The os trigonum is an accessory bone located just behind the talus and is found in only 10% of the population. With extreme plantar flexion, such as in ballet, jumping, or bowling at cricket, the os trigonum may be nipped like a nut in a nutcracker, producing local pain when the subject springs off his toes.[132, 135] The athlete with this disorder should rest his foot until the soreness abates. A talar spur may break off in this region, and the broken piece may have to be removed to relieve pain.

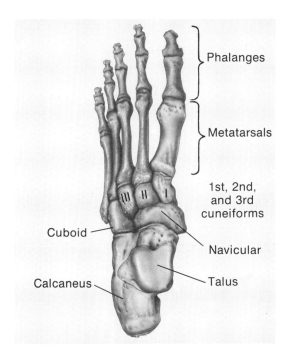

Figure 13-17 The foot comprises 26 bones and numerous joints.

"Black Dot Heel"

Young distance runners may develop "black dot heel," a condition in which painless, irregular, black or bluish-black plaques appear on the posterior or posterolateral aspect of one or both heels[2, 137] (Figure 13-19). The lesion is usually horizontal but may be oval or circular, lying just above the edge of the runner's thick plantar skin, which is often hyperkeratotic in this region. The plaque lies flush with the skin surface and is not palpable.

Black dot heel most likely arises from a shearing stress or a pinching of the heel between the counter and the sole of the shoe at heel strike during running, producing bleeding into the epidermis. When the lesion is pared down with a scalpel, reddish-brown punctate specks of dried blood are uncovered. Under a microscope, clumps of pigment are noted in the stratum corneum. The dark lesion may resemble a melanoma, but individual punctate lesions are usually discernible at the periphery of the main mass. The lesions may also resemble a resolving verruca, but

their position and linear configuration make this diagnosis unlikely.

Black dot heel resolves spontaneously, and recurrence may be prevented by fastening a piece of felt inside the shoe.

Pain Under the Heel

Pain under an athlete's heel can be due to a heel bruise, plantar fasciitis, or pronation neuritis. Anatomically, the heel contacts the ground below the medial tuberosity of the calcaneus. The contour of the tuberosity differs in being sometimes flat, sometimes rounded, and sometimes pointed. The heel pad itself consists of a fatty cushion and fibrous partitions containing little balls of specialized shock-absorbing fat.

The plantar fascia (Figure 13-20) arises from the medial tubercle. The short flexor muscle is just deep to the plantar fascia. Sometimes the flexor pulls bone cells from the calcaneus to form a horizontal bone spur. The abductor hallucis arises medially from the calcaneus and forms a fleshy muscle, but its underside has a very strong fascia that overlies the plantar nerves. The posterior tibial nerve splits into three main branches: the medial plantar nerve, the lateral plantar nerve, and the medial calcaneal nerve. The medial calcaneal nerve can arise proximal to the flexor retinaculum, underneath the retinaculum, or just distal to it. It then travels medial to and then under the heel.

Athletes with heel pain have soreness during running and often even during walking. The heel may be especially painful and stiff in the morning. After a few steps, however, it may feel better. This morning soreness results from transudate that has accumulated from the day before and has settled overnight into glue-like fibrin. These adhesions break with the first steps in the morning and the area loosens up.

As the athlete puts more mileage on his feet, the fat pad flattens and there is less shock-absorbing material. The high-arched foot with a short plantar fascia tugs the plantar fascia and short flexor muscle with each stride, producing a periostitis. The overpronating person usually has an hypertrophied abductor hallucis muscle. Its underlying, firm fascial band then rubs against

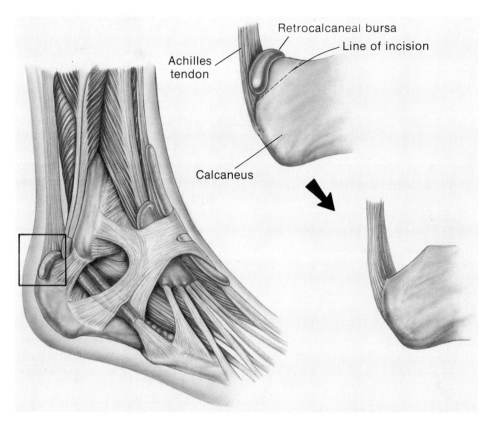

Figure 13-18   Retrocalcaneal pain may be relieved by removing a large piece of bone from the calcaneus *(dotted line)* so that the Achilles tendon no longer rubs against the prominent bone.

the nerves, causing a pronation neuritis characterized by a burning plantar pain and tingling.

Examination   For examination of the sole of the foot, the athlete kneels on the edge of the examining table or lies prone. In this position, the foot is relaxed and can be compared easily to the opposite foot (Figure 13-21).

The foot of a person with a heel bruise will be tender over the medial tuberosity of the heel and will often have a thin or very mobile fat pad. In cases of plantar fasciitis, the tenderness is along the medial edge of the fascia distal to its origin, and over the abductor hallucis. In pronation neuritis, where nerve entrapment predominates, the anteromedial part of the heel pad and abductor hallucis muscle are tender. Tapping over the muscle near the heel may produce lightning-like pains that radiate toward the plantar side of

the heel and advance into the foot. Tenderness over the plantar fascia and its origin is weak or missing. Stretching of the abductor hallucis and shortening of the flexors provoke pain. The symptoms decrease when these muscles are relaxed, suggesting that the nerve compression is dynamic rather than constant or static.

Diagnostic Tests   Treadmill examination is important to show what the athlete is doing dynamically at the subtalar joint and gives a chance to evaluate the shoes. Everyday shoes usually have quite firm heels. In plantar fasciitis and pronation neuritis, the examiner looks for midsole collapse and insufficient counters on the shoes.

On x-ray films, a spur may be seen. The spur itself is probably not the cause of the pain but merely an indication of tugging. In fact, the sev-

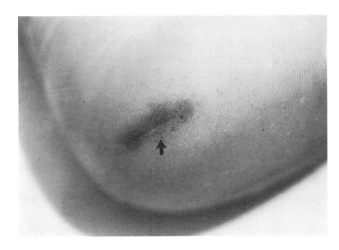

Figure 13-19 Calcaneal petechiae *(arrow)* are noted where the plantar callus joins more normal skin.

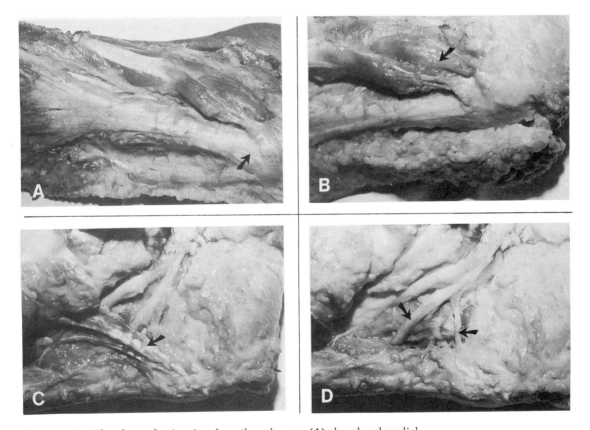

Figure 13-20 The plantar fascia arises from the calcaneus **(A)**; dorsal and medial to it is the abductor hallucis **(B)**. When the muscle belly of the abductor hallucis is stripped away **(C)**, a firm deep fascia is uncovered that overlies the plantar nerves. When this fascia is sectioned and folded back, the plantar and calcaneal nerves are fully seen **(D)**.

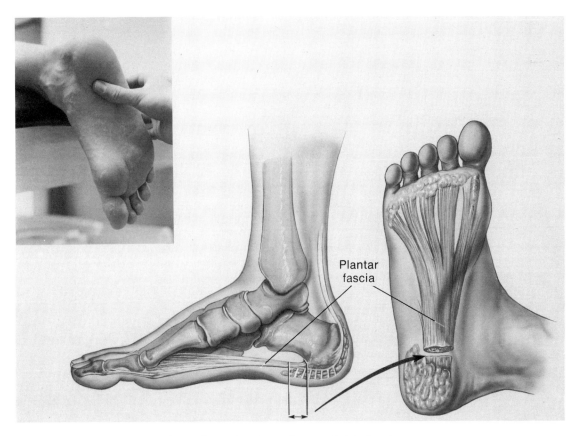

Figure 13-21   The examiner palpates the tender plantar fascia with his thumb. Arrows show the area that is removed.

erest case of plantar fasciitis may have no spur, and many normal feet have large spurs.

Pain under the heel can also be a sign of systemic conditions such as rheumatoid arthritis, gout, Reiter's syndrome, or ankylosing spondylitis. So blood tests may be necessary.

Treatment   Treatment for a heel bruise includes pulsed ultrasound to reduce inflammation and point stimulation to reduce soreness so that deep transverse friction massage may be used to break adhesions painlessly and stimulate healing. A soft pad, heel cup, medial wedged Lynco orthotics, or orthotics with deep heel cups may be used to relieve pressure on the heel (Figure 13-22). The medial wedge takes the pressure off the medial tuberosity, throws it more laterally, and sometimes is effective in curing the problem. A local steroid injection may be curative, but it also may lead to fat necrosis and make the problem worse.

For plantar fasciitis, pulsed ultrasound, point stimulation, and deep friction massage are indicated. The cavus foot should be cushioned with a soft orthotic or runner's mold. A heel lift will reduce the equinus or discrepancy in height between the rear foot and forefoot. A local steroid injection is sometimes curative, but it may endanger the integrity of the plantar fascia. Although it will decrease inflammation, it may also cause tissue degeneration, which would lead to a more intractable problem and may even cause the plantar fascia to rupture. In chronic cases of plantar fasciitis, and especially in patients who have received steroid injections, the athlete may feel a pop or a tear with vigorous activity. The heel often stays sore until a final pop fully ruptures the worn-out plantar fascia. Sometimes, this rupture of the plantar fascia is not bad for the athlete because it breaks the degenerated tissue and is much like doing a plantar fascia release.

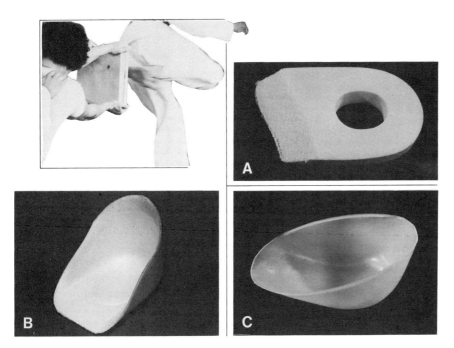

Figure 13-22 A heel bruise may be treated with a foam donut pad **(A)**, a cup of precompressed airplane insulation **(B)**, or a plastic heel cup **(C)**.

In cases of pronation neuritis, a Lynco orthotic with medial wedge will reduce the pronation and prevent the rubbing of the deep band fascia of the abductor against the plantar nerves. In a flat foot, a heel lift will reduce pronation. The lift should be a firm one that tapers to just behind the metatarsal heads. A soft, short lift would compress too easily and also allow the foot to pronate just distal to the lift. If the person has a forefoot varus, then a custom-casted runner's mold orthotic with deep heel cups and metatarsal pad is indicated. The athlete should also wear straight-lasted shoes and do arch-strengthening exercises.

If the athlete has a burning soreness at the heel and positive Tinel's sign along the medial side of the heel, he may have perineural fibrosis around the medial calcaneal nerve. A medial calcaneal nerve block will help with the diagnosis. If the shot alleviates the pain, then perhaps a decompression of the medial calcaneal nerve is indicated. In some heel bruises, however, in which the medial calcaneal end fibers have been contused and have perineural fibrosis, the release will not be effective and a sectioning of the nerve may be needed to relieve the pain.

If therapy, shoe modifications, and orthotics do not alleviate the problem, I recommend a plantar fascia release (see Figure 13-21). The release is performed through a 4-cm transverse plantar incision just distal to the weight-bearing surface of the heel. The plantar fascia is easily exposed and sectioned, a spur may be removed, and the deep fascia of the abductor may be snipped. As soon as the swelling diminishes around the incision, the athlete can begin Poolex. This wound heals fast, and he can begin running with a soft arch support.

Plantar Fascial Tear

An athlete's plantar fascia may tear while he runs in a marathon, while serving in tennis, while running down a ball in squash, or, if he has had a steroid shot for plantar fasciitis, even while walking. Such tears are most common in "middle-aged" athletes. The pain is sudden, sharp, and searing in the midarch, followed by swelling and black-and-blue discoloration.

Ice and Cryotemp reduce the swelling, and pulsed ultrasound decreases the inflammation. If his foot is strapped, the athlete can usually walk without much pain. He can then advance to arch-strengthening exercises. Especially in those persons who have not received treatment for a ruptured plantar fascia, a firm and painful scar may form that may have to be excised.

Midfoot Pain

Midfoot pain is common in athletes who must wear lightweight shoes. Gymnasts, for example, wear only slippers but must run on a hard runway, impact at the takeoff board, and land forcefully. Runners and jumpers wear light and flexible competition shoes. Such light slippers or shoes may cause the feet to pronate excessively, and a midtarsal joint synovitis may develop. To help avoid and to treat this problem, the athlete can add lightweight airplane insulation inserts to the slippers or competition shoes. The runner may also wear his more supportive training shoes in competition, and the intrinsic muscles of the feet may be strengthened with the arch program.

A cross-country runner may develop midfoot pain when training in cold weather on hard ground. When he runs on uneven surfaces in soft shoes, he may also sprain his calcaneonavicular ligament. This "spring ligament sprain" produces a deep medial midfoot aching. An orthosis should be provided to relieve it and the athlete advised to wear firmer, straight-lasted shoes and to resume training on a flat surface.

Navicular Stress Fracture

A stress fracture of the navicular bone is like the broken hock or stress fracture of the navicular in the outside legs of a racing greyhound. Repetitive cyclic loading results in fatigue failure through the relatively avascular central portion of the tarsal navicular. The characteristic fracture is oriented in the sagittal plane and located in the central one third of the bone.[128a] It may be either partial or complete. The incomplete ones are usually confined to the dorsal aspect of the bone.

A navicular stress fracture may produce chronic foot pain. The pain may be vague and diffuse but, like the pain in other stress fractures, increases during the activity. Continued activity may result in a displaced, intra-articular fracture.

Standard x-ray films may not show the fracture. In an anteroposterior x-ray film of the foot, the long axis of the navicular is oriented obliquely to both the x-ray beam and the surface of the film. In this position, partial fractures of the proximal articular border are obscured. The x-ray film should, instead, be taken with the medial side of the forefoot elevated so that the entire foot is everted, setting the widest diameter of the navicular perpendicular to the beam. The sagittal plane of the central one third of the bone is thus parallel to the beam and perpendicular to the film to reveal partial and complete stress fractures. Fluoroscopy may be used to ensure proper positioning of the foot. The foot is then placed on a foam wedge and taped to the cassette in the correct position.

If the area of the navicular is sore but the x-ray films are negative, a bone scan is indicated. If the scan is positive, then tomograms may be done. A navicular stress fracture is treated by placing the athlete's leg in a cast and forbidding weight bearing for 6 weeks.

Cuboid Subluxation

A subluxation of the cuboid bone may produce pain along the lateral side of the foot near the fourth and fifth metatarsals at the dorsal aspect of the cuboid or pain at the calcaneal-cuboid joint.[97a] The peroneus longus passes under the cuboid in the pulley-like peroneal groove from the lateral side of the heel across the arch to its insertion on the first cuneiform and the base of the first metatarsal. Because the cuboid is the fulcrum of this pulley, the tendon may pull the lateral aspect of the cuboid dorsally, allowing the medial aspect to move plantarward. The cuboid may then become locked in this subluxed position.

Subluxations of the cuboid occur most often in athletes who overpronate and are rare in those with pes cavus. With the foot pronated, the midtarsal joint is unstable. The injury usually occurs while the athlete is running on uneven terrain but sometimes results from an acute twist of the foot. The foot then hurts even while walking. On examination, the foot will be tender at the peroneal groove on the plantar aspect of the cuboid. X-ray films will look normal.

To reduce the subluxation, the examiner grasps the athlete's foot with with his fingers and places his thumbs, one over the other, under the cuboid. A quick thumb thrust reduces subluxation and sometimes provides instant relief. The arch is then strapped. Orthotics are provided if the athlete is an overpronator.

Cavus Foot

High-arched "cavus" feet are inflexible and give poor shock absorption (Figure 13-23). Jarring can cause arch pain, heel pain, lateral knee pain, and pains extending up the lateral side of the lower extremity. Repeated tugs on the plantar fascia may produce a plantar fasciitis; however, airplane insulation inserts will cushion the feet and reduce jarring, Flexible heel cords will increase the athlete's shock-absorbing ability, and he should also stretch out his flexor hallucis longus.

An athlete with cavus feet has the highest risk of rupturing his plantar fascia, as when rebounding in basketball. Such a tear can be crippling because this important supporting structure heals with scar tissue that hurts during running and jumping. Soft sock liners should be placed in the shoes of most athletes to reduce the risk of these

injuries. The inserts are especially needed in basketball sneakers, football cleats, and baseball spikes. They not only help to prevent plantar fascia problems, but also prevent calluses and reduce foot fatigue[71, 75]

Tight Calf Muscles

Tight calf muscles can cause many problems. They are often present in athletes with high-arched cavus feet. In these feet, the ball of the foot is lower than the heel (equinous). Tight calf muscles are not limited, however, to athletes with high-arched feet. Flat-footed athletes and those with normal feet can develop tight calves from sitting in a chair with the heels off the floor or just from running, especially up hills.

Tight calf muscles can limit hamstring flexibility. The calf muscles attach to the femur and to the deep fascia behind the thigh. This attachment can be demonstrated by having the athlete bend over, touching toward his toes with his knees straight. When a book or a board is put under his heels, the calf muscles will relax and the freed hamstrings will allow him to flex further.

Many problems are related to tight calf muscles: lower back pain, sciatica, hamstring strains, posterior knee pain, calf pain, posteromedial "shin splints," Achilles tendinitis, Achilles peri-

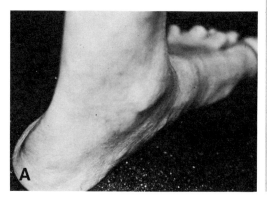
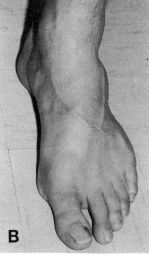

Figure 13-23 The pronated foot is a flat foot **(A)**. Pronation refers to dorsiflexion, abduction, and eversion at the subtalar joint. A cavus foot is high arched and rigid **(B)**.

tendinitis, retrocalcaneal pain, heel spurs, plantar fasciitis, arch strain, metatarsalgia, and metatarsal stress fractures.

Tight calf muscles may cause anterior leg pain, too. The tight calves produce hamstring inflexibility which, in turn, causes the quadriceps to contract more strongly, sometimes producing retropatellar arthralgia. Anterior shin splints may result because the anterior muscles must work against the tight calf muscles so many times an hour while running. In addition to posterior and anterior problems, tight calves can cause medial and lateral trouble. Tendons entering the foot change direction at the ankle under the retinacula. An abnormal angle of entry can result in posteromedial shin splints, lateral leg pain, medial and lateral ankle pain, tarsal tunnel entrapment, and arch pain.

Almost all of the above problems may be solved by calf and hamstring stretches and a heel lift. Stretching should be frequent and gentle. Sitting at a desk should be interrupted often for stretches and walks. Hamstring stretching helps the calves and calf stretches help the hamstrings. However, a person can dorsiflex the ankle only so far before encountering a bony blockage as the talus meets the tibia. Thus if calf stretching does not work even though the athlete has tried hard, there is probably a bony block to extension, and this athlete will not be able to increase calf flexibility and should forget about pushing this stretch.

Heel lifts should be firm because soft ones will just compress. The lift should extend at least one half the length of the shoe, from the back of the shoe beveled to just behind the metatarsal heads. A short heel lift allows the foot to drop and pronate in front of it. A ¼-inch lift can fit into a shoe. If more lift is needed, it should be built into the shoe. To do this, the midsole is cut by running a cast cutter around the shoe. The heel is then opened and the wedge glued in.

Pronated Foot

After heel strike, the runner's leg rotates internally and his foot pronates to achieve a plantigrade position (see Figure 13-23). Pronation combines dorsiflexion, eversion, and abduction at the subtalar joint, motions that provide shock absorption (Figure 13-24). Some pronation is normal, but limited or excessive pronation may lead to injury. Hyperpronation compensates for bowlegs, a tight Achilles tendon, rear-foot varus, and fore-foot varus. The runner with a short leg will overstride on the short side and overpronate.

"Greek Foot"

A "Greek foot" (the ancient Greeks made their statues with feet like these) may pronate excessively. The first metatarsal is short and hypermobile, with the great toe usually not projecting as far as the second toe. The hypermobile first ray takes longer to reach the ground than a normal first ray, and the foot pronates further until the first ray reaches the ground. The second metatarsal head must then bear more weight, remaining

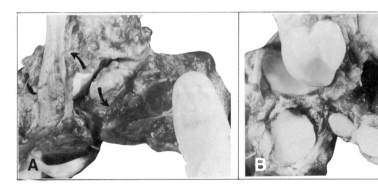

Figure 13-24 When the subtalar joint is opened **(A)**, its complex articulations are revealed **(B)**.

on the ground until the first metatarsal head lands, and the extra weight-bearing may cause painful callus to form under the second metatarsal head.

Treatment of this condition is accomplished with a Morton's extension, a pad placed under the first ray so that it need not travel as far before ground contact (Figure 13-25). The foot may also be taped with the first ray plantar flexed (Figure 13-26).

The Dorsum of the Foot

On the dorsum of his foot, the athlete may suffer an instep bruise, rupture of the extensor hallucis longus tendon, pain at an os supranaviculare, fracture of the base of the fifth metatarsal bone, ski boot compression neuritis, and "surfer's knots."

Instep Bruise

If an athlete's foot is hit by a ball at cricket, struck in field hockey, or stepped on in soccer, his instep may be bruised. There is usually not much swelling, but the area is locally tender; an x-ray film should be taken to rule out a cracked bone. Ice is applied, and, in a few days, whirlpool treatments should be begun. A felt pad or a foam rubber donut pad should be placed over the re-gion to prevent further injury. An instep guard will prevent these bruises in baseball (Figure 13-28).

Os Supranaviculare

Pain and swelling on the dorsum of the foot when running may be due to a mobile accessory ossification center of the navicular, the os supranaviculare. This accessory bone is located at the proximal-superior aspect of the navicular. A local xylocaine injection will relieve the pain and is also diagnostic. If the pain becomes chronic, the os supranaviculare can be resected.[142]

Fracture of the Fifth Metatarsal

The peroneus brevis, cubometatarsal ligament, lateral band of the plantar fascia, and the peroneus tertius all insert into the proximal part of the fifth metatarsal. Weight-bearing places great forces on this bone, and the injuries to it include peroneus brevis strain, hairline fracture, avulsion fracture, and the "Jones fracture."

An inversion twist of the foot may strain the tendon of the peroneus brevis. There will be local tenderness over the tendon and pain with active eversion or passive inversion. An eversion strapping is applied and then ice packs for treatment. A hairline fracture of the fifth metatarsal is caused

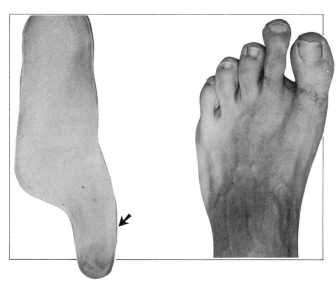

Figure 13-25 The hyperpronation from a short and hypermobile first ray can be restricted with a Morton's extension *(arrow)* that extends under the first ray.

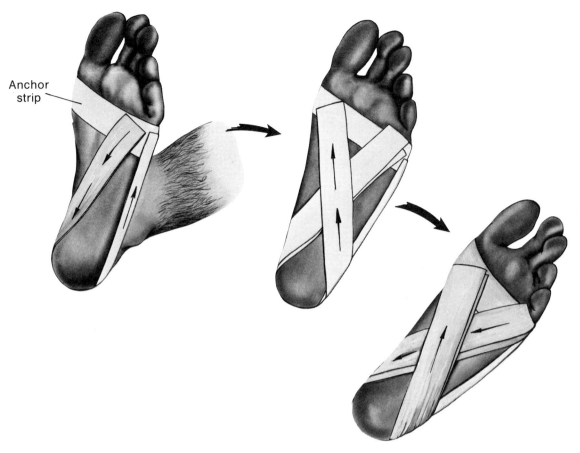

Anchor strip

Figure 13-26   A "teardrop" arch taping supports the athlete's arch and lessens tension on the plantar fascia.

by the same inversion twist mechanism and is also treated with an eversion strapping and ice. Casts should be avoided for these undisplaced fractures because immobilization results in a marked proprioceptive deficit and long rehabilitation. Avulsion fractures, however, demand cast treatment. Occasionally an avulsed piece will become chronically painful and must be excised. Further, an accessory bone at the base of the fifth metatarsal, the os vesalius, may become painful with activity and need to be resected.

The Jones fracture is a fatigue fracture in the diaphysis of the fifth metatarsal[66] (Figure 13-29). In contrast to the injuries described above, this condition is more serious. Nonunion is frequent and may disable and retire the athlete. To compress the fracture site and avoid nonunion, the surgeon should place a malleolar lag screw across the fracture site from the styloid of the fifth metatarsal.[67] If a Jones fracture with an established nonunion is noted late, a bone graft may be needed in addition to the screw fixation.

Ski Boot Compression Neuropathy

Ski boot compression at the front of the ankle may produce a neuritis of the deep peroneal nerve and a synovitis of the extensor tendons. These structures are compressed between the tongue of the boot and the bone.[77] The condition may mimic a compartment syndrome, with decreased web space sensation and poor dorsiflexion of the toes. Boot-top pressure may also cause a numbness and tingling in the soles of the feet.[27] If a skier presents with these symptoms, his leg should be elevated and an ice pack wrapped on.

REHABILITATION PROGRESSION FOR THE ARCH

OBJECTIVES

To strengthen the tibialis posterior and the tibialis anterior
Flexibility: Tibialis posterior, gastrocnemius and soleus
Endurance: Tibialis anterior and tibialis posterior

STAGES

Initial
Cryokinetics in cold water (55°–65°F) with active range of motion and isometrics

Intermediate
Flexibility
    Spread the toes. If the athlete cannot spread his toes, the trainer can hold them apart (Figure 13-27A). As the trainer slowly releases the toes, the athlete should try to keep them spread.
    Flex toes over the edge of the table (Figure 13-27B)
    Extend the toes (Figure 13-27C)
Strength
    Pick up pencils or marbles with the toes (Figure 13-27D)
    Make a fist with the toes (Figure 13-27E). The fist can also be used to gather a towel (Figure 13-27F) or to slide a towel toward the other foot (Figure 13-27G)
    Inversion isometrics and inversion Tubics (see ankle section)
Endurance
Begin EPLEI Goals 1, 2

Advanced
Flexibility: See Intermediate/Advanced ankle section
Strength
    Heel walk
    Toe walk
Endurance
EPLEI Goals 3–8

Anti-inflammatory drugs or a steroid injection will reduce the inflammation. When the skier returns to the slopes, recurrence may be avoided by altering the pressure areas in his boots.

"Surfer's Knots"

Surfing began in Polynesia where the surfers lay prone on the surfboard while paddling out to the waves, but, in colder California waters, surfers kneel on the surfboard when paddling. Sand sticks to a waxed surfboard, and pressure and rubbing will produce hyperkeratotic skin nodules that may be found over the metatarsal–phalangeal joints of the feet and the anterior tibial surface, accompanied by swelling in the synovial sheath of the extensor digitorum longus on the dorsum of the foot. These nodules are painless and do not

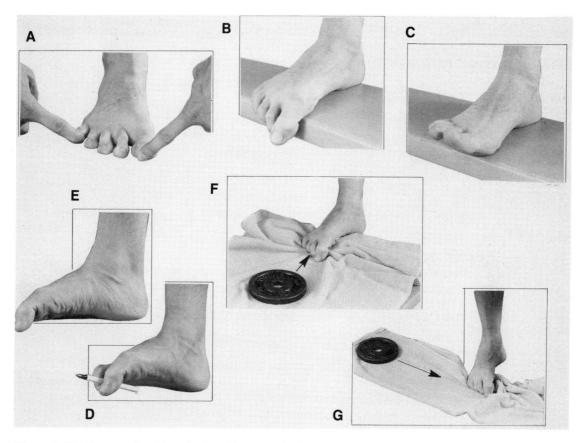

Figure 13-27   To strengthen his arch, the athlete spreads, flexes, and extends his toes and makes "fists" with his foot. He gains agility and foot strength by picking up objects with his foot and by dragging a weight that rests on a towel.

require treatment. Lying prone on the surfboard would prevent knots, but because they are often a status symbol it is doubtful that there will be any change in the paddling technique.

The Forefoot and Toes

Forefoot and toe problems in athletics include metatarsal stress fractures, metatarsalgia, interdigital neuromas, ganglion cysts, hallux valgus, "turf toe," sesamoiditis, sesamoid fractures, claw toes, hammer toes, "tennis toe," and ingrown toenails.

Metatarsal Stress Fracture

A runner pushes off through his second metatarsal head and second toe, and the high forces may cause a stress fracture of the thin diaphysis

of his second, third, or fourth metatarsal. As a response to the repetitive forces of running, the second metatarsal of a distance runner hypertrophies to an extent where it becomes almost as broad as his first metatarsal. Despite this compensation, these runners may suffer a stress fracture if they change shoes or running surfaces, increase the intensity of their training, or run differently because of a blister. Metatarsal stress fractures are not limited to runners, however; swimmers may also develop such fractures from pushing off while practicing turns.

If an athlete sustains a stress fracture, his forefoot becomes painful and swollen (Figure 13-30). The pain is relieved by rest but recurs with weight bearing and pushing off. Early x-ray films may show normal findings, but at about 10 days a cloud of callus can usually be seen around the fracture. Treatment consists of ice, compression,

Figure 13-28 The dorsum of the foot can be protected from bruising.

and a forefoot strapping. To keep fit, the athlete wears a water-skiing vest and runs in the deep water in the diving well of a swimming pool.

Metatarsalgia

Metatarsalgia, or pain and tenderness under the metatarsal heads from bruising, is a common problem in runners. The athlete's training shoes or everyday walking shoes may have worn down, no longer providing a cushion for his metatarsal heads. Pressure builds through the day, and the area is subjected to further stress and becomes painful when the athlete trains. A 0.25-inch foam rubber rocker bottom can be inserted into the sole of the training shoes and street shoes to reduce the forces on the metatarsal heads and allow the inflammation to subside. Shock-absorbing foam inserts in his walking shoes, training shoes, and competition shoes can be worn to prevent this condition.[71]

Intermetatarsal Neuritis

During pronation of the foot, the metatarsals roll and the metatarsal heads and transverse metatarsal ligament may squeeze and pinch a nerve, especially the nerve between the third and fourth metatarsal heads. A sharp, burning pain may then strike out along the opposing surfaces of the toes. This pain is usually relieved when the athlete takes his shoe off and rests his foot. The examiner may be able to reproduce the pain by squeezing the forefoot, and a local anesthetic injected near the nerve will relieve the pain.

An orthosis to reduce pronation usually resolves the problem, but sometimes a hydrocortisone shot may be needed to reduce the inflam-

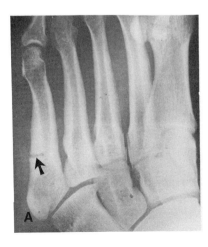
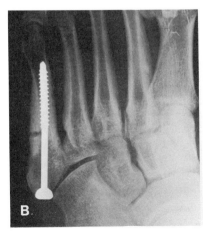

Figure 13-29 A fracture of the diaphysis of the fifth metatarsal **(A)** may be slow healing and may need to be compressed with a lag screw **(B).**

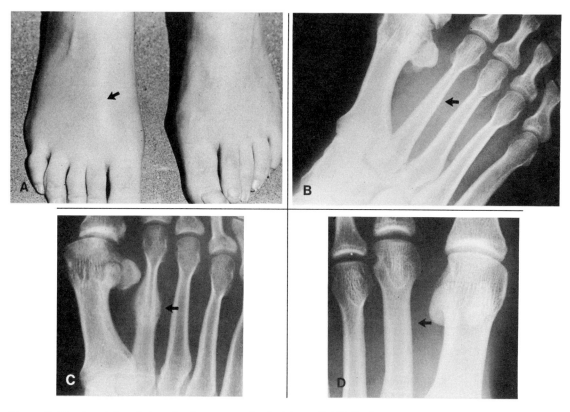

Figure 13-30 A metatarsal stress fracture causes the foot to swell **(A)**; the fracture occurs usually through the very thin bone of the second metatarsal **(B)**. It may not be visible for a few weeks on x-rays; by then callus has developed **(C)**. The second metatarsal of a distance runner hypertrophies because of increased stresses on it **(D)**.

mation. The athlete should switch to shoes that are wider around the forefoot. An operation to remove the neuroma is rarely needed, and such an operation may leave a scar more painful than the neuroma. If a neurectomy is deemed necessary, the surgeon may use a dorsal approach with a small lamina spreader to spread the metatarsals for easy access to the nerve.

Ganglion Cyst

If a firm mass appears dorsally in a web space between the toes with activity and recedes after activity, the athlete may have a ganglion cyst (Figure 13-31).[71] This arises from a flexor tendon sheath, following the path of least resistance between the toes to the dorsum of the foot. If painful, it may be removed completely after tracing it down to its origin.

Hallux Limitis, Hallux Rigidis, and Hallux Valgus

Hallux limitis refers to limited, painful motion of the metatarsophalangeal joint of the great toe. Hallux rigidis is a rigid metatarsophalangeal joint. For best performance, an athlete needs full great-toe, metatarsophalangeal-joint motion because, during pushoff, the great toe must hyperextend about 90° on the first metatarsal. Limitation of this motion may be painful and cause a breakdown at the metatarsophalangeal joint, leading to problems in the rest of the foot.

If an athlete has limited motion in the first metatarsophalangeal joint of the great toe and motion is painful due to arthritis within the joint or a capsular sprain, he should wear a shoe with a rocker sole. Steroids should not be injected into an arthritic metatarsophalangeal joint because

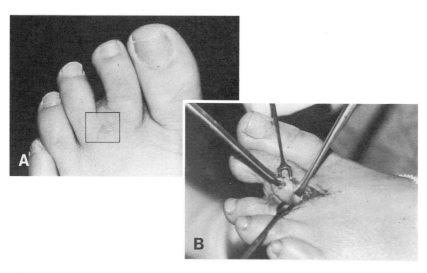

Figure 13-31   Swelling in a webspace **(A)** that follows activity may be caused by a ganglion cyst **(B)** arising from a flexor tendon sheath.

they may hasten the breakdown of the articular cartilage. An arthritic metatarsophalangeal joint is sometimes resected, but the athlete then loses pushoff and he will not jump very well. However, if dorsal spurs are the only problem, they can be removed with good results (Figure 13-32).

The athlete with hallux valgus has poor push-off, and his shoes may irritate the bunion. He may also develop medial knee pain because of abnormal foot mechanics and a valgus stress to the knee. Daily great toe taping will usually benefit the runner with hallux valgus. An anchor strip is first placed around the great toe and another is set proximal to the bunion; these anchors are then spanned by strips of adhesive tape applied with the great toe held in a normal neutral position. An orthosis and the simple taping provide the athlete with a remarkably better gait and restore the feeling of moving straight ahead while running. He can wear shoes with a wider forefoot to prevent rubbing on the bunion or can have his shoes stretched with a shoemaker's swan and wear a bunion shield (Figure 13-33). A bunion splint worn at night can reduce progression of the deformity (Figure 13-34).

There is no ideal operation to correct hallux valgus in an athlete; however, releasing the adductor and applying orthotic correction to reduce the hypermobility of the first ray and pronation

will halt the sesamoid shift and retard progression of the great toe deformity.

Artificial Turf Toe

In tackle football, the metatarsophalangeal joint of the great toe is often sprained, especially when players wear flexible soccer-style shoes on artificial turf[8, 19, 24, 45] (Figure 13-35). Offensive linemen who block or push against a blocking sled and receivers and defensive backs who must cut and make quick stops may forcefully hyperextend and sprain the joint. The sprained plantar capsule of the joint will hurt, especially when the toe is extended; thus the joint should be taped to reduce its motion (Figure 13-36). To reduce forefoot motion, players should wear a firmer shoe with a spring steel or orthoplast forefoot splint.

Sesamoiditis

The two sesamoid bones in the tendon of the flexor hallucis brevis (see Figure 13-35) may be irritated by pressure from a cleat under the first metatarsal head or by bowing in this area that results from faulty cleat placement. The examiner should check the cleat position and fashion a pad that unburdens the first metatarsal head and that may relieve the pain. An orthosis to reduce pron-

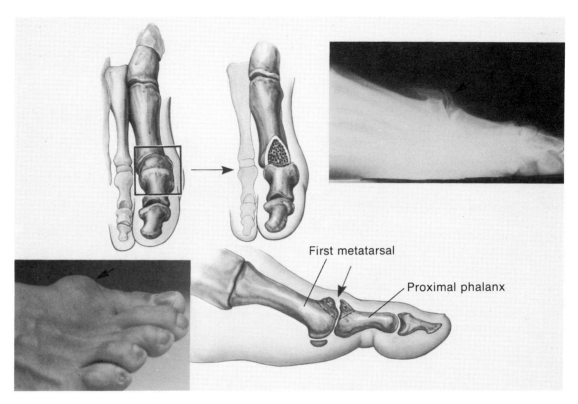

Figure 13-32 Generous pieces of bone *(dotted line)* are removed from the metatarsophalangeal joint.

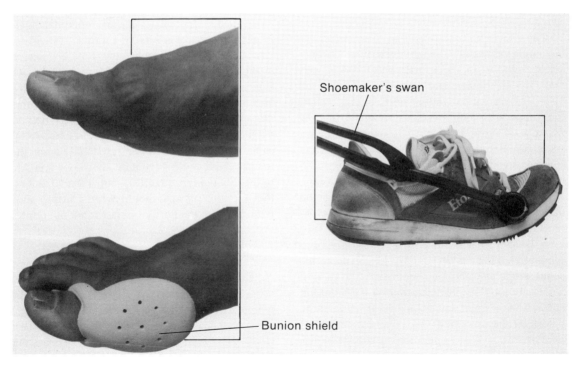

Figure 13-33 Pressure on the painful prominence of a bunion can be relieved by wearing a bunion shield or by stretching the shoe with a shoemaker's swan.

554

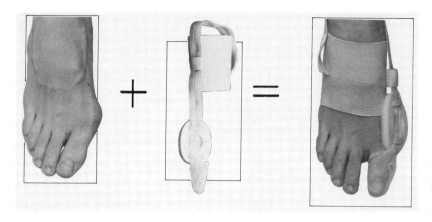

Figure 13-34 A hallux abductovalgus deformity can be countered by wearing a night splint.

ation or a Morton's extension is sometimes curative. A 0.25-inch foam-rubber rocker bottom can be inserted into the sole of the training shoes and street shoes to reduce the forces on the sesamoids and allow the inflammation to subside. The great toe may also be strapped to limit motion, but injections are usually not helpful. In some persons with "sesamoiditis," the medial digital nerve lies just under the medial sesamoid. Their pain may be relieved by transposing this digital nerve.

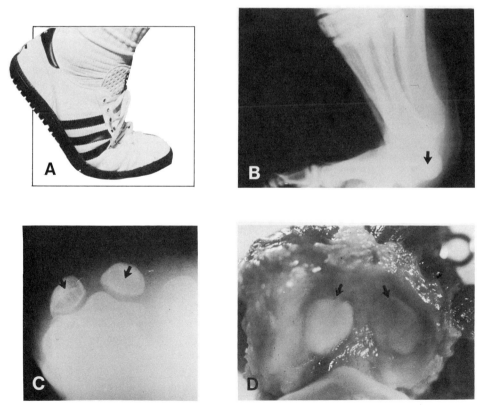

Figure 13-35 Flexible shoes **(A)** worn on artificial turf may lead to a great toe sprain. Weight is borne on the sesamoids **(B)**, small bones that can be seen on a sesamoid bone x-ray view **(C)**. They reside in the tendon of the flexor brevis **(D)**.

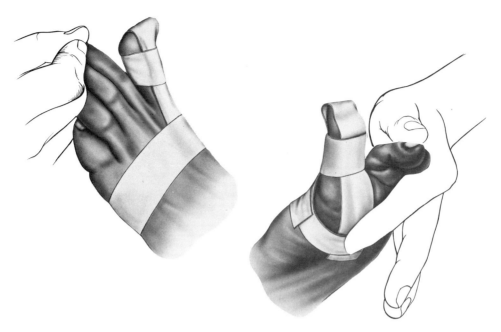

Figure 13-36   ''Turf toe'' taping restricts the motion of the metatarsophalangeal joint of a sprained great toe.

Fractured Sesamoid Bone

When an athlete is down on a knee and another player lands on the back of his heel, the metatarsophalangeal joint of the great toe may be hyperextended violently and a sesamoid bone, usually the tibial, may fracture. Treatment is identical to that for ''turf toe,'' with ice and a strapping. Because a sesamoid is so important to weight bearing, it should be left in place, if possible. If it is painful and suffers arthritic changes, however, it may have to be removed.

''Tennis Toe''

Although the excellent traction of today's tennis shoes and the nonslip court surfaces stop the shoe quickly, the athlete's foot continues to move forward, and the longest toe may jam against the shoe box. Such jamming may produce a subungual hematoma, and the athlete may lose his toenail[47] (Figure 13-37).

Prevention and treatment of tennis toe require a shoe with a larger toe box. Athletes should be advised to wear older, worn shoes when playing on nonslip surfaces so that shoes may slide a bit. If subungual blood has accumulated painfully, it may be removed by puncturing the nail with a sterilized paper clip or a small battery-powered drill point. The nail puncture should be made distally so that the nail grows out fast.

Ingrown Toenail

An ingrown toenail may develop because of pressure from poorly fitting shoes, and this disorder can bench the athlete. A player's feet grow during a high school season, and by the end of the year the shoes may be squeezing his toes. New shoes are needed before his feet outgrow the old shoes, and toenails should be left long enough to keep them from growing in along the borders. If a toenail becomes ingrown and infection appears, hot soaks are started and the edge of the nail is lifted with a cotton bud, allowing it to grow out over the inflamed skin. The skin should be taped back to relieve pressure and to allow the nail to continue to grow. If the condition recurs, the of-

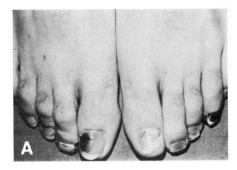
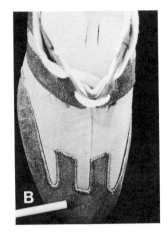

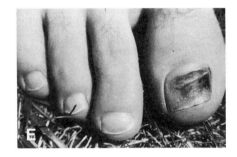
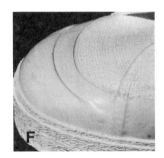

Figure 13-37 "Marathoner's toes" **(A)** may be caused by rubbing from the toe box. Toe box configurations of shoes differ **(B, C)**. Toe clips **(D)** may also irritate the toes. "Tennis toe" **(E)** may be prevented by wearing shoes with a larger toe box **(F)**.

fending portion of the nail should be removed and the nail bed revised under digital block anesthesia.

Claw Toes

Weakness or imbalance of the foot intrinsic muscles may produce a claw toe deformity. In this disorder, the metatarsophalangeal joint of the toe is extended and the proximal interphalangeal joint flexed.

An athlete with claw toes can have his toe box stretched with a shoemaker's swan to reduce rubbing. He can wear a toe shield (see Figure 13-38) to take pressure off the toes.

I like to block these toes with local anesthetic and straighten them manually. This manuever straightens the toe by rupturing the volar plate at the proximal interphalangeal joint. The toe is then more supple, although there is still clawing caused by the tight tendons. Now, however, the toe will be less likely to hold a fixed position against the toe box and the athlete can loosen it even further by stretching the toe each day. If the problem persists, the surgeon can either remove the head of the proximal phalanx or remove the diaphysis of the proximal phalanx.

If the tips of the toes are pressing painfully plantarward, the athlete can place a felt toe crest or foam toe comb just proximal to the distal interphalangeal joint to relieve the pressure.

Hammer Toes

Hammer toes are flexed at the proximal interphalangeal joint and usually result from wearing ill-fitting, tight shoes and sneakers. Painful corns may form over these flexed joints. To relieve pres-

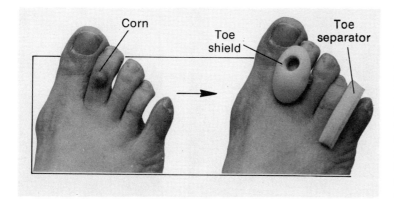

Figure 13-38 Pressure on an athlete's clawed toes can produce "corns" over the PIP joints. These painful places can be protected with a toe shield. Pain between the toes caused by the rubbing of one toe against the bony prominence of another may be relieved with a toe separator.

sure on hammer toes, the athlete needs a shoe with a deep toe box. If the toes still jam, surgical excision of the diaphysis of the proximal phalanx or of the head of the proximal phalanx under local anesthesia will provide complete relief.

Foot Blisters

When an athlete's shoes rub and pinch his skin, the epidermis is soon sheared, and fluid accumulates to separate the epidermal layers (Figure 13-39). Most of these blisters occur early in the season when the skin is soft or when new shoes are being broken in. The sore blister reduces the athlete's efficiency.

The key to dealing with blisters is prevention. Players may be advised to toughen their soles by going barefooted for brief periods during the off-season. Football shoes should be worn occasionally during the summer by football players and breaking-in time allowed for new shoes before formal practices begin. Wrinkles in a sock may also cause blisters, but well-fitted tube socks will help to avoid this problem. Friction may also be reduced by wearing two pairs of socks. A powder or lubricant, such as a thin coating of mineral oil or petrolatum, will aid in reducing friction between foot and shoe. Coating the feet with benzoin must be avoided because a powder and benzoin combination produces a sticky sole with lumps after the foot sweats. Calluses should be kept pared with a callus file after showering because blisters may form under them. An ice cube may be applied to hot spots and friction areas then lubricated with a "friction fighter" to pre-

vent progression. Hot spots behind the heel should be covered with a piece of tape or a Band-Aid, and a donut pad may be taped over a blister.

To avoid infection, blisters should not be unroofed. The blister can be aspirated of fluid with a fine-gauge needle through intact skin outside the blistered area and then covered with tape. If a decision is made to open the blister, a curved incision is made along one border of the blister and the roof left intact. Tape adherent is placed under the roof and the roof then taped down.

A broken blister may become contaminated; thus infection must not be sealed in. A portion of the roof is removed along with any loose skin that cannot protect the area. Dirt is then scrubbed out with soap, an antiseptic applied, and tape placed over the remaining roof for protection while allowing for some drainage.

Calluses

Calluses and corns are protective accumulations of the stratum corneum that results from pressure or pinching. Most calluses form on the ball of the foot or on the heel, and pinch-calluses frequently appear on the great toe (Figure 13-39). Calluses lack the central thrombosed capillaries found in warts.

Calluses may be prevented by wearing cushioned shoes and by orthotically balancing the foot. In addition to his training and competition shoes, the athlete's walking shoes should be inspected, since the soles of these shoes may be too firm. If this is the case, airplane insulation inserts

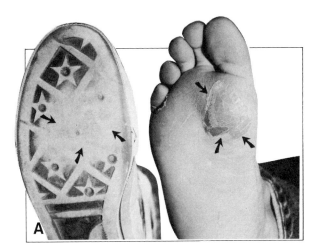
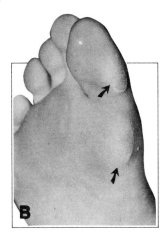
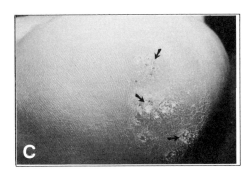
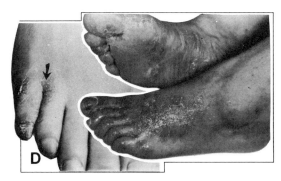

Figure 13-39   Blisters **(A)** form at friction points. "Pinch calluses" **(B)** especially affect runners with a hypermobile first ray. Warts **(C)** may masquerade as calluses, but warts show pinpoint capillaries when they are pared down. Athlete's foot **(D)** is most common in the last web space *(arrow)* but may affect the whole foot as well.

will distribute the pressure under the foot, thus reducing excess pressure on the callused area.

If a callus forms, it should be kept thin and massage lotion used to soften the bottom of the feet for filing. After showering, the callus may be reduced with a callus file, an emery board, or fine sandpaper. Great-toe pinch-calluses disappear when a Morton's extension pad or a rubber forefoot wedge corrects the first ray hypermobility.

Warts

Warts are skin lesions caused by the virus *Verruca vulgaris*, which enters damaged areas such as un-

der the metatarsal heads or at the heel. Pressure forces warts inward on the plantar surface of the foot, whereas in nonpressure areas such as the fingers the warts grow outward. To differentiate a wart from a callus or a corn, the lesion should be trimmed. The wart will show pinpoints of brown, thrombosed capillaries (Figure 13-39), whereas a callus or a corn is clear.

Warts are treated by reducing pressure in the affected area with airplane insulation inserts that spread out the weight-bearing forces. Surface keratin is pared down with a scalpel blade, and a 40% salicylic acid plaster is then applied to the wart. The plaster is removed each day, and the dead tissue is trimmed until the wart finally pushes out. The treatment is continued until the thrombosed capillaries are no longer seen.

There are more aggressive treatments for warts, but all have disadvantages. Cantharidin therapy sometimes leaves warts developing at the edge of the lesion, and electrofulguration and dissection may result in painful scars. Liquid nitrogen or surgical incision may leave the subject with a painful scar that may be worse than the wart itself.

Athlete's Foot

Athlete's foot is an itchy, scaly infestation of the foot caused by a fungus, *Tricophyton rubrum* or *Tricophyton mentagrophytes*, or a yeast, *Candida albicans*.[91] Some persons are especially susceptible to the fungi, which are infectious and can spread from person to person with or without direct body contact. The fungi thrive in dark, warm, moist places, such as shower rooms, humid locker rooms, floors, the inside of lockers, bench surfaces, towels, and sweaty socks.

The lesions of athlete's foot may appear in many forms (Figure 13-39). *Tricophyton rubrum* causes intertriginous scaly webs or squamous, scaly soles. *Tricophyton mentagrophytes* typically produces itchy vesicles and pustules that rupture, ooze, and macerate the skin. Other forms of athlete's foot may be hyperkeratotic and asymptomatic.

Athlete's foot should be diagnosed at the first symptom of itching or when scaly skin or cracks first appear between the toes. It frequently occurs between the fourth and fifth toes, the smallest interdigital space, which is subject to the least movement (Figure 13-39). A scraping is taken from an active-looking skin edge and the roof of the vesicle snipped off. The examiner stains this material with potassium hydroxide and looks for hyphae in the case of the fungi or a combination of hyphae and mycelia in *Candida* infestation.

Some athletes are sensitive to the rubber in athletic shoes, which produces a contact dermatitis with a rash bilaterally over the distal forefoot and toes. Other athletes are allergic to socks or to the detergent in which the socks are cleaned. Contact dermatitis cannot be cured by a fungicidal cream, and conversely a fungal infection will worsen if it is mistaken for a contact dermatitis and treated with a steroid cream. A proper diagnosis must therefore be made by examining a potassium hydroxide preparation to assure appropriate treatment.

Infections should be treated promptly. Dead tissue is removed by careful rubbing with a soft towel, and clotrimazole or miconazole fungicidal cream or solution is then applied. These antifungal agents are also active against the yeast *Candida*. A cream or solution is best, since powder penetrates poorly. Treatment should be continued for 2 weeks; if treatment is stopped early because symptoms have disappeared the infection will recur.

To prevent athlete's foot, all locker room areas must be kept well ventilated to allow moisture to evaporate quickly. Open lockers are recommended, and a disinfectant cleaner should be used frequently. Athletes should be advised to wear rubber shoes, shower clogs, or thongs in the shower room for good foot hygiene. Feet should be dried carefully, especially between the small toes, and dusted with a medicated foot powder. Cotton placed between the toes will keep spaces dry, and clean cotton socks and porous leather shoes or sandals will help to prevent infections.

REFERENCES

1. Arner O et al: Roentgen changes in subcutaneous rupture of the Achilles tendon. Acta Chir Scand 116:496–511, 1958/1959
2. Ayres S, Mihan R: Calcaneal petechiae. Arch Dermatol 106:262, 1972
3. Berndt AL, Harty M: Transchondral fractures (osteochondritis dissecans) of the talus. J Bone Joint Surg [Am] 41:988–1020, 1959
4. Black HM : Roentgenographic considerations in ankle sprains. Am J Sports Med 5:238–240, 1977
5. Black HM: Operative treatment of ankle sprains—acute and chronic. Am J Sports Med 5:256–257, 1977
6. Black HM et al: Improved techniques for evaluation of ligamentous injury in severe ankle sprains. Am J Sports Med 6:276–282, 1978
7. Bosien WR et al: Residual disability following ankle sprains. J Bone Joint Surg [Am] 37:1237–1243, 1955
8. Bowers KD Jr, Martin RB: Turf-toe: A shoe surface related football injury. Med Sci Sports 8(2):81–83, 1976

9. Brady TA, Arnold A: Aspiration injection treatment for varus sprain of the ankle. J Bone Joint Surg [Am] 54:1257–1261, 1972

10. Brand RL et al: The natural history of inadequately treated ankle sprain. Am J Sports Med 5:248–249, 1977

11. Brand RL et al: Repair of ruptured lateral ankle ligaments. Am J Sports Med 9:40–44, 1981

12. Brody DM: Running injuries. Clin Symp 32:4, 1980

13. Brubaker CE, James S: Injuries to runners. Am J Sports Med 2:189–198, 1974

14. Burrows HJ: Fatigue infarction of the middle of the tibia in ballet dancers. J Bone Joint Surg [Br] 38:83–94, 1956

15. Canale ST, Belding RH: Osteochondral lesions of the talus. J Bone Joint Surg [Am] 62:97–192, 1980

16. Chrisman OB, Snook GA: The problems of refracture of the tibia. Clin Orthop 60:217–218, 1968

17. Chrisman OD, Snook GA: Reconstruction of lateral ligament tears of the ankle. J Bone Joint Surg [Am] 51:904–912, 1969

18. Clancy WG Jr: Symposium: Runner's injuries. Am J Sports Med 8:137–138, 1980

19. Coker TP et al: Traumatic lesions of the metatarsophalangeal joint of the great toe in athletes. Am J Sports Med 6:326–334, 1978

20. Collis W, Jayson M: Measurement of pedal pressures. Ann Rheum. Dis 31:215–217, 1972

21. Conniff JCG: James Nicholas: The orthopedic approach. Runner 3(5):62–65, 1981

22. Cooper DL: Contrast bath treatment for sprains. Trainer's corner. Phys Sportsmed 4(4):133, 1976

23. Cooper D, Fair J: Ankle rehabilitation using the ankle disk. Phys Sportsmed 6(6):41, 1978

24. Cooper DL: Turf toe. Phys Sportsmed 6(9):139, 1978

25. Cox JS, Brand RL: Evaluation and treatment of lateral ankle sprains. Phys Sportsmed 5(6):51–55, 1977

26. Cox JS: Surgical treatment of ankle sprains. Am J Sports Med 5:250–251, 1977

27. Crelinsten GL: Ski-boot neuropathy. N Engl J Med 288:240, 1973

28. DeHaven KE: Symposium: Ankle sprains in athletes. Contemp Orthop 2:56–78, 1979

29. Denstad TF, Roaas A: Surgical treatment of partial Achilles tendon rupture. Am J Sports Med 7:15–17, 1979

30. Devas MB, Sweetnam R: Stress fractures of the fibula: A review of fifty cases in athletics. J Bone Joint Surg [Br] 30:818–829, 1956

31. Devas MB: Stress fractures of the tibia in athletes or "shin soreness." J Bone Joint Surg [Br] 40:227–239, 1958

32. Distefano VJ, Nixon JE: Achilles tendon rupture: Pathogenesis, diagnosis and treatment by a modified pullout wire technique. J Trauma 12:671–677, 1972

33. Distefano VJ, Nixon JE: Ruptures of the Achilles tendon. Am J Sports Med 1:34–37, 1973

34. Distefano VJ, Nixon JE: An improved method of taping. Am J Sports Med 2:209–211, 1974

35. Distefano VJ: Ruptures of the Achilles tendon. The 1975 Schering symposium on musculotendinous injuries. Athletic Training 10:195–198, 1975

36. Drez D Jr: Metatarsal stress fracture. Am J Sports Med 8:123–125, 1980

37. Drez D Jr: Running footwear—examination of the training shoe, the foot and functional orthotic devices. Am J Sports Med 8:140, 1980

38. Elmslie RC: Recurrent subluxation of the ankle joint. Ann Surg 100:364–367, 1934

39. Elton RC: Stress reaction of bone in army trainees. JAMA 204:314–316, 1968

40. Emerick CE: Ankle taping: Prevention of injury or waste of time? Athletic Training 14(3):186–188, 1979

41. Erskine L: The mechanics involved in skiing injuries. Am J Surg 97:667, 1959

42. Erskine L: Recent changes in the pattern of skiing injuries. J Trauma 14:92–93, 1974

43. Evans DL: Recurrent instability of the ankle—a method of surgical treatment. Proc Soc Med 46:343–344, 1953

44. Evans DL: Recurrent instability of the ankle—a method of surgical treatment. J Bone Joint Surg [Br] 39:795, 1957

45. Garrick JG: Artificial turf, pros and cons. Phys Sportsmed 3:41–50, 1975

46. Garrick JG: "When can I?": A practical approach to rehabilitation illustrated by treatment of an ankle injury. Am J Sports Med 9:67–68, 1981

47. Gibbs RC: Tennis toe. JAMA 228:24, 1974

48. Gillespie HS, Boucher P: Watson–Jones repair of lateral instability of the ankle J Bone Joint Surg [Am] 53:920–924, 1971

49. Golding D: Tennis leg. Br Med J 4:234, 1969

50. Gray G: Ankle rehabilitation using the ankle disk. Phys Sportsmed 6(6):141, 1978

51. Haggmark T, Eriksson E: Hypotrophy of the soleus muscle in man after Achilles tendon rupture. Am J Sports Med 7:121–126, 1979

52. Harrington KD: Degenerative arthritis of the ankle secondary to long-standing lateral ligament instability. J Bone Joint Surg [Am] 61:354–361, 1979

53. Hlavac HF: The Foot Book: Advice for Athletes. Mountain View, California, World Publications, 1977

54. Hovelius L, Palmgren H: Laceration of tibial tendons and vessels in ice hockey players: Three case histories of a skate boot-top injury. Am J Sports Med 7:297–298, 1979

55. Hullinger CW: Insufficiency fracture of calca-

neous similar to march fracture of metatarsal. J Bone Joint Surg [Am] 26:751–757, 1944

56. Inglis AE: Ruptures of the tendo Achilles. J Bone Joint Surg [Am] 58:990–993, 1976

57. Jackson DW et al: Ankle sprains in young athletes. Relation of severity and disability. Clin Orthop 101:201–215, 1974

58. Jackson DW: Shin splints. Phys Sportsmed 6(10):51–62, 1978

59. Jacobs D et al: Comparison of conservative and operative treatment of Achilles tendon rupture. Am J Sports Med 6:107–111, 1978

60. James SL et al: Injuries to runners. Am J Sports Med 6:40–50, 1978

61. James S, Brubaker DE: Biomechanical and neuromuscular aspects of running. In Wilmore J (ed) Exercise and Sports Sciences Reviews. New York, Academic Press, 1976

62. Johnson MD, Pope MH: Tibial shaft fractures in skiing. Am J Sports Med 5:49–62,1977

63. Johnson RJ et al: Knee injury in skiing: A multifaceted approach. Am J Sports Med 7:321–327, 1979

64. Johnson RJ: Trends in skiing injuries. Am J Sports Med 8:106–113, 1980

65. Jones E: Operative treatment of chronic dislocations of the peroneal tendons. J Bone Joint Surg [Am] 14:574–576, 1932

66. Jones R: Fracture of the base of the fifth metatarsal bone by indirect violence. Ann Surg 35:697–702, 1902

67. Kavanaugh JH et al: The Jones fracture revisited. J Bone Joint Surg [Am] 60:776–782, 1978

68. Kelly RE: An operation for the chronic dislocation of the peroneal tendons. Br J Surg 7:502–504, 1926

68a. Kirby NG: Exercise ischaemia in the fascial compartment of soleus. J Bone Joint Surg [Br] 52:738–740, 1970

69. Kulund DN, Brubaker CE: Injuries in the Bicecentennial Tour. Phys Sportsmed 6:674–678, 1978

70. Kulund DN et al: The long-term effects of playing tennis. Phys Sportsmed 7(4):87–94, 1979

71. Kulund DN et al: Airplane insulation for flying feet. Athletic Training 14(3):144–145, 1979

72. Lagergren C, Lindholm A: Vascular distribution in the Achilles tendon. Acta Chir Scand 116:491–495, 1958/1959

73. Laughman RK et al: Three-dimensional kinematics of the taped ankle before and after exercise. Am J Sports Med 8:425–431, 1980

74. Lea RB, Smith L: Non-surgical treatment of tendo Achilles rupture. J Bone Joint Surg [Am] 54:7, 1972

75. Leach R et al: Rupture of the plantar fascia in athletes. J Bone Joint Surg [Am] 60:537–539, 1968

76. Leach R, Corbett M: Anterior tibial compartment syndrome in soccer players. Am J Sports Med 7:258–259, 1979

77. Lindenbaum BL: Ski boot compression syndrome. Clin Orthop 140:109–110, 1979

78. Lutter LD: Pronation biomechanics in runners. Contemp Orthop 2:579–583, 1980

79. MacCartee CC: Taping treatment of severe inversion sprains of the ankle. Am J Sports Med 5:246–247, 1980

80. MacMahon B, Johnson BA: Function and mechanics of rupture of tendo-Achilles. Its diagnosis and physiological repair. Orthop Rev 8(9):55–60, 1979

81. Mann RA, Hagy J: Biomechanics of walking, running and sprinting. Am J Sports Med 8:345–350, 1980

82. Marks KL: Flake fracture of the talus progressing to osteochondritis dissecans. J Bone Joint Surg [Br] 34:90–92, 1952

83. McBryde AM Jr: Stress fractures in athletes. Am J Sports Med 3:212–217, 1975

84. McLennan JG: Treatment of acute and chronic luxations of the peroneal tendons. Am J Sports Med 8:432–436, 1980

85. McMahon TA, Greene PR: Fast running tracks. Sci Am 239(6):148–163, 1978

86. McMaster PE: Tendon and muscle rupture. J Bone Joint Surg [Am] 15:705–722, 1933

87. McMurray TP: Footballer's ankle. J Bone Joint Surg [Br] 32:68–69, 1950

88. Millar AP: Strains of the posterior calf musculature ("tennis leg"). Am J Sports Med 7:172–174, 1979

89. Miller A: Rupture of the musculotendinous juncture of the medial head of the gastrocnemius muscle. Am J Sports Med 5:191–193, 1977

90. Miller JW: Dislocation of peroneal tendons: A new operative approach. Am J Orthop 9:136–137, 1967

91. Millikan LE: Athlete's foot—scratching beneath surface of fungal ailments. Phys Sportsmed 3(4):51–56, 1975

92. Mital MA, Matza RA: Osgood-Schlatter disease: The painful puzzler. Phys Sportsmed 5(6):60–73, 1977

93. Moore M: Synthetic skin covers blisters, abrasions. Phys Sportsmed 8(12):15, 1980

94. Morris LH: "Athlete's ankle." J Bone Joint Surg [Am] 25:220, 1943

95. Mukerjee SK, Young AB: Dome fracture of the talus. J Bone Joint Surg [Br] 55:319–326, 1973

96. Napier J: The antiquity of human walking. Sci Am 216(4):56–66, 1967

97. Nelson R, Gregot R: Biomechanics of distance running: A longitudinal study. Res Q 47:417–428, 1976

97a. Newell SG, Woodle A: Cuboid syndrome. Phys Sportsmed 9(4):71–76, April 1981

98. Noble HB, Selesnick FH: The Thompson test for ruptured achilles tendon. Phys Sportsmed 8(8):63–64, 1980

98a. Paranen J: The medial tibial syndrome: Exercise ischaemia in the medial fascial compartment of the leg. J Bone Joint Surg [Br] 56:712–715, 1974

99. Peppard A, Reigler H: Ankle reconditioning with TENS. Phys Sportsmed 8(6):105–106, 1980

100. Percy EC, Conochie LB: The surgical treatment of ruptured tendo Achillis. Am J Sports Med 6:132–136, 1978

101. Platt H: Observations on some tendon ruptures. Br Med J 1:611–615, 1931

102. Quigley TB, Scheller AD: Surgical repair of the ruptured Achilles tendon. Am J Sports Med 8:244–250, 1980

103. Radin EL, Paul IL: Importance of bone in sparing articular cartilage from impact. Clin Orthop 78:342–344, 1971

104. Rask MR: Medial plantar neuropraxia (jogger's foot): Report of three cases. Clin Orthop 134:193–195, 1978

105. Rasmussen W: Skin splints: Definition and treatment. Am J Sports Med 2:111–117, 1974

106. Root ML et al: Neutral position casting techniques. Los Angeles, Clinical Biomechanics, 1971

107. Sarmiento A, Wolf M: Subluxation of peroneal tendons: Case treated by rerouting tendons under calcaneofibular ligament. J Bone Joint Surg [Am] 57:115–116, 1975

108. Savastano AA, Lowe EB: Surgical treatment for recurrent ankle sprains. Am J Sports Med 8:208–211, 1980

109. Seder JI: Heel injuries incurred in running and jumping. Phys Sportsmed 4(10):70–73, 1976

110. Seligson D: Ankle instability: Evaluation of the lateral ligaments. Am J Sports Med 8:39–42, 1980

111. Sim FH, Deweerd JH Jr. Rupture of the extensor hallucis longus tendon while skiing. Minn Med 60:789–790, 1977

112. Skeoch DU: Spontaneous partial subcutaneous ruptures of the tendo achillis. Am J Sports Med 9:20–22, 1981

113. Slocum DB: Overuse syndromes of the lower leg and foot in athletes. American Academy of Orthopaedic Surgeons Instructional Course Lectures 17:359–367, 1960

114. Slocum DB, Bowerman W: Biomechanics of running. Clin Orthop 23:39–45, 1962

115. Slocum D, James S: Biomechanics of running. JAMA 205:721–728, 1968

116. Smith WB: Environmental factors in running. Am J Sports Med 8:138–140, 1980

117. Staples OS: Ruptures of the fibular collateral ligaments of the ankle: Result study of immediate surgical treatment. J Bone Joint Surg [Am] 57:101–107, 1975

118. Stein SR, Luekens CA: Closed treatment of Achilles tendon ruptures. Orthop Clin North Am 7:241–246, 1976

119. Steingard PM: Foot failures in basketball. Phys Sportsmed 2(3):64–69, 1974

120. Stewart MJ, Hutchins WC: Repair of the lateral ligaments of the ankle. Am J Sports Med 6:272–275, 1978

121. Stover CN, Bryan DR: Traumatic dislocation of the peroneal tendons. Am J Surg 103:180–186, 1962

122. Subotnick SI: Orthotic foot control and the overuse syndrome. Phys Sportsmed 3(1):75–79, 1975

123. Subotnick SI: Podiatric Sports Medicine. Mount Kisco, New York, Futura, 1975

124. Subotnick SI: The Running Foot Doctor. Mountain View, California. World Publications, 1977

125. Telfer N: Radionuclide bone imaging in stress fractures. West J Med 129:414, 1978

126. Tennis leg (editorial). Br Med J 3:543–544, 1969

127. Thompson TC, Doherty JH: Spontaneous rupture of tendon of Achilles: A new clinical diagnostic test. J Trauma 2:126–129, 1962

128. Torg JS, Quendenfeld T: Effect of the shoe type and cleat length on incidence and severity of knee injuries among high school football players. Res Q Am Assoc Health Phys Ed 43:203–211, 1971

128a. Torg JS et al: Stress fractures of the tarsal navicular. J Bone Joint Surg [Am] 64:700–712, 1982

129. Vainionpaa S et al: Lateral instability of the ankle and results when treated by the Evans procedure. Am J Sports Med 8:437–439, 1980

130. Van der Linden W: The skier's boot top fracture. Acta Orthop Scand 40:797, 1970

131. Van der Linden W et al: Fractures of the tibial shaft after skiing and other accidents. J Bone Joint Surg [Am] 57:321–327, 1975

132. Verne–Hodge N: Injuries in cricket. In Armstrong JR, Tucker WE (eds): Injury in Sport, pp 168–171. Indianapolis, Charles C Thomas, 1964

133. Vine LE: The skier's fracture: A method of treating this and similar leg injuries in country district hospitals. Med J Aust 1:1127, 1968

134. Walsh WM, Blackburn T: Prevention of ankle sprains. Am J Sports Med 5:243–245, 1977

135. Washington ZL: Musculoskeletal injuries in theatrical dancers: Site, frequency and severity. Am J Sports Med 6:75–98, 1978

136. Watson–Jones R: Fractures and Joint Injuries, vol 2, 4th ed. Baltimore, Williams & Wilkins, 1952

137. Wilkinson DS: Black heel: A minor hazard of sport. Cutis 20:393–396, 1977

138. Winfield AC, Dennis JM: Stress fractures of the calcaneus. Radiology 72:415–418, 1959
139. Woodward EP: Ankle ligament surgery: Experience over 18 years. Phys Sportsmed 5(8):49–55, 1977
140. Yvars F: Osteochondral fractures of the dome of the talus. Clin Orthop 114:185–191, 1976
141. Zennis EJ Jr: Lateral ligamentous instability of the ankle: A method of surgical reconstruction by a modified Watson–Jones technique. Am J Sports Med 5:78–83, 1977
142. Zwelling L et al: Removal of os supranaviculare from a runner's painful foot. Am J Sports Med 6:1–3, 1978

Appendix 1

SPORTS MEDICINE JOURNALS

The American Journal of Sports Medicine
  (Official publication of the American Orthopedic Society for Sports Medicine)
The Williams & Wilkins Company
428 East Preston Street
Baltimore, Maryland 21202

Athletic Training
  (Journal of the National Athletic Trainers Association)
Eastern Associates
Post Office Box 1865
Greenville, North Carolina 27834

The Journal of Orthopedic and Sports Physical Therapy
  (Official publication of the Sports Medicine Section, American Physical Therapy
  Association)
428 East Preston Street
Baltimore, Maryland 21202

Medicine and Science in Sports and Exercise
  (Official Journal of the American College of Sports Medicine)
1440 Monroe Street
Madison, Wisconsin 53706

National Strength and Conditioning Association Journal
  (Official Voice of the NSCA)
National Strength and Conditioning Association
211 South Stadium
Lincoln, Nebraska 68588

The Physical Education Index
Ben Oak Publishing Company
Post Office Box 474
Cape Girardeaux, Missouri 63701

The Physician and Sportsmedicine
4530 West 77th Street
Minneapolis, Minnesota 55435

Yearbook of Sports Medicine
Year Book Medical Publishers, Inc.
Chicago, Illinois, and London, England

Appendix ■2

SPORTS MEDICINE ORGANIZATIONS

Academy for Sports Dentistry (ASD)
12200 Preston Road
Dallas, Texas 75230

American Academy of Podiatric Sports Medicine (AAPSM)
1729 Glastonberry Road
Potomac, Maryland 20854

American Alliance for Health, Physical Education, Recreation and Dance
1900 Association Drive
Reston, Virginia 22091

American College of Sports Medicine (ACSM)
Box 1440
Indianapolis, Indiana 46206

American Medical Joggers Association (AMJA)
Box 4704
North Hollywood, California 91607

American Orthopedic Society for Sports Medicine
70 West Hubbard, Suite 202
Chicago, Illinois 60610

American Osteopathic Academy of Sports Medicine
4610 University Avenue, Suite 480
Box 55095
Madison, Wisconsin 53705-8895

American Physical Therapy Association (APTA)
1111 North Fairfax Street
Alexandria, Virginia 22314

Canadian Academy of Sports Medicine (CASM)
c/o Sports Medicine Council of Canada
National Sport and Recreation Centre
333 River Road
Ottawa, Ontario K1L 8H9
Canada

International Federation of Sports Medicine
c/o Allan Ryan, M.D., Secretary General
5800 Jeff Place
Edina, Minnesota 55436

National Athletic Trainers Association (NATA)
1001 East 4th Street
Greenville, North Carolina 27834

National Strength and Conditioning Association
251 Capital Beach Boulevard, Suite 12
Box 81410
Lincoln, Nebraska 68501

President's Council on Physical Fitness and Sports
400 6th Street, S.W.
Room 3030
Washington, D.C. 20201

Appendix ▌3▐

NATIONAL SPORTS ORGANIZATIONS

Amateur Athletic Union
3400 West 86th Street
Indianapolis, Indiana 46268

Association for Intercollegiate Athletics for Women
1201 16th Street, N.W.
Washington, D.C. 20036

National Collegiate Athletic Association
Post Office Box 1906
Shawnee Mission, Kansas 66222

National Federation of State High School Athletic Associations
11724 Plaza Circle, Post Office Box 20626
Kansas City, Missouri 64195

National High School Athletic Coaches Association
3423 East Silver Springs Boulevard, Suite 9
Ocala, Florida 32670

United States Olympic Committee
1750 East Boulder Street
Colorado Springs, Colorado 80909

Appendix ▨

SPORTS ASSOCIATIONS FOR HANDICAPPED ATHLETES

American Athletic Association of the Deaf
3916 Lantern Drive
Silver Spring, Maryland 20902

American Blind Bowlers Association
150 North Bellaire
Louisville, Kentucky 40206

American Wheelchair Bowling Association
6718 Pinehurst Drive
Evansville, Indiana 47711

American Wheelchair Pilots Association
Post Office Box 1181
Mesa, Arizona 85201

Amputee Sports Association
11705 Mercy Boulevard
Savannah, Georgia 31406

Blind Outdoor Leisure Development, Inc. (BOLD)
533 East Main Street
Aspen, Colorado 81611

Braille Sports Foundation
Room 301, 730 Hennepin Avenue
Minneapolis, Minnesota 55402

Canadian Wheelchair Sports Association
333 River Road
Ottawa, Ontario K1L 8B9
Canada

Disabled Sportsmen of America, Inc.
Post Office Box 26
Vinton, Virginia 24179

Handicapped Scuba Association
1104 El Prado
San Clemente, California 92672

International Council on Therapeutic Ice Skating
Post Office Box 13
State College, Pennsylvania 16801

International Foundation for Wheelchair Tennis
1909 Ala Wai Boulevard, Suite 1507
Honolulu, Hawaii 96815

International Sports Organization for the Disabled and International
   Stoke–Mandeville Games Federation
Stoke–Mandeville Spinal Injury Center
Aylesbury, England

International Wheelchair Road Racers Club, Inc.
165 78th Avenue, E.
Saint Petersburg, Florida 33702

National Amputee Golf Association
5711 Yearling Court
Bonita, California 92002

National Foundation for Wheelchair Tennis
3855 Birch Street
Newport Beach, California 92660

National Handicapped Sports and Recreation Association
Farragut Station
Post Office Box 33141
Washington, D.C. 20033

National Wheelchair Athletic Association
2107 Templeton Gap Road
Colorado Springs, Colorado 80901

National Wheelchair Marathon
380 Diamond Hill Road
Warwick, Rhode Island 02886

Sports 'n Spokes (magazine for Wheelchair Sports)
5201 North 19th Avenue, Suite 111
Phoenix, Arizona 85015

United States Amputee Association
Route 2, County Line
Fairview, Tennessee 37062

Wheelchair Pilots Association
11018 102nd Avenue, N.
Largo, Florida 33540

Index

The letter *f* after a page number indicates a figure; *t* following a page number indicates tabular material.

Abdomen
  injury to
    abdominal wall contusion, 410
    examination in, 409–410
    genitourinary, 412–417
    gynecologic, 416
    hematocele, 416
    hematuria in, 413–415
    hemoglobinuria in, 415
    hollow viscus rupture, 411–412, 411f
    kidney damage, 412–413
    muscle tears, 410
    myoglobinuria in, 415
    penile, 416–417, 416f
    solar plexus blow, 410
    spermatic cord torsion, 415–416
    spleen rupture, 410–411
    "stitch in side," 412
    urethral, 416–417, 416f
  muscles of
    strength evaluation of, 19
    strength training of, 23, 24f, 124, 124–126f, 126
Abdominal-thrust maneuver in choking, 287
Abrasion
  on artificial turf, 167
  of cornea, 274–275
  of skin, 67
Acetaminophen, 72
Achilles tendon
  inflammation of, 521
  rubbing against retrocalcaneal bony prominence, 537–538, 540f

  rupture of, 517–521, 519–520f
Acne, 65–66
Acoustic streaming in ultrasound, 220
Acromioclavicular joint
  anatomy of, 301, 302–303f
  arthritis of, 326–327
  separation of
    causes of, 323
    diagnosis of, 323–324
    grades of, 323, 324f
    protection against, 323, 325f
    treatment of, 323–326, 326f
  sprain of
    exercises for, 352
    training after, 149
Acromionectomy, 312, 317f
Acupuncture-like electrical stimulation in pain relief, 205–206
  low-frequency, 199
Acupuncture points, electrostimulation of, 197, 198f, 205–206
  in chronic neck pain, 247
  in lumbar spinal disorders, 251, 254
  in sacroiliac sprain, 264
Acuscope, 206–208
Acute tubular necrosis, 415
Addison's disease, 55
Adenosine triphosphate in metabolism, 81–83
Adhesions, exercise for, 228
Adhesive tape. *See* Tape, types of

Adson's maneuver in shoulder disorders, 303
Adults, fitness programs for, 90–94
  benefits of, 91
  Canadian 5BX exercise plan, 94
  Cooper's aerobic system, 93–94, 94t
  dropouts from, 91
  objectives of, 91
  principles of, 92
  risks of, 91–92
  safety procedures in, 91–92
  stretching-strengthening in, 92–93
  weight control with, 93
Aerobic dancing
  injury prevention in, 39
  shoes for, 39, 40f
Aerobic metabolism, 82–83
  in "second wind," 109
Aerobic points, 93–94, 94t
Aerobic power, maximum (VO$_2$max), 83–85
  in children, 103
  in elderly persons, 95
  vs heart rate, 88–89, 89f
  in women, 99, 100t
Aerobic system, training of
  with Cooper's method, 93–94, 94t
  duration of, 88
  exercise modes in, 87–88
  fartlek running in, 90
  frequency of, 88
  intensity of, 88–89, 89f
  parcours in, 90
Age. *See also* Adults; Children

Age (*continued*)
　developmental, assessment
　　of, 42–43
　of runners, 31
Agility drills in conditioning
　　program, 131–132,
　　132f
Aging, physiology of, 94–95
Agranulocytosis from phe-
　　nylbutazone, 73
Airway obstruction, 287
Alcohol
　abuse of, 75–76
　frostbite and, 62
　in hot atmosphere, 176
Allergy
　to adhesive tape, 183
　contact dermatitis from,
　　66–67
Alum in herpes skin infec-
　　tion, 64
Amblyopia in preseason ex-
　　amination, 10
Amenorrhea in strenuous
　　training, 46, 100–101
American Alliance for Health,
　　Physical Education,
　　Recreation and
　　Dance, fitness test of,
　　104–105, 105t
Ammonia, spirits of, in
　　weight lifter's black-
　　out, 147
Amphetamines, effects of, 77
Amphotericin B in fungal in-
　　fections, 66
Amputee athlete, 51–52
Anabolic steroids, effects of,
　　77–78
Anaerobic glycolysis, 82–83
Anaerobic metabolism, 82–83
Anaerobic threshold, 85
Analgesic balm, 189
Anemia
　aplastic, from nonsteroidal
　　anti-inflammatory
　　drugs, 72–73
　iron-deficiency, 101
　sickle cell, 56
Anesthetics, local, for pain
　　relief, 73–74
Ankle
　anatomy of, 521, 522f
　arthrography of, 525
　instability of, 531, 532f
　peroneal tendon dislocation
　　in, 531, 533
　preseason examination of,
　　16, 17f

rehabilitation of, 534–535,
　　535–538f
　"soccer ankle," 536
　sprain of
　　anterior capsular, 522
　　chronic instability after,
　　　531, 532f
　　diagnosis of, 523, 525
　　lateral, 522–523, 524f
　　medial eversion, 522
　　prevention of, 525–526
　　single *vs* double ligament
　　　tear in, 523, 524f
　　treatment of
　　　acute, 526–528,
　　　　527–528f
　　　surgical, 529, 531
　　　with taping, 528–529,
　　　　529–530f
　　talar fracture in, 533, 533f,
　　　536
　　taping of, 525–526,
　　　528–529, 529–530f
Ankle flip in conditioning
　　program, 131
Ankylosing spondylitis, back
　　pain in, 418
Antihistamines
　before diving, 283
　sweating and, 176
Aorta, coarction of, in pre-
　　season examination, 27
Aplastic anemia from drugs,
　　72–73
Apley test in knee examina-
　　tion, 442
"Apprehension shoulder,"
　　316–317
Arch of foot
　rehabilitation of, 549, 550f
　taping of, 548f
Arm
　nerves to, injury of,
　　294–295
　rehabilitation of, 383,
　　384–385f
　soreness of, after pitching,
　　322
Arndt-Schultz principle, 226
Arteries, injury to, in thoracic
　　outlet syndrome, 305
Arteriovenous oxygen differ-
　　ence in exercise, 84
Arthralgia, retropatellar,
　　455–458, 456f
Arthritis. *See also*
　　Osteoarthritis
　of acromioclavicular joint,
　　326–327

Arthrography
　in ankle sprain, 525
　of knee, 475–476, 476f
　of shoulder, 311, 311f, 339
Arthroscopy
　of knee
　　in anterior cruciate liga-
　　　ment tear, 491–492
　　in meniscal repair,
　　　479–480
　　in torn meniscus, 476
　　training after, 149–150,
　　　149f
　in shoulder dislocation,
　　339–340
Artificial turf. *See under* Turf
Aspiration of knee, 466–467,
　　467f
Aspirin, 72
　in chondromalacia patella,
　　457
　in sore pitching arm, 322
Asthma, exercise-induced,
　　58–60
Astroturf, 167, 170
Athlete's foot, 559f, 560
"Athlete's kidney," 414
Athletic pseudonephritis, 413
Athletic trainer. *See* Trainer
Atlantoaxial area, manual
　　therapy of, 249–250
Atlanto-occipital area, man-
　　ual therapy of, 249
Atlas, fracture of, 291
ATP (adenosine triphosphate)
　　in metabolism,
　　81–83
Atropine
　in asthma, 59–60
　sweating and, 176
Attitudes of injury-prone ath-
　　letes, 160–162
Avascular necrosis
　of femoral head, 427
　of lunate, 378
A-VO$_2$ (arteriovenous oxygen
　　difference) in exer-
　　cise, 84
Axis block, 249–250

Back. *See also* Spine
　evaluation of, 241–242
　　in cervical region, 242,
　　　245–246

in lumbar region,
253–254
in sacroiliac region, 258,
260, 262–264
in thoracic region,
250–251
exercises for
home program, 242
injury from, 22, 22f
injury of, treatment of, 242
intervertebral joint mobilization in, 242
pain in, 417–418, 418f
preseason examination of,
13, 14f
round deformity of, 14
soft-tissue mobilization of,
242
strain of, 242
stretching of, 22, 22f
Back arch exercise with inner
tube, 25, 25f
"Backpack palsy," 304–305,
304f
Bag drill in conditioning program, 131
Ball. *See also* Pitching;
Throwing
orbital fracture from, 277
protection from
eyeguards for, 277–278
face masks for, 273, 273f
helmets for, 272–273
tennis, eye injury from,
275–276, 276f
Ballet. *See* Dancing, ballet
Bankhart operation in shoulder dislocation, 334,
339
Barbells, 127–128, 128f,
144–146, 145f
Barometric pressure on body,
282
Barotrauma, 282–283
Baseball. *See also* Pitching
acromioclavicular arthritis
in, 326–327
ankle sprain in, 522
biceps tendon dislocation
in, 327f, 328
blind athlete in, 50
conditioning for, upper
body plyometrics in,
135
elbow degeneration in, 364
finger injuries in, 397–399,
399f
foot bruises in, 547, 551f
gloves for, 402

hand blisters in, 400
helmet for, 272
patellar dislocation in, 452,
452f
strength training in, 137,
139
thumb ulnar collateral ligament injury in, 384
"Baseball elbow," 364
"Baseball finger," 397–399,
399f
Basketball
ankle sprain in, 522–523
conditioning for, upper
body plyometrics in,
135
finger injuries in, 397
shoes for, 40f, 41
strength training for, 139
Batting, strength training for,
137
Battle's sign in skull fracture,
270
Belladonna, sweating and,
176
"Bell clapper" deformity,
415–416
Belt
shoulder dislocation pre-
vention with, 334,
334f
for weight lifting, 121f,
126–127
Bench crunch for abdominal
strength, 124–125f,
126
Bench press
as competitive sport, 146
with inner tube, 23, 24f
pectoralis major muscle
rupture in, 406
poundage selection for, 126
in strength training,
118–119, 119–120f
Bends in deep diving, 282
Bennett's lesion of shoulder,
318
Benzoin in tape application,
181
Betamethasone for pain relief,
74
Biceps brachii muscle,
strengthening of, 23,
24f
Biceps brachii tendon
dislocation of, 327f, 328
inflammation of, 327–328,
327f
rupture of, 329–330, 329f

Biceps femoris muscle, strain
of, 431
Biceps femoris tendon, anatomy of, 438f, 439
Bicipital groove
anatomy of, 302, 302f
tendinitis at, 327–328, 327f
Bicycling. *See* Cycling
Bipartate patella, 458, 458f
Bite plate, 285–286, 286f
"Black dot heel," 539, 541f
"Black eye," 276
Blackout in weight lifting,
146–147
Bladder
injury to, 412, 414
natural protection of, 412
Blind athlete, 50, 50f
Blisters
on foot, 558, 559f
from frostbite, 63, 63f
on hand, 399, 401
from herpes infection, 64,
65f
from impetigo, 64, 65f
Blood flow
in exercise, 84
ultrasound effects on, 219
Blood pressure
in preseason examination,
27
in weight lifting, 147
Blood vessels, effects of exercise on, 84
Body building, 146
anabolic steroids in, 77–78
Body fat. *See under* Fat
Body rehearsal in coping
with injury, 155
Bone cyst
of femoral neck, 428
in humeral growth plate,
342
Bone spur
of olecranon, 365–366
in "runner's bump," 537
Boot, ski, peroneal nerve
compression by,
548–549
"Boot top fracture," 513–514
Boric acid in swimmer's ear,
280
Bounds in plyometrics,
134–135, 134f
"Boutonnière deformity,"
393–394, 394f
volar plate injury resem-
bling, 395
Bowlegs, cycling and, 446

"Bowler's thumb," 382
Bowling, groin strain in, 425
Bowstring tear of meniscus,
        472–473, 473f, 476,
        477f
"Boxer's elbow," 371
Boxing
    "black eye" in, 276
    elbow disorders in, 371
    facial cuts in, 274
    finger metacarpal injury in,
        390–391
    gloves for, 402
    headgear for, 274
    hematuria in, 413
    "knockout" blow in, 269
    laryngeal injury in, 287
Brace
    knee
        in anterior cruciate liga-
            ment tear, 492, 492f
        in ligament sprain, 489
        in patellar stabilization,
            449–450, 450f
    for scoliosis correction, 14
    for "tennis elbow," 369
Brachial artery damage in el-
        bow fracture,
        359–360, 359f
Brachial plexus injury,
        294–295
    in "backpacker's palsy,"
        304–305, 304f
    in thoracic outlet syn-
        drome, 305
Brachioradialis muscle,
        strengthening of, 23,
        24f
Brain injury
    in concussion, 267–269
    in "knockout" blow, 269
    prevention of, with hel-
        mets, 271–273, 271f
    in skull fracture, 270
    in stroke, 269–270
    in subdural hematoma, 270
Brain stem
    "knockout" blow and, 269
    stroke of, 269–270
Brassiere for sports, 405–406,
        406f
Breast injury in running/jog-
        ging, 405–406, 406f
"Breastroker's knee," 487
Breathing problems
    in asthma, 58–59
    in solar plexus blow, 410
Bridging in neck strength
        training, 297f, 298

Brief-intense transcutaneous
        electric nerve stimu-
        lation, 199–200
Bristow operation in shoulder
        dislocation, 335–336,
        337f, 339
Bronkaid mist in asthma, 60
Brown-Séquard syndrome in
        neck injury, 293
Bunion (hallux valgus),
        552–553, 554–555f
Bupivacaine for pain relief,
        73–74
"Burner," 294–295
Burnout, psychological, in
        children, 104
Burns
    floor, 67
    from sun exposure, 60
    turf, 167
        prepatellar bursitis from,
            447, 448f
Burrow's solution
    in fungal infections, 66
    in swimmer's ear, 280
Bursitis
    greater trochanteric,
        428–429
    of heel, 536–537
    of olecranon, 371
    prepatellar, 447, 448f
    scapular, 346, 348
    scapulocostal, 346
    of shoulder, 307, 308f
    subacromial, 307, 307–308f
Burst mode of transcutaneous
        electric nerve stimu-
        lation, 198f, 200
Butazolidine for sore pitching
        arm, 322
Buttocks
    pain in ("pyriformis syn-
        drome"), 422, 423f
    shaping exercises for, 26
"Buttonhole deformity,"
        393–394, 394f

Cable crunch for abdominal
        strength, 125f, 126
Caffeine, action of, 76
Calcaneal-fibular ligament,
        anatomy of, 521,
        522f
Calcific tendinitis of shoul-

der, 309–310, 309f,
        312
Calcium
    deposit of, ultrasound treat-
        ment of, 221
    loss of, exercise and, 26
Calcium hydroxide in tooth
        damage, 286
Calf muscles
    conditioning of, with ankle
        flips, 131
    shaping exercises for, 27
    soreness in ("tennis leg"),
        517, 518f
    stretching of, 21f, 22
    tight, 545–546
Callus
    on foot, 32, 558–559, 559f
    on hand, 399, 401
Caloric labyrinthitis, 283–284
Camphor
    in herpes skin infection, 64
    in pain relief, 75
Canadian 5BX exercise plan,
        94
Canal of Guyon, nerve com-
        pression in, 382
Cancer, ultrasound and, 222
Candidiasis, 66
    of foot, 560
Canoeing, "oarsman's wrist"
        in, 379
Cantharidin for warts, 560
Capacitance of tissue, 194
Capital femoral epiphysis,
        slipped, 427–428,
        428f
Capitellar-radial articulation,
        357
Capitellum
    anatomy of, 358
    osteochondritis dissecans
        of, 362–363
Capitolunate angle, 376
Capsulorrhaphy in shoulder
        dislocation, 334–335,
        335f
Carbohydrates
    in balanced diet, 68, 69t
    loading of, for endurance
        events, 70
    in precompetition meal,
        71
Cardiac output in exercise,
        83–84
Cardiorespiratory function
    aerobic points and, 94
    in women, 99–100,
        99–100t

Cardiovascular system
  aging effects on, 95
  endurance exercises for, 235
  physiology of, 83–84
  preseason examination of, 27–28
Carpal injuries. *See under* Wrist
Carpal tunnel, nerve compression in, 382
Cartilage of elbow, degeneration of, 365
"Cat and camel stretch," 261f
Cauliflower ear (wrestler's ear), 278–280, 281f
Cavitation in ultrasound, 220
Cavus foot, 545, 545f
Cervical collar, 295
Cervical plexus injury, 294–295
Cervical spine. *See also* Neck
  evaluation of, 242, 245–246
  injury of, 244–250, 245–250f
  sagittal stenosis of, 295
"Charley horse," 429–430
Chest, protective vest for, 407–408, 408–409f
Chest injury
  breast pain from jogging, 405–406, 406f
  costochondral separation, 408
  hyperventilation, 409
  pectoralis major rupture, 406
  pneumothorax, 408–409
  protection from, 407–408, 408–409f
  rib fracture, 406–408, 407–409f
  runner's nipple, 405
Chest pull with inner tube, 23, 24f
Chewing gum, swallowing of, 287
Chilblains, 64
Children
  injury control in, 44–45
  "Little League elbow" in, 361–364
  "Little League shoulder" in, 341–342
  physical education program for, 45, 45t
  training of, 101–105
    epiphyseal injuries in, 104

history of, 101–102
performance limits in, 103
physical fitness and, 104–105, 105t
psychological burnout in, 104
purposes of programs for, 102
rewards in, 104
sexual maturation and, 104
trainability expectations in, 103
weight lifting injuries in, 118
weight training of, 117–118
Chlorothiazide, sweating and, 176
Choking from swallowing of gum/tobacco, 287
Cholinergic urticaria, 61
Chondral fracture of knee, 468–469
Chondromalacia patella, 455–458, 456f
Chrisman-Snook procedure in ankle reconstruction, 531, 532f
Chymotrypsin in pain relief, 75
Cigarette smoking, 76
Circuit training, 90
Clavicle. *See also* Acromioclavicular joint
  dislocation of, 306
  fracture of, 306
Claw toe, 557, 558f
Clean-and-jerk lift in weight lifting as sport, 144–146, 145f
Cleats on shoes, 525
Click test in knee examination, 442
  in torn meniscus, 474, 475f
"Clincher strap" for thumb stability, 386, 387f
"Clipping injury" of knee, 486, 487f
Clotrimazole in fungal infections, 66
Clove, oil of, in tooth damage, 286
Clunk test for glenoid labrum tear, 330–331
Cocaine, 76–77
Coffee, caffeine in, 76
Cold (environmental). *See also* Frostbite; Frostnip

equestrian cold panniculitis from, 61
urticaria from, 61
Cold (treatment). *See also* Ice
  application methods for, 186
  contraindications for, 186
  with heat, 188–189, 526
  indications for, 186
  physiologic effects of, 186
Colds, 56
Collar, cervical, 295
Collateral ligament (elbow), medial
  anatomy of, 357
  injury of, 364
Collateral ligament (finger), injury of, 389, 394f, 395
Collateral ligament (knee)
  lateral, anatomy of, 438f, 439
  medial
    sprain of, 486–498, 487f
    unwanted bone in, 489
Collateral ligament (thumb), ulnar, injury of, 384, 386, 386–388f, 388
Collodion as ear protection, 279–280
Coma
  diabetic, 55
  from heat stroke, 174
Combination drill in conditioning program, 131
Compartment syndrome of leg, 516–517
Competition
  cooling down after, 115
  maturity matching for, 42–43
  return to, after injury. *See* Return to competition/training
  stress in, 87
  training for. *See also* Conditioning; Strength
    cyclic, 135–137, 136f
    "hitting the wall" in, 110
    long-term planning in, 108
    pacing in, 109–110
    peaking in, 109
    in running, 107
    "second wind" in, 109
    staleness in, 108–109
    "stitch," 109
  warm up for, 111–115, 113–114f

Compression fracture of cervical spine, 291
    with flexion, 292, 292f
Compression grind test in knee examination, 442
Compression in injury treatment, 185–187, 185f, 187f
Concussion
    evaluation in, 268
    grades of, 267–268
    return to training after, 268–269
Conditioning, 129–135
    agility drills in, 131–132, 132f
    bounds in, 134–135, 134f
    depth jumps in, 135
    distance running in, 129
    form running drills in, 130–131, 130f
    hops in, 134
    in hot atmosphere, 174–176
    interval running in, 130
    jumps in, 133–134, 133f
    objectives of, 129
    plyometrics in, 132–135, 133–134f
    power development in, 132–135, 133–134f
Condyle, fracture of
    of elbow, 360, 361f
    femoral, 468–469
Cone drill in conditioning program, 131
Confidentiality in doctor-patient relationship, 6
Conjunctival irritation, 274
Contact dermatitis, 66–67
Contact lens, 277
    removal of, in unconsciousness, 270
Contract, physician-sport sponsor, 4
Contrast treatment with heat and cold, 188–189
    in ankle sprain, 526
Contrecoup injury, subdural hematoma in, 270
Contusion
    of abdominal wall, 410
    of quadriceps, 429–430
    treatment of, 184
Cooling down after exercise, 115

Cooper's aerobic system, 93–94, 94t
Coping with injury, 152–156
Coracoacromial arch, anatomy of, 302, 302–303f
Coracoacromial ligament
    anatomy of, 302, 302–303f
    resection of, 311–312
    in subacromial bursitis, 307, 307–308f
Coracoid process
    anatomy of, 301, 302–303f
    injury of, 314
    transfer of, in shoulder dislocation, 335–336, 337f
Cord syndrome in neck hyperextension, 293
Corneal abrasion, 274–275
Corns on foot, 558, 559f
Coronary heart disease, 91
Cortisone in abnormal knee plica, 468, 468f
Costochondral separation, 408
Counterirritants in pain relief, 75
CP (creatine phosphate) in metabolism, 81–83
Cramps, 148
    during relaxation training, 158
Creatine phosphate in metabolism, 82–83
Cricket
    abdominal wall contusion in, 410
    foot bruises in, 547
    groin strain in, 425
    helmet for, 272
    os trigonum pinching in, 538
    rib fracture in, 406–408, 409f
Cromolyn sodium in asthma, 59–60
Crossover cut, 444, 445f
Crossover test in knee instability, 498
Cruciate ligament
    anterior
        anatomy of, 439–440, 439f
        replacement of, 500–501, 500–501f, 503
        stabilization of, 499–500
        tears of, 490–493, 491–493f

testing of, 442–443
    posterior
        anatomy of, 439f, 440
        tears of, 493–494, 494f
Crunches for abdominal strength, 124–125f, 126
Crutches in knee rehabilitation, 484–485, 484–486f
Cryotherapy. See also Cold; Ice
    in ankle sprain, 526
    ultrasound after, 219
Cryptorchidism, 28
Cuboid, subluxation of, 544–545
Curriculum for sports medicine, 166
Cuts, facial, 274
Cutting (directional change)
    bowstring meniscus tear in, 472–473, 473f
    knee effects of, 444, 445f
    patellar dislocation in, 452
Cybex machine
    in rehabilitation, 231–232, 233f
    in strength measurement, 19, 19f
Cyclic training program, 135–138, 136f
Cycling
    Achilles tendinitis in, 521
    biomechanics of, 445–446
    gloves for, 402
    helmet for, 271–272
    knee effects of, 445–446
    laryngeal injury in, 287
    penile injury in, 416, 416f
    saddle height for, 446
    "saddle soreness" from, 67
    safety procedures for, 445–446
    training for, in triathalon, 107–108
    ulnar nerve compression in, 382, 382f
    wind-chill factor in, 446
Cyst
    bone, fracture through, 342, 428
    ganglion, of toes, 552, 553f
    hip, 428
    meniscal
        examination for, 442
        treatment of, 479

Dancing, ballet
    os trigonum pinching in, 538
    stress fracture in
        of leg, 514–515
        of os calcis, 538
"Dead arm" syndrome, 336
Dead lift in power lifting, 146
Deafness. *See* Hearing loss
Dehydration in hot atmosphere, 172–175
Deltoid ligament, 521
Deltoid muscle
    strain of, 306
    strengthening of, 23, 24f
    stretching of, 113f
Dementia pugilistica, 269
Dental care, 286–287
Depth jumps, 135
DeQuervain's stenosing tenosynovitis of wrist, 379
Dermatitis, contact, 66–67
Dermatosis, fungal, 66
Desensitization, systematic, after injury, 159–160
Developmental age, assessment of, 42–43
DeVries program, 97
Diabetes mellitus, exercise in, 54–55
Diet. *See* Nutrition
Dimethyl sulfoxide for pain relief, 74–75
Dipstick screening for proteinuria, 29–30
Discoid tear of meniscus, 474, 479
Discus throwing, strength training for, 139
Disk, intervertebral, rupture of, 417–418
Dislocation
    of clavicle, 306
    of elbow, 360–361, 362f
    of finger
        at distal interphalangeal joint, 397
        at proximal interphalangeal joint, 393, 394f
    of hip, 427
    of knee, 505, 507–508
    of lunate, 377–378
    of peroneal tendons, 531, 533
    of shoulder. *See under* Shoulder

of sternoclavicular joint, 305–306
of thumb metacarpophalangeal joint, 384, 386f
of wrist, 377–378
Diving
    deep, barotrauma in, 282–283
    neck injury in, 289, 290f
        compression fracture, 291
    round window rupture in, 284
Dizziness in weight lifting, 146–147
Dorsal intercalcated segment instability (DISI) of wrist, 376
    with scaphoid fracture, 377
Dot drill in conditioning program, 131
Drawer test
    anterior, of ankle, 523
    of knee, 499
Drop finger, 398–399, 399f
Drugs
    abuse of, 75–78
    in asthma, 59–60
    contraindicated in hot atmosphere, 176
    in fungal infections, 66
    in herpes skin infection, 64
    for pain, 71–75
        iontophoresis and, 209–210, 209f
        phonophoresis and, 221
    for physician's bag, 44
    for sleep induction, 78
Dry needling in jumper's knee, 459, 460f
Dumbbells, 127–128, 128f
Duodenum, rupture of, 412
DuToit operation in shoulder dislocation, 335, 335f
Dynamometer in strength measurement, 19
Dyspnea in asthma, 58–59

Ear
    bleeding from, in skull fracture, 270
    caloric labyrinthitis of, 283–284

hematoma of ("scrum ear"), 278–280, 281f
infection of ("swimmer's ear"), 280, 282
injury to
    from deep diving, 282–283
    from firearm discharge, 284
    from friction ("wrestler's ear"), 278–280, 281f
    osteoma development in, 282
    round window rupture in, 284
    tympanic membrane rupture in, 283
Earguard in wrestling, 278
"Ear squeeze" in diving, 282–283
Ecchymosis, periorbital, in skull fracture, 270
Edema
    heat, 173
    of knee, 466–467, 467f
    of leg in compartment syndrome, 516–517
    prevention of, 185–188, 185f, 187–188f
Efficiency in endurance exercise, 85
Elastic tape. *See* Tape, types of
Elastic wrap, 186–187
Elbow
    anatomy of, 357–358
    articulations of, 357
    "baseball elbow," 361–364
    "boxer's elbow," 371
    bursitis of, 371
    carrying angle of, 357
    cartilage degeneration at, 365
    dislocation of, 360–361, 362f
    fracture of, 358–360, 359f, 361f
    "javelin thrower's elbow," 366
    ligaments of, 357–358
    "Little League elbow," 361–364
    loose bodies in, 366
    medial collateral ligament tears of, 364
    olecranon bone spurs of, 365–366
    "olecranon fossitis" at, 365–366

Elbow (*continued*)
osteoarthritis of, 358
osteochondritis dissecans of, 362–363
preseason examination of, 13
protection of, by taping, 361, 362f
rehabilitation of, 383, 384–385f
"tennis elbow," 366–371, 367–370f
throwing effects on, 361, 363f
ulnar nerve entrapment at, 364–365, 365f
Elderly persons
fitness programs for, 47, 94–97
characteristics of, 96–97, 97f
DeVries program, 97
gerokinesiatrics, 97, 98f
Iowa TOES program, 97
objectives of, 95–96
physiology of aging and, 94–95
risks of, 96
safety procedures for, 96
training in, 95
weight training for, 118
Electrical devices, 192–227. *See also* Lasers; Transcutaneous electrical nerve stimulation; Ultrasound
acupuncture points and. *See* Acupuncture points
biological effects of, 192–196, 193t, 192f
electrophysiology and, 193–196
muscle response to, 192
for muscle stimulation in pain relief, 208
nerve response to, 192–193, 193t, 192f
neuromuscular stimulator, 210–213
Russian, 211
neurophysiology and, 192–193, 192f, 193t
safety procedures for, 213–214
types of, 196
Electric shock, 214
Electro-Acuscope, 206–208
Electrodes of stimulation devices, 194, 197, 198f

interferential unit, 206
for point stimulation, 206
Electrophysiology, 193–196
Elevation in injury treatment, 185–186, 185f
Ellis-Jones procedure in peroneal tendon dislocation, 533
Embolism in deep diving, 282
Emergency care, 5–6
Emotive imagery in coping with injury, 154–155
Endurance events
carbohydrate loading for, 70
pacing in, 109–110
Endurance exercise
physiology of, 84–85
in rehabilitation, 234–235, 234t
Energy
from anaerobic glycolysis, 82–83
ATP-CP system and, 81–83
Enzymes, oral, in pain relief, 75
Epicondyle of elbow, fracture of, 360, 361f
Epicondylopatellar band, 438
Epidermophyton floccosum, 66
Epilepsy, 57–58
Epinephrine in asthma, 59–60
Epiphysis
capital femoral, slipped, 427–428, 428f
injury to, 104
in ankle sprain, 523
in elbow fracture, 360
in finger fracture, 392
in "Little League shoulder," 341–342
tibial, 460–461, 462–463f
ultrasound over, 222
of vertebral end-plates, Scheuermann's disease of, 417
Epstein-Barr virus, 57
Equestrian cold panniculitis, 61
Equestrian sports. See Horseback riding
Equipment. *See also* Protective equipment
for team physician, 43–44
for trainer, 167, 168–169t
"Essential lesion," 333–334

Eugenol in tooth damage, 286
Evans procedure in ankle reconstruction, 531, 532f
Examination
preparticipation
legal aspects of, 5
physician role in, 5
preseason, 6–29
of ankle, 16, 17f
of back, 13, 14f
cardiac, 27–28
of elbow, 13
of eyes, 7, 10–11, 10f
of feet, 16–17
form for, 8–10
group, 7
hemorrhoid diagnosis in, 29
hernia diagnosis in, 28–29
of hips, 14–15, 15f
history in, 7
of iliotibial tract, 15, 15f
individual, 7
of joint flexibility, 17–19
of knee, 15–16, 16–17f
mass, 7
of musculoskeletal system, 11–19, 12–19f
of neck, 11
reasons for, 6–7
for scoliosis, 13–14
of scrotum, 28
setting for, 7
of shoulder, 11–12, 12–13f
of strength, 18–19f, 19
of teeth, 11
timing of, 7
types of, 7
Exercise. *See also* Rehabilitation; Training
asthma induced by, 58–60
for back problems, home instruction for, 242, 252, 253f
effects of, after injury, 228, 228t
endurance, physiology of, 84–85
excessive, inflammation from, 228, 228t
in heat acclimation, 174–175
hematuria induced by, 413–415
after injury, 228
in injury treatment, 187–188, 188f

with inner tube
  for body shaping, 25–27
  in rehabilitation of run-
    ner, 34–35
  strengthening, 23–25,
    24–25f
  of neck, 298
isokinetic, 19, 19f,
    231–232, 233f, 234
isometric, 229, 298
isotonic
  in neck strengthening,
    298
  in rehabilitation, 229
in kidney disease, 415
menstruation and, 46,
    100–101
metabolism and, 81–83
passive, 228
physiology of
  cardiorespiratory func-
    tion, 83–84
  metabolic systems in,
    81–83
during pregnancy, 46–47,
    101
proteinuria in, 29
in renal disorders, 30
resistance, 228
shoes for. *See* Shoes
stretching. *See* Stretching
for warming up. *See* Warm-
    ing up
in water, 34–35, 234–235,
    234t
Exostosis
  in ear, 282
  tackler's, 342, 343f
Extensor carpi radialis brevis
    muscle, anatomy of,
    358
Extensor digitorum com-
    munis extensor
    hood, injury to, 389
Extensor digitorum com-
    munis tendon, "but-
    tonhole deformity"
    and, 393–394, 394f
Extensor mechanism
  of distal interphalangeal
    joint, injury of,
    397–399, 397f, 399f
  of knee, 435–436, 436f
    realignment of, 450–451,
    451f
Eye
  injury to
    "black eye," 276
    conjunctival irritation, 274

from contact lens, 277
equipment for treatment
    of, 275
from finger, 274–275
from foreign bodies,
    274–275
hyphema, 276–277
orbital fracture, 277
periorbital cuts, 274
prevention of, 277–278
retinal detachment, 277
from sunburn, 274
in tennis, 275–276, 276f
from ultrasound, 222
preseason examination of,
    7, 10–11, 10f
Eyeglasses, 277–278
Eyeguard, 277–278
Eyelid
  bruise of, 276
  cuts of, 274

Facemask
  backward leverage of, neck
    injury in, 293, 293f
  emergency removal of, 270
  fit of, 273
  history of, 273
  for hockey, 273
  for lacrosse, 273, 273f
  for motorcycling, 273–274
  visual obstruction by, 273
Facet joint
  fracture of, 292
  sprain of, 254
Facial injury, 273–287
  cuts, 274
  to ear, 278–284, 281f
  to eye, 274–278, 276f, 280f
  fractures, 278, 279f
  to mouth, 285–287, 286f
  to nose, 284–285
  prevention of. *See* Face
    mask
Factor VIII in hemophilia, 56
Fainting from hot atmo-
    sphere, 172–173
Fallopian tube infection, 416
Fartlek running, 90
Fast twitch muscle fibers, en-
    durance exercise
    and, 85
Fat (body)
  determination of, 18f, 19

minimum level of, for
    menses, 46
reduction of, 26
in women, 98–99, 99t
Fat (dietary) in balanced diet,
    68, 69t
Fatigue
  artificial turf and, 167, 170
  from overtraining, 108–109
  "second wind" after, 109
  sudden onset of, 110
Female athlete
  anabolic steroids in, 77–78
  athletic infertility in, 46
  back pain in, from gyne-
    cologic disorder, 418
  genital damage in, in water
    skiing, 416
  greater trochanteric bursitis
    in, 428–429
  injury rate in, 46
  patellar subluxation in, 448
  performance of, in track
    events, 98, 98t
  running shoes for, 38
  training of, 97–101
    body characteristics and,
      98–99, 99–100t
    body fat in, 98–99, 99t
    cardiorespiratory func-
      tion and, 99, 99–100t
    maximal oxygen con-
      sumption in, 99,
      100t
    menstruation and, 46, 70,
      100–101, 104
    muscular function and,
      99
    nutrition in, 101
    pregnancy and. *See*
      Pregnancy
    societal attitudes toward,
      98
    for strength development,
      99–100
  weight training for, 117
Femur
  condyle of, fracture of,
    468–469
  cyst of, 428
  head of, avascular necrosis
    of, 427
  slipped capital epiphysis
    of, 427–428, 428f
  subcapital fracture of, 425
Fencing gloves, 402
Fenoprofen, 72
Fetus, effect of exercise on,
    46–47

Fibrosis of ulnar digital nerve of thumb, 382
Fibula
  fracture of
    in skiing, 513–514
    stress, 514–515
  mechanics of, in ankle movement, 521
Field hockey. *See* Hockey
"Fighter's fracture" of finger, 390–391
Finger
  flexor digitorum profundus avulsion in, 396
  fracture-dislocation of, proximal interphalangeal joint, 393, 394f
  fracture of
    distal phalanx, 399
    metacarpal, 390–391
    middle phalanx, 395–396, 395f
    proximal interphalangeal joint, 392–393
    proximal phalanx, 391–392
  injury of
    rehabilitation after, 400, 401f, 401t
    splinting of, 401t
  interphalangeal joint of
    distal
      dislocation of, 397
      extensor mechanism injuries of, 397–399, 397–399f
    proximal
      anatomy of, 392
      articular fracture at, 392–393
      "buttonhole deformity" at, 393–394, 394f
      collateral ligament injury of, 395, 395f
      dislocation of, 393, 394f
      fracture-dislocation of, 393, 394f
      volar plate injury of, 395
  metacarpal fracture of, 390–391
  metacarpophalangeal joint soft tissue injury of, 388–389, 389f
  phalanx of, fracture of
    middle, 395–396, 395f
    proximal, 391–392
  poked into eye, 274–275

Fingernail, hematoma drainage from, 399
Finkelstein's test in DeQuervain's tenosynovitis, 379
Firearms
  coracoid process injury from, 314
  ear damage from, 284
First aid, 4–5
Fist shape to minimize injury, 390–391, 390f
Fitness
  motor, 104–105
  programs for
    for adults, 90–94
      benefits of, 91
      Canadian 5BX exercise plan, 94
      Cooper's aerobic system, 93–94, 94t
      dropouts from, 91
      objectives of, 91
      principles of, 92
      risks of, 91–92
      safety procedures in, 91–92
      stretching-strengthening in, 92–93
      weight control with, 93
    for children. *See* Children, training of
    for elderly persons, 94–97
      characteristics of, 96–97, 97f
      DeVries program, 97
      gerokinesiatrics, 97, 98f
      Iowa TOES program, 97
      objectives of, 95–96
      physiology of aging and, 94–95
      risks of, 96
      safety procedures for, 96
      training in, 95
    running, 106
  tests for, 104–105, 105t
Flak vest, 407–408, 408f
Flap tear of knee meniscus, 473, 473f, 477–478, 478f
Flexibility. *See also* Stretching
  of ankle, 534, 535f, 538f
  of foot arch, 549, 550f
  of hamstring muscles, 15–16, 16f

of joints, evaluation of, 17–19
  of knee, 502–503, 504f, 508f
  in rehabilitation, 234
  of spine, 13, 14f
Flexion fracture of cervical spine, 291–292, 292f
  with compression, 292, 292f
  lateral, 293
  with rotation, 292
Flexion-rotation drawer test in knee instability, 499
Flexor carpi radialis muscle, anatomy of, 357–358
Flexor carpi radialis tendon, tendinitis of, 380
Flexor carpi ulnaris muscle, anatomy of, 357–358
Flexor carpi ulnaris tendon, tendinitis of, 379–380
Flexor digitorum profundus tendon
  avulsion of, 396
  in extensor mechanism injury, 398
Flexor digitorum sublimis muscle
  anatomy of, 357–358
  in middle phalanx fracture, 395–396
Float phase of running, 31
Floor burns, 67
Fluids and electrolytes
  during exercise, 71
  in hot atmosphere, 172–175
Fluorescein in corneal abrasion, 275
Food. *See* Nutrition
Foot. *See also* Ankle; Heel; Toe(s)
  anatomy of, 536, 539f
  arch of
    rehabilitation of, 549, 550f
    taping of, 548f
  athlete's foot infection of, 559f, 560
  blisters on, 558, 559f
  calluses on, 558–559, 559f
  cavus, 545, 545f
  contact dermatitis of, 66–67
  cuboid subluxation in, 544–545
  dorsal injuries of, 547–550, 551f

"Egyptian," 32
examination of
    preseason, 16–17
    in runner, 32
fracture of
    metatarsal, 547–548,
        550–551, 551–552f
    navicular, 544–545
    sesamoid, 556
fungal infection of, 559f,
    560
"Greek," 32, 546–547,
    547–548f
instep bruise of, 547, 551f
intermetatarsal neuritis in,
    551–552
metatarsal fracture in,
    547–548, 550–551,
    551–552f
metatarsalgia of, 551
navicular stress fracture in,
    544–545
os supranaviculare in, 547
pain in, causes of, 544
pronated, 545–546f, 546
sesamoid fracture in, 556
sesamoiditis of, 553, 555f
shoe boot pernio of, 64
ski boot compression neu-
    ropathy in, 548–549
"surfer's knots" in,
    549–550
warts on, 559–560, 559f
Football
    Achilles tendon rupture in,
        518
    biceps tendon dislocation
        in, 328
    "clipping injury" of knee
        in, 486, 487f
    concussion in, 267–269
    conditioning for
        agility drills in, 131–132,
            132f
        distance running in, 129
        form running drills in,
            130–131, 130f
        interval running in, 130
    cutting (directional change)
        in, knee effects of,
        444, 445f
    deltoid strain in, 306
    finger injury in
        of extensor mechanism,
            397–399, 397, 399f
        of flexor digitorum pro-
            fundus tendon, 396
    glenoid labrum avulsion in,
        330–331
    groin strain in, 425

hamstring strain in,
    431–432
head injury in, 267–269
hematuria in, 413
hip dislocation in, 427
"hip pointer" in, 422
kicking in, knee effects of,
    444–445
kidney injury in, 412–413
knee injury in, 486, 487f
migraine in, 270–271
musculoskeletal injuries in,
    11
neck injury in
    from tackling, 291–293,
        292–293f
    in young players, 289
pants for, 447, 448f
passing in, 314–315
protective equipment for
    facemasks, after facial
        fracture, 278, 279f
    fitting of, 177–179,
        178–180f
    gloves, 402
    helmet, 177–178,
        178–179f, 271, 271f
    hip pads, 422
    knee pads, 447, 448f
    mouthguards, 285, 286f
    silicone wrist splint, 380,
        381f
shoulder dislocation in,
    331, 331f, 334, 334f
skin disorders in, 65–66
spondylolysis in, 418–420,
    419f
strength training for, 138,
    140–142, 142–143f
    for neck, 296, 296–297f,
    298
tackler's exostosis in, 342,
    343f
tackling techniques in,
    288–289
throwing in, mechanics of,
    314–315
thumb ulnar collateral liga-
    ment injury in, 384
toe injury in, 553,
    555–556f
"Football acne," 65–66
"Football finger," 396
Football stance, 130, 130f
Footfire drill in conditioning
    program, 130–131
Forearm injury, rehabilitation
    of, 383, 384–385f
Foreign body
    in airway, 287

in eye
    conjunctival irritation
        from, 274
    removal of, 275
Fracture
    through bone cyst, 428
    of clavicle, 306
    of elbow, 358–360, 359f,
        361f
    of facial bones, 278, 279f
    of fibula, 513–515
    of finger
        distal phalanx, 399
        metacarpal, 390–391
        middle phalanx, 395–396
    of hamate hook, 380–382,
        381f
    of hip, 426–427
    of humerus, 341, 341–342
        in supracondylar region,
            358–360, 359f
    Jefferson's, 291
    Jones, 548, 551f
    of metatarsal, 550–551,
        552f
        fifth, 547–548, 551f
    of navicular, 544
    of neck. *See under* Neck
    of nose, 284–285
    of orbit, 277
    of os calcis, 538
    of patella, 458, 458f
        chondral, 468–469
        osteochondral, 468–469
    of pelvis, avulsion,
        422–423, 424f
    of rib, 406–408, 409f
    of scaphoid, 377, 380, 381f
    of sesamoid, 556
    of skull, 270
    of sternum, 408
    of talus, osteochondral,
        533, 533f, 536
    of tibia
        intercondylar eminence,
            471, 471f
        in skiing, 513–514
        stress, 514–515
    treatment of, 185
    ultrasound over, 222
Friar's balsam in tape appli-
    cation, 181
Friction burns, 67
Frostbite
    deep, 61
    instantaneous, 62
    pathophysiology of, 61–62
    prevention of, 62
    superficial, 61
    treatment of, 62–64, 63f

Frostnip
definition of, 61
prevention of, 62
treatment of, 62
"Frozen shoulder" (calcific
tendinitis), 312
Fungal infection
of ear, 280
of foot, 559f, 560
of skin, 66
Fungo routine in pitching,
323

Ganglion cyst of toes, 552,
553f
Gangrene with frostbite,
63–64
Gastrocnemius muscle strain
("tennis leg"), 517,
518f
Gel pack for cold application,
186
frostbite from, 62
Genitourinary injury
in female athlete, 416
hematocele, 416
hematuria in, 413–415
hemoglobinuria in, 415
to kidney, 412–413
myoglobinuria in, 415
to penis, 416–417
spermatic cord torsion,
415–416
to urethra, 416–417
Gerokinesiatrics, 97, 98f
Glasses, eye, 277–278
Glenohumeral joint
anatomy of, 301–302
stability testing of, 304
subluxation of, 337–338,
338f
Glenoid labrum, avulsion of,
330–331, 330f
Gloves, 402, 402f
contact dermatitis from,
66–67
in frostbite prevention, 62
Glucose monitoring in diabetes, 54–55
Glycogen
anaerobic breakdown of,
82–83
depletion of, sudden fa-
tigue in, 110

storage of, for endurance
events, 70
Glycolysis, anaerobic, 82–83
Goggles, 278
Golf
acromioclavicular arthritis
in, 326–327
hamate hook fracture in,
380–382, 381f
rib fracture in, 406–408,
409f
Grass as playing surface, 170
Gravity stress test in elbow
fracture, 360
Greater trochanteric bursitis,
428–429
"Greek foot," 32, 546–547,
547–548f
Grind test in knee examination, 474, 475f
Grip dynamometer, 19
Griseofulvin in fungal infections, 66
Groin
candidiasis of, 66
intertrigo of, 67
strain of, 425
stretching routine for, 114f
Growth plate. *See* Epiphysis
Guns. *See* Firearms
Guyon, canal of, nerve compression in, 382
Gymnastics
foot pain in, 544
hand calluses in, 399, 401
hand taping in, 180
hollow viscus rupture in,
411, 411f
humeral abnormalities in,
341
spondylolysis in, 419
strength training for,
140–141
wrist synovial cyst in, 374
Gynecologic disease, back
pain in, 418

Hallux limitis, 552–553
Hallux rigidis, 552–553
Hallux valgus, 552–553,
554–555f
Haloprogin in fungal infec-
tions, 66
Hamate hook fracture,
380–382, 381f

Hammer curl with inner
tube, 23, 24f
Hammer throwing, strength
training for, 139–140
Hammer toe, 557–558
Hamstring muscles
conditioning of, with heel-
ups, 131
evaluation of, 15–16, 16f
strain of, 431–432
strength of, *vs* quadriceps
muscles, 431
stretching of, 21f, 22, 114f,
546
Hand. *See also* Finger;
Thumb; Wrist
blisters of, 399–400
calluses of, 399–400
karate injuries of, 389–390,
390f
protection of. *See* Gloves
taping of, to minimize injury, 390–391, 390f
Handball, aerobic points in,
94t
Handicapped athlete, 49–54
amputee, 52–52, 54t
blind, 50, 50f
classification of, for competition, 51, 52–53t
deaf, 50–51
mentally retarded, 52–54,
54f
paralyzed, 51, 52–53t, 53f
sports organizations for,
571–572
Hanging crunch for abdominal strength,
124–125f, 126
Harness drill in conditioning
program, 131, 132f
Head, stretching exercises for,
19, 20f, 21
Headgear. *See also* Face
mask; Helmet
for boxing, 274
for ear protection, 280,
281f
Head injury, 267–273
brain stem stroke in,
269–270
concussion, 267–269
epilepsy and, 58
evaluation of, 270
footballer's migraine,
270–271
knockout blow, 269
prevention of. *See* Helmet
skull fracture, 270

subdural hematoma in, 270
transportation in, 270
Healing process, 183–184
Hearing loss
athlete with, 50–51
from firearm noise, 284
from round window rupture, 284
from tympanic membrane rupture, 283
Heart murmur in preseason examination, 27
Heart rate
aging effects on, 95
in continuous activity training, 89
in exercise, 83–84
in interval training, 89–90
vs training threshold exercise intensity, 88–89, 89f
Heat (environmental)
acclimation to, 174–177
buildup of, on artificial turf, 170
with high humidity, 171
overconditioning during, 175–176
physiologic effects of, 171–172, 174
practice time breaks and, 175, 176t
weight loss from, 175
Heat (treatment)
with cold, 188–189, 189t
in ankle sprain, 526
in frostbite, 63
in pain relief, 75
Heat disorders
cardiovascular effects of, 172
classification of, 172–173
persons predisposed to, 174
prevention of, 173–177
salt depletion in, 173–174, 173t
water depletion in, 173, 173t
Heat edema, 173
Heat exhaustion, 173–174, 173t
artificial turf and, 170
Heat hyperpyrexia, 174
Heat rash, 60–61
Heat stroke, 172, 174
Heel
"black dot," 539, 541f
bone spur in ("runner's bump"), 537

bruise of, 539–540, 542–543, 543f
bursitis of, 536–537
lifts for, 42
in calf muscle stretching, 546
os calcis stress fracture in, 538
os trigonum pinch in, 538
pain under, 539–543, 541–543f
causes of, 539–540, 541f
diagnostic tests in, 540, 542
examination in, 540, 542f
treatment of, 542–543, 542–543f
plantar fascial tear in, 543–544
plantar fasciitis of, 539, 541–542f, 542
pronation neuritis of, 539, 543
retrocalcaneal bony prominence in, 537–538, 540f
Heel cord. See Achilles tendon
Heel strike in running, 31
Heel-ups in conditioning program, 131
Heimlich maneuver, 287
Hein-A-Ken skate aid, 53–54, 54f
Helmet
for baseball, 272
for bicycling, 272
for cricket, 272
emergency removal of, 270, 295
for equestrian sports, 272
for football, 271, 271f
fitting of, 177–178, 178–179f
neck injury and, 288
for hockey, 272–273
for jai alai, 272–273
for lacrosse, 272–273
for motorcycling, 271–272
Hemarthrosis
in ankle sprain, 523
of knee, 466–467, 467f
Hematocele, 416
Hematoma
in ankle sprain, 523
auricular, 278–280, 281f
under fingernail, 399
in groin strain, 425
in nasal septum, 285

ossification of. See Myositis ossificans
in quadriceps contusion, 429–430
in rectus abdominis rupture, 410
subdural, 270
under toenail, 556, 557f
ultrasound treatment of, 221
of vulva, 416
Hematuria, 413–415
Hemoglobin count, 29
Hemoglobinuria, 415
Hemophilia, 55–56
Hemorrhage in eye, 276–277
Hemorrhoids in preseason examination, 29
Hepatitis, 57
Hernia in preseason examination, 28–29
Herpes gladiatorum, 64, 65f
Herpes simplex skin infections, 64, 65f
High pull in strength training, 122
High-voltage pulsed galvanic stimulator, 200–203
classification of, 200–201
pulse parameters for, 201–203, 202f
uses of, 201, 203
Hip. See also Pelvis
adductor tightness of, 14, 15f
bone cysts of, 428
bursitis of, greater trochanteric, 428–429
dislocation of, 427
femoral head avascular necrosis in, 427
flexor tightness of, 14, 15f
fracture of
subcapital, 425
subtrochanteric, 426
iliac crest apophysitis of, 422
iliac crest bruise ("hip pointer"), 422
muscles of, 421
shaping exercises for, 26
stretching of, 428f
preseason examination of, 14–15, 15f
"pyriformis syndrome" of, 422, 423f
rotation of, in runner, 32
slipped capital femoral epiphysis in, 427–428, 428f

Hip (continued)
  strain of
    in groin, 425
    rehabilitation of, 426
  strength of, 14
  stretching of, 21f, 22
Hip circle exercise, 26
Hip pads, 422
Hippocratic reduction of
        shoulder dislocation,
        332, 332f
"Hip pointer," 422
Hip pulse exercise, 26
Hip sled, 149f, 150
History in preseason exam-
        ination, 7
"Hitting the wall," 110
Hockey
  acromioclavicular arthritis
        in, 326–327
  clavicle fracture in, 306
  facemasks for, 273
  foot bruises in, 547
  groin strain in, 425
  helmet for, 272–273
  laryngeal injury in, 287,
        287f
  rib fracture in, 406–408,
        409f
  thumb metacarpal fracture
        in, 383–384
  thumb ulnar collateral liga-
        ment injury in, 384
Hollow viscus rupture,
        411–412, 411f
Hops in conditioning, 131,
        134
Horseback riding
  cold urticaria in, 61
  helmet for, 272
  hollow viscus rupture in,
        411
  neck injury in, 289
  proximal tibiofibular joint
        injury in, 465–466
"Hotshot," 294–295
Humeral-ulnar articulation,
        357
Humerus
  in "apprehension shoul-
        der," 316
  condyles of, 358
  cortical irregularity of, 341
  fracture of, 341–342
    in supracondylar region,
        358–360, 359f
  head of, 301–302
  hypertrophy of, 341
  movement of

  in rotator cuff tear, 312,
        313f
  in throwing, 327
  proximal growth plate of,
    bone cyst in,
        341–342
    tackler's exostosis of, 342,
        343f
Humidity, heat disorders and,
        171–172
Hyaluronidase in pain relief,
        75
Hydra-Gym machine in reha-
        bilitation, 231
Hydrocele, 28
Hydrocortisone for intertrigo,
        67
Hyperextension injury of cer-
        vical spine, 292–293,
        293f
Hyperlordosis, back pain in,
        417
Hyperstimulation trans-
        cutaneous electric
        nerve stimulation,
        199–200
Hypertension, sweating and,
        176
Hyperventilation, 409
  in weight lifting, 146–147
Hyphema of eye, 276–277
Hypoglycemia in diabetes, 55
Hypothalamus, heat regula-
        tion by, 171–172

Ibuprofen, 72, 322
Ice
  for injury treatment,
        185–188, 185f, 188f
  after pitching, 322, 322f
ICE (Ice, Compression, Eleva-
        tion), 30, 31t,
        185–186, 185f
Ice hockey. See Hockey
Ice skating for mentally re-
        tarded persons,
        52–54, 54f
Iliac crest
  apophysitis of, 422
  bruise at ("hip pointer"),
        422
Iliotibial band
  anatomy of, 438–439
  friction syndrome of, 462,
        464, 464f

  stretching exercises for, 21f,
        22
Iliotibial tract, preseason ex-
        amination of, 15, 15f
Ilium, joint of. See Sacroiliac
        joint
Impedance, tissue, 193–194
Impetigo, 64–65, 65f
Impingement syndrome, exer-
        cises for, 352
Indomethacin, 72, 322
Infection
  of blisters, 558
  of ear from swimming, 280,
        282
  prevention of, 184
  skin
    acne, 65–66
    fungal, 66
    herpes simplex, 64, 65f
    impetigo, 64–65, 65f
    molluscum contagiosum,
        64, 65f
    from tape, 183
Infectious hepatitis, 57
Infectious mononucleosis, 57
  spleen rupture in, 410–411
Infertility in women athletes,
        46
Inflammation
  from overexercise, 228,
        228t
  pathophysiology of,
        183–184
Information, medical, release
        of, 6
Inguinal intertrigo, 67
Injection of steroids, 74
Injury
  athletes prone to, 160
  pathophysiology of,
        183–184
  return to competition/train-
        ing after. See Return
        to competition/
        training
  types of, 184–185, 184f
Injury control programs, 4
Insulin, exercise and, 55
Intercondylar eminence frac-
        ture of tibia, 471,
        471f
Interferential stimulation,
        203–205, 204f
Intermetatarsal neuritis,
        551–552
Intermittent compression in
        injury treatment,
        186–187, 187f

Interosseous membrane at elbow, 358
Interphalangeal joint
  distal
    dislocation of, 397
    extensor mechanism injury of, 397–399, 397f, 399f
  proximal
    articular fracture of, 392–393
    "buttonhole deformity" of, 393–394, 394f
    collateral ligament injury at, 395
    dislocation of, 393, 394f
    fracture-dislocation of, 393, 394f
    injury to, 392
    volar plate injury of, 395
Intertrigo from cycling, 67
Intervertebral disk rupture, 417–418
Intervertebral joint mobilization, 242
  in cervical spinal disorders, 248–249, 250f
  in lumbar spinal disorders, 255–258, 263f
  in thoracic spinal disorders, 251–252, 252f
Intervertebral motion, assessment of, 251
Iontophoresis in pain relief, 209–210, 209f
Iowa TOES program, 97
Iron deficiency anemia, 70, 101
Ischemia in compartment syndrome, 516–517
Ischium, soreness at, 67
ISE (Ice, Stretching, Exercise), 187–188, 188f
Isoetherine in asthma, 59
Isoethrane in asthma, 60
Isokinetic exercise in rehabilitation, 231–232, 233f, 234
Isokinetic machine in strength measurement, 19, 19f
Isometric exercise
  in neck strengthening, 298
  in rehabilitation, 229
Isoproterenol in asthma, 59
Isotonic exercise
  in neck strengthening, 298
  in rehabilitation, 229

Itching
  from adhesive tape, 183
  from contact dermatitis, 66–67
  from fungal infections, 66
  in "saddle soreness," 67
  in swimmer's ear, 280

Jai alai, helmet for, 272–273
Javelin throwing
  elbow disorders in, 366
  mechanics of, 315
  strength training for, 139–140
Jaw
  fracture of, 278, 279f
  imbalance of, 285–286, 286f
Jefferson's fracture, 291
Jerk test in knee instability, 498, 499f
Jockey, injury to, 272, 289
"Jock itch," 66
Jogging in rehabilitation of injured runner, 35
Joint(s). *See also specific joint*
  exercise of, after injury, 228
  loose, 17–18
  preseason examination of, 17–19
  tight, 17–18
Jones fracture, 548, 551f
Journals, sports medicine, 565–566
J-stroking in thoracic spine disorders, 251
"Jumper's knee," 459, 460f
Jumping and jumps
  in conditioning, 133–135, 133f
  foot pain in, 544
  os trigonum pinching in, 538
  testing of, 143f

Karate
  hand injuries in, 389–390, 390f

kicking in, knee effects of, 444–445
  laryngeal injury in, 287
Ketoacidosis in diabetes, 55
Kicking
  knee effects of, 444–445
  in swimming, knee injury in, 487
  tibial tubercle fracture in, 461–462, 463f
Kidney
  "athlete's," 414
  disorders of, exercise in end-stage, 415
    after transplantation, 415
  injury to, 412–413
  natural protection of, 412
Kienbock's disease (avascular necrosis of lunate), 378
Knee
  anatomy of, 435–441
    ligaments, 436–440, 437–439f
    menisci, 440–441, 441f
    muscles, 435–436, 436f
    pes anserinus, 441
  ankylosis of, after reconstructive surgery, 504
  arthralgia of, retropatellar, 455–458, 456f
  arthroscopy of, 491–493, 492–493f
    training after, 149–150, 149f
  aspiration of, 466–467, 467f
  bicycling effects on, 445–446
  biomechanics of
    in cutting, 444, 445f
    in cycling, 445–446
    in kicking, 444–445
    in running, 443, 444f
  brace for, 449–450, 450f
    in anterior cruciate ligament tear, 492, 492f
  bursitis of, prepatellar, 447, 448f
  chondromalacia of, 455–458, 456f
  cutting (directional change) effects on, 444, 445f
  dislocation of, 505, 507–508
  examination of, 441–443
    in anterolateral rotatory instability, 497–499, 499f
    arthroscopic, 491–493

Knee, examination of
(*continued*)
in excessive lateral facet
pressure, 453
in ligament tears,
485–486
anterior cruciate, 490,
491f
posterior cruciate, 494
in meniscal tear, 474, 475f
in patellar subluxation,
448–449, 449f
preseason, 15–16, 16–17f
in quadriceps tendon
rupture, 447
excessive lateral facet pressure in, 453–455,
454f
extensor mechanism of,
435–436, 436f
realignment of, 450–451,
451f
fracture of
chondral, 468–469
femoral condylar,
468–469
osteochondral, 468–469
patellar, 458, 458f,
468–469
of tibial intercondylar
eminence, 471, 471f
of tibial tubercle,
461–462, 463f
hemarthrosis of, 466–467,
467f
iliotibial band friction syndrome in, 462, 464,
464f
instability of
combined, 504–505
late, 494, 496
rotary, 496–504
anterolateral, 497–501,
500–501f, 503–504
anteromedial, 496–497
posterolateral, 504
straight, 496–497, 498f
"jumper's knee," 459
kicking effects on, 445–446
ligaments of
anatomy of, 436–440,
437–439f
tears of, 485–494
anterior cruciate,
490–491, 491f
examination in,
485–486
medial collateral,
486–489, 487–488f

pes anserinus,
489–490, 490f
posterior cruciate,
493–494, 494f
loose bodies in, 470
menisci of. *See* Menisci of
knee
Osgood-Schlatter's condi-
tion of, 460–461,
462–463f
osteochondritis dissecans,
469–470, 470f
pads for, 447, 448f
pain in, in slipped capital
femoral epiphysis,
427–428, 428f
patella of
bipartate, 458, 458f
dislocation of, 452–453,
452f
fracture of, 458, 458f,
468–469
subluxation of, 447–451,
449–451f
patellar tendon of, rupture
of, 459–460, 461f
pes anserinus of, anatomy
of, 441
plica abnormalities in,
467–468, 468f
popliteus tenosynovitis in,
464–465, 465f
Q angle in, 448
quadriceps tendon rupture
in, 446–447
radiography of, 443. *See
also specific disorder*
reconstruction of, after late
instability, 494, 496
rehabilitation of, 234–235,
234t
after ligament reconstruction, 495
postoperative, 483–485,
484–486f
"at risk knee," 490–491
"runner's knee," 453
running effects on,
443–444, 444f
stabilizing ligaments of,
437–440, 437f
strength of, 16, 17f
swelling at, 466–467,
467f
synovitis of, 453
tendinitis of ("jumper's"),
459, 460f
tibial epiphysitis in,
460–461, 462–463f

tibiofibular joint of, proximal, injury of,
465–466
wrapping of, in weight lifting, 126–127
Knee bend (squat) in strength
training, 119–121,
121f
Knee lifts in conditioning
program, 130
"Knockout" blow, 269
Kyphosis, back pain in, 417

Laboratory tests, 29–30
Labyrinthitis, caloric,
283–284
Lacrosse
facemasks for, 273, 273f
gloves for, 402
helmet for, 272–273
prepatellar bursitis in, 447
rib fracture in, 406–408,
408–409f
Lactic acid accumulation
in anaerobic glycolysis, 82
in endurance exercise, 85
prevention of, 109
Lactic dehydrogenase in hepatitis, 57
Ladder crunch for abdominal
strength, 124–125f,
126
Laminar release
in lumbar spine disorders,
255
in thoracic spine disorders,
251
Laryngeal injury, 287, 287f
Laséque test for sciatica, 254
Lasers, 222–227
application of, 225–226
contraindications for, 227
frequency of, 224
gallium arsenide, 223–226
gridding with, 224f, 226
helium neon, 223–226
history of, 222
light characteristics of,
223–224, 224f
light production in, 223,
224f
pain management with, 226
penetration of, 225
physiologic effects of, 225

safety procedures for, 226–227
tissue healing and, 226
types of, 223
uses of, 222–223
Lateral facet pressure, excessive, in knee, 453–455, 454f
Lateral quadruple complex of knee, 438–439, 438f
Latissimus dorsi muscle
strengthening of, 23–24, 25f
tightness of, 304
Leg(s). *See also* Calf muscles; Thigh
Achilles tendonitis in, 521
Achilles tendon rupture in, 517–521, 519–520f
compartment syndrome in, 516–517
fracture of
in skiing, 513–514
stress, 514–515
length discrepancy in
back pain in, 417
examination for, 13, 14f
in runners, 32
shin splints in, 515–516, 516f
"tennis leg," 517, 518f
Legal aspects of sports medicine, 2–4
assumption of risk by athlete, 4
athlete's role in, 4
contract, 4
malpractice, 3
negligence, 3–4, 6
tort liability, 3–4
Legg-Calvé-Perthes avascular necrosis, 427
Leg raises
for abdominal strength, 124–125f, 126
in knee rehabilitation, 483–484
in lumbar spine evaluation, 253–254
Lens, contact, 270, 277
Liability of physician, 2–4
Lidocaine for pain relief, 73–74
Ligament(s). *See also under* Ankle; Knee
damaged, treatment of, 185
strength of, 117
Light therapy. *See* Lasers

Little League baseball, helmet for, 272
"Little League elbow," 361–364
"Little League shoulder," 341–342
Liver
hepatitis effects on, 57
rupture of, 412
Local anesthetics for pain relief, 73–74
Locus stimulator in pain relief, 205–206
Long-sitting test in sacroiliac evaluation, 264
Loose bodies
in elbow, 366
in knee, 470
Lordosis
back pain in, 417
examination for, 13
Lower extremity, rehabilitation of, 235–236, 235t, 236–237f, 238
Low-voltage stimulator in pain relief, 208–210, 209f
Lubricant for massage, 190
Lumbar roll, 255, 257, 263f
Lumbar spine
evaluation of, 253–254
injury of, 254–258, 258–263f
spondylolysis of, 418–420, 419f
Lunate
avascular necrosis of, 378
dislocation of, 377–378
impaction of, with triquetal, 374
Lymphocytosis in infectious mononucleosis, 57

Magnuson and Stack operation in shoulder dislocation, 335, 336f
Mallet finger, 398–399, 399f
Malpractice, 3
Mandible
fracture of, 278, 279f
orthopedic repositioning appliance for, 286, 286f

Manual therapy. *See also* Massage
of back
cervical region of, 244–245, 245–247f, 248–250, 250f
intervertebral joint mobilization in, 242
lumbar region of, 255–258, 258f, 262f, 263f
sacroiliac region of, 264–266, 265f
soft tissue mobilization in, 242
thoracic region of, 251–252, 252f
vertebral artery test before, 245–246
Marathon running, training for, 107
"Marathon toes," 32, 556, 557f
March test in sacroiliac evaluation, 263–264
Marijuana, 76
frostbite and, 62
Marksman. *See* Firearms
Mask. *See* Face mask
Massage, 190–191, 191f. *See also* Manual therapy
cross-friction, in thoracic spinal disorders, 251
with ice cup, 187–188, 188f
in lumbar spinal disorders, 255
before pitching, 319–320, 319–321f
Massage hook technique of cervical spine, 250
Mastery rehearsal in coping with injury, 155
Mat burns, 67
Maturation, sexual
competition matching by, 42–43
effects of heavy training on, 104
Medial capsular ligament, anatomy of, 436–437, 437f
Median nerve
at elbow, 358
at wrist, 382
Medical records, 7
Memory deficit in concussion, 268

Menarche
  in competition by maturity
      matching, 42–43
  delayed, in heavy training,
      104
Menisci of knee
  anatomy of, 440–441, 441f
  cyst of, 442, 479
  lateral
    anatomy of, 440–441,
        441f
    tears in, 478–479, 479f
  medial
    anatomy of, 440, 441f
    tears in, 473f, 476–478,
        477–478f
  tears in, 471–483
    arthrography in,
        474–476, 476f
    bowstring, 472–473, 473f,
        476, 477f
    degenerative, 478
    diagnosis of, 474, 475f
    discoid, 474, 479
    flap, 473, 473f, 477–478,
        478f
    horizontal cleavage,
        476–477
    lateral, 478–479, 479f
    medial, 473f, 476–478,
        477–478f
    meniscectomy in
      arthroscopic, 149–150,
          149f, 476
      lateral, 481
      total, 480–481,
          482–483f
      training after, 149–150,
          149f
    repair of, arthroscopic,
        479–480
    types of, 471–472
Menstruation
  body fat proportion and,
      46
  exercise and, 100–101
    strenuous, 46, 104
  iron deficiency and, 70,
      101
Mental retardation
  ice skating therapy in,
      52–54, 54f
  Olympic events and, 52
Metabolism
  aerobic, 82–83
  anaerobic, 82–83
  ATP in, 81–82
  "second wind" and, 109
  in women, 99

Metacarpal fracture
  of finger, 390–391
  of thumb, 383–384
Metacarpophalangeal joint
  of finger, soft tissue injury
      at, 388–389, 389f
  of thumb, dislocation of,
      384, 386f
Metaproterenol in asthma, 59
Metatarsal(s)
  fifth, fracture of, 547–548,
      551f
  neuritis between, inter-
      metatarsal, 551–552
  stress fracture of, 550–551,
      552f
Metatarsalgia, 551
Metatarsophalangeal joint,
      disorders of,
      552–553, 554–555f
Methyl salicylate in pain re-
      lief, 75
Miconazole in fungal infec-
      tions, 66
Migraine, footballer's,
      270–271
Miliaria, 60–61
Molluscum contagiosum, 64,
      65f
Mononucleosis, infectious, 57
  spleen rupture in, 410–411
MORA (mandibular ortho-
      pedic repositioning
      appliance), 286, 286f
Morton's extension, 547, 547f
Motorcycling
  facemasks for, 273–274
  helmet for, 271–272
Motor fitness, 104–105
"Mountain climber" exercise,
      262f
Mouthguard, 285–286, 286f
Mouth injury
  prevention of, 285, 286f
  in temporomandibular joint
      imbalance, 285–286,
      286f
  tooth damage, 286–287
Muscle energy technique in
      sacroiliac disorders,
      264–266, 265f
Muscle fibers
  splitting of, in strength
      training, 115
  types of, endurance exer-
      cise and, 85
Muscles
  breakdown of, myo-
      globinuria and, 415

components of, 115, 116f
contraction of, 115
cramps of, 148
  during relaxation train-
      ing, 158
electrical simulation of,
      192. See also Neuro-
      muscular stimulator
function of, aging effects
      on, 95
hypertrophy of, 115
physiology of, during
      strength training,
      115–117, 116f
soreness of, 148
  prevention of, by warm-
      up, 112
warming-up of. See Warm-
      ing up
in women, 99
Musculoskeletal system, pre-
      season examination
      of, 11–19, 12–19f
Myeloma, back pain in, 418
Myoglobinuria, 415
Myopia in preseason exam-
      ination, 10–11
Myopulse unit, 206–208
Myositis of leg (shin splints),
      515–516, 516f
Myositis ossificans
  vs tackler's exostosis, 342
  traumatic, 430–431, 430f

Nail
  finger, hematoma under,
      399
  toe
    hematoma under, 556,
        557f
    ingrown, 556–557
Naproxen, 72, 322
National Athletic Trainer's
      Association, neck in-
      jury registry of, 288
National Wheelchair Athletic
      Association, classi-
      fications of, 51, 52t
National Wheelchair Basket-
      ball Association,
      classifications of, 51,
      53t
Navicular, stress fracture of,
      544

Nebraska agility drill in conditioning program, 131
Neck. *See also* Cervical spine
circumference of, 11
examination of
preseason, 11
in scapular pain, 348
in shoulder disorders, 303
extension of, 11
flexion of, 11
fracture of
from compression, 291
from compression/flexion, 292, 292f
from flexion, 291–292, 292f
lateral, 293
from flexion/compression, 292, 292f
from flexion/rotation, 292
from hyperextension, 292–293, 293f
from rotation/flexion, 292
spinal structure and, 289–290
x-ray in, 290
injury to
brain stem stroke in, 269–270
in football, 288
helmet construction and, 288
incidence of, 287–288
on-the-field care of, 295
quadriplegia risk and, 288
in rebound tumbling, 171
registry for, 288
transportation after, 295
length of, 11
range of motion of, 245f
strain of, treatment of, 244–245, 245–249f
straps for, 295–296
strength training for, 142f, 296, 296–297f, 298
Neck roll, 293f, 295
Necrosis
acute tubular, 415
avascular
of femoral head, 427
of lunate, 378
Needling in jumper's knee, 459, 460f
Negligence, 3–4, 6
Nerve fibers, 192–193, 193t

Nerve injury
in "backpack palsy," 304–305
pinching, in neck, 294–295
in thoracic outlet syndrome, 305
Nerve root injury from hyperextension, 293
Neuritis
intermetatarsal, 551–552
pronation, 543
Neuromuscular stimulator, 210–213
amplitude for, 212
application of, 211
frequency for, 212
instrumentation for, 211
physiology of, 211–212
pulse duration for, 212
technique for, 212–213
Neurons, 192
Neurophysiology in electrical stimulation, 192–193, 192f, 193t
Nicotine, effects of, 76
Nipple, runner's, 405
Nodules on foot from surfing, 549–550
Noise from firearms, ear damage from, 284
Nonsteroidal anti-inflammatory drugs, 71–73
Nose
bleeding from, 284
fracture of, 284–285
Nutrition, 67–71
balanced, 68, 69t, 70
caloric needs and, 68
carbohydrate loading in, 70
in diabetic athlete, 55
fluids in, 71
in hot atmosphere, 176
poor habits in, 67–68
precompetition preparation, 70–71
supplements in, 68, 69t, 70, 101
for women athlete, 101
Nystatin in fungal infections, 66

"Oarsman's wrist," 379
Obesity, 91, 93

Oblique abdominal muscle, strengthening of, 24–25, 25f
Odontoid fracture, 292
Olecranon
anatomy of, 358
bone spurs of, 365–366
bursitis of, 371
Olecranon fossitis, 365–366
Olympic games for mentally retarded athletes, 52
Oral enzymes for pain relief, 75
Orbit, fracture of, 277
Organizations
sports, 569
for handicapped athlete, 571–572
sports medicine, 567–568
Orthotics for shoes, 42, 43t
Orthotron machine in rehabilitation, 231–232, 232f
Os calcis, stress fracture of, 538
Osgood-Schlatter's condition, 460–461, 462–463f
Os supranaviculare, 547
Osteitis pubis, 423, 425
Osteoarthritis
of elbow, 358
of knee, after meniscectomy, 481, 483f
Osteochondral fracture of patella, 468–469
Osteochondritis dissecans
of capitellum, 362–363
of knee, 469–470, 470f
Osteoma in ear, 282
Osteoporosis, exercise and, 26
Os trigonum, pinching of, 538
Overhead press with inner tube, 23, 24f
Overtraining (staleness), 108–109
Oxygen consumption, maximum (VO$_2$max, 83–85
in children, 103
in elderly persons, 95
vs heart rate, 88–89, 89f
in women, 99, 100t
Oxygen transport during exercise, 83–84
Oxyphenbutazone, 73

Pacemaker, ultrasound over, 222
Pacing for endurance events, 109–110
Pads, protective. *See also* Shoulder pads
  fitting of, 178–179, 179–180f
  hip, 422
  knee, 447, 448f
Pain
  avoidance of, in rehabilitation, 229. 230f, 231
  back, 417–418, 418f
    lower region of, 254–255
  psychological aspects of, 156–159
  relief of. *See also* Electrical devices
    drugs for, 71–75
    physiology of, 197–198
    by self-control, 156–159
  sciatic, leg raise test in, 253–254
  in shoulder injury diagnosis, 11
"Paint the wall" exercise, 252, 253f
Palmaris longus muscle, anatomy of, 357–358
Palumbo patellar brace, 449–450, 450f
"Pancake taping" for thumb stability, 386, 388f
Pancreas, rupture of, 412
Panniculitis, cold, 61
Paperwork, 30
Paralysis. *See* Neck, fracture of
Paralyzed athlete, 51, 52–53t, 53f
Paranasal sinus disorders in deep diving, 282
Paravertebral muscles, strengthening of, 25, 25f
Parcours, 90
Pars interarticularis, spondylolysis and, 418–420, 419f
Partner stretching, 112–115, 113–114f
Patella
  anatomy of, 436
  arthralgia of, 455–458, 456f
  bipartate, 458, 458f
  bursitis of, 447, 448f
  chondromalacia of, 455–458, 456f

dislocation of, 452–453, 452f
  examination of, 442
  fracture of, 458, 458f
    chondral, 468–469
    osteochondral, 468–469
  high, 448
  subluxation of, 447–451
    brace for, 449–450, 450f
    causes of, 448
    examination in, 448–449, 449f
    symptoms of, 448
    treatment of, 449–451, 450–451f
  tendinitis of ("jumper's knee"), 459, 460f
Patella alta, 448
Patellar tendon
  anatomy of, 436
  rupture of, 459–460, 461f
Peaking in training, 109
Pectoralis major muscle
  rupture of, 406
    in pitching, 318
  tightness of, 304
Pectoral muscles
  strengthening of, 23, 24f
  stretching of, 113f
Pellegrini-Steida's disease, 489
Pelvis. *See also* Hip
  fracture of, avulsion, 422–423, 424f
  muscles of, 421
  osteitis pubis of, 423, 425
Pendulum exercise in shoulder rehabilitation, 345, 348f
Penis
  injury to, 416, 416f
  natural protection of, 412
Performance
  limits of, in children, 103
  peaking of, 109
  of women, in track events, 98, 98t
Perilunate dislocation, 377–378
Periodization in strength training, 135–138, 136f
Periostitis of leg (shin splints), 515–516, 516f
Peritoneal lavage in abdominal injury, 410
Permission slips, 30
Peroneal nerve compression by ski boot, 548–549

Peroneal tendons, dislocation of, 531, 533
Peroneus brevis tendon, strain of, 547–548
Pes anserinus
  anatomy of, 441
  examination of, 442
  transfer of, 489–490, 490f
Phalanx fracture
  distal, 399
  middle, 395–396
  proximal, 391–392
Pharmacologic agents. *See* Drugs
Phenylbutazone, 72
  in "tennis elbow," 369
Phonophoresis, 221
Phoresor in pain relief, 209–210, 209f
Physical education program for children, 45, 45t
Physical fitness. *See* Fitness
Physical working capacity, aging effects on, 95
Physician, athletes', 1–47
  consultant team for, 2, 3t
  contract with, 4
  duties of, 2
  emergency care by, 5–6
  equipment of, 43–44
  examination by. *See* Examination
  for female athlete, 46-47
  information release by, 6
  injury control by, 4
  laboratory tests and, 29–30
  legal aspects of sports medicine and, 2–4
  negligence by, 3–4, 6
  for older athlete, 47
  paperwork by, 30, 31t
  responsibility of
    for allowing return to play after injury, 15, 44
    contract for, 4
    on-the-field, 43–44
  treatment explanation by, 6
  for young athlete, 44–46, 45t
Pitching
  adhesion formation in, 317–318
  arm care after, 322, 322f
  "baseball elbow" in, 364
  fungo routine in, 323
  glenoid labrum avulsion in, 330–331, 330f

injury in
    diagnosis of, 316–318,
        318f
    treatment of, 317–318
"Little League elbow" in,
    361–364
"Little League shoulder"
    in, 341–342
mechanics of, 314,
    314–315f, 316, 316t,
    318
rib fracture in, 406–408,
    409f
strength training for, 137,
    139
thoracic outlet problems in,
    305
warming up before,
    318–322, 319–320f,
    353
Pivot-shift test in knee insta-
    bility, 497–498
Plantar fascia of heel
    inflammation of, 539, 541f,
        542
    rupture of, 545, 545f
    tear in, 543–544
Plantar wart, ultrasound
    treatment of,
        220–221
Playing field surfaces, 167,
    170. See also Turf
Plica of knee, abnormalities
    of, 467–468, 468f
"Plow" stretch, injury from,
    22, 22f
Plyometrics
    bounds in, 134–135, 134f
    for children, 117–118
    depth jumps in, 135
    hops in, 134
    jumps in, 133f, 133–134
    mechanism of, 132
    objectives of, 132
    program for, 132–133
    safety tips for, 133
    upper body, 135
Pneumothorax, 408–409
    in deep diving, 282
Point stimulator in pain re-
    lief, 205–206
Pole vaulting, safety precau-
    tions in, 170–171
Pool exercise (Poolex)
    for injured runner, 34–35
    in knee rehabilitation,
        234–235, 234t
Popliteal artery injury in
    knee dislocation, 508

Popliteus muscle, 439, 439f
Popliteus tendon
    anatomy of, 438f, 439
    tenosynovitis of, 464–465,
        465f
Posterior capsule of knee,
    anatomy of, 440
Posterior oblique ligament,
    438
Posture
    correction of, 244, 246f
    screening of, in sacroiliac
        evaluation, 262–263
Potassium loss in heat disor-
    ders, 172
Power
    development of, with ply-
        ometrics, 132–135,
        133–134f
    rehabilitation of, 234
Power clean lift in strength
    training, 121–122,
        123–124f
Power lifting, 146
Power skipping. See Bounds
    in plyometrics
"Prayer stretch," 259f
Precompetition meal, 70–71
Pregnancy
    anabolic steroids in, 77–78
    exercise during, 46–47, 101
    ultrasound during, 222
Prepatellar bursitis, 447, 448f
Priapism, 416, 416f
Primatene mist in asthma, 60
Prixocam, 72
Progressive resistance exer-
    cise, 115
Pronated foot, 545–546f, 546.
    See also "Greek
    foot"
    running shoes in, 37–38
Pronation neuritis, 543
Pronation phase in running,
    31
Proprioception, ankle sprain
    and, 527–528, 528f
Proprioceptive Neuromuscu-
    lar Facilitation
    stretching, 112–115,
        113–114f
Prostaglandin synthesis,
    drugs inhibiting,
        72–73
Protective equipment. See
    also Face mask;
    Gloves; Helmet; Pads,
    protective
    eyeguard, 277–278

    fitting of, 177–179
        football helmet, 177–178,
            178–179f
        shoulder pads, 178–179,
            179–180f
    mouthguard, 285–286, 286f
Protein
    in balanced diet, 68, 69t
    as nutritional supplement,
        68
    in precompetition meal, 71
Proteinuria, 29–30
Pruritis ani from cycling, 67
Pseudoboutonnière deformity,
    395
Psychological care of injured
    athlete, 151–164
    anger and, 163
    childlike behavior and, 163
    coping skills in, 152–156
    dependence/attention-lov-
        ing in, 162
    injury proneness in, 160
    motivation lack in,
        163–164
    pain self-control in,
        156–159
    perception of injury and,
        151–152
    predisposing attitudes and,
        161–162
    resistance in, 162–163
    return to competition and,
        159–160
Psychological factors
    burnout, in children, 104
    injury rate and, 18
    in weight training, 129
Puberty onset, effects of
    heavy training on,
        104
Pubic symphysis, inflamma-
    tion of, 423, 425
Publications on sports medi-
    cine, 565–566
Pudendal nerve irritation in
    cycling, 416
Pull-down exercise with inner
    tube, 23–24, 25f
Pulmonary function, aging ef-
    fects on, 95
Pulse duration of electrical
    devices, 195
Pulse frequency of electrical
    devices, 195
"Punch drunk" athlete, 269
"Punch fracture" of finger,
    390–391
Pushoff phase in running, 31

Putti-Platt operation in shoulder dislocation, 335
Pyriformis muscle, stretching of, 266
"Pyriformis syndrome," 422, 423f

Q angle in Knee, 448
Qmax (maximum cardiac output), 83–84
Quadriceps muscles
  anatomy of, 435, 436f
  conditioning of, with heel-ups, 131
  contusion of, 429–430
  neurostimulation of, 212–213
  in patellar subluxation, 450–451, 451f
  strengthening of, 23, 24f
  strength of, *vs* hamstring muscles, 431
  stretching of, 21f, 22, 114f
Quadriceps tendon
  rupture of, 446–447
  tendinitis of ("jumper's knee"), 459, 460f
Quadriplegia
  competition and, 51
  risk of, in football, 288
Quadruple complex, lateral, 438–439, 438f

"Raccoon eyes" in skull fracture, 270
Race walking, osteitis pubis in, 423, 425
Racing, foot, training for, 107
Racketball
  eye injury in, 275, 276f
  gloves for, 402
Radial head, anatomy of, 358
Radial nerve at elbow, 358
Radial-scaphoid impaction, 373–374, 373f
Radial-ulnar articulation, 357
Radioulnar joint
  action of, 374
  injury of, 374–375

Range of motion
  of cervical spine/neck, 243, 245f
  of thoracic spine, 252
Rash from adhesive tape, 182–183
Rebound tumbling, safety procedures for, 171
Rectus abdominis muscle, strengthening of, 24–25, 25f
Rectus femoris muscle
  anatomy of, 435
  tightness of, 14–15, 15f
Rehabilitation, 227–238
  of ankle, 534–535, 535–538f
    after sprain, 526–528, 527–528f
  cold in, 185–188, 185f, 188f
  of elbow, 383, 384–385f
  endurance development in, 234–235, 234t
  of finger, 400, 401f, 401t
  flexibility development in, 234
  of foot arch, 549, 550f
  of forearm, 383, 384–385f
  goal setting in, 227–228
  heat in, 188–190, 189t
  of hip, after strain, 426
  isokinetics in, 231–234, 232–233f
  of knee, 502–503, 504–508f
    after anterior cruciate ligament tear, 495
    after ligament reconstruction, 495
    postoperative, 483–485, 484–486f
  of lower extremity, 235–236, 235t, 236–237f, 238
  objectives of, 228–229, 229t
  pain avoidance in, 229, 230f, 231
  physiology of, 228, 228t
  power development in, 234
  program for, 229, 230f, 231
  progressions for, 236–238
  psychological aspects of, 227. See Psychological care of injured athlete
  of runners, 34–35
  of shoulder, 345–346, 347–351f

after rotator cuff repair, 313–314
    stages of, 236–237
    strength development in, 229
    trainer's duties in, 166
Relaxation training, 156–159
Respiratory system, physiology of, 83–84
  aging and, 95
  in women, 99–100, 99–100t
Retinaculum of knee, lateral, 438
Retinal detachment
  after eye injury, 277
  in preseason examination, 10–11
Retrocalcaneal bony prominence, 537–538, 540f
Retropatellar arthralgia, 455–458, 456f
Return to competition/training, 15, 44, 148–150, 149f. See *also specific injury*
  after "burner," 294–295
  after concussion, 268–269
  criteria for, 228–229, 229t
  after elbow dislocation, 361
  exercise program for, 229, 230f, 231
  after facial bone fracture, 278
  psychological aspects of, 159–160
Rhomboid muscle, exercises for
  in strain, 352, 353f
  strengthening, 24, 25f
Rib
  costochondral separation of, 408
  fracture of, 406–408, 409f
"Ringman's shoulder," 341
Ringworm, 66
Risks in fitness programs
  for adults, 91–92
  for elderly persons, 96
Rotation fracture of cervical spine with flexion, 292
Rotator cuff
  anatomy of, 302, 302f
  examination of, 304, 310
  injury of, 309–310
    arthrogram of, 311, 311f
    examination of, 310
    exercises for, 352

rehabilitation of, 313–314
treatment of, 312–313, 313f
Round window rupture, 284
Rowing
    hematuria in, 413
    "oarsman's wrist" in, 379
Rubefacients in pain relief, 75
Rugby
    costochondral separation in, 408
    shoulder injury in, 306
"Runner's bump," 537
"Runner's knee," 453
Runner's nipple, 405
Running and runners
    Achilles tendinitis in, 521
    aerobic points in, 94t
    age in, 31
    on artificial turf, 167, 170
    aspirin therapy in, 72
    back pain in, 417–418
    beginning, training for, 106
    "black dot heel" in, 539, 541f
    breast irritation in, 405–406, 406f
    categories of, 30–31
    distance
        in conditioning program, 129
        training for, 105–107
    downhill
        injury in, 462, 464, 464f
        knee mechanics in, 443–444
    examination of, 30–32, 33f, 34
        dynamic evaluation in, 32, 34
        history in, 32
        physical, 32, 33f
    fartlek, 90
    for fitness maintenance, training for, 106
    foot pain in, 544
    greater trochanteric bursitis in, 428–429
    heel bone spur in ("runner's bump"), 537
    hematuria in, 413–414
    hemoglobinuria in, 415
    iliac crest apophysitis in, 422
    iliotibial band friction syndrome in, 462, 464, 464f
    injury in, 31

interval, in conditioning program, 130
knee problems in, 443–444, 444f
leg stress fracture in, 514–515
marathon, training for, 107
mechanics of, knee, 443–444, 444f
metabolism in, 83
metatarsalgia in, 551
metatarsal stress fracture in, 550–551, 552f
osteitis pubis in, 423, 425
plantar fascial tear in, 543
pronated foot in, 545–546f, 546
racing, training for, 107
rehabilitation of, 34–35
retrocalcaneal bony prominence in, 537–538, 540f
retropatellar arthralgia in, 455–458, 456f
sex and, 31
shin splints in, 515–516, 516f
shoes for, 35–39, 36f
    in overpronation, 37–38
    selection of, 37–39
speed development in, 130–131, 130f
"stitch in side" in, 412
stride phases of, 31
subtrochanteric fracture in, 426
toe injury in, 556, 557f
training for, 105–107
    in triathalon, 107–108
uphill, knee mechanics in, 443, 444f
Russian stimulator, 211

Sacral spine
    evaluation of, 258, 260, 262–264
    injury of, 264–266, 265f
Sacroiliac joint
    anatomy of, 258, 260
    biomechanics of, 260
    disorders of, 264–266, 265f
    evaluation of, 260–264
    excessive extension of, 266
    excessive flexion of, 266

Saddle height for cycling, 446
"Saddle soreness," 67
Safety procedures
    in cycling, 445–446
    in diving, 289, 290f
    for electrical stimulators, 213–214
    in fitness programs
        for adults, 91–92
        for elderly persons, 96
    with lasers, 226–227
    in plyometrics, 133
    for rebound tumbling, 171
    in skiing, binding adjustments in, 513–514
    for track and field events, 170–171
    in weight lifting as sport, 145–146
    in weight training, 118–119, 127–129
Salpingitis, 416
Salt depletion heat exhaustion, 173–174, 173t
Scaphoid
    fracture of, 377, 380, 381f
    impaction of, with radius, 373–374, 373f
Scapholunate angle, 376
Scapholunate joint, separation of, 376, 376f
Scapula. See also Coracoid process
    examination of, 304
    pain at, 346, 348
    winging of, 12, 13f
Scapular framing in thoracic spine disorders, 251, 252f
Scapulocostal bursitis, 346
Scapulohumeral joint, motion of, 302–303
Scheuermann's disease, 14, 417
Sciatica, leg raise test in, 253–254
Scoliosis, 13–14
Scrotum
    preseason examination of, 28
    "saddle soreness" and, 67
"Scrum ear," 278–280, 281f
"Second wind," 109
Seizures, 57–58
Semimembanosus ligament, 438, 438f
Serving in tennis, mechanics of, 315–316, 316t, 317f

Sesamoid, fracture of, 556
Sesamoiditis, 553, 555f
Sex before sports, 60
Sexual maturation
    competition based on,
        42–43
    effects of heavy training on,
        104
Shin splints, 515–516, 516f
    from aerobic dancing, 39
    artificial turf and, 167, 170
Shock
    electric, 214
    insulin, 55
Shoe boot pernio, 64
Shoes. *See also* Heel, lifts for
    for aerobic dancing, 39, 40f
    ankle sprain prevention
        and, 525
    artificial turf and, 167, 170
    for basketball, 40f, 41
    "black dot heel" from, 539,
        541f
    blister formation from, 558
    callus formation from,
        558–559
    care of, 41
    cleats on, 525
    contact dermatitis from,
        66–67
    fit of, 38
    for hallux valgus, 553,
        554–555f
    heel bursitis from, 536
    information sources about,
        41
    intermetatarsal neuritis
        and, 551–552
    lacing tricks for, 38–39
    metatarsalgia and, 551
    modifications of, 41
    Morton's extension in, 547,
        547f
    orthotics for, 42, 43t
    parts of
        last, 36
        midsole, 36–37, 36f
        outsole, 36f, 37
    "runner's bump" from, 536
    for running, 35–39, 36f, 106
        modifications of, 41
    sock liners in, 37
    for sore ankles/feet, 38
    for tennis, 39–40, 40f
    toe injury from, 556, 557f
    for volleyball, 40–41, 40f
    for walking, 39
    for weight training, 127
    for women, 38

Shooting. *See* Firearms
Shot-putting
    mechanics of, 315
    scapular pain in, 346, 348
    strength training for,
        139–140
Shoulder
    acromioclavicular arthritis
        in, 326–327
    "apprehension shoulder,"
        316
    arthrogram of, 311, 311f
    "backpack palsy" of,
        304–305, 304f
    biceps tendon dislocation
        in, 327f, 328
    biceps tendon rupture in,
        329–330, 329f
    bicipital tendinitis in,
        327–328, 327f
    bruised, 306
    bursitis in, 307, 308f
    clavicle fracture and, 306
    coracoid injuries of, 314
    deltoid strain in, 306
    dislocation of
        acute, 331–332, 331–333f
        biceps tendon, 327f, 328
        exercises for, 352
        recurrent, 333–340
            anterior subluxation,
                336–340, 338f
            diagnosis of, 338–339
            examination in,
                337–338, 338f
            posterior subluxation,
                340
            protective equipment
                for, 334, 334f
            radiography of,
                333–334
            treatment of, 334–336,
                335–337f, 339–340
        at sternoclavicular joint,
            305–306
        voluntary, 341
    drooped, in tennis, 343,
        344f, 346
    examination of, 303–304
        preseason, 11–12, 12–13f
        for subacromial prob-
            lems, 310–311, 311f
    exercises for, 352, 353f
    frozen (calcific tendinitis),
        309, 309f, 312
    glenoid labrum avulsion in,
        330–331, 330f
    humeral problems in,
        341–342

    instability of, 340–341
    joints of, 301–303, 302f
    "Little League shoulder,"
        341–342
    muscle atrophy in, 11–12
    range of motion of, 347f
    rehabilitation of, 345–346,
        347–351f
    "ringman's shoulder," 341
    rotation of, 12, 13f
    rotator cuff tears in,
        309–310, 312–314,
        313f
    scapular pain in, 346, 348
    separations of, 323–326,
        324–326f
    "shoulder pointer," 306
    sounds of, during move-
        ment, 11
    strength of, 12, 13f
    stretching of, 19, 20f, 21,
        353
    subacromial region of
        examination of, 310–311,
            311f
        pain in, 307, 307–308f
        treatment of problems in,
            311–314, 313f
    subluxation of, 336–340,
        338f
    "swimmer's shoulder,"
        307–309, 311–312
    tackler's exostosis in, 342,
        343f
    tendinitis in, 307, 308f
        calcific, 309, 309f, 312
    tennis effects on, 315–316,
        316t, 343, 344f, 346
    thoracic outlet problems
        and, 305
    throwing and
        after-care of, 322, 322f
        fungo routine for, 323
        injury from, 316–318, 318f
        mechanisms of, 314–315,
            314–315f
        warming up exercises for,
            318–322, 319–321f
Shoulder pads
    fitting of, 178–179,
        179–180f
    neck injury from, 295–296
    shoulder dislocation pre-
        vention with, 334,
        334f
    tackler's exostosis preven-
        tion with, 342, 343f
Shrug exercise with inner
    tube, 23, 24f

Sickle cell trait, 56
Side-bend exercise with inner tube, 23, 24f
Side-gliding of cervical spine, 250, 250f
Side-lying test in knee instability, 498–499
Sidestep cut, 444, 445f
Silicone splint for scaphoid fracture, 380, 381f
Silver nitrate in herpes skin infection, 64
Sinuses, paranasal, effect of deep diving on, 282
Sitting row exercise with inner tube, 24, 25f
Sit-up exercise with inner tube, 24–25, 25f
Skating, ice, for mentally retarded persons, 52–54, 54f
Skiing (cross-country; downhill)
    Achilles tendon rupture in, 518
    by amputee, 51–52, 54f
    by blind athlete, 50, 50f
    boot compression neuropathy in, 548–549
    gloves for, 402, 402f
    knee injury in, to medial collateral ligament, 486–487
    leg fracture in, 513–514
    proximal tibiofibular joint injury in, 465–466
    thumb ulnar collateral ligament injury in, 384, 386, 386–388f, 388
    training for, 514
Skiing (water)
    ear injury in, 283
    gynecologic injury in, 416
Skin care
    in gymnastics, 400
    in taping, 181
Skin damage, 60–67
    abrasions, 67
    from adhesive tape, 182–183
    from allergy, 66–67
    blisters
        of foot, 558, 559f
        of hand, 399, 401
    calluses
        of foot, 558–559, 559f
        of hand, 399, 401
    cholinergic urticaria, 61
    from cold, 61–64, 63f

cold urticaria, 61
contact dermatitis, 66–67
    from cycling, 67
    equestrian cold panniculitis, 61
    from frostbite/frostnip, 61–64, 63f
    from heat, 60–61
    from infection
        acne, 65–66
        fungal, 66, 559f, 560
        herpes simplex, 64, 65f
        impetigo, 64–65, 65f
        molluscum contagiosum, 64, 65f
    miliaria, 60–61
    "saddle soreness," 67
    shoe boot pernio, 64
    "strawberries," 67
    sunburn, 60
    from warts, 559–560, 559f
Skipping, power. See Bounds in plyometrics
Skull fracture, 270
Sleep
    conditions favoring, 78
    drug-induced, 78
    during relaxation training, 158
Slipped capital femoral epiphysis, 427–428, 428f
Slow twitch muscle fibers, endurance exercise and, 85
Smoking, effects of, 76
Soccer
    ankle injury in, 522, 536
    foot bruises in, 547
    hollow viscus rupture in, 411
    kicking in, knee effects of, 445
    migraine in, 270–271
    osteitis pubis in, 423, 425
    strength training for, 141–142
    thumb ulnar collateral ligament injury in, 384
"Soccer ankle," 536
Socks and sock liners, 37, 41
    for cavus foot, 545
Sodium balance in heat disorders, 172
Soft drinks, caffeine in, 76
Soft tissue mobilization, 242
    in cervical spinal disorders, 248, 250f

in lumbar spinal disorders, 255
    in thoracic spinal disorders, 251, 252f
Solar plexus, blow to, 410
Somersaults, safety procedures for, 171
Soreness, 148
    chronic, home treatment for, 30, 31t
    prevention of, by warm-up, 112
Sounds
    of heart, in preseason examination, 27
    of shoulder movement, 11
"Special Olympics," 52
Speed development
    with form running drills, 130–131, 130f
    with plyometrics, 132–135, 133–134f
Spermatic cord torsion, 415–416
Spinal cord
    cervical cord syndrome and, 293
    damage of. See Neck, fracture of
    ultrasound over, 222
Spine
    cervical
        evaluation of, 242, 245–246
        injury of, 244–250, 245–250f
        sagittal stenosis of, 295
        curvature of, 13–14
        flexibility of, 13, 14f
        hyperextension of, spondylolysis in, 418–420, 419f
        length of, 13, 14f
    lumbar
        evaluation of, 253–254
        injury of, 254–258, 258–263f
        spondylolysis of, 418–420, 419f
    sacral
        evaluation of, 258, 260, 262–264
        injury of, 264–266, 265f
    thoracic
        evaluation of, 250–251
        injury of, 251–252, 252–253f
Spleen, rupture of, 410–411
    in mononucleosis, 57

Splint
  in finger injury, 401t
  silicone, for scaphoid fracture, 380, 381f
Spondylitis, ankylosing, back pain in, 418
Spondylolisthesis, 420, 421f
Spondylolysis, 418–420, 419f
Sports
  organizations for, 569
    for handicapped athlete, 571–572
  types of, 1, 2t
Sports medicine
  consultant team for, 3t
  curriculum for, 4t
  journals for, 565–566
  organizations for, 567–568
Spotters for weight training, 118–119, 127
Sprain
  of acromioclavicular joint, 149, 352
  of ankle. *See under Ankle*
  of facet joint, 254
  of sacroiliac joint, 264
  treatment of, 185
Spur, bone
  of olecranon, 365–366
  in "runner's bump," 537
Squash
  eye injury in, 275, 276f
  plantar fascial tear in, 543
Squat
  in power lifting, 146
  in strength training, 119–121, 121f
"Squat jump syndrome," 415
"Squeeze test" in Achilles tendon rupture, 518–519, 520f
Staleness in long-term training, 108–109
Standard of care in liability cases, 3
Stand-up exercise with inner tube, 23, 24f
Steeplechase, injury in, 272
  to neck, 289
Sternoclavicular joint
  anatomy of, 301
  dislocation of, 305–306
Sternum, fracture of, 408
Steroids
  action of, 74
  anabolic, effects of, 77–78
  in greater trochanteric bursitis, 429
  in hip cyst, 428

  injection of, 74
  in "jumper's knee," 459
  for pain relief, 74
  in Pellegrini-Steida's disease, 489
  in popliteal tenosynovitis, 465
  in quadriceps tendon rupture, 447
  in scapular pain, 346
  in ski boot compression neuropathy, 549
  in tennis elbow, 369
"Stinger," 294–295
"Stitch in side," 109, 412
Strain
  of back, 242
  of deltoid muscle, 306
  of gastrocnemius muscle ("tennis leg"), 517, 518f
  of groin, 425
  of hamstring muscles, 431–432
  of hip, 425–426
  of neck, 244–245, 245–249f
  of peroneus brevis tendon, 547–548
  of rhomboid muscle, 352, 353f
  treatment of, 185
Straps
  acne caused by, 65
  neck, 295–296
  in weight lifting, 126–127
"Strawberries," 67
Strength. *See also* Weight lifting/training
  decrease in, with aging, 95
  definition of, 115
  development of. *See also* Conditioning
    in adult fitness programs, 92–93
    with inner tube, 23–25, 24–25f
    in women, 99–100
  in injury prevention, 116–117
  of ligaments, 117
  measurement of, 117
  muscular physiology and, 115–117, 116f
  preseason evaluation of, 19, 19f
  of tendons, 117
  training for
    of ankle, 534–535, 536f

  assistive exercises in, 122, 124, 124–125f, 126
  in baseball, 137, 139
  with bench press, 118–119, 119–120f
  in elbow rehabilitation, 383, 385f
  of foot arch, 549
  in football, 138, 140–142, 142f
  in forearm rehabilitation, 383, 385f
  in gymnastics, 140–141
  with high pull, 122
  of knee, 502–503, 505–508f
  for neck, 296, 296–297f, 298
  with power clean lift, 121–122, 123–124f
  in rehabilitation, 229
  in shoulder rehabilitation, 345–346, 350–351f
  in soccer, 141–142
  with squat, 119–121, 121f
  in swimming, 142, 143f, 144
  in track and field events, 139–140
  in volleyball, 144
  in weight lifting as sport, 144–147, 145f
  in wrestling, 147–148
  in wrist rehabilitation, 383, 385f
  of women *vs* men, 117
Stress, 87
Stretching. *See also* Flexibility
  in adult fitness programs, 92–93
  of calf muscles, 546
  "cat and camel stretch," 261f
  of cervical spine, 246–247f, 248–250, 250f
  of deltoid muscle, 113f
  of groin, 114f
  of hamstring muscles, 21f, 22, 114f
  of head structures, 19, 20f, 21
  of hip, 21f, 22, 428f
  of iliotibial band, 21f, 22
  in injury treatment (ISE), 187–188, 188f

instructions for, 19, 20–22f,
21–23
of lumbar spine, 255–258,
259–263f
with partner, 112–115,
113–114f
of pectoral muscles, 113f
before pitching, 319–320,
319–321f, 353
Proprioceptive Neuro-
muscular Facilita-
tion, 112–115,
113–114f
of pyriformis muscle, 266
of quadriceps muscles, 21f,
22, 114f
of shoulder, 19, 20f, 21,
353
in shoulder rehabilitation,
345–346, 349f, 351f
solo, 112
before swimming, 311
of thigh, 21f, 22
of thoracic spine, 252, 253f
of torso, 20f, 21–22, 113f
in warming-up, 112,
112–115, 113–114f
Stride
length of, 130
rate of, 130
Stride-outs in conditioning
program, 131
Stroke, brain stem, 269–270
Stroke volume in exercise,
83–84
Subacromial bursitis, 307,
307–308f
Subacromial region. *See also*
Rotator cuff
examination of, 310–311,
311f
impingement in, 310
"painful arc" in, 310
pain in, 306, 307–308f
radiography of, 310–311,
311f
treatment of disorders in
calcific tendinitis, 312
rotator cuff tears,
312–314, 313f
"swimmer's shoulder,"
311–312
Subcapital fracture, 425
Subdural hematoma, 270
Subscapularis transfer in
shoulder dislocation,
335, 336f
Subtrochanteric fracture,
426

"Sulcus sign" in shoulder
dislocation, 341
Sunburn, 60
conjunctival irritation from,
274
Supplements, nutritional, 68,
69t, 70
Supraclavicular nerve injury,
294–295
Supraspinatus muscle
atrophy of, 310
examination of, 310
in rotator cuff tear, 310,
312
Supraspinatus tendon
avascular zone of, 308, 309f
calcium deposit in, 309,
309f, 312
inflammation of, 309, 309f
swimming effects on, 307,
307f, 308
"Surfer's knots," 549–550
Sweating
body cooling by, 172
cessation of, in heat stroke,
174
cholinergic urticaria from,
61
after heat acclimation, 175
miliaria from, 60–61
Swelling. *See* Edema
"Swimmer's ear," 280, 282
"Swimmer's shoulder,"
307–309
treatment of, 311–312
Swimming
aerobic points in, 94t
asthma and, 59
biceps tendon rupture in,
329–330
"breaststroker's knee" in,
487
caloric labyrinthitis in,
283–284
cold urticaria in, 61
ear infection in ("swim-
mer's ear"), 280, 282
ear osteoma development
in, 282
hematuria in, 413
shoulder disorders in,
307–308, 311–312
strength training for, 142,
143f, 144
subacromial shoulder pain
in, 307, 307f
training for, in triathalon,
107–108
Syncope, heat, 173

Synovial cyst in wrist, 374
Synovitis of knee, 453

Tackler's exostosis, 342, 343f
Talar tilt test, 523–524
Talocalcaneal ligaments, 521,
522f
Talofibular ligaments, 521,
522f
Talus, osteochondral fracture
of, 533, 533f, 536
Tape, 180–183
application of
for Achilles tendon ten-
sion, 517, 518f
on ankle, 525–526,
528–529, 529–530f
on elbow, 361, 362f
for foot arch support,
548f
on hand, 390–391, 390f
technique for, 180–182,
181t, 182f
on thumb, 386, 387–388f
gaps in, 181, 182f
rash from, 182–183
removal of, 182
skin care with, 181–183
tearing of, 181
types of, 180
uses of, 180
wrinkles in, 181–182
T-bar in upper extremity exercise, 385f
Tea, caffeine in, 76
Teeth
injury to, 286–287
preseason examination of,
11
Temporomandibular joint imbalance, 285–286,
286f
Tendinitis
of Achilles tendon, 521
bicipital, 327–328, 327f
of knee ("jumper's"), 459,
460f
of leg (shin splints),
515–516, 516f
of shoulder, 307, 308f
calcific, 309–310, 309f
in subacromial region, 312
of wrist, 378–379
flexor carpi radialis, 380

Tendinitis, of wrist
(*continued*)
flexor carpi ulnaris,
379–380
Tendons
strength of, 117
transfer of, in medial collateral ligament tear,
364
Tennis
coracoid process injury in,
314
elbow disorders in,
366–371, 367–368f
eye injury in, 275–276, 276f
gastrocnemius muscle
strain in ("tennis
leg"), 517, 518f
gloves for, 402
leg disorders in, 517, 518f
patellar tendon rupture in,
461f
plantar fascial tear in, 543
scapular pain in, 346, 348
serving in, mechanics of,
315–316, 316t, 317f
shoes for, 39–40, 40f
shoulder disorders in, 343,
344f, 346, 352
thoracic outlet problems in,
305
toe disorders in, 556, 557f
"Tennis elbow"
causes of, 366, 367f
pain pattern in, 366–367
prevention of
with exercise, 368–369
with proper grip,
367–368, 367–368f
with proper racket, 368
treatment of, 368–371
"Tennis leg," 517, 518f
Tennis shoulder, 343, 344f,
346
exercises for, 352
"Tennis toe," 556, 557f
Tenosynovitis
of hand, in karate,
389–390, 390f
popliteus, 464–465, 465f
of wrist
DeQuervain's, 379
in "oarsman's wrist," 379
TENS (transcutaneous electrical nerve stimula-
tion). *See under*
Electrical devices
Terbutaline in asthma, 59–60

Testis
maldescended, 28
natural protection of, 412
preseason examination of,
28
rupture of, hematocele in,
416
single, 28
torsion of, 415–416
T-exercise in shoulder rehabilitation, 345, 350f
Theophylline in asthma,
59–60
Thermoregulation, 171–172
Thigh
cold panniculitis of, 61
hamstring strain of,
431–432
myositis ossificans trau-
matica of, 430–431,
430f
quadriceps contusion of,
429–430
shaping of, 26–27
stretching of, 21f, 22
Thoracic outlet problems, 305
in tennis, 343, 346
Thoracic spine
evaluation of, 250–251
injury of, 251–252,
252–253f
Thought stoppage in coping
with injury, 152–154
Throat
foreign object in, 287
laryngeal injury in, 287,
287f
Thrombocytopenia from phenylbutazone, 73
Throwing. *See also* Pitching
elbow mechanics in, 361,
363f
glenoid labrum avulsion in,
330–331, 330f
humerus fracture in, 342
injury in
diagnosis of, 316–318,
318f
treatment of, 317–318
medial collateral ligament
tears in, 364
shoulder mechanics in,
314–315, 314–315f
subacromial shoulder pain
in, 307
Thumb
fibrosis in ("bowler's
thumb"), 382

metacarpal fracture of,
383–384
metacarpophalangeal joint
dislocation in, 384,
386f
taping of, 386, 387–388f
ulnar collateral ligament
injury of, 384, 386,
387–388f, 388
Tibia
epiphysitis of, 460–461,
462–463f
fracture of
at intercondylar emi-
nence, 471, 471f
in skiing, 513–514
stress, 514–515
at tubercle, 461–462,
463f
Tibial collateral ligament,
anatomy of,
436–438f, 437–438
Tibiofibular joint, proximal,
injury of, 465–466
Tibiofibular ligaments, anatomy of, 521, 522f
Tinea cruris, 66
Tinea versicolor, 66
Tissue impedance, 193–194
Tissue resonance-oscillation
theory, 207
Titmus machine, 7, 10, 10f
Tobacco, chewing, swallowing of, 287
Tobogganing, vertebral fracture in, 417, 418f
Toe(s)
claw, 557, 558f
ganglion cyst of, 552, 553f
great, disorders of,
552–553, 554–555f
hammer, 557–558
ingrown nail on, 556–557
injury to, from artificial
turf, 553, 555–556f
"marathon," 32
"tennis toe," 556, 557f
Toenail
hematoma under, 556, 557f
ingrown, 556–557
TOES program, 97
Tolmetin, 72, 322
Tolnaftate in fungal infections, 66
Torsion of spermatic cord,
415–416
Torso, stretching exercises for,
20f, 21–22, 113f

Tort liability of physician, 2–4
Track and field events
  blind athlete in, 50
  conditioning for, upper body plyometrics in, 135
  elbow problems in, 366
  hamstring strain in, 431–432
  metabolism in, 83
  performance in, men *vs* women, 98t
  planning for meet, 170–171
  strength training for, 139–140
  throwing in, mechanics of, 315
Trainer
  certification requirements of, 166
  contest planning by, 170–171
  curricula for, 166
  duties of, 4–5, 166–167
  equipment of, 167, 168–169t
  protective equipment fitting by, 177–179, 178–180f
  taping techniques for, 170–183, 181t, 182f
Training, 81–110
  acromioclavicular sprain in, 149
  in adult fitness programs, 90–94
    benefits of, 91
    Canadian 5BX exercise plan in, 94
    Cooper's aerobic system in, 93–94, 94t
    objectives of, 91
    principles of, 92
    risks in, 91–92
    safety procedures in, 91–92
    stretching-strengthening in, 92–93
    weight control through, 93
  of aerobic system, 87–90, 89f
    circuit training in, 90
    continuous activity in, 89
    duration of sessions in, 88
    exercise modes in, 87–88

fartlek running in, 90
    frequency of sessions in, 88
    intensity of sessions in, 88–89, 89f
    interval training in, 89–90
    parcours in, 90
    repetition training in, 90
  after arthroscopic meniscectomy, 149–150, 149f
  cardiorespiratory function and, 83–84
  of children, 101–105
    epiphyseal injuries in, 104
    history of, 101–102
    performance limits in, 103
    physical fitness and, 104–105, 105t
    psychological burnout in, 104
    purposes of programs for, 102
    rewards in, 104
    sexual maturation and, 104
    techniques for, 103–104
    trainability expectations in, 103
  of competitive athletes, 108–110
  consistency in, 86
  for distance running, 105–107
  of elderly persons, 94–97
    objectives in, 95–96
    physiology of aging and, 94–95
    programs for, 96–97, 97f
    risks in, 96
    safety procedures in, 96
  for endurance performance, 84–85
  exercise physiology and, 81–84
  of female athlete, 97–101
    body characteristics in, 98–99, 99t
    menstruation and, 100–101
    nutritional considerations in, 101
    pregnancy and. *See* Pregnancy

trainability expectations in, 99–100
    individuality in, 86
    injuries during, 148–150
    metabolic systems and, 81–83
    muscle cramps in, 148
    muscle soreness in, 148
    overload in, 86
    periodization in, 86–87
    planning of, long-term, 108
    plateauing in, 87
    progression of, 86
    respiratory function and, 83–84
    return to, after injury. *See* Return to competition/training
    specificity of, 86
    stress in, 87
    for triathalon, 107–108
Trampoline, safety procedures for, 171
Transcutaneous electrical nerve stimulation, 196–214
    acupuncture-like low frequency, 199
    brief-intense, 199–200
    burst mode, 198f, 200
    contraindications for, 200
    conventional high-frequency, 198–199
    electro-Acuscope, 206–208
    electrode placement for, 197, 198f
    high-voltage pulsed galvanic stimulators, 200–203, 202f
    hyperstimulation, 199–200
    interferential, 203–205, 204f
    low-voltage stimulator, 208–210, 209f
    Myopulse, 206–208
    physiology of, 197–198
    point stimulator, 205–206
Transplantation of kidney, exercise after, 415
Transportation, 5–6
    after head injury, 270
    after neck injury, 295
Trapezius muscle, strengthening of, 23, 24f
Treadmill test of runner, 32, 33f, 34
Treatment, explanation of, 6

Triangular fibrocartilage complex, injury of, 375
Triathalon training, 107–108
Triceps muscle, strengthening of, 23, 24f
Trichophyton mentagrophytes, 66
Trichophyton rubrum, 66
Triquetal-lunate impaction, 374
Trochanter, greater, bursitis of, 428–429
Trochlea, anatomy of, 358
Trunk, stretching routine for, 20f, 21–22, 113f
Trypsin in pain relief, 75
Tube, rubber
    for body shaping exercises, 25–27
    for rehabilitation of runner, 34–35
    for strengthening exercises, 23–25, 24–25f
    of neck, 298
Tumbling, rebound, safety procedures for, 171
Turf
    artificial, 167, 170
        toe injury from, 553, 555–556f
    burns from, 167
        prepatellar bursitis from, 447, 448f
    maintenance of, in ankle sprain prevention, 526
Tympanic membrane rupture, 283

Ulnar collateral ligament of thumb, injury of, 384, 386, 386–388f, 388
Ulnar nerve
    at elbow, 358
        compression of, 364–365, 365f
    irritation of, in hamate hook fracture, 381f, 382
    at thumb, fibrosis of, 382
    at wrist, compression of, 382, 382f

Ultrasound, 214–221
    absorption of, 219
    acoustic streaming and, 220
    application of, 217–218
    beam nonuniformity ratio in, 217
    cavitation and, 220
    conducting medium for, 217–218
    contraindications for, 221–222
    after cryotherapy, 219
    effective radiating area in, 216
    with electrical stimulation methods, 221
    energy intensity in, 218–219
    energy production in, 215–216
    equipment for, 215–217, 216f
    frequency for, 215
    indirect, 218
    nonthermal effects of, 220
    with phonophoresis, 221
    therapeutic effects of, 220–221
    thermal responses in, 219–220
    tissue temperatures and, 219
    transmission modes for, 217, 217t
    treatment parameters for, 218–219
    treatment timing in, 221
Unconsciousness in concussion, 268
Urethra, injury to, 416, 416f
Urinalysis, 29–30
    for anabolic steroids, 78
Urine
    blood in, 413–415
    hemoglobin in, 415
    myoglobin in, 415
Urticaria
    cholinergic, 61
    cold, 61
Uterus, injury to, 416

Vagina, injury to, 416
Valsalva maneuver, ear damage from, 284

Varicocele, 28
Vastus intermedius muscle, anatomy of, 435
Vastus lateralis muscle, anatomy of, 435, 436f
Vastus medialis muscle, anatomy of, 435, 436f
Veins, injury to, in thoracic outlet syndrome, 305
Ventilation in exercise, 83
Vertebrae
    disks between, rupture of, 417–418
    epiphysitis of, 14
    fracture of, back pain in, 417, 418f
    slippage of (spondylolisthesis), 420, 421f
Vertebral artery
    occlusion of, in neck injury, 269–270
    testing of, before cervical spine manipulation, 245–246
Vest, protective, 407–408, 408–409f
Visceral injury, 411–412, 411f
Vision, preseason examination of, 7, 10f, 10–11
Visual imagery in coping with injury, 154–156
Vitamins, 68, 70
Volar intercalcated segment instability of wrist, 376
Volar plate of proximal interphalangeal joint, injury of, 395
Volkmann's contracture in elbow fracture, 359–360, 359f
Volleyball
    shoes for, 40–41, 40f
    strength training for, 144
VO$_2$max (maximum aerobic power), 83–85
    in children, 103
    in elderly persons, 95
    vs heart rate, 88–89, 89f
    in women, 99, 100t
Vulva, injury to, 416

Walking
    aerobic points in, 94t

in rehabilitation
of knee, 484
of runner, 35
shoes for, 39
Warming up
effects of, 111–112
exercises for, 19, 20–22f, 21–23
before pitching, 318–322, 319–320f
stretching in
with partner, 112–115, 113–114f
solo, 112
timing of, 112
Wart-like skin disorder, 64, 65f
Wart on foot, 559–560, 559f
ultrasound treatment of, 220–221
Water depletion heat exhaustion, 173, 173t
Water exercise. *See* Pool exercise
Water sports. *See also* Diving; Skiing (water); Swimming
tympanic membrane rupture in, 283
Watson-Jones procedure in ankle reconstruction, 531, 532f
Waveforms of electrical devices, 194
Weight control, 25–27, 93
Weight lifting/training, 144–147
belt for, 126–127
blackout in, 146–147
for body building, 146
errors in, 128–129
facilities for, 127–128, 128f
free weights in, 127–128, 128f
hand blisters in, 400
injuries in, 118, 144–146
lifting aids for, 126–127
lifting *vs* training, 144
machines for, 127–128, 128f
mental aspect of, 129
muscular action in, 116
"oarsman's wrist" in, 379
for older persons, 118

Olympic-style, 144–146, 145f
patellar tendon rupture in, 459–460, 461f
pectoralis major muscle rupture in, 406
power lifting type of, 146
rib fracture in, 406–408, 409f
round window rupture in, 284
rules for, 128–129
scapular pain in, 346, 348
shoes for, 126–127
spotters for, 118–119, 127
starting weight selection for, 126
training for, 144
types of, 144, 145f
for women, 117
wrist straps for, 126–127
for youth, 117–118
Weight room, 127–128, 128f
Wet bulb globe thermometer index, 175, 176t
Wheelchair games, 51, 52–53t, 53f
gloves for, 402
"Whip kick," knee injury in, 487
Wintergreen, oil of, in pain relief, 75
Wound, open, treatment of, 184, 184f
Wrap, elastic, 186–187
"Wrestler's ear," 278–280, 281f
Wrestling
ankle sprain in, 522
brain stem stroke in, 269–270
costochondral separation of, 408
ear injury in, 278–280, 281f
herpes skin infections in, 64, 65f
migraine in, 270–271
pectoralis major muscle rupture in, 406
prepatellar bursitis in, 447
strength training for, 147–148

thumb ulnar collateral ligament injury in, 384
Wrist
examination of, 372–373
hamate hook fracture in, 380–382, 381f
injury mechanisms of, 373
instability of, 375–377, 376f
patterns of, 376, 376f
treatment of, 376–377
ligaments of, 375
lunate avascular necrosis in, 378
lunate dislocation in, 377–378
nerve compression in, 382, 382f
radial-scaphoid impaction in, 373–374, 373f
radiography of, 372–373
radioulnar joint injury in, 374–375
rehabilitation of, 383, 384–385f
scaphoid fracture in, 377, 380, 381f
stabilizing structures of, 375
synovial cyst in, 374
tendinitis of, 378–379
of flexor carpi radialis, 380
of flexor carpi ulnaris, 379–380
tenosynovitis of (DeQuervain's), 379
tenosynovitis of (oarsman's wrist), 379
triangular fibrocartilage complex in, 375
triquetal-lunate impaction in, 374
wrapping of, in weight lifting, 126–127
Wrist wrestling, humerus fracture in, 342

Yeast infection of skin, 66

ISBN 0-397-50765-8

90000